AMERICAN REFERENCE BOOKS ANNUAL
1993 VOLUME 24

AMERICAN REFERENCE BOOKS ANNUAL

1993 VOLUME 24

Bohdan S. Wynar EDITOR IN CHIEF
Anna Grace Patterson EDITOR

ASSISTANT EDITOR
D. A. Rothschild

Comprehensive annual reviewing service for
reference books published in the United States and Canada

1993

LIBRARIES UNLIMITED
ENGLEWOOD, COLORADO

Copyright © 1993 Libraries Unlimited, Inc.
All Rights Reserved
Printed in the United States of America

No part of this publication may be reproduced, stored in a retrieval system, or transmitted, in any form or by any means, electronic, mechanical, photocopying, recording, or otherwise, without the prior written permission of the publisher.

LIBRARIES UNLIMITED, INC.
P.O. Box 6633
Englewood, CO 80155-6633

Library of Congress Cataloging-in-Publication Data

American reference books annual. 1970-
  Englewood, Colo., Libraries Unlimited.

    v. 19x26 cm.

Indexes:
  1970-74. 1v.
  1975-79. 1v.
  1980-84. 1v.
  1985-89. 1v.

    1. Reference books--Bibliography--Periodicals.
I. Wynar, Bohdan S. II. Patterson, Anna Grace.
Z1035.1.A55   011'.02   75-120328
ISBN 1-56308-076-1(1993 edition)
ISSN 0065-9959

Contents

Introduction......................xiii
Contributors......................xv
Journals Cited....................xxvii

Part I
GENERAL REFERENCE WORKS

1—General Reference Works

Acronyms and Abbreviations..............3
Almanacs..............................4
Bibliography..........................5
  Bibliographic Guides..................5
  National and Trade Bibliography........11
    International......................11
    United States......................13
Biography............................15
  International........................15
  United States........................21
Dictionaries and Encyclopedias..........24
Directories..........................31
Government Publications................34
Handbooks and Yearbooks................35
Indexes..............................35
Museums..............................37
Periodicals and Serials................38
Quotation Books......................41

Part II
SOCIAL SCIENCES

2—Social Sciences in General

Social Sciences in General.............47

3—Area Studies

General Works........................51
United States........................52
Africa..............................54
  Angola..............................54
  Central African Republic..............54
  Equatorial Guinea....................54
  Libya................................55
  Mozambique..........................55
  Sub-Saharan Africa...................56
Arctic Regions.......................56
Asia................................57
  General Works........................57
  Afghanistan..........................57
  Bali................................58
  Burma................................58
  China................................59
  Japan................................59
  Laos................................60
  Singapore............................60
  Tibet................................61
Australia............................61
Canada..............................62
Developing Countries..................63
Europe..............................64
  General Works........................64
  Eastern Europe......................64
  France..............................66
  Great Britain........................66
  Northern Ireland....................66
Indian Ocean Region..................67
  Mauritius............................67
Latin America and the Caribbean........68
  General Works........................68
  Argentina............................69
  Brazil..............................69
  Costa Rica..........................70
  Honduras............................70
  Montserrat..........................71
  Turks and Caicos Islands..............71
  Virgin Islands......................71
Middle East..........................72
  General Works........................72
  Egypt................................73
  Jordan..............................74
  Kurds................................74
  Lebanon..............................74
  Saudia Arabia........................75
Pacific Area.........................75
  General Works........................75
  Philippines..........................75

4 — Economics and Business

General Works..........................77
   Acronyms and Abbreviations............77
   Atlases...............................78
   Bibliography..........................78
   Biography.............................80
   Dictionaries and Encyclopedias.........81
   Directories...........................84
   Handbooks and Yearbooks...............88
   Periodicals and Serials...............94
   Quotation Books.......................96
Business Services and Investment Guides....96
Canadian Business.........................99
Consumer Education.......................101
Finance and Banking......................102
Industry and Manufacturing...............106
Insurance................................108
International Business...................109
   General Works........................109
      Dictionaries and Encyclopedias....109
      Directories......................110
      Handbooks and Yearbooks..........113
   Africa...............................117
   Asia.................................118
   Europe...............................119
   Great Britain........................124
Labor....................................125
   Bibliography.........................125
   Dictionaries.........................125
   Directories..........................126
   Handbooks and Yearbooks..............128
Management...............................131
Marketing and Trade......................132
Office Practices.........................134
Real Estate..............................135
Taxation.................................135

5 — Education

General Works............................137
   Catalogs and Collections.............137
   Dictionaries and Encyclopedias.......138
   Handbooks and Yearbooks..............138
   Indexes..............................141
   Periodicals and Serials..............142
Computer Resources.......................143
Elementary and Secondary Education.......144
Higher Education.........................147
   Almanacs.............................147
   Biography............................148
   Dictionaries and Encyclopedias.......148
   Directories..........................149
   Handbooks and Yearbooks..............150
   Indexes..............................156
International Exchange Programs and Opportunities.....156
Learning Disabilities and Disabled.......161
Nonprint Materials and Resources.........161
Reading..................................164
Vocational and Continuing Education......166

6 — Ethnic Studies and Anthropology

Anthropology and Ethnology...............171
Ethnic Studies...........................173
   General Works........................173
   Asian-Americans......................174
   Blacks...............................174
   Hispanic-Americans...................177
   Indians of North America.............178
   Irish-Americans......................181
   Italian-Americans....................182
   Jews.................................182
   Norwegian-Americans..................187

7 — Genealogy and Heraldry

Genealogy................................189
   Chronology...........................189
   Dictionaries.........................189
   Directories..........................190
   Handbooks and Yearbooks..............190
   Indexes..............................192
Heraldry.................................193
Personal Names...........................193

8 — Geography and Travel Guides

Geography................................195
   General Works........................195
   Atlases..............................195
      United States, 195; *Canada*, 197; *International*, 198; *Other Countries*, 201
      Bibliography.....................202
      Biography........................202
      Dictionaries and Encyclopedias...203
      Handbooks and Yearbooks..........204
Place Names..............................205
Travel Guides............................207
   United States........................207
   Asia.................................209
   Canada...............................210
   Developing Countries.................210
   Europe...............................211

9 — History

Archaeology 213
American History 214
    Bibliography 214
    Biography 216
    Catalogs and Collections 217
    Dictionaries and Encyclopedias 217
    Handbooks and Yearbooks 218
Asian History 219
    Chinese 219
    Indic 220
    Vietnamese 221
Canadian History 221
European History 222
    General Works 222
    Armenian 222
    British 223
    Eastern European 225
    French 226
    German 226
    Irish 226
    Spanish 227
Latin American and Caribbean History ... 227
Middle Eastern History 228
World History 229
    Atlases 229
    Bibliography 230
    Chronology 231
    Dictionaries and Encyclopedias 233
    Handbooks and Yearbooks 235
    Indexes 236

10 — Law

General Works 237
    Acronyms and Abbreviations 237
    Bibliography 237
    Dictionaries and Encyclopedias 241
    Directories 244
    Handbooks and Yearbooks 246
    Indexes 249
Criminology 251
Human Rights 256
Victims of Abuse 258

11 — Library and Information Science and Publishing and Bookselling

Library and Information Science 259
    General Works 259
        Acronyms and Abbreviations 259
        Dictionaries and Encyclopedias 259
        Directories 260
        Handbooks and Yearbooks 262
        Indexes 264
        Periodicals and Serials 265
    Careers and Education 265
    Cataloging and Classification 266
    Comparative and International
        Librarianship 270
    Copyright 272
    Indexing 272
    Information Technology 273
    Inter-library Loans 274
    Library Automation 275
    Library Conservation 277
    Public Libraries 277
    School Libraries 278
    Special Libraries and Collections 282
        General Works 282
        Genealogy and Local History 282
        Government Documents 283
        University and College Libraries ... 283
Publishing and Bookselling 284
    General Works 284
    Bibliography 284
    Dictionaries 284
    Directories 285
    Handbooks and Yearbooks 288
    Desktop Publishing 288

12 — Military Studies

General Works 289
    Atlases 289
    Bibliography 289
    Biography 291
    Chronology 292
    Dictionaries and Encyclopedias 293
    Directories 294
    Handbooks and Yearbooks 294
Air Force 296
Army 296
Weapons 298

13 — Political Science

General Works 299
    Almanacs 299
    Atlases 299
    Biography 300
    Dictionaries and Encyclopedias 300
    Directories 300
    Handbooks and Yearbooks 301
    Quotation Books 303

13 – Political Science (*continued*)

Politics and Government..................303
    United States........................303
        Almanacs........................303
        Bibliography.....................304
        Catalogs and Collections............305
        Dictionaries and Encyclopedias.......305
        Directories........................306
        Handbooks and Yearbooks..........308
        Indexes..........................313
    African...............................315
    Asian................................316
    Canadian.............................316
    European.............................318
        General Works....................318
        Eastern European..................319
        Great Britain.....................319
    Latin American and Caribbean........321
    Middle Eastern......................321
Ideologies............................322
International Organizations.............323
International Relations..................325
Peace Movement........................326
Public Policy and Administration........328

14 – Psychology

General Works.........................331
    Bibliography.........................331
    Dictionaries and Encyclopedias.........332
    Directories...........................334
    Handbooks and Yearbooks.............334
Parapsychology........................335

15 – Recreation and Sports

General Works.........................339
    Almanacs............................339
    Bibliography.........................340
    Biography...........................340
    Dictionaries and Encyclopedias.........342
    Directories..........................342
    Indexes..............................343
Baseball...............................344
Basketball.............................344
Cricket................................345
Croquet...............................345
Football...............................346
Golf..................................347
Hiking................................348
Hunting and Fishing....................348
Martial Arts...........................349
Olympics..............................349

Sailing................................350
Track-athletics........................350

16 – Sociology

General Works.........................353
    Bibliography.........................353
    Dictionaries and Encyclopedias.........354
Abortion..............................356
Aging.................................356
Disabled..............................360
Family, Marriage, and Divorce............362
Philanthropy...........................363
Sex Studies............................367
Social Welfare.........................369
Substance Abuse.......................370
Youth and Child Development...........372

17 – Statistics, Demography, and Urban Studies

Demography...........................375
Statistics..............................376
    Bibliography.........................376
    Dictionaries and Encyclopedias.........377
    Handbooks and Yearbooks.............378
    Indexes..............................380
Urban Studies..........................381

18 – Women's Studies

Bibliography............................385
Biography..............................388
Dictionaries and Encyclopedias...........391
Directories.............................391
Handbooks and Yearbooks...............392
Indexes................................393
Quotation Books.......................393

Part III
HUMANITIES

19 – Humanities in General

General Works.........................397

20 – Communication and Mass Media

General Works.........................401
Authorship............................404
Newspapers and Magazines..............410

Radio, Television, Audio, and Video....413	Estonian....459
Bibliography....413	French....460
Biography....414	Georgian....460
Dictionaries and Encyclopedias....414	German....461
Directories....416	Hawaiian....461
Handbooks and Yearbooks....417	Hebrew....462
Indexes....421	Irish....462
	Mahican....463
21 – Decorative Arts	Persian....463
	Portuguese....463
Collecting....423	Russian....464
Coins....423	Sign Language....466
Firearms....424	Somali....467
Crafts....424	Spanish....467
Fashion and Costume....426	Tagalog....468
Photography....426	Vietnamese....469
	Yiddish....469

22 – Fine Arts

24 – Literature

General Works....429
Bibliography....429
Biography....431
Dictionaries and Encyclopedias....432
Handbooks and Yearbooks....433
Indexes....434
Periodicals....437
Architecture....437
Graphic Arts....439
Painting....440

General Works....471
Bibliography....471
Biography....472
Dictionaries and Encyclopedias....473
Handbooks and Yearbooks....474
Children's Literature....476
Bibliography....476
Biography....483
Handbooks and Yearbooks....484
Indexes....486
Drama....486
Fiction....487
General Works....487
Crime and Mystery....488
Science Fiction, Fantasy, and Horror....490
Short Story....492
National Literature....493
American Literature....493
General Works....493
Drama....495
Fiction....496
Individual Authors....496
James Fenimore Cooper, 496; *Stephen Crane*, 497; *William Faulkner*, 497; *Ernest Hemingway*, 498; *Jerzy Kosinski*, 498; *Louis L'Amour*, 498; *Mary McCarthy*, 499; *Herman Melville*, 499; *Walter M. Miller, Jr.*, 500; *Frank Norris*, 500; *Edward Taylor*, 500; *Henry David Thoreau*, 501; *Mark Twain*, 501; *Richard Wilbur*, 502; *Tennessee Williams*, 502
Poetry....502
Wit and Humor....503

23 – Language and Linguistics

General Works....443
Bibliography....443
Dictionaries and Encyclopedias....444
Handbooks and Yearbooks....446
English-Language Dictionaries....447
Abridged....447
Etymology....449
Grammar....450
Idioms, Colloquialisms, and
 Special Usage....450
Juvenile....451
New Words....451
Other English-Speaking Countries....452
Rhetoric....454
Synonyms and Antonyms....454
Terms and Phrases....455
Thesauri....455
Visual....457
Non-English-Language Dictionaries....458
Byelorussian....458
Carolinian....458
Chinese....459

24—Literature (continued)

National Literature (continued)
   British Literature......................504
      General Works......................504
         Dictionaries and Encyclopedias, 504; *Handbooks and Yearbooks*, 504
      Drama..............................509
      Fiction.............................509
      Individual Authors..................510
         Robert Bridges, 510; *George Mackay Brown*, 511; *Joseph Conrad*, 511; *John Fowles*, 511; *Barbara Pym*, 512; *Sir Walter Scott*, 512; *William Shakespeare*, 513; *Bernard Shaw*, 515
      Poetry.............................515
   Canadian Literature...................516
   French Literature.....................516
   German Literature....................517
   Italian Literature.....................517
   Latin American and Caribbean Literature..........................518
   Oceanian Literature...................520
   Russian Literature....................520
   Scottish Literature....................521
   Spanish Literature....................521
   Yugoslav Literature...................522
Poetry.................................522

25—Music

General Works..........................525
   Bibliography.........................525
   Biography...........................527
   Dictionaries and Encyclopedias.........527
   Handbooks and Yearbooks.............529
Composers.............................530
Instruments............................534
   Oboe...............................534
   Piano...............................535
   Voice...............................535
Musical Forms..........................536
   General Works......................536
   Choral..............................536
   Church.............................537
   Classical............................537
   Motion Picture......................538
   Operatic............................539
   Popular.............................540
      General Works......................540
      Band..............................543
      Jazz...............................544
      Rock..............................545
      Soul...............................546

26—Mythology, Folklore, and Popular Culture

Folklore................................547
Mythology.............................550
Popular Culture........................551

27—Performing Arts

General Works..........................555
   Bio-bibliography......................555
   Biography...........................558
   Handbooks and Yearbooks.............559
Dance.................................559
Film...................................560
   Bibliography.........................560
   Biography...........................562
   Catalogs and Collections...............565
   Dictionaries and Encyclopedias.........566
   Directories..........................567
   Filmography........................568
   Handbooks and Yearbooks.............576
   Indexes.............................577
   Quotation Books.....................578
Theater................................578
   Bibliography.........................578
   Biography...........................581
   Chronology.........................582
   Directories..........................582
   Handbooks and Yearbooks.............583

28—Philosophy and Religion

Philosophy.............................585
   Bibliography.........................585
   Dictionaries and Encyclopedias.........586
Religion...............................588
   General Works......................588
      Bibliography.........................588
      Biography...........................590
      Dictionaries and Encyclopedias.......591
      Directories..........................592
      Handbooks and Yearbooks...........592
      Quotation Books.....................594
   Buddhism..........................594
   Christianity.........................595
      General Works......................595
         Almanacs, 595; *Bibliography*, 596; *Biography*, 596; *Dictionaries and Encyclopedias*, 597; *Handbooks and Yearbooks*, 599
      Bible Studies.......................600
   Sikkism............................604

Part IV
SCIENCE AND TECHNOLOGY

29—Science and Technology in General

Bibliography 607
Biography 607
Dictionaries and Encyclopedias 609
Directories 613
Handbooks and Yearbooks 613
Indexes 615
Periodicals and Serials 618

30—Agricultural Sciences

General Works 619
Food Sciences and Technology 621
   Bibliography 621
   Dictionaries and Encyclopedias 622
   Directories 624
   Handbooks and Yearbooks 624
Forestry 625
Horticulture 626
Veterinary Science 628

31—Biological Sciences

Biology 629
Botany 629
   General Works 629
     Bibliography 629
     Catalogs and Collections 630
     Dictionaries and Encyclopedias .. 630
     Handbooks and Yearbooks 632
   Flowering Plants 633
   Fungi 636
   Grasses and Weeds 636
   Liverworts 637
   Marine Flora 637
   Medicinal and Edible Plants 638
   Trees and Shrubs 638
Natural History 641
Zoology 643
   General Works 643
   Birds 646
   Butterflies 650
   Domestic Animals 652
   Fishes 652
   Insects 655
   Mammals 658
   Marine Animals 660
   Reptiles and Amphibians 660

32—Engineering

Astronautical Engineering 663
Chemical Engineering 663
Civil Engineering 664
Electric Engineering and Electronics 665
Genetic Engineering 669
Industrial Engineering 669
Materials Science 670
Plant Engineering 672
Soils Engineering 672
Tools 673
Transportation Engineering 674

33—Health Sciences

General Works 675
Medicine 678
   General Works 678
     Acronyms and Abbreviations 678
     Bibliography 679
     Catalogs and Collections 680
     Dictionaries and Encyclopedias .. 681
     Directories 684
     Handbooks and Yearbooks 685
   Psychiatry 687
   Specific Diseases 687
     AIDS 687
     Birth Related Conditions 689
     Cancer 689
     Hearing Disorders 690
     Heart Diseases 690
     Syndromes 690
Nursing 691
Pharmacy and Pharmaceutical Sciences ... 691

34—High Technology

General Works 695
Artificial Intelligence 696
Computing 696
   General Works 696
     Bibliography 696
     Catalogs 697
     Dictionaries and Encyclopedias .. 697
     Directories 700
     Handbooks and Yearbooks 701
     Indexes 702
   Computer Graphics 702
   Software 703
Optical Storage Devices 703
   CAD/CAM 703
   CD-ROM 704

34 – High Technology (continued)

Optical Storage Devices (continued)
    Imaging Systems......................705
    Microforms..........................705
Telecommunication.....................706

35 – Physical Sciences and Mathematics

General Works........................709
Astronomy............................709
Chemistry............................712
    Dictionaries and Encyclopedias........712
    Handbooks and Yearbooks.............713
    Indexes..............................716
Earth and Planetary Sciences............716
    General Works.......................716
    Climatology.........................718
    Geology.............................718
    Hydrology...........................718
    Mineralogy..........................719
    Oceanography........................721
    Paleontology........................721
Physics..............................722
Mathematics..........................723

36 – Resource Sciences

Energy Resources......................727
    Dictionaries and Encyclopedias........727
    Directories.........................728
    Handbooks and Yearbooks.............728
    Indexes.............................730
Environmental Science..................730
    Almanacs............................730
    Bibliography........................730
    Dictionaries and Encyclopedias........731
    Directories.........................732
    Handbooks and Yearbooks.............735
    Quotation Books.....................740

37 – Transportation

General Works........................741
Air..................................741
Ground..............................742
Water...............................744

    Author/Title Index..................747
    Subject Index......................779
    Contributors' Index................833

Introduction

PURPOSE AND SCOPE

American Reference Books Annual, a far-reaching reviewing service for reference books, is now in its 24th volume. The 1,792 books reviewed in this volume cover imprints from 1992 and some from 1991 that were received too late to be reviewed in the previous volume. In the 24 volumes of ARBA published since 1970, a total of 41,373 titles have been reviewed. Four cumulative indexes for ARBA cover the years 1970-1974, 1975-1979, 1980-1984, and 1985-1989. These indexes facilitate the use of the annual volumes.

ARBA differs significantly from other reviewing media in its basic purpose, which is to provide comprehensive coverage of English-language reference books published in the United States and Canada during a single year. The categories of reference books reviewed in ARBA and the policy regarding them can be summarized as follows: (1) Dictionaries, encyclopedias, indexes, directories, bibliographies, guides, concordances, atlases, gazetteers, and other types of ready-reference tools are routinely reviewed in each volume of ARBA; coverage of this category of reference materials is nearly complete. (2) General encyclopedias that are updated annually, yearbooks, almanacs, indexing and abstracting services, and other annuals or serials are usually reviewed at intervals of three, four, or five years. The first review of such works generally provides an appropriate historical background. Subsequent reviews of these publications attempt to point out changes in scope, editorial policy, and similar matters. (3) New editions of reference books are ordinarily reviewed with appropriate comparisons to the older editions. (4) Traditionally, foreign reference titles have been reviewed only if they had an exclusive distributor in the United States. In 1987 coverage was expanded to include Canadian publications that do not have U.S. distributors. Prices for such titles are in Canadian dollars unless otherwise indicated. Substantial coverage of Canadian reference publications has been achieved and will continue until it is as complete for Canada as it is for the United States. Other foreign title coverage is restricted to English-language publications from Great Britain, Australia, and India. (5) Government publications are reviewed on a highly selective basis because other Libraries Unlimited works, *Government Reference Books* and *Government Reference Serials*, provide the library profession with comprehensive coverage of government reference publications. In ARBA 93 only Library of Congress publications and international publications, such as those of the United Nations, are covered. (6) Reprints are reviewed in ARBA on a selective basis as they often are produced in limited quantities. (7) Titles produced for the mass market in the areas of collectibles, travel guides, and genealogy receive selective coverage.

Certain categories of reference books are usually not reviewed in ARBA: those of fewer than 48 pages, those produced by vanity presses or by the author as publisher, and those generated by library staffs for internal use. Highly specialized reference works printed in a limited number of copies and that do not appeal to the general library audience ARBA serves may also be omitted.

Because there has been a significant increase and interest in electronic publishing, ARBA, with this volume, inaugurates the reviewing of this medium. Approximately twenty CD-ROMs and one disk receive comprehensive and lengthy evaluations. Future volumes will continue to include reviews of these state-of-the-art information storage devices in a variety of subject areas.

REVIEWING POLICY

To ensure well-written and erudite reviews, the ARBA staff maintains a roster of more than 425 scholars, practitioners, and library educators in all subject specialties at libraries and universities throughout the United States and Canada. Because ARBA is not a selective reviewing source, such as *Choice* or *Library Journal*, the reviews are generally longer and more critical and detail the strengths and weaknesses of important reference works. Reviewers are asked to examine a book and provide well-documented critical comments, both positive and negative. Coverage usually includes the usefulness of a given work; organization, execution, and pertinence of contents; prose style; format; availability of supplementary materials (e.g., indexes, appendixes); and similarity to other works and previous editions. Reviewers are encouraged to address the intended audience but not necessarily to give specific recommendations for purchase. An adequate description and evaluation of the reference book are sufficient. All reviews in ARBA are signed.

ARRANGEMENT

ARBA 93 consists of 37 chapters, an author/title index, a subject index, and a contributors' index. It is divided into four alphabetically arranged parts: "General Reference Works," "Social Sciences," "Humanities," and "Science and Technology." "General Reference Works" is subdivided by form: bibliography, biography, catalogs and collections, dictionaries and encyclopedias, handbooks and yearbooks, indexes, and so on. Within the remaining three parts, chapters are organized by topic. Thus, under "Social Sciences" the reader will find chapters titled "Economics and Business," "Education," "History," "Law," and "Sociology."

Each chapter is subdivided to reflect the arrangement strategy of the entire volume. There is a section on general works followed by a topical breakdown. For example, in the chapter titled "Performing Arts," "General Works" is followed by "Dance" and "Film." The latter is divided into sections by format, which include "Biography" and "Filmography." Subdivisions are based on the amount of material available on a given topic and vary from year to year.

ACKNOWLEDGMENTS

In closing, we wish to express our gratitude to the many talented contributors without whose support this volume of ARBA could not have been compiled. We would also like to thank the members of our staff who were instrumental in the preparation: Pamela Getchell, David V. Loertscher, Judy Gay Matthews, Kay Minnis, Jo Anne H. Ricca, and D. A. Rothschild.

Bohdan S. Wynar, Editor in Chief
Anna Grace Patterson, Editor

Editorial Staff

Bohdan S. Wynar, Editor in Chief
Anna Grace Patterson, Editor
D. A. Rothschild, Assistant Editor

Contributors

Stephen H. Aby, Education Bibliographer, Bierce Library, Univ. of Akron, Ohio.

Robert D. Adamshick, Librarian, U.S. Army Corps of Engineers, Chicago.

Walter C. Allen, Assoc. Professor Emeritus, Graduate School of Library and Information Science, Univ. of Illinois, Urbana.

Mary Jo Aman, Education Librarian, Golda Meir Library, Univ. of Wisconsin, Milwaukee.

Byron P. Anderson, Coordinator, Computer Reference Services, Northern Illinois Univ., De Kalb.

Frank J. Anderson, Librarian Emeritus, Sandor Teszler Library, Wofford College, Spartanburg, S.C.

James D. Anderson, Assoc. Dean and Professor, School of Communication, Information, and Library Studies, Rutgers Univ., New Brunswick, N.J.

Robert T. Anderson, Professor, Religious Studies, Michigan State Univ., East Lansing.

Charles R. Andrews, Dean of Library Services, Hofstra Univ., Hempstead, N.Y.

Theodora Andrews, formerly Professor of Library Science and Special Bibliographer, Pharmacy, Nursing and Health Science Library, Purdue Univ., West Lafayette, Ind.

Susan B. Ardis, Head, McKinney Engineering Library, Univ. of Texas, Austin.

Roslyn Attinson, Professor Emerita, College of Staten Island, N.Y.

Lawrence W. S. Auld, Chairman, Dept. of Library and Information Studies, East Carolina Univ., Greenville, N.C.

Bill Bailey, Head of Reference, Newton Gresham Library, Sam Houston State Univ., Huntsville, Tex.

Susan D. Baird-Joshi, Graduate Research Asst., Univ. of Washington, Seattle.

Jack Bales, Reference Librarian, Mary Washington College Library, Fredericksburg, Va.

Robert M. Ballard, Professor, School of Library and Information Science, North Carolina Central Univ., Durham.

Gary D. Barber, Head of Reference, Daniel A. Reed Library, State Univ. of New York, Fredonia.

Helen M. Barber, Reference Librarian, New Mexico State Univ., Las Cruces.

Suzanne I. Barchers, Staff, Libraries Unlimited, Inc.

Donald A. Barclay, Reference Librarian, New Mexico State Univ., Las Cruces.

David Bardack, Professor, Dept. of Biological Sciences, Univ. of Illinois, Chicago.

Pam M. Baxter, Psychological Sciences Librarian, Psychological Sciences Library, Purdue Univ., West Lafayette, Ind.

Craig W. Beard, Head of Reference Services, Mervyn H. Sterne Library, Univ. of Alabama, Birmingham.

Maureen A. Beck, Reference Librarian, Milton S. Eisenhower Library, Johns Hopkins Univ., Baltimore, Md.

Sandra E. Belanger, Reference Librarian, San Jose State Univ. Library, Calif.

Carol Willsey Bell, Head, Local History and Genealogy Dept., Warren-Trumbull County Public Library, Warren, Ohio.

George H. Bell, Assoc. Librarian, Daniel E. Noble Science & Engineering Library, Arizona State Univ., Tempe.

Bernice Bergup, Humanities Reference Librarian, Davis Library, Univ. of North Carolina, Chapel Hill.

John B. Beston, Professor of English, Nazareth College of Rochester, N.Y.

Kerranne G. Biley, Reference Librarian, Univ. of Colorado at Denver.

Terry D. Bilhartz, Assoc. Professor of History, Sam Houston State Univ., Huntsville, Tex.

Ron Blazek, Professor, School of Library Science, Florida State Univ., Tallahassee.

Daniel K. Blewett, Reference Librarian, Cudahy Library, Loyola Univ., Chicago.

Marjorie E. Bloss, Director, Technical Services Division, Center for Research Libraries, Chicago.

George S. Bobinski, Dean and Professor, School of Information and Library Studies, State Univ. of New York, Buffalo.

Bobray Bordelon, Business Reference Librarian, New Mexico State Univ. Library, Las Cruces.

Melvin M. Bowie, Assoc. Professor, Dept. of Instructional Technology, Univ. of Georgia, Athens.

James K. Bracken, Head, Second Floor Main Library Information Services, Ohio State Univ., Columbus.

William Bright, Research Associate in Linguistics, Univ. of Colorado, Boulder.

Robert N. Broadus, Professor, School of Library Science, Univ. of North Carolina, Chapel Hill.

Simon J. Bronner, Distinguished Professor of Folklore and American Studies, Capitol College, Pennsylvania State Univ., Middletown.

Barbara E. Brown, formerly Head, General Cataloguing Section, Library of Parliament, Ottawa.

Judith M. Brugger, Catalog Management & Authorities Librarian, Cornell Univ., Ithaca, N.Y.

Ronald L. Buchan, Lexicographer, NASA STI Facility, Linthicum Heights, Md.

Betty Jo Buckingham, Consultant, Iowa Dept. of Education, Des Moines.

Joanna M. Burkhardt, Librarian, Univ. of Connecticut, Torrington.

Lois J. Buttlar, Assoc. Professor, School of Library and Information Science, Kent State Univ., Ohio.

Hans E. Bynagle, Library Director and Professor of Philosophy, Whitworth College, Spokane, Wash.

Diane M. Calabrese, Research Associate for Planning and Eisenhower Grant Programs, Coordinating Board for Higher Education, Jefferson City, Mo.

John Lewis Campbell, Online Services Coordinator, Univ. of Georgia Libraries, Athens.

Robert A. Campbell, Senior Software Engineer, CIS Department, Weber State Univ., Ogden, Utah.

Esther Jane Carrier, Reference Librarian, Lock Haven Univ. of Pennsylvania, Lock Haven.

James A. Casada, Professor of History, Winthrop College, Rock Hill, S.C.

G. A. Cevasco, Assoc. Professor of English, St. John's Univ., Jamaica, N.Y.

Bert Chapman, Reference/Documents Librarian, Mary and John Gray Library, Lamar Univ., Beaumont, Tex.

John Y. Cheung, Assoc. Professor, Univ. of Oklahoma, Norman.

Boyd Childress, Reference Librarian, Ralph B. Draughon Library, Auburn Univ., Ala.

Eric H. Christianson, Assoc. Professor of History, Univ. of Kentucky, Lexington.

Paul F. Clark, Assoc. Professor, Pennsylvania State Univ., University Park.

Harriette M. Cluxton, formerly Director of Medical Library Services, Illinois Masonic Medical Center, Chicago.

Gary R. Cocozzoli, Director of the Library, Lawrence Technological Univ., Southfield, Mich.

Donald E. Collins, Assoc. Professor, Dept. of Library and Information Studies, East Carolina Univ., Greenville, N.C.

Barbara Conroy, Career Connections, Santa Fe, N.Mex.

Kay O. Cornelius, formerly Teacher and Magnet School Lead Teacher, Huntsville City Schools, Ala.

Paul B. Cors, Catalog Librarian, Univ. of Wyoming, Laramie.

Brian E. Coutts, Head, Dept. of Library Public Services, Helm-Cravens Library, Western Kentucky Univ., Bowling Green.

Richard J. Cox, Lecturer, Univ. of Pittsburgh, Pa.

Kathleen W. Craver, Head Librarian, National Cathedral School, Washington, D.C.

Milton H. Crouch, Asst. Director for Reader Services, Bailey/Howe Library, Univ. of Vermont, Burlington.

Gregory Curtis, Reference Librarian, Univ. of Maine, Presque Isle.

C. B. (Bob) Darrell, Professor of English and Dept. Chair, Kentucky Wesleyan College, Owensboro.

Joseph W. Dauben, Professor of History and History of Science, City Univ. of New York.

Donald G. Davis, Jr., Professor, Graduate School of Library and Information Science, Univ. of Texas, Austin.

Elisabeth B. Davis, Biology Librarian, Univ. of Illinois, Urbana.

Estelle A. Davis, Reference Librarian and Assistant Professor, Science/Engineering Library, City College of the City Univ. of New York.

Dominique-Rene de Lerma, Director, Center for Black Music Research, Columbia College, Chicago.

Bonnie A. Dede, Head, Special Formats Cataloging, Univ. of Michigan Library, Ann Arbor.

Anna L. DeMiller, Social Sciences/Humanities Librarian, Morgan Library, Colorado State Univ., Ft. Collins.

Elie M. Dick, Director of Business Development, ISCO, Inc., Lincoln, Neb.

Donald C. Dickinson, Professor, Graduate Library School, Univ. of Arizona, Tucson.

John B. Dillon, European Humanities Bibliographer, Memorial Library, Univ of Wisconsin, Madison.

Carol A. Doll, Asst. Professor, Graduate School of Library and Information Science, Univ. of Washington, Seattle.

Margaret F. Dominy, Head, Mathematics-Physics-Astronomy Library, Univ. of Pennsylvania, Philadelphia.

Edith M. Dorenfeld, School Psychologist, Denver Public Schools, Colo.

G. Kim Dority, Editorial Director, Jones 21st Century, Englewood, Colo.

Karen Markey Drabenstott, Asst. Professor, School of Information and Library Studies, Univ. of Michigan, Ann Arbor.

Joe P. Dunn, Charles A. Dana Professor of History & Politics, Converse College, Spartanburg, S.C.

Susan Ebershoff-Coles, Supervisor, Technical Services, Indianapolis-Marion County Public Library, Ind.

David Eggenberger, Freelance Writer and Editor, Vienna, Va.

Marie Ellis, English and American Literature Bibliographer, Univ. of Georgia Libraries, Athens.

Claire England, Assoc. Professor, Faculty of Library & Information Science, Univ. of Toronto.

Jonathon Erlen, Curator, History of Medicine, Univ. of Pittsburgh, Pa.

G. Edward Evans, Univ. Librarian, Charles Von der Ahe Library, Loyola Marymount Univ., Los Angeles, Calif.

Andrew Ezergailis, Professor of History, Ithaca College, N.Y.

Ian Fairclough, Music Cataloger, Ball State Univ., Muncie, Ind.

Joyce Duncan Falk, Independent Scholar, Santa Barbara, Calif.

Kathleen Farago, Reference Librarian, Lakewood Public Library, Ohio.

Evan Ira Farber, Librarian, Lilly Library, Earlham College, Richmond, Ind.

Megan S. Farrell, Collection Development Librarian and Asst. Professor, Dupre Library, Univ. of Southwestern Louisiana, Lafayette.

Adele M. Fasick, Dean and Professor, School of Library and Information Science, Univ. of Toronto.

Robin Riley Fast, Assoc. Professor, Division of Writing, Literature, and Publishing, Emerson College, Boston.

Eleanor Ferrall, Librarian Emerita, Arizona State Univ., Tempe.

Joan B. Fiscella, Bibliographer for Professional Studies, Library, Univ. of Illinois, Chicago.

Virginia S. Fischer, Reference/Documents Librarian, Univ. of Maine, Presque Isle.

Jerry D. Flack, Assoc. Professor of Education, Univ. of Colorado, Colorado Springs.

Patricia Fleming, Professor, Faculty of Library and Information Science, Univ. of Toronto.

Michael A. Foley, Honors Director, Marywood College, Scranton, Pa.

Harold O. Forshey, Assoc. Dean, Miami University, Oxford, Ohio.

A. David Franklin, Professor of Music, Winthrop Univ., Rock Hill, S.C.

David K. Frasier, Asst. Librarian, Reference Dept., Indiana Univ., Bloomington.

Suzanne G. Frayser, Social Science Research Consultant and Faculty, Univ. College, Univ. of Denver, Colo.

Sarah A. Freegard, Dept. of Library and Information Science, Northern Illinois Univ., De Kalb.

Susan J. Freiband, Assoc. Professor, Graduate School of Librarianship, Univ. of Puerto Rico, San Juan.

David O. Friedrichs, Professor, Univ. of Scranton, Pa.

Jeanne Friedrichs, Asst. Professor of Occupational Therapy, College Misericordia, Dallas, Pa.

Ronald H. Fritze, Assoc. Professor, Dept. of History, Lamar Univ., Beaumont, Tex.

Ahmad Gamaluddin, Professor, School of Library Science, Clarion State College, Pa.

Joan Garner, Staff, Libraries Unlimited, Inc.

Gregg S. Geary, Music Librarian, Sinclair Library, Univ. of Hawaii, Manoa, Honolulu.

Edwin S. Gleaves, State Librarian and Archivist, Tennessee State Library and Archives, Nashville.

Maya B. Gokhale, Research Staff, Supercomputing Research Center, Bowie, Md.

Lisha E. Goldberg, Technical Writer, Safety Insurance Co., Boston.

Harold Goldwhite, Professor of Chemistry, California State Univ., Los Angeles.

Helen M. Gothberg, Assoc. Professor, Graduate Library School, Univ. of Arizona, Tucson.

Allie Wise Goudy, Professor, Western Illinois Univ., Macomb.

M. Patrick Graham, Reference Librarian, Pitts Theology Library, Emory Univ., Atlanta, Ga.

Marilynn Green, Sciences Reference Librarian, Information Service Dept., Univ. of Houston Libraries, Tex.

Leonard J. Greenspoon, Professor of Religion, Clemson Univ., S.C.

Richard W. Grefrath, Reference Librarian, Univ. of Nevada, Reno.

Arthur Gribben, Professor, Union Institute, Los Angeles, Calif.

Margaret A. Grift, formerly Public Service Librarian, Redeemer College, Ancaster, Ont.

Janice M. Griggs, Mathematics Librarian, Univ. of Minneapolis, Minn.

Jacqueline L. Grossman, Asst. Librarian, Information Services, Littler, Mendelson, Fastiff and Tichy, San Francisco, Calif.

Laurel Grotzinger, Professor, University Libraries, Western Michigan Univ., Kalamazoo.

Stephen Haenel, Staff, Libraries Unlimited, Inc.

Blaine H. Hall, English Language & Literature Librarian, Harold B. Lee Library, Brigham Young Univ., Provo, Utah.

Deborah Hammer, Head, History, Travel and Biography Division, Queens Borough Public Library, Jamaica, N.Y.

Joseph Hannibal, Curator of Invertebrate Paleontology, Cleveland Museum of Natural History, Ohio.

Roberto P. Haro, Director and Professor, Monterey County Campus, San Jose State Univ., Salinas, Calif.

Chauncy D. Harris, Samuel N. Harper Distinguished Service Professor Emeritus of Geography, Univ. of Chicago.

Marvin K. Harris, Professor of Entomology, Texas A & M Univ., College Station.

S. L. Harrison, Assoc. Professor and Coordinator, Advertising Communication and Public Relations, Univ. of Miami, Fla.

Ann Hartness, Asst. Head Librarian, Benson Latin American Collection, Univ. of Texas, Austin.

Joy Hastings, Manager, Technical Library, Hunt-Wesson, Inc., Fullerton, Calif.

Robert J. Havlik, Librarian Emeritus and Exhibit Coordinator, Univ. of Notre Dame, Ind.

Fred J. Hay, Reference and Acquisition Librarian, Tozzer Library, Harvard Univ., Cambridge, Mass.

James S. Heller, Director of the Law Library and Assoc. Professor of Law, Marshall-Wythe Law Library, College of William and Mary, Williamsburg, Va.

David Henige, African Studies Bibliographer, Memorial Library, Univ. of Wisconsin, Madison.

Jean Herold, Business Librarian, General Libraries, Univ. of Texas, Austin.

Mark Y. Herring, Dean of Libraries, Oklahoma Baptist Univ., Shawnee, Okla.

Susan Davis Herring, Reference Librarian, Univ. of Alabama Library, Huntsville.

Janet Swan Hill, Assoc. Director for Technical Services, Univ. Libraries, Univ. of Colorado, Boulder.

Robert Clyde Hodges, formerly Instructor, Univ. of Kentucky, Lexington.

Richard E. Holl, Asst. Professor, History Dept., Lees College, Jackson, Ky.

Deborah D. Hollis, formerly Reference Librarian, Bemis Public Library, Littleton, Colo.

Susan Tower Hollis, Professor, Union Institute, Los Angeles, Calif.

Shirley L. Hopkinson, Professor, Division of Library and Information Science, San Jose State Univ., Calif.

Renee B. Horowitz, Professor, Dept. of Technology, College of Engineering, Arizona State Univ., Tempe.

Valerie R. Hotchkiss, Director, Stitt Library, Austin Presbyterian Theological Seminary, Austin, Tex.

Helen Howard, Assoc. Professor, Graduate School of Library and Information Studies, McGill Univ., Montreal.

Carmel A. Huestis, Editor, Fulcrum, Inc., Golden, Colo.

William E. Hug, Professor, University of Georgia, Athens.

John H. Hunter, Reference/Collection Development Librarian, Fondren Library, Rice Univ., Houston, Tex.

C. D. Hurt, Director, Graduate Library School, Univ. of Arizona, Tucson.

Ludmila N. Ilyina, Professor, Natural Resources Institute, Univ. of Manitoba, Winnipeg.

David Isaacson, Asst. Head of Reference and Humanities Librarian, Waldo Library, Western Michigan Univ., Kalamazoo.

Barbara Ittner, Staff, Libraries Unlimited, Inc.

John A. Jackman, Extension Entomologist, Texas A & M Univ., College Station.

Eugene B. Jackson, Professor Emeritus, Graduate School of Library and Information Science, Univ. of Texas, Austin.

D. Barton Johnson, Professor Emeritus of Russian, Univ. of California, Santa Barbara.

Jennie S. Johnson, Reference Librarian, Carlson Library, Univ. of Toledo, Ohio.

Richard D. Johnson, Director of Libraries, James M. Milne Library, State Univ. College, Oneonta, N.Y.

Dorothy E. Jones, Reference Librarian and Coordinator of Library Services for Persons with Disabilities, Founders Memorial Library, Northern Illinois Univ., De Kalb.

Raymond E. Jones, Assoc. Professor of English, Univ. of Alberta, Edmonton.

Robert L. Jones, Assoc. Professor, Dept. of Family and Community Medicine, Pennsylvania State College of Medicine, Hershey.

Rebecca Jordan, Asst. Professor of English, Wilkes Univ., Wilkes-Barre, Pa.

J. C. Jurgens, Reference Librarian, Northeastern Illinois Univ., Chicago.

Thomas A. Karel, Assoc. Director for Public Services, Shadek-Fackenthal Library, Franklin and Marshall College, Lancaster, Pa.

Edmund D. Keiser, Jr., Professor of Biology, Univ. of Mississippi, University.

John Laurence Kelland, Reference Bibliographer for Life Sciences, Univ. of Rhode Island Library, Kingston.

Dean H. Keller, Assoc. Dean of Libraries, Kent State Univ., Ohio.

Barbara E. Kemp, Consultant, Software AG of North America, Reston, Va.

Cheryl Kern-Simirenko, Asst. Univ. Librarian for Collection Development and Resource Services, Univ. of Oregon Library, Eugene.

Jackson Kesler, Professor of Theatre and Dance, Western Kentucky Univ., Bowling Green.

Vicki J. Killion, Asst. Professor of Library Science and Pharmacy, Nursing and Health Sciences Librarian, Purdue Univ., West Lafayette, Ind.

Norman L. Kincaide, Citation Editor, Shepard's/McGraw-Hill, Inc., Colorado Springs, Colo.

Christine E. King, Reference Librarian, State Univ. of New York, Stony Brook.

Mary Ellen Kollar, Librarian III, Business, Economics, and Labor Dept., Cleveland Public Library, Ohio.

Zsuzsa Koltay, Coordinator of Electronic Reference Services, Bowling Green State Univ., Ohio.

Johan Koren, Lecturer, Library Science Program, Wayne State Univ., Detroit.

Betsy J. Kraus, Librarian/Technical Editor, Environmental Evaluation Group, Albuquerque.

Linda A. Krikos, Head, Women's Studies Library, Ohio State Univ., Columbus.

Colby H. Kullman, Assoc. Professor and Editor, *Studies in American Drama*, Univ. of Mississippi, University.

Peter B. Kutner, Professor of Law, Univ. of Oklahoma, Norman.

R. Errol Lam, Reference Librarian, Bowling Green State Univ., Ohio.

Sharon Langworthy, Production Supervisor/Supplement Editor, Wiley Law Publications, Colorado Springs, Colo.

Renee J. LaPerriere, formerly Reference Librarian, Golden Library, Eastern New Mexico Univ., Portales.

Mary Larsgaard, Asst. Head, Map and Imagery Laboratory Library, Univ. of California, Santa Barbara.

John R. M. Lawrence, Reference and Interlibrary Loan Librarian, College of William and Mary, Williamsburg, Va.

Binh P. Le, Reference Librarian, Pennsylvania State Univ./Ogontz, Abington.

Charles Leck, Professor of Biological Sciences, Rutgers Univ., New Brunswick.

Mary Lou LeCompte, Asst. Professor, Kinesiology and Health Education, Univ. of Texas at Austin.

Hwa-Wei Lee, Dean of Libraries, Ohio Univ., Athens.

Joann H. Lee, formerly Head of Reader Services, Lake Forest College, Ill.

R. S. Lehmann, Rocky Mountain BankCard System, Colorado National Bank, Denver.

Richard A. Leiter, Director and Assoc. Professor of Law, Regent Univ., Virginia Beach, Va.

Bart Lewis, Arts and Sciences, California State Univ., San Marcos, Calif.

Tze-chung Li, Professor, Graduate School of Library and Information Science, Rosary College, River Forest, Ill.

Charlotte Lindgren, Professor Emerita of English, Emerson College, Boston.

Koraljka Lockhart, Publications Editor, San Francisco Opera, Calif.

David V. Loertscher, Staff, Libraries Unlimited, Inc.

Elisabeth Logan, Assoc. Professor, School of Library and Information Studies, Florida State Univ., Tallahassee.

David Lonergan, Librarian, Founders Memorial Library, Northern Illinois Univ., De Kalb.

Jeffrey R. Luttrell, Leader, Humanities Cataloging Team, Princeton Univ. Library, N.J.

Marit S. MacArthur, Serials Cataloger, Auraria Libraries, Univ. of Colorado, Denver.

Sara R. Mack, Professor Emerita, Dept. of Library Science, Kutztown Univ., Pa.

Theresa Maggio, Head of Public Services, Southwest Georgia Regional Library, Bainbridge.

Linda Main, Assoc. Professor, San Jose State Univ., Calif.

Cheryl Knott Malone, History, Government, American Studies, and Australian Studies Bibliographer, General Libraries, Univ. of Texas, Austin.

Judy Gay Matthews, Staff, Libraries Unlimited, Inc.

J. Francis Mattil, President, Climatran Corp., Aurora, Colo.

George Louis Mayer, formerly Senior Principal Librarian, New York Public Library and Part-time Librarian, Adelphi, Manhattan Center and Brooklyn College, N.Y.

James R. McDonald, Professor of Geography, Eastern Michigan Univ., Ypsilanti.

Robert B. McKee, Professor, Mechanical Engineering, Univ. of Nevada, Reno.

Susan V. McKimm, Business Reference Specialist, Cuyahoga County Library System, Maple Heights, Ohio.

T. McKimmie, Reference Librarian, New Mexico State Univ., Las Cruces.

Margaret McKinley, (deceased) Head, Serials Dept., Univ. Library, Univ. of California, Los Angeles.

Marian B. McLeod, Professor of Speech Communication and Theater, Trenton State College, N.J.

Margo B. Mead, Asst. Professor, Library, Univ. of Alabama, Huntsville.

Lillian R. Mesner, Technical Services Librarian, Agricultural Library, Univ. of Kentucky, Lexington.

Michael G. Messina, Assoc. Professor, Dept. of Forest Science, Texas A&M Univ., College Station.

Philip A. Metzger, Curator of Special Collections and Director, Lehigh Univ. Press, Lehigh Univ., Bethlehem, Pa.

Bogdan Mieczkowski, Professor of Economics, Ithaca College, N.Y.

Seiko Mieczkowski, Hobart & William Smith Colleges, Geneva, N.Y.

Zbigniew Mieczkowski, Assoc. Professor, Dept. of Geography, Univ. of Manitoba, Winnipeg.

Edward P. Miller, Payson Public Library, Ariz.

Jerome K. Miller, formerly President, Copyright Information Services, Friday Harbor, Wash.

Richard A. Miller, Professor of Economics, Wesleyan Univ., Middletown, Conn.

Janet Mongan, Research Officer, Cleveland State Univ. Library, Ohio.

Terry Ann Mood, Humanities Bibliographer, Univ. of Colorado, Denver.

Gerald D. Moran, Librarian, Geneva College, Beaver Falls, Pa.

P. Grady Morein, Director of Libraries, Univ. of West Florida, Pensacola.

K. Mulliner, Asst. to the Director of Libraries, Ohio Univ. Library, Athens.

James M. Murray, Director, East Bonner County Library, Sandpoint, Idaho.

Linda A. Naru, Planning and Development Officer, Center for Research Libraries, Chicago.

Charles Neuringer, Professor of Psychology and Theatre and Film, Univ. of Kansas, Lawrence.

Danuta A. Nitecki, Assoc. Director for Public Services, Univ. of Maryland Libraries, College Park.

Joseph Z. Nitecki, Professor Emeritus, School of Information Science and Policy, State Univ. of New York, Albany.

Eric R. Nitschke, Reference Librarian, Robert W. Woodruff Library, Emory Univ., Atlanta, Ga.

Christopher W. Nolan, Head, Reference Services, Maddux Library, Trinity Univ., San Antonio, Tex.

Carol L. Noll, Treasurer and Board Member, Tinton Falls Public Library, N.J.

O. Gene Norman, Head, Reference Dept., Indiana State Univ. Libraries, Terre Haute.

Marilyn Strong Noronha, Reference Librarian, Harleigh B. Trecker Library, Univ. of Connecticut, West Hartford.

Marshall E. Nunn, Professor, Dept. of History, Glendale Community College, Calif.

Herbert W. Ockerman, Professor, Ohio State Univ., Columbus.

Heidi Ann Olinger, Staff, Libraries Unlimited, Inc.

Berniece M. Owen, Coordinator, Library Technical Services, Portland Community College, Oreg.

John Howard Oxley, Halifax, N.S.

Mark Padnos, Adjunct Reference Librarian, Hunter College, City Univ. of New York.

Joseph W. Palmer, Assoc. Professor, School of Information and Library Studies, State Univ. of New York, Buffalo.

Robert Palmieri, Professor Emeritus, School of Music, Kent State Univ., Ohio.

Anna Grace Patterson, Staff, Libraries Unlimited, Inc.

Elizabeth Patterson, Head, Reference and Computer Reference Services, Robert W. Woodruff Library, Emory Univ., Atlanta, Ga.

Gari-Anne Patzwald, Freelance Editor and Indexer, Lexington, Ky.

Harry E. Pence, Professor of Chemistry, State Univ. of New York, Oneonta.

Karin Pendle, Professor of Musicology, Univ. of Cincinnati, Ohio.

Edwin D. Posey, Engineering Librarian, Purdue Univ. Libraries, West Lafayette, Ind.

Daphne Fallieros Potter, Database Specialist, American Mathematical Society, Providence, R.I.

Phillip P. Powell, Asst. Reference Librarian, Robert Scott Small Library, College of Charleston, S.C.

Ann E. Prentice, Assoc. Vice President for Library and Information Resources, Univ. of South Florida, Tampa.

William S. Proudfoot, Aptos, Calif.

Marilyn R. Pukkila, Reference Librarian, Colby College, Waterville, Maine.

Randall Rafferty, Reference Librarian, Mississippi State Univ. Library, Mississippi State.

Kristin Ramsdell, Assoc. Librarian, California State Univ., Hayward.

Lise Rasmussen, Reference Librarian, Dowling College, Oakdale, N.Y.

Jack Ray, Asst. Director, Loyola/Notre Dame Library, Baltimore, Md.

Shulamit Reinharz, Assoc. Professor, Dept. of Sociology and Director, Women's Studies, Brandeis Univ., Waltham, Mass.

James Rettig, Asst. Univ. Librarian for Reference and Information Services, Swem Library, College of William and Mary, Williamsburg, Va.

Diane B. Rhodes, Life Sciences and Agriculture Librarian, Arizona State Univ., Tempe.

Henry J. Ricardo, formerly Program Manager, IBM Corporation, Somers, N.Y.

Jo Anne H. Ricca, Staff, Libraries Unlimited, Inc.

Anne F. Roberts, Adjunct Professor, School of Education, State Univ. of New York, Albany.

William B. Robison, Asst. Professor, History, Southeastern Louisiana Univ., Hammond.

Ilene F. Rockman, Interim Assoc. Dean of Library Services, California Polytechnic State Univ., San Luis Obispo.

Anne C. Roess, Librarian, Peoples Gas, Light & Coke Co., Chicago.

JoAnn V. Rogers, Professor, College of Library and Information Science, Univ. of Kentucky, Lexington.

Deborah V. Rollins, Reference Librarian, Univ. of Maine, Orono.

Bertram H. Rothschild, Asst. Chief of Psychology, V.A. Medical Center, Denver, Colo.

D. A. Rothschild, Staff, Libraries Unlimited, Inc.

Marilyn Rothschild, School Psychologist, Denver Public Schools, Colo.

Samuel Rothstein, Professor Emeritus, School of Librarianship, Univ. of British Columbia, Vancouver.

Emanuel D. Rudolph, Professor of Botany, Ohio State Univ., Columbus.

Louis R. Ruybal, Project Editor, ABC-Clio, Denver, Colo.

Gabriel P. Sabadell, Staff Design Engineer, Environmental Services Group, Morrison Knudsen Corp., Denver, Colo..

Edmund F. SantaVicca, Head, Reference Services, Hayden Library, Arizona State Univ., Tempe.

Jay Schafer, Coordinator of Collections, Auraria Library, Denver, Colo.

Diane Schmidt, Asst. Biology Librarian, Univ. of Illinois, Urbana.

Steven J. Schmidt, Assoc. Librarian, Indiana Univ.-Purdue Univ. at Indianapolis Libraries.

Willa Schmidt, Reference Librarian, Univ. of Wisconsin, Madison.

John P. Schmitt, Head, Social Sciences and Humanities Dept., Morgan Library, Colorado State Univ., Ft. Collins.

Isabel Schon, Director, Center for the Study of Books in Spanish, California State Univ., San Marcos.

Ralph Lee Scott, Assoc. Professor, East Carolina Univ. Library, Greenville, N.C.

Richard A. Scott, Director, Morrison Natural History Museum, Colo.

Robert A. Seal, Director of Libraries, Univ. of Texas, El Paso.

Margretta Reed Seashore, Professor of Genetics and Pediatrics, Yale Univ. School of Medicine, New Haven, Conn.

Charlie Seavey, Univ. of Arizona, Tucson.

Ravindra Nath Sharma, Library Director, Univ. of Evansville, Ind.

Patricia Tipton Sharp, Professor of Curriculum and Instruction, Baylor Univ., Waco, Tex.

Bruce A. Shuman, Assoc. Professor, Library Science Program, Wayne State Univ., Detroit.

Stephanie C. Sigala, Head Librarian, Richardson Memorial Library, St. Louis Art Museum, Mo.

Robert Skinner, Library Network Resource Manager, Alliance for Higher Education, Dallas, Tex.

Jeanette C. Smith, Head, Government Documents, New Mexico State Univ. Library, Las Cruces.

Linda Sue Smith, Staff, Libraries Unlimited, Inc.

Nathan M. Smith, Director, School of Library and Information Sciences, Brigham Young Univ., Provo, Utah.

Natalia Sonevytsky, Head, Reference Dept., Barnard College Library, New York.

Lev I. Soudek, Professor of English Linguistics and Coordinator, Programs in Linguistics and TESOL, Northern Illinois Univ., De Kalb.

Karen Y. Stabler, Head of Information Services, New Mexico State Univ. Library, Las Cruces.

Mary J. Stanley, Acting Head of Periodicals/Liaison to the School of Social Work, Indiana Univ.-Purdue Univ. at Indianapolis.

Allen E. Staver, Assoc. Professor, Dept. of Geography, Northern Illinois Univ., De Kalb.

James Edgar Stephenson, Cataloger, Society of the Cincinnati Library, Washington, D.C.

Norman D. Stevens, Director, Univ. of Connecticut Libraries, Storrs.

John P. Stierman, Reference Librarian, Western Illinois Univ., Macomb.

John W. Storey, Professor of History, Lamar Univ., Beaumont, Tex.

William C. Struning, Professor, Seton Hall Univ., South Orange, N.J.

Bruce Stuart, Assoc. Professor of Health Administration, Pennsylvania State Univ., University Park.

Timothy E. Sullivan, Asst. Professor of Economics, Towson State Univ., Md.

Richard H. Swain, Head of Reference, Fogler Library, Univ. of Maine, Orono.

James H. Sweetland, Assoc. Professor, School of Library and Information Science, Univ. of Wisconsin, Milwaukee.

Nigel Tappin, General Librarian, North York Public Library, North York, Ont.

Deborah A. Taylor, Staff, Libraries Unlimited, Inc.

Lori Elaine Taylor, Asst. Archivist, Smithsonian Institution Office of Folklife Programs, Washington, D.C.

Glynys R. Thomas, Public Services and Bibliographic Instruction Librarian, Emerson College Library, Boston.

Christine E. Thompson, Head, Catalog Department and Assoc. Professor, Univ. of Alabama Libraries, Tuscaloosa.

Mary Ann Thompson, Asst. Professor of Nursing, Saint Joseph College, West Hartford, Conn.

Angela Marie Thor, Information Consultant, Syracuse, N.Y.

Bruce H. Tiffney, Assoc. Professor of Geology and Biological Sciences, Univ. of California, Santa Barbara.

Andrew G. Torok, Assoc. Professor, Northern Illinois Univ., De Kalb.

John U. Trefny, Head and Professor, Dept. of Physics, Colorado School of Mines, Golden.

Ben B. Trotter, Lecturer, Texas Tech Univ., Lubbock.

Carol Truett, Assoc. Professor, Appalachian State Univ., Boone, N.C.

John Mark Tucker, Senior Reference Librarian, Humanities, Social Science and Education Library, Purdue Univ., West Lafayette, Ind.

Dean Tudor, Professor, School of Journalism, Ryerson Polytechnical Institute, Toronto.

Diane J. Turner, Science/Engineering Liaison, Auraria Library, University of Colorado, Denver.

Robert L. Turner, Jr., Librarian and Asst. Professor, Radford Univ., Va.

Arthur R. Upgren, Professor of Astronomy and Director, Van Vleck Observatory, Wesleyan Univ., Middletown, Conn.

Phyllis J. Van Orden, Professor, Library Science Program, Wayne State Univ., Detroit.

Vandelia L. VanMeter, Assoc. Professor and Chair, Department of Library and Information Science, Spalding Univ., Louisville, Ky.

Carol J. Veitch, Regional Library Director, Montgomery-Floyd Regional Library, Christiansburg, Va.

Dario J. Villa, Reference Librarian/Bibliographer, Ronald Williams Library, Northeastern Illinois Univ., Chicago.

Kathleen J. Voigt, Head, Reference Dept., Carlson Library, Univ. of Toledo, Ohio.

Abu N. M. Wahid, Asst. Professor of Economics, Eastern Illinois Univ., Charleston.

Mary Jo Walker, Special Collections Librarian, Eastern New Mexico Univ., Portales.

Lydia W. Wasylenko, Assoc. Librarian, Syracuse Univ. Library, N.Y.

Jean Weihs, Principal Consultant, Technical Services Group, Toronto.

Bella Hass Weinberg, Assoc. Professor, Division of Library and Information Science, St. John's Univ., Jamaica, N.Y.

Darlene E. Weingand, Assoc. Professor, Univ. of Wisconsin, Madison.

Lucille Whalen, Dean of Graduate Programs, Immaculate Heart College Center, Los Angeles, Calif.

Robert A. Wharton, Professor, Dept. of Entomology, Texas A&M Univ, College Station.

Carol Wheeler, Government Documents Reference Librarian, Univ. of Georgia Libraries, Athens.

Cathy Seitz Whitaker, Social Work Librarian, Hillman Library, Univ. of Pittsburgh, Pa.

David L. White, Professor, History Dept., Appalachian State Univ., Boone, N.C.

George M. White, Assoc. Professor, Univ. of Ottawa.

William H. Wiese, Science and Reference Librarian, Parks Library, Iowa State Univ., Ames.

Dorothy M. Williams, Instructor, English/Communications, Front Range Community College, Westminster, Colo.

Lynn F. Williams, Professor, Division of Writing, Literature, and Publishing, Emerson College, Boston.

Robert V. Williams, Assoc. Professor, College of Library and Information Science, Univ. of South Carolina, Columbia.

Wiley J. Williams, Professor Emeritus, School of Library Science, Kent State Univ., Ohio.

Liz Willis, Reference Librarian, Auraria Library, Denver, Colo.

Frank L. Wilson, Professor and Head, Dept. of Political Science, Purdue Univ., West Lafayette, Ind.

Patricia S. Wilson, Public Services Librarian, Agriculture Library, Univ. of Kentucky, Lexington.

Wayne Wilson, Director, Research and Library Services, Amateur Athlete Foundation, Los Angeles, Calif.

Celia J. Wintz, Faculty, Houston Community College, Tex.

Glenn R. Wittig, Director of Library Services, Criswell College, Dallas, Tex.

Randy M. Wood, Assoc. Professor, Baylor Univ., Waco, Tex.

Raymund F. Wood, Editor, *The Westerners*, Encino, Calif.

Hensley C. Woodbridge, Professor of Spanish, Dept. of Foreign Languages, Southern Illinois Univ., Carbondale.

Dorothy C. Woodson, Social Sciences Bibliographer, State Univ. of New York, Buffalo.

Kieth C. Wright, Professor, Library and Information Studies, Univ. of North Carolina, Greensboro.

Bohdan S. Wynar, Staff, Libraries Unlimited, Inc.

Lubomyr R. Wynar, Professor, School of Library Science and Director, Center for Ethnic Studies, Kent State Univ., Ohio.

Martha Miller Yazhari, Belle Mead, N.J.

A. Neil Yerkey, Assoc. Professor, School of Information and Library Studies, State Univ. of New York, Buffalo.

Henry E. York, Head, Collection Management, Cleveland State Univ., Ohio.

Arthur P. Young, Dean of Univ. Libraries, Univ. of South Carolina, Columbia.

Louis G. Zelenka, Public Services Librarian, Southwest Georgia Regional Library, Bainbridge.

L. Zgusta, Professor of Linguistics and the Classics and Member of the Center for Advanced Study, Univ. of Illinois, Urbana.

Oleg Zinam, Professor of Economics, Univ. of Cincinnati, Ohio.

Anita Zutis, Adjunct Librarian, Queensborough Community College, Bayside, N.Y.

Journals Cited

FORM OF CITATION	JOURNAL TITLE
BL	Booklist
BR	Book Report
Choice	Choice
C&RL	College & Research Libraries
CLJ	Canadian Library Journal
EL	Emergency Librarian
JAL	Journal of Academic Librarianship
JOYS	Journal of Youth Services in Libraries
LAR	Library Association Record
LJ	Library Journal
RBB	Reference Books Bulletin
RQ	RQ
SBF	Science Books & Films
SLJ	School Library Journal
SLMQ	School Library Media Quarterly
VOYA	Voice of Youth Advocates
WLB	Wilson Library Bulletin

Part I
GENERAL REFERENCE WORKS

1 General Reference Works

ACRONYMS AND ABBREVIATIONS

1. **Acronyms, Initialisms & Abbreviations Dictionary 1992, Volume 1: A Guide to More Than 520,000 Acronyms, Initialisms, Abbreviations, Contractions, Alphabetic Symbols, and Similar Condensed Appellations.** 16th ed. Jennifer Mossman and others, eds. Detroit, Gale, 1991. 3pts. $215.00/set. LC 84-643188. ISBN 0-8103-5077-7. ISSN 0270-4404.

With 520,000 entries that include 20,000 new terms, this set has comprehensive coverage of acronyms, initialisms, and abbreviations from many different aspects of life. Subjects include everything from aviation to trade shows. There is a slight distinction among the three terms. An *acronym* is defined as having the initial letters or parts of a compound term; an *initialism* is essentially the same, but each letter is verbalized; and an *abbreviation* is a shortened form of a word. As pointed out in an earlier review (see ARBA 88, entry 1), a parenthetical identifier increases the usefulness of each explanation.

Each entry in the set may contain the following elements in addition to the acronym, initialism, or abbreviation: meaning of phrase, translation into English, language (if not English), source code, location or country origin, sponsoring organization, and subject category. Arrangement is letter-by-letter, and if the category has more than one meaning, the subcategories are arranged word-by-word.

With the increasing use of acronyms, initialisms, and abbreviations in everyday conversation, these volumes will enable users to be more aware of the meanings and the uses of these terms. If this work is not the best available, it is certainly close. Recommended for any library that can afford it.
—**Anna Grace Patterson**

2. Buttress, F. A. **World Guide to Abbreviations of Organizations.** 9th ed. Revised by H. J. Heaney. London, Blackie; distr., Detroit, Gale, 1991. 875p. $140.00. 060.14. LC 87-072491. ISBN 0-8103-5544-2.

World Guide is a basic volume for any library that seeks to support a reference function. Consisting of more than 50,000 alphabetically arranged entries, this edition has at least two improvements over the 1988 one. First, there is now cross-referencing between a defunct organization and its successor. Second, more equivalences that link acronyms in different languages for the same organization have been added. All in all, this is a reliable reference work; no errors were found.—**Richard J. Cox**

3. **The Oxford Dictionary of Abbreviations.** New York, Clarendon Press/Oxford University Press, 1992. 397p. $29.95. ISBN 0-19-869172-6.

This well-done, useful abbreviations dictionary will make a good selection for homes and small to medium-sized libraries that are not able to afford the more comprehensive *Acronyms, Initialisms & Abbreviations Dictionary* (see index for entry number). Entries cover a wide range of colloquial, popular, slang, general, and subject-related abbreviations, acronyms, initialisms, shortenings, and symbols for everything from popular catchphrases and general terms to sports and economics. A selection of symbols that are not formed from the letters of the Roman alphabet is given in the appendix. Foreign terms are included, particularly those expected to be encountered by people traveling abroad. Entries are labeled according to nationality or subject field when pertinent. The dictionary also contains some entries of historical interest.—**Donald E. Collins**

ALMANACS

4. **The Guinness Book of Answers.** 8th ed. Clive Carpenter and Tina Persaud, eds. New York, Facts on File, 1991. 768p. maps. index. $19.95. 032.02. ISBN 0-85112-957-9.

With its distinctly British perspective on the world, this latest edition of a ready-reference compendium contains a wealth of information. More than 70 contributors have supplied updated data pertinent to a variety of broad and specific topics. Major sections cover space and time; the Earth; life and physical sciences; technology, industry, and transport; beliefs and ideas; language and literature; visual and performing arts; history; the economic world; the international world; sport; and the United Kingdom. The latter category provides an excellent summary of information relevant to U.K. political geography, history, government, economy, law and law enforcement, defense, transportation, education, religion, and media. The book is heavily illustrated with charts, maps, and graphs.

Similar in style and arrangement to a variety of almanacs, this work differs in its lack of retrospective statistics and its perspectives on specific topics. With the exception of typical historical lists and chronologies (e.g., kings, world events), all information is descriptive and current. Although North American users must contend with the idiosyncrasies of British spelling, this slight inconvenience is overshadowed by the overall high quality of the work. Very affordable, it will be a welcome addition to any ready-reference collection. [R: RBB, 1 Feb 92, p. 1058]—**Edmund F. SantaVicca**

5. **Webster's II New Riverside Desk Reference.** home and office ed. Boston, Houghton Mifflin, 1992. 471p. index. $7.95. AG6.W33. 031. LC 91-41366. ISBN 0-395-59520-7.

This work may be compared to an almanac that does not have a summary of the major events of the past year. The 1990 U.S. Census is used along with other recent Census charts to present characteristics of the U.S. population. Data for each state includes name of governor and a brief history. Similar information is later provided for each nation. A section on U.S. history and government includes names of presidents, lists of cabinet members (past and present), and members of Congress. The Constitution and other historical U.S. documents are printed in their entirety. The remainder of the volume includes a variety of potentially useful information, such as Social Security and Medicare regulations and programs; lists of the world's largest lakes, highest waterfalls, and principal rivers; commodity production and the value of exports and imports by country; and U.S. colleges and universities with their enrollments and costs.

The information is reliable and current for the year. Sources are usually, but not always, given. There are instances in which labels for charts or sections may be misleading. For example, information in the business and economic section pertains only to the United States. Thus, "10 Largest Commercial Banks" refers to U.S. banks. However, on the opposite page the list called "Top 50 Banks in the World" includes only one U.S. bank. It would seem more appropriate for this to have been placed in the World Statistics section.

Information in the "Countries of the World" section appears to be excerpted from the U.S. Department of State Background Notes series. Much of the information in this book can be found in the *Statistical Abstract of the United States* (Bureau of the Census, annual). The *Desk Reference* is better indexed, however. Additionally, a substantial collection of factual information about foreign countries and useful trivia is assembled under one cover. At its price, this book is a bargain.—**Robert M. Ballard**

6. Whitaker, Joseph. **An Almanac for the Year of Our Lord 1992 [Whitaker's Almanac 1992].** 124th ed. London, J. Whitaker; distr., Detroit, Gale, 1991. 1247p. illus. maps. index. $70.00. ISBN 0-85021-220-0.

Published annually since 1868, *Whitaker's* is a treasure trove of information about the United Kingdom and its institutions: the royal family, peerage, parliament and government, education and legal systems, military, media, religion, and more. There are detailed statistics on such topics as gross national product, trade, employment, agriculture, and transportation. The work contains a large number of addresses and telephone numbers for government agencies, public institutions, associations, the press, and publishers. Other features usually associated with an almanac are present, such as important dates, calendars, astronomy, and tidal tables for the upcoming year. There are informative review articles on literature, drama, opera, dance, film, architecture, archaeology, and science. Although most of the work focuses on the United Kingdom, international material is included. A chronology of world events covers the last two years. Alphabetical sections on the Commonwealth and individual countries contain a wide range of political, geographical, and statistical information. The book concludes with an extensive index. *Whitaker's Almanac* is a useful source for collections where an easy to use ready-reference guide to the United Kingdom is needed and for those that cannot afford more specialized works on that area.—**Christine E. King**

BIBLIOGRAPHY

Bibliographic Guides

7. Barker, Keith, ed. **Information Books for Children.** Brookfield, Vt., Ashgate/Gower Publishing, 1992. 245p. index. $43.95. ISBN 1-85742-023-3.

This guide, arranged by topic according to the Dewey decimal classification, assesses slightly more than 500 current nonfiction works for children of all ages. Ten contributors to *The School Librarian* have provided 150-word signed reviews that include British bibliographical details and suggested age ranges. This book also contains a one-page bibliography of articles on selection; lists of regular annual selection guides and major reviewing journals in the United Kingdom; paragraph-long profiles of eight prominent writers and photographers; and complete author, title, and subject indexes. The reviews give a clear view of the content and merits of each text. Where an inferior book is included because alternatives are unavailable, the review indicates both strengths and limitations.

The only major problem with this guide is that, similar to its companion *Children's Fiction Sourcebook* by Margaret Hobson, Jennifer Madden, and Ray Prytherch (Gower Publishing, 1992), it is designed exclusively for the British market. Most listed titles are not available in American editions. Furthermore, the reviews overlook the needs and interests of North American children. For example, the sports section lists books on cricket and soccer but none on baseball, basketball, hockey, or the Olympic Games. Only two books are listed under American history, one on the Korean War and the other on New England mills. Most librarians will be better served by domestic guides.

—**Raymond E. Jones**

8. **Best Reference Books 1986-1990: Titles of Lasting Value Selected from** *American Reference Books Annual.* G. Kim Dority, comp. Bohdan S. Wynar, ed. Englewood, Colo., Libraries Unlimited, 1992. 544p. index. $67.50. Z1035.1.B5344. 011'.02. LC 91-32043. ISBN 0-87287-936-4.

The 1,211 reference works described in this volume were reviewed in volumes 18-22 of *American Reference Books Annual.* They were selected from 10,692 titles included in those 5 volumes as being of lasting value to libraries of all types. All bibliographic citations and reviews have been updated to include the most recent edition of the work described, and prices are current through June 1991. Entries are arranged in four major parts—general reference sources, social sciences, humanities, and science and technology—and then further divided into 37 subsections, which in turn are subdivided. Each review is numbered, and the author/title and subject indexes are keyed to these numbers. Nearly 400 subject specialists prepared the reviews in this volume and are listed with their affiliations. *Best Reference Books 1986-1990* is an excellent resource for librarians who are building or evaluating a reference collection.—**Dean H. Keller**

9. *Booklist*'s **Guide to the Year's Best Books: Definitive Reviews of Over 1,000 Fiction and Nonfiction Titles in All Fields.** 1992 ed. Bill Ott, ed. Chicago, Triumph Books; distr., Detroit, Gale, 1992. 467p. index. $49.95. LC 92-050110. ISBN 1-880141-07-8.

Far more good books are published in one year than anyone has time to evaluate—hence, the need for a book such as this. For librarians who found *The Book Buyer's Advisor* (Triumph Books, 1990) useful, this first annual supplement can be recommended. The change in title reflects what the volume does rather than for whom it is done.

Similar to its initial edition, this guide to books of a popular nature is meant to serve multiple uses. One hope is that the general reader will purchase it as an aid to buying gifts and to selecting books for personal reading. More realistically, it will be used in public libraries to direct readers to the best current books. Its chief value may be to college/university acquisition librarians who wish to double-check recent accessions or to order works they may have missed for their collections.

The original 7,000-odd reviews that appeared in *Booklist* in 1991 have been whittled down to the 1,000 included here. They are organized under such broad subjects as art, biography, business, cookery, crafts, and film and drama. All contain complete bibliographical information, prices, and ISBN. The best books within each category can be quickly spotted because they are indicated by a check to the left of an author's or editor's name. Author and title indexes further enhance this worthwhile reference tool. [R: LJ, 15 Apr 92, p. 84; SLMQ, Fall 92, p. 74]—**G. A. Cevasco**

10. **Canadian Book Review Annual 1990.** Joyce M. Wilson, ed.; Dean Tudor, founding ed. Toronto, Simon & Pierre, 1991. 572p. index. $98.95. ISBN 0-88924-233-X. ISSN 0383-770X.

Now in its 16th year, this work has maintained the format and high standards commended in previous editions of ARBA (see ARBA 88, entry 5 and ARBA 82, entry 2). It is an annual guide to English-language Canadian imprints (on all subjects) presented in the form of reviews and annotations by specialists. For this edition, close to 300 reviewers, the majority academics and librarians from all 10 provinces, have considered the merits and shortcomings of more than 1,200 new books, mostly trade titles with a scattering of federal government publications and educational materials.

Arrangement is by broad discipline divided by subject or genre. Literature is the largest section with nearly 500 titles of creative and critical work, one-fifth of them children's picture books. A single index provides access by author, title, and subject with reference to item number. Broad subjects are closely divided; for example, "Nature" uses 34 subheadings for 46 references. Many titles are indexed under more than one subject. Literary works are grouped in the index by genre, then subject. The next step in subject access would be an index of the DDC numbers already included in each entry.

Because even an excellent source can be improved, the editors should try to shorten the eight-month gap between the end of the year and the date of publication. They should also work to strengthen the reference materials section. Comparison with the listing of 1990 Canadian reference titles in the *Canadian Library Journal* (February 1991) shows additional items that fall within the scope.—**Patricia Fleming**

11. **Children's Reference Plus.** (1992). [CD-ROM]. New Providence, N.J., R. R. Bowker, 1992. Hardware requirements: IBM PC or compatible, 286 or higher, with at least 535K free memory; hard disk, with at least 10MB free; DOS 3.0 or later; CD-ROM drive running under MS-DOS Extensions. $595.00.

R. R. Bowker has created a family of CD-ROM products, all of which have the same front-end engine designed to search the data on the disc. Children's Reference Plus is a composite source that collects bibliographic information, fulltext book reviews, annotations, and plot summaries from a wide variety of tools published by Bowker and some other publishers. Thus, it aims to be the most comprehensive information source of descriptive and critical information about children's literature ever published.

At first glance, the disc seems more comprehensive than it actually is. The product is a subset of a number of larger databases and reference tools—not the complete tools. Thus, only titles for children and young adults are extracted from *Subject Guide to Books in Print* (see ARBA 92, entry 15), *Books Out-of-Print* (see ARBA 90, entry 15), *Ulrich's International Periodicals Directory* (see index for entry number), *Bowker's Complete Video Directory* (see index for entry number), and *Words on Cassette* (see index for entry numbers). Complete information from *El-Hi Textbooks and Serials in Print* (see ARBA 92, entry 285) and *Fiction, Folklore, Fantasy & Poetry for Children, 1876-1985* (see ARBA 85, entry 1128) is also included. Annotations and reviews are taken from ongoing periodicals, including

Publishers Weekly, Library Journal, School Library Journal, Booklist, and *Kirkus Review.* Additional material is drawn from a wide variety of reference tools published by Bowker, such as *Best Books for Children* (see ARBA 91, entry 1111), *Fantasy Literature for Children and Young Adults* (see ARBA 90, entry 1083), and *More Notes from a Different Drummer* (see ARBA 85, entry 1018). The impression is that the disc contains the complete text of these reference tools. It does not.

Updated quarterly and available by subscription either quarterly or annually, Children's Reference Plus is designed as a selection and acquisition tool for school and public libraries. Access to the data is available through every category in the database and through Boolean searching of combinations of the fields (e.g., title, key word, publisher). Simple searches by title or by author are fairly quick; however, Boolean searches are extremely slow and may take a coffee break to assemble.

As a selection tool, the disc contains reviews from the most popular selection sources but is not comprehensive (there are no *VOYA* or *Book Report* reviews, among others). However, for censorship cases and the selection of specific titles, no other source can provide as quick or comprehensive access to reviews. Libraries building in-depth collections in topical areas will benefit from comprehensive searches across in-print and out-of-print bibliographies and the inclusion of films. If the library is linked to major jobbers electronically, this tool can be used to select and transmit actual orders for books and periodicals. In addition, searches can be downloaded to a word processor for editing and use in local projects as long as normal copyright laws are observed.

The front-end engine of Children's Reference Plus and similar Bowker products is not for the novice. An in-depth reading of the manual must accompany the screen and on-disc help sections if a search is to succeed. Bowker could create a much more friendly interface than exists in the current edition. Because the manual is not reprinted each time a new edition appears, sample searches listed in the manual are not duplicated in practice—a confusing aspect for the novice. It will take a number of hours of practice for the user to become comfortable as a searcher and to begin to understand the power of this tool.

For libraries that can afford this product, Children's Reference Plus is a boon to the selection and acquisition process. As the speed of searching on CD-ROM increases and user interfaces become more friendly, it will become even more essential. Right now, it is still in its infancy.—**David V. Loertscher**

12. **Guide to Reference Books: Covering Materials from 1985-1990. Supplement to the Tenth Edition.** Robert Balay, ed. Chicago, American Library Association, 1992. 613p. index. $85.00. Z1035.1.S43. 011'.02. LC 92-6463. ISBN 0-8389-0588-9.

This work has been reviewed in ARBA on several occasions—the 10th edition in ARBA 87 (see entry 17), the first supplement in ARBA 81 (see entry 3), and the second in ARBA 83 (see entry 5). This is the third supplement; it has been prepared by new editor Balay with the assistance of 36 reference librarians from 11 institutions. It covers 4,668 titles published from December 1984 through the end of 1990. Progress in technology has had its impact on this standard source. The supplement has been prepared from the database that maintains records in machine-readable form and adheres closely to the MARC format, following the AACR2 cataloging code as interpreted by the Library of Congress (LC). It should be noted, however, that there are several exceptions—some records depart from LC practice, and some have been created strictly for the supplement and have no counterpart in present cataloging practice. All this is explained in the preface, and in case of problems, the reader should consult these detailed explanations. As is indicated in the preface, the supplement was developed from machine-readable records based on requests from the compilers of the 10th edition to simplify compilation. In this respect Balay indicates: "To what extent that benefit has been realized is not clear at this writing, but the production of this book from the computer-controlled database provides an object lesson in both the power and the limitations of computers" (p. viii). One can only agree.

Despite a significant time lag, this new supplement is somewhat more comprehensive than the earlier ones (there were only 3,000-plus entries in the first supplement and the same number in the second), and there is notable improvement in the inclusion of foreign materials, especially reference sources from Eastern Europe. Given the limitations of space, it is obvious that this guide offers, for the most part, only descriptive annotations. For example, there are two entries on page 416. One deals with Russian and Soviet history (DC208), and the other is an encyclopedia of Ukraine (DC211). The annotations will not make the reader aware of the fact that the first publication is a substandard product edited and published by a little-known individual, while the second, prepared by an internationally known scholar, was published by the University of Toronto Press and was the result of cooperation among some 200 respected scholars and subject specialists. As always, bibliographical descriptions and bibliographic history are very accurate, and the index is excellent.

The guide is a standard publication that will serve libraries as well as previous editions have, although its format and frequency of publication probably need to be rethought. As it stands, it is a very useful publication with limitations well known to its users. Highly recommended for libraries of all types. [R: RBB, July 92, p. 1961]—**Bohdan S. Wynar**

13. Lewis, Audrey. **The New, Completely Revised, Greatly Expanded, Madam Audrey's Mostly Cheap, All Good, Useful List of Books for Speedy Reference.** 5th ed. Saginaw, Mich., White Pine Library Cooperative, 1840 N. Michigan, Suite 114, Saginaw, MI 48602, 1992. 83p. index. $10.00pa.

Imagine Miss Manners as the local librarian, briskly dispensing common sense with uncommon good humor, and you have the tone and technique of this delightful bibliography. Madam Audrey is nothing if not opinionated, but her assessments seem quite reliable and are contained within annotations that are models of brevity (one to three sentences) and clarity.

The approximately 500 titles included, organized by what the author describes as "loose Dewey arrangement," are designed to be useful in the day-to-day reference work of small and rural libraries. Wherever possible, Madam Audrey has chosen the least expensive alternative to fill a reference need; however, upon occasion she claims "bibliographer's prerogative" and cites both inexpensive and expensive works if the latter's quality merits its inclusion.

Given the current exponential increase in information overkill, Madam Audrey is to be commended not only for producing a very useful reference tool but also for doing it economically. Certainly, her work should be included as one of those mostly cheap, all good, useful books for which librarians are always on the lookout.—**G. Kim Dority**

14. Macey, Samuel L. **Time: A Bibliographic Guide.** Hamden, Conn., Garland, 1991. 426p. index. (Garland Reference Library of the Humanities, v.1506). $62.00. Z7876.M33. 016.529. LC 91-25934. ISBN 0-8153-0646-6.

After writing three books on the topic of time, Macey realized that no coherent multidisciplinary guide on this topic existed. As a result, he has produced this work in the form of a single-volume bibliography whose scope incorporates questions of time and timeliness and time as an ordering principle of physical change. Within 100 subdivisions, 6,000 entries on 25 academic disciplines that range from multidisciplinary studies to a final section on time's measurements and divisions make up this work. To accommodate further access, both author and subject indexes are included. The subject entries are accompanied by page numbers. Numbers that appear in boldface type refer the reader to topics that form all or part of the title of a section or subsection. The text is very readable, and the bibliographic entries are logically arranged. This bibliography contains information that will appeal to a fairly wide audience, ranging from the upper undergraduate to the researcher. Recommended for most academic collections. [R: Choice, Apr 92, p. 1210]—**John H. Hunter**

15. March, Andrew L., ed. **Recommended Reference Books in Paperback.** 2d ed. Englewood, Colo., Libraries Unlimited, 1992. 263p. index. $37.50. Z1035.1.R4383. 011'.73. LC 92-15875. ISBN 1-56308-067-2.

This "annotated bibliography of 993 titles selected for their quality, availability, and economy" is a "complete revision and updating" of the 1981 edition, which was edited by Mary Alice Deveny. The 993 titles are organized by section: general reference first, then 36 other sections in alphabetical order, agriculture to zoology. Each title entry provides full bibliographic information and an annotation, ranging from a short sentence to a lengthy paragraph, that includes descriptive and evaluative information, often listing additional, related titles. Reviews in ARBA volumes are also cited.

One can hardly quibble with the individual annotations; they are well done. However, while the editor's "intent is to offer a balanced selection," the finished product hardly meets that goal. The botany section is useful, but too many others have little balance or spread; for example, of the 14 entries in the psychology section, 6 are on parapsychology. In other words, the title is misleading—unintentionally, to be sure. This is not an initial selection tool and should not be used as a guide for building a reference collection. It can be used to supplement a reference collection or to find less expensive alternative titles. One is tempted to ask, though, given the number of paperback reference titles appearing each year, why is this bibliography not a paperback itself?—**Evan Ira Farber**

16. Nilsen, Kirsti, with Alanna Kalnay, eds. **Guide to Reference Materials for Canadian Libraries.** 8th ed. Toronto and Buffalo, N.Y., University of Toronto Press, 1992. 596p. index. $50.00pa. 011'.02. ISBN 0-8020-6004-8.

This work is designed primarily as a guide for students in the University of Toronto's Faculty of Library and Information Science. It is not intended as a buying tool for any library, and listed items are not necessarily in print. Emphasizing a basic and representative approach to reference works in all fields, the volume is divided into four main sections: general reference, humanities, social sciences, and science and technology. The guide cites almost 4,000 reference titles within 3,000 annotated entries. Although the general reference section remains the strongest in view of its instructional goal, the history and environment/energy sections have been significantly expanded for this edition.

Entries are usually arranged alphabetically within subsections by type of reference tool and further subdivided by author or title as appropriate. Balance is evident in the titles selected, and the annotations are generally informative and concisely written. There are troubling exceptions, such as the terse annotation rendered for the *Guide to Reference Books* (see ARBA 87, entry 17), preeminent among national guides. Authors and titles are indexed, but only editors of Canadian works are indexed. This practice is a detriment to the use of the guide and should be remedied in future editions. Overall, this volume is recommended for all collections with an international focus as the most current compilation of Canadian reference sources. [R: CLJ, Aug 92, p. 312]—**Arthur P. Young**

17. **Reference Sources for Small and Medium-sized Libraries.** 5th ed. Compiled by an ad hoc Subcommittee of the Reference Sources Committee of the Reference and Adult Services Division, American Library Association. Jovian P. Lang. Chicago, American Library Association, 1992. 317p. index. $35.00pa. Z1035.1.A47. 011'.02. LC 92-10007. ISBN 0-8389-3406-4.

This work was first published in 1968 and revised in 1973 and 1979 under the title *Reference Books for Small and Medium-sized Libraries*. ALA changed the name to its present title with the 4th edition (see ARBA 1985, entry 6). The growing number of reference sources available online or in microforms and CD-ROM formats is reflected not only by the title change but also by the 75 percent increase in the number of new entries in the 5th edition. Although most of the titles listed are currently available, many significant out-of-print works are also included.

The 22 chapters are arranged by subject in Dewey Decimal Classification system order and are further divided by subtopic and by type of publication. Each annotated entry includes standard bibliographic information, price, and ISBN or ISSN. For government publications, Superintendent of Documents classification numbers and stock numbers are given.

Librarians will find the numerous cross-references invaluable. Another strong point is the quality of the annotations. With each edition the annotations have improved, and even the brief ones are useful and informative. With some titles, such as general encyclopedias, the annotations are a column or more. This work is useful as a collection evaluation checklist and selection tool, not just for public libraries but also for college and large secondary school libraries as well. [R: LJ, 1 Oct 92, p. 126; RBB, 1 Sept 92, pp. 90-91]—**Jack Bales**

18. Rettig, James, ed. **Distinguished Classics of Reference Publishing.** Phoenix, Ariz., Oryx Press, 1992. 356p. index. $55.00. Z1035.1.D57. 011'.02. LC 91-33629. ISBN 0-89774-640-6.

Just as most people can no longer imagine life without photocopiers, today's librarians would have a hard time adjusting to a world without such reference classics as Roget's *Thesaurus of English Words and Phrases*, the *Readers' Guide to Periodical Literature*, or the *Oxford English Dictionary*. For anyone who has ever wondered about the history behind these titles, *Distinguished Classics of Reference Publishing* is a necessity. The volume is composed of 31 essays, each under 20 pages and dedicated to a time-tested reference work. The essays are made up of four main parts. The first, "Development and History," covers such items as the conception of the idea (e.g., *The Guinness Book of Records* originated with an argument among duck hunters about whether the golden plover was the fastest game bird in Europe), the method of compilation, commercial viability, critical reception, imitators, and revisions. The other main parts are a publication history, a bibliography, and notes.

Obviously, no two librarians' list of 31 classics would be identical, and readers will argue about titles excluded from this compilation. However, it is hard to argue about the merits of the reference works that did make it into this volume. The book is well researched, well written, and interesting. [R: C&RL, Sept 92, pp. 465-67; JAL, May 92, p. 132; WLB, June 92, p. 136-37]—**Zsuzsa Koltay**

19. Senecal, A. J. **Canada: A Reader's Guide. Introduction Bibliographique.** Ottawa, International Council for Canadian Studies, 1991. 444p. index. $55.00pa. 016.971. ISBN 0-9691862-4-X.

Designed to meet the needs of Canadianists throughout the world, this bilingual guide recommends 1,500 items in print, microformat, and machine-readable form selected for research in Canadian studies. Subjects covered include reference works, society, economy, political science, language, the arts, literature, geography and environmental issues, and history. Newspapers, periodicals, and scholarly journals form a final section. The scope is international; the focus is recent, with 85 percent of the titles published since 1980. In compiling the guide, Senecal has drawn on the expertise of an advisory board of Canadian librarians and academics; the staff of the International Council for Canadian Studies; and the resources of his own institution, the University of Vermont.

Entries are arranged by broad discipline with appropriate subdivisions of genre, date, or subject. As well as imprint and pagination, each entry includes (where possible) availability, ISBN or ISSN, and price. There are useful notes about earlier editions, title changes, revisions in progress, indexing of serials, and access in all formats. A descriptive annotation (35 to 100 words) in both French and English concludes each entry. There are indexes by authors and titles and a list of cross-references by item number at the end of most subject sections. Despite the shortcomings of limited subject access, a paper binding, and inevitable gaps in coverage (e.g., no newspaper east of Quebec), this guide can be recommended to libraries in Canada and abroad for its detailed entries and breadth of coverage.

—**Patricia Fleming**

20. **Walford's Concise Guide to Reference Material.** 2d ed. Anthony Chalcraft and others, eds. London, Library Association; distr., Lanham, Md., UNIPUB, 1992. 496p. index. $145.00. 011.02. ISBN 1-85604-042-9.

This new edition of the concise guide (see ARBA 82, entry 6 for a review of the first one) abridges the three-volume set of *Walford's Guide to Reference Material* (see index for reviews of volumes 2 and 3 and ARBA 91, entry 1459, for a review of the first volume). Entries in this book retain the basic information from the original volumes, and some entries contain updated material. For example, the entry for *American Reference Books Annual* has updated references to the 1991 edition, and that of *Guide to Reference Books* (see ARBA 87, entry 17) mentions the supplement published in 1992, with further information about a full revision projected for 1995. *Grzimek's Encyclopedia of Mammals* (see ARBA 91, entry 1593), which is not in the parent set, has been added. With some exceptions, prices are no longer included. While the majority of entries refer to printed material, the guide also contains online, microform, and CD-ROM sources. When there are no English-language works available in a subject, foreign titles are listed. Author/title and subject indexes complete the volume.

Subdivided into 10 major sections, the entries are arranged by the Universal Decimal Classification. Each major subdivision is further divided into sections within the classification. The typeface is small, but the book has plenty of leading and is easy to read.

Although there are a number of titles from United States publishers, the guide is compiled for the British user and, therefore, has an understandable British bias. Users in the United States and Canada may find the guide interesting, but they probably will find works specific to their nations more useful.—**Anna Grace Patterson**

21. **Walford's Guide to Reference Material. Volume 3: Generalia, Language & Literature, the Arts.** 5th ed. Anthony Chalcraft, Ray Prytherch, and Stephen Willis, eds. London, Library Association; distr., Lanham, Md., UNIPUB, 1991. 1035p. index. $240.00. 028.7. ISBN 0-85365-549-9.

With the publication of this volume, the 5th edition of this well-known British work is complete. Two earlier volumes, *Science and Technology* (see ARBA 91, entry 1459) and *Social and Historical Sciences, Philosophy and Religion* (see index for entry number) were published not long ago. The previous edition of this volume was published in 1987 and reviewed in ARBA 89 (see entry 12). *Walford's* is the British counterpart of *Guide to Reference Books* (see index for entry number). The three volumes of the 5th edition contain 21,994 entries, and, as the editors claim, "it forms the most substantial work of its kind in the English language." One might point out that since 1970, 39,581 titles have been reviewed in ARBA, and this number pertains only to United States and Canadian imprints, plus some books that have an exclusive distributor in these countries. But *Walford's* coverage is very comprehensive, and in contrast to the supplement to the *Guide to Reference Books* and its predecessors, it contains more evaluative annotations.

Pro domo sua, the following can be said. The author-title index has three works entered under this reviewer's name: *ARBA Guide to Subject Encyclopedias and Dictionaries* (see ARBA 87, entry 52), *Best Reference Books* (see ARBA 87, entry 7), and *Dictionary of American Library Biography* (see ARBA 79, entry 185), but other books could be located only by their titles (e.g., *American Reference Books Annual*, *Recommended Reference Books for Small and Medium-sized Libraries* [see index for entry number], *Library and Information Science Annual* [see ARBA 89, entry 543]). In other words, as was true in the previous editions, the index for *Walford's* is inadequate.

Currency may be questionable when reviews are for older editions, as in the case of the following. ARBA's annotation is for the 1989 edition, and *Recommended*'s is for 1988. In addition, *ARBA Guide to Biographical Dictionaries* (see ARBA 87, entry 25) has been omitted entirely.

The annotations are quite good, and coverage of European material is much stronger than in the supplement to *Guide to Reference Books*. Unfortunately, *Walford's* is not well known or widely used in American libraries. One of the factors is a frequent change of distributors; it has moved from the American Library Association to Oryx Press, back to the American Library Association, and now to UNIPUB. Overall, *Walford's* is a very well constructed reference guide and deserves a place in all academic and most public libraries. [R: LAR, July 92, p. 465] — **Bohdan S. Wynar**

22. Wynar, Bohdan S., and Anna Grace Patterson, eds. **Recommended Reference Books for Small and Medium-sized Libraries and Media Centers 1992.** Englewood, Colo., Libraries Unlimited, 1992. 289p. index. $39.50. Z1035.1.R435. 011'.02. LC 81-12394. ISBN 0-87287-976-3. ISSN 0277-5948.

This is the 12th annual edition of this abridgment of *American Reference Books Annual* (ARBA). ARBA 92 contains 1,806 entries; from it the editors have selected 586 sources most appropriate for smaller libraries. Taken verbatim from the larger volume, the reviews are of good quality for the most part. Entries are divided into 37 chapters under 4 major subdivisions: general reference works, social sciences, humanities, and science and technology. Each source is designated as recommended for college, public, or media center collections.

With a 12-year history, this volume obviously has a market. Small institutions may rely upon its entries as confirmation of purchases most appropriate for their limited budgets. However, the comprehensive ARBA is a much more valuable tool. Most institutions would do better to purchase ARBA rather than this source. — **Joe P. Dunn**

National and Trade Bibliography

International

23. **Cumulative Book Index 1991: A World List of Books in the English Language.** Nancy C. Wong and others, eds. Bronx, N.Y., H. W. Wilson, 1992. 2v. sold on service basis. LC 28-26655. ISSN 0011-300X.

24. **Cumulative Book Index: A World List of Books in the English Language. Volume 95, Number 2.** Bronx, N.Y., H. W. Wilson, 1992. 461p. sold on service basis. ISSN 0011-300X.

The *Cumulative Book Index* (CBI) is an indispensable item for medium and large public and academic libraries. It is a comprehensive list of books in English issued in the United States and Canada, and it also has a selection of publications from other parts of the English-speaking world. Excluded are government documents; books with fewer than 50 pages, except for poetry, plays, bibliographies, juvenile literature, and scholarly works; editions limited to 500 or fewer copies; subsidy press publications; and other fugitive or ephemeral material. While it includes many small presses, the *Small Press Record of Books in Print* (see ARBA 90, entry 22) would likely serve as a supplement for verification of difficult-to-find material.

The CBI arrangement is in one alphabetical list of authors, titles, and subjects; the author entries are the most complete, with full name, complete title, pagination, price, publication year, publisher, ISBN, and LC number. A directory of publishers and distributors appears at the end of each issue and in the cumulative volume. Published periodically since 1928, CBI supplements the *United States Catalog*, and since 1969 it has been issued monthly (except August) with quarterly cumulations and a permanent annual cumulation.—**Byron P. Anderson**

25. **Cumulative Book Index.** (Indexing coverage: 1/82-6/25/92). [CD-ROM]. Bronx, N.Y., H. W. Wilson, 1992. Hardware requirements: WILSONLINE Workstation, IBM PC, or compatible; 640K; hard disk drive. $1,295.00.

Cumulative Book Index (CBI) is one of those venerable publications that every librarian had to be familiar with in the days before bibliographic utilities, such as OCLC (Online Computer Library Center), considerably simplified finding information about recently published English-language titles. The print version of CBI remains the leading international resource for English-language publications, although there are any number of other publications, from *Books in Print* (R. R. Bowker, 1992) to the *National Union Catalog*, that offer some alternative routes to similar information. In the CD-ROM format, however, CBI is one of the few major sources that is general rather than subject-oriented.

The CBI CD-ROM under review covers from January 1982 through June 25, 1992, which is the equivalent of 10 of the annual print volumes and a midyear paper cumulation. In the print version, access is by author, title, and Library of Congress subject heading. The CD-ROM adds several additional access points. In addition to author, title, and imprint information, retrieved records display ISBN, LCCN, Dewey Decimal number, subjects covered, and price.

Installation of the CBI CD-ROM, as well as most other CD-ROMs these days, is fairly trivial on a stand-alone station. (Networks, obviously, are a different matter.) This CD-ROM requires an IBM PC or fully compatible computer, DOS 3.1 or later, 640K RAM, a CD-ROM player, and a hard disk drive with at least 2 MB of free disk space. A printer and modem are optional. MS-DOS extensions are supported but not required if one has a Hitachi, Sony, or Philips CD-ROM player. Users of earlier Wilson CD-ROMs should note that, as of March 1992, some Wilson databases are using compressed data, and CBI is one of them. Versions of WILSONDISC (search software) earlier than 2.4 will seem to work until one tries to retrieve an entry that corresponds to the results of a search. The best one will get is a blank screen; the worst is a frozen computer. Obviously, one must install or upgrade to version 2.4 before using this disc.

Documentation consists of generic materials: an 18-page pamphlet, *The WILSONDISC Quick Reference Guide*; "WILSONDISC Version 2.4 Installation and Setup Guide"; and "WILSONDISC Version 2.4 User Guide to New Features." While the *Quick Reference Guide* is adequate, most users will prefer documentation with examples applicable to a specific CD-ROM. This also applies to Wilson help screens, which are similarly generic. On the other hand, the installation documentation is perfectly adequate.

The strengths of Wilson's interface are its three search modes of differing complexity (BROWSE, WILSEARCH, and WILSONLINE), easy access to the Wilson online version of CBI if desired, and a wide range of customization especially appropriate to public use in a library environment. The BROWSE search interface asks the user for a single search string, either subject, title, or author. WILSONLINE also uses a single string but gives power users access to Boolean logic, truncation, and several viewing options. The WILSEARCH option is more user-friendly than WILSONLINE but still offers the capability of Boolean searching up to three separate subject headings, together with personal name, title words, organization (which can be a publisher as well as a corporate author), Dewey

Decimal classification number, and year. Not searchable, although usually included in a retrieved record, are "other" authors, page numbers, price, ISBN or LCCN, and LC class number. Searches by "other" authors, ISBN, and especially LC class number would be useful; the latter, for example, would facilitate certain types of collection analysis.

While the Wilson interface has much to commend it, there are several areas in which it could be improved. First, no matter how many entries are retrieved by a search, they have to be examined one record at a time (the WILSONLINE interface does offer the option of displaying a list of titles). An intermediate menu display of one entry per line, as is often found in Online Public Access Catalogs, would aid in the navigation of large sets of records and should be available in the BROWSE and WILSEARCH modes as well. Second, it would be better if user-friendly interfaces did not hide the option of downloading to a floppy under the *print* command. For most users, printing and saving data remain conceptually independent, even if the software is not concerned with which device is receiving the information, be it screen, floppy, or printer. — **Robert Skinner**

United States

26. **American Book Publishing Record Cumulative 1991: An Annual Cumulation of American Book Production in 1991....** New Providence, N.J., R. R. Bowker, 1992. 1682p. index. $189.95. LC 66-19741. ISBN 0-8352-3203-4. ISSN 0002-7707.

This edition of *American Book Publishing Record* (ABPR) is the last volume to be compiled from *Weekly Record*, which ceased publication with the December 23, 1991, issue. Future editions will be compiled from the monthly issues of ABPR.

With more than 41,000 entries, this volume catalogs books published in 1991. As in previous volumes (see ARBA 91, entry 8), these titles have been divided into three sections: Dewey Decimal classification, adult fiction, and juvenile fiction. Elements in the Dewey Decimal classification entries generally include the main entry, title in italics, subtitle, author statement, place and date of publication, publisher, collation, series statement, LC classification number, LC card number, and subject tracings. Other information is occasionally provided. All data, including price, are as current as possible. Author and title indexes and a subject guide complete the annual. Although there are some typographical errors and incorrect prices, ABPR remains an excellent resource for librarians.
— **Anna Grace Patterson**

27. **B&T Link Module 2: The Title Source.** world ed. (July 1992). [CD-ROM]. Charlotte, N.C., Baker & Taylor, 1992. Hardware requirements: IBM PC or compatible, DOS 3.3 or higher, hard disk drive with 3-5 MB available, floppy disk drive, CD-ROM drive, up to 9600 baud Hayes compatible modem, 640K RAM. $795.00.

28. **Books in Print Plus with Book Reviews Plus.** (May-June 1992). [CD-ROM]. New Providence, N.J., R. R. Bowker, 1992. Hardware requirements: IBM PC or compatible, 286 or higher, with at least 535K free memory; hard disk, with at least 10MB free; DOS 3.0 or later; CD-ROM drive running under MS-DOS Extensions. $1,495.00.

For libraries that can afford a computer station devoted to CD-ROM databases, having *Books in Print* in electronic form or B&T Link makes a great deal of sense. Books in Print Plus contains all the listings in the various hardcopy volumes that make up *Books in Print*, including *Subject Guide to Books in Print* (see ARBA 92, entry 15) and *Children's Books in Print* (see ARBA 92, entry 16), as well as the database from *Publishers, Distributors & Wholesalers of the United States* (see index for entry number). More than 1.4 million works are listed. In addition, 160,000 book reviews from 10 well-known reviewing sources are easily accessed when a title is searched. The Ingram Distribution Group database cross-references the reviews, which allows the electronic acquisition of more than 160,000 titles.

Books in Print Plus requires some training to use because the front-end search program is not particularly user-friendly. Once the system is learned, however, searching is much easier than using the microscopic print in the paper editions. The advantage of being able to search in any one of 18 different fields and the addition of reviews make this product one of the most logical uses of CD-ROM technology. Searching is relatively fast (speed is governed by the hardware owned), and entries can be printed or stored for editing in a word processor. Automatic links to jobbers for acquisition can be created.

As this product stems from the same database as the print version, it contains both the advantages and the faults of the print version, including comprehensiveness and inaccuracies. Part of the blame for the problems lies with publishers who fail to report to Bowker properly; however, errors made by Bowker seem to be corrected slowly.

B&T Link provides users of Baker & Taylor wholesalers the internal database used at company headquarters. Data for this list is sent by publishers of books and audiovisual materials. Baker & Taylor also adds to the database as invoices requesting materials are sent in by libraries. There is, however, a flaw in the database because the current Baker & Taylor policy is to not return complete listings to publishers for correction, as does R. R. Bowker. Thus the error rate on B&T Link is much higher than on BIP Plus.

B&T Link is a purchasing tool rather than a selection tool because information is briefer than that in BIP Plus; also, the lack of reviews makes it less useful. Because BIP Plus can be interfaced to Baker & Taylor for ordering purposes, it is the better choice even though B&T Link includes audiovisual materials and has a more user-friendly search engine. Librarians should not judge these two products on price alone, but should do sample testing of the types of materials purchased by the library on both systems and then make a decision.

However, in this reviewer's opinion, as BIP Plus grows to include half a million reviews, it will probably be the premier selection tool for in-print materials. Recommended as a replacement of print editions both for the library selection and verification staff and for patrons who need to create bibliographies and who want to choose their own books.—**David V. Loertscher**

29. **Books in Print 1991-92.** New Providence, N.J., R. R. Bowker, 1991. 8v. $374.95/set. LC 4-12648. ISBN 0-8352-3105-4. ISSN 0068-0214.

Books in Print (BIP) continues to be the major information resource for books published and distributed in the United States. It has three volumes of author indexes, three volumes of title indexes, an out-of-print/out-of-stock-indefinitely volume, and a volume of publishers. More than a million books of all kinds—adult, juvenile, popular, scholarly, and reprints—including 136,000 new titles and approximately 350,000 revisions, are a part of the 1991-1992 edition. The out-of-print/out-of-stock-indefinitely volume contains nearly 125,000 titles that have been declared out of print. The volume of publishers contains about 40,000 entries including new and inactive participants.

The author and title indexes are in a word-by-word alphabetical arrangement. Some exceptions do occur. Articles in English, French, German, Italian, and Spanish are omitted from the title index; *M*, *Mc*, and *Mac* are interfiled under *Mac*; and all initials are filed before words under a particular letter. Most abbreviations are filed as if they were spelled out (e.g., U.S.—United States). Each entry for authors and titles contains bibliographic and ordering information with number of pages, prices, publisher, edition notes, binding, and ISBN. The last few editions have relied upon electronic methods in an effort to maintain currency and accuracy. BIP is dependent on individual publishers for information contained in each publication entry.

Although errors are more numerous than one would like, *Books in Print* remains the standard for available book titles. All libraries should have access to this important work.—**Anna Grace Patterson**

30. **The Complete Directory of Large Print Books & Serials 1992.** New Providence, N.J., R. R. Bowker, 1992. 265p. index. $119.95pa. LC 74-102773. ISBN 0-8352-3176-3.

This directory of large-print books and serials is a comprehensive, well-organized (by subject) resource for organizations, libraries, teachers, and individuals who deal with people who use these materials. It addresses a potentially vital need of visually impaired people, the aging population, and children and adolescents with special learning needs. This directory is not likely to be used directly by these individuals, however, due to the miniscule typeface. An earlier review (see ARBA 89, entry 15) pointed out this problem and noted that prior editions had been in 18-point type.

Included in this revised and updated version of the 1991 edition are 6,800 large-type books or serials with print of 14-point type or larger. Subject categories include children's books, general adult reading, textbooks, newspapers and periodicals, and Bibles of different religions and denominations. One hopes that R. R. Bowker will make this valuable resource more usable by the special populations for whom its contents are intended by again publishing a large-print version in the future.

—Jeanne Friedrichs

31. **Paperbound Books in Print: Including Mass Market, Paper, Trade, and Softcover Titles. Spring 1992.** New Providence, N.J., R. R. Bowker, 1992. 6v. index. $179.95/set. LC 71-649559. ISBN 0-8352-3184-4. ISSN 0031-1235.

Growing, growing, grown—to six volumes, twice a year, spring and fall. *Paperbound Books in Print* (PBIP), which began as a single volume in 1955, has grown almost as large as *Books in Print* (BIP) (R. R. Bowker, 1992). The two sources, which differ in coverage, overlap in a good number of cases, but PBIP has found some paperback publishers overlooked by BIP. Because PBIP indexes more than 27,500 publishers, the coverage is quite thorough, although its emphasis is on trade and mass-market books.

The first two volumes are arranged by title, the next two by author. The fifth and sixth volumes give subject listings and a list of publishers. Each entry includes author or editor, translator, title, edition, LC number, illustrations, grade range, year of publication, price, ISBN, publisher's order number, imprint, and publisher. The citation ends with an abbreviation for the type of fiction, such as (My), or a number that represents the book's subject.

This work has already been reviewed in ARBA five times since 1976. (The most recent review was in ARBA 91, entry 10.) The format for subject indexing has not improved. The subject list used is the American Bookseller Association and the National Association of College Stores subject headings. The arrangement by broad subject only (e.g., History - U.S. covers 21 pages with no subheadings) makes a search for a particular time period or event difficult. Juveniles - Fiction covers 77 pages with no aid to the subject content of the book. The publisher's index is arranged by abbreviation rather than name, so in some cases it is difficult to locate a publisher unless the name has already been found by abbreviation in the other volumes.

The high cost of this work must be carefully considered by small libraries for the minimal useful additional material it contains that is not in BIP. However, more and more information is produced by small presses and desktop publishing efforts, and large libraries may have need of some of the special sources listed here.—**Joann H. Lee**

32. Rinderknecht, Carol, and Scott Bruntjen, comps. **A Checklist of American Imprints for 1842: Items 42-1—42-5379.** Metuchen, N.J., Scarecrow, 1992. 424p. $47.50. LC 64-11784. ISBN 0-8108-2533-3.

The latest volume of this checklist lists in alphabetical order (by personal or corporate author) monographs, state and local documents, pamphlets, broadsides, and other material published in the United States in 1842. The new format of the checklists begun in the 1840 volume—larger type and a more informative numbering system—is continued in this one. Each entry contains the author's name, birth and death dates, title, imprint, number of pages, and several locations of copies of the item. There are 5,379 entries in this volume.—**Dean H. Keller**

BIOGRAPHY

International

33. **Biography Index: A Cumulative Index to Biographical Material in Books and Magazines: September 1990-August 1991.** Charles R. Cornell, ed. Bronx, N.Y., H. W. Wilson, 1991. 598p. $115.00/yr. LC 47-6532. ISSN 0006-3053.

Writing a review of *Biography Index* is really an exercise in describing the obvious. Since its inception in 1946 it has been probably the first place to which generations of reference librarians have gone in order to locate material that might contain biographical information. It covers not only the 2,700 periodicals indexed by H. W. Wilson but also selected others; obituaries in the *New York Times*; and current books, including juvenile items. Because requests for biographical information are among the most frequently asked reference questions, and because such information often provides a quick or logical lead into answering more complex reference questions, the *Biography Index* is one of the first items of purchase for a reference collection. The part of it that is often neglected, however, is the index to professions and occupations, the lengthy section at the back of each issue that lists, under each respective profession or occupation, all the individuals who appear in that quarterly, annual, or two-year cumulative issue. One expects to find many names listed under "Conductors (Music)"; "Legislators, French"; and other such well known occupations, but the variety of uncommon ones is fascinating: animal shelter workers, art forgers, balloonists, doll makers, Egyptologists, harmonica players, and transvestites are just a few. Moreover, the section opens up all kinds of interesting projects for students. For example, of the 200 or so architects listed in this annual volume, how many are women? (Only about 14.) Why are there so few, and how does this compare with the proportion 10 years ago?

One could go on about this invaluable work, musing about the information and the possible uses for it. It is clear, however, that it should be in all libraries.—**Evan Ira Farber**

34. **Biography Index.** (Indexing coverage: 7/84-6/25/92). [CD-ROM]. Bronx, N.Y., H. W. Wilson, 1992. Hardware requirements: WILSONLINE Workstation, IBM PC, or compatible; 640K; hard disk drive. $1,095.00.

This disc provides two modes for searching entries contained in Biography Index: personal name and subject. Entering a personal name in BROWSE mode shifts the user to an index screen that identifies the exact or closest match. Once a choice is made from the index, the bibliographic information for each entry may be displayed, printed, or saved to a disk file. Using the subject mode provides a freetext search of the basic index, which includes journal article or book title and assigned subject headings. Boolean searching and truncation are available with this mode. There is also an option, if a modem is available, to access Biography Index at no charge on WILSONLINE, which provides an online interim update between quarterly discs. If other WILSONDISCS are available at the same work station, the search may be repeated in the appropriate files without reentering the terms. The menus and on-screen messages, as well as the in-context help screens available by function key, will guide the novice through the search process. The help screens and brief printed reference guide are generic to WILSONDISC and have no specific references to Biography Index. A password may be set to exit to DOS.

The installation procedure is simple. Some optional configurations are available, such as the number of retrieved entries that may be printed or downloaded and statistics on usage. Technical support is available through a toll-free number, and the optional online system is available at all hours, seven days a week. Because Biography Index is primarily used for personal name searching, the advantages gained with the freetext search capability and multiyear searching may not warrant the price of the subscription. However, if this disc is used in conjunction with other WILSONDISCS and the online capability, larger libraries may wish to offer this service to their users.—**Margo B. Mead**

35. **Biography Today: Profiles of People of Interest to Young Readers. Volume 1, Issue 1.** Laurie Lanzen Harris, ed. Detroit, Omnigraphics, 1992. 166p. illus. index. $10.00pa. (4 issues/yr.); $38.50 (cumulative). ISBN 1-55888-761-X. ISSN 1058-2347.

This quarterly provides short, interestingly written biographies of celebrities, primarily for the use of school children. It has a mixture of individuals of lasting importance and others who are currently enjoying what Andy Warhol termed their "15 minutes" of fame. This first issue contains 29 profiles and a list of future subjects. The great majority are actors, athletes, authors, or musicians. Each profile, a few of which are autobiographical, is accompanied by a photograph and an address where the celebrity can be contacted. The magazine-format reference book provides basic information and the subjects' own views on their lives, without avoiding controversy. The editor does not take sides; for example, the account of Clarence Thomas's confirmation hearings in the Senate mentions Anita Hill's allegations of sexual harassment, but it does not attempt to defend or attack either side's stand. Many of the biographees can be found in other sources, but the choice of celebrities profiled and the tone taken in the essays make *Biography Today* particularly appropriate for young readers. [R: RBB, 15 June 92, p. 1880] – **David Lonergan**

36. Blatherwick, Francis John. **1000 Brave Canadians: The Canadian Gallantry Awards 1854-1989.** Toronto, Unitrade Press, 1991. 414p. illus. index. $29.95pa. ISBN 0-919801-58-7.

This is a specialized reference book about very special people – those who have risked their lives (and sometimes lost them) to save the lives of others. The courageous deeds of more than 1,000 Canadians who have received their country's gallantry awards are recorded here in the exact wording of their official citations.

The arrangement is chronological (by date of incident) under each medal. Part 1 deals with the seven medals (including the Victoria Cross) that originated in England. Part 2 covers, also chronologically, the four Canadian Bravery Awards that have been issued since 1972. In a preface to each section, Blatherwick gives the history of the medal. For each individual listing he provides the citation, data on the present location of the medal, and biographical and other pertinent information about the recipient or incident (where available). There are alphabetical indexes to each section, an illustration of each medal, and a brief bibliography.

1000 Brave Canadians shows evidence of great concern for accuracy and completeness. For libraries interested in Canadian military history and for those that want detailed accounts of many of Canada's most heroic exploits, this book will long serve as the standard work. – **Samuel Rothstein**

37. **Current Biography Yearbook 1991.** Charles Moritz and others, eds. Bronx, N.Y., H. W. Wilson, 1992. 671p. illus. index. $54.00. LC 40-27432. ISSN 0084-9499.

Once again, this work fulfills its promise of providing brief, objective, well-documented articles about living persons worldwide who are generally recognized as outstanding in their fields. All professions are considered for inclusion, but the emphasis in this particular volume falls heavily in the areas of film and music, followed by literature, television, and theater. Of the approximately 160 people profiled this year, only 7 represent the fields of science, technology, and medicine.

As noted in previous reviews (see ARBA 89, entry 20), the work is arranged alphabetically by author. Each entry includes a photograph of the subject, the date of birth, the profession, an address for correspondence, a biographical sketch, and a list of references from which the sketch is drawn. The articles tend to be about three pages long and are consistently well written and generously sprinkled with quotations from interviews published in other sources. The volume includes a list of obituaries for subjects profiled in earlier volumes, an index to the sources consulted, a classification by field or profession, and a cumulated index for 1991. For an index to earlier volumes, *Current Biography Cumulated Index 1940-1990* (see ARBA 92, entry 58) should be consulted. Because coverage is worldwide, the addition of an index by country or geographical location would also prove useful and should be considered for future volumes. A welcome addition since the 1990 edition is an alphabetical list of the subjects and their page numbers at the beginning of the volume. However, this list is sandwiched between the pronunciation key and the key to abbreviations. It would be more logically placed directly before the first entry – an extremely minor flaw in a solid and enduring reference source. – **Janice M. Griggs**

38. **A Dictionary of Twentieth Century World Biography.** Asa Briggs, ed. New York, Oxford University Press, 1992. 615p. $30.00. ISBN 0-19-211679-7.

Biographical dictionaries rise or fall on the basis of the clarity and logic of their selection criteria. In the preface the editor states that the object of this work is to include those "who have had an impact, either directly or indirectly, on the rest of us." This vague announcement is not strengthened by a statement in the foreword that people "about whom it is useful to be able to have easily accessible information" are included.

The editor has listed 1,750 people from all walks of life who have gained prominence in the twentieth century. While the sketches are well written and seem accurate, there are too few of them, particularly when considered against the 5,650 notables in a comparable work, *The International Dictionary of 20th Century Biography* (see ARBA 88, entry 35). For example, the work under review fails to include James Weldon Johnson, W. E. B. Du Bois, Langston Hughes, or Richard Wright. All are included in the older volume. Finally, the book lacks indexing of any kind – a serious flaw. *A Dictionary of Twentieth Century World Biography* cannot be recommended. [R: Choice, Dec 92, p. 600; LAR, Oct 92, p. 672; RBB, 1 Nov 92, p. 545]—**Donald C. Dickinson**

39. **Encyclopedia of World Biography: 20th Century Supplement. [Volume] 17.** David Eggenberger, ed. Palatine, Ill., Jack Heraty, 1992. 624p. illus. index. $69.50. LC 86-63173. ISBN 0-910081-07-7.

More than 100 years ago, Thomas Carlyle wrote that "the history of the world is but the biography of great men." Today, of course, we add "and great women"—some 68 of whom appear prominently in this valuable reference tool. In all, more than 300 individuals are represented in this fourth supplement to the *Encyclopedia of World Biography* (EWB).

Similar to the other supplementary volumes, this addition is a self-contained unit with its own alphabetization and index. All entries have been carefully planned and effectively written by more than 270 authorities. Each essay is followed by its own further reading section, cross-references, and bibliographic notes. Additionally, each has at least one illustration. Special graphics include locator maps and expository tables. To enhance the usefulness of the entire EWB, one section updates important events that have taken place in the lives of the thousands of distinguished people included in previously published volumes. Libraries that already shelve the EWB will, of course, wish to add this supplement.—**G. A. Cevasco**

40. Hoffman, Herbert H., comp. **Faces in the News: An Index to Photographic Portraits, 1987-1991.** Metuchen, N.J., Scarecrow, 1992. 480p. $42.50. CT120.H63. 016.92'0009'048. LC 91-45152. ISBN 0-8108-2530-9.

All photographs indexed in this work are taken from *Newsweek, Time, U.S. News & World Report,* and *People Weekly* (since 1988), as well as *Current Biography* (usually the *Yearbook*). The limited number of sources is more than compensated for by the extremely wide coverage of people in the news from January 1987 to June 1991.

There seem to be no exclusions. If a person was noteworthy enough for a photograph to have been included in one of the sources, it is indexed here. There are more than 6,000 people listed, each with appropriate identification—senator, governor, spy, robber, painter, actress, drug dealer, and so on. Coverage is worldwide; most people are still alive. U.S. presidents have the greatest number of entries, with George Bush having nearly six pages; Mikhail Gorbachev is second with three pages.

The cutoff date of mid-1991 allows Clarence Thomas to be included, but not Anita Hill, as her revelations did not make the weeklies until after June 1991. There are 14 different Kennedys listed, including John Fitzgerald, but there is no cross-reference to William Kennedy Smith, who is listed (Patricia Bowman is not). The work is useful for library patrons as a place to find textual information about some relatively obscure person as well as to obtain a picture or likeness of that person. [R: RBB, 1 Sept 92, p. 85]—**Raymund F. Wood**

41. McGuire, Paula, ed. **Nobel Prize Winners: Supplement 1987-1991.** Bronx, N.Y., H. W. Wilson, 1992. 143p. illus. $35.00. AS911.N9N59. 001.4'4'0922. LC 92-12197. ISBN 0-8242-0834-X.

In 1987, H. W. Wilson published *Nobel Prize Winners* (see ARBA 88, entry 32), a biographical dictionary of the 566 people who received the world's most prestigious award from 1901 to 1986. Now Wilson follows that fine reference book with a 5-year supplement that provides profiles of the 49 notables who received the prizes from 1987 to 1991. Both works are targeted toward students and general readers. The profiles in the supplement are brief but instructive. Each contains a comprehensive account of the research, writing, scholarly work, and political activism for which the nominee won the prize. A photograph of the subject and a bibliography of published work available in English is included with each profile. Separate profiles for each Nobel laureate are provided, even when the prize has been shared. Additional features in this volume include an informative profile of Alfred Nobel and a history of the establishment of the prizes in physiology and medicine, literature, economics, chemistry, and physics. Complete lists of all winners through 1991 are provided by prize category and laureate nationalities. With its portraits of such distinguished individuals as Aung San Suu Kyi, the Dalai Lama, and Nadine Gordimer, this fine volume is a worthy reference book that stands on its own or as an excellent complement to the earlier reference.—**Jerry D. Flack**

42. Park, James. **Icons: An A-Z Guide to the People Who Shaped Our Time.** New York, Collier Books/Macmillan, 1991. 469p. index. $12.00pa. CT103.P157. 920'.009'04. LC 91-36769. ISBN 0-02-047100-9.

Not a typical reference book, with its offbeat tone and unusual contributors, this new biographical dictionary includes a decidedly different array of information about a wide range of political, social, and cultural figures. Symbols scattered throughout indicate such characteristics as "necromantic love-icon" and "almost ended up behind bars." Entries focus on the meaning of an individual's work or the influence someone had on society and history rather than on straight, dry biographical facts.

Intended to serve as a "route map through this postwar world" and to "encapsulate the essence of what 1000 or so" people did to be considered famous, the book's bias is left of center. Also, the varied mix of subjects contains many people who might not be considered quite as famous by the U.S. reader as by the creators of this book (e.g., playwright Dario Fo). But the inclusion of these not-so-obviously influential types is the strong point of this source; information about many of them may not be easy to locate elsewhere. This work will be of interest to those college and university libraries that serve strong programs in twentieth-century history and popular culture. [R: LJ, 1 Sept 92, p. 168; RBB, 15 Nov 92, pp. 626-27] – **Sharon Langworthy**

43. Snodgrass, Mary Ellen. **Late Achievers: Famous People Who Succeeded Late in Life.** Englewood, Colo., Libraries Unlimited, 1992. 286p. $26.00. CT120.S59. 920.02. LC 91-32136. ISBN 0-87287-937-2.

Many books have been written about people who have achieved success, but this book concentrates on those who "took on new challenges in their thirties, their forties, even their sixties and seventies" (p. ix). Some changed careers to become successful, while others started careers or new ventures later in life. This book contains 40 alphabetically arranged biographies of people, both living and deceased, from the eighteenth through the twentieth centuries in Europe and the United States. In many cases readers will be familiar with the subject's achievement (e.g., dumpsters, McDonald's, Outward Bound), but they may not know the name behind the achievement (e.g., George Dempster, Ray Kroc, Kurt Hahn). Others in the volume represent equally diverse fields, such as Peter Mark Roget (thesaurus), Wally Amos (cookies), Vaclav Havel (president), Ethel Waters (actress), and William Griffin Wilson (Alcoholics Anonymous founder).

Six-part narratives about the biographees describe their lives and include important dates. These are followed by footnotes and sources consulted. For recent biographees the sources are mainly magazine and newspaper articles, while for the others the sources are books.

There are some flaws in the work. The date of death for some deceased biographees are omitted; there are several typographical errors; and at times the narrative jumps back and forth in the person's life, making the sequence of events hard to follow. But on the whole, this is a well done, easy to read, and often (with the exception of G. Gordon Liddy) inspiring work. It can be useful as a reference source because information on many of the living biographees is hard to locate elsewhere. – **Kathleen Farago**

44. Sokol, Stanley S., with Sharon F. Mrotek Kissane. **The Polish Biographical Dictionary: Profiles of Nearly 900 Poles Who Have Made Lasting Contributions to World Civilization.** Wauconda, Ill., Bolchazy-Carducci, 1992. 477p. illus. index. $45.00. LC 91-35862. ISBN 0-86516-245-X.

This popular biography includes all the better-known Polish individuals as well as those less familiar outside Polish-American communities. In addition to paragraph-length biographical entries, it includes a short overview of Polish history, a geographical sketch, some portraits, and an index arranged by categories of achievements. Each entry has at least one citation that usually refers to another biographical work.

More than 60 percent of the biographees are classified as artists, musicians, writers, or poets; they are represented by 4 out of 18 portraits in the book. Also included are individuals of different political orientations, communist leaders, and even assassins. Generous tributes are paid to Polish Jews for their contributions to Polish, and in some cases, Israeli culture. Most of the entries concern people born in the nineteenth century; the others are almost evenly divided between pre-eighteenth-century and twentieth-century people. Slightly more than 6 percent of the entrants were still alive at the time of the book's publication. The biography is endorsed by Catholic organizations but is nondenominational in its approach.

This work would benefit from tighter editing. There are a number of typographical errors, mainly in the spelling of Polish words. More serious, however, is the absence of Polish diacritical marks, making the biography useless for verifying the proper spelling of Polish names. The compilation may be useful in library reference collections as a supplement to more comprehensive sources on Polish history, and it will be consulted often in public libraries that serve Polish communities. [R: RBB, 1 Apr 92, p. 1475]—**Joseph Z. Nitecki**

45. Straub, Deborah Gillan. **Contemporary Heroes and Heroines. Book II.** Detroit, Gale, 1992. 559p. illus. index. $49.95. CT120.C662. 920'.009'04. LC 90-132617. ISBN 0-8103-8336-5.

Pop culture authority Ray B. Browne introduces this collection of biographical sketches. He points out that knowledge of heroism provides models of behavior, defines our world, bolsters democracy, nourishes our ideal selves, makes the world one, and inspires us with faith while strengthening our resolve. Straub's sketches demonstrate how these attributes of heroism infuse a life and, in doing so, touch all hearts. The sketches are each approximately five pages in length, with sources listed. A half-page photographic portrait and a compelling quotation preface each entry. The variety of people covered makes for an eclectic but balanced gathering. Grandma Moses, Jim Henson, the Dalai Lama, Vaclav Havel, Simon Wiesenthal, and Stevie Wonder differ dramatically from one another, but all have the common link of heroism. Most of the names will be familiar, although some might not be, such as Corrie ten Boom (she sheltered Jews from the Nazis), Chico Mendes (he fought against the destruction of the Amazon rain forest), and Ben Carson (the Black neurosurgeon). The subjects are as contemporary as Elizabeth Glaser, the AIDS activist, and as renowned as Clarence Darrow. School and public libraries will want to own this book and the previous volume for general reading and classroom assignments.—**Bill Bailey**

46. **Who Was Who 1981-1990: A Companion to** *Who's Who*. New York, St. Martin's Press, 1991. 845p. (Who Was Who, v.8). $99.95. ISBN 0-312-06818-2.

47. **Who Was Who: A Cumulative Index 1897-1990.** New York, St. Martin's Press, 1991. 801p. $99.95. ISBN 0-312-06817-4.

The eighth volume of *Who Was Who*, covering 1981-1990, is a compilation of the biographical entries of people, primarily British, who were previously featured in *Who's Who* (see ARBA 92, entry 31) and who died during the past decade. Biographical information is as current as the latest entry in *Who's Who*; additions include date of death and occasionally information gleaned from obituaries and other sources. Entries are arranged in alphabetical order, and cross-references are provided where necessary (e.g., for pseudonyms, married names, or double surnames). As noted in the last review of this work, on the 1961-1970 volume (see ARBA 73, entry 245), *Who Was Who* allows librarians to dispense with earlier annual volumes of *Who's Who*. In addition, since the last review the format has been much improved: pages are larger, columns are wider, and readability is better.

To assist the user in identifying which volumes to consult, *Who Was Who: A Cumulated Index 1897-1980* was published to accompany volume 7. That cumulation has now been extended to include revisions of earlier volumes of *Who Was Who* as well as the entries in volume 8 (1981-1990). Of course, if one already has the previous index and volume 8, the avoidance of duplication and the restrictions of recessionary budgets may preclude addition of this index to some reference collections.

—**Janice M. Griggs**

48. **Who's Who in Japan 1991-92.** Tokyo, Asia Press; distr., Boca Raton, Fla., CRC Press, 1991. 682p. index. $250.00. ISBN 4-900618-012.

This is the 3d revised edition of *Who's Who in Japan*. It contains more than 27,000 entries, mostly from business, academia, politics, and administration. Information on the order of entries and on abbreviations used precedes the main part. The 12 possible items of information in the entries are rarely complete, but current position, education, and address are emphasized. An index to the volume is arranged by categories, such as diet members, government, bureaucrat/legal, registered or

nonregistered company, communications, culture, natural science, literature, art, music/dance, sports, and fashion/beauty/cooking/hobbies. Under the legal category, the Chief Justice of the Japanese Supreme Court is included, but a check for several other justices revealed a lack of coverage. A directory of public and private institutions completes the volume. The usefulness of this reference source is enhanced by the increasingly close relations between Japan and the rest of the world. It can be recommended to journalists, academicians, business and government executives, and researchers.
— **Bogdan Mieczkowski**

United States

49. Filler, Louis. **Distinguished Shades: Americans Whose Lives Live On.** Ovid, Mich., Belfry, 1992. 278p. illus. index. $24.95; $12.95pa. LC 91-077228. ISBN 0-961527-1-8.

"Distinguished Shades" are Americans who made a difference in history but who were often misunderstood and, in some cases, forgotten. The book consists of 56 biographies of men and women of various races who were born between 1745 and 1903. They were progressives, liberals, politicians, and feminists who were active in civil rights, woman suffrage, and social reform movements. Filler has chosen them because they represent aspects of today's national life and dilemmas. He asserts that we should not forget our shades, for they offer insights to humanity, even today.

The biographies are concise and readable, generally three to five pages long, and include bibliographic notes. Each begins with a statement that covers the impact on society that the person made and continues with a synopsis of the individual's life story. Filler's account goes beyond a factual listing of events; he reiterates the opinions and misconceptions of society at the time and provides the reader with a thought-provoking biography. A comprehensive bibliography would be helpful for those interested in further research, but this makes a good beginning guide.— **Deborah A. Taylor**

50. Serafin, Steven, ed. **American Literary Biographers: Second Series.** Detroit, Gale, 1991. 399p. illus. index. (Dictionary of Literary Biography, no.111). $108.00. LC 91-26672. ISBN 0-8103-4591-9.

Libraries with standing orders to the Dictionary of Literary Biography series have probably already realized that Gale will never exhaust its supply of literary groups to include in this series for undergraduate collections. This recent offering is the second volume in a subseries on American literary biographers. As did the previous volume, this work provides well-written bio-bibliographical essays by recognized scholars. Thirty-five biographers born in the first half of this century are the subjects of articles of about ten pages each. Although many of the best-known biographers (e.g., Richard Ellmann, Edwin H. Cady) appeared in the first volume, this continuation includes important writers such as Virginia Spencer Carr, Walter Harding, Richard S. Kennedy, and Stanley Weintraub. The relation between biographer and subject is a theme that runs through all the articles, with particular emphasis on the circumstances that led the writer to delve into another's life. It becomes clear that the task of the biographer entails not only an enormous amount of research but also a true sense of devotion to the subject, regardless of how many years or centuries might separate the two. If biography is a form of voyeurism, these essays, which obviously use the techniques of the biographer to describe them, are doubly voyeuristic, for one sees into the lives of those who look into the lives of people one admires.— **Valerie R. Hotchkiss**

51. Sinnott, Susan. **Extraordinary Hispanic Americans.** Chicago, Childrens Press, 1991. 277p. illus. index. $30.60. E184.S75S55. 973'.0468. LC 91-13909. ISBN 0-516-00582-0.

Sinnott modestly describes this much-needed book for children and young adults as "a maddening blend of unconnected people and events." While it is by no means comprehensive, it is filled with interesting and meaningful information about Hispanics who stand out in the history of America. (The accuracy of the term "Hispanic" is questioned by Sinnott because it glosses over the fact that there are legitimate historical differences between such groups as Puerto Ricans, Cubans, and Mexicans. Sinnott is, in most cases, careful to mention each biographee's origin.)

The organization of the book is chronological, from the European discovery of America to the modern era. Significant events or periods (e.g., the Zoot Suit Riots of 1942) are covered in brief essays, but much more information is provided in the biographical entries. There are articles on groups, such as the first Angelenos (Los Angeles's first settlers), as well as on individuals. Biographees are from a wide variety of professions, such as the military (e.g., Rafael Chacon, a captain in the Union Army), business (e.g., the Lopezes and the Riveras, colonial merchants), politics (e.g., Dennis Chavez, the first Hispanic U.S. senator), and science (e.g., Luis Alvarez, Nobel prize winner in physics). One nice feature is the emphasis on people who are not sports figures or entertainers, although a few of these are profiled. The text is usually well written and informative, and brief bibliography will interest those who want to explore a subject in greater detail. Illustrations, some a little fuzzy but most sharp, complement the text; they include black-and-white drawings, photographs, and reproductions of stamps. The quality of the paper and binding is excellent. Highly recommended for public and school libraries. [R: SLJ, May 92, p. 28] – **D. A. Rothschild and Dario J. Villa**

52. Smith, Jessie Carney, ed. **Notable Black American Women.** Detroit, Gale, 1992. 1334p. illus. index. $49.95. E185.96.N68. 920.72'08996073. LC 91-35074. ISBN 0-8103-4749-0.

The lives of 501 Black American women are discussed in this handsome volume in an attempt to fill the gap in reference collections in which Black women are inadequately represented. Those responsible for the work acknowledge the omission of many who could have been included. (Notably absent is Katherine Battle, the opera singer.) Criteria for inclusion in this volume hinged around the terms "pioneer," "leader," "major," "noted," "creative," or "distinguished." "The women selected as subjects of biographies do not constitute a list of the five hundred most important African-American women – that would be a foolish and presumptuous goal" (introduction). Those who are included were identified by an advisory board of distinguished contemporary women who come from many areas of endeavor.

Entries cover the lives of selected women from colonial times to the present. The earliest is Lucy Terry Prince, poet (1730), and the latest is Mae C. Jemison, the only Black female astronaut (1956). The range of talents and contributions cover some 200 categories. Many biographees are cross-listed under more than one category (e.g., Nikki Giovanni is listed under both "Publisher" and "Writer"; Fannie Lou Hammer is categorized as a "Sharecropper" and a "Civil Rights Activist"). Some categories overlap in meaning (e.g., "Educator" and "School Founder"; "Author" and "Writer"). It would be more helpful to standardize the list of categories to be used and then explain the reasons governing the choices.

Lengths of the biographies vary according to the amount of material available. For example, there is little known or written about Octavia Albert, who had been a Georgia slave and who wrote *The House of Bondage* in 1890, while entries about Lena Horne and Althea Gibson are lengthy and detailed. One of the best treatments is of Ada Smith, the blues singer and entertainer known from New York to Paris, who was a colleague of Duke Ellington and Cole Porter and who left a collection of her papers to James Haskin, a researcher on African-American life. A list of references accompanies each entry so that researchers and writers can have a ready place to turn. References include journal articles, books, archival materials, and special collections on the subject's life where available. When possible, contemporary biographees were given the opportunity to check over the essays written about them so that inaccuracies could be corrected. Photographs of selected subjects add considerably to the overall appeal of the volume. Entries are arranged alphabetically in a handsome typeface, with good page design and layout. In the front of the volume is an alphabetical list of all entries and lists of contributors, categories, photograph credits, and the members of the Advisory Board. A subject index is found in the back of the volume, where page references to main entries are indicated in boldface type.

Overall, this volume contains well-researched material about African-American women. It should be a welcome addition to many reference collections in school, public, and college libraries. Highly recommended. [R: Choice, June 92, pp. 1524-26; LJ, 1 Mar 92, pp. 84-86; RBB, 15 Apr 92, p. 1552; RQ, Fall 92, p. 121; SLJ, June 92, p. 156; WLB, May 92, p. 128] – **Melvin M. Bowie**

53. **Supplement to Who's Who in America 1991-1992.** 46th ed. Wilmette, Ill., Marquis Who's Who, 1991. 1293p. index. $167.00. LC 4-16934. ISBN 0-8379-7102-0.

This supplement was issued to accompany and update the two-volume 1990-1991 *Who's Who in America* (see ARBA 91, entry 22). It is the third such supplement to a *Who's Who* (see ARBA 88, entry 38 for a review of the first). This supplement contains about 21,000 updates of existing sketches and nearly 3,000 new entries. The format and the standard of admission are the same as for the regular edition. The arrangement is alphabetical, and this volume, similar to the 1989-1990 supplement, contains a geographic index and a professional index arranged by 39 categories. The current supplement also contains an alphabetical new name index, which lists people who appear for the first time and who will therefore also appear in the 47th edition of *Who's Who in America*. This volume may be useful for large reference collections but is not a necessity for smaller libraries. — **Kathleen Farago**

54. Ward, Geoffrey C. **American Originals: The Private Worlds of Some Singular Men and Women.** New York, HarperCollins, 1991. 277p. index. $23.00. CT215.W37. 920.073. LC 90-56401. ISBN 0-06-016694-0.

This collection of well-written short biographical works will interest even readers who usually avoid biography. Most of the pieces were originally written for publication in the monthly *American Heritage*. In the preface Ward identifies and, in some cases, critically discusses the published biographies that helped him in his research. He does not attempt to dryly chronicle entire lives in the 4- to 14-page articles but instead focuses on the private (and not always flattering) side of more than 40 famous Americans. For example, the piece on photographer Margaret Bourke-White illuminates her single-minded dedication to her work, even when "seduction seemed part of the job description." The article on Mark Twain centers on the happy and productive years (1874-1891) Twain spent in the "big curious house" he built for himself and his family in Hartford, Connecticut, before financial woes forced him to move. Ward organizes his subjects mainly by profession: politics, entertainment, writing and art, and the military. There are also sections on "bad men and liars" and the "Delanos and Roosevelts." (Three articles discuss different aspects of Franklin D. Roosevelt, about whom Ward has written two books.) The work is well indexed.

The writing in *American Originals* is fluid and energetic, with warmth and respect for the subjects as human beings. It deserves a place in both public and academic libraries. — **Kerranne G. Biley**

55. **Who's Who in America: Junior & Senior High School Version. [Volume 5 -Volume 8].** Wilmette, Ill., Marquis Who's Who, 1991. 4v. index. $87.00pa./set. LC 04-16934. ISBN 0-8379-1251-2.

These four books are a continuation of the title introduced in 1989 (see ARBA 91, entry 21). The new volumes have the same virtues as the old. In addition, the type size has been more than doubled, and abbreviations have been held to a minimum, making them easier for students to access and to read. The first four volumes provide nearly 6,000 entries about subjects from the fields of science and technology, politics and government, sports, and entertainment. The new volumes have 5,000 more entries on business and industry, literary and visual arts, and world leaders. The final volume also contains a complete index to the subjects of all eight volumes.

Each volume contains a 20-point key to information found in each entry, a table of abbreviations, and an explanation of the alphabetizing practices used. Each entry contains subject's name; vital statistics; occupation; parents; marital status and children; education; professional certification; career patterns and achievements; writings and creative works; civic and political activities; military record; awards and fellowships; political, religious, social, and club affiliations; avocations; and home and office addresses. The business and industry volume profiles such notables as designer Ralph Lauren and Disney head Michael Eisner. In the literary arts volume students will learn about Madeleine L'Engle, Lloyd Alexander, Alice Walker, and Chaim Potok. Andrew and Jamie Wyeth, Peter Max, Yves Saint-Laurent, and Christo are among the subjects in the visual arts volume. World leaders include Boris Yeltsin, Elie Wiesel, Lech Walesa, and Desmond Tutu. The complete set is an excellent resource work. [R: RBB, 15 Mar 92, p. 1400] — **Jerry D. Flack**

56. **Who's Who of American Women 1991-1992.** 17th ed. Wilmette, Ill., Marquis Who's Who, 1991. 1120p. $210.00. LC 58-13264. ISBN 0-8379-0417-X.

This is one of the many who's who publications Marquis produces, and its format and concept are essentially the same as the others. The coverage, however, is specialized. The first edition was published in 1958. Randomly comparing the present edition with that one shows that women now range far beyond the professions once perceived to be traditionally female. It certainly is an indication of women's increasingly varied roles in society. Once the list of more than 30,000 individuals had been determined (and that determination was made on one principle—"reference value"), the candidates were solicited for their personal data. Of the individuals who did not respond but who were considered notable enough for inclusion, Marquis researchers compiled the appropriate information. As in any other who's-who-type publication, the information is not anecdotal. Entries include such bare-bone facts as the woman's occupation, vital statistics, marital and family status, education, and notable contributions to her profession and community. The print is small and the entries can be confusing, but this publication should be included in nearly every collection after *Who's Who in America* (see ARBA 91, entry 22).—**Phillip P. Powell**

DICTIONARIES AND ENCYCLOPEDIAS

57. **Academic American Encyclopedia.** Danbury, Conn., Grolier, 1992. 21v. illus. maps. index. $775.00/set; $599.00/set (schools and libraries). AE5.A23. 031. LC 91-36894. ISBN 0-7172-2041-9.

As has been pointed out in earlier reviews (see ARBA 90, entry 45), *Academic American Encyclopedia* (AAE) is the youngest and most inventive of the major encyclopedias on the market. Known for its short articles, it serves the needs of individuals from early teenage years to adulthood. The information it provides is generally accurate, objective, and current. The set is alphabetical in a word-by-word arrangement, with numerous easy-to-use cross-references that extend accessibility to additional information. Words in small capital letters within a review indicate a cross-reference to an entry elsewhere in the set. (However, there is an error in "Capitance." The cross-reference is "Charges," but the entry is "Charge, Electric.") One of the best features of the encyclopedia is the number and clarity of illustrations, photographs, and maps (most of which are in color).

A policy of extensive revision continues to ensure AAE's currency on a wide range of subjects. The editors of this edition assert that 25 percent of the text and 17 percent of the articles have been revised—more than 220 articles have been changed extensively, and around 4,500 entries have been updated. In addition, some 80 new topics have been added, another 50 have been replaced, and more than 90 maps have been revised (updating illustrations as well as text is a priority).

Some events of the past year that have resulted in major revisions in AAE are the Gulf War, the reunification of Germany, and the disintegration of the Soviet Union. Many revisions reflect the U.S. Census statistics of 1990. New entries related to the Gulf War include the FO1171 Stealth Fighter, H. Norman Schwarzkopf, and Colin Powell. Among replacement articles is one on Germany with new information, new illustrations, and a new map. Other replacement articles include those on foreign policy, the ignition system, and manic-depressive psychosis (which has been cross-referenced from bipolar affective disorder, the more accurate terminology—why not use the new term?).

When compared to other encyclopedias, AAE maintains its integrity. Although the bibliographies lack complete currency—even with more than 2,000 updated titles—most articles have one or more titles for further reading. The work's illustrations are generally better than *World Book Encyclopedia* (World Book, 1992), and its objectivity is better than *Collier's Encyclopedia* (see ARBA 92, entry 39). Admittedly, the articles are succinct, but changes that have been made are significant. The index is more than adequate, providing access to bibliographies, illustrations, maps, and so forth.

This set is now available on CD-ROM and online. The online version is updated on a quarterly basis; the CD-ROM version maintains its currency with annual revisions. Recommended for purchase in school, public, and academic libraries. [R: RBB, 15 Sept 92, pp. 169-70]—**Anna Grace Patterson**

58. **Childcraft: The How and Why Library.** Robert O. Zeleny, ed. in chief. Chicago, World Book, 1991. 16v. illus. maps. index. price not reported. LC 90-70178. ISBN 0-7166-0191-5.

When is an encyclopedia not an encyclopedia? When it is a pre-encyclopedia, meant as a resource for the youngest readers and pre-readers. *Childcraft*, first published in 1934, is the pioneer in this field. The 15 main volumes (an unnumbered sixteenth volume is a children's dictionary, also published separately as the *World Book Student Dictionary*) are not particularly useful as a ready-reference source, because topics are arranged in thematic volumes, based roughly on areas of elementary school curriculum. Furthermore, subjects are chosen for their appeal and interest to children, without too much concern for the complete coverage of human knowledge required of a true encyclopedia. The aim of the work is to capture the attention of children with colorful graphics, clear writing, and stimulating topics, introducing them to the idea that reading can be useful, exciting, and fun.

Volumes 1-3 are an introduction to literature, poetry, and folktales, some meant to be read aloud by parents and teachers, some meant for older children to read themselves. Given the blossoming in children's publishing in recent years, there would seem less need for this type of collection, although parents will find this a handy source for many of the stories and poems they remember from their childhood. Five volumes are introductions to the sciences—4 (geology and astronomy), 5 (zoology), 6 (botany), 7 (oceanography), 12 (physics), and 13 (math). None of these volumes are rigorous treatments of their subject matter, but instead highlight important subjects with snappy, brief articles, do-it-yourself activities and experiments, wonderful illustrations, and even fiction and poetry. All include glossaries, bibliographies (arranged by age of student), and indexes, which increase their reference value. The writing style and treatment level is comparable to the best third or fourth grade science texts. Volume 13 is an interesting look at the science of mathematics, titled "Mathemagic." It consists of puzzles, games, and a little history of the human fascination with numbers.

Volumes 8, 9, and 10 are introductions to the social sciences, presented in ways children can appreciate and understand. Volume 8 looks at family life, religion, work, and play across the spectrum of human cultures, emphasizing similarities as well as differences. Volume 9 does the same, adding some history as well, in a month-by-month look at the calendar called "Holidays and Birthdays." Volume 10 travels the world in search of famous buildings, landmarks, and natural wonders. Volume 11, titled "Make and Do," is an excellent collection of arts and crafts projects. Volume 14, the final volume in the set meant for children, is an introduction to what elementary schools teach as "health"—a little anatomy, a little nutrition, and a lot of reassurance about the physical and mental changes a child experiences in growing up.

Volume 15 is meant for parents and educators. It has an extensive section on child development; a medical guide; and articles on special topics such as adoption, the handicapped child, and day care. As children are not likely to sit down and use these books on their own, volume 15 also includes detailed guides for using each volume of *Childcraft* with children of different ages and a separate guide for using the books to enrich the school curriculum. Finally, there is a general index to the entire set that indexes pictures and stories as well as factual material on thousands of subjects.

Except for the inclusion of the excellent children's dictionary, changes in *Childcraft* since previous editions seem minimal—brighter graphics, more modern illustrations, a little updating of scientific facts and focus. The volume for parents has some changes reflecting contemporary concerns such as children and television, latchkey children, and AIDS. Overall, the set shows two notable trends: an emphasis on learning through doing and exploring, particularly in the science volumes, and a more multicultural look, both in the illustrations and in the choice of stories and folktales.

As in most such publications for children, the world is seen through rose-colored glasses. Wars are long-ago events commemorated at monuments and on holidays; poverty, unemployment, and divorce do not exist. Of the major problems facing the world, only that of environmental pollution is mentioned in any significant way in the children's volumes. Such an approach, while commonplace, underestimates the powers and needs of children to understand reality and to become instruments of change.—**Carol L. Noll**

59. **The Encyclopedia Americana.** international ed. Mark Cummings, ed. in chief. Danbury, Conn., Grolier, 1992. 30v. illus. maps. index. $1,400.00/set; $919.00/set (schools and libraries). AE5.E333. 031. LC 90-23041. ISBN 0-7172-0123-6.

The Encyclopedia Americana has been reviewed many times in ARBA (the last review was in ARBA 90, entry 50), and this standard work again shows a number of changes in text and illustrative material to keep it abreast with new knowledge and rapid political changes in the world. The *Americana* is revised and published annually, and the revision program includes a variety of changes, such as new entries on entirely new subjects, revisions of existing articles, and additions of new illustrative material to accompany changes to the text. The present edition contains approximately 52,000 entries and more than 22,000 illustrations (14 percent in color) on about 26,700 pages, including the index volume. It has a number of important changes: a new editor, Mark Cummings, was appointed in June 1991; 40 new authors have made contributions; and some 3,000 entries have been revised. Of these, approximately

2,000 include new census data (including the 1990 U.S. Census); 415 bibliographies have been updated; and 734 articles show content updating or revision, including 68 with major revisions. There are four new maps: the Persian Gulf War, Berlin (two maps), and the voyages of Christopher Columbus. Nineteen maps have been updated to reflect political changes, including those on Czechoslovakia, Germany, Poland, and the Soviet Union. New articles include "Banks and Banking: North America," "Germany: Germany Reunited," "Homelessness," "Persian Gulf War," "Terrorism," "Union of Soviet Socialist Republics: Gorbachev and Yeltsin" (the breakup of the Soviet Union is not yet represented here), and "United States: Reflections on American Democracy." Many articles have been completely redone, such as those on Algeria, Bulgaria, the Cold War, Canadian health and welfare, Egypt, Pulitzer prizes, Tunis, Tunisia, and Warsaw. Major revisions have occurred in such articles as Andorra and the twentieth century. All in all, *Americana* is one of the best adult encyclopedias and should be found in most libraries. [R: RBB, 15 Sept 92, pp. 174-77] — **Bohdan S. Wynar**

60. **The New Book of Knowledge.** Danbury, Conn., Grolier, 1992. 21v. illus. maps. index. $750.00/set; $559.00/set (schools and libraries). AG5.N273. 031. LC 91-28420. ISBN 0-7172-0523-1.

The New Book of Knowledge (NBK) is a valuable reference work designed by educators and subject specialists for a wide range of student readers, from preschool children to some high school students. Each article has been written or reviewed by one of 1,700 experts in the relevant fields and follows the Dale-Chall readability formula to ensure that the comprehension level matches the age of the intended audience. The text is clarified and supplemented by 1,159 maps and 23,700 illustrations, full-color photographs, artwork, and diagrams.

A five-year program has been initiated with the 1992 edition of NBK that gives emphasis to the revision, redesign, and new illustrations of major articles throughout the set. These changes, both instructive and visually striking, have been implemented with the A, B, C, G, and L volumes and will continue until each volume has been amended. The 1992 edition has updates of important world events through October 1991, with attention given to political changes in China, Germany, the Middle East, the former Soviet Union, and Eastern Europe. (Due to the dynamics of current events, many of these articles will require changes for 1993 as well.) Significant articles in social studies, arts, and sciences have also been added, replaced, or revised. Seventy-five new text articles have been added, including those on Ancient Greece and the Northwest Passage. Fifteen of these articles originally appeared under major subject headings and have been deemed important enough for main entry coverage (e.g., amphibians, biological clock). Biographies comprise 50 of the new articles and include such significant people as Alexander and Carl Jung. Thirty articles have entirely new or rewritten text and have been illustrated with current art and photography. These include those on Berlin, games, and libraries. Another 30 articles that have been substantially revised or updated with new information, illustrations, maps, or photographs include those on education, Kuwait, and the Union of Soviet Socialist Republics. An additional 295 articles have received minor revisions or have been updated to incorporate current information, such as that on Africa, the Middle East, and many cities and states in North America. An earlier review (see ARBA 90, entry 52) noted that internal cross-referencing was not a strength of the set. In answer to this the editors have added 122 cross-references. This system will continue as articles are revised, with the names of important topics listed as cross-references in the main text.

The index is published in two ways. Individual volume indexes reference relevant subjects, illustrations, and photographs contained within the volume. These 85,000 entries are then collected and published cumulatively as volume 21. The individual indexes include dictionary entries that are brief definitional articles on a wide range of subjects that do not appear in the main text. A previous review (see ARBA 84, entries 28 and 29) emphasized the importance of using the dictionary index in order to gain full benefit of the encyclopedia. The ARBA 90 reviewer wondered whether a user would prefer these separate entries to an integrated text structure. A notable and welcome format change to the 1992 edition is the eventual elimination of the dictionary index entries. No new entries have been added, and existing entries will slowly be integrated into the text. The pronunciation guide developed for the NBK uses the Minimal Change System and makes unfamiliar and difficult words immediately recognizable. An example, *gerontology* (ger-on-TOL-ogy), shows that this method makes as few changes as possible to the original spelling and omits the use of special marks, symbols, or extensive phonetic spelling that can be confusing to a child.

The "Home and School Reading and Study Guides" detail the special features of the NBK and includes articles on hobbies, leisure activities, projects, and experiments. Study suggestions are given for the teacher and parent to help extend the information carried in the NBK. A 93-page paperback provides cross-references to articles within the text and includes a bibliography of more than 5,000 quality books for all ability levels. One may prefer that bibliographic entries accompany the articles; however, a separate list provides for yearly revisions, helping to maintain currency. The 1992 bibliography has been updated with more than 900 new titles.

Overall, the NBK is an excellent reference tool for its intended audience, giving accurate and authoritative coverage in a clear writing style. The articles should satisfy curiosity and encourage further reading until the user is ready for the transition to an adult encyclopedia. [R: RBB, 15 Sept 92, pp. 177-80]—**Deborah A. Taylor**

61. **The New Grolier Student Encyclopedia.** Danbury, Conn., Grolier, 1991. 22v. illus. maps. index. $319.00/set. ISBN 0-7172-7137-4. [Also available as *Young Students Learning Library*, Middletown, Conn., Field, 1991. 22v. illus. maps. $199.00/set. ISBN 0-8374-6032-8.]

This children's encyclopedia has been around in one form or another for 20 years. A publication history of the set can be found in the ARBA 90 review (see entry 53) of the 1989 encyclopedia. Since that edition, the number of volumes has shrunk by two, although the number of entries has remained roughly consistent at 3,000-plus. The introduction explains the set's purpose and the symbols used to denote special features, such as "Nuggets" (encapsulated bits of information) and "Learn by Doing" (activities within articles). The latter symbol, a blue box, has unfortunately been omitted in this part.

The articles are designed for elementary and some junior high school children. As in many similar works, the entries start simply and grow more complex. The range of topics is wide and occasionally eclectic; besides the usual entries for major historical figures, countries, animals, and the like are those for obscure Native American tribes (e.g., Athabascan), acupuncture, Abu Simbel (the site of two ancient temples on the Nile River), and chemical weapons, among others. A laudable number of the biographical entries are on women and minorities, and even the smallest countries have a paragraph and a map. The text in each entry is generally clear and written at the level of the student expected to look it up. Most articles define or go into detail about unusual terms; a notable exception is that on abrasives, which mentions powdered coke without explaining that, in this case, *coke* refers to a type of coal. (One can imagine the image that a child might conjure up!) Factual content seems to be appropriate in most cases, and entries can contain harsh facts, such as that millions of people have been displaced or killed in Afghanistan. However, some of the medical articles gloss over their subjects. For example, the entry on cancer neglects to mention that the disease is often fatal, and the entry on AIDS emphasizes the disease's transmittal through needle sharing, with only a quick mention of sexual relations and none at all about blood transfusions. The article on addiction concentrates almost exclusively on drug addiction, with its information rendered largely redundant by the presence of an entry on drug abuse. It would have been better to discuss the varied forms of addiction here, or at least the generic symptoms of addiction. Also, identical cellular life-span charts appear in both the article on aging and the one on growth.

One of the strengths of this set is the large number of really nice illustrations. Some 5,000 photographs, drawings, graphs, maps (from Rand McNally), and diagrams, the majority in full color and all sharp and clear, ground the text in reality and often illustrate concepts that might be difficult for children to grasp. For example, the article on agriculture shows two examples of crop rotation, and the entry on canals gives a clear picture of how locks work. One problem, however, is the frequent placement of illustrations or sidebars next to unrelated articles and even on opposite pages. This results from the format, which is two columns of text per page placed near the center of the book, creating a large outside margin for pictures. An extreme example of the confusion this can cause is that a sidebar on Edwin "Buzz" Aldrin appears next to a lengthy chunk of the article on alcoholic beverages and directly under the running head "Alcott, Louisa May." The article on Aldrin barely starts on that page, taking up more space on the next one, where a large photograph of Aldrin will draw readers' attention. They may not even see the sidebar.

The construction of the books is good. Each volume has its own table of contents, and cross-references are abundant and clear. The index in volume 22 will help users locate more than 22,000 entries. The typeface is sharp and easily read. The books lie flat and are sturdy enough to withstand many manipulations by small hands.

The bottom line with a children's encyclopedia is whether a child will actually use it, and if so, whether the child will glean real facts from it. In the case of this work, the answer is "yes" to both questions. Although its format creates a few problems, and some of the articles are a little coy in their approach to their subjects, *The New Grolier Student Encyclopedia* will attract users with its abundant and interesting pictures and then hold them with its well-written text. Moreover, it contains enough information to satisfy the curiosity of its intended audience, although it may be a bit too simplistic in spots to satisfy junior high students. Elementary schools, children's libraries, and parents will find this work a worthwhile acquisition. Those who deal with older children may want to preview a volume or two before purchase.—**D. A. Rothschild**

62. **New Standard Encyclopedia.** Chicago, J. G. Ferguson; distr., North Bellmore, N.Y., Marshall Cavendish, 1992. 20v. illus. maps. index. $549.95/set. AE5.N64. 031. LC 91-14723. ISBN 0-87392-197-6.

One of the many competitors for the home encyclopedia dollar, *New Standard Encyclopedia* will appeal to families that need a good general set. Although it is meant for adults, children as young as 10 will be able to understand most of the entries. Arranged word-by-word, articles are written largely by the encyclopedia staff and are unsigned; however, each is sent to at least one authenticator, or subject specialist, for review. In all, at least five people go over each article. The text is clearly written, with subjects receiving amounts of space that are appropriate to their importance. A smaller typeface is used for detailed technical information, such as the characteristics of each type of black oak. Most articles have appended bibliographies with books for both adults and children; the two types are clearly separated. Titles generally have a copyright range of 1980 to 1990, with a few older works here and there. Cross-references are plentiful, with subtitles to main articles noted when necessary (e.g., "see also PHYSICS, subtitles *Classical Physics* and *Modern versus Classical Physics*").

In general, the entries provide enough information to answer basic questions. The treatment of United States and Canadian provinces is especially good. One nice feature in these articles is the provision of a list of interesting places and an address for the travel division. (In the case of major cities, such as New York City, the state entry lists interesting places elsewhere in the state, while the city entry incorporates these sights in its text.) Additionally, most cities and towns of any real size—worldwide, not just North American—are profiled in at least a few lines. Articles on pseudosciences (e.g., astrology) are usually careful to point out the unscientific nature of these subjects; however, a few entries on controversial medical practices (e.g., chiropractic) could make their status clearer. The entry on national parks lists every park in the United States and Canada, complete with address.

The encyclopedia has a policy of continuous revision; each year up to 40 percent of the whole set is revised in some way. The next edition will need to update the article on the Olympics to reflect the 1992 games and to convey the results of the breakup of the Soviet Union, both as they apply to the quality of the teams and the reduced sense of tooth-and-nail competition between East and West. Similarly, the entry on Israel is somewhat out of date; it mentions the high birth rate of Arabs and its potential to create an Arab majority in the Jewish state, but it fails to note the enormous influx of Soviet Jews in recent years, which has largely nullified this concern. Some entries are too sparse; for example, the entry on comics has a line about the Comics Code but fails to explain what that entity is and how it has affected comics. Also, the entry on Eugene O'Neill ought to mention the playwright's alcoholism and how it influenced his work. The previous ARBA review (see ARBA 91, entry 32) noted that the bibliography for the entry on computers was out of date. While some of the books have been changed, they still date from the mid- to late 1980s.

Some criticism can be aimed at the illustrations. Although plentiful, many have a certain washed-out look that suggests age, and in general they tend to be small. (The maps are sharp and clear, however.) But as the idea is to pack as much information as possible into the set, the photographs are perhaps less important in this work than they would be in *World Book Encyclopedia* (see index for entry number) or other home encyclopedias.

Neither as sophisticated as *The New Encyclopaedia Britannica* (see ARBA 92, entry 41) nor as colorful as the *World Book, New Standard Encyclopedia* is nevertheless worthy of consideration for its amount of information and its relatively low price. It is appropriate for purchase by families and school and public libraries. [R: RBB, 15 Sept 92, pp. 182-84]—**D. A. Rothschild**

63. **Webster's New World Encyclopedia.** New York, Prentice Hall General Reference, 1992. 1230p. illus. maps. $75.00. AG5.W386. 032. LC 91-43020. ISBN 0-13-947482-X.

Single-volume encyclopedias obviously do not provide the scope or depth of a multivolume set, but they are growing in popularity for two reasons: low cost and currency of data. *Webster's New World Encyclopedia*, the latest (as of October 1992) on the market, has 25,000 alphabetically arranged entries with 2,500 illustrations, most in color. Based partly on the database of *Hutchinson's 9th* (1989), a Commonwealth encyclopedia, almost half of *Webster's* entries have been completely rewritten, and all have been updated and retailored to suit its United States, time-conscious, visually oriented, television-generation audience. Entries are short and to the point; they include pronunciation and are current through March 1992. For example, there is a boxed feature on the breakup of the Soviet Union, information on the AIDS drug AZT, and an entry for Senate confirmation hearings on Clarence Thomas. Other articles range from abortion through civil rights, junk bonds, Georgia O'Keeffe, Yale and other major universities, all 50 states, and 100 Supreme Court cases (e.g., *Roe v. Wade*, *Brown v. Board of Education*, Topeka). One of the book's pluses is its use of 1990 census data, the first encyclopedia to do so.

On the debit side, its articles do little more than skim the essentials. For example, someone seeking information on U.S. automobile history will find a cursory sketch that gives coverage to European and Japanese contributions but nary a nod to William C. Durant, founder of General Motors, or Cadillac/Lincoln founder Henry Leland. The volume has no index and no discernible cross-references, despite claims to many. Although it is well bound and lies flat, the three-column per page print is hard to read at a normal distance.

By way of comparison, *The Random House Encyclopedia* (see ARBA 91, entry 34) has the same number of entries; *The Concise Columbia Encyclopedia* (see ARBA 90, entry 49) has 15,000; *The Cambridge Encyclopedia* (Cambridge University Press, 1990) has 30,000; and *The American Spectrum Encyclopedia* (American Booksellers Association, 1991) has 26,000. The *Random House* has more than three times the number of illustrations as the others (although only its maps are in color) and twice as many pages, but its arrangement is not alphabetical and thus not as accessible. Weighing cost, currentness, and ease of use, *Webster's New World Encyclopedia* looks like a good buy for the money. [R: LJ, Aug 92, p. 92; RBB, 1 Oct 92, pp. 449-50; WLB, Nov 92, pp. 96-97]—**Mary Jo Walker**

64. **The World Book Encyclopedia.** Robert O. Zeleny, ed. in chief. Chicago, World Book, 1992. 22v. illus. maps. index. $599.00-$899.00/set; $520.00/set (schools and libraries). LC 91-65822. ISBN 0-7166-0092-7.

The world's best-selling encyclopedia celebrated its 75th anniversary in 1992 and continues a well-established tradition of outstanding service to its audience in North American schools and homes. With more than 14,000 pages, 22 volumes (including an index), and approximately 17,500 entries, this general encyclopedia provides users with accurate, balanced, up-to-date coverage of the entire field of current human knowledge. Its primary market is students in grades 3-12 and their educators. It is also meant for home use by families. These diverse markets, which span a range of ages and social strata, dictate the topic selection and article format. Emphasis is on those subjects most popular with students (e.g., dog, cat, baseball) and those that are associated with current school curriculum (e.g., moon, Adolf Hitler, United States). In addition, articles have been written at the level of understanding of those most likely to look up that information. For example, the entries on plastics and plate tectonics are more complex than those on dolls and dinosaurs. Overall, the writing style is direct, clear, and concise. Some of the longer articles begin at a basic level and progress to more complex levels of understanding, so it could be said that the content of *World Book* has been customized to the needs of its readership. Another characteristic of the work that makes it especially useful to students is the article format. Longer articles include not only a story and accompanying illustrations but also an outline, cross-references, and a bibliography of resources.

As usual, many articles have been added and updated. The publisher cites some 50 new articles (19 are biographies), more than 450 extensive revisions, and nearly 3,000 partial revisions. Political changes and events are for the most part reflected in updates, as in the article on the Soviet Union, which covers its dissolution and depicts ethnic boundaries on the accompanying maps. According to *World Book* publicity, recent events in the Soviet Union have affected 55 articles across 16 volumes. New entries have been added on the Persian Gulf War, Norman Schwarzkopf, Saddam Hussein, and Clarence Thomas. (There is no article on Anita Hill, although she is referenced in the Thomas article.) Articles in many other areas have been updated as well, including those in areas of art, nature, sports, and religion.

Accessibility is the key to *World Book*'s excellence. A separate index includes more than 150,000 entries, and the entire work is extensively cross-referenced. The index also has reading and study guides for chosen subjects. These list topics for study in the area and a selection of resources organized into two reading levels. A student guide to writing, speaking, and research skills at the beginning of the index volume provides valuable instruction on study methods and skills. Bibliographies list further resources, but as noted in an earlier review (see ARBA 88, entry 53), some resources are dated. For example, the article on alcoholism cites only two resources, both published in 1985.

The 1992 edition of *World Book* has two special features. One is a colorful foldout titled "The Legacy of Columbus: Expanding Views of the World." A general examination of the world in 1492 recounts events and issues of that era in Asia, Africa, the Americas, and Europe. The essay "1492-1592: Voyages of Exploration" offers biographical sketches of a number of explorers and discusses various aspects of navigation. The article "1592: A New View of the World" summarizes the century of exploration and some of its social and political ramifications. Readers may question the amount of space allotted to this topic, but the content is impeccable. For the treatment of material in the feature and in the completely revised summary of Christopher Columbus, the editors deserve commendation for their accuracy and objectivity. The second feature is a special anniversary supplement that appears at the beginning of volume 1. It traces the history of *World Book* from its inception in 1917 to the present, highlighting important events and historical developments over the past 75 years. Reproductions of the original illustrations and text lend historical depth to the content of this piece.

This sturdy and aesthetically pleasing set includes 29,000 photographs and illustrations (24,000 in color). Its chief competitor, *Compton's Encyclopedia and Fact-Index* (see ARBA 90, entry 48), has 22,510 illustrations. Drawings are clear (if somewhat conservative), but unfortunately, many of the photographs are small, pinched, and distant. Also, as the reviewer in ARBA 84 (entry 32) noted, many are out of focus and suffer from poor registration. In general, though, the number of illustrations makes up for their lack of quality. The 3,000-plus contributors include such notables as art critic Dore Ashton and the late author-scientist Isaac Asimov. Major articles contain biographical notations on the authors and list current affiliations.

World Book's many strengths are, unfortunately, offset by persistent weaknesses. As mentioned in earlier reviews, avoidance of controversial subject matter continues to be an obstacle to the work's comprehensiveness. For example, a description of the 1960s in the article on American history cites civil rights, urban unrest, the Vietnam War, and space exploration as issues and events of that period. However, it fails to mention the development of the so-called hippie movement with its rock concerts and its promotion of drug use, free love, and communes. Nor is there a listing for Timothy Leary, an important figure of the era. In some instances the length or lack of treatment betrays a conservative and decidedly Western bias, as in the case of the rather lengthy article on the Roman Catholic Church (approximately 10 pages). The entry for *god* runs several paragraphs, while the entry for *goddess* refers the reader to mythology. In the same vein, the article on the topic of witches concentrates on supposed destructive activities and satanic associations of witchcraft and virtually ignores the simple pagan aspects that, it could be argued, are more important features of modern wicca.

Although *World Book* has a good reputation for science coverage, the 1992 edition has several oversights in this important area. There is no listing in either the encyclopedia or the index for virtual reality (or cyberspace, computer simulation, or flight simulation), a scientific topic of great interest to young people. In addition, an important scientific announcement of 1991 has been overlooked—that of fullerenes, sometimes called "Buckminster Fullerenes" or "buckyballs." Quasicrystals, big news in

1985, are also omitted. Fractals appear, but not Benoit Mandelbrot, the individual who brought them into the public eye.

In spite of its flaws and oversights, *World Book* is a superb encyclopedia, and its purchase is a solid investment in learning. It has more pages than *Compton's*, and, without the index, more entries (17,500 versus 5,234). Its format is more practical, especially for younger students who might have trouble using *Compton's* cumbersome fact index, and the contents of *World Book* are well suited to its intended audiences. Highly recommended for school, public, and home libraries. [R: RBB, 15 Sept 92, p. 184]—**Barbara Ittner**

DIRECTORIES

65. **Associations Canada 1992: An Encyclopedic Directory.** 2d ed. Toronto, Canadian Almanac & Directory Publishing; distr., Detroit, Gale, 1992. 1130p. index. $175.00pa. ISBN 1-895021-07-3.

Associations Canada 1992 has retained some features of its predecessor (see ARBA 92, entry 44); it gives addresses and descriptions of approximately 20,000 associations and information on conventions and conferences. Some associations have been deleted while others have been added. The 2d edition has significant improvements over the previous one. There is now a detailed subject index as opposed to the initial edition's classification under a few general categories. Also, there are a geographic index classified by province and city and an index for serial publications by subject. To improve access to information, a textual reference has been added at the top of each page. Special features of this directory are essays on nonprofit organizations in Canada and association management and brief statistics about giving and volunteering in Canada. This edition is a more worthwhile purchase than the first because of its improvements. However, many entries still only contain name, address, and telephone number, and the work is poorly bound.—**Margaret A. Grift**

66. **Awards, Honors, & Prizes: An International Directory....** 9th ed. Gita Siegman, ed. Detroit, Gale, 1991. 2v. index. $175.00(v.1); $200.00(v.2). LC 85-070620. ISBN 0-8103-5091-2. ISSN 0196-6316.

The information in this guide is organized first geographically (the United States and Canada in volume 1, other countries in volume 2), then alphabetically by name of the awarding agency. Within each volume every agency has a serial identifier. Each award offered by the same agency has a second number added by a dash; the indexes refer to these numbers. In the front of each volume are highlights, an introduction, and a user's guide; these are thorough. Of special value to users is the terse boxed note that advises consultation of the indexes first. Indexes are of organizations (including cross-references), awards, and subjects; the last has a classified list and is well designed with a commendable structure of *see* and *see also* references. Entries are skillfully written, giving a concise and informative description of the award, its functional and commemorative purposes, frequency, value, and history. Addresses, names of contact persons, and telephone numbers are also given. Discontinued awards are so noted.

A search strategy guide that listed the type of question that may be asked of it, and how to proceed to the answer, would be useful. Running heads would help in both the body of the work and the subject index, as some entries cover several columns and pages. A list of awards new to this edition, as well as of discontinued ones, would be worthwhile. Untrained users are likely to miss the classified list of subjects due to its location in the book; this section might be better placed in the front.

This guide is available on diskette and magnetic tape, with all their attendant expanded search strategies. Further, considering the user's need for current information, an online edition is advisable. Meanwhile, those engaged in collection development should weigh the need for slightly dated information against the cost of this work. Major research institutions will wish to acquire this edition; smaller libraries may prefer to live with a superseded one; and all will want to keep abreast of developments that take place after the publication of this edition.—**Ian Fairclough**

67. Caughman, Jennifer T., ed. **Trade and Professional Associations in California: A Directory.** 5th ed. Sacramento, Calif., California Institute of Public Affairs, 1992. 62p. index. (California Information Guides Series). $50.00pa. HD2428.C3T73. 061'.94'025. LC 91-9749. ISBN 0-912102-95-0.

This directory was first published in 1979 and has been revised on a three to four year basis. This edition has been thoroughly revised, and information has been checked by telephone or mail. Included are those associations with statewide or regional scope and national organizations that have offices in the state, plus a few local groups of general interest. Excluded are local chambers of commerce. Numbered entries are listed in alphabetical order and contain the organization's name, address, and telephone number. The index of subjects and key words refers to the entry numbers. The existence of 1,861 entries for one state reflects on our highly organized society and the necessity of a directory such as this.—Sara R. Mack

68. **International Research Centers Directory 1992-93: A World Guide....** 6th ed. Annette Piccirelli, Kelly Crowther, and Christopher Kasic, eds. Detroit, Gale, 1991. 1481p. index. $375.00. ISBN 0-8103-7525-7. ISSN 0278-2731.

The scope of this work is government, university, independent nonprofit, and commercial research and development centers; institutes; laboratories; bureaus; test facilities; experiment stations; research parks; data collection and analysis centers; and foundations, councils, and other organizations that support research. Centers in the United States have been excluded. The arrangement is by country, with multinational bodies in front. The tool is available online and in diskette and tape formats; a mailing label service is also offered.

New this year are the page titled "Highlights" and the improved presentation of the indexes (elements are sharply set off by the use of indentation, bullets, and boldface type). Full explanations are found at the head of each index and in the user's guide section, which expands on the 5th edition's sample entry. Overall, the design has been much improved. In the body of the work, the running title has been changed to present the years of coverage rather than the edition number. Seven hundred entries are new. Use of standardized terms to precede data has increased, resulting in a more concise format. Non-English center names are now listed in the country index, and the use of three-letter geographic codes has been extended to the master index (formerly the name and keyword index). The list of these codes is now placed at the front of the book rather than before the subject index, along with a list of telephone country codes.

Critical to the use of this work is a proper understanding of the indexes. In the subject index, the three-letter country code substitutes for arrangement by country; further, reference is only to entry number. No indication of what source, if any, is used to establish the subject terms; they reflect the scope of the actual centers and include *see* and *see also* references. Except for its references, the country index consists of a list of entries in the same order as the body of work—an indication that it is really an expanded contents list and therefore belongs in front. If the name or acronym of an institute is known, but not its country, access is via the master index—and users should be advised that the order is neither word-by-word nor letter-by-letter but keyword-by-keyword. Thus, the likes of "Centre for" and "Centre de" are interfiled, but "Center for" is filed separately. No list of stopwords is provided.

This work seems to attain its intended scope of comprehensive coverage. However, a library considering its acquisition should weigh both cost and timeliness for the library's community. If usage is sparse, online searching may prove less expensive.—**Ian Fairclough**

69. **The National Directory of Addresses and Telephone Numbers: Containing Phone Numbers, Addresses, Fax Numbers and Toll-Free Numbers....** Steven A. Miles, ed. Detroit, Omnigraphics, 1992. 1472p. index. $69.95; $59.95pa. LC 81-52822. ISBN 1-55888-771-7; 1-55888-760-1pa. ISSN 0740-7203.

The latest edition of this directory, now published by Omnigraphics, is divided into two main sections: an alphabetical listing by company or organization name and a classified listing by subject or SIC (Standard Industrial Classification) code groupings. There are also profiles of top U.S. cities, an index to area and zip codes, and a subject index. Businesses are listed on the basis of size or earnings within industry groupings; criteria for inclusion are provided within each category. The alphabetical listing provides a mailing or street address, telephone number, fax number if available, and some toll-free numbers. A nice feature is the use of a bullet next to the corporate headquarters when there is more than one listing under the same name. The classified listing has a convenient government section that includes federal and state agency addresses and numbers as well as those for all U.S. senators and representatives.

As might be expected with a directory containing "approximately 120,000 unique listings," there are errors. The editor notes that about 25 percent of the listings change over the course of each year, so some incorrect entries are inevitable. Others, however, are avoidable. For example, one of the colleges listed under 4-year institutions for Maine has not been in this category for more than 10 years, and both the name and telephone number of this reviewer's library are listed incorrectly. (Standard directories for educational institutions and libraries provide the correct information.) Also, many existing toll-free business numbers are not listed.

Despite these minor problems, this book offers rapid and usually accurate retrieval of an impressive amount of address, fax, and telephone information. It will find a place on most ready-reference shelves. [R: RBB, 1 Jan 92, p. 847] — **Deborah V. Rollins**

70. Smallwood, Carol, comp. **Free Resource Builder for Librarians and Teachers.** 2d ed. Jefferson, N.C., McFarland, 1992. 313p. index. $24.95pa. Z692.F73S62. 011'.03. LC 92-51211. ISBN 0-89950-685-2.

With budgets in the condition they are today, this work should prove valuable to any collection development specialist. There are 5,435 entries to government agencies and nonprofit organizations that provide free documents. The materials are arranged under 14 topics, from alcohol and drug abuse to women. A detailed list of subgroups in the table of contents provides more specific access, and a full index gives the searcher access by natural language.

This edition expands and updates the first edition by including sections on disabilities, education, alcohol and drug abuse, and women. A particularly valuable section deals with vertical file headings, resources, and management that, according to Smallwood, have received new material listings. Entries have been selected for their usefulness to educators and librarians and for the authority of the source. The limitations of space have required that some sources be left out, but the list is still a long and valuable one. The brief introduction helps one make the best use of the book.

Recommended for reference and collection development librarians, teachers, and other professionals who need free information on specific topics. It can benefit small libraries of all types.

— **Edward P. Miller**

71. **State and Regional Associations of the United States.** 1992 ed. Buck J. Downs, Amy J. Misner, and Judith Tabler, eds. Washington, D.C., Columbia Books, 1992. 489p. $45.00pa. ISBN 0-910416-95-8. ISSN 1044-324X.

Little has changed since the first review of this source in ARBA 90 (see entry 95), except that it now includes publications of the associations listed. It also provides indexes by budget range, executive, acronym, and management firm. A quick comparison with the *Encyclopedia of Associations: Regional, State, and Local Organizations* (see ARBA 90, entry 61) revealed that the item under review is much less comprehensive, as its stated scope would indicate. Because it is also much lower in price than the encyclopedia, smaller libraries might consider it as an alternative purchase. — **Maureen A. Beck**

72. Strangelove, Michael, and Diane Kovacs. **Directory of Electronic Journals, Newsletters and Academic Discussion Lists.** 2d ed. Washington, D.C., Association of Research Libraries, 1992. 241p. $25.00pa. ISSN 1057-1337.

The rapid proliferation of electronic journals and newsletters is seen in the fact that a 2d edition of this directory has appeared only nine months after the initial one. That edition had 627 entries; the new one has 902. Strangelove and Kovacs have attempted to limit themselves to electronic publications with some scholarly interest.

There are two major sections. The first, by Strangelove, lists journals and newsletters; the second, by Kovacs, lists academic discussion and interest groups. There are further subdivisions. Strangelove divides his publications into 3 groups: 36 electronic journals; 80 electronic newsletters; and 17 "Hypercard, digest-newsletters, and others." He does not explain the criteria used for the three groups. For each title he furnishes a short description of contents, information on how to subscribe, and names and addresses of contacts.

Kovacs lists 769 electronic conferences arranged by scholarly interest. For each she gives a brief description and BITNET and Internet addresses. Because there is no overall alphabetical index for the volume, the individual sections must be scanned when searching a title. An introductory essay by Stevan Harnad (reprinted from an electronic journal) attempts a rationale, albeit a wordy one, for such journals. Several notes give information on how to retrieve the directory from networked sources, how to get information about starting an electronic newsletter, and how to secure an ISSN for a journal. Kovacs also supplies instructions on how to address electronic conferences.

The names and electronic addresses, at first view gibberish that is all in capital letters with "@" and "%" symbols tossed in liberally, do not make this work attractive. Even so, this directory is essential in the reference collection of any sizable library. [R: Choice, Apr 92, p. 1205-06; JAL, Sept 92, p. 246]—**Richard D. Johnson**

GOVERNMENT PUBLICATIONS

73. Morehead, Joe, and Mary Fetzer. **Introduction to United States Government Information Sources.** 4th ed. Englewood, Colo., Libraries Unlimited, 1992. 474p. index. (Library Science Text Series). $38.50; $32.50pa. Z1223.Z7M665. 015.73'053. LC 92-13251. ISBN 0-87287-909-7; 1-56308-066-4pa.

This edition of an important work has been given a new title that focuses on the contents of U.S. government publications rather than on their formats. Since the 3d edition was published in 1983 (see ARBA 84, entry 50), online and CD-ROM technology have brought about significant changes in the dissemination of government information. Morehead and Fetzer have done an outstanding job of revising and updating this introductory guide to reflect those changes, as well as changes in printed sources.

This edition has been expanded by more than 150 pages and reorganized. Chapters that cover reference, legislative, and regulatory sources are now more prominent, and a separate chapter has been created for statistical sources, including extensive information on the 1990 Census and the federal budget. Coverage of patent, trademark, copyright, and General Accounting Office sources is a welcome enhancement. The title/series index has been made comprehensive, and subjects and names are newly divided into separate indexes.

This text continues to be the most comprehensive introduction to the bibliographic structure of federal government information. Although it is not intended as a commentary on issues of information policy, it does provide background necessary for understanding the issues. Not only is it a valuable text on government information for library and information studies students, but it also serves librarians as an important ready-reference tool. [R: JAL, Nov 92, p. 317]—**Carol Wheeler**

74. Schwarzkopf, LeRoy C., comp. **Government Reference Books 90/91: A Biennial Guide to U.S. Government Publications.** 12th biennial ed. Englewood, Colo., Libraries Unlimited, 1992. 393p. index. $65.00. Z1223.Z7G68. 015'.73. LC 76-146307. ISBN 0-87287-913-5.

The form of this volume remains essentially the same as previous editions (see ARBA 91, entry 43). The table of contents outlines 4 general subject categories—general library reference, social sciences, science and technology, and arts and humanities—within which 1,345 brief annotated entries are arranged. Entries are also accessed through entry numbers in the author/title/subject index. The compiler's information section provides a detailed explanation of each element of every bibliographic citation and annotation. Many entries now include ISBNs, which the GPO began assigning to sales publications in early 1991. The two-year period covered by this volume represents the date of distribution to depository libraries rather than the imprint date. While most government serials appear in this book's sister volume *Government Reference Serials* (see ARBA 89, entry 58), serials published less frequently than biennially, as well as a small number of other irregular and regular serials, continue to appear in *Government Reference Books*. Because of the backlog in GPO distribution of microfiche, this edition reverts to the practice of the first 10 editions in including works distributed in paper format only. Despite the descriptive rather than critical nature of the annotations, both federal depository and nondepository libraries will find this volume helpful as a collection management and reference tool and as a starting place for the development of subject bibliographies of government publications.

—**Jeanette C. Smith**

HANDBOOKS AND YEARBOOKS

75. **Yearbook of International Organizations 1991/92.** Edited by Union of International Associations. Munich, New Providence, N.J., K. G. Saur, 1991. 3v. index. $825.00/set. LC 49-22132. ISBN 3-598-22209-2. ISSN 0084-3814.

Volume 1 of this set is divided into two sections. Section 1 is an index of organizations. The entries are arranged alphabetically, and each is assigned an entry number (e.g., EE1056). Letters refer to the section; numbers refer to the order of the entry listed in a particular section. Section 2 provides full descriptions of the organizations, arranged according to entry number. Typically, each entry consists of the name of the organization, officers, address, telephone and fax numbers, history, aims, activities, events, structure, relations to other organizations, consultative status, finance, languages, publications, members, and cross-references. More than 28,000 organizations are listed in this volume, which is the easiest to use and the most useful of the entire set.

Volume 2 is also divided into two sections. Section 1 lists the organizations which each country is a member of or to which it belongs. Entries in this volume are organized by continents; within each continent, countries (entries) are listed in alphabetical order. Section 2 lists organizations that have secretariats in every country. Also included is a country index, in which each country is assigned an entry number.

Volume 3 consists of two sections as well. The first is an index of organizations arranged according to subject. Each entry is accompanied by an entry code that can be used to locate more information either in this or the other volumes. The second section provides more detailed information for each organization. Entries in this part are arranged according to subject category. This volume is useful when the organizations are not known, but inexperienced users may take a while to learn how to use volumes 2 and 3 due to their unconventional arrangement.

The print, although small, is clear, and the binding is sturdy; the only drawback is the cost. All in all, this is an indispensable reference tool for college, research, and large public libraries.—**Binh P. Le**

INDEXES

76. **Book Review Digest.** (Indexing coverage: 1/83-6/25/92). [CD-ROM]. Bronx, N.Y., H. W. Wilson, 1992. Hardware requirements: WILSONLINE Workstation, IBM PC, or compatible; 640K; hard disk drive. $1,095.00.

Compact disc (CD) technology is eminently well suited to *Book Review Digest* (BRD). Most users of this source have particular books or authors in mind when they come to use it, and they want to get in and out quickly, gathering the maximum number of reviews in the shortest possible time. The print version of BRD does an admirable job of this, but the CD version is even better. A few keystrokes allow one to search a disc that contains some 10 years of book reviews and very quickly bring up the reviews for a particular title. All reviews in the printed version are displayed in the CD version, with some minimal rewriting of abstracts. No information is lost.

As in all WILSONDISC products, there are three levels of searching that vary in difficulty and sophistication. BROWSE is the most straightforward approach. WILSEARCH demands more sophistication, and WILSONLINE requires a fair amount of study and practice time. For most BRD searches, BROWSE will be most useful. One can input either an author's name or a book's title and display a mingled list of titles, authors, and subjects that alphabetically surround the term inputted. One can then choose the desired term and display all records related to it. WILSEARCH allows the searcher to enter multiple subject terms. With BRD, this is most useful when looking for books on a topic rather than for reviews of one particular book. It is also the WILSEARCH level that allows one to search for an author in the personal-name field only, rather than—as in BROWSE—finding all references to an author, whether as author or subject. When using WILSEARCH and entering an author's name with the suffix ":(au)," the computer will find only records with that name as the author, not references to books about that author.

Title searching in the BROWSE mode can be tricky, as it demands that the exact title be inputted. For example, searching for the best-seller *—and Ladies of the Club* as a title resulted in nothing until the hyphen was entered as part of the title. Neither *Ladies of the Club* nor *And Ladies of the Club* got results. However, by moving to the WILSEARCH mode and doing a multiterm search on *ladies* and *club*, the title was found.

A useful feature is the truncation key, the "#" key. The operator can use this key in the middle of a word or at the end, thus asking the computer to search both *women* and *woman* by typing in *womfln*. The program will truncate automatically, without being asked, in the case of plurals. A feature that would be useful (it is present in CD products from other companies) is the mark feature, by which a user can scroll through all records from a search, marking those of interest. At the end, one command will cause all the marked records to print. WILSONDISC requires either that each desired record be commanded to print at the time of display or that all records be printed.

In general, instructions on each screen and the easily retrieved help screens are helpful and will lead a user through the search process. However, as with any computer application (or with any printed reference book, for that matter), the user must make the effort to read the screens and follow the directions rather than randomly striking keys. So far, even WILSONDISC's more-than-average user-friendly program cannot guarantee that everyone will be able to use it without guidance.

Installation is reasonably simple, with documentation that gives step-by-step instructions. Again, the installer needs to take the time to read instructions carefully and follow all steps. In general, for the first-time user of this technology, the WILSONDISC products are a good choice.—**Terry Ann Mood**

77. **Essay and General Literature Index.** rev. ed. (Indexing coverage: 1/85-12/26/91). [CD-ROM]. Bronx, N.Y., H. W. Wilson, 1991. Hardware requirements: WILSONLINE Workstation, IBM PC, or compatible; 640K; hard disk drive. $695.00.

The beauty of CD-ROMs from H. W. Wilson is that all are born equal. This classic title on CD-ROM looks comfortingly familiar to one who has used Social Sciences Index, MLA International Bibliography, or any other Wilson CD-ROM product. Commands, indexing structure, and screen format are all similar. Three levels of searching exist: BROWSE; WILSEARCH, for multiterm subject searching; and WILSONLINE, the disc version of Wilson's online searching. BROWSE is the most straightforward approach. WILSEARCH demands a bit more sophistication, and WILSONLINE requires a fair amount of study and practice time. The trade-off is in results: WILSONLINE, with its Boolean logic capability, accomplishes much more complicated searching than does either of the other forms.

For the majority of searches and searchers, the WILSEARCH function will be the most useful. With it the user can input more than one subject term and the computer will then search all fields of each record. This is helpful when—as is often the case—the user is uncertain of the particular subject heading to enter. Inputting several subject words will allow the computer to locate those words even if they are separated in the record; it can find one in a title and another in an abstract. This approach usually calls up one or two relevant records. Such records, in turn, display subject headings that can be used for a more complete search. Sometimes using BROWSE and WILSEARCH in tandem is useful. BROWSE can be used to display the list of subject terms that alphabetically surround the term inputted; a more specific subject term can then be selected from the displayed list.

A useful feature is the truncation key, the "#" key, for wild-card searches. The operator can use this key in the middle of a word or at the end, thus, for example, asking the computer to search both *women* and *woman* by typing in *womfln*. The program will truncate automatically, without being asked, in the case of plurals. A feature that would be useful is the ability to mark records so that a user could scroll through all records from a search, marking those of interest and printing them when the search was complete. WILSONDISC requires either that each desired record be commanded to print at the time of display or that all records be printed.

A feature of the CD-ROM version that is not replicated in the print version is the list of a book's contents. When the entry displayed is that of an entire book rather than a separate chapter or section, the display includes a list of chapter titles or headings. This can lead to further "hits" (further search terms).

In general, instructions on each screen and the easily retrievable help screens are helpful and will lead users through the process. However, as with any computer application (or with any printed reference book, for that matter), the user must make the effort to read the screens and follow the directions rather than randomly striking keys. So far, even WILSONDISC's more than average user-friendly programs will not guarantee that every user will be able to use it without guidance. Installation is reasonably simple and the documentation gives instructions. (Again, the installer needs to read the instructions carefully and follow all the steps.) For the first-time installer and CD-ROM user, the WILSONDISC products are a good choice. — **Terry Ann Mood**

MUSEUMS

78. Cleaver, Joanne. **Doing Children's Museums: A Guide to 265 Hands-On Museums.** Charlotte, Vt., Williamson Publishing, 1992. 229p. index. $13.95pa. AM11.C56. 069'.054025'73. LC 92-8280. ISBN 0-913589-63-2.

The rise in the number of children's museums across the country helps to justify the publication of this reasonably priced work. The book includes sites in both the United States and Canada; both traditional (e.g., Boston, Detroit) and newer (e.g., San Jose, Vancouver) museums are listed. The directory is preceded by four thoughtful essays that provide background information on the development of children's museums since the turn of the century and that differentiate between discovery rooms, science laboratories, and participatory exhibits that may be found in some children's museums. Also included are tips to help parents prepare children for a museum visit and follow-up questions to continue the learning process at home.

Directory information is alphabetically arranged by state and subdivided by city and name of museum. Each entry includes a descriptive paragraph that notes age-appropriate exhibits, address and telephone number, hours of operation, admission fee, parking logistics, and special features (e.g., gift shop, access for strollers/wheelchairs, nearby attractions). The well-organized indexes provide access by name of museum and list all museums by state. Both the main entry information and the indexes are graphically attractive and easy to use, as they are printed in large type and include the city/state at the top and bottom of each page. Unfortunately, Cleaver provides no criteria for inclusion.

Although *Children's Museums, Zoos, and Discovery Rooms* (see ARBA 88, entry 61) covers some of the same territory, it is less extensive in scope and coverage and more expensive. Libraries on a budget will appreciate this newer paperback guide. — **Ilene F. Rockman**

79. **The Official Museum Directory 1992.** Wilmette, Ill., National Register Publishing, 1991. 1474p. index. $159.95pa. (with *The Official Museum Products and Services Directory 1992*). LC 79-144808. ISBN 0-87217-956-7.

This directory to museums in the United States and its territories includes over 7,000 institutions arranged alphabetically by state, then city. Each entry provides the museum's name, address, telephone number, fax number, and founding date. In addition, the following information is given: U.S. congressional district, key administrative and curatorial personnel, governing authority, a profile of collections, research fields, a description of physical facilities, educational and other activities offered by the museum, publications, hours information, admission costs, and membership fees. More than 200 new museums are included in this edition.

The major section is prefaced by a profile of the American Association of Museums and a list of staff and services offered. Affiliate professional organizations, regional museum associations and state representatives, federal agencies that provide museum support, state museum organizations, regional arts organizations, state humanities councils, and other organizations are also listed. Supplementary material includes an alphabetical list of all institutions, an alphabetical list by name of director or department head, and a list of museums by category. A companion volume to *The Official Museum Products and Services Directory* (National Register Publishing, 1991), this work should remain a key reference tool in every museum, academic, and public library collection. — **Edmund F. SantaVicca**

80. **The Official Museum Products and Services Directory 1992.** Wilmette, Ill., National Register Publishing, 1991. 210p. $159.95pa. (with *The Official Museum Directory 1992*). LC 79-144808. ISBN 0-87217-956-7.

From computer software to taxidermy, from shipping and moving companies to conservation supplies, most basic services and products needed by museum staff are to be found in this directory. Designed as a companion volume to *The Official Museum Directory 1992* (National Register Publishing, 1991), this alphabetically classed arrangement is complemented by a one-page index to classifications and an alphabetical list of entries by name of company or business. Entries in the main section are much briefer than those in *Official Museum Directory*. Included here are name, address, and telephone number, followed by a brief description of type of business or services offered and key personnel. If the company has placed an advertisement in the volume, the reader is cross-referenced to that page. Unlike its companion volume, which will likely be found in a variety of library collections outside of museums, this excellent resource directory's limited scope will prove most useful to museum and gallery staff. — **Edmund F. SantaVicca**

PERIODICALS AND SERIALS

81. **Australian Periodicals in Print 1991.** 9th ed. Port Melbourne, Austral., D. W. Thorpe; distr., New Providence, N.J., K. G. Saur, 1991. 782p. $75.00. ISBN 0-909532-82-6. ISSN 1030-2476.

This guide to some 5,000 Australian and Australia-related periodicals provides comprehensive information in an easy-to-use format. The text covers periodicals published up to July 1991. Magazines, directories, yearbooks with ISSNs, newspapers, proceedings, and trade publications are included, but most government publications are excluded. Readers can track desired entries by publishers, titles, or subjects. The introduction provides sufficient information for readers to readily comprehend the abbreviations in the various entries. Considerably larger than the previously reviewed 7th edition (see ARBA 90, entry 25), but not much more expensive, this work will be useful primarily to Australian libraries and those with a strong focus on the country. — **Dorothy M. Williams**

82. **CD-ROM Periodical Index: A Guide to Abstracted, Indexed, and Fulltext Periodicals on CD-ROM.** By Pat Ensor and Steve Hardin. Westport, Conn., Meckler, 1992. 420p. (Supplements to Computers in Libraries, no.48). $95.00. PN1.E57. 025.04. LC 92-6948. ISBN 0-88736-803-4.

CD-ROM products for libraries are becoming a hydra-headed monster. No sooner is one purchased than nine more appear, some better than the ones already purchased. Nor does there seem to be an end. This work lists 30,000 periodical titles indexed or included fulltext in more than 77 major CD-ROM databases. Part 1 lists the databases alphabetically and gives the name of the publisher, price, years covered, operating software, search capabilities, and an alphabetical list of the periodicals included. Part 2 lists the 30,000 periodical titles alphabetically and indicates the database in which each is listed.

The work is well done and easy to use, but because the authors give no explanation as to the source of their information, a few problems with the periodical listings for the *MLA International Bibliography* are mystifying. The journal *ELH* (Johns Hopkins University Press, 1931-), for instance, does not appear in the list, yet it appears in both the CD-ROM and print versions. There is also an MLA indexer's error in the list: "Eng. Song & Dance" should be *English Dance and Song*. Future editions should have more careful information verification.

Despite these problems, this index will help reference librarians direct users to appropriate CD-ROM databases (and their print versions) for their periodical searching. In addition, librarians will also find the periodical lists and other information on each database helpful both for purchase decisions on the CD-ROM products most useful to their users and for subscription decisions on periodical titles to correlate with their indexing sources. Recommended for libraries with periodical bibliographic and fulltext databases on CD-ROM. [R: RBB, 1 Oct 92, p. 364; WLB, Oct 92, p. 103] — **Blaine H. Hall**

83. **Index to Commonwealth Little Magazines 1987-1989.** Troy, N.Y., Whitston Publishing, 1991. 434p. $40.00. LC 66-28796. ISBN 0-87875-416-4.

This is the eighth volume of an index to literary magazines published in the British Commonwealth or in former Commonwealth countries. The number of publications covered has shrunk to 15 from 17 in the 1985-1986 volume and 36 in the 1983-1984 book. All but six of them are published in Great Britain.

A journal list at the beginning of the volume indicates which issues of each title are covered in the index. Two of the publications have since ceased publication. There is no explanation as to how the magazines were selected for inclusion, but selection seems to have been based primarily on the fact that they are published in English and are not indexed elsewhere, as none from such large countries as India and Canada is included. Similar to the previous volumes, this one is arranged in a single interfiled author-subject index. Book reviews are included, with access by author, reviewer, and subject. The small number of titles covered detracts from the value of the work, but as the only access point to these magazines, it is an appropriate purchase for those libraries that own the earlier volumes.
—**Christine E. King**

84. Katz, Bill, and Linda Sternberg Katz. **Magazines for Young People.** 2d ed. New Providence, N.J., R. R. Bowker, 1991. 361p. index. $34.95. ISBN 0-8352-3009-0. ISSN 0000-1368.

Given the number of new periodicals being published each year, the latest edition of this work, formerly *Magazines for School Libraries*, should be considered an essential purchase by all school and public librarians. Modeled after *Magazines for Libraries* (R. R. Bowker, 1992) in format and style, this volume lists more than 900 young adult titles; about 100 children's titles; and 200 professional journals suitable for librarians, educators, and parents. Entries contain the date founded, frequency, price, editor, publisher and address, illustrations, index, advertising, circulation, sample, whether refereed, date volume ends, existence of microform reprint, whether indexed, and presence of book reviews. The annotations are critical and have been rewritten since the last edition. Those that overlap with *Magazines for Libraries* have also been edited with a view toward a younger audience.

One of the new features of this edition is the notation of first choice to designate the editors' ratings of periodicals considered best within their genre. For librarians who have to make cost-beneficial purchases, this improvement will be welcomed. A second positive aspect of this volume is the completeness of the titles listed within each subject category. A perusal of the literature, fiction, journalism, and writing sections reveals a wealth of titles to choose from and excellent evaluative comments that help to distinguish between magazines. This edition also provides access from an index of titles and major subjects (e.g., various ethnic groups). A final index furnishes a list of titles by age group, beginning with ages 1-5 and ending with professional journals.

The only works that compete with this volume are *Magazines for Children*, 2d ed. (American Library Association, 1991) and *Magazines for Young Adults* (see ARBA 85, entry 563). While the annotations in those works are longer and more informative, and the volumes cite a significant number of titles that are not listed in *Magazines for Young People*, the number of titles covered does not match the work under review. Librarians who acquire this volume will receive excellent value for their money. [R: SLMQ, Fall 92, p. 74]—**Kathleen W. Craver**

85. **Magazines for Libraries.** 7th ed. By Bill Katz and Linda Sternberg Katz. New Providence, N.J., R. R. Bowker, 1992. 1212p. index. $139.95. LC 86-640971. ISBN 0-8352-3166-6. ISSN 0000-0914.

In an era of shrinking acquisitions budgets and a universe of some 70,000 serials to choose from, this publication has become a familiar and reliable resource for libraries of all sizes. It focuses on about 6,600 general-interest magazines, 20 percent of which, according to the editors, are new to this edition. Additionally, nine new subject classifications have been included: aquaculture, classroom magazines, college and alumni, comic books, food and wine, hospitality/restaurant, music reviews, new age, and women: feminist and special interest. Organization is by 145 subject classifications, within which are found 148 specific subcategories. Each subject classification begins with a brief subject introduction and is followed by a list of basic or core periodicals. In addition to the basic bibliographic data provided for each entry, the work also notes each title's purpose, scope, and audience.

For those who use the guide for serious reference and acquisitions work, it would be helpful if the subcategories were subdivided and organized a bit more tightly. However, this is a minor annoyance, because the strength of this work lies in its descriptions. For people who love magazines for all their glorious diversity and breadth of information, *Magazines for Libraries* is a joy to peruse. A good example is the section on personal computer magazines. Clearly written and user-friendly, this section does an excellent job of drawing useful distinctions between competing titles for the novice computer user as well as the acquisitions librarian. In all, the 7th edition continues to be an excellent, reliable resource of value to all libraries, regardless of size. [R: RBB, 1 Sept 92, p. 87; SLMQ, Fall 92, p. 74]

— G. Kim Dority

86. **New Periodical Title Abbreviations: Volume 3 of** *Periodical Title Abbreviations*: Supplement. 7th ed. Leland G. Alkire, Jr., and Cheryl Westerman-Alkire, eds. Detroit, Gale, 1991. 201p. $140.00pa. LC 84-640700. ISBN 0-8103-6961-3. ISSN 0737-7843.

This volume supplements the 7th edition of the 2-volume set *Periodical Title Abbreviations* (Gale, 1989) by adding 8,500 newly coined or recently discovered abbreviations from indexes, abstracts, and bibliographies. Volume 1 of the basic set arranges the entries by abbreviation and helps scholars, researchers, information specialists, and librarians translate magazine, journal, and newspaper title abbreviations into their full forms. Volume 2 arranges the entries by title and indicates the abbreviations used. The supplement contains both the abbreviation and the title sections in the same volume and performs the same function as the parent volumes. It will be needed in libraries that own the basic volumes so as to broaden and deepen their coverage. — **Sara R. Mack**

87. Richardson, Selma K. **Magazines for Children: A Guide for Parents, Teachers, and Librarians.** 2d ed. Chicago, American Library Association, 1991. 139p. index. $20.00pa. PN4878.R5. 051'.083. LC 90-45152. ISBN 0-8389-0552-8.

This edition of an already popular reference work is a useful evaluative bibliography of more than 100 children's magazines. School and public librarians, teachers, and parents who are searching for such magazines will find this a well-organized and informative resource. It focuses on a wide range of magazines written for children through 14 years of age in elementary, middle, or junior high school, although some grade levels are indicated through senior high school.

Magazines that were evaluated in the 1983 edition of this work have been reassessed for this edition, and many new titles have been added. In addition to subscription information for each magazine, Richardson devotes at least one-half page, and more often one to three pages, to a comprehensive assessment of each periodical's characteristics and potential for classroom, library, and leisure uses. Both content and format are examined, and comments about recent articles, illustrations, covers, and typefaces are typical within entries. Ages and grade levels reported are always those specified by the publisher, although Richardson cautions users to consider these designations as "rough estimates or general indicators of the reading difficulty." If a magazine is indexed in *Children's Magazine Guide* (see ARBA 86, entry 1117), that guide's title is found immediately following the annotation.

Appendixes include a useful list of 16 magazines from religious publishing houses with denominational affiliation indicated. No evaluation is given for these periodicals, but subscription information is provided. This hard-to-find data will be appreciated, and it is hoped that descriptions will be added in future editions. Appendix B is a list of periodical editions for the visually impaired. Appendix C provides lists of magazines by age and by grade level suggested by the publisher. Appendix D is a list of magazines chronologically organized by year of initial publication, and Appendix E cites circulation figures for the magazines. A subject index is provided, but with only one subject used for each periodical, it is general in nature. *Magazines for Children* provides thorough, thoughtful annotations with an effective organizational scheme. — **Patricia Tipton Sharp**

88. **Ulrich's International Periodicals Directory 1992-93.** 31st ed. New Providence, N.J., R. R. Bowker, 1992. 3v. index. $364.00/set. LC 32-16320. ISBN 0-8352-3264-6. ISSN 0000-0175.

To say that *Ulrich's* is an accurate, comprehensive, user-friendly informational source is an understatement. The readability of this edition has been greatly improved by the use of boldface print for entry titles and a change in punctuation for data elements. In addition, access to back issues and hard-to-find serials has been provided; years of coverage of serials by specific abstracting indexing services are given; online and CD-ROM titles (about 4,000) are included; and serials from the former Soviet Union and Yugoslavia have been updated to reflect the emergence of 19 new countries.

The set follows the general arrangement of past editions. Nearly 126,000 serials are listed in the first 2 volumes under 788 subheadings. About 10,000 of these are new, and more than 66,000 have been updated. Information is given for more than 3,800 serials that began publication after January 1, 1990, and for 8,304 titles that have not been published in the last 3 years. In addition, there are vendor file names or numbers for 2,941 titles found only online or in addition to hardcopy, and 558 serials available online. A full entry contains all the elements found in the previous edition (see ARBA 92, entry 65), with the addition of British Library Document Supply Centre shelfmark numbers, the name of the advertising contact, and the rate for a full-page advertisement.

If tradition holds, *Ulrich's* will be even better next year. It is a necessary tool for anyone involved in serials research and for all librarians who deal with serials acquisitions.—**Jo Anne H. Ricca**

QUOTATION BOOKS

89. Bartlett, John. **Familiar Quotations: A Collection of Passages, Phrases, and Proverbs....** **Justin Kaplan, ed.** 16th ed. Boston, Little, Brown, 1992. 1405p. index. $40.00. PN6081.B27. 808.88'2. LC 91-21170. ISBN 0-316-08277-5.

Who said "Go ahead, make my day"? Clint Eastwood or Ronald Reagan? Did either one write it? The answers are "both" and "no." The attribution can be found in this completely revised and updated edition that will continue to "make the day" for those users who have found the earlier editions of *Familiar Quotations* (or *Bartlett's*, as it is more commonly known) a source of information and pleasure. Although 340 new authors have been added since the 1980 15th edition (e.g., Russell Baker, Leonard Bernstein, Annie Dillard, Stephen Hawking, Alice Walker), bringing the total to 2,550 and the number of quotations to more than 20,000, many of the familiar, often-searched-for sources remain. Among them, the Bible and Shakespeare are still the most heavily quoted, with 1,591 and 1,960 entries respectively.

The format remains the same, with authors appearing chronologically in the order of their birth dates and anonymous quotations following the last dated author. Again, copious and helpful footnotes appear at the bottom of the page. The alphabetical index of authors, with birth and death dates, follows Kaplan's interesting preface, and the massive keyword index closes the volume. One might say about each *Bartlett's* editor, from Kaplan back to John Bartlett himself, what Robert Schumann said on first hearing Chopin's music—"Hats off, gentlemen—a genius!" [R: RBB, 1 Nov 92, p. 547]

—**Charles R. Andrews**

90. Colombo, John Robert. **The Dictionary of Canadian Quotations.** Toronto, Stoddart Publishing, 1991. 671p. index. $29.95. 818'.02. ISBN 0-7737-2515-6.

This completely new collection of more than 6,000 quotations covers a wide range of topics, largely current issues. Chosen for inclusion are quotations by Canadians and by non-Canadians about Canada. Colombo states that the themes of the sayings are about contemporary society and humanity, not culture and history (his earlier works emphasized the latter two qualities). Approximately one-half of the quotations refer to topics that have emerged since the 1970s, and one-third cover issues since 1984. Quotations about the past offer new perspectives on earlier events.

Entries are arranged alphabetically by subject. There are many *see* and *see also* references. Quotations are followed by the sources from which they originate, which is helpful for those who wish to do further reading. At the back of the book is an index of the 2,500 contributors, including for each a short phrase that describes the quotation and a page reference. For some important contemporary issues there are disappointingly few quotations. For example, only four quotations about AIDS appear. However, this collection contains enough new and unique material to warrant its addition to most reference collections.—**Margaret A. Grift**

91. **The Merriam-Webster Dictionary of Quotations.** Springfield, Mass., Merriam-Webster, 1992. 501p. index. $4.99pa. ISBN 0-87779-904-0.

Published by the largest U.S. publisher of dictionaries, this new book is a compilation of more than 4,000 historical and contemporary quotations. Arranged alphabetically by subject, the 400 categories cover a wide range of writers, thinkers, and public figures. There is a mixture of the traditional and the modern (e.g., Emily Dickinson, Nancy Reagan), the well known and the not so well known (e.g., Mark Twain, Marquis de Vauvenargues), and the literary and the popular (e.g., William Shakespeare, Graham Greene). The quotations are both new and familiar ones, and many can be found in other quotation books. Each is listed with its author (either known or attributed) and source. The source listings are often incomplete; they contain the title and sometimes the format (e.g., a speech, a letter) and year. Some quotations have notes that provide additional information about them or the author. The subject headings contain numerous cross-references, and there is an author index, but there is no separate list of the subject headings, which would be useful. Considering the price and the coverage, this title is recommended for libraries of all kinds.—**Byron P. Anderson**

92. **The Oxford Dictionary of Quotations.** 4th ed. Angela Partington, ed. New York, Oxford University Press, 1992. 1061p. index. $35.00. ISBN 0-19-866185-1.

When the judges gather to vote on the best reference books of the year, the *Oxford Dictionary of Quotations* should be high on all their lists. Thoroughly revised from the 1979 edition, carefully edited, well indexed, clearly organized for easy use, and attractively printed and bound, this book meets all the criteria for reference excellence. Beyond that, the quotations have been intelligently selected, representing both the familiar and the obscure, the new and the old, the witty and the apposite. As a body, they fulfill the splendid definition provided by Partington in the preface: "Ideally, a quotation should be able to float free from its moorings, remaining buoyant when detached from its original context." This volume includes some 17,500 such quotations and emphasizes many more non-English authors, thinkers, and public figures than were included in the previous editions. In the case of these non-English figures, the quotations are given in the original language along with an English translation.

Two features are entirely new to this edition: Quotations are included from hymns and songs, and each author entry is enhanced with a brief biographical summary that gives nationality, date of birth, and some designation of the person's chief area of importance. Ian Dury, for example, is called an "English rock singer and songwriter," while Edna Ferber is identified simply as an "American writer." Following each quotation, the editors have provided a full citation to the source from which the extract was drawn. Finally, users will be pleased with the carefully constructed 300-page keyword index.

As an update to the 1979 edition and as a supplement to *The Oxford Dictionary of Modern Quotations* (see ARBA 92, entry 68), this volume will serve to answer a common problem for reference workers—finding very recent quotations. In this work, for example, it is possible to identify not only Euclid's "A line is length without breadth" (c300 B.C.) but also Margaret Thatcher's "We have become a grandmother," (1989). *The Oxford Book of Quotations* continues to be the standard in the field and belongs in all libraries. [R: RBB, 1 Dec 92, p. 690]—**Donald C. Dickinson**

93. **Tuttle Dictionary of Quotations for Speeches.** Rutland, Vt., Charles E. Tuttle, c1989, 1992. 198p. index. $9.95pa. PN6081.T87. 082. LC 91-67339. ISBN 0-8048-1779-0.

First published as *Quotations for Speeches* (London: Bloomsbury, 1989), this is a compilation of 1,000 quotations under 214 categories that range from abstinence to youth by way of insensitivity, love, and Ireland. The quotations have been selected on the basis of their probable appeal to those who have to make a speech and who want something amusing to loosen up the audience. Two indexes, one by key word and one by name (e.g., Churchill, Winston; Parker, Dorothy), help users locate entries by their favorite wits or by subjects other than the main categories. Spelling and selections reflect a British bias, although there is an entire category on Goldwynisms. This is a delightful little book to keep handy behind the reference desk and sneak a peek at between questions.—**Mary Jo Walker**

94. **Webster's II New Riverside Desk Quotations.** By James B. Simpson. Boston, Houghton Mifflin, 1992. 420p. index. $8.95. PN6081.S475. 082. LC 91-43811. ISBN 0-395-62024-4.

This collection contains 6,000 notable quotations attributed to nearly 4,000 individuals from 1950 to the present. Quotations are divided into 3 major sections (world, humankind, and communications and the arts), 25 subsections, and 54 subcategories. Authors, brief identifications, and source names appear in alphabetical order with each quoted selection. Browsing the volume reveals humor and profundities in this eclectic assemblage, which includes Ted Turner, Lee Iacocca, Malcolm Forbes, Coretta

Scott King, Sandra Day O'Connor, Margaret Thatcher, and Andrew Tobias. The main text is supplemented by two very helpful indexes. In the source index, the reader will find an alphabetical list of quotations, authors, and cited sources. The index by subject and key lines will simplify access by topics, phrases, and lines from famous and less well known individuals. Numerous cross-references enhance the index's value. Although source documents are provided for each quotation, page numbers are omitted, requiring users to read substantial portions of a source document to locate the quotation and collateral text.

Speakers, writers, and students of American culture will find much of interest in this balanced compendium of memorable remarks. Recommended for all types of libraries. [R: RBB, 15 Nov 92, p. 626] – **Arthur P. Young**

Part II
SOCIAL SCIENCES

2 Social Sciences in General

95. O'Donnell, Timothy S., and others. **World Quality of Life Indicators.** Santa Barbara, Calif., ABC-Clio, 1991. 199p. $35.00. ISBN 0-87436-657-7.

This book provides data taken from ABC-Clio's Kaleidoscope: Current World Data database for 171 countries and territories. Data are arranged in uniform format for each country and territory under 12 topics: location, area, population, vital statistics, health care, ethnic composition, religion, language, education, economic data, travel notes, and government. Most of the information contained herein can be found in other reference sources. *Worldmark Encyclopedia of the Nations* (see ARBA 85, entry 78) provides some 50 topics of information that are more detailed in many aspects. The *Encyclopaedia Britannica*'s (see ARBA 92, entry 41) "World Data" gives general information in small print for more than 180 countries and territories, and its data on national economies (and other subjects) are plentiful. However, the availability of other reference sources does not detract from the value of this book. It is concise for quick reference, and its line-by-line listing of data is convenient for use. The book can complement other reference sources of a similar nature. In the next edition, a list of countries and territories would be useful.

One error was noted. For the Republic of China in Taiwan, it is stated that "the institutions of the government are headed by a National Assembly." According to the Chinese Constitution (not amended in 1992), the National Assembly is empowered only to elect and recall the president, to amend the Constitution, and to vote on proposed constitutional amendments submitted by the Legislative Yuan. It does not function as a governing body. – **Tze-chung Li**

96. **Social Sciences Index: April 1990 to March 1991.** Cheryl Ehrens and Louise J. Hoffman, eds. Bronx, N.Y., H. W. Wilson, 1991. 2138p. sold on service basis. LC 75-649443. ISSN 0094-4920.

Last reviewed in ARBA 88 (see entry 106), *Social Sciences Index* (SSI) is an invaluable tool for people doing research in periodical literature concerned with the social sciences. This edition has expanded by 318 pages, including 312 extra pages of subject and author citations and 6 extra pages of book reviews. Covering a wide range of areas, from anthropology to urban studies, SSI provides thorough indexing of 353 key international English-language periodicals. Alphabetically arranged, this author and subject index makes it easy to find information and is excellent for use by undergraduates. To link subject headings, an extensive cross-reference structure is provided. *See* and *see also* references move the user from unused terms to common ones. Having this valuable source available online and through the CD-ROM version is an added benefit. Unlike the print SSI, which abbreviates the periodical title in the citation, the online and CD-ROM versions give the complete title. This enhancement makes it much easier for users to find periodical titles on local online catalogs that do not recognize abbreviations. Unfortunately, if this option were added to the print version, libraries would not have enough shelf space for the expanded indexes.

With budgets decreasing, the problem of print versus nonprint purchase becomes even more crucial. In any format, SSI will remain an indispensable tool for public libraries. – **Diane J. Turner**

97. Social Sciences Index. (Indexing coverage: 2/83-6/25/92). [CD-ROM]. Bronx, N.Y., H. W. Wilson, 1992. Hardware requirements: WILSONLINE Workstation, IBM PC, or compatible; 640K; hard disk drive. $1,295.00.

The WILSONDISC system has been in existence for several years, and the interface is well known to most patrons and librarians because H. W. Wilson has donated hardware and software to all accredited library schools. This new version does not change that interface appreciably but adds several other enhancements, notably in the installation and setup phases, making both somewhat easier. An interesting simplification in the search commands is the ability to substitute the "$" and "?" truncation for the traditional WILSONLINE ":" for multiple characters.

However, what appears not to have changed are the large memory requirements: a minimum of 487K of free conventional memory is required. With all the device drivers and TSRs (terminate-and-stay-resident) that are necessary for various programs, it becomes exceedingly difficult to use WILSON-DISC with other CD-ROM software unless one has a dedicated computer for Wilson products or creates a special boot disk. Perhaps Wilson needs to consider implementing a Windows version of their software or providing some means of using extended memory. — **Johan Koren**

98. Walford's Guide to Reference Material. Volume 2: Social and Historical Sciences, Philosophy and Religion. 5th ed. Alan Day and Joan M. Harvey, with Marilyn Mullay, eds. London, Library Association; distr., Lanham, Md., UNIPUB, c1990, 1991. 942p. index. $180.00. 011.02. ISBN 0-85365-539-1.

This review is one year late because of some communication problems. The 4th edition of this volume was published in 1982, and previous editions appeared in 1975 (see ARBA 77, entry 15), 1968, 1963, and 1959. As before, volume 2 of *Walford's* covers social and historical sciences, philosophy, and religion. This new edition significantly increases the coverage of U.S. imprints, with substantial expansion in such subjects as tourism and travel, genealogy, and family history. The quality of annotations is somewhat better than in Sheehy, and many annotations contain quotations from a wide variety of reviewing sources and provide occasional references to related works. In general, the selection seems to be sound; for example, in the chapter on philosophy there are five entries under the section "Encyclopedias, English." Omitted are such works as *Dictionary of Philosophy* (see ARBA 84, entry 1010) and *New Encyclopedia of Philosophy* (see ARBA 73, entry 1124). Similar omissions can be found in other sections, but the selection of material is quite adequate. Most libraries should have *Walford's* because it offers good coverage of reference materials published outside the United States, with its special emphasis on British, Australian, and Indian sources. — **Bohdan S. Wynar**

99. Weinberg, Meyer, ed. **The World of W. E. B. Du Bois: A Quotation Sourcebook.** Westport, Conn., Greenwood Press, 1992. 282p. index. $65.00. E185.97.D73A25. 305.896'07302. LC 92-15481. ISBN 0-313-28619-1.

Weinberg — historian, bibliographer, and educator — has compiled more than 1,000 quotations drawn from the published and unpublished writings and correspondence of W. E. B. Du Bois. A few excerpts from the Du Bois FBI file are also included. Quotations are arranged into 20 subject chapters and subdivided by topic. The 957 topic headings are arranged alphabetically within individual chapters. The quotation's source is presented with each entry. There is an index to topics, titles, and personal names (when they are part of the bibliographic citation).

Topic headings have been devised by Weinberg and are, where possible, derived from Du Bois's text. Unfortunately, topic headings are almost useless in retrieving quotations on a particular subject from the index. For example, quotations about John Brown or from the book *John Brown* are indexed under "John Brown," not Brown, John; Fordham University is accessible only under "Catholic Colleges"; and Kate Richards O'Hare appears only under "Socialist Party." Some of Du Bois's most famous quotations are not included (e.g., "sorrow songs," "double-consciousness"). Other quotations are included for no apparent reason (e.g., "Garbage" from a routine note about garbage pickup.)

Weinberg is correct when he asserts that Du Bois "stands preeminent among intellectuals of the United States in this century" (p. 1). For this reason, a collection of memorable quotations from Du Bois is a welcome and important contribution. Due to the problems outlined above, this book is better for reading or browsing than for reference. — **Fred J. Hay**

100. Wepsiec, Jan. **Social Sciences: An International Bibliography of Serial Literature, 1830-1985.** New York, Mansell/Cassell, 1992. 486p. index. $130.00. Z7161.A15W38. 016.3'005. LC 90-20252. ISBN 0-7201-2109-4.

The need for bibliographic control in the social sciences is evident by the large number of serial publications. One example of control is this work, which is current through 1985 and retrospective to 1830. The starting date represents the first published journal on economics, the first established social science discipline. In addition, coverage includes political science, cultural anthropology, sociology, international public law, and comparative law. Journal titles were selected if they contained information about either theories or methods or social, political, economic, and cultural systems of any society. Excluded are titles with geographic coverage smaller than a U.S. state or corresponding entity. Scholarly and international organizations' publications are included. The 5,254 entries are arranged alphabetically, followed by dates of existence, place of publication, publisher, frequency, previous title, language, and where indexed. Two appendixes composed of short essays help define the social sciences. There is a subject index.

This bibliography is valuable for title verification, dates of publication, and knowledge of journals in a social sciences subject area. Its shortcoming is the ending date. Given the economic situation over the past seven years, many titles will have ceased. It would be best to supplement this work with *World List of Social Sciences Periodicals 1991* (UNIPUB, 1991), a comprehensive list of current titles. Although limited in current coverage, this bibliography will be of value to social sciences researchers and research collections. [R: Choice, Nov 92, p. 451]—**Byron P. Anderson**

101. **World List of Social Science Periodicals 1991. Liste Mondiale des Periodiques Specialises dans les Sciences Sociales. Lista Mundial de Revistas Especializadas en Ciencias Sociales.** 8th ed. Paris, Unesco; distr., Lanham, Md., UNIPUB, 1991. 1264p. index. (World Social Science Information Directories). $40.00pa. ISBN 92-3-002734-0.

This is a valuable reference tool for students in the social sciences who wish to become more aware of periodicals in their area of study. The book provides information on scholarly periodicals in the main social science disciplines, such as economic and social history; human, economic, and political geography; linguistics; and social and cultural anthropology. Also listed are secondary bibliographic and abstracting periodicals that provide coverage of the primary periodicals. This edition has 1,450 more entries than the previous one. The introductory section is in English, French, and Spanish, but the remaining text is in English only.

The volume is divided into sections, beginning with an alphabetical index of titles and former titles. The full-entry section is arranged alphabetically by country, then alphabetically by periodical. The full entries include proper name, date of first appearance, ISSN, editors, address, publisher, average number of pages and articles, and a brief description. A detailed subject index includes geographic areas and topics such as aging, folklore, and sex roles. No other list as comprehensive exists, although one could laboriously explore *Ulrich's International Periodical Directory* (see ARBA 92, entry 65) for basic title and address information. *World List* does not claim to be exhaustive, but it likely comes close. Highly recommended for larger academic and research libraries.—**Byron P. Anderson**

102. Young, Copeland H., Kristen L. Savola, and Erin Phelps. **Inventory of Longitudinal Studies in the Social Sciences.** Newbury Park, Calif., Sage, 1991. 567p. index. $55.00. H62.Y667. 300. LC 91-11195. ISBN 0-8039-4315-6.

Although this excellent inventory contains information that is of interest to medicine, sociology, and other disciplines, psychology is its primary focus. It includes United States and Canadian studies from two Social Science Research Council publications—Susan Migdal, Ronald P. Abelas, and Lonnie R. Sherrod's *An Inventory of Longitudinal Studies of Middle and Old Age* (1981) and Frederick Verdonik and Sherrod's *An Inventory of Longitudinal Research on Childhood and Adolescence* (1984). (European studies will be included in a new inventory being prepared under the auspices of the European Science Foundation.) The editors of this volume have added new studies and have updated and standardized entries for the previously indexed studies. Criteria for inclusion are that data had to be collected at least twice across a span of a year, that there had to be a low attrition rate of the sample population, that there had to be extensive information on the sample, and that it had to be an active study or one that is now available for secondary analyses by others. Studies on language acquisition have been excluded. Qualitative research studies, especially the many high-quality longitudinal ethnographies, are not included. Each of the more than 200 studies indexed includes project title; dates; chief investigators; contact person/institution address and telephone number; brief description of study topic; size, ethnicity, age, gender, and socioeconomic class of sample; sample selection process; data on sample attrition; current status of study; whether data are in machine-readable form and available for secondary analyses; and selected references. Entries are arranged alphabetically by chief investigator's name. The work includes lists of studies by investigator and by title and an adequate subject index. [R: Choice, July/Aug 92, p. 1663]—**Fred J. Hay**

103. Young, Michael L. **Dictionary of Polling: The Language of Contemporary Opinion Research.** Westport, Conn., Greenwood Press, 1992. 266p. index. $55.00. HM261.Y684. 303.3'8'03. LC 91-24198. ISBN 0-313-27598-X.

This book defines approximately 400 significant terms in contemporary public opinion research. The definitions are approximately one-half to one page or more in length. Technical and highly specialized terms are excluded. The format is alphabetical with extensive cross-referencing; text references lead to an extensive bibliography in the back of the book. The introduction contains a good overview of the literature of polling, and there is a comprehensive topical index. This is an excellent source for definition of polling terms and jargon, something not usually found in other dictionaries. A great deal about public polling can be learned simply by reading through the terms (e.g., *sugging* [Selling Under the Guise of a Poll or Survey]). Highly recommended for research and academic libraries, and other libraries with collection responsibilities in political science. [R: Choice, Nov 92, pp. 451-52]—**Byron P. Anderson**

3 Area Studies

GENERAL WORKS

104. **Names of Countries and Their Capital Cities Including Adjectives of Nationality and Currency Units. Nomes de Pays. Nombres de Paises.** Rome, FAO of the United Nations; distr., Lanham, Md., UNIPUB, 1991. 216p. index. (FAO Terminology Bulletin, no.20). $20.00pa. ISBN 92-5-003059-2.

This multilingual guide gives the names of member nations of the Food and Agriculture Organization (FAO) of the United Nations and other specialized UN agencies, as well as those of certain other countries mentioned in FAO documents. The entries are arranged in English alphabetical order. Each page contains five sections with information in English followed by the same in French, Spanish, Arabic, and Chinese. The entry name—a short, commonly used name—is followed by the full name as used in official documents. Entries also give the nationality; the name of the capital city; and the unit of currency, followed by its symbol. Entries for FAO member nations include the symbol recommended by the International Organization of Standardization for the official language of communication for the country. There are three indexes in English, French, and Spanish; a short list of bibliographical sources; and a list of documents issued by the FAO Terminology and Reference Section from 1966 through 1991, with classification numbers and language codes. This compilation will be a useful authority for general reference and subject collections. It should also be of interest to those involved in business, commerce, and international trade.—**Shirley L. Hopkinson**

105. **The World Factbook 1991-92.** By the Central Intelligence Agency. McLean, Va., Brassey's (US), 1992. 405p. maps. $28.00. ISBN 0-02-881033-3. ISSN 0277-1527.

This annual publication from the CIA is excellent for answering quick reference questions on the nations of the world (e.g., "How many airports are there?"). Brief information on each country's governmental structure, leadership, geography, and defense forces can be found here. Statistical data on a nation's economy, communications, and demographic makeup are also included.

Brassey's is known for publishing excellent (if expensive) titles in the defense/national security fields. This one is just a reprint of a federal government document with a hard cover and a nice jacket. Gale also offers a reprint of this title under the name *Handbook of Nations* (see ARBA 92, entry 676). Much of this same information can, of course, be found in other annual publications, such as *Europa World Year Book* (see ARBA 90, entry 91) and the *World Almanac and Book of Facts* (see ARBA 90, entry 3). While this work is certainly suitable for all public, academic, and school libraries, institutions will want to consider whether the duplication of information with other annual directories is worth the expense. If a decision is made to purchase this title, it is suggested that it be bought from the U.S. Government Printing Office; that version is less expensive.—**Daniel K. Blewett**

UNITED STATES

106. **Florida Almanac 1992-1993.** 9th ed. Del Marth and Martha J. Marth, eds. Gretna, La., Pelican Publishing, 1992. 432p. illus. maps. index. $11.95pa. ISBN 0-88289-886-8. ISSN 0361-9796.

Since 1972 this guide to the facts and figures of all phases of life in Florida has grown and prospered as an excellent reference tool (see ARBA 89, entry 85 for a review of a previous edition). During the last few years it has established an identity as a reliable and predictable biennial publication. The new edition is similar to those that preceded it, rendering comprehensive and (in some cases) detailed information on a variety of topics in 30-odd categories. The volume is essentially an update of information in those categories for which new data are available (e.g., demographics, vital statistics, prices); the population figures for counties and cities are based on the 1990 federal census. Those categories that remain unchanged (e.g., history, geography, archaeology) have simply been reprinted. One subcategory added is exotic pest plants (in the agriculture section). The new edition begins with a section on climate and weather and ends with a detailed index and a selective bibliography. Throughout the work, information is presented in a quick, easily retrievable manner. Especially useful for ready-reference are the sections that include county maps, toll-free numbers, zip codes, and the mileage chart for 43 of the most important cities in the state. — **Ron Blazek**

107. **Florida Statistical Abstract 1991.** Shermyen, Anne H., ed. Gainesville, Fla., University Press of Florida, 1991. 736p. maps. index. $31.95; $19.95pa. ISBN 0-8130-1085-3; 0-8130-1086-1pa. ISSN 0071-6022.

Similar to *Florida Almanac* (Pelican Publishing, 1992) in terms of topical coverage, this annual *Abstract* provides more in-depth coverage of statistical data about the state of Florida. It serves as a convenient vehicle for up-to-date statistics and also as a guide or index to more detailed reports. Source notes are given for each table used in any of the five divisions: human resources, physical resources and industries, services, public resources and administration, and economic and social trends. These divisions are subdivided into different sections, each of which is numbered sequentially, from 1.00 — "Population" (human resources) — to 25.00 — "State Comparisons" (economic and social trends). The middle three divisions (sections 9.00 to 23.00) furnish information on establishments involved in economic, social, and political activities. These are classified according to Standard Industrial Classification (SIC) number and include both profit making and not-for-profit organizations. At the back of the volume is a segment on explanatory notes and sources for each of the sections covered. There are a glossary of terms, a detailed index to the volume, and an index to censuses of various details covered in previous editions of this work. — **Ron Blazek**

108. **The Indiana Factbook 1992.** Terry Creeth, ed. Bloomington, Ind., Indiana University Press, 1992. 413p. maps. $44.95pa. ISSN 0886-330X.

As were the two previous editions, this is a valuable compendium of statistical data on Indiana. The oversized volume contains more than 200 easy-to-read graphs, charts, and tables that detail the state of the state. Topics addressed include population, education, employment, earnings, vital statistics, business manufacturing, and agriculture. The *Factbook* is drawn from the EDIN (Economic Development Information Network) online database and uses 1990 census data whenever possible.

The volume is divided into four sections. The first shows Indiana in relationship to the nation and adjoining states. The second offers county-level data arranged by subject. The third repackages the information from the previous chapter into miniprofiles of each county. The fourth, a new feature in this edition, offers a series of useful directories for local economic development organizations, chambers of commerce, and general assembly members. — **Steven J. Schmidt**

109. **The Kentucky Encyclopedia.** John E. Kleber, ed. Lexington, Ky., University Press of Kentucky, 1992. 1045p. index. $35.00. F451.K413. 976.9'003. LC 91-26146. ISBN 0-8131-1772-0.

This is the source for almost anything one would want to know about the Commonwealth of Kentucky. A project of the Kentucky Bicentennial Commission, this massive undertaking includes 2,000-plus entries written by more than 500 contributors. The span of subjects runs from prehistoric settlements to contemporary headlines with emphasis on such things as art, architecture, business, education, history, literature, politics, religion, science, and sports. Biographical sketches are included on all Kentucky governors, U.S. senators, noted congresspersons, state and local politicians, and Kentuckians of note in all areas of endeavor. Every county and county seat, as well as each community with a population of at least 2,500, has an entry. Many of the narratives are followed by bibliographic citations for further information. Other important features include the outstanding "Kentucky: A Historical Overview," written by the state's historian laureate, Thomas D. Clark (who also contributed nearly 100 entries and served as one of the volume's 3 associate editors); a fine bibliographic essay; a thorough index; a list of authors and consulting editors for the various topics; and a pair of useful maps—one of counties and geographic regions and the other of landmarks and pioneer trails.

This attractive volume is a model work that other states should emulate. It should be in all libraries that include state histories and other such reference sources. It has an amazingly modest price for such a valuable tool. [R: Choice, Dec 92, p. 602; LJ, 1 June 92, p. 112]—**Joe P. Dunn**

110. **Louisiana Almanac 1992-93.** Milburn Calhoun and Susan Cole Dore, eds. Gretna, La., Pelican Publishing, 1992. 622p. maps. index. $19.95; $13.95pa. ISBN 0-88289-797-7; 0-88289-796-9pa.

This is an excellent example of a state almanac. It was first published in 1949, and in recent years a new edition has appeared approximately every four years. Information is organized into 26 sections in no particular order. In the general information section there is a table for sunrises and sunsets in New Orleans and a correction list for other Louisiana cities. Peculiar land measurements used in Louisiana, such as the arpent and the vara, are also noted. Louisiana's State Parks and Preservation and Commemorative Areas are listed in the section on touring and recreation, as are famous gardens and plantations. Prominent tourist attractions for New Orleans, Cajun country, and other parts of the state are listed with directions, admission fees, and telephone numbers. Population figures by county include the latest from the 1990 census. A chapter on parishes and cities gives an economic profile and vital statistics. A section on Louisiana superlatives highlights a series of the state's firsts. There is even a list of the largest remaining live oak trees arranged by girth. Some of the longest sections concern state government and have long lists of officials and details of elections since 1812. A helpful list of Louisiana ZIP codes is also included. Surprisingly, Louisiana sports coverage focuses primarily on Louisiana State University and Tulane football. Basketball is scarcely mentioned save for Pete Maravich's scoring records.

With the exception of a few charts (the one on precipitation requires a magnifying glass to read) and maps of Senate and House districts (which probably cannot even be read with a magnifying glass), this is an excellent reference work. It will be eagerly purchased by all libraries with an interest in this unique state.—**Brian E. Coutts**

111. **Texas Almanac and State Industrial Guide, 1992-93.** Mike Kingston and Mary G. Crawford, eds. Dallas, Tex., Dallas Morning News; distr., Houston, Tex., Gulf Publishing, 1991. 656p. illus. maps. index. $15.95; $10.95pa. LC 10-3390. ISBN 0-914511-14-9; 0-914511-15-7pa.

The *Texas Almanac* has been called the "Encyclopedia of Texas." From big cities to small towns, this work not only looks at geography but also reviews science, technology, literature, history, industry, agriculture, sports, politics, and weather. A Texas tradition since 1857, it traces the history and development of the Lone Star state in statistics and narrative. Inside the 1992-1993 edition readers will discover the people, places, events, and trivia that describe the diverse world that is Texas. As in previous editions, it continues to have regular sections on politics and government, the environment, population, and education. Some of the special features included are the birds of Texas, a review of dinosaurs that roamed Texas, a brief history of Spain in celebration of the quincentennial, a look at mystery writers in Texas, courageous Texans (65 have won the Congressional Medal of Honor), archaeology (the first Texans), and political scorecards and expanded demographics on each of the 254 Texas counties. Numerous graphs, charts, and photographs enhance the narrative descriptions. This volume will benefit any home or library where information about Texas is needed.—**Randy M. Wood**

AFRICA
Angola

112. Broadhead, Susan H. **Historical Dictionary of Angola.** 2d ed. Metuchen, N.J., Scarecrow, 1992. 296p. maps. (African Historical Dictionaries, no.52). $39.50. DT611.5.B76. 967.3'003. LC 91-44889. ISBN 0-8108-2532-5.

Similar to its predecessor, this edition was compiled by a long-standing historian of Angola. Its strong points are a useful introduction, good maps, currency (events from late 1991 are included), copious cross-references, and an excellent bibliography. Its weak point is the entries. This is no reflection on the qualifications of Broadhead, but a reminder that five centuries of history cannot be distilled into a series of large-print alphabetical entries that fill fewer than 200 small pages. Anyone interested in the famous Nzinga will find several hundred words (under "Njinga") and a few citations in the bibliography. The former might be useful for elementary term papers; the latter, of much more value, can readily be found in bibliographies of African history. Fortunately, Broadhead does not shrink from including foreign-language materials in her bibliography, but anyone who would benefit from these citations will be unlikely to find the entries useful. A possible exception is the series of capsule biographies of pre- and postindependence political personages. In this reviewer's opinion, librarians should ask whether they need to purchase this work when 3d editions cannot be far behind.—**David Henige**

Central African Republic

113. Kalck, Pierre. **Historical Dictionary of the Central African Republic.** 2d ed. Metuchen, N.J., Scarecrow, 1992. 188p. maps. (African Historical Dictionaries, no.51). $32.50. DT546.35.K353. 967.41'003. LC 91-45671. ISBN 0-8108-2521-X.

Kalck is a recognized authority—perhaps the major one—of this obscure landlocked nation in the heart of Africa. As the Central African Republic has a past only one century long and Kalck is not interested in prehistory or protohistory, the work consists largely of two sets of collective biographies. The first covers explorers and administrators in the early period; the second deals with politicians since independence. Although the book is fairly up-to-date, the careers of many politicians are left hanging; for instance, what has become of Jean-Bedel Bokassa since 1987? There is a list of governors and other chief administrators. A few maps are provided, none historical. The bibliography is, perhaps unavoidably, shorter than usual for this series.

It is odd to see a work published in 1992 that has been reproduced from typed copy. Throughout the book the letter *i* is misaligned, and all accents have been added by hand (rather obtrusively). Surely these problems are preventable. Also, the translation from the French is quite stilted—sometimes to the point of amusement—leading to a kind of *franglais* in reverse. There is, for instance, far too much of the French impersonal formation.—**David Henige**

Equatorial Guinea

114. Fegley, Randall, comp. **Equatorial Guinea.** Santa Barbara, Calif., ABC-Clio, 1991. 118p. index. (World Bibliographical Series, v.136). $64.00. 016.9671803. ISBN 1-85109-167-X.

It would be hard to find a country more obscure than Equatorial Guinea, formerly Guine Espanola, a small coastal enclave and two islands in west-central Africa. Anomalously Spanish during its colonial period, it became formally independent in 1968. Both before and after independence, its history has been one of the most violent and tragic in all Africa. This work serves to introduce readers to the literature of Equatorial Guinea. In all, 339 items are arranged into 34 classifications, which is too fine a breakdown because several categories have only 1 or 2 items each. The largest category is history with 53 items, and there is an unusual (but welcome) section on the newspapers published in the country. A useful geographical and historical introduction of nearly 50 pages begins the work; a map and an author/title/subject index close it. Fegley has properly included a good percentage of Spanish-language titles despite the series' typical orientation toward English-language materials.

Paradoxically, Equatorial Guinea is bibliographically perhaps the most comprehensively researched country in Africa, thanks to the industry and many volumes of Max Liniger-Goumaz, all duly noted by Fegley. In some ways, though, this volume mirrors the constraints imposed by a series that adopts the questionable policy of one volume per country, whether it be the enormous (former) Soviet Union or tiny Equatorial Guinea. The unusually large number of classifications and the arrangement of cross-references represent wasteful use of space, contributing to the feeling that, for barely 100 pages of bibliography (minus the empty spaces), this is an overpriced book. Still, for those who do not have (or need) access to the monumental oeuvre of Liniger-Goumaz, this volume should prove useful.
— **David Henige**

Libya

115. St John, Ronald Bruce. **Historical Dictionary of Libya.** 2d ed. Metuchen, N.J., Scarecrow, 1991. 192p. (African Historical Dictionary, no.33). $25.00. DT223.3.S7. 961.2. LC 91-27764. ISBN 0-8108-2451-5.

A different compiler was responsible for the first edition of this title in 1981. The present edition is about 40 percent longer in terms of entries and includes a bibliography that is nearly four times as big as its predecessor's. Despite this, the number and length of historical (preindependence) entries has actually decreased, which means that the volume's title is more a misnomer than ever. The work is well cross-referenced, but there is no index at all, which is inexcusable (but all too common in this series).

In a work as distilled as this one (fewer than 110 small-size, large-print pages cover 2,500 years of Libyan history), criteria of inclusion and exclusion must necessarily be subjective. Even so, one can only wonder at such entries as "Fly, Screwworm," which is longer than average but makes no effort to justify itself as "historical." (In fact, readers are told that the fly "was first spotted ... in July 1988.")

In a previous review (*Africana Journal* 10 [1979]: 120-28) the justification for this series was questioned by this reviewer. While the bibliography could be useful to students unfamiliar with Libya, and this edition is better than the first, libraries should appraise volumes in this series individually before acquisition. [R: Choice, May 92, p. 1376] — **David Henige**

Mozambique

116. Azevedo, Mario. **Historical Dictionary of Mozambique.** Metuchen, N.J., Scarecrow, 1991. 250p. index. (African Historical Dictionaries, no.47). $29.50. DT3337.A94. 967.9'003. LC 91-15423. ISBN 0-8108-2413-2.

This historical dictionary is undoubtedly better than its counterpart for Libya (Scarecrow, 1991). Azevado is a historian; more attention is paid to the past; there are more substantial entries; and there is even an index. The bibliography is substantial, although not as much so as the bibliography for Mozambique in ABC-Clio's World Bibliographical Series (see ARBA 89, entry 100). Still, the emphasis in the bibliographies in this series on recent, popular, and ephemeral materials means that they tend to complement rather than duplicate other such works devoted to the same countries.

There are organizational and epistemological problems with the structure of this volume. The index entries largely duplicate the main entries rather than provide access to materials within these entries. There is virtually no cross-referencing and no attempt to be syndetic. For example, there are entries for a couple of rulers of Quitongonha but no entry—either in the main listing or in the index—to Quitongonha itself. For some reason the Nguni people are granted an entry—a very short entry—under the rather peculiar form "Anguni," with no cross-reference to the index for finding the entry (except by serendipity). Another peculiarity is that alphabetization of names with "van" and "de" is by these elements rather than by the surnames. All in all, it is easier to recommend this volume than that on Libya, but this is not in itself enough to justify the acquisition of every book in the series. [R: Choice, June 92, p. 1514] — **David Henige**

Sub-Saharan Africa

117. Moss, Joyce, and George Wilson. **Peoples of the World: Africans South of the Sahara: The Culture, Geographical Setting, and Historical Background of 34 African Peoples.** Detroit, Gale, 1991. 443p. illus. maps. index. $39.95. ISBN 0-8103-7942-2.

While sources that survey governments and economies of the world or a region abound, handbooks that describe cultures are rare. Yet any enthusiasm that might greet this book should be tempered by doubts about its reliability. (For a review of its Latin American counterpart, *Peoples of the World: Latin Americans*, see ARBA 90, entry 139.) The book has three sections: "Old Cultures," which describes five ancient African civilizations; "African Societies Today," which explores 34 contemporary cultures; and "African Countries Today," with short overviews of 41 countries. Sections on cultures range from 3 to 14 pages, while each country is allotted 2 to 3 pages. Crude maps try to show where different cultures are predominant. A bibliography and a glossary (each two pages long with no discernible rationale for what is included) and an index conclude the book.

The country section provides very basic information readily found elsewhere. The "cultural" content in this section is a list of each country's major ethnic groups. The "African Societies Today" section presents information on geographical setting, historical background, and "Culture Today," which includes paragraphs on such things as clothing, shelter, family life, social life, religion, economy, health, and the arts. Accuracy of this information is not assured. This reviewer lived among the Wolof of Senegal for two years and noticed errors in the section on this culture. Among other things, the assertion that Wolof houses have no windows is false, and the description of women's dress is inaccurate.

There is no information on the credentials of the two authors. Future books in this series should have each culture written about by authorities of the area. That sort of painstaking care is far from evident here. This book leaves one wanting to use it, because sources on culture are rare, but hesitant to do so because its accuracy is suspect.

—Cathy Seitz Whitaker

ARCTIC REGIONS

118. **Directory of Arctic Science and Technology Research in Canada. Repertoire Canadien des Recherches Arctiques en Science et en Technologie.** Ottawa, Indian and Northern Affairs Canada, 1991. 297p. index. free spiralbound.

The first edition of a directory that will be updated periodically, this work summarizes the results of a 1990 questionnaire sent to Canadian researchers with active programs in the Canadian Arctic, almost all of which are conducted in the field. The body of the volume is arranged alphabetically into 34 disciplines, from administration/logistics to strategic studies. Each entry gives the researcher's name, telephone and fax numbers, subdisciplines, a short description of the research, field work locations, and key words related to the research. Three indexes provide access by names, field work locations, and key words. The volume has a bilingual preface and introduction.

—Emanuel D. Rudolph

119. Miller, Kenneth E., comp. **Greenland.** Santa Barbara, Calif., ABC-Clio, 1991. 111p. index. (World Bibliographical Series, v.125). $55.00. 016.9982. ISBN 1-85109-139-4.

The world's largest island, Greenland has a population of Inuit and mostly Danish Europeans; it hosts two American air bases. This very useful reference for English readers to a country about which most people know very little should be a help to librarians. The nine-page introduction gives basic background information. The categorized list of books, reports, and articles is succinctly annotated and well indexed and cross-referenced. When a book has several different titles in its various printings, these are noted and indexed also. This reference should be in every library with an interest in international affairs. [R: Choice, Mar 92, p. 1052]

—Emanuel D. Rudolph

ASIA

General Works

120. Lee, Thomas H., comp. **A Guide to East Asian Collections in North America.** Westport, Conn., Greenwood Press, 1992. 158p. index. (Bibliographies and Indexes in World History, no.25). $45.00. Z3001.L4. 016.95. LC 91-46698. ISBN 0-313-27397-9.

The first East Asian-language materials arrived in the United States in 1869. Since then the number of East Asian collections has grown tremendously; a 1991 survey showed holdings of the larger collections at more than 10 million volumes and half a million microforms. This guide covers 52 United States and 3 Canadian collections that hold 20,000 volumes or more. Information for the directory was collected by questionnaire and supplied by the institutions. (The response was 100 percent!) Entries are arranged alphabetically by the key words in the name of the parent institution. Each supplies address, telephone number, year founded, hours, holdings and areas of strength, special collections, access, travel grants, interlibrary loan services, participation in a bibliographic utility, network or consortium affiliations, local catalogs, publications, and information on East Asian materials in other libraries of the institution. Collections are also listed under geographical regions. There is a list of abbreviations used in the entries; an index combines subjects, personal names, and variant names of libraries. Special collections and files are thoroughly noted in the entries. However, a large number are not listed in the index and therefore cannot be accessed easily.

This directory is the first comprehensive guide to East Asian language collections. As such, it fills a serious gap. Scholars, researchers, and students of Asian studies will find it extremely useful.

—Shirley L. Hopkinson

Afghanistan

121. Adamec, Ludwig W. **Historical Dictionary of Afghanistan.** Metuchen, N.J., Scarecrow, 1991. 376p. (Asian Historical Dictionaries, no.5). $39.50. DS356.A27. 958.1'003. LC 91-31544. ISBN 0-8108-2491-4.

Funds for the Afghanistan section of most reference collections are not as plentiful as those for the United States section, and most Americans only know about the Soviet presence there. Thus, it is important to have reference material on the country that is both bereft of intellectual flaws and yet endowed with a flexible, historical impetus. Adamec, who is also the author of the *Historical and Political Who's Who of Afghanistan* (Akademische Druck, Groz-Austria, 1975), has produced such a volume.

Besides being concise and informative, the 800-plus entries support the 67-page chronology, which is itself a major contribution to Afghan studies. Brief users' notes explain the romanization scheme used. Geographical names are given etymological analysis. For example, in the *Garmsir* entry, Adamec explains that *garm* means *warm*, so the fact that *Garmsir* is a "low-lying, hot country" does not surprise the reader. Despite the regular inclusion of geographical information, the volume's focus is unwaveringly historical, not cultural or sociological. There are no entries on *pushtunwali* (women), for example, although a section of the 42-page bibliography is devoted to sociology. However, *Umma*, the concept of Pan-Islamic unity, merits a two-line entry. The dictionary is replete with wonderful articles on various political vehicles (e.g., *Parcham*) or on historically significant individuals (e.g., Abdullah Qari, poet laureate). The articles almost always contain a reference to another entry, so that reading this dictionary can give one the feeling of having tackled a tar baby (but a tar baby that feeds the mind). [R: Choice, June 92, p. 1513]—**Judith M. Brugger**

122. Jones, Schuyler, comp. **Afghanistan.** Santa Barbara, Calif., ABC-Clio, 1992. 279p. index. (World Bibliographical Series, v.135). $130.00. ISBN 1-85109-140-8.

Written by an anthropologist of Nuristan, this bibliography is a useful first source for research on Afghanistan, whether by the novice or the scholar. The book has more than 1,000 entries, including scholarly monographs and articles, government reports, coffee-table books, and *National Geographic* articles. The bibliography was constructed for an English-speaking audience, but there are references to important works in German, French, and Russian. While most of the material identifies dates from the nineteenth and twentieth centuries and includes works written on the Soviet incursion and effect on Afghanistan, there are references to earlier works (e.g., translations of Persian-language material written during the Mughal period). Numerous works also deal with the Northwest Frontier area of present-day Pakistan, the trans-Oxus region of central Asia, and eastern Iran because these areas are ethnically, linguistically, culturally, and religiously connected.

After an informative and interesting introduction to Afghanistan's geography, history, and geopolitical importance, the book is divided into 37 categories such as history, geography, economy, politics, customs, religion, social organization, education, statistics, and calligraphy. There is even a section of children's books. Each entry is annotated, and the best works in each category are specified. One interesting section identifies currently published journals that emphasize material on Afghanistan. The book concludes with indexes of authors, titles, and subjects, which should make this addition to the World Bibliographic Series useful for scholars as well as the general public. — **David L. White**

Bali

123. Stuart-Fox, David J. **Bibliography of Bali: Publications from 1920 to 1990.** Leiden, Netherlands, KITLV Press; distr., Detroit, Cellar Book Shop, 1992. 708p. index. $47.00. ISBN 90-6718-040-8.

Compiled by a respected scholar, this extensive 8,000-entry bibliography is a comprehensive update of C. Lekkerkerker's compilation for the Bali Instituut of Amsterdam, *Bali en Lombok* (Rijswijk, Netherlands: Blankwaard & Schoonhoven, 1920). While its dramatically larger size (the original contained 800 entries) has precluded the annotations provided by Lekkerkerker and narrowed the scope to Bali alone, its breadth and depth should serve and challenge scholars around the world. Entries are divided among sections that include natural sciences, social sciences, tourism and travel, health and medicine, economy and agriculture, history, religion, language and literature, arts, and serials. Special sections are included on *Memories van Overgave* (end-of-service reports by colonial officials) and village monographs and other Indonesian series. Entries are largely in Balinese, Dutch, English, or Indonesian, but other languages are also represented.

Bali is best known as one of the select "laboratories" for anthropological fieldwork, ethnomusicology and dance, and art, having attracted such scholars as Margaret Mead, Gregory Bateson, and Colin McPhee before World War II and, more recently, C. Hooykaas and Clifford Geertz and Hildred Geertz. Yet these individuals increasingly have relied on solid bodies of research conducted by students, scholars, officials, and perceptive observers—all well represented here. Most libraries are unlikely to have many of the items cited; however, users should be advised that notable collections can be found in a few academic libraries in the United States, as well as in the Library of Congress (cited by the author). Because of Bali's unique culture and importance for research in a wide variety of fields, this invaluable bibliography should find an appreciative audience among serious researchers in many fields.

— **K. Mulliner**

Burma

124. Herbert, Patricia M., comp. **Burma.** Santa Barbara, Calif., ABC-Clio, 1991. 327p. index. (World Bibliographical Series, v.132). $85.00. 016.591. ISBN 1-85109-088-6.

In her introduction Herbert states that her bibliography is the "first and most fully annotated multidisciplinary guide to English-language publications about Burma to appear in twenty years"; she is quite correct. Her closest competition is *Burma: A Study Guide* (Wilson Center Press, 1988), a nice bibliography that contains articles in other languages but that is not, unfortunately, annotated. (For a more informative discussion of this competitor, see Herbert's annotation. In fact, the 30 or so candidates for best bibliography of Burma are succinctly discussed in her chapter on bibliographies and research guides.)

Herbert's work is divided into subject and form chapters of the most wide-ranging nature, as are many of the other excellent volumes in the World Bibliographical Series. The British Library's

magnificent collections have furnished her with material on such things as flora and fauna, history, population and minorities, periodicals, transport and communications, education, cuisine, and the arts. Entries that fit into more than one area are cross-referenced in the secondary area. Annotations range from a line or two to a dozen sentences. Herbert gives the uncanny impression that she is equally expert in all areas. For example, her remarks on the agricultural title *Farm Household Economy under Paddy Delivery System* provide a bibliographical reference within the body of the entry, and her entry on the first of Cecil Champain Lowis's Burmese novels, *The Treasury-Officer's Wooing*, includes a bit of biography on Lowis himself. The volume concludes with author, title, and subject indexes and a map of Burma. The only way to improve this work would be to supplement it with a bibliography of materials produced in the Burmese language since 1962 (at which point Burma's researchers were encouraged by the newly installed military government to cease publishing in English). [R: Choice, Dec 92, p. 602]
—**Judith M. Brugger**

China

125. **The Cambridge Encyclopedia of China.** 2d ed. Brian Hook and Denis Twitchett, eds. New York, Cambridge University Press, 1991. 502p. illus. maps. index. $49.50. DS705.C35. 951'.003. LC 91-18600. ISBN 0-521-35594-X.

This single-volume, comprehensive reference work on ancient and modern China is a welcome addition to the literature, despite many rivals since the first edition appeared in 1982 (see ARBA 84, entry 300). The three-volume *Information China* (see ARBA 90, entry 121) is more extensive in coverage, but it is far more expensive and reflects the official views of the Chinese government.

The encyclopedia arranges its contents under seven broad subject areas: land and resources, peoples, society, the continuity of China, the mind and senses of China, art and architecture, and science and technology (a historical perspective). (The section on the continuity of China, which treats the entire history of China to the present, comprises nearly one-third of the volume.) Each of the subject areas is divided into many sections and subsections. For example, under the mind and senses of China, there are sections on beliefs, customs, and folklore; philosophy and religion; words and signs; literature; drama, music, and cinema; cuisine; and time and quantities. Subsections for the latter include hours; the traditional calendar; the cycle of the years; coins and currencies; and dimensions, weights, and measures. Numerous illustrations, maps, tables, and charts enhance the text. Eight appendixes, suggestions for further readings, a select glossary, and an index conclude the volume.

One major change in this edition is the replacement of the Wade-Giles romanization by the pinyin system. A shortcoming mentioned in the review of the first edition, the lack of cross-references in the index, remains. For example, "Forbidden City" and "Tiananmen Square incidents (1976)" are listed under the subject "Beijing" but not separately. Despite the inadequate index, the encyclopedia's authoritative coverage and reasonable price make it a useful addition to most libraries. [R: BR, May/June 92, pp. 59-60; LJ, 1 Feb 92, p. 78; RBB, 15 Feb 92, pp. 1127-28]—**Hwa-Wei Lee**

Japan

126. Perren, Richard, comp. **Japanese Studies from Pre-History to 1990: A Bibliographical Guide.** New York, Manchester University Press; distr., New York, St. Martin's Press, 1992. 172p. index. (History and Related Disciplines Select Bibliographies). $79.95. Z3301.J36. 016.952. LC 91-37386. ISBN 0-7190-2458-7.

This book provides Western students of Japan with information on relevant publications in English. The volume, which groups the studies covered under broad historical and thematic headings, consists of six sections and an index of authors and editors. The book starts with general works (545 entries). Next comes the premodern period to 1868 (609 entries), 1868 to 1914 (673 entries), 1914-1945 (853 entries), 1945-1965 (636 entries), and 1965-1990 (753 entries). The annotated entries in each section are listed under such categories as bibliographies, historiography, and methodology; population and demography; money, prices, and public finance; the military; education; labor; urban life; and women.

Perren's annotations of book (but not article) entries are useful and have cross-references where a work overlaps more than one subject area.

While female authors are listed with full first names, male authors are given only initials. Some Japanese authors, who according to Japanese custom have used their last name first in their publications, are treated as if their first names were their last names. Translations of Japanese novels are not covered, and at least one bibliography has been omitted. Overall, the volume is a helpful guide to sources on Japanese studies. [R: Choice, Oct 92, p. 275] — **Seiko Mieczkowski**

Laos

127. Cordell, Helen, comp. **Laos.** Santa Barbara, Calif., ABC-Clio, 1991. 215p. index. (World Bibliographical Series, v.133). $74.50. 016.9594. ISBN 1-85109-075-4.

Similar to its predecessors in this series, the coverage of this work is comprehensive, stretching from archaeology to politics to cookery. The entries, however, are selective and mostly in English or French; few works written in Laotian are included. This is due to two factors: Western scholars have shown a lack of interest in Laos, and Laos lacks a strong literary tradition. For example, the National Library of Laos is no more than 30 years old, and it was built primarily with the help of Western scholars and private American foundations. Library services have not been widely available to the public. Similarly, Laotian higher education is not as advanced as that of its neighbors (e.g., Vietnam, Thailand).

The work under review consists of 548 items divided into 34 subject areas and then arranged alphabetically by author. Although entries are arranged thusly, the titles are printed in boldface type and appear before the authors, a rather confusing practice. The annotations are descriptive, adequate, and brief. Most of the materials cover the period from 1945 to 1973. (Locating these sources in U.S. academic libraries will be a challenge.) A highly informative introductory chapter explains the history of Laos, and there are three indexes. The cover, paper, printing, and binding are excellent.

This work is intended to introduce users to major and significant sources about Laos, and it does so successfully. Highly recommended for college and research libraries. [R: Choice, Dec 92, p. 598]
— **Binh P. Le**

128. Stuart-Fox, Martin, and Mary Kooyman. **Historical Dictionary of Laos.** Metuchen, N.J., Scarecrow, 1992. 258p. maps. (Asian Historical Dictionaries, no.6). $35.00. DS555.5S78. 959.4'003. LC 91-36215. ISBN 0-8108-2498-1.

This work attempts to list the major events in the history of Laos. The entries, each about one-third of a page in length, focus on the important political forces and personalities of modern Laos. The information presented is accurate and objective, but entries could have been more selective. For example, entries on such topics as corruption, electricity, alcohol, health, and historians and historiography seem to have little "historical" significance, yet have been included. On the other hand, entries that seem pertinent to Laotian history have been omitted or are discussed only briefly (e.g., John F. Kennedy, the Vichy Colonial Government, the Village Cluster Program, the National Progressive Party, the National Union Party). Furthermore, some of the entries could have been discussed jointly rather than separately (e.g., cooperatives and collectivization, Vietminh and the Vietminh invasions). Also included are maps, appendixes, and a lengthy bibliography. The items listed in the latter will not be easy to find because most are either in French or were published elsewhere. There are no indexes. Still, this book should prove useful for students and scholars of Southeast Asia. [R: Choice, Sept 92, p. 92] — **Binh P. Le**

Singapore

129. Mulliner, K., and Lian The-Mulliner. **Historical Dictionary of Singapore.** Metuchen, N.J., Scarecrow, 1991. 251p. index. (Asian Historical Dictionaries, no.7). $32.50. DS610.4.M85. 959.57'003. LC 91-35697. ISBN 0-8108-2504-X.

An excellent addition to Scarecrow's growing series of Asian Historical Dictionaries (see ARBA 90, entries 117 and 526), this work follows their general pattern. There are a note on spelling, a short chronology, an excellent overview of the history of Singapore, the dictionary itself, appendixes, an extensive bibliography, maps, and an index. The dictionary portion comprises about three-fifths of the work and includes short entries on people, events, organizations and other terms relevant to the history and cultures of Singapore. The entries range in length from a couple of sentences to over two pages. Fittingly, the entry on Lee Kuan Yew is the longest, and the dictionary provides excellent coverage of the ins and outs of Singapore's recent political history. The authors seem scrupulously fair and accurate, and they go to great pains to point out the contrast between the restrictions imposed on Singapore's citizens and the official desire of the government to make Singapore into "a world information hub."

The classified bibliography occupies almost one-fifth of the encyclopedia. It is preceded by an excellent bibliographical note that not only points out the standard historical works but also notes "lighter" works of literature and commentary that give insights into the complex politics and culture of this modern city-state. Appendixes list heads of government since 1891, population by ethnic group, the percentage distribution of Chinese by dialect, and election results and cabinet members since the mid-1950s. This is a solid reference work suitable for general readers and experts alike and is recommended to all libraries. [R: Choice, Oct 92, pp. 276-77]

– Richard H. Swain

Tibet

130. Pinfold, John, comp. **Tibet.** Santa Barbara, Calif., ABC-Clio, 1991. 158p. index. (World Bibliographical Series, v.128). $66.00. 016.9515. ISBN 1-85109-158-0.

Produced in the familiar format and style of previous volumes in this useful series, *Tibet* is arranged in broad subject headings that include such topics as the country and its people, travel and exploration, and flora and fauna. There also is an unusual group of works under "Tibetan Medicine." The book contains a list of periodicals devoted to the study of Tibet and a list of other bibliographies. The introduction has a useful survey of the history, geography, and religion of Tibet. There is an author/title index. The convenience of this bibliography should make it a welcome addition for most large and academic libraries. [R: Choice, Jan 92, p. 725]

– J. C. Jurgens

AUSTRALIA

131. **The Australian Reference Dictionary.** Anne Godfrey-Smith and others, eds. New York, Oxford University Press, c1986, 1991. 911p. illus. maps. $55.00. 032. ISBN 0-19-553296-1.

Computer technology, which has helped create many wonderful new reference tools, can also be the bane of the unwary reference librarian. *The Australian Reference Dictionary* is simply a derivative of the excellent 1986 *Oxford Reference Dictionary* (ORD) (see ARBA 88, entry 51). Through the wonders of technology, the textual database of the ORD has been manipulated by the addition of dictionary entries for more common Australianisms; the abridgment of many of the British encyclopedic entries; and the addition of southeast Asian, Pacific, and Australian encyclopedic entries. The result is a reference dictionary tailored for the Australian audience that still contains much of the original ORD. For Australian audiences this is an extremely useful variant edition. For audiences in other countries, especially the United States, it has little real value. Most of its non-Australian information is readily available in other sources, such as the ORD, and the Australian information is too brief to meet the needs of even those library users with only a passing interest in the country. For just about the same price, *Concise Encyclopedia of Australia* (see ARBA 90, entry 124) will provide substantially greater information about Australia and will meet the needs of a great many more library users. [R: Choice, Nov 92, p. 437] – **Norman D. Stevens**

CANADA

132. Cencig, Didier, and Christian Pouyez. **International Directory of Canadian Studies. Repertoire International des Etudes Canadiennes.** Ottawa, International Council of Canadian Studies, [1992]. 525p. index. $95.00pa. 971'.007. ISBN 0-9691862-6-6. ISSN 0846-5495.

One of the original purposes of the International Council for Canadian Studies (ICCS) was to promote the exchange of information between the growing number of Canadian studies associations outside Canada. This directory came about through the efforts of the organization's membership and supersedes two publications that appeared in 1989: the *Directory of Canadianists* and the *International Directory to Canadian Studies* (see ARBA 91, entry 106). This greatly expanded version contains 12 chapters, each with a short introduction that explains the content and method used to compile the data. The two most helpful sections are the lists of Canadian studies publications for 33 subject fields (from anthropology to women's studies) and 3,500 Canadianists worldwide with their business/home addresses and telephone/fax numbers. Also included are worldwide Canadian studies and affiliated associations; courses taught; journals, proceedings, and directories for the field; Canadian studies centers and programs; and grants and scholarships available.

Canadian studies is a flourishing field. Consequently, this directory should be in all academic libraries that support area studies programs.—**Gary D. Barber**

133. **Encyclopedia of Newfoundland and Labrador. Volume Three.** St. John's, Nfld., for Joseph R. Smallwood Heritage Foundation by Harry Cuff, 1991. 687p. illus. maps. $90.00. 971.8'003. ISBN 0-9693422-2-5.

Volume Three (Hu-M) continues the publication of what should become the standard reference work on Newfoundland and Labrador. The first two volumes were published in 1981 and 1984; publication ceased until the Smallwood Heritage Foundation was able to complete a fund-raising campaign to finish the encyclopedia and endow a research center at Memorial University. The work will be completed with the publication of volumes four and five in 1993 and 1994.

Smallwood, premier of Newfoundland from 1949 to 1972, conceived and published the first two volumes of the encyclopedia as a means to make "Newfoundland better known to Newfoundlanders." The third volume not only substantially advances the achievement of that goal but also provides a remarkably comprehensive picture of the history, geography, natural history, cultures, daily life, communities, and personalities of the region. Articles range from a single short paragraph to more than 10 pages, and the work is notable for its extensive coverage of people and places. General topics are not neglected; for example, the "L" section includes excellent articles on libraries, lighthouses, liquor, literacy, literature, and logging camps. The work is well illustrated by photographs, drawings, and maps. The photographs are particularly notable as they range from superb modern aerial photographs of geographical features and places to nineteenth-century pictures of people and the activities of daily life. The information provided is authoritative and comprehensive, and the book is well bound. Highly recommended to all libraries with an interest in Newfoundland and Labrador.—**Richard H. Swain**

134. Jones, Linda M., comp. **Canadian Studies: Foreign Publications and Theses, Etudes Canadiennes.** 4th ed. Ottawa, International Council for Canadian Studies, 1992. 525p. index. $30.00pa. 016.971. ISBN 0-9691862-7-4.

This work is intended for researchers and for librarians doing collection development in Canadian studies. It lists 3,300 books, serials, and theses about Canada or Canadians, all produced outside of Canada. Explanatory text is written in English and French, while titles are in their language of origin. Although the majority are in English or French, quite a few are in other languages, such as Spanish, German, and Russian. The list was compiled by the International Council for Canadian Studies (ICCS) where it is stored on the INMAGIC database. In the paper copy, access is provided through name and title indexes only. Unfortunately, there is no subject index, making it necessary to go through entire sections of the book to find a relevant item. Sources are organized by broad subject categories only (e.g., "Geography and Travel," "History and Civilization"). Specific subject searches can be requested from ICCS, as can information about individual articles, addresses, lectures, and essays that have been excluded from this bibliography.—**Margaret A. Grift**

135. Stephen, Marg, with Merle Harris and Karen Pinkoski. **Alberta Bibliography: Books by Alberta Authors and Alberta Publishers.** Edmonton, Alta., Young Alberta Book Festival Society, 1992. 73p. $10.00pa. 016.97123. ISBN 0-9693147-3-6.

This bibliography lists books published in Alberta between 1988 and 1992 or written by authors who were permanent residents of Alberta during that period. The works are arranged alphabetically by author (or by title, if there is no author) under Dewey Decimal Classification System categories. Entries include author, title, place, publisher, date, and ISBN. When appropriate, a suggested reading level is appended to an entry. There is a one-sentence annotation for each entry. Coverage is broad, including trade books, university press publications, juvenile books, and works from various organizations and institutions. This book is primarily of regional interest, although some libraries that specialize in Canadiana may find it useful.—**Gari-Anne Patzwald**

DEVELOPING COUNTRIES

136. Hadjor, Kofi Buenor. **Dictionary of Third World Terms.** London, I. B. Tauris; distr., New York, St. Martin's Press, 1992. 303p. $49.95. ISBN 1-85043-346-1.

Hadjor (professor, University of California) has created a most useful and readable collection of words and terms associated with the Third World. His book draws information from many disciplines to provide definitions that are necessary to understand and analyze less-developed countries. The book could also be used to obtain succinct definitions of many modern economic expressions, such as monetarism and purchasing power parity, and political terms such as colonization and Peronism. Many of the entries extend well beyond definition and include historical perspectives and analyses. Tables are used to summarize extensive information. Although the selection of terms and the point of view lean to the Third World, the definitions are remarkably neutral. A number of entries include references for further reading. Numerous world organizations and leaders associated with the Third World are profiled.

Although other dictionaries offer definitions of terms associated with Third World nations, this one is probably the most comprehensive and authoritative work in the field. It fills an information gap by providing reasoned insights for better understanding of the Third World. [R: Choice, Dec 92, p. 602; WLB, Oct 92, p. 106]—**William C. Struning**

137. Kurian, George Thomas, ed. **Encyclopedia of the Third World.** 4th ed. New York, Facts on File, 1992. 3v. illus. maps. index. $225.00/set. HC59.7.K87. 909'.09724. LC 92-3544. ISBN 0-8160-2261-5.

The problems of Third World countries (e.g., deteriorating economies, political violence, terrorism, destruction of the environment, foreign debt) are topics that continue to be the focus of much scholarly and governmental attention. With this edition of the *Encyclopedia of the Third World*, Kurian once again provides the interested student/scholar with a compendium of vital information necessary to an understanding of these countries. The focus of the information is on the political, social, and economic factors that impact on—but are by no means exclusive to—the underdeveloped or developing world. Kurian has made every effort to provide readers with an objective view of the subject matter; "evaluations of men and events are deliberately avoided...."

Some of the topics covered include geographical features, population, ethnic composition, languages, human rights, economy, currency and banking, and legal systems. Each entry has a bibliography of books and films, a valuable addition for teachers who want to encourage students to further explore countries of interest. The encyclopedia also provides an array of other relevant information, such as a list of organizations and their associated agencies. Numerous appendixes indicate per capita income, population trends, agriculture, finance, exports, and more. A selected bibliography lists other relevant works on the Third World, although this reviewer was unable to locate citations for any of Immanuel M. Wallerstein's important works on Third World issues (e.g., *The Capitalist World-Economy* [Cambridge University Press, 1979]). Overall, this expensive encyclopedia is a worthwhile addition for all academic and public libraries, especially for those whose clientele includes Third World patrons.—**Dario J. Villa**

EUROPE

General Works

138. **Directory of Pan-European Organizations 1992.** London, Euromonitor; distr., Detroit, Omnigraphics, 1992. 258p. index. $335.00. ISBN 0-86338-405-6.

With European unity close to becoming a reality, the appearance of this work is particularly timely. It covers 500-plus groups in Europe and offers basic information on them, including addresses, telephone and fax numbers, and other necessary contact data. In addition, the work provides capsule coverage of each organization's objectives along with other salient information, such as the nature of membership, any publications, and date of founding. Most of the work, more than 200 pages, is devoted to an alphabetical list of these organizations and the provision of this type of information. Section 2 contains a brief list of statistical data compiled by the organizations, followed by sections that index acronyms and subjects. All sorts of organizations—official, semiofficial, and voluntary groups—are included.

This is a work of great utility, and ideally every library should own a copy. However, in a time of tightening budgets, the price seems rather high.—**James A. Casada**

Eastern Europe

139. Collins, David N., comp. **Siberia and the Soviet Far East.** Santa Barbara, Calif., ABC-Clio, 1991. 217p. index. (World Bibliographical Series, v.127). $75.00. 016.957. ISBN 1-85109-157-2.

This is an annotated, thorough bibliography of English-language works about Siberia. The word "Soviet" in the title, although by now an anachronism, does not diminish the bibliography's usefulness. The work is subdivided into 27 categories; travel, flora and fauna, history, languages, ethnography, economy, transportation, and literature are among the major ones. The annotations about the works are very informative, giving users a good sense of the scope of literature on Siberia available in English. In all, 735 titles are listed. The work also contains valuable cross-indexes of authors, titles, and subjects. [R: Choice, Jan 92, p. 716]—**Andrew Ezergailis**

140. **Eastern Europe: A Directory and Sourcebook 1992.** London, Euromonitor; distr., Detroit, Omnigraphics, 1992. 436p. index. $390.00. ISBN 0-86338-410-2.

This volume is a treasure trove of information that can strengthen economic and political ties between what used to be called "the West" and "the East." The volume has 2 maps and 221 statistical tables that cover all of Eastern Europe, including the former Soviet Union but excluding Albania. Under Yugoslavia, Slovenia is discussed separately. Information ends with 1990-1991.

There are five sections and an index of companies covered. Section 1 provides an exhaustive overview with a discussion of structural changes, including foreign trade, manufacturing, agricultural policies, demographic trends, and the economics of the German unification. It also deals with key issues such as emigration, debt, the energy crisis, technology, ecology, labor and employment, inflation, and tourism; Eastern Europe (much of which is now called Central Europe) as a consumer market, with data on the growth of consumption; selling within Eastern Europe; area; and problems and prospects by countries. Section 2 provides information on access to markets by individual countries. Section 3 gives data on major companies within the individual countries and by industries. Section 4 covers sources of information for those interested in Eastern European markets, both international and single country, including official, research, advertising, publishers, major libraries, trade associations, economic journals, and information databases. Section 5 reviews the statistical datafile with the help of statistical tables.

The volume is thorough, ingenious, and imaginative, and is potentially quite useful for business. Because of the rapidly changing business conditions in Eastern Europe, the book is not, of course, completely current, but it gives more than enough to establish working relations within Eastern Europe. Highly recommended for business and general libraries.—**Bogdan Mieczkowski**

141. **Eastern Europe and the Commonwealth of Independent States 1992.** Detroit, Omnigraphics, 1992. 583p. maps. $375.00. ISBN 0-946653-77-1. ISSN 0962-1040.

  To begin this work, eight essays discuss regional issues, such as nationalism, religion, international relations, and the environment. A ninth essay covers the end of the German Democratic Republic. Chapters on the East European countries follow a common outline. Sections include geography, statistics, chronology, signed essays on history and economy, and a brief bibliography. "Directory" sections provide information on a range of topics, such as government and politics, religion, the media, culture and education, business and finance, and the environment. The chapter on Yugoslavia includes an essay on nationalism and politics and separate sections for each republic that cover geography, history, economy, and directory information.

  Coverage of the former Soviet Union is more extensive but follows the same basic format. Each member country of the Commonwealth of Independent States, plus Georgia and the Baltic countries, has separate geography, history, economy, statistics, and directory sections. The text of the treaty that established the Commonwealth is also included. Twelve signed essays provide a more comprehensive assessment of political and economic questions. Among the topics covered are the August Revolution, nationalism, foreign policy, agriculture, energy, and foreign trade. A biographical dictionary closes the volume. Brief sketches with addresses are given for some 175 prominent political figures. An outline of headings used in the directory sections, a list of full-page maps, a key to abbreviations, and some updated information on government figures are included in the front matter. There is no index.

  Greater detail in the table of contents would improve access. The topics included in the directory sections, for example, are not listed. However, the systematic and consistent presentation of information compensates for this lack of guidance. Overall, this volume should prove an excellent source of ready-reference information and a solid introduction to current issues in the study of this region. [R: Choice, Nov 92, p. 440; LJ, Aug 92, p. 86; RBB, 1 Oct 92, pp. 365-66; WLB, Sept 92, p. 112]
  — **Cheryl Kern-Simirenko**

142. Pockney, B. P. **Soviet Statistics since 1950.** New York, St. Martin's Press, 1991. 333p. $55.00. HA1444.P63. 314.7'09'045. ISBN 0-312-04003-2.

  Recent political events have increased the value of this volume as a major source of data on what used to be the Soviet Union. Much of the information gathered by Pockney (University of Surrey) has come from primary Soviet sources and from unclassified data released during the period of glasnost in the late 1980s. Other statistics have been provided by the OECD (Organization for Economic Cooperation and Development), the European Community, the Stockholm International Peace Research Institute, and the U.S. Arms Control and Disarmament Agency. Pockney has collected as much data as possible; very little is available prior to 1950, and many of the tables in this volume do not cover the entire period after 1950.

  The statistics are grouped into five broad categories: population and labor, industry, energy, agriculture, and foreign trade. An explanatory section accompanies each table or cluster of tables, and a source is given for each table. The variety of data is impressive and quite detailed in many categories. For example, the national composition of the republics is given, and there is data on the number of pensioners, educational levels of the labor force, death rates by age groups, divorce statistics by republics, investment data for each major industry, growth rates, energy statistics for agriculture, data on power stations, the utilization of agricultural land, engineering imports, and trade statistics with selected countries. This compilation is an essential resource for academic libraries and complements other standard Soviet statistical sources, such as the *East European and Soviet Data Handbook* (see ARBA 82, entry 363), which covers 1945 to 1975, and the *USSR Facts and Figures Annual* (see ARBA 82, entry 364). [R: Choice, Mar 92, p. 1054; WLB, May 92, pp. 129-31] — **Thomas A. Karel**

France

143. Ardagh, John, with Colin Jones. **Cultural Atlas of France.** New York, Facts on File, 1991. 240p. illus. maps. index. $45.00. ISBN 0-8160-2619-X.

This profusely illustrated, up-to-date survey for the general reader was compiled by a journalist and a historian. It is organized into four main parts: geography; history; contemporary society and culture; and the regions, including the politics and economics of regionalism. History, although greatly condensed, still takes up the largest portion of the text. The contemporary section seems ample, but only an enticing introduction is given to the history and characteristics of each region. The basic narrative is interspersed with 33 essays on special topics such as peasant life, Paris through the ages, delicacies of the Southwest, and the hill villages of Provence. Currency varies among the topics. For example, coverage extends through the 1988 elections, 1989 wine production, and 1990 cultural and intellectual life, but only through 1986 or 1987 for transportation, unemployment, and immigration figures.

The text is accompanied by maps, photographs, tables of rulers, a chronological table, a bibliography, a gazetteer, a list of illustrations, and an index. There are, however, no exact citations of sources of statistics and less commonly known facts. The 42 maps are attractive and legible in most cases, although some gradations of pale green and white are difficult to distinguish. The captions of the numerous, excellent photographs are used effectively to supplement the text, but they can occasionally be confusing by covering too much material. For example, the caption for the St. Paul de Vence fountain refers to the Maeght Foundation, which is well beyond the village of St. Paul and is in no way related to the picture. Not only is the theater at Orange mistakenly identified as the amphitheater at Nimes, but the reference to the use of a statue in an amphitheater is also misleading. The Bonaparte dynasty chart erroneously shows Hortense de Beauharnais married to Napoleon III (as well as correctly showing her to be his mother). On the whole, however, this is an authoritative and well-presented survey of French history and culture at a very reasonable price. [R: BR, May/June 92, p. 60; Choice, Apr 92, p. 1203; RBB, 15 May 92, p. 1714; SLJ, Mar 92, p. 270] – **Joyce Duncan Falk**

Great Britain

144. **Contemporary Britain: An Annual Review 1992.** Peter Catterall and Virginia Preston, eds. Cambridge, Mass., Basil Blackwell, 1992. 492p. index. $74.95. 941.0859. ISBN 0-631-18494-5. ISSN 0957-5960.

This annual review is the third yearbook created by the Institute of Contemporary British History. Its aim, which is fulfilled admirably, is to act both as an analysis of contemporary Great Britain and as a record of events and developments. Arranged by subjects such as politics, the economy, the Gulf War, the environment, religion, and culture, it contains 41 essays written by scholars and political journalists. The essays review and analyze relevant legislation, reports, speeches, and events of the previous year. Each is followed by a detailed chronology of major events in that subject area. The work concludes with an index.

The reader will certainly get a sense of the prevailing trends and themes in British society from these essays. Some of them reflect the opinion of the writers but still give a thorough overview of the material. Recommended for all academic libraries with a clientele interested in modern British history or politics. – **Christine E. King**

Northern Ireland

145. Shannon, Michael Owen, comp. **Northern Ireland.** Santa Barbara, Calif., ABC-Clio, 1991. 603p. index. (World Bibliographical Series, v.129). $70.00. 016.9416. ISBN 1-85109-032-0.

One of a long series of bibliographies, *Northern Ireland* has a classified arrangement that contains the headings one would expect in a bibliography of a country, such as geography, history, biography, and population. There are also not so obvious, but still expected, categories, such as politics, government, law, trade, education, and employment, as well as the pleasant surprises of folklore, food and drink, publishing, libraries, and the book trade.

Most items were published between 1920 and 1990, although some earlier classic works are included. While Shannon has tried not to repeat titles included in his earlier volume *Irish Republic* (ABC-Clio, 1986), there is some overlap, mostly of books that cover both countries. Only a few official reports and periodical articles are included.

The supplementary material is useful, including a map and indexes of authors, titles, and subjects. Most helpful is the glossary, which explains political and historical terms used in the various annotations, some peculiar to this country. Most interesting is the introduction, which gives a concise history of the country. It explores the relationship of Northern Ireland to both the United Kingdom and the Republic of Ireland, and it sets the present tensions and disagreements in historical context.

All in all, this appears to be a thorough examination of the literature on Northern Ireland. It is useful for librarians wishing to check their collections of works on this subject or for students researching in the area. [R: Choice, Dec 92, p. 604]

—**Terry Ann Mood**

INDIAN OCEAN REGION

Mauritius

146. Bennett, Pramila Ramgulam, with George John Bennett, comps. **Mauritius.** Santa Barbara, Calif., ABC-Clio, 1992. 151p. index. (World Bibliographical Series, v.140). $65.00. 016.96982. ISBN 1-85109-153-X.

Perhaps best remembered as the setting for the French novel *Paul and Virginie*, exotic Mauritius has had a colorful history. Part of a series that will eventually cover every country in the world, this bibliographic introduction to Mauritius is a fine addition. Bennett acknowledges that the 537 annotated entries are selective in light of Auguste Toussaint's 8,000-entry *Printed Record*, which covers the years 1502-1954. Toussaint, Chief Archivist of Mauritius, competently laid the groundwork that Bennett draws from and updates. A good part of the literature is in French, because French cultural influence was (and still remains) pervasive. All French titles have been rendered into English; if an English translation of a book exists, it has been noted. The Dutch and British periods are also dealt with, although the French found the islands more alluring.

Bennett's opening essay on Mauritius crowds a lot of history into a few pages, and for the beginning researcher it unveils a fascinating panorama of hectic sugar trade and European exploitation. Contained in the bibliography are not only the standard offerings of works about social conditions, politics, and the economy but also the arts, cuisine, and literature. The annotations are deftly written and convey a personal knowledge of the literature. The section on government reports and statistics directs the researcher to unexpected sources. Recommended for libraries with an interest in world geography. —**Bill Bailey**

147. Selvon, Sydney. **Historical Dictionary of Mauritius.** 2d ed. Metuchen, N.J., Scarecrow, 1991. 253p. (African Historical Dictionaries, no.49). $35.00. DT469.M455S45. 969.8'2'003. LC 91-38866. ISBN 0-8108-2480-9.

A jewel of an island set squarely in the Indian Ocean, Mauritius has been a sparkling success amidst the widespread economic and political failures that have plagued post-Independence Africa. This work, an extensive update of the volume first published in 1982, is essential for academic libraries that support African or Third World studies. The fact that its author resides on the island while serving as editor in chief of *Le Mauricien* adds to its appeal. Even those who own the original edition will need to acquire the book, if for no other reason than to give readers access to the considerably expanded and updated bibliographical entries. Anyone who wishes to know or understand more about Mauritian life and history will find the volume invaluable. —**James A. Casada**

LATIN AMERICA AND THE CARIBBEAN

General Works

148. Covington, Paula H., and others, eds. **Latin America and the Caribbean: A Critical Guide to Research Sources.** Westport, Conn., Greenwood Press, 1992. 924p. index. (Bibliographies and Indexes in Latin American and Caribbean Studies, no.2). $115.00. Z1601.L3225. 016.98. LC 91-34622. ISBN 0-313-26403-1.

This comprehensive annotated guide to library reference and bibliographic sources on Latin America and the Caribbean will be an invaluable resource for students, librarians, and scholars of the region. The volume provides access to approximately 6,000 citations that are multidisciplinary in scope. The emphasis is on English, Spanish, and Portuguese materials. Regions covered include Mexico, Central America, South America, and the Caribbean. The annotations vary in length from one line to one paragraph and provide the reader with essential descriptive information.

The volume is divided into 15 chapters, the first dealing with general bibliography and the remaining ones addressing disciplines from anthropology to women's studies. The chapters on history, literature, and performing arts are divided into subsections. What makes this reference book a valuable addition to any library are the introductory essays that outline scholarship trends for each discipline. A notable feature is that each chapter contains a section of resources that lists special collections, such as clippings files, film collections, and primary research materials. For example, the chapter on art and architecture cites the University of Miami Library as a major resource for Cuban posters (1959-1985), "primarily from Cuba but also from exiled Cuban artists." The editor contends, and rightly so, that the purpose for listing these resource sections is to alert the reader to "pockets of specialized collections." The subject, author, and title indexes are thorough. This excellent guide is highly recommended for all academic and public libraries with substantial Latin American collections. [R: Choice, Nov 92, pp. 444-46; RBB, 1 Dec 92, p. 688; WLB, Oct 92, p. 111]—**Dario J. Villa**

149. Grow, Michael. **Scholars' Guide to Washington, D.C. for Latin American and Caribbean Studies.** Revised by Craig VanGrasstek. Baltimore, Md., Johns Hopkins University Press, 1992. 427p. index. (Scholars' Guide to Washington, D.C., no.2). $60.00; $19.95pa. Z1601.G867. 026.98. LC 92-12589. ISBN 0-943875-36-6; 0-943875-37-4pa.

This work continues to be a valuable, if not indispensable, tool for anyone in Washington, D.C., preparing a research project on Latin America. The guide provides a detailed description of the resources available, including special collections at public libraries, universities, and research centers and materials from federal agencies and international organizations. Topical coverage is on the social sciences and the humanities, with some limited coverage of the sciences. Geographically, the guide deals with all of Iberic Latin America and the former and current possessions of Great Britain, France, and the Netherlands.

More than 500 collections, organizations, and agencies are listed in this guide. Each entry provides basic information such as name, address, telephone number, specifics about the collection, and individuals to contact. The material is organized under two major sections—collections and organizations—with appropriate subheadings. Several appendixes list bookstores, housing, and so forth that a visitor to Washington would find useful. Overall, this revised and updated edition is recommended for all major academic and research collections, particularly those that support Latin American Studies.—**Dario J. Villa**

150. Schon, Isabel. **A Hispanic Heritage, Series IV: A Guide to Juvenile Books about Hispanic People and Cultures.** Metuchen, N.J., Scarecrow, 1991. 165p. index. $22.50. Z1609.C5S364. 016.973'0468. LC 91-26335. ISBN 0-8108-2462-0.

Schon's guide to books about Hispanic people and cultures is a welcome source of bibliographic information about juvenile and young adult books that sensitize readers to the cultures of Spanish-speaking peoples. Extensive and well annotated, it includes materials that focus on understanding the people; history; art; and political, social, and economic problems of Central and South America, the

Caribbean, Spain, and the Hispanic-heritage people in the United States. Books are arranged alphabetically by country and author. There are chapters on Central America and Latin America as a whole. The annotations are lengthy, well written, and useful for selecting appropriate titles. Each annotation includes a recommendation that indicates the appropriate reading level of the material. An author/title/subject index aids the reader. This book is recommended for public and academic libraries that have strong teacher education collections. [R: BL, 1 Jan 92, p. 839; VOYA, June 92, p. 140; SLMQ, Fall 92, p. 74]—**Dario J. Villa**

151. **Statistical Yearbook for Latin America and the Caribbean. Anuario Estadistico de America Latina y el Caribe.** 1991 ed. Santiago, Chile, Economic Commission for Latin America and the Caribbean; distr., Lanham, Md., UNIPUB, 1991. 774p. $65.00pa. ISBN 92-1-021030-1. ISSN 1014-0697.

This edition of a well-known compendium contains 385 tables of statistical data on the 33 Latin American and Caribbean countries that are members of the United Nations' Economic Commission for Latin America and the Caribbean (ECLAC). Through the years the ECLAC has worked diligently to standardize indicators and measurements for all the countries of the region and to make them comparable with the statistics that UN bodies collect in other areas of the world.

Part 1 consists of six chapters of "derived socioeconomic indicators," such as rates and ratios, and part 2 consists of 10 chapters in absolute figures on such topics as population, finance, natural resources, industrial production, infrastructure, and employment. Both sets of statistics usually present historic data (back to 1970) as well as more recent figures. An annex includes 14 tables of economic projections for 1991. Most tables give comparable statistics for each country. All text and table headings are in both Spanish and English. Explanatory pages are adequate and clearly describe the statistics presented in each chapter. This yearbook remains the standard reference work for socioeconomic (especially economic) statistics for Latin American and the Caribbean.—**Fred J. Hay**

Argentina

152. Biggins, Alan, comp. **Argentina.** Santa Barbara, Calif., ABC-Clio, 1991. 460p. index. (World Bibliographical Series, v.130). $85.00. 016.982. ISBN 1-85109-109-2.

This annotated bibliography of Argentina, intended for English-speaking users, has 1,350 entries that describe and evaluate books, serials, and periodical articles. It is arranged by broad subject, with author, title, and detailed subject indexes. A wide range of subjects is covered, from the traditional academic disciplines (e.g., archaeology, history, philosophy, the arts, science and technology) to agriculture, urbanization, sports, and health and medicine. It also includes chapters on subjects specific to Argentina, such as gauchos and the Falkland Islands/Malvinas dispute. The literature chapter covers biography and criticism of 21 major writers in addition to titles on Argentine literature in general.

This work suffers from the uneven coverage inherent in bibliographies largely limited to works in English about a country that uses another language. Subjects popular with the English-speaking audience are well covered, while others of equal importance are given short shrift, and significant works in other languages are omitted. Nevertheless, this is a useful bibliography. Recommended for academic and large public libraries. [R: Choice, Dec 92, p. 597]—**Ann Hartness**

Brazil

153. Hartness, Ann. **Brazil in Reference Books, 1965-1989: An Annotated Bibliography.** Metuchen, N.J., Scarecrow, 1991. 351p. index. $39.50. Z1671.H39. 016.981. LC 90-28356. ISBN 0-8108-2400-0.

Brazil is a country with a long and complex history (e.g., colonialism, race and ethnic relations) and has recently become the concern of environmentalists around the world. It provides the interested student with an array of opportunities for rewarding intellectual research. But, as is the case with other Latin American countries, comprehensive bibliographic tools on literature about the country are unavailable or are difficult to use. Access to important data thus becomes a major obstacle for any but the most determined researcher. *Brazil in Reference Books* is designed to alleviate the problem. It is a comprehensive list of 1,669 entries about literature on Brazil in reference books from 1965 to 1989, and works in progress have also been cited. Hartness limits her inclusion of relevant entries to the humanities, the fine arts, and the social sciences. Entries are arranged in 29 broad subject categories that range from general bibliographies to labor and industry. Although the annotations are brief, they are clear and very helpful. Also of note are the author index, which includes corporate authors, and the subject index. *Brazil in Reference Books* is highly recommended for all academic libraries that have significant Latin American collections, especially for universities that offer programs in Latin American studies. [R: C&RL, Sept 92, pp. 424-25; Choice, Feb 92, p. 874] — **Dario J. Villa**

Costa Rica

154. Stansifer, Charles L., comp. **Costa Rica.** Santa Barbara, Calif., ABC-Clio, 1991. 292p. index. (World Bibliographical Series, v.126). $83.50. 016.97286. ISBN 1-85109-027-4.

This volume is one in a series—a very long series—that is planned to cover every country in the world. The keynote of the series is to provide an interpretation of each country that will aid in the understanding of that country's culture, its place in the world, and its uniqueness.

Among all the world's countries, Costa Rica is indeed special. It is easily the Latin American country with the longest and most respected democratic tradition. The reasons for this and other traditions are explored lightly in the introduction, which is followed by more than 700 annotated bibliographical entries. All volumes in the series are intended primarily for the English speaker, and therefore most of the titles cited (books and periodicals) are in English. Even so, Stansifer has wisely included a generous sampling of Spanish-language titles (with English translation), most of them published in Costa Rica. The subject coverage is broad and includes all areas except the hard sciences. The work concludes with three very useful indexes of authors, titles, and subjects. Many titles are also cross-referenced from chapter to chapter, making access even easier. This is an excellent introductory bibliography to a country worth the attention of all North Americans. [R: Choice, Apr 92, p. 1214] — **Edwin S. Gleaves**

Honduras

155. Howard-Reguindin, Pamela F., with Martha E. McPhail, comps. **Honduras.** Santa Barbara, Calif., ABC-Clio, 1992. 258p. index. (World Bibliographical Series, v.139). $70.00. 016.9728. ISBN 1-85109-137-8.

Honduras was frequently in the news in the 1980s as the central staging area for the Reagan administration-backed contras in the Nicaraguan civil war. Howard-Reguindin, a librarian with the U.S. Information Agency, has organized this bibliography into 37 chapters that list 788 books, articles, and dissertations current through 1990. All entries are critically annotated. Her introduction varies from the series format by focusing on Honduras history, geography, society, and economy. Interestingly, she notes that despite receiving $1 billion of United States aid between 1980 and 1987, Honduras remains one of the poorest countries in the Western Hemisphere.

While the chapter on history is the longest (75 entries), there is extensive coverage of such topics as foreign relations, prehistory and archaeology, politics, and economics. The chapter on human rights provides coverage of a broad range of sources, including many critical of the U.S. role in violations. The plight of refugees from Nicaragua and El Salvador is described in a chapter on ethnic groups and refugees although there are no listings for the several Central American agreements on this topic. Honduras's famous "soccer war" with El Salvador in 1969 and their continuing boundary disputes are described in several entries under foreign relations.

Overall, this useful bibliography will be a helpful introduction to easy-to-find materials on any Honduran topic. A detailed table of contents and author, title, and subject indexes make it easy to use. — **Brian E. Coutts**

Montserrat

156. Berleant-Schiller, Riva, comp. **Montserrat.** Santa Barbara, Calif., ABC-Clio, 1991. 102p. index. (World Bibliographical Series, v.134). $70.00. 016.72975. ISBN 1-85109-154-8.

What is Montserrat—an island, a place, a state, or a republic? All of the above. Montserrat is an island in the Caribbean, specifically part of the Lesser Antilles. This slight volume is a good introduction to the state. It provides valuable information on the history, geography, economic, social, and political aspects of the island. The bibliography is in alphabetical order under broad subjects. There are three separate indexes: author (personal and corporate), title, and subject. The information provided is from standard sources and includes materials from serials, journals, governmental reports, and monographs. Each citation is numbered, and some of the entries have considerable information in their annotation. More cross-references would be desirable.

Given the limited knowledge that most people have about Montserrat, it is surprising that this work does not have a map to locate it for the user. Not even the state's latitude and longitude are given. These would make this work more useful. Because of its specificity, smaller public libraries and community colleges may want to pass it by and purchase a more comprehensive work on the Lesser Antilles.
—**Roberto P. Haro**

Turks and Caicos Islands

157. Boultbee, Paul G., comp. **Turks and Caicos Islands.** Santa Barbara, Calif., ABC-Clio, 1991. 97p. index. (World Bibliographical Series, v.137). $50.00. 016.97296. ISBN 1-85109-162-9.

Volume 137 in the World Bibliographical Series is the first attempt to compile the elusive and scanty literature (English materials only) on this small (193 square miles) archipelago of islands southeast of the Bahamas. At first, these islands were populated by Arawak Indians enslaved by the Spanish conquistadores. The first Europeans to inhabit the islands were salt rakers from Bermuda. These and other interesting points of historical narrative are covered in the excellent introductory essay. The Turks and Caicos islands are of significance because, according to the literature cited in this excellent work, recent underwater archaeology seems to indicate that they were the initial landfall for Christopher Columbus. Although new evidence is still inconclusive, and will probably remain so, this bibliography is invaluable for any serious research on the topic. It lists 305 entries, each placed under a general subject heading that is standard for the World Bibliographical Series. These include geography, geology, flora and fauna, and history. Books, journal articles, government documents, and dissertations are listed. For the English-speaking student this bibliography will be an essential starting point for any serious research. Highly recommended.—**Dario J. Villa**

Virgin Islands

158. Moll, Verna Penn, comp. **Virgin Islands.** Santa Barbara, Calif., ABC-Clio, 1991. 210p. index. (World Bibliographical Series, v.138). $60.00. 016.972972. ISBN 1-85109-165-3.

The comprehensiveness and authority—and hence the utility—of this series have long been established; however, the organization of the contents (which follows a standard pattern) could be improved. One wonders, for example, why theses and dissertations are listed separately rather than under the appropriate subject and why tourism is located between geographical and historical studies rather than with trade, industry, agriculture, and transportation. While all the other chapters provide item numbers, titles in boldface type, and annotations, that on university theses does not. Items that concern the British Virgin Islands are listed immediately after those of general application; although the United States Virgin Islands population is almost five times that of the British Virgin Islands (and the economy more viable), the number of entries selected for each territory is roughly the same. A longer introduction would have been an advantage; the history of the islands jumps from Columbus's arrival to 1690. (Blank pages in the final signature could have been used for this expansion.)

Most of the entries have descriptive annotations, but few are evaluative. A strength is the inclusion of materials up to November 1991. Some of the entries have only the most tenuous association with the Virgin Islands, such as *Party Politics in the West Indies* by C. L. R. James (1962) and *The Negro in the Caribbean* by Eric Williams (1942). But by way of compensation, Moll, born in the Virgin Islands and long a professional librarian there, has unearthed and included many (even ephemeral) items that seem to have eluded other bibliographers. In addition, there seems to be only a single disparity in an exhaustive index. This work will be useful to libraries interested in the subject.—**Marian B. McLeod**

MIDDLE EAST

General Works

159. **Bibliographic Guide to Middle Eastern Studies 1990.** New York, G. K. Hall, 1991. 617p. (Bibliographic Guides). $195.00. ISBN 0-8161-7151-3. ISSN 1058-644X.

This interdisciplinary bibliographic guide to publications published in and about 17 Middle Eastern countries provides a comprehensive guide to works on the region from 1987 to 1990. Books, serials, and nonbook materials are included. The bibliography is arranged alphabetically, integrating subject, title, author, and series entries. The main entry for each source provides complete Library of Congress cataloging information including call number and tracings. Appropriate cross-references are provided (e.g., "Coptic Art" *see* "Art, Coptic"). Researchers, acquisitions personnel, and interlibrary loan staff will find the guide particularly useful for verification of titles in Arabic, Persian, Hebrew, and Turkish and titles published in the Middle East. Because it is not annotated, the guide may not be as useful to collection librarians in need of evaluative information.

A few typographical errors and lapses in editing are minor annoyances. For example, the subject heading "Egpt-Economic Policy" causes one title to be separated from several others on "Egypt-Economic Policy." It is likely that the *Turkey Cook Book* deals with fowl rather than Turkish cookery, and another title, *L'Enigma Pirandello* by Persi-Haines, written in Italian and published in Canada, appears unrelated to the targeted subject matter. This source is recommended as a resource for acquisitions and collection development and as a current awareness tool on the region.—**Ahmad Gamaluddin**

160. Moss, Joyce, and George Wilson. **Peoples of the World: The Middle East and North Africa: The Culture, Geographical Setting, and Historical Background of 30 Peoples....** Detroit, Gale, 1992. 437p. illus. maps. index. $39.95. ISBN 0-8103-7941-4.

This handbook brings together considerable information, both historical and current, on Middle Eastern peoples. Starting with the Sumerians at about 5000 B.C., the authors explore the growth of civilization in the region and the impact of Arabism, Islam, nationalism, and oil.

Information is grouped in four sections—ancient cultures, Middle Eastern regions, culture today, and countries today. Entries for ancient cultures are arranged chronologically and provide an overview of the history, geography, and culture of each people. Religions considered include Islam, Christianity, and Judaism. Thirty major cultures of the region are covered; a 10-page summary on Arabs provides a foundation for more specific entries. The last section includes maps and brief descriptions of 20 Middle Eastern countries. An index and glossary enhance use of the resource.

Information that the student or general reader might otherwise consult several sources for has been consolidated. Written at a basic level, the text can easily be understood by secondary school students; it could also be useful as a ready-reference or starting point for research for adult public and academic library users.—**Ahmad Gamaluddin**

161. Shimoni, Yaacov. **Biographical Dictionary of the Middle East.** New York, Facts on File, 1991. 255p. illus. maps. $40.00. DS62.4.B56. 920.5694. LC 90-32553. ISBN 0-8160-2458-8.

This work contains more than 500 short biographies of twentieth-century rulers, party leaders, government heads, religious figures, and military leaders who have played significant roles in countries from Morocco in the west to Iran in the east and from Turkey and Cyprus in the north to Yemen and Oman in the south. Although not as exhaustive as a who's who, the book does include literary figures such as Mahmud Darwish and Nagib Mafouz. It is organized in a convenient alphabetical order and is excellent as a reference tool for quick, basic information on these individuals. In addition, a number of terms, such as *Abu, Bilu, Gush Emunim*, and *al-Nashashibi*, are explained. Three addendums include the Arab and Israeli delegates to the 1992 Madrid Peace Conference, seven pages of maps, and tables of the Hashemite dynasty and the Egyptian ruling family. The biographies contain much historical information, including birthplace, education, and employment, and they place the individuals within the political contexts in which they lived. Although there is no overt attempt to interpret an individual's positions or actions, the biography does contain a perspective. For instance, in the 1956 Suez Crisis, Shimoni writes that Israel coordinated its attack because of "Egyptian aggression."

This book will be very useful for those who are students of the modern Middle East. However, finding some entries will be difficult for those who are not conversant with variant transliterations of Middle Eastern languages to English. Still, Shimoni has provided an essential volume for almost all libraries and for all students of the modern Middle East. [R: Choice, July/Aug 92, p. 1661; RBB, 15 May 92, p. 1712; SLJ, June 92, p. 156] – **David L. White**

162. Silverburg, Sanford R. **Middle East Bibliography.** Metuchen, N.J., Scarecrow, 1992. 564p. index. (Scarecrow Area Bibliography Series, 1). $69.50. Z3013.S54. 016.956. LC 91-26074. ISBN 0-8108-2469-8.

This bibliography contains 4,435 entries for books, the majority published after 1980. Most of the entries identify English-language works, but some in other European languages and a few in Middle Eastern languages are also listed. The entries cover the geographical region bounded by Egypt, Iran, Turkey, and the Indian Ocean. The book opens with a useful introduction that lists other bibliographies, sources for reprinted titles, bibliographies on subjects not covered in this volume, research material available on microfilm and microfiche, and lists of photographic essays and travelogues. Entries in the main body are listed alphabetically under topics such as "Arab World-History," and there are some currently popular topics, such as Salman Rushdie. Most of the topics cover personalities, countries of the Middle East, cities, commodities, ethnic/religious/political groups, activities (e.g., art, commerce, education), and movements (e.g., the Gusg Emunim, the Intifada). The largest entries are for Egypt (36 pages), Iran (54 pages), Islam (65 pages), and Israel (70 pages). The books are listed in common bibliographic form without comment as to their quality. The work concludes with an author index. – **David L. White**

Egypt

163. Kalfatovic, Martin R. **Nile Notes of a Howadji: A Bibliography of Travelers' Tales from Egypt, from the Earliest Time to 1918.** Metuchen, N.J., Scarecrow, 1992. 427p. index. $49.50. Z3685.2.K34. 016.916204. LC 92-10286. ISBN 0-8108-2541-4.

This 1,150-entry annotated bibliography provides a selective overview of travelers' accounts of the Nile Valley and nearby deserts from antiquity to the close of World War I. The author indicates that works with a strictly archaeological, anthropological, political, or instructional focus have been excluded. Entries are arranged chronologically, then alphabetically by traveler's name. Each entry includes complete bibliographic data, a well-written annotation, and an indication as to the traveler's nationality when possible. An extensive introduction reviews major phases of Egyptian history, describes a typical travel itinerary, and lists well-known visitors to the region. A name index of all major travelers and a title index simplify access to entries.

Kalfatovic states that he has attempted to examine the first edition of each work in the original language and in English or French translation when possible. The Library of Congress catalog, the British Library catalog, and the Brooklyn Institute of Arts and Sciences' "Catalogue of the Egyptological Library and Other Books from the Collection of the Late Charles Edwin Wilbour" are among the sources credited as resources for completion of the bibliography. The volume is well organized and will provide scholars, armchair travelers, and future visitors to the region with a well-organized source list and miniature travel history. – **Ahmad Gamaluddin**

Jordan

164. Gubser, Peter. **Historical Dictionary of the Hashemite Kingdom of Jordan.** Metuchen, N.J., Scarecrow, 1991. 140p. (Asian Historical Dictionaries, no.4). $22.50. DS154.G83. 956.9504'3'03. LC 91-25171. ISBN 0-8108-2449-3.

   This title is a combination of dictionary, history, chronology, and bibliography. A 14-page introduction and a 9-page chronology provide a capsulized regional history and some context for the dictionary entries, 75 pages of which follow. The length of the entries varies from a brief description to several-page essays on topics such as "Hussein Ibn Talal, H.R.M. King" and Palestinians.

   The dictionary provides useful information, but in some instances it might have been further enhanced by guides to pronunciation. The 51-page bibliography that follows the entries is intended to provide the reader with a "substantive listing of major works on Jordan." Most works cited are written in English; however, a few are in other languages, including Arabic. The bibliography offers numerous citations on the history, archaeology, economy, politics, and social development of Jordan, as well as the Arab-Israeli conflict. This title offers a good research source for individuals studying or teaching about Jordan and the Arab world. [R: Choice, May 92, pp. 1368-70]—**Ahmad Gamaluddin**

Kurds

165. Izady, Mehrdad R. **The Kurds: A Concise Handbook.** Bristol, Pa., Taylor & Francis, 1992. 268p. maps. $15.95pa. DS59.K86I93. 956'.0049159. LC 92-8174. ISBN 0-8448-1727-9.

   According to the preface, Izady has written this book as a reference manual for the public, the press, teachers, students, scholars, and travelers because there are too few reference works on the Kurds. He claims that this lacunae is due to the Kurds not having a national government, which would give them a national identity in the world's eyes. Consequently, the book tries to be all things for all people; but similar to most works of this sort, it does not meet the needs of any group. This does not mean that it is not valuable; it does mean that the book could have accomplished more if Izady had identified the needs of one audience and written primarily for it. As it is, the book has too much for the general reader and too little for the specialist.

   The work is divided into 10 chapters on geography, land and environment, history, human geography, religion, language/literature/the press, society, political and contemporary issues, the economy, and culture/arts. Each chapter is further subdivided and contains interesting, sometimes interpretive, explanations of the Kurds or Kurdistan. Yet the language and approach used will be difficult for the nonscholar, and the chapters and sections are not self-contained but require reading and understanding previously introduced material. Assisting the reader, though, are many illustrative maps and charts; also, each section and chapter is followed by a thorough bibliography of other sources. Coupled with the thorough introduction to many aspects of Kurdish society, the book will be a good starting point for those beginning a study of the Kurds.—**David L. White**

Lebanon

166. Bleaney, C. H., comp. **Lebanon.** rev. ed. Santa Barbara, Calif., ABC-Clio, 1991. 230p. index. (World Bibliographical Series, v.2). $84.00. 016.95692. ISBN 1-85109-150-5.

   Lebanon is an annotated bibliography on works that deal with almost all aspects of the country. Subjects covered include history, geography, politics, mass media, religion, education, economy, banking and finance, agriculture, industry, energy, transportation, literature, the arts, plants, and animals. The book starts with an excellent but brief overview of the history, geography, and politics of Lebanon. This is followed by the 32-chapter bibliography, which takes up most of the book and is certainly the most comprehensive bibliography available in the English language about Lebanon. Each entry includes title, author, publisher, place and date of publication, number of pages, and a short but clear annotation. The last part of the book is an extensive index that would please any user. *Lebanon* is highly recommended to all university libraries and to all students of the Middle East and Lebanon. [R: Choice, Nov 92, p. 438]—**Elie M. Dick**

Saudia Arabia

167. Ricks, Stephen D. **Western Language Literature on Pre-Islamic Central Arabia: An Annotated Bibliography.** Denver, Colo., American Institute of Islamic Studies, 1991. 163p. index. (Bibliographic Series, no.10). $10.00pa. Z7835.M6A54. 016.9538. LC 90-28859. ISBN 0-933017-01-4.

Well conceived and well executed, this work can stand as a model for others preparing an annotated bibliography. Ricks has clearly and reasonably defined both a geographical-chronological framework (Central Arabia in the pre-Islamic period) as the subject of his study and a body of literature (works in Western languages) as the object of the bibliography. Moreover, he has divided the more than 250 entries into categories and subcategories that make this material easily accessible to beginning as well as seasoned researchers. Major divisions include general reference works, studies on the history and geography of pre-Islamic Central Arabia, studies on its religious institutions, and studies on social and political institutions. Ricks has provided a helpful and impartial annotation for each item, often making judicious use of its author's own words. Author and title indexes are supplied. In short, Ricks's bibliography can be confidently recommended to all libraries that cater to its intended audience.
—**Leonard J. Greenspoon**

PACIFIC AREA

General Works

168. **Who's Who of the Asian Pacific Rim.** 1992 ed. Laguna Beach, Calif., Barons Who's Who, 1991. 705p. index. $175.00. LC 91-061765. ISBN 0-9620943-5-8. ISSN 1059-5392.

More than a who's who, this volume is an up-to-date source of information on business and government leaders; principal Asian Rim corporations; government agencies; and religious organizations in China, Hong Kong, Indonesia, Japan, Malaysia, the Philippines, Singapore, South Korea, Taiwan, and Thailand. The 6,145 biographies of leaders are alphabetized by surname in the first and largest section. They include business addresses, telephone and fax numbers, current job title, and function. Many also give personal and professional data, and a few are accompanied by a photograph of the biographee. The corporation directory lists 4,262 corporations grouped by country. Each entry gives address, telephone and fax numbers, and names and titles of the chief executives. Government agencies are provided in a third section by country and include ministries, consulates, embassies, officials, and courts. Major religious organizations and churches of each country appear in a separate section. An index to the directory sections is organized under 68 professional or subject categories, then by country, and finally by corporate name. No page references are given; the user must look under the appropriate section and under each country. Because the directories are basically alphabetical in arrangement, this should cause no major difficulty.

This compilation will be extremely useful for persons in business and commerce who need to make contact with or learn about key individuals and corporations in the Asian Rim countries. It will be an essential part of any business collection and also of use in general reference or Asian studies collections.
—**Shirley L. Hopkinson**

Philippines

169. Muijzenberg, Otto van den. **Dutch Filipiniana: An Annotated Bibliography of Dutch Publications on the Philippines.** Leiden, Netherlands, KITLV Press; distr., Detroit, Cellar Book Ship, 1992. 135p. index. (Koninklijk Instituut voor Taal-, Land- en Volkenkunde: Working Papers, 9). $20.00pa. ISBN 90-6718-050-5.

What accounts for Dutch interest in the Philippines? It is a by-product of Dutch historical, political, and economic interests in Indonesia; this interest intensified after World War II, when the former Dutch colony gained its independence and Dutch scholars were not as welcome there as before. The main purpose of this bibliography is to provide access to articles and books written by Dutch authors on the history, sociology, and anthropology of the Philippines. There are also entries on economic, linguistic, and geographic themes. Most of these works were published in the Netherlands or the former Netherlands Indies (now Indonesia).

Dutch scholarly publications on the Philippines have increased in numbers in recent years. The bibliography consists of 349 annotated titles, two-thirds of them dating from the 1970s and 1980s. About 200 of these titles appeared in Dutch. The list of titles is presented alphabetically, with the title of each Dutch publication also given in English. The annotations are quite complete and scholarly. There are geographic and subject indexes to enhance the book's usefulness and accessibility. The author, a Southeast Asia specialist at the University of Amsterdam, has produced a bibliography of value (albeit somewhat limited in scope) to Southeast Asian and Philippine scholars. — **Marshall E. Nunn**

4 Economics and Business

GENERAL WORKS

Acronyms and Abbreviations

170. **McGraw-Hill Dictionary of Business Acronyms, Initials, and Abbreviations.** By Jerry M. Rosenberg. New York, McGraw-Hill, 1992. 352p. $29.95; $14.95pa. HF1002.5.R67. 650'.03. LC 91-23464. ISBN 0-07-053734-8; 0-07-053935-9pa.

Rosenberg, professor at the Graduate School of Management at Rutgers University and a consultant to the *Oxford English Dictionary* (see ARBA 90, entry 1006) and the *Random House Dictionary of the English Language* (see ARBA 88, entry 1095), has scoured 40 subject areas to compile his dictionary. The acronyms represent the fields of marketing, insurance, management, retailing, banking, accounting, economics, statistics, and trade. About 25 percent of the 15,000 entries are ticker symbols and newspaper abbreviations for publicly held companies. Government agencies and international associations are also included.

Given the proliferation of acronyms today, subject-specific dictionaries such as this tend to be more useful than very large, general sources. The economical price and size of this dictionary will make it attractive to both large and small libraries. [R: LJ, 15 Mar 92, p. 80; RBB, 1 Jan 92, p. 851; WLB, Jan 92, p. 128]—**Mary Ellen Kollar**

171. **McGraw-Hill Dictionary of Wall Street Acronyms, Initials, and Abbreviations.** By Jerry M. Rosenberg. New York, McGraw-Hill, 1992. 235p. $24.95; $12.95pa. HG4513.R68. 332.6'32'03. LC 91-24841. ISBN 0-07-053934-0; 0-07-053736-4pa.

If one wishes to decode a symbol representing a corporation traded on one of the three major U.S. stock exchanges, abbreviations found in the stock listings in some newspapers, or abbreviations used in the financial world, this handbook can help. Its usefulness is limited, however, because a much more common quest for investors and professionals is to discover which symbol is associated with a company whose name is known. This book does not answer that question. For example, one can determine that the symbol RTRSY represents Reuters Holdings, but there is no entry for Reuters Holdings with its associated exchange and newspaper symbols. Different stock issues of the same corporation are not indicated. With approximately 10,000 entries, the majority represent stock symbols. The remaining abbreviations include items such as "XO: Executive Officer" but omit, for example, stock indexes such as XMI (Seymour-Moss International). While it is suggested that this tool might be used with a "related dictionary," no bibliography is appended. The information here can be found elsewhere in tools that provide additional useful information. [R: LJ, 15 Mar 92, p. 80; RBB, 1 Jan 92, p. 851; WLB, Jan 92, p. 128]—**JoAnn V. Rogers**

Atlases

172. **The *Economist* Atlas.** Ian Castello-Cortes, ed. New York, Henry Holt, 1991. 384p. illus. maps. index. $47.50. LC 91-58152. ISBN 0-8050-1987-1.

Although this work is detailed, it is well laid out and easy to understand, combining physical, thematic, and political maps with more than 800 country and regional profiles. Businesspeople, students, and educators will find it to be a good resource with which to start an investigation into past and current economic, political, social, and trade matters.

The text begins with a list of world maps and then moves on to world comparisons of such matters as economic strength, energy, foreign debt, populations, education, and language. Most of the work consists of regional and detailed breakdowns of each country, covering such elements as climate, geography, language, economy, and religion. Some of the information is already dated; for instance, the Soviet Union no longer exists. However, this is offset by the atlas's breakdown of the Soviet empire into regions (e.g., the Baltic States, the Russian Federation). The book concludes with a brief glossary, an explanatory note on the data, a short general word index, and a detailed map index. Affordably priced, this edition of a well-recognized atlas is recommended for public, academic, and business libraries. [R: Choice, Oct 92, p. 271; RBB, July 92, p. 1958] – **James M. Murray**

Bibliography

173. Danesh, Abol Hassan. **The Informal Economy: A Research Guide.** Hamden, Conn., Garland, 1991. 420p. index. (Research and Information Guides in Business, Industry, and Economic Institutions, v.2; Garland Reference Library of Social Science, v.624). $55.00. Z7164.C81D14. 016.33. LC 91-9975. ISBN 0-8240-3419-8.

In spite of the florid language of the introduction and the awkward prose of the author, this annotated bibliography is a useful tool for researchers and others interested in the somewhat shadowy world of informal economies. Covered topics include theory, labor market structure, household economy, moonlighting, small businesses, subcontracting, the underground and black markets, tips and gratuities, and unorganized street economy. The focus is international and includes works in languages other than English.

The major problem with the work is the fragmentation of the basic literature into the chosen categories. In some cases the author seems unaware of related materials in other disciplines. Likewise, the topical divisions are a confusing mix of the types of informal activity, the roles of the informal economy in developing nations versus those in developed countries, and the impacts of these economies on the participants. There is the additional problem in some annotations of conclusions summarized without identifying the contexts (developing countries, large cities, rural areas, or industrialized national economies) from which they have been taken. In these cases the conclusions are less than useful. Overall, however, the work makes a contribution to the literature on the informal economy and should be useful to those doing formal research or making a casual investigation. [R: Choice, Mar 92, p. 1042] – **Elisabeth Logan**

174. Nasrallah, Wahib. **United States Corporation Histories: A Bibliography 1965-1990.** 2d ed. Hamden, Conn., Garland, 1991. 511p. index. (Garland Reference Library of Social Science, v.807). $67.00. Z7164.T87N37. 016.3387'4'0973. LC 91-28858. ISBN 0-8153-0639-3.

This edition contains over 3,000 citations to U.S. corporation histories that appeared between 1965 and 1990. Companies listed include sports teams, newspapers, small banks and savings and loans, and major corporations. The citations come from a wide variety of sources: newspapers, magazines, company-produced reports, monographs, and dissertations. Criteria for inclusion in the bibliography are not clear, and the quality of the sources in several instances seems doubtful. Some cited articles are only two to three pages in length and may prove of little value to researchers. Arrangement is by company name in alphabetical order, with an industry index. Some cross-referencing is provided (e.g., Estee Lauder *see* Lauder, Estee); however, some references are sorely lacking (e.g., there is no entry for USX [US Steel Corp.], but there are entries for United States Steel). No locations are provided for the

sources, and some, such as company-produced brochures and promotional pieces, may be very difficult to locate. This work is for research libraries rather than popular business collections.
—**Robert D. Adamshick**

175. Redman, Deborah A. **A Reader's Guide to Rational Expectations: A Survey and Comprehensive Annotated Bibliography.** Brookfield, Vt., Edward Elgar/Gower Publishing, 1992. 182p. index. $59.95. HB199.R43. 330'.01. LC 91-34832. ISBN 1-85278-567-5.

This is a concise and balanced overview of the theory of rational expectations and its impact upon modern macroeconomic analysis. It describes the origins, evolution, and applications as well as the criticisms and limitations of a theory that has been at the center of many theoretical and public policy debates since it was first proposed in 1961.

The text begins with a well-organized, well-written, and nontechnical introduction into rational expectations that draws many useful comparisons between Keynesian economics and the new classical economics. Users will benefit by the author's efforts to define and categorize the various versions of hypotheses that carry such labels as *strong, weak, narrow, generalized, extreme*, and *dogmatic* in the literature. Because many of these concepts have ambiguous definitions and interpretations, this book will be of great assistance to a variety of users. The author even addresses the semantic difficulties inherent in hypotheses that use terms such as *rational, natural*, and *expected*. (It is interesting to ponder how people would react if words such as *correct, consistent*, and *anticipated* were used instead.)

The text also includes a comprehensive, although nonexhaustive, list of major and influential books, articles, and reviews of rational expectations published from 1961 through 1989. Because these 476 annotated entries are concise and informative, users will be able to trace both the developments and limitations of a theoretical approach that remains revolutionary to some and controversial to others.
—**Timothy E. Sullivan**

176. **Wilson Business Abstracts.** (Indexing coverage: 7/82-5/31/90. Indexing & abstracting coverage: 6/90-6/25/92). [CD-ROM]. Bronx, N.Y., H. W. Wilson, 1992. Hardware requirements: WILSONLINE Workstation, IBM PC, or compatible; 640K; hard disk drive. $2,495.00.

Taking Business Periodicals Index (BPI) on disc one step further, Wilson has added abstracts. The result is Wilson Business Abstracts (WBA), updated monthly, which provides two years of abstracted articles from BPI with 10 years of indexing. As with Wilson's other CD-ROMs, hardware requirements are minimal and software installation is simple. Both printed steps and on-screen instructions are provided. Backup support is available through Wilson's toll-free number. New software versions (WILSONDISC version 2.4 was provided for review purposes) are easily installed over existing versions, and both parameters and defaults are set during installation.

There are three search modes in WBA: BROWSE, WILSEARCH, and WILSONLINE. Each has advantages, and the level of the user determines the search mode. BROWSE is a list of index terms complete with references to subheadings. WILSEARCH is a menu-driven mode that provides several unique access points, including journal title and date in addition to subject, corporate, and personal name access. Perhaps the best feature is the capability to search by author, SIC (Standard Industrial Classification) code, or journal, all unavailable in the print product. WILSONLINE mode allows for Boolean searching and is the logical choice for experienced users. Wilson also provides a 30-page pamphlet that details WBA and its features. Instructions for specific search techniques are clearly illustrated for each mode, including printing and downloading, as well as search qualifiers, content and descriptive codes, and the expand command, all essential for effective WILSONLINE searching.

WBA includes only two years of abstracts, but these are excellent, providing a capsule summary of the article (what most abstracting services refer to as nonevaluative abstracts). WBA abstracts, 50 to 150 words in length, are written by librarians and subject specialists. While letters to the editor and articles of less than one column are excluded, these and book reviews are, nevertheless, indexed. Articles, biographical sketches, company profiles, interviews, product reviews, and prominent obituaries are abstracted.

WBA abstracts compare favorably with ABI/INFORM, the primary competition for Wilson's product. For the purpose of this review, 20 WBA abstracts were compared to the same articles abstracted in ABI/INFORM. While abstract length varies slightly, abstract content varies not at all, and WBA abstracts some articles ABI/INFORM does not. Abstracts in WBA include article title; author; source; citation; abstract; assigned subject headings; companies referenced; and, when applicable, SIC codes and personal name entries. Indexing coverage begins in July 1982, and abstracting begins in June 1990. File size (by June 1991) is 383,000 records, and 5,500 records are added monthly.

The price of WBA is $2,495 annually; BPI on disc costs $1,495 a year; and the basic annual price of ABI/INFORM is $5,250 and now includes almost six years' worth of abstracts on two discs. Librarians and information scientists will have to decide—coverage versus cost, WBA versus ABI/INFORM. For the price, WBA offers a viable alternative and strong competition for the more established ABI.

—**Boyd Childress**

Biography

177. Arestis, Philip, and Malcolm Sawyer, eds. **A Biographical Dictionary of Dissenting Economists.** Brookfield, Vt., Edward Elgar/Gower Publishing, 1992. 628p. $139.95. HB76.B5. 330'.0922. LC 91-16267. ISBN 1-85278-331-1.

Unfortunately, the writings of numerous economists who are in substantial disagreement with basic assumptions about the nature, scope, methods, and significance of orthodox theorizing have not received adequate recognition within the economics profession. This dictionary has been compiled to provide a guide to the writings of 90 illustrious dissenting economists who have made significant attempts to broaden and deepen the understanding of economics. Although the listing is far from complete, it has some special, useful features. Some entries on living dissidents are in the form of autobiographical essays that cover how they developed their innovative thinking, the extent to which they disagree with economic orthodoxy, and the sociopolitical influences on their theories. Some dissidents asked another to write about their work. A small number declined the invitation to contribute. Most dissidents can be classified as post-Keynesian, Marxists or neo-Marxists, Sraffian, Kaleckian, institutionalists, or behaviorists, but few defy an exact categorization.

On the whole, this is a clearly written, well-organized biographical dictionary. Highly recommended to all members of the economics profession, especially those whose primary interest lies in research or the history of economic thought.—**Oleg Zinam**

178. Aronoff, Craig E., and John L. Ward, comps. **Contemporary Entrepreneurs: Profiles of Entrepreneurs and the Businesses They Started....** Detroit, Omnigraphics, 1992. 488p. index. $85.00. HC102.5.A2C66. 338'.04'092273. LC 91-7637. ISBN 1-55888-315-0.

This volume gives brief discussions of 79 individuals and their 74 entrepreneurial ventures. There is little attempt at economic analysis, no synthesis or summary or conclusions, and no indication of the criteria that produced this selection of entrepreneurs. With only a few exceptions (e.g., Donald C. Burr, Steven P. Jobs) the individuals are not household names, but their products and services fall in the expected markets: computers and software, construction and building, food, clothing, and communication. Some of the products or firms are well known (e.g., Mrs. Fields' Cookies, L. A. Gear, Blockbuster Entertainment, WordPerfect, Sun Microsystems). Each entry covers basic topics: biographical information on the entrepreneur/founder, the business's origin and growth, obstacles encountered, keys to success, future vision, and entrepreneurial lessons (with a brief bibliography of relevant articles in the business press). Much of this information comes directly from the biographees. The writing is light and informative, with generous quotations, and is similar in style to the *Wall Street Journal, Forbes,* and *Business Week.* The entries were written by more than a dozen different authors who are identified only by initials. [R: RBB, 1 Oct 92, p. 365; WLB, Sept 92, p. 111]—**Richard A. Miller**

179. **Who's Who in Finance and Industry 1992-1993.** 27th ed. Wilmette, Ill., Marquis Who's Who, 1991. 942p. $220.00. LC 70-616550. ISBN 0-8379-0327-0.

This biennial directory provides brief biographical sketches of persons possessing "current business reference value," based upon a prominent position held or a notable accomplishment. The 27th edition contains more than 25,400 entries, a significant increase over the 25th edition (see ARBA 88, entry 161).

This directory has great breadth of U.S. coverage. Biographees represent not only major corporations in all business sectors but also in areas of education, government, and media that significantly relate to business. Coverage of other countries is proportionally small and should be expanded. Sketches average around 20 lines in length and follow the typical Marquis Who's Who format. The amount and diversity of information supplied is exemplary. The sketches of executives compare favorably with those in directories that focus only on corporations. They contain not only the detailed job history found in *Reference Book of Corporate Managements* (see ARBA 87, entry 274) and the complete list of directorships held in other corporations found in volume 2 of *Standard & Poor's Register of Corporations, Directors, and Executives* (see ARBA 87, entry 182), but also substantially more information than either one on memberships in professional, political, and civic organizations; on publications authored; and on awards and honors.

Two checks were conducted to determine if persons whom one would reasonably expect to find were absent. The first check, for the chief executive officers of the largest 100 publicly held U.S. companies, found 11 CEOs missing, among them those of Chevron, Johnson & Johnson, and Woolworth. In a second (random) check for persons often mentioned in the business press, the following were missing: Richard Darman, William Gates, Ted Turner, and Peter Drucker.

Overlap with other Marquis publications should not be large. A spot-check of the 1991 *Index to Who's Who Books* discovered that one-half of the persons in the 26th edition were not in any other Marquis Who's Who publications. Despite the absence of some important persons from this directory, its breadth of U.S. coverage and the fullness of its sketches continue to make it an essential purchase for business reference collections. — **John Lewis Campbell**

Dictionaries and Encyclopedias

180. Cole, Don, ed. **The Encyclopedic Dictionary of Economics.** 4th ed. Guilford, Conn., Dushkin Publishing, 1991. 270p. illus. $12.95pa. LC 90-81960. ISBN 0-87967-884-4.

This encyclopedic dictionary is written for use in an introductory survey of economics course and will serve that purpose admirably. But its thoughtful and diverse approaches to presenting economic information make it a helpful resource to have on hand for any reader not familiar with the "language, institutions, and practices unique to the study of economics" (preface).

There are 1,400 entries and articles. Most are brief and concise, but major concepts, products, and processes (e.g., market operation, business cycles) are treated in lengthier signed articles. Of the 1,400 entries, 69 are biographies. The definitions frequently include current statistics that further clarify the concept under review. The writing is clear and jargon-free, and the contributors do a good job of explaining complex topics, such as the landmark 1982 case of United States v. American Telephone & Telegraph. The section on business cycles is especially informative.

The dictionary provides a wealth of supplementary material, including 33 topic guides (boxed text that accompanies the regular definition and recommends related topics and subject maps); 21 subject maps; and numerous maps, diagrams, organization charts, tables, and photographs. In addition, three types of cross-references are used: the standard *see* and *see also* references and a defining cross-reference, which gives a simple definition and then refers the reader to another article for more complete information if necessary.

As always in a work of this kind, what has been selected for inclusion is interesting. The contemporary phrases "service economy," "information revolution," "law of the commons," "trickle-down theory" and "voodoo economics" are not included, but "Buddhist economics" (popularized by E. F. Schumacher's 1970s counterculture classic, *Small Is Beautiful*) appears.

In all, Cole has done an excellent job of providing access to a frequently confusing and daunting area of study. This is a useful work that, given its reasonable price, can be recommended to all libraries.
— **G. Kim Dority**

181. Knopf, Kenyon A. **A Lexicon of Economics.** San Diego, Calif., Academic Press, 1991. 314p. $29.95. HB61.K57. 330.'03. LC 91-19658. ISBN 0-12-416955-4.

In a world where an increasing number of politicians, commentators, consultants, and columnists are using (or misusing) basic economic terms and concepts to influence public and private decisions, it is essential that consumers and citizens be well informed. Professional jargon, while useful to those already informed, too often acts to intimidate and exclude those who are initially uninformed. This concise and straightforward dictionary of many of the most commonly used terms, concepts, and institutions in business, finance, and economics is a handy and useful guide that will help make the jargon more understandable. It is contemporary and as easy to use as it is informative.

The dictionary begins with a useful list of commonly used abbreviations, acronyms, and foreign phrases. This is followed by the definition and explanation of more than 800 terms and concepts. The entries are concise yet detailed enough to provide a basic understanding. Several entries have simple and informative diagrams that help to illustrate concepts, and, whenever appropriate, concepts are cross-referenced with related entries.

This concise dictionary is unable to include all of the words and phrases that might confront potential users. Even a few of the terms that are included will undergo some redefinition over time. But despite these unavoidable limitations, this dictionary will be a useful guide to anyone looking for simple and understandable definitions. [R: Choice, June 92, p. 1520; RBB, 1 June 92, p. 1777]

—Timothy E. Sullivan

182. **NTC's French and English Business Dictionary.** By Michel Marcheteau and others. Lincolnwood, Ill., National Textbook, c1988, 1992. 620p. $39.95. ISBN 0-8442-1479-5.

This carefully researched, thorough work has been compiled by people who are knowledgeable about French business. The target audience includes novices as well as experienced businesspeople. Pronunciation is given for specific English words, but for French words the pronunciation is consistent enough that one page about French pronunciation suffices. An especially useful feature is the inclusion of phrases and some sentences. English, United States, and legal usage are presented when these differ from each other. For instance, the French term for a British corporation is not the same as for a United States corporation.

This dictionary is admirably up-to-date and topical, including such terms as *junk bond, laptop computer*, and *fax*. (A few of the most recent terms are listed in an appendix, which might prove a minor inconvenience.) There are several appendixes that should prove invaluable to anyone trying to prepare business correspondence in French. These cover the format of a French business letter, common sales contract terms, numbers, weights and measures, the names for countries and their inhabitants, and abbreviations. These tables, and the words in the body of the dictionary, are so well selected and so well defined that this work should be invaluable to those needing to conduct business with someone who speaks French. There are a number of specialized English/French-French/English dictionaries available, but none seems as well designed to meet the needs of businesspeople.

—Susan V. McKimm

183. Pearce, David W., ed. **The MIT Dictionary of Modern Economics.** 4th ed. Cambridge, Mass., MIT Press, 1992. 474p. $40.00; $15.95pa. HB61.P4. 330'.03. LC 91-45008. ISBN 0-262-16132-X; 0-262-66078-4pa.

The 2,800 entries in this work cover the vocabulary and concepts of modern economics with clear and concise definitions and explanations. This is a true dictionary: entries are definitions rather than brief expository articles (as in *The New Palgrave Dictionary of Money & Finance* [see index for entry number]). The coverage is wide and includes entries on standard economics (e.g., marginal cost, economic rent), analytics (e.g., net present value, offer curves), institutions (e.g., international payments system, Group of Seven), mathematics (e.g., function, exponential), statistics (e.g., vector auto regression, likelihood ratio test), economists (e.g., all Nobel prize winners), laws (e.g., Single European Act, Monopolies and Mergers Act 1965), and events (e.g., Kennedy Round, green revolution). Included is a list of 80-plus acronyms and 4 tables of annual data. The definitions are clear, accurate, and helpful. More detail, naturally, is available in *The New Palgrave*, which has a much higher price.

This dictionary is an excellent acquisition for public, academic, and personal libraries. The audience ranges from undergraduate economics majors through senior academic economists.

—Richard A. Miller

184. Room, Adrian. **Corporate Eponymy: A Biographical Dictionary of the Persons behind the Names of Major American, British, European and Asian Businesses.** Jefferson, N.C., McFarland, 1992. 280p. $35.00. HC29.R66. 338.7'4'0922. LC 92-53502. ISBN 0-89950-679-8.

This work provides brief biographical descriptions of individuals whose names adorn major commercial enterprises in the English-speaking world. Room gives dates, places, family, and career history of nearly 1,000 people whose names have become familiar to us because they identify a company or product, such as Henry Ford of Ford Motor Company or James L. Kraft of Kraft cheeses. The names are presented in a dictionary arrangement. To assist in identifying similar names, a short descriptive phrase indicates the company's general area of business. Within each biography a name with its own entry is in boldface print. The 100- to 200-word biographical sketches generally supply the answer to where the name of the company originated and provide a starting point for more detailed research if desired. While the work's scope is worldwide, the majority of companies listed are of British origin. Emphasis is on names currently in use.

The introduction states that composite names are entered in all their forms with appropriate *see* references to the main entry, but this practice is executed inconsistently. For instance, Philip Morris is referred from "Morris, Philip," but Melson Wingate is not referred from "Wingate, Melson." Companies with names derived from two or more persons (e.g., Dow Jones, Merrill Lynch) are generally not cross-referenced.

A bibliography provides sources for the better-known eponyms. Also included is an exhaustive list of people who provided information about the lesser-known firms. This list is arranged by personal name, not company, which reduces its value. [R: RBB, 1 Dec 92, p. 687] — **William S. Proudfoot**

185. Rutherford, Donald. **Dictionary of Economics.** New York, Routledge, Chapman & Hall, 1992. 539p. index. $75.00. ISBN 0-415-06566-6.

Rutherford, lecturer in economics and associate dean of the faculty of social sciences at the University of Edinburgh, has compiled an easily read, comprehensive dictionary of current economic terms. Coverage of subject areas is unusually broad: names of leaders and movements in the history of economic thought; acronyms used in both the United States and the United Kingdom; and terms from applied economics, domestic and international finance, and the policy sciences. There are more than 200 biographical entries as well as citations for major works. An effort has been made to include female economists. Because of the breadth of coverage, the entries are necessarily brief, and many contain only a sentence or two. The author, however, conveys considerable information in a very few words (e.g., worker "alienation" covers both the Marxist and sociological aspects of the term). There are few gratuitous uses of jargon, and circular definitions are rare. Often the initial definition is followed by discussion of how the term is commonly used, a simple graph, cross-references and lists of related terms in boldface type, and citations to related sources. Definitions sometimes assume a good deal of background knowledge from the reader and hence may not be helpful to U.S. high school students. Terms are listed alphabetically but are accompanied by three-digit subject codes that correspond to those used by the *Journal of Economic Literature* (American Economics Association, 1963-) and the *Economic Journal* (Basil Blackwell, 1891-). An appendix lists terms arranged by subject area. Although British spelling is used, the broad focus of this book makes it as useful for the reader of the *Wall Street Journal* (Dow Jones, 1889-) as for the reader of British journals. [R: Choice, Sept 92, pp. 90-92; LAR, June 92, p. 411] — **Elisabeth Logan**

186. Thomsett, Michael C. **The Little Black Book of Business Words.** New York, AMACOM; distr., Detroit, Gale, 1991. 161p. $14.95pa. HF1001.T46. 650'.03. LC 91-53061. ISBN 0-8144-7753-4.

The Little Black Book Series (same author) includes volumes on budgets and forecasts, letters, math, reports, meetings, speaking, statistics, management, and etiquette. This volume defines about 800 words in accounting, automation, bookkeeping, finance, human resources, insurance, law, marketing and sales, and math. The intended audience is middle-level managers interested in using a single book as a resource for business terminology. The selection of business words is reasonable. Most definitions are clear but very short, so they will likely serve only as a starting point in the search for meaning. Several puzzling omissions are *mortgage* and *cost of capital. Current yield* (for bonds) is included, but *yield to maturity* is not. *Ex-dividend* appears, but not *settlement date.* More disturbing are entries that are unclear or wrong, such as *annual compounding, discounted cash flow, internal rate of return, normal distribution, off-balance sheet items, present value, range, simple interest,* and *variance.* The arithmetic of corporate finance is not this volume's strength.—**Richard A. Miller**

Directories

187. **Books & Periodicals Online: The Guide to Business and Legal Information on Databases and CD-ROMS.** 1992 ed. Nuchine Nobari, ed. New York, Library Alliance, 1991. 820p. $149.00pa. ISBN 0-9630277-0-0. ISSN 0951-838X.

This is a comprehensive directory of computerized databases and business and legal publications that are available either directly from producers, on networks, or on other online services. It alphabetically lists some 22,000 entries and 12,800 periodicals, serials, and other databases that deal with such diverse subjects as business, law, the sciences, medicine, the arts, literature, and general interest topics. The directory identifies which publications and databases are accessible online, how far back that information is available, and how to go about acquiring it from its publisher.

Entries include such detailed information as name and origin of the publication, former and continuing names, dates of publication, publisher, names of databases in which the publication is included, the scope of editorial coverage, names of vendors, file names or numbers, and whether the database is currently available in CD-ROM. The directory also lists the names and addresses of publishers and of producers and vendors, as well as the books and periodicals included in each database.

Access to these databases has obvious advantages for libraries and researchers alike, but to be useful, they must also be accessible. This directory helps to make them just that. The advantages of having such a comprehensive directory of available data and publications are not just the savings in time and storage but also the ability to determine whether or not an article can be selectively indexed and the format of an article in a database. This directory should thus be of interest to any library that wants to maintain or electronically expand its collection in the face of shrinking shelf space and tightening budgets.—**Timothy E. Sullivan**

188. **Brands and Their Companies 1992: Consumer Products and Their Manufacturers with Addresses and Phone Numbers.** 10th ed. Susan L. Stetler and Allison K. McNeill, eds. Detroit, Gale, 1992. 2v. $355.00/set. LC 84-643242. ISBN 0-8103-7542-7. ISSN 1047-6407.

189. **Companies and Their Brands 1992: Manufacturers, Their Addresses and Phone Numbers, and the Consumer Products They Produce.** 10th ed. Susan L. Stetler and Allison K. McNeill, eds. Detroit, Gale, 1992. 2v. $355.00/set. LC 84-643242. ISBN 0-8103-7541-9. ISSN 1047-6393.

Now in its 10th edition, this pair of sets, formerly the *Trade Names Dictionary*, remains the definitive source when researching consumer brands and their manufacturers. Despite recent developments in global marketing and free trade, the volumes continue to focus on U.S. companies and U.S. operations of foreign companies. Foreign brands and companies must be researched in the *International Brands and Their Companies* and *International Companies and Their Brands* (Gale, 1992).

Although different approaches are used, both works present similar information with some organizational variations. *Brands and Their Companies* displays brand names in one alphabetical sequence. Consumer products (e.g., Blue Ice) are emphasized, with some commercial, industrial, generic (e.g., aspirin), and out-of-production items (e.g., Studebaker-Packard) listed. Entries offer a one- or two-word product description, company name, and source code. A typical search can produce single or multiple references from which to choose. As with previous editions, data have been verified with questionnaires and industry sources (e.g., magazines, directories, annual buyers' guides), and sources are clearly identified. Company names are listed in the "yellow pages" with addresses, source codes, and telephone numbers. Fax and toll-free numbers are new in this edition.

Companies and Their Brands is a basic directory that repeats the contents of the "yellow pages" section of the other. Relevant trade names have been added, resulting in entries of one product name or several pages of them (e.g., Congoleum). Both sets incorporate separate entries for divisional offices but fail to trade subsidiaries completely (e.g., Best Foods and CPC International). Serious competitive analysis between brands or companies would benefit from the presence of SIC (Standard Industrial Classification) codes or international SITC (Standard Industrial Trade Classification) numbers, a geographic index for regional name changes (e.g., Hellmans, Best Foods), and subsidiaries.

With these works, Gale continues its long-standing tradition of providing finely crafted, usable reference tools. But as library resources shrink further, economic conditions will force choices among available sources. Although both works are worthy of consideration for purchase, one directory of worldwide brands and companies would better serve the user. For some libraries, searching the database equivalent on DIALOG may be a more cost-effective alternative.—**Sandra E. Belanger**

190. **Business Organizations, Agencies, and Publications Directory: A Guide to Approximately 26,000 New and Established Organizations, Agencies, and Publications....** 6th ed. Catherine M. Ehr and Kenneth Estell, eds. Detroit, Gale, 1992. 1423p. index. $330.00. ISBN 0-8103-2949-2. ISSN 0888-1413.

This edition continues the monumental and ambitious proportions of its predecessors. More than 25,000 entries cover a wide variety of sources such as trade and business associations, labor unions, commodity and stock exchanges, federal and state agencies, franchise companies, convention bureaus, conference centers, schools of business, business publishers, newspapers, and computer databases. These entries are grouped into U.S. and international organizations, government agencies and programs, facilities and services, research and educational facilities, and publications and information services. Information provided varies from category to category and from entry to entry. A preliminary feature entitled "Section Descriptions" supplies content and selection criteria, type of data arrangement, sources of data, and indexing information. This is an excellent introduction for reference librarian use. The directory can be used to find names, addresses, telephone and toll-free numbers, brief textual information, fax numbers, personal names, dates, frequency of publications, and more. The excellent master name and keyword index ties this work together, enabling the reader to find most any entry. A superior typeface and judicious use of bolding combine with permanent paper to add to the usefulness of the directory.

The directory does not aim at being the most complete compendium of this information. It is easy to find omissions; for instance, the breakup of the Soviet Union is not noted (there are entries only for the USSR, not individual republics), and only one bank is listed for the state of Oklahoma. However, one should generally use this excellent source as a starting point in a reference search (although in many cases it will also be the ending point). As a quick ready-reference source, this is a must-own title.
—**Robert D. Adamshick**

191. **Corporate Yellow Book: Who's Who at the Leading U.S. Companies. Vol. 8, No. 3.** Laura Gibbons and others, eds. New York, Monitor Publishing, 1992. 1092p. illus. index. $185.00pa./yr. ISSN 1058-2908.

This is one of a series of "Yellow Books" from Monitor Publishing. Companies are listed alphabetically. Included for each are address; ticker symbol; telephone and fax numbers; number of employees; a brief statement about the nature of the business (including annual revenue); lists of officers and management (sometimes with telephone numbers); major subsidiaries, divisions, and affiliates (with addresses and telephone numbers); the Board of Directors (with titles); and a shareholder relations contact (with address and telephone number). There are indexes for parent company, subsidiary and division, geographical location, and name; a list of additions, deletions, and name changes is also included. This is clearly a work aimed at the business communities rather than libraries; for one thing, there is a small picture of each chief executive officer with the person's titles and academic degrees.

Updated quarterly, this title includes many more names and telephone numbers than appear in such works as *Standard and Poor's Corporation Register*. It could adequately serve any library not able to afford a comprehensive business directory. It would be a truly superb acquisition if it also included SIC (Standard Industrial Classification) codes and the names and telephone numbers of personnel departments and officers. As it stands, it is a solid work that should be seriously considered by any library that serves the business community.—**Richard H. Swain**

192. **The Directory of Business Information Resources, 1992.** Leslie Mackenzie, ed. Lakeville, Conn., Grey House Publishing, 1992. 674p. index. $135.00; $120.00pa. ISBN 0-939300-11-7; 0-939300-15-Xpa.

This directory is intended to provide "information every business needs to stay current and competitive" in a single volume. It lists trade associations, newsletters and other such publications, and trade shows. The book's organization is by "major" industry group, in alphabetical order—accounting to wholesalers—in 90 categories. A SIC (Standard Industrial Classification) table is provided by general SIC, with reference to industry chapters. An index by "entry" name and company name completes the directory.

The associations section contains name, address, telephone and fax numbers, executive director, and membership count. The newsletters and journals section gives publisher name, address, telephone number, current price, editor, whether advertising is included, and a brief description of the publication. Data provided varies widely from entry to entry. Trade show information includes show name, address of sponsor, telephone number, number of exhibitor booths, attendee count, and director. Most of this information can be obtained from other sources, such as *Encyclopedia of Associations* (see ARBA 91, entries 37-38) or the *Gale Directory of Publications* (see ARBA 91, entry 61). Librarians can also go to online sources for this information, and the directory is available in computer-readable format. There are notable omissions (e.g., *ENR* [McGraw-Hill Information Systems, 1874-]) in the publications section for engineering information.

At its price, this directory will give many libraries pause before purchase. Perhaps a small business library with a limited budget might want to purchase this one book in lieu of several on different subjects. [R: Choice, Dec 92, p. 600; RBB, 15 Sept 92, p. 188]—**Robert D. Adamshick**

193. **Directory of Merger and Acquisition Firms and Professionals 1992.** 2d ed. New York, Walker; distr., Homewood, Ill., Business One Irwin, 1992. 395p. index. $150.00. ISBN 0-8027-4896-1. ISSN 1048-6097.

This directory contains four sections. The first (company profiles) lists information for each of about 900 companies that specialize in mergers and acquisitions: name, address, telephone and fax numbers, parent, year established, number of employees and staff, services offered, names of staff, geographic area, types of clients, industry expertise, value of deals handled, number of deals completed (recent years), and fees (including equity interest). Many company entries contain most of these items, but some contain much less, occasionally only name, address, and telephone number. The second section lists 2,700 professional biographies. Data include individual's name, position, employer, birth date, marital status, specialization, professional history, education, publications, affiliations, and memberships. However, most of these biographies are limited to only the first three items. The third section arranges companies alphabetically within broad geographic areas. The fourth section lists companies alphabetically within areas of industry expertise and service (e.g., acquisition financing, agriculture, automotive, biotechnology, business broker/finder). The gathering of information apparently stopped in mid-1991. A 3d edition is promised.—**Richard A. Miller**

194. Lignor, Amy, and Donna Vanicky, eds. **The Directory of Business to Business Catalogs, 1991: A Comprehensive Source of Suppliers to Meet Most Day-to-Day Business Needs.** Lakeville, Conn., Grey House, 1991. 387p. index. $110.00pa. ISBN 0-939300-08-7.

For more than 10 years Grey House has successfully published *The Directory of Mail Order Catalogs* (see ARBA 91, entry 193). It has now produced *The Directory of Business to Business Catalogs*. This new work follows a generally similar format to its older sibling, presenting a detailed catalog/producer list grouped by broad subject categories (e.g., automobile parts and supplies, building supplies) and then subdivided by narrower elements (e.g., car care, insulation). Each entry may contain company name; address; toll-free, regular telephone, and fax numbers; names of specific products and of company officials; catalog price, size, and frequency; sales; availability of mailing lists; credit cards accepted; and more. Data varies widely, no doubt the result of the level of completeness with which questionnaires were returned to the publisher. Indexes are by state and company name. A sample entry guides the user through the information in each entry. The typeface is quite good, with boldface type used to highlight and delimit information. A few errors in street name spellings were noted. Although

not inexpensive, the directory is worth the price for libraries that serve the business community and for businesses themselves. It will be useful for locating catalogs to aid the purchasing actions of companies.
—**Robert D. Adamshick**

195. **National Directory of Nonprofit Organizations 1992. Volume 1: Organizations with Annual Revenues of $100,000 or More.** Rockville, Md., Taft Group; distr., Detroit, Gale, 1992. 2pts. index. $285.00/set. ISBN 1-879784-59-9. ISSN 1048-8154.

Formerly titled *Taft Directory of Nonprofit Organizations*, this 2-part directory is designed to provide brief information on 176,194 U.S. nonprofit organizations whose income exceeds $100,000 annually. A companion volume supplies information on another 80,305 organizations with reported incomes between $25,000 and $99,000.

This directory is divided into three sections. The first is the main body, which is arranged alphabetically by the name of the organization and includes its address, telephone number, IRS filing status, employer identification number, charitable deduction eligibility, annual reported income, and activity identifier code. The second section is an activity index that lists organizations by one of 270 specific activity descriptions; it is supplemented by numerous *see* references. The third section is a geographic index arranged by state, with zip codes as a further breakdown; it also includes a number code that denotes income range.

For those seeking more detailed information on larger nonprofit organizations or access to the largest, *Encyclopedia of Associations* (see ARBA 91, entries 37-38) will probably better serve their needs. However, for its sheer number of listings, the work under review is excellent. Recommended for large public and university libraries that need access to nonprofit listings.—**Bobray Bordelon**

196. **Owners & Officers of Private Companies, 1992.** Rockville, Md., Taft Group; distr., Detroit, Gale, 1992. 2v. index. $260.00pa./set. ISBN 1-879784-49-1. ISSN 1056-3326.

This publication brings together hard-to-find information on executives, more than 100,000 of them, from 44,000-plus private companies with $5 million or more in annual revenue. Data were gathered from a variety of sources, including annual reports, questionnaires, banks, trade commissions, newsletters, government documents, and telephone interviews.

Volume 1 presents listings by state, with executives' names arranged alphabetically therein. Each entry provides executive position held, company name and contact information, sales, number of employees, SIC (Standard Industrial Classification) code, and principal product or service. The revenue figures are not strictly comparable, as many companies (e.g., advertising agencies) report another figure (e.g., gross billings, assets, operating revenues). An asterisk preceding the financial figure indicates an estimated value. The method used is described briefly in the introductory pages. Volume 2 contains an alphabetical SIC list, an index by company name (with the names of the executives given), a numeric SIC index, and a geographic index (with company name and annual sales).

This work is useful for all collections. Possible applications include development activities, job seeking and executive searches, and sales prospecting. [R: LJ, July 92, p. 78]—**Maureen A. Beck**

197. **Pratt's Guide to Venture Capital Sources.** 1992 ed. David Schutt and Judith Grover-Lizardi, eds. Phoenix, Ariz., Oryx Press, 1992. 662p. index. $195.00. LC 85-644764. ISBN 0-914470-62-0. ISSN 0884-1616.

This work is the 16th edition of a handbook and directory on venture capital firms. Most of the 800 investment organizations listed are based in the United States, but a significant number are located in Canada, Europe, or the Far East.

The book is organized into two main sections. The first gives a series of 14 short essays by experts that are intended to aid the entrepreneur seeking funds. Topics include an overview of the industry, business plans, legal considerations, and the relationship between the entrepreneur and the investor. The second part, considerably longer, is devoted to a directory of venture capital companies, including those that provide buyout and acquisitions financing. After an explanatory note, it is organized alphabetically under each U.S. state, with a separate section for foreign firms. The non-U.S. section includes cross-references to U.S. entries from foreign affiliates. In addition to directory and officer information, data include preferred industries, geographical areas, size of financing, and industry. The entries are derived from questionnaires sent to the companies. Access is provided by indexes of company names, officer names, and industry preferences, and also through the table of contents.

This work is a professionally produced business tool that should prove useful to emerging companies that want to raise funds from the venture capital industry. It should be considered as an acquisition by special or larger business libraries where funds and client demand warrant. —**Nigel Tappin**

198. **Ward's Business Directory of U.S. Private and Public Companies 1992.** Detroit, Gale, 1992. 5v. index. $1,150.00/set. ISBN 0-8103-7559-1. ISSN 1048-0707.

One of the best all-around printed business directories is now even better. With the 1992 edition, *Ward's Business Directory of U.S. Private and Public Companies* now covers more than 133,000 companies, an increase of 26,000 over last year's edition. Since last reviewed (see ARBA 90, entry 182), the set has gone from three volumes to five. The first three volumes list companies alphabetically, the fourth lists them geographically by state and ZIP code, and the fifth ranks them by sales within Standard Industrial Classification (SIC) codes. The information given in each part of the directory is concise but useful. The first three volumes give the most data elements: company name, address, telephone and fax numbers, financial information, fiscal year end date, number of employees, public or private status, ticker symbol, stock exchange, year founded, import/export designation, SIC codes, description of business, and top officers. Volumes 4 and 5, while providing slightly less data on the same companies as do the first three volumes, are helpful for their organization. In addition to geographic listings, volume 4 includes several top 1,000 lists. One important new feature is that there is no longer any minimum sales cutoff for inclusion in the directory, so many more small companies are listed.

The publisher should be applauded for selling the volumes individually, allowing libraries to choose those that are most appropriate for their needs. Unlike some directories that use flimsy paper, *Ward's* is printed on high-quality paper that will outlast other high-use business directories. Highly recommended for all libraries whose clientele request company information. [R: LJ, 1 Apr 92, p. 114]
—**Kerranne G. Biley**

199. **Ward's Sales Prospector: A Directory of Leads by State and by Industry.** Kenneth Estell, ed. Detroit, Gale, 1992. 5v. $750.00pa./set. ISBN 0-8103-8888-X. ISSN 1059-9266.

Ward's Sales Prospector (WSP) is a directory of more than 133,000 companies arranged in 5 volumes. Each volume covers companies (arranged by ZIP code) in a certain region of the United States. At the end of every volume, companies are ranked by sales using their 4-digit Standard Industrial Classifications (SICs). Most entries include such information as company name, address, telephone and fax numbers, sales data, number of employees, parent company, officers' names, and SIC code.

The introduction states that "market researchers, sales managers, job seekers, telemarketers, fundraisers, and others will find WSP a useful prospecting tool and information source." This is true, but readers will find it very difficult to use. For example, it is extremely difficult to locate a company unless its ZIP code is known, a major weakness. Also, many entries are out of date, especially in regard to financial data and personnel information. Serious users will be better off relying on other sources.
—**Elie M. Dick**

Handbooks and Yearbooks

200. Berle, Gustav. **Business Information Sourcebook.** New York, John Wiley, 1991. 374p. $75.00. ISBN 0-471-52976-1.

According to Berle, the audience for this work is the businessperson trying to find information on various business-related topics. He suggests that the book is intended to be stimulating rather than informational and hopes that "these reference selections, covering a spectrum of current business information, will spark your curiosity to seek further." In other words, the book presents a hodgepodge of information, without any apparent selection rationale.

The work is divided into six sections: business books (including that famous and ever-popular title, *Kindergarten Teacher's Month-by-Month Activities Program*); periodicals (with the notation that "some publications are free; others might cost or are available by subscription"); directories (e.g., the Library of Congress); government business sources (some entries have telephone numbers, some do not); newsletters, associations, and corporate publications (including the sales section of the United Nations); and electronic business references (which inexplicably lists *Encyclopedia of Associations* [see ARBA 91, entries 37-38]).

There is no consistency in the type, placement, or manner of presentation of data. Sometimes marketing materials are listed under marketing, other times under finance. Sometimes costs are given, sometimes not. (And sometimes the costs given are of no use to the reader; under the periodicals section, for example, the costs listed are not for subscriptions but for advertising.) The presentation of other information is equally inconsistent. For instance, *Business Periodicals Index* (see index for entry number) is listed under directories, and in the same section, which is organized by topic, the *Thomas Register* (Global Engineering Documents, 1991) is listed as its own topic heading between "Textiles" and "Tire Business."

Although clearly geared to an information novice, the book offers no guidelines for identifying what types of information might be needed, what resources are available, or how to evaluate information that is obtained. Perhaps the best advice given, in fact, is the frequent admonition to check with one's local librarian for more in-depth information. When one considers the excellent business information publications that are already available, such as *Business Information Sources* (see ARBA 86, entry 1158), the fact that this work was published by a major, respected business publisher known for its quality books is surprising. [R: RBB, July 92, p. 1957] — **G. Kim Dority**

201. Bernstein, Jake. **The Handbook of Economic Cycles: Jake Bernstein's Comprehensive Guide to Repetitive Price Patterns....** Homewood, Ill., Business One Irwin, 1991. 282p. index. $67.50. HB3711.B46. 338.5'42. LC 91-8285. ISBN 1-55623-294-2.

The use and significance of cyclical theories in analyzing and interpreting economic activity is an interesting and controversial subject — interesting because the ability to identify, define, and benefit from cyclical patterns potentially offers great advantage and insight to investors and policymakers, and controversial because the reliability of cyclical economic phenomena is not universally accepted. It is clear that repetitive patterns in natural or economic data series do exist and will likely continue to exist well into the future. Unfortunately, observed qualitative changes in a given economic model may or may not be able to consistently explain quantitative fluctuations. This book attempts to bridge the gap between the existence of repetitive patterns and the explanatory power that these patterns portend. It is a comprehensive guide to both the theory and the application of cycles in various markets and over varying time periods.

This self-described "catalog of cycles" is well organized and easy to follow. It is filled with descriptive examples, definitions, and more than 150 useful charts and diagrams. The text outlines not only the practical and theoretical considerations of cyclical phenomena but also provides an overview of the operation of economic cycles and details on the seasonal tendencies and patterns of stocks, commodities, and other economic cycles. Because it consciously avoids more rigorous mathematical models and the corresponding terminology, this handbook will appeal to a fairly wide audience.

— **Timothy E. Sullivan**

202. **Business Rankings Annual, 1992: Lists of Companies, Products, Services, and Activities....** Compiled by Brooklyn Public Library Business Library Staff. Detroit, Gale, 1992. 878p. index. $155.00. ISBN 0-8103-4295-2. ISSN 1043-7908.

This volume ranks the top (largest) business firms, products, or other entities (usually the largest 10) for each of 4,498 categories (e.g., best-selling snack products [potato chips win], largest U.S. multinational corporations, leading foot-care products, 10 best mutual funds for 1990). Information for each listing includes title, criterion for ranking (e.g., sales, total return on investment, market share), number listed in the source, names of the top items (e.g., firms, funds, brands) with sizes (e.g., dollars, percent, pairs), and source (e.g., *Wall Street Journal*, trade association reports, *Advertising Age*). There is an excellent index for the firms, products, and other entities. A bibliography lists names, addresses, telephone numbers, frequency of publication, subscription rate, and ISSN for each of about 350 sources of the categories. — **Richard A. Miller**

203. Cousins, Jill, and Lesley Robinson, eds. **The Online Manual.** Cambridge, Mass., Basil Blackwell, 1992. 626p. $195.00. HF5548.2.C695. 020.06'65. LC 92-5920. ISBN 0-631-18228-4.

More than three-fourths of this work consists of a list of periodical titles, telling what database file covers them and which vendors offer that file. The editors acknowledge that not all vendors are covered, but that efforts at complete coverage will be made in future editions. This title is British, which has influenced the initial choice of vendors. These include BRS, Data Resources, DIALOG, IRS/DIALTECH, Kompass Online, Leatherhead, MAID, NEXIS, ORBIT, PFDS, Profile, and Textline. A large portion of these are either British or European. A number of well-known U.S. vendors, such as Westlaw, Datatimes, and VU/TEXT, do not appear. The book reveals that vendors' coverage overlaps extensively. For instance, *Forbes* is covered by 14 files and carried by a total of 9 vendors. At least one vendor, DIALOG, already provides an online database where the searcher can check periodical names to see which files carry that periodical.

This manual will be most useful to institutions that carry several of the vendors covered. For such subscribers, the book has a number of useful features, such as specific subject indexing. Also, a lengthy table tells which files contain what company financial information and on which countries. The subject index characterizes databases as E, M, T, F, or S. If the meaning of these initials is spelled out in the book, it is very well hidden, although it can be deduced by readers already familiar with the files. *The Online Manual* can be recommended for large institutions doing online searches in a variety of subject areas and international databases. — **Susan V. McKimm**

204. Darnay, Arsen J., comp. and ed. **Economic Indicators Handbook: Time Series, Conversions, Documentation.** Detroit, Gale, 1992. 1056p. index. $145.00. HC103.E26. 330.973. LC 92-13545. ISBN 0-8103-8400-0.

This handbook presents statistical time series used to measure the U.S. economy. Most series are obtained directly from federal agencies rather than from published sources. (The other major sources of data are the American Stock Exchange, the National Association of Security Dealers, and the New York Stock Exchange.)

The book is very well planned and researched. Librarians will love the lucid explanations of what these series mean and how they are calculated. The bibliographies, agency citations, and detailed index are benefits to be appreciated. A great deal of attention has been given to the Consumer Price Index (CPI). The inclusion of historical data for individual cities is especially welcome, as many sources that give historical CPI figures include only national data. The use of the new base years 1982-1984 is also welcome, as many sources now on library shelves have historical data based on 1967 equals 100. Producer Price Indexes are reported in commendable detail. Use of the index is essential, because some series, such as the Standard and Poor's 500 or prime rate, are listed under economic indicators so that their location is not immediately obvious. The calculation of rates of change for each year is valuable, as the rate of change is asked about as often as the index itself.

The real strength of this work is that it assists the user who may have trouble with statistics. Most others of its type are meant for people with more training. [R: RBB, 15 Oct 92, p. 452]

—**Susan V. McKimm**

205. **The *Economist* Desk Companion: How to Measure, Convert, Calculate and Define Practically Anything.** Penny Butler, ed. New York, Henry Holt, 1992. 272p. maps. index. $40.00. LC 92-53161. ISBN 0-8050-2380-1.

The introduction states that this work has been developed from the *World Measurement Guide* (WMG), 4th ed. (Economist, 1980). However, a more accurate description is that it is a revised, enlarged, and reorganized version of the earlier work; it contains much of the same data. The publication information for the *Economist Desk Companion* (EDC) does not identify this relationship. As in the WMG, the EDC is full of information on a wide range of subjects, including accountancy, agriculture, health, sound and music, textiles, and weapons. Although it is intended for use in the home, office, or library, an understanding of many of the definitions and explanations requires some basic knowledge of a topic, particularly for specialized areas such as economics and engineering.

The work is divided into four sections: a brief description of the metric, British, and United States systems of measurement; a subject arrangement of definitions, measurements, formulas, and calculations; conversion tables; and appendixes of abbreviations, rough conversions, and weights and measures around the world. The table of contents clearly lists the individual subareas of parts 2 and 3 within each larger area or discipline. This feature, in conjunction with the fairly detailed index, makes the information highly accessible. The emphasis on arranging material by subject is an improvement over the organization of the WMG, where sections were arranged by type of data (e.g., systems of measurement, general tables). Instead, in part 2, definitions, formulas, and measurements are all combined under a particular subject, and subjects are then listed alphabetically. However, the conversion tables for individual subjects have been moved to a separate section (part 3). In those sections that have been revised and expanded (and not just reprinted), the prose appears to be tighter and more concise; many more cross-references have been added. In addition, the EDC has larger print and tables, making data easier to read. Boldface headings are also used, again improving readability. This resource is a handy compilation of facts and figures and offers a number of welcome improvements over the WMG.

—Janice M. Griggs

206. **Encyclopedia of Business Information Sources: A Bibliographic Guide to More Than 24,000 Citations....** 9th ed. James Woy, ed. Detroit, Gale, 1992. 1176p. $235.00. LC 84-643366. ISBN 0-8103-7489-7. ISSN 0071-0210.

This bibliographic encyclopedia contains more than 24,000 citations that cover 1,100 business, financial, and industrial subjects. The majority of items are in print, and those that are out of print are typically available in libraries. An outline of contents provides a quick list of subject areas and cross-references. An alphabetical subject index is divided by source type (17 categories) and then by publication title or organization name. Entries usually include the title, publisher's information, frequency of issuance or publication date, and price. Brief descriptive information is often provided. The inclusion of online databases, CD-ROMs, and trade associations and professional societies is particularly useful, but the lack of a title index is a drawback.

Due to the massive amount of topics and publications included, this work is not able to offer the detail or evaluation provided in such standards as *Business Information Sources* (see ARBA 86, entry 158) or Michael Lavin's *Business Information: How to Find It, How to Use It*, 2d ed. (Oryx Press, 1992). However, as a starting point for information on a fairly specific topic, it is an excellent source, although the price is a major deterrent. Thus, while useful, it is not an essential source.

—Bobray Bordelon

207. **The Guide to Campus & Non-Profit Meeting Facilities 93.** Denver, Colo., AMARC, 1992. 128p. illus. index. $19.95pa. ISBN 1-881761-04-5. (Publisher's address: 2150 W. 29th Ave., Ste. 500, Denver, CO 80211).

Included in this work are approximately 400 college and university campuses and nonprofit retreat centers in the United States and Canada that have facilities to host conferences, seminars, training sessions, or workshops. Selection criteria are not stated, and a number of large universities with conference facilities have been omitted. The entries are arranged by state and subdivided by institution; the format is consistent and easy to use. Location, availability, facilities, contacts, and recreational information are given. An index with tables that detail the facilities is particularly useful, and there is also an institutional index. Advertisements are included.

A more comprehensive source would be welcome. However, given this work's low price and ease of use, it will be helpful for hospitality collections with a planning emphasis and for business and association libraries. —**Bobray Bordelon**

208. **Hoover's Handbook of American Business 1992.** Gary Hoover, Alta Campbell, and Patrick J. Spain, eds. Austin, Tex., Reference Press; distr., Emeryville, Calif., Publishers Group West, 1991. 630p. index. $24.95pa. HF3010. 338.7. ISBN 1-878753-01-0. ISSN 1055-7202.

This handbook lists 500 enterprises, including 24 governmental and nonprofit ones, that range from the United States through the University of Chicago, two professional sports teams, Wal-Mart stores, the Teamsters Union, and General Electric. Firms have been selected on the basis of size, growth, visibility, and breadth of coverage. Attractive one-page entries include an overview and sections on when (history), who (management, auditors, and work force), where, what (products), rankings, key competitors, and how much (financial data). The entries are lively and read well. Introductory material includes the setting of *Hoover's Handbook*: an illuminating explanation of the business world, comparisons between industries and companies, enterprise evolution, and the importance of the human element; and a lesson on the interpretation of important financial figures, with a caution about pitfalls in interpretations. Attention is drawn to supplementary sources. There are also some 40 separate listings of top, largest, leading, and similar companies, which are generally grouped according to their industries. One of the obvious uses of this handbook is for career selection. The search for leaders is made easy, and industrial histories are lively and relevant. Three indexes close this eminently practical reference guide. [R: LJ, 1 Apr 92, p. 112]—**Bogdan Mieczkowski**

209. Lavin, Michael R. **Business Information: How to Find It, How to Use It.** 2d ed. Phoenix, Ariz., Oryx Press, 1992. 499p. index. $49.95; $38.50pa. HF5356.L36. 650'.072. LC 91-28129. ISBN 0-89774-556-6; 0-89774-643-0pa.

This edition of Lavin's guide to business information resources continues the strengths of the previous one. It is a valuable source of information for novice business researchers who need to know not only what information resources are available but also how to compare and evaluate their strong and weak points.

The guide is made up of 22 chapters organized within 5 sections. The first two sections are an overview of types of business information and a survey of the directories, indexes, bibliographies, and catalogs that lead the researcher to other business sources. The third section covers the resources available to investigate both public and private companies: directory data, financial profiles, investment information, and specialized news. The fourth section focuses on statistical data (demographic, economic, and industrial) and includes an introduction on general statistics concepts and research issues. The concluding section covers four special topics: local area information, business and labor law, marketing, and taxation and accounting. Each chapter leads off with a brief outline of topics covered and identification of the major sources described, followed by a lengthy explanation of the concepts addressed by the sources under review. An annotated (and, Lavin admits, somewhat idiosyncratic) list of books and articles for further reading concludes each chapter. Supplementary materials include subject and title indexes and an appendix that recommends titles for ongoing reading. New to this edition are a stronger emphasis on research strategy (especially helpful to inexperienced searchers) and, as would be expected, much more extensive coverage of electronic resources, including online databases and CD-ROMs. The materials are current through 1991.

Lavin has not attempted a sophisticated, comprehensive bibliography along the lines of *Business Information Sources* (see ARBA 86, entry 158); instead, he has chosen more of a teaching approach that walks the reader through the vagaries and intricacies of business and corporate research. Intended as both a classroom text and a hands-on manual, the guide's coverage, organization, and "user-friendly" tone for the most part successfully reflect this objective. (Occasionally Lavin over- or underdefines his terms; for example, *abstract* is defined, but *Boolean logic* is not.) Especially useful are Lavin's evaluative comparisons of similar works and alternative formats (e.g., print versus online) of the same product. Lavin should consider greatly expanding the materials on markets and industry information with the next edition. Although this book will probably be considered too basic by most experienced business researchers, beginners will sigh with relief upon discovering it. [R: JAL, May 92, p. 134; JAL, Nov 92, p. 308; LJ, 15 May 92, p. 86; RQ, Fall 92, p. 134]—**G. Kim Dority**

210. Lesko, Matthew. **Government Giveaways for Entrepreneurs.** 3d ed. Kensington, Md., Information USA, 1992. 638p. index. $33.95pa. ISBN 1-878346-01-6.

In this work Lesko offers some 9,000 sources of money, information, and other types of free help available to entrepreneurs from federal, state, and local government sources. As much a how-to guide as a directory of resources, the book is organized into 26 sections that fall into 3 broad categories: general information on entrepreneuring and how government resources can help small businesses, federal and state monies available to entrepreneurs, and special topics (e.g., help for inventors, selling overseas, free experts [more than 6,500], resources for women entrepreneurs). Also included within the special topics grouping is a section devoted to market studies, demographics, and statistics. Anyone who has purchased market studies recently can testify that the information included here could easily save entrepreneurs thousands of dollars.

Although the book's listings will be valuable to any entrepreneur or person involved in small business, Lesko has also taken the time to provide other useful information that will help encourage success. The book leads off with a well-documented chapter arguing that there is still an abundance of government money available to both large and small entrepreneurs and that it is well worth one's time and energy to investigate the options. Other topics include "What Entrepreneurs Don't Need," "Key Pointers When Applying for Money," and (probably the most important item) "The Art of Getting a Bureaucrat to Help You."

Information specialists might quibble with the rather random manner in which the special topics section is organized, and the index could use some attention by a professional skilled in the ways of cross-referencing. However, this work contains such a wealth of useful information for entrepreneurs and small businesses, at such a reasonable price, that all public libraries will want it. [R: RBB, 1 May 92, pp. 1620-23]—**G. Kim Dority**

211. **The National Book of Lists 1992.** San Ramon, Calif., Local Knowledge, 1992. 106p. index. $39.95pa. ISBN 0-9632232-0-8. ISSN 1060-8435.

Exxon Corporation ranks first in assets of oil and gas companies. Money Store Investment Corporation ranks first in the number of Small Business Administration loans. If items such as these are of interest to one's library, this compilation of top-40 lists provides an easy way to access data on 50 industries that encompass 2,000 U.S. companies. The criteria for compiling the lists vary by industry. For example, the number of rooms is used for hotels; revenue is used for market research companies; and average daily circulation is used for newspapers. Names, addresses, telephone and fax numbers, revenues, key personnel, and other relevant data are given.

The limited scope of 50 industries somewhat lessens the usefulness of this compilation. A glaring addition mistake (probably a typographical error) was found in the "Colleges and Universities" section for the enrollment at Louisiana State University (an extra 10,000 students were added). Overall, this source is convenient but not essential.—**Bobray Bordelon**

212. Nixon, Judith M., ed. **Organization Charts: Structures of More Than 200 Businesses and Non-Profit Organizations.** Detroit, Gale, 1992. 240p. index. $129.00. ISBN 0-8103-8497-3.

This volume prints the organization chart for each of more than 200 large corporations and other organizations, showing lines of authority and responsibility within each. Because individuals shift jobs frequently, each box gives only job title, divisional area, or affiliated company. Many companies consider their organization charts to be proprietary, so the selection represents those firms whose charts are public or who were willing to divulge them. Companies are primarily from the United States (e.g., Bell & Howell, IBM, Merrill Lynch, Nalco, McGraw-Hill), with selections from other countries (e.g., Scottish & New Castle Breweries in Scotland, SKF Group in Sweden). Some nonprofit organizations are also included (e.g., Sycamore Girl Scout Council, Sunnybrook Medical Center Cancer Program, World Bank, Yale-New Haven Health Services). All charts are quite recent, generally from 1990 or 1991. John G. Maurer of Wayne State University has written an interesting foreword that discusses the history, forms (shapes), and uses of organization charts. The intended audience is students, job seekers, researchers, and businesspeople who wish to compare structures, identify positions and areas within an organization, analyze the span of control and lines of communication within various corporations, and study how competitive companies organize their activities. The index is excellent. [R: RBB, 1 Nov 92, p. 552]—**Richard A. Miller**

213. **Small Business Sourcebook: The Entrepreneur's Resource.** 5th ed. Carol A. Schwartz and Kathleen E. Maki, eds. Detroit, Gale, 1992. 2v. index. $210.00/set. ISBN 0-8103-5482-9. ISSN 0883-3397.

This edition of a popular two-volume reference work includes expanded Canadian sources, SIC (Standard Industrial Classification) codes for the small businesses profiled, and broader coverage of audiovisual information sources. Volume 1 contains specific profiles for more than 200 different small businesses. Volume 2 contains information on topics of interest to small business entrepreneurs, such as taxation, unions and labor relations, credit, and collection. Also included are state listings of small business organizations and programs, Canadian listings, and federal government assistance organizations and programs. The small business list in volume 1 runs from accountants to yogurt shops and includes computer stores, sewing centers, cocktail lounges, fur farms, dry cleaners, and tattoo parlors. In volume 2, state agency listings include development centers, assistance programs, financing and loan programs, minority business assistance, education programs, and legislative assistance. A glossary of business terms and a combined index to both volumes make the information in this extensive reference work easily accessible to all users. Recommended as a comprehensive, user-friendly resource for those taking a first look at small business ventures, although libraries would do well to supplement it with more detailed small business information.—**Elisabeth Logan**

214. **Walker's Manual of Western Corporations 1992.** 83d ed. San Mateo, Calif., Walker's Manual, [1992]. 2v. index. $380.00/set. ISBN 1-879346-05-2.

The corporations and financial institutions covered in this manual share the following attributes: they are headquartered in the 13 western states; they are publicly owned; their stock is traded on the New York Stock Exchange, American Stock Exchange, or National Association of Securities Dealers Automated Quotations (NASDAQ); they have a 10K filed with the Securities and Exchange Commission since January 1990; and their assets are greater than $3 million. For each of the 1,100 firms listed, the following information is included: address, telephone number, state and year of incorporation, annual meeting, ticket symbol, number of employees, SIC (Standard Industrial Classification) number, business description, subsidiaries, counsel, officers, directors, number of shares and shareholders, transfer agent, and auditor. There is a summary of financial data for each of the most recent 5 years, including stock data (e.g., dividend, price range, splits), balance sheets (9-10 asset classifications and 20-25 liability and net worth entries), income statement data (12-14 items), and business ratios (6 for the latest year). The introduction defines the terms. There are indexes by company name, by geographic location of principal corporate offices, and by primary SIC code (four-digit).—**Richard A. Miller**

Periodicals and Serials

215. **Business Periodicals Index: August 1990-July 1991.** Walter Webb, Hiyol Yang, and Chris Gerolemou, eds. Bronx, N.Y., H. W. Wilson, 1991. 2531p. sold on service basis. LC 58-12645. ISSN 0007-6961.

Even with all its electronic competition, this work (BPI) remains one of the best indexes of business periodicals. Since BPI was last reviewed (see ARBA 89, entry 170), it has seen a few changes, notably the approximately 10 percent increase in the number of periodicals indexed (from 310 to 343). Some new additions to the list reflect the growing interest in global business: *Asian Business, Business Mexico*, and *Europe*. Also notable is a greater focus on technology, reflected in the addition of *International Journal of Technology Management, Journal of Information Systems Management*, and *Technology Review*. The publisher has increased the number of indexers from six to nine, and the result is tighter indexing of more articles, with more subject headings and cross-references. BPI still covers a broad range of subject fields but now does so with greater depth. For example, one previously had to look under the heading "Investment Companies" to find articles on mutual funds, but this subject now has its own entry. The indexers also use more geographic subheadings, again reflecting the greater focus on international business in the literature. The explanatory notes at the front of the index have been replaced by a clear diagram of a sample entry.

With more journals and deeper indexing, one would expect the volume size to have grown correspondingly, but this is not the case. H. W. Wilson has decided to decrease the point size of the type to keep the page count down. The publisher is still advised by the Committee on Wilson Indexes of ALA's Reference and Adult Services Division on matters of indexing and editorial policy, and the list of periodicals indexed still comes from subscriber votes.—**Kerranne G. Biley**

216. **Business Periodicals Index.** (Indexing coverage: 7/82-6/25/92). [CD-ROM]. Bronx, N.Y., H. W. Wilson, 1992. Hardware requirements: WILSONLINE Workstation, IBM PC, or compatible; 640K; hard disk drive. $1,495.00.

In the 7th edition of *Magazines for Libraries* (R. R. Bowker, 1992), *Business Periodicals Index* (BPI) is described as the standard source for all libraries; thus, the CD-ROM version serves the same purpose—a reliable resource for indexing nearly 400 business magazines. Begun in 1987, BPI on disc is a relatively easy-to-install, easy-to-use source that extends access points found in the paper source. Two examples help to illustrate this point. The print format of BPI provides no author access, nor can the user search by journal easily. The CD-ROM version provides both of these as search points and adds title words and date (year) access, as well as SIC (Standard Industrial Classification) code searching, making BPI on disc a user-friendly reference tool that expands the print BPI. Coverage is also quite good, as the two discs provided for review purposes span from July 1982 to May and June 1992. Thus, coverage is now for 10 years with monthly updates. Now for the not-so-good news—the price. BPI on disc is $1,495 a year, compared to $160 for the paper version—greater access, greater costs. Yet for the library wishing to create an automated atmosphere for its clientele, BPI on disc is certainly a viable option.

Wilson software is easily installed, and, as with most CD-ROM installation software, the user is asked to set parameters and default functions. Experienced users will have no trouble, others will need to pay close attention to instructions and make use of the toll-free number when necessary. Generally, installation help is excellent and appropriate for the novice. Hardware requirements are minimal.

The initial screen offers three search modes: BROWSE, WILSEARCH, and WILSONLINE. BROWSE lists subject words alphabetically on the screen, providing immediate access to the index. Subject terms can either be selected from a BROWSE screen or entered on the WILSEARCH screen. In WILSEARCH, actual searching is simple—if one reads the on-screen instructions. For example, the user is instructed to use the END key after entering search terms. This function is used in all Wilson CD products and may create a problem. Another difficulty may come when attempting to use subheadings. While subheadings are indicated on each record by a slash (/), searching is cumbersome. In most cases such a search results in a null set (e.g., REAL ESTATE BUSINESS/FAILURE found no records when entered, but records exist for the heading), but when each concept is entered as a subject, relevant citations are retrievable.

For users familiar with Wilson's online service, the WILSONLINE mode is the choice, as WILSONLINE provides Boolean logic (AND, OR, NOT connectors) and more specificity. However, the infrequent or novice user may want to avoid this mode.

One of the true user-friendly aspects of BPI on disc is the help screens, which are well designed and readily accessible. Additionally, these screens provide help as the user encounters a problem; that is, the screens are designed for a specific step in the search process. Printing and downloading features are provided, although marking citations for these are not. Documentation is excellent. Wilson provides both an installation and setup guide and another to new features. The latter, dated April 1992, illustrates disc enhancements. When used in tandem, the two provide clear instructional support. A toll-free support number is also available; responses to two random calls were cordial and patient, and answers were adequate. In general, BPI on disc is a system with many useful features that outweigh those few that could be enhanced by the producer. Ideal for the academic or public library, it is another fine Wilson product (as is its print counterpart).—**Boyd Childress**

217. Riley, Sam G., ed. **Corporate Magazines of the United States.** Westport, Conn., Greenwood Press, 1992. 277p. index. (Historical Guides to the World's Periodicals and Newspapers). $75.00. PN4888.E6C67. 070.4'86. LC 91-33481. ISBN 0-313-27569-6.

Hundreds of corporate (or company) magazines are published in the United States; they are, by definition, sponsored by and produced for a single business firm. Some are house organs, meant for employees only; others are designed for customers; and still others are aimed at both. This volume profiles 52 corporate magazines. Some are free; others are available by subscription. Some are well known, such as *Ford Times* (Ford Motor Company, 1908-). Some are easily linked with the sponsoring corporation, such as *Boise Cascade Insight* (Boise Cascade Corporation, 1986-). Others are less widely known, such as *The Furrow* (Deere, 1895-). Each three- to five-page profile reviews the magazine's history, philosophy, evolution, circulation, objectives, and audience, usually with some selected topics and titles of past articles. Each also lists publication history: title, volume and issue (frequency) data, publishers, editors, and circulation. The appendixes provide a list of profiled magazines by founding date; the location, by state, of magazines profiled; and corporate magazines not profiled, with title, sponsoring corporation, and location. The well-written profiles have been contributed by 29 academics, usually professors of communication and journalism. [R: RBB, Aug 92, p. 2034]—**Richard A. Miller**

Quotation Books

218. Boone, Louis E. **Quotable Business: Over 2,500 Funny, Irreverent, and Insightful Quotations about Corporate Life.** New York, Random House, 1992. 338p. index. $13.00pa. PN6084.B87B66. 082. LC 92-10190. ISBN 0-679-74080-5.

219. Zera, Richard S. **1001 Quips & Quotes for Business Speeches.** New York, Sterling Publishing, 1992. 160p. illus. index. $6.95pa. PN4193.I5Z47. 808.5'1. LC 91-40120. ISBN 0-8069-8486-4.

Quotable Business is intended for audiences at all levels in any type of organization. Boone states that in order for a quotation to be included it must be "relevant to organizations, their people, and their dreams," and it must be funny or profound or both. The work is divided into five parts that are further subdivided into chapters and then sections. Extra care is given to attribution, and the dates and profession of the person being quoted are included. Author and subject indexes are provided.

1001 Quips focuses on selectivity. An alphabetical arrangement by approximately 140 categories mixes stories, quotations, and cartoons. Many of the quotations are not attributed; however, an author index is included.

Both works emphasize modern English and draw from a variety of sources that range from classic authors to celebrities to business moguls. Although Zera's work contains less than half the number of quotations that Boone's book has, its mix provides a broader base. However, the arrangement of Boone's work provides a better flow. Both are reasonably priced and should prove useful additions to any business reference collection.—**Bobray Bordelon**

BUSINESS SERVICES AND INVESTMENT GUIDES

220. **The Business One Irwin Business and Investment Almanac, 1992.** Sumner N. Levine and Caroline Levine, eds. Homewood, Ill., Business One Irwin, 1992. 709p. index. $49.95. ISBN 1-55623-532-1. ISSN 1057-5014.

This work is a truly comprehensive source of business information. It starts with a brief review of significant business activities from September 1990 to September 1991. The second section provides surveys of some 16 industries, followed by business and economic indicators, performance of leading economic indicators, U.S. demographics, government budget data, stock market performance, and taxes. The book even covers the European Community and provides a detailed business information directory.

This work is very brief yet well written. It should appeal to all businesspeople, although the investment sections are of limited value as the information they contain is generally too old to be useful for investment decisions. Recommended to all university libraries as a general business reference.

—**Elie M. Dick**

221. **Directory of Incentives for Business Investment and Development in the United States: A State-by-State Guide.** 3d ed. By the National Association of State Development Agencies. Washington, D.C., Urban Institute Press; distr., Lanham, Md., University Press of America, 1991. 778p. maps. index. $149.50; $75.00pa. HC110.I53N4. 332.6'732273. LC 86-15714. ISBN 0-87766-515-X; 0-87766-501-Xpa.

This volume is intended for business and government decision makers concerned with state incentives for business, an area of increasing importance in the drive to strengthen state economic bases. The introduction discusses trends based on the NASDA (National Association of State Development Agencies) State Economic Development Expenditures survey. The body of the work is a well-formatted description of each state's direct financial incentives; basic business taxes; and tax exemptions, deductions, credits, and special treatment. The direct incentives are consistently presented in a short narrative that covers program goals, eligibility, volume, application process, and contact person. The typography and layout of information in the other categories makes information easy to locate. The index of incentives follows the three general categories. By further breaking down programs into broad categories, it is also possible to find, for example, an alphabetical list of states that offer a particular program such as loan guarantees. This is an essential tool for business, policymakers, and interested citizens. — **JoAnn V. Rogers**

222. **The Handbook of World Stock and Commodity Exchanges, 1992.** Cambridge, Mass., Basil Blackwell, 1992. 518p. index. $245.00. HG4551.H32. 332.64'2. LC 90-14393. ISBN 0-631-18309-4.

This is a comprehensive list of stock and commodity exchanges by country. Useful information is provided for each exchange: address; telephone, telex, and fax numbers; principal officers; history; structure; trading hours; description of futures contracts traded or number of equities listed; trading volume; trading systems; method of setting and clearing; commission rates; tax information; investor protection; and prospective developments. The handbook also contains lists of abbreviations; an acronyms glossary; indexes of personnel, contracts, exchanges, and information vendors; and a list of relevant international organizations. Preceding the list of exchanges are 33 brief essays on current issues and on activities of specific exchanges. Featured are a foreword by Rudiger von Rosen (Frankfurter Wertpapierborse) and an introduction by William J. Brodsky (Chicago Mercantile Exchange).

This book is more comprehensive than *St. James World Futures and Options Directory 1991-92* (see ARBA 92, entry 168). But the St. James directory has at least one feature not included in the Blackwell handbook — membership lists for 35 large exchanges. The book under review is highly recommended as a comprehensive guide to the world's stock and commodity exchanges. [R: Choice, Feb 92, p. 869] — **William C. Struning**

223. **Moody's Handbook of Common Stocks: Spring 1992.** Robert P. Hanson, Martin Schulman and Elizabeth J. Wall, eds. New York, Moody's Investors Service, 1992. 1v. (unpaged). $70.00pa. ISSN 0027-0830.

This quarterly handbook covers more than 900 of the most popular stocks and furnishes quick access to basic financial data derived from quarterly and preliminary annual reports. Information ranges from brief narratives to charts and statistical tables. The work opens with an introductory segment that clearly explains the use of the handbook. This is followed by a section of special features that offer analyses of stock price movements by company, industry price charts, and classification of companies by type of industry. The following section furnishes charts that enumerate the long-term averages of the major stock market indexes, such as Dow Jones and the New York Stock Exchange. As over-the-counter stocks are not treated in the work, the National Association of Securities Dealers Automated Quotations (NASDAQ) index has been omitted. The addenda section identifies the latest developments, such as companies added and dropped in the handbook, dividend changes, earning reports, and pending dividends and splits. There is also a feature article on Moody's 1991 dividend achievers ranked by 10-year dividend growth.

The major part of the text is an alphabetical arrangement of the common stocks. Entries are a page in length and begin with a chart that shows the volume of trading along with figures on capitalization, earnings, and dividends. This is followed by a brief narrative on background, recent developments, and prospects and a 10-year table of such factors as P-E ratios, yield, and assets. The entry concludes with a directory-like list of officers, addresses, annual meeting dates, and shareholders. — **Ron Blazek**

224. **Moody's Handbook of Dividend Achievers 1992.** Robert P. Hanson and others, eds. New York, Moody's Investors Service, 1992. 1v. (unpaged). $19.95pa. ISSN 0737-1586.

Since 1979, Moody's has kept track of companies that have increased their cash dividends annually for at least 10 years. Moody's calls these companies "dividend achievers" and believes they should be attractive to conservative investors, who want solid investments with little risk. In the early 1980s Moody's published a similar handbook, and it has been resurrected now as a premium to be sent to individual investors and as a low-cost reference work. It is very similar in format to *Moody's Handbook of Common Stocks* (see ARBA 87, entry 207) and begins with a ranking of 313 dividend achievers in order of growth of their dividends over the past 10 years, rankings of the top companies by other criteria (including return on equity and yield), a classification of dividend achievers by industry, and various other charts and tables. For the most part these rankings, charts, and tables are the same as those appearing in the annual special feature on dividend achievers in *Common Stocks*. One chart contains comparative monthly dividend changes from 1982 to 1991 based on the dividend activity of 8,500 stocks. The body of the work consists of page-long summaries of each company's performance on the model of summaries given in *Common Stocks*.

Much of the information is similar to that found in other Moody's publications, but according to a telephone conversation with the associate director in charge of the data in the *Dividend Achievers*, its data was not copied from any of the other publications but was assembled especially for the work. The data is organized somewhat differently, and there are some curious discrepancies between the data in the *Dividend Achievers* and *Common Stocks*. For example, the figures given in *Dividend Achievers* for Hasbro Incorporated net revenues are the same as the figures given in *Common Stocks* for Hasbro's gross revenues. Nonetheless, the book is remarkably inexpensive for such a useful work. While it is not a necessary purchase for a library that subscribes to *Common Stocks*, it is recommended to libraries that cannot afford expensive investment guides but that still want to offer works that give reliable investment information. — **Richard H. Swain**

225. **NASDAQ Yellow Book: Who's Who at the Leading Younger Growth Companies in the U.S. Vol.4, No.1.** Catherine Shih and others, eds. New York, Monitor Publishing, 1992. 662p. index. $125.00pa. ISSN 1058-2886.

Formerly titled *Over-the-Counter 1000 Yellow Book* (see ARBA 90, entry 214), this annual directory focuses on management personnel at more than 1,100 publicly traded companies on the National Association of Securities Dealers Automated Quotation (NASDAQ) system. Coverage emphasizes leading younger growth companies and excludes financial services. Arrangement is alphabetical. Parent company data include address, telephone and fax numbers, business description, annual sales, top officers (with job titles), and directors (with affiliations). Data for major subunits (e.g., subsidiaries, affiliates, divisions, regional offices) vary and may include address, telephone and fax numbers, and one or more officers. The companies themselves verified the data. There are four thorough, accurate indexes: names of parent companies and subunits, their location by state, names of their 20,000 officers and directors, and industries (for parents only). An excellent layout and format permit quick location of information.

Management personnel for 10 companies were compared with Dun & Bradstreet's *America's Corporate Families* (see ARBA 84, entry 755) and National Register Publishing's *Directory of Corporate Affiliations* (see ARBA 91, entry 142) and *International Directory of Corporate Affiliations* (see ARBA 90, entry 178). The *NASDAQ Yellow Book* tends to have as many parent company officers as those from National Register but a few more than Dun & Bradstreet, and, unlike both, it indicates affiliations of noncompany directors. It lists only major subunits, having half as many as the other two. More often than the National Register work, but less often than Dun & Bradstreet, it indicates an officer for a subunit.

This directory well fulfills its limited focus on contacting management personnel. A decision to purchase it must weigh the need for this type of information on so many NASDAQ companies against the purchase of other directories that cover a broader range of companies, but fewer NASDAQ ones, and that provide more detail on parents and subunits. — **John Lewis Campbell**

226. Olsen, M. A., and Alison Matthews. **The Gold Book: A Guide to Commonly Traded Gold Bullion Coins and Bars.** Westminster, Colo., Westminster Publishing, 1992. 117p. illus. index. $19.95pa. ISBN 0-9630498-4-4.

This detailed, illustrated guide to gold coins and bars serves those interested in these objects for their trading rather than their numismatic value. It provides a range of information for more than 80 gold coins issued by 20 countries and approximately 20 bullion bars. A brief introduction gives some useful background information about buying and selling such items and discusses other factors that may influence their value. The main section of the book is a country-by-country listing that illustrates and describes each of the coins. This is followed by a short list of bars arranged by commercial firm of issuance. A series of six appendixes provides additional listings by characteristics that are of particular interest to traders, such as diameter, thickness, gold content, purity, total weight, and fineness. A short glossary, a list of weights and measures, gold prices from 1972 to 1991, conversion tables, a bibliography, and an index round the book out. Almost all the information of interest on these (and many more) gold coins can be found in the wide assortment of standard coin books that appears in most library collections.—**Norman D. Stevens**

CANADIAN BUSINESS

227. Albala, Leila. **Catalogue of Canadian Catalogues.** 3d ed. Chambly, Que., Alpel, 1992. 168p. illus. $12.50pa. 381'.142'02571. ISBN 0-921993-05-6.

In this work 800 Canadian mail-order catalogs are described. Each entry lists the company and its address, telephone number, fax and toll-free numbers (if appropriate), product list, an indication of how long it has been in business, and a "mission statement" (which should be taken at face value). The arrangement is by subject; there are about 100 categories, such as basketry, fabric, food, knitting, docking facilities, organic gardening, weather instruments, wigs, and winemaking. Most are for home crafts and family life. There are also 11 pages of advertisements between the text and the index; most are from the publisher. This is a useful tool for Canadian libraries, perhaps less so for United States ones.—**Dean Tudor**

228. **Business Connexions 1992: Canada's Business Directory. Connexions d'Affaires.** Toronto, Telinfomatic; distr., Detroit, Omnigraphics, 1992. 1v. (various paging). index. $59.95pa. ISBN 1-55888-791-1.

This is a handy, quick guide to business-related addresses in Canada. The white page information (section 1) alphabetically lists names of businesses, trade offices, charitable institutions, and other such places. Brief address, telephone, and fax data is given, and some branch offices are included. The blue page section gives federal, provincial, and local municipal government agency data. In some cases, multiple numbers are given with no information as to what they stand for. The third section is the gold (yellow) page listings; these are subject lists of products and services, with separate lists in English and French. A list of subject headings precedes the actual information. Within each subject heading the names of the provinces come first followed by alphabetical names of companies. The listings in French are considerably fewer than those in the English subjects. For instance, under bath equipment the English listing has more than 20 companies while the French *bains* lists only 3, with none in common.

Reference librarians may prefer other Canadian business and government sources, such as the *Canadian Key Business Directory* (Dun & Bradstreet Canada, 1991), the *Canadian Trade Index* (Canadian Manufacturers Assoc., 1991), or the *Canadian Almanac & Directory* (see ARBA 92, entry 98). These provide much more detail and better organized sources for Canadian information needs. [R: Choice, Oct 92, p. 268]—**Robert D. Adamshick**

229. **Canadian Master Tax Guide, 1992.** 47th ed. Don Mills, Ont., CCH Canadian, 1992. 906p. index. $36.95pa. ISBN 0-88796-705-1.

This work is one of a number of rival Canadian income tax guides for the assistance of professionals and taxpayers. The text is made accessible through a thorough, 47-page, double-columned index; tables that refer the user to passages where sections of the Income Tax Act, tax regulations, and rules are cited or explained; tables that indicate where court decisions, information circulars, and interpretation bulletins are mentioned; and a detailed table of contents. The text is set out in numbered paragraphs. In addition to the main parts, which analyze and interpret income tax provisions, other features of the work include highlights of changes after December 31, 1991; a tax calendar; tax rates for all 10 provinces and the territories; sample forms; and summaries of the United Kingdom-Canada and United States-Canada tax conventions. CCH Canadian is a leading producer of looseleaf business and legal manuals, and there are numerous references to sections of its corresponding looseleaf service.

This standard annual is a well-executed guide to the maze of Canadian income tax provisions. It should be considered by collections with relevant client interest.—**Nigel Tappin**

230. **Directory to International Business Education in Canada. Repertoire Canadien pour la Formation au Commerce International.** Montreal, Corporate-Higher Education Forum, 1991. 240p. free pa. 650'.071'171. ISBN 0-920429-10-6.

This directory of educational venues will help businesses gain access to graduates of Canadian universities who possess international expertise. It should also help them identify sources of further education and training for current employees. Listed are courses, seminars, exchanges, and college programs relevant to the conduct of international business. No private-sector training is included. Each entry has a mission statement of sorts, lists of degree programs, exchange programs, research activity, publications, and level of scholarship. These entries are arranged by type of institute (university, college, association, and government organization). There are indexes by subject, region of the world, and languages spoken. A quick check shows some thoroughness in coverage, but a look at Ryerson Polytechnical Institute in Toronto revealed an incorrect street address. Still, the price is reasonable.

—**Dean Tudor**

231. **Glossary of Finance and Debt. Glossaire des Finances et de la Dette. Glosario de Finanzas y de Deuda.** Washington, D.C., World Bank, 1991. 213p. (World Bank Glossary). $11.95pa. HG151.G629. 332'.042'03. LC 90-44772. ISBN 0-8213-1644-3.

This useful glossary gives English banking and finance terms followed by their French and Spanish equivalents and their definitions in English. The terms are those found in current use by the World Bank. French and Spanish indexes lead the user to the English terms. The foreword is in the three languages. Phrases are entered in direct order, not under the noun (e.g., *open market*, not *market, open*). References lead the reader to the entry with the definition.

The choice of terms is excellent, and the definitions and translations are clear. The layout is good, and the volume is easy to use. There is one detail lacking, however: the indication of any grammatical gender, which is essential for creating the correct agreement of adjectives and related pronouns. [R: Choice, Jan 92, p. 729]—**Barbara E. Brown**

232. **The Guide to the Canadian Financial Services Industry 1991.** Toronto, Financial Times; distr., Detroit, Gale, 1991. 1v. (various paging). index. $305.00. ISBN 0-920838-20-0. ISSN 0827-0864.

This guide is a very useful source of information on Canadian financial institutions. Initially published by Flagship, it has been produced annually since 1989 by Financial Times.

The different sections are printed on color-coded paper for rapid access. They present corporate profiles, line of business and geographical indexes, government regulators, industry associations, and the top 20 accounting firms in Canada. The corporate profiles, arranged alphabetically by firm, provide details of ownership, main office, directors, executives, regional and international offices, subsidiary companies, other interests, total assets, net income, number of branches and employees, auditing firm, SIC (Standard Industrial Classification) code, and line of business. The alphabetical list of executives and directors has the names of the companies worked for and the positions held. Some entries also contain pertinent biographical information.

All the data are clearly and accurately presented. This work is a must for large business libraries, particularly in Canada.—**Barbara E. Brown**

233. Hutcheson, Helen. **Vocabulary of Free Trade. Vocabulaire du Libre-Echange.** Ottawa, Department of the Secretary of State of Canada, 1991. 445p. (Terminology Bulletin, 204). $28.95pa.; $34.75pa. (U.S.). 382'.71'03. ISBN 0-660-56518-8.

This dictionary is part of an ongoing project by the Translation Bureau in the Department of the Secretary of State of Canada to provide tools to simplify and standardize translation in the federal civil service and in business, law, and other relevant fields. It primarily focuses on the terminology of the U.S.-Canada Free Trade Agreement but also includes words drawn from the European Communities, the General Agreement on Tariffs and Trade (GATT), and the United Nations Conference on Trade and Development (UNCTAD). Thus, the potential audience is extended beyond the bilateral context. About 2,500 terms are included.

The text is divided into two main parts. The first is an English-French vocabulary in two columns that is arranged alphabetically by English term. For some phrases the list only provides synonyms, but many entries for more complex concepts give bilingual definitions. Some listings also supply contextual notes, such as those that indicate GATT usage. The second section, the French-English glossary, is a straight list of French terms, arranged by the most prevalent French synonym, and their English equivalents. In both parts *see* and *see also* references are used. The quality of the production and editing appears to be good.

In summation, this useful work will be of significant help to government and other professionals who deal in English-French translation in the context of trade. For others, and for libraries with little pertinent demand, it will be of lesser interest. – **Nigel Tappin**

CONSUMER EDUCATION

234. **Consumer Reports 1992 Buying Guide Issue.** Yonkers, N.Y., Consumer Reports Books, 1991. 396p. index. (*Consumer Reports*, v.56, no.12). $8.95pa. ISSN 0010-7174.

This work covers major test reports, brand-and-model ratings, and general buying advice from the last few years of *Consumer Reports*. Major product reports from the 1991 issues of the magazine (November 1990-October 1991) have been summarized; earlier summaries have been reviewed and, where necessary, revised. Reports are grouped in chapters according to product category. Last year's *Buying Guide* chapter on "Kitchen and Laundry" has been expanded to three chapters: major kitchen appliances, small kitchen appliances, and laundry appliances and detergents. A new chapter, "Recreation and Exercise," has been added. As in previous *Buying Guides*, there are details of dangerous products recalled from the marketplace, a section on repair histories on major appliances and electronic gear, and automobile frequency-of-repair records. The index is in two parts this year: an index to the *Buying Guide* and one to the last four years of *Consumer Reports*. This annual continues to be an accessible, reliable information guide for consumer reference and decision making. – **Roslyn Attinson**

235. **Consumer Sourcebook 1992-93: A Subject Guide....** 7th ed. Shawn Brennan, ed. Detroit, Gale, 1991. 627p. index. $185.00. ISBN 0-8103-2999-9. ISSN 0738-0518.

This work is divided into 26 chapters on topics of interest to consumers, such as aging, money management, food, health, housing, occupational safety, and travel. The extensive user's guide lays out the plan of the work and carefully defines what is included within the scope of each chapter and the issues of concern. Each section follows the same pattern of organization: federal, state, and local governmental agencies; national and local associations; corporation contacts (e.g., complaint or customer service departments); and, in many sections, tips or cautions for consumers. Many of the entries for national associations look similar to Gale's other association books, but the entries often give more in-depth description of interest to laypeople and less information about professional aspects. Entries list consumer-oriented monographic and periodical items published by these agencies. More than 2,300 publications are noted, but journals intended for professionals or association members are excluded. The majority of local associations, organizations, and agencies have no description, just basic directory data. More toll-free and fax numbers have been added to this edition.

The categories of the work are broadly encompassing but do not lend themselves to browsing. For example, American National Standards Institute (ANSI) appears under the chapter on housing and home improvements, the reason for which is not immediately clear. Therefore, it is important to rely on the index for access to this work. The index is not a full keyword style but does rotate some of the main words of the title. However, the City of Albuquerque Area Agency on Aging appears under "City" but not under "Albuquerque" or "Aging," indicating that not all of the entries are indexed as expected. Because of the limited use of added subject terms, there is little subject approach to the entries via the index. The indexing of acronyms seems very erratic. Sometimes a well-known acronym is included in the entry but not indexed; sometimes the acronym is indexed but not included in the entry; sometimes it is in both; and sometimes even well-known acronyms are not included in either. The index would be more effective if it had more consistency and more subject words.

Despite its imperfections, this work will no doubt be useful for many libraries. The convenience of so much information in one place, especially for governmental agencies and their telephone numbers, is perhaps its greatest strength. But it is also true that much of this information can be found in basic

reference tools already at most libraries. In a comparison with the local associations books published by Gale, there were very few duplicate entries. Why there was not a greater number of duplicates should perhaps concern reference librarians, who may be under the assumption that these works are more inclusive than they are. However, the lack of duplication provides another reason to consider this title. Recommended for public libraries, especially those that may not have a full array of association or business directories, and for comprehensive reference collections in larger libraries of other types.
—Gary R. Cocozzoli

FINANCE AND BANKING

236. *American Banker*'s **Banking Factbook 1991: The Comprehensive Guide to Banking in the U.S. and the World.** 1991 ed. Edwin A. Finn, Jr., ed.. Naperville, Ill., Sourcebooks, 1991. 152p. index. $75.00. ISBN 0-942061-37-3. ISSN 1057-8854.

American Banker is a respected and long-established daily journal that serves the banking community. This work contains more than 100 tables that rank commercial banks, bank holding companies, thrifts, and mortgage companies by characteristics such as assets, loans, and deposits. Primary attention is given to U.S. institutions, with breakdowns provided by state. However, data for the world's largest 500 banks are included, with special attention to the position of U.S. banks. Each section of tables is introduced by a brief overview that has an analysis of recent developments. New features have been added to the 1991 edition, including information on the highest-paid bank and thrift executives. Every company listed in the guide can be easily accessed by reference to an index.

This book provides a broad perspective of the banking and financial services industries, particularly with respect to the largest companies. It must be noted, however, that the title year, 1991, refers to the period of time during which the data were gathered—1990 is the latest year covered in the book. [R: Choice, Sept 92, p. 71; WLB, Apr 92, p. 119]—**William C. Struning**

237. **Collection Agency Directory.** 2d ed. Warren, Mich., First Detroit, 1992. 191p. index. $185.00pa. ISBN 0-9630819-8-5.

The American Collectors Association, the American Commercial Collectors Association, and the American Recovery Association publish membership directories. Except for the latter association, these directories are available to members only, precluding any comparison of the *Collection Agency Directory* to them. It is, therefore, considered solely on its own merits. The work includes 481 agencies ranked by dollar amount of placements. Other rankings include the top 25 agencies by numbers of employees, of computer terminals, of predictive dialer workstations, and of branches. Definitions of these terms are not provided, which would have helped a credit novice trying to use the book. The chief standard for inclusion is that the agencies were willing to reveal information about themselves. (It is stated in the preface that agencies who refused to respond could be viewed with "some caution.")

Each agency's collection specializations, such as credit cards or commercial credit, are listed. This could be very useful to someone trying to hire an agency. Other information given, such as size and contact persons, could also be helpful. For libraries serving businesses that wish to employ an agency, this would be a useful source, giving information that is not readily available elsewhere about a large number of firms.—**Susan V. McKimm**

238. **The Corporate Finance Sourcebook 1991.** Wilmette, Ill., National Register Publishing, 1991. 1463p. index. $377.00pa. LC 86-642719. ISBN 0-87217-930-3.

Introduced in 1979 and published annually in March, this is a comprehensive guide to sources of capital funding. Included are venture capital firms, private lenders, banks, trusts, commercial financing and factoring firms, pension managers, accounting firms, and more. Each entry contains extensive information, such as lending criteria, industry preference, minimum and preferred size of investment, and year established, as well as names, addresses, and telephone numbers of officers. More than 3,400 firms and 20,000 executives are listed. Also included are a geographical index and indexes to firms and personnel.

An extraordinary amount of information is contained in this publication. The data are well organized and clearly presented under various groupings. Anyone involved in securing or raising investment funds will find the work useful. It will be a worthwhile resource to academic and public libraries that serve business communities.—**P. Grady Morein**

239. **Financial Yellow Book: Who's Who at the Leading U.S. Financial Institutions. Vol.5, No.2.** James L. Marcus, Jr., and others, eds. New York, Monitor Publishing, 1992. 685p. index. $160.00 (2 issues). ISSN 1058-2878.

This semiannual directory provides access to the names, titles, addresses, telephone and fax numbers, and functional responsibilities of more than 32,000 board members and executives in more than 1,000 public and private U.S.-based financial institutions. A very useful feature is the inclusion of more than 2,500 subsidiaries and how their executives can be reached. In some cases the editors felt that a subsidiary's size and scope warranted a separate, unabridged listing. When this occurs, a cross-reference to the parent company alerts the user that this is a subsidiary. Access is provided by company name (parent or subsidiary), geographically, by financial services rendered, and by individuals' names. A quick guide to the relationship among the companies can also be found.

The work is useful for ready-reference and job hunters. For libraries that need detailed financial statistics, a service such as *Moody's Bank & Finance Manual* (Moody's Investors Service, annual) would be better. Due to its cost and the limited amount of data provided, this work is recommended strictly as a supplementary reference item.—**Bobray Bordelon**

240. Katz, Bernard S., ed. **Biographical Dictionary of the Board of Governors of the Federal Reserve.** Westport, Conn., Greenwood Press, 1992. 385p. index. $75.00. HG2563.B46. 332.1'1'092273. LC 91-11329. ISBN 0-313-26658-1.

The 70 biographical entries in this dictionary cover everyone who has served on the Board of Governors of the Federal Reserve System from its inception in 1914 through January 1991. The work's brief introduction sets the stage for the biographies, describing the board's creation, changing structure, and policy tools. The biographies present standard who's-who-type information on the members, along with a discussion of their service on the board. This may include a few or all of the following topics: the politics surrounding the appointment; confirmation hearings; key votes; relations with other members, Congress, the president, and interest groups; philosophical stance on board policy; major speeches; economic conditions prompting board action; effects of that action; and assessment of the member's overall contribution to the board. A bibliography accompanies each entry. The length of the biographies ranges from 18 pages for William McChesney Martin, Jr., to 2 pages for less-prominent figures. Chairs average 11 pages; other members, 4. Practically all of the entries' 40 authors have academic affiliations with business or economics departments. The dictionary has an index of every person mentioned in the book.

The quality of the biographies is generally good but varies considerably. The best entries (e.g., Eugene Meyer, Eugene Black, Abbott Mills, Preston Martin) skillfully interweave the who's-who data with a balanced, detailed, and insightful discussion of the topics that relate to the member's board service. The weakest entries commonly convey an inadequate sense of the member's role on the board.

Stylistically, authors sometimes lapse into jargon or present an extended recital of facts when a judicious summary would suffice. There are several typographical, factual, and indexing errors. Finally, because the profiles are arranged alphabetically, a list of members by dates of board service would help put them in historical context. Although the dictionary fulfills its purpose sufficiently well to warrant a recommendation for purchase by business and economics collections, tighter editorial control would have improved it. [R: Choice, Apr 92, p. 1204; WLB, Apr 92, p. 120]

—**John Lewis Campbell**

241. **The McGraw-Hill Pocket Guide to Business Finance: 201 Decision-Making Tools for Managers.** By Joel G. Siegel, Jae K. Shim, and Stephen W. Hartman. New York, McGraw-Hill, 1992. 354p. index. $29.95; $14.95pa. HG4027.3.S54. 658.15. LC 91-40332. ISBN 0-07-057577-0; 0-07-057576-2pa.

For each of 201 decision-making tools (or concepts used in financial analysis in the business world), the authors present a definition and answers to two questions: "How is it (the tool) computed?"

and "How is it used and by whom?" Tools include those in accounting (e.g., accounts payable ratios, inventory ratios), statistics (e.g., regression statistics, median, normal distribution), finance (e.g., Beta, present value, earnings per share), and management (e.g., decision tree, learning curve, reorder point). The computation discussion usually includes an algebraic expression that embodies the definition, and the algebra is explained by several clear and very helpful examples. In most cases, however, some familiarity is necessary to fully understand the meaning of the definition and the explanation of the tool.

Although this volume does not substitute for courses in finance and accounting, it does allow businesspeople to look up topics where their information is uncertain or rusty. The sections on computations and examples are considerably more detailed and informative than those found in a business dictionary, but they lack the breadth of definitional coverage of topics found in such a work. The cross-references among related tools could be better. [R: Choice, Nov 92, p. 450]—**Richard A. Miller**

242. **The New Palgrave Dictionary of Money & Finance.** Peter Newman, Murray Milgate, and John Eatwell, eds. New York, Stockton Press, 1992. 3v. index. $595.00/set. 332.03. ISBN 1-56159-041-X.

Rapid advancement in electronic data processing has sharply reduced transaction costs in financial markets. Changes in regulations and taxation have also contributed to extensive innovations in financial instruments, and the wave of deregulation has reduced the distinction between financial institutions. A major consequence of this is that retail banks have lost their central role as principal intermediaries in Great Britain and North America. Many of these changes were rapid and unanticipated. Both practitioners and policy-makers must know how credit institutions work and how they change. This comprehensive dictionary provides a solid basis for broadening such knowledge.

The New Palgrave Dictionary of Money & Finance represents the most extensive reference source in the fields of monetary and financial theories. It has been compiled by more than 800 of the very best specialists from various universities' economics departments, the most prestigious business colleges, research and financial institutions, and private and public banks. They come from 30 countries and are doing research in both analytical and applied areas. Nineteen advisory board members were selected from the most distinguished scholars and government and business leaders in the United States and abroad. No other dictionary covers the kind of invaluable information on money and finance that this one does. Newman, Milgate, and Eatwell are distinguished economists with long careers in teaching, research, publishing, and consulting. All three have served as editors of the standard reference source *The New Palgrave: A Dictionary of Economics* (see ARBA 88, entry 165), the companion work to the present compilation.

This monumental reference source contains 1,008 essays that average more than 2,000 words each and deal with a wide range of topics on money and finance. At the beginning of each volume is a list of entries that includes 420 cross-references shown in italics, glossarial entries in roman type, and essays in boldface letters, followed by a list of acronyms. Subject classification of the essays, which contains 12 major groups and 104 subheadings, and the list of contributors appear at the end of the third volume. Each essay is accurate and balanced, containing comprehensive, insightful information that is documented by a full bibliography. Despite the dictionary's impressive size, its editors do not claim that it provides a comprehensive treatment of the historical and geographic aspects of monetary and finance theories. At best, it is only a sample of a vast field of the world's monetary and financial history. And while efforts have been made to cover some 30 countries, the main geographic foci are still North America and Great Britain.

The trend toward specialization, carried beyond the point of diminishing returns, has separated "money" from "finance," placing the former in the economics departments and the latter in the departments of finance in business and management schools. Due to differences in methodology, monetary economists tend to use aggregative general equilibrium models, while financial economics applies disaggregate partial equilibrium analysis to study financial markets. The need to integrate monetary and financial theories is an important task facing economic theorists. These subjects are essentially complementary and need a stronger common empirical-statistical basis to test analytical models developed separately in the monetary and financial areas. The editors of this set are convinced that this extensive dictionary will facilitate the process of the convergence and eventual integration of these two theories. An ideal union of monetary and financial studies can be attained only by a thorough reconstruction of the neoclassical economic paradigm. The presentation of such a large number of essays in both fields should help in making financial economics an important part of training general economists.

Another significant contribution of this dictionary lies in the promotion of interaction between theoretical and applied work, which is greatly facilitated by the relative abundance of quantitative data in these two branches of economics. However, because statistical testing in social sciences cannot prove, but can only fail to disprove, a hypothesis, no listing of information, no matter how plentiful, can eliminate the numerous conflicting explanations of the same phenomena. As a result, several theoretical essays on the same subject and under different titles are connected by cross-references. This is especially true of numerous applied topics seen by the quite distinct points of view of the authors. Most of the differences are caused by such factors as diverse geopolitical perspectives, different mixtures of deductive and empirical inferences, varying balances of positive and normative theorizing, and alternative choices among the levels of analytical complexity. In such cases duplication is a small price to pay for the broader theoretical perspective.

On the whole, this magnificent three-volume compilation is an up-to-date, authoritative reference work in money and finance, with numerous potential users. It will aid the efforts of teachers, researchers, and businesspeople conducting institutional research by providing them with a broad overview of specific subjects and an extensive source for quotations in reports, speeches, and presentations. Moreover, the combination of contributions from outstanding theoreticians and successful market practitioners makes this publication fascinating reading not only for specialists in the field and researchers but also for the general public interested in money and finance. — **Oleg Zinam**

243. Siegel, Joel G., Jae K. Shim, and Stephen Hartman. **Dictionary of Personal Finance.** New York, Macmillan, 1992. 391p. $70.00. HG151.S427. 332.024'003. LC 91-14276. ISBN 0-02-897393-3.

This dictionary is designed to aid the layperson in interpreting terminology encountered when reading popular press business serials and in planning personal financial affairs. More than 3,500 terms help define concepts in consumer economics, money management, and personal finance. Technical jargon is avoided. The arrangement is alphabetical and word-by-word. Cross-references and synonyms are given. If a concept defined elsewhere in the dictionary is included, the term appears in all capital letters. Concepts that differ according to field are numbered and defined appropriately, and definitions are sometimes compared and contrasted. Checklists, graphs, illustrations, tables, applications, and practical examples help clarify the terms. The appendix consists of time value of money tables, sources of consumer help, and consumer tips. In addition, addresses are given for federal information centers, selected federal agencies, state government protection offices, and state utility commissions.

While not a comprehensive business dictionary, this is a useful ready-reference source for personal finance. It is a bit expensive for its intended audience, but it should prove to be a welcome addition for public and academic libraries looking for easily understood personal finance terminology. [R: BR, Sept/Oct 92, p. 68; LJ, 1 June 92, p. 118; RBB, 15 June 92, p. 1880; WLB, June 92, p. 108]

— **Bobray Bordelon**

244. **World Debt Tables 1991-92: External Debt of Developing Countries.** Washington, D.C., World Bank, 1991. 2v. $125.00pa./set. HJ8899.W672. 336.3'435'091724. LC 82-642205. ISBN 0-8213-1984-1.

For more than 20 years the World Bank (WB), one of the major loan-making, economic development agencies, has annually published detailed data on the external long-term debt of developing countries. The current edition covers 114 countries. The WB compiles its data from reports submitted by the countries to whom it lends, from other agencies, and from staff estimates. Volume 1 has 2 parts: a 100-page analysis of the current developing-country debt situation and summary tables for the world, 6 regions, and 10 country groups based on income (low/medium) and debt burden (moderate/severe) levels. Volume 2 consists of tables for individual countries.

Each table is four pages long and has data for 1970, 1980, and each of the last seven or eight years, along with a 1991 projection in the summary tables. Annual editions have rolling coverage, deleting a year and adding a year, but they always provide a historical perspective. The 200-plus data elements in each table paint a very complete picture of the types of debt, categories of lenders, debt burden, interest/principal payments, and ratios of debt service capacity. Data is usually in U.S. dollars. These tables are very readable. The sources of the data and the methodology are described, countries are listed according to their income and debt burden levels, and terms used in the tables are defined. Informative ancillary charts and graphs abound. Two supplements are issued per year to update some tables.

In every respect this is a first-class work. Data is also available on magnetic tape and diskette.

—John Lewis Campbell

INDUSTRY AND MANUFACTURING

245. **American Wholesalers and Distributors Directory: A Comprehensive Guide Offering Industry Details....** Deborah M. Burek and Holly M. Selden, eds. Detroit, Gale, 1992. 1745p. $150.00. ISBN 0-8103-8248-2. ISSN 1061-2114.

This directory lists 18,000 wholesalers and distributors of all types in the United States. It is arranged in three parts: alphabetically by company name; geographically by state, then city; and by Standard Industrial Classification (SIC) code. The entries in this latter section are actually listed alphabetically by industrial area. Most entries contain the following information when available: company name; address; telephone, fax, and toll-free numbers; primary and additional SIC codes; year established; annual estimated sales; number of employees; names and titles of principal officers; and product lines. Information for the directory was obtained from companies directly through questionnaires, from other Gale databases, and from miscellaneous secondary sources. A guide for users discusses the organization of the directory and the quick location of a specific company; it also provides illustrated entries with each element identified.

Approximately 25 books on wholesale trade are in print, but only 3 directories are listed. Most are limited to specific product lines such as printing and office supplies, consumer electronics, food service, and home furnishings. *American Wholesalers and Distributors Directory* is one of the few directories that covers a broad spectrum of wholesale companies. It will be useful for academic, large public, and special libraries that need this type of information and can afford it. [R: Choice, Nov 92, p. 437; LJ, 15 Oct 92, p. 60; RBB, 1 Sept 92, p. 82]—**O. Gene Norman**

246. **Corporate Technology Directory 1992.** 7th ed. Woburn, Mass., Corporate Technology Information Services, 1992. 4v. index. $445.00pa./set. LC 86-642570. ISBN 0-936507-31-4. ISSN 0887-1930.

This is an impressive collection of data on more than 35,000 U.S. firms that manufacture or develop high-tech products. Three of the volumes contain an alphabetical listing of each company with pertinent information such as fax, telephone, and telex numbers; address; sales; volume; number of employees; names and titles of executives; product line; a brief overview of services provided; year of formation; and type of ownership. The first volume contains indexes of the profiled companies by name and associated names, of listed companies by city within states (with city and zip code maps), and of listed units that are foreign owned. Also provided are suggestions for using the directory and a demographic summary of the included companies. Not only is the printed version available, but the publisher also makes available mailing lists and electronic databases.

The directory is revised on an annual basis (this is the 7th edition). But if more timely data are required, monthly updates on employment trends are available. The publisher can also provide custom and regional directories, custom reports and analyses, and a list of the fastest-growing firms. The directory can save an immense amount of search time for those who wish to locate and contact firms in high-tech industry, not only for sales purposes but also for conducting research and for suggesting names of prospective employers.—**William C. Struning**

247. Darnay, Arsen J., ed. **Manufacturing USA: Industry Analyses, Statistics, and Leading Companies.** 2d ed. Detroit, Gale, 1992. 1884p. index. $169.00. ISBN 0-8103-7574-5. ISSN 1044-7024.

This volume presents comprehensive statistical information from a variety of government and private sources on the manufacturing sector of the U.S. economy. Using the Standard Industrial Classification (SIC) system as revised in 1987, *Manufacturing USA* covers 459 manufacturing industries. Data is presented for the period 1982 through 1988 in all cases, and through 1991 in selected industries.

The guide is organized by industry. Each separate listing includes eight tables and two graphics. The tables cover general industry statistics, including establishments, employment, compensation, and production; indexes of change within each industry for these general statistics; selected personnel, production, and financial ratios; name, address, sales, and employment data for the leading companies in that industry; purchases of materials and products; product categories within the industry; occupational data; and industry data by state. The graphics depict shipment and employment trends and states and regions where the industry predominates. The work has a very helpful user's guide, and it indexes industries by SIC, product, company, and occupation.—**Paul F. Clark**

248. **Encyclopedia of American Business History and Biography: The Airline Industry.** William M. Leary, ed. New York, Facts on File, 1992. 531p. illus. index. $85.00. TL509.E54. 387.7'0973. LC 92-17993. ISBN 0-8160-2675-0.

This book is part of a series of eight volumes, five of which deal with the American transportation industry. This volume on the airline industry starts with an informative historical introduction. The main section consists of two basic types of entry: the most important leaders and agents of change and development, with brief biographies; and institutions, whether airlines, federal agencies, or organizations (e.g., air traffic controllers, the International Air Transport Association, the International Civil Aviation Organization). The airline histories seem more synoptic than the biographies, but references provided at the end of all entries allow for deeper research. The main outlines of people and organizations are adequate and competently done. The experiments, the risks, the failures, and the successes are cogently depicted without histrionics but with statistical figures and factual descriptions. A large number of photographs of various airplane models and biographees are provided. Recommended for all business libraries and for reference libraries of organizations in the transport (especially air transport) industry.—**Bogdan Mieczkowski**

249. Pennell, Allison A., Patricia E. Choi, and Lawrence Molinaro, Jr., eds. **Business and the Environment: A Resource Guide.** Washington, D.C., Island Press, 1992. 364p. index. $55.00. HD69.P6P46. 016.6584'08. LC 91-38369. ISBN 1-55963-159-7.

This work is intended as a resource guide for educators. It can assist those wishing to incorporate environmental issues in business courses or business issues in natural resources management training. There are three major sections that list different types of resources: publications, case studies, and educators with professional interests in environmental issues. All three sections are subdivided under the same six general headings (e.g., accounting and finance, natural resources management). The publications and case studies sections also list keyword descriptors that apply to the item.

The publications section includes annotated references to journal articles, chapters of textbooks, books, government reports, and newspaper articles published since 1980. The case studies section lists sources of such studies that describe a situation requiring a decision with some environmental repercussions; these can be used to teach business school students. There is also an annotated list of environmental videos. For most materials an address is given for acquisition.

The directory of educators is a source of information frequently not published and can act as a source for networking. For each educator the university affiliation, publications, courses taught, research activity, educational background, and employment history are listed. There are indexes by key word, general subject heading, author, reference number, educator, and university.

This is a useful sourcebook in an area of urgent and wide concern. Because of its specific orientation as a resource for educators, it will be of most interest to academic libraries, although it will probably also be useful to business corporations and public libraries with many business clients. [R: Choice, Nov 92, p. 438; LJ, 1 May 92, p. 74]—**Marit S. MacArthur**

250. **Service Industries USA: Industry Analyses, Statistics, and Leading Organizations.** Arsen J. Darnay, ed. Detroit, Gale, 1992. 925p. maps. index. $170.00. 338.40973. ISBN 0-8103-8397-7. ISSN 1058-1626.

This directory covers 151 of the 4-digit service industries (SIC [Standard Industrial Classification] 7xxx and 8xxx), collecting data almost exclusively from four sources: *Census of Service Industries* (Bureau of the Census, 1987), the *Industry-Occupation Matrix* (Bureau of Labor Statistics), *Ward's*

Business Directory of U.S. Private and Public Companies (see ARBA 90, entry 182), and the *National Directory of Nonprofit Organizations* (Taft Group, 1991). The introduction, overview, and user's guide provide useful information on the use of this directory. The tables in part 1 cover each of the industries by state, general statistics, and indexes of change (all giving establishments, payroll, revenue, and ownership); 22 selected ratios (e.g., employees and payroll per establishment); leading companies; occupations employed; and representative nonprofit organizations. Part 2 lists the major service industries in each of 623 cities and metropolitan areas (there is some overlap). Data supplied are 4-digit SIC code (and name), tax status, number of establishments, employment, payroll, receipts, and numbers of proprietorships and partnerships. There are indexes of SIC industries covered, services included, companies listed (more than 3,500), cities and metro areas, and occupations. [R: Choice, May 92, pp. 1374-76; LJ, 1 Feb 92, p. 82; RBB, 1 Mar 92, pp. 1308-09; WLB, Mar 92, pp. 117-18]

—**Richard A. Miller**

251. **Who Knows about Industries and Markets.** 13th ed. By Washington Researchers Publishing. Washington, D.C., Washington Researchers, 1991. 118p. $85.00pa. LC 88-656305. ISBN 1-56365-009-6. ISSN 1042-0215.

This directory to industry experts in governmental agencies provides names and telephone numbers of analysts in the International Trade Administration, Bureau of the Census, U.S. International Trade Commission, Federal Trade Commission, U.S. Department of Justice (Antitrust Division), U.S. Customs Service, Congressional Budget Office, Congressional Research Service, and Office of Technology Assessment. Within each agency, commodities or industries are listed alphabetically, indicating an analyst's name and telephone number. For the Census Bureau industries, two-digit SIC (Standard Industrial Classification) codes are provided. An appendix has a brief explanation of the SIC codes; an alphabetical list of industries and products with their two-, three-, or four-digit codes; and a numerical list of the most relevant codes and their products. The introduction discusses the value of governmental experts for research on industries and suggests ways to use them. Each agency also has its own specific introduction that indicates the kinds of information the analysts can provide. The general introduction could be improved with an outline of how to prepare for a productive conversation with experts. Although it suggests reviewing reports done by the agencies prior to interviewing such individuals, some researchers would benefit from guidelines to finding published industry analyses available through public and academic libraries.

This directory does a good job of providing brief, specific listings organized in a useful way. The print size and the amount of white space between columns make for easy reading. *Who Knows* will be useful for special libraries or for public and academic libraries that serve business researchers.

—**Joan B. Fiscella**

INSURANCE

252. Johnston-Des Rochers, Janeen, with Denise Langlois. **Unemployment Insurance Glossary. Lexique de l'Assurance-Chomage.** Ottawa, Department of the Secretary of State of Canada, 1992. 421p. (Departmental Glossary Series). $35.95pa. (U.S.). 368.44'003. ISBN 0-660-57314-8.

This well-executed vocabulary of English/French and French/English equivalents for terms in the unemployment insurance field follows the standard format of Terminology and Linguistic Services Directorate publications. Updating a 1984 edition, it focuses on the usage of Employment and Immigration Canada in administering the Canadian Unemployment Insurance scheme. About half of the 3,400 entries are said to be new since the earlier version.

Access is aided by the foreword, introduction, user's guide, and table of contents—all brief but helpful. Text is arranged in double columns, French on one side and English on the other, a style common in Canadian government publications at the federal level. (For nondictionary and nonlegislation publications, two separate texts in the single document is perhaps more common.) The main body of the dictionary is organized in two parts. The first gives a straight list of English terms with synonyms in one column and French equivalents in the other. The second is the mirror of the first, arranged alphabetically by the French version. There are no definitions although a few contextual notes are provided.

Entries are repeated under each synonym. In sum, this is a handy tool for translators interested in the subject. — **Nigel Tappin**

253. **Who's Who in World Insurance.** Harlow, England, Longman Group; distr., Chicago, St. James Press, 1991. 280p. index. $150.00. ISBN 1-55862-168-7.

Unlike many directories that use "World" in their title, this one is truly international. It includes insurance executives from even the smallest countries and does not overrepresent either the United Kingdom, where it is published, or the United States. The major portion of the book is an alphabetical list of executives, their titles, and contact information. A few entries include brief information on qualifications, memberships, directorships, areas of expertise, and previous employment history. As a biographical dictionary, the information is generally too sketchy—or nonexistent—to be of use. However, as a way of contacting these executives, the book is quite useful, as it provides, when available, business address, telephone number, telex, fax, and cable information. The number of personnel listed per company ranges from 1 to 22. An index that lists executives and firms by specialty might enhance the usefulness of this title.

Unfortunately, the price is high in relation to the amount of information. This directory is recommended for comprehensive business collections or for insurance or international firms that can afford it. — **Susan V. McKimm**

INTERNATIONAL BUSINESS

General Works

Dictionaries and Encyclopedias

254. **IMF Glossary: English-French-Spanish.** Washington, D.C., International Monetary Fund; distr., Lanham, Md., UNIPUB, 1992. 341p. index. $26.00pa. HG3881.5.I58I63. 332.4'5'03. ISBN 1-55775-267-2.

The International Monetary Fund's (IMF's) Bureau of Language Services has prepared this glossary primarily as an aid for IMF language personnel. However, it can be used as an English/French/Spanish glossary for money and banking; public finance; balance of payments; economic growth; and IMF organization, structure, and staff titles. Words, phrases, and institutional titles are included, and some entries denote the term's origin or context. Color indexes are used to find French and Spanish terms. An IMF organization chart is appended, and another appendix provides information on the spelling and abbreviations of currency units of various countries and areas.

This is an inexpensive way of obtaining a foreign-language glossary for international finance and economics. Recommended for academic libraries with collections in multinational business.

— **Bobray Bordelon**

255. Presner, Lewis A. **The International Business Dictionary and Reference.** New York, John Wiley, 1991. 486p. $45.00. HF1359.P74. 658'.049'03. LC 91-9328. ISBN 0-471-54594-5.

Presner reveals the extent to which we belong to a global economy. Terms used every day in U.S. business, such as *total quality*, have international repercussions. In general, many terms are treated in commendable depth, referring to legislation, relevant agencies, and derivation. Substantial research has gone into the longer entries, which are really brief articles. It is disconcerting, however, to find the Baldrige Award referred to in the total quality entry as Japanese and the Deming Award as American when the reverse is true. Sometimes definitions of general terms concentrate only on trade aspects of the term. For instance, *shrink wrapping* is defined as a technique used by export packers. It is a technique used by other packers as well, and the word "export" in the definition could confuse an individual who has no knowledge of the term's general applicability.

Although primarily an alphabetical dictionary, this title also has a directory of international organizations and a lengthy bibliography. There are 7 appendixes and 10 geographical indexes. For the

reference librarian, it would be better to have as much as possible in one alphabet. The arrangement could be useful, however, to a person who uses the book often and learns its organization. This work can be recommended for business collections because of the useful background information provided, as it goes beyond mere definitions. [R: Choice, July/Aug 92, p. 1660; RBB, 1 Mar 92, p. 1307]
—Susan V. McKimm

Directories

256. **Bergano's Register of International Importers 1992/93.** Fairfield, Conn., Bergano Book, 1992. 214p. index. $95.00pa. ISBN 0-917408-06-3.

Directed at businesses seeking firms outside their own market to import or distribute their products, this directory lists a cross-section of importers in countries worldwide (other than the countries of the Commonwealth of Independent States). A brief introduction includes information about how to initiate contact with the firms and how to evaluate each importer's ability to market selected products.

The directory is organized by country within broad geographic areas. More than 2,000 firms are listed alphabetically within country categories. The company entry provides information derived from questionnaires and telephone interviews, including firm's name and address; contact person and title; telephone, fax, telex, and cable numbers; year of establishment; number of sales offices; number of employees; and bank. Finally, the entry lists any companies the importer represents, indicates if it provides technical or maintenance service, and lists the kinds of products in which it is interested. Each importer's product list is based on, but is not limited to, a product category list that is located after the country/company directory. An index of companies by product category completes the volume. An alphabetical index of companies would be a helpful addition. This directory is particularly useful for libraries that serve businesses who wish to make direct contact with importers in other countries, or libraries that wish to supplement material found in the Department of Commerce's *Foreign Trader's Index*.—**Joan B. Fiscella**

257. **European Wholesalers and Distributors Directory.** Linda Irvin and others, eds. Detroit, Gale, 1992. 677p. $175.00. ISBN 0-8103-8354-3. ISSN 1063-8288.

This directory lists European wholesalers of consumer and industrial products in Eastern and Western Europe, the Balkan States, and the Commonwealth of Independent States. Although the introductory material is in English, French, and German, the listings and indexes are only in English. The main section is arranged by Standard Industrial Classification (SIC) codes 50 and 51 (wholesale trade of durable and nondurable goods). Alphabetically within this arrangement are the countries and companies. Each company listing provides name, address, and telephone number; primary and secondary SICs; revenue in the home country's currency; year of establishment; number of employees and key people; territories served; and products provided. Given the need for language expertise in international business transactions, it is unfortunate that the editors have omitted the category of language competency. The product listing is based on the Harmonized System of goods classification. Concise sections adequately explain the use of SICs and Harmonized Codes; material covering the latter also includes a hierarchical index of four-digit codes and an alphabetical index by the names of goods.

The first index is a product key based on primary two-digit Harmonized Codes. Product descriptors used in the company descriptions are based on the more specific four-digit codes. Consequently, one must narrow the field of appropriate firms considerably from the list provided in the product-key index. An index to territories served cross-references companies under the countries they serve. Within each country the companies are alphabetized under the appropriate SIC, with the headquarters' location and entry number noted. The final index is an alphabetical list of companies.

All in all, this directory is well planned and well explained. It will make a welcome addition to the international business collection of any library—special, public, or academic.—**Susan D. Baird-Joshi**

258. **IEG Directory of Sponsorship Marketing, 1991.** 4th ed. Lesa Ukman, ed. Chicago, International Events Group, 1991. 718p. index. $175.00 spiralbound. ISBN 0-944807-03-8. ISSN 0894-0649.

This is the most comprehensive reference guide to sponsorship marketing. Almost every significant event, domestic or international, is included. The book consists of eight sections. The first covers events by location in the United States and in foreign countries. The second lists events by category, by month, and alphabetically by name. The third has details about attendance and budget, and the fourth deals with information about new opportunities for sponsorship. Sections 5, 6, and 7 cover agencies, suppliers, and vendors who serve the sponsorship industry. The last section is an excellent index of telephone numbers for events, organizations, and individuals. This directory is highly recommended to all businesses, especially large agencies, involved in the sponsorship industry.—**Elie M. Dick**

259. **International Corporate Yellow Book: Who's Who at the Leading Non-U.S. Companies. Vol.5, No.1.** Catherine Shih and others, eds. New York, Monitor Publishing, 1992. 768p. index. $125.00pa. ISSN 1058-2894.

As its title suggests, this directory provides company names and acronyms, addresses, executive names and titles, telephone and fax numbers, subsidiaries, and other important data about international corporations. The information, arranged by geographical area, is easily accessible and clearly presented. The various indexes are helpful, as they include alphabetical lists by company, subsidiary, country, industry, and individual. The book also furnishes charts of time zones and world holidays.

With close to 800 pages of information, this reference work appears to be a comprehensive who's who of international corporations. However, when one begins to look for specific companies, major omissions become evident. One such example is Scandinavian Airlines System (SAS) and its internationally known CEO, Jan Carlzon. Although the editors list criteria for inclusion, they are not specific enough to explain such omissions. Nevertheless, this work will prove useful to researchers in the field of international trade and to people interested in establishing contact with the listed companies.

—**Renee B. Horowitz**

260. **International Directory of Company Histories. Volume IV.** Adele Hast and others, eds. Chicago, St. James Press, 1991. 847p. index. $125.00. 338.7409. ISBN 1-55862-060-5.

Dissatisfied with the brief descriptions in most investment tools, students and others researching company and industry performance will welcome this series with joy. Ultimately covering the world's largest and most influential companies, this work is the fourth in a set of volumes begun in 1988 (see ARBA 92, entry 148; ARBA 91, entry 132; and ARBA 90, entry 177). The highly detailed articles provide a condensed story of the major individuals, events, changes, and acquisitions that have influenced the development of more than 200 companies in 5 industries, ranging from mining to real estate. Here, for example, the relationship between Dow and Jones and Barron can be examined.

Compiled from publicly accessible sources, the articles consist of basic data (e.g., address, telephone and fax numbers, ownership), a lengthy essay, names of subsidiaries, and a list of further reading. Changes instituted since the first volume include longer, signed essays and more extensive identification of the contributors. The index to companies and persons is cumulative. Unfortunately, topics (from the contents page), products, subsidiaries, contributors, and geographical areas cannot be searched; their inclusion would have enhanced the work's usefulness. Recommended, particularly for libraries that serve an active business clientele. [R: LJ, 1 Mar 92, p. 84]—**Sandra E. Belanger**

261. **World Business Directory: Detailed Information on More Than 100,000 Businesses Involved in International Trade.** Meghan A. O'Meara and Kimberley A. Peterson, eds. Detroit, Gale, 1992. 4v. index. $395.00/set. 338.7025. ISBN 0-8103-7715-2. ISSN 1062-1172.

To assist the business community, government officials, and economists in their efforts to expand trading activities among nations, the World Trade Centers Association and Gale have published this directory, which provides business information, valuable assistance opportunities, and the names and location of potential business partners needed to succeed in future international endeavors. This outstanding compilation covers numerous world enterprises, including the Pacific Rim region, the European Community, Eastern Europe, the nations emerging after the disintegration of the Soviet Union, and Communist China. Listed are more than 100,000 companies in 190 countries chosen because of their interest in global trade. In each country the extent of coverage is proportionate to the nation's involvement in such trade. Specific efforts have been made to include small and medium-sized businesses with the potential to become future business leaders.

World Business Directory is printed in four attractively bound large reference volumes that contain 5,314 pages of direct information on businesses and more than 250 introductory pages of explanatory materials in different languages at the beginning of each volume. Every geographic section is introduced by a complete list of the 244 cities that have world trade centers. Each company's listing may contain such data as telephone, fax, and telex numbers; names, titles, and financial data of company executives; type of business; fiscal year end; year company was established; industry activity and products traded; parent information; world trade center affiliation; and world trade center network code. The first three volumes of the directory contain an alphabetical list of all nations with world trade centers. Within each country the businesses are presented in alphabetical order. The 4th volume rearranges all company listings in indexes by products and industries, and it also has an alphabetical index.

The product index uses the Harmonized System (HS) codes based on numerical and alphabetical reference lists developed under the auspices of the Customs Cooperation Council in Brussels, Belgium. The HS standardizes the commodity classification that is used by trade associations, government agencies, research organizations and business professionals. It consists of three levels of codes. First, a two-digit code depicts a given family of products. For example, code 10 represents cereals, while code 39 stands for plastics. Second, a four-digit code represents a subdivision of the product designated by the first two digits. For instance, 10.04 stands for barley and 39.10 is silicones. Third, a six-digit code represents even more specific commodity information. For example, 49.11 stands for printed matter, while 4911.91 designates "printed matter including pictures, designs and photographs." To allow easy identification of products, the product index in volume 4 is immediately preceded by two reference lists in which all commodities are arranged first by numeric code and then alphabetically by product description. The product index lists codified products alphabetically, then subdivides them by countries and by company names within each country. A page reference is provided for each company. In the industry index section, the industries are listed alphabetically, then subdivided by countries and within them by company name, and followed by a page number. In the alphabetical index, all firms listed in the directory are printed alphabetically, with their locations placed in brackets.

The World Business Directory provides information on international markets by identifying potential trading partners, locating firms and their commodities that compete for foreign markets, conveniently classifying commodities and firms with precise product information by means of an internationally accepted coding system, and by providing information on global job opportunities. It is an outstanding reference source for all people and organizations interested in promoting international trade in an emerging global economy.—**Oleg Zinam**

262. **World Retail Directory and Sourcebook 1991.** London, Euromonitor; distr., Detroit, Gale, 1991. 770p. index. $390.00. ISBN 0-86338-435-8.

This new international retail directory covers a wide variety of materials from many sources. Geographical areas represented include Europe, North America, Central and South America, the Middle East and Africa, the Far East, and Oceania. The book is divided into four sections. Section 1 lists public organizations, government offices, consultants, publications, trade fairs, conferences, and seminars that are related to marketing. Information provided for each entry consists of address; telephone number; fax and telex numbers, if available; training courses available; hours open; name of publications; and circulation figures of publications. Section 2 contains information on more than 2,000 companies from 75 countries; the introductory part profiles 330 retailers with sales exceeding $1 billion. Each entry includes, when available, the ownership, subsidiaries, officers, number of outlets, number of employees, sales, recent developments, and notes. Section 3 presents detailed statistical data on retail trade, including trends in retail sales by country and international comparisons. Retail legislation is covered by country in section 4. A general index in the back of the volume provides quick access to materials.

Few comprehensive directories of this nature are available. *Fairchild's Financial Manual of Retail Stores* (Fairchild Books, annual) has a detailed list of retail stores, but it is limited to the United States. Although the price is high, *The World Retail Directory* will be quite useful and timesaving for academic, special, and large public libraries that have a demand for this kind of information. [R: Choice, Oct 92, p. 282]—**O. Gene Norman**

Handbooks and Yearbooks

263. **CIFAR's Global Company Handbook.** 1992 ed. Vinod B. Bavishi, ed. Princeton, N.J., Center for International Financial Analysis & Research, 1992. 2v. index. $395.00pa./set. ISBN 1-877587-04-4. ISSN 1060-8710.

This set consists primarily of tables on the world's leading companies and how they are performing. Volume 1 contains information on introduction and research design; sections include 500 of the world's top performing companies measured by a global uniform standard. Information is divided both by country and industry. Another section indicates global, country, and industry rankings of the leading 7,500-plus companies in the areas of sales, assets, net income, market value, and employees. In another section, industry and country averages are indicated. Data are divided into country overall; industries overall and by country; banks, insurance companies, and other financial organizations in each country; and by industry classification. Volume 1 also contains one appendix that is a synthesis of accounting standards and another that indicates capital market characteristics in 44 countries. Volume 2 has detailed profiles by country for the 7,500-plus companies in volume 1. The print is fairly small in this document, but because it is not meant to be read straight through, it is acceptable. Recommended. [R: Choice, Nov 92, p. 438; LJ, 15 Sept 92, p. 58] — **Herbert W. Ockerman**

264. **Craighead's International Business, Travel, and Relocation Guide to 71 Countries 1992-93: The Most Comprehensive Reference Source Available....** 6th ed. Detroit, Gale, 1991. 1603p. maps. $425.00. ISBN 0-8103-8455-8. ISSN 1058-3904.

Rapid technological advances have induced revolutionary changes in communication and transportation. These have contributed to an unprecedented expansion in international travel, which can be rewarding but also hazardous, even dangerous. While travel for recreational purposes can be postponed or canceled, business travelers do not always have these options. This volume is a most comprehensive reference source for travelers abroad. It contains such vital information on each of 71 countries as social customs, political situation, economic conditions and trends, climate, health matters, custom regulations, airline connections, telecommunications, currency rates, business opportunities, and personal safety. While previous editions were written for traveling businesspeople and those intending to relocate in a foreign country, this edition is focused on the broader goals of serving students and vacationers (as well as businesspeople) interested in cultural, social, political, and economic conditions abroad.

The first of the work's five sections covers precautionary measures recommended to minimize the risks of international travel. In the next two sections the reader is provided with vital data on technical aspects of problems that concern personal and business trips abroad and the relocation of individuals and their families — information useful for human-resource executives. The final two sections provide five regional reports on Africa, Asia, Europe, the Middle East, and the Americas as well as comprehensive information on travel and relocation in each of the countries covered. Vividly written, with fascinating details, this beautifully bound hardcover volume is an indispensable reference book for the shelves of public, college, or private collections. — **Oleg Zinam**

265. Estell, Kenneth, ed. **World Trade Resources Guide: A Guide to Resources on Importing from and Exporting to the Major Trading Nations of the World.** Detroit, Gale, 1992. 891p. maps. index. $169.00. ISBN 0-8103-8404-3. ISSN 1058-1618.

The purpose of this guide is to bring together sources for international trade data arranged by country name. Each chapter covers a country, and all begin with a profile that includes the capital, major cities, languages, currency, trade statistics, and major types of commodities traded. This information was selected from the *World Factbook 1990* (Central Intelligence Agency). Each country's profile is followed by a directory of information source, such as banks and other financial institutions, chambers of commerce, trade associations, business libraries, statistical sources, free trade zones, and shipping lines. Eighty-two countries have been selected for inclusion based on their gross national product, geographic location, and natural resources and exports. All major countries are listed along with others such as Cuba, Gambia, Mauritius, Jamaica, and Vietnam. Some of the countries not included are Bolivia, Guatemala, Iceland, Syria, and Tanzania.

This competent directory would be helpful in libraries that serve users who frequently need quick access to sources of trade information, such as international business students and journalists. However, people who need information in order to actually import or export specific commodities or goods may be better served by contacting the Trade Office in each embassy or the consular offices located in most American port cities. This work, however, is a good place to start. [R: Choice, May 92, p. 1378; LJ, 1 Feb 92, p. 82; RBB, 15 Jan 92, p. 980]—**Susan B. Ardis**

266. Fraser, Robert, ed. **The World Trade System.** Harlow, England, Longman Group; distr., Detroit, Gale, 1991. 435p. $165.00. ISBN 0-582-08696-5.

This work emphasizes the parts that comprise the world trade system rather than the overall system. The major portion of the book consists of an overview of trade for each country of the world—principal exports and imports, major trading partners, notes on the economy and political structure, international memberships, the address of the principal government agency responsible for trade, and other pertinent data. The second largest section discusses each of 54 major commodities in international trade, including significant trading organizations (where they exist) that serve each commodity. A third section provides descriptions of each of the major international trade-related organizations. The introduction gives historical perspective on the world trade system since World War II.

The book is a highly useful and authoritative reference volume on world trade, bringing many pertinent facts together succinctly. It also serves as a point of departure for further research on a particular country or commodity. In future editions it would be desirable to have a section on the scope and magnitude of world trade. A brief note on the background of the editor and the contributors would also be of interest. [R: Choice, June 92, p. 1531]—**William C. Struning**

267. **Global Texas: International Trade Information Sourcebook.** Raymond J. Brimble, ed. Austin, Tex., Bureau of Business Research, Graduate School of Business, University of Texas, 1992. 227p. index. $29.95pa. LC 91-76185. ISBN 0-87755-326-2.

Many businesses, large and small, are seeking to compete in the global market, but before any products can be exported, an understanding of a whole new trading structure is necessary. Information is available in many publications, but locating the right organization or person to contact is not an easy task. This directory makes it easy by including a wide variety of information sources not only essential for the beginning exporter but also useful for companies already engaged in international trade. Although aimed at Texas businesses, any company researching foreign markets can locate needed information in this publication. It is a list of a variety of governmental and UN agencies and private organizations. Some of the areas covered are addresses of U.S. and foreign embassies and consular offices and chambers of commerce in foreign countries; financial assistance banks and agencies; patent, trademark, licensing, and product standards contacts; trade data sources; and travel and transportation services. Most entries include a brief explanation for clarification of services offered. Because it consolidates in one volume the names of organizations and agencies that provide international trade assistance, this inexpensive directory is recommended for purchase by businesses and libraries.

—**Jean Herold**

268. **Global Trade White Pages 1992.** Karen L. Holloway, ed. Washington, D.C., Carroll Publishing, 1992. 728p. index. $295.00pa. ISSN 1054-8742.

Designed as a customized international trade telephone directory, this work provides access to contacts in the U.S. federal government; Congress; state governments; countries of the world; and international, intergovernmental, and nongovernmental organizations. Contacts have been included according to two general criteria: they must be knowledgeable about individual countries or they must provide assistance to U.S. businesspeople in international trade. Included are experts in business, economic, political, or cultural relations. There also are selected governmental and private-sector organizations that assist exporters, importers, and foreign investors; regulate exports and imports; and work to encourage foreign investment in the United States. For each of 170 countries, an information snapshot covers language, exports, imports, current trading partners, currency, exchange rate, industries, agriculture, and natural resources. Also listed are embassy and consulate offices in the United States by state, U.S. embassy and consular staff in that country, government and business organizations in that country and in the United States, and the International Airport Authority. Three quick-reference, useful appendixes include holidays by country, a matrix of state and port offices in foreign countries, and a matrix of foreign consular offices in the United States. A comprehensive keyword index includes the acronym used to denote agency, state, or country, as well as the section in which the entry can be located. In general, information is current as of January 1, 1991. This is an easy-to-use, valuable source for individuals and organizations seeking international trade contacts.—**Roslyn Attinson**

269. **The Henry Holt International Desk Reference: A Guide to Essential Information Resources of the World's Major Trading Nations.** By Gary McClain. New York, Henry Holt, 1992. 606p. index. $39.95. LC 91-58028. ISBN 0-8050-1852-2.

According to the author's introduction, *The Henry Holt International Desk Reference* seeks to be a springboard in the search for information about the world's major trading nations. As such, it succeeds. The handbook is an excellent one-volume starting point for access to organizations and publications in 63 countries. It is organized by region and then by country. The country chapters average about seven to eight pages in length and list resources under uniform subject headings. The subject headings primarily deal with business or political topics (e.g., embassies, business development offices, import/export organizations), although headings for cultural and educational resources are also included. Types of resources include associations, institutes, societies, newsletters, directories, government publications, and books. The handbook makes liberal use of cross-referencing to avoid duplication of multinational organizations under different countries or headings. Most chapters conclude with a brief bibliography for background reading. An appendix lists organizations and publications with a global focus.

This work pulls together useful information into an easy-to-understand format. It will serve as a good alternative to more expensive political or trade guides such as *Europa World Year Book* (see ARBA 90, entry 91). Subject access to international associations, institutes, and societies is easier with this guide than in the keyword index to the *Encyclopedia of Associations: International Organizations* (see ARBA 90, entries 59 and 60), but fewer organizations are covered.—**Kerranne G. Biley**

270. **International Trade 90-91.** Geneva, General Agreement on Tariffs and Trade; distr., Lanham, Md., UNIPUB, 1992. 2v. $30.00pa./v. ISBN 92-870-1070-6(v.1); 92-870-1071-4(v.2). ISSN 0072-064X.

These up-to-date volumes concentrate on trade data for 1989 and 1990 but also include some 10-year trends. Trade is divided by regions, by countries, and by groups of similar countries, such as leading traders, LDCs (least developed countries), highly indebted countries, and ex-communist countries. There are separations into merchandise and services, general current account trends, and the impact of the Gulf War. An effort is also made to forecast the near future. A novel feature is the attention to environmental issues, in the form of a long chapter in volume 1 and in scattered references. More general statistics are found in volume 1 (with 14 tables, 4 charts, and 6 boxes), together with descriptions of changes, 2 appendixes, and 5 appendix tables. Volume 2 contains 133 statistical tables, several charts, technical notes, and an additional 20 appendix tables. The data, conveniently and thoughtfully arranged, are useful for tracing aggregate changes and changes in commodity groups or in individual commodities. (This reviewer used the material in these volumes in his international economics class.) Values are uniformly presented in U.S. dollars. Some of the conclusions, both for trade prospects in the West and for the chances of successful integration of former communist countries into the world trade network, inspire optimism. One can even find satisfaction in some of the changes among the LDCs. Highly recommended for college libraries.—**Bogdan Mieczkowski**

271. Leslie, John, ed. **European Accountancy Yearbook 1992/93.** London, Graham & Trotman; distr., Detroit, Gale, 1992. 375p. maps. $235.00pa. ISBN 1-85333-610-6. ISSN 0963-0538.

This first edition contains three major sections: eight articles titled "Looking Back Over 1991: The Year in European Accounting," European accountancy groups, and European accountancy firms by country. The articles cover such topics as "Management Consulting: Boosting Your European Management Team" and "Cross-Border Accounting: Transfer of Skills." The focus of these seems to be for European firms themselves rather than for clients seeking European firms. The European accountancy group section provides valuable information about the history and present scope of operations of the various groups. It includes names, telephone and fax numbers, a professional head count, addresses of principal national offices, and the history and structure of some 40 groups. In a few cases fee income is included, although this data is presented in a variety of formats.

The largest section is the one on accounting firms by country. For each country there is a quarter-page summary of geographic, political, and economic information (e.g., area, population, Gross Domestic Product, official language, currency, professional accounting body). This summary is followed by a one-page article about corporate tax data for the country and a list of firms practicing in each country, whether or not they are members of a group listed earlier. For each firm are listed principal office location, European affiliation, contact information by functional specialization (e.g., audit, tax), client services, major clients, and other offices and associated firms. A final short section contains a summary of professional bodies by country. This information is included in the firms by country section, but it is useful here.

The data was supplied by the practice or group and therefore lacks uniformity. More consistency in future volumes would enhance its usefulness. Despite its high price, this volume should prove a valuable tool for those seeking information about European accountancy services.—**Ben B. Trotter**

272. Mattera, Philip. **World Class Business: A Guide to the 100 Most Powerful Global Corporations.** New York, Henry Holt, 1992. 763p. index. $50.00. HD2755.5.M384. 338.8'8'025. LC 91-45585. ISBN 0-8050-1681-3.

This guide provides a synoptic introduction to the nature and distribution of multinational corporations on which the sun never sets. Size was not the only criterion for inclusion, the other criteria being the extent of international activity, growth potential, and Mattera's desire to provide a broad representation by industry and geography. United States companies number 43; Japanese, 16; and European, 32. (Japanese and Korean entries are actually multiple-firm entries with major affiliates within the *keiretsu* and *chaebol* conglomerate groupings.) The coverage for individual firms includes basic data (e.g., name, address, year of founding), an overview, history, operations, top executives, outside directors, financial data (e.g., revenues, net income), a geographical breakdown of revenues and income, labor relations, the environmental record, and a bibliography of books and major reports. Six appendixes and an index of names complete the guide. This work is useful for a quick identification of, and introduction to, top businesses for students and as a reference for businesspeople. Recommended for schools of business and large public libraries.—**Bogdan Mieczkowski**

273. O'Donnell, Timothy S., and others, eds. **World Economic Data.** Santa Barbara, Calif., ABC-Clio, 1991. 261p. $35.00. ISBN 0-87436-658-5. ISSN 0891-4125.

Providing a broad overview of current economic data for 171 countries throughout the world, this reference guide is an excellent resource for basic or initial research on single countries and economic comparisons between two or more countries. Data and information were compiled from ABC-Clio's Kaleidoscope: Current World Data database. The text is divided into data from countries of the world, covering 225 pages, and data concerned with U.S. indicators. A very good glossary of economic terms and a brief but useful bibliography conclude the text. It is likely another edition will be published in the near future, as economic and political conditions have changed dramatically in parts of the world. Most notably the Soviet Union has ceased to exist.

This publication is intended for librarians, teachers, students, and others seeking information on factors that influence world economics. However, while it is particularly suited for use in secondary schools and libraries, the data is limited and selective, so researchers may need to consult more extensive resources. Overall, many public libraries that cannot afford more expensive world economic statistical reference sources will find this a very good bargain.—**James M. Murray**

274. **Who Knows about Foreign Industries and Markets.** 13th ed. By Washington Researchers Publishing. Washington D.C., Washington Researchers, 1992. 102p. index. $85.00pa. LC 86-659605. ISBN 1-56365-010-X. ISSN 1052-4134.

This work lists the names of country experts and their specialties and affiliations with their office addresses. Individuals have been arranged separately by foreign countries (including foreign embassy personnel in Washington, D.C.) and by U.S. institutions or agencies. Despite its sweepingly general title, the work actually has a rather narrow geographical and institutional pool of talent. The listings refer only to the Washington, D.C., area and cover talent found in various governmental bodies. Some of the people listed represent years of specialization, while some are (according to this reviewer's sources among independent researchers) mere functionaries. Excluded are various research organizations, including those connected with universities, and business and financial area specialists. But as a first stop for information about foreign opportunities, this book is potentially useful.

—Bogdan Mieczkowski

275. **World's Greatest Brands: An International Review by Interbrand.** New York, John Wiley, 1992. 255p. illus. index. $49.95. ISBN 0-471-57283-7.

This is a beautifully designed book on brands and branding. Interbrand has chosen more than 300 of the most distinctive brands from around the world. There has been no attempt at formal ranking of the brands, although the top 10 and top 50 are indicated by asterisks. Graphs compare brands in certain subject areas for international brands or in certain countries for national brands. These cover leadership, stability, market, internationality, trend, support, protection, and total, with symbols that show the ranking of the brand in each category.

Individual brands are described in detail, with their history and a picture of their logo. Illustrations, most of them in color, show the advertisements that make use of the logos. In some cases a logo is shown in various scripts and still remains recognizable, and logos are also shown as they have appeared over the years (some have gone unchanged). An index by brand name is provided at the end. In addition, there is advice on how to choose a brand name and how to register it and protect it as a trademark. This book will be most useful for those with a new product line who have to choose a name and a logo design. [R: LJ, Aug 92, p. 92]—**Barbara E. Brown**

Africa

276. **Transnational Corporations in South Africa: List of Companies with Investments and Disinvestments 1990.** New York, United Nations, 1991. 282p. $22.00pa. ISBN 92-1-104363-9. S/N E.91.II.A.9.

This book provides a list of companies that have had or still have interests in South Africa. Table 1, which is 237 pages long, provides a list of companies that have divested themselves of their interests in South Africa. It is arranged alphabetically by country, then by company. For each entry are given the name of the company, sector, type of nonequity link (if known), method of disinvestment, and remarks. Table 2 provides a list of companies with equity interests in South Africa of more than 10 percent. Arranged alphabetically by country, this table gives the name of the company and the sector.

This book was compiled by the United Nations Centre on Transnational Corporations from publicly available material such as annual reports, directories, specialized publications, and business newspapers and magazines. It is current as of January 31, 1991, and updates previous lists published in 1985, 1988, and 1989. It is a very useful and reliable source for those seeking this information.

—**Barbara E. Brown**

277. **The Urban Informal Sector in Africa in Retrospect and Prospect: An Annotated Bibliography.** Washington, D.C., International Labor Office, 1991. 86p. index. (International Labour Bibliography, no.10). $14.00pa. ISBN 92-2-107747-0. ISSN 1010-8106.

Who better to compile a bibliography of the informal sector in African cities than the International Labor Office (ILO)? The present work has 188 entries, all annotated—some quite extensively (200 or more words)—and arranged in 10 "chapters." With very few exceptions the coverage is from 1980 to 1991. Most of these chapters contain lists for additional reading, and each has a brief introduction. There are author, subject, and geographical (country only) indexes; from the last we learn that 44 African countries are represented.

By and large, the items included consist of the publications of the ILO and other international organizations. Page numbers are not included in references to articles, which will hinder researchers in acquiring these materials efficiently. Otherwise, in terms of mechanics, the bibliography is exemplary.

There is a hint, though, that the work was compiled largely (if not solely) on the basis of database searching. We are told that it was compiled "within a short period of three to four months" (p. vi), and there is an unusually frequent recurrence of the phrase "informal sector" in the titles cited. It would seem likely that the concept would also turn up in many articles without necessarily appearing in the title of those articles. However, this is a useful source—particularly for the annotations—on the subject at hand. [R: Choice, Feb 92, p. 880]—**David Henige**

Asia

278. **The China Business Directory 1992.** New York, Asiatic Publishing, 1992. 361p. $149.00pa. ISBN 0-9625143-0-6.

This directory has been published annually since 1985. According to the publisher, it covers 15,000 Chinese companies grouped under 40 broad categories, from accounting to travel services. About 60 percent of the listings have been revised or updated, and there are also 1,000 new entries. In the main directory each listing includes company name; address; telephone, fax, telex, and cable numbers; management personnel; products; and services. Four appendixes list foreign companies in China and Chinese firms in Europe, Hong Kong and Macau, and in North America. (The appendix that lists foreign companies is new.) Unlike in the main directory, the listings in the appendixes are not grouped by category, making it difficult to find companies in a particular type of business. Overall, this directory provides more information than the *China Phone Book and Address Directory* (see ARBA 85, entry 93) and is more up-to-date than *Trade Contacts in China* (see ARBA 89, entry 246) and *China Directory of Industry and Commerce and Economic Annual* (see ARBA 84, entry 716).—**Hwa-Wei Lee**

279. **Directory, 1991-1992: Japanese-Affiliated Companies in USA & Canada.** Tokyo, Japan External Trade Organization; distr., Detroit, Gale, 1991. 821p. maps. index. $150.00pa. ISBN 4-8224-0514-1.

This directory lists almost 10,000 Japanese-affiliated companies with operations in North America. All fields except religion are covered (although at least one religious organization was found on page 260), including subsidiaries of companies. Puerto Rico is included, but Guam is not. Fields represented include medical and law offices, travel agencies, tour operators, local transport, land development, real estate, construction, restaurants, hotels, insurance, accounting, distributors, and golf courses. Naturally, import, export, and trading companies; banking; and manufacturing also appear. The entries are highly abbreviated but informative. The main part of the directory is divided into the United States (by state) and Canada (by province or territory). Additionally, there are lists of companies (arranged by country) by product category, an alphabetical list of the companies included in the directory, and a separate list of sources of information on Japan (e.g., governmental, chambers of commerce, industry and trade associations, Japan societies). This work is excellent for contacts, whether on a local or national level. [R: CLJ, June 92, p. 241]—**Bogdan Mieczkowski**

280. **Inside Japanese Support 1992: Descriptive Profiles and Other Information....** Katherine E. Jankowski, ed. Rockville, Md., Taft Group; distr., Detroit, Gale, 1992. 250p. index. $195.00pa. ISBN 1-879784-20-3. ISSN 1058-8671.

Inside Japanese Support contains a guide to funding of research and educational programs, profiles of major Japanese foundations and their grant-making activities, and profiles of contribution programs administered by major United States subsidiaries and affiliates of Japanese companies. The first descriptive section of the volume provides information on the history and current status of Japanese foundations. It contains aggregate data, where available, on their historical growth, types of donors, assets at the disposal of foundations, and grants programs; there is separate data on grants that promote international exchanges. A glossary is included. Indexes, found in the second section, cover companies by state of headquarters, operating location, grant types (particularly useful), nonmonetary support type, recipient type (another good indicator for prospective applicants), major products or industry, Japanese parent company, officers and directors, and grant recipients by state.

This work is useful for any educational or research institution as a guide to potential sources of grants. It provides enough information about making applications, additional inquiries, and past giving performance to be of sufficient assistance to grant seekers.—**Seiko Mieczkowski**

281. **Major Companies of the Far East and Australasia 1991/92. Volume 1: South East Asia.** 8th ed. Jennifer L. Carr, ed. London, Graham & Trotman; distr., Detroit, Gale, 1991. 342p. index. $1030.00/set. ISBN 1-85333-604-1. ISSN 0961-3226.

This work is part of an 11-volume set that covers major (and some medium) companies throughout the world. In each case information includes address; telephone, fax, and telex numbers; names and titles of directors and senior executives; principal activities; subsidiaries and parent company; principal banks; number of employers; dates of establishment; and, where available, key financial data. Companies are listed alphabetically and indexed in three ways: alphabetically for all of southeast Asia, alphabetically within each country of southeast Asia, and alphabetically by business activity by country in southeast Asia. Lists of companies on disk, labels, or hardcopy printouts (e.g., telephone, fax, and telex numbers) are available. Information is supplied largely by the listed companies, and the editors check the data received to ensure accuracy.

Major Companies of the Far East and Australasia is updated and published each year. It would be useful to provide data about company size—perhaps the number of employees—in future editions. Also, users may find summary data on a country or industry to be of interest. This volume has one small flaw: the index page references are consistently off by two pages; thus, an entry indicated as being on page 101 will actually be found on page 103.—**William C. Struning**

Europe

282. **The Book of European Forecasts.** London, Euromonitor; distr., Detroit, Gale, 1992. 311p. $295.00. 658.8094. ISBN 0-86338-401-3.

This work provides an excellent overview of the possible changes in European markets in the coming years. A good introduction describes the scope of the handbook, the methodologies used, and the nature of forecasting. A 40-page essay describes various trends and events that will influence European markets, such as environmental issues, the unification of Germany, the fragmentation of the Soviet Union, changes in Eastern Europe, and the development of a single European market. The data sections cover more than 110 pages and include figures and charts on the sales of various goods and services as well as basic demographic and trade statistics. A 12-page section gives country-by-country responses to 10 questions on social, political, and economic issues, such as the possibility of a single European currency and the political unification of Europe. The final section of the work is a country-by-country directory of sources for forecast data; this includes addresses; telephone, telex, and fax numbers; and descriptions of the major publications.

Although expensive, this work compiles and clearly presents information not available elsewhere. It is definitely recommended to libraries that serve patrons interested in European business, economics, and politics.—**Richard H. Swain**

283. **Consumer Eastern Europe 1992.** London, Euromonitor; distr., Detroit, Gale, 1992. 300p. $550.00. ISBN 0-86338-423-4.

The revolutions in Eastern Europe in 1989 and 1990 have created a fertile ground for new business marketing initiatives and have started to yield a series of specialized reference sources in support of these efforts. *Consumer Eastern Europe* is a surprisingly rich resource that provides demographic and economic data that goes far beyond the scope of most "marketing" reference sources. Data is provided for Bulgaria, Czechoslovakia, Eastern Germany, Hungary, Poland, Romania, the former Soviet Union, and the former Yugoslavia. The volume is primarily intended to be a statistical sourcebook and, as such, does not present much analysis of business trends in these nations. Most of the data was gathered from 1988-1990, although for some categories the latest figures are from the early 1980s. A section on regional marketing parameters provides statistics on economic growth, employment, income, inflation rates, trade, and consumer expenditures. Another major section focuses on 13

consumer markets, giving consumption data for categories such as food, clothing, electrical appliances, personal goods, automotives, and tourism. There is brief background information and economic analysis in the introductory chapter; some trends are considered, new regional groupings are anticipated, and the future is tentatively charted. This will be an extremely useful reference tool for most business and academic libraries, as it pulls together much hard-to-find data. [R: LJ, 1 Oct 92, p. 78]
—Thomas A. Karel

284. Didik, Frank X., ed. **Eastern European Business Directory: A Guide to More Than 8,000 of the Largest Businesses, Commercial Enterprises, and Special Interest Associations....** Detroit, Gale, 1992. 962p. $275.00. HF3500.7.A48E23. 338'.0029'447. LC 92-13756. ISBN 0-8103-8401-9.

This directory is a must for any businessperson who wants to establish relations with the new, potentially rewarding market for Western goods or production facilities in the former communist countries. The coverage of more than 8,000 enterprises extends from agriculture and defense through tourist and business services and trade representatives. The wealth of business categories reveals, among others, substantive interest by several Japanese trading companies; the rich and varied industrial and service potential of the region; and facilities for foreign businesses, such as translation, financial, and computer services.

The introductory material is clear and helpful. The main part of the volume covers five East European countries and "western USSR," which includes even Vladivostok and Siberian locations. It is divided into three sections that list businesses by product and service categories, by geographical location (subdivided into regions and cities), and alphabetically. All entries give address; telephone, telex, and fax numbers; and main activities, while some include additional information. A final part of the directory provides the same three sections for the former East Germany. Although the book contains some minor spelling errors, it is informative and very useful. Highly recommended. [R: Choice, Apr 92, pp. 1206-08; RQ, Summer 92, pp. 567-68]—**Bogdan Mieczkowski**

285. **European Advertising Marketing and Media Data 1992: A Directory and Sourcebook.** 2d ed. London, Euromonitor; distr., Detroit, Gale, 1992. 771p. $390.00. ISBN 0-86338-412-9.

This substantive volume has almost 900 tables that provide a wealth of useful information. Its outstanding feature is the large amount of data on Eastern Europe and the integration of that information into the book. All country data are brought up to 1990, with trends indicated for the last four to seven years. A European overview that introduces the volume details the trends in advertising and lists the main companies, regulations, agencies, and regions. The first principal part of the volume consists of statistical tables. The section on pan-European comparisons gives the key economic indicators for all countries, population data with emphasis on markets, consumer spending, trends in advertising expenditures, and information on the media. Sections on individual countries provide information on marketing geography, marketing data (demographics, economic indicators, spending and ownership of key durables, retail sales, and market size), advertising data, and media data. The second principal part of the volume lists comprehensive information on advertising agencies by countries, with the top 10 featured separately; leading newspaper and magazine publishers and other media operators; advertising, marketing, and business associations; and market research companies. The volume concludes with advertising regulations, both pan-European and by country. The usefulness of this reference source is particularly strong for non-European marketing units, for all businesses that seek the European market or that intend to increase their sales on that market, and for schools of business and communications. Highly recommended.—**Bogdan Mieczkowski**

286. **European Compendium of Marketing Information.** London, Euromonitor; distr., Detroit, Gale, 1992. 421p. index. $335.00pa. ISBN 0-863-38440-4.

This work provides a splendid opportunity to obtain a broad overview of trends in consumer purchasing in the countries of Europe. Because the amount of detail is limited, broad patterns emerge for product/service groups that permit comparison among countries. Most of the book consists of analyses of 50 consumer markets—related groups of products and services, such as snack foods, small electrical appliances, and car rental. Preceding these analyses is a section on marketing parameters (demographic, socioeconomic, and retailing trends) to provide perspective in evaluating the performance of a particular product/service group. More than 300 tables summarize key data and contain source notes if a reader requires further details. A table of contents, a list of tables, and a subject index facilitate the location of information on a specific topic. Although categorized as a directory, the book is so well presented and edited that browsing is invited.—**William C. Struning**

287. **European Consultants Directory.** Karin E. Koek, ed. Detroit, Gale, 1992. 1038p. index. $225.00. ISBN 0-8103-8313-6. ISSN 1060-1880.

This text attempts to do for a new Europe what its companion volume, *Consultants and Consulting Organizations Directory* (CCOD) (see ARBA 92, entry 128), does for North America. Unlike its English-speaking cousin, the *European Consultants Directory* (ECD) provides the book's highlights; an introduction; and a user's guide in English, French, and German. The substance of the book, though, is in English. The book covers 34 geopolitical divisions within a less-divided Europe, including the new Russian republic, the former Eastern Europe, and Latvia. Information from some countries is more plentiful than from others; agency listings total more than 5,000, but 9 of the countries have a description for only a single organization.

The organization descriptions are grouped geographically by country, then subdivided by the 14 major subject headings used in CCOD plus a general consultants category. A subject terms master list provides a more detailed understanding of the occupations that these headings include. Unfortunately, the user's guide fails to explain the master list. The geographic section also lists branch offices in most countries and refers readers to the appropriate main office for a full description. In addition to location and consulting activities, two nice features in the descriptions are the language competencies and geographic areas that firms serve. Indexes to key personnel, consulting activities, and firm names provide cross-references to the main descriptive information. Another useful tool is the appendix of U.S. consulates, embassies, and trade administrations.

For those familiar with CCOD, the similarities between it and its European companion will make ECD easy to comprehend. This text will be an excellent addition to any business library—academic, public, or special—that serves a clientele with international interests. [R: LJ, July 92, p. 76]
—**Susan D. Baird-Joshi**

288. **The European Directory of Consumer Brands and Their Owners 1992.** London, Euromonitor; distr., Detroit, Gale, 1992. 823p. index. $335.00. 380.1029. ISBN 0-86338-465-X.

After an introduction that points out the value of product brands as company assets, this directory provides an alphabetical listing, by country, of more than 12,500 European brands. A major section of the directory lists brands and their owners by product sector, ranging from alcoholic drinks, bakery products, breakfast cereals, and consumer electronics to tobacco products. Another valuable section offers alphabetical lists of European brand-owning companies. Each entry gives the company name and address followed by its telephone, telex, and fax numbers. A brief indication of the company's recent financial performance and a list of its brands are included.

Researchers may find the directory's format confusing: product categories in section 5 (Europe's leading brands) and section 6 (European market size breakdown) do not match each other or the product sector classifications used earlier in the book. In addition, the directory title fails to indicate its major limitation: it deals only with Western European countries. Nevertheless, with current emphasis on improving U.S. competitiveness in foreign trade, researchers and business organizations will find this work to be an important reference source.—**Renee B. Horowitz**

289. **European Markets: A Guide to Company and Industry Information Sources.** 4th ed. By Washington Researchers Publishing. Washington, D.C., Washington Researchers, 1992. 598p. index. $275.00pa. LC 82-62886. ISBN 1-56365-012-6. ISSN 1044-9280.

According to Lester Thurow of MIT, Europe is the main future competitor of the United States. Consequently, the importance of this book for United States users lies in its ability to identify new and existing markets in Europe, to inform about European competitors in United States and European markets, and to locate appropriate trade partners. The emphasis is on sources of information rather than on information itself (Washington Researchers specializes in identifying such sources in their various publications).

This volume has three parts. The first indicates organizational sources of information, from the Congress, the Library of Congress, the Government Printing Office, and the like, to the U.S. International Trade Commission and the U.S. Trade Representative. When appropriate, there are lists of local offices; ports; international organizations; and private sector organizations, such as banks, business associations, universities, and information services. Part 2 contains published sources and databases, including a compendious directory of the latter, while part 3 lists information sources for individual countries in the European Community and the European Free Trade Association, with separate lists of publications for each country. The form and amount of information provided are both convenient and useful, including telephone and fax numbers, local holidays, and brief descriptions of the kind of data obtainable from individual sources. The index includes subjects. Highly recommended for researchers and business organizations. — **Bogdan Mieczkowski**

290. Fraser, Robert, ed. **Western European Economic Organizations: A Comprehensive Guide.** Harlow, England, Longman Group; distr., Detroit, Gale, 1992. 448p. index. $145.00. ISBN 0-582-06845-2.

This book covers the overall economic position of Western Europe both internationally and from a regional context. The political, economic, and structural conditions are given for Austria, Belgium, Denmark, Finland, France, Germany, Greece, Iceland, Ireland, Italy, Liechtenstein, Luxembourg, the Netherlands, Norway, Portugal, Spain, Sweden, Switzerland, and the United Kingdom. There is also a section on international organizations. The work describes the country's history, principal personnel, organizations, and objectives. It also provides details about major institutions that helped to shape the economic policy (e.g., principal ministries, the stock exchange, political parties). For each of these it gives the history, structure, personnel, aims, and objectives in factual outline style. Telephone and fax numbers are listed. The book is current to the end of 1991. Recommended for anyone interested in understanding the complexity of the rapidly changing economic conditions of European countries.
— **Herbert W. Ockerman**

291. Newman, Oksana, and Allan Foster, comps. **European Business Rankings: Lists of Companies, Products, Services and Activities....** Detroit, Gale, 1992. 437p. index. $140.00. ISBN 1-873477-00-7.

This book compiles data from hundreds of business sources, including periodicals, financial services, and directories. The compilers then rank this information, listing the top 10 under each of the various subject categories. With prefaces in three languages — English, French, and German — and an outline of the contents to help, the serious researcher will find information easily accessible. Throughout the volume, categories are organized alphabetically, and they are followed by a comprehensive index that includes company names and countries, as well as subject headings. Thus, the researcher whose primary interest is in a specific corporation can use the index to look up that company. Du Pont, for example, is listed under the following subject headings: Capital Market; Chemical Industries, International; Companies, International; Corporate Mergers and Acquisitions — Finland; Industry, International; and Paint Industry, International. Sources for all data follow each list of rankings.

In addition to its value for business researchers, this book will provide browsers with a fascinating view of European industry at a time when interest in the European Economic Community is high. Further, this careful compilation underlies the internationality of corporations today. [R: LJ, 1 Sept 92, p. 166; RBB, 1 Nov 92, pp. 546-47] — **Renee B. Horowitz**

292. **Short-Term Economic Statistics: Central and Eastern Europe. Statistiques Economiques a Court Term.** Washington, D.C., OECD Publications and Information Center, 1992. 390p. $32.00pa. ISBN 92-64-03523-0.

This statistical compendium has been compiled by the Centre for Co-operation with the European Economies in Transition, created in March 1990 by the OECD (Organization for Economic Cooperation and Development), an international organization composed of 24 developed market economies. To help the postcommunist countries of Bulgaria, the Czech and Slovak federal republics, Hungary, Poland, and Romania, these short-term statistics (monthly and quarterly) will enable specialists to determine trends and tendencies in the development of these struggling economies that would be difficult to ascertain by studying annual data.

The book is published in the two official languages of the OECD, English and French. It opens with a discussion of general, mainly methodological, issues, followed by general tables and charts that contain data on area, population, and annual economic indexes from 1980 to 1990. Subsequent chapters are devoted to separate countries in alphabetical order. Each of these chapters is composed of two parts: sources and methods, and the statistical tables. The material covered is limited to indexes that represent changes in the output of mining, manufacturing, construction, and energy sectors. Data on the agriculture and service sectors are lacking. Absolute figures are provided for such items as coal, natural gas, steel, and cement. Other absolute figures pertain to housing construction, domestic trade, employment, wages, and salaries. Next follow the fluctuations in the Consumer Price Index. The money supply and bank deposits are given in domestic currencies. The statistics close with the variations in exchange rates against the U.S. dollar, foreign currency reserves, foreign debt, and foreign trade. The book will be useful to economics professors and researchers. — **Zbigniew Mieczkowski**

293. **SIBD 92-93: The Business Directory for the Soviet Region.** Washington, D.C., FYI Information Services, 1992. 2v. index. $240.00pa./set. ISBN 0-9632263-0-4. ISSN 1052-8156.

The editors claim that this set is the fullest business directory of the Soviet region. Giving the chaotic circumstances of the area, it can be counted as a major accomplishment, and no doubt it will help Western businesspeople orient themselves in the region. The information in the volumes is organized into an alphabetical list of enterprises, an index of products, a business activity index, a geographical index, an index of leaders, and the 500 largest enterprises. On another level, however, the directory represents the confusion of the collapsed Soviet Union. Although business may be the wave of the future in the newly liberated lands of the East, the editors, by calling this work "The Business Directory for the Soviet Region," have committed a politically retrograde step. In spite of the title, the set is very Russian centered, and no respect is shown for the alphabets and languages of the newly independent countries. A major editorial cleanup is necessary for the next edition. — **Andrew Ezergailis**

294. **Ukraine Top 100 Exporters.** Washington, D.C., FYI Information Resources, 1991. 87p. $75.00pa.

In recent years Eastern Europe has shared an increased number of business activities, and contacts with Western countries have shown substantial gains. This is especially true of the former Soviet Union. As a result, many business directories have been published, including this one, prepared by the Information Industry Association Sistema-Reserve.

According to the preface, it comprises more than 100 of the largest key state enterprises registered for foreign trade. Each entry provides name, address, key officials, main products, value of sales and export, and size of labor force. However, information is almost two years old and for all practical purposes obsolete. Names of corporation, officers, and even cities are Russified. Some street names, such as "Lenin Street" and "Chekistov Street," no longer exist (they were changed a long time ago). Acquisitions planned are only for 1991.

This directory needs to be used with caution. In general, current information about business activities in Ukraine can be obtained from a number of newspapers and newsletters (with some published in English) and *Ukrainian Business Digest*. — **Bohdan S. Wynar**

295. Valverde, Antonio Martin. **European Employment and Industrial Relations Glossary: Spain.** London, Sweet and Maxwell; distr., Lanham, Md., UNIPUB, 1991. 247p. index. $35.00pa. ISBN 0-421-44840-7.

As the third glossary in a series that will cover all of the European Community (EC) member countries, this volume attempts to define major terms from the field of industrial relations. The purpose is not to translate the terms from Spanish to English but "to communicate the substantive importance of the institutions and processes described."

After two alphabetical lists of entries, one in Spanish and one in English, a comprehensive introduction discusses employment and industry in Spain. Topics include the formation of Spain's system of industrial relations, its economic context and legal framework, collective bargaining and industrial conflict, and the role of the Spanish government. A number of tables provide data in areas such as employment and salaries.

The glossary, which is the main part of the work, includes concepts and issues that help in understanding the economic and social context of Spanish industry. However, of the hundreds of terms, many, such as "absentismo—absenteeism," seem unnecessary. Other entries, particularly the summaries of laws that affect industry and the lists of government departments and institutes with industrial responsibilities, could prove valuable to researchers interested in the EC and Spain's potential role.—**Renee B. Horowitz**

Great Britain

296. **Industrial Research in the United Kingdom: A Guide to Organizations and Programmes.** 14th ed. Harlow, England, Longman Group; distr., Detroit, Gale, 1992. 543p. index. $255.00. ISBN 0-582-08273-0.

This guide is a directory of research and development (R&D) centers and funding bodies in the United Kingdom. The R&D laboratories covered are in the fields of science and technology; other areas of research, such as social science or management, are generally beyond the scope of this book. A major purpose of the work is to locate experts in various technical fields.

The first four chapters cover R&D laboratories. These entries are fully annotated, with many having lengthy descriptions of research activity as well as budget, contact persons, number of research staff, and some client names. The last two chapters cover associations, giving only address, telephone, and fax number. Fortunately, the indexing is extremely detailed and complete, making it possible to quickly locate organizations that specialize in such specific topics as AIDS or thyristors. Otherwise, since this book is arranged by organization type rather than subject, it could prove hard to use. The chapter on universities and polytechnics covers university research by department, giving many faculty names, and is by far the longest chapter in the book. Information is a little more sketchy on some of the industrial firms, perhaps reflecting the fact that what they do is proprietary in nature.

This title seems to be a useful, well-researched one for all who need R&D contacts in the United Kingdom. Entries are densely written and chock-full of information.—**Susan V. McKimm**

297. Terry, Michael, and Linda Dickens. **European Employment and Industrial Relations Glossary: United Kingdom.** London, Sweet and Maxwell; distr., Lanham, Md., UNIPUB, 1991. 261p. index. $35.00pa. ISBN 92-826-2600-8.

As one of the inaugural volumes in a series, this glossary is a useful reference work about British industrial relations. A comparable glossary will be produced for each of the 12 European Community member states based on a recognized "need for clarity and mutual understanding" (preface) across borders. The series, funded by the European Foundation for the Improvement of Living and Working Conditions, will present an important alternative to polyglot dictionaries that translate but do not explain.

The range of topics covered includes British industrial relations, employment law, and labor markets. An informative introductory essay discusses the history of British industrial relations since the end of World War II. The 812 entries, arranged alphabetically, offer more than simple definitions; most contain jargon-free explanations of terms, leaving the reader with a basic understanding of the institution or process discussed. Entries contain numerous cross-references that help to highlight interchangeable terms. The glossary covers the entire United Kingdom, and most terms can be applied in all locations; however, a few technical differences are cited where appropriate.

Particularly noteworthy is the inclusion of many important British labor laws and acts with which foreigners may not be familiar. The majority of terms are recognizable to North Americans, but terms such as "London weighting" (higher pay for London residents) or "golden hello" (a one-time bonus to entice someone into employment) are not as well known. Supplementary materials include statistical tables, a short bibliography, and an index. The primary audiences for this and other volumes in the series are students, researchers, and practitioners of labor relations in all countries.—**Kerranne G. Biley**

298. **Who's Who in Business and Industry in the UK 1991.** Juliet Margetts, ed. Chicago, St. James Press; distr., Detroit, Gale, [1991]. 964p. index. $250.00. LC 90-64379. ISBN 1-55862-155-5.

This reference contains almost 10,000 entries that include companies in distribution, advertising and consulting, chambers of trade, senior civil servants in the Department of Industry, trade associations and unions, and leading industrial journalists and academics. (Banking and insurance companies are not included because they can be located in other reference works.) Some of the longer entries include such things as dates and positions held, education, personal data, professional organizations, and types of recreation. The work has a companies index that includes addresses, communication numbers, and senior executive officers; a sector index that breaks companies down into services or products they provide; and a regional index that lists companies by geographical location. This monumental undertaking will be extremely valuable for people doing business with the larger companies in the United Kingdom. — **Herbert W. Ockerman**

LABOR

Bibliography

299. **Labour and Population Programme: An Annotated Bibliography.** Washington, D.C., International Labor Office, 1991. 209p. index. (International Labour Bibliography, no.11). $22.00pa. ISBN 92-2-107748-9.

For anyone interested in International Labor Office (ILO) publications, this bibliography provides a list of materials that are located in the ILO Central Library so that they can be borrowed, if not purchased. About 500 ILO titles, including monographs, books, and journals, published between 1972 and 1990 are indexed. The ILO Labordoc database was the basis for production of this bibliography, which supersedes the one published in 1982. The four divisions cover labor and population programs; ILO series; population and family welfare education in the work setting; and reports from meetings, seminars, and workshops, divided by areas of the world. Each entry has the title in boldface type and includes author, imprint, ISBN, indexing descriptors that give a brief explanation of content, language, and some prices. An author index is provided, but there is no subject index, so locating a publication on a particular topic is difficult. Libraries interested in international labor material will find this bibliography useful for collection development. — **Jean Herold**

300. Weiss, Carla M., comp. **Plant Closings: A Selected Bibliography of Materials Published 1986 through 1990.** Ithaca, N.Y., ILR Press, 1991. 85p. index. $8.95pa. Z7164.U56W46. 016.3386'042. LC 91-8328. ISBN 0-87546-801-2.

This bibliography is an update to an earlier, similarly titled work that covered material published through 1985 (see ARBA 89, entry 231). Following the same pattern, the entries include citations to books, dissertations, government reports, working papers, journal articles, and labor union publications. The emphasis is on public policy, research policy, and case studies.

The 347 entries, arranged alphabetically by author, are numbered, and each has subject headings that are related to topics associated with plant closings. To find information on a specific topic, the subject index must be consulted. That index includes state names as part of a form entry (e.g., Geographic Locations Study — United States — Utah). Inverted entries are used for industries (e.g., Industry, Chemical). No company names are indexed, and no cross-references are given. An author index is also provided.

While the book is useful as a starting point when researching this topic, one should be aware that the citations are intended to be comprehensive only for materials in the Cornell University Library System. If the original bibliography is owned, this inexpensive update should be considered for addition to the library's collection. — **Jean Herold**

Dictionaries

301. **Dictionary of Occupational Titles.** 4th ed. By U.S. Department of Labor Employment and Training Administration. Lanham, Md., Bernan Press, 1991. 2v. index. $49.95/set. LC 91-76504. ISBN 0-89059-000-1.

In 1939 the U.S. Department of Labor published the first edition of this dictionary (DOT) to provide standardized occupational information. Each new edition documented the changes in U.S. job characteristics. This reprint of the Labor Department's revised 4th edition reflects the rapid technological advances in the United States. The changing job market makes this an important source of information for anyone associated with personnel work and job placement. It also gives insight into training needs, career guidance, and wage restructuring.

All of the job definitions are in volume 1 and are arranged by numeric code, cascading from one digit (broad categories) to nine digits (specific jobs). As an example, the first three digits in entry 301.137-010 indicate that this job is "Housekeeper, Home." The second three digits are worker functions in relation to data, people, and things. The last three digits distinguish this job from all others. At the end of the job definition is a definition trailer that uses letters and numbers to indicate the last update of information, the time required to learn the job, and the education needed. Volume 2 contains a glossary of technical terms and appendixes that explain the meaning of various designations. An alphabetical index of occupational titles and an index of the titles arranged by industry are also provided.

This hardback reprint of the paperback Labor Department publication costs about $6. Hardback editions are preferable for any library. Another advantage of this publication is the separate volume of indexes and appendixes instead of having definitions split as in the original publication. The new version of the DOT is a welcome addition to academic and public libraries because it includes all the supplements and provides up-to-date information on U.S. jobs. — **Jean Herold**

302. Tracey, William R. **The Human Resources Glossary.** New York, AMACOM; distr., Detroit, Gale, 1991. 416p. index. $49.95. HF5549.A23T73. 658.3'003. LC 90-56195. ISBN 0-8144-5011-3.

This volume includes more than 3,000 terms central to major human resource management responsibilities such as benefits, recruitment and hiring, communications, training, employee development, labor-management relations, organizational design and development, and testing. It includes entries for common human resources abbreviations and acronyms as well as relevant laws and regulations. There are definitions of key terms from areas such as finance, computer science, law, marketing, and education. In addition, names, addresses, purposes, and other pertinent data are provided for more than 130 associations and societies of interest to human resource practitioners.

The work is divided into two parts. The body of the glossary contains acronyms, abbreviations, and terms arranged alphabetically. The entries range in length from a single line to paragraphs of about 20 lines. *See* and *see also* references are liberally supplied. The next section consists of an index to key terms that is designed to assist the user in recalling or locating terms in a given area of interest. Entries are arranged under 45 main headings. Comprehensive, well organized, and up-to-date, this tool should be a boon to human resource professionals and others who wish to obtain a definition to answer questions related to the human resources field. Recommended for public, special, and academic library collections. — **Helen Howard**

Directories

303. **The Hidden Job Market: A Job Seeker's Guide to America's 2,000 Little-Known, Fastest-Growing High-Tech Companies.** Compiled by CorpTech. Princeton, N.J., Peterson's Guides, 1991. 268p. index. $16.95pa. HF5382.7.H53. 620'.0023'73. LC 91-29096. ISBN 1-56079-110-1.

Today's bleak economy has forced more people to compete for fewer jobs. This directory of high-growth manufacturers and developers of technology products may give some job seekers a head start on the competition. Although the 2,000 firms included were selected from CorpTech's database, the entries are more geared toward job seekers than that company's annual publication, *Corporate Technology Directory* (see ARBA 89, entry 211). In addition to address and telephone and fax numbers, *The Hidden Job Market* lists for each company the number of employees, number of job openings in the past year, percentage of employment growth, year founded, sales, and line of business. The firms are listed by state and cover a wide range of industries, including biotechnology, computers, environment, medical, telecommunications, and transportation. Two indexes list companies by industry and name.

The introduction gives readers job-seeking tips on identifying, contacting, and interviewing with potential employers.

The Hidden Job Market should only be used as a guide, because the current economy may have rendered some figures (e.g., number of job openings, annual sales) out of date since CorpTech last interviewed the companies. The companies are mostly smaller, privately held firms, which often present the greatest difficulty when doing company research. The work is a welcome addition to any library's high-tech career materials. [R: RBB, 15 Apr 92, p. 1531] – **Kerranne G. Biley**

304. Kuman, Arthur, Jr., and Richard D. Salmon. **The Job Hunter's Guide to 100 Great American Cities: A National Employment Directory.** Latham, N.Y., Brattle Communications, 1991. 117p. $17.95pa. LC 91-070424. ISBN 0-918938-04-X.

Serious job hunting requires thorough research well before the all-important interview. The authors of this guide have pulled together key information on 100 U.S. cities to help lessen the legwork of job seekers. Expanding *The Job Hunter's Guide to Eight Great American Cities* (see ARBA 79, entry 864), this guide now includes information on at least one city in each state. The preface states that the authors selected cities that offer diverse employment opportunities and an appealing quality of life.

Each city's one-page profile includes information on population, average housing price, unemployment rate, climate, public transportation, and attractions, as well as a brief overview of the city's economic outlook. Perhaps the most useful part of the profile is the list of local publications and organizations. Federal, state, and local employment offices; chambers of commerce; and libraries are also supplied. Special offices for women, minorities, disabled persons, veterans, and senior citizens are listed for most cities. Where available, the authors have included an address for obtaining a relocation packet. In addition, major employers (not necessarily the largest) in each city are provided, with address, telephone number, and line of business. While the format is concise, the reader is supplied with enough information to start researching employment in a given city. The section "How to Get a Good Job in Tough Times!" is an excellent, although brief, overview of the job search process; it includes a bibliography. The informal style of writing will appeal to a wide audience. – **Kerranne G. Biley**

305. Marsh, Arthur. **Trade Union Handbook: A Guide and Directory to the Structure, Membership, Policy and Personnel of the British Trade Unions.** 5th ed. Brookfield, Vt., Gower Publishing, 1991. 424p. $83.50. HD6663.M37. 331.88'0941. LC 91-25138. ISBN 0-566-02975-8.

This manual and directory is a well-done, factually dense work. It will be an important reference source for industrial relations collections with client interest in British, international, or comparative concerns. Compiled by an Emeritus Fellow at St. Edmund's Hall, Oxford, the book is divided into four parts. In the first part there is a series of background essays (with numerous statistical tables) plus a description and listing of the Trades Union Congress, related bodies, and officers. Articles deal with union membership, structure, finance, governance, and legal status. Material appears to be current as of late 1990 or early 1991; the departure of Margaret Thatcher as Prime Minister is mentioned, but John Major does not figure significantly. Statistics end in 1988 or 1989. The second part is divided between directories of international union organizations and of British union associations. The third part, the main directory, lists and characterizes individual unions and also gives a roster of acronyms. Besides address and telephone number, the directories in the second and third parts usually indicate named officers – for large unions down to regional level – and some affiliations. The fourth part is a directory of "other industrial relations institutions." This is a must buy for organizations with relevant constituencies. – **Nigel Tappin**

306. Spomer, Cynthia Russell, ed. **American Directory of Organized Labor: Unions, Locals, Agreements, and Employers.** Detroit, Gale, 1992. 1638p. index. $275.00. ISBN 0-8103-8360-8.

The *American Directory of Organized Labor* (ADOL) provides information on the organizations that make up the U.S. labor movement, as well as descriptions of selected collective bargaining agreements that these organizations have negotiated with employers. The ADOL is divided into four major sections. The first section provides fairly detailed information about 230 national or parent labor organizations. Included in each union's profile are addresses and telephone numbers; organizational data; information about key officials; union financial data; a discussion of the union's history and background; and sections on present activities, current agreements, and special services provided by the union. Section 2 has contact information for nearly 40,000 regional, state, and local labor organizations. The last two sections provide general information on 1,500 current bargaining agreements. Section 3 lists these agreements by union and section 4, by employer. The entries in the directory are indexed by industry, by state and city, by AFL-CIO affiliates, and by key words. Included is a helpful "how to use" section.

The ADOL is a convenient reference source for locating information about national unions, their subordinate bodies, and the contracts these organizations negotiate. The data has been gathered directly from unions and from government records and reports. Because of its nature, some of the information in the directory is already, or will quickly become, outdated. Relatively frequent updates of the directory will be necessary to keep it current. — **Paul F. Clark**

307. **Training and Development Organizations Directory: A Descriptive Guide to More Than 2,300 Firms, Institutes, Other Agencies, and Approximately 11,500 Training, Professional, and Personal Development Programs....** 5th ed. Janice McLean, ed. Detroit, Gale, 1991. 677p. index. $295.00. LC 81-643973. ISBN 0-8103-4349-5. ISSN 0278-5749.

Training and Development Organizations Directory (TDOD) lists more than 2,300 firms, institutes, and university programs that offer training and development programs and services for private organizations, government agencies, and individuals. A typical entry includes certain basic information about the organization: name, address, fax and telephone numbers, date of founding, staff size, principal officials, target audience, and course descriptions. The 5th edition has added a "Special Note" (e.g., information about additional consulting services) to some entries and has renamed the "Pre-produced Training Programs" section, "Packaged Training Programs." Entry information came from the firms, either by questionnaire or company publications.

The arrangement in this edition is alphabetical by firm name, followed by a geographic index, a personal name index, and a subject index thesaurus (2,000-plus terms) that will simplify the search for the correct term in the 600-term subject index. Selected topics illustrate the wide variety of today's training and development interests: administrative assistants, birth control, burnout, computer applications, counseling, human resource development, leadership, union relations, and women and employment.

This work provides useful descriptive information, making it worthy of consideration by libraries that serve corporate and governmental training managers and other personnel. It is to be remembered, however, that TDOD has not attempted to indicate the credentials of the persons named. Nor should users forget to consult area telephone books to see whether there are other trainers not listed in TDOD. — **Wiley J. Williams**

Handbooks and Yearbooks

308. Arden, Lynie. **The Work-at-Home Sourcebook.** 4th ed. Boulder, Colo., Live Oak; distr., Emeryville, Calif., Publishers Group West, 1992. 279p. illus. index. $14.95pa. HD2336.U5A73. 338.7'4'02573. LC 91-30758. ISBN 0-911781-09-9.

The only such guide in publication, this sourcebook on working from the home is well written and easy to read. As in previous editions (see ARBA 89, entry 223), Arden examines factors that affect the work force (e.g., technology), work styles (e.g., freelancing), and the employment process. A section on how to get started (e.g., regulations, restrictions) is followed by a job bank with listings in six topical areas (e.g., arts, crafts, computers). Companies appear alphabetically with address; available positions; experience and residency requirements; and provision of training, equipment, and earnings. Interspersed throughout are quotations, cartoons, and pictures of successful workers and entrepreneurs that illustrate both accomplishments and difficulties overcome (e.g., outdated zoning restrictions). The indexes are by company name, state, and activities for persons with disabilities. Several resource chapters identify books, periodicals, and accredited home-study courses.

This edition adds two useful sections on telecommuting and home business opportunities. These examine converting a present position into a work-at-home one through technology and buying into an existing business. Entries for the 150 franchise and turnkey opportunities, ranging from automotive to

travel, disclose franchise status and profit potential along with basic information. This source will prove a desirable addition to career development collections, especially in areas of high unemployment.
— **Sandra E. Belanger**

309. **The Encyclopedia of Career Choices for the 1990s: A Guide to Entry Level Jobs.** By Career Associates. New York, Walker, 1991. 862p. index. $75.00. HF5382.5.U5E46. 331.7'02'0973. LC 90-49527. ISBN 0-8027-1142-1.

This handbook profiles 42 fields such as broadcasting, data processing, and real estate. Each profile contains specific sections that describe various functions in the field, such as its administration, development, and research. Together these sections provide a broad, concise overview and the field's areas of specialty, giving the job outlook, geographic profile, qualifications, salaries and working conditions, and resources.

Although comparable information can be found in other sources, the presentation in this work is fresh and appealing. Written in an informal and energetic style, it gives somewhat less information than *The Encyclopedia of Careers and Vocational Guidance* (see ARBA 91, entry 374) and a different point of view than the *Occupational Outlook Handbook* (see ARBA 91, entry 249), but it fits the adult as well as the student career seeker. It extends the traditional coverage to qualifications, career paths, major employers, and key trade and professional associations. Where relevant, many profiles have information on intrapreneuring (positions that include the autonomy of the entrepreneur within the organizational structure). Interviews with individuals in the field are also supplied; they not only personalize the information but also serve to illustrate a range of personal interests and motivations and reveal interesting approaches to work life. Together, these aspects are likely to stimulate creative thinking about careers in ways that the other sources will not. This excellent guide to individuals seeking a first-time career or career change is highly recommended for schools, libraries, and career professionals at all levels. — **Barbara Conroy**

310. **Job Seeker's Guide to Private and Public Companies.** Charity Anne Dorgan and others, eds. Detroit, Gale, 1992. 4v. index. $350.00/set. ISBN 0-8103-7810-8. ISSN 1061-3285.

This guide is intended to serve as a resource for those seeking prospective employers in a particular region or industry. It is issued in four regional volumes, with each containing identical indexes that cover all volumes. Separate volumes can be purchased according to need. The more than 15,000 companies included are drawn from various ranking lists such as the Fortune 500 and the *Inc.* 500 (44 percent are private companies). Arrangement is geographical. The amount of information given for each company is highly variable but often includes address, date founded, type of company, subsidiaries and affiliated companies, business description, corporate officers, basic financial information, number of employees, and names of human resources contacts. The industry index lists company names under 300 or so primary industries, such as commercial fishing and child day-care services. This index has no cross-references. There are also a corporate name index and a "Job Titles Key to the Industry Index" that lists job titles and industries where such jobs may be found.

Coverage of companies in a particular region seems to be somewhat arbitrary; at least one company with only four employees is listed, and major employers such as IBM can not always be found by geographical location. General business directories such as *Ward's Business Directory of U.S. Private and Public Companies* (see ARBA 89, entry 160) give similar information on a far greater number of companies. *The Career Guide: Dun's Employment Opportunities Directory* (Dun's Marketing, 1991) gives much more information about the professional groups the companies are actively seeking as well as training opportunities and benefits information, but the number of companies included is far smaller. Perhaps *Job Seeker's Guide* would be of most use to libraries that either want a relatively inexpensive single-volume guide to their region, or to large libraries that can afford many alternative sources of information. [R: LJ, 15 Sept 92, pp. 60-62; RBB, 15 Oct 92, p. 456] — **Marit S. MacArthur**

311. Kleiman, Carol. **The 100 Best Job$ for the 1990s and Beyond.** Chicago, Dearborn Trade, 1992. 362p. index. $19.95pa. HF5382.75.U6K54. 331.7'02'0973. LC 92-256. ISBN 0-79310-420-3.

This is a useful addition to existing literature on careers, companies, and business opportunities. Knowledge is portrayed as a powerful tool that enhances job seeking through the 1990s. The first of two sections is an excellent overview of the changing workplace, its problems (e.g., illiteracy), developments (e.g., flexible scheduling), and globalism (e.g., overseas workers). The text, with success stories and folksy tips, is oversimplified in places. The discussion of disabled workers, for example, seems almost demeaning in tone, neglects newer terminology (e.g., mobility-impaired), and does not explain adequately what recent legislation means for employees with disabilities.

One hundred top careers are examined in part 2. The absence of page or chapter numbers in the list of positions necessitates the use of the index or cross-reference chart (chapter 8). Career segments focus on education, skills, employment outlook, career paths, and salaries (with projections to the year 2000). The intuitive analysis of the effect of educational level on employability and career advancement is most valuable; however, some industry combinations are confusing (e.g., radio/television technician within manufacturing, agriculture, and transportation), and sources for most quoted salary figures are lacking. Referral to resources on individual careers, beyond the meager bibliography provided, would correct deficiencies in both sections of the book.

This volume will attract a wide readership among those facing layoffs and a stagnant economy. It has a place in any career library along with more detailed works on resume production and the job search. [R: LJ, 1 Sept 92, pp. 186-88]—**Sandra E. Belanger**

312. Morgan, Hal, and Kerry Tucker. **Companies That Care: The Most Family-Friendly Companies in America—What They Offer and How They Got That Way.** New York, Simon & Schuster, 1991. 351p. index. $12.95pa. HF5549.5.D39M67. 331.25. LC 91-6655. ISBN 0-671-73598-5.

In order to attract and retain the best employees, companies are having to look beyond traditional benefits to family-supportive options, including flexible leave, flexible work policies, and child and elder care. *Companies That Care* examines the 124 firms that offer comprehensive family-supportive packages.

A general history of family benefits is presented along with a section of information for firms interested in starting or improving such a plan. The major portion of the book is composed of 16 in-depth profiles and 108 short (typically single-page) sketches. The profiles provide directory data, a brief policy statement, a history of the company's program development, and interviews with executives and employees. Indexes by company size, state, and industry provide quick access for job hunters.

The price is unbeatable, as is the service. This is a must for any library whose patrons may be job seeking or are trying to remain or become competitive employers.—**Bobray Bordelon**

313. **Trade Unions of the World 1992-93.** 3d ed. Revised by Martin Upham. Harlow, England, Longman Group; distr., Detroit, Gale, 1991. 579p. index. $130.00. ISBN 0-582-08194-7.

This updated and revised edition is an extremely valuable resource for anyone interested in the comparative study of industrial relations systems or labor organizations around the world. In a country-by-country format, 186 countries are profiled, ranging from highly developed capitalist nations to current and former members of the Marxist bloc to the countries of the largely undeveloped Third World.

Each entry provides a synopsis of the nature and status of that country's political and economic system. Most of the entries also supply a breakdown of the work force, usually giving specific data on the agriculture, industry, and service sectors within a nation's economy. Also included are sections on the industrial relations system in operation and on trade unionism. The first of these sections describes the legal framework within which labor-management relations are conducted and provides specific information as to whether the government has ratified relevant International Labor Organization Conventions within each nation. The trade unionism section discusses the evolution and current structure and status of the labor movement in each country. The most significant unions and labor federations are identified, and a useful synopsis of these groups is provided at the end of each entry, including addresses, current leaders, and membership levels.

A final section identifies the major worldwide organizations of national unions and national labor federations (the two largest being the International Confederation of Free Trade Unions and the World Federation of Trade Unions). It also provides information about membership levels and affiliates. A useful index has the acronyms of the major trade union centers for the nations included in the volume. Highly recommended, especially for academic and research collections with substantial holdings in economics and business.—**Paul F. Clark**

314. **Year Book of Labour Statistics 1991. Annuaire des Statistiques du Travail. Anuario de Estadisticas del Trabajo.** 50th ed. Washington, D.C., International Labor Office, 1991. 1132p. index. $120.00. ISBN 92-2-007339-0.

This reference work brings together in one volume vital data on conditions of work and employment for some 180 countries, areas, and territories. The statistics are drawn from data sent to the International Labor Office by national statistical services or from official publications of these services. The data are divided into nine general headings including total and economically active population, employment, unemployment, hours of work, wages, labor cost, consumer prices, occupational injuries, and strikes and lockouts. Each of these headings contains several tables, with each table dividing the data into relevant categories. For example, the unemployment statistics for each country are first reported for the entire population and are then broken down by age, sex, industry, and occupation. In most cases the individual statistics are reported for the last 10 years. The volume lists all entries and explanations in English, French, and Spanish. It includes an index by countries and a list of all sources.

The data in this volume are unavailable in any other single publication, making it a valuable reference work. It is most useful for locating work and employment-related statistics for a single country. Due to the different definitions accorded many of the categories covered, as well as the differences in how the statistics are compiled, the use of the data reported for cross-national comparisons is problematic. — **Paul F. Clark**

MANAGEMENT

315. Caelli, William, Dennis Longley, and Michael Shain. **Information Security Handbook.** New York, Stockton Press/Grove's Dictionaries of Music, 1991. 833p. index. $165.00. 658.4. ISBN 1-56159-018-5.

To minimize the misuse of sensitive information, information security has become an important concern of government agencies; commercial, industrial, and banking corporations; and others. This handbook consists of 11 chapters, each credited to experts from Australia and the United Kingdom. The chapters cover an overview of security, security management and policy, risk management, contingency planning and damage avoidance, information security and the law, monitoring and audit control, applications and theory of cryptography, access control, security of stored data and programs, communications security, and formal models of secure systems. Each chapter has its own appendixes and references. Because of its comprehensive scope, this work, although expensive, has merit for large reference collections and for individuals dealing with problems of information security. — **Hwa-Wei Lee**

316. Hitt, William D., ed. **Thoughts on Leadership: A Treasury of Quotations.** Columbus, Ohio, Battelle Press, 1992. 294p. index. $29.95; $19.95pa. HD57.7.T47. 303.3'4. LC 91-15106. ISBN 0-935470-66-2; 0-935470-61-1pa.

Thoughts on Leadership is more than a book of quotations. Hitt, who has written extensively on the intertwined topics of management and leadership, has created a theoretical framework within which he has organized selective quotations that he has noted over many years as a researcher, practicing manager, and teacher. His purpose for organizing the quotations within a theoretical framework is to provide a set of guidelines for effective leadership in the words of the original authors. Two sections with quotations on "The Model Leader" and "A New Leadership Model" introduce the book. A fully effective leader is described as "first and foremost, a fully functioning person" (p. xii). Hitt then develops this thesis within the framework of humanistic psychology and formulates a prototype composed of 5 leadership dimensions and 25 specific leadership competencies: reasoning (e.g., conceptual skills, logical thinking); coping (e.g., people, information networks, excellence integrity), knowing (e.g., oneself, the job); believing (e.g., valuing, visioning); and being (e.g., identity, courage). The book concludes with a 12-page bibliography of sources, an index to the authors of the quotations, and a 3-page subject index that runs from "accountability" to "world peace."

The content and organization of this volume are novel, providing considerable insight into different views of effective leadership. However, since there is no connecting narrative or evaluation of the quotations' content, the book cannot be considered as providing guidelines. Nevertheless, it is not only a useful source of quotations on leadership but also an encapsulated overview of much of the field's literature. —**Helen Howard**

317. Statt, David A. **The Concise Dictionary of Management.** New York, Routledge, Chapman & Hall, 1991. 163p. $12.95pa. 658. ISBN 0-415-05569-5.

Designed to be a quick reference guide for students and professionals, this dictionary defines, in extremely concise fashion, common management terms and concepts, as well as some related terms drawn from psychology and sociology. In addition, the dictionary lists a number of historical developments and individuals significant in the evolution of modern management theory and practice. Thus, for example, there are entries for Hawthorne studies, the Industrial Revolution, scientific management, Chris Argyris, Peter Drucker, and Douglas McGregor. Quite up-to-date, the work lists current, popular, and even slang terminology, including, for example, *brainstorming, golden handshake,* and *whistle blowing.*

The fact that this is a British publication is apparent both in some spellings (e.g., "behavioural science") and in the presence of certain entries (e.g., *constructive dismissal, milk round*). This could be an asset for the individual seeking explication of British English. Occasionally, terms in wide use in the United States are lacking, a glaring example of this being the absence of the acronym TQM (total quality management) (which, however, is covered conceptually in the entry "total quality").

The dictionary lacks a preface but is fairly self-explanatory. Most acronyms and abbreviations are handled through cross-references, and whenever a given definition makes use of a related term that has a separate entry of its own, the related term is printed in all capital letters. Illustrations that accompany such entries as "Gantt chart" could be helpful. However, overly general terms (e.g., *ability, anthropology*) seem out of place in a specialized management dictionary.

The Concise Dictionary of Management appears to be intended primarily for personal use, but it would not be out of place in a library reference collection. Although not a source in which to seek in-depth explanations, it might often prove useful as a starting point for quick reference purposes.
—**Lydia W. Wasylenko**

MARKETING AND TRADE

318. **American Export Register 1992.** New York, Thomas Publishing, c1989, 1991. 2v. maps. index. $120.00/set. LC 80-648882. ISBN 0-937200-74-3. ISSN 0272-1163.

This international directory of U.S. companies provides a rich source of information for individuals and companies that wish to purchase American products or services. The publication is written in English, but it includes product indexes in French, German, Italian, Portuguese, Spanish, Arabic, Chinese, Japanese, and Russian. Specific products can be located in the alphabetically arranged index. A reference is made from the product to its eight-digit classification number and to the page numbers, which begin in volume 1 and continue in volume 2. In the classification section, companies are listed alphabetically within every classification number. Information for each company includes address, telephone and fax numbers, and an occasional description of products. The company profile section in volume 2 also lists key executives in export sales. An array of special information services for exporters can be found in volume 2, including lists of embassies, consulates, banks, railroads, steamships, ports, international chambers of commerce, and freight forwarders.

The United States Importers & Exporters Directory (see ARBA 90, entry 286) is similar to the *American Export Register.* It covers both importing and exporting information and provides more detailed information about each company, but its price is almost three times higher. Libraries that need only export information should find the *American Export Register* sufficient. —**O. Gene Norman**

319. **Associations Yellow Book: Who's Who at the Leading U.S. Trade and Professional Associations. Vol.2, No.1.** Despina Laudati and others, eds. New York, Monitor Publishing, 1992. 939p. index. $160.00 (2 issues). ISSN 1054-4070.

A semiannual publication, this work profiles approximately 1,200 leading trade and professional organizations that are vocational, that operate nationally, and that have a minimum budget of

$1 million. Each entry contains a description of the association; name and address; telephone and fax numbers; numerous officers, managers, and governors; publications; number of members and employees; year founded; and tax status. Indexes provide varied access through industry, officer, and political action committee names; acronyms; budgets; and locations. Fifty new associations have been added to this edition, and the geographical index is also new.

In comparison, the *Encyclopedia of Associations* includes more than 22,000 organizations that cover a broad range of subject areas. Entries contain similar information, but usually with only one officer listed and only a brief statement about annual meetings. The *Yellow Book* notes numerous officers and detailed meeting information projected up to six years. Most libraries that already have the *Encyclopedia of Associations* will find it sufficient for their needs, but the *Yellow Book* complements the *Encyclopedia* with expanded information for organizations listed.—**O. Gene Norman**

320. Salvatore, Dominick, ed. **National Trade Policies.** Westport, Conn., Greenwood Press, 1992. 574p. index. (Handbook of Comparative Economic Policies, v.2). $95.00. HF1411.N34. 382'.3. LC 91-11332. ISBN 0-313-26489-9.

In this work, data is included on only the most important trading nations of the world. An overview of national trade policies in part 1 is followed by chapters on GATT (General Agreement on Tariffs and Trade), the EEC (European Economic Community), and the Council for Mutual Economic Assistance. Parts 2 through 6 discuss trade policies in the main industrial countries; selected countries in Latin America, Asia, and Africa; and the former Soviet Union, Poland, and China. The approximately 20-page sections by 29 contributors are written by economists from those countries or (in several cases) by World Bank economists. Some of the 84 tables that are particularly interesting are those that present support for agricultural production and average post-Tokyo round tariff rates of the United States, the European Community, and Japan. (Note that U.S. trade policy is described on page 103 as "bad mercantilist" and "closet welfare" economics.) The volume is a useful reference source, especially for students of comparative economic systems.—**Karen Y. Stabler**

321. Taucher, Frank A. **The $upertrader's Almanac (Reference Manual).** 2d ed. Tulsa, Okla., Market Movements, 1991. 536p. index. $30.00pa. ISBN 1-879591-01-4.

This almanac addresses business and trading people in general, not specific kinds of traders (e.g., stock, gold). The purpose of the book is twofold: to lay down some basic rules and principles that successful traders have used, and to help individuals choose the best rule or principle to suit a particular trading environment or condition. In order to fulfill the first objective, Taucher attempts to build optimism, self-confidence, high expectations, and courage in the minds of his readers, making it clear that determination and motivation are the roots of success. He then familiarizes readers with the jargon of finance such as *brokerage, solvency, margin, speculation,* and *trading limits.* Next he teaches readers the basics of financial management and investment strategy by explaining asset allocation, equity cycle theory, modern portfolio theory, self-evaluation, analysis of track record, reward to risk, and more.

Taucher's analyses are clear enough to relate these financial principles to general trade and business problems. However, he fails to address specific issues, such as how a person or a firm should adopt an optimum policy under a certain set of business conditions. The book would benefit from a chapter that described some possible business or trading problems and offered solutions derived from the general framework.—**Abu N. M. Wahid**

322. **Tradeshow Week Data Book, 1992: The Annual Guide to Marketing and Statistical Data on U.S. and Canadian Tradeshows and Public Shows.** New Providence, N.J., R. R. Bowker, 1991. 1v. (various paging). index. $279.00pa. ISBN 0-8352-3140-2. ISSN 0000-1023.

Tradeshow Week Data Book is a comprehensive guide to shows that are to be held from 1992 to 1996. Its desired target audience is corporate exhibit managers. The main section covers show listings by industrial classification and comprises most of the book. More than 4,000 shows are arranged alphabetically under 104 industrial classification codes. Each show is covered in detail, with most entries including such information as show management, show location and dates, a profile of show attendees and exhibitors, show history, and costs. The remaining sections provide valuable geographical, chronological, and show management indexes. This work is highly recommended to all businesses involved in shows and to all large libraries with significant business sections.—**Elie M. Dick**

OFFICE PRACTICES

323. **Elsevier's Dictionary of Office Automation: In Four Languages: English, German, French and Dutch.** Compiled by Centre de Terminologie de Bruxelles, Institut Libre Marie Haps. New York, Elsevier Science Publishing, 1991. 462p. index. $157.00. HF5548.E49. 651.8. LC 91-27525. ISBN 0-444-88065-8.

This work is a compilation of more than 4,500 terms used in office automation. The entries represent, for the most part, applications of data processing on microcomputers to business office procedures. They have been drawn largely from software manuals and journals devoted to microcomputing. An extensive bibliography lists those sources.

Each entry is clearly and briefly defined in English, followed by equivalents in German, French, and Dutch. Also included are separate lists of terms in each of the languages (except for English, because entries are alphabetized in that language), with references to appropriate definitions. Extensions of many terms are given and are directed to relevant definitions. The entries are remarkably comprehensive, with a surprising number of statistical terms. This straightforward book will be useful to translators, information systems specialists, technical writers, and office employees who require quick and current understanding of automation terms.—**William C. Struning**

324. **Professional Secretaries International Complete Office Handbook: The Secretary's Guide to Today's Electronic Office.** By Susan Jaderstrom, Leonard Kruk, and Joanne Miller. New York, Random House, 1992. 573p. illus. index. $25.00. HF5548.J34. 651.8. LC 91-43208. ISBN 0-679-40080-X.

Even though the subtitle implies that secretaries will be the ones to find this work useful, this book provides valuable information for all office professionals who wish to be successful in their jobs. It is divided into five parts that give in-depth analyses of the subjects treated. The first section considers professional development. It begins with an overview of career opportunities for office professionals and includes everything from the types of jobs available and how to get one (e.g., resumes, interview skills) to office politics, ethics, and etiquette. The next section deals with equipment and supplies. All sorts of business machines are discussed, with helpful information about different features, applications, and how to select the most appropriate ones. An entire chapter is devoted to the selection and use of computer software; another lists supplies and explains their application, how to choose the correct ones, how to evaluate suppliers, and the correct storage and maintenance of materials. Inventory control and the office environment are also covered here.

Section 3, on specialized office procedures, emphasizes the importance of office manuals and pertinent reference materials for an office and explains how to decide which ones are appropriate for a given office and considerations for, and preparation of, specialized materials. Records management, accounting and bookkeeping, travel and meeting planning, and mailing procedures are also explained in detail. The fourth section gives information on office communication, dealing with everything from written correspondence to telephone etiquette. Examples of various formats for letters, memorandums, reports, and charts are given, along with useful timesaving tips on general correspondence. The chapter on office publishing is particularly helpful, as it discusses various typefaces, column requirements, and software and design criteria. The final section is a grammar and punctuation review that provides easily understood definitions of terms and examples of proper usage. The clearly worded text is accompanied by relevant checklists, tables, charts, forms, and examples that are truly useful, and a good index concludes the book.

This comprehensive handbook, as the authors state, "sets the standard for developing and maintaining a responsive office," emphasizing the high-tech nature of today's workplace. The information provided will lend comfort and confidence to anyone who deals with the variety of skills needed in a modern office. Recommended for all offices as a guide for standard procedures; individual office professionals will probably want their own copies.—**Jo Anne H. Ricca**

REAL ESTATE

325. Tosh, Dennis S., Jr. **Handbook of Real Estate Terms.** rev. ed. Englewood Cliffs, N.J., Prentice-Hall, 1992. 522p. $19.95pa. HD1365.T67. 333.333'03. LC 90-21461. ISBN 0-13-376070-7.

Tosh's book is designed as a handy desk book for those who are, or aspire to be, real estate professionals. It offers clear, but sometimes very short, definitions. Many abbreviations (which abound in real estate) are spelled out and defined. Especially welcome is the inclusion of slang, such as *handyman's special*, as these terms do not appear in many other dictionaries. Appendixes give addresses of real estate organizations and state real estate commissions, but no addresses are given for the many federal agencies covered.

Coverage is up-to-date enough to include terms from the recent savings and loan bailout. However, many entries could be longer and could present more background information. Many definitions are too simple to be truly useful. For instance, *useful life*, defined as "the period of time over which property is expected to have utility," is spelled out more specifically in U.S. Treasury guidelines. It might have been too much to spell out what these guidelines are, but the tax implications of the term could at least have been mentioned. On other subjects, such as the Equal Credit Opportunity Act, much more useful information is provided, including legislative history and a list of 10 legal "dos" and "don'ts" for lenders.

This title is adequate and reasonably priced, but the entries are too uneven for it to be an outstanding work. It is recommended for libraries that serve real estate professionals and that need an updated, inexpensive source. — **Susan V. McKimm**

TAXATION

326. Esanu, Warren H., and others. **Guide to Income Tax Preparation.** Yonkers, N.Y., Consumer Reports Books; distr., New York, St. Martin's Press, 1992. 696p. index. $13.95pa. KF6369.6.G84. 343.7305'2044. LC 87-71005. ISBN 0-89043-550-2.

Librarians have come to rely on *Consumer Reports* for expert information at a reasonable price, and this topical tax guide is no exception. Users will appreciate its jargon-free approach and easy-to-use arrangement. Chapter 1 outlines the 1991 tax law changes and is followed by sections on filing and dependents, income, alimony, business, depreciation, sale or exchange of property, pensions, other income, limitations on losses, deductions, homes, computing tax, credits against taxes, paying taxes, choosing a tax preparer, audit, estate planning, tax planning for older Americans, and planning for tax savings. Useful appendixes include sample tax forms, a glossary, a list of IRS publications, where to file, IRS toll-free numbers, a 1992 tax table, and an index. This one-stop source will be extremely popular at tax time in all libraries. — **Maureen A. Beck**

327. **J. K. Lasser's Your Income Tax 1993.** By the J. K. Lasser Institute. New York, Prentice Hall Press, 1992. 511p. index. $14.00pa. ISBN 0-13-513896-5.

One dreaded date in the United States is April 15, tax day. To help solve the taxpayer's problems with IRS forms, deductions, and instructions, this publication, in its 56th year, provides detailed explanations that are as understandable as possible when dealing with the complex U.S. Tax Code. Income tax basics are covered in part 1; reporting your income is discussed in part 2; deductions, credits, and how to figure one's taxes appear in part 3; personal tax computations are listed in part 4; tax savings plans are described in part 5; business tax planning is the concern of part 6; and part 7 details what happens after a return is filed. The explanation for each subsection has references to other applicable sections and is accompanied by a clarifying example. Red type is used for potential problems of deductions, changes in the tax laws, and other court decisions. A tax organizer, a glossary, and an index are also provided. Worksheets and examples of tax forms have a table to indicate which number is needed for a specific tax entry.

Individuals filling out tax forms need their own copies of this work to refer to when questions arise. Most libraries can afford a copy, but changes in the tax code will necessitate a new volume each year.

— **Jean Herold**

5 Education

GENERAL WORKS

Catalogs and Collections

328. **Educators Index of Free Materials.** 101st ed. Mary P. Parent, ed. Randolph, Wis., Educators Progress Service, 1992. 392p. index. $45.95 looseleaf w/binder. LC 44-32700. ISBN 0-87708-238-3.

This catalog lists 1,870 items from previous editions and 712 new titles for a total of 2,582 entries. The addition of three new indexes—title, subject, and source—greatly improves the usefulness of this edition. The subject index is especially useful for finding materials on a specific topic. Another marked improvement over some previous editions is the careful attention given to omitting obsolete, inappropriate, unavailable, or discontinued titles. The introductory sections offer sound advice for obtaining and evaluating free materials sponsored by professional associations (e.g., the National Council of Teachers of English), governmental agencies (e.g., the Federal Trade Commission), nonprofit organizations (e.g., the March of Dimes), and business and industry. The evaluation form included is especially valuable for assessing materials produced by business and industry.

This index remains a valuable resource for teachers and other educators, librarians, and audiovisual directors, not only because the educational materials are free but also because the index provides information not available from other sources. Annotations provide meaningful information, including the number of free copies that may be obtained, appropriate grade level, and whether or not the material may be reproduced. — **William E. Hug**

329. **The ETS Test Collection Catalog. Volume 6: Affective Measures and Personality Tests.** Compiled by Test Collection, Educational Testing Service. Phoenix, Ariz., Oryx Press, 1992. 165p. index. $54.50pa. LB3051.E79. 016.3712'6. LC 86-678. ISBN 0-89774-248-6.

The sixth volume of this catalog lists more than 1,500 affective measures and personality tests. The catalog's intended audience includes "those in research, advisory services, education, counseling, business, and other activities." Professionals in these fields will find this volume useful in identifying instruments that assess such traits as anxiety, self-esteem, depression, and emotional adjustment.

Descriptive entries for tests are listed in accession number order and include test title, author, descriptors and identifiers, age or grade level, and an abstract. Abstracts do not include evaluation or criticism of the tests; other sources should be consulted for this purpose. Availability information, such as the ERIC document number, a full bibliographic citation for journal articles and monographs, and mailing addresses for authors and publishers, is also provided. Entries do not include cost information. All tests were available at the time of printing. The catalog has author, title, and subject indexes; the latter uses ERIC descriptors as well as some Educational Testing Service-assigned identifiers. Academic and other libraries that serve patrons in education, psychology, and business will want to purchase this volume. — **Deborah V. Rollins**

Dictionaries and Encyclopedias

330. **American Educators' Encyclopedia.** By David E. Kapel, Charles S. Gifford, and Marilyn B. Kapel. Westport, Conn., Greenwood Press, 1991. 716p. index. $95.00. LB15.D37. 370'.3. LC 90-41510. ISBN 0-313-25269-6.

The best test of a reference book is to use it while immersed in a research project, and the *American Educators' Encyclopedia* passed the test with strong marks. It contains nearly 2,000 brief entries that range from *abacus* to *z-score*, an abbreviations and acronyms list, and 27 appendixes. For the reader who wants to verify information on education, the volume is particularly useful. However, while terms such as *Writing to Read* and *schema theory* appear, surprising omissions are *Reading Recovery* and *scaffolding*. For the researcher who needs more information, the references provide a starting point. For the browser who enjoys sampling educational tidbits, the entries provide pleasant reading. The appendixes, which range from the Caldecott and Newbery winner lists to past presidents of many national organizations, are useful but soon outdated. This is a concise, functional resource. [R: RBB, 1 Jan 92, p. 846; WLB, Apr 92, pp. 119-20] – **Suzanne I. Barchers**

331. **Encyclopedia of Educational Research.** Marvin C. Alkin with others, eds. New York, Macmillan, 1992. 4v. index. $330.00/set. LB15.E48. 370'.3. LC 91-38682. ISBN 0-02-900431-4.

This useful set provides the reader with an excellent overview of the current status of research in education. The articles, on relatively broad topics and largely from U.S. contributors, explore the research in a variety of subjects, from AIDS education to military education to women's education in the Third World. The casual browser will enjoy sampling the extensive number of current topics. The serious researcher will appreciate the bibliographies that accompany each article, the extensive index that leads the user to more specific topics, and the article entitled "Doing Library Research in Education." Because there is no table of contents, a useful addition to the next edition would be the inclusion of page numbers in the list of articles. A feature that is particularly welcome, however, is the list of acronyms in the index that will assist users when reading about this subject area, which is rife with jargon. [R: Choice, Nov 92, p. 440; LJ, July 92, p. 74; RBB, Aug 92, p. 2037] – **Suzanne I. Barchers**

332. Williams, Leslie R., and Doris Pronin Fromberg, eds. **Encyclopedia of Early Childhood Education.** Hamden, Conn., Garland, 1992. 518p. index. (Garland Reference Library of the Social Sciences, v.504). $95.00. LB1139.23.E53. 372.21'03. LC 92-4579. ISBN 0-8240-4626-9.

This work is not an encyclopedia in the usual sense. Instead, it delves into every aspect of early childhood education: historical, philosophical, sociocultural, political, and economical. It also encompasses curricula, educators, children (from conception to classrooms), observation methods, literature, and peer culture. Each chapter is preceded by a short introductory essay, followed by articles written by experts in all fields related to the child. Each article has references and sources for further study. Many of the pioneers in early childhood education, from Mary Ainsworth and Jean Piaget to Stanley Greenspan and Burrhus Skinner, are given extensive coverage. Although this work is devoted to research, it also has other sorts of information, such as a list of national advocacy organizations, the definition of cuisenaire rods, families and their impact upon children, curriculum preparation, achievement tests, demographics regarding pregnant teens, and school desegregation and the concomitant court cases. This is truly a work that speaks to the whole child. The information contained here justifies the cost of the book. Highly recommended for anyone working with any aspect of early childhood education. [R: Choice, Nov 92, p. 518; RBB, 1 Sept 92, p. 85] – **Mary Jo Aman**

Handbooks and Yearbooks

333. Hammill, Donald D., Linda Brown, and Brian R. Bryant. **A Consumer's Guide to Tests in Print.** 2d ed. Austin, Tex., Pro-Ed, 1992. 197p. $27.00pa. LB3060.32.N67H36. 371.2'6. LC 92-3041. ISBN 0-89079-548-7.

This work fills a gap in the literature of test criticism in that it is the only source in which all tests covered are reviewed by means of a standardized evaluation form. The authors suggest that the book may be used to select an appropriate test, to teach the process of test evaluation, and to improve the quality of tests; it should fulfill these roles admirably.

The more than 250 tests reviewed are norm-referenced tests for K-12 students, with "a focus on tests that are individually administered for diagnostic, screening, or identification purposes." Thus, a test such as the Wechsler Intelligence Scale for Children is evaluated, but the Stanford Achievement Test is not. The authors give a detailed yet clear overview of the principles of measurement for norm-referenced tests and also discuss the development of evaluative criteria for those principles. Based on ratings of norms, reliability, and validity, each test is given an overall rating of A (highly recommended—very few merit this rating), B (recommended), or F (not recommended). The tables also provide information on nontechnical characteristics of the tests reviewed, such as age of intended use, administration, scoring, and input and output formats. Tests are classified according to a taxonomy, with 4 general domains (achievement, aptitude, effect, and general intelligence) and 86 content areas; an appendix lists ratings of tests within each content area. Other appendixes list members of the review board, a bibliography of tests reviewed, test publishers, and the reviewer evaluation form. *A Consumer's Guide to Tests in Print* should be in every academic library that supports programs in education and psychology. Public and other libraries that make use of *Mental Measurements Yearbook* (see ARBA 90, entry 751) or *Test Critiques* (Pro-Ed, 1992) will also want to add this to their collection.—**Deborah V. Rollins**

334. **Handbook of Research on Curriculum.** Philip W. Jackson, ed. New York, Macmillan, 1992. 1088p. index. $65.00. LB1570.H264. 375'.00973. LC 91-12373. ISBN 0-02-900385-7.

The American Educational Research Association has produced a comprehensive overview of the status of, and issues in, the curriculum field from nursery school through high school. The handbook includes essays by 52 prominent university curriculum specialists, from Richard L. Allen to Karen Zumwalt. The 34 chapters are grouped into 4 parts: conceptual and methodological perspectives, how the curriculum is shaped, the curriculum as a shaping force, and topics and issues within curricular categories. The volume contains both author and subject indexes. Some information on countries other than the United States is included. The chapter bibliographies are extensive and current.

The editorial intent is that each chapter should contain a historical perspective on its topic; present the best available scholarly and empirical knowledge; offer an up-to-date bibliography; and point investigators, particularly graduate students in education, toward needed research. This approach has given consistency to chapters on diverse topics although it has led to some duplication of historical background. The author index lists more than 70 references to John Dewey and 30 to J. Franklin Bobbitt.

This exemplary volume will be indispensable to those seeking to expand and update their backgrounds in almost all aspects of the complex that is curriculum. It will be, as intended, particularly valuable for graduate students in education, although, perhaps also as intended, their imaginations will be stretched in designing research. If the volume has a flaw, it lies in being much more retrospective than prospective. American education—and curriculum is its heart—is in ferment. This handbook details where we have been but provides only hints about where we may be going. [R: RQ, Fall 92, p. 114]—**Richard A. Scott**

335. McMillon, Bill. **Wilderness U: Opportunities for Outdoor Education in the U.S. & Abroad.** Chicago, Chicago Review Press; distr., Chicago, Independent Publishers Group, 1992. 281p. illus. index. $12.95pa. LB1047.M38. 371.3'8. LC 92-19616. ISBN 1-55652-158-8.

For the person who wants to learn from and about nature, either informally or formally, *Wilderness U* describes classes, workshops, expeditions, programs, and tours offered by universities, colleges, institutes, clubs, and other organizations. The book is divided into three parts. The first part, grouped by type of sponsoring institution, describes each institution and its aims, its range of offerings and their costs and requirements, and telephone numbers and addresses. However, no contact person or position is included for those who prefer writing to calling. The second section includes articles that provide longer portraits of selected programs. These articles originally appeared in various magazines and have been adapted by McMillon for inclusion in this book. While interesting in themselves, they might more effectively have been included with McMillon's own sketches in the first part to avoid flipping back and forth between sections and to balance the objective with the subjective. Unfortunately, the first section includes far more programs than there are articles about them, suggesting that these vignettes are either incomplete or unnecessary. The third section includes a topically arranged index and a bibliography of additional sources, as well as an indication of relevant state agencies. This final list is enough to suggest sources beyond the scope of McMillon's book. [R: LJ, 1 Nov 92, p. 80]

—Rebecca Jordan

336. Shaver, James P., ed. **Handbook of Research on Social Studies Teaching and Learning.** New York, Macmillan, 1991. 661p. index. $65.00. LB1584.H275. 300'.7'073. LC 90-38751. ISBN 0-02-895790-3.

In the past few years, a number of major collections of research, such as *The International Encyclopedia of Curriculum* (see ARBA 92, entry 274), have tried to present various viewpoints and meta-analysis of the research in curricular areas of contemporary K-12 education. This work has been compiled as a project of the National Council of the Social Studies. The editor has drawn together 53 originally written summaries of research that are divided into 8 major topical divisions: research methodology, the student of social studies, the social studies teacher, society's influence on social studies, current issues, methods of teaching, integration with other teaching fields, and international concerns and perspectives. Each article is written by a specialist; almost all are professors of education in the United States and Canada. Articles are structured roughly parallel and examine the research background of a topic, look at methodology, synthesize results across studies, suggest topics for future research, and look at newer techniques for research that are likely to yield information results.

While balance in such a hefty collection is difficult to achieve, Shaver has succeeded in looking at a broad spectrum of education issues of current interest through the eyes of social studies. The reader discovers, for example, that the methods of teaching social studies have changed little over the years but that current technologies and social views of equity are having an impact. Recommended for university and school libraries. —**David V. Loertscher**

337. **Test Critiques. Volume IX.** Daniel J. Keyser and Richard C. Sweetland, eds. Austin, Tex., Pro-Ed, 1992. 749p. index. $89.00. LC 84-26895. ISBN 0-89079-521-5.

There are extraordinary numbers of psychological, educational, and industrial tests available, but it is almost impossible for anyone to know about all of them. The information largely resides in test publisher's catalogs and research articles; finding and studying them is often daunting. Worse, it is hard to know if a test exists that might solve a particular clinical or research problem.

This book is representative of the first eight in the noteworthy series, providing professionals with clear, useful information about currently used tests. The critiques are written by well-known people who are experts not only in the use of the tests but also in their technical development. Each critique follows the same format: introduction, practical applications and uses, technical aspects, critique, and references. Although each author was required to write within those reference points, each was also given latitude so as to make the work as scholarly as possible. As a result, the writing is crisp and to the point, providing readers with enough information to determine if they wish to pursue a test further. The indexes are extremely useful, covering not only the contents of this volume but also those of previous volumes. Readers can examine them to learn of all the tests critiqued, all test publishers, all authors/reviewers, and all subjects. The subject index, divided into major headings (psychology, education, and business and industry), is further subdivided into secondary categories so that locating specific tests, or the tests critiqued in a particular dimension, is quite easy.

Perhaps the only criticism of this volume (and the series) is that there does not seem to be a unifying principle that determines which tests will be in a particular volume. To examine all the tests in a subcategory will require access to all of the volumes, which may not always be possible.

This work is designed for professionals who need information about tests. Clinicians, researchers, and their students will most likely be its users. For others, it would be a formidable task to try to understand the issues discussed. Thus, the work belongs in departments of psychology and reference libraries. —**Bertram H. Rothschild**

338. **Tests: A Comprehensive Reference for Assessments in Psychology, Education, and Business.** 3d ed. Richard C. Sweetland and Daniel J. Keyser, eds. Austin, Tex., Pro-Ed, 1992. 1250p. index. $79.00. BF176.T43. 150'.28'7. LC 89-78495. ISBN 0-89079-255-0.

This reference work is a quick guide to tests available in the areas of psychology, education, and business. Around 700 new or revised tests have been added to this edition, bringing the number of citations to more than 3,500. The information is restricted to tests written in English.

The measurement instruments are presented alphabetically within topical subsections of the three aforementioned areas of interest. Each entry consists of test title and author, whether the test is self- or examiner-administered, intended population, purpose, brief description, timing information, scoring method, cost and availability, and publisher. Several useful indexes and appendixes are supplied: an index of test titles; a list of out-of-print tests; tests for the hearing, physically, and visually impaired; foreign-language versions of cited tests; a new index of computer-scored tests; a test author index; and a publisher and test distributor index.

Test users will not want to make final decisions about what measuring devices to select based only on the information in this volume. The entries are severely condensed, and no evaluations nor reviews are offered. However, this reference work is an excellent starting point for searching out potentially useful tests. — **Charles Neuringer**

339. Wicker, Gerald L. **Gifted & Talented Information Resources: A Comprehensive Guide for Parents and Educators....** Snellville, Ga., Cardinal Publishing, 1991. 95p. $8.95pa. LC 91-77523.

Any educator, parent, librarian, or official who needs information on resources for the gifted and talented should begin with this guide. It includes not only expected information, such as appropriate associations, periodicals, publishers, and programs, but also the unexpected, such as descriptions of federally funded projects for fiscal years 1989 and 1990. The World Council listings at the end of the book (omitted from the table of contents) are not to be missed. The guide is well organized, with brief but informative annotations and easy-to-reference lists. Of particular interest is the inclusion in the appendix of Public Law 100-29, Title IV, Part B—Gifted and Talented Children. Although the book could benefit from better copyediting, it is a valuable resource. [R: RBB, Aug 92, p. 2030]
—**Suzanne I. Barchers**

Indexes

340. Defty, Jeff. **Creative Fingerplays & Action Rhymes: An Index and Guide to Their Use.** Phoenix, Ariz., Oryx Press, 1992. 255p. illus. index. $29.50pa. GV1218.F5D44. 793.4. LC 92-9655. ISBN 0-89774-709-7.

The introduction to this work defines fingerplay and action rhyme and combines the two under one heading: active verse. A core repertoire of active verse is provided. There are chapters devoted to a specific age group (infants, toddlers, storytime, and older children); other chapters cover materials for special-needs children and English as a Second Language (ESL). Extensive bibliographies at the end of each chapter list not only books but periodicals and audiovisual materials as well. Each chapter addresses evaluating, selecting, and teaching active verse and at the same time exhorts the user to be mindful of racial and sexual bias found in many of the older active verses. Each chapter is replete with verses and illustrated teaching techniques. Also covered are holidays, languages (e.g., Japanese, Arabic, French, German, Turkish), concepts, adapting active verse to story hours, writing active verse, and teaching children to write verses. The chapter on working with special-needs children (e.g., learning impaired, emotionally disturbed) and ESL children is especially informative and helpful. Some of the references that deal with language and mainstreaming go back to 1966, which seems dated for this topic. However, there are also references to active verse dated earlier, which is acceptable.

A first-line and subject index to active verses and their sources is supplied so that users can select materials suitable for a particular subject or need. There is also a separate index for the body of the text.

The author is an experienced preschool teacher, children's librarian, and storyteller; much of his information has been gleaned from his work with children. This informative and helpful tool for all levels of storytellers is highly recommended for all storytelling collections.—**Mary Jo Aman**

341. **Education Index.** (Indexing coverage: 6/83-6/25/92). [CD-ROM]. Bronx, N.Y., H. W. Wilson, 1992. Hardware requirements: WILSONLINE Workstation, IBM PC, or compatible; 640K; hard disk drive. $1,295.00.

Education Index on CD-ROM is the electronic companion to the print *Education Index* (see ARBA 88, entry 333) produced by H. W. Wilson since 1929. The indexing on the improved version (2.4) of WILSONDISC covers educational publications in the English language from June 1983 to June 1992. This disc, along with other WILSONDISC products, such as Social Science Index, Index to Legal Periodicals, and MLA International Bibliography, includes new searching features not available on previous discs. A custom message can be assigned to each tagged periodical; new truncation characters enhance search capabilities; expanded search capabilities in the BROWSE mode are now available; and reported problems in the WILSEARCH mode have been corrected—and these are just a few of the improvements. The toll-free helpline and detailed documentation make instructions easy to use and understand for even the novice installer, so a computer-literate person should have no problem.

Likewise, a beginner should be able to use the BROWSE search mode with little or no instruction, while the more sophisticated user can proceed directly to the WILSEARCH mode. As with the Wilson print indexes, the WILSONDISC CD-ROMs are popular with users and librarians because there is minimal need for instruction, and many of the periodicals indexed can be found in academic libraries.

Although the searching capabilities are not yet as powerful as those on SilverPlatter's ERIC system, Education Index on WILSONDISC is still recommended because it is user-friendly and reasonably priced. Once the new software is loaded, the various WILSONDISC products can be searched just by changing the CD-ROM disc. Recommended for academic libraries that serve clientele doing research in education.—**Diane J. Turner**

342. **John Dewey: The Collected Works, 1882-1953. Index.** Anne S. Sharpe, Harriet Furst Simon, and Barbara Levine, eds. Carbondale, Ill., Southern Illinois University Press, 1991. 526p. $50.00. B945.D45Z85. 016.191. LC 90-20120. ISBN 0-8093-1728-1.

John Dewey's productive years totaled an astonishing three score and ten; he started publishing at 23 and was still writing when he died at 93. This volume is an index to *The Collected Works of John Dewey*, edited by Jo Ann Boydston, now available in 37 volumes (with this essentially the 38th). It consists of a compendium of tables of contents from the set, followed by extensive title and subject indexes to the volumes. The compendium covers 52 pages, while the title index covers 47 and the subject index 425. The level of indexing is detailed and a little complex, with coded references that may require some practice before the user feels comfortable with them. The volume will be indispensable to owners of *The Collected Works* and useful to nonowners and all interested in this significant American philosopher/educator.—**Mary Jo Walker**

Periodicals and Serials

343. Richardson, Michael D., and Robert L. Prickett. **Publication Sources in Educational Leadership: A Compilation of Publication Outlets for the Creative Exchange of Information....** Lancaster, Pa., Technomic Publishing, 1991. 116p. index. $29.00pa. LC 90-72122. ISBN 0-87762-789-4.

Faculty members in higher education are usually expected to make ongoing contributions to research and scholarship in their fields. Once a piece of research has been carried out and the results have been presented in manuscript form, authors must select the periodical publication to which their work will be sent for publication consideration. Selection can be based on several considerations, such as information about the audience to whom a particular periodical in the field is addressed; whether the journal is a refereed publication, where the evaluation process is conducted using peers instead of the editor or an editorial board; the turnaround time required for notice of acceptance or rejection; and whether the periodical is research-based.

Richardson and Prickett have included 1,013 education periodical titles organized alphabetically by title in this compilation. An index arranged into 35 subject categories allows the user to consult journals in a specific field. Information provided in each entry includes periodical title; editor; address; frequency of publication; sponsoring organization, if any; and intended audience and orientation of articles. Refereed periodicals are so noted.

There are four chapters in this work. Chapter 1 is titled "The Trojan Horse" and refers to the "publish or perish" mandate that has become associated with university teaching. In it the authors give some advice about getting started in research and tips for getting the results published. Chapter 2 is the major portion of the work and includes the periodical descriptions. Chapter 3 is called "Publishing a Book," and chapter 4, "Millennial 2000: Prospering through Publications," discusses reform and restructuring of education in the 1990s and how educators can respond.

Comparing this tool to a similar one for the field of library and information science, *Librarian/Author*, edited by Betty-Carol Sellen (Neal-Schuman, 1985), the latter is much more useful to prospective authors. It includes additional useful information about where the periodical is indexed or abstracted, specific style requirements, average desired length of articles, number of copies needed for submission, whether an abstract is required, whether a query letter is advised, manuscript acceptance rate, estimated time for acceptance or rejection notice, and estimated time from acceptance to publication. However, in spite of the lack of this kind of information, *Publication Sources in Educational Leadership* is a starting place and will benefit scholars interested in writing for publication in any field of education. — **Lois J. Buttlar**

COMPUTER RESOURCES

344. Lamb, Annette C. **Emerging Technologies and Instruction: Hypertext, Hypermedia, and Interactive Multimedia.** Englewood Cliffs, N.J., Educational Technology, 1991. 64p. (Educational Technology Selected Bibliography Series, v.4). $14.95pa. Z5814.E34L35. 016.3713'078. LC 91-4704. ISBN 0-87778-234-2.

This bibliography lists publications under eight somewhat overlapping descriptive titles: historical and background information; general information on hypermedia and multimedia; hypermedia, multimedia, and instruction; hypermedia and multimedia in the content areas; hypermedia and multimedia: design, development, and evaluation; hypertext, hypermedia, and information exploration; educational applications of CD-ROM; and current directions and the future of emerging technologies. Most entries are from periodicals, although books, chapters in books, conference proceedings, and the like are included.

The basic problem with the bibliography is that information in the publications does not naturally fall into the eight categories. Consequently, to find out about particular applications of hypermedia and multimedia requires a search through most of the eight sections. A content index and subject descriptors after each entry could help resolve this problem. Professionals working in these areas should be able to make their own database searches to produce bibliographies that meet specific needs; such a search would produce more data about individual information resources.

The bibliography could have been published on approximately 25 rather than 67 pages. It would be easier to use if it were printed on both sides of the page and had single-spaced entries separated by a double space, arranged in two columns. The unusually wide margins also increase the amount of paper used. — **William E. Hug**

345. Romiszowski, Alexander J. **Computer Mediated Communication: A Selected Bibliography.** Englewood Cliffs, N.J., Educational Technology, 1992. 55p. (Educational Technology Selected Bibliography Series, v.5). $14.95. Z5814.A85R66. 016.3713'34. LC 91-43966. ISBN 0-87778-243-1.

This volume lists various conference proceedings, books, and journal articles on computer-assisted communication. Sections provide citations to an overview of the field, research and development, applicable hardware and software, databases, and libraries. The usefulness of this bibliography is seriously compromised by its content. Nowhere does the bibliographer offer a basis for his choices. In a discipline that evolves almost every year, why does the research and development section contain citations for books published 20 years ago? While these listings may be significant in the overview section, it is mystifying to find selections from 1972, 1980, and 1985 in a division devoted to new research and projects.

The searching capabilities of computers have spawned a host of machine-generated bibliographies. Using the term "selected," compilers can affix their names to a loosely organized list of citations produced as a result of various search sets. The usefulness of these citations when they are neither annotated nor examined critically by the compiler is questionable for any library's collection. A search of relevant computer periodical indexes and online databases will serve the researcher much better than this type of material. A library science library that collects at the doctoral level may feel the need to purchase this item. It is not recommended for other collections.—**Kathleen W. Craver**

ELEMENTARY AND SECONDARY EDUCATION

346. **Brown's Directory of Instructional Programs, 1992: K-8.** Compiled by Brown Publishing Network. Mendham, N.J., Infinity Impressions, 1992. 6v. index. $99.75pa./set. LB1028.35. 371.32. ISBN 1-879339-22-2.

This multivolume directory is designed to provide information about textbooks and other instructional programs in reading, whole language/literature, language arts/spelling/handwriting, social studies, mathematics, and science/health for grades K-8. Entries are arranged under divisions such as basal programs, supplementary programs, and software (they vary a little depending on the volume) and then in alphabetical order by company name. According to the introduction, "BROWN'S DIRECTORIES do not attempt to evaluate, critique, or review any of the programs in any subjective way." Individual entries give a description of the program, textbook series, or software, listing the features and components of the texts, teachers' materials, and supporting materials.

These volumes were examined by six educational consultants who were united in their opinion that such directories could be helpful to curriculum consultants in school district offices and regional service centers. They were also universally convinced that the series would be much more useful if it did provide critical analysis or evaluations of the material. Also, one consultant was concerned that the basal and supplementary programs in health seemed limited. As this is only the third year that this set has been published, the latter criticism may be corrected in time.—**Betty Jo Buckingham**

347. **Brown's Directory of Instructional Programs, 1992: 7-12.** Compiled by Brown Publishing Network. Mendham, N.J., Infinity Impressions, 1992. 6v. index. $99.75pa./set. LB1028.35. 371.32. ISBN 1-879339-333-3.

One of the more tedious aspects of selecting school textbooks is gathering sufficient information to make an informed decision. Relevant details and evaluations are scattered in a variety of sources, such as journal reviews, publisher catalogs, and *El-Hi Serials & Textbooks in Print* (see ARBA 92, entry 285). *Brown's Directory of Instructional Programs* is intended to expedite the review process by providing "unbiased descriptions" of textbooks, textbook series, videos, and software available from many major and some minor publishers.

Each volume of the set is dedicated to a different subject area: social studies, language arts, foreign languages, technology/vocational education, science/health, and mathematics. The instructional program descriptions, organized by publisher within specific subject categories, include publication date, appropriate grade level, and "Features" and "Components" of the material. The "Features" section provides a brief description of the organization, emphases, and strengths of the title, while the "Components" section usually describes supplementary teaching materials, such as workbooks or resource books. For pricing information, one is referred to an alphabetical directory of publishers in the back of the volume, which includes fax and toll-free numbers. There is also an index to titles.

While the descriptions of the instructional programs are usually thorough, some are too superficial to be of much help. One sociology textbook is described as showing students the "relevance" of sociology, sharpening "their critical thinking skills," and teaching them "to think like sociologists." Entries such as this, although the exception, point to the need for consistently thorough descriptions, especially as they are not evaluative or critical. Also, users should be aware that not all appropriate publishers or instructional programs are included. These caveats aside, this directory should help shorten the process of identifying appropriate textbooks, and, for the price, it should be worthwhile to curriculum coordinators, school libraries, and college curriculum centers.—**Stephen H. Aby**

348. Grant, Mary A., and Thomas C. Hunt. **Catholic School Education in the United States: Development and Current Concerns.** Hamden, Conn., Garland, 1992. 296p. index. (Source Books on Education, v.31; Garland Reference Library of Social Science, v.474). $46.00. LC501.G55. 377'.82'73. LC 92-14907. ISBN 0-8240-6342-2.

Grant and Hunt provide a brief history and an extended bibliography of Catholic education in the United States, written from a Catholic point of view. Most of the bibliographical entries and the opinions of the authors are favorable toward parochial education. For example, Hunt writes in the introduction that "these schools have made, and continue to make, major contributions to American society in a myriad of ways."

The book offers nine chapters, beginning with an overview. The remaining chapters are in chronological order, from "Colonial Times to 1840" to "Current Concerns 1982-1991." Each chapter offers a brief history of Catholic education in the United States for the stated time period, including careful endnotes, and then presents an annotated bibliography of books and articles on the topic. There are a total of 527 bibliographical entries, not counting endnote entries, which do not necessarily overlap. Author and subject indexes follow.

While the brief historical essays will be of interest to a wide audience, the primary appeal of this volume will be to those universities and programs in which there is strong interest in Catholic education. Scholars interested in the overall private school picture or in the opinion of non-Catholic educators on parochial education will probably need to look beyond this list. – **Betty Jo Buckingham**

349. **The Handbook of Private Schools: An Annual Descriptive Survey of Independent Education.** 73d ed. Boston, Porter Sargent, 1992. 1440p. illus. maps. index. $70.00. LC 15-12869. ISBN 0-87558-129-3. ISSN 0072-9884.

This informative volume gives data parents and advisors need to know on 1,715 leading independent schools in the United States. The school profiles are listed geographically by state, from east to west across the country, and alphabetically by city within each state. Every city or town is briefly described with relevant or interesting information. Included for each school are names of admissions officer, grades offered, academic orientation, number of yearly admissions in each grade, total student enrollment, and number of faculty. Also provided is a graduate record that specifies the total number of students in the previous year's graduating class and the number who entered college. The section on academic orientation provides specific facts for the prospective student as to whether the basic curriculum is college preparatory, pre-preparatory, general academic, or specialized. (In some cases, schools are vocational, business, technical, or secretarial.) Regularly offered advanced or accelerated courses are also pointed out. Following each school's statistical information is a paragraph that describes its history and administration as well as academic and extracurricular programs. In addition, 300 schools have purchased space in the "Private Schools Illustrated" section, where they are able to stress significant features in their programs and aims. This work is a necessary resource for all libraries.
– **Randy M. Wood**

350. Harrison, Charles. **Public Schools USA: A Comparative Guide to School Districts.** 2d ed. Princeton, N.J., Peterson's Guides, 1991. 483p. index. $44.95. LA217.2.H37. 371'.01'0973. LC 91-30607. ISBN 1-56079-081-4.

This guide was first published in 1988 (see ARBA 89, entry 277). The introduction states that it is the only guide in a print or electronic medium to provide "so much information about so many school districts." It profiles more than 400 public school districts in 41 major metropolitan areas in 26 states and the District of Columbia. All school districts within 25 miles of a city core that have at least 2,500 students were given an opportunity to complete the survey form.

An Effective Schools Index (ESI) compares the school districts to state averages on percentage of students in average daily attendance, expense per student, percentage of students that took ACT tests and their average score, percentage of each class of graduates enrolled in college, teacher-student and counselor-student ratios in secondary schools, music and art specialist-student ratios in elementary schools, ratio of computers for instruction to students, and average teacher salary and average years of experience. Ethnic population, languages taught, classes for gifted students, and Advanced Placement (AP) classes are also noted. A major test of quality – the extent, recency, and support of the library media collections and the provision of adequate professional and support staff in library media centers – does not appear to be addressed. Terms that affect the ESI score are totaled to provide a quick comparison between schools. Those scores range from 21 to 100, with inner-city schools usually receiving the lowest ratings and recording the highest percentage of nonwhite students, indicating once again that inner-city students frequently receive poorer schooling than suburban ones.

In addition to the specific ESI charts, there are tables that give such state averages as current expenses per pupil for all 50 states. Appendix F gives each district name; the number of teachers; the number of schools; relative wealth indicator and rate of instructional materials dollars (high, medium, low); and each school's name, principal, grade span, enrollment, address, and telephone number. Indexes by state/metropolitan area and by district are provided.

It is difficult to avoid errors in a book of this nature, but inaccuracy diminishes the value of the book. The reviewer questions, for example, whether Atlanta really had only 152 students suspended or expelled out of 60,275 while 14,377 students were reported expelled out of 44,977 from Fulton County, a suburb of Atlanta.

Users of this work will probably be rising executives with children who are likely to attend school in a major metropolitan area within the United States. Libraries and counselors serving such families will also find it useful. [R: RBB, 1 Apr 92, p. 1474; WLB, May 92, pp. 128-29]

— Betty Jo Buckingham

351. Lamme, Linda Leonard, and Suzanne Lowell Krogh, with Kathy A. Yachmetz. **Literature-Based Moral Education: Children's Books & Activities....** Phoenix, Ariz., Oryx Press, 1992. 145p. index. $24.50pa. LC311.L36. 370.11'4'0973. LC 92-3190. ISBN 0-89774-723-2.

Two university professors who teach in the field of education and an elementary school guidance counselor have combined their experience to compile this annotated resource list of books and instructional activities related to moral education. The authors begin by providing a brief overview of the theoretical knowledge available in the literature, including the research findings and conclusions of Jean Piaget, Lawrence Kohlberg, William Damon, and Robert Selman. Based on their stage-related concepts of moral development, they also present some strategies for helping children respond to the values and moral dilemmas that are prevalent in children's literature.

The books selected for inclusion are arranged by thematic chapters and include those that focus on self-esteem; responsibility; sharing; truthfulness; solving conflicts peacefully; respecting and appreciating others; ecological values; diligence, perseverance, and patience; and unconditional love. Each chapter begins with a rationale for the inclusion of that particular value or moral issue, followed by a classroom vignette that provides a model by which the moral lesson can be exemplified. The section on book reviews and curricular extensions is followed by a summary section that integrates objectives, titles, and strategies related to the moral value. The majority of the books reviewed in each chapter are picture books; the annotation also includes ideas for use in the classroom, library, or home setting. Grade levels at which the books are appropriate are designated.

Parents, teachers, librarians, and other educators will find this compilation a very useful resource. While it does not claim to be a comprehensive list, it will stimulate thinking about additional examples of children's literature that may have application in moral education. — **Lois J. Buttlar**

352. Long, Kim. **Encyclopedia of Field Trips & Educational Destinations.** Santa Barbara, Calif., ABC-Clio, 1991. 355p. index. $45.00. LB1047.L63. 371.3'8. LC 91-632. ISBN 0-87436-585-6.

This attractive encyclopedia provides a state-by-state guide to destinations of interest to educators or people who work with children. In spite of the author's claim that this resource is for those who are tired of the same old field trips, destinations are predictable: zoos, nature centers, museums, historical buildings, planetariums, and unique natural history sites. Sadly, Long limits inclusions to those destinations found in metropolitan areas with a population of 100,000 or more. This policy results in South Dakota, a state rich in field trip opportunities, having only four entries, all from Pierre, with no mention of Mount Rushmore or Badlands National Park.

Although the facilities are described and a limited schedule is provided, the volume would be more useful if the author had included suggested grade, age, or interest levels and noted the availability of program brochures. While limited in scope, this encyclopedia is useful for residents of major metropolitan areas. [R: Choice, May 92, p. 1370; RQ, Summer 92, pp. 568-69; SLJ, May 92, p. 26]

— **Suzanne I. Barchers**

353. **NCEA/Ganley's Catholic Schools in America 1992.** 20th ed. Mary Mahar, ed. Montrose, Colo., Fisher Publishing, 1992. 333p. $37.50pa.

Since 1969-1970 the National Catholic Educational Association (NCEA) has published a statistical report on Catholic elementary and secondary schools in the United States. Prior to this time, extensive data did not exist for these schools. This edition contains the core school enrollment and staffing data of the NCEA historical file. Additionally, data have been collected on the following new programs: extended care programs, Chapter I services, and state certification and accreditation. (This information is found in appendixes B and C.) The first part of the report presents a comparison of Catholic schools with other private schools and with the public sector. The second part of the report discusses Catholic education 1991-1992. The report is based upon information submitted by 174 archdiocesan and diocesan offices of education and, in some instances, state Catholic conferences. The directory is divided by states and territories of the United States and subdivided by Catholic diocese. Each diocesan listing is headed by the names, addresses, telephone numbers, and position codes of diocese-wide administrators. Listings include school names, addresses, and telephone numbers as well as grades, enrollment, and principals' names.

The introduction and statistical graphic presentations are particularly useful for understanding the growth and work of Catholic schools. This directory will be helpful for education students and researchers. — **Randy M. Wood**

354. Van Scotter, Richard D. **Public Schooling in America: A Reference Handbook.** Santa Barbara, Calif., ABC-Clio, 1991. 240p. index. (Contemporary World Issues). $39.50. LA217.2.V36. 371'.01'0973. LC 91-28497. ISBN 0-87436-595-3.

This volume is designed to serve as a general handbook on the American public school. Ambitiously conceived, it contains a synopsis of significant issues, factual data, and several lists of information resources. Modern educational reform, frequently viewed as a recurrent struggle between equality and excellence, is introduced in the first section. The reform movement is then analyzed within the framework of specific issues facing the public school. Prominent among these issues are media, desegregation, finances, safety and order, creationism, censorship, public school choice, and the school structure. A chronicle of educational landmarks, from the founding of the Boston Public Latin School in 1635 to the Charlottesville education summit in 1989, distills the essential story of educational reform. Further historical context is provided by biographical sketches of several dozen educational leaders, such as Ernest Boyer, John Goodlad, Diane Ravitch, and Theodore Sizer.

Recommendations from the major educational reports published during the past decade add perspective to the issues and personalities. Statistical data in the form of charts and graphs cover a variety of areas, including school population, behavioral problems, school performance, curriculum, teaching profession, and financial support. A selective list of national organizations, associations, and government agencies that contribute to the field of education is furnished. Rounding out the volume are two bibliographic sections that enumerate reference materials and journal titles.

Van Scotter's goal of producing a brief, readable guide to the themes, leaders, reports, data, and information resources that define the American public school has been realized. Concisely and gracefully written, this volume is appropriate for all types of libraries, especially those with a strong demand for career information. [R: Choice, Apr 92, p. 1214] — **Arthur P. Young**

HIGHER EDUCATION

Almanacs

355. **The Almanac of Higher Education 1992.** By the editors of the *Chronicle of Higher Education*. Chicago, University of Chicago Press, 1992. 342p. $18.95pa. ISBN 0-226-18457-9. ISSN 1044-3096.

Each year the *Chronicle of Higher Education* publishes, either as a supplement or as a full issue, its almanac, which contains mostly statistical and tabular information about many aspects of higher education — students, faculty and staff, institutions, and governmental matters — but not about programs or curricula. Another major portion is devoted to summaries of the higher education situation in each state. The almanac under review is a repackaging of that information from a tabloid format into a much handier one, along with some additional material—in particular, a table that shows the racial and ethnic enrollments for 3,100 colleges and universities. Any library that has frequent calls for such information about higher education will want this almanac, even if it receive the *Chronicle*, because the book is much easier to handle.—**Evan Ira Farber**

Biography

356. **Princetonians 1784-1790: A Biographical Dictionary.** By Ruth L. Woodward and Wesley Frank Craven. Princeton, N.J., Princeton University Press, 1991. 618p. index. $59.50. LD4601.P75. 378.749'67. LC 81-47074. ISBN 0-691-04771-5.

357. **Princetonians 1791-1794: A Biographical Dictionary.** By J. Jefferson Looney and Ruth L. Woodward. Princeton, N.J., Princeton University Press, 1991. 577p. index. $59.50. LD4601.P75. 378.749'.67. LC 81-47074. ISBN 0-691-04772-3.

These volumes bring to a close the series of biographical sketches of Princeton University students (1748-1794) first published in 1976. The fourth and fifth volumes contain biographies of 355 men who attended Princeton (College of New Jersey) classes during the period 1784 to 1794. Each volume includes a substantial introduction, sketches (often illustrated) by class year, appendixes that tabulate geographical and occupational variables of students, and a detailed index. Volume 5 also furnishes sketches omitted from previous volumes as well as errata and additions for these volumes.

The post-Revolutionary decade was one of great change for the Princeton community. Fiscal problems, demands for a more relevant curriculum, the loss of many New England students and a shift to heavy recruiting in the South, and the dramatic increase in the number of students entering the legal profession rather than the ministry were some of the issues that faced the university during this period. Notable graduates are found throughout the volumes: William Johnson, Jr., associate justice of the United States Supreme Court; John Taylor, governor of South Carolina; John Randolph of Roanoke, Virginia congressman; and Joseph Caldwell, a founder of the University of North Carolina. All of the sketches are carefully researched, clearly written, and accompanied by extensive bibliographies that identify primary and secondary sources. The history of Princeton University is so intertwined with the nation's experience that these unique biographical volumes deserve a high priority for education and history collections.—**Arthur P. Young**

Dictionaries and Encyclopedias

358. **The Encyclopedia of Higher Education.** Burton R. Clark and Guy R. Neave, eds. Tarrytown, N.Y., Pergamon Press, 1992. 4v. index. $1500.00/set. LB15.E49. 378'.003. ISBN 0-08-037251-1.

With more than 300 articles and essays contributed by almost an equal number of scholars from many countries, this encyclopedia attempts "a far-reaching, extensive integration" of "the current international knowledge about higher education." It is most successful in achieving that purpose. Volume 1 is devoted to individual national systems of higher education. To be included, a country had to have at least 3,000 students in higher education institutions. Each of the 138 countries within is treated in a single article that ranges from 2 pages (e.g., Mali) to 19 (e.g., Germany, Federal Republic of) in length. Each article contains five sections: "Higher Education and Society"; "The Institutional Fabric of the Higher Education System"; "Governance, Administration, and Finance"; "Faculty and Students—Teaching, Learning and Research"; and a conclusion, which in a number of cases is refreshingly candid. Many of the articles contain useful statistical tables, and all conclude with a bibliography, some quite extensive.

Volumes 2 and 3, "Analytical Perspectives," use as a framework the first four sections treated for each country in volume 1. Under these sections are analytical papers on many specific (and occasionally unexpected but useful and interesting) topics. For example, under "Higher Education and Society" are such topics as credentialism, equality and higher education, and student mobility (international); under "The Institutional Fabric" are liberal arts colleges, distance education at postsecondary level, and universities from 1500 to 1900; and under "Governance" are accreditation, institutional autonomy, and deans and heads of departments. These examples do not really indicate the variety, originality, and readability of the essays. A final section in volume 3 includes 19 essays that look at higher education from the perspective of a particular discipline. These two volumes are especially valuable, as the topics they treat are much less likely to become dated soon, the discussions are well written and frequently have informative or provocative observations, and information and sources not easy to find quickly elsewhere have been pulled together. A good example is the essay on faculty recruitment, promotion, and tenure, which includes a clear discussion of a complex issue, tenure—its history, pros and cons, and alternatives, with a selective, up-to-date bibliography—all in fewer than 10 pages. Volume 4 contains 40 fine up-to-date essays on individual disciplines, their "development and structure, orientation and thought." A name index and a detailed subject index complete the set.

There are many differences between this set and the 1977, 10-volume *International Encyclopedia of Higher Education* (see ARBA 79, entry 638). A primary one is that all articles are now grouped under major topics and within particular themes or categories rather than alphabetically. It is impossible to say whether this changed structure or the totally different set of contributors and editors has made the difference, but there is no question that the present set is more interesting to browse and more pleasurable to read. Many of the articles and essays are more than just overviews or summaries of present knowledge; they offer useful insights and interpretations. Even the essays that introduce the various sections are worth reading.

Overall, all the differences between the two sets favor the new one. Of course, with the number and variety of contributors, there is some unevenness in quality, but the editors have done a masterful job in keeping it to a minimum. This encyclopedia makes an important contribution to the field and should be a useful addition to any large reference collection.—**Evan Ira Farber**

Directories

359. **AACJC Membership Directory 1992.** Jim Mahoney and Lela Sallis, eds. Washington, D.C., American Association of Community and Junior Colleges, 1992. 206p. index. $44.00pa. ISBN 0-87117-242-9.

As of February 1, 1992, the American Association of Community and Junior Colleges (AACJC) had a membership of 1,140 community, technical, and junior colleges. The purpose of this annual directory is to serve as a quick reference guide of basic information about these schools.

The book has two parts plus appendixes and indexes. Part 1 contains information on the mission, leadership, and components of the AACJC. Part 2 is the main section of the book; its list of AACJC institutional members, arranged alphabetically by state, is quite valuable. The entry for each college contains address, telephone and fax numbers, names of chief executive officers, year established, credit enrollment, type of control, and number of campuses. The appendixes give the names, addresses, and telephone and fax numbers of state directors of two-year colleges; the texts of the AACJC constitution and bylaws; and various policy statements. This publication is an authoritative and basic reference book for all libraries.—**Marshall E. Nunn**

360. **Directory of Faculty Contracts and Bargaining Agents in Institutions of Higher Education. Volume 18: January 1992.** By Joel M. Douglas with Michael Sandorfy. New York, National Center for the Study of Collective Bargaining in Higher Education and the Professions, Baruch College, City University of New York, 1992. 167p. index. $35.00pa. ISSN 0276-7805.

This is a sourcebook for those engaged in either the practice or study of faculty unionization in higher education. The major portion of the directory is a status report on collective bargaining activity among college faculty during 1991. It covers faculty contracts and bargaining agents in public and private institutions in the United States, listed in alphabetical order by states. The statistical analyses cover full- and part-time faculty, administrators, chairs, and other professional staff bargaining units. Excluded are academic support staff (nonprofessional), health care support staff, and graduate and teaching assistants. Data is broken down by public and private and 4-year and 2-year institutions, as well as for recognized faculty agents and collective bargaining agreements. Also included is a roster of bargaining agents cited in the directory. The index covers institutions. This work should be of interest to practitioners, researchers, and students of collective bargaining in higher education.—**Roslyn Attinson**

361. **Faculty White Pages 1991: A Subject-Classified Directory....** Compiled by CMG Information Services. Detroit, Gale, 1991. 2181p. $130.00pa. ISBN 0-8103-7178-2. ISSN 1040-1288.

Essentially similar to the 1989 edition (see ARBA 90, entry 327), this book is a directory to more than 537,000 university and college faculty in the United States, American Samoa, Guam, Puerto Rico, the Trust Territories of the Pacific Islands, and the Virgin Islands. What makes it different from other faculty directories is its arrangement by discipline: individuals are listed alphabetically within 41 categories, from agriculture to vocational education. Each entry contains the person's name, department, college, and telephone number. Entries can be duplicated; for example, C. Elise Albert appears in the astronomy and the physics sections (in both cases, her discipline is listed as physics). The front matter consists of an introduction, a how-to-use section, a list of subjects covered, a list of abbreviations, and a roster of colleges and universities. This last seems unusually complete, as it includes small religious colleges as well as larger institutions.

Because of the subject arrangement, it is not possible to search for someone by name unless one knows that person's field; even then, one may have to search through several related disciplines (e.g., allied health, nursing). Thus, this competently produced, attractive work is probably best used as a supplement to the larger, name-arranged faculty directories. – **D. A. Rothschild**

Handbooks and Yearbooks

362. **The ACCC Directory of Canadian Colleges and Institutes. Repertoire ACCC des Colleges et Instituts Canadiens.** Concord, Ont., Irwin Publishing; distr., Don Mills, Ont., General Publishing, 1992. 359p. index. price not reported. 378'.05202571. ISBN 0-7725-1930-7.

This softcover directory of ACCC (Association of Canadian Community Colleges) member, postsecondary, non-degree-granting schools is organized by Canadian province. Each section contains a description of the characteristics of the provincial school system and a map that shows general campus locations. Institution profiles are arranged alphabetically and include a college overview and information about the calendar system, enrollment, admission requirements, tuition, application deadlines, financial assistance, and campus life. The profiles also list areas of expertise and academic programs. The entries for institutions in Quebec are presented in both French and English. The index contains a detailed list of specific educational programs and identifies the institutions that offer each program. The utility of this book could be enhanced by additional general and how-to information for prospective students; however, it is a valuable resource for identifying Canadian institutions that offer vocational and college preparatory education. – **J. Francis Mattil**

363. **American Universities and Colleges.** 14th ed. Hawthorne, N.Y., Walter de Gruyter, 1992. 1991p. index. $149.95. LC 28-5598. ISBN 0-89925-861-1. ISSN 0066-0922.

This latest edition of a title that has become a mainstay of education reference collections includes information on more than 1,900 institutions of higher education. A series of introductory essays profiles the growth and current status of higher education in the United States, presenting statistics on funding, undergraduate and graduate professional education, and foreign student enrollment. Projections for higher education and a discussion of the structure of higher education are also included. A second section profiles academic and professional programs according to institution and degrees offered. The third and major section of the work, arranged alphabetically by state and institution, presents summary profiles of each institution, with information on characteristics, history, admission requirements, degree requirements, financial aid, library resources, student housing, and the like. Appendixes include essays on academic codes and ceremonies, tables of earned doctorates, ROTC programs, summary data on institutions included in the major section, and a brief description of the American Council on Education. Institutional and general indexes are included. Highly recommended for high school, public, and academic library reference collections, especially those that cannot afford a variety of general or specialized guides to higher education. – **Edmund F. SantaVicca**

364. **Barron's Best Buys in College Education.** 2d ed. By Lucia Solorzano. Hauppauge, N.Y., Barron's Educational Series, 1992. 680p. index. $13.95pa. L901.S567. 378.73. LC 92-12265. ISBN 0-8120-4860-1.

This work is touted as the "student's #1 choice" for those seeking a source that discusses good values in higher education. Included are 300 colleges and universities from all 50 states; they range from small private colleges to large state universities. In addition to the usual statistics on enrollment, test scores, and tuition, each entry is divided into such categories as student body, academics, facilities, and campus life. All of the information in these is reported anecdotally. It appears that Solorzano has made a considerable effort to ensure accuracy. A random sampling of familiar schools found *Best Buys* to be quite accurate. The entries that make this guide special are "Cost Cutters," "Payoff," and "Bottom Line." These sections cover financial aid, the results of attending a school, and a brief summary of the institution. Particularly impressive are the quotations by students about their schools. These comments put a human face to the discussions and are both supportive and critical.

This guide will prove invaluable to prospective undergraduates and their parents. In addition to being most informative, it is very readable and even entertaining. Highly recommended.
—**Phillip P. Powell**

365. **Barron's Profiles of American Colleges.** 19th ed. Compiled and edited by the College Division of Barron's Educational Series. Hauppauge, N.Y., Barron's Educational Series, 1992. 1606p. index. $18.95pa. LC 87-640099. ISBN 0-8120-4862-8.

One of Barron's many progeny, *Profiles* provides comprehensive, analytical coverage of all four-year colleges in the United States and its protectorates (plus large universities in Canada, Mexico, and abroad) that offer a bachelor's degree and are accredited or recognized candidates for accreditation. Consisting of capsules and critical essays, the profiles comprise the main section. Capsules give at-a-glance data on application deadlines, student size and composition, average ACT and SAT scores, tuition and expenses, percent of faculty with doctorates, salary level, faculty/student ratio, and more. Under bold headings, essays cover information summarized from 1991-1992 data on student life, principal areas of study, financial aid, computers available to students, library holdings, and so forth. A brief history of the school begins each essay. Arrangement is by state, then alphabetical by college name. A map heads each state section.

Blue pages at the beginning of the volume provide useful charts. One allows users to compare data from the capsules geographically. Another reviews 600 majors: which schools offer what, along with tuition and rating. Still another lists institutions under the categories "Very Competitive" through "Non-Competitive." An introduction gives sensible advice on how to choose a college, score high on entrance exams, make a good interview impression, find the money, survive the freshman year, and decide on a major. This work's information is more critical and more easily scanned than its competitors.—**Mary Jo Walker**

366. **Barron's Top 50: An Inside Look at America's Best Colleges.** Tom Fischgrund, ed. Hauppauge, N.Y., Barron's Educational Series, 1991. 682p. $12.95pa. L901.B34. 378.73. LC 91-11846. ISBN 0-8120-4744-3.

Selecting a college frequently involves visiting campuses, reviewing catalogs and guides, talking with guidance counselors, and conversing with currently enrolled students. None of these sources alone will reveal the total learning environment of an institution. The fit and feel of a college is perhaps best conveyed through the insights of recent graduates who comment on their collegiate experience. This volume is designed to furnish that student-based perspective through essays about the nation's top 50 institutions of higher education. The schools were selected on the three-fold criteria of percent accepted, percent enrolled, and SAT scores. Essays average a dozen pages and cover the following areas: overall program, financial aid, academic environment, social life, extracurricular activities, graduates, and summary overview. Following the profiles is a section of tips on selecting colleges, getting in, filling out the application, financing, and succeeding. The volume is rounded out by appendixes that provide statistical comparisons of the colleges, notes on contributors, and schools by regions.

These profiles are crisply written, informative, and evocative of the special atmosphere associated with each institution. Serious commentary leavened with humor is found throughout. Recommended for all types of libraries, especially those catering to college-bound patrons.—**Arthur P. Young**

367. **Chronicle Financial Aid Guide for 1991-92 School Year.** Moravia, N.Y., Chronicle Guidance, 1991. 461p. index. $19.95pa. 378.3. LC 79-640360. ISBN 1-55631-169-9. ISSN 0190-339X.

An excellent source of noncollegiate financial aid, this guide contains current information on 2,050 financial aid sources offered nationally or regionally. Information is also provided on federal aid programs, state-sponsored programs, and aid available from national and international labor unions. The scope of the aid listed is broad, covering high school to postdoctoral students. Aid presented includes competitions, contests, essay awards, loans, scholarships, grants, internships, work-study programs, postdoctoral fellowships, and research grants.

The main body of the work alphabetically lists the sponsoring agency and all pertinent information: level of student, eligibility, amount, selection information, and when and where to send applications. Essential to using the volume is the "Cross-Reference to Programs" that lists subject areas and the aid available for each one. The index lists names of sponsoring agencies and specific programs. Most useful here are the lists of aid programs that individual states offer scholars. There is also a bibliography of additional publications on the topic. For those people who may not be able to attend college or who wish to receive training in a trade, there is a list of regional and state offices that may be contacted to learn where training is available. This annual publication is one of the most comprehensive sources of noncollegiate aid available and should be on the shelves of all school, college, and public libraries.—**Marilyn Strong Noronha**

368. **Chronicle Four-Year College Databook for 1991-92 School Year.** Moravia, N.Y., Chronicle Guidance, 1991. 550p. index. $19.99pa. 378.1. LC 79-644820. ISBN 0-55631-168-0. ISSN 0191-3670.

369. **Chronicle Two-Year College Databook for 1991-92 School Year.** Moravia, N.Y., Chronicle Guidance, 1991. 441p. index. $19.96pa. 378.1. LC 79-644821. ISBN 1-55631-167-2. ISSN 0191-3662.

These college guides are easy to use and provide quick access to basic factual information. Data was gathered from institutions of higher education listed in the *hep Higher Education Directory* (see ARBA 88, entry 358). The 4-year guide covers more than 2,000 institutions; the 2-year guide lists 2,300. Each volume contains a brief introduction on how to use the book, followed by two sections: college majors or programs of study, and college charts. In the college majors section, the type of degree offered (e.g., bachelor's, master's, doctoral, certificate, associate) is indicated after each school's name. The main strength of these books lies in the number of detailed listings for majors, with the 4-year volume giving 920 fields of study and the other giving 980. In comparison, the *Index of Majors* (see ARBA 91, entry 333) lists only 580 majors for degree levels from certificate to doctorate. *The College Blue Book* (see ARBA 88, entry 372) also contains a very comprehensive index of majors. Still, one may need to check all three guides to obtain a comprehensive list for any given field of study. For instance, under Native American/American Indian studies, *The College Blue Book* lists 16 colleges, *Index of Majors* lists 34, and the *Databooks* list 29, yet only 6 schools are common to all 3 lists.

The college chart section of each *Databook* is arranged by state. Charts give the name, address, and telephone number of each college, followed by information about the calendar system, enrollment statistics, admissions requirements (e.g., exams, application deadlines, fees), college costs, and financial aid data. The tabular arrangement makes it especially easy to compare data for different institutions. An appendix contains additional information on accreditation and may list fax and toll-free numbers for some of the schools. A second appendix lists accrediting associations.

Most reference librarians would agree that you can never have too many college guides. While Chronicle databooks do not provide the longer narrative descriptions such as those found in *The College Blue Book*, they will prove useful as indexes to majors, as directories, and as sources of comparative data.—**Deborah V. Rollins**

370. **College Admissions Data Handbook 1992-93: West Region.** Concord, Mass., Orchard House, 1992. 770p. index. $48.00pa. ISBN 1-878172-18-2.

This handbook is the 33d edition of an annual directory first begun in 1960 by the Educational Research Corporation of the Harvard Graduate School of Education. Created to help counselors, parents, and college applicants select schools best suited to students' needs and resources, the directory offers information about nearly 400 accredited colleges and universities in the 19 states west of the

Mississippi River; in the Canadian provinces of British Columbia, Alberta, Saskatchewan, and Manitoba; and in Guam and Mexico. Three companion volumes provide similar data for colleges in the midwest, the northeast, and the southeast.

For each institution there is a two-page entry. The entries, which are listed alphabetically by the principal word in the name of the college, follow a standard format that allows for easy comparisons between schools. The descriptions include data on student enrollments, admissions policies, student body characteristics, expenses and financial aid opportunities, academic and extracurricular offerings, campus housing and automobile regulations, the academic calendar, and other miscellaneous items. The editors do not attempt to recommend or rate the comparative quality of the institutions.

Every November the editors send questionnaires to the college's admissions offices with instructions to update the data presented in the previous year's edition. Readers should be aware, however, that while the statistical data generally is current and correct, the descriptive information may be out of date. For instance, the information on this reviewer's home institution appears to have been derived from a university catalog published a decade ago, and thereby contains several inaccuracies. Despite this problem, the directory is a valuable source for college-bound individuals searching for a school to match their interests, abilities, and pocketbooks.

—Terry D. Bilhartz

371. Dennis, Marguerite J. **Complete College Financing Guide.** 2d ed. Hauppauge, N.Y., Barron's Educational Series, 1992. 251p. index. $13.95pa. LB2337.4.D455. 378.3'0973. LC 91-42484. ISBN 0-8120-4950-0.

This is a revised edition of *Dollars for Scholars*, first published in 1989. The book is a how-to manual written primarily for students and their parents who are looking for undergraduate college financing. It also contains general advice and selective funding sources for graduate education.

The book is divided into three parts. The first deals with how to apply for aid and how financial need is determined. Section 2 has information on federal, state, individual school, and employment programs. It also includes chapters on financial aid for specific types of students, such as minorities, women, and graduate students. The last miscellaneous section covers such topics as the rights and responsibilities of students who receive financial assistance; tips on reducing college costs; and a list of all the colleges in the United States, arranged by state, with the cost of tuition, room and board, and books and supplies, as well as the telephone numbers of their financial aid offices.

Because it has much more information about different types and sources of financial aid, this publication complements other well-known guides, such as the College Board's *College Cost Book* and *Peterson's College Money Handbook*, which concentrate primarily on the cost and aid profiles of individual schools. It is a useful addition to all college guide collections.

—Christine E. King

372. **The Insider's Guide to the Colleges 1993.** Compiled and edited by the staff of the *Yale Daily News*. New York, St. Martin's Press, 1992. 751p. index. $26.95; $15.99pa. ISBN 0-312-08507-9; 0-312-08224-Xpa.

There are many reputable college guides available today, so why is another one needed? *The Insider's Guide to the Colleges* is unique in that it is still the only one written and edited exclusively by students. It has established itself as a lively and valuable source as it has grown over the years. The latest edition contains profiles of more than 300 colleges and universities, so it is selective; only those colleges the editors believe to be the best and noteworthy are included. Each entry begins with standard statistical and descriptive information on enrollment, costs, admission, and SAT scores. This section is followed by an essay that gives the insider's view of each campus. The heart of the guide, these essays are the source of its enduring appeal; they are of uniform quality and bring a distinctly human touch to what can be an impersonal description. The book also has information on college admissions, choosing a school, and disabled student services, along with an introduction for international students; a glossary of college admission terms; and "The College Finder," which helps students identify the right school in dozens of categories, such as small liberal arts colleges. The guide concludes with a short section on Canada that describes eight of the better Canadian universities.—**Marshall E. Nunn**

373. Kirby, Debra M., with Christa Brelin. **Fund Your Way through College: Uncovering 1,100 Great Opportunities in Undergraduate Financial Aid.** Detroit, Visible Ink Press/Gale, 1992. 454p. index. $19.95pa. ISBN 0-8103-9422-7.

For prospective college students and their parents, this work provides guidance in confronting the financial maze that surrounds higher education. The preface has general information on preparing to finance a college education, and the introduction explains how to use the book, which is divided into three main parts: "Vocational Paths," "Vocational Pathfinders," and "Great Opportunities." The first section simply lists 30 fields of study and specific career goals encompassed by each field. The second lists awards grouped under career titles, and the third arranges these awards alphabetically by sponsor and describes them. Once a vocational title has been selected, the second section indicates general requirements and restrictions for each award. For a complete description of the purpose, aims, availability, and application procedures of each award, the third section must be consulted.

Although the introduction adequately explains the book's layout, the shift from organization by vocational title to organization by sponsoring agency seems arbitrary and unhelpful. This forces the reader to flip back and forth between the second and third sections or use the index to find each agency. Students are probably more interested in vocational titles than in sponsoring agencies; having complete descriptions in one section rather than scattered throughout the book would simplify their search. Nonetheless, the information on each award is satisfactory and clear. [R: RBB, 1 Dec 92, p. 688]
— **Rebecca Jordan**

374. **Peterson's Grants for Graduate Study.** 3d ed. Princeton, N.J., Peterson's Guides, 1992. 365p. index. $59.95pa. ISBN 1-56079-052-0. ISSN 1058-6377.

Generally considered the standard for graduate study grant information, *Peterson's Grants for Graduate Study* describes more than 700 programs that offer financial support for master's and doctoral students. Arranged alphabetically, the work provides well-written profiles for each program that focus on dollar amounts available for an applicant, eligible fields of study, special features, eligibility requirements, application deadlines, and contact names and addresses (occasionally including telephone numbers). Special indexes furnish lists by field of study and by administering (sponsoring) agency. Especially helpful is the 22-page chapter on the grant-seeking process. This is the most useful guide to grants for graduate study available. — **C. B. (Bob) Darrell**

375. **Peterson's Grants for Postdoctoral Study.** Princeton, N.J., Peterson's Guides, 1992. 373p. index. $54.95pa. ISBN 1-56079-053-9. ISSN 1058-9287.

Produced from the nation's best grants database for graduate and postgraduate study (the same database produced the unparalleled *Peterson's Grants for Graduate Study* [Peterson's Guides, 1991]), this work describes more than 700 fellowships, scholarships, grants, awards, and prizes. A first edition, it profiles dollar amounts available for each successful applicant; eligible fields of study; special features; eligibility requirements; application deadlines; and contact names, addresses, and telephone numbers. The work also includes indexes that list fields of study and administering or sponsoring agencies. There is an excellent chapter on seeking and winning postdoctoral grants and awards. No more complete directory on money for postdoctoral study exists. — **C. B. (Bob) Darrell**

376. Purcell, Catherine. **Guide to MBA Programs in Canada.** Toronto, ECW Press, 1991. 225p. maps. $14.95pa. 650'.071'171. ISBN 1-55022-131-0.

The strengths and weaknesses of 26 Canadian MBA schools are delineated in this useful educational guide. Introductory sections address the value of, and preparation required for, the MBA degree. Admission requirements and suggestions for submitting a strong dossier are covered. Profiles of the individual schools, usually 7 to 10 pages, are based on a survey of administrators and 10 percent of the student population. Institutional profiles furnish class data related to average GPA, average GMAT, number of applicants, size of incoming class, percentage of women, percentage of students with full-time work experience, distribution of undergraduate degrees, and part-time student data. Placement information and a description of the local area are included. A detailed profile of one or two currently enrolled students accompanies the description of each school.

Several informative appendixes round out the volume: major trends in the applicant pool and the MBA curriculum, percentage of women MBA students, average age of entering students, ratio of applications to acceptances, unique school characteristics, and school addresses. The guide is crisply written, up-to-date, and organized for easy use. Recommended for all reference collections that serve students interested in graduate business education. — **Arthur P. Young**

377. **Scholarships, Fellowships and Loans, 1992-93: A Guide to Education-Related Financial Aid Programs for Students and Professionals.** 9th ed. Debra M. Kirby and Eric G. Carlson, eds. Detroit, Gale, 1992. 769p. index. $110.00. ISBN 0-8103-8347-0.ISSN 1058-5699.

The 9th edition of one of the best guides to scholarships has been revamped under the auspices of Gale. Covering grants, awards, contests, and loans, the work has added about 1,200 new awards for a total of 2,600. Some governmental sources are included, but the majority of benefactors are private corporations and foundations, religious groups, and professional associations. The funds are applicable for a variety of educational purposes, from the high school level through postdoctoral and professional study.

The descriptive entries give all the pertinent information necessary for applicants: qualifications, selection criteria, award amount, addresses, and telephone and fax numbers. What sets this guide apart from other sources, however, is the fine set of indexes. A vocational goals index lists financial aid sources under a number of career objectives, then charts the educational level, award type, and any special requirements (e.g., citizenship, religious affiliation) for each aid source. Most of the additional indexes — field of study, legal residence, place of study, special recipients, and sponsoring organization — also list the study level and type of award next to the award name. The ability to zero in on appropriate sources and avoid those that are not is a great timesaver.

As is typical of Gale sources, this one is well edited and attractively produced. The price is not low compared to various paperback sources, but the book's sturdiness and comprehensiveness serve reference purposes well. It compares favorably with similar hardbound titles, such as *The Scholarship Book* (see ARBA 91, entry 314) and the scholarship volume of *The College Blue Book* (see ARBA 88, entry 372). [R: LJ, 1 May 92, p. 76; RBB, 1 Feb 92, p. 1058]

— **Christopher W. Nolan**

378. Thorson, Marcie Kisner. **Campus-Free College Degrees.** 5th ed. Tulsa, Okla., Thorson Guides, 1992. 158p. index. $16.95pa. LC6251.T6. 378.2'4. ISBN 0-916277-32-1.

This guidebook focuses on nontraditional degree programs that accept credit for prior learning, both formal and informal, with the remainder of study for the degree completed through off-campus directed study with little or no residency required. Thorson lists different governmental accreditation agencies and identifies them as institutional accreditation, specialized (professional) accreditation, and state recognition. This list is very helpful in determining which programs have achieved high levels of academic excellence. Each state agency for higher education is also listed as a reference for students wanting to know more about specific institutions.

Several sections of the book give different ways students can gain credit. Credit for examination, military experience, experiential learning, education completed in other countries, and correspondence study are all discussed in detail, along with specific information on how to learn more about these areas. Special sections also discuss high school diplomas, specialized home study schools, Bible colleges, and the learning contract.

The largest section of the book lists, in alphabetical order, schools that grant bachelor's, master's, and doctoral degrees with either no residency or a short residency required. Each school entry provides address, telephone number, accreditation, residency requirement, and degrees offered, as well as specific information about credit hours, tuition, and requirements for graduation. The directory of colleges by state and the index of schools are particularly helpful.

— **Randy M. Wood**

Indexes

379. **College Admissions Index of Majors & Sports 1992-93.** Concord, Mass., Orchard House, 1992. 448p. $28.00pa. ISBN 1-878172-19-0.

This title is touted as an important source of information that will help students, their parents, and counselors identify four-year institutions. However, although it cites majors and sports and lists institutions that offer them, it provides no addresses or other information about the schools. It must be used along with the *College Admissions Data Handbook* (see index for entry number), which has pertinent information about the campuses cited and what they are like.

The index also suffers from several weaknesses. There are no cross-references. There is a cross-index of interest areas, but these categories are too few and too broad. In some cases the majors listed are too broad (e.g., engineering). Some fields, such as comparative language and literature, are not listed, and some disciplines are absent, such as Asian-American and Mexican-American studies. The tuition information included may be useful but must be updated annually. Unless the companion works are available, this book is not a practical purchase. — **Roberto P. Haro**

INTERNATIONAL EXCHANGE PROGRAMS AND OPPORTUNITIES

380. **Access to UK Higher Education: A Guide for Overseas Students.** London, Her Majesty's Stationery Office; distr., Lanham, Md., UNIPUB, 1992. 155p. $36.95pa. ISBN 0-11-701508-3.

This directory of opportunities for overseas students in the United Kingdom covers a wide range of programs, from undergraduate bridging courses to jointly supervised doctoral programs. It also lists summer school, junior year abroad, and external degree programs. The information for the entries was supplied by the institutions.

Entries are arranged alphabetically by key word in the institution's name under 10 categories of study possibilities. A typical entry gives information on entry qualifications, subjects offered, degrees or certification granted upon completion, admission requirements, length and dates of programs, fees, and availability of accommodations. Some entries are quite specific, with lists of courses and fee ranges; others are extremely brief. One section lists scholarships available to overseas students at each institution. Another gives information on nonacademic services such as housing for families, child care and health facilities, welfare services, and clubs and societies for overseas students. A list of abbreviations used in the guide identifies organizations, degrees, and other relevant names.

There are no indexes. Access is provided only through the 10 categories and the alphabetical lists of institutions in each. The work lacks introductions that explain the scope or characteristics of each category, and major terms (e.g., "sandwich courses") are not defined. However, the guide does have much information that will be helpful to prospective students. — **Shirley L. Hopkinson**

381. Altbach, Philip G., ed. **International Higher Education: An Encyclopedia.** Hamden, Conn., Garland, 1991. 2v. index. (Garland Reference Library of the Social Sciences, v.506). $150.00/set. LB15.159. 378'.003. LC 90-46952. ISBN 0-8240-4847-4.

This set is not really a comprehensive reference work; rather, it is an impressive anthology. Altbach acknowledges this fact and makes no apology for it.

The principal source for comparison is the 10-volume *International Encyclopedia of Higher Education* (see ARBA 79, entry 638). That work is much more comprehensive in scope and more objective in style. Many of its articles, written from a comparative perspective, are aimed at students and novices, not merely faculty specialists. As a reference encyclopedia that will introduce the user to basic facts, ideas, and events, that work has established the standard, although a thoroughly revised edition is much needed.

Albach's work consists of 67 essays about major issues, themes, nations, and regions. (Seventy percent of the entries discuss a nation or a region.) Contributions are analytical and interpretive, representing up-to-date scholarship from authorities throughout the world. Each nation is represented by a comprehensive narrative, detailed notes, and a bibliography; additionally, statistical tables and charts are often provided.

The initial section of volume 1 treats general topics from historical, political, and intellectual perspectives. These 15 essays range in subject from academic freedom to women in higher education and could well stand alone as a separate volume. Most entries attempt an international approach, but North America is predominant. One would like to see essays on libraries, computers, philanthropy, and research. A topic and name index provides some insight into subject coverage; a number of entries appear under "research" and "private sector." Taken as a whole, this work is a good sourcebook for political and economic issues in higher education.—**John Mark Tucker**

382. Boswick, Storm. **Guide to the Universities of Europe.** New York, Facts on File, 1991. 296p. index. $35.00. L914.5.B67. 378.4. LC 90-19169. ISBN 0-8160-2359-X.

A study experience in Europe has many advantages for the North American student, not the least of which, surprisingly enough, is financial. Many European universities charge foreign students no tuition or much less than some United States institutions. Another advantage, of course, is the opportunity for a truly international education. Under two sections that cover Western and Eastern Europe, a sampling of every country's university and college level institutions is listed. Provided for each are address and type of institution; date founded; enrollment; degrees awarded; academic and special programs; language of instruction; admission requirements; tuition (if any); number of faculty; library collections; publications; and the name of the rector, president, or chancellor. For some countries, such as Germany, France, and the United Kingdom, general information on such important topics as visa requirements, application procedures, deadlines, and cost of living is given. The 1991 publication date means that full details of the dramatic changes in Eastern Europe could not be accommodated. In particular, the work predates the dissolution of the Soviet Union.

A number of typographical errors are likely the result of a lack of familiarity with the languages involved, and the book is most helpful in a geographical sense, less so for the task of selecting schools by subject (although some subjects are included in the index). Nevertheless, this is a very valuable resource, the more so as the work was the result of personal initiative on the part of Boswick. [R: Choice, Sept 92, p. 72]—**Johan Koren**

383. Brickman, William W., and John T. Zepper. **Russian and Soviet Education 1731-1989: A Multilingual Annotated Bibliography.** Hamden, Conn., Garland, 1992. 538p. index. (Reference Books in International Education, v.9; Garland Reference Library of Social Science, v.200). $83.00. Z5815.S66B75. 016.37'0947. LC 91-45874. ISBN 0-8240-9052-7.

Educational development is a subject of ongoing concern to individual countries as well as states and municipalities. The history of education in Russia and the Soviet Union is the subject of this bibliographic study. The authors open with a historical survey of Russian and Soviet educational trends, covering medieval, tsarist, and Soviet eras. Particular emphasis is placed on the tension between Russian officials desirous of modernizing Russia and expanding ties to the West and policymakers who wanted to maintain Russian isolation and prevent national and ideological "contamination" from foreign influences. Examples of individuals who played significant roles in Russian educational history, representing both these viewpoints, include Peter and Catherine the Great, Konstantin Pobedonostsev, Andrei Zhdanov, and Trofim Lysenko.

The center of this compilation is an annotated bibliography of 1,755 entries featuring monographs, articles, dissertations, and government documents compiled through the use of library resources on a global scale. Entries are arranged in alphabetical order by author, with citations and annotations covering scholarship in numerous languages including English, Russian, German, Hebrew, and French.

Despite incorrectly listing the Soviet invasion of Afghanistan in 1981 instead of 1979 (p. 45), Brickman and Zepper have produced a substantive bibliographic chronicle of Russian and Soviet education that will benefit students and scholars. It belongs in the collections of university libraries with significant comparative education and Russian history holdings. [R: Choice, Oct 92, p. 268]

—**Bert Chapman**

384. El-Sanabary, Nagat. **Education in the Arab Gulf States and the Arab World: An Annotated Bibliographic Guide.** Hamden, Conn., Garland, 1992. 572p. index. (Reference Books in International Education, v.17; Garland Reference Library of Social Science, v.689). $75.00. Z5815.A69E4. 016.37'0953. LC 91-21261. ISBN 0-8240-8249-4.

This extensive but selective annotated bibliography includes English-language books, journals, articles, chapters in handbooks, encyclopedia articles, and doctoral dissertations on education in the Arab Gulf states. El-Sanabary indicates that only material with substantial information on education in the Arab Gulf states or the Arab world as a whole is listed. She has also excluded sources that she believes to be biased or stereotypical in their treatment of Arabs, Islam, or Arab society.

The bibliography covers 1950 to 1989, which the author indicates was a period of significant educational expansion in the region. Resource lists are grouped together in 23 chapters on various aspects of education (e.g., preschool and primary education, literary and adult education, higher education). Each chapter is subdivided by country as appropriate. Detailed subject and author indexes provide appropriate access points. Coverage of the topic appears to be comprehensive although not all-inclusive. (At least one area of study—education for librarianship—could not be located in the index.) This title provides an excellent overview of education in the Arab Gulf states and will aid research in comparative education. [R: Choice, July/Aug 92, pp. 1653-54]—**Ahmad Gamaluddin**

385. **European Education Thesaurus.** 1991 ed. Brussels, Office for Official Publications of the European Communities; distr., Lanham, Md., UNIPUB, 1991. 473p. $65.00pa. ISBN 92-77-72423-4.

This is the 3d edition of a work originally titled *EUDISED Multilingual Thesaurus for Information Processing in the Field of Education.* The new title is to some extent misleading because *European* in this context refers to the 12 countries of the European Community (EC). Nevertheless, because Danish is very close to Swedish and Norwegian, the thesaurus still has great value for searchers in those languages. In addition, the introduction notes that a Slovak edition was published in 1985, that a Finnish version exists, and that Turkish and Serbo-Croatian versions are in preparation.

The thesaurus is similar in construction to the *ERIC Thesaurus*, with descriptors (in all nine languages, designated by language indicators; Greek is not transliterated); an indication of category (e.g., MT for microthesaurus) to which the term is assigned; the occasional scope note; and a listing of broader, narrower, or related terms. Each of the nine language versions provides cross-references from unofficial terms in its own language only. Thus, for the English version, there are only references from unofficial English terms, with a strange mixture of American and British terminology (e.g., city USE town; building industry USE construction industry). As in ERIC, there is a rotated listing of descriptors, but this thesaurus also provides terminographs, graphical representations of relationships between the descriptors. Because several of the languages represented are world languages, this work has clear application and value even outside of the EC.—**Johan Koren**

386. **Higher Education in the United Kingdom 1992-93: A Handbook for Students and Their Advisers.** 25th ed. Harlow, England, Longman Group; distr., Phoenix, Ariz., Oryx Press, 1991. 312p. illus. index. $32.95pa. ISBN 0-582-08195-5. ISSN 0306-1744.

This annual is published specifically for foreign students considering study in the United Kingdom. It includes universities, polytechnics and colleges, and degree and nondegree courses. The book is divided into two parts. The first describes in general terms the various types of programs available in different sorts of educational institutions, including "junior year abroad," vacation and continuing education study, and formal degree courses. It also covers admission requirements and procedures, tuition, and student life in the United Kingdom.

The second part is arranged by subject, reflecting the British system of primarily studying in only one field. It is then subdivided, first by qualification awarded and then by type of institution. Each school that has a course in the featured subject area is listed. A bibliography of other books to consult is provided, as are appendixes of college and professional association addresses and a subject index.

Anyone starting to investigate possibilities for study in the United Kingdom will find this book useful. The introductory material will be especially helpful as the higher education system there is quite different from that in the United States. However, for students interested in graduate programs, the annual guides *Graduate Studies* (Cambridge: Hobsons) and *British Universities Guide to Graduate*

Study (London: Association of Commonwealth Universities) are more comprehensive sources. Recommended for academic and public libraries. — **Christine E. King**

387. **International Exchange Locator: A Guide to U.S. Organizations, Federal Agencies, and Congressional Committees....** New York, Institute of International Education, 1991. 183p. index. $25.00pa. ISBN 0-87206-189-2.

International exchange is a form of educational experience very different from a simple year or semester abroad, as it involves a counterpart who takes one's place in the home country and institution, often in one's own home. The result is often a more intimate acquaintance with the people of another country.

Information about educational exchanges is available from a number of different sources, including *Guide to International Education in the United States* (see ARBA 92, entry 314). *International Exchange Locator*, on the other hand, is exclusively concerned with organizations that operate exchange programs, provide support services, or have a specific interest in international educational exchange. Thus, more details can be supplied about the organizations: statement of purpose, types of programs offered, availability of financial support, and so on. Besides standard directory information, therefore, readers learn that the Asian Cultural Council provides fellowships to artists and specialists from Asia and their counterparts in the United States for research, study, travel, and creative pursuits; that its geographical focus is Asia, from Afghanistan eastward; that it covers certain academic levels and exchange areas; that it does offer financial assistance; and that it publishes an annual report. *International Exchange Locator* does not stop there, however. As well as providing information about organizations, the source has tables that list the organizations by region, academic level, exchange area, extent of financial support, and so forth, and a section about government (executive and legislative) agencies related to educational exchange. This is an extremely helpful resource!

— **Johan Koren**

388. Kirk, Mary E. **Where Walls Once Stood: U.S. Responses to New Opportunities for Academic Cooperation with East Central Europe.** New York, Institute of International Education, 1992. 109p. (East Central Europe Information Exchange, no.2). $7.00pa.

"May you live in interesting times." This ancient Chinese curse has been fulfilled with a vengeance in this final decade of the twentieth century, which has seen more changes in political history than several of the preceding decades combined, particularly in Eastern Europe. The result is that new vistas have been opened for exploration of export from the United States of commodities, from technology and money to expertise and culture. This report provides some information on the efforts of academia to reach out to East Central Europe, officially defined here as including Bulgaria, Czechoslovakia, Hungary, Poland, Romania, and Yugoslavia (or what is left of Yugoslavia).

At first this book appears to be less a reference source than a report of research. Nevertheless, most of the report is, in fact, made up of several appendixes with lists of cooperation programs as reported in replies to questionnaires. Associations and institutions, from the American Bar Association to Yeshiva University, have reported involvement in a total of 333 programs. These programs are listed by group or institution, by country and partner institution, and by field of study. Information is also provided on availability of grants from the United States Information Agency or the Agency for International Development, with a final appendix giving suggested references. Continuing changes in the region, with the impending "velvet divorce" between the Czech and Slovak republics and, more violently, the war among the former Yugoslav republics, make some of this information somewhat tenuous but still of interest. — **Johan Koren**

389. **Open Doors 1990/91: Report on International Educational Exchange.** Marianthi Zikopoulos and Elizabeth Sutton, eds. New York, Institute of International Education, 1991. 194p. $36.95pa. ISBN 0-87206-190-6. ISSN 0078-5172.

390. **Profiles 1989-1990: Detailed Analyses of the Foreign Student Population.** Marianthi Zikopoulos, ed. New York, Institute of International Education, 1991. 139p. $34.95pa. ISBN 0-87206-187-6.

As the number of overseas students attending U.S. institutions of higher education continues to increase, it is critical to have current, comprehensive sources that analyze and characterize this phenomenon. These two books fit the bill quite well and include data collected by the Institute of International Education (IIE) from voluntary contributions of members of the American Association of Collegiate Registrars and Admissions Officers and the National Association for Foreign Student Affairs: Association of International Educators.

Open Doors is the annual census of international students from data collected by IIE. Data represent more than 400,000 students from 186 nations, and statistics by geographic origin and field of study are interpreted and arranged in graphs and charts. Users can easily find that more than 2,800 institutions enrolled foreign students, the majority from Japan (22.7 percent), studying education (9.5 percent), and in California (13.5 percent). Gross statistics such as distributions by public and private schools, cost of living expenditures, and institutions with the largest number of foreign students are also provided. In addition, there is information on the more than 70,000 Americans studying abroad.

Profiles, the companion volume, examines the characteristics of individual foreign students by providing relationships among the data. Users can quickly determine how many foreign students from a certain country are studying a specific discipline. Arrangement of data is by region/national origin, subdivided by field, academic level, and gender. Comparative and cross-tabulated data permit users, for example, to discover differences between foreign students studying in various regions of the United States. Also of interest are comparative charts for foreign student characteristics for the last 40 years.

Together or separately, these two sources provide accurate and detailed data difficult to find in other sources. The ease of use and nominal costs should be attractive to international educational policymakers, researchers, students, and foreign student admissions personnel.—**Ilene F. Rockman**

391. Raza, Moonis, and Nirmal Malhotra. **Higher Education in India: A Comprehensive Bibliography.** New Delhi, Concept Publishing; distr., Columbia, Mo., South Asia Books, 1991. 477p. index. $44.00. ISBN 81-7022-346-6.

The first comprehensive bibliography on higher education in India, this work contains 2,485 entries arranged under 50 topics. It includes citations to books, articles, committee and commission reports, and research studies. Topics range from administration to women and cover all aspects of higher education. The entries, which give standard bibliographical information, are arranged in each category first by type of material, then alphabetically by author (or by title when no author is named). They are also classified by a system that the authors carefully explain and illustrate. Charts show the number of items in every category within each topic. The reader can see at a glance, for instance, the areas that have had many research studies and those that have had none. Entries for books and articles are not annotated; those for committee and commission reports and research studies are. Annotations vary from short paragraphs to about two pages and provide access to the ideas and facts in publications that are not normally available outside India. The bibliography is indexed by author names, by regions in India, and by universities. Index entries refer to pages rather than to the classification entry numbers, which makes direct access somewhat slow. In general, the compilation appears to have been carefully prepared and to be comprehensive. It should be useful in subject collections.—**Shirley L. Hopkinson**

392. Steen, Sarah J., ed. **Academic Year Abroad.** New York, Institute of International Education, 1992. 482p. index. $39.95pa. ISBN 0-87206-192-2.

The Institute of International Education (IIE) is the largest U.S. higher education exchange agency. Its guide gives information on more than 2,000 postsecondary study-abroad programs that are open to U.S. citizens and that take place during the academic year. Seventy-five percent of the programs are sponsored by U.S.-accredited colleges and universities.

Entries are arranged by country, then by city, then alphabetically by name. They give information on location, host institution, dates, subjects, eligibility, credits, language and format of instruction, costs, housing, deadlines, contacts, and other miscellaneous pieces of information, including financial aid. Indexes provide access by sponsoring institution or consortia, fields of study, special options, and cost ranges. A section on planning study abroad gives suggestions and recommendations on evaluating educational programs, interpreting advertisements, and living and working abroad. Some advertisements for programs are included. Information for the guide was obtained from the sponsoring institutions.

This is the largest and most complete compilation of its kind. It will be of interest in all collections used by prospective overseas students. A companion volume is the IIE's *Vacation Study Abroad* (1992).—**Shirley L. Hopkinson**

393. Steen, Sarah J., ed. **Vacation Study Abroad.** 42d ed. New York, Institute of International Education, 1992. 321p. index. $31.95pa. ISBN 0-87206-191-4. ISSN 1046-2104.

This guide gives information on summer programs of varying lengths and on short courses in the fall, winter, and spring that are open to U.S. citizens of postsecondary age and educational level. About 60 percent of the programs are sponsored by U.S.-accredited colleges and universities. Information is given on the offerings of many foreign universities, language schools, and other organizations that are open to U.S. students as well as to those from other countries. Many of the programs combine study with travel over short periods of time, or focus on topics of broad interest that are slanted toward adults.

Entries are grouped by country, then by city, then by name of program or sponsor. They include data on location, dates, subjects, eligibility, credit, instructional methods, costs, availability of housing, deadlines, and contacts. The information was obtained directly from the sponsoring program contacts. Indexes provide access by name of sponsoring institution, consortia, fields of study, special options, cost ranges, and duration time. There are suggestions for prospective students on options, language proficiency requirements, locations, facilities for disabled students, internships, travel, and living abroad. Another section covers how to read and interpret advertisements for study programs and study-abroad literature.

This guide is carefully prepared and thorough. It will be useful in any collection used by postsecondary and adult students.—**Shirley L. Hopkinson**

LEARNING DISABILITIES AND DISABLED

394. Lantzy, M. Louise, comp. **Individuals with Disabilities Education Act: An Annotated Guide to Its Literature and Resources, 1980-1991.** Littleton, Colo., Fred B. Rothman, 1992. 147p. index. $37.50 looseleaf w/binder. KF4210.A1L36. 344.73'0791. LC 92-9676. ISBN 0-8377-9274-6.

In 1975, federal law mandated the right of children with disabilities to a free and appropriate public education. This law, although challenged, has to date been upheld. Professionals and advocates with a personal interest in protecting or advancing these rights will find a concise, selective compilation of the pertinent laws in this book. One section lists print and nonprint articles and resources related to different dimensions of the right-to-education issue. This section includes a list of materials about advisement, advocacy, instruction, media coverage, past history, practical matters, and scholarly research. Another section includes brief profiles of various support groups, both government mandated and privately run, with the emphasis on national organizations. Six information clearinghouses are also listed, with brief profiles.

Lantzy comments on the contradictory nature of past rulings that have affected the implementation of the basic right to education for disabled children. There is an implicit expectation that a body of case law challenging this right will continue to evolve. The binder format of this valuable reference work, which allows for insertion of future legal cases and resource information, is a reminder of the ongoing threats to this long-neglected civil right.—**Jeanne Friedrichs**

NONPRINT MATERIALS AND RESOURCES

395. **AFVA Evaluations 1991.** Fort Atkinson, Wis., Highsmith Press, 1992. 340p. illus. index. $40.00. ISBN 0-917846-07-9. ISSN 1051-5925.

While the 1,200 films, videotapes, and interactive videos in this work were not selectively chosen, all entrants in the 1991 American Film and Video Festival appear, and the work does include the fine jury evaluations for each title. These assessments "represent the collective insight of at least four professionals from several relevant viewpoints, rather than an individual reviewer." Among these people are at least one subject specialist and at least one production specialist, plus "programmers, media selectors, professional media specialists, and audiovisual librarians who regularly use film and/or video." For this edition 400 people have contributed their expertise and evaluations. Thus, as a media evaluation source, this work is one of the best.

Other features that make this directory commendable include its excellent and highly readable format, with film titles that appear in large dark print; the fact that productions for all levels of audiences are included; and the rating system based on the jury assessments. Finalists as well as actual award winners are indicated. Entries fall into 100 subject categories and include educational and nontheatrical films and videos. Under each title are found time, format, prices for sale and rental, director, producer and distributor, a synopsis, comments (from jurors' evaluations), age level, uses, awards (if any), and subject areas. There are black-and-white pictures from some of the highly rated films. Basic arrangement follows that of most film and video catalogs (i.e., alphabetical by title), and there are indexes by distributor (including addresses), director, and subject.

The only criticisms that can be made about this work are that a few rating stars appear somewhat detached from their entries and that an index or a list of the most highly rated titles would be useful, as would separate listings by format, especially for interactive video. An examination of 10 sample pages did not disclose a single title in the latter category. Otherwise, this seems to be an excellent general audience film and video rating and selection tool that anyone who needs such an evaluative work should purchase. [R: Choice, Nov 92, p. 437; LJ, 15 June 92, p. 68; RBB, Aug 92, pp. 2030-32; RQ, Fall 92, p. 106] — **Carol Truett**

396. Berger, James L., ed. **Educators Guide to Free Videotapes.** 39th ed. Randolph, Wis., Educators Progress Service, 1992. 628p. index. $24.95pa. LC 55-2784. ISBN 0-87708-243-X.

This annual guide first appeared in 1955 as the *Educators Guide to Free Tapes, Scripts, and Transcriptions*. From 1977 through 1991 it was the *Educators Guide to Free Audio and Video Materials*. The present edition marks a significant change in both scope and title. Audio materials have been removed and are now found only in the publisher's multimedia subject guides (e.g., *Educators Guide to Free Social Studies Materials*). The present volume contains 2,581 free-loan videos from 179 sources, including 874 titles that are new to this edition. A disproportionate number of videos in all subject categories are from religious organizations and government agencies. About a quarter of the total videos (more than 650) are from NASA. More than 165 are from Church World Services, and there are substantial numbers from Dawn Bible Students, Gospel Films, and half a dozen similar groups. Industries and professional associations are also well represented. In marked contrast to the 1992 *Educators Guide to Free Films*, there are only a handful of videos from foreign governments and tourist bureaus, probably reflecting a lack of new materials from such sources.

The preface states that every title has been reviewed by the editor and the only videos included are those that provide authoritative current information that will help meet some accepted and socially useful curriculum goal. However, sectarian bias appears to be a problem in some controversial areas. All of the 11 titles listed in the subject index under sex education are from Gospel Films, and, except for several videos from NASA, all of the titles listed under evolution are from religious groups or Eden Films, an antievolution distributor. Educators may wish to contact agencies listed in *Current Issues Resource Builder* (see ARBA 90, entry 88) to inquire about the availability of free-loan videos that present other points of view. — **Joseph W. Palmer**

397. Diffor, John C., and Elaine N. Diffor, eds. **Educators Guide to Free Films.** 52d ed. Randolph, Wis., Educators Progress Service, 1992. 344p. index. $27.95pa. LC 45-412. ISBN 0-87708-240-5.

The 1992 edition of this familiar guide to 16mm films available on free loan to schools and other groups lists 1,876 films from 122 sources. This is down from the 2,215 listed in the 1991 edition even though 126 new listings have been added. This reflects the dwindling popularity of the 16mm format and the weeding of aging titles. (Some of the current listings, while probably still useful, are decades old.) The editors stress the importance of not using superseded editions of this reference tool, and, given the large number of deletions, this seems good advice.

Sponsors range from the National Gallery of Art to the National Rifle Association and include U.S. government agencies, foreign consulates and tourist bureaus, industries, religious groups, educational organizations, and professional associations. A majority appear to be worthwhile films. Few appear to be outright propaganda; those that are will usually be detected by the combination of subject matter and sponsorship. Naturally, educators will want to preview the films before use. Entries are well annotated and identify any restrictions on availability (usually geographic). There are title, subject, source, and Canadian-availability indexes. Introductory materials include a sample request letter and a guide for evaluating industry-sponsored materials. — **Joseph W. Palmer**

398. **Educational Media and Technology Yearbook. Volume 18: 1992.** Donald P. Ely and Barbara B. Minor, eds. Englewood, Colo., published with the ERIC Clearinghouse on Information Resources and the Association on Educational Communications and Technology by Libraries Unlimited, 1992. 369p. index. $55.00. LB1028.3.E372. 370.778. ISBN 1-56308-015-X. ISSN 8755-2094.

Begun in 1974, this standard work highlights the recent history of the field of educational communications and technology, and it has numerous noteworthy features to recommend it. Especially commendable are the articles on cable in the classroom, interactive multimedia computer systems, and technology and school restructuring. The latter article, by Michael Molenda, is especially helpful. Two noteworthy biographies included are those on Robert Gagne and Robert Heinich. There are also two nice reviews of Paul Saettler's 1991 updated edition of his monumental history of instructional technology, *The Evolution of American Educational Technology*, a work that, according to Saettler, represents the culmination of more than 40 years of study and research and more than 400 personal interviews with key figures in the field.

Also present are the usual features of this yearbook, from reports on seven major media organizations to the directory of more than 200 professional organizations and associations; graduate programs in instructional technology (including a special directory of programs in educational computing); scholarships and awards; and the mediagraphy, which lists books, periodicals, and ERIC documents. One could criticize the fact that 10 pages are devoted to an article on machine technology that appears to be primarily a historical review of teaching machines, while more current and important topics receive much less attention. Otherwise, this new edition appears to live up to its usual high standards and should certainly be purchased by all libraries and individuals that want to continue their collections of these yearbooks and that desire an overview of the previous year. — **Carol Truett**

399. Lankford, Mary D. **Films for Learning, Thinking, and Doing.** Englewood, Colo., Libraries Unlimited, 1992. 228p. index. $24.50. LB1044.L29. 371.3'352. LC 92-17077. ISBN 0-87287-626-8.

Films and videos can be appealing and invaluable instructional resources, provided they are of good quality and are used effectively. This handbook provides teachers and librarians with models and techniques of effective film and video use as well as an annotated bibliography of representative titles. The first four chapters discuss a rationale for film and video use, characteristics of visual literacy, techniques involved in film and video usage, and equipment operation. The last seven chapters cover techniques involved in using more specific types of films: biographical, children's literature, narrationless, folklore, science, visual literacy, and cultural understanding. These chapters also include a selective, annotated bibliography of relevant films and videos, with information on length, date, current distributor, and appropriate grade levels. Many of the brief annotations are excerpts from reviews. There is also a name/title/subject index.

The book's strengths are its models of active viewing, including previewing, viewing, and postviewing activities; its "idea boxes" of suggested classroom activities; and its related library activities. On the other hand, the bibliographic citations do not indicate whether titles are available in film, video, or both formats (this information is only provided for the few films and videos used as instructional models), and no laser disc titles are listed. However, the book should be of use to teachers and educational media specialists. — **Stephen H. Aby**

400. **Educators Guide to Free Guidance Materials.** 30th ed. Mary H. Saterstrom, ed. Randolph, Wis., Educators Progress Service, 1991. 528p. index. $25.95pa. LC 62-18761. ISBN 0-87708-233-2.

Completely revised, this new edition has stylistic changes that should make use easier. The headings are in boldface type, capitalized, and underlined, and titles are also in boldface type. Included are 758 films, 64 filmstrips, 167 slide sets, 2 transparency sets, 250 audiotapes, 429 videotapes, 47 audiodiscs, and 463 print (e.g., charts) items. Of the 2,180 titles included, 515 are new. As with other titles in the series, this source includes sample letters, color-coded indexes (title, subject, source, and availability), descriptive annotations, and an evaluation form. Of particular interest to counselors and teachers will be the sections on relationships, career planning, health, and leisure. Current information on AIDS, family life, and nutrition is offered.

Users need to understand that "free" in this context may mean that the material is loaned without charge, not given away. Often, items must be returned to their sources within a specified period of time, with the user paying the return postage. Suppliers of materials vary from consulates and universities to government agencies and private foundations. Some suppliers will lend only to individuals in certain states. Others request that items be reserved at least a month in advance. Suggestions for future editions include the addition of telephone numbers in the source and availability indexes and the indication of new items (now noted only in the main body of the work) in the title and subject indexes.
— Ilene F. Rockman

401. Nehmer, Kathleen Suttles, ed. **Guide to Free Computer Materials.** 10th ed. Randolph, Wis., Educators Progress Service, 1992. 464p. index. $37.95pa. ISBN 0-87708-237-5.

The latest edition of this guide has several features to recommend it. The shareware section, added just a few years ago, has now expanded to include 220-plus pages of software listings, not counting the source index, and more than 2,000 titles. This should prove a real boon to those with tightened or reduced school budgets. Apple, Amiga, Atari, Commodore, IBM, and Macintosh software are all represented.

More than half of the free items listed in the regular section are new to this edition, and most of the materials may be kept. Close to 300 products are represented in the 11 sections and include films, videotapes, disks, pamphlets, booklets, magazines, posters, and books. Three indexes (title, subject, and source) speed access to desired materials. Some sample subjects are aeronautics, astronomy, business, chemistry, compilers, desktop publishing, DOS, foreign languages, and programming. There is an extensive glossary of computer terminology that could practically serve as a textbook for a computer literacy class.

On the down side, many entries are only for catalogs or descriptions of products. For example, under software the first entry is for a catalog of Apple educational software. Other listings are only for demo disks. However, it is understandable that most software companies are in business to make money. And certainly the extensive shareware section more than makes up for the paucity of truly free software in the regular section.

One change that would greatly enhance the usefulness of this guide would be the addition of a separate index by format of material (e.g., books, disks, films) to better serve the needs of educators with specific requirements. Alternately, format designations could be included as part of each entry in a prominent and standardized position. While many entries do clearly indicate media format and even underline this information, others do not, and this makes the catalog harder to use. Also, a summary by format that gives total numbers included for each, similar to the one that the publisher provides for general categories, would be helpful. In the final analysis, the shareware alone makes this catalog well worth the purchase price. — **Carol Truett**

READING

402. Canavan, Diane D., and Lavonne Hayes Sanborn. **Using Children's Books in Reading/Language Arts Programs: A How-To-Do-It Manual for Library Applications.** New York, Neal-Schuman, 1992. 206p. index. (How-to-do-it Manuals for School and Public Librarians, no.3). $29.95. Z718.1.C24. 025.2'1878. LC 92-3861. ISBN 1-55570-101-9.

If one book were to be recommended for a school librarian or teacher with limited funds, this is the book. A great many annotated booklists are carefully organized to reinforce concepts, skills, vocabulary, comprehension, and literary awareness for reading and language arts programs in grades K through 8. For example, the teacher who would like to enliven a grammar program can turn to "Trade Books Illustrating Parts of Speech" and find illustrated books that not only entertain but also reinforce instruction. The teacher building a unit on letter writing can save hours of research by consulting the list of books that feature that subject. The librarian who wants to involve children in early reading experiences will treasure the sections titled "Books with Repetitive Language," "Books with Rhythm and Rhyme," and "Rebus Books."

The format is easy to read, with ample margins for notes. The annotations are informative and interesting, and the variety of categories and titles is particularly impressive. Teachers and librarians who are using whole language or who wish to supplement the basal reader program through literature will find this resource invaluable and will learn from using the recommended titles.
—Suzanne I. Barchers

403. Gilbar, Steven, ed. **The Reader's Quotation Book: A Literary Companion.** New York, Penguin Books, c1990, 1991. 193p. illus. $7.00pa. Z1003.R27. 808.88'2. LC 91-16619. ISBN 0-14-015839-1.

When one picks up this undersized paperback, which collects quotations on reading, books, libraries, and bookstores, the first thought that comes to mind is that these quotations ought to be easy to find in the standard sources. Wrong! Gilbar has brought together a fascinating collection of tidbits, both familiar and unusual, drawn from such individuals as Percy Bysshe Shelley, Robert Browning, Hilaire Belloc, Maya Angelou, John Cheever, John Updike, and Ralph Waldo Emerson. These notables describe their experiences with favorite genres, children's reading, the role of libraries and bookstores, book collecting, the future of books and reading, and books as friends. Nineteenth-century illustrations add some interest to each of the sections.

Any reader or librarian will enjoy this work, and it will be useful to those preparing talks and brochures where a quip or quotation, a short anecdote, or a sound bite about books and librarians is needed. Highly recommended. —**David V. Loertscher**

404. Hladczuk, John, and William Eller, eds. **International Handbook of Reading Education.** Westport, Conn., Greenwood Press, 1992. 510p. index. $75.00. LB1050.2.I58. 428.4. LC 91-10420. ISBN 0-313-26253-5.

The issue of literacy in this country and abroad is one of growing interest, as nearly one billion adults are illiterate and more than 100 million children do not attend school. The editors, authors of other literacy bibliographies published by Greenwood Press, have compiled 26 case studies from countries as diverse as Australia and Zaire. Each contribution, written by an indigenous scholar, discusses reading in the context of goals, programs, research, materials, teacher qualifications, and parental involvement. The chapter on the United States was written by two professors of education at Millerville University of Pennsylvania. Countries have been selected to provide a geographic, economic, and political balance, but no further criteria are mentioned. The source concludes with brief biographical sketches of the authors.

Absent from the introductory essay is any discussion of the work of the International Reading Association or the International Federation of Library Associations. In addition, a separate recent study of reading literacy by the International Association for the Evaluation of Educational Achievement noted that students in Finland outperformed youngsters in 30 other countries, yet Finland is not featured as a chapter.

While there are several unanswered questions about the selection of countries and contributors, the work does expand and supplement the discussions of literacy and reading published in the *International Encyclopedia of Education* (see ARBA 86, entry 292) and serves to complement *Cross-Cultural Literacy: Global Perspectives on Reading and Writing* (Prentice-Hall, 1992). For those libraries collecting at a comprehensive level for comparative education titles, this is a useful book.
—**Ilene F. Rockman**

VOCATIONAL AND CONTINUING EDUCATION

405. **Chronicle Career Index.** Moravia, N.Y., Chronicle Guidance, 1991. 90p. $14.25pa. 331.7. LC 79-640396. ISBN 1-55631-149-4. ISSN 0276-0355.

Published for 31 years, this work indexes print and audiovisual materials useful to individuals making career decisions. Intended for school-based career counselors and students, it lists materials available as of spring 1991. The list is alphabetical by source (e.g., publisher). Indexes by job (e.g., chefs, dentists, journalists) and publisher key words guide users to main entries.

Most entries include descriptive information, cost (many are free), and source of material. Many publications are lists of educational and training programs accepted by professional/trade associations publishers. Most list narrowly defined materials, but some provide broader guidance, inventories, and assessments to assist counselors and students through the career selection and job search processes.

Although coverage is comprehensive, from paperhanging to floral wholesaling, some high-interest fields are not included (e.g., hospice work, fundraising). The strongest representation is in more traditional fields.

Because students and counselors most often seek information about particular career fields, much use will be made of the works index. It not only leads to the main entry/description but also keys the field to *Dictionary of Occupational Titles* (Employment and Training Administration, 1977) and other such designations, which enables easy access to other key resources of career information.
— **Barbara Conroy**

406. **Chronicle Vocational School Manual for 1991-92 School Year.** Moravia, N.Y., Chronicle Guidance, 1991. 407p. $19.98pa. 378.1. LC 82-643014. ISBN 1-55631-166-4. ISSN 0276-0371.

Chronicle Guidance publications consistently provide sources of essential information for school guidance counselors and students at a reasonable price. This guide leads to occupational education programs currently available in the United States, Guam, and Puerto Rico as of early 1991. The first section lists 897 programs and 4,000-plus schools that offer programs of study and training that lead to specific occupations. Some are vocational schools that offer accredited postsecondary occupational education; others are commercial trade schools, teaching hospitals, or other professional learning sites. Since multiple names for jobs and fields exist, a helpful and comprehensive cross-reference listing leads from various terms used for a field to the more common name under which it is listed in the first section. The second section consists of charts arranged by state. These provide brief data on each school's address, admissions requirements, costs, enrollment, student services, job training, and financial aid. Although this book is intended for use in school settings, public libraries and career counselors can make good use of these materials, given the degree of job mobility in more mature workers and the needs of business and industry for training programs. — **Barbara Conroy**

407. **The Guide to Academic Travel.** 2d ed. Coral Gables, Fla., ShawGuides, 1992. 246p. index. $16.95pa. LC 90-61178. ISBN 0-945834-12-8.

For those who want to enrich their travel experiences by learning more about the culture, history, and language of the places they visit, ShawGuides offers a comprehensive sourcebook to adult study and language vacations throughout the world. Arranged geographically by sponsor location, the guide contains detailed descriptions of 450 programs offered by 307 sponsors (schools, colleges, museums, educational and cultural organizations, travel companies, and learned individuals) and vital statistics for 145 language schools worldwide. The section on language programs is new to this edition.

Each of the listings in the main section of the book ("General Interest Programs") contains specific details such as length and number of programs offered each year, approximate dates, maximum number of participants, scope of educational content, sample itineraries, faculty credentials, lodging arrangements, costs, and contact person. This section accounts for more than 80 percent of the book, with the language programs section and the appendix completing the work. Most of the entries are quite detailed and present a significant amount of information. The general format of the book, while not attractive, nonetheless makes for easy access for the reader. The number of programs in this edition represent a 20 percent increase from the previous edition. Of special interest are the programs that focus on ecological concerns; some even actively involve participants in saving endangered species. There are also programs for the whole family.

The appendix is really an index that lists the programs geographically and by subject. The master index lists each program by name. If one is looking for a particular program, one must go to the master index because the programs are arranged by sponsor location, which is not necessarily the program location. Thus, the Journeys East program in Japan is listed under "California." It would have been more useful to have the contents list each program rather than lumping them into three separate indexes. A currency conversion table is also provided, with rates as of October 1991. As it is outdated (and could never be otherwise), it does not seem necessary. These are, however, minor quibbles; this is a solid, useful reference book. — **Carmel A. Huestis**

408. Iglitzin, Lynne B. **Focus on Careers: A Reference Handbook.** Santa Barbara, Calif., ABC-Clio, 1991. 160p. index. (Teenage Perspectives). $35.00. HF5381.I36. 650.14. LC 91-31047. ISBN 0-87436-588-0.

Iglitzin has written an intelligent, practical, useful, and imaginative book to help teenagers and guidance counselors make their way through the difficult world of careers. Her approach is unusually perceptive and helpful. She permeates her work not only with good doses of reality but also with some high-minded insights. She points out that discrimination still exists, that there is no one perfect job, that the skills of career planning may occupy one forever, and that juggling home and work life is not always easy. Along the way she incorporates some excellent, unusual, and surprising fiction resources which are very much welcome in a book such as this: Amy Tan's *The Joy Luck Club*; Beryl Markham's *West with the Night*; and works by Aldous Huxley, Bruce Coville, and Barbara Werbsa that depict careers in fiction. She also includes many good biographies and autobiographies that should captivate young adult readers interested in various careers.

This handy reference has well-organized chapters that cover the basics: the world of work and the world beyond high school, understanding careers, careers in the twenty-first century, career awareness, career preparation (traditional and nontraditional), practical tips, and moving towards an equal-opportunity workplace. Iglitzin predicts trends for the future, such as that more workers will be older, women, minorities, and immigrants, and that more jobs will be in services and information and will require more education. Solid practical exercises are offered, and there is an index. This is a worthwhile book. [R: SLJ, May 92, p. 31] — **Anne F. Roberts**

409. Jones, Lawrence K., ed. **The Encyclopedia of Career Change and Work Issues.** Phoenix, Ariz., Oryx Press, 1992. 379p. index. $67.50. HF5381.E516. 650.1. LC 91-33913. ISBN 0-89774-610-4.

Work issues and problems frequently arise in an individual's life, often creating a need for quick background information about various situations. This source supplies brief overviews of topics that range from occupational health and safety to testing. Each is written by an acknowledged authority in the field and includes a brief bibliography of references that are usually in accord with the author's perspective.

The treatment of topics is excellent — concise, well written, and easy to understand. Articles include facts and suggest alternative remedies for problems and issues that often arise in the workplace. A section expanding on the four-line suggestion in the introduction, which offers general advice and resources for those seeking more information on workplace topics, would have been helpful.

Access is provided through the basic alphabetical listing and is supplemented by in-text referrals, an excellent index, and a guide that groups the 159 articles under 20 general areas. The articles are usually 2 to 3 pages long, with "Law in the Workplace" and "Resume" rating 16 and 5 pages respectively. Because terms in the career development field are somewhat slippery, index coverage of topics varies; "workaholic" is included but not "headhunting" or "executive recruiting." An excellent resource for managers, supervisors, and personnel departments, this work is recommended for public, school, and corporate libraries. [R: RBB, 1 Oct 92, p. 366] — **Barbara Conroy**

410. Rowe, Fred A. **The Career Connection: A Guide to College Majors and Their Related Careers.** rev. ed. Indianapolis, Ind., JIST Works, 1991. 261p. index. $15.95pa. HF5382.5.U5R68. 331.7'023. LC 91-22629. ISBN 0-942784-82-0.

This is a useful tool that allows career counselors, academic advisers, and school and public librarians to help people explore alternative areas of study in relation to career fields and majors. The guide enables the selection of relevant high school and college courses targeted at a future occupation. It will be most helpful in building familiarity prior to looking into college catalogs.

More than 100 career majors, such as finance and banking, environmental health, and journalism, are outlined. Two pages for each major offer a description of the field in general terms, the most commonly required courses, options offered within the major, and desirable high school courses. Concluding the data on each major is a list of possible associate, bachelor, and graduate degrees, each with an indication of its general employment outlook, average initial salary, and code from the *Dictionary of Occupational Titles* (DOT) (Bernan Press, 1991).

Various appendixes support this material with an overview of DOT, descriptions of educational alternatives and interest areas, a personal summary (to be filled in by the reader), and a planning guide to follow once a major is selected. In addition, a job title index of 100 occupations leads to the most suitable college majors.

Coverage is comprehensive and accessible through a combination of the body and index of the book. However, this is only one tool to be used in conjunction with others, such as current editions of *The Encyclopedia of Careers and Vocational Guidance* (see ARBA 91, entry 374) and *Occupational Outlook Handbook* (see ARBA 91, entry 249) for fuller career considerations. Its appeal is in its concise approach. With many career fields undergoing change, it warrants a comment about the need for initiative and adaptation for adults changing careers. — **Barbara Conroy**

411. Savage, Kathleen M., Annette Novallo, and Joseph M. Palmisano, eds. **Professional Careers Sourcebook: Where to Find Help Planning Careers That Require College or Technical Degrees.** 2d ed. Detroit, Gale, 1992. 1166p. index. $75.00. ISBN 0-8103-7573-7. ISSN 1045-9863.

In this edition of *Professional Careers Sourcebook*, the editors have apparently decided not to meddle with a good thing. Although seven new career profiles have been added, the format is the same as in the 1990 edition, which was very well received (see ARBA 91, entry 378). Each of the 118 profiles lists up to 11 categories of career information, including career guides, professional associations, meetings and conventions, awards and scholarships, and professional and trade periodicals. The incorporation of so much information into one source makes this an especially useful career planning tool.

Those concerned with currency and convenience should welcome many of the changes in this edition. Toll-free and fax numbers have been added, new and revised sources are listed, and changes in financial awards are noted. The editors, in fact, claim that thousands of changes have been made. The thoroughness and methodology of revision is of some concern, however. The profile on librarians, for example, lists the 4th edition of the excellent *Introduction to Reference Work* by William Katz (McGraw-Hill, 1992); that work is now in its 6th edition. With a little tightening of its revision standards, this source has the potential to become a career reference classic. — **Liz Willis**

412. **Vocational Careers Sourcebook: Where to Find Help Planning Careers in Skilled, Trade, and Nontechnical Vocations.** Kathleen M. Savage, Karen Hill, and Joseph M. Palmisano, eds. Detroit, Gale, 1992. 1129p. index. $75.00. ISBN 0-8103-8405-1. ISSN 1060-5630.

This new publication provides an outstanding bibliographic resource on 135 vocational careers that may require specialized training, certification, or examination but do not require an advanced degree for one who is skilled to be considered for employment. The volume is not primarily a direct source of occupational information. Rather, it provides an excellent bibliographic index to information sources, supplementing other sources with more extensive references and resources than are easily available. Although it does briefly indicate job descriptions, salary data, and employment outlook, its strength lies in its exhaustive guides to key information such as associations, standards and certification agencies, test guides, educational directories and programs, scholarships and grants, and meetings and conventions. Printed resources are annotated and cited fully, often complete with telephone and fax numbers.

Coverage of fields is generally good and clearly organized. Included are marketing and sales, administrative support, services (e.g., health, personal, food and beverage), the armed forces, and production (e.g., metalworking, transportation, handlers). However, similar to *Occupational Outlook Handbook* (see ARBA 91, entry 249), coverage does not include hospice workers, hazardous waste cleanup fields, estate managers/caretakers, or artists (e.g., commercial, graphic).

Indexing is excellent, with an alphabetical list of all occupations mentioned and a separate index to all information sources and titles. An appendix provides a full list of state governmental agencies that grant professional and occupational licenses. Highly recommended for libraries and career/guidance counselors. [R: LJ, 15 Sept 92, p. 62; RBB, July 92, pp. 1963-66; SLJ, Nov 92, p. 138]

—**Barbara Conroy**

6 Ethnic Studies and Anthropology

ANTHROPOLOGY AND ETHNOLOGY

413. **Encyclopedia of World Cultures. Volume III: South Asia.** Paul Hockings, ed. New York, G. K. Hall, 1992. 379p. maps. index. $100.00. GN307.E53. 306'.03. LC 90-49123. ISBN 0-81611-812-4.

South Asia, as defined by Hockings, consists of Bangladesh, Bhutan, India, Maldives, Mauritius, Nepal, Pakistan, and Sri Lanka. His nine-page introduction provides an excellent overview of the region and some basic explanation of issues such as language, castes, and tribes. It would be very useful for a person unfamiliar with the region to read the introduction before reading any of the "cultural summaries." Fifty-nine scholars from around the world contributed one or more summaries. These follow the structure established in volumes 1 and 2 of the set (see ARBA 92, entries 334-35). As in the previous volumes, entries range from a single paragraph (e.g., Bihari) to five-plus pages (e.g., Bhil and Irula). There are even entries for nonindigenous peoples, such as Europeans in South Asia, the French of India, and the Chinese of South Asia. In addition to the concise factual material, one of the major values of the volume is that each entry contains at least one reference to further information about the group described. Another feature is the 31-page appendix of additional castes, caste clusters, and tribes that also contains cross-references to appropriate sections of the main text. This is important as most castes have many subgroups that are not covered by individual summaries. There are a bibliography and an ethnonym index for this appendix. A short glossary, a filmography, and an ethnonym index to the summaries round out this excellent volume. Highly recommended. [R: Choice, Dec 92, p. 601]
– **G. Edward Evans**

414. Steele, Philip. **The People Atlas.** New York, Oxford University Press, 1991. 64p. illus. maps. index. $16.95. GN333.S84. 305.8. LC 91-7242. ISBN 0-19-520846-3.

Designed for children, this book contains adequate illustrations, with a writing style that is definitely British. It has a helpful glossary, an abbreviated index, and some 50 pages of simple text with many illustrations and a few poorly prepared maps. The price is reasonable, but the text and maps need to be updated.

It was rather difficult to prepare an up-to-date atlas in 1991 as a result of the changes in Eastern Europe. Steele's labor is no exception. Regarding the Soviet Union, for example, the reader will find obsolete information, some of it dating to the Brezhnev-Kosygin era. – **Bohdan S. Wynar**

415. Stevenson, Joan C. **Dictionary of Concepts in Physical Anthropology.** Westport, Conn., Greenwood Press, 1991. 432p. index. (Reference Sources for the Social Sciences and Humanities, no.10). $85.00. GN50.3.S74. 573'.03. LC 90-22815. ISBN 0-313-24756-0.

This series offers dictionaries of concepts in disciplines and subdisciplines of the social sciences and humanities. The purpose of the series is to provide current working definitions for the concepts most basic to the discipline in question, to discuss the etymological development of the concept, and to provide bibliographic sources of information relating to the concept. Each volume contains approximately 100 entries. Every entry contains four parts: the concept's current meaning or definition; a history of its origins and connotative development; sources for its origins and development, plus other notes of interest; and sources of additional information. This volume, dedicated to physical anthropology, begins by giving a brief definition for the broad topic. Concepts, selected from introductory texts on the subject, are listed in the table of contents. Entries are cross-referenced where appropriate. The volume contains both subject and name indexes.

This volume adheres to the charge of the series admirably. The concepts are basic; the definitions are clear and concise. Histories offer highlights of the development of the concepts but are not intended to be exhaustive. Sources of information, although somewhat dated, are plentiful. Overall, this volume will prove useful to those new to the field and will be a basic review for the more knowledgeable. [R: Choice, Mar 92, p. 1056]—**Joanna M. Burkhardt**

416. Strijp, Ruud. **Cultural Anthropology of the Middle East: A Bibliography. Volume 1: 1965-1987.** Kinderhook, N.Y., E. J. Brill, 1992. 565p. index. (Handbuch der Orientalistik. Erste Abteilung, Der Nahe und Mittlere Osten, 10). $165.75. Z3014.E85S77. 016.306'0956. LC 92-100. ISBN 90-04-09604-3.

Begun as an effort to compile a list of monograph sources to be used in a specific course on North Africa and the Middle East, the project grew to its present parameters—a survey of social and cultural anthropological studies on the Middle East published in English, French, and German between 1965 and 1987. The author promises a supplementary volume that will bring the project up to the present. The bibliography is divided into 6 sections: anthropological monographs and volumes (451 references) and articles (2,780 references), relevant books (223) and articles (340) by nonanthropologists, and subject and author indexes. The first four sections are subdivided by country, and most of the books are annotated. Even though the volume makes no effort to touch the vast anthropological literature in the native languages of the area (Arabic, Turkish, Persian, and Hebrew—one hopes that someone will undertake this larger task), it is still a very valuable contribution that, despite its excessive price, should be acquired by all research libraries. [R: Choice, Oct 92, p. 281]—**Joe P. Dunn**

417. Van Willigen, John. **Anthropology in Use: A Source Book on Anthropological Practice.** Boulder, Colo., Westview Press, 1991. 254p. index. (Westview Special Studies in Applied Anthropology). $32.50pa. Z5118.A54V37. 016.301. LC 90-25495. ISBN 0-8133-8250-5.

Enlarged from 322 to 530 entries, this bibliography is a new edition of the compiler's *Anthropology in Use: A Bibliographic Chronology of the Development of Applied Anthropology* (see ARBA 82, entry 789). Van Willigen has rearranged the entries into six chapters: predisciplinary activities (starting in 596 with Pope Gregory I's recommendations not to destroy the pagan temples in Britain), early disciplinary events (1852-1930), ethics, publications, research and professional organizations, and cases of application and practice (subdivided by 42 subjects). Within each chapter (and subdivision), entries are arranged chronologically and include title, place-name current at time of project, date, brief annotation, and one or more bibliographic citations to documents that refer to described activity. The subject categories used to divide most of the entries are broad and overlapping. Entries are listed only once, and there are no cross-references.

The title is misleading; this bibliography contains entries only for those items that have been voluntarily sent to the Applied Anthropology Documentation Project of the University of Kentucky Library. Van Willigen admits that coverage is biased toward agriculture and forestry and that almost no archaeology or physical anthropology is included. This bibliography does not systematically cover the fugitive literature of applied anthropology (e.g., that sponsored by federal, state, local, and foreign governments; private consulting firms; and universities). A general index provides access to personal, institutional and place-names, and some subject terms. Although limited in coverage, this work is useful as the annotated accession list of the important Applied Anthropology Documentation Project. [R: Choice, May 92, p. 1376]—**Fred J. Hay**

418. Winthrop, Robert H. **Dictionary of Concepts in Cultural Anthropology.** Westport, Conn., Greenwood Press, 1991. 347p. index. (Reference Sources for the Social Sciences and Humanities, no.11). $65.00. GN307.W56. 306'.03. LC 91-6283. ISBN 0-313-24280-1.

This reference takes a middle ground in its approach to explaining anthropology. It lies somewhere between heady historical tomes, such as Marvin Harris's *The Rise of Anthropological Theory* (Crowell, 1968), and breezier references, such as Charles Winick's *Dictionary of Anthropology* (see ARBA 72, entry 783). The former probes theories with an eye toward promoting a vision of anthropology's future, while the latter surveys the discipline's terms. "Evolutionism," for example, receives more than 100 pages of discussion in Harris's work, while Winick gives barely 2 pages to the idea and subdivides it into 19 terms that students may encounter.

Winthrop's dictionary may answer a need for a useful desk reference. In it, evolution receives seven pages of unbiased attention. After a concise definition in general and anthropological usage, the entry elaborates on the concept's philosophical background, its historical context in the Victorian period, its application by prominent Victorian anthropologists, critiques of the concept, and later developments to the present day. The entry has a list of references and sources of additional information appended. Within the entry, cross-references are made to concepts covered separately elsewhere in the volume.

The entries ring with clarity and authority; in place of extended treatment of the fine points within the concepts or an extensive list of terms, the entries offer a basic grounding for the user. Aiding in the volume's ease of use are a list of concepts at the beginning of the volume and indexes for names and subjects at the end. [R: Choice, May 92, pp. 1376-78; LJ, 15 Feb 92, p. 162; RBB, 15 May 92, p. 1714; WLB, Sept 92, pp. 112-15] – **Simon J. Bronner**

ETHNIC STUDIES

General Works

419. Duryea, Michelle LeBaron. **Conflict and Culture: A Literature Review and Bibliography.** rev. ed. Victoria, B.C., UVic Institute for Dispute Resolution, 1992. 135p. index. $14.95pa. 016.3036'9.

This work focuses on cultural assumptions, premises, and practices related to mediation and conflict among Canadian immigrants. Duryea is director of the Multiculturalism and Dispute Resolution Project at the University of Victoria's UVic Institute for Dispute Resolution. Coverage is both multicultural and multidisciplinary and includes intercultural communication, cross-cultural psychology, diversity management, social conflict, minority group acculturation, and other topics in anthropology, psychology, sociology, communications, management, and law. The work is prefaced with a list of related subject headings, pertinent abbreviations used, an introduction to the field of dispute resolution, and operational definitions of terms adopted by the Multiculturalism and Dispute Resolution Project. The main body of the work is evenly divided between a review of the research literature and an annotated bibliography. Categories of the literature review include multiculturalism, dispute resolution and the mediation model, cultural awareness and service provision, dispute resolution and culture, client-centered process design, research on conflict and culture, and the future. The bibliography lists journal articles, books, and chapters in books. Arrangement is alphabetical by author. Entries range from two or three sentences to two or three paragraphs and are both descriptive and critical. Indexes of authors and editors, titles, and subjects conclude the work. This reference tool is timely in that it helps to provide bibliographical control of the burgeoning material in two relatively new cross-disciplinary fields: conflict resolution and multicultural diversity. – **Lois J. Buttlar**

420. Mageli, Paul D. **The Immigrant Experience: An Annotated Bibliography.** Pasadena, Calif., Salem Press, 1991. 183p. index. (Magill Bibliographies). $40.00. Z1361.E4M334. 016.973'04. LC 91-32964. ISBN 0-89356-671-3.

Most bibliographies on immigration to the United States, such as *The New American Immigration* (see ARBA 88, entry 707), narrow their focus either by ethnic or population group (e.g., Europeans, Chinese-Americans, women) or time period. Given the vastness of the subject, this is understandable. Mageli's scope is broader, covering both past (starting with 1840) and present immigration and a wide variety of groups and topics. His work is preceded in ambitiousness of content perhaps only by *Immigration and Ethnicity* (see ARBA 78, entry 375), which it partially updates but does not replace.

Mageli states in his introduction that his compilation is aimed at high school and college students as well as the interested nonspecialist. While it does include scholarly articles and books, it is by no means comprehensive. Dissertations are omitted, and very few reference works are cited. Annotations are informative and evaluative, often indicating appropriate audiences. Divisions and subdivisions by area (e.g., Europe, Asia, Middle East) and group (e.g., Dominicans, Cape Verde Islanders) facilitate access. Topical sections such as "The Immigrant and Urban Ills" are interesting but often contain fewer than a dozen entries. The last of these sections covers critical assessments of ethnic autobiography and fiction; with only seven listings, it hardly seems worth including. An author index is appended; adding titles to it would have been helpful.

This is very much an introductory work. Public and school libraries and collections that primarily serve undergraduates will find it useful. [R: Choice, June 92, p. 1522; RBB, 1 June 92, p. 1776]
— **Willa Schmidt**

Asian-Americans

421. **Asian Americans Information Directory: A Guide to Organizations, Agencies, Institutions, Programs, Publications, and Services....** Karen Backus and Julia C. Furtaw, eds. Detroit, Gale, 1992. 461p. index. $75.00. ISBN 0-8103-8332-2. ISSN 1059-2458.

This comprehensive directory of information sources is an invaluable resource that serves the fastest-growing minority group and the resultant increase in the number of organizations, institutions, and agencies for Asian-Americans. The 19 ethnic groups covered range from Bangladeshi, Burmese, Cambodian, and Chinese through Sri Lankan, Thai, and Vietnamese. More than 5,200 listings guide the user to organizations, agencies, institutions, programs, publications, and services. Also included are museum collections, research centers, Asian studies programs, library collections, publishers, broadcast media, and videos. A typical entry contains descriptive information and contact data (name, address, and telephone number). A master name and keyword index allows ready access to entries under any key word or subject.

Indexing of inclusive terms such as "Indochinese" and "Southeast Asian" may be overlooked due to the great diversity of Asian groups. The "Pacific Islander American" section would have been better placed after the "Asian American" section. (Better yet, the book could have been titled "Asian/Pacific Islander Americans Information Directory.") This new directory is highly recommended for purchase by all public, academic, and special libraries because of its singular coverage of an important minority group. [R: LJ, 15 Feb 92, p. 156; RBB, 1 Mar 92, p. 1304; RQ, Summer 92, pp. 562-63] — **R. Errol Lam**

Blacks

422. **The Black Resource Guide.** 10th ed. Washington, D.C., Black Resource Guide, [1992]. 390p. $69.95. LC 85-91077. ISBN 0-9608374-8-5.

This directory includes names, addresses, and some telephone numbers for 35 categories of African-American specialists, professionals, and organizations. A brief but useful summary of the demography (1990 Census) of Black America is included as the 36th chapter. The publisher also sells mailing labels for the lists in this directory. Chapters on sports agents, union leadership, and scholarship assistance programs have been added to this edition. It is an eclectic and extremely selective listing (e.g., there are only 28 entries for church denominations and organizations and only 12 entries for civil rights organizations; the Association of Black Sociologists is included, but not the Association of Black Anthropologists). In some chapters essential information is omitted (e.g., the list of U.S. Representatives does not include the district or state represented). There is unnecessary duplication between chapters, especially egregious in the chapters titled "National Associations" and "Resource Organizations." Too frequently information is either out of date or simply incorrect. For instance, in the list of African-American studies programs, both the director and the department address are wrong for Kansas State and Harvard Universities; the name of the program is incorrect for Kansas State and Northeastern Universities; and Harvard's important W. E. B. Du Bois Institute for Afro-American Research is not included at all. There is no index. — **Fred J. Hay**

423. Hawkins, Walter L. **African American Biographies: Profiles of 558 Current Men and Women.** Jefferson, N.C., McFarland, 1992. 490p. illus. index. $39.95. E185.96.H38. 920'.009296073. LC 91-50938. ISBN 0-89950-664-X.

This biographical dictionary contains 558 biographical sketches of African-Americans residing in the United States. Many include black-and-white photographs. Occupational and geographic (by state of birth) indexes are included. Hawkins specified three criteria that he used in determining who should and should not be included in this work. First, individuals must have been born or have spent their childhood in the United States (a few exceptions are admitted). Second, they must be good role models for African-American children (an undefined quality). Third, they must not have died prior to 1969 (although Malcolm X, who was assassinated in 1965, is included). In terms of occupation, the most entries are for government employees (appointed and elected), attorneys, and educators. In spite of this, prominent African-Americans in government (e.g., Grace Hamilton, Julian Bond) and in education (e.g., Harvard's W. E. B. Du Bois Professor, Henry Louis Gates, and dean of African-American historians, John Hope Franklin) are excluded. The selection for other occupations, such as music and athletics, is similarly idiosyncratic. Hawkins does include entries for individuals in the military, law enforcement, and nursing, occupations not usually covered in works of this kind. Geographic coverage is also uneven, with more entries for persons associated with Georgia than for any other locale. This book will not be a useful addition to a general reference collection but may be a helpful supplement to other biographical sources in collections that specialize in African-American or United States genealogy. [R: LJ, 15 Apr 92, p. 86; RBB, Aug 92, p. 2030; SLJ, Nov 92, p. 137; VOYA, Dec 92, pp. 318-19; WLB, June 92, p. 107]—**Fred J. Hay**

424. **Hippocrene U.S.A. Guide to Black America: A Directory of Historic and Cultural Sites Relating to Black America.** By Marcella Thum. New York, Hippocrene Books, 1991. 384p. index. $11.95pa. ISBN 0-87052-045-8.

Because the comprehensive directory to American museums, *The Official Museum Directory* (National Register Publishing, 1991), does not index the ethnic content of collections, the door has been left open for guides to the ethnic landmarks and museums in America. Hippocrene's guide is a directory of historic and cultural sites that include or devote themselves to African-American material. After an all-too-brief introduction (three pages) the directory is divided by states and subdivided by cities. Each site, usually a museum or public facility (e.g., parks, churches, cemeteries, monuments), is highlighted in capital letters, with information on its location and the significance of its material, often accompanied by a historical background. Details of admission hours and prices are given, but telephone numbers and contact personnel are not provided.

This guide, while serviceable, falls short when compared to *Historic Landmarks of Black America* by George Cantor (see ARBA 92, entry 440). Cantor's guide has a fuller historical introduction, maps, photographs of figures and sites, more extensive listings and descriptions, and coverage of Canada in addition to the United States. [R: BL, 1 Feb 92, p. 1005; Choice, June 92, p. 1529]—**Simon J. Bronner**

425. **The Kaiser Index to Black Resources, 1948-1986.** Brooklyn, N.Y., Carlson Publishing, 1992. 5v. $595.00/set. Z1361.N39K34. 016.973'0496073. LC 92-11493. ISBN 0-926019-60-0.

The publication of this index is a monumental event in the history of bibliographic access to African-America. It began in 1948 as a "Reference Aids" file for the staff of the Schomburg Center for Research in Black Culture, a unit of the New York Public Library. Schomburg staff recorded bibliographic data—discovered while helping library patrons—on handwritten slips of paper. These slips were filed by subject in a card catalog. Added to this reference file were slips for articles, reviews, obituaries, and the like from more than 150 Black journals (academic and popular) and newspapers, periodicals dealing primarily with African-America (including the Caribbean), and selected articles from a wide array of general interest publications. By 1986 *Kaiser Index* (named for long-time Schomburg employee and distinguished bibliographer, Ernest Daniel Kaiser) had more than 174,000 unique citations classified by more than 15,000 subject headings. Many of these titles have not been included in other indexes, making the index a unique and essential resource for African-American studies.

Citations are arranged alphabetically by subject, within subject by date (most recent first), within date by periodical title, and within periodical title by first word of reference (usually title). They usually include title or explanatory note, journal title, date, pagination, and author. Often a note field is also included, supplying information about photographs or illustrations, Schomburg staff annotations on content, or other relevant data. Notes also contain cross-references to materials included in the *Schomburg Center Clipping File* (Chadwyck-Healey, 1986, microfiche). The subject headings are structurally similar to those of the Library of Congress (LCSH); many are identical. Other subject headings have been devised where LCSH was found inadequate.

The *Kaiser Index* has many of the drawbacks common to any in-house reference file. It is, as Alice Adamczyk states, "idiosyncratic" (p. xv). Citation style and completeness and subject classification are inconsistent. Users are encouraged to look under as many subject headings as possible. For instance, articles on Bobby "Blue" Bland are found under BLUES (SONGS, ETC.) and BLUES (SONGS, ETC.) – BIOGRAPHY, not under BLAND, but articles on bluesman Howlin' Wolf are found under WOLF, HOWLIN', 1910-1976 rather than BLUES ..., HOWLIN' WOLF, or BURNETT, CHESTER. These inconsistencies, the frequent omission of standard bibliographical data, and the lack of cross-references are certainly disadvantages, but the advantages of making this index available far outweigh them. *Kaiser Index* is an essential acquisition for all U.S. libraries. [R: RBB, 1 Nov 92, pp. 548-49] – **Fred J. Hay**

426. LaBlanc, Michael L., ed. **Contemporary Black Biography: Profiles from the International Black Community. Volume 1.** Detroit, Gale, 1992. 263p. illus. index. $39.95. ISBN 0-8103-5546-9. ISSN 1058-1316.

The title of this volume leads one to think that only living persons are included between its covers. This, however, is not the case. Biographical sketches of African-Americans who are currently making headlines appear, along with those who have recently died (e.g., Ralph Abernathy) and those who died long ago (e.g., Henry Ossawa Tanner, Marcus Garvey). The latter group was selected because, in the words of the editor, their "influence continues to impact on contemporary life" (introduction). A small number of the personalities are from other countries (23 out of 78, although one might argue that James Baldwin and Henry Tanner were not French), but the majority are American.

The endeavors of the personalities cover a broad spectrum, from politics to music to art to education to sports. Each entry is accompanied by a photograph and a boxed summary of the person's life titled "At a Glance." Additional photographs are often included, which add to the value of some entries. The writing is contemporary and upbeat, sometimes too much so, particularly when the subject is a recording artist. For example, Regina Belle has "dazzled critics and fans alike...." Similarly, Queen Latifah is "one of the hottest artists on the burgeoning Tommy Boy label" and became that way by "not stepping on her fellow rappers on her way to the top." Much of the text is taken directly from sources in the popular media, which could diminish the volume's usefulness as a scholarly work. However, the treatment of personalities is sincere and well written.

The volume is full of pleasant surprises as to individuals included. This reviewer recently needed information about Jennifer Lawson, the executive vice president for programming at PBS. When turning to *Notable Black American Women* (Gale, 1992) and similar sources proved fruitless, a check of *Contemporary Black Biography* proved successful. Not only does this volume include African-American personalities who are not readily found in other biographical handbooks but it also places each personality's contributions into some context of significance. For example, the discussion on Jennifer Lawson reveals that her appointment at PBS was a landmark for the network because it centralized programming decisions in one major office for the first time. Other "surprises" include Manute Bol (professional basketball), Harvey Gantt (politician from North Carolina), Sinbad (comedian and actor), Lori McNeil (tennis player who upset Chris Evert), Erroll McDonald (executive editor at Pantheon Books), and Mae C. Jemison (astronaut).

Entries are in alphabetical order, and coverage of profiles is fairly even throughout the volume. There are a nationality index, an occupation index, a subject index, and a name index. Thus, the user is provided many routes to the information. Page layout and design are attractive, although on first glance the pages look much like a computer-generated newsletter. The print is large and the photographs are of excellent quality. This book should be a welcome addition to many reference collections, particularly those in schools and small public libraries. [R: BR, Sept/Oct 92, p. 67; Choice, May 92, pp. 1363-64; LJ, 1 Apr 92, p. 110; RBB, 1 Apr 92, p. 1470; RQ, Summer 92, pp. 564-66; VOYA, June 92, p. 141] – **Melvin M. Bowie**

Hispanic-Americans

427. Fernandez-Shaw, Carlos M. **The Hispanic Presence in North America from 1492 to Today.** New York, Facts on File, 1991. 375p. illus. maps. index. $45.00. E169.1.F375. 973'.0468. LC 91-10786. ISBN 0-8160-2133-3.

Detailing the role of Hispanics in the United States, this ambitious survey covers the period from the fifteenth century to the present in a most unusual way. It is in part a narrative, descriptive analysis of well-known data replete with dates, important personages, and significant events. The first part of the book provides the reader with an introduction to the discovery and subsequent exploration of the North American continent, including the influential role played by missionaries, the cultural attributes of the colonizers (Spaniards), and the process of colonization. The work then proceeds to a state-by-state analysis of the role of Hispanics in the history of each state. The appendixes include lists of Spanish governors, missions and forts, National Parks and other sites of interest, a list of North American universities that have chapters of the National Association of Spanish Students, a list of periodicals published in Spanish, and a brief bibliography. There are numerous maps and black-and-white photographs.

A major flaw of the book is the lack of any mention of the treatment of and the atrocities perpetrated on the indigenous populations during the conquest. Also, in the index there is no entry for Bartolome de las Casas. This book is not recommended for academic libraries and will be of dubious use to the beginner seeking a historically accurate survey of the influence and significance of Spanish-speaking individuals in the United States. – **Dario J. Villa**

428. **Hispanic Americans Information Directory 1992-93: A Guide to Approximately 4,900 Organizations, Agencies, Institutions, Programs, and Publications....** 2d ed. Julia C. Furtaw, ed. Detroit, Gale, 1992. 486p. index. $75.00. ISBN 0-8103-7536-2. ISSN 1046-3933.

Census extrapolations indicate that the Spanish-speaking populations in the United States will increase dramatically, particularly in and around metropolitan areas. Consequently, publishers are producing numerous reference publications that address issues and concerns expressed by the myriad groups of Spanish-speaking people in the United States. This edition of the *Hispanic American Information Directory* (HAID) continues, as its predecessor did, to list approximately 5,000 entries on cultural and civic organizations, government agencies and programs, educational opportunities, publications and publishers, research centers, and special libraries. The organizations are alphabetical under descriptive categories such as national associations and libraries. Each entry provides name, address, telephone number, contact person, and a descriptive paragraph that outlines the characteristics of the organization. Also included are fax and toll-free numbers. There is a chapter on audiovisual materials and where to obtain them. This information is not readily available elsewhere. For ease of access, there is a master name and keyword index. Overall, this excellent publication is recommended for all libraries. – **Dario J. Villa**

429. Schorr, Alan Edward. **Hispanic Resource Directory 1992-1994: A Comprehensive Guide to Over 6,000 National, Regional and Local Organizations, Associations, Agencies, Programs and Media....** Juneau, Alaska, Denali Press, 1992. 380p. index. $47.50pa. ISBN 0-938737-26-0.

This guide lists 6,167 national, state, and local Hispanic organizations and associations. Included are research centers, libraries and museums, state and local Hispanic commissions, Hispanic studies programs, educational institutions with significant Hispanic enrollment, migrant and bilingual education, migrant health, human rights agencies, Hispanic chambers of commerce, minority and small business programs, Hispanic employment programs, print and electronic media, and Latin American diplomatic offices in the United States. Excluded are organizations and agencies principally concerned with Hispanic refugee and immigration issues, and those involved with United States policy in Latin America.

The information is arranged into 16 chapters. In addition, there is a statistical appendix, including four tables with breakdowns in Hispanic population nationally, by region and state, and by state and city. The statistical information is based on the 1990 census data from the Ethnic and Spanish Statistics Branch of the Bureau of the Census. There are separate indexes by organization name, by state and city, and by contact person. The term "Hispanic" as used in this directory refers to those persons of Mexican, Puerto Rican, Cuban, Central and South American, and Spanish descent. Most of the entries represent nonprofit organizations. Arrangement is generally alphabetical by name, or is by state and then alphabetical by name. The information included under each entry is generally limited to the name, address, telephone number, and contact person (if available). (It is important to keep in mind that information in directories, especially names of contact persons, goes quickly out-of-date.) A brief description is included for each research center, library, and museum. The chapter on media also briefly identifies each item included in the list of "periodicals and reference serials."

Because the scope of the directory is so broad, the amount of information for each item is general and minimal. This limits the directory's usefulness. However, because such a variety of material is included in one easy-to-use volume, the work is a convenient, practical, and valuable resource. A user's guide clearly explains the compilation and organization of the material and indicates, chapter-by-chapter, the number of entries, arrangement, and source of the information. Although the type impression is dark and easy to read, the paper could have been thicker; type from the other side of the page is visible. The margins, especially the inside margin, could have been wider for easier photocopying. However, the directory remains a valuable reference book for public, academic, special, and secondary school libraries, especially those in states with large or growing Hispanic populations. [R: Choice, Feb 92, p. 880; RQ, Spring 92, pp. 418-19] — **Susan J. Freiband**

Indians of North America

430. **Biographical Dictionary of Indians of the Americas.** Newport Beach, Calif., American Indian, 1991. 2v. illus. index. $285.00/set. E89.B56. 920'.009297. LC 91-41400. ISBN 0-937862-29-0.

The publisher's flyer, enclosed with the review copy, states that this work has more than twice the number of entries as did the first (1983) edition. Checking the entries for *B*s and *P*s shows this claim to be correct. However, in the foreword it is stated that the first edition was a 1975 imprint. Moreover, this reviewer has a two-volume set from American Indian with the title *Biographical Dictionary of Indians of the Americas* that gives no copyright date, but the invoice for the review copy indicates it was shipped in 1985. Also owned is a 1978 three-volume set from Scholarly Press with the title *Dictionary of Indians of North America* (see ARBA 80, entry 29). The content of these two sets is identical. It is thus not surprising that the current compilers have trouble determining the date of the first edition.

A spot check shows that everything from the first editions, whatever their dates, appears in this one. In some cases the entry's sentence order has been changed, and in two sample entries one or two sentences have been rewritten. Most of the new entries are for contemporary persons. However, part of the increased entry count is for one-line entries (17 of 107 in the *P*s) that are linked to illustrations—or at least they should be. For example, "Pachtuwa-chta (Arikara; fl. 19th century) was an Arikara warrior. This drawing was done in 1834. (See portrait)" (p. 507). No illustration is identified as Pachtuwa-chta. On page 508, one of three illustrations lacks any identification label, so one might assume this is the person in question. For some of the twentieth-century entries that were relatively short in the earlier versions, there has been substantial increase in length. Entries for people such as Leonard Peltier, Lou Diamond Phillips, and Elvis Presley do make this a somewhat useful resource. In general the contemporary entries are accurate; however, there are occasional editorial lapses. For example, Samuel W. Brown (Yuchi) did not serve with both the Confederate and Union armies. He joined the "Loyal Creeks"; in fact, much of his later life was devoted to getting compensation for the Loyal Creek.

For nineteenth-century individuals, a better publication is *Who Was Who in Native American History* (see ARBA 91, entry 402). *Reference Encyclopedia of the American Indian* (see ARBA 91, entry 398) lists more twentieth-century personages, but the entries are shorter than those in this set. The set's price is very high, but it does contain new material and may be appropriate for some libraries with major collections of American Indian material. — **G. Edward Evans**

431. Gattuso, John, ed. **Native America.** New York, Prentice Hall General Reference, 1991. 389p. illus. maps. index. (Insight Guides). $19.95pa. ISBN 0-13-467119-8.

As the latest entry into the crowded field of travel guides to "Indian Country," what does this book offer that others do not? Perhaps the most obvious difference is the abundance of crisp color photographs, some of which are very striking. A more substantive difference is that 10 of the 30 contributors (writers and photographers) are American Indians, and the other contributors have extensive backgrounds in American Indian studies or activities. Thus, the material provides a more balanced picture of the contemporary Indian situation than is found in some of the other guides.

The format is that of a series of essays that incorporates travel information into a narrative about a particular region. Some of the essays address historical concerns, such as the arrival of Europeans or nineteenth-century Indian-Caucasian conflicts. Other essays deal with contemporary issues, such as the federal government's Indian policy. Unlike other guides, this one concentrates on the western United States (310 pages out of 389). There are only two short essays on Northeast and Southeast Indians. The last section covers basic travel information—destinations and directions, where to stay, things to do, proper behavior, travel essentials (e.g., visas/passports), event dates, and other useful data. A short index assists in locating specific places and tribes.

There are at least four other national travel guides currently in print: *Indian America Companion* (see ARBA 91, entry 395); Ralph and Lisa Woo Shanks's *North American Indian Travel Guide* (Costano Books, 1986); *America's Ancient Treasures* (see ARBA 84, entry 328); and *A Guide to America's Indians* (see ARBA 75, entry 805). Each has its merits and drawbacks. All four provide broader coverage of the United States than does *Native America*; however, this title contains solid essays on the areas it does cover. Also, its color photographs will attract many users. If none of the other titles are in the collection, this one would be a reasonable first choice. It would also be desirable in areas of high user interest in the subject.—**G. Edward Evans**

432. Hirschfelder, Arlene, and Paulette Molin. **The Encyclopedia of Native American Religions: An Introduction.** New York, Facts on File, 1992. 367p. illus. index. $40.00. E98.R3H73. 0299'.7'03. LC 91-21145. ISBN 0-8160-2017-5.

Maintaining a balance between providing accurate, relevant information and violating the wishes and concerns of Native American religious practitioners is a difficult feat. That may be why this is the first encyclopedia of Native American religions. The authors have done an admirable job of balancing both needs. Entries are based upon published material; however, they do not include references to those sources. A 15-page section on further reading provides some leads to more detailed information. The bibliography has a few topical divisions so the search can be narrowed a little more quickly. Entries range in length from 75 words to several pages. The compilers take a broad view of religion; thus, one will find material on what some might consider social ceremonies/activities (e.g., girls' puberty rites). There is biographical information about both Native American religious practitioners and non-Indian missionaries. There is also information about disease and native medicine because many illnesses are viewed as an imbalance of the mind, body, and spirit. However, the authors did not include myths, tales, and stories about deities and spirits, nor are there tribal cosmologies. The texts of prayers, songs, and poetry that relate to spirits and deities are also omitted. An excellent subject index completes the volume. This work is a worthwhile addition to any general reference collection. [R: BR, Nov/Dec 92, p. 57; Choice, Oct 92, p. 274; LJ, July 92, p. 76; RBB, 15 May 92, p. 1716]—**G. Edward Evans**

433. Slapin, Beverly, and Doris Seale. **Through Indian Eyes: The Native Experience in Books for Children.** Philadelphia, New Society, 1992. 312p. illus. index. $49.95; $24.95pa. ISBN 0-86571-212-3; 0-86571-213-1pa.

The authors have gathered together a collection of articles and reviews that showcase the Native American point of view. From articles on Columbus and Thanksgiving to reviews of children's and young adult books featuring Native Americans to bibliographies of recommended books, this title discusses various aspects of Native life and experiences. The list of resources, which includes publishers, organizations, and educational groups, will be especially helpful.

The articles are interesting and generally well written. The comments about storytelling stress the need for tellers to understand and respect the culture that generated the stories—certainly an important point when dealing with any culture, and a legitimate theme central to this title. The section identified as a checklist of criteria for evaluating materials with Native lifeways is actually a series of questions. With a little more guidance for readers and the development of an actual checklist, it could be very useful. The book reviews, done by Seale, evaluate children's and young adult titles in terms of their racism and sensitivity. While writing in a personal and informal manner, Seale makes many sound criticisms. For example, *The Indian in the Cupboard* by Lynne Reid Banks (Avon, 1980) and its sequels may be literary successes, but Banks's portrayal of the Indian is stereotyped and negative. In spite of its usefulness, this section could have been stronger if Seale had indicated how or why titles were chosen for the extended reviews and if more current titles had been included in this edition. There are no books later than 1988 and only four with a copyright in that year.

This book's greatest strength is also its greatest weakness. *Through Indian Eyes* is biased, as reflected in such statements as the comment about contemporary Native writers and illustrators, "many of whom are so gifted that they would be famous, if they were not Indians" (p. v), or, "We hope readers will not take the anger personally: no one of us individually caused the horrendous conditions that assault the People today, but, at the same time, we bear the collective responsibility for correcting it" (p. 4). However, this title does have value for consciousness raising precisely because it presents this point of view. Overall, if *Through Indian Eyes* were more current and less biased, it would be an important book for school, public, and academic libraries. As it stands, it is primarily useful as a tool for consciousness raising. [R: SLJ, July 92, p. 32]—**Carol A. Doll**

434. Tiller, Veronica E., ed. **Discover Indian Reservations USA: A Visitors' Welcome Guide.** Denver, Colo., Council Publications, 1992. 402p. illus. maps. index. $19.95pa. LC 92-071259. ISBN 0-9632580-0-1.

One wonders how many more guides to "Indian Country" the market will support. Each of the five existing in-print national guides claims to have some special feature. In the case of *Discover Indian Reservations USA*, the special feature is that all the information about the reservations comes from the tribes themselves and was published by a tribal consortium. What this book contains, therefore, is information that the tribes want known about tourist activities available on reservations.

The overall arrangement is by state (only the lower 48) and then in alphabetical order by reservation or rancheria. Entries range from less than a half page for the Coeur d'Alene to 12 pages for the Navajo. The minimum information provided is a tribal profile and an address and telephone number. Most entries include directions to the reservation, cultural institutions, special events, recreational opportunities, and accommodations. Longer entries include information about archaeological/historical sites, businesses and industries, tribal organizations, and restrictions and special conditions on access. Unfortunately, not all the tribes who have restrictions have listed them. For example, there is no indication in the Haulapai (Arizona) entry that one needs to get permission to drive on the tribally maintained roads. An excellent index with cross-references provides subject access to widely scattered information. As an example, many people may be surprised to see that there are more than 120 reservations listed under the heading "Bingo and Casinos." Questions such as "Where can I camp, boat, hunt, attend a tribal fair, and play golf" are answered as well.

If one has *Indian America* (see ARBA 91, entry 395), *Native America* by John Gattuso (Prentice Hall General Reference, 1991), or a recent edition of Ralph and Lisa Woo Shanks's *North American Indian Travel Guide* (Costano, 1986), this title may be a luxury. But if one needs an accurate, up-to-date guide to reservations, *Discover Indian Reservations* is an excellent choice.—**G. Edward Evans**

435. Trafzer, Clifford E. **Yakima, Palouse, Cayuse, Umatilla, Walla Walla, and Wanapum Indians: An Historical Bibliography.** Metuchen, N.J., Scarecrow, 1992. 253p. index. (Native American Bibliography Series, no.16). $32.50. Z1209.2.U52N697. 016.9795'00497. LC 91-41052. ISBN 0-8108-2517-1.

Unlike the other tribal bibliographies in the series, this one contains a 14-page introduction that provides a historical overview of the groups covered, and it does not clearly state what is included or excluded. Trafzer provides only general statements such as "newspapers should be examined since they contain numerous stories...." A careful examination shows that a few newspaper articles are included.

The 939 descriptive annotated entries (ranging from 15 to 127 words in length) are arranged in sections that cover general information; prehistory, language, and geography; culture, customs, and religion; the fur trade; missions; exploration, transportation, and surveys; treaties, policies, and reservations; the Plateau Indian War; white settlement, agriculture, and ranching; and the Nez Perce War. A personal name, place, and subject index provides a useful means of access.

If a user wants comprehensive coverage, it will be necessary to check both the 4th edition and its supplement of *Ethnographic Bibliography of North America* (see ARBA 77, entry 738 and ARBA 91, entry 380). Of 35 items from *Ethnographic Bibliography* used to check the coverage of this book, 15 were not found. Theses and dissertations are given, but Trafzer omits chapters in books and apparently has not covered education, as none of the education items used in the spot-check appear. If one does not need comprehensive coverage, this is certainly an easy volume to use. Given the price, it may be limited to libraries with a high interest in Plateau Indians. [R: Choice, Sept 92, p. 94]
— G. Edward Evans

436. Webber, Bert. **Indians along the Oregon Trail: The Tribes of Nebraska, Wyoming, Idaho, Oregon and Washington Identified.** expanded ed. Medford, Oreg., Webb Research Group, 1992. 208p. illus. maps. index. $17.95pa. E78.W5W39. 978. LC 91-39448. ISBN 0-936738-60-X.

Of the 172 pages used to describe the tribes along the Oregon Trail in this book, 129 cover the Native Americans of Oregon and Washington. Kansas is not included, despite the fact that the map illustrating the Trail's route shows it going west along the Kansas River before swinging north into Nebraska. Some tribal entries provide information about the tribe's name and a little background data about the group and its population (one or two brief paragraphs). The entries in the Oregon and Washington section are the longest and include the most information (e.g., listing village sites).

There are some disconcerting aspects to the text. In the Nebraska section there is a one-sentence entry for the Arikara that ends with a *see* reference to North Dakota. However, there is no chapter or section for North Dakota, nor is there such an entry in the index. The entry for Dakota (also in the Nebraska section) states that the group was commonly known as the Sioux; it ends with a *see* reference to South Dakota, which also does not exist in the book. Further, there is no reference to the entry *Sioux*.

This book is of limited interest outside Washington and Oregon. For those needing general information about the tribes along the Oregon Trail, *Encyclopedia of Native American Tribes* (see ARBA 89, entry 364) is better; for more scholarly material, the *Handbook of North American Indians* (see ARBA 91, entry 396) or *Encyclopedia of World Cultures. Volume 1: North America* (see ARBA 92, entry 334) is recommended. — **G. Edward Evans**

Irish-Americans

437. Blessing, Patrick J. **The Irish in America: A Guide to the Literature and the Manuscript Collections.** Washington, D.C., Catholic University of America Press, 1992. 347p. index. $49.95. Z1361.I7B54. 016.973'049162. LC 90-1667. ISBN 0-8132-0731-2.

Blessing has created a bibliography of printed sources on a wide variety of subjects that relate to the Irish experience. Among the topics are dictionaries, guides, statistics, ethnicity, politics, religion, labor, reminiscences, writers, and literature. All are arranged by author in each section. Also covered are manuscript collections in 48 states, arranged by state and then by city. Many of the descriptive entries are quite detailed, but some contain only a sentence or two. Some states could have been more thoroughly covered (the author requests additions). Another section presents government manuscripts and publications. Details for many specific agencies, such as the Bureau of Customs, the Immigration and Naturalization Service, and the Bureau of Prisons, are cited in the entries. The index covers only the sections on manuscript collections and government materials. Overall, this publication is a treasure trove of sources about the Irish. Highly recommended. [R: Choice, Nov 92, p. 438] — **Carol Willsey Bell**

Italian-Americans

438. Hobbie, Margaret, comp. **Italian American Material Culture: A Directory of Collections, Sites, and Festivals in the United States and Canada.** Westport, Conn., Greenwood Press, 1992. 173p. index. (Material Culture Directories, no.4). $45.00. E184.I8H64. 973'.0451. LC 91-36601. ISBN 0-313-27200-X.

The study of material culture is relatively new, as are ethnicity studies. This volume joins previously published books on Irish-American, Hispanic-American, and East and Southeast Asian-American material cultures. Data for the entries was collected by questionnaire; the work assembled from them is inclusive of only those entities that responded.

Material culture within this volume is represented by lists of photographic and oral history collections, societies, festivals, neighborhoods, houses, commercial buildings, gardens, monuments and other sites arranged by state or province within broad topic area (e.g., festival, site). Represented among the 252 listings are 31 states and provinces. A typical entry consists of the state or province's postal abbreviation code, a sequential number, the address or vicinity, a contact person, dates of inclusion, hours of operation, and possibly a *see also* reference to another entry in the volume and a brief description. The entry for the Feast of Our Lady of Mount Carmel in Passaic, New Jersey, for example, includes the information that traditional foods (meaning "zeppole, sausage, pizza, and Italian ices") are served and that "several thousand people attend the four day festival." Events associated with the voyages of Christopher Columbus, while currently topical, were not avidly sought by Hobbie, who wisely saw them as not specific to Italian-American ethnicity. The entries are preceded by a succinct essay on the demographics of the Italian immigration to North America. The subject index, which includes broad concepts such as "saints' festivals" and places such as "Latium," excludes "Lodi" and fails to list "music (live performances)" when "music (photographs)," "music (sheet music)," and "music (sound recordings)" are all represented. – **Judith M. Brugger**

Jews

439. **American Jewish Year Book 1992. Volume 92.** David Singer, ed. Philadelphia, Jewish Publication Society and New York, American Jewish Committee, 1992. 670p. index. $30.00. LC 99-4040. ISBN 0-8276-0429-7.

The *American Jewish Year Book* is an essential reference for Jewish social studies, and the volume for 1992 may be the most significant yet published. The strength of the series has been its surveys of Jewish demographics and sociology. The yearbook carries an emphasis on the United States, but its scope is global, with coverage extending to Canada, Europe, Australia, South Africa, and Israel. It summarizes major events and issues of Jewish populations around the world and offers valuable directories of Jewish organizations and periodicals. Other useful features are Jewish calendars and obituaries of important Jewish figures.

Articles on Jewish intermarriage patterns and population trends make this work particularly newsworthy. Pointing to a new population survey that reveals a quickening pace of dispersion and a loss of ethnic association, the future survival of Jewish ethnicity is openly questioned. Tables lay out figures for a number of essential categories, including denominational association, education, occupation, and identity. The figures invite interpretation and discussion; one author, for example, commends the success Jews have had in melding into American life but raises concerns about the consequent loss of Jewishness. The studies are bound to attract immediate attention from Jewish leaders and laypeople alike – not to mention scholars and students of contemporary Jewish studies – and they should also concern scholars of ethnic, religious, and American studies and sociology. – **Simon J. Bronner**

440. Beinart, Haim. **Atlas of Medieval Jewish History.** New York, Simon & Schuster Academic Reference Division, 1992. 144p. illus. maps. index. $55.00. G1034.B413. 909'.04924'00223. LC 92-995. ISBN 0-13-050691-5.

For far too many libraries, the shelves of Jewish history have a conspicuous gap from the biblical period to the beginnings of Zionism in the nineteenth century. In between these milestones were a complex series of social movements by Jews and interactions with Christians that affected the course of European and world history. It is an often overlooked saga of persecution, migration, and adaptation. A few classic studies and collections of documents have brought out the socioeconomic situations of Jews and Christians during the medieval era, but Beinart, a professor of Jewish history at Hebrew University who specializes in the Middle Ages, has vividly brought the significance of the era's human geography to life with the first English-language atlas of medieval Jewish history. As the atlas visibly reveals, it is a history inexorably linked to the major movements of Europe—the Crusades, invasions, divisions, massacres, empires, plagues, and expulsions. And there are many sections of special concern to Jewish sociology that demand study, such as the Kabbalistic and Shabbatean movements.

The maps, more than 100 in all, begin with the barbarian invasions of Europe during the fifth century and end with the settlements of Poland and Russia during the seventeenth century. Accompanying each map is explanatory text and many illustrations that depict key artifacts or figures. Rather than highlighting maps of individual countries, the atlas mostly contains maps of broad areas on a light blue background with black lettering. The effect is to emphasize the transnational social movements of Jews during the period. The maps are abundant in detail; in several cases they would have benefited from enlargement. All are labeled and nicely framed, with the exception of the final two-page map of the Jewish diaspora and their languages, in which the binding splits the central map of Europe. Users of the atlas will find the index to subjects and place-names useful, and a select bibliography offers a guide to further reading. One shortcoming in the atlas is the introduction, which is only a few paragraphs long; users would benefit from an overview of the themes of Jewish social geography and sociology during this significant period of world history.

Overall, these maps will demand reinterpretation of medieval history, which all too often gives short shrift to the influence of ethnic-religious tension on the course of the world's social, economic, cultural, and religious life. Although the atlas may be most appealing to academic collections of geography, world history, religious studies, Jewish studies, and sociology, it is also suitable for public library use. [R: LJ, 15 Apr 92, p. 84; RBB, Aug 92, p. 2034]—**Simon J. Bronner**

441. Chernofsky, Ellen, ed. **Traveling Jewish in America: The Complete Guide for Business & Pleasure.** 3d ed. Lodi, N.J., Wandering You Press, 1991. 493p. $11.95pa. LC 91-065733. ISBN 0-9617104-2-X.

An indispensable guide for the kosher tourist, student, or business professional, *Traveling Jewish in America* lists the locations of, and pertinent facts on, more than 3,000 synagogues; 800 kosher food stores and restaurants; and numerous hotels, bookstores, and day schools that cater to the Jewish population. Now in its 3d edition, it covers not only the United States but Canada as well. Listings are alphabetized according to state or province and city. Details are provided about the denomination of synagogues, the types of food available in restaurants and grocery stores, and the walking distance from hotel to synagogue (for those who do not drive on the Sabbath). The guide also furnishes the Jewish populations of cities (where known) and the addresses of mikvehs (ritual baths). A form in the back of the guide allows readers to contact the editor about changes that have occurred since the book's publication.

Surprisingly, the guide makes almost no mention of one of the most dominant institutions in the Jewish community: the Jewish Community Center (JCC). If the guide refers to a JCC at all, it is only in passing. For example, readers are told that kosher sandwiches are available in the JCC snack bar in Newton, Massachusetts. What the guide does not say is that the Newton JCC is the largest such institution in the greater Boston area. Despite the limited coverage of JCCs, the guide has invaluable information for Jewish travelers.—**Lisha E. Goldberg**

442. Fischel, Jack, and Sanford Pinsker, eds. **Jewish-American History and Culture: An Encyclopedia.** Hamden, Conn., Garland, 1992. 710p. index. (Garland Reference Library of the Social Sciences, v.429). $95.00. E184.J5J48. 973'.04924'003. LC 91-14188. ISBN 0-8240-6622-7.

This superb reference tool, designated an "encyclopedia" by its editors, is in fact a work that defies easy categorization. Many of its finest entries, on broad topics that range from academe to Zionism, are minimonographs of the type that graced turn-of-the-century editions of the *Encyclopaedia Britannica*. Other extended essays, with rather unexpected titles such as "Movie Moguls" and "Television," bring critical perspectives to discussions of popular culture that might otherwise descend to the level of "But I Didn't Know That He (She) Was Jewish." In between is a vast assortment of biographical, institutional, geographical, and historical entries that chronicle Jewish life in America from colonial to contemporary times. All entries are up-to-date and include intelligently selected bibliographies.

For the most part, contributors to this volume are well-known and highly regarded specialists in their chosen field. They write knowledgeably and entertainingly in a style appropriate to the general audience for whom this work is intended. Ease of use is also furthered by an introductory list of entries and a concluding index. There is sure to be disagreement over the inclusion of certain individuals for whom Judaism was of marginal importance, and some will debate the wisdom of omitting other figures who are less well known outside of a particular religious constituency. But all things considered, this is a groundbreaking work that commends itself to almost all academic and public libraries. (And is there any other source that refers, even in passing, to Elvis Presley's "rabbinic" connection?) [R: C&RL, Sept 92, pp. 419-20; Choice, May 92, p. 1370; LJ, Aug 92, p. 90; RBB, 1 May 92, p. 1629]

—Leonard J. Greenspoon

443. Frankel, Ellen, and Betsy Platin Teutsch. **The Encyclopedia of Jewish Symbols.** New York, Jason Aronson, 1992. 234p. illus. index. $35.00. BM50.F74. 296.4'03. LC 91-39033. ISBN 0-87668-594-7.

This collection of 266 entries and about 100 illustrations is the first work of its kind and results from the collaboration of an accomplished writer (Frankel) and artist (Teutsch). An essay on the significance of symbols, a guide to the use of the work, and a complete list of symbols introduce the volume; a glossary, appendixes, a chronology of Jewish history, a bibliography, and an index conclude it. Entries are listed alphabetically by their English translation or transliteration and include the Hebrew equivalent, a discussion of the symbol, footnotes to sources, cross-references, relevant generic categories, and pertinent abstract concepts. The margins are narrow, and the print is set in double columns.

The text is well written, and illustrations are clear and attractive. Although in general the text has been edited carefully, a few problems were found. The Hebrew form of the first entry is misspelled; the Hebrew equivalent of "Hare" is omitted; and occasionally the English entry name does not accurately reflect the Hebrew equivalent (e.g., "Eden" versus "Garden of Eden," "Exodus" versus "Exodus from Egypt," and "Gate" versus "Gates"). In addition, some of the etymologies appear to be based more on popular beliefs than sound scholarship (e.g., the name "Esther" probably derives from the Akkadian "Ishtar" rather than from the Hebrew construction "I will hide" [p. 103]). Nevertheless, the book should prove helpful to nonspecialists with interests in Judaica and should be a welcome addition to the shelves of public and synagogue libraries. —M. Patrick Graham

444. Frazier, Nancy. **Jewish Museums of North America: A Guide to Collections, Artifacts, and Memorabilia.** New York, John Wiley, 1992. 242p. illus. index. $12.95pa. E184.J5F63. 970.004'924. LC 91-44026. ISBN 0-471-54202-4.

As recognition of America's ethnic diversity has grown in scholarship, popular guides have appeared that concentrate on special collections of ethnic material. Judaica collections date to the nineteenth century, and new collections and exhibits have arisen to cover the Holocaust and contemporary immigration. In this work listings are given for museums in states under the headings of American regions (Northeast, Midwest and South, and West), with a separate category for Canada. Indicative of its popular feel, the book offers a cute headline for each institution. Essential information is then given: address, telephone number, and hours. Besides providing a rundown of the institutions' collections and displays, Frazier offers observations (often colorful and opinionated) based on personal visits. The entries thus become more like essays than information sheets.

In addition to listing Jewish museums, Frazier identifies art and history museums with Jewish collections. Photographs with examples of artifacts from various collections enliven the text, but shots of the institutions or exhibits might have been more useful. The reference includes a valuable index, glossary, and bibliography. Although this book has popular appeal, it could also be useful to students and scholars looking for sources and to public libraries. [R: RBB, 1 May 92, pp. 1629-30]

—Simon J. Bronner

445. Gross, David C., and Esther R. Gross, comps. **Jewish Wisdom: A Treasury of Proverbs, Maxims, Aphorisms, Wise Sayings, and Memorable Quotations.** New York, Walker, 1992. 216p. index. $9.95pa. BM43.G75. 296. LC 91-46069. ISBN 0-8027-2667-4.

In large-type format, this book contains more than 1,000 proverbs, sayings, and quotations from varied Jewish sources. The compilers have arranged the entries under subject headings that range from "ability" to "Zion." After each entry only a general source is given, such as "Talmud." The compilers claim to have scoured many volumes to select the entries, but they list only nine titles in the acknowledgments. Notable in its absence is *Words Like Arrows*, compiled by Shirley Kumove (Warner Books, 1984), a focused cultural collection of Yiddish folk sayings that offers much more to the reference librarian for annotating examples of folk wisdom. At best, *Jewish Wisdom* gives a smattering of quotations from figures as different as Benjamin Disraeli and Maimonides. There is a list of references that explain figures and terms used in the book. Considering that the book is arranged alphabetically by subject, the index of topics after the list of references is redundant, but an index of authors, absent from the work, would have been helpful. Indeed, better annotation generally would have made this work more useful to reference shelves. As it stands, the book is meant more for browsing than for reference. – **Simon J. Bronner**

446. Herbsman, Yael. **Index to Florida Jewish History in the *American Israelite* 1854-1900.** Gainesville, Fla., George A. Smathers Libraries, University of Florida, 1992. 118p. $30.00pa. F320.J5H47. 975.9'004924. LC 92-12102. ISBN 0-929595-01-7.

This tool provides access to information found in the weekly Jewish newspaper, *American Israelite*, about Jews in Florida during the second half of the nineteenth century. All references to Florida Jewry from 1854 to 1900 are abstracted and indexed. These include not only articles but also betrothal announcements, advertisements, lists of contributions, correspondence, and miscellaneous reports. There are indexes to personal names, place-names, congregations, and organizations and societies. Each index entry includes date, location, name, and page. The abstracts section is arranged chronologically by date, followed by title and location, page, and column. The abstracts are brief, generally one or two sentences. A short preface describes the organization and content of the index and its scope and limitations. (A more detailed description of how to use the index would have been helpful.) There is also a short historical account of Jews in Florida.

This index improves access to primary sources of information about Florida Jewry. Because Florida has become an important center of Jewish life and activity over the years, the early history of Jews in Florida is of increasing interest. This specialized tool will be useful in Judaica collections of large academic libraries and in reference collections of temple, synagogue, and community center libraries, especially those in Florida and neighboring states. – **Susan J. Freiband**

447. Luckert, Yelena. **Soviet Jewish History, 1917-1991: An Annotated Bibliography.** Hamden, Conn., Garland, 1992. 271p. index. (Garland Reference Library of Social Science, v.611). $44.00. Z6373.R9L83. 016.947'004924. LC 92-1682. ISBN 0-8240-2583-0.

This work identifies the wide variety of materials available in the field of Soviet Jewish studies. It includes 1,446 numbered bibliographic citations to scholarly works, bibliographies, periodical articles, political propaganda pamphlets, personal narratives, memoirs, biographies, court transcripts, literature, and musical scores. In the introduction Luckert briefly sketches the history of the Jews in the Soviet Union from earliest times to the present day. She also discusses the scope, purpose, and arrangement of the bibliography. Most of the items included are annotated, except those she was unable to obtain. The annotations are short and descriptive, generally one or two sentences. The materials cover the period from the revolution and early years of the Soviet Union to the post-Gorbachev and Glasnost periods. They include items published in 10 different languages and countries. Library of Congress transliterations are used when possible for Russian material, and some English titles of non-English publications are included. However, Luckert's intention was not to include everything published in this field, but rather to incorporate material of different kinds. (The criteria used to determine which titles were to be included needs further discussion in the introduction.)

The organization of the book is by broad subject, arranged chronologically and then subdivided into topics. The scope is wide, including historical, literary, political, military, intellectual, cultural, and religious aspects. Two chapters are devoted to special topics common to all periods from 1917 to 1991. A table of contents divided by topic presents the arrangement. Although there is an author index, title and subject indexes would have helped improve access to individual items.

This book is an important contribution to Soviet Jewish history and scholarship. It will be a significant and useful addition to reference collections of temple, synagogue, and Jewish community center libraries as well as to those of public and academic libraries with Jewish studies programs or that serve Jewish clientele.—**Susan J. Freiband**

448. **The New Standard Jewish Encyclopedia.** 7th ed. Geoffrey Wigoder, ed. New York, Facts on File, 1992. 1001p. illus. $59.95. DS102.8.S73. 909'.04924'003. LC 92-18351. ISBN 0-8160-2690-4.

In the review of the previous edition of this work (see ARBA 78, entry 285), several shortcomings were pointed out. Although some of these—merely matters of wording, interpretation, or choice rather than matters of fact—did not merit revision, others were substantial deficiencies. The editors have remedied a number of them in this edition. For example, the Sephardic, German, and Soviet immigration periods are now mentioned in the United States entry; there is now an entry on Belorussia ("White Russia"); there is a table of the Jewish population in the Commonwealth of Independent States; and the entry on Jacob Sverdlov now mentions that he played a role in organizing the central Soviet committee. One problem that remains is the blind cross-reference from "Federations" to "Welfare Funds" (an entry that does not exist).

Spot-checking reveals several other revisions. Jewish population figures and other statistical data have been updated where possible, in some cases to 1991; biographical entries include death dates for persons who have died since the previous edition; and such events as the reunification of Germany and the dissolution of the Soviet Union are included. Another change that will be immediately obvious to those who are familiar with the earlier editions of the encyclopedia is the use of page numbers instead of column numbers.

Although *The New Standard Jewish Encyclopedia* is not perfect, it is a useful source of brief information on things that are part of, and that have affected, the Jewish experience. Recommended.
—**Craig W. Beard**

449. Olitzky, Kerry M., and Ronald H. Isaacs. **A Glossary of Jewish Life.** Northvale, N.J., Jason Aronson, 1992. 254p. index. $40.00. BM50.045. 269'.03. LC 91-12399. ISBN 0-87668-547-5.

Olitzky and Isaacs envisioned this work to be a ready-reference of terms, names, and assorted other data "essential to an American-Jewish culture code" that would assist communication and mitigate misunderstanding. So lofty and praiseworthy a goal deserves far better than it receives in this work.

The major problem is that the authors have attempted to do far more than is possible or advisable in the relatively few pages allotted to them. How, in just more than 200 pages, can one expect to provide meaningful definitions or descriptions for more than 2,400 items in areas as vast as the Bible, Rabbinic literature, world Jewish history, philosophy, theology, and Israel (and this list of major sections is not complete)? Superficiality, incompleteness, and misplaced emphasis abound, none of which is compensated for by a bibliography (which is lacking) or a useful index or system of cross-referencing. Moreover, the volume is physically unattractive. Given the fact that there are a number of fine Bible dictionaries and easily accessible reference tools on every aspect of Judaism and Jewish life, it is hard to imagine an audience for this particular book. [R: Choice, Sept 92, pp. 86-88]—**Leonard J. Greenspoon**

450. Polner, Murray, ed. **Jewish Profiles: Great Jewish Personalities and Institutions of the Twentieth Century.** Northvale, N.J., Jason Aronson, 1991. 410p. illus. index. $40.00. DS115.J38. 920'.0092924073. LC 90-28237. ISBN 0-87668-793-1.

The 40 profiles in this book are more than encyclopedia essays and less than biographical chapters. They are magazine articles taken from the now defunct *Present Tense*, which was devoted to the tradition of Jewish liberalism. As befitting the source of the profiles, the articles exhibit a journalistic crispness and an engaging quality that derives from interviews. They also have a reference appeal because the figures and institutions covered, while enjoying renown, are often absent from Jewish biographical references. Checking *Dictionary of Jewish Biography* (see ARBA 92, entry 381), for example, reveals that only two of the figures in Polner's book are covered in the dictionary.

The profiles are arranged in alphabetical order and typically run from 6 to 18 pages. They prominently feature artistic, political, and educational figures and institutions, such as Brandeis University, Jewish Daily Forward, Amos Oz, Ariel Sharon, and Elie Wiesel. A detailed index is included to add coverage to the many names mentioned in the profiles. As a reference work, this book is idiosyncratic in its selection and content, but it complements other existing texts and provides some enjoyable reading. — **Simon J. Bronner**

Norwegian-Americans

451. Thompson, Harry F., comp. **Guide to Collections Relating to South Dakota Norwegian-Americans.** Sioux Falls, S.D., Center for Western Studies, Augustana College, 1991. 65p. index. $10.95pa. Z1335.T46. 016.9783'0043982. LC 91-3761. ISBN 0-931170-50-8.

There are only 44 pages of listings in this thin but useful guide. It covers 55 institutions, libraries, museums, and historical societies from across the United States that responded to Thompson's questionnaire about holdings on Norwegian immigrants and Norwegian-Americans. As he indicates, his mailing was selective; it would have been helpful if a list of all the institutions contacted had been provided to save researchers time and effort.

The work is a guide to collections held, not individual items in a collection. Entries are in alphabetical order by institution name. Information provided ranges from single-sentence entries (e.g., the Sterling Library at Yale University) to 17 pages (for Augustana College, Thompson's home institution). Data contained in each entry are apparently taken directly from the questionnaire, and some is of little use to a researcher. For example, for the Lead Public Library (S.D.), the complete entry reads, "The library has some books in Norwegian." For libraries with this subject interest, the price and content of this work make it a satisfactory addition to the collection. — **G. Edward Evans**

7 Genealogy and Heraldry

GENEALOGY

Chronology

452. Coldham, Peter Wilson. **The Complete Book of Emigrants 1700-1750: A Comprehensive Listing Compiled from English Public Records....** Baltimore, Md., Genealogical Publishing, 1992. 743p. index. $44.95. LC 91-77741. ISBN 0-8063-1334-X.

This work is a continuation of the excellent series of the same title by Coldham. The previous volumes covered the years 1607 to 1660 and 1661 to 1699 (see ARBA 88, entry 429 and ARBA 91, entry 416).

Among the records examined for this volume are Acts of the Privy Council, Calendar of State Papers—Colonial Series, Lord Mayor's Court of London Depositions, and Liverpool Town Books. The entries are arranged by year and thereunder by date of record. Information includes name, age, occupation, residence, ship, destination, and a precise source citation. The information varies depending upon the source. Indexes of persons and ships make this work easy to use.

This important series is a must for any genealogical collection and a wonderful addition to the ever-growing collection of emigration sources. Highly recommended. [R: LJ, 15 Apr 92, p. 84]

—**Carol Willsey Bell**

Dictionaries

453. Thode, Ernest. **German-English Genealogical Dictionary.** Baltimore, Md., Genealogical Publishing, 1992. 286p. illus. maps. $29.95pa. LC 92-70580. ISBN 0-8063-1342-0.

Thode, the author of *Address Book for Germanic Genealogy* (Genealogical Publishing, 1991) and a professional genealogist specializing in German-American lineages, has designed his dictionary for the family researcher who has little or no knowledge of German but who nevertheless needs to make a translation of German-language documents. With simplicity in mind, he covers thousands of German terms and defines them in single words or brief phrases. All words, symbols, and abbreviations in the dictionary have been chosen on the basis of their association with genealogy. They have been used in church records, civil registration records, family correspondence, genealogical journals, ships' passenger lists, and emigration records. In conjunction with a standard German-English dictionary, the user of this work should be able to make a word-by-word translation of any German document for genealogical purposes.

Thode has collected words from several sources. These include genealogical publications and German-English and German-German dictionaries, from which he has selected words under key categories such as family, birth, and death. Additionally, the author has included a few terms of genealogical and cultural significance (e.g., FANA, a genealogical research source; Baedeker, a famous European guide series) that might be difficult to find elsewhere.

The dictionary's categories include family relationships; days of the week; map terms; months; legal terms; cardinal and ordinal numbers; roman numerals; signs of the zodiac; coins; liquid and dry measures; measures of length; historical territories; place-names (with Latin versions of major places); genealogical terms; occupations; military ranks; types of taxes and tithes; ecclesiastical terms; illnesses; genealogical and historical societies; calendar days; male and female given names; heraldry; abbreviations; books of the Bible; and common genealogical words from Danish, Dutch, French, Latin, and Polish. The German-English tables presented in the front of the work are crucial tools in deciphering documents written in German script. These include the German alphabet with script variations (printed alphabet with script equivalents), German genealogical terms (script with modern German equivalents and English translation), genealogical symbols, male and female given names, surnames and occupations, months/signs of the zodiac, planets/metals/days of the week, ordinal numbers, cardinal numbers, suffixes, a reverse suffix index, a key to German dialect pronunciations, and the German empire 1871-1918 (a map depicts all German provinces). Thode's work is highly recommended for public libraries and will be a welcome addition to academic and institutional library collections as well. [R: LJ, Aug 92, p. 92]—**Mark Padnos**

Directories

454. Thode, Ernest. **Address Book for Germanic Genealogy.** 4th ed. Baltimore, Md., Genealogical Publishing, 1991. 218p. $24.95pa. LC 91-74047. ISBN 0-8063-1321-8.

This edition takes into account the sweeping changes that have occurred in Germany since December 1989. With the reunification of Germany in 1990, every address in the two German areas had to be changed with respect to prefix. There were literally thousands of changes.

The "Table of Contents and Research Guide" is the key to accessing addresses. Although the basic organization of addresses is easy to follow, the research guide aspect of these two pages is in need of improvement. The paragraphs devoted to genealogical research in the table of contents are insufficient for carrying out such research, which requires a specific book on the subject.

The sections on German national, regional, and specialized archives are the most useful features of this work and contain easy-to-follow cross-references. Some sections also include introductory material (e.g., the Heimatortskarteien for formerly German areas that are now parts of Czechoslovakia, Poland, the former Soviet Union, and Yugoslavia). Users of the work will be especially pleased by the map of the German Empire 1871-1918 (with the names of all provinces), the map of German postal codes, and German form letters for church parishes and registration offices that include useful phrases for insertion. Thode's work is recommended for all genealogy collections as well as for German collections in public and academic libraries.—**Mark Padnos**

Handbooks and Yearbooks

455. **Ancestry's Red Book: American State, County & Town Sources.** rev. ed. Alice Eichholz, ed. Salt Lake City, Utah, Ancestry Publishing, 1992. 858p. maps. index. $39.95. CS49.A55. 929'.1'072073. LC 91-30311. ISBN 0-916489-47-7.

The purpose of *Ancestry's Red Book* is to help genealogists locate family history data in and on each of the 50 states of the Union. Attractive in appearance, the volume is organized in a consistent, easy-to-use format. States are treated in separate, alphabetically arranged chapters of 8 to 20 pages. For each state several elements are given. First, brief essays treat history; vital and census records; background sources; maps; land, probate, and court records; tax, cemetery, church, and military records; periodicals, newspapers, and manuscript collections; archives, libraries, and societies; special focus groups (particularly Black and Native American); and county resources. Second, a map identifies counties in the state and adjacent counties in bordering states. Third, a tabular section provides for each county the address; date formed; parent county; and beginning dates for birth, marriage, death, land, probate, and court records.

In reviewing this work, attention must be paid to the previous edition. Although selected as one of the outstanding reference books of 1990 by the American Library Association, it was severely criticized by genealogists and librarians, who found it error-filled and poorly written. The present edition shows substantial improvement. Most errors appear to have been corrected, and extensive revision is evident. The index remains, however, merely a table of contents arranged in alphabetical order. Material that should be indexed is omitted, while most indexed subjects may be found easily without the index. The binding is weak and may not stand up to constant use by library patrons or genealogists (the review copy was received with the covers almost torn off). With continued improvements, this may become one of the standards of genealogical reference. Recommended for genealogists and libraries with genealogical or local history interests. – **Donald E. Collins**

456. Baxter, Angus. **In Search of Your Roots: A Guide for Canadians Seeking Their Ancestors.** rev. ed. Toronto, Macmillan Canada, 1991. 331p. index. $18.95pa. 929'.1'072. ISBN 0-7715-9134-9.

The subtitle of this work is the clue to its usefulness to anyone searching for information about research in Canada. Revised and updated, this edition covers many topics, including the National Archives of Canada, Canadian church records, and the various provinces, with brief paragraphs on land records, census, genealogical societies, libraries, and civil registrations. Only the first 141 pages cover records in Canada; the balance of the book deals with the rest of the world. The British Isles, the United States, and France are given the most space, while "the rest of Europe" finishes the recitation.

Although an index is included, it is deficient in subjects that genealogists seek. Topics such as land records, births and deaths, and civil registrations are not listed, and there is no table of contents. Despite these drawbacks, the work will be useful and is recommended. – **Carol Willsey Bell**

457. Clark, Murtie June, comp. **The Pension Lists of 1792-1795: With Other Revolutionary War Pension Records.** Baltimore, Md., Genealogical Publishing, 1991. 200p. index. $21.50. LC 91-73507. ISBN 0-8063-1318-8.

The publication of this volume – by the same firm that has just published a reprint of a 1935 work, *The Pension Roll of 1835*, which claims to be "the most complete roll of Revolutionary War pensioners ever published" – raises a serious problem. If that four-volume reprint is actually "the most complete," is this new volume really needed? According to the publisher, the 1835 roll was "legally" the most complete. However, because of the fires of 1800 and 1814, certain "replacement" records were inserted wherever the original files were destroyed. These replacements were taken from letters, applications for pensions, and so forth and were often incomplete, inaccurate, or impossible to locate. So the statement of 1835 may well be true. It was – at that time – the most complete. But subsequent research has located pre-1800 records, and these are what constitute the present volume.

The text of section 1 is arranged by judicial district and is printed in columnar form, giving name, residence, monthly allowance, arrearages, and a wide column of remarks. Section 2 differs somewhat in that it is an 1810 relisting of claims previously not allowed by reason of a statute of limitations. It gives name, date (between 1792 and 1796), name of claimant, unit of service, "interest date," and amount of claim. Section 3 lists officers killed in action prior to May 1778. A 15-page index of names completes the work.

The book is very valuable to genealogists as it gives the rank or occupation of hundreds of men who lived in the 1780s and 1790s, with such entries as "Seaman, frigate, 'Boston'"; "Gunner, 4th S.C. Regiment"; and "Treasurer of Society of Cincinnati." Other information includes the place of, date of, and type of wound suffered by the pensioner. – **Raymund F. Wood**

458. Stern, Malcolm H., comp. **First American Jewish Families: 600 Genealogies, 1654-1988.** 3d ed. Baltimore, Md., Ottenheimer; distr., Baltimore, Md., Genealogical Publishing, 1991. 442p. index. $75.00pa. CS59.S76. 929'.2'0973. LC 78-17341. ISBN 0-87068-443-4.

The name of Stern is well known in the field of Jewish genealogy. Genealogists working in this field are probably familiar with most of his major publications, such as *Americans of Jewish Descent* (Hebrew Union College Press, 1960). His latest contribution – this specialized area of genealogical study – is a revised and updated version of an earlier publication, *First American Jewish Families: 600 Genealogies 1654-1977* (American Jewish Archives, 1978). That work was an exhaustive compilation of pedigree charts of 600 Jewish families that were established in the United States by 1840. The current edition is identical in format (although issued in paperback), size, and scope to the former edition. It includes a list of abbreviations, an "Addenda et Corrigenda," a bibliography, and an index of names. An "Update" section is appended to the new edition and provides the latest research data on these families from 1978 to 1988. These entries include not only new births, deaths, and marriages within these families but also earlier events as well.

Stern is likely to produce future volumes of this impressive work as these families continue to grow and as he uncovers new material. *First American Jewish Families* is a unique contribution to the field of genealogy.—**J. C. Jurgens**

Indexes

459. Clark, Murtie June. **Index to U.S. Invalid Pension Records 1801-1815.** Baltimore, Md., Genealogical Publishing, 1991. 132p. $18.50. LC 91-70240. ISBN 0-8063-1304-8.

The preface to this work makes it clear that it is an index to a ledger and does not contain much information beyond name, rank, page references, and an occasional remark. The preface goes on to give the dimensions of the bulky ledger that survived the 1814 fire in Washington (and also an 1833 fire in the Treasury Department) and points out that its existence is remarkable, considering its size and the difficulty involved in preserving it from danger. (The original ledger is now in the National Archives.) There is also an introduction of some dozen pages, which gives useful information about early pension law, documentation required, and the value of money in Revolutionary times. It supplies a table of pay and rations for all ranks of the army in December 1776, from the Commander-in-Chief ($500.00 a month) to privates ($6.66).

The work is organized geographically, from New Hampshire to the Carolinas and then westerly to Kentucky, Tennessee, Ohio, and the Territories. Entries in the "Remarks" column are brief, usually no more than the date pension began, date of death, or occasional transfer of pensioner to another state's rolls. There is a name index. Because this work contains many names not found in other listings, it will prove invaluable to researchers looking for Revolutionary War ancestors.—**Raymund F. Wood**

460. **Passenger and Immigration Lists Index: A Guide to Published Arrival Records of More Than 2,029,000 Passengers.... 1992 Supplement.** P. William Filby with Dorothy M. Lower, eds. Detroit, Gale, 1992. 628p. $170.00. LC 84-15404. ISBN 0-8103-7603-2. ISSN 0736-8267.

This volume is the 11th supplement to a continuing series. Included are more than 125,000 citations found in 105-plus published passenger and naturalization lists between the sixteenth and mid-twentieth centuries. Arranged in alphabetical order by passenger names, entries include age (if given), port of arrival, year, and a code number that leads to the bibliographic citation. The "Sources Indexed" section lists the title, author, and publisher of each work examined. Among some of the interesting sources included are naturalizations from Bucks County, Pennsylvania; Ripley County, Indiana; Riverside County, California; and Erie County, Ohio. Also listed are immigrants from the village of Till, West Germany, and transportees from the London Workhouse. This series is a necessity to any serious genealogical collection.—**Carol Willsey Bell**

461. Saul, Pauline, and F. C. Maxwell. **The A-Z Guide to Tracing Ancestors in Britain.** 4th ed. Baltimore, Md., Genealogical Publishing, 1991. 256p. index. $17.95pa. LC 92-70312. ISBN 0-8063-1341-2.

This marvelous resource for British genealogy emphasizes sources of information in book form or indexes and articles to which the family historian can refer in a search. Arranged in alphabetical order, the work contains definitions, explanations, bibliographies, sources, addresses, and guides to nearly every conceivable topic that could be of interest. Excluded are a number of words that are still in common usage and can be found in any good dictionary. Medieval terms and more obscure occupations have also been omitted. Some entries are bibliographic essays that detail sources and how to use them, including their quirks. There are also tips on how to search the records and what to look for.

There are five appendixes. The first gives a breakdown of the records in the various divisions of the Public Record Office. The second lists Public Record Office leaflets that summarize information on particular records or subjects. The third covers the units of the British Army; the fourth lists the

Chapman County codes; and the fifth contains maps that show counties and their boundaries before and after April 1, 1974. There is also an index with cross-references. This work is not a textbook for British family history and therefore is not meant for the novice. However, it should be consulted frequently by those experienced in genealogical research in Great Britain.—**Robert L. Turner, Jr.**

HERALDRY

462. Rubinstein, W. D., comp. **The Biographical Dictionary of Life Peers.** New York, St. Martin's Press, 1991. 386p. index. $75.00. DA28.8.R83. 929.7'2. LC 91-17740. ISBN 0-312-01911-4.

A peer is defined in this book as an English or Irish noble with the rank of baron or higher who has been elevated either by heredity or by action of the Crown and who is entitled to sit in the House of Lords. This biographical directory is limited to those peers who were ennobled by royal action "for life," meaning that their title is not hereditary. In 1958 the structure of the House of Lords was considerably changed by the passing of the Life Peerage Act of 1958, an attempt to modernize the ancient House of Lords by bringing in many Labour leaders and others who, by reason of their prominence in the business, political, intellectual, or social world of England, deserved this type of recognition.

The 562 peers "for life" are listed here, not by alphabet but by the date of the Patent to their title, so that use of the index is necessary. The work begins with Baron Fraser of Lonsdale, title patented August 1, 1958, and ends with Baron Tombs, who received his title on February 28, 1990. In addition, there are some 30 Lords of Appeal in Ordinary, who have had their titles since a prior Act of 1876, which decreed that certain judges should be ennobled to the rank of baron in order to form the High Court of Parliament. In 1958 it was decided to include all such peers in the category of "life peers."

Each peer receives a rather complete biography. Family name, date of birth, marriage, children, education, affiliations, and major accomplishments fill up the first few paragraphs, followed by occasional footnotes that amplify some point or add personal accounts. These are often pithy; Baron Boardman, for example, is described as a "Bright, rightish businessman-politico; lined, greying, friendly, tough." No photographs are included.

Most of these peers are leaders in governmental committees, international commerce, journalism, ambassadorial appointments, or other areas of importance in today's world. Their lives and achievements should be as well known to Americans as to Britons. This book will help achieve that end.
—**Raymund F. Wood**

PERSONAL NAMES

463. Benson, Morton. **Dictionary of Russian Personal Names, with a Revised Guide to Stress and Morphology.** New York, Cambridge University Press, 1992. 174p. $44.95. CS2811.B4. 929.4'0947. LC 91-34064. ISBN 0-521-41165-3.

Cambridge University Press has republished, with minor changes, the 2d revised edition of the standard reference work *Dictionary of Russian Personal Names*, first issued in 1967 by the University of Pennsylvania Press. The dictionary lists some 23,000 stressed surnames plus an inventory of stressed first names and their diminutives. It also includes a sketch of the stress rules for Russian surnames and the formation of patronymics. Because the name lists are only in Cyrillic, the volume is, practically speaking, useful only to those who know at least some Russian. The new version differs from the 1967 edition in only three minor respects: a new three-page section of simplified rules for assigning names to declensional types and stress patterns to inflected names, a new "Table 2" that gives transliteration systems in addition to the "popular" system, and a copy of the Cyrillic alphabet to facilitate locating names in the listings. The selected bibliography has been expanded and updated.—**D. Barton Johnson**

464. **The Penguin Dictionary of Proper Names.** By Geoffrey Payton. Revised by John Paxton. New York, Penguin Books, 1991. 562p. $29.95. ISBN 0-670-82573-5.

This eclectic collection of proper names, ancient and modern, was first published in 1969, with U.S. incarnation as *Webster's Dictionary of Proper Names* in 1970 (see ARBA 72, entry 381). For this edition more than 1,000 new entries have been added, and some of the original entries have been edited or dropped. The purpose of these entries, which have been selected as "useful or interesting," is to help modern readers deal with the abundance of proper names they are likely to encounter in the various media, to provide information when "only a roomful of reference books can save us from embarrassment." There is a marked preference for British terms over United States ones, although both appear in this international compendium. Titles of literary works are included because of their allusive use, not necessarily because of any literary merit. The entries are arranged in double columns, with headwords in boldface type. These main words are then explained briefly, with only occasional pronunciations given. Dates of publication of literary works are provided, as are those of historical events and periods. Cross-references are indicated by words in small capitals.

In an ambitious dictionary of this kind, a reader can always nitpick. Would a New Yorker recognize the apostrophe in the entry *Triboro' Bridge*? Where are entries for Nelly Bly and the Lone Ranger? Superman's creators are not mentioned, but Batman's creator is. The explanation of the ubiquitous initials *OK* is not current.

Despite such quibbles, the general reader, puzzle fan, and player of word games would be hardpressed to find *Abbots Bromley Horn Dance*, *Chappaquiddick*, *Monty Python's Flying Circus*, *Scotch woodcock*, *Ricardo's theory of rent*, and *Sing-Sing* in a single volume of this size. It is informative and fun to browse through this book, which belongs in personal and library collections near such works as *Brewer's Dictionary of Phrase and Fable* (see ARBA 83, entry 1058), *Grand Allusions* (see ARBA 91, entry 1055), and *The Facts on File Dictionary of 20th Century Allusions* (see ARBA 92, entry 878). [R: RBB, 15 Apr 92, pp. 1552-54] – **Henry J. Ricardo**

465. **Tuttle Dictionary of First Names.** By Julia Cresswell. Rutland, Vt., Charles E. Tuttle, c1990, 1992. 248p. $14.95pa. CS2377.C74. 929.4'03. LC 91-67340. ISBN 0-8048-1780-4.

This British export, reprinted by Tuttle, is larger and has more information than the usual dictionary of first names, which is often targeted at young parents. With half a dozen entries per page that run from about 6 to 20 or even 30 lines, and with innumerable cross-references (usually from pet names or diminutives), Cresswell covers almost all British and Welsh names; many biblical names; and a few French, German, and Russian ones. Each explanation for a name's origin includes not only the meaning (if known) but also the source – popular movie or novel (e.g., Scarlett), national hero (e.g., Nelson), royal family (e.g., Eugenie), and so on. Also useful are the many, sometimes remote, variants. The name Margaret, for example, has 28 derivatives, which are all cross-indexed to their source. Many of the names have long entries to explain their origin. Sometimes unusual tidbits of information are included, such as that Swinburne's poem "Felice" was written to settle a bet as to who could find the most words that rhymed with the name, or that the name *Imogen* owes its present form to a misprint in Shakespeare's First Folio edition.

Readers from the United States will find the book useful, especially for information about names in British and Welsh literature. They may wish, however, that more Hispanic and Italian names had been included. In cities with large ethnic populations, such names as Felipe, Jorge, Socorro, and Luigi are frequently mentioned in the media, as well as many diminutives, such as Paco (Francisco), Pepe (Jose), or Chewey (Jesus). And other languages fairly common in the United States, such as Armenian, also give us names (e.g., Avedis, Manoog, Vartiter), none of which appear in the book. Additionally, Israeli names such as Yuri or Yona are scarce (although Yehudi is included).

The typesetting is unusual, the customary punctuation for quotation marks having been replaced by single acute accents. This symbol is also occasionally used to indicate stress but unfortunately is not placed directly over the stressed syllable; instead, it appears to the left of it. Thus, a three-syllable word stressed on the second syllable shows the mark over the first one, which will be a little puzzling to the reader. [R: RBB, Aug 92, p. 2041] – **Raymund F. Wood**

8 Geography and Travel Guides

GEOGRAPHY

General Works

Atlases

United States

466. Balder, A. P. **Marine Atlas of the Hawaiian Islands: Complete Charts for Mariners....** Honolulu, University of Hawaii Press, 1992. 120p. illus. maps. index. $39.00pa. G1534.21.P5B3. 633.89'2249. LC 91-45699. ISBN 0-8248-1444-4.

Newest in a line of marine atlases begun in 1966 by the author, this volume of Hawaiian Islands' nautical charts is intended to be used as a planning guide, not as a substitute for the most current NOS (National Ocean Service) charts. This value-added atlas provides excerpts from the *United States Coast Pilot #7*, various lists (e.g., Hawaii state boating facilities), helpful hints from local sources (e.g., "When entering the Bay, favor the W shore to avoid a reef, covered 2 feet, in the entrance"), and safety information. The atlas is composed of reproductions (in some cases with scale altered) of the NOS charts that cover the main Hawaiian Islands; these segmented reproductions include the aforementioned helpful hints. A resealable plastic pouch is included with the book as it is intended for use in the cockpit of a boat. The design of the book is very busy and cluttered, but this is preferable to scanty information. Recommended for collections that cater to sailors of Hawaiian waters. – **Mary Larsgaard**

467. **Gousha New Deluxe Road Atlas: United States, Canada, Mexico.** New York, H. M. Gousha/Simon & Schuster, 1992. 160p. maps. index. $7.95pa. ISBN 0-13-213331-8.

468. **Rand McNally Road Atlas: United States, Canada, Mexico.** Skokie, Ill., Rand McNally, 1992. 128p. maps. index. $7.95pa. LC 79-62950. ISBN 0-528-81000-6.

A road atlas is probably second only to a dictionary as the most popular home reference source. Both Rand McNally and Gousha (a division of Simon & Schuster) update their road atlases annually and encourage travelers to keep the current edition in a handy place. Both are high-quality tools and are recommended for library and home use, but as they vie for sales, a comparison of features is in order.

While both atlases are the same size, the maps in the Gousha atlas are slightly larger and use a somewhat bigger typeface than the Rand McNally, making it easier to read. Colors in the Gousha are a lighter shade, making details within a national forest or a city area easier to read; however, the Rand McNally uses colors to better advantage in borders of states and counties. Main roads and city locations are virtually identical in both atlases, but country roads and location of tiny communities are not consistent. (Neither atlas could be trusted to get one through wilderness or sparsely settled areas.) Both atlases use grids to help locate specific cities from the alphabetical listings. The Gousha grids are easiest to follow. Both are arranged alphabetically by state, with detailed maps of major cities usually positioned close to the state in which they are located. Not all metropolitan areas are featured in both atlases. For example, Rand McNally includes a map of Manhattan but Gousha does not. Local points of interest are indicated in both atlases in varying detail (one does not seem superior to the other).

A typical page in each book contains the state map, insets of larger cities, mileage charts, and a legend. In addition, the Gousha atlas has a list of place-names (not complete) on the page with the state map for quick identification of major cities and towns. The index in the back of Rand McNally lists place-names alphabetically by state whereas the Gousha atlas has a master index in straight alphabetical order across the United States. Both indexes are printed in microscopic type. Each atlas includes detailed maps of Canada and Mexico, large mileage charts, a big freeway map of the United States (the Gousha one is more detailed and easier to read). The Rand McNally atlas includes commercial coupons for hotels and vacation spots. It also features general information for travelers about such things as travel plans, climate, road conditions, telephone numbers, and calendars of events, making it a little more useful for the person on vacation.

Both atlases are standard tools for the family, the traveler, and the library. For ease of use, particularly in the car at night, the Gousha wins for clarity. Neither is superior overall. Families on extended vacations would benefit from owning both atlases when proceeding into unfamiliar areas.

—David V. Loertscher

469. Smith, Kathie Billingslea. **United States Atlas for Young People.** Mahwah, N.J., Troll, 1991. 128p. illus. maps. $14.95; $9.95pa. G1200.S6. 912.73. LC 90-675059. ISBN 0-8167-2195-5; 0-8167-2196-3pa.

This atlas is written in a perky, straightforward style geared to the youngest readers making their first acquaintance with an atlas. Each state gets a two-page "spread." One side is a narrative offering a variety of facts, from the origin of the state name and nickname to major cities, industries, and places of interest. It is illustrated by three small color photographs. The maps on the facing page are simple outlines drawn to scale. Triangles indicate mountains, dots denote deserts, and blue lines are rivers. Cities are shown with circles; the capital has a star. The map page also lists the state nickname, bird, flower, tree, motto, and song. There is a small color picture of the state flag. Topographic, time zone, and political maps, along with charts on major products and industries, are at the back of the book.

By the time children are ready to do research in an atlas, they deserve more information than is offered here and maps that more closely conform to what they will use as adults. (This reviewer's 10-year-old son said the charts were good, but he needed more information.) This is a marginal purchase for a library serving the very young.

—Deborah Hammer

470. Suarez, Thomas. **Shedding the Veil: Mapping the European Discovery of America and the World.** River Edge, N.J., World Scientific, 1992. 203p. maps. $65.00. E121.S87. 970.01. LC 92-6466. ISBN 981-02-0869-3.

The intent of this work is to illustrate the history of the European discovery of America with reproductions of maps from the Sidney R. Knafel collection of early maps, atlases, and globes (1434-1865). After a list of maps in chronological order, with location in chapters noted, the work is divided into "A World Called Europe," "A New World," and "Early Colonization." These are followed by a 4-page index, about 25 pages of color plates, and a 3-page bibliography. The text is enjoyable to read (even the footnotes—of which there are a good number—are entertaining to an early-map aficionado); the color plates are very good; and the work gives a valuable look into a private collection (whose location seems not to be given anywhere in the book). The black-and-white illustrations are a bit dark. The bibliography does not consistently give place of publication or page numbers for periodical articles, making it difficult for the eager reader to follow up on citations of interest.

This is certainly an appropriate publication for the year of the Quincentennial. Joining many other works on the history of cartography of this time period, it is appropriate for collections specializing in this area. —**Mary Larsgaard**

Canada

471. **The Macmillan School Atlas.** 3d ed. By Ronald C. Daly. Toronto, Gage Educational Publishing, 1992. 140p. illus. maps. index. $24.95. 912. ISBN 0-7715-8269-2.

Last revised 10 years ago to reflect the conversion to metric measurement, this latest edition of *The Macmillan School Atlas* is designed for the Canadian educational market at the elementary and middle school levels. Well organized and clearly detailed maps, graphs, and photographs illustrate sections that deal with Canada, each of the continents, and the world. Explanatory material introduces basic geographic concepts and gives a brief history of maps and mapping. The inside front cover features quick facts about Canada's provinces and territories, while the back cover gives facts about the world and the continents. Maps are colorful and clear, with a level of detail appropriate for the intended audience. A substantial gazetteer of places included completes the volume. An interesting footnote to the publication: boundary and name changes that took place just as the book went to press precluded revision of political designations.

Visually appealing and easy to use, the work's only major drawback is its lack of a comprehensive index. The table of contents is adequate, but arrangement seems a bit disjointed (e.g., students may miss an excellent section on contemporary native peoples, which is included at the end of the volume under the heading "World Exploration—Canada"). Despite this, students and teachers in Canada will welcome this revised edition. —**Virginia S. Fischer**

472. McCalla, Robert J. **The Maritime Provinces Atlas.** Halifax, N.S., Maritext/Formac, 1991. 96p. illus. maps. index. $29.95. 912'.715. ISBN 0-921921-05-5.

This revised edition expands only slightly on the original, which was published in 1988. However, this publication is one of the most comprehensive graphic representations available of the geography of these Canadian provinces. Organized in 5 thematic sections, the publication contains 40 plates that delineate the diverse physical and human aspects of the region. The combination of graphs, tables, and maps present relationships with little textual explanation but are clear, detailed, and up-to-date. Following the thematic sections, a detailed gazetteer of the region with index and distance matrix is included. A glossary and a list of bibliographic references complete the volume.

Some minor corrections have been made to this edition, and updated statistical material has been included (e.g., 1988 federal election results and household income data). The rail and water transportation plate has been redrawn to reflect changes in regional transportation networks. For those possessing the original edition of this atlas, this revision will not be an essential purchase. However, for others interested in any aspect of Canadian maritime geography, it is a fine choice. —**Virginia S. Fischer**

473. McManus, Gary E., and Clifford H. Wood. **Atlas of Newfoundland and Labrador.** St. John's, Nfld., Breakwater, 1991. 77p. illus. maps. index. $49.95. 912.718. ISBN 1-55081-000-6.

Appealing to a broad spectrum of potential users, this provincial atlas of Newfoundland and Labrador consists of 22 plates that depict an array of elements that represent the distinctive features of this easternmost province of Canada. A project that has been almost 20 years in the making (according to the authors, who are both with MUNCL [Memorial University of Newfoundland Cartographic Laboratory]), the atlas demonstrates the professional design and production services provided by this facility. The initial plates place Newfoundland geographically in relation to the rest of Canada and the world, graphically comparing land area and population data. Subsequent plates position towns and communities and indicate the various transportation routes throughout Newfoundland, Labrador, and the Avalon Peninsula. Relief maps indicate height and depth from sea level within and without the province. Climatic and seasonal changes for various areas of the province are also graphically illustrated.

Several pages are devoted to tracing the cultural heritage of the provinces' people, presenting archaeological evidence of early migrations through the periods of European exploration and settlement to present-day cultural patterns. A helpful feature included at the bottom of these pages is an ongoing timeline of significant events and activities that have shaped the character of Newfoundland. Plates that pinpoint population, labor force, and economic data detail changes that have taken place primarily since the area's entrance into the Confederation in 1949. The largest sections summarize the components of the various resource bases on which the province has supported growth and development. A gazetteer of more than 500 names concludes the volume, providing feature classification and geographic coordinates.

Much needed and long overdue, this provincial atlas will have wide appeal for Canadian readers and those with interest in Canadiana. In light of recent Canadian political developments, this graphic picture of the tenth and newest province may generate substantial interest south of its borders as well. [R: Choice, July/Aug 92, p. 1659]—**Virginia S. Fischer**

International

474. **Hammond Gold Medallion World Atlas.** Maplewood, N.J., Hammond, 1992. 1v. (various paging). illus. maps. index. $85.00. G1021.H2685. 912. LC 91-675781. ISBN 0-8437-1291-0.

The earlier editions of this atlas were favorably reviewed (see ARBA 87, entry 433). The 1992 edition updates material. The 15 successor states to the Soviet Union are shown as Russia and neighboring countries, with new names and a separate map for the Baltic states. Constituent republics of disintegrating Yugoslavia are depicted as republics in transition. The reunited Germany is portrayed with its new internal boundaries within the territory of the former German Democratic Republic. Finally, the two Yemens are joined. Changes to former pre-Soviet names are reflected in St. Petersburg for Leningrad, Nizhniy Novgorod for Gor'kiy, Samara for Kuybyshev, and Bishkek for Frunze. Population data have been revised to record final figures from the 1990 census for the United States. A new 24-page section of thematic maps displays important world features, such as distributions of religions, languages, and economic production.

The essential features of earlier editions are retained. Maps of countries or states show internal political boundaries and have indexes to names on the same page, making for easy reference. Basic political-administrative maps are supplemented by maps of topography and land use. Each state of the United States or province of Canada has a separate map. The consolidated name index locates more than 100,000 places by map number and a grid. Separate sections are devoted to world history (72 plates), United States history (72 plates), and terrain maps of the continents and the ocean floors (24 plates). Altogether, the atlas contains 516 pages of map plates and 158 pages of indexes and tables.

The maps are distinguished more for their utility than their beauty. Some of the colors are rather garish. The thematic maps are highly simplified; the major patterns are easy to recognize, but the thematic maps in the smaller *Rand McNally Goode's World Atlas*, 18th ed. (see ARBA 91, entry 429) show more detail and are generally superior. The number of place-names is less than in the *National Geographic Atlas of the World*, 6th ed. (see ARBA 92, entry 402), but internal political subdivisions of countries and states are depicted more clearly. The atlas is a handy reference source with a wide range of information and with the time-saving feature of having map, index, and summary information for a country or state together on facing pages. [R: WLB, Feb 92, p. 107]—**Chauncy D. Harris**

475. Kidron, Michael, and Ronald Segal. **The New State of the World Atlas.** 4th ed. New York, Simon & Schuster, 1991. 159p. maps. $27.95; $15.00pa. G1021.K46. 912. LC 91-6798. ISBN 0-671-74639-1; 0-671-74556-5pa.

If a picture is worth a thousand words, this kaleidoscopic collection of colorful maps and graphs is equivalent to numerous scholarly volumes. It is a masterpiece of "cartojournalism," a new genre of cartographic art befitting the revolutionary changes in the field of instant communications. Kidron and Segal claim to provide a rapid visual survey of the global socio-politico-economic changes. In their view, the major source of endurance and relative stability lies in the world of states with their concentration of economic, political, and cultural power. Yet, under the apparent surface of relative stability are at least four slowly emerging deep cracks at the very foundation of the global system. These cracks reveal inherently dangerous stresses and the need to devise national and international policies to prevent detrimental future scenarios.

The maps are followed by a world table that lists the most fundamental statistical data about 160 nations at the end of the 1980s. (This list would have been substantially longer if the atlas had been compiled after the disintegration of the Soviet Union and Yugoslavia.) This imaginatively compiled, multicolored atlas is highly recommended for all persons interested in global problems. [R: LJ, 15 Mar 92, pp. 76-78]—**Oleg Zinam**

476. **Macmillan First Atlas.** By Nicola Wright and others. New York, Macmillan, 1991. 39p. illus. maps. index. $12.95. ISBN 0-02-774920-7.

Given the geographic illiteracy at almost all levels of U.S. citizenry, the appearance of atlases for children is a good sign. Although the pages of this effort seem very busy, the large, clear type and cheerful colors and design seem likely to attract the young eye and mind. Each map page gives the scale in kilometers and miles; unfortunately, "km" is never explained, and it is doubtful that young U.S. readers of the atlas will know what it means. Interestingly enough, the maps show vegetation rather than topography, which may well be a good decision; the only problem here is that as an illustration of tundra areas, penguins are shown on ice floes. Occasionally the text becomes almost surrealist in nature (e.g., "Eagles and vultures live in the Pyrenees"), but generally it is straightforward and focuses on notable characteristics of areas. Although the work shows the Soviet Union as an entity, it does note that the constituent parts are splitting off. In summary, this is a good work for juvenile collections. [R: RBB, 15 June 92, p. 1884; SLJ, Nov 92, p. 138]—**Mary Larsgaard**

477. **The New Cosmopolitan World Atlas.** census/environmental ed. Skokie, Ill., Rand McNally, 1992. 304p. illus. maps. index. $60.00. G1021.R35. 912. LC 91-14589. ISBN 0-528-83442-8.

This edition of a popular atlas is perplexing, for while the cartographics are aesthetically incomparable, many of the maps, particularly the regional ones, are not easy to read. The practice of placing country names in nearly imperceptible letters within colored lines that demarcate national boundaries is particularly bothersome.

Although the publishers purport to display maps that reflect the sweeping geopolitical changes in Eastern Europe (effective to October 31, 1991), this is not the case. While it is true that Estonia, Latvia, and Lithuania are now set off by colored borders on the main map of the region (p. 26), all other maps displaying these nations show them clearly as part of the Soviet Union (pp. 28, 52, 158, and 160). Furthermore, the index of place-names lists Riga, Tallin, and Vilnius as cities in the Soviet Union. And, contrary to claims that changes have been made to reflect the resumption of the use of the name "St. Petersburg," several maps (pp. 3, 4, 22, and 26) and the main index of place-names show the city as "Leningrad." Eastern Europe is not the only region that presents difficulty for users. Oddly, the main map of Africa displays Transkei, Ciskei, and Bophuthatswana as independent states.

Although there are serious flaws, the publisher is to be commended for the relatively accurate depiction of the troubled borders in the Middle East and for the many indexes, which are very good and extremely useful. An index to U.S. cities, including zip codes, is a nice feature. [R: WLB, Feb 92, p. 107]—**Dorothy C. Woodson**

478. **Rand McNally World Atlas.** [Rand McNally International Geographic Atlas]. Skokie, Ill., Rand McNally, 1992. 240p. illus. maps. index. $19.95. G1021.R21. 912. LC 91-16938. ISBN 0-528-83440-1. [Published in paperback under *Rand McNally New Century World Atlas*, 1992. $11.95pa. ISBN 0-528-83440-1].

The price and size of this atlas reflect its intended audience—offices and homes. Moreover, the focus of geographic coverage (the United States is the object of 40 percent of the maps, which is substantial given that the country covers only about 6 percent of the Earth's land surface) clearly indicates who the book is meant for. The maps are clear, pleasant to the eye, and supplied with projection and scale. While the map of Germany reflects that nation's reunion, the maps of the former Soviet Union do not show the recent changes, although the borders of the republics are clearly shown. The gazetteer is 63 pages long (about half as many pages as the number of maps, which is a good ratio), and an additional 50 pages of text include populations (1990 Census) for U.S. cities. One bibliographically puzzling feature is that while the title on the dust jacket indicates that this is the *Rand McNally International Geographic Atlas*, the title on the title page, spine, and CIP is *Rand McNally World Atlas*. This atlas is appropriate for the home, small office, or small library.—**Mary Larsgaard**

479. **The Random House Compact World Atlas.** rev. ed. New York, Random House, 1992. 1v. (various paging). maps. index. $12.00pa. G1021.R523. 912. LC 92-357. ISBN 0-679-74330-8.

This small paperback atlas, published in the United States by Random House, is produced by the British mapmakers Bartholomew. Its 120 pages of maps are of high quality and are well distributed among the world's continents. Most of the maps are done in the familiar green-to-brown shading for elevation and encompass regions of a continent rather than specific nations or groups of nations. The rectangular area covered by each map is displayed in the table of contents. The maps are reasonably detailed but are not cluttered.

Inclusion of the 80-page, 20,000-name index in a paperback atlas of modest size is commendable. However, less sophisticated users of the index and map pages will be frustrated by the use of national languages rather than English for the names of most regions and various islands. Thus, there is no Bavaria, only Bayern, and neither Rhodes nor Crete is found on the map of the Balkans although they are in the index (cross-referenced to Rodhos and Kriti). There is also some inconsistency in the treatment of national subdivisions. The names and boundaries of some important subdivisions, such as the republics of Yugoslavia, are omitted while others of considerably less importance, such as the ASSRs (Autonomous Soviet Socialist Republics) of the former Soviet Union, are included.

This would be an excellent atlas to keep on an office shelf or in a student's bookbag for ready-reference use if it were up-to-date. Unfortunately, it is not. Any atlas of the world that does not reflect the changes of various countries cannot provide the information that its users are most likely to want. [R: VOYA, Feb 92, p. 407] — **Peter B. Kutner**

480. **The Reader's Digest Children's World Atlas.** Pleasantville, N.Y., Reader's Digest Books, 1991. 128p. illus. maps. index. $20.00. G1021.R57. 912. LC 90-28667. ISBN 0-89577-388-0.

This contribution, aimed at 7- to 12-year-olds, has many attractive features. Based on an earlier atlas published in Australia, it makes excellent use of full color and combines maps, text, photographs, and graphics in visually attractive compositions that should interest young readers. The text is accurate and simple, although not insultingly so, and such controversial topics as population growth, hunger, and the relative poverty of many nations are mentioned. An introductory section on world patterns (including the seemingly obligatory "world animals") is followed by materials on the various continents, in which North America (roughly 20 percent of the total pages) unsurprisingly takes much of the space.

As has nearly every other geography textbook and atlas published in 1991, this book has been caught behind by the rapid pace of world events. Germany is suitably reunified, but the Soviet Union remains whole; its 15 ex-republics still reside within a unitary framework. Nonetheless, this is a well-printed and well-produced atlas. Its modest price should ensure it a share of the increasingly competitive market for children's atlases. [R: BR, Mar/Apr 92, pp. 53-54] — **James R. McDonald**

481. **Today's World: A New World Atlas from the Cartographers of Rand McNally.** Skokie, Ill., Rand McNally, 1992. 192p. maps. index. $29.95. G1021.R4867. 912. LC 92-16250. ISBN 0-528-83500-9.

The dissolution of the Soviet Union and Yugoslavia and the reunification of Germany have created a demand for atlases that portray the new nations that have taken the place of the old. Rand McNally has risen to the occasion with the publication of *Today's World*. It is primarily a political reference atlas, as distinct from an atlas that highlights elevations, vegetation, and other physical features. The 128 large pages of maps present clearly delineated international boundaries (as of 1992), principal towns and villages, and (in most cases) political subdivisions (states and provinces) of new and old nations around the world. Rivers, main roads, railways, and other familiar atlas features are also included. At some points the details result in a cluttered presentation, but this is acceptable because of their value. The maps are accompanied by an index that contains 69,000 entries. In the index and on the maps, both English and national-language names are given for major cities, regions, and islands.

The map plates are well apportioned among the world's continents and include sizable maps of countries such as Korea and Madagascar, which are often seen only at small scale in atlases of comparable size. However, there are some significant regions, such as Central and East Africa, for which there is no detailed coverage. Also, the political subdivisions of much of the former Soviet Union are not shown, so one cannot readily locate places such as South Ossetia that are present areas of conflict and potential secessionist states.

These are minor flaws in what overall is a high-quality product. A collection of older atlases with a different geographical emphasis (e.g., Europe, North America) or more detail on physical features will be complemented rather than duplicated by acquisition of this reasonably priced atlas. — **Peter B. Kutner**

482. **Troll Student Atlas.** By Michael Dempsey. Mahwah, N.J., Troll, 1991. 127p. illus. maps. index. $14.89; $9.95pa. G1021.D48. 912. LC 90-675152. ISBN 0-8167-2253-6; 0-8167-2254-4pa.

While this work nowhere states for which age group it is intended, it seems to be—even given the geographic illiteracy of students—for sixth or seventh grade students. It starts with a large-type, 60-page gazetteer that unfortunately does not contain map references; these are left for the small-type map index at the end. This seems wasteful; why not put the locations in the front listing? Further, the two do not seem to be the same listing, and no clue is given as to what the criteria were for either one. At the same time, the atlas does follow the good guideline of having an equal number of place-location and map pages. A 15-page section after the gazetteer covers the United States and the physical processes of the Earth. Europe receives by far the largest number of pages (12), six times more than the United States. Possibly, as are so many other atlases, this one was originally put together in Europe. Maps are pleasantly colored, clear, and easy to read; the occasional color photographs make the book enjoyable to scan. For elementary and secondary school libraries.—**Mary Larsgaard**

483. **The World Book Atlas.** rev. ed. Chicago, World Book, 1992. 432p. illus. maps. index. $69.00. LC 91-65696. ISBN 0-7166-2692-6.

In the highly competitive market for atlases, it seems important to find a niche. Thus, recent publications have tended to focus on the country in which they expect most of their sales, on a narrow price range, or on some systematic specialty (e.g., history, physical features, environment). Another possible niche is age group. *The World Book Atlas* aims at the young adult audience.

This is a relatively new entry in the atlas field (this is its eighth printing), and much of its content has been modified from other publications to which Rand McNally holds the copyright, such as the classic *Goode's World Atlas* (see ARBA 91, entry 429) or the 1982 *Great Geographical Atlas* published in Italy. A highlight of the work is an 88-page section that in text, stunning photographs, and useful thematic maps illustrates the world's biomes, major geographical regions, and basic patterns of production and trade.

The legend is printed in five languages (English, French, German, Spanish, and Italian), and the maps are detailed and well printed in unobtrusive colors with topography as a backdrop. North America is the featured continent, spread over 114 pages of maps and information, while the rest of the world is covered in just 72 pages. Geographical data, populations, a glossary, and an extensive index occupy the final 142 pages.

Content is about as up-to-date as the rapid march of events will allow, given publication lag time. Germany is suitably reunited, but the "Soviet Union" still appears to be unitary, with all its former "S.S.R.s," and an occasional leftover from Eastern Europe (Czechoslovakia is still an "S.S.R." on at least one map) merely emphasizes the speed of transition. Nevertheless, this is a very respectable large atlas at a moderate price. It is an attractive selection for libraries as well as individuals.
—**James R. McDonald**

Other Countries

484. Brawer, Moshe. **Atlas of South America.** New York, Simon & Schuster Academic Reference Division, 1991. 144p. illus. maps. index. $65.00. G1700.B7. 912.68. LC 90-675175. ISBN 0-13-050642-7.

There is much that is useful in this compact atlas of one of the world's least-known continents. Its two-part arrangement, consisting of 10 survey chapters on the continent as a whole and 14 chapters on each of the South American republics plus French Guiana and the Falkland Islands, provides a healthy balance of the general and the specific. Each chapter on a specific country includes a useful introductory table with basic statistical information. The essays on each country treat the natural regions, population, economy, history, government and politics, and national capital, as well as other subjects of importance to that country (e.g., the Inca Empire of Peru, the Galapagos Islands of Ecuador). The annotated bibliography, prepared by Linda S. Vertrees of the Chicago Public Library, is timely and wide-ranging. Finally, the book provides a field day for those readers fascinated by maps, tables, and graphs.

Unfortunately, there is also much to question about these very assets. To begin with, the atlas suffers from the lack of an introduction, nor does it provide acknowledgments beyond the picture credits. The graphs, as useful as they are, are not consistent from chapter to chapter; some carry legends, some do not. Some of the capital city maps, such as the one of Bogota, Colombia, are too sketchy to be useful. None of these maps, nor the text itself, is represented in the index of place-names, which appears to refer only to the principal maps of each country. (A brief index of about 60 persons does reference the text.) Finally, for a 144-page book of two-color maps, the price may be an obstacle to purchase by the small library in times of economic stress.

The options available among atlases on Latin America are few. This volume, as imperfect as it is, meets an important need and is worthy of consideration by all libraries that need to fill a void in this area. [R: Choice, June 92, p. 1514; LJ, 15 Feb 92, p. 157; RBB, 15 Feb 92, p. 1127]—**Edwin S. Gleaves**

Bibliography

485. Dufour, Pierre, and Michelle Guitard. **Passages: A Treasure Trove of North American Exploration.** Ottawa, National Library of Canada, 1992. 119p. illus. price not reported. 917.04. ISBN 0-660-57343-1.

A catalog to an exhibition of rare books that deal with North American exploration (it is currently [to October 4, 1992] on display at the National Library of Canada), this volume provides fascinating background to the materials. *Passages* does not attempt to describe the content of the exhibition but rather to enhance it. The volume encompasses a selection of the works that demonstrates the diversity of those on display. The focus chosen for the exhibition is threefold (concentrating on what was deemed to be three relatively neglected themes): native guides, the hardships of exploration voyages, and the sense of wonder experienced by the explorers. In addition to National Library of Canada rare books, historical artifacts on loan from various Canadian and United States institutions are included in the display.

The arrangement of *Passages* is chronological, beginning with the fifteenth-century voyages of Columbus and encompassing various northwest passages through the beginning of the twentieth century. Entries typically contain basic bibliographic data for each rare book, with a text, map, or illustration reproduced. Following each entry is a short summary, usually a page or two, with English and French text in parallel columns. Written by a historical consultant, these focus on the explorers' lives and accomplishments in the New World. A chronological outline by name with dates precedes the entries. Several pages of bibliographic sources consulted conclude the volume. For those interested in exploration throughout North America or in Canada's national heritage, this volume provides an excellent opportunity to delve into these treasured publications.—**Virginia S. Fischer**

Biography

486. Bohlander, Richard E., ed. **World Explorers and Discoverers.** New York, Macmillan, 1992. 531p. illus. maps. index. $85.00. G200.W67. 910'.922. LC 91-23156. ISBN 0-02-897445-X.

Exploration and *discovery* are words that conjure up images of adventure. It is therefore not surprising that many readers seek biographical information about explorers. Fortunately, *World Explorers and Discovers*, with its 313 entries, will help fulfill that demand. Significant explorers from all times and places have been included, such as the Chinese Zhang Qian (d. 107 B.C.), the Arab Ibn Battuta (1304-1368/9), the English Mary Henrietta Kingsley (1862-1900), and the Norwegian Thor Heyerdahl (1914-present). People involved in space exploration, aviation, and mountaineering are excluded (except for Sir Edmund Hillary), while people whose work as geographers, inventors, and historians has helped advance exploration are included (e.g., the historian Herodotus).

Individual entries are listed alphabetically and vary in length from about 400 to 4,000 words. All entries have a headnote that supplies the person's nationality, vital dates, and major accomplishments. Longer entries include a bibliography. Also supplied are a glossary of terms, a list of explorers by nationality, a list of explorers by area of exploration, and a bibliography that is further subdivided by the names of some explorers. In this regard, it would have been better if each entry included at least one item of bibliography. (This reviewer has no idea where to find more information on the fascinating

Johan Schiltberger [1380-1440?], and the main bibliography is not much help.) Finally, an index of personal names, places, and subjects concludes the volume.

On the surface, *World Explorers and Discovers* appears to be quite similar to *The Discoverers* (see ARBA 81, entry 3), which contains about 200 mostly biographical entries (although many are topical). In fact, the two books should be seen as complements rather than as rivals. For example, *The Discoverers* lists 13 entries in the letter *D* and *World Explorers* contains 17, but only 8 entries are common to both volumes. The amount of unique material in *World Explorers* makes it worth purchasing even if a library already owns *The Discoverers*. [R: BR, Sept/Oct 92, p. 68; RBB, 1 June 92, p. 1780; WLB, June 92, p. 158]—**Ronald H. Fritze**

487. Dunmore, John. **Who's Who in Pacific Navigation.** Honolulu, University of Hawaii Press, 1991. 312p. index. $34.00. DU19.D78. 910'.91823. LC 91-19280. ISBN 0-8248-1350-2.

The term *navigation* as used as a criterion for inclusion in this biographical dictionary is restricted to those who led or played a major role in voyages of exploration and research in the Pacific Ocean. Some secondary figures whose names occur in accounts of voyages, their origin or aftermath, are also included. Well-known names, such as Bligh, Bougainville, Cook, Drake, and La Perouse, will be found as well as those of lesser-known explorers. American, British, Dutch, French, Spanish, and other nationalities are represented. Sketches are mostly short, the longest being about two pages in length; they are not complete biographies. When available, information on date and place of birth, parentage, education, and notable accomplishments is given, but the entries are mainly devoted to the person's Pacific explorations and discoveries. A selected bibliography lists general works and reference sources as well as specific titles that are alphabetically arranged under the country with which the voyage is associated. A name index provides reference access not only to the main entries but also to places within the sketches where the explorer is mentioned. There are also indexes to the names of ships and to broad subjects. This thoroughly researched and well-prepared work will be an excellent source of information for historians, subject specialists, and others who are interested in the Pacific area. [R: Choice, July/Aug 92, p. 1653]—**Shirley L. Hopkinson**

488. Waldman, Carl, and Alan Wexler. **Who Was Who in World Exploration.** New York, Facts on File, 1992. 712p. illus. maps. $65.00. G200.W24. 910'.922. LC 91-21277. ISBN 0-8160-2172-4.

More than 800 entries and 120 illustrations make up this timely and easy-to-read biographical dictionary. Its scope extends from ancient to modern times, but most of the entries deal with those persons from the so-called "Age of Exploration" (the fifteenth to the nineteenth centuries). Fortunately, the authors consider cartographers important to the history of discovery and have included them in this volume. With each person's name are given the years of birth and death, a sentence or two that describes the person's place of origin and importance, and a brief chronological list of the highlights of the individual's contributions to world exploration. The real meat of the book lies in several paragraphs of historical narrative about the person. Cross-references to other entries in the book are in heavier type. However, the entries lack suggested readings. Appendix 1 lists the explorers by region of exploration, while appendix 2 is composed of 15 maps of the world that show countries and important locations in the history of exploration. Additionally, black-and-white prints of old maps are scattered throughout the volume. A 14-page bibliography arranged by geographic region rounds out the book, but there is no index.

Reference librarians will want to compare the coverage of the item under review with that of two other new publications: *World Explorers and Discoverers*, edited by Richard E. Bohlander (Macmillan, 1992), and *Old Worlds to New: Age of Exploration and Discovery*, edited by Steven Anzovin and Janet Podell (H. W. Wilson, 1992). Recommended for the reference collection of all libraries. [R: RBB, 15 Oct 92, p. 460; SLJ, Nov 92, p. 146; WLB, Oct 92, p. 115]—**Daniel K. Blewett**

Dictionaries and Encyclopedias

489. **The Concise Oxford Dictionary of Geography.** By Susan Mayhew and Anne Penny. New York, Oxford University Press, 1992. 247p. $8.95pa. G63.M39. 910.3. LC 91-30530. ISBN 0-19-282565-8.

The key word is *concise* when describing this book. A relatively short work, it attempts to cover terms relating to both human and physical geography. The dictionary is clearly arranged and organized. A profusion of asterisks within definitions denotes liberal cross-referencing. Coverage is limited in the 5,000 entries, especially when comparison is made with other dictionaries of geography, such as *Longman Dictionary of Geography* (see ARBA 87, entry 436). Also, there are no illustrations except for a few basic statistical equations. This is a British dictionary with British usage and spellings, although allowance is made for United States readers, especially when a particular concept is given for two seemingly unrelated designations. This dictionary will be useful in an individual's collection or in a small library that wants low-cost coverage of geography terms. — **Phillip P. Powell**

490. **The World Book Encyclopedia of People and Places.** Chicago, World Book, 1992. 6v. illus. maps. index. $149.50/set. LC 91-68041. ISBN 0-7166-3492-9.

This set supplements and complements a number of reference sources published in recent years, such as *The Europa World Year Book* (see ARBA 90, entry 91) or *World Fact File* (see ARBA 92, entry 83). It can be classified as a "convenience tool" that covers most countries and regions; it serves primarily as a cultural and physical geography reference work. The text is accompanied by some 2,000 full-color photographs, drawings, maps, and other graphic material, and is readable and easy to use. In many respects the work is reminiscent of *The World Book Encyclopedia* (see ARBA 90, entry 54). The material is recent and updated, notably in articles about Croatia, Macedonia, Serbia, Slovenia, Ukraine, and other newly established countries in Eastern Europe. In addition to a narrative of some two to four pages, each entry provides a "text box" with brief information about basic geographical data, government, people, religion, and the like. All in all, this is a well-executed work suitable for elementary schools. Most general encyclopedias will provide more information on individual countries, including *The Encyclopedia Americana* (see ARBA 90, entry 50) or even *The World Book Encyclopedia*. [R: RBB, 1 Sept 92, p. 91; WLB, Nov 92, p. 97] — **Bohdan S. Wynar**

Handbooks and Yearbooks

491. **International GIS Sourcebook, 1993: Geographic Information System Technology in 1992.** 4th ed. Derry Eynon, ed. Fort Collins, Colo., GIS World, 1992. 482p. illus. maps. index. $179.95pa. ISBN 0-9625063-5-4. ISSN 1057-3348.

Geographic Information Systems (GIS) deal with place-specific data. Using a bewildering variety of computer hardware and software, they depict locational patterns on the Earth's surface and help analysts discover relationships among computer-readable, geographically referenced sets of data. This annual sourcebook, first published in 1989, is a gold mine of information on such systems and their applications. Section 1 is an introduction to GIS and what has happened between editions. Section 2, the annual GIS survey, provides information on GIS-related companies with foldout tables that compare products and services; there are also extensive vendor profiles. Section 3 includes a series of directories of 436 firms from 27 countries that are grouped by fields of specialization. Section 4, "GIS Technology and Applications," contains 13 fields of specialization. Section 4, "GIS Technology and Applications," contains 13 informative articles by experts on use of GIS in programs as diverse as civil engineering, emergency management, utilities, land regulation and taxation, terrain analysis, marketing, environmental studies, and international policy. Incidentally, the 23 similar chapters by another group of experts in the previous 1991-1992 sourcebook are still of value for their coverage of a wide range of geographic applications, such as the U.S. Bureau of the Census TIGER (Topologically Integrated Geographic Encoding and Referencing system), which provides detailed census data tied to a map base. Section 5 surveys GIS in 23 countries. Section 6 (new to this edition) lists programs and courses in 180 educational institutions. Section 7 has information on digital data sources, particularly the U.S. Geological Survey, companies processing TIGER files of the U.S. Bureau of the Census, and Canadian sources. Section 8 covers professional associations, and section 9 includes a bibliography of GIS literature.

This sourcebook is both an industrial catalog and a state-of-the-art review of a rapidly evolving technology with numerous practical and theoretical applications. It is a valuable reference tool.

— **Chauncy D. Harris**

PLACE NAMES

492. Karamitsanis, Aphrodite, ed. **Place Names of Alberta. Volume II: Southern Alberta.** Calgary, Alta., University of Calgary Press, 1992. 152p. illus. $18.95pa. 917.123'003. ISBN 0-919813-95-X.

This second volume of a proposed four-volume series covers southern Alberta, including the cities of Calgary, Lethbridge, and Medicine Hat. As in the first volume (see ARBA 92, entry 424), entries are arranged alphabetically by place-name. Each entry includes (where available) type of feature (e.g., hill, town); number of the National Topographic System Grid Reference map that contains the feature; location by section, range, township, and meridian; latitude and longitude; approximate location in relation to the nearest population center; and the origin or probable origin of the feature's name. There are 11 black-and-white and 16 color photographs, 2 maps, and a bibliography. An introduction includes a brief history of southern Alberta. The entries are attractively printed on cream-colored paper, and the text is concise, well written, and interesting. Recommended wherever there is interest in Alberta, Canadian history or geography, or toponymy. — **Gari-Anne Patzwald**

493. Mills, A. D. **A Dictionary of English Place Names.** New York, Oxford University Press, 1991. 388p. $29.95. DA645.M55. 914.2'003. LC 90-28522. ISBN 0-19-869156-4.

This dictionary is deceptively simple, having both more and less information than expected. Included are more than 12,000 place-names culled from maps prepared by various organizations, including the Ordnance Survey. The dictionary breaks down each place-name into its elements, giving the etymology of the elements, an approximate date of early use and a source for this use, and a definition of the name. Much is left out: alternate derivation if the given derivation is unlikely, information on individuals for whom a place is named, and explanations of alternate spellings.

The brief definitions tantalize, but the supplementary material is even more fascinating: a 20-page introduction, a glossary of common terms, and a bibliography of further sources. The introduction is a discussion of the historical origin of names, rich in explanation. The glossary gives meanings of common name elements and their modern manifestations, such as *caster*, meaning "Roman station or walled town," or *wic*, an Old English word for *settlement* or *dwelling* that shows up at the end of modern names as *week* or *wyck*. The real treasure trove is in the bibliography, which lists such invaluable sources as the Domesday Book (often the first record of a name), *Concise Dictionary of Modern Place-Names in Great Britain* (see ARBA 85, entry 409), and the many publications of the English Place Name Society.

For the serious scholar, *A Dictionary of English Place Names* will be only a starting point, if that; for satisfaction the scholar will have to consult the listed sources. For the person with an immediate interest in a particular name, this work will be of use. Casual readers, however, should beware. Looking up one name, or leisurely paging through the erudite introduction, triggers curiosity that may lead to looking up name after name. [R: Choice, Sept 92, pp. 84-86; WLB, May 92, p. 122] — **Terry Ann Mood**

494. Mokotoff, Gary, and Sallyann Amdur Sack. **Where Once We Walked: A Guide to the Jewish Communities Destroyed in the Holocaust.** Teaneck, N.J., Avotaynu, 1991. 514p. illus. $69.50. DS135.E83M65. 914.7'0003. LC 91-70405. ISBN 0-9626373-1-9.

In the crowded field of Holocaust literature and reference material, any new entry must struggle to obtain even a foothold. Success is achieved only by those volumes that meet a real need in a responsible manner and in a format responsive to its intended audience. By these measures, *Where Once We Walked* succeeds admirably.

The basic concern of Mokotoff and Sack, as revealed in the subtitle, is to provide a guide to more than 21,000 Jewish communities in Central Europe (from Estonia to Greece, north to south; from Germany to Ukraine, west to east) that suffered during the Holocaust. A (perhaps *the*) major deterrent to research on these communities by nonacademicians is the fact that most of these towns have changed names several times over the past centuries as a result of political and social upheavals that have continued in the region to this day. Moreover, the spelling of many towns is devilishly tricky even for experts, especially when the residents rarely felt the need to impose restrictions on how they wrote the name of their settlement.

Mokotoff and Sack cut through all of these difficulties by devising and implementing a system that, although it initially appears distressingly complex, in actual use turns out to be simple, workable, and—what is best—perfectly suited to the needs of those most likely to use the volume. There is even a section organized according to sound rather than alphabetical order. Those who succeed in locating a desired town (although success is not guaranteed, it will be achieved in a high percentage of cases) will be rewarded with a raft of useful data about that community and a list of resources to consult for further information.

It is indeed unfortunate that an entire generation knows of its recent forbearers only as names and numbers. But it is fortunate that, through reference tools such as this, members of this and succeeding generations can at least call to life thousands of communities whose very existence might otherwise be doubted or forgotten.—**Leonard J. Greenspoon**

495. **Omni Gazetteer of the United States of America.** [CD-ROM]. Detroit, Omnigraphics, 1992. Hardware requirements: IBM PC or compatible; 640K; PC-DOS or MS-DOS 3.1 or better; or Apple Macintosh; MacPlus, SE, or II series; 2 MB RAM; hard disk drive; system 6.02 or better; CD-ROM drive. $2,000.00. ISBN 1-55888-418-1.

The Geographic Names Information System (GNIS) is a monumental, ongoing project developed by the Geographic Names Information Section of the United States Geological Survey (USGS). Information derived from the GNIS is available from the USGS, on the Internet, and as value-added commercial products, the most comprehensive of which is *Omni Gazetteer*. Phase 1 of the GNIS comprises all names shown on USGS large-scale topographic maps (7.5 minute, 1:24,000 scale). Phase 2 is still in progress and adds names found in federal, state, and other sources as well as historical materials, including the FIPS (Federal Information Processing Standards) codes for named populated places, the 1990 U.S. census, and the National Register of Historic Places. In 1991 Omnigraphics produced the print version of *Omni Gazetteer* (see ARBA 92, entry 425), which conflated the information from all of phase 1 and phase 2 of the GNIS into 11 volumes. The set references almost 1.5 million places, structures, facilities, locales, historic places, and named geographic features in the 50 states, the District of Columbia, Puerto Rico, and U.S. territories. The CD-ROM version of *Omni Gazetteer*, produced by SilverPlatter using their standard interface, offers a number of capabilities over the printed versions. Its principal disadvantage is that where one could, for under $300 in most cases, buy the printed index from Omnigraphics and a print volume for a particular state from the USGS, the CD-ROM is all or nothing. The CD-ROM version also omits the generally excellent essays found in the printed volumes.

Omni Gazetteer CD-ROM is available for both the IBM PC or compatible and the Apple Macintosh. Installation of the SPIRS (SilverPlatter Information Retrieval System) version 3.1 search software is simple. Although the combined installation/user manual is helpful and nicely printed, it is generic to all SilverPlatter CD-ROMs. Only a tri-fold, single-page "Quick Reference Guide" references the Omni Gazetteer CD-ROM. Fortunately, the online help is specific to the Gazetteer and includes several examples of sample searches.

SilverPlatter provides a single search interface (as opposed to the four on H. W. Wilson's products, for example). A word or phrase is input at the FIND: prompt, and SPIRS does an intermediate search on each individual term and then reports the number of records that contain the phrase. All of the search results are numbered to facilitate combining intermediate searches. Users may mark records as they go along, and display, download, or print an easily customizable variety of fields and records. Omni Gazetteer recognizes 75 feature types, including airports, beaches, bridges, cemeteries, churches, craters, dams, forests, geysers, islands, levees, oilfields, parks, postal stations, reservoirs, schools, trails, and woods. It is important for users to realize that they may get vastly different results by inputting a word with and without a type. For example, the search "FIND: state in typ" combined with "FIND: California" limits the results only to those items physically associated with the state of California; the search "FIND: California" by itself will retrieve any place, school, cemetery, and the like in the United States or its territories that has California in its name.

The research possibilities—geographical, geological, historical, and statistical—of this CD-ROM are impressive. It is possible, for example, to search for all locations with a population of between 10,000 and 99,000 in Massachusetts within a certain range of ZIP codes, to locate chapels in California, or to find dams below a certain elevation throughout the country. Retrieved records will display the following fields (if relevant): place-name, state, county, type, ZIP code, population value, latitude, longitude, USGS map name, elevation, date added by the Board of Geographic Names, and the source. Because the map name is included, Omni Gazetteer could serve a bibliographic function as an access point to a collection of USGS topographical maps.

The SPIRS software for searching this database does not seem as robust as with Silver Software's bibliographic CD-ROMs. Two searches retrieving a large amount of records in a specific type did not work. On one, the software unhelpfully noted that it had searched 252 percent of the database and was still finding additional records before control + break aborted the search. In another, the software reported a system error and the computer had to be rebooted. Both searches, however, were completed without incident on a machine with more RAM. Regardless of memory, searching by ZIP code is capricious (e.g., "FIND: zip = 92000-92999" sometimes returned no results, sometimes 43, sometimes 296). Other types of numeric data, such as longitude, seem to work without a problem.

The growing privatization of government information has led to some resources, such as the GNIS, being available in a variety of ways, most of which are not exactly comparable in terms of either format or content. The USGS sells all of phase 1 as individual volumes, with most available either in bound, microfiche, or magnetic tape formats. The completed volumes of phase 2, known as the *National Gazetteer*, are only available in print or tape format. The total cost of buying the GNIS from the government varies as not all volumes are available in all formats, but the cost is approximately $1,650 for phases 1 and 2 as bound volumes. (More fiche, where available, are $2 per state or territory.)

The $350 difference in cost between either the print or CD-ROM version of *Omni Gazetteer* and the print version the USGS sells buys a considerable amount of convenience. With computer-based resources, there are more choices. The GNIS database can be searched interactively at the USGS's information offices, or the USGS will perform a computer search at a modest cost. It is possible to purchase GNIS on magnetic tape from the USGS at approximately a fourth of the cost of Omni Gazetteer, but one must be prepared for the difficult task of efficiently extracting information from these large machine-readable datafiles. The USGS has also made its own CD-ROM version of GNIS available to state affiliates and reputedly will do so soon to other depositories (the cost is not yet known). The Geographic Name Server at the University of Michigan and the shareware software program GeoDex, both available on the Internet, offer other alternatives. In none of these cases, however, is one able to perform the range of searches offered by Omni Gazetteer. The cost, however, is considerably less. To increase its value, SilverPlatter could consider including the option of purchasing any future edition of Omni Gazetteer at a greatly reduced price (the GNIS Board meets annually; the latest names represented on the CD-ROM are from 1990). SilverPlatter could also follow the lead of Wilson and eliminate network licensing fees, which would increase the value of the product to libraries.—**Robert Skinner**

TRAVEL GUIDES

United States

496. Frome, Michael. **National Park Guide 1992.** New York, Prentice Hall General Reference, 1992. 247p. illus. maps. index. $15.00pa. ISBN 0-13-625070-X. ISSN 0734-7960.

Frome, who has visited all of the 49 U.S. national parks, introduces each area with a brief essay that combines his personal experience in the park with historical and geological facts. This is followed by the "Practical Guide"—what every serious visitor needs to know about weather, facilities, and programs. Frome also comments on specific hiking trails and roads; tours offered; and opportunities for such things as fishing, bird-watching, and photography. A photograph of each park is included; modest maps are given for 19 areas. Additional chapters briefly cover archaeological, historical, natural, and recreational areas throughout the United States. There are suggestions for the disabled traveler and (new this year) sections on activities for children and on parks that are celebrating the Hispanic and/or Native American aspects of the Columbus Quincentennial. Although this work does not replace trail guides or books on the individual parks, it is a concise overview good for the traveler looking for vacation ideas or doing preliminary planning.—**Deborah Hammer**

497. Jones, John Oliver. **The U.S. Outdoor Atlas & Recreation Guide: A State-by-State Guide to Over 5,000 Wildlife and Outdoor Recreation Areas.** Boston, Houghton Mifflin, 1992. 191p. illus. maps. index. $16.95pa. ISBN 0-395-56334-8.

For anyone contemplating travel to outdoor recreation areas in the United States, this atlas should be part of their planning. It outlines national, state, local, and private wildlife and recreation areas for each state. Also included are information charts with statistics on various questions that range from accessibility for the handicapped to animals within the area to types of vehicles allowed. Many other questions are covered as well. Each state location is presented on a one-page map with a code to designate the type of area it is. Some accompanying states are treated on one map (e.g., New Hampshire and Vermont). Other states with significant areas located near major population areas have inset maps for a clear presentation. The atlas ends with a discussion of the BLM (Bureau of Land Management), USFS (United States Forest Service), and USGS (United States Geological Survey) maps and information on where to write for more information. A city and location index provides quick and easy access when locating a particular area.

Much of the introductory material on state, federal, and nonprofit agencies is available elsewhere. For instance, the *Conservation Directory* (see ARBA 92, entry 1788) provides greater detail than the atlas. However, the atlas certainly is helpful if more specialized sources are not available. A minor irritant in the state profiles is the amount of information on one page. With all of the information listed, the arrangement results in some pages having small type in an odd format. Most states would benefit from a three-page layout instead of the current two, thus providing a less cramped setting. However, this problem should not detract from purchase of this work. Any library should include it on its shelves. Ease of use, a reasonable price, and comprehensiveness make this book an excellent choice in this age of increased awareness of natural resource areas.—**Gregory Curtis**

498. Robertson, Dave, and June Francis. **National Parks: The Family Guide.** Pt. Roberts, Wash., ON SITE!, 1991. 388p. illus. maps. index. $12.95pa. 917.304'928. ISBN 0-9692549-3-8.

Similar to *Whiz Trips with Kids: The Best of the Rockies and the Southwest* (ON SITE!, 1990), *National Parks* emphasizes educational and recreational opportunities through family travel. The authors, along with their children, nephews, and grandmother, visited America's national park sites so they could provide the traveler of any age with a first-hand evaluation. The focus is entirely on national parks, including parks, monuments, memorials, battlefields, seashores, lakeshores, historical parks and sites, parkways, rivers, scenic trails, and recreation areas.

The introduction gives the reader an explanation of how to use the guide, information on the National Park Service, family travel tips, a map of the United States that shows the park sites, and a table of contents for quick reference. Cross-referencing by a park's historical, geological, or archaeological significance makes the index useful in planning. The guide is arranged alphabetically by state, then alphabetically by park site within the state. A state map locates each site. Park information includes times, dates, cost, highlights, special events, accessibility, camping information, and group information. A special section on "Kid's Stuff" focuses on a park's special features for kids. "For Info" at the end of each entry gives names, addresses, and telephone numbers of key contacts. The black-and-white photographs used throughout the book provide a glimpse of the nation's history and culture. This travel guide should be a favorite with families of all ages.—**Jennie S. Johnson**

499. Roth, Wendy, and Michael Tompane. **Easy Access to National Parks: The Sierra Club Guide for People with Disabilities.** San Francisco, Calif., Sierra Club Books; distr., New York, Random House, 1992. 404p. illus. maps. index. $16.00pa. E160.R5. 917.304'928'087. LC 91-34274. ISBN 0-87156-620-6.

The authors, one of whom uses a wheelchair for mobility, visited 45 national parks and more than 100 campgrounds to research the information for this guide. Concerned with access for the physically disabled, for those with small children, and for seniors, this work goes beyond the National Park System's own guides by providing personal experience and practical advice. Fifteen National Parks that met the criteria for accessibility, significance, and scenic beauty are described in detail, followed by a section with briefer descriptions of fifty national parks. The descriptions include access highlights, activities, terrain, climate, accessible trails and sites, accommodations, and services. There are a glossary, an index, lists of park recreation groups and support groups, and a list of parks arranged by state. Maps and photographs supplement the narrative descriptions. Information for the visually or hearing impaired, for those with deafness or blindness, and for those with developmental disabilities is also provided. Because of the passage of the Americans with Disabilities Act, it is possible that some of the access information may change, but this guide will still have value because the authors have so openly shared their own experiences and solutions.

This is a book for anyone who enjoys the outdoors, especially people with physical limitations. The format is more conventional than *Access America* (see ARBA 89, entry 406), which may account for the difference in price. This title will be useful in a personal or public library and in any library that serves the disabled. [R: LJ, 15 Apr 92, p. 86] — **Margo B. Mead**

500. Smith, Darren L., ed. **Parks Directory of the United States: A Guide to 3,700 National and State Parks ... and Other Designated Recreation Areas....** Detroit, Omnigraphics, 1992. 525p. index. $85.00. E160.S65. 917.304'928. LC 91-45072. ISBN 1-55888-765-2.

While cruises, foreign travel, and other expensive jaunts constitute the general image of "tourism" to most Americans, the reality is that nearly everyone spends most of their leisure and recreation time much closer to home. The average American visits a national or state park about five times per year (nearly a billion total visits), and this does not include patronage of regional or local parks. This level of interest in state and national parks stems from three realities. First, with 3,700 of these facilities described in this book (slightly more than one per county), few people in the United States are far away from such a park. Second, the relatively low cost of enjoying the parks (e.g., modest entry fees, inexpensive camping) brings the experience within the economic range of nearly everyone. Third, the "outdoors," as exemplified by the parks, is increasingly appreciated by a largely urban and environmentally conscious population.

The book lists national parks alphabetically and state parks alphabetically by state. The consistent format provides name, address, telephone contact, size, establishment date and historic background, entry fee, facilities, activities, and special features for each entry. There are a comprehensive index and a useful list of park-related organizations and agencies, including each state's tourism office. In a work of this scope, individual entries obviously cannot be described in much detail, but a basic location map for each state seems an unfortunate omission. Nonetheless, this will be a useful reference volume for prospective park visitors and for anyone contemplating research on the U.S. park system. [R: Choice, Nov 92, p. 448; RBB, 1 Dec 92, pp. 690-91; WLB, Oct 92, p. 111] — **James R. McDonald**

Asia

501. **Hippocrene Insiders' Guide to Nepal.** 9th ed. By Prakash A. Raj. New York, Hippocrene Books, 1992. 136p. illus. index. $9.95pa. ISBN 0-87052-026-1.

This is an inexpensive, friendly guide to the country of Nepal, birthplace of the author. It provides the tourist/traveler and new resident the necessary orientation and essential information needed to enjoy and survive in the country. The guide contains the standard fare found in most guidebooks; chapters cover such things as facts about the country, facts for the visitor, and getting there. Useful information is provided on excursions, walking tours, hiking and rafting opportunities, and housing. The black-and-white line-drawing maps are not detailed, so the visitor will need additional country and city maps. Accurate and current information on this country is difficult to obtain, so this small book fills a gap. — **J. C. Jurgens**

502. **South Asian Handbook, 1992: India, Pakistan, Nepal, Bangladesh, Sri Lanka, Bhutan, the Maldives.** Robert Bradnock, William Whittaker, and Roma Bradnock, eds. New York, Prentice Hall General Reference, 1991. 1528p. maps. index. $35.00. ISBN 0-13-457359-5.

An informative, well-written travel guide for Westerners traveling to the countries listed in the subtitle, this British-based publication combines historical facts, places of interest, and practical information (e.g., climate, nearest airport) about the cities in each country. Also included is a selection of services such as local transportation facilities, banks, principal shopping areas, entertainment, restaurants, and hotels. Unlike Fodor's travel guides, this handbook offers the traveler a greater variety in accommodations. A good selection of hotels, hostels, and other lodgings are listed, from the most to the least expensive. Information on alternative housing is especially welcome for lesser-known, less-traveled areas of these countries. Although the guide does include small black-and-white maps of the major cities that highlight principal attractions, they cannot be relied upon for direction since their lack of detail can be confusing, especially given the urban complexity of a major city such as Hyderabad in India.

This handbook is useful not only as a travel guide but also as a ready-reference source on the history of the individual countries. It contains glossaries of architectural terms, names, and other terms. Three indexes are provided to personalities, places, and maps. Even suggested trekking routes in the Himalayas are offered. Highly recommended for all libraries. — **J. C. Jurgens**

Canada

503. Nanton, Isabel, and Mary Simpson. **Adventuring in British Columbia.** San Francisco, Calif., Sierra Club; distr., New York, Random House, 1991. 365p. illus. maps. index. (Sierra Club Adventure Travel Guides). $15.00pa. GV191.46.B74N36. 790'.09711. LC 91-10193. ISBN 0-87156-674-5.

British Columbia, Canada's westernmost province, is bigger than California, Oregon, and Washington put together but has less than one-tenth of the population of those states. Obviously, the province has a huge amount of wilderness and is an ideal subject for "adventure travel." The would-be adventurer in British Columbia will find in this book (as the reputation of the publisher and series implies) a valuable guide. Dividing the province into 11 regions, the work gives for each some background data on such things as history and geography; descriptions of outdoor adventures available (e.g., rafting, fishing); information on transportation and accommodations; advice on clothing and equipment; and addresses and telephone numbers for pertinent government departments, associations, and clubs. Maps (small but clear) are provided for each region, and there are some attractive black-and-white photographs.

It should be noted that the book is not limited to outdoors adventures. Cities and towns are covered, as well as such features as suspension bridges, gardens, and fish hatcheries. Whether as a take-along travel guide or as a semiencyclopedic description, the book will serve its users well.

— **Samuel Rothstein**

Developing Countries

504. Theuns, Leo. **Third World Tourism Research 1950-1984: A Guide to Literature.** New York, Peter Lang, 1991. 282p. index. $57.80pa. ISBN 3-631-42955-X.

This bibliography, authored by a well-known expert in the field, is an important and welcome contribution to the literature. It will be of significant assistance to anyone dealing with the issues of Third World tourism, as it reflects the rapidly increasing interest in the sustainable development of the economies of this part of the world. The importance of this work is enhanced by the introduction by Jafar Jafari, the editor in chief of the *Annals of Tourism Research*.

After a list of abbreviations and acronyms come the bibliographical entries, arranged by consecutive years. The book contains 2,166 entries in English (72 percent), French (10 percent), German (15 percent), and Dutch (3 percent), covering economic, sociocultural, and environmental issues of tourism. The absence of titles in Spanish and Portuguese is not a major problem because there is excellent coverage of Latin America in English. The work closes with indexes of authors and editors, areas, and subjects.

The scope of the coverage raises some questions. Greece, Yugoslavia, Portugal, Spain, and even the Canadian Arctic (5 inadequate entries) are covered, but the republics of the ex-Soviet Union, the postcommunist states of Europe, Alaska, and the Australian outback are excluded. The audience for the book is almost everybody interested in the subject matter, from casual reader to researcher. A follow-up that included more recent literature would be welcome. — **Zbigniew Mieczkowski**

Europe

505. **Hippocrene Insider's Guide to Hungary.** By Nicholas T. Parsons. New York, Hippocrene Books, 1992. 366p. illus. maps. index. $16.95pa. ISBN 0-87052-976-5.

In the all too often superficial world of tourism, travelers think they have to be able to define a country by differences that can only be based on sweeping generalizations. This guide represents a real departure from that notion. Parsons opens his book with a 50-page summary of Hungarian history and culture that skillfully blends elementary introduction, data, and the author's objectively sympathetic personal insights into the national character and psyche. Then comes the actual guide, which covers the country thoroughly. Besides sights, Parsons also discusses local history with a good feel for the different characteristics of regions. Half-page special features interrupt the text periodically to introduce famous historical or cultural figures and events in more detail. The third part of the book is dedicated to useful information on food, seasonal events, activities, practical information, and language for emergencies. The volume is illustrated with a good selection of black-and-white photographs.

This edition is based on the original 1990 British text. It is unfortunate that Hippocrene Books did not attempt any updating, especially in this era of accelerated changes. Street and square names have been changed recently in a number of cities; old public holidays have been replaced by new ones; and visa and registration requirements have been eased, among other things. Still, this guide is recommended for its insights and user-friendly comprehensiveness, but users must get some up-to-date street maps before they embark on the big journey. – **Zsuzsa Koltay**

506. **Spain: 1001 Sights: An Archaeological and Historical Guide.** By James M. Anderson. Calgary, Alta., University of Calgary Press, 1991. 359p. illus. maps. index. $27.95pa. (U.S.). 914.6'04'83. ISBN 0-919813-93-3.

The main purpose of this book is to provide information about historical and archaeological sites in Spain that are not marked by road signs and that are not easily found in maps and tourist books. A study of such sites tells much about the various cultures that have influenced Spain over the centuries. Sites that are famous and well documented elsewhere, such as the Alhambra and the Generalife in Granada, are given only brief mention (or no mention).

The main part of the book is divided into the major regions of Spain – 15 in all. Each region is subdivided into provinces and then into cities, towns, and villages. Within the latter, entries tell of historical and archaeological sites and their locations. Sites included cover dwellings, fortifications, arches, portals, temples, caves, bridges, and cemeteries. The directions given are very specific, and an effort is made to put the sites into historical context. Photographs of many of the sites are included; some are in color.

The introduction contains several good historical essays on the various cultures that have created the Spain of today (e.g., prehistoric, Celts, Iberians, Romans, early Christians, Moslems, Jews). The book concludes with a glossary of Spanish terms and their English equivalents, a bibliography, and an index of towns and villages.

This work serves three useful purposes. It will assist reference librarians in trying to find obscure information on historical and archaeological sites in Spain; it provides succinct historical essays on the multiple cultures that influence Spain; and it will serve as an excellent guide book for those who like to get off the beaten track when on vacation. – **Linda Main**

9 History

ARCHAEOLOGY

507. McMillon, Bill. **The Archaeology Handbook: A Field Manual and Resource Guide.** New York, John Wiley, 1991. 259p. illus. index. $24.95; $14.95pa. CC76.M38. 930.1. LC 91-10973. ISBN 0-471-55015-9; 0-471-53051-4pa.

Designed to help would-be archaeologists discover how they can become part of this popular avocation, this guide offers information on how an excavation is run, what volunteers with limited experience can and cannot do on professionally staffed excavations, and where to find excavations that use volunteers. Part 1 provides a brief introduction to archaeology; part 2 is subdivided into chapters on the preparation of a site, artifacts, recording finds, and writing the final site report. Part 3 discusses (and discourages) working on one's own, following laws and regulations, and beginning a survey. Part 4 (the most useful part of the book) lists travel agencies that specialize in archaeological tours, museums with special exhibits, field schools, volunteer placement agencies, locations of ongoing digs where volunteers are welcome, and government agencies that can direct volunteers to places around the world where they can contribute time and talent to uncovering the secrets of lost civilizations. Periodicals that list fieldwork opportunities, a bibliography (latest copyright 1981), and a subject index conclude the book.

Practical information is limited. Dating techniques are covered in less than one page; staffing and tools and equipment are covered in three and a half pages. Mediocre black-and-white photographs are scattered throughout. McMillon points out that all excavations are destructive in nature, then covers preparation of a site in only five pages: two pages of text and three pages of symbols and signs, a grid method for determining square corners, and a sample grid map with natural and human-made features visible on the surface of the site plotted in the appropriate squares.

McMillon's goal to produce a brief, practical guide for amateur archaeologists has been realized. Concisely written, this volume is appropriate for all types of libraries, especially those in archaeologically rich areas of the United States and Canada.—**Judy Gay Matthews**

508. Patterson, Alex. **A Field Guide to Rock Art Symbols of the Greater Southwest.** Boulder, Colo., Johnson Books, 1992. 256p. illus. maps. $15.95pa. E78.S7F54. 979'.01. LC 92-883. ISBN 1-55566-091-6.

This unusual field guide discusses about 140 symbols found in Indian rock art that are mainly from the Southwest but also from California, Wyoming, and northern Mexico. The symbols are arranged alphabetically by simple descriptions, from "Arrow" to "X-Ray Style." Usually one, but sometimes two or three, pages are devoted to any one symbol. Four or five petroglyphs or pictographs are shown on one page. Their location is given, together with a description and interpretation taken directly from a published archaeological source. As a help in finding the symbol, the book includes three pictorial "Finders" sections that are arranged alphabetically under type of symbol, and two other indexes. Maps show the general location of rock art sites, and directions are given to 18 sites open to the public. There are a brief list of general books for recommended reading, a bibliography of sources used, and picture credits.

A drawback of the book is its lack of consistency. Because the comments are from disparate sources, the depth and content differ considerably. Some are just brief descriptions; others contain some interpretation. This book covers only a few of the existing symbols, and it would be helpful to know why these particular symbols were chosen. However, because of its unique approach, the book can be useful for visitors to areas with rock art and for students who need to identify such symbols. The bibliography is also helpful for further study.—**Kathleen Farago**

AMERICAN HISTORY

Bibliography

509. Frederick, Richard G., comp. **Warren G. Harding: A Bibliography.** Westport, Conn., Greenwood Press, 1992. 386p. index. (Bibliographies of the Presidents of the United States, no.28). $59.95. Z8386.2.F74. 016.97391'4'092. LC 92-8211. ISBN 0-313-28186-6.

This bibliography contains 3,386 citations to books, journal articles, and dissertations, as well as to newspapers and manuscript and archival sources that relate to Warren G. Harding's life and political career. The work is arranged in 13 subject-oriented chapters. The coverage is broad and includes biographical materials, political analyses, and—an unfortunately fertile ground for Harding—popular writings about his personal scandals. Citations are to materials about Harding, his political associates, his administration, and events during his presidency. The iconography section lists citations to printed works and films, and there is one citation to a recording of Harding's speeches. All entries are briefly and helpfully annotated. Other features of the work are a chronology of Harding's life, an introduction that briefly summarizes his contributions to history and his presidential reputation, a list of periodicals consulted (including almost 300 titles), and author and subject indexes. This bibliography is recommended for public and academic libraries; it will be particularly useful for undergraduate political science and history programs.—**Linda A. Naru**

510. Jones, Lewis P. **Books and Articles on South Carolina History.** 2d ed. Columbia, S.C., University of South Carolina Press, 1991. 178p. $24.95. Z1333.J65. 016.9757. LC 91-19772. ISBN 0-87249-649-X.

Jones, emeritus professor of history at Wofford College, has been studying, teaching, and writing about South Carolina history for most of his life. The first edition of this book was published in 1970 during South Carolina's tricentennial. It has now been revised, expanded, and updated. The purpose of the bibliography is to suggest titles to those who want to learn about South Carolina history—the items listed are those that might generally be available in bookstores and libraries.

The book is arranged in 21 chapters, each of which covers a particular era from 1521 to the present. Within each chapter the books and articles are categorized into special studies, general studies in Southern and American history, general histories of South Carolina, special topics, contemporary descriptions, and older accounts by early historians. Order of entry in each category is usually alphabetical by author. There is some overlap of titles cited. The annotations are both descriptive and critical, and sometimes dryly humorous; for example, the annotation to *Dictionary of American Biography* calls it "almost Holy Writ for biographical sketches on notable Americans." There is no index. The work is well laid out, nicely printed, and sturdily bound.—**Frank J. Anderson**

511. Quebedeaux, Richard. **Prime Sources of California and Nevada Local History: 151 Rare and Important City, County and State Directories 1850-1906.** Spokane, Wash., Arthur H. Clark, 1992. 237p. illus. $65.00. LC 91-74139. ISBN 0-87062-213-7.

City, county, and state directories are valuable as research tools. They provide access to information, much of it unavailable elsewhere, about the earliest development of communities. Among the first printed works about a region, they frequently contain the initial histories of the area covered, typically based on written and oral sources no longer extant. The first directories in California appeared in 1850, and in Nevada in 1862. This new reference tool will be a useful addition to library collections that are interested in local history in these states. An annotated bibliography of 151 city, county, and state directories, it provides important information on each directory. An ideal entry includes publisher, noteworthy contents, significance, location of the item, references to key citations, and interesting excerpts.

This work represents considerable research and careful preparation of sources by Quebedeaux. It is a welcome addition to bibliographical literature that focuses attention on the early local history of California and Nevada. – **Roberto P. Haro**

512. Shuffelton, Frank. **Thomas Jefferson, 1981-1990: An Annotated Bibliography.** Hamden, Conn., Garland, 1992. 238p. index. (Garland Reference Library of the Humanities, v.1217). $40.00. Z8452.S54. 016.9734'6'092. LC 92-6846. ISBN 0-8240-5347-8.

It is truly remarkable that the nature of the religious, intellectual, and private life of one of the American Revolution's most prominent figures is still the topic of such abundant scholarship and historical investigation. This comprehensive bibliography is the best evidence available of the importance of Thomas Jefferson as a figure in U.S. history. It covers all books published in a 10-year period and includes nearly 750 entries; it is hard to imagine that it could be lacking in any detail.

As a companion to the author's earlier volume, *Thomas Jefferson: A Comprehensive Annotated Bibliography of Writings about Him (1826-1980)* (see ARBA 85, entry 444), it is an indispensable supplement. However, this is not to say that the book has no faults. One important difference between this edition and the earlier volume is that this one has the entries arranged chronologically instead of by subject. This has the advantage of showing the reader the trends in publishing of material about Jefferson, but it says nothing about the type of research actually done. The introduction says that the subject index is intended to help the reader get into the material topically. However, certain subjects, such as religion, have about 50 entries, causing the researcher who wishes to examine all material on the topic to have to flip through the entire book.

Despite this shortcoming, the book is a rich source of information about a most important American. Owners of the earlier volume will want it, and any library that boasts a collection of Americana or that supports even casual research of American history should have both.

– **Richard A. Leiter**

513. Socolofsky, Homer E., and Virgil W. Dean, comps. **Kansas History: An Annotated Bibliography.** Westport, Conn., Greenwood Press, 1992. 587p. $65.00. Z1285.S59. 016.9781. LC 91-46959. ISBN 0-313-28238-2.

Socolofsky is professor of history at Kansas State University, and Dean is a research historian with the Kansas State Historical Society. *Kansas History* is very broad in its coverage of time periods and subject matter. The work consists of citations to a wide variety of written materials about Kansas that have appeared in more than 200 periodicals, plus books, master's theses, doctoral dissertations, and state and local publications. Entries are included for many older materials, but recent publications, including some 1991 items, are also represented. Many of the citations have brief but helpful descriptive annotations. Separate subject and author indexes are provided. Worthy of special attention is a 100-page chapter on local and county history that is arranged alphabetically by county or region and includes numerous references to locally published items.

Arrangement of the chapters is a bit confusing. Several of the beginning chapters cover historical periods from prehistory and indigenous population (Native Americans) to Kansas since 1898. Next are some chapters on assorted topics such as agriculture, economic and cultural life, and social history, followed by Kansas general histories, historiographical materials, and historic sites.

Although no book of this type could accurately be called complete, the compilers have gathered into a single work more than 4,500 references to writings on Kansas. The first in a new series, Bibliographies of the States of the United States, *Kansas History* should be of considerable value to researchers of Kansas and U.S. western history as well as to anyone who has a personal interest in the state.

– **William H. Wiese**

Biography

514. DeGregorio, William A. **The Complete Book of U.S. Presidents.** 3d ed. New York, Dembner Book/Barricade Books, 1991. 740p. illus. index. $30.00; $19.95pa. E176.1.D43. 973'.0992. LC 91-19325. ISBN 0-942637-37-2; 0-942637-38-0pa.

This book is a trivia buff's delight and a treasure for reference librarians in search of otherwise difficult-to-find information on U.S. presidents. In a well-organized, easy-to-use format, historian DeGregorio presents major and minor facts about the presidents, from Washington through the first 27 months of the Bush administration. Subcategories for each president provide answers to questions about name, physical description, personality, family, ancestry, relatives, childhood, education, religion, recreation, romances (including extramarital), marriage, and career prior to the presidency. History students will be pleased with the detail provided on presidential administrations, including campaigns, campaign issues, political opponents, cabinet members, Supreme Court appointments, and other historically pertinent information (both favorable and unfavorable). Articles are footnoted and identify books for further reading. Three appendixes give data on the political composition of Congresses from 1789 to the present, presidential curiosities, and historians' rankings of the presidents. Access is excellent through the logical arrangement of chapters and a good subject index.

Historians and individuals may disagree with some of the author's interpretations of history. Lincoln himself would disagree that slavery was the main cause of the Civil War (p. 238). And, considering the importance of secession to his administration, Lincoln's little-known 1848 argument in favor of the right of revolution in general, and the right of Texas to separate from Mexico in particular, perhaps should be included. Nevertheless, the book is quite good, and historians do not always present varying viewpoints. *The Complete Book of U.S. Presidents* is highly recommended for anyone with an interest in American history and for school, public, college, and university libraries.

—**Donald E. Collins**

515. O'Neal, Bill. **Fighting Men of the Indian Wars: A Biographical Encyclopedia of the Mountain Men, Soldiers, Cowboys, and Pioneers....** Stillwater, Okla., Barbed Wire Press, 1991. 255p. illus. index. $26.95. E81.053. 978'.00992. LC 91-36114. ISBN 0-935269-07-X.

Although this work is billed as an encyclopedia, O'Neal admits that it is an arbitrary selection of more than 100 men who fought Native Americans during the nineteenth century. Even so, it is a valuable collection of biographies, made even more interesting by the frequent inclusion of graphic details of the fighting and occasionally of actual conversations, as recorded in Army field notes or diaries.

Preceding the biographical sketches are some interesting preliminaries: an introduction; an essay on "What the Indians Called Them"; chronological statistics from 1810 to 1898; "Extraordinary Exploits of Warriors, and of Indians"; combat techniques; and "The Medal of Honor," with tables of recipients by year. After all this (and yet another short introduction) the biographies begin, running from one double-columned page to three or four pages in length, although George Custer is assigned nearly eight pages.

Each entry starts with biographical information, followed by detailed combat data. Each combat has a separate entry; some have three or four paragraphs. At the end of each biographee's entry is a brief list of sources; there is also a full-length bibliography at the end of the book. In addition, a good index lists not only the biographees but also cross-references to other persons. For example, William T. Sherman does not have an entry, but there are 10 cross-references from his name in the index. A few other omissions were noted. Marcus Reno does not have an entry, although he has eight cross-references in the index; the cases are similar for Edward Canby (perhaps because he was pursuing peace when he was killed in the Modoc War) and John Chivington (perhaps because his men slaughtered defenseless women and children at Sand Creek). Some 35 black-and-white illustrations, mostly of individual fighters but occasionally of groups, add to the value of the book. [R: RBB, July 92, pp. 1958-60]—**Raymund F. Wood**

Catalogs and Collections

516. Lester, DeeGee. **Roosevelt Research: Collections for the Study of Theodore, Franklin, and Eleanor.** Westport, Conn., Greenwood Press, 1992. 194p. index. (Bibliographies and Indexes in American History, no.23). $55.00. CD3029.5.R66L47. 016.973917'092-2. LC 92-10072. ISBN 0-313-27204-2.

This reference source serves as a guide for researchers to the lives and careers of Theodore, Franklin, and Eleanor Roosevelt. It opens with a succinct introduction of the historical significance of these individuals, directions on using this work, and a list of important abbreviations used throughout the volume. The heart of *Roosevelt Research* is a list of American libraries and repositories with significant Roosevelt collections, compiled from responses to questionnaires sent to various libraries. Libraries are listed alphabetically by state and city and provide the address, telephone number, hours, and significant features of individual collections delineated between holdings for Franklin, Theodore, and Eleanor. Lester mentions that the most significant Roosevelt research collections are at the Library of Congress; the National Archives; the FDR Library in Hyde Park, New York; and the Theodore Roosevelt Collection at Harvard University's Houghton Library. The work concludes by also listing British and Dutch repositories with significant Roosevelt collections.

This will be a useful reference source for students and scholars of the Roosevelts. It could have been strengthened further by listing the names of the relevant librarians, archivists, and subject experts at these respective institutions. Recommended especially for libraries with strong twentieth-century American history collections.—**Bert Chapman**

Dictionaries and Encyclopedias

517. Eckhart, Mary Lawrence. **Columbus' Dictionary.** Boston, Branden Publishing, 1992. 92p. $11.95pa. E111.E25. 970.01'5'03. LC 92-11733. ISBN 0-8283-1993-6.

This dictionary of terms and definitions that pertain to the life and travels of Christopher Columbus will be of interest to readers grades four and up. Definitions vary from a few lines to nearly a page. A wide assortment of personal names, places, events, customs, objects, and dates are included in this compact, informative work. A bibliography is appended.

Some definitions are choppily written and simplistic, and some of the entry terminology seems idiosyncratic. A statement to explain the use of italicized entries is needed, and pronunciation guides throughout the work would have been helpful. This is, nonetheless, a unique work that will find an appreciative audience in most schools. The volume's size and attractive cover art will appeal to the intended readers.—**Vandelia L. VanMeter**

518. Gale, Robert L. **The Gay Nineties in America: A Cultural Dictionary of the 1890s.** Westport, Conn., Greenwood Press, 1992. 457p. index. $75.00. E169.1.G26. 973.8. LC 91-47061. ISBN 0-313-27819-9.

Students of the Gay Nineties will be happy to know that Gale, an emeritus professor of American literature, has introduced a reference book on the subject. Arranged alphabetically, the dictionary (which could be more accurately described as a handbook or one-volume encyclopedia) contains approximately 500 entries that range from a few sentences to 3 pages. The entries fit into the following categories: general subjects (e.g., crime, homosexuality), key events (e.g., Wounded Knee, Homestead Lockout), groups (e.g., the Anti-Saloon League of America), titles of significant literary works or publications (e.g., *A Connecticut Yankee in King Arthur's Court*), and people who shaped the Gay Nineties (e.g., Thomas Edison). Because Gale does not provide a list of references with each entry, the user will have to consult the lengthy classified bibliography at the back of the book for more information. An occupational index and a general index are included.

The source's strength is also its weakness. More than half of the entries focus on a writer, editor, journalist, poet, playwright, or critic (or their work). This is not surprising considering the author's area of expertise. On the positive side, the entries on specific titles include plot summaries and criticism, which, depending on the title, can be hard to locate elsewhere. However, Gale dedicates too much space to some literary entries, such as Lafcadio Hearn, an Irish-Greek writer, and too little to others, such as

Lincoln Steffens. A good example of the source's literature bias is the entry on George Cabot Lodge, a poet and son of Henry Cabot Lodge. While George has an entry, Henry is only mentioned in connection with his son. Gale could have excluded a few writers and included such topics as nativism and nativist groups (e.g., the American Protection Association which had a significant impact on the first half of this decade).

In a world of shrinking book budgets, a book restricted to the 1890s in the United States will not be a high priority for many academic libraries. Research libraries with strong American studies or American literature collections will want it. [R: LJ, 1 Sept 92, pp. 166-68; RBB, 15 Oct 92, p. 453]

—John P. Stierman

Handbooks and Yearbooks

519. Connolly, Thomas, and Michael D. Senecal, eds. **Almanac of American Presidents from 1789 to the Present: An Original Compendium of Facts and Anecdotes about Politics and the Presidency....** New York, Facts on File, 1991. 485p. illus. index. $35.00. E176.1.A584. 973'.0992. LC 91-18895. ISBN 0-8160-2219-4.

This compendium of miscellaneous facts consists primarily of a series of 20 topical chapters with the addition of a number of lists and 2 short bibliographies. Several chapters are more or less biographical, dealing with such things as military careers, family relationships, occupations of the men before their elevation to office, and what they did after they left the presidency. Others include discussions of the various official residences, the homes of the presidents through McKinley, "critical" elections, and religion. There are chapters on "memorable" first ladies and the vice presidents. Two more general chapters include "Fear in National Politics" and "Secession Movements in American History." After a list of books by presidents published during their lifetimes, there is a 12-page list of basic reference sources, primarily biographies; otherwise, there is no documentation. The book concludes with a useful and reasonably complete index. Many articles contain illustrations, mostly rather informal photographs.

While all chapters are well written, this book does not add to the standard reference literature on the presidents. The topical organization, with subarrangements by president, inevitably leads to a degree of overlap. The inclusion of a number of "unpresidential" chapters and such specialized ones as "Presidents and the Civil War" adds to the feeling that this is a book for casual browsing rather than reference. Libraries should invest their money in William A. DeGregorio's *Complete Book of U.S. Presidents* (3d edition, Barricade Books, 1991) and Joseph Kane's *Facts about the Presidents* (see ARBA 90, entry 479). These titles both have more and a greater variety of facts. [R: BR, Sept/Oct 92, pp. 61-62; SLJ, Nov 92, p. 136; WLB, Mar 92, p. 113]—**James H. Sweetland**

520. **The United States.** Godfrey Hodgson, ed. New York, Facts on File, 1992. 3v. maps. index. (Handbooks to the Modern World). $150.00/set. E156.U54. 973. LC 91-494. ISBN 0-8160-1621-6.

This set presents an overview of various aspects of life in the United States, partially in traditional political handbook format but mostly through 50 interpretive essays written by leading scholars and experts. Volume 1 treats each of the 50 states, plus the District of Columbia. Readers are presented with brief facts in the following areas: recent history, geography, population, economic aspects, employment and income, agriculture, education, health and social services, crime and criminal justice, media, state government, biographical sketches of state political leaders, and addresses and telephone numbers for other information sources. Some of these areas are further subdivided, such as population, which includes information on ethnic composition, religion, and miscellaneous other topics. A long appendix provides comparative statistics about the states.

Volumes 2 and 3 are devoted to a variety of essays, including descriptions and interpretations of political, social, economic, and intellectual aspects of life in the United States. The articles are generally well written and encyclopedic in nature, providing readers with basic introductions, historical perspective, current situations, and analyses. They are footnoted, and some contain significant bibliographies. A detailed index gives the user excellent access to the data in all three volumes.

In general, this work is likable. The articles provide good overviews on topics in which there is much interest. However, there are things to criticize. Except for volume 1, the term "handbook" hardly applies, and without it, the set probably would be found in the general collection rather than on the reference shelves. Also, certain entries display a political bias. For example, volume 1 mentions North Carolina's "dubious exports—cigarettes and Jesse Helms" and refers to the former as a "carcinogenic product" sold to a "nationwide population of addicts." And in volume 2, a conservative author writes of the "clever electioneering" of Jimmy Carter; "Lyndon Johnson, [the] wheeler-dealer [and] hard-grasping Texan"; and "the mass media of opinion" (not defined) that, with the Democrats, harassed Richard Nixon out of office. Fortunately, the vast majority of authors avoid this approach, and balanced views generally prevail. Recommended for college and university libraries. [R: LJ, 15 May 92, p. 88]—**Donald E. Collins**

ASIAN HISTORY

Chinese

521. Chang, Sidney H., and Leonard H. D. Gordon, comps. and eds. **Bibliography of Sun Yat-sen in China's Republican Revolution, 1885-1925.** Lanham, Md., University Press of America, 1991. 349p. index. $57.50. Z8854.4.B53. 016.95104'1'092. LC 90-42959. ISBN 0-8191-7961-2.

The fundamental role Sun Yat-sen played in the revolution that ended two-and-a-half centuries of Manchu rule in China is historic on its own terms. But more remarkable still, many of his most basic principles came to influence both Mao Tse-tung's communist movement and its antithesis, Chiang Kai-shek's nationalist government. Scholarly editions of Sun's "selected" and "complete" works published in Taiwan and China since the 1950s have made it possible to reassess Sun's pervasive role in virtually every aspect of Chinese society—whether nationalist, communist, or simply overseas in Chinese communities around the world.

The focus of this 2,216-item bibliography, compressed into 300 pages, is the period of Sun's life beginning in 1885. It encompasses the evolution of his social and political thought, covering its development and influence until his death in 1925. Both primary works by Sun and secondary studies about him are covered. The bibliography is drawn from commonly available publications and rare archival documents in all major libraries and archives, East and West, known to the compilers.

Works in 16 languages are included (although Chinese, English, and Russian predominate). English translations are given for most foreign titles. Although Chinese is transliterated using the Wade-Giles system, original characters are given for authors, titles, and publishers of all works in Chinese, Japanese, and Korean, which serves to eliminate any ambiguity for Asian-language readers. Sun was known by at least 50 different names and titles, making research on his life and work somewhat confusing at first, but these are all listed, along with the relevant characters, which will be of considerable use to readers. Two indexes are provided, one by author and another by subject. Primarily a research scholar's reference tool, this work is made all the more attractive by the provision of Library of Congress catalog numbers (when known) and University Microfilm numbers for dissertations, both United States and foreign. Some items are also given brief annotations.—**Joseph W. Dauben**

522. Lawrance, Alan. **Mao Zedong: A Bibliography.** Westport, Conn., Greenwood Press, 1991. 197p. index. (Bibliographies of World Leaders, no.3). $55.00. Z8548.3.L38. 016.95105. LC 91-8424. ISBN 0-313-38222-6.

This bibliography surveys more than 1,000 titles, almost all in English, devoted to the Chinese revolutionary and reformer, Mao Zedong. Some major—but not many—works in European languages are also included. All transcriptions are made in pinyin, the official spelling for Chinese adopted by Mainland China, but to help avoid confusion with earlier (pre-1979) works that used the Wade-Giles system, a conversion glossary has been included. For many readers this will prove indispensable in recognizing equivalents that had been more commonly used (e.g., Peking instead of Beijing). Names and places universally familiar in their Wade-Giles spelling, however, such as Sun Yat-sen and Hong Kong, are not transliterated from Wade-Giles (which in pinyin are Sun Zhongshan and Xiang Gang, respectively).

In addition to a useful chronology of Mao's life, there is also a list of his 3 wives and 11 children (1893-1976). The bibliography runs to 185 pages and covers Mao's life, his published works, general biographies, and works according to six successive chronological periods. Concluding sections deal with works on Mao's thought, his military strategy and poetry, and historiography. Both author and subject indexes are included. Most entries are annotated; the critical comments offered often prove to be the most useful and interesting feature of this bibliography. [R: Choice, Apr 92, p. 1210]

—Joseph W. Dauben

523. Leung, Edwin Pak-wah, ed. **Historical Dictionary of Revolutionary China, 1839-1976.** Westport, Conn., Greenwood Press, 1992. 566p. index. $85.00. DS740.2.H57. 951. LC 91-15990. ISBN 0-313-26457-0.

In his introduction Leung notes several works that treat China from 1839 to 1976 in great detail. While these works are far more comprehensive, they are often dated, biographical in their approach, and limited to shorter time periods. Of greater importance, however, they also fail to address the fundamental problem that faces the beginning student, who can easily be intimidated by the vast scope of Chinese history and its myriad events and leaders of significance. For that student, Leung has created a useful selective guide on perhaps the most turbulent period of Chinese history. The 277 topics covered in this volume represent the key events, people, organizations, and ideas that shaped China from the beginning of the Opium War in 1839 to the death of Chairman Mao in 1976. The focus is on political and military affairs; and, as the title suggests, emphasis is placed on the continuity of the civil wars and reform movements of the nineteenth century with the revolutions of the twentieth century. More than 70 scholars have contributed thorough, well-written articles that make lively reading and almost always provide cross-references and additional readings for each topic. A lengthy bibliography identifies more sources for the student, and a chronology provides an overview of the period. The editor addresses the problem of two standards for Romanizing Chinese with cross-references in the index and with a glossary of phrases in Chinese. Despite a weak index that occasionally fails to connect related topics (e.g., there are no index entries for World War II or Chinese relations with foreign powers), this volume will make a valuable addition to academic libraries. [R: Choice, Oct 92, pp. 247-75; RBB, 1 Oct 92, p. 369]

—John R. M. Lawrence

Indic

524. Dewey, Clive. **The Settlement Literature of the Greater Punjab: A Handbook.** New Delhi, Manohar; distr., Westwood, Mass., Riverdale, 1991. 107p. index. $44.50. ISBN 81-85425-22-1.

This book should prove very useful in helping researchers of northwest India and Pakistan familiarize themselves with the assessment and settlement reports, district gazetteers, and codes of customary law produced between 1803 and 1947. Dewey provides an avenue into the settlement literature for social and economic historians and anthropologists who are concerned with any area of what was the greater Punjab Province of 1858-1900. The book includes material from the Northwest Frontier Province and the Delhi territory but excludes the native states.

After two lists of additional bibliographic and biographical material, an introduction explains the genesis, uses, and value of the different kinds of agrarian reports produced by East India Company and British Raj officials. This section could be used to introduce students to the kinds of primary materials available for the study of India. Included in the introduction is a good brief history of British settlement policy and its results. After a section on reading the entries, most of the book groups (in chronological order) all assessment reports, settlement reports, district gazetteers, and customary law reports for a given *tehsil* (district). Each entry indicates the tehsil covered, year of report, author, location, date, and India Office Library call marks.

The final section of the book is an author index that groups all contributions made by officials. Because of its comprehensive nature, format, and introductory explanation, *The Settlement Literature of the Greater Punjab* will be very useful for anyone interested in the history of the Indian and Pakistani Punjab or the provinces of Haryana, Himachal Pradesh, the Northwest frontier, and Delhi.

—David L. White

Vietnamese

525. McDonald, Ben. **The Vietnam Book List.** Conifer, Colo., Bibliographies Unlimited, 1991. 224p. index. $23.95. Z1227.M37. 016.8108. LC 90-81201. ISBN 0-9626437-3-4.

   A listing of 3,343 book citations should have some value, but this particular source has little. Lacking categorization and annotation, the volume is nothing more than a long numbered list of titles of nonfiction, reference works, poetry, anthologies, personal narratives, and government sources. The reader is left to guess the nature of each listing by the title. This is particularly problematic when trying to ascertain whether a book is fiction or nonfiction. (An appendix does cite the entry numbers of all works of fiction.) The volume includes obscure presses and self-published works as well as those by recognized publishers, but it is difficult to judge which books are serious and which are frivolous. The index does list the citation numbers of all entries, arranged under various topics, but this is only minimally helpful. Finally, many important books, especially scholarly works, are not included. While Vietnam aficionados may find some use for this volume, it is not a reference source on which a library should spend its resources. — **Joe P. Dunn**

CANADIAN HISTORY

526. **The Acadiensis Index, 1971-1991.** By Eric L. Swanick with David Frank. Fredericton, N.B., Acadiensis Press; distr., Fredericton, N.B., Goose Lane, 1992. 177p. $19.95pa. 971.5. ISBN 0-919107-35-4.

   Since its inception in 1971, *Acadiensis* has been recognized as one of the leading Canadian scholarly publications with an interdisciplinary focus on research and study of the Atlantic region. This latest edition of the index covers a 20-year span through 1991, updating the previous edition, which covered the first 12 volumes through the spring issue of 1983. Arranged in the same format, it is divided into two major sections. The first is a comprehensive author-subject index that includes articles, documents, essays, bibliographies, and other items. Each has a complete bibliographic citation for locating materials and a note on material type. As materials in both French and English are accepted for publication in *Acadiensis*, citations are in the language of the text. Part 2 supplements the initial section by providing an index to all books reviewed, arranged alphabetically by author, and to other materials (e.g., films, theses) discussed in reviews. Cross-references to pertinent citations are included in both parts. For libraries that possess the original index, this volume will supersede that one. Libraries that do not will find this work a valuable source in locating these regional materials. — **Virginia S. Fischer**

527. **From the Past to the Future: A Guide to the Holdings of the University of Alberta Archives.** Edmonton, Alta., University of Alberta Archives, 1992. 284p. illus. index. $15.00pa. 016.3787123'34. ISBN 0-88864-770-0.

   This guide to the holdings of the University of Alberta archives is an outstanding addition to the growing body of guides to primary source materials in Canadian repositories. The guide's introduction describes the archives' program, facilities, and services and provides information on the arrangement and contents of the guide. The work has three sections: university records, arranged by office or department; records of organizations both within and outside the university; and records of individuals, most of whom are or were associated with the university. Entries include name of collection, entry number (for use in conjunction with the index), a history and description of the creating body or biography of the individual, media of records (e.g., text, moving images), inclusive dates of the collection; extent in linear meters; descriptions and dates of individual categories of records; and any restrictions on use. A name and subject index is included. The work is illustrated with black-and-white photographs from the archives' collections.

   The guide has an attractive and readable format. Its arrangement is sensible and its index is excellent. The reasonable price should make it affordable for institutions and individuals interested in the University or Province of Alberta, higher education, or Canadian studies. Highly recommended.

   — **Gari-Anne Patzwald**

EUROPEAN HISTORY

General Works

528. Ringelheim, Joan, comp. **A Catalogue of Audio and Video Collections of Holocaust Testimony.** 2d ed. Westport, Conn., Greenwood Press, 1992. 209p. (Bibliographies and Indexes in World History, no.23). $69.50. D804.3.R55. 940.53'18. LC 91-43368. ISBN 0-313-28221-8.

Video and audio tapes taken of Holocaust survivors fit remarkably well into an assessment of historical memory for teaching and research. This reference provides a real service by pointing to the repositories of the tapes in the United States and in many cases offering detailed summaries of their holdings. The repositories are listed by state, and appendixes index the type of collection; nation of birth; survivors hiding or passing as non-Jews; survivors in ghettos; survivors in concentration, extermination, and transit camps; rescuers; liberators; and additional groups represented in the catalog. Summaries include information such as total number of interviewees, nature of experiences, religious and ethnic affiliations, and (in some cases) the names of specific camps covered. The information was compiled through questionnaires sent to 70 Holocaust repositories, which resulted in 43 responses. In this edition, 8 new repositories are represented, 2 from the first edition have been dropped, and 16 have been updated.

In sum, this guide reveals a resource of 11,641 interviews housed in the United States. There are more interviews available, to be sure; perhaps future editions will rely on visits as well as questionnaires to make a more comprehensive survey. Ringelheim, a consultant to the United States Holocaust Museum, is on target when she states that "the testimonies must not be overlooked if the Holocaust is to be fully explored." This reviewer would add that they must not be overlooked if our humanity is to be fully explored. [R: Choice, Dec 92, pp. 604-05]—**Simon J. Bronner**

529. Stevenson, John, ed. **The Columbia Dictionary of European Political History since 1914.** New York, Columbia University Press, 1992. 437p. $69.50. D424.C65. 940.2'8. LC 91-29693. ISBN 0-231-07880-3.

As a record of major world events from a European perspective, this dictionary will serve both the scholar and the layperson. Approximately 1,500 entries survey the events, people, and concepts prominent in twentieth-century political history from 1914 to the present. Because of the quality and objectivity reflected, users may well wish for a broader scope. The vast range of material, however, has determined that choices be selective. For example, U.S. presidents Franklin D. Roosevelt, Harry Truman, John F. Kennedy, and Ronald Reagan appear, but Lyndon Johnson, Richard Nixon, and Jimmy Carter do not, the former group presumably having had a greater impact on Europe and Great Britain than the latter. Similar reasoning explains why the Cuban Missile Crisis warrants an entry but Vietnam does not. Although military history is not the major focus, considerable coverage is given to World Wars I and II.

The entries are clearly written and succinct, ranging in length from a single paragraph to several pages, with two or more bibliographic references provided for the longer articles. Cross-references are identified by all capital letters. The material is very current; the entry for Mikhail Gorbachev notes the attempted coup of August 1991.

Larger history collections will find this an excellent and convenient reference. To avoid possible duplication, selectors should be aware that the work was originally published in the United Kingdom as *Dictionary of British and European History since 1914* (Macmillan, 1991). [R: Choice, Sept 92, p. 74; RBB, July 92, pp. 1957-58; RQ, Fall 92, pp. 108-09]—**Bernice Bergup**

Armenian

530. Vassilian, Hamo B., ed. **The Armenian Genocide: A Comprehensive Bibliography and Library Resource Guide.** Glendale, Calif., Armenian Reference Books, 1992. 103p. $24.95pa. Z3461.V37. 016.9566'2015. LC 92-25048. ISBN 0-931539-10-2.

The bibliographical material compiled in this volume supports the claim that between 1894 and 1923 the government of the Ottoman Empire was responsible for the destruction of more than one and a half million Armenians who resided in its territory. Although the Turkish government categorically denies it, several international organizations officially recognize that Turkey was indeed responsible for the Armenian genocide. Numerous books and articles have been published on this subject.

The first annotated bibliography about it, by Richard G. Hovannisian, was titled *The Armenian Holocaust: A Bibliography Relating to the Deportations, Massacres, and Dispersion of the Armenian People, 1915-1918* (Armenian Heritage Press, 1980). Vassilian's volume, representing an important part of the total evidence, is limited to publications in the English language. (Some contributions in foreign languages are depicted in this collection as "Bibliographies.") On the scholarly level, it includes works in comparative studies on genocide. It also contains, on the humanistic level, writings that urge that Turkey be punished for the crimes of genocide and provide solace for the descendants and relatives of the victims. The main body of this volume contains 1,189 entries. Alphabetically arranged by author, title, and subject, the listing provides bibliographic information and other relevant notes, such as subject headings. Among the various materials are historical accounts, analytical studies, eyewitness reports, official documents, teaching guides, bibliographies, fiction, poetry, and even publications that deny the genocide. Each contribution represents an effort to present a variety of responses to this holocaust and to deepen public awareness of its tragic consequences.

The last eight pages provide a list of libraries that hold books and other publications related to the Armenian culture. This work is recommended for everyone interested in the tragic past of Armenians.
— Oleg Zinam

British

531. Dabundo, Laura, ed. **Encyclopedia of Romanticism: Culture in Britain, 1780s-1830s.** Hamden, Conn., Garland, 1992. 662p. index. (Garland Reference Library of Social Science, v.1299). $95.00. DA529.E53. 941.07'3. LC 92-2682. ISBN 0-8240-6997-8.

Romanticism is an often ill-understood literary, artistic, and historical movement that dominated Western society and culture from the French Revolution to the advent of Victorianism. Thanks to Dabundo, her 140 contributors, and their more than 400 entries, Romanticism will now be far better understood. The encyclopedia focuses chronologically on the 50 years from the 1780s to the 1830s. As the work's subtitle indicates, Great Britain is its geographical focus, although essays describing Romanticism in various other countries, such as America, Italy, and Russia, are included. Germany receives additional entries, such as "Grimm Brothers" and "Kant and Theories of German Idealism," due to its particularly strong contribution to the development of British Romanticism. Literary, cultural, and social matters form the topical focus of the work; political and military events are ignored. Biographical overviews form more than half the entries and range from the well known, such as William Wordsworth and Sir Walter Scott, to lesser figures, such as the children's author Sarah Kirby Trimmer and the playwright and translator Margaret Wrench Holford Hodson. Topical entries include the expected ones, such as the French Revolution, the Industrial Revolution, and novels; then they go even further and include such intriguing topics as androgyny, prophecy and apocalypse, vampire, and vegetarianism. Individual entries are clearly written, signed, and are from 200 to several thousand words long; they are followed by a bibliography of works consulted. A modest personal name and subject index closes the volume.

The *Encyclopedia of Romanticism* is a fine work that rightly deals with ideas and not just facts. The only complaints are that Dabundo decided to limit cross-references a bit too much and that the book lacks a general bibliography and chronology to supplement the entries. [R: Choice, Oct 92, pp. 271-72; LAR, Oct 92, p. 669; LJ, July 92, p. 74; RBB, 1 Nov 92, pp. 545-46; WLB, Sept 92, p. 112]
— **Ronald H. Fritze**

532. Fritze, Ronald H., ed. **Historical Dictionary of Tudor England, 1485-1603.** Westport, Conn., Greenwood Press, 1991. 594p. index. $85.00. DA315.H5. 942.05. LC 91-9153. ISBN 0-313-26598-4.

Although several dictionaries cover the entire span of British history, Fritze decided that there was a need for a specialized one just for the age of the Tudors. There is considerable interest in this period, and a great deal of revised Tudor scholarship has been produced in recent years. The primary geographical focus is England, although Scottish and Irish histories are included, particularly where they had an impact on England. Most of the entries cover political, diplomatic, military, and religious topics, although some on social, economic, and cultural topics are also included.

The dictionary consists of 295 entries written by 66 international scholars. Sixty-six of the entries are biographical. (*Who's Who in Tudor England* [see ARBA 92, entry 482] covers many more people in greater detail.) The remainder of the entries concern events, laws, institutions, and special topics such as coinage and monetary policy. The individual articles, ranging from 250 to 2,000 words in length, are signed and include selected bibliographies for additional reading. A detailed chronology, a bibliography of further readings, and a subject index conclude the book. Unfortunately, some of the references in the index seem to be blind or incorrect. Also, the subject headings assigned are very selective. For example, there is an entry for Newfoundland but not one for the Netherlands, an important area in Elizabethan foreign policy. Access to the Netherlands is through such subject headings and dictionary entries as "Leicester's Expedition to the Netherlands" and "Flushing and Brill" (two Dutch ports), thus assuming a prior knowledge of the topic.

This work will be most useful to those who are already conversant with the Tudor period, as there are no cross-references in either the text or the index. For those individuals it will provide succinct synopses of topics and helpful bibliographies for further study. [R: LJ, 15 Apr 92, p. 44]

— Christine E. King

533. Propas, Sharon W. **Victorian Studies: A Research Guide.** Hamden, Conn., Garland, 1992. 334p. index. (Garland Reference Library of the Humanities, v.1068). $50.00. Z2019.P76. 016.941. LC 91-45048. ISBN 0-8240-5840-2.

The Victorian period (1832-1900) in all its myriad aspects forms the subject of this useful interdisciplinary guide, which is intended primarily for use by graduate students. Propas, a librarian with extensive experience in research libraries, has divided her guide into parts that cover using the library and tools of research. The first part provides some elementary but often neglected advice on developing research strategies; using the library catalog; using bibliographies, indexes, and abstracts; and using interlibrary loan. The tools of research consist of 678 annotated items arranged in 8 broad categories of reference materials: guides and bibliographies; union lists, catalogs, and guides to collections; manuscripts, archives, and unpublished sources; general reference sources; multidisciplinary reference sources; reference sources for various specific disciplines; microform sources; and electronic formats. The first four sections largely list general reference tools that appear in most reference guides for the humanities and the social sciences. It is in the fifth and sixth sections that specialized Victorian items appear. Among the various disciplines appearing in the sixth section are architecture, decorative arts, medicine and health, and the history of science and technology. The sections that deal with microform sources and electronic formats provide useful introductions to reference sources that have been relatively neglected by scholars of the humanities. There is an index to titles, authors, editors, and compilers. *Victorian Studies* is a must for any collection that supports graduate studies in that era.

— Ronald H. Fritze

534. **The Times London History Atlas.** Hugh Clout, ed. New York, HarperCollins, 1991. 191p. illus. maps. index. $45.00. LC 91-55208. ISBN 0-06-270042-1.

This lavishly illustrated historical atlas traces the growth of the great city from its establishment in Roman times to the present day. The work was compiled by an impressive list of archaeologists, historians, and geographers and contains not only excellent maps but also many reproductions of paintings, engravings, and photographs. Perhaps the most impressive illustrations are the skillfully drafted reproductions of what London probably looked like in the past.

The work is divided into 11 chapters and arranged by period, with the first chapter concentrating on London's geology and the important role the river Thames has played in its history. Chapter 10 covers themes such as pollution, parks, leisure, and royal London. The final chapter looks at specific places in London and includes the Underground, the docklands, bridges, monuments and cemeteries, and such fanciful topics as plans for the city that never came to fruition and the London of the future.

The text and descriptive captions complement the illustrations. Cross-references are printed at the side of the text in order to make them stand out. A useful chronology has a topical arrangement: history and politics, commerce, architecture, institutions of popular culture, and science and the arts. There is also an etymology of London place-names, an extensive bibliography, and an index of place-names and subjects. All in all, this is a beautifully produced work and a major scholarly achievement that will delight browsers, travelers, and serious researchers. [R: RBB, 15 Apr 92, p. 1555]—**Christine E. King**

Eastern European

535. Edelheit, Abraham J., and Hershel Edelheit, eds. **The Rise and Fall of the Soviet Union: A Selected Bibliography of Sources in English.** Westport, Conn., Greenwood Press, 1992. 430p. index. (Bibliographies and Indexes in World History, no.27). $65.00. Z2510.3.R57. 016.94708. LC 92-24470. ISBN 0-313-28625-6.

This timely bibliography provides a list of 2,016 books and journal articles that cover the entire scope of Soviet history, politics, and culture. The Edelheits have limited their book selection to only the best and the standard sources, supplemented by articles from 28 scholarly journals. The bibliography is divided into 12 sections that range from reference works and background studies to specific time periods of Soviet history. Each section contains several subdivisions, although there is just one consecutive numbering for the entries. Two of the most extensive and useful sections are on the Cold War and the age of Perestroika (this last section concludes with 18 items on the demise of the Soviet Union). The Edelheits have provided brief annotations for many of the entries, and content notes are listed for most of the edited books. Within each section of the bibliography, cross-references are inserted to relevant items found in other sections.

Many familiar names appear in the bibliography: popular journalists (e.g., Hedrik Smith, Robert Kaiser, David K. Shipler), historians (e.g., E. H. Carr, Edward Grankshaw, Richard Pipes), and political scientists (e.g., Stephen F. Cohen, Jerry Hough, Marshal Goldman). There are also countless less-familiar scholars. Even John LeCarre is included (for his recent novel *The Russia House*). Author are indexed with their titles, but the index is arranged only by authors' names. A subject index uses fairly broad headings (e.g., capitalism, Cold War, Bolsheviks, dissidents) as well as names of individuals and places. Also appended is a useful glossary of terms.

Given the amount of interest in this area, *The Rise and Fall of the Soviet Union* will be in high demand in most academic libraries. It is a worthy complement to Stephan Horak's ongoing bibliography, *Russia, the USSR, and Eastern Europe* (see ARBA 88, entry 132).—**Thomas A. Karel**

536. White, Stephen, ed. **Handbook of Reconstruction in Eastern Europe and the Soviet Union.** Harlow, England, Longman; distr., Detroit, Gale, 1991. 407p. index. $115.00. ISBN 0-582-08502-0.

This collection of essays focuses on the events of 1989 and 1990 and is intended to update and supplement the editor's *Political and Economic Encyclopaedia of the Soviet Union and Eastern Europe* (see ARBA 92, entry 104). Country chapters follow a common format, with sections devoted to chronology, overviews of political and economic developments, more detailed information with some statistics for key economic sectors, foreign trade, brief biographical information on prominent political figures, the media, and foreign policy. Two additional chapters discuss Comecon and the Warsaw Treaty Organization. Texts of the May 1990 and August 1990 German unification treaties and the text of the Soviet Constitution as amended through December 1990 are provided.

An index consists primarily of personal names and country names with topical subdivisions. It is neither thorough nor consistent. For example, the Council for Mutual Economic Assistance is indexed as CMEA but not as Comecon; Charter 77 and Civic Forum appear as separate entries but not as subdivisions under Czechoslovakia; and each page that contains a reference to Civic Forum is listed, but only the first reference to the Christian Democrats is listed.

Because this work focuses on two momentous years in the history of this region, it will be useful for a general collection. The 33d edition of the *Europa World Year Book* (Gale, 1992) or the new *Eastern Europe and the Commonwealth of Independent States* (Gale, 1992) can provide more up-to-date, extensive, and readily accessible data for reference purposes. [R: Choice, Jan 92, p. 722]

—**Cheryl Kern-Simirenko**

French

537. Northcutt, Wayne, ed. **Historical Dictionary of the French Fourth and Fifth Republics, 1946-1991.** Westport, Conn., Greenwood Press, 1992. 527p. index. $85.00. DC401.H57. 944.082. LC 91-17387. ISBN 0-313-26356-6.

French history since World War II has been a subject composed of rapidly shifting political philosophies, a full range of ideas and intellectual posturing, and a seemingly endless parade of personalities. No fewer than 21 governments came to power and fell under the Fourth Republic (1947-1958); the more stable Fifth Republic has seen 15 since that time. Keeping track of the context and contributions of individuals, and of the multitude of organizations and key events that have influenced the national scene over 45 years, is a daunting task that will be made much easier by this book.

In about 250 entries, some of them quite detailed (the average is nearly 2 pages per entry), the players and concerns of postwar France are delineated. The arrangement is alphabetical, but there is an excellent cross-referencing system, bibliographic notes for each entry, and a comprehensive index. Every entry is signed by one of the 63 contributors, and the overall editing is smooth and skillful. Heavy emphasis is placed on political affairs, social history, and culture, while science and technology, which have played such a significant role in modern France, are given sketchy treatment. France's recent Nobel laureates in literature are, for example, discussed in detail; those in physics and medicine are not mentioned. Moreover, there is an uneven scale to the entries that can be unsettling; a page of information on a relatively obscure politician or playwright can be followed by an entry of similar length on a large, complicated topic (e.g., agriculture, inflation, leisure). Nonetheless, this is an impressive reference and should be of great value to scholars attempting to unravel the complexities of modern France. [R: Choice, Nov 92, p. 442; LJ, 15 Feb 92, p. 160]—**James R. McDonald**

German

538. Doerr, Juergen C. **The Big Powers and the German Question, 1941-1990: A Selected Bibliographic Guide.** Hamden, Conn., Garland, 1992. 403p. index. (Canadian Review of Studies in Nationalism, v.9; Garland Reference Library of Social Science, v.518). $55.00. Z2240.3.D63. 016.943087. LC 91-45118. ISBN 0-8240-0696-8.

With the conclusion of another era in modern Germany's tumultuous history, the time is ripe for summation and assessment. The present bibliography would appear to be part of that trend. Doerr, cocompiler (with Dieter Buse) of *German Nationalisms* (Garland, 1985), has employed a similar arrangement here: the list of 530 continuously numbered entries is divided into 8 chapters, each with its own substantial introductory essay. The first six, which form most of the book, cover German policy of the Allies as a body and individually (Great Britain, the Soviet Union, the United States, and France) from 1941 to 1949. The brief final chapters document the Allies' *Deutschlandpolitik* from 1949 to 1990 and their stance on Berlin over the 50-year span. The emphasis is on political rather than social or cultural questions, making Doerr's work quite different from *The Germans after World War II* (see ARBA 91, entry 531). German- and English-language books, articles, and collections of official documents are included; they are updated through 1989 and generously annotated. Although the listing is alphabetical by author, accessibility is enhanced by direct references to bibliography items in the introductory essays and a limited subject index. Narrative portions are extensive, leaving less room for bibliography, but the selection seems adequate for basic research, and students will probably find this combination history-bibliography approach helpful. [R: Choice, Oct 92, p. 271]—**Willa Schmidt**

Irish

539. Newman, Peter R. **Companion to Irish History 1603-1921: From the Submission of Tyrone to Partition.** New York, Facts on File, 1991. 244p. maps. $27.95. ISBN 0-8160-2572-X.

The 318 years covered by this work are among the most turbulent in Irish history. They saw the flight of the Earls and the opening up of Ulster to English rule, the settlement of English and Scottish colonists on land that belonged to the native Irish, the United Irishmen, Charles Stewart Parnell, the

Potato Famine and subsequent mass immigration, the land wars, the rise of Sinn Fein, the Easter Rising, and the events leading to the creation of the North Ireland state. Newman covers all these subjects and many more in this excellent reference book.

Topics are arranged in one alphabetical sequence, with extensive *see* and *see also* references. Each topic has a brief entry that ranges from one paragraph to one page. In the text of the entry, other topics that have their own entry are in capital letters. The entries are clearly written, concise, and informative. An excellent three-page introduction serves as a background to the period. Appendixes list the viceroys of Ireland from 1603 to 1921, the deputies in Ireland from 1603 to 1800, and the chief secretaries in Ireland from 1603 to 1921. The book concludes with a chronology of events; a comprehensive bibliography; and a series of six maps that show the ancient provinces of Ireland, the counties of Ireland from the Middle Ages to the seventeenth century, the plantations, the land war activities from 1879 to 1882, the areas of Sinn Fein support in 1919, and the six counties of North Ireland from 1921. The *Companion to Irish History* is a first-rate reference aid for anyone needing brief information on Irish history between 1603 and 1921. [R: Choice, Apr 92, p. 1211; SLJ, June 92, p. 155] – **Linda Main**

Spanish

540. Olson, James S., and others, eds. **Historical Dictionary of the Spanish Empire, 1402-1975.** Westport, Conn., Greenwood Press, 1992. 701p. index. $89.50. DP56.H57. 909.'0971246'003. LC 91-8250. ISBN 0-313-26413-9.

Over the past decade, Greenwood Press has addressed a serious need on the part of U.S. students of history and produced several excellent historical dictionaries that cover different periods of modern history. The majority have been well-researched, clearly written guides by experts in the fields. This new work is no exception. It represents the collaborative effort of 39 scholars, although most of the entries were written by Olson and his four associate editors, Sam L. Slick, Samuel Freeman, Virginia Garrard Burnett, and Fred Koestler. More than 1,200 brief essays describe Spain; her colonies; and the people, events, laws, institutions, and groups that shaped Spain's empire. The majority of the entries cover the sixteenth through the early nineteenth centuries, although the early colonial period and the revolutionary era are emphasized heavily. This slight imbalance is corrected with lengthy historical overviews of various jurisdictions and places. Coverage of Spain's African and Pacific colonies is not neglected, and entries documenting the native peoples that the Spanish encountered are common. Most entries include citations to additional readings, and the appendix includes a chronology and a list of colonial viceroys.

However, no effort is made to relate Spain's colonial empire to its important holdings in Europe and the Mediterranean. Also lacking are overviews of Spain's relations with its rivals (Great Britain, France, Portugal, and the United States). An extremely useful feature would have been maps that showed the extent of Spain's empire and changes in the administration of the viceroyalties over time (e.g., one showing the audencias in 1650, another showing the intendencies in 1800). Both the chronology and the bibliography could use subdivisions by period or subject. The index, little more than a reiteration of the alphabetical entries with some additional place-names and persons, is inadequate. Mexico, Great Britain, the United States, and Portugal are not cited in the index, nor are most general concepts such as agriculture, bureaucracy, industry, or trade. Despite frequent cross-references in the texts, users will miss related entries because of the failure of the index to provide connections. Nonetheless, students and scholars will find this a useful reference tool. [R: Choice, Apr 92, p. 1209; LJ, Jan 92, p. 108; RBB, 15 Mar 92, p. 1403; WLB, Apr 92, p. 125] – **John R. M. Lawrence**

LATIN AMERICAN AND CARIBBEAN HISTORY

541. Handler, Jerome S. **Supplement to *A Guide to Source Materials for the Study of Barbados History, 1627-1834*.** Providence, R.I., Barbados Museum and Historical Society and John Carter Brown Library, 1991. 89p. illus. index. $22.50. ISBN 0-916617-35-1.

Unless Handler's excellent 1971 parent work is available, this supplement will be of little use to a researcher. However, if the earlier work can be consulted, this one will fill several minor lacunae. That there are no major additions attests to the expertise and comprehensiveness of the original; it contains more than 650 published titles, whereas the supplement lists 270, almost all of which are new (some are revised or amended). It would have been of great help to researchers if the work had been brought closer to the present, for there has been an exponential expansion of interest and research on Barbadian history since 1834. The tripartite organization of the documents (printed books, pamphlets, broadsides, and maps; newspapers; and manuscripts) is helpful and traditional, as is the chronological division of the first category. However, from such a renowned archivist, it is disappointing to so often find modifiers such as "some of which were examined" and "none were examined" in reference to items. Other entries (frequently garnered from others' allusions) are qualified by "there is no information on the latter" and "this could not be located," which both show the extent of Handler's efforts and the weaknesses of the product. A large number of the entries carry the notation that Barbados is merely mentioned in the text but given no treatment; this is especially frequent in mariners' logs, commercial records, and sermon texts. Rhetoricians and social historians will be pleased to find a number of sermons that allude to the slave trade—including one that argues that it is not inconsistent with Christianity. The index is most comprehensive. The typeface is good; the casing will guarantee long life under arduous use.—**Marian B. McLeod**

MIDDLE EASTERN HISTORY

542. **BBC World Service Gulf Crisis Chronology.** Compiled by BBC World Service. Harlow, England, Longman Group; distr., Detroit, Gale, 1991. 454p. index. $115.00. ISBN 0-582-09005-9.

This is an excellent reference book—well planned, comprehensive, easy to use, and accurate (many entries were checked against the chronology prepared by the U.S. Army Command and General Staff College). It provides day-to-day coverage of the seven month crisis/war in the Persian Gulf, from the August 2, 1990, Iraqi invasion of Kuwait to the March 3, 1991, signing of the cease-fire. Each day carries a number of entries, averaging 10 to 12 for every 24 hours.

The work contains all the diplomatic maneuvers, U.N. resolutions, effects on the home fronts (particularly the Islamic world), and military events as well as the many ambiguous happenings that permeated the period. For example, on August 10, 1990, in allying himself with Iraq, King Hussein called for a Jihad to protect Mecca from the Americans and Zionists; 13 days later the U.N. Security Council agreed on a package of short-term financial aid to Jordan. And two days after the November 6, 1990, elections, President Bush suddenly raised the ante by doubling the U.S. forces in the Gulf to 460,000.

Two features make the chronology more than ordinarily useful: an 82-page name index (Tariz Aziz has 77 citations, General Schwartzkopf has 27) and an 80-page general index. Both are equally well done. [R: WLB, May 92, p. 126]—**David Eggenberger**

543. Mikdadi, Faysal. **Gamal Abdel Nasser: A Bibliography.** Westport, Conn., Greenwood Press, 1991. 148p. index. (Bibliographies of World Leaders, no.5). $55.00. Z8614.74.M54. 016.96205'3'092. LC 91-21168. ISBN 0-313-28119-X.

Of all the Middle Eastern leaders of the twentieth century, Gamal Abdel Nasser arguably has had the greatest impact on the politics and society of the modern Middle East. After the revolution of 1952, Nasser attempted to develop a modern industrial economy and to break the hold of the landed elite on Egyptian agriculture and society. Along with Nehru and Sukharno, he helped found the nonaligned movement. Yet it has been 20 years since the last major biography of him was published. Mikdadi's bibliography is an attempt to goad historians and political scientists into reassessing Nasser's character and impact on the world.

The volume begins with a less-than-successful summary biography of Nasser's life. For instance, the depiction of the 1930s is confusing; Nasser's date of birth is not mentioned; and gratuitous remarks about his smoking detract from the quality of this section. The rest of the volume is divided into sections that detail manuscript, newspaper, periodical and archival sources; works by Nasser; general biographies; background reading on Egypt, the Middle East, and the Israeli-Palestinian problem; Nasser's youth and his acquisition of power; his foreign policy; Suez; the nonaligned movement;

pan-Arabism; the Palestine conflict; Nasser's later life; assessments of his historical importance; and theses, bibliographies, and reviews about Nasser. The bibliography is designed primarily for readers and writers of English; therefore, most of the referenced material is in English, although there are a few French, German, and Arabic works included. Some of the more important references in these sections are annotated, but most of the material appears without comment. Mikdadi's division of the material into these categories makes the work useful for neophytes. However, the lack of comment on the cited material detracts from the volume's value. [R: Choice, Apr 92, p. 1211] – **David L. White**

544. Purvis, James D. **Jerusalem, the Holy City: A Bibliography. Volume II.** Metuchen, N.J., Scarecrow, 1991. 525p. index. (ATLA Bibliography Series, no.20). $49.50. Z3478.J4P87. 016.95694'4. LC 87-4758. ISBN 0-8108-2506-6.

Volume 2 of *Jerusalem, the Holy City* significantly expands the bibliography in the previous volume (see ARBA 88, entry 143). The current volume includes books and articles published since 1986, works previously unknown to Purvis, titles not included in volume 1, and titles included in volume 1 for which additional information is provided. A new feature is the inclusion of reviews.

An expanded system of classification within the original framework enhances the accessibility of the listings in volume 2. Although containing the same number of major subdivisions (8) and chapters (40), the number of subsections of chapters has been significantly increased, so that the total number of discrete units has grown from 48 to 134. In addition, Purvis has included at the end of each chapter subsection a list of the entry numbers in his first volume that relate to the same category.

Although the author indicates he has included some titles in this volume that might have been included in the first volume but were not, he does not amplify his criteria for inclusion, which were minimally spelled out in volume 1. Some expansion of concern with Islamic Jerusalem is evident, but such attention remains limited in comparison to Christian and Jewish Jerusalem. The omission of works in Arabic and, for the most part, Hebrew, while justified on the basis of the lack of accessibility to those works in North American libraries, limits the comprehensiveness of the bibliography. [R: Choice, Sept 92, p. 90] – **Harold O. Forshey**

WORLD HISTORY

Atlases

545. **Rand McNally Atlas of World History.** 1992 ed. R. I. Moore, ed. Skokie, Ill., Rand McNally, 1992. 192p. illus. maps. index. $39.95; $24.95pa. 01030.R38. 911. ISBN 0-528-83499-1; 0-528-83498-3pa.

This atlas is being simultaneously published in Great Britain as *Philip's Atlas of World History* and is a slightly revised edition of the *Rand McNally Historical Atlas of the World* (see ARBA 82, entry 383). The chief changes for this edition are updated bibliographies at the end of each chapter and revisions to some maps of the world and the United States since 1945. Otherwise, this edition preserves the strengths and weaknesses of its predecessor. Nearly 100 chronologically arranged maps trace the progress of humanity from various "isolated societies" at the dawn of history to what approaches a single "global community" in 1990. The maps, although often detailed in terms of the places and physical features included, are uncluttered, attractive, and easy to interpret. The well-written text accompanying them may be read as an introductory survey to world history. Both the maps and the text emphasize the development of European cultures and, with the exception of India and China, give only selective coverage of the rest of the world. A special section on the United States appended at the end of the text is generally redundant and is not covered by the index. The general index of people, "important places," and subjects is very selective, inconsistent (e.g., appearances of London and Paris are indexed; Washington, D.C., and Madrid are not), and occasionally inaccurate. Additional place-names can be located using a special index of alternative place-names, but the majority of places identified on the maps are not referenced in either index. Despite these faults, the well-executed maps and text, and the convenient size and price make this atlas a good buy for students and libraries. – **John R. M. Lawrence**

Bibliography

546. Pok, Attila, ed. **A Selected Bibliography of Modern Historiography.** Westport, Conn., Greenwood Press, 1992. 284p. index. (Bibliographies and Indexes in World History, no.24). $55.00. Z6208.H5S45. 016.9'072. LC 91-46699. ISBN 0-313-27231-X.

Pok's main objective is to list important works on the development of historical science. As opposed to *Historiography* (see ARBA 76, entry 292), it covers materials through 1990 and is not limited to English-language publications. Its arrangement is according to geographical regions: Europe, North America, Africa and the Middle East, Asia, and Australia. A separate chapter is devoted to general works on historiography.

Pok's selection criteria are subjective, an approach that has resulted in uneven coverage of various regions. For example, the section on Hungarian historiography consists of more than 50 entries, as compared with 3 on Norway, 5 each on Portugal and Canada, and 2 on Australia. Such uneven coverage limits the reference value of this work. The subject index does not list Lithuania, Latvia, or Estonia, and in the section on "Russia, Soviet Union," there is no indication as to how many former Soviet republics are covered. There is no entry for the major publications by D. Doroshenko and O. Ohloblyn that deal with Ukrainian historiography, and the outstanding Ukrainian historian Michel Hrushevsky, a founder of a new historiographical scheme of East European history, has been omitted. In addition, some transliterations and translations of a listed entry are incorrect; bibliographic citations are not complete (publishers' names are omitted from entries); and there are no annotations in this bibliography. Overall, the book has limited reference value. [R: Choice, Nov 92, pp. 448-50] – **Lubomyr R. Wynar**

547. Rollins, Alden. **Rome in the Fourth Century A.D.: An Annotated Bibliography with Historical Overview.** Jefferson, N.C., McFarland, 1991. 324p. index. $48.50. Z2340.R653. 016.937'06. LC 91-52762. ISBN 0-89950-624-0.

In comparison to those who specialize in other periods of ancient history, the student of the fourth century is at a disadvantage. Having commonly been viewed as a transitional period, the fourth century is often given cursory treatment in surveys, and literature on the period is widely scattered in publications on ancient, medieval, Byzantine, and early Christian studies. Rollins has assembled a substantial bibliography of works on the fourth century from these disparate sources. Included are twentieth-century articles, books, dissertations, and conference papers published in English through 1990. The annotations vary considerably in length and quality; in the case of more general works, they illuminate the work's relevance to the study of the fourth century. One-fifth of the entries lack annotations and represent titles that the author was unable to review. However, most entries for books are enhanced with citations to reviews, meaning the amount of material cited far exceeds the 1,408 enumerated entries. The citations are arranged by author within 11 subject categories, and a subject index provides additional access. Predictably, most entries relate to politics; government; the military; or religion, particularly Christianity. Other subjects emphasized include foreign relations, economic issues, science, literature, education, and art. Not included (by deliberate design of the author) is any survey of primary sources for the period. Considering that most in the intended audience are students, a selective list of important translations, plus an author index, would have improved the utility of the volume. In addition, while the brief historical overview introduces some of the topics covered, separate chapter introductions would have served this purpose better. Nonetheless, students and scholars will find this a useful compendium. [R: Choice, Mar 92, p. 1054] – **John R. M. Lawrence**

548. Totten, Samuel. **First-Person Accounts of Genocidal Acts in the Twentieth Century: An Annotated Bibliography.** Westport, Conn., Greenwood Press, 1991. 351p. index. (Bibliographies and Indexes in World History, no.21). $55.00. Z6207.G44T67. 016.90982. LC 91-20600. ISBN 0-313-26713-8.

First-person accounts serve as an antidote to the incomprehensibility and numbness felt by readers in the face of the magnitude of genocide. This compilation, unique in its focus on first-person accounts, lists statements by individuals who survived or witnessed genocidal acts (except as perpetrators). The 1,275 numbered and annotated entries are primarily of diaries, letters, memoirs, autobiographies, oral histories, interviews, and newspaper articles, the majority of which are in English. They also include notices of essays, reports, films, microfilm collections, archives, and bibliographies related to first-person accounts. The author is careful to define the scope of this work and to credit other work used.

The substantial introduction discusses the literature of genocide, especially the values and limitations of first-person accounts and the issues involved in collecting and cataloging them. Chapters cover specific genocidal events, from the well-known Jewish Holocaust (about 60 percent of the entries), the Ottoman genocide of the Armenians (11 percent), and several Soviet genocides (15 percent) to ones in southwest Africa, Uganda, Pakistan, Burundi, Cambodia, Bangladesh, Brazil, Guatemala, and Paraguay. The chapters are subdivided by type of material (e.g., first-person accounts, accounts in reports and studies, films, essays about accounts). There are subject and author indexes.

The entries are clear and bibliographically adequate (except for a couple of entries for items in a collection). Annotations are generous, ranging from a sentence to three-quarters of a page. They include a citation of the source of information taken from other bibliographies. Despite the author's sometimes awkward style, infatuation with the phrase "vis-a-vis," and overuse of the virgule, the commentary and annotations provide valuable context and explanation for the list of resources.

—**Joyce Duncan Falk**

Chronology

549. Asimov, Isaac. **Asimov's Chronology of the World.** New York, HarperCollins, 1991. 674p. index. $35.00. D11.A76. 902'.02. LC 91-55007. ISBN 0-06-270036-7.

Asimov's chronology of world history, one of his last published works, begins with a concise overview titled "Over 15,000,000,000 Years of History at a Glance," setting the stage for 600-plus pages of narrative. In brief essays Asimov discusses the events of early geological periods and the development of life forms. This segues naturally into essays on early civilizations. At 4000 B.C. the narrative begins to be divided according to geographic area and nation. The order of arrangement within a given time period is determined by "the necessity of telling a connected story so that a region of central importance will be considered first. Naturally, I will have to be the judge of what is of particular importance" (p. 30). In his usual informative and informal style, Asimov covers political, military, social, and cultural events. He closes his chronology with 1945, explaining that the monumental events of that year caused such changes in human history that another style of book is required to cover subsequent events properly.

The readable narrative will appeal to students in grades 8 and above, and to adults. Allowing for the limitations of space, which leads to oversimplification, this is a valuable reference book. The primary difficulty in using this work is that the indexing is very uneven. Once a nation becomes important within a given time period, one must simply turn pages to find all of the appropriate entries. Although the index does identify more isolated entries on nations, many people named in the narrative are not indexed.

Asimov's work compares favorably to *Encyclopedia of World History*, 5th ed. (see ARBA 73, entry 309). *The Columbia History of the World* (Columbia University Press, 1990), a collaborative effort by many scholars, provides maps and more detailed information. [R: Choice, Apr 92, p. 1203; WLB, Feb 92, p. 105]—**Vandelia L. VanMeter**

550. Edelheit, Hershel, and Abraham J. Edelheit. **A World in Turmoil: An Integrated Chronology of the Holocaust and World War II.** Westport, Conn., Greenwood Press, 1991. 450p. index. (Bibliographies and Indexes in World History, no.22). $75.00. D804.3.E34. 940.53'18'0202. LC 91-22265. ISBN 0-313-28218-8.

This is the third collaborative Holocaust reference work by the Edelheits. The previous volumes — *Bibliography on Holocaust Literature* (see ARBA 87, entry 522) and its *Supplement* (see ARBA 91, entry 519) — were well received by reviewers. The chronology, which spans nearly 16 years (January 1933 to May 1948), attempts to integrate general world and European events with a more precise record of anti-Jewish measures by Nazi Germany and other European governments (e.g., Fascist Italy, Romania, Vichy France). It therefore seeks to provide Holocaust researchers with clear and concise data describing those events. The entries in the chronology emphasize political events in Europe, the

Middle East (especially Mandatory Palestine), and the Americas; intellectual trends; and specific descriptions of Holocaust events. For example, the researcher might read through January 1942 to find entries for the Wannsee Conference (January 20), the founding of the United Partisans of Vilna (January 21), the massacre of Jews and Serbs by Hungarian troops in Yugoslavia (January 21-23), and the decree by Hitler that gave Martin Bormann control over all Nazi party directives and laws (January 24). The next entry is for Thailand's declaration of war on the United States (January 25).

The Edelheits include the original terminology used in virtually all European countries of Holocaust interest. Most foreign terminology is also provided in English translation, either in the entry or in the excellent glossary following the chronology. Usually, German organizational names are provided in the original with their abbreviations and an English equivalent (e.g., Wirtschafts und Verwaltungshauptamt [WVHAS] is the SS Economic and Administrative Office).

Access to the Holocaust chronology is provided by the three indexes—name, place, and subject. Although the place index does not include all locations of Holocaust importance in Central and Eastern Europe, it has lengthy entries for major extermination camps and mass killing sites, providing immediate access for researchers.

A selective bibliography lists English Holocaust titles as well as some titles in other languages. Hebrew titles are indicated. However, readers should note that the Memorial books listed in the bibliography are virtually all in Hebrew or Yiddish, although this is not indicated.

This work is recommended for undergraduate and graduate collections as well as larger public libraries. It is, additionally, a useful acquisition for research centers that deal with twentieth-century European history. [R: Choice, Apr 92, p. 1208; RBB, 1 Jan 92, pp. 850-51]—**Mark Padnos**

551. Gray, Randal, with Christopher Argyle. **Chronicle of the First World War. Volume II: 1917-1921.** New York, Facts on File, 1991. 383p. maps. index. $45.00. ISBN 0-8160-2595-9.

The detailed tabular arrangement begun in volume 1 of this chronology (see ARBA 92, entry 504), which covered July 1914 to December 1916, is continued here for the latter war years, through December 1918. (A more concise chronology arranged in simple columns follows for the period labeled "Towards Peace: 1919-1921.") A day-by-day account of events is given across a double page for nine areas of operation, including the three main fronts, Turkish and African operations, the sea and air wars, international events, and various home fronts. This crossing of areas with dates makes it easy to zero in on what was happening where on any given day. It also makes for a good deal of white space and a bigger book, but the price is not high by today's standards. Other useful sections of the work include statistical tables on a wide variety of topics related to the war and society of the time in general; a who's who of important persons; a series of pertinent maps; a list of sources arranged by subject; an extensive glossary; and an index to main events, places, and people.

The authors correctly emphasize that this work is the first English-language general chronology of World War I to appear since 1922. Oddly, they make no mention of *World War I in the Air* (see ARBA 78, entry 1566), a specialized but complementary effort. Nonetheless, ease of use and the amount of information provided make this title a recommended purchase for collections on modern history. [R: RBB, 1 Feb 92, p. 1058]—**Willa Schmidt**

552. Herman, Gerald. **The Pivotal Conflict: A Comprehensive Chronology of the First World War, 1914-1919.** Westport, Conn., Greenwood Press, 1992. 800p. index. $125.00. D522.5.H43. 940.3'02'02. LC 91-22245. ISBN 0-313-22793-4.

As a turning point that in many ways marked the real beginning of the twentieth century, World War I continues to present the student of history with compelling material. However, much of the available literature is not particularly precise about dating events or placing them in context, according to Herman, who proposes to do both. Beginning with the assassination of Austria-Hungary's Archduke Ferdinand on June 28, 1914, and ending with the signing of the Treaty of Versailles on June 28, 1919, the chronology provides day-by-day accounts arranged in three columns that cover military, inter-national-diplomatic, and domestic developments. The column on the military is coded A, B, C, and D for the western, eastern, and southern fronts and colonial/sea/air events, respectively. Similarly, the international section has four lettered subdivisions for formal agreements, conferences, other contacts, and declarations. Under the domestic heading are divisions for political, economic/social, and cultural/technical events. A helpful introduction explains the arrangement. The material itself, although brief, allows the war and related events to unfold in all their complexity. The subject index offers dates rather than page numbers as access points for information in the volume.

The author, an assistant professor of history, has compiled an impressively detailed chronology of World War I. Unfortunately, the type is too small, columns too narrow, divisions by date too faint, and a volume too thick for any but the most determined user. Simply put, the information is too much for the format. More appropriate and stimulating would have been a multimedia CD-ROM with illustrations, maps, music, and extracts from speeches. Recommended for history collections with a devoted World War I clientele. [R: Choice, Sept 92, p. 78; WLB, Nov 92, p. 95] — **Cheryl Knott Malone**

553. Stewart, Robert. **The Illustrated Almanac of Historical Facts: From the Dawn of the Christian Era to the New World Order.** New York, Prentice Hall General Reference, 1992. 320p. illus. maps. index. $40.00. LC 91-66999. ISBN 0-13-276395-8.

Stewart's chronology of significant events on all continents will be very useful to readers asking the common question, "When X was happening in the United States, what was happening in Asia (or other area of the world)?" The body of the text consists of chronologically arranged descriptions of thousands of historical events. The pages are divided into three vertical columns, each providing a concise narrative of one or more significant occurrences of a given year, enhanced by photographs, engravings, and maps. Brief comments on other events and social issues are included in occasional sidebars. An overview of significant events and issues is provided by the colorful picture essays in the introduction. Well-planned historical charts display a wealth of information on international leaders and elections, Nobel Peace prize winners, inventions, and statistics.

This work is an excellent review for persons with some background in world events. The brevity imposed by the format and the complexity of the issues and events presented will encourage the reader to look elsewhere for fuller explanations. The biographical and geographical dictionaries, which provide brief information, would be more useful if the entries included reference to the year or page where each is included in the chronology (if it is); one must use the index for this purpose. A useful supplement to other chronologies of world history, the work is suitable for advanced high school students and adults. [R: BR, Sept/Oct 92, p. 64; RBB, Aug 92, p. 2037] — **Vandelia L. VanMeter**

554. Trager, James. **The People's Chronology: A Year-by-Year Record of Human Events from Prehistory to the Present.** rev. ed. New York, Henry Holt, 1992. 1237p. illus. index. $45.00. D11.T83. 902'.02. LC 91-36734. ISBN 0-8050-1786-0.

This must be the most ambitious chronology ever attempted. Trager endeavors to squeeze the whole of human history into 1,237 pages. In general, this is a one-volume history book. For the most part the data are broken down into conventional categories such as politics, economics, religion, arts, education, communications, technology, and sports. A more contemporary sensibility of the author appears in the inclusion of information about nutrition, consumer protection, and the environment. Inasmuch as the author is from the United States, most of the pages are filled with information of interest to the U.S. populace. The work contains 110 pages of a cross-index that magnifies its usefulness.

Although the most frequent user of this work may be journalists digging up background information, it may also be of use to biographers and novelists who need to fill in the cultural and political events of a particular year. In addition to being informative, the compendium is often entertaining, and readers may consult it for nostalgia (e.g., reading about the year of one's birth). [R: LJ, 1 Mar 92, p. 86; RBB, 15 May 92, p. 1717; WLB, Sept 92, p. 121] — **Andrew Ezergailis**

Dictionaries and Encyclopedias

555. **The Blackwell Companion to the Enlightenment.** By John W. Yolton and others. Cambridge, Mass., Basil Blackwell, 1992. 581p. illus. index. $74.95. CB411.B57. 940.2'53'03. LC 91-30201. ISBN 0-631-15403-5.

This attractive reference book will be of enormous value to anyone interested in virtually any aspect of the Enlightenment. Following a useful introductory essay by Lester G. Crocker are interpretive essays on a wide variety of subjects, including the arts, science, history, philosophy, and religion, as well as shorter entries on specialized topics, several hundred biographical entries, and more than 80 illustrations. Many of the more lengthy entries are accompanied by bibliographies that contain the essential works on the subject or person in question. The work concentrates on the period from 1720 to 1780, although some attention is given to the late seventeenth, late eighteenth, and early nineteenth centuries. In geographical scope it goes beyond France—the center of the Enlightenment—to include the rest of Europe and North America. It should be noted that the entries are all intended to relate conceptually to the Enlightenment; this is not a reference for eighteenth-century studies in general. Thus, one will find the writer Horace Walpole, but not his father, Sir Robert, the English prime minister.

Inevitably one can quibble with some items. There is, for instance, an anachronistic entry on feminism but not one on women (there is one on "literature, women in"), and it is twice the length of the entry on democracy—not the dominant ideology of the age but certainly no anachronism. On the whole, however, the depth and breadth of coverage is extremely impressive. Arbitrarily choosing the *A*s as an illustration, one finds entries on absolutism, academies of art and science, John Adams, Joseph Addison, aesthetics, agriculture, Jean d'Alembert, Alexander I, the Alps, the American Revolution, anatomy, ancients and moderns, astronomy, and many, many more. This is an essential volume for libraries, Enlightenment scholars, and anyone interested in the age. [R: Choice, Nov 92, pp. 437-38]
— **William B. Robison**

556. Polmar, Norman, and Thomas B. Allen. **World War II: America at War 1941-1945.** New York, Random House, 1991. 940p. illus. maps. index. $35.00. D743.5.P56. 940.53'02'02. LC 91-16212. ISBN 0-394-58530-5.

The most important parts of this book are the prolog, the war chronology, the war guide, and the epilog. The prolog provides context, stressing that German, Italian, and Japanese aggression culminated in World War II. The war chronology runs from January 1, 1941, to December 19, 1945, headlining notable events of the conflict. The war guide features brief summaries of strategy, tactics, campaigns, battles, weapons, and soldiers. The epilog portrays the Cold War as the aftermath of World War II, wherein the Soviet Union eventually collapsed under American pressure. Polmar and Allen sum it up this way: "Economically—and probably politically—the Soviet Union could no longer compete."

War buffs will enjoy this encyclopedia, but others might not be as pleased. The military aspects of World War II—particularly weaponry—receive excellent coverage. To cite just one example, the American Fido Torpedo "was 84 inches long and 19 inches in diameter"; it also possessed the capability to execute "a circular search pattern before finding its target." Treatment of industrial mobilization and the home front is less salutary although adequate. There is considerable information on war production and civilian life, but separate entries for the Office of Production Management, price controls, and "Rosie the Riveter" are omitted. A careful reader will find references to all three subjects under different headings, but it takes some digging. All told, *World War II* is a useful contribution that is well worth the occasional inconvenience it causes. Recommended for high school and college libraries. [R: LJ, 1 Feb 92, p. 82; RBB, 15 Jan 92, p. 980]—**Richard E. Holl**

557. Teed, Peter. **A Dictionary of Twentieth Century History 1914-1990.** New York, Oxford University Press, 1992. 520p. $30.00. ISBN 0-19-211676-2.

In one alphabetical arrangement, Teed provides nearly 2,000 entries that cover worldwide political, military, social, cultural, and technological movements; events; and people that have marked the era. Entries vary from a few sentences to a page or more in length. While the book has been published in Great Britain, there appears to be little material that will confuse North American readers; for example, the entry on Judaism uses United States terms for its three major forms.

As might be expected, a single volume on a topic of such magnitude cannot avoid gaps in coverage. The vast majority of entries are political, geographic, or military in nature, with popular culture and science and technology all but ignored. The article on Albert Einstein is short and gives no indication that he is considered one of the most influential people of the century; and there seem to be no other profiles of scientists. Also, there are no entries on television or telephones; these significant inventions are relegated to a short paragraph on telecommunications. There are entries on each of the countries of the world and on a wide variety of non-Western individuals, but most U.S. Supreme Court justices, including Thurgood Marshall and Sandra Day O'Connor, are not profiled. Some of the entries appear to be of minor interest from a global perspective (e.g., the Cod War [antagonism between Great Britain and Iceland over fishing rights], *Meanjin* [an Australian literary journal]).

Entries that do appear are clearly written and include cross-references (asterisks) so that one can read the entry on a nation and identify people and movements that merit further study. The small print precludes extensive reading at one sitting, but this work would be a worthwhile addition to most collections, largely for its coverage of non-Western material. Similar in intent (and also from a British perspective) is *The Facts on File Dictionary of 20th Century History, 1900-1978* (see ARBA 81, entry 404). [R: WLB, Nov 92, p. 92]—**D. A. Rothschild and Vandelia L. VanMeter**

Handbooks and Yearbooks

558. **The Guinness Book of Records 1492: The World Five Hundred Years Ago.** Deborah Manley, ed. New York, Facts on File, 1992. 192p. illus. maps. index. $24.95. AG243.G863. 031.02. LC 91-58588. ISBN 0-8160-2772-2.

This book is a joy to hold and gets better when one begins to sample its entries and to savor its well-chosen, full-color illustrations and maps. It is a collection of records from the human and natural world as they stood around 1450-1550. References to events that occurred after 1550 appear occasionally, and, of course, many of the records listed are quite ancient. It is important to keep in mind that this collection of records has been compiled from a modern point of view and not the point of view of someone living at the time of Columbus. The geographical scope of the entries is truly worldwide. Records have been garnered from Ming China, Ashikaga Japan, Mogul India, Mameluke Egypt, Timbuktu, the Aztec Empire, and the Incan Empire, among many other places, although entries for England are the most common.

The entries are organized into 11 topical chapters: "The World and Beyond," "The Human Being," "Transport," "Exploration and Discovery," "Industry and Commerce," "Science and Technology," "Buildings and Structures," "The Arts and Entertainment," "Sport," "Religion and Popular Belief," and "Rulers and Law Makers." Individual chapters are further subdivided into appropriate categories. A brief bibliography provides guidance for further reading on a chapter-by-chapter basis, while a simple index of persons, places, and subjects provides the reader with some help in locating entries.

Among the many fascinating facts listed: The first good calendar was compiled by the Egyptians before 420 B.C. (although the most precise calendar was developed by the Maya in the sixth century A.D.). The title for being the vilest nobleman is given to the fifteenth-century Frenchman, Gilles de Rais, who murdered more than 100 children in satanic rites and is possibly the origin of the Bluebeard legend. (The Aztecs, however, hold the record for the largest human sacrifice; in 1487 they killed between 20,000 and 84,000 captives during the dedication of the new temple complex at Tenochtitlan.) Sponsorship of the largest beauty contest belongs to the Russian Tsar Vassily III, who looked at more than 1,500 maidens before picking a wife.

The price of this attractive book makes it affordable for the smallest college, public, or school library as well as individual purchasers. It is not a ready-reference tool, but it is a browser's delight. [R: RBB, 1 Sept 92, p. 85; SLJ, July 92, p. 98]—**Ronald H. Fritze**

559. **The Longman Handbook of World History since 1914.** By Chris Cook and John Stevenson. New York, Longman, 1991. 539p. maps. index. (Longman Handbook to History). $39.95. D421.C64. 909.82. LC 89-77970. ISBN 0-582-48588-6.

This handbook strives for contemporaneity. As far as publishing goes, it achieves that goal. Contained between its covers are all historical events (e.g., the Intifada, Tiananmen Square) that have occurred since 1914. The book is arranged in sections such as political history (e.g., Europe, the Middle East, Africa), heads of state, wars and international affairs, and economic and social conditions. A glossary of terms, a bibliography, a section of biographies, and a map section round out the volume.

The difference between this work and *Facts on File World Political Almanac* (1992) is one of taste. The Facts on File book lacks a bibliography section and covers fewer years. Acquisition of both volumes would be superfluous.—**Mark Y. Herring**

560. **The Timetables of History.** 3d ed. By Bernard Grun. New York, Simon & Schuster, 1991. 724p. index. $20.00pa. ISBN 0-671-74271-X.

Simon and Schuster waited 12 years to bring out the 3d edition of this popular reference work instead of the mere 4 years between the previous editions. Those familiar with the earlier editions will find that the book continues to consist of the same seven parallel chronologies of events in the areas of history and politics; literature and theater; religion, philosophy, and learning; visual arts; music; science, technology, and growth; and daily life. The chronology still begins at 5,000 B.C. but has been updated to the end of A.D. 1991. The volume concludes with a substantial index of persons, places, and subjects.

When Hans E. Bynagle reviewed the 2d edition in ARBA 81 (see entry 398), he rightly criticized it for merely adding on 13 pages of new material at the end without revising any of the earlier entries where it was appropriate. In the 3d edition, the editors have reacted to some of these criticisms. When the *Timetables of History* lists a person's birth, it also indicates the year of that person's death in parentheses. The 2d edition did not update that information for people who had died between 1974 and 1978, but the 3d edition has brought it current for 1974-1991. Unfortunately, if the addition of new information would have meant adding new lines and changing pagination, it has been ignored. So the reader still does not know when presidents Gerald Ford, Jimmy Carter, Ronald Reagan, or George Bush were born. Still, *Timetables of History* remains a useful, interesting, and inexpensive work of reference that belongs in most libraries and in the private collection of any history buff. [R: WLB, Mar 92, p. 119]
—**Ronald H. Fritze**

Indexes

561. VanMeter, Vandelia. **World History for Children and Young Adults: An Annotated Bibliographic Index.** Englewood, Colo., Libraries Unlimited, 1992. 266p. index. (Libraries Unlimited Data Book). $32.00. Z6201.V28. 909. LC 91-43521. ISBN 0-87287-732-9.

World History for Children and Young Adults brings under one cover recent titles (1980-1989) that have received at least one good or one mixed review. Nine journals were searched for reviews, including *Library Journal, Booklist, Horn Book,* and *School Library Journal.* Selection of titles was made for their maximum usefulness to teachers, librarians, parents, and authors. Some political correctness is evident but it is not all-pervasive. The bibliography may be used by those who teach gifted students, by those whose students need remediation, and everyone in between.

Each entry lists author, title and subtitle, publisher, cost, physical description, series, and grade level, followed by a very brief annotation. While the annotations are not critical, a symbol has been placed in the description of the title to indicate the critical reception of the book at the time of review. Author, title, subject, series, and grade level indexes close out the volume. Supplements are planned. [R: Choice, Sept 92, p. 94; RBB, 15 May 92, p. 1717; VOYA, Dec 92, pp. 317-318]—**Mark Y. Herring**

10 Law

GENERAL WORKS

Acronyms and Abbreviations

562. Kavass, Igor I., and Mary Miles Prince, eds. **World Dictionary of Legal Abbreviations.** Buffalo, N.Y., William S. Hein, 1991. 1v. (various paging). $75.00 spiralbound. ISBN 0-89941-781-7,

This work fills an important gap in the bibliography of legal research. It consists of an alphabetical list of 8,400 abbreviations to foreign legal materials of 5 countries (Great Britain, France, Italy, Portugal, and Spain) with the "translation" of these abbreviations into full titles. For many years *Dictionary of Legal Abbreviations Used in American Law Books* (see ARBA 86, entry 536) has faithfully served the needs of people in the United States researching American law. That work's only shortfall has been its lack of coverage of foreign materials, which is hardly a fair criticism; as the title indicates, the book was never intended to cover foreign materials in the first place. The present work does for the particular countries covered what the other book does with American law materials. For the most part it is done well. The only troubling feature of the dictionary is that abbreviations are arranged by country, requiring the researcher to check five separate lists to find an abbreviation unless the country of origin is known. Given the looseleaf format of the book, the country lists can be easily expanded and updated, greatly increasing the value of this work.

Any library supporting the research needs of legal researchers would do well to have this book in their reference collection. In addition, any library with *Dictionary of Legal Abbreviations Used in American Law Books* should have this current volume as a companion. – **Richard A. Leiter**

Bibliography

563. Avalos, Francisco A. **The Mexican Legal System.** Westport, Conn., Greenwood Press, 1992. 254p. index. (Reference Guides to National Legal Systems, no.1). $49.95. KGF150.A95. 016.34972. LC 91-39512. ISBN 0-313-27565-3.

This is a guide to the legal literature about Mexican law. It concentrates primarily on federal legislation but also deals with state legislation. The 41 subject headings include 1,100 entries. Headings such as commercial laws, contract laws, customs laws, foreign exchange laws, property laws, and others that would pertain to investment and trade with the United States are listed. Most entries are under banks and banking laws, foreign investment laws, tax laws, and transfer of technology laws. For example, the 9 pages on foreign investment laws contain 4 citations on primary materials, 5 citations on the location of legislation, 34 citations on secondary source materials (of which 10 are from 1990 and 6 are from 1989), and 13 citations on secondary monographs. English and Spanish sources are included; they are indexed by author and subject.

The 23-page introduction to the Mexican legal system is especially helpful. In it the author concludes that the three steps in Mexican legal research are finding the relevant articles in the appropriate

code, finding the relevant *doctrina*, and finding the correct *jurisprudencia*. Mexican-trained lawyers usually undertake only the first two steps, while American-trained lawyers undertake all three. Avalos attributes this to the fact that Mexican lawyers are trained in the civil law tradition and American lawyers in the common law tradition. Recommended for academic and large public libraries.
— **Karen Y. Stabler**

564. Bouckaert, Boudewijn, and Gerrit de Geest, eds. **Bibliography of Law and Economics.** Norwell, Mass., Kluwer Academic, 1992. 667p. index. $179.00. K38.B525. 016.34. LC 92-250. ISBN 0-7923-1645-2.

This scholarly work encompasses both traditional (e.g., social security) and nontraditional (e.g., family, criminal law) areas of law and economics. Its 7,000 citations are arranged in 2 parts. The primary section employs a numbered classification system to distinguish general works from specific topics, while the other section lists non-English publications for European countries. Entries consist of standard citations without annotations; the legal form, in which the volume number appears first, is used for journal entries. The high percentage of non-English items is ameliorated somewhat by title translations.

The editors' aim was to provide students with references for papers, but they have neglected to supply access to their extensive, unique collection. The bibliography lacks annotations, section introductions or explanations, and an adequate subject index. A more detailed index could solve some of the work's problems: citations repeated in the text and the author index, overlapping topics that refer to disparate categories, and the inability to locate important current topics in the bibliography. As it stands, the wealth of data contained here is lost to all but those who are well acquainted with the field. The high price and structural weaknesses limit this work's usefulness to the most scholarly collections. — **Sandra E. Belanger**

565. **Bowker's Law Books & Serials in Print 1991: A Multimedia Sourcebook.** New Providence, N.J., R. R. Bowker, 1991. 3v. index. $525.00/set. ISBN 0-8352-3050-3.

R. R. Bowker's various indexes to in-print publications have long been standard resources for libraries and bookstores. This compilation follows the familiar *Books in Print* format but limits its contents strictly to books and serials that fall within Library of Congress legal subject headings. The editors have fine-tuned the coverage by eliminating items from the social sciences that are not, strictly speaking, law publications. In addition to books and serials, all types of legal media appear in separate listings: microforms, audio and video cassettes, computer software, and online databases. New to this edition are brief annotations for some entries. Attorneys with legal writing experience provide information on a title's content, coverage, audience, and focus. Bowker promises that future issues will include notes for all entries.

Each type of publication has its own index, with access by author, title, and subject for books and access by title and subject for serials and other media. Each volume in the set includes instructions on how to use the guide and a list of abbreviations. Quarterly cumulative supplements come with the subscription price. — **Berniece M. Owen**

566. Epstein, Lee, Tracey E. George, and Joseph F. Kobylka. **Public Interest Law: An Annotated Bibliography and Research Guide.** Hamden, Conn., Garland, 1992. 213p. index. (Organizations and Interest Groups, v.4; Garland Reference Library of Social Science, v.693). $30.00. KF299.P8E67. 016.34973. LC 91-45119. ISBN 0-8240-7636-2.

Recognizing the difficulty in precisely defining public interest law, the authors have annotated publications by and about organizations and societies dedicated to conducting public interest litigation. These are organizations for which the ultimate motive of the suits they pursue is the enhancement of a broad public good—for the United States or for groups of U.S. citizens who have certain similarities or mutual concerns. The American Civil Liberties Union (ACLU) and the National Association for the Advancement of Colored People (NAACP) are two examples of well-known public interest organizations.

The longest sections of the book's seven chapters cover specific organizations (e.g., ACLU, NAACP) and areas of law (e.g., children's rights, poverty, religion). If an item falls into more than one category, the authors provide a cross-reference. Full annotations appear only once for each title. The notes, descriptive rather than critical, are usually one or two paragraphs long. The book concludes with appendixes about key organizations and authors; a list of the Solicitors General of the United States; an outline of the U.S. legal system, including the Supreme Court's calendar; a subject index; and an author index.

The authors emphasize that this resource is a starting point for research on public interest law. As such, it serves its audience well. — **Berniece M. Owen**

567. Goedan, Juergen Christoph. **International Legal Bibliographies: A Worldwide Guide and Critique.** Ardsley-on-Hudson, N.Y., Transnational, 1992. 388p. index. $95.00. K37.G63. 016.01634. LC 91-43259. ISBN 0-941320-09-X.

The primary objective of this book is to inform "the user of the special features, advantages, and weaknesses of each bibliography" (p. 1). This objective is realized. The works reviewed are limited to international bibliographies — that is, those with worldwide coverage that have been published since World War II and that are generally available in large law libraries. The means by which the bibliographies are examined and criticized come primarily from book reviews. All sources are cited, and the reviews and critiques are presented clearly and carefully. Each review offers general background information on the bibliography, the manner and frequency of publication, an evaluation, instructions for use, and a summary, among other things. Chapter 1 provides a brief statement about the purpose and function of the work. Chapter 2 offers an analysis and evaluation of 17 international bibliographies, including *Law Books Recommended for Libraries* (see ARBA 71, entry 532), the *Index to Foreign Legal Periodicals* (IFLP) (University of California Press, 1960-), the *Index to Legal Periodicals* (ILP) (see ARBA 88, entry 583), and the *Current Law Index* (CLI) (see ARBA 88, entry 582). The conclusion to chapter 2 provides useful advice on how to avoid duplication of indexing among the IFLP, the CLI, and the ILP. Chapter 3 offers a narrative review of the 17 bibliographies considered, including an analysis of problems common to legal bibliographies and recommendations for their improvement. For law librarians and legal researchers, this reference work will be most useful. — **Michael A. Foley**

568. Harding, Jim, and Beryl Forgay. **Breaking Down the Walls: A Bibliography on the Pursuit of Aboriginal Justice.** Regina, Sask., Prairie Justice Research, University of Regina, 1991. 108p. (Aboriginal Justice Series, no.2). $20.00pa. ISBN 0-7731-0191-8.

This is a classified list of more than 1,000 items on the relationship between Canadian native peoples and the criminal justice system. The work also contains a limited number of comparative sources on United States and developing country experiences. The bibliography is divided first into six main subject classes (e.g., judicial inquiries, self-government) and further divided by subject where merited. Each subcategory is finally divided by type of material (e.g., newspaper article, film/video). Due to funding/space constraints, there are no annotations. Materials for the work were generated primarily through computer searches of eight major (largely Canadian-based) bibliographic databases of books, periodicals and newspapers, government documents, and research reports. The concepts used were native/Inuit/aboriginal, correction/prison, and Canada/Canadian. Additional searches were performed on specific cases and issues. The dates covered are concentrated in the 1980s, particularly after 1982. There are a detailed table of contents, an introduction, and a five-page methodological note.

In its field, this work should prove important. Organizations collecting materials and research aids on native issues, particularly within a Canadian context, should strongly consider acquiring it. [R: CLJ, Oct 92, p. 404] — **Nigel Tappin**

569. Harding, Jim, with Bruce Spence. **An Annotated Bibliography of Aboriginal-Controlled Justice Programs in Canada.** Regina, Sask., Prairie Justice Research, School of Human Justice, University of Regina, 1991. 89p. (Aboriginal Justice Series, no.3). $20.00pa. ISBN 0-7731-0190-X.

This is a list of 28 publications that deal with native-controlled justice programs in Canada. In addition to the entries, the report includes a detailed table of contents, a 3-page introduction, 11 pages on methods used, 7 pages of conclusions, and 4 appendixes that list (inter alia) other sources of aboriginal justice information and Native-delivered justice programs in Canada.

The bibliography is arranged in five sections (general, policing, courts, corrections, and diversion), and each subject is further subdivided by one added level of subheadings. The annotations average more than 2 pages in length (68 pages for 28 entries). The programs/documents are discussed under nine standardized headings, such as program profile, aboriginal control, funding, and recommendations. The comments are critically evaluative and seem well executed.

Aboriginal issues have gained public and media interest in Canada in the past few years. In part this stems from the police-Mohawk standoff at Oka, Quebec, in 1990; the role of an aboriginal provincial legislator in derailing constitutional reform; and some prominent miscarriages of justice. In consequence, the work may be of interest to general Canadian studies collections as well as its natural constituencies among libraries and other institutions with client interest in aboriginal issues. Highly recommended to these groups. [R: CLJ, Oct 92, p. 404]—**Nigel Tappin**

570. **Law Books in Print 1990: Law Books in English Published throughout the World....** 6th ed. Nicholas Triffin with Alice Pidgeon, comps. and eds. Dobbs Ferry, N.Y., Glanville/Oceana, 1991. 6v. $750.00/set. ISBN 0-87802-032-2.

The compilers of this ambitious undertaking strive to list all law books published in English throughout the world that were in print as of December 31, 1990. They include many titles that cross disciplinary lines, but all entries are law related. This edition also includes nonbook materials for the first time: microforms, computer files, audiovisual works, and CD-ROM titles. Continuations and periodicals are specifically omitted, but looseleaf services are included.

The first and last volumes include a publishers' directory, which is the key to the abbreviations for publisher names and has publisher addresses. The first section is an intermingled author/title list. Next is a subject list, with titles repeated under as many relevant headings as necessary. The third section is arranged by publisher, and the final section has titles arranged by series. Every entry has full bibliographic information, plus subject headings and price, in a clear, easy-to-read format.

Triffin cautions users that the information is based mainly on publisher input, but he and Pidgeon have made heroic efforts to be comprehensive and current. Revised sets are scheduled every three years, with supplements called *Law Books Published* appearing twice a year between editions.

—**Berniece M. Owen**

571. Martin, Fenton S., and Robert U. Goehlert. **How to Research the Supreme Court.** Washington, D.C., Congressional Quarterly, 1992. 140p. index. $22.95; $13.95pa. KF8741.A1M36. 1016.34773'26. LC 91-46903. ISBN 0-87187-697-3; 0-87187-633-7pa.

Although not the definitive manual for Supreme Court researchers (one does not yet exist), this new book offers a basic introduction to researching the Court. Included are lists of both primary and secondary materials that will assist Court watchers. Bibliographic information and brief abstracts follow entries of biographical and encyclopedic works; bibliographies; and major print, online, and CD-ROM indexing and abstracting services. Important periodicals and newspapers containing articles on the Court are listed, as are selected articles and books on the Court and its justices. A chronological list of nominations to the Court, brief biographies of the justices, and a glossary are included as appendixes.

Although the authors acknowledge the selectivity of the entries, some important source materials have been omitted. Furthermore, many sources cited in the text cannot be found in the author or title indexes. Nevertheless, this is a useful handbook for Supreme Court researchers. It will certainly get them started in the right direction, which is no small feat. At its modest price, the book is recommended for most academic and law libraries. [R: Choice, Oct 92, p. 276; RBB, 1 Sept 92, pp. 85-86; WLB, Oct 92, p. 110]—**James S. Heller**

572. Matthews, Elizabeth W. **The Law Library Reference Shelf: Annotated Subject Guide.** 2d ed. Buffalo, N.Y., William S. Hein, 1992. 209p. index. $42.50. KF1.M33. 016.34973. LC 92-2275. ISBN 0-89941-796-5.

Matthews is the law librarian and a professor in the School of Law at Southern Illinois University at Carbondale. She applies her experience in the library to her selection of titles for this ready-reference bibliography. Her emphasis is on books that supply simple facts, addresses, definitions, and names. Many titles relate to the law only indirectly.

Titles appear alphabetically by author or title within 15 broad topics (e.g., almanacs and encyclopedias, bar associations, occupations, finance). Where the quantity of materials justifies it, Matthews subdivides her topics. Under research and bibliography she has separate categories for federal and state governments, foundations, and style manuals. The table of contents is a guide to the topics in the list; the index includes both authors and titles. Citations provide author, title, place of publication, publisher, date, collation, Library of Congress classification number, and a concise annotation. Each title appears under only one topic. If an item is available online or in another format, such as CD-ROM, Matthews notes the fact. She does not show if titles are in print or what they cost. This is a neat and orderly guide to locating the answers to "who, what, when, and where" questions in any law library and a handy supplement to format guides to legal research.—**Berniece M. Owen**

573. Miller, Oscar J., and Mortimer D. Schwartz, comps. **Recommended Publications for Legal Research 1990.** Littleton, Colo., Fred B. Rothman, 1992. 158p. index. $37.50pa. ISSN 0898-266X.

A crucial law library development tool, this work is a must for any academic law library that desires to be thorough and comprehensive. It is nearly the only list that can be used as a checklist to assess general acquisition policies in an academic setting. The book is very practically laid out. The format is clearly designed for utility and ease of use. Virtually all important law titles are evaluated by the compilers. They are categorized into three groups: "A," for material recommended for a basic collection; "B," for an intermediate collection; and "C," for an in-depth research collection. If the book has any weaknesses, they are in the lack of a sublist by classification and the omission of a detailed description of the methodology upon which such recommendations are made.—**Richard A. Leiter**

Dictionaries and Encyclopedias

574. Burton, William C. **Legal Thesaurus.** 2d ed. New York, Macmillan, 1992. 1011p. $40.00; $21.00pa. KF156.B856. 340'.14. LC 91-37968. ISBN 0-02-897077-2; 0-02-897079-9pa.

Members of the legal profession need to express themselves accurately, persuasively, and plainly. This work is intended to provide them with more specific vocabulary than is available in a general thesaurus. Originally published in 1979, this edition has added more words generally used by lawyers but not specifically limited to law.

The work is organized in two parts: a main listing and an index of all words included that leads readers to the proper entry term. The main alphabet of entries includes both English words and a few foreign words and phrases. If one word or term has multiple parts of speech or meanings, each is listed separately. Under each entry is given the part of speech, a one-word definition if there are multiple meanings, and a wide assortment of synonymous or related words and terms. For many entries an "associated concepts" section lists related legal terms, and another section covers related foreign phrases, usually legal Latin. Because many terms included are related rather than synonymous, the author cautions the user to also use a legal dictionary for precise meanings.

West's Legal Thesaurus/Dictionary (see ARBA 87, entry 551) may be preferred by those relatively new to law, as it gives more complete definitions and lets the user use one reference source instead of two. But this work gives many more choices of related terms and should be very useful to anyone involved in extensive legal writing. Recommended for any library with patrons in legal fields.

—**Marit S. MacArthur**

575. Byrne, W. J. **A Dictionary of English Law.** London, Sweet & Maxwell, 1923; repr., Littleton, Colo., Fred B. Rothman, 1991. 942p. $97.50. KD313.B97. 349.42'03. LC 91-34705. ISBN 0-8377-1952-6.

In the *Oxford Companion to Law* (see ARBA 81, entry 582), *A Dictionary of English Law* is described as one of the four principal modern law dictionaries. Byrne was a member of both the English and the Irish Bars (the "senior" branch of the legal profession that provides advocacy services before the higher courts). He confines the scope of this work to law as used in England. The book apparently was intended as a revision of Sweet's *Dictionary of English Law* (1882), but this last became so altered as to justify the new attribution. A pleasant feature is the table of regnal years (used instead of calendar years until 1963 for formal statute citation) with an interesting explanation of the distinction between them and historical and legal (or ecclesiastical) years.

The dictionary is both a useful (although dated) reference and a marvelous treasury to browse. The reproduction affords libraries and individuals the opportunity to acquire an acid-free edition.

—**Nigel Tappin**

576. **Encyclopedia of the American Constitution. Supplement I.** Leonard W. Levy, Kenneth L. Karst, and John G. West, Jr., eds. New York, Macmillan, 1992. 668p. index. $90.00. KF4548.E53. 342.73'023'03. LC 86-3038. ISBN 0-02-918678-1.

This volume supplements the four-volume *Encyclopedia of the American Constitution* (see ARBA 87, entry 711). Its contents include more than 300 signed articles, 247 new entries, updates to various articles, and cross-references to pertinent articles in this volume and the original compendium. Topics covered are as broad as the law's jurisdiction. They include biographical sketches of Supreme Court justices such as Anthony Kennedy; significant U.S. Supreme Court cases of recent years, including Bowers v. Hardwick, Missouri v. Jenkins, and Webster v. Reproductive Health Services; and ongoing subjects of constitutional debate, including separation of church and state, search and seizure, property rights, judicial review, and habeus corpus. Emerging issues of constitutional concern are also examined and analyzed, including drug testing, Critical Legal Studies, the impact of computers, sexual orientation, and the apparent emergence of a field of constitutional inquiry focusing on the impact of science and technology.

This supplement to the *Encyclopedia of the American Constitution* is an excellent introduction to American constitutional law. It is presented in a thoughtful and analytical manner by a diverse group of scholars. A weakness is the absence of articles on Clarence Thomas and his tumultuous confirmation hearings, sexual harassment, and the impact of political correctness on First Amendment rights. It is hoped that these omissions will be corrected in subsequent supplements and further enhance the value of this compilation. [R: RBB, 1 June 92, pp. 1774-75; WLB, May 92, p. 123]—**Bert Chapman**

577. Fox, James R. **Dictionary of International & Comparative Law.** Dobbs Ferry, N.Y., Oceana, 1992. 495p. $65.00. JX1226.F69. 341'.03. ISBN 0-379-20430-4.

This dictionary is an outgrowth of answers to questions about international law at the Dickinson School of Law. In addition to words and phrases, the book features defining agencies, organizations, events, cases, and documents. Most of the definitions are documented, but the book's coverage of comparative law is quite limited.

Definitions are concise, and in some instances, completeness has been sacrificed for brevity. For example, the book defines the United for Peace Resolution as the General Assembly resolution "urging the Security Council to act to maintain peace." Actually, the resolution says that if the Security Council "fails to exercise its primary responsibility for the maintenance of international peace and security ... the General Assembly shall consider the matter...." Also, the book defines specialized agencies of the United Nations and gives one example. However, it does not mention the Universal Postal Union as one of the specialized agencies.

One also wonders why some terms have been excluded. For example, *veto* is defined, but not *double veto*. *Treaties and Other International Acts* (ITAS) appears, but not *United States Treaties and Other International Agreements* (UST); nor is the difference between treaties and other international agreements mentioned. The term *compulsory jurisdiction* is cross-referenced but not defined. In spite of its flaws, the book is a fine addition to law collections.—**Tze-chung Li**

578. Johnson, John W. **Historic U.S. Court Cases 1690-1990: An Encyclopedia.** Hamden, Conn., Garland, 1992. 754p. index. (American Law and Society, v.2; Garland Reference Library of the Social Sciences, v.497). $150.00. KF385.A4J64. 349.73'0264. LC 91-40175. ISBN 0-8240-4430-4.

This collection of 171 essays covers 197 cases, from the Salem witch trials to recent challenges to flag-burning laws. While passages from the decisions are quoted, these are not annotated case excerpts but thoughtful discussions that place the cases in their historical and social contexts and identify their significance in U.S. legal history. Coverage and treatment are aimed at a broad audience; most of the 80 contributors teach history or political science, not law. Concluding bibliographical references are often to general historical/biographical works.

The arrangement is by subject rather than case name (there are indexes at the end). Six subject divisions—crime and criminal law; governmental organization, power, and procedure; economics; race and gender; civil liberties; and law in critical periods in American history—are divided into numerous subtopics, within which cases are arranged chronologically. A number of cases could have been placed in more than one subject area, and the last major division is not a subject area in the same sense that the others are. Careful scanning of the table of contents will be necessary. Despite these shortcomings (and the book's high cost), these are useful essays for students and general readers. [R: Choice, Sept 92, p. 82; LJ, 15 June 92, p. 70; RBB, 1 June 92, p. 1776; WLB, June 92, p. 112]—**Jack Ray**

579. Mellinkoff, David. **Mellinkoff's Dictionary of American Legal Usage.** St. Paul, Minn., West Publishing, 1992. 703p. $39.95. KF156.M45. 349.73'014. LC 92-281. ISBN 0-314-00068-2.

This is an easy-to-use source for clear definitions of often complex legal concepts in U.S. common law. Although similar in intent to other dictionaries of modern legal usage, this work employs nonlegal terminology to precisely define words and cross-references to identify relationships (e.g., *criminal lawyer, litigator*). Clearly an extension of Mellinkoff's previous work on legal writing and the development of legal language, it is an excellent addition to the many dictionaries already published on English and United States law.

The alphabetical entries vary in length from short paragraphs (e.g., *for the record*) to several pages (e.g., *judge*). They are clarified by the notation of the origin, a translation for foreign words (e.g., *profit a prendre*), and the addition of cross-references for slang expressions (e.g., *mouthpiece, shyster*) and other alternate usages (e.g., *trial jury, advisory jury*). Mellinkoff has injected humor into definitions of such terms as *know*, a word that has no precise legal meaning. The index of entries, printed on green paper, repeats all terms, variant spellings, and cross-references found in the main section. However, its purpose is unclear as it lacks page references or other search aids usually associated with an index. This dictionary belongs not only in law collections but also in libraries that serve the legal needs of the general public.—**Sandra E. Belanger**

580. Nash, Ralph C., Jr., and Steven L. Schooner. **The Government Contracts Reference Book: A Comprehensive Guide to the Language of Procurement.** Washington, D.C., George Washington University, 1992. 445p. $40.00pa. KF846.4.N37. 346.73'023'03. LC 92-8925. ISBN 0-935165-19-3.

Nash is the founder of the Government Contracts Program at the George Washington University National Law Center and a professor at the law school; Schooner is an attorney with the U.S. Justice Department. Together they have compiled a very helpful dictionary of public contracts law terminology. Although designed for attorneys, most definitions are written in language that can be understood by laypeople. In addition to defining more than 1,100 terms and phrases, the list of nearly 300 acronyms and abbreviations is particularly helpful because of the frequency with which short terms are used in the government contracts field.

The definitions typically range from 75 to 150 words in length, and most entries cite other documents (e.g., *Federal Acquisition Regulations*) as their source. Cross-references to terms found elsewhere in the book are common, and some entries make reference to the United States Code, court decisions, and Board of Contract Appeals Decisions, as well as to secondary sources such as dictionaries, journal articles, and treaties.

Although *Keyes Encyclopedic Dictionary of Contract and Procurement Law* by Noel Keyes (Oceana, 1980) is more comprehensive, its higher price may make it less attractive for many consumers. For the price, *The Government Contracts Reference Book* has to be considered a "Best Buy," and it is recommended for all law libraries and large academic and public libraries.—**James S. Heller**

581. **West's Tax Law Dictionary: Definitions of Terms, Words, and Phrases Used in Modern American Tax Law.** 1992 ed. By Robert Sellers Smith. St. Paul, Minn., West Publishing, 1992. 798p. index. $33.00pa. ISBN 0-314-00560-9.

This work is a user-friendly aid for the professional or taxpayer seeking assistance in unraveling the tangled skein of modern U.S. federal tax terminology. If regularly updated, it should become a standard tool in the field. After a brief (but interesting) preface, Smith provides 628 pages of definitions, from *abusive tax shelters* through *zero bracket amount* and *zinc sulfate*. Each entry includes references to the Internal Revenue Code of 1986 and Interpreting Treasury Regulations (where appropriate) in existence at the beginning of the 102d Congress, 1991. Entries range in length from a brief sentence (e.g., *receipts for payment of tax*) to half a page for more complex phrases (e.g., *qualified preretirement survivor annuity*). Under the names of the states, the appropriate state government addresses are supplied for inquiries about state tax provisions. No references to cases are given, but there are *see* and *see also* references.

Addresses for sources of free Internal Revenue Service publications and forms are provided in one appendix. Others list federal tax (and related) forms, federal tax form instructions, and free federal tax publications, all in numerical order. Indexes of publications and forms provide the numbers. A helpful addition is a "margin index" that serves the same function as lettered tabs. The typeface is easy to read and nicely laid out. Headers indicate first and last entries on each page pair.

In sum, the publication seems well thought out and efficiently executed. It merits strong consideration by individual professionals as well as libraries and information centers with relevant client interests. — **Nigel Tappin**

Directories

582. **BNA's Directory of State and Federal Courts, Judges, and Clerks: A State-by-State and Federal Listing.** 4th ed. Compiled by Kamla J. King and Judith Springberg with the BNA Library Staff. Washington, D.C., BNA Books, 1992. 497p. index. $85.00pa. KF8700.A19K56. 347.73'3'25. LC 92-18961. ISBN 0-87179-758-5.

Those who have business with the court system need a convenient source of contact information. This directory has expanded its coverage to include appellate and general jurisdiction federal courts as well as state and territorial ones. There are charts for the federal and state systems that list each court structure, jurisdiction, and path of appeal. For every court there are a summary of geographic jurisdiction (generally counties) and the names, addresses, and telephone numbers of court clerks and judges. There are also personal name and geographic jurisdiction indexes and lists of chief federal and state court administrators. A very useful and unusual feature of this directory is that it includes fax numbers where available. There is also a list of the new electronic and voice information and filing services that are increasingly available in many court systems.

If biographical information about judges is needed, a source such as *The American Bench* would need to be consulted. Such works as the *Judicial Staff Directory* (see ARBA 91, entry 576) give more detailed information on the staffing of federal courts. The *National Directory of Courts of Law* gives the names and addresses of courts down to county and some municipal courts, but it does not supply personal names of clerks or judges. *Want's Federal-State Court Directory* (see ARBA 91, entry 582) and *Directory of State Court Clerks & County Courthouses* (see ARBA 91, entry 574) together have similar information to that in *BNA's Directory*, but they do not include names of judges and clerks at all levels.

This work gives more complete information in one source than its competitors if what is needed are federal and state court listings with clerks' and judges' names, addresses, and telephone and fax numbers. It should be in the reference collection of general collection and law libraries.

— **Marit S. MacArthur**

583. **Canada Legal Directory 1992.** 82d ed. Georganne Burke, ed. Scarborough, Ont., Carswell, 1992. 1v. (various paging). index. $105.00.

This directory of lawyers, law firms, and related institutions has been published annually since 1911. Its rival, *The Canadian Law List* (Canada Law Book, annual), commenced publication in 1883.

The volume is divided into three major sections and four minor ones. The main listing of firms and lawyers is arranged by city and firm. This is supplemented by a list of lawyers by surname, with references to city and partnership. The third principal section is a directory of courts and judges, law societies and associations, law schools, and government agencies organized by jurisdiction (federal, provincial, and territorial). The other sections include advertisers and nonlegal associations, "professional cards" of Canadian lawyers and international law firms, and in-house counsel. Access is provided by a detailed table of contents, a general index by topic, and section indexes. This is a high-quality, professionally produced tool that—along with its rival—should be considered for general and specialized collections with the relevant client interest in Canadian legal affairs.—**Nigel Tappin**

584. **Law Firms Yellow Book: Who's Who in the Management of the Leading U.S. Law Firms. Vol.II, No.1.** Alice K. Thompson and others, eds. New York, Monitor Publishing, 1992. 941p. index. $160.00 (2 issues). ISSN 1054-4054.

This title is a directory of managers in law firms, including both attorneys and other administrators. It purports to cover the largest firms that practice general corporate law; it includes both United States and foreign firms, although international coverage is skimpy (eight Canadian firms are listed). This edition covers 659 U.S. firms. Information given for each includes address, number of attorneys, committee chairs, chairpersons or contact persons in departments, names of various administrative personnel, and branch offices. Law school name and graduation date are given for each attorney listed; telephone numbers are given for everyone. Indexes provide access by law school, management, administrators, geographic location, personnel, and firms, subsidiaries, and affiliates. There is also an index by department, such as bankruptcy, equine law, or workers' compensation.

This work seems to be of limited usefulness because of its inadequate coverage of law firms compared to more inclusive directories such as the *Martindale-Hubbell Law Directory* (see ARBA 91, entry 581). It lists managers rather than prominent legal practitioners in specialized areas, and because it lists firms that practice general corporate law, it is not very useful for finding firms with particular specialties. For this a better source would be the *Law & Business* directories (see ARBA 91, entries 577-579). Perhaps this work would be useful to new attorneys seeking contacts with hiring authority from their own law schools and for those interested in marketing their products to large law firms. [R: LJ, 1 June 92, p. 112]

—**Marit S. MacArthur**

585. **Tennessee Attorneys Directory, 1992.** Joseph L. White, Mary K. Weber, and Deborah Brannan, eds. Nashville, Tenn., M. Lee Smith, 1991. 1v. (various paging). $42.00 looseleaf w/binder.

When matters turn litigious, Tennesseans will want to turn to this source first. More than 9,000 attorneys are listed. Similar to *Tennessee Government Officials Directory* (M. Lee Smith, 1991), the work has an alphabetical attorney list, a section on law firms, a geographic section, federal and state court judges, paralegals, legal secretaries, and a "Buyer's Guide" (complete down to its "yellow pages"). The sections are separated by tab-dividers.

One cannot imagine a more comprehensive guide than this. All Tennessee libraries, law libraries, and legal entities will want it. Reference librarians in Tennessee will discover that legal questions about individuals in the profession or types of services offered by law firms will usually be answered by this directory.—**Mark Y. Herring**

586. Yannone, Mark J. A., comp. **The National Directory of Courts of Law 1991.** Arlington, Va., Information Resources Press, 1991. 888p. $90.00. ISBN 0-87815-060-9. ISSN 1054-9471.

This new directory aims to list nearly every United States court in one place. It is organized in four parts: federal courts (from the Supreme Court to special courts such as the Court of International Trade), state courts (from each state's highest appellate court to local courts), territorial courts (from American Samoa to the Virgin Islands), and Indian tribal courts (from the Absentee Shawnees to the Zunis). Entries include the court's name, address, and central telephone number.

The *National Directory of Courts of Law* (NDCL) offers both less and more than other court directories. Not included are the names and telephone numbers of the clerk of court and the judges. That information is found in *BNA's Directory of State Courts, Judges and Clerks* (see ARBA 89, entry 511), as is a chart of each state's court structure and, occasionally, the court's fax number. The BNA directory does not include as many lower state court listings as the NDCL, however. A lesser competitor to the NDCL is *Want's Federal-State Court Directory* (see ARBA 91, entry 582). Although the Want directory is quite comprehensive in listing federal courts and their officers, its state court section is less a directory than a description of the state's court organization. Other state court directories include *Directory of State Court Clerks and County Courthouses* (see ARBA 91, entry 574) and the *County Courthouse Book* (see ARBA 91, entry 584). If a comprehensive directory of federal courts and their officers is desired, the best bet is the semiannual *United States Court Directory* (Administrative Office of the United States Courts). It is free to federal depository libraries.

The definitive court directory does not exist. For comprehensive (yet basic) listings, the NDCL cannot be beat; 445 federal, 19,334 state and local, 122 territorial, and 229 Indian tribal courts are listed. However, the reader who wants more than merely the name, address, and telephone number of the court will have to use one of the other directories.—**James S. Heller**

Handbooks and Yearbooks

587. Auger, C. P., ed. **Information Sources in Patents.** Munich, New Providence, N.J., K. G. Saur, 1992. 187p. index. (Guides to Information Sources). $75.00. ISBN 0-86291-906-1.

Intended for researchers in any discipline who make use of patent literature, this small book purports to give "detailed coverage of the available sources of worldwide patent literature." Separate chapters are devoted to the European patent, patents in the United States, and patents in the United Kingdom. While it is not surprising that a book published in Europe would devote more space to patents from the United Kingdom and Europe and less to United States patents, the coverage for the rest of the world is even slighter, with Germany, Japan, and Australia having one page each, and with Canada not covered at all. (Canada is mentioned only when the work mentions licensing pharmaceuticals.)

The United States has one of the largest and most important patent systems in the world, so it is somewhat unusual that the section on that country does not list or mention the 80-plus U.S. Patent and Trademark depository libraries. Also, the search tools are listed without discussion or any real comment. However, a small example of the classification system used in the United Kingdom that is also used under the Patent Cooperation Treaty (PCT) is reproduced, as is a map showing the location of patent libraries in the United Kingdom.

Online searching is given cursory treatment. The important concept of searching for patent equivalents in patent families is covered in only five paragraphs. At the end of this section is a short list of patent files on DIALOG, ORBIT, STN, Questel, and Data-Star. Interestingly, LEXIS/NEXIS, a fulltext U.S. file, is not listed; however, the file Spacepatents, produced from 1984 to 1990 and no longer updated, is mentioned.

This work is too expensive to be purchased by most libraries, especially when there are better sources for this type of information—*Patents throughout the World* (Trade Activities, 1978-) and a book of interest to more than chemists, *Patents for Chemists* by Philip W. Grubb (Oxford University Press, 1982). Both cover worldwide patents in more detail.—**Susan B. Ardis**

588. Biskupic, Joan. **The Supreme Court Yearbook 1990-1991.** Washington, D.C., Congressional Quarterly, 1992. 273p. illus. index. $27.95; $16.95pa. ISBN 0-87187-637-X; 0-87187-638-8pa. ISSN 1054-2701.

The 1990-1991 *Supreme Court Yearbook* is the second to appear in this new annual series. While each yearbook can stand alone, the series is designed to update *Congressional Quarterly's Guide to the U.S. Supreme Court*, 2d edition (see ARBA 91, entry 746). There are six chapters in this volume, beginning with a brief overview of the Clarence Thomas nomination. These are followed by summaries of major cases heard by the Court; summaries of all signed opinions, arranged alphabetically by subject;

excerpts from major cases; a preview of cases to be heard during the 1991-1992 term; and a detailed description of the inner workings of the Court. (This final section appears in each yearbook.) The excerpted cases account for one-third of the volume's length.

Appendixes include brief biographies of the justices, a glossary of legal terms, and the text of the U.S. Constitution. More readable type and photographs improve the book's overall appearance. It is also well bound and will stand up to heavy reference use. Geared to nonlawyers, this moderately priced reference will be useful in all academic, high school, and public libraries. — **Gary D. Barber**

589. Canter, Laurence A., and Martha S. Siegel. **The Insider's Guide to Successful U.S. Immigration: Discover How to Make the New Immigration Act Work for You.** New York, HarperPerennial/HarperCollins, 1992. 281p. index. $30.00; $15.00pa. KF4819.6.C36. 342.73'082. LC 92-9238. ISBN 0-06-271558-5; 0-06-273166-1pa.

Siegel and Canter have produced another edition of their 1990 classic, *U.S. Immigration Made Easy* (Sheridan Chandler). The nearest thing to competition that the authors have comes from *Immigration Made Simple* (see ARBA 91, entry 780). That work does indeed challenge this one, but it cannot stand up to *U.S. Immigration Made Easy*. Neither does the new edition.

In a comparison of the two Siegel and Canter works, it can be seen that what may once have been a research theme enhanced by the fruit of experience and a bent for the compendious has been replaced with a large-print manual of dubious thoroughness. The 1990 book is exhaustive. It contains, for example, 103 pages of forms. The 1992 book adheres more strictly to the one-chapter/one-kind-of-visa formula and has only 57 pages of forms. However, neither its brevity nor its emendations significantly enhance the text. The passages taken from the 1990 text are generally reprinted verbatim, and the authors rarely add more than an admonition to check with the nearest office if one thinks one may be an exception. Moreover, it is not clear why only portions of the 1990 book have been selected for reprinting. Perhaps the reason is that the law (and precedents based on it) has evolved, although the authors did not give this as an explanation. The 1992 volume could be made more useful with the addition of legislative histories, even anecdotal information on the order of, "Yes, you did this legally in 1989, but it cannot be done legally now." However, if one has never seen the 1990 volume, the present one is quite satisfactory. — **Judith M. Brugger**

590. Dworsky, Alan L. **User's Guide to the** *Bluebook***.** Littleton, Colo., Fred B. Rothman, 1991. 54p. $5.50pa. KF245.D853. 348.73'47. LC 91-31634. ISBN 0-8377-0558-4.

This is the perfect reference tool for the legal professional who is a novice in legal writing. The guide explains the basic rules needed for writing memoranda and briefs and is meant to be used in conjunction with the *Bluebook*. It provides a discussion of the rules, distinguishing between some of the finer points of citation and pointing out significant exceptions. It covers how to cite cases, statutes, and other commonly cited sources, such as law review articles, administrative rules and regulations, rules of procedure and evidence, and restatements. It is a wonderful complement to the *Bluebook* and makes it user-friendly. — **Jacqueline L. Grossman**

591. Eis, Arlene L., comp. and ed. **The Legal Researcher's Desk Reference 1992.** Teaneck, N.J., Infosources, 1991. 406p. maps. $50.00pa. ISBN 0-939486-21-0. ISSN 1050-3056.

The Legal Researcher's Desk Reference is one of the best legal research tools on the market. It provides quick access to information on the federal government, legislation, states, foreign countries, law library suppliers, associations and organizations, law librarianship, law schools in the United States and Canada, bar admissions, legal periodicals, and finances and economics. The information for the federal government includes such things as the Declaration of Independence, the Constitution, addresses for all major agencies and departments, lists of senate and house committees, and names of all judicial circuits and federal judges. State information includes governors and their addresses, attorneys general, banking authorities, secretaries of state, chief justices, court structure charts, and the death penalty and the states. Under legal periodicals are lists of all legal periodicals indexed in current law indexes and of legal newspapers in the United States. Other sections provide information on used law book dealers; U.S. government bookstores; state bar associations; law schools approved by the ABA (as well as those not approved); countries of the world and their capitals, currencies, and official languages; and a list of state codes, reporters, regulations, and registers. The information is current, timely, well organized, and attractively presented. This tool will be used often by anyone who does legal research and reference work.—**Michael A. Foley**

592. Grant, Todd W. **Resources for Research in Legal Ethics.** Buffalo, N.Y., William S. Hein, 1992. 50p. (Legal Research Guides, v.13). $35.00. KF306.G73. 174'.3'072073. LC 92-20434. ISBN 0-89941-802-3.

Hein's Legal Research Guides will be familiar to most librarians. The other guides cover such timely topics as teenage pregnancy, surrogate motherhood, and women in sports. Grant's guide provides quick and easy research strategies for practicing attorneys making their way through the complex underbrush of the legal jungle. In this case, the subject is legal ethics (perhaps the reason for the tenuity of size?); the courses covered are hiring decisions, advertising, mergers, handling of clients and funds, bar codes and disciplinary action, malpractice, and much more. Each section begins with a bibliographic essay and ends with selected sources that are thoroughly abstracted. Although designed to help practicing attorneys, the volume is a definite aid in selecting materials for reference and general collections, and it will also guide the reference librarian in helping patrons with legal questions. The book should be in most libraries.—**Mark Y. Herring**

593. Greene, Thurston. **The Language of the Constitution: A Sourcebook and Guide to the Ideas, Terms, and Vocabulary Used by the Framers of the United States Constitution.** Westport, Conn., Greenwood Press, 1991. 1045p. index. $99.50. KF4548.5.G74. 342.73'02'014. LC 91-29197. ISBN 0-313-28202-1.

Eighty-five selected words and phrases from the U.S. Constitution and Bill of Rights have been arranged alphabetically and presented with extracts from other documents and writings that contain the word or phrase and to which the founding fathers would have had access. Prominent among these sources are state constitutions; colonial charters; grants and ordinances; and political writings such as *The Federalist*, "Brutus," "Fabius," and "The Federal Farmer." Some of these sources were already in electronic form; others were scanned optically and added to the database from which this book was created. The relevant extracts were then identified by searching each word or phrase in the database. Each extract is referenced to a source that contains the full text of the document or writing. Included as an appendix is the 1872 concordance to the Constitution by Charles W. Stearns. There is also a subject/source index.

While it is useful to the historian to have gathered in one place other instances of these words and phrases, Greene is perhaps claiming too much when he asserts that these extracts will illuminate their meanings as the founding fathers understood them. For example, repeated usages of the terms "arms" and "bearing arms" do not bring us much closer to knowing exactly what was meant by the term in Article II of the Bill of Rights, let alone what the right to bear arms was intended to encompass. What this book provides are examples of usage, not definitions, but it does this very well and will be of value to students and scholars.—**Jack Ray**

594. King, Martha P. **Maternal and Child Health Legislation: 1991.** Denver, Colo., National Conference of State Legislatures, 1991. 87p. $15.00 spiralbound. ISBN 1-55516-696-2.

This guide summarizes 350 laws related to maternal and child health that were enacted in the 50 states, the District of Columbia, and Puerto Rico in late 1990 and 1991. The laws are arranged alphabetically by jurisdiction under headings such as access (to health care), financing, insurance, Medicaid, minority health, nutrition, and special health care needs. Laws appear under more than one heading when necessary. Summaries are succinct, clearly written, and informative. Key words are underlined to aid users in identifying specific issues of interest. This will be a useful resource for health planners, legislators and their staffs, maternal and child health advocates, and others in the legal and health care fields. Recommended.—**Gari-Anne Patzwald**

595. **The Legal Assistant's Notebook: A Reference Guide for California Courts (Including Independent Calendaring and Fast Track).** Sandra L. Quarles, ed. San Diego, Calif., ASAP, 1991. 1v. (various paging). $85.00 looseleaf w/binder. ISBN 0-9629697-4-5.

Updated quarterly, this is a practical handbook for attorneys, legal assistants, and legal secretaries who must find their way through the complicated maze of rules that govern the filing of documents in federal and state courts. The *Notebook* covers the U.S. Supreme Court and those branches of other federal courts that sit in southern California. The California Supreme Court, the Second and Fourth Appellate Districts of the California Court of Appeal, and the Superior and Municipal courts in southern California are also covered. Information on filing fees, pleading form requirements, timetables for filing documents, court venues, citation formats, tables of civil statutes of limitations, and calendaring guidelines is set out in clear tables. Citations to the applicable rules are included. A handy index of courts in California cities lists which superior and municipal courts sit in the city and also gives the county where the city is located. The table of citations covers the bluebook citation for commonly cited reporters as well as frequently used abbreviations. This handbook is recommended for southern California law libraries, both public and private.—**Jacqueline L. Grossman**

596. Shimpock-Vieweg, Kathy, and Marianne Sidorski Alcorn. **Arizona Legal Research Guide.** Buffalo, N.Y., William S. Hein, 1992. 330p. $38.50. KFA2475.S55. 340'.0720791. LC 91-40052. ISBN 0-89941-784-1.

This research guide will prove indispensable to all libraries in Arizona, whether they have legal collections or not. Any library with patrons who might pose legal questions will want to have this book handy, although it is far more suited to the needs of experienced legal researchers. The guide does an exemplary job of directing the user to the best and most efficient resources available for particular types of information. The material is meticulously explained and carefully laid out for optimum utility and readability. It is written by known experts in the field, a fact reflected by the overall quality of the book. The only shortcoming is one that is common for works of this sort: there is a need for a topical, issue-oriented guide to legal research. Additionally, an index would be helpful, as would a description of the information production/publishing industry in Arizona. Overall, this outstanding research guide is highly recommended for all Arizona libraries and out-of-state ones with strong interests in Arizona research.—**Richard A. Leiter**

597. Stelbecker-Pountney, Barbro E., ed. **The Legal Desk Book 1992: Being a Compendium of Information Useful to the Practice of Law in Ontario.** Scarborough, Ont., Carswell, 1991. 663p. index. $108.00pa. ISBN 0-459-36303-4.

This is an annual handbook of addresses, legal facts, general information, and materials useful to those involved in legal practice or related activities in Ontario. The work begins with a brief overview of legal research and sources of information, followed by lists of law libraries, legal publishers, and online databases. It then provides a synopsis of the federal and Ontario court structure, a directory of judges and court officers, a guide on where to obtain unreported court judgments, and a 250-page table of statutory limitation periods. An added feature is a list of miscellaneous municipal fees that relate to real estate transactions. Other sections include the legal profession in Ontario and entry requirements; a directory of federal, Ontario, and municipal governments; directories of information sources and referrals on business, family, and criminal law and on real estate and litigation; abbreviations; and legal etiquette. Access is enhanced by a detailed table of contents, a brief general index, and a marginal index. The cutoff date for the 1992 edition was November 1991. In addition to its primary audience in the Ontario legal community, this well-designed tool should be considered by libraries and information centers.—**Nigel Tappin**

Indexes

598. **Canadian Law Symposia Index.** J. McRee Elrod, comp. Victoria, B.C., Special Libraries Cataloguing, 1991. 1v. (various paging). $225.00 spiralbound. 016.34'00971. ISBN 1-895024-10-2.

The *Canadian Law Symposium Index* provides a list of symposia papers with Canadian content or held in Canada after January 1, 1990. (The material is available in semiannual cumulations contained in looseleaf binders.) The work contains three parts. First, an author index lists the speakers, along with the title of the paper, symposium name, publisher abbreviation, and year. Second, a title index presents the symposia papers by their titles and subtitles. Third, a subject/keyword index arranges symposia under Library of Congress headings and symposia and papers under keyword. The most useful part of this work is undoubtedly the latter section. If there is a specific topic to research, this is the place to begin, for every listing can be found in these subdivisions. For example, in the list of symposia there is a citation for "ERISA Aspects of Soft Dollar Arrangements." Under "ERISA" in the subject/keyword index there are not only that symposia piece but four additional entries relevant to ERISA as well. Some sections, however, are so all-encompassing that it might help to search specific symposia first. For example, under "Family Law" in the subject/word index, it will take some time to locate "Family Law and Estate Planning," but there is a separate listing for it in the symposia index. For anyone needing information about recent Canadian law or in areas that relate to Canadian law, such as United States commerce activities, this is the index to use. It is comprehensive and incredibly easy to use.

—**Michael A. Foley**

599. **Hein's Cumulative Index to Interim Precedent Decisions of the Board of Immigration Appeals: August 1940-March 1991.** Buffalo, N.Y., William S. Hein, 1992. 389p. $75.00. KF4812.7.H45. 342.73'082. LC 92-20058. ISBN 0-89941-801-5.

This subject index is likely to be useful to, and usable by, only those who are extremely well versed in immigration law. There are many subheadings within general headings that are alphabetically arranged by nondescript words, such as "applicability," "by," and "no"; other subheadings are arranged by statute section. Clearly, a lot of scanning will be necessary, even for experts. There are numerous *see* and *see also* references, but it is perplexing that some *see* references are followed by citations, while some *see also* references have none. Under marriage the subheading "divorce" has a *see* reference to divorce as a primary index entry, but the running head "divorce" continues for four more pages over the subheadings for marriage. Recommended only for the thoroughly initiated, particularly those who have the decisions that are indexed. —**Jack Ray**

600. **Index to Legal Periodicals: September 1990-August 1991.** Stephen Rosen and Joy London, eds. Bronx, N.Y., H. W. Wilson, 1991. 886p. $220.00. LC 41-21689. ISSN 0019-4077.

Once, purchasing an index on a specific subject area or type of material was a simple matter because there was only one real choice. Now there are often several choices and different index formats. This index, which began in 1926, continues to be a basic source in the field of law. But it now has formidable, and in many ways superior, competition in the *Current Law Index* (CLI) (see ARBA 88, entry 582) and its even more comprehensive CD-ROM version, *LegalTrac*.

Unlike CLI, the *Index to Legal Periodicals* (ILP) includes fewer titles, covering exclusively legal periodicals that the editors consider to regularly publish legal articles of high quality and permanent reference value. In addition, student contributions, articles shorter than five pages, and such features as case notes and bibliographies that are shorter than two pages are not indexed. The ILP uses its own subject headings, which tend to be rather general and infrequently subdivided. The Library of Congress subject headings in CLI are much more specific, so that one can find entries such as "Pit Bull Terriers" or "Golden Parachute Payments"; in ILP one must look under "Animals" or "Corporate Acquisitions and Mergers."

In addition to these time-consuming limitations, the ILP has failed to incorporate other time- or effort-saving features found in CLI. The subject and author index entries give only an abbreviation of the periodical title; a separate list must be consulted to find the full title. There are no annotations or explanatory notes for cryptic article titles (as are found in CLI). The index of book reviews gives no indication of whether the review is positive or negative, and the case table does not give any notes about the subject matter of the case. The preface gives less specific information than that of its competitor, which may work to its detriment. For instance, CLI says its case table is very selective. The case table of ILP appears to be more complete, but the preface is silent as to its scope.

Law is a very distinctive discipline, one whose practitioners have their own needs, preferences, and vocabulary. A library whose subject area is exclusively law may have patrons who prefer ILP's selectivity and familiar terminology. A general library may favor CLI's greater coverage and ease of use, particularly for users familiar with Library of Congress subject headings or for those who are not legal specialists. A law library of any size should contain both indexes.—**Marit S. MacArthur**

601. **Index to Legal Periodicals.** (Indexing coverage: 8/81-8/27/92). [CD-ROM]. Bronx, N.Y., H. W. Wilson, 1992. Hardware requirements: WILSONLINE Workstation, IBM PC, or compatible; 640K; hard disk drive. $1,495.00.

The print version of the *Index of Legal Periodicals* has long been a standard reference source in the field of law. This CD-ROM version offers better and quicker access to the same information. Currently it indexes more than 570 legal journals, yearbooks, law reviews, and the like published in English-speaking countries. Coverage for the CD-ROM version begins with August 1981 and is updated monthly. Its chief CD-ROM competitor, LegalTrac, begins with 1980, is also updated monthly, and indexes 800-plus legal publications and selected law-related articles from more than 1,000 other business and general-interest publications. However, LegalTrac costs more than twice as much as the Index of Legal Periodicals.

Searching software used on all WILSONDISC CD-ROMs offers three separate and increasingly sophisticated searching modes. BROWSE mode allows the user to search subjects, authors, case names, and statutes simply by typing in a word or citation; the software will find the closest match. If a valid subject term is located, a prompt to hit a key to view *see also* references appears. BROWSE mode is easy but allows only one search at a time for a term or a citation, thus abandoning a major advantage of CD-ROM over print indexes. Its usefulness is also severely limited by the same overly general subject headings used in the print version. If a specific term is searched, such as pit bull terriers, the program goes through all the references under "animals," which also cover such things as genetic engineering and animal experimentation. With a popular topic such as corporate acquisitions and mergers, more than 1,000 unsubdivided entries may be listed. LegalTrac's Library of Congress subject headings and subdivisions offer much better and more specific access by controlled vocabulary descriptors.

The WILSEARCH mode is much more useful than BROWSE and will be preferred by most users. A user-friendly fill-in-the-blanks screen allows the input of multiple terms, using Boolean logic terms. Terms indexed include subject words, personal names, journal titles, title words, and organizations. The software translates a search into WILSONLINE command language and displays it on screen, which could be helpful to those who want to learn it.

The WILSONLINE mode provides the most specific and powerful search mode for those who are willing to learn its command language. Searches executed in WILSEARCH and WILSONLINE modes on this CD-ROM index can also be re-executed online in WILSONLINE to get the most current references if this option has been chosen and a computer has been set up accordingly.

The installation procedure for the WILSONDISC software is easy, and it does not require unusual hardware. During setup a file of journals held can be created so ownership information will show when records are printed or displayed.

CD-ROM indexes are definitely superior to their print versions in power and ease of use, if their time coverage limitations and higher prices are acceptable. Libraries with a high interest in law may prefer LegalTrac for its wider coverage and superior subject access. But the Index of Legal Periodicals has the advantages of a lower price and the long-standing reputation of its print version. It is also easy to learn and use in some modes, and it uses the same familiar software as other Wilson CD-ROM indexes, such as MLA International Bibliography and Social Sciences Index.—**Marit S. MacArthur**

CRIMINOLOGY

602. Beirne, Piers, and Joan Hill, comps. **Comparative Criminology: An Annotated Bibliography.** Westport, Conn., Greenwood Press, 1991. 144p. index. (Research and Bibliographical Guides in Criminal Justice, no.3). $42.95. Z5703.B44. 016.364. LC 91-27306. ISBN 0-313-26572-0.

Beirne and Hill have prepared a very useful annotated bibliography for those pursuing studies and research in comparative criminology. The bibliography contains three parts: "Meaning and Measurement in Comparative Criminology," "Cross-National Crime Rates," and "Social Control and Criminal Justice." Each part is then subdivided into chapters. In part 1 are found chapters that address general issues in comparative criminology, cross-national data, and perceptions of crime. Part 2 deals with violent crime, crimes against property, economic and political crime, and correlates of crime (age, class, gender, and race). Part 3 covers social control, dispute resolution, and criminal justice and penal policies. The book is made additionally useful by the presence of author and subject indexes. Appendixes include lists of countries in cross-national data sets, addresses of United Nations Regional Institutes for Crime Prevention, and miscellaneous research aids. The compilers are quite consistent in that all cited works involve two or more cultures. The works were, for the most part, published after 1960, and the majority of the publications appeared after 1970. Finally, the bibliography contains works originally published in English.

Overall, this bibliography will prove quite useful. The coverage is good, and the annotations are clear and direct. For research into works in comparative criminology, this is one of the best places to begin the search. [R: Choice, Apr 92, p. 1204] — **Michael A. Foley**

603. Bentley, William K., and James M. Corbett. **Prison Slang: Words and Expressions Depicting Life behind Bars.** Jefferson, N.C., McFarland, 1992. 120p. index. $25.95. LC 91-52763. ISBN 0-89950-646-1.

The rapid growth of the prison population makes this dictionary of prison slang used by inmates particularly timely. The terms are arranged alphabetically in categories related to various aspects of the prison experience (e.g., serving time, inmates, sexuality, drugs and alcohol). The definitions are well written and informative.

The authors, themselves ex-prisoners, recognize that language is not static and that the constant changes in prison language make it impossible to be completely up-to-date. Prison language is also regional, and some regional terms and variations are not included. For example, in some states the term *seg* (segregation) is used for what the authors call *adjustment center* or *sol*, and *fish* may be used not only for a new inmate, as the authors indicate, but also for a new prison employee. However, given the need for a resource of this kind, this flaw is minor. The work will be an essential resource for personnel in corrections, criminal justice, and law as well as a useful tool for journalists, etymologists, fiction writers, and anyone seeking a better understanding of prison life. [R: Choice, Nov 92, p. 437; RBB, 1 June 92, p. 1778; RQ, Fall 92, pp. 121-22; WLB, June 92, p. 116] — **Gari-Anne Patzwald**

604. Birkenhead, Frederick Edwin Smith, Earl of. **Famous Trials.** London, Hutchinson, 1926; repr., Littleton, Colo., Fred B. Rothman, 1991. 567p. illus. $45.00. KD370.B57. 345.41'05. LC 91-18551. ISBN 0-8377-1906-2.

The author of this book was Lord Chancellor of England from 1919 to 1922. A lawyer by profession, he was clearly a talented writer as well. The present volume combines two works that were originally published separately and contains accounts of varying length of some 50 famous trials. Some of these trials are historically well known, including those of Mary, Queen of Scots; Charles I; Marie Antoinette; Joan of Arc; Francis Bacon; Captain Kidd; and Roger Casement. Most of the other trials are English cases that typically involved prominent political figures, notorious murderers, professional criminals, or embezzlers. The author writes in a florid style that will strike many contemporary readers as old-fashioned. The accounts are nevertheless entertaining and reasonably informative on some of the historical circumstances involved in these trials, as well as the principal legal issues.

Since the original publication of this volume, numerous books and articles (both scholarly and popularly oriented) have examined these famous trials. It is likely that this work will be of interest to only a small number of contemporary scholars and readers. It should be considered a low-priority acquisition for law libraries and criminal justice collections. — **David O. Friedrichs**

605. Flynn, Robert A. **The Borden Murders: An Annotated Bibliography.** Portland, Maine, King Philip Publishing, 1992. 113p. illus. index. $19.95. LC 91-075384. ISBN 0-9614811-3-7.

Lizzie Borden's parents were murdered with an axe in 1892; in a sensational trial, Lizzie was accused of the crime. Since that time, journalists and writers from many disciplines have debated the results of the trial. Flynn has collected books and articles about the case for many years and has reprinted several rare items about it; now he has compiled this bibliography to mark the centennial anniversary of the murders.

The book cites most of the known writings on the subject, including references in encyclopedias, songs, stories, and plays. Items appear alphabetically by author under 10 categories: books, articles, reference works, miscellaneous (including the official trial transcript), novels, short stories, plays, operas/ballets, poetry, and music. Listings include author's name, title, source or publisher, and date of publication. Brief notes about each title highlight the viewpoint or focus of its author. Flynn does not hesitate to give his opinion of the value and accuracy of titles included. He also features the story of a "bibliographical ghost," a history of the Borden murders that appeared in *Books in Print* but apparently was never published. A brief index to names and magazine titles completes the bibliography. Borden researchers will welcome this compilation because it draws together hard-to-find material from the last 100 years.—**Berniece M. Owen**

606. Gladstone, Jane, Richard V. Ericson, and Clifford D. Shearing, eds. **Criminology: A Reader's Guide.** Toronto, Centre of Criminology, University of Toronto, 1991. 275p. $17.95pa. 364. ISBN 0-919584-67-5.

In recent years some of the most interesting criminological scholarship and research has been produced in Canada. This work, however, has not received the attention it merits from those in the United States. The Centre of Criminology at the University of Toronto is one of the major contributors to the Canadian criminological enterprise. The Centre is especially committed to an "institutional" approach to crime and criminal justice, which seeks to identify decision making, organizational, and institutional mechanisms that contribute to social order and disorder.

The present volume contains essays by 10 of the leading scholars associated with the Toronto Centre. These essays focus on such topics as historical developments in British and Canadian policing and criminal justice, penology, relations between politics and crime, narcotics law, formal charters, the mentally ill in the criminal justice system, juvenile justice, and the feminist perspective in criminology. Each author attempts to briefly identify some of the principal themes of the literature on the assigned topic, with particular emphasis on recent trends or scholarship. A fairly extensive list of readings, annotated in most cases, is appended to each essay.

Criminology certainly has the potential to serve as a point of departure for further investigation of the topics covered. Less advanced students will find most of the included essays quite accessible. The institutional perspective promoted here persuasively responds to some of the limitations of alternative criminological perspectives. There is no index, but this is a relatively minor inconvenience given the clearly focused nature of the essays.—**David O. Friedrichs**

607. Lambert, Jean L. F., comp. **International Illustrated Vocabulary of English-French Fingerprint Terminology with a Short Index in Six Languages (Serbian, Japanese, Dutch, Italian, Spanish, German).** Ottawa, Canada Communication Group; distr., Portland, Oreg., ISBS, 1991. 1v. (various paging). index. $59.95pa.; $71.95pa. (U.S.). 363.258. ISBN 0-660-56562-5.

Fingerprint analysis continues to be a significant investigatory tool for police agencies, although new techniques (e.g., DNA analysis) have also been introduced to replace or supplement this form of identification. This volume is principally a massive list of fingerprint terminology in English and French. It also includes a short index of this terminology in a number of other languages (those shown in the title), which are incorporated into the listing where appropriate. The Solicitor General of Canada was a major sponsor of this project, which is part of a larger effort to address problems of communication in a bilingual nation. A brief chronology of fingerprinting, a bibliography, and a number of illustrations are included.

This volume will be used primarily, if not exclusively, by police personnel directly involved in fingerprint identification and as a resource to assist in translation of relevant documents from English to French or from French to English (with some usefulness for the other languages mentioned as well). Only libraries that directly serve police investigative personnel should consider obtaining it.

—David O. Friedrichs

608. Nash, Jay Robert. **Dictionary of Crime: Criminal Justice, Criminology, & Law Enforcement.** New York, Paragon House, 1992. 433p. $39.95. HV6017.E5425. 364'.03. LC 91-38107. ISBN 1-55778-509-0.

609. Nash, Jay Robert. **Encyclopedia of Western Lawmen & Outlaws.** New York, Paragon House, 1992. 571p. illus. index. $49.95. F591.N38. 978'.00992. LC 91-46116. ISBN 1-55778-507-4.

610. Nash, Jay Robert. **World Encyclopedia of Organized Crime.** New York, Paragon House, 1992. 624p. illus. index. $49.95. HV6017.E54. 364'.03. LC 91-40697. ISBN 1-55778-508-2.

611. Nash, Jay Robert. **World Encyclopedia of 20th Century Murder.** New York, Paragon House, 1992. 693p. illus. index. $49.95. HV6515.E5325. 364'.03. LC 91-40492. ISBN 1-55778-506-6.

These works are genre extractions made by Paragon House from Nash's six-volume *Encyclopedia of World Crime* (see ARBA 92, entry 552). The intent is to appeal to all buyers, from libraries with large criminal justice collections to the individual fan of crime literature. Nash is first and foremost a crime reporter; he does not attempt to study his subjects from any scholarly footing.

To compile *Dictionary of Crime*, Nash culled entries from more than 50 general sources and from his private archives. The reader will find a profusion of slang, drug lingo, law enforcement terminology, and legal language that is among the most colorful speech anywhere. When known, the entries are dated to establish a time period of usage. Most entries are brief.

The entries in *Encyclopedia of Western Lawmen & Outlaws* are identical with those in the parent set up to the supplemental sections. The first two of these sections, "Western Lawmen" and "Western Outlaws and Gunmen," are favorites of Nash but of little value, as they contain alphabetical listings of meager information. For example, the entry "Allen, Frank, a gunman, was shot and killed in El Paso, Texas, in March 1881" leaves one as cold as Frank Allen. The next section, "The Wild West in Photos & Illustrations," will hold readers' attention with the photographs but may lose their interest with the stylized Currier-&-Ives-like illustrations.

World Encyclopedia of Organized Crime contains good crime journalism; it sticks to the facts and creates fast-paced biographies without mulling over cause and effect. The crime lore is heightened with several hundred illustrations scattered throughout the book—mostly a rogues' gallery rather than grisly crime scene photographs. Because the crime figures were organized or linked together, Nash uses cross-references to keep the linkages intact. The international guide to organized crime simplifies identification of the country of origin for the crime figures.

In several ways, *World Encyclopedia of 20th Century Murder* is a better product than the volume from which it was extracted. The many abbreviated entries that cluttered the multivolume set have been deleted. Also absent are the sources (which mostly referred to Nash's private CrimeBooks Archive) that he had appended to the end of each entry. The unwieldy unclassified bibliography in the set has been reduced to suit the special focus of this volume and is no longer so daunting. The print is larger and clearer than in the set; otherwise, the text and illustrations remain the same.

The major problem with these spinoff volumes is that the references are not included at the end of each entry as was done in the parent set. Instead, they have been tossed together in a rambling bibliography in each volume, which will be very disconcerting for readers. But as always, Nash's material is interesting and easy to read. These volumes are recommended for libraries that did not purchase the six-volume set. [R: BR, Nov/Dec 92, p. 59; Choice, July/Aug 92, p. 1659; LJ, 15 Mar 92, p. 78; RBB, 15 Jan 92, p. 964; RBB, 15 Apr 92, p. 1556; RBB, 1 Oct 92, pp. 367-68; WLB, June 92, p. 116]—**Bill Bailey**

612. Segrave, Kerry. **Women Serial and Mass Murderers: A Worldwide Reference, 1580 through 1990.** Jefferson, N.C., McFarland, 1992. 327p. index. $39.95. HV6515.S44. 364.1'523'092. LC 91-50949. ISBN 0-89950-680-1.

Women perpetrators of serial and mass murder receive little attention in the literature except for occasional sensationalism. As Segrave points out in her introduction, women commit "multicides" for reasons entirely different from men. These excuses include an intense hatred of men, a dead-end marriage, money, and a simple slight. Women also differ from men in their method of murder—in most cases they employ poison or suffocation (deemed more humane), whereas men prefer methods such as bludgeoning or throat-slitting (deemed more violent). Women keep silent about their crimes; men brag about theirs. On the other hand, few men kill babies, which women often do because of the infants' powerlessness. These notions and others gleaned from the 80-plus profiles of women murderers in this work will certainly stimulate debate.

The profiles average three pages in length with sources appended. Unless the reader is steeped in crime lore, these women will be unknown and darkly fascinating. Each profile is concise, objective, and riveting. They are, however, historical reporting only, not true psychological profiles. What inferences accrue about the nature of female serial and mass murderers are from singular facts, not from in-depth study. Thus, a statement that arsenic figures in many of the murders can be verified by reading the entries, while the idea that women's inferior position in society and hatred of males leads to murder is a hasty conclusion. Recommended for crime collections; a marginal purchase for criminal justice academic studies. [R: Choice, Oct 92, p. 280]—**Bill Bailey**

613. **USSR Crime Statistics and Summaries: 1989 and 1990.** Joseph Serio, ed. Chicago, Office of International Criminal Justice, University of Illinois, 1992. 114p. index. $18.00. HV7013.U17. 364'.042'0947021. LC 92-50141. ISBN 0-942511-53-0.

Credit Mikhail Gorbachev for this book. His policy of glasnost opened the door to many Soviet secrets, among which the prevalence of crime was one of the darkest. At the dawn of communism, Lenin envisioned a perfect society free from crime. For anyone thereafter to suggest that crime occurred in the Soviet Union was heresy. Of course, it did occur, but not in official records. And of the so-called official records, those crime statistics that did appear were at best suspect. Serio worked in the Soviet Ministry of Interior from 1990 to 1991. During that time he was able not only to compile accurate crime statistics but also to get them out of the country for publication in the West.

The data are for 1989 and 1990, with some tables retrospective. In many cases the tables show a precipitous increase in crime over previous years, which is no surprise, as the earlier data was incomplete or disregarded. (Naturally, the false increase in crime made Gorbachev look bad, when in fact nothing had changed except for glasnost. This historical irony was partially responsible for Gorbachev's downfall.) The statistics cover the field from general to unsolved and juvenile crime. Charts and tables mix with text that alerts the reader to missing data and problems of analysis. The text is reportorial, and other than the introductory mention of Gorbachev, it presents the data without socio-political commentary. That Soviet women have engaged in extensive bootlegging activities or that robbery has doubled since 1980 are facts left to the reader to glean.

For readers used to studying the FBI's *Uniform Crime Reports*, this volume will seem sketchy. But given what was available before, it is a cornucopia of information. Recommended for all criminal justice collections.—**Bill Bailey**

614. Vandome, Nick. **Crimes and Criminals.** New York, Chambers Kingfisher Graham, 1992. 248p. illus. index. $9.95pa. ISBN 0-550-17012-X.

This reference work is the latest addition to a series of compact reference books on topics that range from the occult to space exploration. It consists of some 200 articles from 1 to 3 pages long on celebrated criminals (e.g., Billy the Kid, Al Capone) or crime cases (e.g., the Lindbergh kidnapping, the Watergate scandal). The criminals covered range from pirates and highwaymen of several hundred years ago to contemporary assassins and serial killers. Although some celebrated cases of forgery, theft, fraud, corruption, and similar crimes are included, the largest number of selections deal with murderers. Many of the cases are the famous and familiar ones, including Lizzie Borden, Jack the Ripper, and the Manson family. Insofar as the book has an English publisher, it is not surprising that British cases are disproportionately represented.

This book probably has greater entertainment than reference value. The entries generally provide lively, if concise, accounts of some crimes and criminals, but the number of entries is relatively small for a reference work, and there is no bibliographical information. The entries are also too short to explore complex elements of the crimes described in any depth. Furthermore, there are other encyclopedias that cover much of the same ground more fully, including *Bloodletters and Badmen* (see ARBA 74, entry 745). The present volume is hardly an essential acquisition, although it is an inexpensive and harmless alternative to other, more substantial reference works. — **David O. Friedrichs**

HUMAN RIGHTS

615. Langley, Winston E., ed. **Human Rights: Sixty Major Global Instruments Introduced, Reprinted and Indexed.** Jefferson, N.C., McFarland, 1992. 369p. index. $65.00. K3238.H859. 341.4'81. LC 92-53503. ISBN 0-89950-669-0.

All of the major UN human rights instruments, including a few that originally came into existence through the League of Nations, are included in this volume. The primary human rights instrument, adopted by the United Nations on December 10, 1948, is the Universal Declaration of Human Rights. Together with the covenants on civil and political rights and economic, social, and cultural rights, it forms the International Bill of Rights, which is considered the foundation for all of the other human rights instruments. The editor has brought these together in one handy volume, not in chronological or alphabetical order as is found in some collections, but under general topics such as employment and freedom to associate; marriage, family, and children; and socioeconomic welfare and peace. A few other documents that do not fit these general topics, such as "two instruments on implementation," are found in the appendixes, which are followed by an index. Of particular use are the single-page introductions presented for each of the 10 topical sections. These include valuable information about the background of the collective group of instruments and specific suggestions for further reading. It might have been useful to indicate which of the instruments have been ratified by the United States. The fact that the government has been so slow in ratifying any of the instruments might serve as a basis for further study of these important documents. This is a very useful work that should make these global instruments more easily accessible to many people. [R: WLB, Nov 92, p. 93] — **Lucille Whalen**

616. Lowery, Charles D., and John F. Marszalek, eds. **Encyclopedia of African-American Civil Rights: From Emancipation to the Present.** Westport, Conn., Greenwood Press, 1992. 658p. illus. index. $59.95. E185.61.E54. 305.896'073. LC 91-27814. ISBN 0-313-25011-1.

This reference work is meant to be used for obtaining quick and useful information about people, places, legislation, events, and constitutional cases relating to civil rights during the past 130 years. It can also be read for sheer pleasure and review. The more than 800 entries are usually short but well-defined. There are entries on such individuals as Thurgood Marshall, Alex Haley, Malcolm X, Jesse Jackson, and Fannie Lou Hamer (along with a reprint of a Hamer campaign poster). The only reference to Clarence Thomas, however, is in the entry on the Equal Employment Opportunity Commission (EEOC), where we read that Thomas, who chaired EEOC during the Reagan years, "criticized the agency for pursuing affirmative action quotas." Other types of entries include the one on affirmative action. All entries contain cross-references. Useful selected bibliographies for each entry provide direction for additional research. The work concludes with a 10-page chronology that covers the period 1861 to 1990, a 5-page selected bibliography, and a 41-page index. Every college, university, and public library will benefit from the addition of this work. Highly recommended. [R: Choice, Dec 92, p. 600; LJ, 1 May 92, p. 74; RBB, Aug 92, p. 2036; WLB, Oct 92, p. 107] — **Michael A. Foley**

617. Magill, Frank N., ed. **Great Events from History II: Human Rights Series.** Pasadena, Calif., Salem Press, 1992. 5v. index. $375.00/set. K3240.6.G74. 341.4'81'0904. LC 92-12896. ISBN 0-89356-643-8.

Dionysius of Halicarnassus, the great Greek historian, taught that history, with its myriad names, faces, and facts, underscored what abstract philosophy tried to teach. History provided us with the examples, he said, that are so often missing from the austere cerebration of philosophy. It is hard to think of any better confirmation of this fact than *Great Events from History* (GEFH). The complete set now chronicles history's examples from 4,000 B.C. to the present.

The original set of GEFH included ancient and medieval, European, American, and worldwide twentieth-century events. Taking a cue from the *GEFH II: Science and Technology Series* (see ARBA 92, entry 1465), this new series adumbrates the newsmaking episodes relating to human rights. The volumes are veritable newspapers in miniature. Similar to its predecessors, *Human Rights Series* follows a typical pattern. Beginning with the 1900 Boxer Rebellion, the volumes proceed apace to the downfall of the Soviet regime and the consequent restructuring of its republics. More than 25 issues in human rights are covered, including children's rights, education, the rights of the homeless, gray rights, gay rights, the peace movement and its organizations, racial and ethnic rights struggles, women's rights, voting rights, and reproductive rights. One improvement made in this set is the lengthening of individual articles. Articles now run 2,500 words or more, assuring readers that epochal matters will be dealt with in the detail they deserve and require.

Each event begins with a category description, usually a subject or key word, plus its range of years and geographic location. Subsequent to these facts are one to three lines of summary information about the event for ready-reference. An especially helpful feature is a kind of personae dramatis in which the names of people appearing in the text are identified with respect to who they are and the importance of their presence to the event. A summary of the event, which runs more than half the length of each article, puts the event in its historical place and outlines conditions that led up to it or were subsequent to it. These are especially informative, crisp, and clear.

"Impact of the Event," another new feature, describes in several hundred words why the event is important. For example, under the event "The Pure Food and Drug Act," the impact statement points out that the 1906 legislation was a landmark decision that led to the later and more familiar consumer rights of today. Further, it takes the reader on a quick tour of the protestations against the act and how these fears were eventually allayed. The impact statements do not tell readers what to think. In random and small sampling, no partisanship of any kind was detected. For example, the article on gay rights reports the facts directly and correctly. It does not pander to either side of this controversial issue.

Librarians considering this set will argue that the material offered here is readily available in other sources, such as encyclopedias and specialized handbooks. But having so much information in one place, so handy, so neatly arranged, and so carefully researched and organized is especially convenient. [R: RQ, Spring 92, pp. 417-18] — **Mark Y. Herring**

618. Weinberg, Meyer, comp. **World Racism and Related Inhumanities: A Country-by-Country Bibliography.** Westport, Conn., Greenwood Press, 1992. 1048p. index. (Bibliographies and Indexes in World History, no.26). $99.50. Z7164.R12W5. 016.3058. LC 92-4094. ISBN 0-313-28109-2.

For those in need of bibliographic information on racism throughout the world, this book provides a useful and fascinating beginning. It covers some 135 countries and includes studies of racism from ancient times to the present. The coverage is broad, based on the understanding that racism cannot be seen in isolation from the humanities. By "humanities" Weinberg means "all the ways that present-day societies have of denying systematically the equal worth of some groups of people in the interest of others." Thus, the "inhumanities" include racism, slavery, class domination, sexism, national oppression, imperialism, colonialism, and anti-Semitism.

The first 10,028 references are to single countries and may be further subdivided as necessary. For example, there is a section on Australia (general) and Australia-Aborigines. Listings for Canada are subdivided into such subjects as anti-Semitism, Asians, Blacks in Canada, and first nations. Peculiarly enough, however, there are no subdivisions for the United States. The remaining entries (approximately 2,100) cover areas and regions (e.g., Africa, the Caribbean, Europe, Latin America) and do not duplicate any references found in the list of individual countries. The bibliography concludes with an author index and a very useful subject index that cross-references entries according to such categories as affirmative action, bilingual education, fascism, nationalism, and Zionism. The bibliographic citations focus on material published in the 1980s, with some cites from 1990. Overall, researchers should find this collection quite helpful. [R: Choice, Nov 92, p. 451] — **Michael A. Foley**

619. **World Directory of Human Rights Research and Training Institutions.** 2d ed. Paris, Unesco; distr., Lanham, Md., UNIPUB, 1992. 290p. index. (World Social Science Information Directories). $30.00pa. ISBN 92-3-002794-4.

There are 348 numbered entries in this title (first reviewed in ARBA 89, entry 531), 66 of them at the beginning under international organizations. The remaining entries are grouped alphabetically by country. All entries provide basic directory information along with the names and types of publications, types of research activity, and names of senior staff. Also included is an outline of the human rights education program at the institute, with data on fees, target groups, subjects taught, admission requirements, and diplomas offered. Naturally, the completeness of the data varies among the entries. There are separate indexes for courses and subjects taught, senior staff, country, research subjects, and names and acronyms of the institutions. There is also a list of abbreviations of the diplomas awarded for completion of an institution's educational program. Easily recommended for all academic and larger public libraries. — **Daniel K. Blewett**

VICTIMS OF ABUSE

620. Barnes, Dorothy L., comp. **Rape: A Bibliography 1976-1988.** Troy, N.Y., Whitston Publishing, 1991. 326p. index. $38.50. LC 77-8964. ISBN 0-87875-261-7.

This continuation of Barnes's previous rape bibliography (see ARBA 78, entry 673) cites books, pamphlets, dissertations, and periodical articles on virtually all aspects of rape (including legal, medical, sociological, psychological, and feminist) published between 1976 and 1988. Monographs and dissertations are listed alphabetically by author; articles are listed alphabetically by author or title under subject headings as diverse as capital punishment, parking garages, rape in literature, and principals in noteworthy rape cases. Entries include all necessary bibliographic information including ISBN numbers for monographs. There are lists of subject headings and journals cited, along with an author index.

To compile the bibliography, Barnes consulted 55 indexes and abstracts as well as catalogs and bibliographies in an attempt to be comprehensive. Consequently, this bibliography will save researchers considerable time and effort usually devoted to searching reference sources. It will be particularly helpful for locating more obscure materials, such as pamphlets and articles in feminist magazines. Recommended for all academic and larger public libraries and specialized libraries where interest warrants. — **Gari-Anne Patzwald**

11 Library and Information Science and Publishing and Bookselling

LIBRARY AND INFORMATION SCIENCE

General Works

Acronyms and Abbreviations

621. Sawoniak, Henryk, and Maria Witt. **New International Dictionary of Acronyms in Library and Information Science and Related Fields.** 2d ed. Munich, New York, K. G. Saur, 1992. 497p. $135.00. ISBN 3-598-10972-5.

Acronyms in the fields of library and information science and fields related to them (e.g., publishing, printing, archive management) are being created at a prodigious rate. Because of this, a new edition of this work (the first was published in 1988) is welcome indeed.

Conceptually, there is no difference between the two editions. Both are international in scope, focusing on institutions, library and information systems, professional problems and equipment, programming languages, and titles of publications that relate to these subjects. A wide variety of sources was consulted for this compilation from both the obvious and less-obvious countries and languages. The 1988 edition of this work contained 28,500 entries; this new edition, 33,600.

The acronyms are displayed in the language of the official name when known. Acronyms in the Cyrillic alphabet are transliterated into the Roman alphabet and are marked with an asterisk. Variant acronyms for the same organization and acronyms of related and parent organizations are also included. Arrows are used to indicate preceding and succeeding names, and dates that indicate when an organization or a title began are also given. Finally, an abbreviation that represents the country or language of the organization or title is provided.

All in all, this is a very easy work to use. It provides the user with concise information in a clear manner. As is always the case, a work of this nature becomes outdated very rapidly. This should be viewed as a fact of life and should in no way dissuade potential buyers from purchasing this work. Although the price is high, this volume is a valuable tool for anyone who has ever been stymied by the "alphabet soup" used in the fields of library and information science.—**Marjorie E. Bloss**

Dictionaries and Encyclopedias

622. Watters, Carolyn. **Dictionary of Information Science and Technology.** San Diego, Calif., Academic Press, 1992. 300p. $29.95. Z1006.W35. 020'.3. LC 91-29644. ISBN 0-12-738510-X.

Over the years the term *library science* has evolved into *library and information science*, with a growing emphasis on information science. Consequently, librarians have had to expand their technical vocabularies as the computerization of library activities becomes the norm. This dictionary brings together many of those terms and concepts that are essential for librarians to meet today's technological demands.

The terms in this work are arranged in a single alphabet, reflecting the interdisciplinary nature of information and its uses. The author states that "time and space constraints necessarily limit the number of terms included" (preface) but never gives a clear-cut indication of the criteria used either for inclusion or exclusion. The definitions are concise, usually running six or seven lines; frequently they are diagrammed, and formulas are included where appropriate. The volume concludes with a section called "Subject Outlines" (in which terms found in the volume are used in conjunction with one another in outline form) and references. The author relates these two sections to the terms by including the numbering in the subject outline and the primary related reference in abbreviated form after each term. The subject outline concept is especially useful in that it clusters related terms together, thus providing the user with a broader context for the individual term.

Although this is a useful quick reference, the author (and subsequently the user) would have been better served by tighter editorial work. As examples, some of the writing is awkward (e.g., *Chinese test*), the abbreviations for the references are not always obvious, and this reviewer has yet to figure out the order of entries under the letter "X" (e.g., X.400, X.75, X.21, X.25). Even so, this is a reasonable tertiary source, good especially for quick reference. [R: Choice, Oct 92, p. 282] – **Marjorie E. Bloss**

Directories

623. **American Library Directory 1992-93.** 45th ed. New Providence, N.J., R. R. Bowker, 1992. 2v. index. $215.00/set. LC 23-3581. ISBN 0-8352-3157-7. ISSN 0065-910X.

American Library Directory (ALD) is the answer to finding and documenting changes in areas such as the incomes, personnel, and expenditures of libraries in the United States and Canada. The main portion of the set is arranged geographically by state or province and alphabetically by city, then by institution or library. Each entry is coded by type of library (e.g., P for public) and ideally includes the following data: official name, other name by which it may be known, address, SAN (Standard Address Number), telephone numbers, personnel, number and status of staff, library history, library income and expenditures, projected income, library holdings, collections, library automation, library system to which the library belongs, networks in which the library participates, any special services, branches (with pertinent information), and available bookmobile program.

Information for the directory has been obtained from the cited library or from public sources. The criteria for inclusion are vague. Some special libraries (e.g., business libraries) are included; others have been omitted. For instance, the Marathon Oil Research Center Library in Colorado is not listed. Several unlisted church libraries would seem to qualify for inclusion as well.

Additional information in ALD includes library counts for public, academic, government, armed forces, and special libraries; library award recipients for 1991; libraries in areas administered by the United States (e.g., Guam); libraries in Canada; library data on networks; library schools; and libraries for the blind and physically handicapped and for the deaf and hearing impaired. An alphabetical list of libraries included completes the volume. As pointed out in an earlier review (see ARBA 91, entry 607), some facts are dated, but ALD continues to be an excellent resource of information on libraries.
– **Anna Grace Patterson**

624. **FID Directory 1991-1992.** The Hague, Netherlands, FID, 1991. 141p. index. $38.00pa. ISBN 92-66-00-699-8. ISSN 0379-3680.

The International Federation for Information and Documentation (FID) was founded in 1895. It is an active organization dominated by Western professionals in the field of information management. Members come from 84 different countries. This directory is a fact-finding book about this important organization. Each of 18 chapters deals with a special aspect of the organization, such as structure, committees, regional commissions, national and international members, sponsoring members, and international affiliates. There are a good chapter on the history of the organization and a list of all its presidents, honorary fellows, secretaries general, and executive directors. There is also a complete list of FID conferences and meetings (with dates) held in various cities around the world.

The list of members is arranged alphabetically by country and includes for each individual the full name; complete address; telephone, telex, and fax numbers; and date of joining the organization. Short biographies of all officers of the Council and Councilors are supplied. A comprehensive persons and institutions index leads to page numbers and has addresses of individuals in the index. A subject index also leads to page numbers. Full of information, this work is recommended for libraries, librarians, and information specialists interested in FID and its activities. — **Ravindra Nath Sharma**

625. Grant, George C., comp. **The Directory of Ethnic Professionals in LIS (Library and Information Science).** Winter Park, Fla., FOUR-G, 1991. 254p. index. $52.95. Z720.A1D5. LC 90-85845. ISBN 0-9625423-3-4.

Compiling a biographical directory of ethnic library and information science professionals that is comprehensive and international in scope is an enormous undertaking. Grant has made a good start on creating an interesting and useful tool. However, the title is somewhat misleading inasmuch as about 80 percent of the entries are devoted to African Americans, Africans, and other Blacks. Asians, considered in a broad sense to include Chinese, Japanese, Koreans, Filipinos, and East Indians, constitute the second largest group (approximately 11 percent), followed by Hispanics, who make up somewhere between 5 and 6 percent. Native Americans and all other miscellaneous groups are subjects of the remaining 3 percent of the entries.

Grant indicates in the introduction that his original interest in compiling such a reference work came about as a result of his frustration in "being unable to locate biographical and professional data about several Black librarians," and his methodology reflects this emphasis. Several obvious omissions are evident, such as Roberto Haro, an LIS faculty member who writes about Hispanic librarians and library users, and Salvador Guerena, who edited *Latino Librarianship*. There are slightly more than 1,400 sketches, only a small percentage of the 25,000 ethnic librarians that Grant claims should be included.

Information provided in the entries includes name; ethnic heritage; current employer, title, dates, address and telephone number; employment history; employment status; preferred mailing address; education; professional memberships, appointments, and years; professional publications, exhibits, and works; professional awards, honors, fellowships, and the like; professional specializations; and areas of consulting or lecturing. Entries range in length from two lines to three pages, with the average typically being about one-third of a column on a two-column page. An index lists biographees' names under the names of their employers and alma maters. A geographical index would be helpful.

A data sheet is included in the back of the directory so that unlisted ethnic professional librarians can reproduce it, complete it, and return it to Grant. It is hoped that they will do so to help create more comprehensive and better balanced representation in the 2d edition. This directory has the potential to fill a critical gap in the reference literature of both the fields of library and information science and ethnic studies. [R: C&RL, Sept 92, p. 417] — **Lois J. Buttlar**

626. Kessler, Jack. **Directory to Fulltext Online Resources 1992.** Westport, Conn., Meckler, 1992. 138p. index. (Supplements to Computers in Libraries Series, no.55). $30.00pa. Z674.3.K47. 025.04'025'73. LC 91-38584. ISBN 0-88736-833-6.

Directory is much too prosaic a word to describe this friendly, disarming, and chatty guide to the bewildering, chaotic world of the global Internet. It is "written for someone who has not yet used a computer e-mail network," although "even dedicated hackers" will find it useful. Its goal is to make the enormous resources (and the fun!) of the internet available to all, especially librarians. "To some of us — this warning to managers — network-hacking becomes so much fun that it replaces working: but so much the better if a manager or a hacker can figure out a way to combine the play with real work" (p. xvi). A great deal of good advice is given, such as "The best thing to do with the voluminous and obscure 'documentation' which accompanies computer hardware and software is to ignore it: it is written by and for computer geniuses and they are not normal people. Ask someone. Ask your kids." You can start with this book!

Separate chapters address the nature of fulltext in the network environment, commercial fulltext, CD-ROM, OPACs, bulletin board systems, interest groups, electronic conferences, electronic journals, electronic libraries, and universally available local resources. Each chapter includes lists or examples of possibilities, along with suggestions on how to access them and commentary. The book concludes with more editorials on "information overload" and "taming the nightmare and the dream," plus references, a bibliography, and a skimpy index that has only slightly more than 200 headings.

This valuable introduction is especially appropriate for librarians who have not yet ventured into this new information world that will likely dominate our future. The author, a "techno-skeptic," has succeeded in giving "patient and clear explanations of techno-wizardry terms" (to paraphrase his description of John Ober at UC Berkeley). An underlying theme is the future role of librarians: "The area does need a catalyst, however: a group dedicated to easing the 'information overload' problem, by acting as an intermediary between users and the new information systems.... For the last fulltext medium, the book, this intermediary was the librarian. For fulltext online it has yet to be shown who the intermediary will be" (p. 4). In this regard the author succeeds in giving "users an overview to help them grasp this tool and use it to shape the future, rather than let the tool do the shaping" (p. xi).

—**James D. Anderson**

Handbooks and Yearbooks

627. **Advances in Librarianship. Volume 15.** Irene P. Godden, ed. San Diego, Calif., Academic Press, 1991. 292p. index. $55.00. LC 79-88675. ISBN 0-12-024615-5.

Through the years this series has proven an important barometer of the profession—its concerns and values. The challenge, therefore, is for subsequent volumes live up to expectations. In this case, these expectations have been met.

The subject matter is broad and covers a wide range of topics, including "The Transfer of Library Skills to Nonlibrary Contexts" (Michael E. D. Koenig), "The Scholarly Vocation and Library Science" (Mary Biggs), "Ethnic Libraries and Librarianship in the United States" (Stephen Stern), and "Area Studies in United States Libraries" (Marianna Tax Choldrin and others). Each of these essays is approximately 50 pages in length. The authors, therefore, are able to discuss their topics in some depth. While the essays are carefully researched, readers should not expect to be overwhelmed by tables, graphs, and numerical data. The essays are all well written, scholarly, and very readable, without the unevenness often found in this type of work. Extensive bibliographies conclude each section and provide readers with excellent citations for furthering their reading. This work should appeal to librarians in libraries at many different professional levels. It is a credit to the continuing series.—**Marjorie E. Bloss**

628. **Annual Review of Information Science and Technology. Volume 26: 1991.** Martha E. Williams, ed. Medford, N.J., Learned Information, 1991. 515p. index. $87.00. LC 66-25096. ISBN 0-938734-55-5. ISSN 0066-4200.

The 26th edition of this guide (popularly known as ARIST) continues the tradition of earlier volumes. Although published annually, ARIST does not treat the same subjects year after year. Contents change to mirror the dynamics of information technology. Individual chapters present "scholarly reviews of specific topics as substantiated by the published literature," some updating earlier articles and others reporting for the first time on a new subject. This edition includes nine chapters. They deal with cognitive research in information science, information pricing (a new subject), standards in information technology, expert systems, human-computer interface, optical disk technology, information technology in schools (another new subject), information systems and technology for the humanities, and human networks in organizational information processing (another first). The chapters require intense concentration, laden as they are with detailed information and numerous citations. Substantial bibliographies accompany each chapter. There is a lengthy index for the individual volume and an author and keyword index to all 26 volumes published to date. This extra index gives a special reference value to the guide. The introduction lists the secondary services that index or abstract the series. Except in a specialized library, ARIST will probably not find a place in the reference collection, but the series remains an invaluable resource for all academic, research, and large public libraries. [R: JAL, Mar 92, p. 56; JAL, Sept 92, p. 233]—**Richard D. Johnson**

629. **The Bowker Annual Library and Book Trade Almanac.** 37th ed. Catherine Barr, ed. New Providence, N.J., R. R. Bowker, 1992. 766p. index. $129.95. LC 55-12434. ISBN 0-8352-3224-7. ISSN 0068-0540.

Published annually for more than 50 years, this core reference work summarizes library and book trade trends for the past year and provides vital, statistical, industry-related information on such items as book sales and costs, library budgets, and library organizations. This edition follows the format of previous ones by dividing the contents into six sections. The first, titled "Reports from the Field," features new reports on the state of the homeless, the unemployed, after-school children, immigrants, and the disabled vis-a-vis libraries. It also includes information about the second WHCLIS (White House Conference on Library and Information Services) meeting, the status of the Nixon and Reagan libraries, the economic conditions that affect academic and public libraries, and censorship repercussions. Two articles highlight the latest developments with the libraries of Eastern Europe.

Part 2 analyzes various legislative works and rules that affected libraries in 1991 and lists numerous institution grant recipients. Part 3 furnishes employment and salary information to aspiring and practicing librarians. Part 4 contains budget justification information on library expenditures, book prices, and sales. Included this year is a report by Marilyn Miller and Marilyn Shontz that summarizes school library expenditures for fiscal year 1989-1990. Part 5 supplies publishers' toll-free numbers, instructions for obtaining ISBNs and ISSNs, and various lists of literary prize winners. The last section includes demographic data for various network consortia and state, regional, and international library associations. A newly added index of organizations and an acronyms list make this edition even more accessible than previous ones.

The 39th edition of *The Bowker Annual* should be a mandatory acquisition for all academic, public, and large school libraries. It is a fundamental resource for anyone employed in the information science field. – **Kathleen W. Craver**

630. **Guide to the Information Activities of European Development Networks.** Paris, Unesco; distr., Lanham, Md., UNIPUB, 1991. 259p. index. $25.00pa. ISBN 92-3-102737-9.

This work provides a comprehensive list of European organizations that engage in the dissemination of information with respect to activities aimed at assisting developing countries. Profiles of some 270 development networks based in western Europe comprise most of the book. They include addresses, telephone numbers, key contacts, services offered, aims, activities, working languages, countries in which they operate, and other pertinent comments. Several articles that precede the profiles provide a useful overview of the current status of development networks in Europe and offer definitions of key terms used in the guide. Organizations are listed by the country in which they are based and alphabetically by acronym. Networks are listed alphabetically. Also included are a table of contents; indexes of activity focuses, geographical coverage, activities in Europe, and information activities; and a bibliography. Obviously, every effort has been made to enable the reader to locate information of specific interest. – **William C. Struning**

631. **Librarianship and Information Work Worldwide 1991.** Graham Mackenzie and Ray Prytherch, eds. Munich, New Providence, N.J., K. G. Saur, 1991. 240p. index. $95.00. ISBN 0-86291-626-7.

In past years, library and information studies has had two good annual reviews of the literature: *Annual Review of Information Science and Technology* (see ARBA 92, entry 569) and *Advances in Librarianship* (Academic Press, 1991). Now, thanks to the work of the publisher and the editors, there is another good collection of review essays. And this one fills a gap not adequately covered by the other two: attention to the worldwide literature of the field.

The organizational format of the volume is fairly traditional: 10 chapters on topics familiar to the profession, an introductory overview chapter, and a closing brief summary. Each chapter is in essay form, covers the most recent literature, and includes a complete bibliography of all cited materials. While traditional, the topics are also of continuing high interest to the profession worldwide, covering academic libraries, public libraries, national libraries, business and industrial information services, collection development, reference services, cooperation, access, management, and education for the profession. An introductory thematic essay by Charles Oppenheim, which provides an overview of recent trends in the library and information professions worldwide, and a closing summary essay by Prytherch, who speculates on the convergence/divergence of the professions, act as nice "bookends" to the other specific topical chapters. A modest subject index and a complete author index to all cited works close the volume.

The complementary goals of this work are to cover both librarianship and "information work" worldwide. While the worldwide aspect is covered better than any other existing compilation, there is a decided British flavor in most of the essays (9 of the 12 writers are from the United Kingdom), and the cited literature is not as international as the topics demand. Librarianship is well covered, but the writers only occasionally venture into the other areas of "information work," such as information systems, information resource management, archives, records management, and related areas. Despite these weaknesses, however, it is refreshing—and needed in the field—to see these topics treated with some deliberate concern for international developments. U.S. writers almost always write on these topics as if their literature was the one and only word. Here, the topics are not always covered worldwide, but they are almost always internationally focused.—**Robert V. Williams**

Indexes

632. **Library Literature.** (Indexing coverage: 12/84-6/25/92). [CD-ROM]. Bronx, N.Y., H. W. Wilson, 1992. Hardware requirements: WILSONLINE Workstation, IBM PC, or compatible; 640K; hard disk drive. $1,095.00.

Library Literature, the main index to the literature of librarianship in the United States, is available from H. W. Wilson on one CD-ROM disc that covers December 1984 to the present. This review will focus on the latest version of the operating software (2.4). As in previous versions, there are two options on the WILSONDISC main menu: a disc search and an online search. The Online Search allows access to the online database and can be used to retrieve the most recent information. The disc product is updated quarterly; the online database, monthly. Given this difference, there may be less need for the dialup option. Besides, online time connect costs must be taken into consideration.

The instructions for loading the software are easy to follow. Once loaded, version 2.4 presents a number of enhancements over the previous version. The journal holdings manager has a new customized message option. A new screen-saver option allows libraries to turn off the flashing multiple-box screen after three minutes of display or altogether. The "Print Brief" feature allows the printing of a shortened version of the citation; however, entries are still displayed on the screen one at a time.

WILSONDISC products have three search modes: BROWSE, WILSEARCH, and WILSONLINE. Each mode has its own set of search steps or commands to access information, which can be confusing to new or infrequent users, most of whom will want to use BROWSE. BROWSE searches by subject, one heading at a time. The subjects must match the authority headings assigned by Wilson, and subheadings must follow the main heading with a slash. Little instruction in the use of proper subject headings is provided, and there is no thesaurus, which requires the user to identify proper terms related to the information sought. However, the disc is easy to browse either with the page up or page down keys or by typing another term.

The WILSEARCH mode searches by subject heading, author, key words, title words, journal name, organization, Dewey decimal number, year (single year only), or a combination of the above. Up to three subject terms can be combined per search. Compared to BROWSE, WILSEARCH is more comprehensive. A search of "rare books" in WILSEARCH retrieved 425 hits; in BROWSE, the search retrieved the main heading with 18 subheadings for a total of 181 hits. A search on "online information retrieval," not found in BROWSE, retrieved 410 hits in WILSEARCH. In both BROWSE and WILSEARCH, retrieval time is good, although WILSEARCH is slower. The use of function keys makes it easy to move between screens or citations, to print or download records, or to move to another database product.

The WILSONLINE mode uses commands and will almost always require an experienced searcher. Command mode is powerful and fast. For example, typing the search statement "ethic: and (electronic or technolog: or automat: or computer#)" retrieved 20 hits in less than a minute.

Context-sensitive help screens throughout provide minimal instructions and will assist some users. Wilson has provided a quick reference guide and individual instruction sheets that briefly outline each of the search modes. While helpful, they do not explain broader retrieval concepts (e.g., positional operators, controlled versus free text terms).

Any library or library school that can afford the Library Literature CD-ROM should purchase it. An excellent tool for librarians, it represents the best way to keep up with the literature, which could result in better service and collections.—**Byron P. Anderson**

Periodicals and Serials

633. Miller, Shelley, comp. and ed. **Latin American Serial Publications Available by Exchange: Mexico, Central America and Panama.** Albuquerque, N.Mex., SALALM Secretariat, General Library, University of New Mexico, 1991. 86p. (Bibliography and Reference Series, no.29). $20.00pa. ISBN 0-917617-29-0.

Over the past 20 years, the Seminar on the Acquisition of Latin American Library Materials (SALALM) has made a major contribution to the identification and acquisition of Latin American publications by North American libraries. In addition to the Bibliography and Reference Series, SALALM has published its final reports and working papers as well as a newsletter that began in 1973. Much of the material found in these publications is highly specialized and can be found nowhere else.

Serial Publications Available by Exchange continues this tradition by unearthing information about Latin American periodical publications—in this case, those in Mexico, Central America, and Panama. Latin American serial publications are notoriously difficult to identify and to acquire on a regular basis by North American libraries. On the other hand, exchange of publications has been one of the most successful means of acquiring those publications from organizations and libraries that often are not set up to handle subscriptions on a regular basis. This work lists institutional addresses in Mexico, Central America, and Panama through which serials are available on exchange. Each institution carries at least one serial title, some as many as four.

Although useful to librarians who need to acquire Latin American serial publications not otherwise available, this economically published directory will not win any awards for format. It is arranged alphabetically by country and by state for Mexico, but no such divisions are indicated in the directory other than in the table of contents. More puzzling in a publication of this kind is the total lack of Spanish accents and diacritical marks, which are easily reproduced these days by word processors. However, the editor's suggestion that all correspondence with institutions listed in the directory be conducted in the language of the country is well taken. In sum, this is a useful publication for a specialized market, published by an organization that has opened many doors to Latin American publications.
—Edwin S. Gleaves

Careers and Education

634. Johnson, Karl E. **An Annotated Bibliography of Faculty Status in Library and Information Science.** Champaign, Ill., Graduate School of Library and Information Science, University of Illinois, 1992. 66p. (University of Illinois Graduate School of Library and Information Science Occasional Papers, no.193). $8.00pa.

Improvement in professional status has been a concern for all librarians, particularly academic librarians, for many of whom attainment of full, coequal faculty status has been a long and desperate battle. The professional literature is replete with opinion pieces, research articles, and editorials, starting with H. A. Sawtelle's 1878 article on "The College Librarianship." Nancy Huling, as Johnson points out, previously published a comprehensive bibliography on the subject in *College and Research Libraries* 34, no. 6, November 1973, and his bibliography is intended as a continuation of her work.

Johnson does not mention, although the title is included in his bibliography, that another, more selective chronological bibliography was published in 1985 by Emily Werrell and Laura Sullivan (*Faculty Status for Academic Librarians* [ED 274 364]). This work included 121 items the authors considered relevant, appropriate, and useful that were published between 1974 and 1985. As many as 26 items from Werrell and Sullivan's bibliography have not been included in Johnson's, however. This illustrates a problem with definition as Johnson's aim is similar—to include items directly pertaining to the topic. Johnson does not state his criteria for direct pertinence, nor does he attempt to define faculty status—but, then, neither did Huling, who instead included a call for the profession to unite around a common, acceptable definition. Johnson would have done well to have repeated that call, considering the need for such agreement. Nevertheless, his bibliography is valuable as a documentation of the ongoing debate regarding faculty status for academic librarians. [R: JAL, July 92, p. 186]
—Johan Koren

Cataloging and Classification

635. **Art & Architecture Thesaurus. Supplement 1.** New York, Oxford University Press, 1992. 221p. $50.00. Z695.1.A7A76. 025.4'97. LC 91-36537. ISBN 0-19-507656-7.

In 1990 Oxford University Press published the three-volume *Art & Architecture Thesaurus* (see ARBA 91, entry 618) on behalf of the Getty Art History Information Program. The function of this work was to present a controlled vocabulary to ease the use of databases in the fields of art and architecture. This gigantic task used hundreds of experts and specialists who examined thousands of sources for terms. The result was a monumental work that is of benefit to all who are interested in the arts, the cataloging of objects and their reproductions, and the literature of art history. A thesaurus is a living thing, however, constantly changing and growing. This supplement is the first of a series of updates to be used in conjunction with the original set. It contains changes to terms, to hierarchy structure, and to bibliographic sources. Because the number of changes is so large and continuous, a new fulltext edition is scheduled for 1994.—**Robert J. Havlik**

636. **ERIC Identifier Authority List (IAL) 1992.** Carolyn R. Weller and James E. Houston, eds. Phoenix, Ariz., Oryx Press, 1992. 497p. $55.00. ISBN 0-89774-738-0. ISSN 1062-0508.

Thesauri and lists of subject headings do not generally include names of persons, organizations, institutions, products, places, diseases, languages, equipment, documents, and similar entities. If such names are controlled or monitored at all, they are maintained in some kind of authority list, in the hopes that consistency can be maintained. ERIC calls such terms "identifiers," and lists them in its Identifier Authority List (IAL). Although maintained since 1980, this 1992 edition is the first published for wide distribution in print form by a commercial publisher. In addition to names of particular entities, events, and similar phenomena, ERIC includes all "candidate descriptors" for the ERIC thesaurus. Such terms are transferred to the thesaurus once their "scope, definition, authoritativeness, and 'staying power' have been established."

This edition includes 44,000 names. Each name is classed into one of 20 categories by type of entity (e.g., conferences/meetings, curriculum areas). The only other information provided in entries are occasional cross-references from alternative forms, such as "C SPAN, UF (used for) Cable Satellite Public Affairs Network, CSPAN Series," and a scope note or two. Classification into categories is problematic in some cases, because many names consist of "bound terms" representing more than one facet. "Black writers" is listed in the "groups (other)" category rather than the "groups (ethnic)" or "groups (occupations)" categories. Some errors in classification are apparent; for example, Pennsylvania (Monroeville) is in the "groups (ethnic)" rather than the "geographic locations" category. Most names of religious groups are in "groups (other)," but "General Conference Mennonites" has been placed in "groups (ethnic)." Every term has the number of postings (or uses) in the two ERIC database files, Resources in Education (RIE) and Current Index to Journals in Education (CIJE). Most terms have very few postings.

This compilation will be useful to ERIC searchers, who will be able to verify the standardized form of identifier terms before beginning a search; it will also help indexers, catalogers, and thesaurus editors, who must establish terms for the kinds of entities included in the IAL. The editors caution, however, that not all identifiers in currently available ERIC database files conform to the forms listed here. [R: WLB, Sept 92, p. 112]—**James D. Anderson**

637. **The GRANTS Subject Authority Guide.** Phoenix, Ariz., Oryx Press, 1991. 80p. $29.50pa. Z695.1.R46G7 025.4'900144. LC 91-27852. ISBN 0-89774-720-8.

The problem of subject authority control is one that not all publishers of indexes have cared to tackle, despite the fact that without that control, users are at a severe disadvantage as they root around for those subjective subjects. Therefore, Oryx Press is to be congratulated on the appearance of this volume. The intended purpose of *The GRANTS Subject Authority Guide* is to provide a cross-reference structure for the subject terms that have recently been added to the GRANTS Database. Benefits, however, also accrue to the annual paper counterpart of the database, *The Directory of Research Grants* (DRG) (see ARBA 90, entry 339), which has long enjoyed a "very extensive subject index", despite its lack of cross-references.

Approximately 3,000 terms are included in the new authority guide, with cross-references and *see also* references approaching 18 percent. The guide is not a faceted thesaurus of overwhelmingly significant structure (e.g., there are no broader term/narrower term listings). It is a good and thorough list nonetheless, based not only on what the current database and DRG have to offer but also on the possibility of a listing. No grants are reported to the heading "Guyana," for example (DRG 1991, p. 954), but "Guyana" exists as a legitimate term between "Guinea" and "Haiti" in the guide (p. 34).

By way of comparison, *The Foundation Grants Index* (see ARBA 90, entry 823) uses no cross-references in its large subject index. On the other hand, users of the *Annual Register of Grant Support* (see ARBA 89, entry 802) enjoy not only the large subject index, complete with *see also* and cross-references, but also a text arranged alphabetically within broad subject categories, a search-enhancing feature. Neither *The Foundation Grants Index* nor the *Annual Register of Grant Support*, however, has online versions; and it is the GRANTS Database that the guide is (successfully) intended to enhance.

—**Judith M. Brugger**

638. Harrison, Harriet W., comp. and ed. **The FIAF Cataloguing Rules for Film Archives.** Munich, New Providence, N.J., K. G. Saur, 1991. 239p. index. (Film, Television, Sound Archive Series, v.1). $55.00. ISBN 3-598-22590-3.

The Federation Internationale des Archives du Film (FIAF) has promulgated these rules to increase the consistency of description among film archives. Coverage includes description and choice of entry but not form of entry or subject analysis. The rules generally follow ISBN(NBM) (Nonbook Materials) where there is overlap. Differences from ISBN(NBM) may be wordy, syntactically odd, or unclear (e.g., "The expansion may be either short or long—a condition which will be determined by [1] the staff and space [either computer or manual files] available to the archive for creating and storing long summaries ..."). Some rules are missing; some locate information inappropriately. There are no general instructions on the use of abbreviations. Instructions for abbreviating place-names appear in the rule for "Place" in the "Production, Distribution, etc. area," but the rule is not indexed under "Abbreviations" or "Place", or noted in the appendix. There are an appendix of 35 complete descriptions, a glossary, the ISO standard for dates, measurement conversion charts, abbreviations, FIAF Archive codes, a bibliography, and an index. The latter is flawed, as it includes references to the glossary (e.g., "Trailer ... definition, Appendix B"), is incomplete, and may use unexpected terms (e.g., the rule for "Abridging or omitting other title information" is indexed under "Abbreviation" but not "Abridging" or "Omission"; "Probable dates ..." is indexed only under "Probable ...").

In addition to content problems, the book is poorly produced in ways that affect its usability. The boards of the review copy were warped to double the width of the text block, and the casing is poor. Pages must often be creased to lie open. Clarity is reduced because the publisher did not use boldface type, italics, changes in type size, or similar style characteristics. Copyright symbols and some diacritical marks are hand drawn. This work fills an acknowledged gap, but it is unfortunate that the content and production could not have been more polished. —**Janet Swan Hill**

639. Howarth, Lynne C., comp. **AACR2 Decisions & Rule Interpretations.** 5th ed. Ottawa, Canadian Library Association and Chicago, American Library Association, 1991. 2v. index. $90.00/set looseleaf with binder. 025.3'2. ISBN 0-88802-237-9.

This work consolidates the decisions and rule interpretations that the Library of Congress, the National Library of Canada, the British Library, and the National Library of Australia have composed to govern their use of *Anglo-American Cataloging Rules*, 2d edition, 1988 revision. It is intended to assist librarians in understanding the policy decisions issued by the national agencies. It will also aid catalogers in interpreting the rules for their own use, guide cataloging instructors in teaching the rules and how to apply them, and assist those interested in the comparative cataloging developments in these national agencies.

This edition, in two standard three-ring binders to maximize ease of use, has been compiled by Howarth, who continues the work of C. Donald Cook (see ARBA 84, entry 145 for a review of the 2d edition of this work). Official decisions and interpretations of the national agencies are revised to

March 1991. When there is concurrence on decisions, only one resolution appears, with an indication of which agencies concur. Variant decisions have been included. [R: CLJ, Feb 92, pp. 79-80]

—Bonnie A. Dede

640. Intner, Sheila S., and William E. Studwell. **Subject Access to Films and Videos.** Lake Crystal, Minn., Soldier Creek Press, 1992. 125p. $25.00pa. Z695.64.I55. 025.3'473. LC 91-32024. ISBN 0-936996-60-9.

A challenge some catalogers face is assigning media-specific subject headings to film and video materials. To assist such catalogers, the authors have compiled and reprinted relevant Library of Congress (LC) subject headings and cross-references, including such varied headings as DISTANCE EDUCATION, DOCUMENTARY FILMS, DOCUMENTARY MASS MEDIA, DOCUMENTS IN OPTICAL STORAGE, DOGS IN TELEVISION, DONALD DUCK, DONKEY KONG, DRAMATIC CRITICISM, and DRIFTERS IN MOTION PICTURES. The volume also contains a few interesting short articles. Intner contributes a brief overview of issues related to form and genre headings for film and video and current LC practices as well as a good annotated bibliography on subject access to film and video. In a particularly interesting article, David P. Miller describes his experiences using both LC subject headings and descriptors from the thesaurus *Moving Image Materials: Genre Terms*, compiled by Martha M. Yee (Library of Congress, 1987), on records added to the online union catalog of a Massachusetts consortium. He discusses problems encountered when using multiple thesauri in a single system and suggests some strategies for dealing with resulting conflicts. The book also contains a chapter that offers worthwhile suggestions to the novice developing a video collection. The rationale offered for including this chapter is that in small libraries the video cataloger must sometimes assist in collection development.

This is one of more than 20 publications and workbooks available from Soldier Creek Press that deal with cataloging specialized materials. The intended audience should find it useful.

—Joseph W. Palmer

641. **Macrothesaurus for Information Processing in the Field of Economic and Social Development.** New York, United Nations, 1991. 375p. $40.00pa. ISBN 92-64-13450-6. S/N E.91.I.3.

This 4th edition was prepared by Alan Gilchrist, a British expert in vocabulary management, and the consulting firm of GAVEL under the direction of the Organisation for Economic Co-operation and Development (OECD), the United Nations (UN) Department of International Economic and Social Affairs, the UN Advisory Committee for Co-ordination of Information Systems (ACCIS), and the International Development Research Center (IDRC). Thus it is truly an international, authoritative thesaurus of terms for indexing and retrieval of texts that deal with economics and social development. Approximately 350 terms have been added to those in the 3d edition, but no terms have been removed and no changes in the previous structure have been made (no new categories have been added, and no changes in hierarchical relationships have occurred).

This is a fairly standard thesaurus. An effort has been made to use terms that represent single concepts, but many bound terms (e.g., "access to culture," "accident investigation") are included for clarity and convenience. The typical entry in the alphabetical list includes the descriptor, equivalents in French and Spanish, a category notation, an occasional scope note, synonyms or equivalent terms, broader terms, hierarchical top terms (unless the immediately broader term is the top term), narrower terms, and related terms. Supplemental displays include 19 broad subject categories (further subdivided into three levels), hierarchies, and a KWOC (keyword-out-of-context) index that provides direct access to all key words in descriptors. An appendix lists all new terms in this edition.

Many hierarchies are shallow and disconnected, and the relationship between subject categories and hierarchies is unclear. For example, there is a separate, isolated hierarchy for "youth organizations: Student movements," but it is not linked to the larger "groups" hierarchy, which includes "associations," "interest groups: occupational organizations," and "social groups." Individuals who deal with databases or collections that deal with economics or social development will want to consider this thesaurus for possible use in indexing and searching, especially because its publishers are committed to continuous maintenance and future revisions.—**James D. Anderson**

642. Scriven, Michael. **Evaluation Thesaurus.** 4th ed. Newbury Park, Calif., Sage, 1991. 391p. $45.00; $22.00pa. AZ191.S37. 025.4'9. LC 91-9264. ISBN 0-8039-4363-6; 0-8039-4364-4pa.

Evaluation as a field of inquiry received intense interest in the late 1960s. After 20 years of development, it is beginning to show signs of maturity. Scriven, a recognized authority in the field, has collected and defined its terms into this much expanded edition. Each term is described in a miniessay, some as long as several pages. Terms in the essay that are defined elsewhere are boldfaced, and cross-references are often listed at the entry's end along with articles or books to check for further information. Terms come from a broad range of fields, such as education, public administration, business, and social institutions in general. Thus, the thesaurus is valuable to all areas where evaluation strategies and research methods are important. The terms are very current, with excellent descriptions of such techniques as meta-analysis and naturalistic research.

Scriven is both descriptive and critical in his judgments about various methods of evaluation. However, while the educated layperson or beginning graduate student will be able to understand most of the text, Scriven occasionally launches into jargonistic prose that will turn away all but the seasoned expert. Of immense help would be a list of main terms or areas of evaluation that the beginner could use to search the text in a systematic way using the existing cross-reference structure. Still, *The Evaluation Thesaurus* is highly recommended for any library, student, or professional interested in evaluation. [R: Choice, Apr 92, p. 1214]—**David V. Loertscher**

643. **Sears List of Subject Headings: Canadian Companion.** 4th ed. By Lynne Lighthall. Bronx, N.Y., H. W. Wilson, 1992. 88p. $18.00. Z695.S43. 025.4'9. LC 92-27740. ISBN 0-8242-0832-3.

The 4th edition of this useful work follows the format and purpose of earlier editions. Begun in 1978 by Ken Haycock and with subsequent editions coauthored by Lighthall, the *Canadian Companion* serves as a supplement to *Sears List of Subject Headings* (see ARBA 92, entry 585) for works with Canadian content. This edition relates to the 14th edition of *Sears* and draws its classification numbers from *Abridged Dewey Decimal Classification and Relative Index*, 12th edition (see ARBA 91, entry 617). It also reflects some of the changes and additions found in the recently published 3d edition of *Canadian Subject Headings* (CSH). It has a slightly larger introduction, and the list of subject headings has been expanded from 72 to 88 pages.

As in previous editions, the subject headings deal with topics related to Canadian history, politics, the nature of Canadian society, and terminology where these differ from the United States or need more depth in subject access (e.g., POSTAL CODE - CANADA versus ZIP CODE - CANADA; TOTEM POLES versus TOTEMS AND TOTEMISM). *Canadian Companion* follows CSH in listing Canada's two founding peoples (e.g., CANADIANS, FRENCH-SPEAKING rather than FRENCH CANADIANS) and in subdividing various types of Canadian literature into the official languages (e.g., YOUNG ADULTS' LITERATURE, CANADIAN [English]). This work is an essential purchase for any library that uses the main Sears list and has materials with Canadian content in its collection.
—**Jean Weihs**

644. **Unreal! Hennepin County Library Subject Headings for Fictional Characters and Places.** 2d ed. Jefferson, N.C., McFarland, 1992. 145p. index. $29.95. Z695.1.F47H45. 025.4'980883. LC 92-53596. ISBN 0-89950-733-6.

Unreal! is an alphabetical list of subject headings and references established at the Hennepin County Public Library for fictional characters and imaginary places. Up to four elements are given under individual entries for established subject headings: *see* references from other names by which characters and places may be known, including uninverted forms for characters entered under their surnames; cataloger's notes describing who or what the subject heading is, such as "fictional character," "fictional group," and "imaginary place"; cataloger's notes giving the name's creator; and public notes to display in the public catalog to library users. An alphabetical index of creator names concludes the volume.

Unreal! will provide library catalogers with a rich source of names that they can consult when establishing subject headings for fictional characters and places. If libraries are not using the Hennepin County subject headings system, catalogers will have to consult practice manuals for the particular subject headings system they are using to choose the correct form of heading, assign MARC tags and subfield codes to headings in online systems, and index and display established subject headings and references. Reference librarians will also find this work a valuable resource for identifying the creators of fictional characters in response to patron requests.—**Karen Markey Drabenstott**

645. Walker, Alvin, Jr., ed. **Thesaurus of Psychological Index Terms.** 6th ed. Washington, D.C., American Psychological Association, 1991. 332p. $65.00. Z695.1.P7T48. 025.4'915. LC 90-14520. ISBN 1-55798-111-6.

This thesaurus lists and describes terms used to index *Psychological Abstracts*, PsycINFO, and PsycLIT. Two introductory sections describe the development of the thesaurus throughout its six editions. Other sections explain the construction of the thesaurus and its use. Search strategies for *Psychological Abstracts*, PsycINFO, and PsycLIT are outlined in additional sections. There are lists of index terms new to this edition and new terms not used (referred from). In the relationship section of the thesaurus, each index term includes date first used; scope notes; number of times used in citations; broader, narrower, and related terms; and index number for use in online searching. The rotated alphabetical terms section places, in alphabetical order, each word in indexed and nonindexed (referred from) terms. A final section lists indexed terms in broad clusters, such as educational, legal, geographical, and treatment terms, and subclusters, such as counseling, attitude and interest measures, occupational groups, criminal offenses, special education, and symptomatology. The explanations given in the introductory material are clear, lucid, and thorough.

This is an essential tool for effective use of the online and print abstracts produced by the American Psychological Association. As such, any library that has access to these reference sources should own this thesaurus. In other libraries it could be used to define psychological terms and place them in chronological and subject contexts. The thesaurus is very easy to use with a few minutes' instruction.—**Margaret McKinley**

Comparative and International Librarianship

646. **Directory of Special Collections of Research Value in Canadian Libraries. Repertoire des Collections Specialisees Utiles a la Recherche dans les Bibliotheques Canadiennes.** Ottawa, National Library of Canada, 1992. 1v. (various paging). index. $32.25pa; $41.90pa. (U.S.). 026'.00025'71. ISBN 0-660-57302-4. [Editor's note: this work is no longer in print.]

This tool can be used to discover which Canadian library has a strong collection of works by Thomas Hobbes, on the Mormon Church, in women's studies, or on vulcanology. Some 245 special collections held at 45 locations (principally universities) are described. They are arranged by broad subject, and a subject index is provided. The entries come from questionnaires; each source has described its collection on the basis of a variety of scopes. These include subjects, history of collection, description, language, holdings, bibliographic access, physical access, and any publications that further describe the collection. The work is useful, but it is twice the size it should be because the text is in both French and English.—**Dean Tudor**

647. Gupta, B. M., ed. **Handbook of Libraries, Archives & Information Centres in India. Volume 9: Humanities Information Systems and Centres.** Delhi, India, Aditya Prakashan; distr., Columbia, Mo., South Asia Books, 1991. 2pts. index. $74.00/set. ISBN 81-85179-53-0.

648. Gupta, B. M., ed. **Handbook of Libraries, Archives & Information Centres in India. Volume 11: Libraries, Archives & Information Technology: An Annotated Bibliography 1970-1990. Part 1.** Delhi, India, Aditya Prakashan; distr., Columbia, Mo., South Asia Books, 1991. 454p. index. $49.50. ISBN 81-85179-68-9.

Gupta has filled a major gap in the library literature by producing this set of books. Volume 9 of the proposed 12-volume handbook has been published in two separate volumes. Part 1 has 31 articles written by well-known authors on various special libraries in India. The long list includes many old libraries, such as the Asiatic Society of Bombay, Khuda Baksh Oriental Public Library, the Asiatic

Society Library of Bengal, the Adyar Library, and Deccan College: Archives and Library. Part 2 has 36 articles on various research institutes, libraries, and archives. All articles are descriptive, and a few are more scholarly. The state archives of many Indian states, including Delhi, Rajasthan, Tamil Nadu, and West Bengal, have been included in this volume. There are special articles on the Indira Gandhi National Centre for Arts; university archival programs; and various research institutes, including the Indian Institute of Islamic Studies, the Central Institute of Buddhist Studies, and the Sikkim Research Institute of Tibetology. Both volumes have good, useful indexes.

Volume 11, part 1, is an annotated bibliography of literature on libraries, archives, and information technology and covers the period from 1970 to 1990. It is divided into 16 chapters under various subjects, such as acquisition and book selections, classification, collection development, information and reference sources, interlibrary loan, librarianship, and library and information management. The 2,957 entries have been arranged alphabetically under each subject heading. More than 80 percent of the entries are annotated. There are indexes to authors, publishers, corporate subjects, and subjects to help users find material by entry numbers.

The book includes three appendixes: a list of publishers, distributors, and exporters; a list of library and information science serials; and a list of books and reports published between 1980 and 1990. In addition, there are three lists in front of the bibliography: journals indexed, abbreviations of periodicals indexed, and abbreviations used in the book. One of the special features of this volume is an introduction in which Gupta traces a short history of the development of all types of libraries in India. These works are excellent additions to the library literature and are highly recommended for all librarians, library educators, and library school libraries interested in Indian libraries and librarianship.

—**Ravindra Nath Sharma**

649. Nunn, Hilary, comp. **Industrial Group Index: Members Classified by Name, Employer, Industry, Geographic Location and Software Used.** London, Library Association; distr., Lanham, Md., UNIPUB, 1992. 396p. index. $55.00pa. 020.6. ISBN 1-85604-008-9.

This is an excellent directory of the backgrounds and capabilities of the 1,600 members of the Library Association's Industrial Group. Although it has been a long time in coming, the tool has benefited from comparison with similar works from earlier years of related ASLIB, ALA, SLA, and ASIS groups. Also, the stated intention of Nunn to provide an inquiry service upon the database now at hand will lead to further improvements in the content. The presentation is clear, clean, and complete for each of the subarrangements mentioned in the title. As an example, "Indexes of Members by Software" has these categories: cataloging, communications, database construction, library management, programming, spreadsheets, text retrieval, and word processing. One might quibble that the index to postal addresses will be more useful to Continentals accustomed to the peculiarities of the Postal Service's practices rather than to North Americans. Highly recommended.—**Eugene B. Jackson**

650. Penney, Barbara, comp. and ed. **Music in British Libraries: A Directory of Resources.** 4th ed. London, Library Association; distr., Lanham, Md., UNIPUB, 1992. 97p. index. $80.00. 026.00025. ISBN 0-85365-739-4.

The 4th edition of this work differs in its physical presentation from the 3d. It has larger pages and is much thinner; it is also colorful, attractive, and sturdy. However, the scope and arrangement are similar. Both editions are based on a questionnaire mailed to "all public libraries, universities and polytechnics with music courses or music collections, cathedrals, colleges of music, museums with music collections, and individuals with known specialist collections." Data sought includes name, address, chief music/audio librarian (or contact person), hours, registered users, manuscripts, stock (e.g., statistics), sound recordings (description of genres held), publications, listings (e.g., in *British Union Catalogue of Orchestral Sets*), services, restrictions on services, automation, special collections, and comments. Arrangement of the 340 entries is alphabetical. Those who wish to borrow material can find public lending libraries in appendix 2; sound recordings are found in appendix 3. The county index provides a useful geographical prospectus. Where the main entry differs from the name of the library's location, it is listed in the index of place-names. Finally, access to special collections is through the index of composers, types of music, and names of collections.

The result is a comprehensive, although not exhaustive, inventory of music libraries throughout Great Britain and Northern Ireland. It is the tool of first recourse to discover addresses, fax and telephone numbers, and personnel data. Penney has been liberal in including small collections, such as Worcester Cathedral (a highly specialized collection of church music). Note that universities and the like are listed under place-name. In some cases individual collections (e.g., the various constituents of London University) are given separate entries; in others, mention is made of other collections, but no entry is given. It is regrettable that nonresponding libraries are listed separately under contact addresses, as users seeking the address and telephone number may not think to look beyond the main section.

Penney's uniform treatment of both major and minor collections has produced a work broad in coverage. For those planning scholarly study, it is a starter tool to find contact information. Any library with an interest in music in Great Britain should acquire it. [R: LAR, Nov 92, p. 735] – **Ian Fairclough**

Copyright

651. Jasion, Jan T. **The International Guide to Legal Deposit.** Brookfield, Vt., Ashgate Publishing/Gower Publishing, 1991. 210p. $69.95. K1426.J37. 344'.092. LC 91-12842. ISBN 1-85742-001-2.

There is no uniform definition of *legal deposit*, but in broad terms it describes laws and regulations that require publishers to deposit a specified number of copies of each publication in designated libraries. This applies to private and corporate publishers as well as to government agencies. Legal deposit is sometimes called "copyright deposit," but legal deposit is broader than the deposit portions of copyright laws and regulations.

This work is a worldwide summary of legal deposit laws and regulations. Part 1 is a 10-page overview of legal deposit, from the 1645 Polish deposit law to the most recent. Part 2 contains a tabular survey of legal deposit, a list of legal deposit libraries, and citations to current laws and regulations. Part 3 summarizes past and present legal deposit practices in each nation and state. For example, government agencies in Manitoba must deposit one copy of each official publication in the Library of Congress.

This well-documented book appears to provide a thorough treatment of the subject. Recommended for comprehensive collections in international law, publishing, government publications, and library administration. [R: JAL, Mar 92, p. 58] – **Jerome K. Miller**

Indexing

652. Gorman, G. E., and J. J. Mills. **Guide to Current Indexing and Abstracting Services in the Third World.** Munich, New Providence, N.J., K. G. Saur, 1992. 260p. index. $65.00. 025.3'09171'4. LC 91-44499. ISBN 0-905450-85-X.

Gorman and Mills, of the School of Information Studies, Charles Sturt University, Australia, have filled an important gap in Third World bibliographic control by compiling this descriptive and critical bibliography of indexing and abstracting services. Ranging in length from 1 to 3 pages, entries describe 123 services, providing the date of first publication; ISSN; frequency and cumulation data; subscription information; publisher; descriptions of scope, arrangement, and content; and an overall assessment. Information is based on examination of one or more actual issues, with the exception of online databases, for which published documentation was used. An appendix lists 48 services for which issues or documentation were unavailable. The great majority of services are printed publications. In the main section, only three online databases and one CD-ROM database are identified. Unfortunately, the index does not provide access to services by medium.

The presentation of this compilation ignores a basic tenet of subject bibliography: the main arrangement of entries should reflect the principal purpose of the listing. Most users will want to discover services from particular countries or regions or on particular subjects. Hence, the main arrangement should have been by country and region and then by subject. Instead, entries are arranged alphabetically by service title, something that most users are unlikely to know. Consequently, the subject index is even more important, but it suffers from two related defects: too many undifferentiated entries (e.g., 39 under India, 26 under social sciences) and too many headings without subheadings to provide context for selecting entries. Entries under countries should have been subdivided by topic, as was well done under such regions as the Caribbean and Latin America. Similarly, entries under topics should have been subdivided by country and region. This valuable compilation can be made even more useful by aligning its arrangement and indexing more closely to expected use.

—James D. Anderson

653. Wellisch, Hans H. **Indexing from A to Z.** Bronx, New York, H. W. Wilson, 1991. 461p. index. $35.00. Z695.9.W45. 025.3. LC 90-26933. ISBN 0-8242-0807-2.

Organized not by chapter but by alphabetically arranged topical heads, Wellisch's indexing book presents the prospective indexer, librarian, library student, or editor with a comprehensive and frequently humorous study of indexing. Its broad, in-depth discussion, while often light in tone, is clearly written and well researched by this past president of the American Society of Indexers. The syntax, tone, and organization of the book make it superior to similar texts (e.g., *Introduction to Indexing and Abstracting*, 2d ed., by Donald B. Cleveland and Ana D. Cleveland, [Libraries Unlimited, 1990] or *Indexing Concepts and Methods* by Harold Borko and Charles L. Bernier [Academic Press, 1978]) as both an introductory guide to preparing indexes and as a reference source for the inexperienced indexer. The large type flows through a simple and pleasing page design, and the book is filled with many examples, each keyed with abbreviations to authoritative sources in the indexing field (ranging among *Anglo-American Cataloging Rules*, 2d ed. [see ARBA 80, entry 204]; British Standards Institution; National Information Standards Organization sources; the *Chicago Manual of Style* [see ARBA 83, entry 85]; and others).

While on the whole a complete and wide-reaching resource, this work has some interesting minor aberrations. Although published by a United States publisher, it uses the British convention of placing punctuation marks, such as commas and periods, outside quotation marks—neither publisher nor author comment on this. The well-prepared index to this book violates at least two of the author's own general rules for preparing indexes. Several headings with more than seven locators are not broken down into subcategories, and *see* references are sometimes used rather than double entries when only a few locators are involved. In addition, in at least one entry to an abbreviation (BGN [Board of Geographic Names]), only the abbreviated form appears as an entry. These nominal errors do not detract from the strength of the book, which is a must for any school, research, or public library. [R: WLB, Mar 92, p. 115]—**Louis R. Ruybal**

Information Technology

654. Burwell, Helen P., and Carolyn N. Hill, eds. **The Burwell Directory of Information Brokers 1992.** Houston, Tex., Burwell Enterprises, 1992. 442p. index. $59.50pa. ISBN 0-938519-08-5.

This directory is an annual compilation designed to link those who need information with professional information retailers. Prior to 1991 it was called the *Directory of Fee-based Information Services*, but the publisher changed its name because people in the industry were referring to it as *Burwell Directory* and because the term *information broker* has become more widely recognized in the nine years of the directory's publication. The directory contains 1,300 entries, an increase of more than 200 entries from the previous year, for information brokers, freelance librarians, independent information specialists, information packagers, public and academic libraries, and other information retailers in the United States and 44 other countries. Retailers offer fee-based research and document retrieval through primary and secondary sources and public and private computer databases. Entries are arranged alphabetically by state in the U.S. section and alphabetically by country in the international section. They are numbered consecutively across the two sections to enable users to find entries when consulting the directory's indexes to cities, companies, contact names, subjects, and services.

The Burwell Directory is a standard reference source in academic, public, and special libraries. Small and medium-sized businesses that have no library but an occasional information need will also find the directory a useful acquisition.—**Karen Markey Drabenstott**

655. **Directory of Japanese Technical Resources in the United States 1992.** By the U.S. Department of Commerce, National Technical Information Service, Office of International Affairs. Springfield, Va., National Technical Information Service, 1992. 115p. (Japanese Directories Series). $40.00pa. ISBN 0-934213-32-1.

This 5th annual edition was prepared by the Secretary of Commerce in compliance with the requirements of the Japanese Technical Literature Act of 1986. Listed alphabetically are 165 commercial services, 19 nonprofit organizations, 5 professional and trade associations, 41 government agencies, 18 libraries, 2 universities, and 2 other organizations that acquire, translate, or disseminate Japanese technical information. Further access is provided by indexes of organizations grouped by type, services grouped by function, expertise grouped by product or area, and geographic locations within the United States. Directories of federally funded translations (8 items) and university programs (9 sites) are also included. Relatively few libraries will need to purchase this specialized item, particularly if they already have an earlier edition. – **Lawrence W. S. Auld**

656. Williams, Brian. **Directory of Computer Conferencing in Libraries.** Westport, Conn., Meckler, 1992. 429p. (Supplements to Computers in Libraries, v.36). $65.00. Z674.8.W55. 021.6'5025'73. LC 91-39968. ISBN 0-88736-771-2.

The focus of this book is computer conferencing, with the information it contains gathered through a survey conducted in 1990. It provides a great deal of very useful data on computer conferences available and the networks used to access the conferences. The directory begins with a definition/description of computer conferencing that focuses on the differences between electronic mail, bulletin boards, teleconferencing, and video conferences. This section also discusses the applications and selection of a conferencing solution. The introduction is followed by a description of conferencing system software, including hardware and operating system requirements, costs, and a list of the commands used by the software; conferencing systems, including instructions on how to log on and a list of the different conferences that can be accessed; and networks such as BITNET, the Internet, SPRINTNET, and TYMNET (with a resource list of where to find more information). The book concludes with several appendixes, of which the most useful are the list of library catalogs accessible through the Internet and the databases and online catalogs that can be accessed without charge. There is also a comprehensive bibliography.

This informative directory is not for the novice computer user; it assumes a comfortable degree of computer literacy. It will be extremely useful for those users who have that literacy but who need technical instruction on how to access networks and the computer conferences and online catalogs through the networks. [R: CLJ, Oct 92, p. 410; JAL, July 92, pp. 191-92; WLB, Sept 92, p. 111]
– **Linda Main**

Inter-library Loans

657. Morris, Leslie R., and Sandra Chass Morris. **Interlibrary Loan Policies Directory.** 4th ed. New York, Neal-Schuman, 1991. 785p. index. $95.00. Z713.5.U6M67. 025.6'2. LC 91-31443. ISBN 1-55570-090-X.

The use of online bibliographic databases has expanded the world of information resources for library patrons just when their local libraries' acquisitions budgets have contracted. One of the results of these developments is that interlibrary loan has become a more important source of information delivery to the patron. For librarians, accurate, easily accessible interlibrary loan (ILL) policies are essential for the rapid and efficient processing of ILL requests.

This edition of the *Interlibrary Loan Policies Directory* will be of limited usefulness, mostly because of the small number of libraries represented in it. Although the *American Library Directory* (R. R. Bowker, 1992) includes more than 35,000 public, academic, special, governmental, and Canadian libraries, and OCLC (Online Computer Library Center) lists more than 12,000 participating libraries, this directory has entries for about 1,550 lending libraries. This edition has been minimally expanded compared to the 3d (1988) edition, which included about 1,500 entries.

The amount of information collected on each library's policies is extensive and well presented. The directory is arranged by state, with libraries listed alphabetically. Each entry includes the interlibrary loan department's address and telephone number, acceptable methods of request transmission, fees, average turnaround time, and policies for specific types of materials. This edition no longer includes the NUC (National Union Catalog) codes for libraries, but it does have an institutional name index and a list of fax numbers.

 A paper directory such as this is handy. However, the use of the online Name-Address Directory (NAD) in OCLC really is more convenient than the preface to this volume would indicate—at the OCLC terminal, the user can search the NAD without leaving the ILL subsystem. A library doing a substantial volume of ILL transactions will need more than this directory for adequate information. Considering the price of the 4th edition, the rapid changes in ILL policies and pricing, and the limited number of additions to this work, a library could satisfactorily use other sources. [R: LJ, 1 May 92, p. 126]—**Linda A. Naru**

 658. **WLN Interlibrary Loan Policies Directory.** Lacey, Wash., WLN, 1991. 1v. (unpaged). index. $45.00 looseleaf w/binder.

 This directory, derived directly from the WLN (Western Library Network) online ILL (Interlibrary Loan) policy file, provides access to information about the interlibrary lending policies of more than 230 libraries of all types throughout the Pacific Northwest with holdings in the WLN database. Update pages, which include both new policies and updates to existing policies and which can easily be inserted in the binder, will be issued at least annually and are included in the directory price.

 Policies in the directory are arranged alphabetically by institution name, followed by the National Union Catalog (NUC) symbol so users may rearrange by this symbol if they so desire. Policies are marked with the "last updated" date and with the "printed" date so that the currency of policy information for a specific library can be easily determined. From the directory information submitted by the libraries in an easily read format and the 14 indexes, the user can find not only the standard items (e.g., address, ILL contact name, telephone and fax numbers, loan services provided, charges) but also such information as which libraries will lend certain material types (e.g., videocassettes, genealogy materials, printed music, government documents), whether a library accepts subject requests, and what the major collections and subject or language specialties of a library may be.

 Although libraries with online access to WLN can search the ILL policy file for updated information, data on interlibrary loan policies in a quick, convenient format is always useful. Therefore, this directory should be of interest to libraries that work with WLN institutions. [R: LJ, July 92, p. 133]
—**Esther Jane Carrier**

Library Automation

 659. Desmarais, Norman, ed. **CD-ROM Reviews 1987-1990: Optical Product Reviews from *CD-ROM Librarian*.** Westport, Conn., Meckler, 1991. 300p. $40.00. Z681.3.067C325. 025.3'0285. LC 91-25365. ISBN 0-88736-733-X.

 660. Ensor, Pat. **CD-ROM Research Collections: An Evaluative Guide to Bibliographic and Full-Text CD-ROM Databases.** Westport, Conn., Meckler, 1991. 302p. index. (Supplements to Computers in Libraries). $55.00. Z675.R45E57. 025.2'1877. LC 91-23710. ISBN 0-88736-779-8.

 As libraries begin to create CD-ROM stations, they need to learn about the best applications geared to the clientele of a library. Two publications may help until CD-ROM reviews and basic lists are commonplace. *CD-ROM Reviews* provides a cumulation of the reviews printed in *CD-ROM Librarian* since the beginning of CD-ROM as a library technology. The reviews have merely been reprinted with no attempt at updating to reflect new versions of the product. However, if the product was reviewed twice in *CD-ROM Librarian*, both reviews are included. The book has 73 reviews and contains titles such as PsycLit, Ulrich's Plus, Oxford English Dictionary on Compact Disk, LaserCat, Moody's 5000 Plus, and Books in Print Plus. A typical review includes a description of the product, hardware and software, searching requirements, a description of a test search, a critical summary, and product information.

CD-ROM Research Collections is a companion volume to *CD-ROM Reviews* that contains Ensor's critical evaluations of 114 CD-ROM databases. Databases are included if they are useful in bibliographic research across a wide spectrum of fields. Thus, Library Literature, Medline, and GPO Monthly Catalog are included, but fulltext sources such as Oxford English Dictionary on Compact Disk are not. Each review contains title with bibliographic description and price, equipment and software requirements, arrangement, searching capabilities, licensing arrangements, and a description of the product.

Taken together, the two sources would cover the major titles on CD-ROM that might be considered of reference value. As a beginning, they are valuable as a source list of major tools available and as a collection of somewhat critical descriptions. But they are only the beginning. After reading the review, the librarian must search for more recent reviews, check current product literature, and test the disk before purchase. Even the most recent review will not cover changes and updates made by the producers as the industry is evolving so rapidly. These books are recommended for purchase if their contents fill a need. [R: CLJ, June 92, p. 243; LJ, 1 Mar 92, p. 124; RQ, Summer 92, p. 593]

—David V. Loertscher

661. Henry, Marcia Klinger, Linda Keenan, and Michael Reagan. **Search Sheets for OPACs on the Internet: A Selective Guide to U.S. OPACs Utilizing VT100 Emulation.** Westport, Conn., Meckler, 1991. 195p. index. (Supplements to Computers in Libraries). $39.50. Z699.35.C38H46. 025.3'132. LC 91-31065. ISBN 0-88736-767-4.

Search Sheets for OPACs on the Internet consolidates the command capabilities of online public access catalogs (OPACs) administered by 25 institutions into 6 functional areas: search, limit, display, moving around, edit, and help. Overlap is evident between functional areas. For example, the call-number browse capabilities of Polycat and LCS/Ohio State are comparable, but they are classified in two different search-sheet functional areas. One-half of the book gives examples of online help screens for 7 of the 15 OPACs. More than half of these screens come from HOLLIS and MELVYL online catalogs that have been developed separately for Harvard University and nine University of California campuses. The two indexes that conclude the book are alphabetical lists of the 1,000 libraries that can be searched by the commands given on the search sheets.

The authors acknowledge that the material documented in their work is subject to change. For example, the implementation of version 5.0 of the NOTIS system may change searching in the six OPACs based on the NOTIS system that are included in the book. The authors have made a proposal to Meckler to announce changes in the newsletter *Research and Education Networking*.

Library staff and patrons may be using OPACs on the Internet to perform their own research. Library staff may also be involved with interlibrary loan, reference, or the enhancement or selection of a stand-alone automated system. This work will help both groups get started searching the 25 OPACs mentioned. Seventeen of these OPACs are based on seven turnkey systems (i.e., ATLAS, CLSI, GEAC, INNOPAC, NOTIS, CARLYLE, VTLS), and their search sheets may be used as guides to many more OPACs on the Internet. [R: WLB, Feb 92, pp. 111-12]—**Karen Markey Drabenstott**

662. Schuyler, Michael. **Dial In 1992: An Annual Guide to Online Public Access Catalogs.** Westport, Conn., Meckler, 1992. 282p. index. $55.00pa. ISBN 0-88736-808-5. ISSN 1047-3424.

The book consists of single-page lists of libraries and their online catalogs accessible by network. Each page contains name of the library; number of volumes; contact person; and telephone number, dial-in number and parameters for connection, hours of operation, Internet address, and type of online system.

Although the intent of this work is laudable, it falls short of being a comprehensive reference source. Because it relies upon voluntary cooperation for listings, the coverage is spotty and the information for individual listings is often incomplete. The listings are from public libraries as well as college and university libraries. Unfortunately, many important online university catalogs are not listed. Noticeably absent are the University of Colorado, the University of Michigan, Harvard, University of California at Los Angeles, and the University of California at Berkeley, which limits the potential of this printed list. A much more comprehensive collection is available online via Internet or BITNET. The informal and chatty introduction is full of useful information for the novice, but be forewarned—the polemics are strong. It is hoped that at a future date a more complete and comprehensive volume will be possible. However, because lists of catalogs on the networks are available online and are updated frequently, a handbook of directions and procedures for network connection might serve the purpose more effectively.—**Elisabeth Logan**

Library Conservation

663. DePew, John N., with C. Lee Jones. **A Library, Media, and Archival Preservation Glossary.** Santa Barbara, Calif., ABC-Clio, 1992. 192p. $59.00. ISBN 0-87436-576-7.

According to the cover blurb, this is a comprehensive source on the terminology of conservation and preservation of library, archival, and media center materials, with concise but comprehensive definitions of more than 1,500 terms. In the preface the authors' claims are more modest; they indicate that they have attempted to select terms primarily for the nonspecialist in conservation that reflect the state of technology in the 1980s and early 1990s. Some of the definitions have been supplied by the authors themselves; others are identified as having been revised by the preservation librarian of Princeton University; and others have been abstracted from 54 sources listed at the end of the book. For these, source and page citations are supplied in the text.

In actuality, this is a highly uneven glossary, with entries that vary from the superficial to the solid to the technical. For instance, there is no entry for *mass deacidification*, only a reference to *deacidification*. This, in turn, receives a rather cursory definition that equates deacidification with neutralization and makes no mention of mass deacidification or its techniques. When specific techniques were searched, good detailed technical explanations with source citations were found for DEZ and the obsolete morpholine process, but the entry for the important, widely used WEI T'O process merely states that it is Richard Smith's trademarked nonaqueous book deacidification system and that the name derives from an ancient Chinese god. There is no discussion of the chemistry involved even though there is a reference in the text (magnesium methoxide *see* WEI T'O). Also disappointing is the lack of an entry for the much-touted lithco process that promises to both deacidify and strengthen brittle paper.

While these examples illustrate the unevenness of this glossary, the book does contain much useful information. It seems strongest for media and binding terminology and for older preservation techniques. While this will be a worthwhile addition to the preservation bookshelf, it will often need to be used in conjunction with other sources. [R: RBB, 15 Sept 92, p. 188]—**Joseph W. Palmer**

Public Libraries

664. **University Press Books for Public and Secondary School Libraries 1991.** New York, Association of American University Presses, 1991. 114p. index. free pa. ISSN 1055-4173.

A cooperative venture between the American Association of School Librarians (AASL) and the Public Library Association (PLA) has produced this bibliography for the use of school and public librarians. (In separate publications for their respective constituencies, there had been much overlap.) Publications from 62 university presses have been examined and evaluated by committees from both organizations to determine what to include. Types of materials listed are publications of interest to secondary school students, scholarly titles that require a moderate knowledge of the subject, books that have broad applicability, and new editions or paperbacks of works previously published. Titles that appear to be textbooks, journals, or other serial publications have been omitted. Each entry contains, in addition to full bibliographical information, an annotation and a letter designation (O-Outstanding, G-General Audience, S-Special Interest, RG-Regional General, or RS-Regional Special Interest). Arrangement is by Dewey decimal number with an author and title index. This combined list should be very useful to librarians in their book selection for both secondary schools and small and medium-sized public libraries.—**Sara R. Mack**

665. Van Orden, Phyllis. **Library Service to Children: A Guide to the Research, Planning, and Policy Literature.** Chicago, American Library Association, 1992. 141p. index. $25.00pa. Z718.1.V336. 016.02762'5. LC 92-3823. ISBN 0-8389-0584-6.

Although an extensive body of literature about public library services to children exists, it is scattered in a number of journals and other sources and is therefore difficult to locate. Van Orden has performed a valuable service in compiling this annotated bibliography to "policy literature, historical works, research studies, reports, and conference proceedings relating to public library services to children and children's librarianship." The time frame covered is long: the earliest article is Harriet H. Stanley's 1901 "Reference Work with Children," and each decade of the twentieth century is represented in the list. However, most of the material comes from the 1980s and 1990s. Each entry includes the standard bibliographic information; a concise descriptive annotation; and notes on the type of literature, funding source, research method, and subject headings. Appendixes give access by research method and type of literature. One of the strengths of the book is that it includes a number of guidelines statements published by individual states. These documents are valuable for librarians trying to set up their own service guidelines, but they are often difficult to locate. Other types of materials included are periodical articles, reports, books, and theses. Van Orden has provided invaluable help for children's librarians and library school students in compiling this useful list.—**Adele M. Fasick**

School Libraries

666. ***The Book Report & Library Talk* Directory of Sources.** By Renee Naughton. Worthington, Ohio, Linworth Publishing, 1991. 1v. (various paging). illus. $15.95 spiralbound. ISBN 0-938865-09-9.

Naughton has worked to gather a potentially valuable list of materials and services for practicing school library media specialists. To meet the wide-ranging needs of media centers, the entries are necessarily diverse. The 20 chapters include lists of professional materials; bibliographies for audiovisual, storytelling, art and graphic, and automation resources; and addresses for publishers, jobbers, library supply firms, and security systems. The intent is to provide working professionals with information about products and services important in managing today's media centers.

The main strength of this work is its diversity. Naughton has succeeded in identifying many of the needs associated with media centers and then suggesting appropriate resources to help meet those needs. The first chapter, a bibliography of recommended professional materials, is especially well balanced. Naughton has tried to include resources for audiovisual media, but this coverage is weaker than for print media and especially lacking in references for educational microcomputer software. For example, of nearly a hundred titles in chapter 1, only one is a multimedia listing and only three are on videos. The chapter on teaching students library skills does have more audiovisual items, but only one software program is listed. Also, in the chapter on reviewing journals, it would have been helpful to identify those titles that review books, those that review audiovisual materials, and those that review both types.

Inevitably, there are some mistakes. Mildred Knight Laughlin and Kathy Howard Latrobe are library educators, not practicing school library media specialists (p. 10.3). Bound to Stay Bound puts durable bindings on hardback books and does not specialize in "hardcover paperbacks" (p. 19.10). Many of the chapters are merely nonevaluative listings of all sources Naughton could identify. It would have greatly increased the utility of this book if critical annotations that identified strengths and weaknesses of the items listed were included. Finally, chapter 20 reproduces reviews of professional books that were originally published in *Book Report* or *Library Talk*. Unfortunately, there is no indication of how these reviews were chosen for inclusion, the original date of publication of the review, or why Naughton felt it was valuable to reprint them here.

While this directory of sources could have been much stronger and the material in it has a limited life span, its comprehensiveness, practical approach, and occasional listing of lesser-known resource certainly make it useful, especially for beginning media specialists. For more in-depth coverage of this topic, volumes of *School Library Media Annual* (see ARBA 92, entry 612) should be consulted. [R: RBB, 1 Apr 92, p. 1469; SLMQ, Summer 92, p. 242; VOYA, June 92, p. 138]—**Carol A. Doll**

667. **The Elementary School Library Collection.** 18th ed. Lauren K. Lee and Gary D. Hoyle, eds. Williamsport, Pa., Brodart, 1992. 1254p. index. $99.95. Z1037.E4. 011.62. LC 91-23193. ISBN 0-87272-095-0.

This edition of *The Elementary School Library Collection* (ESLC) has been prepared by a new editor and is a basic, essential selection tool for school libraries. It includes works published before

June 1, 1991. More than 2,800 new titles have been added, making it the largest collection yet published. The current edition adds recommended CD-ROM products and CD sound recordings to the wide array of books and audiovisual materials included. Titles have been selected by an impressive advisory committee as well as a selection committee of school librarians and school district library directors. As with previous editions, strict qualitative criteria must be met for inclusion, and titles selected must reflect respect for, and understanding of, the multiethnic, pluralistic nature of the United States and Canada. Titles are annotated and arranged by Dewey Decimal number, and books and other media are interfiled. Adequate indexing provides sufficient access to the list. In addition, each title in the list is given a phase 1-3 designation that indicates a purchase priority.

This work is without peer as a general selection tool for elementary schools. It is more frequently updated than *Children's Catalog* (see ARBA 92, entry 610), it is larger, and it includes multimedia materials that reflect the needs of the elementary school curriculum. Public libraries that seek materials beyond books should purchase this work. For school libraries, it is recommended as often as the budget will allow. [R: RBB, 1 June 92, pp. 1773-74; SLMQ, Summer 92, p. 241]—**David V. Loertscher**

668. Kelly, Melody S. **Using Government Documents: A How-To-Do-It Manual for School Librarians.** New York, Neal-Schuman, 1992. 160p. (How-to-do-it Manuals for School and Public Librarians, no.5). $29.95pa. Z688.G6K44. 025.2'8. LC 92-11729. ISBN 1-55570-106-X.

The acquisition and use of government publications by school and public librarians will be greatly simplified by the purchase of this book. Designed to blaze a path through the bureaucratic confusion inherent in ordering government materials, it provides comprehensible access to the information published not only by the U.S. Government Printing Office but also by other federal agencies.

The introduction furnishes librarians with a cost-saving rationale for ordering government documents and clear instructions on acquisitions procedures. The first four chapters include government catalogs that contain books and periodicals; federal agencies and information clearinghouses, such as ERIC (Education Resources Information Center) and NTIS (National Technical Information Service); catalogs for nonprint materials available from the National Audiovisual Center; and catalogs for maps and atlases. The remaining six chapters contain information on using the nearest Federal Deposit Library; government subscriptions appropriate to elementary and secondary schools; 31 essential documents suitable for school and public libraries; documents recommended in support of various curricula, such as English, foreign languages, and science; documents that pertain to career information; and important publications related to education. Appendixes A to D include regional depository libraries, U.S. government book stores, the Superintendent of Documents classification system, and further reading on government documents.

While well organized and easy to use, Kelly's manual does not offer the quantity of citations that *U.S. Government Publications for the School Library Media Center* (see ARBA 92, entry 611) provides. School and public librarians who already have that guide should consider Kelly's manual only a supplementary acquisition. [R: SLJ, Dec 92, p. 38; VOYA, Dec 92, p. 316]—**Kathleen W. Craver**

669. Latrobe, Kathy Howard, and Mildred Knight Laughlin, comps. **Multicultural Aspects of Library Media Programs.** Englewood, Colo., Libraries Unlimited, 1992. 217p. index. $27.50. Z675.S3M83. 027.6'3'0973. LC 92-5385. ISBN 0-87287-879-1.

The changing demographics of U.S. cities have greatly influenced the nation's schools and school library media centers. School media specialists are faced with demands for programs that address the special needs of students in multicultural classrooms. In addition, educators were given a mandate in 1977 by the National Council for the Accreditation of Teacher Education to incorporate multicultural components into their curricula. This useful and pertinent collection of readings helps to fill the gaps in information sources and will help school media specialists and other educators understand cultural diversity and to design programs relevant to their individual school settings.

The readings are arranged in four major sections. Part 1, the introduction, emphasizes the multicultural library media center and provides background information on multiculturalism, the multicultural movement, and ethnicity. Part 2, "Gaining Perspective," includes a series of essays related to understanding and appreciating the unique needs of individual cultural groups. Melvin M. Bowie writes about African-Americans; Rose Mary Flores Story, Mexican-Americans; Lotsee Patterson,

Native Americans; Donna S. Richey, European-Americans; and Katheryne A. Averette, Jews. These essays cover the cultural, language, and personal needs and characteristics of each group, and its history and literature. In part 3, "Meeting Multicultural Needs within the Curriculum and the SLMP (School Library Media Program)," seven different essays cover topics related to theory, research, literature, and multicultural curricula. In part 4, "Multicultural Issues in Collection Development," the essays discuss access and intellectual freedom as well as collection development. Included here is a bibliography compiled by Isabel Schon on Spanish-language books. All essays are concluded with a reference list that provides a selective supporting bibliography of information sources on the topic. Other features include a glossary of definitions of terms that occur repeatedly in the literature and an author/subject/title index. While this work is by no means comprehensive and is limited in the information and approaches it presents, it is a timely presentation and represents a good start in developing a professional collection of similar resources. — **Lois J. Buttlar**

670. Nichols, Margaret Irby. **Guide to Reference Books for School Media Centers.** Englewood, Colo., Libraries Unlimited, 1992. 463p. index. $38.50. Z1037.1.W95. 011'.02. LC 91-45242. ISBN 0-87287-833-3.

This basic resource for school librarians, educators, and students has been updated and now contains 189 more entries than the 1986 edition. It is divided into media services, general reference, social sciences, humanities, and science and technology. Each of these areas is further divided into 54 subject categories. Within a subject are section headings for dictionaries and encyclopedias, handbooks and almanacs, biographies, indexes, and bibliographies when relevant. The format of this edition is similar to that of the 1986 work with the exception of the last three divisions. These are arranged by subject category. A chapter heading has been changed from "The Disabled" to "Handicapped," and an additional subject, "Etiquette," has been included. This edition still includes mostly works that adhere to the standard definition of a reference book, but it also cites titles that provide essential information when no reference works are available. Entries are consecutively numbered throughout the text. Each provides the user with full bibliographic data plus grade level codes that indicate suggested audience levels.

The quality of the annotations is excellent. All titles are marked either "recommended" or "highly recommended," thus enabling prospective purchasers to choose critically between similar works. Cross-references, where appropriate, are noted at the start of a specific topic or subtopic. Author/title and subject indexes complete the text.

A sampling of various subject categories yields a completeness that is normally difficult to achieve in one volume. For example, the section on ethnic minorities is replete with excellent references to various groups. Librarians wishing to increase their collections in this area will discover a wide selection of good sources. Given the rapid increase of references available on CD-ROM and disk, this reviewer was pleased to note how many in those formats were listed and evaluated, such as Grolier's *Electronic Encyclopedia* and several college software references.

This outstanding aid to the acquisition of reference materials for young people is highly recommended. School librarians should make frequent use of it for all subject areas. [R: LJ, 15 June 92, p. 107; WLB, Sept 92, p. 115] — **Kathleen W. Craver**

671. Paulin, Mary Ann. **More Creative Uses of Children's Literature. Volume I: Introducing Books in All Kinds of Ways.** Hamden, Conn., Library Professional Publications/Shoe String Press, 1992. 621p. index. $57.50; $35.00pa. Z675.S3P247. 027.8. LC 92-8916. ISBN 0-208-02202-3; 0-208-02203-1pa.

The enormous number of children's books published since Paulin's *Creative Uses of Children's Literature* (see ARBA 84, entry 1126) appeared in 1982 has required a two-volume update. Volume 1, based on the first chapter of the previous book, focuses on children's works published from the early 1980s to 1990. In 13 chapters Paulin discusses such subjects as booktalks, multimedia, genres, basal readers, and television tie-ins as keys to introducing books. Appendixes, 2 of which are bibliographies, comprise more than 40 percent of the book. The first bibliography, arranged by author and cross-referenced to the other, combines children's books and reference works. The second is an alphabetical and numbered list of nonprint materials. Title and subject indexes complete the volume.

Although an independent work, this volume cross-references topics in the first edition. Its one new element is an excellent discussion of resources for understanding whole language and literature-based curricula. The earlier volume received good reviews. This one is not, however, a particularly creative part of that work. Too often Paulin does little more than group books by topic to provide annotated bibliographies in essay form. She scatters bits of practical advice, but her techniques and uses are sketchy. The book's real weakness is that, instead of illustrating methods, Paulin randomly and irregularly attaches methods to illustrations. In general, many librarians and media specialists looking for hints for presentations will appreciate this work, but teachers looking for creative classroom activities will be disappointed. – **Raymond E. Jones**

672. **School Library Media Annual. Volume Ten: 1992.** Jane Bandy Smith and J. Gordon Coleman, Jr., eds. Englewood, Colo., Libraries Unlimited, 1992. 290p. index. $37.50. Z675.S3S291158. 027.805. ISBN 1-56308-068-0. ISSN 0739-7712.

This annual volume continues the established tradition of providing timely information and opinions on current topics of concern to school library media specialists. After a brief discussion of *America 2000*, articles concentrate on trends and issues, constructivism, and working with advanced placement teachers. The second section starts with an article, and responses to it, about the impact of online and CD-ROM databases on the way users search for information. Then there is a detailed article that describes and elaborates the decision-making process involved in implementing ACCESS PENNSYLVANIA. Ten research articles range from reviews of the literature to the New Christian Right and the public school curriculum. Finally, updates are included on such topics as pertinent professional organizations, the White House Conference on Library and Information Services, the Treasure Mountain Research Retreat, and book awards. The useful annual index of professional articles and a list of sources for identifying notable materials conclude the volume.

The emphasis in this volume is, appropriately, on the school library media center. Sixty percent of the thirty-eight contributors are from education, and the rest have a connection to school librarianship. The entire volume reflects the awareness of current trends and issues that are, or should be, of interest to school library media specialists. However, the research articles are not as strong as the rest of the work. For example, while the review of the ERIC material is well done, the analysis of selected research and of earlier editions of the *School Library Media Annual* are more superficial. The article about the attitudes of professors of educational administration toward school library media programs is based on a survey with a 35 percent return rate. The report on CD-ROM technology in secondary school library media centers does not give specifics on the inferential statistical tests and results, and there are no bibliography or references to the professional literature. Finally, there is an eastern bias to this volume; 18 of the 38 contributors are from the South, 8 are from the Northeast, and 7 are from the Midwest. Only three are from the West. Potentially valuable because the information here is timely and not always readily accessible in the library literature, this volume is useful for school library media specialists, youth librarians, and library educators. – **Carol A. Doll**

673. **Senior High School Library Catalog.** 14th ed. Brenda Smith and Juliette Yaakov, eds. Bronx, N.Y., H. W. Wilson, 1992. 1467p. index. (Standard Catalog Series). $115.00. Z1037.S435. 011.62. LC 92-26946. ISBN 0-8242-0831-5.

More than 1,000 new titles have been added to the recommended core collection for senior high school libraries in this edition of *Senior High School Library Catalog,* for a total of 5,762 titles. In addition to the initial volume, four paperbound supplements will be provided for 1993, 1994, 1995, and 1996. For easy use, the first part of the catalog consists of entries arranged in Dewey Decimal order (based on the 12th edition of *Abridged Dewey Decimal and Relative Index Classification* [1990]) with separate sections for fiction and short story collections. The committee of book selectors for this edition was composed of book reviewing personnel, library science faculty members, and senior high school librarians (most of whom work directly with students) from all parts of the United States. Most books have publication dates of 1985 or later, with some classics predating that time. The second part of the catalog is an author/title/subject/analytical index. Subjects include teenage suicide, teen pregnancy, AIDS, the environment, World War II, and science. Some subjects are better covered than others. For example, authors have extensive biographical coverage, whereas biographees in other fields of endeavor receive less attention. The analytical index provides access to parts of books, which will be useful in some libraries but not necessarily in others. Concluding the volume is a directory of publishers and distributors.

This catalog has been designed as an acquisition tool, a reference source, and an instructional aid in library schools. It can also be used for information verification, curriculum support, and collection maintenance. Although this work serves a definite purpose in these areas, it is not intended, nor should it be used, as the only such resource.

As was pointed out in ARBA 88 (see entry 640), most high school libraries are now multimedia, and a core selection of titles should reflect this. Publications suitable for use in school libraries in CD-ROM format, online, microform, and other media are available and need to be considered. However, while one may quibble with the selection process, this volume remains the standard for a good core list of titles. — **Anna Grace Patterson**

Special Libraries and Collections

General Works

674. **Tools of the Profession.** 2d ed. Jane Taylor, ed. Washington, D.C., Special Libraries Association, 1991. 192p. $19.00pa. ISBN 0-87111-378-3.

This volume is composed of 16 subject bibliographies prepared by divisions of the Special Libraries Association; it includes more than 1,000 titles. The first edition was published in 1988 (see ARBA 89, entry 571). Each bibliography lists basic reference sources for a given specialty, beginning with advertising and marketing and concluding with transportation. Although a uniform bibliographical style is employed for titles, there is no consistency in the organization of the individual bibliographies. Lengths of bibliographies vary, such as 24 pages for biological sciences versus 11 pages for chemistry. Annotations are erratic, with the best ones in the aerospace, education, library management, pharmaceutical, physics/astronomy/mathematics, and publishing bibliographies. The library management bibliography covers management in general, even listing *Business Week* as a title. There is no index; items are located by scanning the titles in each bibliography. In this way the volume may possibly serve as a training device for new library staff members, and it can also be used as a checking tool for collection development. As a basic reference source its use is limited.

— **Richard D. Johnson**

Genealogy and Local History

675. Kokernak, Jane, ed. **Prospect Researcher's Guide to Biographical Research Collections.** Rockville, Md., Taft Group; distr., Detroit, Gale, 1992. 339p. index. $79.00pa. LC 91-075405. ISBN 0-930807-26-X.

This directory attempts to list special collections, chiefly in genealogy and local history, held by libraries and information centers throughout the United States. According to the preface, the volume was prepared chiefly to assist those engaged in "prospect research" — apparently an endeavor to locate potential donors for fund-raising efforts. The descriptive information given in the state-by-state listings for each library looks much like that provided by the *American Library Directory* (see ARBA 91, entry 607) and by *Encyclopedia of Associations* (see ARBA 91, entries 37 and 38). In fact, these two sources could supply much of the same material presented here. Finally, it is not clear why certain institutions were included and others left out. For example, the Phoenix (Arizona) Public Library is here, but the Tucson (Arizona) Public Library is not. Neither the University of Arizona nor Arizona State University is included. There are few listings for local historical society libraries. The only library listed for the entire state of Wyoming is the Church of Jesus Christ of Latter-Day Saints collection in Byron. With its uneven treatment of libraries and considerable overlap with existing sources, this work cannot be recommended for purchase.

— **Donald C. Dickinson**

Government Documents

676. **Directory of Government Document Collections & Librarians.** 6th ed. Judy Horn and others, eds. Bethesda, Md., Congressional Information Service, 1991. 650p. index. $57.50pa. Z1223.Z7A43. 027.7'0973. LC 74-10760. ISBN 0-912380-15-2.

The 6th edition of this work contains updated directory information about government documents collections and librarians. Coeditors followed up on libraries that did not respond to questionnaires soliciting information for this edition, which resulted in more accurate and up-to-date information and in the inclusion of listings not in the 5th edition (see ARBA 88, entry 642). In fact, all libraries currently designated as federal depositories are listed.

The basic format of the directory remains the same although several sections have been renamed and a new section added. The main section, which is arranged by state and then by city, provides addresses, telephone numbers, staff names, and information about collections and services. Fax numbers and E-mail addresses have been added. Other sections of the directory include indexes by library name; type of collection (e.g., state, local, international, foreign); subject, agency, or organization strengths; and personal name. In addition, there are lists of library schools' documents instructors, libraries/agencies responsible for administering state documents programs, Bureau of the Census State Data Centers, organizations and agencies of primary importance for documents librarians, and individuals who are active in documents librarianship but not currently employed as documents librarians (a new section).

This attractively laid out and well-indexed directory provides a wealth of information useful to documents librarians. Names of staff members inevitably change, but basic information about documents collections and listings of other contacts make this an important ready-reference tool for anyone working with government documents. [R: JAL, May 92, p. 118]

—Carol Wheeler

University and College Libraries

677. Nisonger, Thomas E. **Collection Evaluation in Academic Libraries: A Literature Guide and Annotated Bibliography.** Englewood, Colo., Libraries Unlimited, 1992. 271p. index. $35.00. Z675.U5N58. 025.2'1877. LC 92-11037. ISBN 0-87287-925-9.

Aimed both at practitioners and educators, this work includes about 600 English-language books, chapters, articles, and other publications. Semipublished formats, such as dissertations, theses, and ERIC and NTIS documents are excluded. While nominally covering 1980 through most of 1991, the book also includes important items from earlier years (e.g., the "Pittsburgh Study" by Allen Kent and colleagues). All aspects of macro-evaluation are included; micro-evaluations that discuss title-by-title decisions are generally excluded, which means the coverage of selection and weeding is very sparse.

Material is arranged in 12 sections, beginning with general overview material and items related to methods. There is a section each on case studies, use studies, availability, overlap, and citation studies; there are also sections on standards, the use of a conspectus, and the use of automation. Reflecting current interests, there are two sections on serials. Each item is listed only once, and cross-references are rather sparse. There are detailed author-title and subject indexes, a useful introduction, short chapter introductions, and a brief glossary. Perhaps the most useful feature, however, is the annotations, which provide excellent summaries of the material and cogent evaluations.

Within Nisonger's limits, the choice of entries appears reasonably comprehensive; the exclusion of dissertations and ERIC and NTIS documents, which are readily available, is less reasonable. Lack of collocation in the index suggests overreliance on an automated indexing program; for example, "SCIsearch" and "Science Citation Index" are separate (and nonoverlapping) entries. Given the sparse cross-references, this flaw is most unfortunate. Despite these caveats, this work will stand for some time to come both as a record of the state of the art in academic library collection evaluation and as a guide to the researcher, teacher, and practitioner.

—James H. Sweetland

PUBLISHING AND BOOKSELLING

General Works

Bibliography

678. Armstrong, Robert D. **Nevada Printing History: A Bibliography of Imprints & Publications, 1881-1890.** Reno, Nev., University of Nevada Press, 1991. 403p. index. $50.00. Z1309.A74. 015.793. LC 88-33955. ISBN 0-87417-124-5.

The present volume continues Armstrong's earlier work, *Nevada Printing History: A Bibliography of Imprints & Publications, 1858-1880* (University of Nevada Press, 1981), and has over 1,400 entries. Official state documents are included, as are invitations, playbills and programs, printing for organizations, special publications of newspapers, broadsides, circulars, speeches, directories, and technical publications. Presses in 16 Nevada communities and 6 cities outside the state (many large printing jobs were sent to printers in other states) are represented. Each entry includes information on title pages, content summaries, and locations. Some descriptions also include extensive printing and production histories and accounts of related contemporary events in Nevada. An extended introduction summarizes Nevada printing history, while briefer introductions precede entries for each year. There are a subject index and an index of printers and publishers. Full-page photographs of some broadsides and title pages are also included.

Having examined each item described, Armstrong has prepared an exceptionally careful and detailed analysis of Nevada printing for a single decade. In addition, he has a talent for bringing history to life. The book itself is a fine example of printing. Libraries with an interest in printing history or in the history of the southwestern United States will find this volume a valuable addition to their collections. — **Margaret McKinley**

Dictionaries

679. Joyce, Donald Franklin. **Black Book Publishers in the United States: A Historical Dictionary of the Presses, 1817-1990.** Westport, Conn., Greenwood Press, 1991. 256p. index. $55.00. Z471.J68. 070.5'089'96073. LC 91-10528. ISBN 0-313-26783-9.

Joyce, director of the Felix G. Woodward Library at Austin Peay State University in Clarksville, Tennessee, and Greenwood Press should be congratulated for making this important book available. With an alphabetical arrangement and thorough indexes, the book is indispensable for any research into Black book publishing. Its interest extends beyond the scholar to the ordinary citizen, who will find this book most useful.

Although there may be some omissions, Joyce has scoured the land in search of his topic. Many publishers produce religious works; others are limited to Black topics; and some also work with fiction and poetry. Many of these publishers are landmarks in Afro-American history, including Howard University, the DuSable Museum, Hampton Institute, and the Afro-American newspaper.

The consistent arrangement of the text provides a clean approach to information. Each entry is broken down into the institution's publishing history and publications, a conclusion, notes, information sources, selected published titles, libraries holding titles, and officers. In addition to standard indexes such as name, subject, and title, Joyce includes a geographical index. This book should see extensive use. [R: Choice, Mar 92, p. 1048; LJ, 1 Feb 92, p. 80] — **Ronald L. Buchan**

680. **Multilingual Dictionary of Publishing, Printing and Bookselling.** Alan Isaacs, Elizabeth Martin, and Fran Alexander, eds. New York, Mansell/Cassell, 1992. 439p. $95.00. ISBN 0-304-32612-7.

More than 2,000 terms used in the international book trade are included in this dictionary and translated into English (both American English and British English when there are differences), French, German, Italian, Portuguese, Spanish, and Swedish. For example, the English-speaking reader who wants to know the equivalent of *paperback book* in German would look for that term in alphabetical order and find that the German word is *Taschenbuch*. The translations in the other included languages are also found in the entry. The selection of terms appears to be up-to-date (computer terms are included), and the book is well designed, clearly printed, and easy to consult. As the international character of printing, publishing, and bookselling increases—which it shows every sign of doing—this multilingual dictionary will become very significant to those in the trade.—**Dean H. Keller**

Directories

681. **Books and Magazines: A Guide to Publishing and Bookselling Courses in the United States.** Princeton, N.J., Peterson's Guides, 1992. 124p. $24.95pa. Z285.35.U5B66. 381'.45002'07073. LC 91-41014. ISBN 1-56079-088-1.

This is an alphabetically arranged guide to various study programs related to book and magazine publishing and bookselling. Programs include writing, editing, acquisition of publishable materials, author/editor relations, production, and management. The bookselling programs include those aimed at wholesalers, retailers, bookstore owners, and staff. Listings range from formal university programs that lead to a degree to topic-specific, one-day seminars for those already employed in bookselling or publishing. Eighty-one such programs are listed. The offering institutions are profiled in a standard manner, with name and location, program name, level of instruction, time needed to complete program, fees, contact person, and so on. The data was compiled in 1991 from information supplied by the institutions or associations that offer the classes. There are geographical and subject indexes.

Although this is a potentially useful directory, it is far from comprehensive and could probably be expanded to 150 institutions and associations without too much trouble. For instance, in the subject category of book arts, the seven listings merely scratch the surface. There are numerous other book arts programs, including such well-established ones as Nexus Press in Atlanta, the printing program at the University of Iowa, the King Library Press at the University of Kentucky, Pyramid Atlantic in Maryland, the Minnesota Center for Book Arts in Minneapolis, and Ohio State University's Logan Elm Press Arts of the Book Laboratory. [R: Choice, July/Aug 92, p. 1652; LJ, 15 May 92, p. 84; WLB, May 92, p. 121]—**Frank J. Anderson**

682. Clark, Bernadine. **Fanfare for Words: Bookfairs and Book Festivals in North America.** Washington, D.C., Library of Congress, 1991. 108p. index. $6.95pa. Z475.C57. 381'.45002074'7. LC 90-21318. ISBN 0-8444-0711-9.

The first third of *Fanfare for Words* is devoted to an enthusiastic essay that details the virtues of book fairs and also provides some practical advice on how to organize and run one. The rest of the book supplies information on, and descriptions of, some 60 book fairs in the United States and abroad. For each one there is information on attendance, audience, admission, and sponsors, as well as the names and addresses of contact persons. The dates for the 1990 and 1991 editions of each book fair are given to provide readers with an idea of when a particular book fair is normally held. Most of the ones listed in this work are not listed in *Chase's Annual Events* (see ARBA 91, entry 2) or the somewhat dated *A Guide to Fairs and Festivals in the United States* (see ARBA 86, entry 49), so this work could prove to be a useful source for libraries that serve serious bibliophiles or members of the publishing industry.—**Donald A. Barclay**

683. **The Colorado Book Guide.** Denver, Colo., Bloomsbury Review, 1991. 116p. $7.95pa. ISBN 0-9631589-0-2.

Colorado is hardly New York when it comes to publishing, but the state does support a lively and thriving book community, including what has been called the best bookstore in the Western Hemisphere, the Tattered Cover. *The Colorado Book Guide* covers most of the bookstores, libraries, publishers, agents, writing/book organizations, literacy programs, bookbinders, and book-related services (e.g., editing, retreats) to be found in the Centennial State. Each entry includes directory information, plus a line or two appropriate to the subject; for example, most bookstore listings include owner or manager and type of books sold. The typeface is clear and crisp, although there are a number of typographical errors.

The list of bookstores, while nearly complete for smaller and independently owned shops, omits some of the chain stores, especially in the city of Aurora (e.g., The Carpenter's Shop and Hatch's

Bookstore, both in Buckingham Square Mall). A few mall-based bookstores are not noted as such (e.g., Fantasy Works in Buckingham Square, Family Bookstore in Aurora Mall), and wholesale book dealers are not listed at all. The list of "Publishers/Other: A Selection of Literary and Consumer Publications ..." could be longer. An index, while not essential, would help lead the user to specialty stores (e.g., those that sell comic books).

This guide is a necessity for all Colorado libraries and bookstore owners, and is inexpensive enough that publishers and other such services in the Rocky Mountain region should also have a copy. Finally, those libraries around the country that serve a community of writers would find it useful.

—D. A. Rothschild

684. **Computer Publishers & Publications: An International Directory and Yearbook.** 1992-93 ed. Larchmont, N.Y., Communications Trends; distr., Detroit, Gale, 1991. 579p. index. $205.00. ISBN 0-88709-024-9. ISSN 0740-4085.

This directory lists more than 250 book publishers and 1,500 English-language periodicals, most from the United States, Canada, and Great Britain. It begins with a status report of the year in publishing, an interesting analysis of a decade of computer publishing trends. The listed publishers range from small houses with only one title to industry giants with dozens of titles. The listings detail the audiences (consumer, professional, and educational), number of current and projected titles, a list of representative and best-selling books, machine coverage, and language and software coverage. In some cases distributors are listed, as are the publishers' vertical markets (e.g., accounting, telecommunications, law). The periodicals include both obscure user group newsletters and well-known trade and consumer magazines. Each entry provides the type of periodical, format, circulation, frequency, coverage, price, advertising rates, and whether the periodical buys articles. There are numerous indexes, but there is no subject index, which would enhance the directory's usability.

In general, this comprehensive directory is an excellent source of information on computer publishing. It will appeal to consumers, computer and marketing professionals, and freelance writers.

—Stephen Haenel

685. **Information Marketplace Directory, 1993: A Directory of Information Industry Publishers and Their Suppliers.** Wilton, Conn., Simba/Communications Trends, 1992. 635p. index. $375.00. ISSN 1065-0393.

The scope of this work is fully expressed by the subtitle—it lists information firms and characterizes them by relevant market segments (e.g., finance and investing), by products (e.g., newsletters, databases), by formats (e.g., print, diskette), and by suppliers (e.g., fax/voice response systems). The volume lists these firms but does not evaluate them.

A typical entry includes name, mailing address, telephone and fax numbers, date of founding, number of employees, sales volume in 1991, name of "Ultimate Parent" (many firms are subsidiaries of well-known firms), a brief scope statement, name of contact person, distribution (format) used, markets, and products. The variety of firms and products ranges from John Wiley to "EDI Spread the Word." The preference for communication by telephone or fax is evident, as is some padding of entries. It is unlikely that many users would need the listing of a Cleveland suburban tabloid or a small-town Southern member of the Kidder-Ridder chain.

Included among the many indexes are those to products of information companies, distribution (format), markets, geographical location, and ownership. The lists that cover vendors useful to information companies begins with an alphabetical section and varies from such veterans as Dictaphone Corporation (1,200 employees) to the young Enterprise Corporation of America (5 employees). Other vendor information includes a section on products that is divided into 58 categories.

Despite the fact that the majority of firms and services listed have one or more products in print format, there are enough listings of newer items to make *Information Marketplace Directory* worthy of consideration. Libraries most likely to purchase it are those that serve graduate programs in the information industry, marketing, and library and information science, and those that serve small businesses.

—Eugene B. Jackson

686. **MLA Directory of Scholarly Presses in Language and Literature.** James L. Harner, ed. New York, Modern Language Association of America, 1991. 285p. index. $75.00; $25.00pa. ISBN 0-87352-391-1; 0-87352-392-Xpa. ISSN 1057-2899.

Much time can be wasted by submitting a manuscript to a publisher for whom it is inappropriate. Toilers in the field of literary criticism, literature departments, and libraries will find this volume very helpful in assisting in the most efficient submission of manuscripts. In addition to directory information for 283 university and commercial scholarly presses worldwide, there is data on particular subject interests, manuscript style, method of submission, and other useful topics. Especially helpful is the list of presses that did not respond to the questionnaire, or that responded but failed to meet the selection criteria (that of more than casual interest in literary or linguistic works). One drawback is that the information was gathered in 1989 and 1990 and so may already be out of date in some cases. Thus, this work needs to be updated frequently. [R: Choice, Sept 92, p. 86]

— Philip A. Metzger

687. **Publishers Directory, 1992: A Guide to New and Established, Commercial and Nonprofit, Private and Alternative, Corporate and Association, Government and Institution Publishing....** Linda S. Hubbard and Wendy S. Van de Sande, eds. Detroit, Gale, 1992. 1914p. index. $245.00pa. LC 84-645506. ISBN 0-8103-4908-6. ISSN 0742-0501.

The 12th edition of this work continues to provide comprehensive coverage of publishing information in the United States and Canada. Almost 18,000 publishers and 600 distributors are listed. Among them are publishing companies, small presses, special interest groups, museums and societies, divisions within universities, religious institutions, corporations whose principal activity is not publishing, and government agencies. Information has been derived from questionnaires sent to the publishers and from other sources when publishers have failed to respond. More than 1,000 entries have been added since the 11th edition. Changes in addresses and so forth have been noted.

Entries are entered numerically in an alphabetical word-by-word arrangement under the complete name of the publisher. Directory information includes the following when available: name of organization, address, telephone and fax numbers, founding date, ISBNs, Standard Address Number, CIP, affiliation with another publisher, persons of responsibility in the company, number of new titles published during the past three years, company policy on marketing and sales, subject area of publishing, sales market distribution, return policy with addresses, imprints or divisions or subsidiaries, and representative titles.

As is generally true with directories of this nature, *Publishers Directory* is already somewhat out of date. However, it complements *Literary Market Place* and *Publishers, Distributors, and Wholesalers of the United States* (R. R. Bowker, 1991) and is useful when a variety of directories is needed.

— Anna Grace Patterson

688. **Publishers, Distributors & Wholesalers of the United States 1991-92.** New Providence, N.J., R. R. Bowker, 1991. 2v. index. $139.95/set. ISBN 0-8352-3103-8. ISSN 0000-0671.

A standard in publishing for years, this work has seen a major and most welcome format change: it has been split into two volumes. Volume 1 contains the name index to publishers and the list of imprints, subsidiaries, and divisions. Volume 2 holds the key to abbreviations, toll-free and fax numbers for publishers and distributors, entries for wholesalers and distributors, a geographic index to the publishing industry, a list of ISBN prefixes with their publishers, a list of publishers by their fields of activity, and entries for inactive and out-of-business publishers. The new format makes it much more convenient to search for an entity as each volume is considerably smaller than the single book used to be (although together they are larger than the previous edition).

With some 58,000 active U.S. publishers, distributors, wholesalers, associations, museums, software producers, and audiocassette producers, this set is likely to answer most directory questions about these businesses. Highly recommended.

— D. A. Rothschild

Handbooks and Yearbooks

689. Rose, Jonathan, and Patricia J. Anderson, eds. **British Literary Publishing Houses, 1881-1965.** Detroit, Gale, 1991. 420p. illus. index. (Dictionary of Literary Biography, v.112). $108.00. LC 91-31918. ISBN 0-8103-4592-7.

In addition to publishing more than 100 volumes of short biographies of European and North American writers, Gale includes in the Dictionary of Literary Biography series several volumes of "biographies" of British and American literary publishing houses from the nineteenth century to the present. For scholars these are essential for the study of the commerce of literature, and for librarians they can make the task of pinning a date on an undated imprint an easy one. The present volume is the second of two on British firms, the first having covered the years 1820-1881, the beginning of the modern period in publishing. As before, entries include crucial dates, name changes, and up to several pages that recount the history of the particular firm. Illustrations of founders, key persons, house trademarks, and other subjects are frequently provided. A bibliography and list of sources are also included where possible. [R: Choice, Jan 92, p. 716; Choice, Sept 92, pp. 72-74] – **Philip A. Metzger**

Desktop Publishing

690. Berger, Sidney E. **The Design of Bibliographies: Observations, References and Examples.** Westport, Conn., Greenwood Press, 1992. 198p. index. (Bibliographies and Indexes in Library and Information Science, no.6). $85.00. Z1001.B4537. 010'.44. LC 91-34485. ISBN 0-313-28425-3.

One of the traditional ways of gaining access to information is through reference materials, and this work attempts to discuss and define bibliographies from a physical and intellectual perspective. Beginning with a brief chapter on book design (e.g., type selection, layout, legibility), Berger offers sound research references and figures tied to the 52-page bibliography (the heart of this project). The shape and content of bibliographies are addressed in subtopics such as audience, subject matter, organization, punctuation, annotations, use of abbreviations and symbols, numbering of entries, and coding (control of appearance of the bibliography). The overview of computers and desktop publishing is too brief to be useful. Examples abound: both the truly ugly and the aesthetically pleasing are reproduced. Berger correctly points out that there is no single right way to produce a usable bibliographic entry, but that book designers should concentrate on the physical elements of which bibliographies are composed as well as provide logical access to the data. Chapter 2, the annotated bibliography, lists some 300 works that cover the broad fields of book design, literary research, bibliographic style manuals, theory of national and international bibliographies, preparation of indexes, use of electronic composing systems, and criteria for readability. The appendix includes examples of various forms of bibliographies prepared on typewriters, on computer systems, and by photoreproduction. The index lists all the issues considered in the main text and the bibliography.

While the index appears to be adequate in terms of the range of topics covered, examination of a specific entry causes some concern. Under "cross-references" (pp. 39, 119) one finds a single sentence: "The index should contain as many cross-references as are necessary to guide the reader to the proper heading." An example of this process is not provided. Page 119 is an example (in Italian) from another source, with the caption material referring to the various page elements displayed; nowhere, however, does it mention cross-referencing. A discussion of bibliographies, which often rely heavily on cross-referencing, should devote more substantial material to the topic and its preparation.

Few would quarrel with the selection or quality of the annotated bibliographic items presented here. However, writers, editors, book designers, and publishers who wish to improve their bibliographic formats should read the original sources cited for a more thorough understanding of the complexities and vagaries of the bibliographic process. – **Judy Gay Matthews**

12 Military Studies

GENERAL WORKS

Atlases

691. Symonds, Craig L. **Gettysburg: A Battlefield Atlas.** Baltimore, Md., Nautical & Aviation Publishing, 1992. 103p. illus. maps. index. $19.95. G1264.G3S5S8. 973.7'349'0223. LC 91-40093. ISBN 1-877853-16-X.

The bloody, no-quarter American Civil War melded the United States into a seamless nation and holds a unique place in the hearts and minds of every succeeding generation. The ferocious battle among the rolling hills of Gettysburg, Pennsylvania, stands out as the best-known conflict of that war. The decisive victory of the Union forces ranks with such crucial battles in world history as Marathon, Waterloo, and Midway. Happily for the novice reader, this book does a job worthy of its subject in illustrations, text, and 24 maps. Symonds, who teaches history at the U.S. Naval Academy, has created atlases of the American Revolution and the Civil War. Cartographer William J. Clipson collaborated with Symonds on the two earlier atlases.

Paving the way to the three-day battle (July 1-3, 1863) are 23 pages of text and maps. The action itself is covered in 52 pages—again, text and maps—including separate graphics of place-names burned into the nation's conscience: Devil's Den, Little Round Top, Culp's Hill, the Angle, and Cemetery Ridge. General Lee's retreat and General Meade's limpid pursuit take seven pages. One appendix gives the order of battle for both the Army of the Potomac and the Army of Northern Virginia; a second presents the casualty figures for both sides. [R: LJ, 15 Feb 92, p. 162]—**David Eggenberger**

Bibliography

692. Floyd, Dale E., comp. **Military Fortifications: A Selective Bibliography.** Westport, Conn., Greenwood Press, 1992. 360p. index. (Bibliographies and Indexes in Military Studies, no.4). $59.50. Z6724.F67F56. 016.3557. LC 91-24840. ISBN 0-313-28220-X.

Floyd, a historian for the National Park Service, specialist in military architecture, and compiler of two previous military bibliographies, offers the first English-language general bibliography on military fortifications. His 2,155 briefly annotated citations cover books (including a few novels), articles, pamphlets, essays, master's theses, doctoral dissertations, and videos. Arrangement is by geographical region with listings under more than 100 countries. A miscellaneous chapter covers topics such as castles, the Middle Ages, the Russo-Turkish and Russo-Japanese Wars, and World Wars I and II. An author and subject index is helpful, and the compiler's introduction makes a case for the study of fortifications and the import of this reference tool.

The specialized subject of this fine volume limits its appeal to large research libraries. On the other hand, its reasonable price allows smaller libraries to consider it as a source for high school and college student research papers. However, a high percentage of the listings are in obscure or esoteric sources not readily available. [R: Choice, July/Aug 92, p. 1655]—**Joe P. Dunn**

693. Rasor, Eugene L. **The Battle of Jutland: A Bibliography.** Westport, Conn., Greenwood Press, 1992. 176p. index. (Bibliographies of Battles and Leaders, no.7). $45.00. Z6207.E8R38. 016.9404'56. LC 91-24368. ISBN 0-313-28124-6.

The seventh volume in the series is the first to tackle a World War I battle. Rasor, of Emory and Henry College, is an expert on British naval affairs. His other published volume in this series is *The Falklands/Malvinas Campaign* (Greenwood Press, 1992).

Superior to many bibliographies examined by this reviewer, this one devotes 52 of 170 text pages to a historiographical survey of the battle of Jutland (called the battle of Skagerrak by Germany). Rasor points out that it was the first serious challenge to British sea power since Lord Nelson's decisive victory of Trafalgar in 1805. (Happily for Great Britain, Sir John [Jacky] Fisher had built up the Grand Fleet from the earlier force said by Churchill to suffer from "rum, sodomy, and the lash.") Here are trenchant discussions of the diplomatic situation, warships, strategy and tactics of the battle itself, various assessments and critiques of what was really a standoff engagement, sources Rasor used, and a glossary of the naval leaders on both sides.

The crux of the volume lies in the 528 annotated sources, alphabetized by author. It is scholarly and comprehensive, giving credit to the best works and speaking plainly if the citation is weak or wrong. The German side of the battle is well represented. Although the Public Record Office, National Maritime Museum, and other British sources naturally predominate, a few United States authors are also represented. Published too late for inclusion here is Robert Massie's masterful *Dreadnought*. Its addition in the next edition will make a good book even better. — **David Eggenberger**

694. Rasor, Eugene L. **The Falklands/Malvinas Campaign: A Bibliography.** Westport, Conn., Greenwood Press, 1992. 196p. index. (Bibliographies of Battles and Leaders, no.6). $45.00. Z1945.R37. 016.99711. LC 91-24365. ISBN 0-313-28151-3.

This compact volume divides into two roughly equal parts: a critical/evaluative historiographical narrative and an annotated bibliography of 554 works, 17 of which are addenda. Intended coverage is all publications in a variety of media in English, Spanish, German, or French, including some items that cover subjects such as electronic warfare which, while relevant to the topic, do not discuss Falklands operations specifically. Excluded are daily newspapers, popular magazines, service journals, works on the natural history of the Falklands, and references to some atlases and all simulation war games that cover this campaign.

While providing an adequate general background overview in a brisk, well-organized, and easily read format, the narrative is marred by a number of factual errors (e.g., in the 1914 Battle of the Falklands, four German cruisers were sunk rather than the three cited; torpedoes *were* used at the Battle of the River Plate) and misspellings (e.g., *fuzes* is consistently misspelled "fuzzes"). The bibliography has problems as well. The compressed format makes accessing some articles unduly difficult and uses a nonstandard form of citation for the *U.S. Naval Institute Proceedings*. Checking a sample revealed a 46 percent error rate, with mistakes ranging from overlooking joint publishers to incorrect pagination, title, or location information. Nor is the bibliography complete; among other things it omits John Keegan's *World Armies* (see ARBA 85, entry 595) and *Modern Naval Combat* by David Miller and Chris Miller (London: Salamander Books, 1986).

Clearly, this book is neither definitive nor comprehensive. Nevertheless, it does provide a good introduction to its subject, and with its chronology and index it can serve equally well as a ready-reference source or a background companion to serious research. Clearly printed on paper conforming with the Permanent Paper Standard, this sturdily bound volume is a useful addition to any library that deals with modern military topics. [R: Choice, July/Aug 92, p. 1660] — **John Howard Oxley**

695. Smith, Myron J., Jr. **The Battles of Coral Sea and Midway, 1942: A Selected Bibliography.** Westport, Conn., Greenwood Press, 1991. 157p. index. (Bibliographies of Battles and Leaders, no.5). $55.00. Z6207.W8S5628. 016.94054'26. LC 91-20673. ISBN 0-313-28120-3.

696. Smith, Myron J., Jr. **Pearl Harbor, 1941: A Bibliography.** Westport, Conn., Greenwood Press, 1991. 197p. index. (Bibliographies of Battles and Leaders, no.4). $55.00. Z6207.W8S5625. 016.94054'26. LC 90-49167. ISBN 0-313-28121-1.

These annotated bibliographies will be welcomed by librarians who serve a population interested in the attack on Pearl Harbor and the pivotal battles of the Coral Sea and Midway. Both bibliographies are organized in a similar and useful format. Smith first surveys primary source collections in the United States and abroad—national and service archives, university archives and collections, and research centers—noting the strengths and focus of each. Following a list of printed reference works, both standard and specialized, is the subject bibliography. In each work this begins with citations to general studies of the war, followed by works on ship and aircraft types involved in the actions and then by biographies of key individuals. The core of each work is devoted to citations that concern, in the case of Pearl Harbor, the political, diplomatic, and military conditions leading up to the attack; the attack itself; and its immediate aftermath. For the battles of the Coral Sea and Midway, the bibliography covers the events leading up to the battles and the actual battles. Both works contain a chronology; an author index; and an index to individuals, units, ships, and aircraft. Materials cited include books, articles from a wide range of magazines and journals, dissertations and theses, government documents, and service reports. Most materials are in English, with Japanese the second most common language; some European languages are also represented. Citations date from 1941 (in the case of Pearl Harbor) to 1989.

Both bibliographies will serve high school and undergraduate research well. For advanced projects they will provide an excellent outline of and introduction to the literature and a guide to repositories of primary material. Recommended for all libraries. [R: Choice, Mar 92, p. 1056]—**Eric R. Nitschke**

Biography

697. Bishop, Arthur. **Courage in the Air.** Toronto, McGraw-Hill Ryerson, 1992. 307p. illus. index. (Canada's Military Heritage, v.1). $35.00. 355'.00971. ISBN 0-07-551376-5.

This volume, by a writer with a deep knowledge of his subject, both personal and professional, presents brief profiles of selected Canadian airmen from World Wars I and II and the Korean War. The entries are arranged alphabetically by conflict. As Bishop admits, the coverage is selective rather than comprehensive, but most major fighting figures (and many people distinguished for administrative services) are discussed.

The straightforward descriptions relate each man's wartime activities in varying length and detail (a few contain personal remarks that could be controversial). Every entry is followed by a citation of awards, publications, date of death, and (most valuably) the archival citations on which the accounts were based. This provides an ideal starting point for further research. Some biographies are accompanied by photographs; these are clear and of good size, but most lack captions (and one that has a caption misidentifies a German "Panther" tank as a "Tiger" tank). A few other inaccuracies were noted (e.g., no German light cruiser was sunk off Wilhlemshaven in early April 1945, by "Typhoon" attack; the "Sunderland" flying boat is repeatedly called "Sutherland" and credited with a cannon armament it did not have; the heavy cruiser KM *Prinz Eugen* is persistently designated a battleship), but these do not detract substantially from the book.

Crisply printed on good-quality paper in a sturdy binding, this is a useful initial guide to its topic. While a name index enhances its value as a ready-reference tool, the absence of an analytic index to the variety of significant historical detail it contains is regrettable.—**John Howard Oxley**

698. **The Harper Encyclopedia of Military Biography.** By Trevor N. Dupuy, Curt Johnson, and David L. Bongard. New York, HarperCollins, 1992. 834p. $65.00. U51.D87. 355'.0092'2. LC 89-46526. ISBN 0-06-270015-4.

Dupuy is one of the world's most renowned military historians. He has written more than 90 books, and his *Encyclopedia of Military History* (coedited with his father) (see ARBA 87, entry 656) is a classic in the field. This latest volume promises to take its place alongside the *Encyclopedia* and be the standard reference on the subject.

A massive volume, it consists of profiles on more than 3,000 world military leaders and thinkers, from Sun Tzu and Julius Caesar to Colin Powell and Norman Schwarzkopf. The entries follow a common format. Most run between 200 and 1,000 words and have a brief bibliography of sources. The 32 contributors admittedly include only a few major military history scholars. Some leaders receive no more than a sentence or two. One would expect, for example, that Sun Tzu would merit more than a few lines. Although the volume includes many Asian leaders, especially Japanese, they tend to have brief listings. One assumes this is because most of the source material on these individuals is in languages that the authors cannot read. Also, the brief lists of sources at the end of each entry are far too limited, and many do not include the latest or best works. But these points aside, this is an impressive undertaking and an important contribution that should be a basic reference source in virtually every library in the country. [R: LJ, Aug 92, p. 86; RBB, 15 Oct 92, pp. 453-56] – **Joe P. Dunn**

699. Windrow, Martin, and Francis K. Mason. **A Concise Dictionary of Military Biography: The Careers and Campaigns of 200 of the Most Important Military Leaders.** New York, John Wiley, 1991. 337p. $24.95. U51.W53. LC 90-44696. ISBN 0-471-53441-2.

Combining factual details with clear analysis, this dictionary presents the careers of 200 of the most important personalities in military history, covering tribal chiefs, warrior kings, and field marshals as well as influential theorists, innovators, and administrators. Here the conquests of such great leaders as Genghis Kahn and Napoleon, whose wartime successes changed the world and its maps, may be followed as well as the incompetence of others, such as George Armstrong Custer and Benedict Arnold. Popular culture heroes such as Joan of Arc and El Cid may also be investigated. Cross-cultural in design, this biographical study of careers and campaigns makes a valid effort to include great leaders of non-Western culture, such as Hideyoshi Toyotomi and Shaka. Even people such as the Baron Friedrich von Steuben and Lazare Carnot, whose careers were relatively obscure because they never held a major field command, are presented and analyzed because of their theoretical or administrative mastery of the art of warfare.

These biographical essays are fascinating studies that proceed chronologically according to major events in the subject's life. Summary remarks about the unique and significant contributions of each military leader provide important analytical information. For example, the authors point out that King Henry V of England is noteworthy not only for his considerable personal courage, tactical sound sense, and appeal to the common soldier but also for "the sense of national pride and national identity which his victories engendered among the English people of all classes." Particularly informative are the presentations of major military campaigns and the leaders involved.

Not only is this dictionary a valuable basic reference tool for anyone interested in military history, but it also makes for enjoyable armchair and bedside reading. "Coeur de Lion" Richard I, "Law-giver" Suleyman I, John Joseph "Black Jack" Pershing, George Smith "Old Blood and Guts" Patton, Yamashita "Tiger of Malaya" Tomoyuki – they are all properly introduced. – **Colby H. Kullman**

Chronology

700. Chant, Christopher. **The Military History of the United States.** North Bellmore, N.Y., Marshall Cavendish, 1992. 16v. illus. maps. index. $449.95/set. T181.C52. 973. LC 90-19547. ISBN 1-85435-361-9.

This is a large and very impressive undertaking, a chronologically arranged military history of the United States from the Revolutionary War through the Gulf War. Each of the 135-page volumes artfully combines narrative text, illustrations, maps, and drawings to tell its story. Some conflicts, such as the Civil War, World War II, and Vietnam, necessitate two volumes; other wars are treated in one; and volumes such as "Wars of Consolidation and Expansion," "The Indian Wars," and "Wars in Peace and the Cold War" cover spans of time.

The more than 1,500 annotated illustrations – contemporary photographs, engravings, and paintings augmented with abundant maps and pictures or drawings of important weapons and weapons systems – most in color, are the heart of the volumes. Particularly interesting are the dozens of full-page color drawings of military men from each war in the uniforms of the day (with complete annotations about characteristics of the uniforms). Also valuable are the cutaway drawings of weapons that show the inner workings of tanks, airplanes, artillery pieces, munitions, and the like. The high-quality slick paper, the abundant color, and the skillful display of text and visual on every page make these most attractive volumes.

Each book has a helpful table of contents, a brief glossary, an excellent short bibliography, cross-reference panels, and a complete index. Volume 16 contains a general glossary for the set, a repeat of each volume's individual bibliography, and a fully comprehensive cross-reference index for the set. All of this makes the composite set easy to use and quite valuable.

The narrative histories of the various conflicts by Chant, who has compiled several previous military encyclopedias, handbooks, and pictorials, are well done. The scholarship is up-to-date, and the accounts address the central issues of each war.

In sum, this series is a valuable source for students at all levels, from junior high to college, and for the general public as well. The volumes are not likely to become dated soon, and it is doubtful that a better single set will be forthcoming in the near future. Were it not for the high price, this set would be recommended for all school, undergraduate college, and public libraries. However, individual libraries must give serious thought to the cost-use ratio prior to purchase.—**Joe P. Dunn**

Dictionaries and Encyclopedias

701. **The Penguin Encyclopedia of Modern Warfare: 1850 to the Present Day.** By Kenneth Macksey and William Woodhouse. New York, Penguin Books, 1991. 373p. maps. index. $29.95. LC 90-72128. ISBN 0-670-82698-7.

This volume, by two retired British military officers-turned-historians, enters a rather crowded field of military encyclopedias, dictionaries, and handbooks. Some of these reference works focus on individual wars; others treat specific aspects, such as air war, tanks, or other weapons; and a few are general sources. Macksey and Woodhouse's volume includes brief entries on the principal wars, campaigns, battles, and personalities of the last 150 years, as well as treatment of strategy, tactics, intelligence, weapons, logistics, technology, military philosophy, law, training, and education. Fully cross-referenced, the book is readable and easy to employ. Its best features are the 80 maps and diagrams, and it also includes a limited bibliography and a chronology of war and technology/weapons innovations. Although the individual entries are far too brief for more than a basic introduction to the topics, at its reasonable price, most libraries will find it a useful addition to their other military references. However, if one must chose, clearly the more comprehensive, detailed, and authoritative forthcoming 4th edition of *The Harper Encyclopedia of Military History* (formerly *The Encyclopedia of Military History* [see ARBA 87, entry 656]) and its companion volume, *The Harper Encyclopedia of Military Biography* (HarperCollins, 1992), are the superior reference tools. [R: Choice, June 92, p. 1522; RBB, 15 Feb 92, p. 1132]—**Joe P. Dunn**

702. Tobias, Norman, ed. **The International Military Encyclopedia. Volume I.** Gulf Breeze, Fla., Academic International Press, 1992. 244p. $57.00. ISBN 0-87569-159-5.

Academic International Press is the publisher of several multivolume encyclopedias, all of which are still in progress. Among these are *The Modern Encyclopedia of Russian and Soviet History* (MERSH) (see ARBA 79, entry 442); *The Modern Encyclopedia of Russian and Soviet Literature* (see ARBA 90, entry 1210); *Encyclopedia USA* (see ARBA 87, entry 500); and *The Modern Encyclopedia of Religions in Russia and the Soviet Union* (see ARBA 90, entry 1381). Typically (and the title under review promises to follow the pattern), the 240-250 page volumes are issued at the rate of three or four per year. For example, MERSH began in 1976, and volume 54 was issued in 1991.

This first volume of *The International Military Encyclopedia* covers topics from A-1 Skyraider to the Siege of Acre in 1799. The editor intends that the range of subject matter in the work be quite broad, although naval history is not covered, unfortunately. In this volume military leaders, weapons, campaigns, and battles predominate. Geographically, coverage is generally worldwide, and chronologically, it goes back to classical Greece. Tobias says the work will emphasize the twentieth century, but that is not apparent in this volume. Articles vary in length from 2 or 3 sentences (e.g., *Ablecti*) to 10 pages (e.g., *Abwehr*); all articles have bibliographies.

One volume cannot a set predict; but based on the publisher's other titles, this work should provide a useful reference and means of entry to military (although not naval) subjects. Libraries at all levels will want to consider it.—**Eric R. Nitschke**

703. **The Visual Dictionary of Military Uniforms.** New York, Dorling Kindersley; distr., Boston, Houghton Mifflin, 1992. 64p. illus. index. (Eyewitness Visual Dictionaries). $14.95. UC460.E94. 355.1'4'03. LC 91-58206. ISBN 1-56458-010-5.

This chronological and topical dictionary provides an introduction to a good cross-section of military uniforms, equipment, and accoutrements from ancient times to the present. "Visual dictionary" is certainly the appropriate term to use for this enjoyable (although not exhaustive) work. Obscure as well as more common items of military apparel and weapons are identified (but not always explained) in beautifully laid out and organized color plates, accompanied by a brief narrative. English and ancient terms are provided for older military items, as are modern foreign-language terms. Not all nationalities are represented, and notably absent is reference to any military force in North America other than that of the United States; there are no references to Native American and South American armed forces. But this is only a representative work, and in that sense it offers an excellent introduction to military uniforms and paraphernalia. This thin, large-format volume is an excellent addition to secondary, public, and personal reference collections. [R: LJ, 15 May 92, p. 90; SBF, Aug/Sept 92, p. 180; SLJ, Sept 92, p. 288]—**Norman L. Kincaide**

Directories

704. Cragg, Dan. **Guide to Military Installations.** 3d ed. Harrisburg, Pa., Stackpole Books, 1991. 470p. illus. index. $17.95pa. UC403.C7. 355.6'025'73. LC 91-10791. ISBN 0-8117-3019-0.

This guide describes 227 domestic and 102 overseas Army, Navy, Marine Corps, and Air Force facilities. It differs from the 2d edition (see ARBA 90, entry 656) by seven additions, one deletion, five name changes, and other new material. It is written for military or civilian personnel who have been assigned to, or are considering work at, a particular installation. A typical entry discusses the facility's history, mission, location, availability of schools, medical and recreational facilities, and other personnel services. Maps show locations of all bases mentioned, and all entries give the address and telephone number of the base Public Affairs Office for those seeking more detailed information.

This guide does not list museums or other tourist attractions on the bases, nor does it give details about facility budgets, manning levels, or attached commands or units. William R. Evinger's *Directory of Military Bases in the U.S.* (see ARBA 92, entry 650) does list these items and, while omitting overseas installations, includes Coast Guard, National Guard, and Reserve facilities, which Cragg does not. Evinger's work is columnar while Cragg's is narrative. The titles complement each other, the main difference between them being geographical: Cragg's more complete worldwide coverage versus Evinger's more complete domestic coverage. Evinger, for example, lists 20 military installations in Georgia; Cragg lists 10. Cragg's edition went to press before Congress designated (in July 1991) 24 domestic and 72 European facilities for closure and before Clark Air Force Base and the Naval Facility at Subic Bay, both in the Philippines, were abandoned. But until bases are actually shut down, this edition will remain highly useful for all public and most academic libraries.—**Eric R. Nitschke**

Handbooks and Yearbooks

705. **Handbook on Japanese Military Forces.** By U.S. War Department. Novato, Calif., Presidio Press, 1991. 403p. illus. $39.95. UA847.H36. 355'.00952'09044. LC 91-20930. ISBN 1-85367-102-9.

Few reference works have served such a vital purpose as this handbook. The original edition was hastily compiled and issued in September 1942 as a classified War Department technical manual (TM-E-30-480) and was revised throughout the war. This reprint of the final October 1944 edition represents a distillation of Japanese Army manuals and three years of Allied intelligence and combat reports. Its purpose was to help save lives and win the war by providing Allied officers with an understanding of their enemy in the Pacific. The handbook details the organization, tactics, training, weapons, and equipment employed by the Japanese Army during World War II. The assessment of the potential of both personnel and equipment is remarkably impartial and, with numerous illustrations, documents the Japanese military in great detail. Because the original manuals were classified and issued in a looseleaf format, few copies have been available in libraries. This moderately priced edition provides a more convenient format than the original and includes a brief essay and afterword that places the handbook in proper context. As an artifact documenting the Japanese military and United States attitudes and intelligence gathering during the war, this volume will prove interesting to historians and students of military history. Recommended for academic libraries that support programs in history. – **John R. M. Lawrence**

706. Holt, Dean W. **American Military Cemeteries: A Comprehensive Illustrated Guide to the Hallowed Grounds of the United States....** Jefferson, N.C., McFarland, 1992. 512p. illus. maps. index. $55.00. UB393.H65. 353.0086. LC 91-51215. ISBN 0-89950-666-6.

The United States has been an independent democracy for more than 200 years. The cost of winning and keeping the resultant freedoms can be calculated in many ways. In this book Holt indirectly but poignantly describes one specific cost: the more than three million U.S. servicepeople who now lie buried in military cemeteries.

As the book's subtitle indicates, Holt, a 16-year official of the governing National Cemetery System (NCS), provides a wide-ranging reference work. Each of the 113 national military cemeteries is described as to location, founding, history of interest, notables buried within, and all superintendents and directors. In addition, there are briefer accounts of 7 Confederate cemeteries, 22 soldiers' lots (only partially developed), 3 monuments, and 33 "lost" cemeteries (no longer maintained by the NCS). Holt also includes cemeteries under other jurisdictions. For example, the Department of the Army administers Arlington National Cemetery in Virginia, across the Potomac River from the nation's capital. Here are the Tombs of the Unknowns and the burial sites of presidents William H. Taft and John F. Kennedy. The Army also supervises the Soldiers' Home National Cemetery in Washington, D.C. The National Park Service has jurisdiction over 11 cemeteries, almost all Civil War battlefields. The American Battle Monuments Commission administers 24 permanent U.S. burial grounds and 14 separate monuments overseas, most of the acreage devoted to the 93,240 war dead of World War II. Finally, there are 40 state veterans cemeteries established or being planned. The appendix includes a list of the 3,409 recipients of the Medal of Honor and the cemeteries in which they are buried. This book is well planned, comprehensive, accurate, and easy to use. [R: LJ, 1 Oct 92, pp. 78-80]

– **David Eggenberger**

707. Seeley, Charlotte Palmer, comp. **American Women and the U.S. Armed Forces: A Guide to the Records of Military Agencies in the National Archives....** Washington, D.C., National Archives and Records Administration, 1992. 355p. illus. index. $25.00. U21.75.S44. 355'.0082. LC 91-40430. ISBN 0-911333-90-8.

This is a comprehensive guide to sources located in the National Archives in Washington, D.C., and in presidential libraries on women in the military. It is comparable to others published by the National Archives on selected record groups in the collection, such as *Guide to Federal Records Relating to the Civil War* (1962), *Guide to Records in the National Archives Relating to American Indians* (1981), and *A Guide to Civilian Records in the National Archives* (1984). Seeley has gathered together record and series groups (records are filed under the name of the office from which the records originated) in the National Archives that are on U.S. women in the military from the Revolutionary War through the Vietnam War. She has also included a brief section of materials housed in the presidential libraries of Herbert Hoover, Franklin D. Roosevelt, Dwight D. Eisenhower, John F. Kennedy Library, Lyndon Baines Johnson, and Gerald R. Ford. Summaries of the records are provided. The guide contains four appendixes that list the most frequently used acronyms used by these libraries, the War Department decimal classification scheme, a list of records available on microfilm, and the addresses of the branches of the National Archives. An index is included. Recommended for all libraries with an interest in locating primary sources for studying the changing role of women in the United States. – **J. C. Jurgens**

708. Wildhaber, Michael E., and others. **Veterans Benefits Manual: An Advocate's Guide to Representing Veterans and Their Dependents.** Washington, D.C., National Veterans Legal Services Project, 1991. 2v. maps. index. $125.00pa./set. LC 91-67115. ISBN 1-878902-01-6.

The subtitle of this work is important because this is not a list of benefits and how to get them. Rather, it is a handbook for lawyers, veterans' organizations workers, paralegals, and state and county veterans administration employees who help veterans file claims with or appeal decisions to the Department of Veterans Affairs (VA). (The authors admit that the set may be used by the knowledgeable veteran, but they discourage this practice.)

The manual concentrates on the various disability and death benefits offered veterans, their dependents, and their survivors, because these are the most complex cases from both procedural and legal standpoints. It also provides the attorney/advocate with an overview of VA rules of procedure, the law and literature of veterans' benefits, the correction of military records, and the relation between Social Security and VA benefits. It is a subject guide; yet, in its detail, it provides more than a mere entry to the subject. Relevant forms are reproduced, as are pertinent parts of various important publications. There are a list of court cases, a glossary, and an index.

There are several publications available that describe veterans' benefits, but all are aimed at the veteran. This manual will find a welcome place in libraries that specialize in law, public advocacy, or veterans' affairs. [R: WLB, Apr 92, p. 128]—**Eric R. Nitschke**

AIR FORCE

709. Watson, Bruce W., and Susan M. Watson, eds. **The United States Air Force: A Dictionary.** Hamden, Conn., Garland, 1992. 861p. (Garland Series on U.S. Military Affairs; Garland Reference Library of Social Science, v.696). $110.00. UG633.U624. 358.4'00973. LC 91-42269. ISBN 0-8240-5539-X.

This is a specialized dictionary of Air Force terms that deal with warfare, personnel administration, supply, materiel, intelligence, operations, research, and weaponry. It does not include proper nouns; for example, there is an entry for fighter aircraft but not for specific aircraft, such as the F-15. Likewise, biography is excluded. The definitions have been slightly reworded and taken from, for the most part, the *Department of Defense Dictionary of Military and Associated Terms* (1984) (incorrectly cited as the *Department of Defense Dictionary of Military and Related Terms*); many specialized Air Force manuals are also used as sources. Unfortunately, the definitions are awkward and frequently obscure. The editors fail to clarify the more contorted definitions derived from military sources and in many cases render ambiguous the intelligible ones. *See also* references often connect terms that lack any comprehensible relation, and the introduction is filled with spelling and grammatical errors.

Samuel Johnson is said to have remarked that dictionaries are like watches; the worst is better than none, and the best cannot be expected to go quite true. Well, a poor, cheap dictionary may be better than none, but a poor, expensive dictionary is folly. Libraries that require definitions of Air Force arcanum should consider the dictionary previously cited or *Encyclopedia of the U.S. Military*, edited by William M. Arkin and others (Harper & Row, 1990), a serviceable yet specialized dictionary of terms, organizations, and weapons. [R: Choice, Oct 92, pp. 281-82; LJ, 15 June 92, p. 72]—**Eric R. Nitschke**

ARMY

710. Shrader, Charles R. **U.S. Military Logistics, 1607-1991: A Research Guide.** Westport, Conn., Greenwood Press, 1992. 356p. index. (Research Guides in Military Studies, no.4). $65.00. Z6724.S9S48. 016.3554'11'0973. LC 92-9263. ISBN 0-313-27246-8.

Logistics refers to the supply and upkeep of armed forces. It entails the purchasing, storage, transportation, distribution, and repair of materials needed by the fighting forces when they need them, where they need them, and in the proper amounts. Shrader has produced a model bibliography on this important and overlooked aspect of warfare.

This is a selective but well-defined work. It concerns only U.S. Army logistics and contains citations primarily to studies published in books and articles, omitting the large number of Army technical manuals, most unit histories, and most works that deal with medical support and the Corps of Engineers. Publication dates of the sources cited range from the mid-nineteenth century to 1991. Periodical sources are primarily history journals and military titles (e.g., *Army Logistician* [GPO, 1969-]).

Shrader begins with an essay that defines the topic, lists his own top 50 works on logistics, and continues with a fine chapter that outlines sources in the National Archives, other manuscript collections, published government documents, periodical sources, and works that identify unit histories. The main part of the bibliography lists works in several areas: theory, doctrine, and organization of logistics; general works and those that deal with specific periods; procurement and mobilization for war; the Quartermaster Corps (clothing, fuel, and all equipment except food and weapons); Transportation Corps; Subsistence Supply (food supplies); and Ordnance. Appendixes give army expenditures and strength from 1775 to 1989 and key names in Army logistics. There is an author and subject index. This is a fine example of a subject bibliography and will be much appreciated in libraries that support research in this specialty. [R: Choice, Dec 92, p. 605]—**Eric R. Nitschke**

711. Sifakis, Stewart. **Compendium of the Confederate Armies: Alabama.** New York, Facts on File, 1992. 144p. index. $24.95. E546.S58. 973.7'42. LC 90-23631. ISBN 0-8160-2287-9.

712. Sifakis, Stewart. **Compendium of the Confederate Armies: Florida and Arkansas.** New York, Facts on File, 1992. 143p. index. $24.95. E546.S58. 973.7'42. LC 90-23631. ISBN 0-8160-2288-7. [R: RBB, 1 Jan 92, p. 848]

713. Sifakis, Stewart. **Compendium of the Confederate Armies: North Carolina.** New York, Facts on File, 1992. 187p. index. $24.95. E546.S58. 973.7'42. LC 90-23631. ISBN 0-8160-2289-5.

714. Sifakis, Stewart. **Compendium of the Confederate Armies: Tennessee.** New York, Facts on File, 1992. 197p. index. $24.95. E546.S58. 973.7'42. LC 90-23631. ISBN 0-8160-2286-0.

715. Sifakis, Stewart. **Compendium of the Confederate Armies: Virginia.** New York, Facts on File, 1992. 287p. index. $24.95. E546.S58. 973.7'42. LC 90-23631. ISBN 0-8160-2284-4.

These books are meant to be the Confederate companion to Frederick H. Dyer's work, *A Compendium of the War of the Rebellion* (Dyer Publishing, 1908). This work is organized into volumes by state. Chapters in each volume cover artillery, cavalry, and infantry. Units that had a numerical designation are listed first, followed by those that used the name of their commander, home region, or other designation. Units are then broken down alphabetically by size—battalions, batteries, companies, and regiments. They are also listed by special designation, if any, such as regulars, reserves, or sharpshooters. Also named for each unit are the first commanding officer and other field-grade officers. Battles and campaigns in which the units saw service are noted, and some entries provide information on when and where the unit was disbanded or surrendered, as the case may be. Suggested reading is included for some units; all volumes contain an annotated bibliography. Each volume also contains indexes of battles and names of officers, but none has an index of local units. Also missing is information about casualties that individual units suffered or the outcomes of the battles in which the units participated.

The serious student of Civil War history probably already knows where to find the information contained in these books, while those less conversant with the topic will likely find little of use. Perhaps the greatest contribution of these volumes is to provide points of departure for further research into the subject. [R: RBB, 1 Jan 92, p. 848]—**Kay O. Cornelius**

716. Sigler, David Burns. **Vietnam Battle Chronology: U.S. Army and Marine Corps Combat Operations, 1965-1973.** Jefferson, N.C., McFarland, 1992. 184p. index. $42.50. DS557.7.S57. 959.704'34'0202. LC 91-50941. ISBN 0-89950-683-6.

Frustrated by his inability to place the myriad individual personal stories of Vietnam War combatants into the larger overall picture of the conflict, Sigler started his research to better understand the participant literature that intrigued him. The end result is this useful reference tool, which traces the flow of specific combat operations and incidents throughout the war.

Sigler pored through unit operational reports and other government documents to identify more than 600 Army and Marine ground combat operations between 1965 and 1973. As he proceeds year by year, his format for each operation includes dates, code names, location in South Vietnam, specific goals or targets, Allied and enemy units involved, important events in the operation, and reported casualties. He admits that the hundreds of small actions that were not given code names are not included, but this is the most comprehensive accounting available.

The excellent appendixes and indexes are the best features of the volume. They include an alphabetical list of Army and Marine combat operations; a chronological list of operations by major command units; a bibliography that provides the Operational Reports of each command, complete with the codes to locate these at the National Archives (this is a particularly valuable feature for researchers); and complete name, subject, and military unit indexes.

This work is an important companion resource to the three classic military references: Stanley Stanton's *Vietnam Order of Battle* (U.S. News and World Report, 1982), *The Vietnam War Almanac* (see ARBA 86, entry 519), and John S. Bowman's *The World Almanac of the Vietnam War* (World Almanac/St. Martin's Press, 1986). It is essential for all research libraries and useful for any library with a Vietnam collection. Moreover, students at all levels will find that the book does fulfill the author's original purpose. — **Joe P. Dunn**

717. Zurick, Tim. **Army Dictionary and Desk Reference.** Harrisburg, Pa., Stackpole Books, 1992. 263p. $12.95pa. UA25.Z86. 355'.003. LC 91-28377. ISBN 0-8117-2435-2.

Each discipline and profession possesses its own jargon and terminology. One purpose of such terms is to prevent outsiders from understanding, analyzing, and evaluating the practices unique to the field. The military is an especially prominent example of this. Zurick's compendium of army terminology is an effort to make this often arcane subject comprehensible to civilians.

Zurick opens with a dictionary list of acronyms from various army branches. The heart of his work is an alphabetical list of army acronyms and terms cross-referenced to the branch acronyms under which they fall in current army operational practice. Examples of these acronyms and terms include APO (Army Post Office), *counterinsurgency, order of battle*, and SECDEF (Secretary of Defense). The dictionary section is supplemented by a series of rating tables that include the phonetic alphabet, Morse Code, a wind chill factor chart, platoon formation diagrams, listings of enlisted personnel and officer occupational specialties, and a spectrum chart for electronic warfare. The work concludes with the "Code of Conduct for Members of the U.S. Armed Forces" and samples of military correspondence.

Zurick has presented a valuable compilation of army acronyms and terminology that will benefit readers in all varieties of libraries. His work is strengthened by the cross-references between the dictionary and the introductory listing of branch acronyms and by his ongoing service as an army officer. It is hoped that this effort will stimulate the production of dictionaries of comparable quality for other branches of the armed forces and that it will be updated to incorporate future developments in army terminology. [R: LJ, 1 Feb 92, p. 82; RBB, 15 May 92, pp. 1711-12] — **Bert Chapman**

WEAPONS

718. **The International Defense Electronic Systems Handbook.** Englewood, Colo., Cardiff Publishing, 1992. 239p. index. $195.00pa. ISBN 1-881289-00-1.

A collection of almost every conceivable type of electronic defense system, this handbook is divided into 11 sections, which include simulation and training equipment, space-based systems of seven countries and NATO, antisubmarine warfare systems, navigation systems, and radar systems. Each section alphabetically lists and describes various systems with their applications and service histories and their manufacturers (where applicable). The information in each entry, as well as that in the index, is intended for a sophisticated, technically knowledgeable readership.

Interspersed throughout the volume are numerous advertisements for equipment, hardware and software, and subscriptions to defense-oriented periodicals and handbooks. They would be less of a distraction to the user if they were placed at the end. The steep price of this glossy paperbound volume will likely put it out of reach of all but the most highly specialized technical libraries, probably its primary audience. — **Charles R. Andrews**

13 Political Science

GENERAL WORKS

Almanacs

719. **The Facts on File World Political Almanac.** 2d ed. Chris Cook, comp. New York, Facts on File, 1992. 490p. index. $45.00. D843.C5797. 909.82'02'02. LC 91-44943. ISBN 0-8160-2603-3.

Facts on File publications have long been library staples. It is a delight to report that the present volume represents no departure from the excellence librarians and scholars have come to expect from the company. This work contains political information from 1945 to the beginning of the 1990s, covering information on international organizations, treaties, elections, political parties, and much more. The material is not so unusual or recondite as to be unavailable elsewhere; *The Statesman's Year-Book* (see ARBA 92, entry 77), for example, covers much of the same information. What makes this work so important is that it identifies so much under one cover—the librarian's "Sam Walton's Wholesale of Reference." Even though it will not settle many issues for the scholar or the freshman political science student, this work will put to rest many nagging details, such as the identification of terms, the names of heads of state, and the political parties throughout the world. No ready-reference shelf should be without this volume. It should also be found on the shelves of journalists and political science professors. [R: BR, Nov/Dec 92, p. 58]—**Mark Y. Herring**

Atlases

720. Boyd, Andrew. **An Atlas of World Affairs.** 9th ed. New York, Routledge, Chapman & Hall, 1991. 240p. maps. index. $49.95; $14.95pa. G1035.B6. 911. ISBN 0-415-06624-7; 0-415-06625-5pa.

This atlas consists of 72 essays on the major events that happened in various regions of the world (e.g., Indochina, India and Pakistan, Morocco and Western Sahara), from World War II up to 1990. Although recent events such as the Iran-Iraq war, the withdrawal of Russian troops from Afghanistan, and the unification of Germany are covered, such events as the dissolutions of the Soviet Union and Yugoslavia, the downfall of Mikhail S. Gorbachev, and the American-led coalition against Iraq are not included. Besides adding the events that took place since the last edition (see ARBA 89, entry 478), this new edition includes an essay on the environment. The essays, averaging two pages in length, are concise and balanced. Accompanying the text are small but clear maps. Also included are an appendix of countries and currencies and a subject index.

The paperback edition is perhaps a better choice for acquisition as it costs considerably less than the hardcover one. Overall, this work should prove useful as a quick reference tool for every reference collection.—**Binh P. Le**

Biography

721. **Chambers Dictionary of Political Biography.** John Ransley, ed. New York, Chambers Kingfisher Graham, 1991. 436p. $30.00. ISBN 0-550-17251-3.

In one concise volume the editor has brought together short biographies of 1,150 prominent political leaders who have had or are having lasting effects on world politics, from Alexander the Great to John Smith. The biographies are very short but nonetheless useful in identifying key figures and their relationships with other political leaders. There is also a separate collection of quotations from some of the leaders in the biographical dictionary. Finally, Ransley provides a glossary of terms and foreign phrases often used in political discourse.

In a book as small as this with as large a scope, there is often concern about the selection criteria and comprehensiveness. This is not a problem with the current volume. There is a slight bias toward contemporary political figures and Anglo-American leaders, but there is still very good coverage of politicians from other parts of the world, including a respectable number of important leaders in Asia and Africa. The quotations are highly selective but useful. The glossary is even more discriminating and most useful in understanding foreign phrases that are not usually included in other political dictionaries. This volume is recommended for all libraries and the personal collections of historians, political scientists, and others interested in political history. – **Frank L. Wilson**

Dictionaries and Encyclopedias

722. Raymond, Walter John. **Dictionary of Politics: Selected American and Foreign Political and Legal Terms.** 7th ed. Lawrenceville, Va., Brunswick Publishing, 1992. 760p. maps. $60.00. JA61.R39. 320'.03. LC 92-14215. ISBN 1-55618-008-X.

This is a revision of the 1978 volume of the same title. It does not seem to have a systematic approach to the unavoidable tasks of selecting what to include. For example, there is an entry on political theory but not one for other subfields of political science; the unimportant PIAGC of Guinea-Bissou is included but not the governing PRI from Mexico. Despite the entry "Grassroots Perot," many of the entries are dated. For example, "Parti Quebecois" stops in 1977, and the entry on the right to privacy ends in the same year. Other entries are inaccurate, such as the entry on French republics, which has the Fifth Republic being modeled "after the American pattern." Still other entries are incomplete or provide misleading information. For example, the entry on political theory, one of the longest entries in the entire volume, is not an accurate reflection of key issues in that field. There does not appear to be an underlying ideology to explain the selections or differential coverage. Instead, the entries seem idiosyncratic, as exemplified by the lengthy entry on "Virginia: Mother of Presidents." Not recommended. [R: LJ, 1 Nov 92, p. 81; RBB, 1 Nov 92, p. 545] – **Frank L. Wilson**

Directories

723. **The World Directory of Diplomatic Representation.** London, Europa; distr., Detroit, Gale, 1992. 671p. index. $375.00. ISBN 0-946653-78-X. ISSN 0965-3783.

This new Europa publication may be the ultimate diplomatic directory. More than 7,000 embassies, consulates, and delegations are listed for every country of the world and several major international organizations (e.g., the United Nations, European Community, European Free Trade Association, OECD, and NATO). The directory is arranged by country, with the diplomatic breakdown covering more than 33,000 names. Most of the entries include the names of lower-level diplomatic staff as well as ambassadors, high commissioners, and consuls. Each listing provides the person's name; job title; address; and telephone, telex, and fax numbers. A substantial index section is appended to the directory; it is an alphabetical list of personal names arranged by country of origin.

Although the diplomatic information found in other standard sources (e.g., *The Statesman's Year-Book* [see ARBA 92, entry 77]) will be sufficient for most libraries' needs, this is a valuable resource that major university and other research libraries should consider purchasing. Publication frequency is not indicated in this first volume, but annual updates are essential for this kind of information. [R: LJ, July 92, p. 79; WLB, Nov 92, p. 97] – **Thomas A. Karel**

724. **Worldwide Government Directory 1992: With International Organizations.** Washington, D.C., Belmont; distr., Detroit, Gale, 1992. 1190p. $325.00. LC 83-641103. ISBN 0-9629283-2-1. ISSN 0894-1521.

The format of this political directory, formerly titled *Lambert's Worldwide Government Directory*, has not changed significantly since the previous ARBA review (see ARBA 91, entry 721). In this edition 173 countries are covered, plus more than 100 international organizations. The directory information is quite detailed; for example, undersecretaries and department heads are listed within the section on cabinet members. Brief background information is provided for each country, but this is minimal compared to the material and data provided in other standard sources such as *Europa World Yearbook* (see ARBA 90, entry 91) and *The Statesman's Year-Book* (see ARBA 92, entry 77). The publication time lag has improved with this edition, but even so, many of the names of individuals are no longer accurate. Libraries with a need for very extensive directory listings will want to purchase this book on a regular basis; for most other libraries this will be an unnecessary resource if *Europa* or *The Statesman's Year-Book* is in the reference collection. — **Thomas A. Karel**

Handbooks and Yearbooks

725. **The Annual Register 1991: A Record of World Events.** Alan J. Day with Verena Hoffman, eds. Harlow, England, Longman Group; distr., Detroit, Gale, 1992. 618p. index. $147.00. 909.82'8'05. LC 4-17979. ISBN 0-582-09585-9.

The arrangement of the first 10 sections of this work will be familiar to anyone who has ever used *Europa World Yearbook* (see ARBA 90, entry 91) or *The Statesman's Year-Book* (see ARBA 92, entry 77). It differs from those two, however, in that the discussion is entirely about significant events that occurred during the year. The final nine chapters cover, in relatively few pages, significant and related subject or discipline areas: international organizations, defense and arms control, religion, the sciences, law, the arts, government, economic and social affairs, and documents and reference. Preceding the volume is an editorial about the significant events of the year. Concluding it is an obituary followed by a chronicle of principal events of the year. As near as can be determined, there is an entry for every established nation. Contributors and their qualifications are listed; they are primarily British.

For the review of the *Register*, several knowledgeable persons were asked to evaluate sections in their areas of expertise. The opinions were overwhelmingly favorable. Should a library purchase this reference book? (Rather, is this the best source of the information provided?) The answer is probably yes, as long as one is looking for significant events of the year or those that occurred in Western-oriented and major nations. (One would not consult this work for routine information about systems of government or characteristics of the inhabitants of a country.) Purchase will thus probably be restricted to larger academic and public libraries or those with a specialized and internationally oriented clientele. — **Robert M. Ballard**

726. **Federal Systems of the World: A Handbook of Federal, Confederal, and Autonomy Arrangements.** By Daniel J. Elazar and the staff of the Jerusalem Center for Public Affairs, comps. and eds. Harlow, England, Longman Group; distr., Detroit, Gale, 1991. 402p. maps. $105.00. ISBN 0-582-08694-9.

According to the editors, democracy is the wave of the future, and federalism is the means most often used to achieve it in heterogeneous nations. This volume is designed to provide information on the formal and informal arrangements of self-rule and autonomy. Organized into two major sections, the book lists, categorizes, and supplies information on federal states and confederations around the world. In a brief introduction the editors explain the various flavors of both, define their terms, and outline recent developments (as of late 1991) in the Soviet Union and eastern Europe.

This hardcover book presents information clearly and concisely, although some areas of the world are changing too rapidly for accuracy to prevail in any handbook not updated hourly. The entry for each state is arranged alphabetically and includes an introduction with information on when and how the state came to exist, its precise governmental structure and constitution, and its political culture (often with charts detailing significant factors, such as ethnic composition). From three to eight pages are given on each federation and confederation.

While the book does exactly what it set out to do, it is hard to see how very many libraries will need it. Furthermore, much of the information presented can be garnered (with slightly more effort) from any high-quality encyclopedia. Only university libraries at institutions with major political science or diplomacy programs should consider it. [R: Choice, June 92, p. 1518] — **Robert Clyde Hodges**

727. Lane, Jan-Erik, David McKay, and Kenneth Newton. **Political Data Handbook: OECD Countries.** New York, Oxford University Press, 1991. 257p. (Comparative European Politics). $61.00. HA155.P65. 320'.021. LC 91-4022. ISBN 0-19-827718-0.

Comparative statistics are frequently troublesome to find and interpret as one must look in many different sources that have their data arranged in various ways. This expensive title rearranges data from many United Nations, Organization for Economic Cooperation and Development (OECD), World Bank, and other publications for easier use by researchers. First come statistics grouped by subject (e.g., government structure, employment) and then by country (19 from Western Europe, plus the United States, Canada, Japan, Australia, and New Zealand). The sources are cited at the bottom of the tables. Each national section is further subdivided and includes political information (e.g., who served as Prime Minister and when), the names of major newspapers and economic interest groups, the address of the country's central statistical office, and a list of further readings. Because of the time period covered, usually 1950 to 1985, there are data for historical comparisons. There are a bibliography of reference sources and a directory of data archives, but there is no index. According to the introduction, the authors sifted through nearly 230 sources and 450 tables of statistics to find the data for this volume. Note that the other titles in this series, such as Stephen George's *Politics and Policy in the European Community*, 2d ed. (1991), are texts and not reference books.

As one expects from the Oxford University Press, this is a quality publication. Recommended for all academic and larger public libraries. [R: Choice, Sept 92, p. 88] — **Daniel K. Blewett**

728. **Revolutionary and Dissident Movements: An International Guide.** 3d ed. Harlow, England, Longman Group; distr., Detroit, Gale, 1991. 401p. index. $145.00. ISBN 0-582-08692-2.

This work provides the required information on the underground movements that make today's world such an uncertain place in which to live. The main arrangement of the book is by country, of which 163 are included. Each section has a short description of the country and its political structure, as well as a historical narrative of the nation's major political events for the past several years (mainly from 1987, when the previous edition ended its coverage, to 1991). Some countries, such as Denmark, have small sections because they have no organized opposition movements, while others, such as India, have longer sections due to the many political groups that oppose the government.

Each of the more than 800 individual group entries usually has an identifying acronym and native-language name as well as transliterated name. The aims, history, tactics, and leadership of the movements are included, and illegal or semilegal groups from all shades of the political spectrum are covered. Information on many of the better-known groups, such as the Palestine Liberation Organization, can be found in other reference books, but this book is really valuable for its data on the less well known groups (e.g., the Bougainville Revolutionary Army). The introduction is much shorter than that found in the previous edition, which offered a brief discussion of terrorism and revolutionary activities. There is an index of organization names but no general index or list of acronyms, which would have been useful.

The original edition of this work was entitled *Political Dissent* (see ARBA 85, entry 625), and its present title was adopted with the 2d edition (see ARBA 89, entry 664). Patrons may also want to consult its companion volumes, *Political Parties of the World* (see ARBA 86, entry 666) and the 2d edition of *Communist and Marxist Parties of the World* (see ARBA 92, entry 728). This title meets the publisher's standards of quality, and it is easily recommended for the reference collections of all libraries. [R: Choice, June 92, pp. 1526-28] — **Daniel K. Blewett**

729. Sullivan, Michael J., III. **Measuring Global Values: The Ranking of 162 Countries.** Westport, Conn., Greenwood Press, 1991. 423p. index. $65.00. HN25.S85. 301'.072. LC 90-25209. ISBN 0-313-27649-8.

This work compares 162 countries, using more than 100 indicators that measure 5 global values: peace, economic well-being, ecological balance, social justice, and political participation. These five are considered by scholars to be sufficiently abstract and desirable so they can be accepted by states from all cultural milieus and political ideologies.

The goal of this study is to develop a set of political and social indicators of the values as well as a set of measures by which policies can be analyzed and performance judged. Because statistical data can vary from source to source, the author has selected sources that are widely available, comprehensive, and potentially usable for widespread scholarly collaboration in future research. Geographic divisions group the states into five zones (Europe, Islamic, Africa, Asia, and Latin America) that are broadly representative of historic centers of civilization. Each zone is further subdivided into three regions. Chapter text explains at length the general value indicators and specific statistical and narrative measures for each value. Tables rank countries within zones and summarize statistical data compiled. Bibliographies of resources used to compile data are presented at the end of each chapter. An index of geographic names and a general index provide the user with access to the data in both narrative and tabular forms.

Measuring Global Values should be of interest to students in world politics, international political economy, global ecology, international law, and comparative government. Academic and other research libraries will have the most use for this volume.—**Carol J. Veitch**

Quotation Books

730. Baker, Daniel B. **Power Quotes: 4,000 Trenchant Soundbites....** Detroit, Visible Ink Press/Gale, 1992. 387p. index. $15.95pa. ISBN 0-8103-9416-2.

This work reproduces all of the 4,014 numbered quotations from about 1,000 persons from the author's *Political Quotations* (see ARBA 91, entry 724) and adds some 25 quotations from 1990, 1991, and earlier years. It retains the alphabetical arrangement of 53 categories (e.g., bureaucracy, democracy, economics/the economy), within each of which quotations are entered chronologically. The source note (e.g., book, article, letter, speech, court decision, newspaper item) has been moved from the end of the quotation to the margin. Readers will see at a glance that documentation for a book is usually the author's name and book title (e.g., Adolf Hitler, *Mein Kampf*, 1924); for a journal/newspaper reference it is the publication's title and date.

Power Quotes has retained the author index of the parent volume but has replaced the entry numbers with page numbers. It has also preserved the inclusion of birth and death dates, brief background description, and category name and page number, but the valuable entry number keyword index (nearly one-fourth of the text) has been dropped. As before, the same 14 twentieth-century quotation books have been used as a base to which many sources, particularly those from the post-World War II era (about 40 percent of the citations), have been added.

High school, public, and academic libraries with *Political Quotations* will not need *Power Quotes*. Other libraries will find it a useful complement to their collection of general and specialized books of quotations.—**Wiley J. Williams**

POLITICS AND GOVERNMENT

United States

Almanacs

731. Haas, Lawrence J. **The Washington Almanac: A Guide to Federal Policy.** New York, Henry Holt, 1992. 653p. index. $50.00. JK271.H23. 320'.6'0973. LC 91-37577. ISBN 0-8050-1761-5.

This guide, which focuses especially on recent years through 1991, describes how U.S. federal policies have been made and profiles the policymakers. Twenty-three chapters that cover such topics as education, housing, farmers, taxes, environment, and defense are grouped into five broad sections. Each of the chapters includes a poorly formatted list of people profiled, an essay on key issues, and profiles of key players in policy-making. The essay provides historical background on legislation and regulations and discusses the ramifications of an issue and the political maneuvering that surrounds it. The profiles are divided into the public sector (e.g., officials in the White House and cabinet departments, officials at regulatory and independent agencies) and the private sector (e.g., lobbyists, lawyers, members of the business community). Some individuals are covered in more than one of the almost 400 profiles. The sources of information, which are not specifically cited, include interviews; biographical information provided by individuals; and such secondary sources as newspapers, magazines, and a variety of published almanacs and directories. A table of contents and a detailed index of subjects and names provide access.

This guide is intended to assist anyone who wants to change a law or regulation or to influence the course of national debate. With a publication date shortly before a presidential election and the election of many new members of Congress, one has to wonder whether this guide will fulfill its intended purpose or be rendered obsolete by new key policymakers and a new policy agenda. Nevertheless, this work by a writer at *National Journal* provides a fascinating snapshot for students of the policy-making process. [R: LJ, 1 Sept 92, p. 168; RBB, 1 Nov 92, p. 555]—**Carol Wheeler**

732. **The World Almanac of Presidential Campaigns.** By Eileen Shields-West. New York, World Almanac/St. Martin's Press, 1992. 250p. illus. index. $21.95; $10.95pa. JF285.S55. 324.973. LC 91-28734. ISBN 0-88687-610-9; 0-88687-609-5pa.

From the first American presidential election of 1788 through the Bush/Dukakis campaign of 1988, this paperback almanac supplies an interesting array of "facts, anecdotes, scandals, and mudslinging" related to the races for the White House. Each campaign is covered by a chapter with a standard outline and similar contents. For each major candidate the chapters discuss credentials, conventions, campaigns, party symbols, songs, examples of name-calling, slogans, and other "curious facts." The vote and campaign expenditures are documented. Each chapter closes with a two-page narrative of the highlights of the campaigns that concentrates on media coverage, tactics, and examples of the style, strategy, and mistakes of the candidates as campaigners. The candidates have been illustrated by Pulitzer prize-winning cartoonist Jeff MacNelly.

This title is a useful addition to reference collections on the U.S. presidency as it concentrates specifically on the campaigns rather than on biographical information on the presidents or historical coverage of the administrations. It covers basically the same ground as *Presidential Campaigns* by Paul F. Boller, Jr. (Oxford University Press, 1984), but there is little overlap in the information used to portray the nature and color of the presidential campaigns and the candidates. [R: RBB, 15 May 92, p. 1716]—**Henry E. York**

Bibliography

733. Brune, Lester H., and Richard Dean Burns. **America and the Indochina Wars, 1945-1990: A Bibliographical Guide.** Claremont, Calif., Regina Books, 1992. 286p. index. (New War/Peace Bibliographical Series, no.1). $39.95. Z3226.B89. 016.959704'3. LC 91-32259. ISBN 0-941690-43-1.

With this title the Center for the Study of Armament and Disarmament of California State University, Los Angeles, begins its New War/Peace Bibliography series. The work deals with the United States involvement in Indochina's three wars since 1945. It supplements, but does not replace, two related earlier volumes by Burns and Milton Leitenberg, the most recent of which is *The Wars in Vietnam, Cambodia, and Laos, 1945-1982* (see ARBA 85, entry 475).

The bibliography emphasizes books, articles, and dissertations published since 1980. The 3,550 citations are organized into 9 chapters that cover the background, history, and military events of the conflicts in Indochina between 1945 and 1990. The last chapter deals with reference aids, including guides to printed documents, archival collections, and oral histories. There are also chapters on postmortems of the war and the war's impact on U.S. life. The only annotations are one-line descriptions for some of the entries. There are author and subject indexes and a number of useful tables on such topics as casualties and expenditures. The general and chapter introductions are short but provide useful orientations to the materials included. For the person in search of comprehensive, well-organized, thoughtful coverage of the literature, this excellent bibliography will be a valuable asset.—**Henry E. York**

734. **State Reference Publications 1991-1992: A Bibliographic Guide to State Blue Books, Legislative Manuals and Other General Reference Sources.** Lynn Helleburst, ed. Topeka, Kans., Government Research Service, 1991. 211p. $55.00 spiralbound. ISBN 1-879929-00-7.

The first edition of this title was published as *State Blue Books, Legislative Manuals, and Reference Publications* (see ARBA 91, entry 730). Under the new title the plan is to publish annually in June. This straightforward, comprehensive guide covers blue books, directories of state governments, and other state government reference sources for the 50 states, the District of Columbia, and Puerto Rico. A substantial number of these publications, especially the increasing number produced by private publishers, are difficult to identify or obtain. And many state publications present difficulties simply because they are published beyond state borders.

In addition to the blue books, legislative manuals and handbooks, directories, biographic profiles, statistical abstracts, texts on governments and politics, and other reference sources are included. There are roughly 12 to 40 entries for each state. Each entry contains a one- or two-line description of the content; full bibliographic description; price; and name, address, and telephone number of the publishing agency or firm. An appendix includes a bibliography of 52 reference books, directories, and periodicals that deal with state issues generally or across all the states. This annual guide will be a valuable tool for researchers, librarians, and government officials who need current information on state reference publications. — **Henry E. York**

Catalogs and Collections

735. Reilly, Bernard F., Jr. **American Political Prints 1766-1876: A Catalog of the Collections in the Library of Congress.** New York, G. K. Hall, 1991. 638p. illus. index. $150.00. E183.3.R45. 320.973'0207. LC 90-43029. ISBN 0-8161-0444-1.

This work fully reveals the art form of editorial cartooning and displays the rich array of prints that are housed in the Library of Congress. Unrivaled for its insight into U.S. history, *American Political Prints* provides a visual political commentary of the years 1766 to 1876 unmatched elsewhere. Similar to the papers in which they appeared, cartoonists could be hateful, biased, and propaganda-laden. A number of the plates reflect these qualities, vilifying minorities and drawing them grotesquely to "prove" a point. The pictures of Abraham Lincoln and other presidents are also revealing. Many of the plates occupy a full page; all are well displayed. The text that accompanies the prints is interesting and educational, and there are excellent notes.

This magnificent collection belongs on the shelves of college or university libraries that have any interest in political literacy. Many individuals will also want this work. — **S. L. Harrison**

Dictionaries and Encyclopedias

736. **The HarperCollins Dictionary of American Government and Politics.** By Jay M. Shafritz. New York, HarperCollins, 1992. 656p. illus. $50.00. JK9.S43. 320.973'03. LC 91-55389. ISBN 0-06-270031-6.

Shafritz has compiled short entries on a variety of themes related to American politics. Entry types include political science jargon and the slang expressions of politicians, technical legal and legislative terms, court cases and major legislation, federal agencies and nongovernmental institutions, and biographies of government figures and key political scientists who have made major contributions to the understanding of American politics. The material is presented in an encyclopedic format; numerous photographs, charts, cartoons, and tables illustrate the various entries. The author often injects a bit of gentle humor into the entries.

The work is readily accessible to the nonspecialist and will benefit scholars and those tracking down obscure agencies or laws. Students, journalists, scholars, and laypeople interested in politics will find this an invaluable resource in understanding the sometimes obscure terms of political discourse. Highly recommended for community, college, and research libraries. [R: Choice, July/Aug 92, p. 1661; LJ, 1 June 92, p. 118; RBB, 1 May 92, p. 1623; WLB, Apr 92, pp. 124-25] — **Frank L. Wilson**

737. Wellek, Alex, ed. **The Encyclopedic Dictionary of American Government.** 4th ed. Guilford, Conn., Dushkin Publishing, 1991. 338p. illus. $12.95pa. LC 90-81964. ISBN 0-87967-883-6.

This work is a dictionary of terms, events, concepts, and individuals that lists and explains the significance of a variety of ideas, organizations, and personalities essential for understanding the U.S. system of governance. Entries include biographical sketches of presidents, prominent congressional leaders, and Supreme Court justices; important concepts in U.S. political theory and practice, such as presidential succession, legislative veto, and grand jury; various federal agencies, such as the General Accounting Office and the Office of Management and Budget; major Supreme Court cases, such as Marbury v. Madison and Mapp v. Ohio; and terms and concepts unique to foreign affairs and national security policy.

This is generally a succinct, objective, and well-produced volume. One exception to this is an editorial error in the entry on absolutism (p. 3), which repeats the first paragraph of what appears to be an article on rainforests that does not appear under the headings "rainforest," "environment," or any other pertinent subject heading. Despite this weakness, *The Encyclopedic Dictionary of American Government* is a useful addition to the political science collections of all libraries. [R: RBB, 15 Apr 92, p. 1549] — **Bert Chapman**

Directories

738. Baker, Jennifer, and Mary Noel Rees, comps. **State Legislative Staff Directory 1991: Key Policy and Fiscal Contacts.** Denver, Colo., National Conference of State Legislatures, 1991. 114p. $25.00pa. ISBN 1-55516-982-1.

As are other publications of the National Conference of State Legislatures (NCSL), this directory of key policy and fiscal contacts is authoritative and informative. Any library whose patrons need current information on their state governments and need to know how to receive updates on key political issues should keep a copy of this publication.

This volume contains more than 3,600 listings for key state policy and fiscal contacts in 18 major issue areas. The information is taken from a February 1991 questionnaire sent to legislative research and fiscal directors within each state, the District of Columbia, Puerto Rico, and the Virgin Islands. The directory is arranged alphabetically by major issue and then subarranged within each issue section by state. These sections include policies concerning children, youth, and families; education; the elderly; environment and natural resources; and telecommunications. Within each listing, information is provided on name; address; telephone number; and whether the person is a principal contact, specialist, secondary contact, or partisan/nonpartisan staff. For specialists, the specialty is listed with the directory information. An appendix gives information on the state survey coordinators responsible for returning the questionnaire.

This directory is part of an annual set of reports prepared by the NCSL State Issues and Policy Analysis Program. Other volumes in the set are *Selected State Enactments, State Issues: Priority Issues for State Legislatures*, and *Leaders' Outlook*. All are recommended purchases for libraries.
— **Christine E. Thompson**

739. **Directory of Legislative Leaders 1991-92.** Denver, Colo., National Conference of State Legislatures, 1991. 112p. $15.00 spiralbound. ISBN 1-55516-737-3.

Arranged alphabetically by state and presented in a visually pleasing format, this directory provides addresses and telephone and fax numbers for all state senators and representatives from the 50 states and Puerto Rico. The same type of information is provided for the legislative bodies of the District of Columbia, American Samoa, Guam, the Northern Mariana Islands, and the Virgin Islands. Party affiliation is indicated, and information is given on current position in the legislature, committee memberships, occupation, and names and addresses of key staff members. As a single source of useful information, this is a must for public and academic libraries. — **Sharon Langworthy**

740. **The Government Directory of Addresses and Telephone Numbers: Your Comprehensive Guide to Federal, State, County, and Local Government Offices....** Detroit, Omnigraphics, 1992. 1290p. $89.00. ISBN 1-55888-799-7. ISSN 1062-1466.

While most reference departments may not relish the thought of yet another directory to the U.S. government, this new publication may well be worth considering as a supplement to the standard sources. *The Government Directory*, in one large (but convenient) volume, provides a comprehensive list of government offices and positions, from city level to federal agencies and most areas in-between.

The directory is arranged by broad level of authority. Federal offices include the Executive Office of the President, the Cabinet departments, administrative agencies, other federal organizations (e.g., the Smithsonian Institution, the National Academy of Sciences), and the U.S. Congress. Federal regional offices primarily include the administrative agencies but also list the federal courts. State offices are arranged by state, with a keyword index to topics, and the section on city and county offices includes a separate list of municipalities with a population of less than 15,000 (although just a brief address and a single telephone number are provided). A typical entry in the directory gives the address, a list of top administrative positions by title only (e.g., director, deputy director, legislative specialist), and telephone numbers. Divisions and branches of a large department are also listed. Only the names of individual officeholders are provided for most of the city and county positions.

This directory is much more comprehensive than *The United States Government Manual* (Office of the Federal Register, annual) or *The Book of the States* (see ARBA 91, entry 743), although it does not include any descriptive information about the departments or positions. A comparable reference source is the series of Yellow Books published by Monitor Publishing (see ARBA 91, entries 736 and 738). The Yellow Books have the advantage of being more current (they are updated quarterly) and of listing the names of the current officeholders. However, to duplicate the coverage in *The Government Directory*, a library would have to subscribe to four different editions of Yellow Books: *Federal*, *Congressional*, *State*, and *Municipal*. Thus, libraries that either lack the Yellow Books or that seek a more convenient resource are encouraged to consider this directory. [R: LJ, 15 Nov 92, p. 70] – **Thomas A. Karel**

741. **Municipal Yellow Book: Who's Who in the Leading City and County Governments and Local Authorities. Vol.II, No.1.** Mary Flanigan Forrester and others, eds. New York, Monitor Publishing, 1992. 746p. index. $160.00 (2 issues). ISSN 1054-4062.

This is a directory of municipal governments in the United States. It covers the 100 largest cities; the 100 most populous counties; a few additional cities and counties with smaller populations; and some major governmental authorities responsible for transportation, power, water supply, and other such services. The *Yellow Book* lists the departments of each city, county, and authority; the address and principal officials of each department; and the title and telephone number of each official. This work is quite comprehensive with respect to the municipal governments included. It is neither limited to the most important departments nor to the top one or two administrators in the department. It includes the elected officials (e.g., mayors, city council members, county commissioners) of each municipal government as well as appointed officials. Elected officials' political parties are given in some instances.

There are separate sections for cities, counties, and authorities. Within each section the governments are listed alphabetically, not grouped by state. A state-by-state list of cities and counties in the book is provided, as is a table of contents. There is also an alphabetical index to the name of each official listed. Most people will use this book only for information about a government or officials in their area, but it will be very helpful to those who work in or with municipal governments and who want to communicate with officials in another region. – **Peter B. Kutner**

742. **Tennessee Government Officials Directory, 1991.** Joseph L. White and Mary K. Weber, eds. Nashville, Tenn., M. Lee Smith, 1991. 1v. (various paging). $37.00 looseleaf w/binder.

If one is looking for the name of a person or an agency in Tennessee government, such will be found in this directory – mayors, police chiefs, board of county commissioners, public works directors, district attorneys, planning commissioners, and more. Also included are higher education institutions, state associations, chambers of commerce, lobbyists, media outlets (print and nonprint), and political party representatives. The volume is arranged by subject (e.g., state department and agencies, general assembly, state judiciary), with tab dividers separating each section and allowing for easy access. State senatorial and representative districts are also given.

The directory is a must buy for all Tennessee libraries and for most libraries in states contiguous to Tennessee. The only criticism is the quality of printing, which is uneven throughout. Some sections are excellent and clearly legible; others are too tightly compacted and use very tiny print. — **Mark Y. Herring**

743. **Washington Information Directory 1992-1993.** Ann Davies, ed. Washington, D.C., Congressional Quarterly, 1992. 1118p. index. $89.95. F192.3.W33. 975.3'0025. LC 75-646321. ISBN 0-87187-692-2. ISSN 0887-8064.

The 1992-1993 annual update of this directory continues Congressional Quarterly's (CQ) excellent guide to information sources available in Washington, D.C. Some 5,000 entries are divided into 18 chapters that cover prominent organizations in such fields as business, health, national security, science, and transportation. Within each of these chapters the entries are grouped into more specific subject areas for which the tables of contents serve as guides. The information sources are further divided into three categories: executive branch agencies, congressional committees, and nongovernmental organizations. For each source there is a paragraph that offers the name of the principal officer, address, and telephone and fax numbers, plus a useful short statement on the purpose, interests, and activities of the organization. In addition, this guide contains a clearly written introductory section on how to use the directory efficiently; detailed subject and name indexes; and many ready-reference lists that cover the major administrative and congressional officials, and mayors of major cities. As with all CQ publications, there is a wealth of additional related information in boxes, charts, maps, and lists. Although no longer inexpensive, this title remains an essential resource for information on governmental agencies and organizations in Washington, D.C. — **Henry E. York**

744. **Washington Representatives 1992.** 16th ed. Arthur C. Close, J. Valerie Steele, and Curtis W. McCormick, eds. Washington, D.C., Columbia Books, 1992. 826p. index. $60.00pa. LC 76-21152. ISBN 0-910416-97-4.

Special-interest groups are probably as important as the politicians they attempt to influence. This directory lists the names, addresses, and telephone numbers of more than 14,000 individuals and firms representing those interests. The directory's information has been compiled from lists of registered lobbyists and foreign agents and from public documents.

Lobbyists, consultants, and foreign agents are listed in alphabetical order in the first section. The next section compiles the names of businesses, trade and professional associations, and various advocacy groups in alphabetical order, providing addresses, telephone numbers, and the names of the persons or firms that represent each organization. A third section lists (by executive branch department or agency) the staff members responsible for legislative affairs. Subject and foreign-interests indexes round out the volume.

The publishing time lag associated with print means that this material can become out-of-date fairly quickly. As electronic formats become more affordable and available, the publisher may want to investigate such an alternative. For now, *Washington Representatives*, with its focus on federal government and its inclusion of foreign countries and business firms, is recommended as a complementary companion to *American Lobbyists Directory* (see ARBA 91, entry 742). — **Cheryl Knott Malone**

Handbooks and Yearbooks

745. Bickers, Kenneth N., and Robert M. Stein. **Federal Domestic Outlays 1983-1990: A Data Book.** Armonk, N.Y., M. E. Sharpe, 1991. 294p. $45.00. HJ275.B47. 336.1'85. LC 91-651. ISBN 0-87332-840-X.

This compilation by two political science professors at Rice University reports federal outlays by congressional district for fiscal years 1983 (the first year in which comparable district data from the Federal Assistance Award Data System [FAADS] were available) through 1990. It is thus a supplement to the data presented in *Federal Expenditures by State*, *Consolidated Federal Funds Report*, and annual publications of the Bureau of the Census.

This volume consists of five chapters and four appendixes. The introduction (chapter 1) is a brief history of federal data collection efforts and pinpoints certain limitations of FAADS, such as situations where counties encompass more than one congressional district. Chapter 2 contains histograms for each recipient category (e.g., local governments, special districts, private universities, small businesses, individuals), showing monies going to each of the four major regions of the country—Northeast, Midwest, West, and South. Separate tables in chapter 3 provide the data for 13 recipient categories for each congressional district for each year. The bar graphs in chapter 4 display outlays in all regions year by year for each of 12 functional policy categories (e.g., agriculture, community development). Chapter 5 reports outlays for the policy categories by congressional district year by year.

Appendix A lists the congressional districts that represent the state capital county and those districts that represent only portions of a county. Appendixes B and C list the programs in each recipient category and each functional category, using the catalog number sequence employed in the *Catalog of Federal Domestic Assistance* (Office of Management and Budget, 1989). The states included in each U.S. region are listed in appendix D. Scholars, government officials, and citizens interested in the creation, maintenance, and expansion of federal programs will welcome *Federal Domestic Outlays*. [R: Choice, Mar 92, p. 1038]—**Wiley J. Williams**

746. Bosnich, Victor W., comp. **Congressional Voting Guide: A Ten Year Compilation.** 4th ed. Bronx, N.Y., H. W. Wilson, 1992. 637p. index. $34.95pa. JK1051.B67. 328.73'0775. LC 92-12140. ISBN 0-8242-0833-1.

As a 10-year compilation of the voting records of members of the 102d Congress, this guide covers 144 major bills, including nominations, amendments, and veto overrides, from the U.S. House of Representatives and Senate. The measures examined have been selected to reflect public interest and to reveal how members voted on major issues of the day. The majority selected are from 1988 to 1992 to focus on the positions of recently elected members of Congress.

The major part of the guide lists, in House and Senate sections, the measures covered and provides a short description of the bill, the date and result of the vote, and a breakdown of the vote by political party. Following each of these sections of measures is a list of members of Congress, arranged alphabetically by state, that records how each member voted on each issue. There is a short biographical paragraph at the beginning of each member's voting record. Support of the president by members of congress is indicated in percentage terms.

Similar information is, of course, available in more piecemeal fashion from government documents and such commercial publications as *Congressional Quarterly Weekly Report* and *Congress and the Nation*. But for a systematic and convenient study of congressional treatment of major issues of the last decade, or for an overview of the voting record of particular members of Congress, this is an invaluable resource. [R: SLMQ, Fall 92, p. 75]—**Henry E. York**

747. **Congressional Quarterly's Guide to Congress.** 4th ed. Mary Cohn, ed. Washington, D.C., Congressional Quarterly, 1991. 1v. (various paging). illus. index. $179.95. JK1021.C565. 328.73. LC 91-19946. ISBN 0-87187-584-5.

The U.S. Congress is an imperfect body, but a potent and valuable one. Legislative gridlock occurs when Congress is divided against itself or collides with another branch of the federal government. Sometimes unduly influenced by outside organizations that are motivated by a desire for economic gain, Congress occasionally loses sight of the public well-being. Scandals such as those that involved Speaker of the House Jim Wright and the Keating Five have brought the institution into disrepute. Yet Congress has also made great contributions to America's development, passing beneficial legislation in virtually every sphere of human endeavor.

This volume contains a vast amount of information on the origins, history, powers, procedures, and politics of Congress. After describing the constitutional beginnings of the legislative branch, the extent of its authority, and the great events of the past, the editor shows how Congress interacts with the president, the Supreme Court, and constituents. Especially relevant are sections on the war powers debate, judicial review, special-interest groups, political action committees, and congressional ethics. The House of Representatives and Senate receive approximately equal coverage. Although a small amount of repetition appears, it is of passing concern (e.g., the same quotation by Dave McCurdy is found on both page xviii and page 73).

Straightforward, generally well written, and comprehensive, *Guide to Congress* is the best single-volume treatment of Congress available. Cohn and her assistants have proven particularly adept at fitting the House and Senate into their proper institutional and political settings. Selected readings at the back of each chapter are helpful, as is the list of congresspeople who served between 1789 and 1991. Every citizen of the republic should read this nearly flawless effort. Highly recommended for public, high school, and college libraries.—**Richard E. Holl**

748. Day, Glenn. **Minor Presidential Candidates and Parties of 1992: A Reference.** Jefferson, N.C., McFarland, 1992. 192p. illus. index. $25.95pa. E884.D39. 324.973'0928. LC 91-51228. ISBN 0-89950-653-4.

The quadrennial presidential election cycle produces candidates from Democratic and Republican ranks who receive a preponderance of media attention and financial support. However, presidential aspirants are not limited to establishment figures from the two major parties. Candidates also come from minor parties, the fringes of the major parties, nonpartisan campaigns, and ambitious individuals. The unheralded candidates for 1992 are chronicled in this work.

Day opens with criticism of what he sees as the undue legal restrictions placed upon unconventional presidential campaign aspirants by the two established parties. He proceeds to list the names and platforms of candidates, representing a mosaic of opinions, who responded to his requests for information about their candidacies. The platforms of these individuals vary in length and quality, with some espousing plausible solutions to national problems and others drifting into the absurd, as evidenced by one candidate who contends that 4 space travelers have been imprisoned at Ohio's Wright-Patterson Air Force Base for the last 40 years.

Day's portrayal is entertaining but fails to qualify as serious scholarship or analysis of minor party presidential candidates. While this portrait includes individuals who have received no media recognition, it also has coverage of Patrick Buchanan, whose campaign saw considerable national press. This compilation will be most useful for collections that want comprehensive coverage of presidential campaigns or that promote unconventional or "alternative" political viewpoints to their users. [R: RBB, 15 June 92, p. 1876; WLB, Sept 92, p. 116]—**Bert Chapman**

749. Fritz, Sara, and Dwight Morris. **Handbook of Campaign Spending: Money in the 1990 Congressional Races.** Washington, D.C., Congressional Quarterly, 1992. 567p. index. $105.00. JK1991.F75. 324.7'8'0973. LC 92-8597. ISBN 0-87187-735-X.

This authoritative and informative handbook gives an overview of the costs of the 1990 congressional campaigns and includes an analysis of 972 candidates and more than 400,000 separate expenditures. For the House candidates, the two-year cycle from January 1989 through December 1990 is analyzed. For the Senate candidates, the six-year cycle from January 1985 through December 1990 provides the basis for information. The Federal Election Commission (FEC) reports were obtained from the *Los Angeles Times* for this extensive report.

The work contains 43 tables that illustrate such interesting facts as categories of expenditures, the top 25 spenders in both the House and the Senate campaigns, and expenditures for Phil Gramm's 1989 presidential gala (which was the most lucrative fund-raiser of the cycle). A guide to the tables explains the categories of expenditures and the source for the figures. The section on individual candidates is arranged by state for both House and Senate, then by district for the House races. An excellent index is provided in the appendix. Also included in the work are several narratives on raising and spending money, such as a discussion on the reasons for campaign costs, the cost for television exposure, and campaign expenditure reform.

Works complementary to *Handbook of Campaign Spending* are *Almanac of Federal PACs: 1990* by Edward Zuckerman (Amward Publications, 1990) and *Open Secrets* by Larry Makinson (see index for entry number). Both of these excellent works give an extensive analysis of campaign contributions, thereby providing information on both the fund-raising and the spending activities of all candidates in the 1990 congressional races. [R: RBB, 1 Nov 92, pp. 547-48]—**Christine E. Thompson**

750. Helleburst, Lynn. **State Legislative Sourcebook 1992: A Resource Guide to Legislative Information in the Fifty States.** Topeka, Kans., Government Research Service, 1991. 531p. $135.00 looseleaf with binder. ISBN 1-879929-02-3. ISSN 0898-7297.

The 7th edition of this familiar source follows the publication of several reference books on the 50 states (see ARBA 91, entries 730 and 897). A section on each state, arranged alphabetically, describes that state's legislative process and cites government and commercial sources on all aspects of legislation, legislators, and lobbying. Also included are more general sources such as blue books, newspapers and journals, and state telephone directories. This information is presented in the same outline format for each state and made clear with indentations, boldface type, and good spacing. Appendixes list telephone numbers for learning the status of a bill, addresses and telephone numbers for "bill rooms" (where copies of documents can be obtained), and an extensive bibliography on influencing state legislation.

This is much more than a bibliography, as pertinent facts are pointed out in the description of each source, such as requirements for legislators' financial disclosures. It is more complete (and more expensive) than *State Blue Books, Legislative Manuals and Reference Publications* (see ARBA 91, entry 730). Its binding is the only drawback; the looseleaf/binder format makes it prone to stolen pages and difficult shelving. [R: RBB, July 92, p. 1963] – **Cathy Seitz Whitaker**

751. **Inside the Legislative Process: A Comprehensive Survey of the American Society of Legislative Clerks and Secretaries....** 1991 ed. Denver, Colo., National Conference of State Legislatures, 1992. 167p. $20.00 spiralbound. ISBN 1-55516-739-X.

This spiralbound survey was conducted by the American Society of Legislative Clerks and Secretaries in cooperation with the National Conference of State Legislatures. It is the sixth since 1975. Much of the information has not been repeated, so the earlier editions are still useful. The book consists largely of tables that set forth the responses to a questionnaire sent to each legislative house in each U.S. state, commonwealth, or territory. (Unfortunately, a few of the houses did not respond to this 1991 survey.) The tables are grouped in seven chapters: general legislative procedures, committee procedures, bill processing, public information, printing of legislative documents, the office of the chief clerk and secretary, and benefits and personnel policies.

The tables reveal an interesting array of diversity of practice throughout the United States on such matters as the procedure for selecting the presiding officers of state legislative houses; the options legislative committees have in disposing bills; the requirement for open meetings; the indexing of bills; charges for legislative documents; and the selection, duties, and work benefits of chamber officers. There is a total of 60 tables. The survey will be useful for legislators, staff, lobbyists, media representatives, and the general public who want to know specifically the rules or procedures for a particular legislative house. It could also be useful for students, politicians, or members of the public who wish to do comparative studies across the various states. – **Henry E. York**

752. Makinson, Larry. **Open Secrets: The Encyclopedia of Congressional Money and Politics.** 2d ed. Washington, D.C. Congressional Quarterly, 1992. 1339p. index. $136.00. JK1991.M26. 324.7'8'0973. LC 92-5802. ISBN 0-87187-689-2.

Makinson presents a bipartisan analysis of contributions from more than 3,200 political action committees (PACs) to candidates in the 1990 congressional elections. The work is divided into five sections: overall PAC spending patterns, profiles on industries and interest groups, contributions to members of specific congressional committees, contributions to each candidate elected in 1990, and profiles of PACs that contributed at least $20,000 to federal candidates in 1990. The analysis is based on a classification system (outlined in appendix A) that links the primary or secondary legislative interests of PACs with the committee assignments of candidates receiving contributions. A brief explanation is provided in the introduction. *Open Secrets* includes more than 3,000 charts and graphs that visually represent patterns of PAC contributions. Narrative analysis is provided where clarification is needed. For ease of use, state delegation and name indexes are included.

Another work comparable to *Open Secrets* is *Almanac of Federal PACs* by Edward Zuckerman (Amward Publications, 1990). Zuckerman provides excellent background on individual PACs but does not have the extensive analysis found in Makinson's work. The Center for Responsive Politics plans to continue publication of this information. Although the cost is not low, the book is a valuable source of information on campaign finances. Highly recommended for any library that needs political campaign information. [R: RBB, 1 Nov 92, pp. 547-48] — **Christine E. Thompson**

753. Nelson, Michael, ed. **Historic Documents on Presidential Elections 1787-1988.** Washington, D.C., Congressional Quarterly, 1991. 902p. index. $72.95. JK1965.H56. 324.973. LC 91-18729. ISBN 0-87187-607-8.

The return of America's quadrennial presidential election in 1992 is a good time to focus on past presidential campaigns and important statements and documents that influenced those races. This material and focus are provided in the book under review. Nelson provides chronological coverage of key documents, debates, and speeches from most presidential campaigns and from other significant influences on the presidency. Each entry opens with a contextual introduction and proceeds with generally verbatim textual coverage of source materials, with modest editorial changes to enhance clarity. Events covered include George Washington's farewell address (1796), Martin Van Buren's letter on Texas annexation (1844), William Jennings Bryan's "Cross of Gold" speech (1896), the 103d ballot of the 1924 Democratic Convention, House debate on the 22d Amendment (1947), Barry Goldwater's 1964 Republican Convention acceptance speech, and numerous other portraits of political skill and ineptitude by presidential aspirants. Nelson also includes an appendix that lists presidential birth and death dates, terms of service, vice-presidential terms of service, and presidential election returns. The cumulative result is a substantive yet succinct portrait of major documents from American presidential campaigns. [R: RBB, 15 May 92, p. 1716; WLB, May 92, pp. 126-28] — **Bert Chapman**

754. Ornstein, Norman J., Thomas E. Mann, and Michael J. Malbin. **Vital Statistics on Congress, 1991-1992.** Washington, D.C., Congressional Quarterly, 1992. 275p. index. $29.95; $19.95pa. LC 87-659232. ISBN 0-87187-620-5; 0-87187-621-3pa. ISSN 0896-9469.

Vital Statistics is much more than a compendium of charts and tables. It fulfills its authors' promise to chronicle the turmoil of the past decade in an institution commonly perceived to be relatively static and entrenched.

The requisite charts and tables do appear. Statistics on membership, occupations, elections, committees, spending, staffs, work load, votes and voting alignments, and much more are usually broken down into microscopic detail for researchers. Also, despite the book's title, it presents more than just a compendium of information for 1991 and 1992; most charts span many years. The information is clearly presented and well organized and indexed. Of greater importance is the fact that the editors succinctly analyze the statistics presented in each chapter in readable chapter introductions. They assemble a fascinating portrait of an institution that has changed over time and that underwent particularly rapid change through the 1980s. (In the 1990s the Congress seems to be stabilizing.)

Vital Statistics succeeds at its mission: to bring a wealth of statistics on the legislative branch quickly and easily to the fingertips of any researcher. Research libraries need it; public libraries will probably want it too. [R: WLB, Jan 92, p. 132] — **Robert Clyde Hodges**

755. **State Issues 1992: A Survey of Priority Issues for State Legislatures.** Denver, Colo., National Conference of State Legislatures, 1991. 116p. $65.00 spiralbound. ISBN 1-55516-987-2.

This work undertakes an annual survey of issues that confront state legislatures. The universe surveyed consists of 1,400 legislators and staff members who were asked to rank each of 18 items, from agriculture through transportation, in order of priority for each state. Results are ranked for each responding state and displayed in a graphic chart. (The top items are, in order of priority: education finance, health care [especially Medicaid], reapportionment and redistricting, economic development, and campaign finance and ethics.) The reader must assess each of the rankings (these are published in the separate *Leaders' Outlook*), which is a bother. More disconcerting is the lack of data from states that failed to respond to selected sections. For example, Florida, a state with grave fiscal problems, did not indicate any priorities. This book has limitations, but interested readers may find useful the overview of each of the topic areas with a brief focus on each state's outlook. — **S. L. Harrison**

756. Surrency, Erwin C., comp. and ed. **Consolidated Treaties & International Agreements: Current Document Service: United States.** Dobbs Ferry, N.Y., Oceana, 1991. 827p. index. $125.00pa. ISSN 1053-9905.

This volume contains the text of recent U.S. treaties and international agreements. Each is listed and explained; typically, background information on negotiations, the effect of the agreement, and the legal authority for it are provided. The treaties and international agreements are organized according to Department of State (DOS) document number, from DOS 90-1 to DOS 90-82. The time period covered ranges from January 4, 1990, to March 29, 1990. Subsequent volumes in this series treat later agreements; together, they offer the most up-to-date text of U.S. treaties and international agreements available. Six appendixes are located at the back, the most important of which indexes the treaties and international agreements by country and subject (e.g., agricultural commodities, debts, defense, trade and commerce).

Remarkably, Surrency and Oceana present these documents to the public *before* the government does. Because the State Department is behind in its publication of international agreements, *Consolidated Treaties & International Agreements* brings them to the reader even before they become official. Just as important, Surrency arranges this material in a systematic manner that simplifies the finding process. Modern treaties and international agreements are therefore collected in one place and put in logical order, and the various indexes permit the researcher to try several different approaches to locating the required document. Timeliness and ease of use may well make this expensive book a worthwhile purchase. Recommended for college, university, and law libraries. — **Richard E. Holl**

757. Trattner, John H. **The Prune Book: The 60 Toughest Science and Technology Jobs in Washington.** Lanham, Md., Madison Books; distr., Lanham, Md., National Book Network, 1992. 545p. index. $37.50. Q149.U5T73. 353.07'4. LC 91-35960. ISBN 0-8191-8419-5.

Candidates seeking federal appointments to "policy and supporting positions" often refer to the congressional publication of these executive branch jobs as the "Plum Book." The ironically titled *Prune Book* describes the responsibilities, programs and objectives of 62 scientific and technical appointive positions in Washington, D.C. First published in 1988 (see ARBA 89, entry 658), the work's main goal is to attract experienced and competent people to manage these important positions. A uniform format is followed for each position profiled. The major responsibilities of the position are outlined; the training, experience, and skills needed to manage the position are noted; and a discursive "insight" segment offers an in-depth analysis of each position's role within the federal bureaucracy. This narrative portion also addresses various problem areas and provides historical context and critical commentary by past and present managers. Each profile ends with an outline of key relationships (e.g., reports to ..., works closely with ...), a brief sketch of the current manager, and a list of past managers.

Among the 62 profiles, 4 come under the Executive Office of the president, 20 are executive departments and agencies, and 6 are either congressional committees or offices that report to Congress. The more than 200 interviewees include present and former holders of the positions described as well as informed "observers," usually members of congressional committee staffs, think tanks, or trade associations. This edition of the *Prune Book* is a valuable reference tool that students and scholars of American public policy will need to consult. — **Gary D. Barber**

Indexes

758. **CIS Four-Year Cumulative Index, 1987-1990.** Bethesda, Md., Congressional Information Service, 1991. 4v. $1,840.00/set. LC 79-158879. ISBN 0-88692-226-7.

This fifth multiyear cumulation revises and supersedes *CIS/Annual* index volumes for 1987 through 1990 (see ARBA 86, entry 697 for review of the 1984 *CIS/Annual*). It covers hearings, committee prints, House and Senate reports and documents, Senate treaty documents, Senate executive reports, public laws, and special publications CIS has been able to obtain. Using CIS's accession number system based on issuing congressional body and type of publication, the four-volume cumulative index leads the user to the previously published abstract and legislative history volumes for the years covered. Numerous access points are provided. The subject headings and cross-references in the index of subjects and names are based on a controlled vocabulary developed by CIS. The policy is to index using the most specific subject term applicable from the controlled vocabulary, and multiple subject access points are provided whenever warranted by the content of the publication. Because "hot topics" may not have found their way into the controlled vocabulary, broader subject headings may have to be consulted. The convenience of having four years of indexing together occasionally pales when a specific subject heading has as many as eight pages of listings.

Other indexes provide access by bill, report, document, hearing, or print number; by Superintendent of Documents number; and by title. There is also an alphabetical list of committee and subcommittee chairs that provides accession numbers for their committees and subcommittees and indicates the dates during 1987-1990 that the individual served as chair.

CIS continues to be *the* provider of legislative indexing. This cumulative index represents another source of well-presented and relatively easy-to-use (once the system is understood) information. It should be noted, however, that two of the volumes received for review were already coming apart in back, where the material holding the text block to the spine was not sturdy enough for the size and weight of the volumes. Libraries interested in cumulative indexing to congressional information should also investigate CIS's Congressional Masterfile 2 on CD-ROM. — **Carol Wheeler**

759. **United States Treaty Index: 1776-1990 Consolidation.** Igor I. Kavass, comp. and ed. Buffalo, N.Y., William S. Hein, 1991. 11v. $1,500.00/set. ISBN 0-89941-770-1.

Treaties are major components of diplomacy, and the ability to access and examine them is vital for those studying diplomatic history, international law, and international economics. Kavass seeks to provide "a comprehensive index of all documented treaties and agreements entered into by the United States from 1776 through 1990." Two Department of State publications, *Treaties in Force* (annual) and *United States Treaties and Other International Agreements*, are the principal governmental publications for locating the text of treaties entered into by the U.S. government. While these two sources are reasonably useful, neither (particularly the latter) is a repository of the most current information about U.S. treaties.

The set opens with a historical note concerning superseded U.S. treaty indexes produced by William S. Hein. The initial volume also lists the names of five series under which U.S. treaties have been classified, a glossary of pertinent American and international treaty reference sources, and numerical and chronological citations to treaties classified under these divergent series. These citations continue through volume 5.

Volumes 6 and 7 feature chronological lists of U.S. treaties, starting with 1776, and include references that indicate the countries and subjects involved, the series and number citation, and the dates on which the treaties were signed or entered into force. (The increasing number signed by the United States in recent years becomes particularly apparent in these volumes.) Volumes 8 and 9 include an alphabetical list of countries and multilateral organizations with whom the United States has signed treaties. The listings for individual countries are arranged alphabetically and in chronological order, from the first treaty signed by the United States with that country, group of countries, or organization to the most recent compacts between these parties. Each entry is cross-referenced to the appropriate series citation and classification and contains a brief subject description. The final two volumes contain a subject index. Subjects include agreements named for specific individuals (e.g., the Hay-Pauncefote Treaty); the names of international negotiations and organizations, including the General Agreement on Tariffs and Trade and International Atomic Energy Agency; and individual subject headings and subheadings, such as a 1950 treaty between the United States and Canada on halibut fishing vessels.

Kavass has prepared an exhaustive and usable index to the complexities involved in researching American treaties. Its greatest strengths include its multiple access points and cross-references, timeliness, and overall arrangement. Users must still consult *United States Treaties and Other International Agreements* to examine the text of individual treaties and *Treaties in Force* to determine which treaties remain in force during a given calendar year. *United States Treaty Index* is a valuable addition to any library with significant American diplomatic history, international relations, international law, and international business holdings. Unfortunately, its price will make it accessible only to research libraries and other relatively affluent institutions. — **Bert Chapman**

African

760. Rake, Alan. **Who's Who in Africa: Leaders for the 1990s.** Metuchen, N.J., Scarecrow, 1992. 448p. index. $59.50. DT18.R35. 920.067. LC 92-8166. ISBN 0-8108-2557-0.

Biographical sketches of political and military leaders from 47 African nations and principalities are presented in this handbook-size volume. Sketches range in length from several paragraphs to fewer than 200 words. It is stated that the book treats the most important and the most populated countries in greater depth than it does smaller and island nations. No sketch, however, is longer than two-and-a-half pages, even those of Nelson Mandela and Desmond Tutu. In most instances the biographies resemble news reports from the Associated Press or other news agency. Rake is the managing editor of *New African* (based in London), so the journalistic flavor is understandable.

This edition is the first such work from Rake since 1973, when many African countries had just won independence from European colonial powers. Since that earlier volume, many new leaders have been swept in and out of power. The biographees represent countries and political principalities south of the Sahara Desert. Many of these countries are prominent in today's international headlines; thus, informed citizens need to become better acquainted with the personalities shaping events in those countries. This volume covers those who currently hold political leadership roles, those who were leaders in the recent past, and those who stand on the immediate horizon. Rake takes particular pride in having been able to build profiles of figures from some Marxist countries (e.g., Angola, Mozambique, Ethiopia, Somalia) where published information about such personalities is practically nonexistent. Cultural, artistic, religious, and business leaders are not included unless they are visibly concerned with politics. Apparently no women met either of these criteria as none are included in the book.

Who's Who in Africa is arranged alphabetically by country and then alphabetically by last names of persons within the country. Each country receives a brief profile with essential facts about population and type of government. Biographies are chronological in nature, highlighting the subject's major accomplishments so the reader can quickly scan the discussions. An italicized paragraph at the beginning of each biography summarizes the political or military activities that established the person as a central figure in his country. As a serious spectator of African affairs, Rake has interspersed editorial comments throughout the biographical data.

One of the real values of this volume is that when taken collectively, the biographies provide a sweeping view of the turmoil and political intrigue that have engulfed this part of the world over the last 35 to 40 years. At the same time, many of the personalities have contributed much to the social and economic progress of their countries. This is particularly true of people such as Kwesi Botchwey of Ghana, who is credited with turning the collapsing Ghanian economy around and who has seemingly helped to create a stable society in spite of many adverse conditions. Serious students of world history should gain valuable insight and knowledge about not only the political history of this part of Africa but also about the men and the circumstances that are directly and indirectly contributing to these conditions.

There is no map of Africa in this work, so the reader must turn to an up-to-date atlas to locate countries. Nor are there photographs of the personalities discussed. Otherwise, this is a well-done book. It should be a welcome addition to most reference collections in secondary school, college, university, and public libraries. [R: Choice, Oct 92, p. 280; LJ, 1 June 92, p. 116; RBB, 1 Sept 92, p. 92; WLB, Sept 92, p. 122] – **Melvin M. Bowie**

761. Wiseman, John A. **Political Leaders in Black Africa: A Biographical Dictionary of the Major Politicians since Independence.** Brookfield, Vt., Edward Elgar/Gower Publishing, 1991. 248p. index. $74.95. DT352.8.W57. 967.03'2'0922. LC 91-3753. ISBN 1-85278-047-9.

Prosopographical studies of current political leaders run the risk of becoming rapidly obsolete. The present work diminishes that risk by incorporating individuals from the 1950s to the present, thereby retaining a historical dimension. Every African country is represented in the 485 brief biographies, 3 of them (Cape Verde, Djibouti, and Sao Tome and Principe) only once and 2 of them (South Africa and Nigeria) a total of 105 times. This apparently disproportionate coverage simply reflects the relative population, importance, and intrinsic interest of the respective countries. Although the selection of entries is not likely to satisfy every potential user, this reviewer was able to find an entry for every political figure sought. However, information is not as current as it might be and seems to end about two years before the date of imprint.

In addition to the biographies, *Political Leaders in Black Africa* includes an alphabetical list of entries, which merely wastes eight pages by duplicating the listings of the biographies themselves; a much more useful list of some 225 acronyms; and an even more useful index of leaders arranged by country. A country-by-country political chronology, too sketchy to be helpful, completes the work. Unfortunately, all accents are missing from French names, and there are no bibliography nor cross-references. As it is, libraries will need to decide whether the volume is worth the price, even though there is no comparable source for quick information on such a large array of postindependence political figures in Africa. [R: Choice, May 92, p. 1378] – **David Henige**

Asian

762. **Who's Who in Asian and Australasian Politics.** Munich, New Providence, N.J., Bowker-Saur, 1991. 475p. $175.00. DS35.2.W48. 920.05. LC 91-15868. ISBN 0-86291-593-7.

This fine tool combines a political who's who and a government directory for Asia, Australasia, and Oceania, excluding the Middle East and the former Soviet Union. The main body of the work is divided into two parts. The first is an alphabetical biography section with over 3,000 entries. Entry criteria limit subjects to current heads of state, members of governments or national legislatures, leaders of parties or trade union federations, regional leaders, and a few other prominent figures. Information on each entrant is arranged under 24 categories and includes birth date; education; family; career; offices and honors; recreations; address; and telephone, telex, and fax numbers when possible. The cutoff for updates was late March 1991.

The second part is organized by country name. Under each state there is a governmental list with addresses of major ministries and then a list of the legislature, the main parties, and union federations, again with directory data. There is an index to the country's entries in the biography section. The directory part seems to contain fewer fax and telephone numbers than such sources as the *International Directory of Government* (see ARBA 91, entry 719) or the *Europa World Yearbook* (see ARBA 90, entry 91), but it is still a very useful feature in a basically biographical tool.

The prefatory material is well done and the physical production is good with high-contrast printing, although the print is a little small. This work is an important, well-executed source and deserves serious consideration as an acquisition where budgets allow. [R: Choice, Apr 92, p. 1214; LJ, 1 Feb 92, p. 82] – **Nigel Tappin**

Canadian

763. Bejermi, John. **Canadian Parliamentary Handbook.** Ottawa, Borealis Press, 1992. 546p. illus. index. $50.95. 328.71'002'02. ISBN 0-88887-902-4. ISSN 0714-8143.

Revised early in 1992, this edition is an excellent reference source that deals with Canada's parliamentary government and its current members. Prefaced by a brief description of the parliamentary process as it operates in Canada, the volume is primarily a biographical compilation of the membership. Each entry includes a photograph and basic political (and personal) information as well as individual parliamentary address. Organized by major legislative divisions, a brief history and description of role within the government introduces sections on the Governor General, the Senate, and the House of Commons. For the latter section, personal entries also contain the 1988 election results. A short descriptive entry is presented for the Library of Parliament, and there are lists of current Canadian ministries and parliamentary secretaries. An alphabetical constituency listing, a complete name index, and a fax directory complete the volume. Presented in bilingual format, this handbook is up-to-date and accurate, making it a most valuable reference source for Canadian politics and government. – **Virginia S. Fischer**

764. Eagles, D. Munroe, and others. **The Almanac of Canadian Politics.** Peterborough, Ont., Broadview Press, 1991. 675p. $75.00. 324.971'0647. ISBN 0-921149-89-1.

Tapping into a tradition of political almanacs, the authors have compiled a comprehensive profile of Canada's current parliamentary democratic system. As a primary statistical source for a myriad of public affairs details, the volume gives a verbal descriptive summary for each constituency, including election history and composition.

After a brief introduction that outlines the authors' intent to examine constituency-level political units and the significance of this focus in Canadian democratic tradition, the almanac is arranged by province. Following each provincial overview, a riding-by-riding narrative and statistical profile is presented. While each profile comprises just a few pages, the information contained is in greater detail than standard sourcebooks, such as the *Canadian Almanac and Directory* (see ARBA 92, entry 98), which typically devote a section to government and politics. Using 1981 population statistics, the recent election results are analyzed with reference to changes since 1984.

A number of appendixes are listed in the table of contents, of which only two are actually included in the volume. Constituency rankings compile the 15 best/worst finishes for each party, winning margins, vulnerable seats, and other interesting election information as well as more general income, employment, and population data. A second appendix details by-election results to November 1991. Missing are the appendixes that contain the alphabetical list of candidates, cartograms, and summary definitions of measures. The candidate list would certainly be an asset to the usefulness of the work. Without examination of omitted material, though, it is difficult to comment on the other appendixes. Compiling information from a number of sources, the authors rely heavily on data from both Election and Statistics Canada. To explicate provincial and regional aspects that are integral to any discussion of Canadian politics, the authors have also consulted various area media reports and political sourcebooks.

The expectation is that this work may be published in the future on a regular basis, as it will likely be of great value both before elections and in interpreting results afterwards. With corrections as previously noted, this unique almanac will be a prime reference source for anyone interested in the Canadian political scene. — **Virginia S. Fischer**

765. McDougall, D. Blake, John E. McDonough, and Kenneth W. Tingley. **Lieutenant-Governors of the Northwest Territories and Alberta 1876-1991.** Edmonton, Alta., Alberta Legislature Library, 1991. 106p. illus. price not reported.

Part of a publication project intended to record developmental aspects of the parliamentary process in the Canadian province of Alberta, this volume is a companion to the 1987 Legislative Assembly publication *The Alberta Legislature*. Part of the Northwest Territories until it became a province in 1905, Alberta's struggle for political sovereignty may be traced by looking at the governmentally appointed Lieutenant-Governors of the region and the part they played in shaping the history of self-government in the area. This collection of biographies of the men and one woman who held this position from 1869 to 1991 is the focus of the volume. Each biographical entry consists of a page or two of text that outlines the individual's period of service and basic personal information: birth date and place, education, family, and death date and place (if applicable). Several paragraphs are devoted to the history and term of appointment, with a portrait or photograph of each person in ceremonial apparel. The entries are prefaced by several pages of an introductory history on Alberta's political administrators and followed by appendixes that contain biographies for individuals who served during the period immediately preceding the establishment of the Northwest Territories as a separate administrative area. Completing the publication is a section designated "notes" that includes diverse and fascinating information about the various seats of government, coats of arms, flags, residences, and other details, as well as illustrations and photographs. For an unusual perspective on Alberta history, this volume is well worth the reading. — **Virginia S. Fischer**

European

General Works

766. Cook, Chris, Tim Kirk, and Bob Moore. **Sources in European Political History. Volume 3: War and Resistance.** New York, Facts on File, 1991. 176p. $35.00. 22000.C57. 016.9402. LC 82-7365. ISBN 0-8160-1757-3.

This is the third in a series of guides to the location of the private papers of personalities in European political history between 1870 and 1945. The first volume dealt with the European Left; the second covered the personal papers of diplomats. The present volume provides a directory of personal papers of approximately 1,000 individuals who had roles in conflict and war. Included are not only the major wars but also civil wars, resistance movements, and the Zionist movement and the Holocaust. Collections in major libraries and archives in Europe, the United States, and Israel are listed.

In most cases the entries are brief, giving only the location of the papers without describing their contents or how many of them are available. In some cases there are also short descriptions of the events covered by the papers and the size of the collection. It should be stressed that the directory includes only private papers. For public and governmental papers researchers will need to consult D. H. Thomas and L. Case's *The New Guide to the Diplomatic Archives of Western Europe* (University of Pennsylvania Press, 1975). The present volume represents an important reference for major research libraries and historians working on contemporary Europe. [R: Choice, Sept 92, p. 74] — **Frank L. Wilson**

767. Cox, Andrew, and Paul Furlong. **A Modern Companion to the European Community: A Guide to Key Facts, Institutions and Terms.** Aldershot, England, Edward Elgar; distr., Brookfield, Vt., Ashgate Publishing/Gower Publishing, 1992. 327p. $59.95. ISBN 1-85278-516-0.

This is a short but comprehensive guide to the European Community (EC). It includes a very brief survey of the development of the EC, the Single European Act, and a description of its key institutions. There are separate country studies for each of the members that focus on postwar economic developments and the challenges of the 1990s. Another section provides key addresses of EC offices in Europe and the location of libraries and information centers where EC documents can be located. Finally, there is a glossary of EC terms and acronyms. Most of the material in this small volume is available in greater detail in other reference volumes and trade books. It will be especially useful for people who have little background on the EC and who are bewildered by the myriad of acronyms they encounter when reading about it, especially in its official documents. — **Frank L. Wilson**

768. Philip, Alan Butt, ed. **Directory of Pressure Groups in the European Community.** Harlow, England, Longman Group; distr., Detroit, Gale, 1991. 415p. $165.00. ISBN 0-582-08697-3.

In recent years the policy-making powers of the European Community (EC) have grown as the Community has assumed greater control over matters that once were the prerogatives of individual countries. Those powers are expected to continue to expand, drawing more attention to how decisions are made by EC institutions. This directory is valuable in identifying some 800 of the several thousand pressure groups that have emerged to influence the EC policymakers.

This work provides information on each group's location, officers, goals, resources, organization, scope, and activities. Despite the proliferation of acronyms and multilingual group names, the directory is easy to use due to its lists of groups by sectors (e.g., agriculture, industrial, voluntary associations, professional associations). It also provides the names and addresses of consulting firms that engage in lobbying EC institutions. It does not list the interest groups that represent single member states or the plethora of representatives from individual firms seeking to influence EC policies. It does, however, provide a useful step toward identifying the major EC-wide pressure groups. [R: Choice, Oct 92, pp. 270-71] — **Frank L. Wilson**

Eastern European

769. Parrish, Michael. **Soviet Security and Intelligence Organizations 1917-1990: A Biographical Dictionary and Review of Literature in English.** Westport, Conn., Greenwood Press, 1992. 669p. $75.00. JN6529.I6P37. 327.1'2'092247. LC 91-34996. ISBN 0-313-28305-2.

The recent collapse of the Soviet Union and the ambivalent role played by elements of the Soviet security forces in the August 1991 coup attempt that contributed to this demise provide an appropriate backdrop to Parrish's bibliographic review. *Soviet Security and Intelligence Organizations* features material obtained through systematic searches of Soviet documents and books as well as reference books, newspapers, and magazines. It opens with a historiographical and analytical portrait of the Soviet security system. The work proceeds with biographical synopses of significant intelligence and internal security officials; an annotated review of monographic works in English (non-English works will be covered in a forthcoming compendium); and appendixes that feature a glossary of selected acronyms, various reference sources including Soviet journals and newspapers, an organizational chart of Soviet security and intelligence leadership, and an addenda to the biographical dictionary.

Parrish's efforts are exhaustive and will prove beneficial to students and scholars beginning research on this titanic and foreboding subject. Those consulting this source should be aware, as Parrish is, of lingering questions about the reliability of narratives about Soviet intelligence personnel, organs, and operations due to the secrecy and deception inherent in the operational aspects of this profession. One criticism is the use of only the first name initials of the officials and operatives portrayed. Another weakness is Parrish's criticisms concerning the efficacy of intelligence organizations, which overlook the vital and positive role such entities can play promoting national security and intellectual advancement. These caveats excepted, this timely work should stimulate further research on the organizations foundational to the Soviet state and their undetermined role in the Soviet Union's successor entities. [R: Choice, June 92, p. 1526]—**Bert Chapman**

770. Szajkowski, Bogdan, ed. **New Political Parties of Eastern Europe and the Soviet Union.** Harlow, England, Longman Group; distr., Detroit, Gale, 1991. 404p. index. $95.00. ISBN 0-582-08575-6.

This well-executed survey and directory is a thoughtful, useful entry in the efforts to fill the reference vacuum left by the collapse of Stalinist regimes in the former Soviet empire. It provides background and electoral data on the party political situation in the ex-Soviet Union and its former satellites up to summer or fall 1991.

The book is divided into chapters on each state, including eastern Germany and the three Baltic countries. The basic format provides an introductory essay of background and analysis, followed by an alphabetically arranged list of parties with brief descriptive, leader, address, and communication information. For present or former federal states there are separate national and republican sections within the chapter.

The country sections are compiled by British-based academics. The standard format is not uniformly followed by all contributors; for example, there are few addresses or telephone numbers in the Soviet section, and those on the Baltic states are very brief (about two pages each). This, however, is atypical; the less-turbulent majority of countries are treated more thoroughly (e.g., 38 pages on Hungary, 75 pages for Yugoslavia). Access is simplified by a 35-page index, a preface, a table of contents, and a handy alphabetical list of party acronyms.

Dated information is inevitably a concern for tools on this region. However, the survey essays on the events of 1989-1991 and their background, plus the electoral information and party lists, make this work a valuable acquisition. [R: Choice, June 92, p. 1524]—**Nigel Tappin**

Great Britain

771. Cowie, Leonard W. **William Wilberforce 1759-1833: A Bibliography.** Westport, Conn., Greenwood Press, 1992. 146p. index. (Bibliographies of British Statesmen, no.17). $49.95. Z8973.7.C8. 016.326'092. LC 92-5351. ISBN 0-313-28283-8.

One of history's most vivid examples of persistent dedication to a cause is William Wilberforce's dogged and ultimately successful effort to outlaw slavery in the British Empire. Determining which sources are available for research on the life and career of this prominent abolitionist is a focus of Cowie's bibliographic compilation. The work opens with a biographical essay on Wilberforce and a chronology of his life. It proceeds to list manuscript and archival sources with significant Wilberforce materials, with Perkins Library at Duke University being the most prominent U.S. repository. Subsequent chapters provide biographical sketches and bibliographic citations of Wilberforce's contemporaries, such as William Cobbett, Charles James Fox, and William Pitt the Younger; the religious and political background of Wilberforce's era, with particular emphasis on his involvement with the evangelical movement; accounts of Wilberforce's life; his House of Commons speeches; caricatures; places associated with his life; and author and subject indexes.

This is a useful source for researching Wilberforce's life and career and for stimulating research on the British abolitionist movement. It is a valuable addition to college and university libraries with substantive British political history and slavery holdings, despite the excessive price for such a slender volume. — **Bert Chapman**

772. Crewe, Ivor, Neil Day, and Anthony Fox. **The British Electorate, 1963-1987: A Compendium of Data from the British Election Studies.** New York, Cambridge University Press, 1991. 500p. $160.00. JN956.C74. 324.941085. LC 90-36080. ISBN 0-521-32197-2.

It is astounding how much statistical data on British society has been jammed into this impressive data sourcebook for the eight general elections held between 1964 and 1987. Questionnaires were administered to sample respondents from the general population, and the raw data has then been organized into tabular form. These tables have been organized into 12 topical chapters: the vote; party identification; party membership; electoral decisions; interest in elections; party image; the economy; business, trade unions, and strikes; nationalization and privatization; the welfare state; issues of citizenship; and newspaper readership. Within the chapters the data has been analyzed by party affiliation, gender, age, geographical region, and social class. Among the interesting statistics found in these chapters is the fact that 42.9 percent of the British population in 1987 felt that attempts to ensure sexual equality had not gone far enough. It is also surprising to note that in 1987, 3.4 percent of the British population claimed to read the *Times*, 6.6 percent read the *Guardian*, and 17.2 percent read the *Sun*.

This reference collection of electoral data is extremely well done and authoritative. It belongs in the collection of any library with a special interest in modern British politics, society, or history. [R: Choice, May 92, p. 1364] — **Ronald H. Fritze**

773. Schweitzer, David. **Charles James Fox 1749-1806: A Bibliography.** Westport, Conn., Greenwood Press, 1991. 209p. index. (Bibliographies of British Statesmen, no.4). $65.00. Z8312.159.S28. 016.94107'3'092. LC 91-8425. ISBN 0-313-28118-1.

Charles James Fox was one of the most colorful and significant figures in the political history of the second half of the eighteenth century in Great Britain. As such, he makes a worthy choice for inclusion in Greenwood Press's excellent series. Compiled by an expert on the period, this volume begins with a helpful biographical essay that describes Fox's life and career. This is accompanied by a detailed chronology of events in his life and the history of Great Britain. Following are eight bibliographical chapters that list hundreds of annotated entries. The first and longest chapter covers manuscripts and archival sources that include published collections of Fox's papers and of individuals with close associations to Fox. A second and briefer chapter lists Fox's published writings and the commentaries of others on those writings. Chapters 3 through 6 provide information on relevant secondary writings in books and journals that deal with Fox's general biography, his early life, his political and official career, and his personal and professional life. Chapters 7 and 8 cover caricatures and satires about Fox and iconography portraying Fox. The work concludes with separate author and subject indexes.

This bibliography serves the needs of a wide audience. Its identification of manuscript collections in archives will be of interest to advanced researchers, while its listing of appropriate secondary materials will be an aid to scholars, students, and general readers using academic libraries. — **Ronald H. Fritze**

Latin American and Caribbean

774. Calvert, Peter, ed. **Political and Economic Encyclopedia of South America and the Caribbean.** Harlow, England, Longman Group; distr., Chicago, St. James Press, 1991. 363p. index. $85.00. ISBN 0-582-08528-4.

A useful addition to the sources of information about South and Central America and the Caribbean, this one-volume encyclopedia provides general information about prominent leaders, the different countries in the region (including the United States), and matters and movement of political-economic importance. While historical information is included, the emphasis is on current developments.

The format for this encyclopedia is a strict alphabetical arrangement that includes proper names, places and people, and movements (e.g., Farabundo Marti National Liberation Front [FMLN]). A very limited general index is provided, along with two maps for the region that are on the inside front and back covers. The maps will be of little value if libraries need to add any items to either parts of the book.

This work suffers from several limitations. It will quickly be out of date, as economic and political changes in these parts of the world are constant. (Conditions in Haiti and El Salvador seem to change almost overnight.) There are no cross-references and no entries from Spanish to English or Portuguese to English. The same is true for other languages used in the Caribbean. While the index needs to be consulted regularly, it is questionable as to why some items receive separate entries and others are merely mentioned. The lack of sources for further information is a serious limitation. Recommended only for smaller public libraries that cannot afford the more standard and comprehensive works on South and Central America and the Caribbean. [R: Choice, May 92, p. 1374] – **Roberto P. Haro**

775. Camp, Roderic A. **Mexican Political Biographies, 1884-1935.** Austin, Tex., University of Texas Press, 1991. 458p. $75.00. F1233.5.C28. 920.72. LC 90-39352. ISBN 0-292-75119-2.

This is Camp's fifth book of Mexican biographies. His purpose is to provide short, accurate biographies of public figures, especially the leaders of political institutions. Unfortunately, intellectual, religious, and guerrilla figures are not included. The sections on criteria for inclusion and how to use the book are especially helpful. More than 700 biographies are included, followed by 8 appendixes that separate the political leaders by positions held, such as federal deputies and directors of federal departments and agencies. Hence, an individual can be found if one knows either the name or the position held. Camp admits to possible mistakes as he believes some of his sources were inaccurate. Recommended for academic and large public libraries. [R: LJ, 1 Feb 92, p. 78] – **Karen Y. Stabler**

Middle Eastern

776. Ziring, Lawrence. **The Middle East: A Political Dictionary.** Santa Barbara, Calif., ABC-Clio, 1992. 401p. index. (Clio Dictionaries in Political Science). $56.50; $29.95pa. DS61.Z58. 956'.003. LC 92-15379. ISBN 0-87436-612-7; 0-87436-697-6pa.

Included in this volume are 271 numbered entries on events, movements, diplomacy, conflict, culture, and characteristics relevant to Middle East politics in the second half of the twentieth century. Entries are grouped in seven broad categories (e.g., ethnicity and culture, Islam) and then arranged alphabetically within the sections. Each entry includes a definition of the topic and a synopsis of its significance in the political schema. Many entries include cross-references to related information, and a detailed index facilitates access.

Although this volume includes a helpful regional map on the lining papers, it does not include the appended maps and tables and selected bibliography that supplemented the text of the author's earlier work, *Middle East Political Dictionary* (see ARBA 85, entry 623). The current volume does include updated information and new entries (e.g., Desert Storm) and will be a useful reference tool for students, librarians, and the general public. [R: LJ, July 92, p. 79; RBB, 1 Sept 92, p. 87; SLMQ, Fall 92, p. 76] – **Ahmad Gamaluddin**

IDEOLOGIES

777. Alexander, Robert J. **International Trotskyism 1929-1985: A Documented Analysis of the Movement.** Durham, N.C., Duke University Press, 1991. 1125p. index. $165.00. HX313.8.T76A7. 335.43'3. LC 90-38617. ISBN 0-0223-0975-0.

Trotskyism offered an important alternative to the Stalinist model of Marxism-Leninism as implemented in the Soviet Union and other communist countries. It focused attention on the international aspects of the movement and on the need for permanent revolution. As traditional communist parties around the world falter or change their nature as a result of the collapse of communism in Eastern Europe and the Soviet Union, Trotskyism may endure as a small, still untested, but purer form of Marxism-Leninism. This volume offers a useful and comprehensive survey of Trotskyist movements. After brief chapters on the origins and characteristics of Trotskyism, Alexander provides separate chapters on this movement in more than 65 countries. For those countries where it had a greater impact, two or more chapters give full coverage. In addition, there are chapters devoted to such Trotskyist organizations as the Fourth International, the Spartacist tendency, and the International Workers League.

Alexander has written extensively on communist internationalism and on Trotskyism in Latin America. He provides here a valuable survey of Trotskyist movements around the world that fills an important gap in the literature. Specialized indexes of names, organizations, and publications assist in using this valuable resource. Strongly recommended for research libraries. – **Frank L. Wilson**

778. Nursey-Bray, Paul, with Jim Jose and Robyn Williams, comps. and eds. **Anarchist Thinkers and Thought: An Annotated Bibliography.** Westport, Conn., Greenwood Press, 1992. 284p. index. (Bibliographies and Indexes in Law and Political Science, no.17). $55.00. Z7164.A52N87. 016.335'83'0922. LC 91-33407. ISBN 0-313-27592-0.

The editors of this useful bibliography want to demonstrate that the anarchist tradition has much more to offer than the stereotypical "cloaked, mustachioed figure with the smoking bomb" (p. xiii). They provide an annotated list of works by and about significant anarchist thinkers, from Mikhail Bakunin and Louise Michel to Noam Chomsky. In addition, there are brief annotated lists of works on anarchism in 18 countries. The editors also note the titles and main themes of major anarchist journals of the past and the addresses of contemporary anarchist publications. In addition, there is an unannotated listing of doctoral theses on anarchism.

The annotations are brief and the listings are largely English-language works (with a few in French and Italian). Apart from these limitations, this is a useful bibliography for major research libraries. [R: Choice, Oct 92, p. 278] – **Frank L. Wilson**

779. Simoncini, Gabriele. **Revolutionary Organizations and Revolutionaries in Interbellum Poland: A Bibliographical Biographical Study.** Lewiston, N.Y., Edwin Mellen Press, 1992. 278p. $99.95. Z7164.S67S55. 016.3242438'092'2. LC 92-7441. ISBN 0-7734-9487-1.

This is a specialized but valuable bibliographic reference tool for library collections that support research on Eastern European history and politics. It is divided into two major sections. Part 1 has more than 3,000 entries in 10 languages (but primarily in Polish) on the Communist Party of Poland and on other revolutionary organizations in Poland from 1918 to 1990. Sources listed include books, articles, documents, archives, catalogs, and a variety of other materials not usually found in major bibliographical studies. Part 2 is an extensive listing of 600-plus Polish revolutionaries with accompanying bibliographic entries. An introductory essay provides a historical background to this period and an analysis of the sources listed. – **George S. Bobinski**

780. **Yearbook on International Communist Affairs 1991: Parties and Revolutionary Movements.** Richard F. Staar, ed. Stanford, Calif., Hoover Institution Press, 1991. 689p. index. $59.95. LC 67-31024. ISBN 0-8179-9161-1. ISSN 0084-4101.

After the monumental changes that shook the communist parties of Eastern Europe in 1989, Moscow lost much of its influence in the Third World. Many African nations are turning away from their imported Soviet models, while "vanguard revolutionary democratic parties" in Nicaragua and South Yemen are no longer in power. In the former Soviet Union, the communist party membership declined by 2.7 million in a 15-month period, while the Komsomol's (Union of Communist Youth) membership dropped from 42 to 23.6 million. In Asia, China's communist party still claims 48 million in membership, but North Korea has lost one-third of its members. In Latin America, nonruling communist parties expanded their membership in Chile, Ecuador, Nicaragua, and Uruguay.

This volume is the 25th consecutive edition published by the Hoover Institution on War, Revolution and Peace, founded by Herbert Hoover at Stanford University in 1919. It contains information on communist parties and "national liberation" movements, detailing their domestic and international activities in 1990. Eighty-one authors have contributed to this magnificent compendium that covers 125 countries, with 3 articles on international communist organizations and an essay on Soviet foreign propaganda. Most materials included have been collected throughout the year, drawn from sources already published in newspapers, journals, transcripts of monitored broadcasts, and communist party publications. This well-organized, clearly written, and well-bound reference is highly recommended for all readers who desire to keep up with the flow of information on the global communist movement. — **Oleg Zinam**

INTERNATIONAL ORGANIZATIONS

781. Ali, Sheikh R. **The International Organizations and World Order Dictionary**. Santa Barbara, Calif., ABC-Clio, 1992. 283p. index. (Clio Dictionaries in Political Science). $55.00. JX1995.A4595. 341.2'03. LC 91-38953. ISBN 0-87436-572-4.

Unlike the traditional format for this series—subject-based chapters—this title features one alphabetical sequence throughout for all entries. This arrangement enhances this title as a dictionary or ready-reference guide. For those who wish to use it as a study guide or supplement to a course on international organizations, many subsidiary terms have been grouped under the major concepts. A detailed general index covers all terms.

The nearly 300 entries attempt to comprehensively cover all important aspects of international organizations and world order. The United Nations and its related agencies are emphasized. Other important contemporary international organizations (e.g., the Western European Union) and ancient organizations (e.g., the Achaean League) are included. World order, the second focus of this dictionary, seems a somewhat more ambiguous subject. Arms control, nuclear proliferation, and self-determinations are examples of terms placed under this topic. The definitions are usually a page long. Each includes (as do all entries in this series) a very useful "Significance" paragraph that interprets and analyzes the information in the basic definition. [R: Choice, June 92, p. 1513] — **Henry E. York**

782. Greenfield, Stanley R., ed. **Who's Who in the United Nations and Related Agencies**. 2d ed. Detroit, Omnigraphics, 1992. 850p. index. $185.00. JX1977.W467. 341.23'092'2. LC 92-28304. ISBN 1-55888-762-8.

This directory provides brief biographical information, most of which cannot be found in other sources. The criteria for inclusion have changed slightly since the 1975 edition (see ARBA 76, entry 471). Retired officials now seem to be excluded. Individuals who served the United Nations (UN) in 1991 are covered, including high-level officials of the Secretariat, agencies, and UN missions of specific countries, as well as a few leaders of related organizations. Also included are the book's editor and most of the members of its advisory panel, some of whom do not meet other criteria for inclusion. Two appendixes describe the 1992 reorganization of the UN Secretariat and list new senior officials.

In addition to biographical entries, this work provides a number of listings (e.g., presidents of the General Assembly; secretaries-general of the UN; permanent missions to the UN in New York, Geneva, and Vienna; UN depository libraries). The most extensive and useful listings are those for the UN system of organizations and specialized agencies and related organizations, which provide directory-type information and list individuals in specific positions. The first edition had a list of UN offices by country all over the world, including liaisons of specialized agencies at UN headquarters in New York and in other countries. It is unfortunate that this hard-to-find information has been omitted from the new edition.

Additional access to the alphabetically arranged biographical entries is provided through indexes by organization (new to this edition) and by nationality. It would be helpful if the indexes indicated an individual's specific position, because the names in the index by organization do not necessarily match the names in the lists of organizations and specialized agencies, and also because the index by nationality includes at least one nationality with more than 300 names. — **Carol Wheeler**

783.   Hajnal, Peter I., comp. **Directory of United Nations Documentary and Archival Sources.** New York, United Nations and Millwood, N.Y., Kraus International, 1991. 106p. index. (Reports and Papers/The Academic Council on the United Nations System; 1991-1). $12.50pa. JX1977.8.D6H34. 026'.34123. LC 91-61735. ISBN 92-1-100455-1 (United Nations. S/N 91.I.14). ISBN 0-527-37321-4.

This annotated guide provides information on more than 500 titles and series published by the United Nations, its specialized autonomous agencies, and publishers of related reference works. The Academic Council on the United Nations System enlisted Hajnal, a recognized expert on international documents, to prepare this work. Hajnal's introduction, which is based on material he has contributed to other publications, provides a wealth of information on the UN system, the nature of material published by its bodies, distribution of and access to the material, and bibliographic tools.

The main part of the guide is divided into two sections: subjects and research resources. Numbered entries within these two sections are further divided into categories. Each entry gives complete bibliographic information, including any sales or publication number, and an annotation. Cross-references are provided to avoid reprinting complete entries in more than one category. A table of contents and an author/title index are also included.

While the arrangement seems straightforward, it is not entirely satisfactory. Some of the subject categories (e.g., "Structural and Institutional Issues," "Other Topics and General Information") and some of the research resource categories (e.g., "Statistics," "Catalogs, Indexes, Guides, and Other Bibliographic Tools") contain too many entries for easy browsing. A detailed subject index or further division of some of the subject and research resource categories would greatly enhance access to the bibliographic entries. Also, while this guide brings together a vast array of sources, there are some questionable omissions: for example, the 2d edition of the UN's *Blue Helmets*, the Economic Commission for Africa's *African Statistical Yearbook*, and the UN Department for Disarmament Affairs's *Disarmament Topical Papers* and *Disarmament Study Series*. Editorial problems include indentation inconsistencies and errors in the author/title index and incorrect cross-references in the main body. It is unfortunate that organizational and editorial problems impede access to the valuable content of this work. [R: Choice, Sept 92, p. 78; LJ, Jan 92, p. 184] — **Carol Wheeler**

784.   Jenkins, Jon C., with Cecile Vanden Bloock, eds. **Who's Who in International Organizations: A Biographical Encyclopedia of More Than 12,000 Leading Personalities.** Munich, New Providence, N.J., K. G. Saur, 1992. 3v. index. $400.00/set. ISBN 3-598-10908-3.

More than 12,000 entries for eminent individuals appear in this set prepared by the Union of International Associations. These people are many of the principals involved in the management and operation of the institutions and networks listed in the association's *Yearbook of International Organizations* (K. G. Saur, 1991). Many of them are not well known enough to appear in most of the standard international biographical reference works.

To develop this publication, questionnaires were sent to 10,000 major international organizations. The editors had difficulties with incomplete and illegible returns, and in some cases did not receive any. This first edition, therefore, does not claim to be complete or representative of all important organizations that could have been included. Complete entries for individuals consist of full name and title, nationality, date and place of birth, spouse's name, number of children, religion, languages spoken, education, current positions in international organizations, main field of work, career, publications, memberships, honors, and residential and mailing addresses. The minimum acceptable entry provides name, organization, position, and address.

The first two volumes contain the alphabetical entries for the individuals. Volume 3 indexes their names by country, profession, and organization. Given the price of this set, it would seem to be most appropriate in collections with a particular focus on international organizations for which the standard international biographical sources are not sufficient. — **Henry E. York**

INTERNATIONAL RELATIONS

785. Petersen, Neal H. **American Intelligence, 1775-1990: A Bibliographical Guide.** Claremont, Calif., Regina Books, 1992. 406p. index. (New War/Peace Bibliographical Series, no.2). $49.95. Z6724.I7P48. 016.3271273'09. LC 92-16324. ISBN 0-941690-45-8.

This bibliographical compilation contains 6,166 entries on espionage, covert action, counterintelligence, domestic intelligence, technical collection, cryptology, research and analysis, policy and process, organization and oversight, and other aspects of U.S. intelligence operations. Petersen includes books, articles from scholarly and professional periodicals, and selected items from newspapers and news/opinion magazines.

The work is arranged chronologically and further subarranged by specific historical event. There are chapters devoted to the period 1775-1939, World War II, the Vietnam War, the congressional investigations of the 1970s, and presidential administrations. Many of the periods (e.g., the Bush administration, 1989-1990) and historical events (e.g., the intervention in Panama, 1989) covered begin with a short narrative that explains major events or significant intelligence occurrences during the period. Other chapters discuss intelligence production, gathering, and investigation and related topics on American intelligence activities (e.g., proliferation of weapons of mass destruction, international broadcasting, economic intelligence). An excellent chapter on counterintelligence and internal security concentrates on the House Un-American Activities Committee during the McCarthy era.

The work is balanced by an excellent index to both authors and subjects, making it easy to use. Highly recommended for academic and research libraries, especially those with an extensive international law or political history collection.—**Christine E. Thompson**

786. Shavit, David. **The United States in Latin America: A Historical Dictionary.** Westport, Conn., Greenwood Press, 1992. 471p. index. $75.00. F1418.S494. 303.48'28073'03. LC 91-32403. ISBN 0-313-27595-5.

This volume claims to provide "comprehensive coverage of persons, institutions, and events that brought the United States into contact with Latin America." The body consists of short (80- to 350-word) entries arranged alphabetically, each with one or more references. In addition, there are a list of abbreviations, a chronology, a list of American diplomatic mission chiefs from 1823 to 1990, a list of individuals by occupation, a bibliographic essay, and a subject index. The preface states that the geographical scope includes all Latin American countries south of the United States but says nothing about the time period covered.

The author is not a Latin American specialist but rather an associate professor in library and information studies. He has written three similar books on other regions. The references cited in each entry and the bibliographic essay suggest that the book has been compiled carefully with adequate research. It is essentially a biographical dictionary, however, despite the stated scope; about 19 out of every 20 entries are on individuals. Within this limitation, the book is an easy-to-use, authoritative work. [R: Choice, Nov 92, p. 450; RBB, 15 June 92, pp. 1890-91]—**Cathy Seitz Whitaker**

787. Wright, Peter. **The Spycatcher's Encyclopedia of Espionage.** Toronto, Stoddart Publishing, 1991. 265p. $14.95pa. 327.12'03. ISBN 0-7737-5517-9.

Perhaps no profession contains jargon as esoteric as that of intelligence. Attempting to decipher the arcane terminology of this field is a challenging effort for nonpractitioners. *The Spycatcher's Encyclopedia of Espionage* attempts to provide greater clarity about what has been described as the world's second oldest profession. Wright gained notoriety a few years ago when the British government unsuccessfully sought to prevent publication of his book *Spycatcher*, which chronicled his version of his career in British intelligence.

Spycatcher's Encyclopedia is arranged alphabetically and features discussion of individuals, organizations, concepts, equipment, and procedures involved in intelligence operations. Many of these entries feature Wright's pointed commentary and analysis of their value. Unfortunately, this effort contains numerous flaws. No mention is made of longtime American counterintelligence head James Jesus Angleton or KGB London resident Oleg Gordievsky (who defected to the United Kingdom in 1985). British Labour MP Tam Dalyell is incorrectly identified as Tam "Dalziel" during discussion of the

Ponting case. More serious flaws include Wright's echoing of leftist charges of CIA responsibility in the 1973 overthrow of Chilean President Salvador Allende; his failure to address intelligence analysis and its implications for policymakers; and the glib and self-serving tone of his writing throughout much of the work (influenced, no doubt, by bitterness over the tumultuousness of the *Spycatcher* affair and the unpleasant termination of his own career).

A compact yet comprehensive dictionary of intelligence terminology is a worthy goal in order to achieve partial demystification of this enigmatic and complicated profession. However, polemical, subjective, and contrived works such as this only spread misinformation and confusion about intelligence operations and activities. Not recommended. — **Bert Chapman**

788. **Yearbook of Soviet Foreign Relations.** 1991 ed. Alex Pravda, ed. London, I. B. Taurus; distr., New York, St. Martin's Press, 1991. 347p. $89.95. ISBN 1-85043-242-2.

The publication of this new annual comes at an inconvenient time, given the political situation in the former Soviet Union. A few years ago (when the idea for this kind of yearbook was undoubtedly conceived) it would have been received as a major new resource for the field of international relations; now, it is almost an anomaly. Nevertheless, this first volume will be a valuable acquisition for most libraries. It provides, in 12 lengthy chapters, a comprehensive and detailed look at the foreign policy events of 1990, which climaxed with the resignation of Soviet Foreign Minister Shevardnadze on December 20. The editor notes that the "remarkable progress" in foreign affairs during 1990 were threatened by the "economic and political dislocation" that dominated the final months of the year. Indeed, 1991 proved to be a tumultuous year for the Soviets.

The yearbook is organized geographically, with additional chapters covering military and security issues, economic relations, and the United Nations. Each chapter is written by a subject specialist and includes reference notes and a chronology of events. There is also a general chronology of key events for the year; however, the volume lacks a general index. Some statistical tables are provided, especially in the chapter on economic factors and relations. Because of the abundance of text, most libraries will prefer to place this book in the general collection. It is highly recommended for academic libraries. — **Thomas A. Karel**

PEACE MOVEMENT

789. Blumberg, Herbert H., and Christopher C. French, eds. **Peace: Abstracts of the Psychological and Behavioral Literature 1967-1990.** Washington, D.C., American Psychological Association, 1992. 229p. index. (Bibliographies in Psychology, no.10). $27.50pa. Z6464.Z9P39. 016.3271'72'019. LC 91-33902. ISBN 1-55798-137-X.

Similar to the previous titles in this series (e.g., *Homelessness: Abstracts of the Psychological and Behavioral Literature, 1967-1990*, reviewed in ARBA 92, entry 835), the abstracts in this book are derived from the PsycINFO database, with a few earlier publications (pre-1967) included. The main abstract section of this bibliography is arranged alphabetically by author and contains 1,472 entries. The indexing is especially helpful; in addition to a detailed subject index (which uses the terms found in the *Thesaurus of Psychological Index Terms*, 5th ed. [see ARBA 89, entry 701]), there is a title index arranged by classifications in which the abstracts are grouped into 19 fairly broad categories, such as aggression, conflict resolution, feminist aspects of peace, genocide, peace movements, and psychodynamic aspects. There is also an index of coauthors and coeditors. The brief introduction to this volume includes an interesting overview of the American Psychological Association's involvement with peace-related research and organizational activities, and the editors provide a description of the search strategy they used to retrieve the citations from the database. This work will be a useful supplement to the more general bibliographies on peace and is recommended for most academic library collections. — **Thomas A. Karel**

790. Esenwein, George, comp. **Guide to the John D. Crummey Peace Collection in the Hoover Institution.** Stanford, Calif., Hoover Institution Press, 1991. 140p. index. (Hoover Press Bibliography, 75). $16.95pa. Z6464.Z9J57. 086.3271'72. LC 91-16234. ISBN 0-8179-2752-2.

The Hoover Institution on War, Revolution and Peace (located at Stanford University) contains "one of the earliest and largest repositories of peace materials in North America." The Peace Collection, named after John D. Crummey, founder of the FMC Corporation (which funded the formal establishment of the collection in 1977), houses more than 8,000 books, 300 serials, 838 posters, and 2 million pages of archival materials related to peace. Esenwein, of the International and Americas staff at the Institution, traces the growth of the Peace Collection and highlights notable acquisitions in the introduction to this guide.

This work is a descriptive survey of certain major collections rather than a comprehensive listing of the entire Peace Collection. Part 1 provides information on more than 200 of the special collections, listed alphabetically by the name of the individual or organization. Brief identification and a summary of the archive holdings are given. Within this section are found the official publications of the League of Nations, 1920-1946; the New Left Collection, 1964-1988; records of the Paris Peace Conference, 1919-1921; the archives of the War Resisters' International, 1921-1974; records of the Women's International League for Peace and Freedom, 1919-1959; and the papers of a wide variety of American and European peace activists and diplomats. Part 2 contains an alphabetical list of the organizations whose papers are included in the Peace Collection, and part 3 is a list of the collection's serials, plus a select bibliography and an index.

This guide is recommended for university libraries with strong holdings in peace studies or international relations; it will be most useful for libraries with easy access to the Hoover Institution. Other academic libraries will be better served by more general guides to peace resources, such as *Peace and War* (see ARBA 84, entry 419), *The American Peace Movement* by Charles F. Howlett (G. K. Hall, 1991), and *Peace Movement Organizations and Activists in the U.S.* (see ARBA 92, entry 751).

—**Thomas A. Karel**

791. Howlett, Charles F. **The American Peace Movement: References and Resources.** New York, G. K. Hall, 1991. 416p. index. (Reference Publications on American Social Movements). $40.00. Z6464.Z9H7. 016.3271'72'0973. LC 91-2992. ISBN 0-8161-1836-1.

This ambitious bibliography fills an important void in collections of peace resources. Howlett has surveyed three centuries of American peace activism, scanned existing bibliographies, perused the Swarthmore College Peace Collection and other archives, and devoured hundreds of books on the peace movement in the United States. His lengthy historical introduction (which boasts 116 reference notes) and concluding historiographical essay are testimony to his dedication and mastery of the subject—and can stand alone as a fine overview of the American peace movement. He has limited his exhaustive research to 1,600 entries, all with brief annotations, divided into 12 sections: general reference works; general histories of the American peace movement; international peace movements; leaders and thinkers; women and peace; religious pacifism; the history of peace and antiwar groups; pacifism, nonviolence, and related theoretical positions; peace and the judicial process; arbitration, internationalism, and disarmament; peace education; and the sociology of peace. Each chapter contains listings for primary sources, books, articles, biographies, historical accounts, anthologies, dissertations, and a few government documents. They also include a brief introduction that explains their scope and content. Author and subject indexes are especially useful in tracking specific ideas, writers, and events. Howlett appends a list of peace organizations with brief descriptions.

As with any selective bibliography, there are some puzzling omissions. In the section on religious pacifism, for example, there are sufficient entries for Daniel Berrigan and Philip Berrigan and for A. J. Muste but only a passing reference to Thomas Merton. Also, within the entire bibliography the writings of such influential figures as William Sloane Coffin, David Dellinger, Michael Harrington, and Tom Hayden are not mentioned (although their names show up in the subject index and within annotations). However, this is generally an exceptional reference work. Except for the bibliographies found in some of the major studies on American peace movements (a more general and highly selective recent bibliography [unannotated] can be found in volume 4 of *The World Encyclopedia of Peace* [see ARBA 88, entry 760]), this is the first comprehensive bibliography available. Most academic libraries will need to own it. It is a worthy complement to *Peace and War* (see ARBA 84, entry 419). [R: RQ, Summer 92, p. 510]—**Thomas A. Karel**

792. **World Directory of Peace Research and Training Institutions. Repertoire Mondial des Institutions de Recherche et de Formation sur la Paix. Repertorio Mundial de Instituciones de Investigacion y de Formacion sobre la Paz.** 7th ed. Paris, Unesco; distr., Lanham, Md., UNIPUB, 1991. 354p. index. (World Social Science Information Directories). $35.00pa. ISBN 92-3-002752-9.

This publication of the United Nations complements the Unesco Studies in Peace and Conflict series and is published within the context of "Unesco's Contribution to Peace, Human Rights and the Elimination of All Forms of Discrimination" (p. v). This series of directories is based on the DARE Data Bank of the Unesco Social and Human Sciences Documentation Centre in Paris. Previous editions of this reference tool have appeared since 1966, with the last one coming out in 1988 (see ARBA 89, entry 685).

Preceded by a 39-page section of international and regional organizations, most of the book is organized by country, with entries listed alphabetically. There are 418 entries, 100 more than were in the 6th edition. Each entry has the standard directory data of address, founding date, director's name, types of publications, and telephone and fax numbers. Also included are notations on the subject and geographical coverage of research and teaching, titles of recent publications, a description of the organization, and the method of data processing (seeing how many groups still do manual data processing is a good reality check). The indexes deal with institutional names and acronyms, research interests, geographical location, senior staff, courses taught, and scholarships offered. A copy of the DARE peace questionnaire for institutions to complete and send in accompanies the directory.

This book complements *The International Peace Directory*, edited by T. Woodhouse (Plymouth, England: Northcote House Publishers, 1988), which contains more entries (almost 600) and more textual discussion on a broader range of peace organizations. This useful title is recommended for all academic and large public libraries. – **Daniel K. Blewett**

PUBLIC POLICY AND ADMINISTRATION

793. Allswang, John M. **California Initiatives and Referendums 1912-1990: A Survey and Guide to Research.** Claremont, Calif., Regina Books, 1991. 211p. index. $29.95. JF495.C24A43. 328.794'09'04. LC 91-36188. ISBN 1-878644-02-5.

Since 1970 California's increasing use of voter initiatives has caused controversy. The initial intent of this type of direct democracy was to safeguard citizens from corrupt public officials. However, policy analysts have found that the democratic process has been compromised by media-oriented campaigns financed by private interest groups. This research guide, published by the Edmund G. "Pat" Brown Institute of Public Affairs, provides a thorough summary of all state-level initiatives and referendums voted on in California between 1912 and 1980. Since 1912 a total of 226 initiatives and 40 referendums have come before California voters, and about one-third of them have been passed. Most were about taxation or economic regulation issues, while others addressed elections, education, health, morals, the environment, and civil rights.

The book's main purposes are to help researchers and policy-makers evaluate the efficacy of this form of democracy and to determine whether the process needs to be reformed. It includes a 20-page overview of the origin and development of California direct democracy, followed by chronologically arranged summaries of the propositions. Each entry indicates the type of proposition (e.g., referendum initiative, constitutional amendment), outcome, arguments for and against the proposed legislation, and endorsers' names. A selected bibliography includes books, articles, government documents, master's theses, and doctoral dissertations.

This compilation will be especially helpful to college students who wish to explore this public policy area. Scholars will use it as an aid for further research. – **Gary D. Barber**

794. Cherry, Virginia R., and Marc Holzer. **Public Administration Research Guide.** Hamden, Conn., Garland, 1992. 253p. index. (Public Affairs and Administration, v.26; Garland Reference Library of Social Science, v.537). $35.00. Z7164.A2C48. 016.35. LC 91-43812. ISBN 0-8240-7643-5.

The authors have done a thorough job of leading the reader/student through the process of research in the field of public administration. There are 15 chapters, each dealing with a particular aspect of the research process. All chapters begin with a brief description of how library research is done and how that section relates to such research. Guides to the literature and how to use it are the main focus of each chapter. Every entry is numbered for easy location through the index at the back of the book. A total of 767 items are cited and annotated. The entries are to literature that will aid the public affairs/public administration researcher in finding whatever is needed for any topic in the field. The book has an added value for library staff members, as it will help library users find information in this field. It is also a fine example of illustrative material that describes the reference function in a library. The introductory paragraphs of the chapters would serve well as a brief textbook for this purpose. The book is highly recommended for public affairs and public administration special collections in academic or public libraries. — **Edward P. Miller**

795. **Public Interest Profiles 1992-1993.** Washington, D.C., Congressional Quarterly, 1992. 988p. index. $159.00. JK1118.P8. 322.4'025'73. LC 86-645195. ISBN 0-87187-461-X.

Now published every 3 years, this updated directory by the Foundation for Public Affairs provides in-depth profiles of approximately 250 organizations that have influence on U.S. public policy. While the number of groups covered is about the same as in the 1988-1989 edition (see ARBA 90, entry 736), many of the specific ones selected for inclusion have changed. The selections reflect changes in a group's influence on national policy.

The organizations are grouped into 12 chapters, such as "Civil/Constitutional Rights," "Consumer/Health," "Environmental," and "Think Tanks." The profiles, which range in length from two to eight pages, include basic information taken from questionnaires filled out by the organizations (if they responded), as well as other sources. New to this edition are fax numbers and information about conferences held by each group. Especially useful parts of the profiles are lists of current concerns and publications, as well as media quotations that attest to an organization's effectiveness and political orientation.

Completing the volume are name, subject, and group indexes. The useful subject index is new to this edition. There is, however, room for improvement here. The explanatory note for the group index appears before the name index, causing the user to have to hunt for explanations of boldface type, italics, and asterisks. Also, some of the groups profiled in the volume appear in both the subject and group indexes. Combining those two indexes and highlighting the page number of a group's profile might be a solution for future editions.

This work is a useful resource for any library serving the public, academic, or business communities. Since only approximately 13 percent of the organizations covered are or have political action committees (PACs), this volume covers different territory from directories of PACs. And the extent of information provided sets it apart from other directories of lobbyists or associations. — **Carol Wheeler**

14 Psychology

GENERAL WORKS

Bibliography

796. Dyer, Donald R. **Cross-Currents of Jungian Thought: An Annotated Bibliography.** Boston, Shambhala, 1991. 489p. $35.00. Z8458.75.D94. 016.15019'54. LC 90-53379. ISBN 0-87773-904-8.

This extensive bibliography focuses on works written by and about Carl G. Jung and those influenced by him. The nearly 800 books cover materials published through 1990 and are arranged topically in 12 subject classifications that closely mirror Jung's own arrangement of topics in his *Collected Works*. Within each topic, books are arranged chronologically to give a historical perspective on the development and influence of that theme. Each citation is followed by a descriptive annotation of varying length and a list of book reviews for that work. A list of works arranged by author and title follows this subject section. Appendixes include the abbreviations used in the citation and book review listings, a checklist of publishers that specialize in Jungian literature, and a list of Jungian organizations.

Only book-length works in English are covered in this volume. No journal articles or dissertations are included, a disappointing omission. Selection criteria are subjective but appear to have ensured extensive coverage in all 12 subject sections. Certain sections, particularly those on feminine and masculine psychology and religion, would have been enhanced by the addition of journal literature, but even as they stand they represent a thorough picture of recent extensive studies and interpretations. This work is a thoughtful complement to other Jung bibliographies, particularly Lisa Ress's *General Bibliography of C. G. Jung's Writings* (Princeton University Press, 1992), which omits related works in favor of Jung's writings. Together, these books are a formidable resource for scholars in the field. [R: Choice, May 92, pp. 1364-66] — **Elizabeth Patterson**

797. Schuker, Eleanor, and Nadine A. Levinson, eds. **Female Psychology: An Annotated Psychoanalytic Bibliography.** Hillsdale, N.J., Analytic Press, 1991. 678p. index. $59.95. RC451.4.W6F45. 155.6'33. LC 91-4562. ISBN 0-88163-087-X.

This is more than an annotated bibliography; it is a chronicle of articles, papers, and books pertinent to psychoanalytic views of female psychology. Female psychology was not one of Freud's major emphases, and perhaps this is the reason that few psychoanalytic institutes have offered specialized courses in the area. Editors Schuker and Levinson have compiled more than 2,000 annotations not only to aid psychoanalysts in planning curricula and programs in female psychology but also to provide a major resource for scholars, teachers, and clinicians in allied fields. They have succeeded in producing a well-conceived, well-organized, comprehensive, easy-to-use volume.

Spanning the period from Freud to 1990, the book concentrates on materials in English, primarily drawn from contemporary American sources. It includes not only psychoanalytic views but also alternatives, revisions, reactions, and dissent from them. The first three sections—"Historical Views"; "Developmental Perspective"; and "Female Sexuality, Character, Psychopathology"—highlight important psychoanalytic aspects of female psychology. They cover such diverse topics as Freud's writing and early analytic views; gender differences, menstruation, and the relationship between the sexes; and narcissism, eating disorders, and sexual abuse. Each of the 24 chapters is introduced by a short commentary that places materials in theoretical and historical context, highlights major themes, and assesses their relevance to contemporary psychoanalytic material. Some annotations were written by the authors of the articles or books cited. Many of the entries are lengthy and quite informative. Frequent use of cross-references, subject and author indexes, and well-organized content simplifies the use of the volume. All entries are placed in chronological order within the chapters "so that readers can develop a frame of reference." However, some conceptual guidance would help.

Overall, the volume is well conceived and conceptually integrated. The more than 60 psychoanalysts who contributed to this bibliography should be proud of this work. It will benefit not only psychoanalysts but other professionals who cast a critical eye at analytic theory and therapy. [R: Choice, May 92, p. 1366]—**Suzanne G. Frayser**

Dictionaries and Encyclopedias

798. **The Blackwell Dictionary of Cognitive Psychology.** Michael W. Eysenck, ed. Cambridge, Mass., Basil Blackwell, 1991. 390p. index. $69.95. BF311.B535. 153'.03. LC 90-34225. ISBN 0-631-15682-8.

This ambitious book purposes to "provide the reader with the scope and diversity of contemporary cognitive psychology." The emphasis is on traditional cognitive science, cognitive neuropsychology, and cognitive science (artificial intelligence). Applied cognitive science is somewhat de-emphasized because its methods are not perceived to be distinctly different. Still, applied cognitive psychology was a force well before the renewed interest in cognitive science.

Although this is a dictionary, it is more like an encyclopedia, with each entry written by an identified expert in the field and with appropriate references for further investigation. This is of particular advantage for those who might wish to further their knowledge about a specific topic. However, the references are often old and at times do not represent current thinking. Because of the different authors, the writing varies from perfectly clear to clearly difficult. Sentences of 45 words are difficult to digest by even the most learned readers. The user is warned that it would be "prudent to assume that there will be some minor omissions." Still, it is hard to see how omitting John Bargh, Martin Seligman, Daniel Wegman, and James Pennebaker—to name a few—could be construed as minor. The field of unintended thought is missing; attribution theory is given little attention; learned helplessness is not mentioned at all.

While the goal is to encompass cognitive psychology, there is a bit of overreaching. Humor is included, although Eysenck says that cognitive scientists have not done research in that area. Hypnosis is given as much space as cognitive therapy; eidetic imagery is present despite the author's point that its classification is difficult; and auditory perception is described, although the content of that entry is purely mechanical with no mention of cognitive influences. The de-emphasis of applied cognitive psychology permits the reader to conclude that not much is going on in that area. In that topic, Albert Ellis, Donald Meichenbaum, and Aaron Beck are each referenced only once (!), and George Kelly, not at all; Beck appears only twice in the section on mood disorders and cognition. Further, U.S. readers will be surprised to learn that mood disorders encompass anxiety and depression; in this country they are clinically separate categories.

This is not a book for the layperson. The language is often technical, and the omissions and strange emphases would not be apparent to the nonprofessional. Still, professionals might find it useful. A wide range of useful topics covers the huge domain of cognitive psychology. For the most part the cross-references are helpful (but subliminal perception for cognitive therapy but not for mood disorders?), and the index is useful, although the type is somewhat small and a bit difficult to read.

—**Bertram H. Rothschild**

799. Noll, Richard. **The Encyclopedia of Schizophrenia and the Psychotic Disorders.** New York, Facts on File, 1992. 374p. index. $45.00. RC514.N63. 616.89'003. LC 91-19999. ISBN 0-8160-2240-2.

No other work provides the kinds of information offered in this one. It gives a "panoramic view of the ... belief(s) regarding the nature of madness over the years" and does so splendidly. While the title is a bit misleading (it might better have been titled "The Dictionary of Psychotic Disorders"), nothing pertaining to the purpose of the work seems to have been left out.

All theories that account for psychosis are presented with equal emphasis; but better still, the mythologies of mental illness are also presented. For example, readers learn the word *cacodemonomania*, the belief that one is inhabited by evil spirits, and that witches burned at the stake were not madwomen, but rather poor old people who were disliked by their neighbors. All sorts of such fascinating tidbits are embedded in a surround of solid and useful information. It is also of great interest to discover the sources of some recently current practices. Before the advent of neuroleptics, the treatment of psychosis was cruel in the extreme. For example, patients were tied to "bed-saddles," given wet-pack treatments and convulsive therapies, or strait-jacketed. (Some of these practices can be traced to Johann Christian Reil, a German physician who advocated noninjurious torture as the correct treatment.) The definitions are crisp with an appropriate number of lines per topic and hardly any jargon. Except for the index, the type is appropriately sized and easy to read. There are three appendixes: the care of persons with schizophrenia in the United States, National Institute of Mental Heath schizophrenia-related research grants, and resources.

Some minor problems exist. Phrases such as "An infrequently observed but not uncommon behavior" leaves one confused about the prevalence of the disorder (e.g., trichtillomania). Australia is a topic, but the content of the entry refers only to that continent's aborigines. Nevertheless, this valuable work will be useful to professionals, academicians, students, the lay public, and journalists. [R: Choice, Oct 92, pp. 277-78; RBB, 1 Apr 92, p. 1472]—**Bertram H. Rothschild**

800. Pettijohn, Terry F., ed. **The Encyclopedic Dictionary of Psychology.** 4th ed. Guilford, Conn., Dushkin Publishing, 1991. 298p. illus. $12.95pa. LC 90-81963. ISBN 0-87967-885-2.

The goal of this work is to easily answer "specific questions ... and to demonstrate the nature of the interrelationships among the elements of psychological study." The book is well organized, with cross-references (three kinds), illustrations, topic guides, subject maps, and subject directories. There is even a list of the biographical entries. Each of the entries has been prepared by an authority on the topic, and longer ones are signed. What is particularly good is that the entries are appropriately skeptical about specific areas. This is not a work that, in a superficial way, presents psychology in all its glory. The tone is scholarly, and the scope is comprehensive, if not deep. The entries are in alphabetical order and the reader will not miss an index, but there are no references. While this is not a fatal flaw, it reduces the book's usefulness.

Some of the entries are too brief. Only 13 lines discuss bipolar disorder, and there is no mention of lithium, the treatment of choice. Cognitive-behavioral therapy might have been better served by one long entry that discussed the various theories rather than the multiple entries that require a reader to shift back and forth. Post-traumatic stress disorder is another that is only briefly touched, and it is incorrect to call it an "anxiety disorder." There is a funny mistake on how psychologists are trained; the internship is a condition for receiving the doctorate and is not taken afterwards.

This will generally be a useful book for those interested in getting a brief glimpse of psychology. Most of the entries are informative in spite of their brevity. [R: RBB, 15 Apr 92, p. 1549]
—**Bertram H. Rothschild**

801. Wright, Elizabeth, ed. **Feminism and Psychoanalysis: A Critical Dictionary.** Cambridge, Mass., Basil Blackwell, 1992. 485p. index. $59.95; $19.95pa. BF175.4.F45F462. 150.19'5'082. LC 92-6812. ISBN 0-631-17312-9; 0-631-18347-7pa.

Wright has developed an unconventional dictionary—one that does not define terms in an objective way but that seeks to generate a critical dialogue between feminism and psychoanalysis and to conceptualize a field of feminist psychoanalytic practice. The contributors and entries were chosen with these twin goals in mind. More than 70 international scholars working in the areas of both feminism and psychoanalysis have written lengthy entries that reflect the concepts and themes, applications and descriptions, and theorists and practitioners relevant to the intersection of these domains, particularly those that repeatedly appear in contemporary feminist studies. In an effort to facilitate the assessment of psychoanalysis's impact on feminism, the text of the dictionary focuses on three major dimensions: historical, psychoanalytic, and political.

Arranged alphabetically, the entries span such themes and concepts as androgyny, desire, essentialism, feminists, libido, postmodernism, science, sexual differences, and women's development; such applications and disciplines as biology, anthropology and cross-cultural analysis, philosophy, and personal and autobiographical criticism; and theorists and practitioners. The text of each entry focuses on the theme of the book and is followed by a helpful bibliography. Entries are clear, succinct, informative, and to the point; the volume as a whole is easy to read and to use. A detailed index of content, names, and bibliographical entries makes the location of information easy.

This dictionary is both a reference work and a guide to dialogue between feminism and psychoanalysis. It is an important contribution not only because it clarifies terms and concepts but also because it acknowledges the difficult process that is a part of, and that precedes, such clarification. Readers can learn from and respond to the legitimate debate surrounding the intersection of these fields.

—Suzanne G. Frayser

Directories

802. **APA Membership Register, 1991.** Washington, D.C., American Psychological Association, 1991. 785p. $35.00pa. LC 72-623170. ISSN 0737-1446.

This membership register supplies names, addresses, telephone numbers, and membership status data for 72,202 current fellows, members, and associate members of the American Psychological Association (APA). More detailed information on members who joined the APA between February 1990 and January 1991 is found in a separate section. The citation format for that listing follows that of the 1989 edition of the *Directory of the American Psychological Association* (see ARBA 90, entry 749). Divisional membership and diplomate rosters are also included as well as definitional and abbreviation sections. The current membership register serves as a supplement to the more detailed directory. These lists should be of great use to those needing information about the activities of psychologists.

—Charles Neuringer

Handbooks and Yearbooks

803. **The Eleventh Mental Measurements Yearbook.** Jack J. Kramer and Jane Close Conoley, eds. Lincoln, Nebr., Buros Institute of Mental Measurements; distr., Lincoln, Nebr., University of Nebraska Press, 1992. 1183p. index. $125.00. LC 39-3422. ISBN 0-910674-33-7.

This distinguished series is designed to be a compilation of all commercially published psychological, educational, and vocational English-language tests. For each test at least one review is provided. Criteria for inclusion require that the test be new or revised (older ones can be examined in earlier editions of this work). No attempt is made to screen the tests to determine if they have value; the reviewers, experts in their fields, are expected to give honest appraisals of the tests' designs and their psychometric merit and usefulness. They do their job exceedingly well. Even well-known tests, highly regarded and widely used, do not escape appropriate criticism.

The book contains just about everything one might wish to know about each of the tests. It includes a bibliography of 477 commercially available tests; 703 test reviews; bibliographies related to the construction, use, and validity of specific tests; a cross-referenced title index; a publisher's index; a name index that lists reviewers and authors of tests and references; an index of test acronyms; and an index that refers readers to tests that use scores of particular interest to them. The tests are alphabetically arranged so that finding them is easy if their names are known.

This work is well constructed and logically organized, with a typeface that is comfortable to read. It contains much technical material and would be daunting for those unfamiliar with the complexities of mental measurement, but for those knowledgeable about such matters, it is splendid. While it is somewhat expensive for an individual, it is the sort of work that belongs in libraries and departments of psychology, education, business, psychiatry, and social work.

—Bertram H. Rothschild

804. Reed, Jeffrey G., and Pam M. Baxter. **Library Use: A Handbook for Psychology.** 2d ed. Washington, D.C., American Psychological Association, 1992. 179p. index. $19.95pa. BF76.8.R43. 025.5'6'02415. LC 91-31704. ISBN 1-55798-144-2.

Updating its 1983 predecessor (see ARBA 85, entry 673) in many areas, this new edition will prove as useful and informative as the original handbook. Following the same topical organization as the initial edition, this work expands its coverage in many areas, such as psychological testing and computing technologies. A new section on *PsycBOOKS* (see ARBA 91, entry 788), an index to chapters in books, has been included, and virtually every section has been updated with new resources. Within each chapter, sample search topics serve to illustrate the value and application of the titles discussed. This is a particularly valuable way to demonstrate applications, and it is reinforced by the inclusion of a new appendix that lists several additional search topics that can be used by instructors or students for practice exercises in library research.

While still an excellent introduction to college-level library research in psychology, this work does show some unevenness, especially in its discussion of computers and electronic technologies. The chapter on locating a book goes into an extensive discussion of locating materials through the card catalog, but it gives only a glancing mention to the now-common use of online systems and Boolean logic as the increasingly standard way to organize and locate information. While a slightly longer discussion of controlled vocabularies using the *Thesaurus of Psychological Index Terms* (see ARBA 89, entry 701) is included in the subsequent chapter, a longer review and explanation would have been in order given its key place in electronic retrieval of data. Similarly, the passing references to the CD versions of *Psychological Abstracts* and numerous other CD products that have all but supplanted their older print counterparts indicate a somewhat myoptic view of current research practices. Electronic technologies have revolutionized the way in which students approach research in almost all fields, particularly in psychology, and they deserve more extensive coverage. Despite these drawbacks, this work still should prove an immensely helpful guide to the field for both beginning and advanced students.

—Elizabeth Patterson

PARAPSYCHOLOGY

805. Angelo, Joseph A., Jr. **The Extraterrestrial Encyclopedia: Our Search for Life in Outer Space.** rev. ed. New York, Facts on File, 1991. 240p. illus. index. $40.00. QB54.A523. 574.5999. LC 90-22192. ISBN 0-8160-2276-3.

The search for extraterrestrial life is a legitimate scientific pursuit. However, nearly all books on the subject geared to a popular audience focus on UFOs, alien kidnappings, and similar dubious phenomena. Happily, *The Extraterrestrial Encyclopedia* eschews such pseudoscience and concentrates on the tools, terms, and theories of matters beyond the surface of Earth. In addition to the search for life, the book covers astronomy, the space program, astrophysics, and such subjects as can be reasonably considered "extraterrestrial."

Arranged in an A-to-Z format, the entries include discussions of everything from the Moon to ethical questions that might arise if aliens were encountered. Information has been updated from the 1985 original to cover developments such as the *Challenger* disaster and the Hubble Space Telescope. When a controversial or speculative topic is mentioned, Angelo makes its status clear. (The entry on unidentified flying objects presents a thoughtful and convincing set of reasons why these things are unlikely to be of extraterrestrial origin.) Interesting black-and-white photographs are scattered throughout, and a section of color photographs appears in the center of the book. Good cross-references and a comprehensive index make it easy to find information.

Angelo, director of advanced technology at Science Applications International Corporation in Florida, has created a fascinating reference work that combines good science with intelligent, clear writing. Readers with a casual interest in the topic will immediately understand anything they read, while those with more expertise will be led to related topics. Highly recommended for school, college, and public libraries. [R: RBB, 1 Jan 92, p. 849; SLJ, Nov 92, p. 135]

—D. A. Rothschild

806. Bjorling, Joel. **Channeling: A Bibliographic Exploration.** Hamden, Conn., Garland, 1992. 363p. index. (Sects and Cults in America. Bibliographic Guides, v.15; Garland Reference Library of Social Science, v.589). $57.00. Z6878.S8B56. 016.1339'1. LC 91-13554. ISBN 0-8240-5691-4.

Trance channeling is the conveyance of a message from the spirit world through a chosen human. The New Age researcher will delight in this thorough bibliography of 2,715 items that focuses on trance channeling. The purpose of the book is to be a research guide, to outline the historical roots of channeling, to explain its major teachings, and to consider its significance as a spiritual movement. The book does not attempt to either prove or debunk channeling, and it does not endorse any particular group or philosophy.

The information is presented in chapters that cover the history of channeling, channel revelations presented in books, UFO contactees with messages from extraterrestrials, and contemporary channelers and channeling groups. The essays that precede each chapter are one of the most valuable features of the work. These provide supporting information on the literature of channeling, prominent mediums, the history of movements, entities, prominent authors, foundations and institutes, and other aspects of the topic. The essays are well written, very readable, and cross-referenced to items in the bibliography. Two appendixes and an author index are found at the end of the book. Appendix 1 is a directory of mediumship and channeling groups. Appendix 2 lists critical sources that consist of persons or groups who have done scholarly or critical studies on the topic.

This work appears to be the only source that brings together so much information on all aspects of channeling. Public libraries will find it a useful source, as will libraries that collect in new or esoteric religions. [R: Choice, Sept 92, p. 72]—**Marilyn Strong Noronha**

807. Clark, Jerome. **The UFO Encyclopedia. Volume 2: The Emergence of a Phenomenon: UFOs from the Beginning through 1959.** Detroit, Omnigraphics, 1992. 433p. illus. index. $75.00. TL789.U13. LC 91-37611. ISBN 1-55888-301-0.

Volume 1 of this set, focusing on UFO phenomena in the 1980s, received a favorable review (see ARBA 91, entry 797). Based on examination of the second volume—and if the forthcoming final volume, covering 1960 to 1979, is of similar quality—this set is one that school, public, and academic libraries will rely on for many years.

Most of the 115 lengthy essays discuss the investigations, controversies, individuals, and organizations associated with UFO phenomena after the first sighting of "flying saucers" in 1947. Others focus on earlier time periods, including legends and folklore and reports of unexplained phenomena (e.g., the Fatima miracle, flying serpents) now viewed by some ufologists as evidence of contact established by extraterrestrial life. Twenty-six of the essays are biographical, profiling both serious researchers and charlatans. Others cover publications and organizations important in the history and development of UFO investigation. As the previous review noted, Clark approaches the subject matter from a believer's perspective, yet he considers obvious hoaxes and inconsistencies of research and reporting. Essays not only demonstrate balanced treatment, they are extremely well written and enjoyable.

Reference lists appended to each article cite substantive recent works. Many also contain citations to popular works and published accounts contemporaneous with the topic or event at hand. The detailed index and liberal use of cross-references make the volume easy to use. This work is a solid contribution on often sensationalized subject matter. [R: Choice, Oct 92, p. 270; RBB, July 92, p. 1958]—**Pam M. Baxter**

808. Drewes, Athena A., and Sally Ann Drucker. **Parapsychological Research with Children: An Annotated Bibliography.** Metuchen, N.J., Scarecrow, 1991. 226p. index. $27.50. Z6878.P8D64. 133.8'088054. LC 91-39046. ISBN 0-8108-2514-7.

Drewes and Drucker cite 463 journal articles, conference proceedings, books, and other works that represent English-language publications from the 1880s to 1990. The citations are arranged under seven categories according to paranormal experience: clairvoyance, telepathy, precognition, psychokinesis, poltergeists, reincarnation, and items not otherwise classified (e.g., research issues, near-death experiences). The first three sections further organize entries under age groups: infancy to 12, 13 to 15, and 15 to 17. Annotations are descriptive and, in the case of book entries, often cite published reviews. In lieu of cross-references, entries appropriate to more than one category are reproduced, resulting in a small amount of duplication. Most citations are from core journals in parapsychology, with about 30 percent of all entries derived from one journal title. However, relevant literature from philosophy, religion, anthropology, developmental psychology, and psychiatry is also included. Emphasis throughout is on substantive scholarship and case studies, not popular or sensational literature. Among the volume's other features are a glossary, a list of parapsychology resource centers and degree programs, and an author index. The bibliography proper is preceded by six papers delivered at the 1990 Parapsychological Association meeting that specifically address research on parapsychological phenomena and children.

A publisher's blurb calls this bibliography the only one of its kind, which is probably true. The panel papers reproduced are interesting, the selection of bibliographic entries is good, and the whole is well organized. However, the subject matter will appeal to a narrow audience, making the book's purchase most appropriate for specialized collections.—**Pam M. Baxter**

809. Fitzherbert, Andrew. **The Palmist's Companion: A History and Bibliography of Palmistry.** Metuchen, N.J., Scarecrow, 1992. 236p. illus. index. $27.50. BF921.F58. 133.6. LC 92-5150. ISBN 0-8108-2524-4.

An Australian who first learned palmistry from reading books on the topic has prepared this guide to the history and literature of palmistry. It contains information of interest to all hand readers. The first half of the book has essays on several aspects of palmistry, including a discussion of scientific research and a bibliography of scholarly articles; medical palmistry, and Indian, Chinese, and other forms of palmistry. There are also biographical essays on famous people in the field. Black-and-white photographs and illustrations are interspersed throughout the text. The rest of the book is primarily an annotated bibliography of 560 entries, arranged alphabetically by author's last name. At the end of the volume are reviews by Fitzherbert of classic books on palmistry and a title index to all the books cited or listed in the volume.

This esoteric and fascinating work is well researched and clearly written. It brings together in one volume most of the pertinent information on palmistry. This book will be of interest in public libraries and libraries with occult collections, and it will be an invaluable resource for amateur and professional palmists. [R: Choice, Dec 92, p. 601]—**Marilyn Strong Noronha**

810. Guiley, Rosemary Ellen. **The Encyclopedia of Ghosts and Spirits.** New York, Facts on File, 1992. 374p. illus. index. $40.00. BF1461.G85. 133.1'03. LC 91-37427. ISBN 0-8160-2140-6.

This excellently written encyclopedia is a compendium of information on supernatural activity worldwide, including explanations of strange phenomena from folklore and scientific research. Some of the topics discussed are Ouija boards, apparitions of the Virgin Mary, levitation, and famous ghosts or hauntings. Biographical information is provided for well-known individuals involved in spiritual activity or research. There are 400 entries and 70 illustrations. Each entry is followed by a short bibliography of books or articles to supply additional sources for research. A topical index assists the reader in finding specific information. Informative and fascinating, this encyclopedia will be a valued source in libraries with collections on the occult or supernatural. [R: Choice, Dec 92, p. 601; LJ, 1 Sept 92, p. 168; RBB, 15 Oct 92, p. 452; WLB, Nov 92, pp. 92-93]

—**Marilyn Strong Noronha**

811. Melton, J. Gordon, and Isotta Poggi. **Magic, Witchcraft, and Paganism in America: A Bibliography.** 2d ed. Hamden, Conn., Garland, 1992. 408p. index. (Religious Information Systems, v.3; Garland Reference Library of Social Science, v.723). $65.00. Z6878.M3M44. 016.299. LC 91-45867. ISBN 0-8153-0499-4.

In the review of the first edition of this work (see ARBA 83, entry 1431), the work was declared essential to any collection of the subject of witchcraft and magic. The same review could be written for this edition. Melton and Poggi have compiled an excellent bibliography of the literature produced by and about the American magical community. It is divided into eight major topics, including ceremonial magic; traditional Earth religions; and periodicals devoted to magic, witchcraft, and paganism. The first 7 sections contain 2,540 entries for books and articles, while the last section has lists of current American and foreign periodicals. There is an excellent index of authors, editors, translators, and compilers. Appendix 1 lists the works on witchcraft bound in the New York Public Library in 1908, and appendix 2 contains the curriculum of the A.A. (Argenteum Astrum), most commonly used by OTO (Ordo Templi Orientis) magical lodges. Excluded from the work are the "secret" works of various magical groups, which are held by the Institute for the Study of American Religion but released only to serious scholars of the subject of witchcraft.

Excellent complementary works that may be useful to a library collection are *The Encyclopedia of Witches and Witchcraft* (see ARBA 90, entry 755) and *The Encyclopedia of Magic and Magicians* (see ARBA 89, entry 738). These and the book under review are highly recommended.
—**Christine E. Thompson**

15 Recreation and Sports

GENERAL WORKS

Almanacs

812. Hitzges, Norm. **The Norm Hitzges Historical Sports Almanac.** Dallas, Tex., Taylor Publishing, 1991. 376p. illus. index. $17.95pa. GV707.H57. 796'.0207. LC 88-12171. ISBN 0-87833-621-4.

Hitzges, a television baseball announcer, set out to produce a volume "that combined history, trivia, nostalgia, and the bizarre from every sport" (p. vii). He only partly succeeds. The book is somewhat reminiscent of *Facts and Dates of American Sports* (see ARBA 89, entry 709) turned sideways, but that work has many more significant facts and less trivia. The book begins on January 1 and ends on December 31, with an average of five entries per date. Most are twentieth-century incidents, and fewer than one percent concern women. Hitzges's knowledge of the Olympics is at best limited. For example, the Greek Spiridon Louis won the premier event of the 1896 games, the marathon. He became and remains a hero for this feat, yet he fails to appear in this book; his accomplishment is accorded to the second-place finisher (p. 70). Also, winners at the 1896 Olympics received silver medals, not gold as Hitzges suggests. The index contains names only, so one can find the Quenemo, Kansas, high school but cannot look up football, baseball, basketball, or the Olympic Games. Many of the photographs have no captions, and the drawings often bear no relationship to the text.

This is more of a humor book than a reference or history book; it will be of little use to scholars or libraries. It may be useful to sportscasters; when a score is 40-0 in the first quarter, they can fill the time with humorous anecdotes (e.g., "Did you know that on this date in 1962, all five members of the Coors men's handicap bowling team at Miami, Arizona, bowled games of 192?" [p. 278]).
— **Mary Lou LeCompte**

813. **The *Sports Illustrated* 1992 Sports Almanac.** By the editors of *Sports Illustrated*. Boston, Little, Brown, 1991. 656p. illus. $8.95pa. ISBN 0-316-80799-0.

For the serious sports fan, this compact, inexpensive volume provides team and individual records and highlights for all major sports. Included are not only the popular spectator sports of baseball, football, basketball, hockey, and golf but also swimming, figure skating, and bowling. Not ignored are tennis, boxing, horse racing, and motor sports, as well as track and field, the Olympics, and miscellaneous sports—archery, cycling, and polo, to name a few. A brief essay opens the section on each sport, followed by page upon page of records, both current and retrospective. Interspersed throughout the book are black-and-white and color photographs and notable quotations by sports figures. Two special sections that conclude the volume are profiles of widely recognized sports personalities (e.g., Larry Bird, Satchel Paige, Secretariat) and 1990-1991 obituaries.

The accompanying narrative reflects the best of the writers of *Sports Illustrated*—Jay Greenberg on hockey and Phil Taylor on college basketball, for example—but the strength of the book is its records. While the emphasis is on professional sports, college basketball and football are included as well as amateur track and field and swimming. Other works may provide more in-depth one-sport coverage, but this one stands alone as an all-sports source. — **Boyd Childress**

Bibliography

814. Cox, Richard William. **Sport in Britain: A Bibliography of Historical Publications 1800-1988.** Manchester, England, Manchester University Press; distr., New York, St. Martin's Press, 1991. 285p. index. $59.95. Z7515.G7C69. 016.796'0941. LC 89-49179. ISBN 0-7190-2592-3.

There has long been a paucity of reference works on sport in general, and this is especially true as regards historical aspects of the subject. However, with the blossoming of interest in sport history over the last decade, there have gradually been positive changes in this situation. The present work is a case in point, and it does a reasonably good job of covering books (and some articles) on British sport that have appeared since 1800. There are, however, some shortcomings. There are no annotations for the 7,154 entries, and in the fields known best to this reviewer (hunting and fishing), some noteworthy works are missing. Also, the price is high, particularly for a book with a binding that can (at best) be described as indifferent. (On the review copy, one corner of the binding was not even squared.) These problems aside, it should be noted that this is the best work of its type available, and it will certainly serve as a solid building block for future efforts. Larger academic collections or those with an interest in sport should acquire it. — **James A. Casada**

Biography

815. Condon, Robert J. **Great Women Athletes of the 20th Century.** Jefferson, N.C., McFarland, 1991. 180p. illus. index. $25.95. GV697.A1C68. 796.092'2. LC 91-52633. ISBN 0-89950-555-4.

Condon presents biographical sketches of 50 female athletes of the twentieth century. Each biographical essay is two or three pages long and is accompanied by a black-and-white photograph. The work does not include footnotes or other bibliographic citations.

Condon's writing style is simple and easy to follow. In most essays he does a good job of describing the historical and situational contexts of an athlete's life and accomplishments. A few historical and factual errors appear but do not constitute a major problem. For instance, in discussing the pioneers of women's marathon running, Condon mistakenly says that Katherine Switzer was ejected from the Boston Marathon course in 1967. He also fails to mention that in 1966 Roberta Gibb Bingay became the first woman to complete the Boston race. The entry on Katarina Witt states that Olympic figure skating competition now includes a compulsory figures competition. In fact, 1988 marked the last time that compulsory figures appeared in the Olympics.

The entries are well chosen. Readers may wonder why basketball star Cheryl Miller and volleyball player Flo Hyman are omitted, but there is no question that all of the entries deserve inclusion. This book will serve as a useful source of concise biographical information on many of the top female athletes of this century. [R: BR, Nov/Dec 92, pp. 59-60; Choice, Mar 92, pp. 1119-20; SLJ, May 92, pp. 28-29] — **Wayne Wilson**

816. **Great Athletes.** Pasadena, Calif., Salem Press, 1992. 20v. illus. index. (Twentieth Century). $400.00/set. GV697.A1G68. 796'.092'2. LC 91-32301. ISBN 0-89356-775-2.

As the first in a series that is intended to give young adults a broad perspective on the events, ideas, and people of the twentieth century, *Great Athletes* gets things off to a sound start. Its multivolume, oversized format, with only about 35 entries per volume, seems, at first glance, inappropriate for a reference set. In fact, the set is most likely to be used either as a source for student papers or simply for entertainment. Under those circumstances, a set of large volumes with text that is easy to read and that can be used by several students at once is a distinct advantage. On the other hand, while the price per volume seems reasonable, the decision to publish the set in so many volumes has probably driven the price up to the point where many libraries, especially school libraries (to whom the set is targeted), will think carefully about adding it to their collection.

Great Athletes has much to recommend it. It provides brief (typically two-page) biographical sketches of 738 outstanding athletes who were active in this century. Every entry is accompanied by a full-page black-and-white photograph and a separate body of tabular materials. Each sketch is broken down into basic biographical information, initial career development, contributions that made the person a superstar, and later career developments and other aspects of the person's life. The texts, which have been written by experts who have strong academic credentials, are carefully organized and highlight the challenges and opportunities that motivated the biographees. This kind of balanced presentation—coupled with the representation of 61 different major and minor sports and the inclusion of men and women from 42 different countries—makes *Great Athletes* a set of substantial value that should find wide acceptance and use.

The individuals covered represent the best in their fields. Each volume includes the name, sport, and country index for the entire set, making it easy for a student using one volume to locate information in others. The final volume contains an excellent glossary that explains sport-specific terminology (e.g., chip shot) used in the entries that is not likely to be found in a standard dictionary. It also includes a less useful timeline section that simply lists each of the individuals chronologically by their date of birth. Unfortunately, this feature often fails to reveal much about rivals or stars who were active at the same time. All in all, *Great Athletes* offers a comprehensive, diverse, and useful series of biographical sketches of a splendid body of athletes. Despite its seemingly high price, it represents a sound purchase. [R: BR, Sept/Oct 92, p. 72; RBB, July 92, pp. 1960-61; WLB, June 92, p. 112]—**Norman D. Stevens**

817. Porter, David L., ed. **Biographical Dictionary of American Sports: 1989-1992 Supplement for Baseball, Football, Basketball, and Other Sports.** Westport, Conn., Greenwood Press, 1992. 752p. index. $79.95. GV697.A1B494. 796'.092'2. LC 91-28742. ISBN 0-313-26706-5.

This work supplements the previously published four volumes of this dictionary: *Baseball* (see ARBA 88, entry 798); *Football* (see ARBA 89, entry 735); *Outdoor Sports* (see ARBA 90, entry 757); and *Basketball and Other Indoor Sports* (see ARBA 90, entry 769). More than 600 profiles of American sports personalities have been included in this volume. In addition to athletes, others such as coaches, officials, administrators, and media figures are also included.

The quality of the profiles varies, but in general they are presented in an interesting fashion, not simply as a recounting of statistics. Early years and family life are covered as they relate to the individual's personal and athletic development. Career progression and accomplishments as well as later years of life are covered. A short bibliography accompanies each entry. Those profiled are in various stages of their careers. An index is included. Appendixes cover entries alphabetically, by sport, and by state of birth; women by sport; U.S. Sports Halls of Fame; and sites of Olympic Games. [R: RBB, July 92, p. 1957]—**T. McKimmie**

818. Woolum, Janet. **Outstanding Women Athletes: Who They Are and How They Influenced Sports in America.** Phoenix, Ariz., Oryx Press, 1992. 279p. illus. index. $39.95. GV697.A1W69. 796'.0194'0922. LC 92-199. ISBN 0-89774-713-5.

Woolum's work is the latest, and probably the best, of new books featuring biographical sketches of women athletes. It is certainly superior to Robert J. Condon's *Great Women Athletes of the 20th Century* (McFarland, 1991). Besides providing sketches of 60 women who represent 19 sports, *Outstanding Women Athletes* includes a brief history of American women's sports and women's Olympic participation, a bibliography, a directory of some relevant organizations, and a list of all female Olympic medalists by sport.

Having all this data under one cover is excellent. However, this is not primarily a scholarly reference. As the quotation on the back cover indicates, it is intended for young readers. The bibliography, which contains numerous scholarly monographs, is therefore inappropriate. The biggest problem, however, is with the biographies themselves. Unlike standard biographical dictionaries, which have for every entry standard facts such as birth date, parentage, education, marriage, divorce, offspring, and career, this book is uniform only on the first two. For example, entries for Patricia McCormick and Joan Benoit Samuelson mention that they became pregnant and had children, but their husbands are never mentioned. Worse, many women appear to have no life beyond the pool or gym, and many significant achievements are ignored. Better biographies of many of these women are available elsewhere, including in the 20-volume *Great Athletes* (Salem Press, 1992), which is also intended for the youth market and lists the victories and records for each athlete. Woolum's book is a worthwhile addition to public school and public libraries but not for colleges. [R: RBB, 1 Nov 92, pp. 552-54]—**Mary Lou LeCompte**

Dictionaries and Encyclopedias

819. Hickok, Ralph. **The Encyclopedia of North American Sports History.** New York, Facts on File, 1992. 516p. illus. index. $50.00. GV567.H518. 796.'097. LC 91-6667. ISBN 0-8160-2096-5.

For general interest in sports in North America, this is a solid choice for a one-volume reference book. Coverage includes Canada because of hockey—the Canadian-dominated National Hockey League—and football. Virtually all sports are covered, both college and professional, but the focus is on the major ones—football, baseball, basketball, hockey, and golf. There are more than 1,600 entries, with cross-references, numerous photographs, and a good index. Many entries for team leagues (e.g., the National League in baseball, the Canadian Football League) include franchise addresses, as do organizations such as the Championship Auto Racing Teams (CART) and the Professional Bowlers Association (PBA). Generally, the entries are concise and well-written. In many instances award winners are listed (e.g., the Prince of Wales Trophy in hockey, the Butkus Award in college football). Coverage is historical and current—even the fledgling World League of American Football is included.

Within its seemingly exhaustive approach, the book has curious omissions. For example, there is no mention of legendary college football coach Paul "Bear" Bryant, baseball record-setter Pete Rose, or basketball great Jerry West. Nevertheless, this is a good contribution to any reference collection. [R: LJ, Jan 92, p. 108; RBB, 15 Feb 92, p. 1130; SLJ, May 92, p. 155]—**Boyd Childress**

Directories

820. Gelbert, Doug. **Sports Halls of Fame: A Directory of Over 100 Sports Museums in the United States.** Jefferson, N.C., McFarland, 1992. 176p. illus. index. $34.50. GV583.G45. 796'.06'873. LC 92-53506. ISBN 0-89950-660-7.

The days when a sports museum was an unorganized collection of memorabilia are gone. The hall of fame has become an integral part of sports and a leading tourist attraction in many communities. The Baseball Hall of Fame in Cooperstown, New York, averages a quarter of a million visitors each year, and the PGA World Golf Hall of Fame in Pinehurst, North Carolina, enjoys 100,000 square feet of display space. More than 100 sports museums are included in this small volume. The book is divided into three sections on national halls of fame, museums devoted to an individual sport and multisport halls, and local attractions devoted to sports. More than half of the entries are in part 1, 9 are listed in part 2, and nearly 30 local halls or museums are in the final part. A geographic listing by state and an index conclude the volume.

Each entry provides relevant information on location, hours of operation, and admission charges. The museum is described briefly, including its purpose, contents, and special attractions. The result is a volume that should interest sports fans, archivists, and librarians.—**Boyd Childress**

821. Glanville, Martyn P., ed. **Directory of European Sports Organisations. Repertoire des Associations Europeennes Sportives. Handbuch der Europaischen Sportverbande.** Beckenham, England, CBD Research; distr., Detroit, Gale, 1992. 136p. index. $100.00. ISBN 0-900246-56-1.

This is a comprehensive directory, arranged in alphabetical order, of the sport organizations active in 36 European countries. For each entry the organization's address, a description of the sport with which it is involved, its representative status (e.g., governing body), publications, membership data, affiliations with other bodies, and the like are given. *Sport* is defined in a broad sense so that field sports and fishing, along with athletics, are covered. A subject index makes the work much easier to use, and there is also a detailed abbreviations index. The work is, overall, quite useful, but the price is so inflated, especially for a volume of only 136 pages, that none save the most affluent of libraries will be able to acquire it.—**James A. Casada**

822. **Sports Fan's Connection: An All-Sports-in-One Directory....** Bradley J. Morgan and Peg Bessette, eds. Detroit, Gale, 1992. 584p. index. $59.95. ISBN 0-8103-7954-6. ISSN 1059-0862.

This directory serves as a finding aid to specialized sources of information about all professional, collegiate, and Olympic organizations and teams. It is arranged in three major sections—professional sports, collegiate sports, and Olympic sports—and then by organization or sport within each section. For each category (e.g., professional baseball), information is provided, as appropriate, about leagues and individual teams or institutions; associations, fan clubs, and halls of fame; sports services and fantasy camps; radio and television stations; sports videos; and books, magazines, newsletters, and newspapers.

While brief factual information is provided about the organization or the team, the strength of this directory is the information it provides about how to obtain more information. Data include names and addresses, telephone and fax numbers, key personnel and their positions, and accessibility of information through online services. The lists of reference sources, media guides, books, videos, and serial publications are quite useful because information about much of that material, especially that produced by leagues or teams, is not readily available elsewhere. A lengthy master name and keyword index simplifies access to most of the information. The two major weaknesses are the lack of price information about most of the materials and the failure to include the names of key personnel (e.g., coaches) in the index.

Many sports reference books are aimed at individual fans, but this one is a carefully prepared, well-organized, useful directory aimed primarily at libraries. As such, it is worth serious consideration even by libraries that do not normally purchase sports books or that do not have a large sports reference collection. [R: BR, Nov/Dec 92, p. 60; Choice, July/Aug 92, p. 1662; LJ, 1 Apr 92, p. 114; RBB, 15 Apr 92, p. 1554]—**Norman D. Stevens**

Indexes

823. **Index to the *Sporting News* [A Subject Index from 1975-1990].** Ned Kehde, comp. and ed. Evanston, Ill., John Gordon Burke, 1992. 446p. $40.00; $24.95pa. ISBN 0-934272-18-2; 0-934272-28-Xpa. ISSN 1041-2859.

The *Sporting News*, frequently referred to as the "Bible of Baseball," also provides excellent coverage of other major professional and college sports and the Olympic Games. This index covers a 16-year run of the publication, from 1975 through 1990. It is not comprehensive. Columns and other regular features that offer short snippets on a wide variety of topics are excluded. Still, there are more than 65,000 citations in the index, and a random check indicates that they are accurate.

There is not much depth of indexing. In fact, most stories have been assigned only one subject heading. However, given the editorial content of the *Sporting News*, which consists largely of items about individuals and specific teams, this does not present a problem. Although *Magazine Index* (Information Access, n.d.) covers the *Sporting News* beginning with 1977, printed hardcopy indexes such as *Readers' Guide to Periodical Literature* (H. W. Wilson, 1990-), *Biography Index* (H. W. Wilson, 1946-), and *SportSearch* (Gloucester, Ont., Sport Information Resources Centre, 1974-) ignore it. This index will be a valuable tool for sports fans and others seeking recent sports information from a basic source of sports reporting. [R: RBB, 15 June 92, p. 1882]—**Wayne Wilson**

824. **The Neal-Schuman Index to Sports Figures in Collective Biographies.** By Paulette Bochnig Sharkey. New York, Neal-Schuman, 1992. 167p. (Neal-Schuman Index Series, 2). $35.00. GV697.A1S475. 796'.092'2. LC 90-30605. ISBN 1-55570-055-1.

Young readers maintain a high interest in athletes, past and present. Whether Michael Jordan, Stan Musial, or Chris Evert, sports personalities are popular subjects for term papers, oral reports, and leisure reading. This small volume provides access to biographies of 1,670 sports figures in 225 collective biographies published from 1970 to 1988. The arrangement is alphabetical, listing name, dates (if available), sport, and at least one reference to a biographical source. Abbreviations are used to indicate the sources, which are listed by four-letter codes. Indexes are by sport, by women covered in the volume, and by nation of origin. Surprisingly, athletes from 45 nations are included, although many countries are represented by only 1 or 2 names. The vast majority represents the United States, Canada, and Great Britain. Virtually all sports are included; there are more than 100 auto racers, 36 ice skaters, and more than 50 wrestlers, most professionals. Sports figures from the early twentieth century are also included. A useful volume intended for school and public libraries, this selection is a pleasant surprise (if somewhat expensive). [R: SLJ, May 92, p. 28]—**Boyd Childress**

BASEBALL

825. Fournier, Marion, and others, eds. **The Baseball File: A Comprehensive Bibliography of America's National Pastime.** Gloucester, Ont., Sport Information Resource Centre, 1992. 176p. index. $39.95pa. 016.796357. ISBN 0-921817-03-7.

The Baseball File is just what it says it is: a just-the-facts book that lists alphabetically by subject the majority of articles and some books written about baseball in the past dozen years. All have bibliographic information. Some could benefit from a line or two of annotation; not all the titles are self-explanatory (e.g., "The Dreamlife of Johnny Baseball"). The articles are graded by complexity. "A," for instance, is only for the very advanced scholar. Many of the entries are definitely "A" material.

The work has a few problems. In the biographical selections, it would be better to use an individual's nickname if is more commonly used than the real name (e.g., "Happy" Chandler instead of Albert Chandler). Joe Morgan, the Cincinnati Reds Hall of Famer, is confused with Joe Morgan, the former Red Sox manager. Cross-references (e.g., from "Injuries" to "Medicine") would be helpful. Finally, the index could either be expanded or eliminated; currently, it is simply the contents list with page numbers added. Libraries at colleges that offer courses in sports history, sports administration, and especially sports medicine will find this bibliography useful.—**R. S. Lehmann**

826. Skipper, James K., Jr. **Baseball Nicknames: A Dictionary of Origins and Meanings.** Jefferson, N.C., McFarland, 1992. 374p. index. $45.00. GV867.3.S55. 796.357'03. LC 91-43690. ISBN 0-89950-684-4.

Baseball has produced some truly colorful and inspired nicknames. Many players became so well known by their nicknames that their real names were forgotten, such as Cy Young, Babe Ruth, and Duke Snider. This book lists almost all of the names awarded throughout the history of baseball. The nicknames are listed alphabetically by individual's last name, with the origin of the first name and the person's primary nickname given. Any secondary nicknames are also listed. For example, Ted Williams was primarily known as "The Splendid Splinter," but he was also called "The Kid" and "Teddy Ballgame." Skipper noticed a decline in nicknames in the 1970s and 1980s. It will be interesting to see if future editions show any effects from the new nicknaming craze created by ESPN sportscaster Chris Berman.

The book is, in many ways, a typical McFarland baseball offering: a meticulously researched niche filler that contains numerous annoying typographical and grammatical errors. For example, Bobby Thomson's name is spelled "Thompson" at one point, and "uninhabited" is used for "uninhibited" and "banded" for "banned." Also, there are no cross-references to players' real names. However, the book is recommended because strengths outnumber weaknesses. Nineteenth-century players, Negro Leaguers, umpires, fans, owners, and media members are all included. In addition, there is a welcome section on the All American Girls Baseball League, which existed from 1943 to 1954. [R: Choice, Nov 92, p. 450]
—**R. S. Lehmann**

BASKETBALL

827. **NCAA Basketball's Finest: All-Time Great Man's Collegiate Players and Coaches.** Laura E. Bollig, ed. Chicago, Triumph Books; distr., Detroit, Gale, 1991. 211p. illus. index. $24.95. ISBN 1-880141-04-3.

For those interested in the college careers and statistics of some of the all-time best college coaches and players at major institutions, this may be a useful guidebook. Because it concentrates on the individual statistics of players only in a narrow stage of their careers, only the most avid fan, friends and relatives, or alumni of a particular school or college are likely to make much use of it. Compiled by the National Collegiate Athletic Association's (NCAA) research staff, it is a frustrating book to rely on because the criteria for inclusion are as complex and arcane as the NCAA's rules for eligibility for current players. It takes almost a page to explain those criteria. The title is misleading; the main body of entries that provides detailed player-by-player statistics covers only 301 players who have participated since 1948—the first year that the NCAA kept official statistics. For those players, year-by-year regular season and tournament statistics are included; for some of the players—selected at random—a black-and-white college-era photograph is also included. Pre-1948 players are relegated to a list of 1,050 players from 204 colleges who, during the whole 100 years, qualified by another set of rules. There is also a list of 97 coaches, with their year-by-year won and lost records, who qualified by meeting one of five different criteria. Because even the most experienced reference librarian will have difficulty figuring out which players and coaches may or may not be included, this useful-seeming guidebook is, in fact, almost worthless. [R: LJ, 15 Mar 92, pp. 78-80]—**Norman D. Stevens**

CRICKET

828. **Padwick's Bibliography of Cricket. Volume II.** Stephen Eley and Peter Griffiths, comps. London, Library Association; distr., Lanham, Md., UNIPUB, 1991. 251p. index. $68.00. 796.358016. ISBN 0-85365-528-6.

In the 2d edition of *A Bibliography of Cricket* (London: Library Association, 1984), E. W. Padwick expressed hope that it would be continued by 10-year supplements. This work fulfills that hope and shares the earlier work's scope and organization. The physical format has changed to a broader page, allowing the presentation of more information in one view—especially noticeable in the contents pages. General works, including those on content and technique of the game, are listed first. The organization then proceeds to coverage by nation through the British Isles and those of Great Britain's former colonies to which the sport has been successfully exported. Cricket in the rest of the world follows, with a subsection on cricket in America, wherein some 10 entries for the United States are found, further subdivided by state. Next, international cricket is covered, again by nation. Cricket in literature and various other sections follow. The work concludes with a title and author/title index, which refers to entries by number.

The work is remarkably easy to consult; access is enhanced by the variety of typefaces and by indentations. The bibliographical style is clear, precise, and detailed. A page or so of explanatory notes precedes the entries. The scope is expressly limited to print materials, both monographic and serial. Individual articles in serials are out of scope, as are audiovisual and other nonprint materials. A reminder to American users: the work is a bibliography, not a dictionary, and so uses expressions, such as "limited overs," without explanation. Needed, however, is explanation of the abbreviations CC and CCC. Three sections—"Sports and Games," "Miscellaneous," and "Appendix"—have headings so vague and entries so diverse that they could be combined into one without loss of access.

The work is a tool of first recourse for all who would delve into the lore of the sport whose name is a metaphor for fair play. Libraries that specialize in sports or British culture should acquire it, especially if the earlier work is in the collection. A companion work dealing with nonprint formats would be a welcome addition to the literature.—**Ian Fairclough**

CROQUET

829. Rhoades, Nancy L. **Croquet: An Annotated Bibliography from the Rendell Rhoades Croquet Collection.** Metuchen, N.J., Scarecrow, 1992. 214p. illus. index. $29.50. Z7514.C73R46. 016.79635'4. LC 92-12217. ISBN 0-8108-2571-6.

This comprehensive (but extremely idiosyncratic) bibliography of croquet provides a detailed list of the nearly 1,000 items in the Rendell Rhoades Croquet Collection, which is housed in the Rutherford B. Hayes Presidential Center. The 679 references cover everything, from books to trading cards, that has anything even remotely to do with croquet. An interesting introduction tells a great deal about both the history and practice of the game as well as about the material in the collection. The bibliography is presented in sections whose headings give a good picture of the odd nature of the collection and the bibliography. These include croquet in literature, in biography, in art and music, and in social etiquette and cookery; government regulations; and ephemera (e.g., scrapbooks). The text also contains a brief chronological list of books on croquet published through 1966, taken from a British journal on the game. A useful index contains some amusing entries (e.g., "Croquet first, then a salad").

The nature of the collection is such that most of the material is not readily available in other libraries. Thus, in large measure it will be of interest only to historians of the game.

— Norman D. Stevens

FOOTBALL

830. Adler, Larry, comp. **Football Coach Quotes: The Wit, Wisdom and Winning Words of Leaders on the Gridiron.** Jefferson, N.C., McFarland, 1992. 212p. index. $29.95. GV959.F56. 796.332'0973. LC 91-52630. ISBN 0-89950-542-2.

Adler has collected 2,357 quips, comments, opinions, one-liners, and thoughtful commentary from football coaches across the nation — college and professional alike. Individuals range from current coaches, such as Don Shula, Lou Holtz, Joe Gibbs, Mike Ditka, and Hayden Fry, to those recently retired, such as Bo Schembechler, Ara Parseghian, Tom Landry, and Darryl Rogers, to the grand names of the game — Amos Alonzo Stagg, George Halas, John Heisman, Paul "Bear" Bryant, Knute Rockne, and Vince Lombardi. Some quotations are a single line; others are longer. Quotations are listed alphabetically under the last names of the coaches. Each quotation is numbered, and the subject index refers to these numbers. A bibliography lists additional material about some of the coaches. Most of the citations are to magazine or newspaper articles.

With any book of this type, discussions will range around coaches that have not been included. One of the most quotable coaches omitted, at least from this reviewer's perspective, is Jack "The Ripper" Mollenkopf of Purdue. Occasionally someone will miss a favorite quotation. The book is still a worthy addition to sports collections everywhere. [R: BR, Nov/Dec 92, p. 60]

— Susan Ebershoff-Coles

831. **NCAA Football's Finest: All-Time Great Collegiate Players and Coaches.** Laura E. Bollig, ed. Chicago, Triumph Books; distr., Detroit, Gale, 1991. 232p. illus. $24.95. ISBN 1-880141-03-5.

College football remains one of the most popular spectator sports, and record books maintain a prominent place in reference literature. This small volume is loaded with records of All-American (AA) college players from 1904 through 1989, 343 stars in all. The book is divided into two major sections: players before 1970 and those from 1970 to 1989. Only offensive players are profiled. Complete collegiate records are listed: rushing yards, passing yards, percentages, kick return yards, touchdowns, kicking points, punting yardage, and games played. Many players are pictured (Texas A & M placekicker Tony Franklin kicked barefooted, not with a shoe as shown in his photograph), and all are briefly profiled to include position, high school, size, brief postseason bowl notes, and year AA honors were gained. Another brief section lists all players by school. A coaches' section concludes the volume with regular season coaching records and bowl game scores. All of the great players are here, from Texas Christian University's Davy O'Brien to modern stars such as Herschel Walker of Georgia and Ozzie Newsome of Alabama. Casual fans may be surprised to find Supreme Court Justice Byron "Whizzer" White (Colorado, 1935-1937) and Chicago Bears coach Mike Ditka (Pittsburgh, 1958-1960).

Future volumes are planned for basketball, college baseball, and professional hockey. One hopes that editors of those books will strive to eliminate the typographical errors and incomplete sentences found in this one. [R: LJ, 1 Feb 92, p. 80]

— Boyd Childress

GOLF

832. Campbell, Malcolm. **The Encyclopedia of Golf.** Scarbourough, Ont., Prentice-Hall Canada, 1991. 336p. illus. maps. index. $55.00. 796.352'03. ISBN 0-13-276445-8.

This lavish encyclopedia is substantially better as a library reference tool, as well as considerably more up-to-date, than either *Golf Magazine's Encyclopedia of Golf* (see ARBA 80, entry 710) or *The Hamlyn Encyclopedia of Golf* (see ARBA 87, entry 769). While its oversized format and multitude of color plates suggest it is little more than a coffee-table book, it is, in fact, full of useful information.

The first two sections describe the early development of golf and the modern game, including commentary on balls, clubs, other accessories, and course architects. Next there are detailed descriptions of 50 of the world's most famous courses—primarily in Great Britain and the United States—that provide a narrative description of each course, its history, an excellent color visual representation of the layout, and color photographs. That section also includes one-paragraph descriptions, color visual representations, and hole-by-hole distances and pars of another 50 championship courses throughout the world. Another section describes and illustrates 100 men and women who, as champions, administrators, or architects, have contributed to the game. This is followed by a brief section about the four major golf championships (the British and United States Open, the United States Masters, and the United States Professional Golf Association championship), the leading amateur and women's championships, and the world's principal team events. For each are provided year-by-year information, through 1991, on the winners and their scores. The text concludes with an inadequate two-page glossary that lists fewer than 90 of the many specialized terms of the sport and a short index that primarily covers courses and individuals. Given the widespread interest in golf and its rich history, this encyclopedia represents a good investment for many libraries.

—**Norman D. Stevens**

833. Campbell, Malcolm. **The Golfers Almanac.** Moffat, Scotland, Lochar; distr., Cincinnati, Ohio, Seven Hills Book, 1991. 144p. illus. index. $12.95. 796.35206841. ISBN 0-948403-84-5.

Millions of American golfers dream of playing the famed courses of the United Kingdom and Ireland. For those who can translate dreams into an actual British/Irish golfing holiday, this book is a valuable guide to planning and a pleasurable companion. In a page for each club, it offers information that the would-be golfer will need to have about some 100 courses available to nonmembers and deemed "worth the trip." Campbell is the long-time editor of *Golf Monthly*; the reliability of the information can thus be safely assumed. For each course he gives not only standard directory data but also such worthwhile extras as an account of the course's history and features of special interest. Color photographs are provided for some two dozen of the courses. Campbell has included not only the famous and obvious courses but also lesser-known places that "are well worth rooting out."

The Golfers Almanac is pocket size but sturdily bound. It will tuck nicely into the lucky golfer-traveler's bag; for the rest of us, it is still useful for reference and wishing. Recommended.

—**Samuel Rothstein**

834. **The Guide to Golf Schools & Camps.** Coral Gables, Fla., ShawGuides, 1991. 142p. index. $16.95pa. LC 91-60659. ISBN 0-945834-10-1.

This guide presents information on 137 golf schools and camps in 41 states and 10 countries. The arrangement is alphabetical by state and country. Each entry includes dates, costs, program and facility descriptions, information on teaching techniques, and student-to-teacher ratios. An added feature is an 11-page list of domestic and international golf organizations. There is a master index to the guide and an appendix that can be used to look for particular types of schools (e.g., programs for disabled golfers, parent/child programs). The book is easy to use and provides thorough information in each listing.

—**Wayne Wilson**

HIKING

835. Cook, Charles. **The Essential Guide to Hiking in the United States.** New York, Michael Kesend Publishing; distr. New York, Talman, 1992. 228p. illus. maps. index. $18.95pa. GV199.4.C66. 917.3. LC 92-34801. ISBN 0-935576-41-X.

Although the word "Essential" in the title seems a bit self-laudatory, it is probably well deserved. The work begins with some short chapters that cover about 40 pages of useful, carefully written, and perhaps "essential" information about hiking in general; enjoying the wilderness; clothing, equipment, and food; the various seasons of the year and how they affect the hiker; the varying types of terrain (desert, brush, forest, alpine heights, open country, canyons, and lake and river country); safety on and off the trail; and minimizing the impact of the human presence on the natural habitat of wild animals.

Part 2, titled "Where to Hike," is arranged by state, with a sketch-map of each one that shows areas suitable for hiking in grey and principal trails in black. The accompanying text lists major trails, best hiking trails, and other recommended locations. These short, descriptive paragraphs are followed by a list of hiking resources for each state, often running to 30 or 40 items. There is also a summary chapter on the various types of public lands: national forests, national parks, refuges, state parks, BLM (Bureau of Land Management) lands, private lands, and brief accounts (with maps) of the principal national trails (e.g., the Appalachian, the Pacific Crest, the still incomplete Continental Divide Trail). This book is recommended for almost every type of library, as it is written for, and will be enjoyed by, all would-be outdoors enthusiasts.—**Raymund F. Wood**

HUNTING AND FISHING

836. Jolma, Dena Jones, comp. **Hunting Quotations: Two Hundred Years of Writings on the Philosophy, Culture and Experience.** Jefferson, N.C., McFarland, 1992. 232p. index. $29.95. PN6084.H84H86. 639.1. LC 91-51214. ISBN 0-89950-668-2.

The 629 quotations on hunting found here constitute a sort of mini-*Bartlett's* for those interested in hunting, conservation, and related subjects. This is, in one sense, a wonderfully useful book, but it is to some degree marred by Jolma's apparent lack of familiarity with many of the greatest spokespersons for the hunting ethos in the United States. There are no quotations from such eloquent voices as Havilah Babcock, Nash Buckingham, Archibald Rutledge, or Hal Borland. Likewise, the biographical notes on individuals quoted are singularly uneven. Robert Ruark did work as a columnist for the *Washington Daily News*, but his considerable fame as an outdoor writer did not come from this position. Similarly, to describe Humberto Fontova as an "outdoor sportswriter" is to miss the mark by a wide margin. These and many other irritations notwithstanding, the work belongs in public libraries serving appreciable numbers of hunters, in academic collections supporting study in areas such as conservation and wildlife management, and on the desks of serious outdoor writers.—**James A. Casada**

837. Price, Taff. **Fly Patterns: An International Guide.** 2d ed. London, Ward Lock/Cassell; distr., New York, Sterling Publishing, 1992. 192p. illus. index. $17.95pa. ISBN 0-7063-6898-3.

Price is a highly skilled, gregarious flytier who has fished widely and learned techniques from across the globe. In this work, an updated version of the 1986 edition, he melds his skills at the vise with solid literary abilities and the artistic work of George Thomson. This book belongs on the shelves of all serious fly fishers who enjoy the delights of producing their own creations of feather and bluff, hair and hackle. Of particular note is the fact that the book is truly international in scope, and while its primary focus (and rightly so) is trout flies, patterns designed specifically with other species in mind—sea trout, grayling, salmon, bass, and saltwater sportfish—also come in for their fair share of coverage. Highly recommended for libraries serving areas where fly-fishing and fly tying are popular recreations.—**James A. Casada**

MARTIAL ARTS

838. **The *Aiki News* Encyclopedia of Aikido.** By Stanley A. Pranin. Tokyo and Albany, N.Y., Aiki News, 1991. 217p. illus. index. $29.95pa. GV1114.35.P7. 796.8'154. ISBN 4-900586-12-9.

The creation of aikido as a modern Japanese martial art is credited to Morihei Ueshiba in 1942. However, its development has been greatly influenced by numerous individuals from other martial arts systems. This biographical encyclopedia provides one of the most accurate descriptions of persons currently involved in or contributing to the development of modern aikido. The work is a milestone in the English-language literature on martial arts. Although limited to aikido, it does not suffer from the bias inherent in many other martial arts books or from poor translations of foreign sources. While drawing heavily on materials published in the journal *Aiki News*, Pranin has done a tremendous job of pulling together current information often scattered throughout various English and foreign-language sources.

The main section of the book presents illustrated biographies of important individuals from several countries. For living people, addresses and telephone numbers are provided. A detailed chronology for Ueshiba is presented in a separate section. The main section also includes definitions of terms and brief subject entries for important concepts. Indexes include tables of contents from back issues of *Aiki News*, an annotated subject bibliography, an author index, and the *Aiki News* videotape catalog. An international directory of aikido schools, with addresses, telephone numbers, and names of the head instructors, is also provided.

This up-to-date book is recommended for all serious martial arts collections. It provides a good model for background books on other martial arts systems.—**Andrew G. Torok**

839. Frederic, Louis. **A Dictionary of the Martial Arts.** Rutland, Vt., Charles E. Tuttle, c1988, 1991. 276p. illus. $29.95; $19.95pa. LC 91-061445. ISBN 0-8048-1753-7; 0-8048-1750-2pa.

Originally published in French in 1988, this work will be welcomed by both tyros and serious students of the martial arts. "Dictionary" in the title notwithstanding, the book is in many ways an encyclopedia, with some of its more significant entries running to several pages. Some 40 martial arts, ranging from *aikido* to *yamato-ryu*, are covered, and a good number of useful drawings and photographs are included. The translation from the original French into English is quite good. Recommended for acquisition by public and academic libraries in areas where there is an interest in martial arts. [R: RBB, 1 Feb 92, p. 1053]—**James A. Casada**

OLYMPICS

840. Connors, Martin, Diane L. Dupuis, and Brad Morgan. **The Olympics Factbook: A Spectator's Guide to the Winter and Summer Games.** Detroit, Visible Ink Press/Gale, 1992. 613p. illus. $16.95pa. ISBN 0-8103-9417-0.

The authors and contributors, all journalists, pose the first serious challenge to the premier Olympic Games source book, David Wallechinsky's *Complete Book of the Olympic Games* (Little, Brown, 1992). However, their approach is quite different. The first section, "Opening Ceremonies," gives a brief Olympic history, a profile of IOC (International Olympic Committee) President Samaranch, a discussion of Olympics on television, and the 1992 network television schedule. There follow sections on the winter and summer games. Each provides an introduction to the host city and a discussion of each of the events, in alphabetical order, as well as the following sections: "Warmup," which covers history; "Spectator's Guide," the rules; and the self-explanatory "Hopefuls," "Schedule," "Highlights," and "Medalists."

There are quite a few errors. Mitch Gaylord did not compete in gymnastics at the 1988 Games (p. 332), Betty Watanabe is not a member of the IOC (p. 443), gymnastics was not included in the Ancient Greek Games (p. 321), and it is very doubtful that track and field meets took place in Ireland in 1829 B.C. (p. 475)! The best part of the book is the inclusion of rules and history for each sport. There are a lot of good photographs, although a picture of Jim Thorpe in a football uniform seems out of place. Notably absent are details of each Olympiad, including number of participating countries and medals won. Also missing are key details of the finals: date, number of participants, and top eight finishers. This book is suitable for its intended purpose—a guide for television viewers. As a research and record book, Wallechinsky's is far superior in both detail and accuracy. [R: Choice, June 92, p. 1516; WLB, Apr 92, p. 126]—**Mary Lou LeCompte**

841. Wallechinsky, David. **The Complete Book of the Olympics.** 1992 ed. Boston, Little, Brown, 1991. 763p. illus. $29.95; $14.95pa. GV721.5.W25. 796.48. LC 91-13275. ISBN 0-316-92054-1; 0-316-92053-3pa.

Wallechinsky's work is the premier reference book for laypersons, students, teachers, and scholars interested in the Olympic Games. For every single event in every Olympiad since 1896, it includes the time, place, and date of the finals, with the numbers of countries and individuals participating and the results for the top eight finishers. This information is rarely found elsewhere. It also gives the overall results of each Olympiad and a brief history of the games, both ancient and modern. Vintage photographs are scattered throughout the book, along with anecdotes about notable individuals.

While a few of the stories are more folklore than fact, the book holds up well to scrutiny. The only real drawback is that the format makes it almost impossible to quickly analyze what happened at any particular Olympiad. Virtually all other Olympic books, most recently *The Olympics Factbook* by Martin Connors and others (Gale, 1992), organize their data Olympiad-by-Olympiad rather than event-by-event. Wallechinsky could add this feature fairly simply by using charts for each Olympiad that give medal counts for each country and sport, but it is hardly needed. Other items that could be included are Olympic governance, International Olympic Committee presidents and current members, and names and addresses of international sports federations. Even a simple rearrangement of pages would improve the book. For example, the first page of the section on women's track and field is separated from the second page by over thirty pages of photographs and a blank page. Why not put the "lost" text on the blank page? But these are minor matters. This is the most complete book on the Olympics available and is an excellent source for home, classroom, and library.—**Mary Lou LeCompte**

SAILING

842. Dear, Ian, and Peter Kemp, eds. **An A-Z of Sailing Terms.** New York, Oxford University Press, c1987, 1992. 216p. illus. $11.95pa. GV811.P63. 797.1'24'03. LC 91-30595. ISBN 0-19-286147-6.

This work is an abridgment of the well-known *Oxford Companion to Ships and the Sea* (see ARBA 78, entry 1549). The abridgment was first issued as the *Pocket Oxford Guide to Sailing Terms* in 1987. This latest edition appears to be little changed from the earlier one; most of these maritime terms have passed into English language nautical lore and consequently have not changed much over time.

Some 1,500 nautical and maritime terms are covered in this volume. The work is compact and designed to be carried aboard even the smallest vessel. A few entries are illustrated, but most of the work is in standard dictionary format. Entries are best described as ample and full. A number of diagrams portray various aspects of vessel and sail construction. Other extensively covered topics include rigging and navigation. Libraries that do not own the *Oxford Companion to Ships and the Sea* will benefit by the purchase of this handy little work.—**Ralph Lee Scott**

TRACK-ATHLETICS

843. Davis, Michael D. **Black American Women in Olympic Track and Field: A Complete Illustrated Reference.** Jefferson, N.C., McFarland, 1992. 170p. illus. index. $24.95. GV697.A1D38. 796.42'092'2. LC 91-50946. ISBN 0-89950-692-5.

This book celebrates the achievements of more than 90 athletes. A valuable "Olympic Checklist" includes every Black U.S. female track athlete for each Olympiad since 1932. For each woman it lists event, year of competition, time or distance, and place of finish. This is followed by alphabetically arranged profiles that vary in length from a sentence to 8 or more pages for superstars, 20 of whom Davis personally interviewed. Several profiles merely repeat information listed in the checklist. Davis should have provided more data about those individuals or omitted them from the profiles. He also calls some of the women "Amazons" and makes derogatory comments that add nothing to the book. Most of the profiles end abruptly with the subject's last Olympics, never going into later life and career, or even reporting if the athlete is still alive. The introduction includes glaring errors; for example, women first competed in the Olympics in 1900, not 1928. David seems unaware of the dramatic changes in U.S. sports since the passage of Title IX in 1972 and the Amateur Sports Act of 1978, as well as the radical changes in Olympic eligibility rules since 1980. The result is a series of errors, inaccuracies, and omissions that undermine his credibility and call the validity of the entire work into question. The book has neither notes nor bibliography. On the plus side, Davis lists the women who qualified for the 1980 boycott team. His well-written appendix discusses gender testing and makes several excellent and often overlooked points.

In the final analysis, the negatives of this book overwhelm its assets. It is a good idea that falls far short of its potential. [R: Choice, Oct 92, p. 270; LJ, 15 May 92, p. 84; RBB, 1 Oct 92, pp. 364-65; SLJ, Nov 92, p. 136]—**Mary Lou LeCompte**

16 Sociology

GENERAL WORKS

Bibliography

844. Deegan, Mary Jo, ed. **Women in Sociology: A Bio-Bibliographical Sourcebook.** Westport, Conn., Greenwood Press, 1991. 468p. index. $75.00. HM19.W59. 016.301'092'2. LC 90-43376. ISBN 0-313-26085-0.

Deegan begins her introduction by stating that female sociologists have shaped and changed the world, often without the recognition given to males in the profession. This book documents the major themes of their work and their impact on sociology from 1840 through 1990. It encompasses a broad range of specialization, from marriage and the family to race relations, research methods, social psychology, and aging. The 51 women selected for inclusion cover the entire era of women's sociological influence. All were born before 1927. Some notable Americans, such as Alice Paul, have been omitted to provide more balanced international coverage, although the majority of women included are from the United States. Each entry includes a brief summary of the individual's contribution to sociology, biographical information, important themes and critiques of her writing, and a bibliography. The latter includes selected writings, coauthored works, and studies about the woman. An appendix contains the names of additional notable women sociologists. Name and subject indexes provide access for users. *Women in Sociology* will be most useful to academic and large public libraries.
— **Carol J. Veitch**

845. Fairchild, Halford H., and others, comps. and eds. **Discrimination and Prejudice: An Annotated Bibliography.** San Diego, Calif., Westerfield Enterprises, 1991. 312p. index. $59.95pa. LC 91-65024. ISBN 0-942259-02-5.

This work includes articles, books, and dissertations on discrimination and prejudice. Arranged in five separate bibliographies, material covers Afro-Americans (1,568 records); American Indians (210 records); Asian-Americans (406 records); Hispanic-Americans (582 records); and multiethnic discrimination, which deals with two or more ethnic or racial groups (1,521 records). The bibliographies include most of the following content areas: attitudes/bias, criminal justice, civil rights, education, employment, housing, immigration, land, economic rights, electoral politics, public services, treaties, women, and miscellaneous. For the American Indians additional content areas focus on treaties and land. The citations in each content area are in alphabetical order by the senior author's surname. Every section is numbered separately and has its own index.

Most of the articles were published in the 1960s and 1970s, with some dating back to the 1920s. There are very few citations after 1982. The majority of the entries have brief annotations. In order to get this information, several indexes, such as *Psychological Abstracts, America: History and Life, Social Sciences Citation Index,* the *Federal Register,* and the *Congressional Record,* were searched, as well as a number of online retrieval services. This will be a good starting place for researching discrimination. [R: Choice, Sept 92, p. 76] — **Robert L. Turner, Jr.**

846. Larson, Olaf F., Edward O. Moe, and Julie N. Zimmerman, eds. **Sociology in Government: A Bibliography of the Work of the Division of Farm Population and Rural Life, U.S. Department of Agriculture, 1919-1953.** Boulder, Colo., Westview Press, 1992. 301p. index. $40.00pa. Z7164.S688L37. 016.30772'0973. LC 92-2514. ISBN 0-8133-8529-6.

This work lists all the publications of the Division of Farm Population and Rural Life. From these 1,507 citations (chronological by author, with a keyword index) emerges a pattern of social and geopolitical change in the United States between 1919, when the unit of Farm Life Studies was established, and 1953, when Ezra Benson, Secretary of Agriculture, dissolved the unit. The years between the inception of this subgroup of the Bureau of Agricultural Economics and the late 1930s saw books published that were both far-flung (e.g., *Rural Life in Argentina*) and basic (e.g., *Fundamental Concepts of Sociology*). Research publications chronicled farm family life, including its dimensions of rural hospitals, libraries, community centers, and population trends. (However, congressional testimony centered on wages, employment, and patterns of laborer demand and supply.) A flurry of unpublished, confidential papers in the early 1930s tells the story of Ohio farm bureaus. Publications between 1939 and 1941 signal a country on the verge of war: democracy and national strength figured heavily. And from 1943 to 1945, the topics of mobilizing for, leading during, and going to war consumed many pages; the notable exception was a robust series of papers on Latin America by Charles P. Loomis. After the war, research returned to traditional topics and encompassed veterans.

These entries will be eagerly mined. (The intrigue the papers of Loomis suggest ought to ignite someone!) The editors promise an analytical volume soon. — **Diane M. Calabrese**

Dictionaries and Encyclopedias

847. **Encyclopedia of Sociology.** Edgar F. Borgatta, eds. New York, Macmillan, 1992. 4v. index. $340.00/set. HM17.E5. 301'.03. LC 91-37827. ISBN 0-02-897051-9.

The four volumes of this excellent encyclopedia provide the first comprehensive introduction to the field of sociology. Prior to its publication, scholars and students had to rely on a number of sources that are now more than several decades old. One of these is the 17-volume *International Encyclopedia of the Social Sciences*, edited by David L. Sills (Macmillan, 1968). Its format of alphabetically arranged, lengthy articles, each written by an authority in the subject area and accompanied by a substantial bibliography, provides the pattern for the present work. Other sources that serve as a foundation for this set are the series of sociology handbooks issued by Rand McNally in the 1960s and 1970s and for which Borgatta served as advisory editor.

For this encyclopedia Borgatta enlisted the assistance of a distinguished board of advisory and associate editors who then selected the article authors. The 339 contributors who wrote and signed the 370 articles are scholars based mostly in United States and Canadian universities and research centers. Of the handful of those from other countries, nearly all serve as authors for the articles on the national sociologies of their countries or area of the world (e.g., Germany, India, Japan, Scandinavia). A list of authors that includes their affiliated institutions and the titles of the articles they wrote appears at the beginning of volume 1.

The editors wanted the encyclopedia to be accessible not only to sociologists reading outside their areas of specialization but also to other scholars, students, and the uninitiated. Thus, a goal was to make the articles readable by a broad range of literate audiences. This goal has been achieved with the exception of some presentations that deal with technical areas. Articles typically begin with background information, placing the topic in context within the discipline. They then discuss issues, theory, and research findings if appropriate. Often they conclude with questions for further investigation. Many entries are 5 to 6 pages long, but they can range in length from 2 to 18 pages, with the longer ones often divided into subtopics. Most articles are followed by a list of cross-references and a bibliography that in some cases is very substantial. Readers wishing to do further study will find classic works along with research results as recent as 1991.

The articles deal with both traditional concepts and theories and newer theoretical approaches (e.g., feminist theory, new structuralism). Social problems are addressed (e.g., homelessness, incest, organized crime) and brought up to date with information on such recent developments as the failure of the savings and loan companies in the late 1980s and the 1991 research reports on AIDS. Other types of articles deal with subfields of sociology (e.g., urban, applied), various area studies (e.g., Africa, the Middle East, Latin America), multicultural studies (e.g., African-American, Native American, Asian-American), and the sociology of other disciplines (e.g., law, education). The articles that cover technical aspects are liberally illustrated with black-and-white line drawings, equations, charts, and graphs. There are no biographical articles on sociologists, although material on their contributions to the field can be found in the topical articles by using the index.

The encyclopedia has a number of useful features. Readers seeking an overview can turn to the beginning of volume 1 and browse the list of articles. To find a particular topic they can either go directly to an entry in the main body of the encyclopedia and find what they want or use the index at the end of volume 4. The 76-page index is detailed and well designed but unfortunately has a few errors (although not more than would normally be expected in a work of this magnitude). The spelling of the name for the American sociologist Samuel A. Stouffer proved particularly troublesome. There is an entry for both "Stouffer, Sam" and "Stougger, Samuel," and under the entry for "*American Soldier, The*" his last name is spelled "Souffer."

In spite of such minor flaws, this is an important work that should endure as a standard reference in the field for years to come. Highly recommended for purchase by all libraries that can afford it. [R: Choice, July/Aug 92, pp. 1654-55; LJ, July 92, p. 76; RBB, 1 May 92, p 1619; RQ, Fall 92, pp. 112-13; SLJ, May 92, p. 31; WLB, May 92, p. 123] – **Anna L. DeMiller**

848. **The HarperCollins Dictionary of Sociology.** By David Jary and Julia Jary. New York, Harper-Perennial/HarperCollins, 1991. 601p. $13.00pa. LC 91-55446. ISBN 0-06-461036-5.

This is the United States version of a similar dictionary issued in Great Britain under a slightly different title. Although most of the definitions are short enough to merit the "dictionary" label, this work includes a considerable number of short biographies; many definitions that are not usually considered within the concept "sociology"; and a considerable number of definitions, with illustrative tables, of statistical concepts used by social scientists. Although the work does include a 40-page bibliography, the individual entries do not have any citations. They do, however, contain a large number of cross-references.

There are some possible competitors which should be mentioned. *Critical Dictionary of Sociology* (see ARBA 91, entry 841) is excellent in what it does but has a limited number of definitions, being more of a handbook or even, perhaps, an encyclopedia, than a dictionary in the conventional sense. *Penguin Dictionary of Sociology* (London: A. Lane, 1984) is more comparable to the present work but has much shorter definitions and appears to have fewer biographical entries. On the other hand, it does include a few bibliographic references with many entries and generally has more cross-references per entry than does *HarperCollins*.

Ironically, the most successful competitor to the work under review is the British edition of this very same title: *The Collins Dictionary of Sociology* (London: HarperCollins, 1991). By the same compilers, the British edition includes many more definitions and more short biographies than the United States version. Because there is no difference in common entries (all are from a mildly British perspective), logic suggests buying the British over the United States edition. [R: Choice, June 92, p. 1520; LJ, 15 Mar 92, p. 76; WLB, May 92, p. 123] – **James H. Sweetland**

849. Lachmann, Richard, ed. **The Encyclopedic Dictionary of Sociology.** 4th ed. Guilford, Conn., Dushkin Publishing, 1991. 321p. illus. $12.95pa. LC 90-81962. ISBN 0-87967-886-0.

This compilation is the fourth updated and revised edition of the original *Encyclopedia of Sociology*, published in 1974. Written to facilitate access to the terminology, institutions, and practices that prevail in the field of modern sociology, it contains more than 1,350 entries, each prepared by one of 120 authorities. A major difficulty in the work's compilation was deciding what to include and what to leave out of the enormous body of information available. Rather than to provide exhaustive information on particular topics, the goal of this encyclopedia is to answer specific questions on the interrelationship among sociological concepts. An attempt has been made to produce a reference volume of the greatest value for the general reader. This desideratum, combined with the limitation of available space, has resulted in the exclusion of some specific sociological terms and theories. Entries are arranged alphabetically, with some containing cross-references to either connect interrelated items or to deepen comprehension of the subject. Most of the longer articles cover some major products of sociology, such as theories, research, and fundamental processes. This volume is highly recommended for everyone interested in the study of sociology. [R: RBB, 15 Apr 92, p. 1549]—**Oleg Zinam**

ABORTION

850. Clements, Bonnie L., comp. **Abortion and Family Planning Bibliography for 1989-1990.** Troy, N.Y., Whitston Publishing, 1992. 526p. index. $55.00. LC 72-78877. ISBN 0-87875-420-2.

Formerly called *Abortion Bibliography*, this volume is the twentieth annual list of world literature on abortion for the preceding year (with a few late additions, mostly books and dissertations, from 1987-1988). Some peripheral subjects previously covered in *Population Bibliography*, such as birth control, family planning, contraceptives, fertility, and sterilization, are included. The preface lists 55 indexes and abstracts searched. Analysis of the list of journals cited indicates many outside medicine and the health sciences (e.g., legal, religious, general interest, women's magazines). While there is an author index, subjects must be deduced from the periodical literature by the subject heading list in the table of contents. Article citations are arranged alphabetically by title under these fairly specific headings.

The expanded scope and broad journal coverage add to the significance of this extensive and carefully compiled bibliography. Now that social concern about all aspects of the abortion issue is so great, many different kinds of libraries will find it an important and useful reference for a variety of patrons, and they should retain it for historical purposes.—**Harriette M. Cluxton**

851. Costa, Marie. **Abortion: A Reference Handbook.** Santa Barbara, Calif., ABC-Clio, 1991. 258p. index. (Contemporary World Issues). $39.50. HQ767.5.U5C67. 363.4'6. LC 91-15231. ISBN 0-87436-602-X.

For those who want to inform themselves on the issue of abortion, Costa's handbook is an excellent guide to the debate's issues, events, personalities, organizations, and publications. The book begins with a chronology on abortion, which traces the history of the subject from the Roman Empire through the middle of 1991. Most of the entries, many of which are quite substantive, fall within the last 30 years. The second chapter provides page-long biographical sketches of almost two dozen key figures in the contemporary development of the abortion debate, including such well-known individuals as Congressman Henry Hyde; Planned Parenthood's Faye Wattleton; and lawyer Sarah Weddington, who successfully argued the Roe v. Wade case. Chapter 3 covers United States and foreign laws on abortion, statistics on the incidence of abortion, the demographic characteristics of women who receive abortions, deaths caused by illegal abortions, incidents of antiabortion violence, abortion techniques, and much more. Chapter 4 is a directory of organizations, with information on each organization's address, telephone number, purpose, services, and publications. The last two chapters provide an annotated bibliography of print and nonprint materials on the debate. There are an appended glossary of terms and a combined name/title/subject index.

Costa's handbook is similar in content and organization to Carl N. Flanders's *Abortion* (Facts on File, 1991), which has an excellent introduction and good descriptions of key court cases. Both are more user-friendly than *The Abortion Debate in the United States and Canada* (see ARBA 92, entry 805), which has sections on philosophical, religious, and legal/political positions on the debate. Overall, Costa's book is well done and recommended for public and academic libraries. [R: BR, Sept/Oct 92, p. 60; Choice, Apr 92, p. 1205; LJ, 15 Apr 92, p. 42; SLJ, May 92, pp. 29-30]—**Stephen H. Aby**

AGING

852. Aboussafy, David. **Bibliography of Seniors and the Family Research 1980-1991.** Vancouver, B.C., B.C. Council for the Family, 1991. 42p. index. $5.00 spiralbound. 016.30687'084'6. ISBN 1-895342-32-5.

This bibliography will be most useful for social workers, students, and those in the caregiving professions who deal with senior citizens and their role in society. It has been divided into 12 categories that include care issues, childless elderly, divorce, elder abuse by family, grandparenting, long-standing marriages, remarriage, senior parent-adult child relationships, sibling relationships, social support and families of choice, widowhood, and general seniors and the family research. Within these categories are lists of articles, chapters, and books related to the subject area. An author index gives the author's name and the page reference within the bibliography.

This is a valuable tool for those institutions that have schools of social work, but public libraries and elementary or secondary school libraries probably do not have immediate access to the resources cited. Researchers in the area of aging and the elderly will find it helpful since it reflects current issues of concern. (Several of the articles cited would have been most helpful for questions received at this reviewer's institution in the past year.) The spiral binding may not stand up to much handling; however, this is a minor problem and should not influence the decision to purchase. Recommended for academic institutions or agencies directly associated with the elderly, geriatrics, and caregiving. — **Mary J. Stanley**

853. Cheney, Walter J., William J. Diehm, and Frank E. Seeley. **The Second 50 Years: A Reference Manual for Senior Citizens.** New York, Paragon House, 1992. 445p. illus. index. $21.95pa. HQ1064.U5C44. 305.26'0973. LC 91-42339. ISBN 1-55778-531-7.

Retirement years can generate at least as many challenges and anxieties as opportunities. Those approaching their "second 50 years" are confronted with such issues as retirement planning, living on a fixed income, health care, insurance, nutrition and fitness, housing, and personal security. This reference manual provides them with much of the basic information needed to understand and negotiate these challenges.

The manual is composed of one- to six-page essays arranged under approximately two dozen broad subject categories that cover such topics as financial matters, assistance for seniors, nutrition and diet, health problems, legal concerns, and retirement. Each broad category is divided into a number of constituent essays written by one of the manual's three authors. Not surprisingly, the two categories that receive the most coverage are assistance for seniors and health problems. The former deals with a variety of community services for senior citizens, while the latter includes essays on physiology, specific diseases and disorders, drugs, coping with illnesses, and related subjects. All of the essays are clearly written and are accompanied by addresses and telephone numbers for important organizations and services. Also, the large page size and 12-point type should aid those with less than perfect vision. A good subject index, which includes organization names and book titles, provides additional access to information.

There are a number of reference books that supply more detailed information on specific topics covered here, such as the *National Continuing Care Directory* (see ARBA 90, entry 789) or *Paying for Health Care after Age 65* (see ARBA 92, entry 1640); however, they lack this manual's breadth of coverage. *The Retirement Sourcebook* (see ARBA 90, entry 791) does cover a similar range of topics, but it mostly provides references to relevant publications and organizations. *The Second 50 Years*, with its informative discussions of a variety of topics, fills an important information need among senior citizens. [R: LJ, 1 May 92, p. 74; RBB, 15 June 92, pp. 1888-90] — **Stephen H. Aby**

854. Coyle, Jean M., comp. **Families and Aging: A Selected, Annotated Bibliography.** Westport, Conn., Greenwood Press, 1991. 208p. index. (Bibliographies and Indexes in Gerontology, no.14). $45.00. Z7164.O4C67. 016.6467'8. LC 91-29593. ISBN 0-313-27211-5.

The swelling of the proportion of aged Americans compared to other population groups has led to a national debate about who should care for the elderly. Some put the responsibility on the elders themselves, others on the government, and others on the families of the elders. This annotated bibliography provides many relevant sources for understanding what is known about family involvement in the lives of elderly Americans. The introductory essays provide an overview of various subject matters: middle-aged families, single life, older couples, widowhood, grandparents, adult children, intergenerational relationships, family care giving, racial and ethnic minority groups, and living arrangements of older persons. With these topics in mind, the reader can select items in the related bibliographic listings. Noteworthy in this reference work are the clear organization of the items; the useful annotations; and the inclusion of books, films, government documents, articles and chapters, and dissertations. The volume concludes with separate author and subject indexes. [R: Choice, June 92, p. 1516]—**Shulamit Reinharz**

855. **The Henry Holt Retirement Sourcebook: An Information Guide for Planning and Managing Your Affairs.** By Wilbur Cross. New York, Henry Holt, 1991. 330p. index. $35.00. HQ1063.2.U6C75. 646.7'9. LC 91-17184. ISBN 0-8050-1760-7.

The purpose of this book is to help individuals locate organizations that publish materials, provide referrals, or offer other assistance related to aging and retirement. The author's goal is readily met in this comprehensive, well-organized, easy-to-use sourcebook. Short introductory chapters give an overview of living arrangements and health, economic, legal, leisure, and social issues that concern older adults. Each chapter ends with a list of organizations that specifically deal with the topic discussed. An alphabetized directory of these organizations follows the introductory section. The names of the resources (and their abbreviated titles, where appropriate) are highlighted and spaced to provide easy reference. More than 400 entries are included. Along with the customary directory information, a short profile of the organization is supplied along with a brief summary of types of publications it makes available. An index cross-references the organizations by subject area or title of publications, and a short bibliography highlights classic texts or other references specific to each subject area. Overall, the book is an excellent resource for anyone—not just retirees—seeking information about organizations for older adults. [R: LJ, 1 Mar 92, pp. 80-82]—**Mary Ann Thompson**

856. McLeish, John A. B. **Creativity in the Later Years: An Annotated Bibliography.** Hamden, Conn., Garland, 1992. 149p. index. (Garland Reference Library of Social Science, v.552). $20.00. Z7204.C8M38. 016.15567. LC 91-32398. ISBN 0-8240-4645-5.

Gerontology and related specialties concerned with the growing number of elderly in this country are generating a large amount of literature. However, no one has examined this material for the relationship between creativity and the over-60 segment of the public. McLeish's brief, partially annotated bibliography is intended to fill this void. It covers selected items from monographic, scholarly journal, magazine, and newspaper publications as well as doctoral and master's theses, diaries, and films. While some of the entries focus on the broad topic of creativity, most of the citations have at least some relationship to creativity in the elderly. Special attention is paid to the female and Black portions of this population group. Unfortunately, McLeish has failed to explain his selection criteria, thus making it difficult to evaluate the comprehensiveness of this bibliography. Were items selected after being reviewed or merely chosen from a computer-generated list? Why are only some citations annotated?

Despite these flaws, this short reference tool will be a useful starting point for specialists and scholars interested in the subject of creativity in the elderly. It should not, however, be considered the definitive study on this topic.—**Jonathon Erlen**

857. Mori, Monica. **Palliative Care of the Elderly: An Overview and Annotated Bibliography.** Vancouver, B.C., Gerontology Research Centre, Simon Fraser University, 1991. 213p. index. $21.00 spiralbound. ISBN 0-86491-106-8.

This resource and reference bibliography is for service providers, trainers, researchers, and students caring for the elderly. Its scope is that of North America, although there are several British references. The sources of the references are several online databases, such as Ageline, Medline, and ERIC. The majority of references are journal articles, with 30 percent having been published between 1985 and 1990, the cutoff date.

The focus of the 438 references is primarily palliative (hospice) care and the team that supports the patient and family at the point of terminal illness and impending death. Hospice staffing, facilities, and services each have separate sections. The organization is clear, logical, and useful, and annotations are brief but descriptive. A comprehensive table of contents and three indexes (keyword, related-keyword, and author) give easy access to the contents. Key words are indicated on each entry.

The beginning section presents a narrative overview of the hospice movement—its past, present, and future. The initial section of the bibliography includes references on the need for such care, the hospice movement as such, and future directions. For this section alone, the volume will be helpful for hospice administrators and service providers. – **Barbara Conroy**

858. Roy, F. Hampton, and Charles Russell. **The Encyclopedia of Aging and the Elderly.** New York, Facts on File, 1992. 308p. index. $45.00. HQ1061.R69. 305.26'03. LC 91-23435. ISBN 0-8160-1869-3.

This encyclopedia is coedited by an M.D. and a Ph.D., an ideal combination for assembling information about aging. The book has a brief preface, an introduction that covers physiological changes connected with aging, alphabetically grouped entries, a bibliography, and an index. The entries typically are a column in length and are written on a fairly sophisticated level in easily readable type. Each entry is followed by at least one bibliographic item for further reference, with no citations in the entries. There is extensive cross-referencing among entries and use of multiple terms, such as "Hair, Excessive (Hirsuitism)" and "Hair Transplants (Baldness)." The entries offer a mix of medical, sociological, and cultural items. For example, under *H* one will find happiness, Hatha Yoga, hearing aids, Hottentot elderly, hobbies, and age-segregated housing.

Some of the cross-referencing would benefit from fuller explanations. For example, "Japanese Americans" has the following entry: "*See also* Stress of Life." However, the explanation for "Stress of Life" does not mention any link to Japanese-Americans. The appendixes contain 28 tables and 4 graphs with a wide variety of data and a list of national and state organizations concerned with the welfare of the elderly. The exact readership for this encyclopedia is not specified, and it is unclear whether laypeople would be interested in the appendixes or if professionals would find the entries sophisticated enough for their purposes. [R: Choice, Dec 92, pp. 604-05; LJ, 15 Oct 92, pp. 62-64; RBB, Aug 92, pp. 2036-37; WLB, Oct 92, p. 104] – **Shulamit Reinharz**

859. Simmons, Henry C., and Vivienne S. Pierce, comps. **Pastoral Responses to Older Adults and Their Families: An Annotated Bibliography.** Westport, Conn., Greenwood Press, 1992. 218p. index. (Bibliographies and Indexes in Gerontology, no.15). $49.95. Z7761.S55. 016.259'3. LC 91-43560. ISBN 0-313-28039-8.

This bibliography is intended for researchers in the field of religion and the elderly as well as for practicing clergy, educators, lay professionals, and laity. It begins with an informative introduction that provides an overview of trends in religion and aging. The 736 entries include books, journal articles, and dissertations on religion and aging. Most of the items are scholarly; however, works of interest to the general reader are also included. The large majority of the entries are from the Jewish and Christian traditions. The bibliography is subdivided into church and synagogue; empowerment; ethics; personal spiritual life; life review and written reminiscences; death and dying; theology, Bible, and other religions; religious professionals; special populations; and health and religion. Divisions have been designed to reflect the materials available and their uses. Descriptive annotations are concise and clear so that the researcher can determine the usefulness of the original work. Author and subject indexes allow easy access to this reference tool. *Pastoral Responses* will be most useful to theological, church/synagogue, academic, and public libraries with extensive religious collections. – **Carol J. Veitch**

860. Van Tassel, David D., and Jimmy Elaine Wilkinson Meyer, eds. **U.S. Aging Policy Interest Groups: Institutional Profiles.** Westport, Conn., Greenwood Press, 1992. 258p. index. $59.95. HQ1064.U5U22. 305.26. LC 91-29198. ISBN 0-313-26543-7.

Offered as "a reference guide to organizations that influence U.S. public policy regarding aging and the aged," this work will be a valuable source for libraries that have an emphasis on aging or that support academic programs with this emphasis. Eighty-three organizations are profiled, from AARP (American Association of Retired Persons) to Zonta International. To be included, an organization must devote more than 50 percent of its resources towards influencing national policy on aging and the aged. Omitted are government agencies and organizations that focus more on recreation, research, or service (e.g., Elderhostel). (Many of these latter organizations are included in appendix A, which gives their names, addresses, and telephone numbers.) Some organizations are part of coalitions on aging, and these are listed under their coalitions in appendix B. A preface sets the tone for the book, and an introduction describes the changes that have been effected by these groups over the years. A chronological list of federal legislation enacted provides further help in understanding the positions held by many of the organizations. A valuable selected bibliography completes the text. The index provides excellent access by subject and name as well as principal emphasis of individual organizations. The book will prove valuable to academic, large public, and special libraries that deal with the topic. [R: WLB, Sept 92, p. 121]—**Edward P. Miller**

861. Wallace, Steven P., and John B. Williamson, with Rita Gaston Lung. **The Senior Movement: References and Resources.** New York, G. K. Hall/Macmillan, 1992. 204p. index. (Reference Publications on American Social Movements). $40.00. Z7164.O4W38. 016.30526'0973. LC 91-40851. ISBN 0-8161-1841-8.

Senior citizens are a major economic, political, and social force in the United States. This valuable resource provides access to 800 expertly cited books, journals, dissertations, and primary sources on the senior movement. For the most part the information is national rather than regional or local and has been gleaned from numerous databases.

Especially noteworthy is the well-written, comprehensive, 30-page introductory essay that provides a scholarly overview of the major issues and debates in a historical perspective. Following this is a section of general works, most of which are relatively recent; these offer breadth of coverage rather than depth. Each citation is well annotated and addresses the movement's leaders, organizations, advocacy positions, and political strategies since the 1930s. Major specific issues are highlighted, with separate sections devoted to public policies, social security, economic health, ageism, intergenerational conflict, and the legal system. A relatively brief section profiles major resources for research and advocacy, and an appendix provides specific names, addresses, and telephone numbers for advocacy organizations. The indexes of authors and subjects are well done, with an adequate level of specificity to lead the user to the resource needed.—**Barbara Conroy**

DISABLED

862. **The Complete Directory for People with Disabilities, 1992.** Leslie Mackenzie and Amy Lignor, eds. Lakeville, Conn., Grey House; distr., Detroit, Gale, 1991. 580p. index. $99.95. ISBN 0-939300-12-5. [Paperback available from Lakeville, Conn., Grey House, 1991. $69.95pa. ISBN 0-939300-09-5.]

The purpose of this title is to provide a single information resource for people with disabilities, their families and friends, and the professionals who provide services for them. The editors have come fairly close to fulfilling that purpose. The directory is divided into institutions, media, products, and programs. Under associations there are additional categories (e.g., hearing impaired, hotlines, mentally disabled, physically disabled, visually impaired). In the products section, each of the items has a brief description and price code, which can be very useful for individuals as well as libraries and helping organizations. In the program section, addresses, telephone numbers, and directors/administrators are included along with a brief description of the program. Indexes to entry/organization/name, disability/need, and geographic location of institutions and organizations are included.

This title will be helpful since it covers so many of the needs of disabled persons. The media section can be useful in collection development. Highly recommended for all libraries. [R: BR, Sept/Oct 92, p. 67; Choice, July/Aug 92, p. 1653; LJ, 1 Apr 92, p. 110; RBB, 15 Jan 92, pp. 968-72; RQ, Fall 92, p. 109; WLB, Apr 92, pp. 120-21]—**Mary J. Stanley**

863. **The Illustrated Directory of Handicapped Products 1991-92.** Marion S. Behzad, ed. Lawrence, Kans., Trio, 1991. 306p. illus. $12.95pa.

With an emphasis on products that assist the physically handicapped, this revised and updated catalog provides information for the disabled person, the caregiver, and the professional seeking sources for a wide variety of aids and necessities. Most of the product descriptions also include a black-and-white photograph or drawing, but only a minimum of price information is provided. The catalog is divided into 21 categories that range from mobility and transportation items to clothing and recreational aids. Lists of catalogs and organizations are also included. Each section has its own index of suppliers, which comes complete with addresses and telephone numbers (some toll-free), including those suppliers that did not submit descriptions to the catalog. There is no cumulative index to the volume, which would be helpful in locating a particular distributor. Many of the products and some auxiliary services are featured in the advertising, which has its own index.

This volume complements *The First Whole Rehab Catalog* (see ARBA 91, entry 853), which provides some of the same material but also includes more services, organizations, and other information. Because of their reasonable prices and the growing interest in the needs of the disabled, libraries, especially public and health science institutions, should have both of these works to maximize the information provided. [R: BR, Nov/Dec 92, p. 39]

—Margo B. Mead

864. Shrout, Richard Neil. **Resource Directory for the Disabled.** New York, Facts on File, 1991. 392p. index. $45.00. HV1569.5.S57. 681'.76. LC 91-10244. ISBN 0-8160-2216-X.

This resource directory is divided into four sections, from general resources for persons with physical disabilities to resources for the mobility impaired, the visually impaired, and the hearing impaired. Within each section, categories are appliances and devices; travel helps; recreation and social opportunities; organizations, associations, and sport groups; employment/training opportunities; education; publications of interest; and miscellaneous. There is a topical index. Each entry provides address and telephone information and an extended annotation that is descriptive, not evaluative, of the services or functions of agencies and publications. Each section also contains a list of addresses for various types of agencies and manufacturers. A selected check of addresses and telephone numbers confirmed that the listings are up-to-date as of the publication date.

This valuable resource will be useful in general and academic reference departments for helping users find where to go next for more information or assistance. Association, agency, and manufacturer addresses and telephone numbers will change, but the directory is a good starting point. Facts on File publications of this sort are usually updated regularly. [R: LJ, 1 June 92, p. 118; RBB, 15 Jan 92, pp. 968-72; SLJ, July 92, p. 100; WLB, Apr 92, pp. 120-21]

—Kieth C. Wright

865. Sobsey, Dick, and others. **Disability, Sexuality, and Abuse: An Annotated Bibliography.** Baltimore, Md., Paul H. Brookes, 1991. 185p. index. $24.00pa. HV6626.7.D57. 364.1'53. LC 90-15042. ISBN 1-55766-068-9.

In response to the need to provide a better way to identify the assault and abuse of people with disabilities and to assure "accessible, appropriate" services for victims, the authors have provided an annotated bibliography of more than 1,100 materials related to disability, sexuality, and abuse. The variety and scarcity of materials in this area indicate the cultural biases that influence attention to and research on this problem. The authors think that so few materials have been produced because people with disabilities were assumed to be asexual; because the recognition of abuse is recent, as is work in the area; and because research has been rare, limited in distribution, and not identified as a scholarly research area for electronic literature searches. Therefore, the development of this bibliography is a significant contribution to the field. Primarily written in the 1980s, sources include newspaper and journal articles, books, reports, newsletters, legal cases and acts, and cassettes. Abstracts are full, informative, and useful. Subject and author indexes follow the text.

The format of the volume is somewhat unwieldy for accessing information. Sources are arranged alphabetically by author rather than by topic because of overlap in subject matter. However, the indexes are often not helpful in finding material because the categories are too broad (e.g., neglect, abuse, therapy). Arrangement of sources by category with cross-references would improve access to information.

This is an important bibliography for all professionals who are serious about developing appropriate programs for and responses to confronting this much too invisible, important issue. Therapists can use it to treat and counsel victims; physicians, to diagnose problems; teachers, to identify sexual abuse; and lawyers, to prepare cases and legislation.

—Suzanne G. Frayser

FAMILY, MARRIAGE, AND DIVORCE

866. Adamec, Christine, and William L. Pierce. **The Encyclopedia of Adoption.** New York, Facts on File, 1991. 382p. index. $45.00. HV875.55.A28. 362.7'34'0973. LC 91-4629. ISBN 0-8160-2108-2.

The entire scope of adoption, from agencies to zygote adoption, and all the social, legal, economic, psychological, and political issues are covered in over 400 definitions and 4 appendixes. Some of the important topics discussed are who adopts and why, drug-addicted babies, gay and lesbian adoption, surrogate parenthood, teenage parents, and transracial adoption. The introduction presents a concise overview of the history of adoption.

The extensive appendixes provide, through tables and charts, information on the demographics of adoption in the United States. Other listings found here are state adoption agencies, adoptive parent groups, adoption-related organizations, and periodicals and newspapers relevant to adoption. A lengthy bibliography at the end of the volume and bibliographies that follow many definitions provide the researcher with additional sources on the topics. Entries are cross-referenced in the text and indexed at the end of the volume, which allows for easy access to specific topics. This well-written and well-researched work will serve as the primary source for the topic and should be a part of every collection of adoption material. [R: BR, May/June 92, p. 59; Choice, Sept 92, p. 71; LJ, Jan 92, p. 104; RBB, 15 Feb 92, p.128; SLJ, June 92, p. 150]—**Marilyn Strong Noronha**

867. Chadwick, Bruce A., and Tim B. Heaton, eds. **Statistical Handbook on the American Family.** Phoenix, Ariz., Oryx Press, 1992. 295p. index. $59.50. HQ536.S727. 306.85'0973'021. LC 91-44175. ISBN 0-89774-687-2.

This book looks at the American family in great detail. Data is presented in more than 400 tables and graphs that discuss marriage rates, the quality of marriage and family life, divorce, children, sexual attitudes and behaviors, contraceptive use, living arrangements and kinship ties, working women, wives and mothers, family violence (including child and spouse abuse), and elderly families. The data was obtained from federal and state government agencies, Gallup polls, professional journals, research monographs, various public domain national databases (e.g., the *National Survey of Families and Households*), and some unpublished sources. The editors often use the various data sets to calculate the material presented in the tables. Sources of information in each table are given in a separate section. The tables include the latest data at the time of publication; however, most of the 1990 census materials were not available. This valuable source on the American family should be in every library where such topics are studied. [R: Choice, Nov 92, p. 450; RBB, 1 Nov 92, pp. 554-55; WLB, Oct 92, p. 113]
—**Robert L. Turner, Jr.**

868. Miles, Susan G. **Adoption Literature for Children and Young Adults: An Annotated Bibliography.** Westport, Conn., Greenwood Press, 1991. 201p. index. (Bibliographies and Indexes in Sociology, no.21). $39.95. Z7164.A23M55. 016.3627'34. LC 91-31854. ISBN 0-313-27606-4.

This work covers literature, published since 1900, that deals with adoptees and adoption. It is divided into four categories based on the age and grade of readers: preschool and primary (preschool to 3d grade), intermediate (grades 4 to 6), junior high school (grades 7 to 9), and high school (grades 10 to 12 and beyond). Each category is further divided into fiction and nonfiction, with fiction predominating (except in the high school category). Many adoption situations are discussed, including search and reunion; racial identity; age of arrival; adoption by siblings, single parents, foster parents, stepparents, and relatives; and transracial, intercountry, minority family, special needs, large family, and open adoption. The annotations for each of the 503 books are excellent. There are two appendixes, one suggesting further reading and the other a directory of adoption-related organizations. There are indexes of authors/illustrators, titles, and subjects (the latter detailed and very effective). The review copy had one signature out of place (pages 133-64 are between pages 172-73). This work will be very useful to those who are either adopted or who are thinking of adopting. [R: RBB, 1 Apr 92, p. 1468]
—**Robert L. Turner, Jr.**

869. Paul, Ellen. **Adoption Choices: A Guidebook to National and International Adoption Resources.** Detroit, Visible Ink Press/Gale, 1991. 590p. index. $24.95pa. ISBN 0-8103-9403-0.

This title is the result of Paul's efforts to work through the adoption maze. The entries have been compiled from questionnaires and telephone interviews with agencies and organizations, all conducted over a two-year period. The first section is an alphabetical state-by-state listing of public, private, and independent agencies, associations, and support groups for adoptive parents. It includes an agency profile, procedures, fees, and home study protocol. The second section is devoted to adoption exchanges; the third and fourth sections cover Canada and selected foreign countries; and the final section deals with foster care. Information panels in the margins have state statutes and other bits of information (e.g., "In Connecticut, stepparents wishing to adopt the children of their spouses must undergo a study process as would any other adoptive applicant"). There is an organization index.

This is quite an unusual title as it covers many adoption alternatives for prospective parents. It will be useful for any public library reference collection or an academic library that supports social service programs. – **Mary J. Stanley**

PHILANTHROPY

870. **America's New Foundations 1992: The Sourcebook on Recently Created Philanthropies.** 6th ed. Bohdan R. Romaniuk, ed. Rockville, Md., Taft Group; distr., Detroit, Gale, 1992. 672p. index. $137.00pa. ISBN 1-879784-25-4. ISSN 1048-4965.

Rearranged and expanded from its previous incarnation as *America's Newest Foundations* (see ARBA 88, entry 838), this directory lists, in alphabetical order by state, more than 3,300 foundations established since 1987. Included are community, corporate, and private foundations whose total donations or assets meet the directory's $100,000 criterion. Such a low figure means that most of those listed do not appear in *The Foundation Directory* (see ARBA 91, entry 866), which includes only foundations with assets of at least $1 million whose yearly giving reaches or exceeds $100,000.

Each foundation profile provides name and address, government-issued Employer Identification Number, and year established. When available from sources such as telephone surveys and annual reports, additional data are provided, including the foundation's geographic or financial limitations, major priorities, assets, total giving, and number of grants awarded. The "Other Things You Should Know" portion of the profile notes deadlines, application guidelines, and restrictions.

Many of these smaller and newer giving institutions are focused locally; the state-by-state arrangement facilitates identification. Indexes offer other access points: foundations by grant type and by recipient type, officers and directors, grant recipients by location, and the alphabetical master list of foundations. Recommended for libraries that support the work of fundraisers and the research of philanthropy studies scholars. – **Cheryl Knott Malone**

871. **The Awards Almanac 1992: An International Guide to Career, Research, and Education Funds.** Karen P. Singson, ed. Detroit, St. James Press/Gale, 1991. 794p. index. $85.00. ISBN 1-55862-082-6. ISSN 1052-2220.

While resources abound for organizations that seek grants-in-aid, individuals have usually had few places to turn. Now, this compendium identifies more than 2,000 worldwide awards available to faculty, graduate and postgraduate students, and individuals pursuing career-related activities. Details include award purposes, areas of study, requirements, deadline, amount of award, contact person, and directory information for the grantee. Of special interest is the ratio (for the most recent year available) of the number of awards to the number of applicants, giving applicants a sense of the competition.

The master index is to the awards listed under both grantee institution and award name. The index by subject is subdivided by levels or types of awards, such as student, professional, competition, or scholar. There is also a useful quick reference guide that lists general awards not restricted to a field of study and international opportunities by country, as well as a list of awards for specific populations, such as ethnic groups, blind individuals, and citizens of developing countries. The entries and double-columned pages are user-friendly, with rich use of contrasting type intensity and white space. Although not so labeled, the preface indicates this to be the 2d edition of the title. This streamlined, one-volume resource will serve well the needs of scholars and professionals seeking funds. – **Eleanor Ferrall**

872. **The Directory of Corporate and Foundation Givers 1992: A National Listing of the 8,000 Major Funding Sources for Nonprofits.** Katherine E. Jankowski, ed. Rockville, Md., Taft Group; distr., Detroit, Gale, 1992. 2v. index. $195.00pa./set. ISBN 1-879784-18-1. ISSN 1054-108X.

Imagine a directory that lists, in one alphabetical sequence, not only private foundations but also corporate foundations and corporate direct givers. This is it. Jankowski interfiles 8,000 philanthropic programs available in the United States. Of these grant givers, more than 4,100 are private foundations, 1,500 are corporate foundations, and 2,400 are corporate direct givers. Grant seekers may find the latter group enticing because such information has been sparse in the past. For users interested in the philosophy undergirding philanthropy and examples of its application, the preface offers a discussion of seven current issues, from education to family to environment to volunteerism. Under the grant giver's official name, a profile provides sufficient details to enable grant seekers to carefully evaluate its applicability to their needs. In addition to financial data, grants data, contact persons, and application information, the profiles provide biographical data on officers and brief but encompassing exposes of the donors' interests, priorities, and limitations. Entry names in boldface type with dividing liners and adequate white space create effective legibility despite small type and four columns of entries per page.

The directory devotes 933 pages to its indexes by headquarters state, operating location, grant type, nonmonetary support, recipient type, major SIC (Standard Industrial Classification) products/industry, officers' and directors' names, and grant recipient arranged by state. There is also a final master index to corporations and foundations. Placing the list of recipient categories adjacent to the recipient type index rather than in the preface, and providing a separate list of grant types adjacent to the index by grant type, would save time. And one always hopes for a master subject index that cross-indexes by types of grants available, fields of giving interest, and giving limitations. For now, this is the latest word in directories. Large public and university libraries, development offices, and nonprofits will find this innovative resource to be a valuable investment, not an expense. – **Eleanor Ferrall**

873. **Directory of Research Grants 1992.** Phoenix, Ariz., Oryx Press, 1992. 1156p. index. $118.00pa. LC 76-47074. ISBN 0-89774-698-8. ISSN 0146-7336.

As salaries and operating budgets decrease and the need for supplemental funds increases, individuals and organizations are turning to external sources of revenue. One such tool to assist in the process is this directory, the print equivalent of the online GRANTS database. Information is current as of November 1991. Contained within are research-related projects, scholarships, fellowships, conferences, and internships for funding opportunities in the health, physical, and social sciences; the arts and humanities; and education.

Arrangement is alphabetical by title of grant (5,963 are included), with indexes for subject, sponsoring organization, and type of sponsor. Each entry contains an extensive description of the purpose, requirements, restrictions, amount, deadline, and sponsor. The currency of this information may be maintained with an online search of the data, which is updated monthly and available via DIALOG. In addition, because there are no cross-references in the subject index, users will want to explore each topic in depth. For example, entries under "Libraries" and "Academic Libraries" contain different information.

The scope of this tool sets it apart from *The Foundation Directory* (see ARBA 91, entry 866), the *International Foundation Directory* (see ARBA 88, entry 843), and the *Taft Corporate Giving Directory* (Taft Group, 1991). Its price will warrant careful consideration, in light of the currency of the information and the ability to access online information. Useful for comprehensive collections and those with healthy serials budgets. – **Ilene F. Rockman**

874. Dumouchel, J. Robert. **Government Assistance Almanac 1992-93: The Guide to Federal Domestic Financial and Other Programs....** 6th ed. Washington, D.C., Foggy Bottom and Detroit, Omnigraphics, 1992. 810p. index. $84.00. LC 86-658073. ISBN 1-55888-769-5. ISSN 0883-8690.

This title was previously reviewed in ARBA 90 (see entry 806). This edition has updated the information very carefully. Eighty-seven programs have been added and 24 have been deleted. Abbreviations are clearly defined in the early pages of the volume. A section on field office contacts will be useful for readers to learn who to contact in various areas; for example, each State Energy Office is listed with its address and telephone number. One new feature with the index is a notes section that explains entry codes, subject headings, program titles, and references. This is a most comprehensive tool for domestic assistance, much easier to use than its government counterpart. Recommended for any library that needs information on financial assistance. — **Mary J. Stanley**

875. **EHR Directory of Awards: Fiscal Year 1990.** Washington, D.C., National Science Foundation, [1992]. 531p. index. price not reported.

To support excellence and progress in research and education in science, mathematics, and engineering is the avowed mission of the National Science Foundation's (NSF) Directorate for Education and Human Resources (EHR). This report, published annually, verifies this support through its abstracts of awards presented during fiscal year 1990. The abstracts provide succinct descriptions of each award project. For the first time, programs are included as they are named, rather than at year's end. The introduction presents an informative, detailed description of the units and programs within EHR at publication time. The abstracts are grouped by EHR program title, then under recipient's name. Transition from one program to another is clearly labeled by the EHR program name as a heading, but to determine which of EHR's five divisions or one office sponsors the program, the user must laboriously search the introduction to the book. Adding the EHR unit to the heading would present a clearer picture of its structure. Congress-mandated changes in this structure are forthcoming. Supplementary materials, not listed in the table of contents, include Presidential Awards for Excellence in Teaching; graduate, minority graduate, and NSF-NATO postdoctoral fellowships awards; Presidential Young Investigators awards; and program activity by EHR division. Perusal of the contents clearly indicates trends in subject viability and research, giving the user a better understanding of award possibilities. The report is an excellent summary of EHR activities. — **Eleanor Ferrall**

876. **Guide to Federal Funding for Volunteer Programs.** Cheva Heck, ed. Arlington, Va., Government Information Services, 1991. 1v. (various paging). index. $68.00 looseleaf w/binder. ISBN 0-933544-43-X.

This first edition provides detailed descriptions of 21 federal programs that assist volunteer projects. These programs are concentrated in the areas of education, job training, health, and social services. Instead of being organized by grant program function, this work is organized by agency, necessitating a detailed subject index (which is supplied). The agencies either require the use of volunteers or have volunteerism as a central focus. Among other things, the work contains the first comprehensive description of the new volunteer programs to be administered by the Commission on National and Community Service.

For each program are listed the program title, the Catalog of Federal Domestic Assistance (CFDA) (GPO, 1971-) number, a quick check box, and a detailed description of the program. The quick check box summarizes the most important facts about the program, including how federal dollars go to grantees, who may receive aid under the program, type of aid provided, and key requirements. (A wise caution is given that those interested in applying for aid should check with the program administrator to make sure of the current requirements.) This work is to be updated by a supplement.

The publisher offers three other guides that together cover all of the federal aid programs open to state and local governments, community organizations, and nonprofit organizations of all types. This one will be very useful for those wanting funds for volunteer programs. — **Cheryl Knott Malone**

877. Hodgkinson, Virginia Ann, and others. **Nonprofit Almanac 1992-1993: Dimensions of the Independent Sector.** 4th ed. San Francisco, Jossey-Bass, 1992. 628p. index. $49.95pa. ISBN 1-55542-746-4. ISSN 1060-7889.

A thick assemblage of data that describes the so-called independent sector of the economy, the *Nonprofit Almanac* pulls together statistics from a variety of government and private sources. The almanac's first part quantifies the not-for-profit arena's industries, entities, and workers in four chapters. The second part, with three sections, provides data on nonprofit organizations in summary form and in a classified arrangement based on purpose (e.g., education, medical research) as well as state-by-state figures on independent sector activities. Each chapter features a clearly written introduction followed by tables of data that include citations to the sources of those data. Appendixes offer a discussion of methods used to calculate and compile the information, a description of the classification scheme employed in part 2, and a glossary. An index provides an additional access point for the tables.

A product of Independent Sector, an umbrella organization that promotes charitable giving and volunteering, this almanac documents the range and depth of a largely ignored but nevertheless influential segment of the economy. Recommended for any library that serves students, professionals, and policymakers in the growing field of philanthropy. [R: Choice, Sept 92, p. 78] – **Cheryl Knott Malone**

878. Maxfield, Doris Morris, and Joseph M. Palmisano, eds. **Charitable Organizations of the U.S. 1992-93: A Descriptive and Financial Information Guide.** 2d ed. Detroit, Gale, 1992. 565p. index. $139.50. ISBN 0-8103-8081-1. ISBN 1052-3979.

From A to Zonta, this useful reference tool gathers descriptive information and (usually) financial data on 783 of the almost 450,000 entries that meet the Internal Revenue Service's legal definition of a public charity. Arranged in alphabetical order by organization name, the entries cover such essentials as the history and purpose, charitable activities, administration, fundraising techniques, and tax status of the charity described. The organizations themselves provided the information and in some cases declined to make financial data available. The criteria for inclusion in the guide is unclear. The amount of funds raised apparently was not a selection factor, since both the Shriners Hospitals for Crippled Children ($414 million) and the Salvadoran Medical Relief Fund ($168,000) are represented. An overview of standards for judging the worthiness of charitable organizations and a clear user's guide are included, as are subject, geographic, and personal name indexes.

Designed to assist people making decisions about their charitable contributions, this directory will also be of interest to researchers in the growing field of philanthropic studies. Recommended for academic and large public libraries. [R: Choice, July/Aug 92, p. 1652; RBB, 1 Apr 92, pp. 1469-70]
– **Cheryl Knott Malone**

879. **National Data Book of Foundations: A Comprehensive Guide to Grantmaking Foundations.** 16th ed. Compiled by the Foundation Center. C. Edward Murphy and Joan Seabourne, eds. New York, Foundation Center, 1992. 1916p. index. $135.00pa. ISBN 0-87954-436-8.

It is often difficult to make something good even better, but the Foundation Center consistently finds ways to improve this valuable reference. Now in a single volume, it proves useful in two primary ways. It serves as an index to the 990-PF returns filed annually with the Internal Revenue Service by each private foundation, and it functions as a resource for locating preliminary information on funding sources. Its basic details on four types of foundations are preceded by explanations of what constitutes a foundation and what distinguishes one type of foundation from another.

Section 1 lists 30,461 private or company-sponsored and 328 community foundations by state and in descending order by total grants paid. Section 2 notes 3,200-plus operating foundations arranged by state and, within each state, by descending order of total assets. Section 3, an appendix, alphabetically lists those foundations that have ceased to exist since January 1, 1988. Both sections 4 and 5 are indexes, the first to private foundation names and the second to community foundation names. Placing these indexes in the main volume simplifies user access to the material. As with previous editions, introductory materials provide efficient usage suggestions, foundation characteristics, statistical analyses, titles of state and local foundation directories, and computer availability of information. – **Eleanor Ferrall**

880. Olson, Stan, Ruth Kovacs, and Suzanne Haile, eds. **Guide to Funding for International and Foreign Programs.** New York, Foundation Center, 1992. 245p. index. $75.00pa. ISBN 0-87954-441-4.

Produced by the Foundation Center, this specialized funding guide targets foundations and corporate giving programs that have demonstrated an interest in international and foreign programs, either by stated intent or the awarding of funds. The guide is not intended to be comprehensive, but it does identify 464 potential funding sources. A comparison of the *Foundation Directory* (see ARBA 91, entry 866) and this guide shows a large number of duplicate entries; however, the international guide provides supplementary information on many funding sources. Nearly two-thirds of the guide's entries are enhanced with lists of recent grant recipients, grant amounts, and project focus.

Similar to the *Foundation Directory*, arrangement is by state, with each entry assigned a number. Indexes by foundations and corporate giving programs, subject, type of support (e.g., student aid, equipment, building funds), and donor/officers/trustees facilitate access to entries. A selected bibliography of other funding resources for international and foreign programs complements the rest of the data provided.

This well-organized guide will be of interest to those working on programs with an international focus, whether in the United States or abroad. Recommended for libraries with large grantsmanship collections or those collecting in the area of international business or foreign development.

— **Ahmad Gamaluddin**

881. Olson, Stan, Ruth Kovacs, and Suzanne Haile, eds. **National Guide to Funding for the Environment and Animal Welfare.** New York, Foundation Center, 1992. 332p. index. $75.00pa. ISBN 0-87954-440-6.

Foundations and corporate contributors in the United States awarded almost $13 billion in donations in 1990. In profile format, this volume introduces 1,028 (among 32,000) foundations and 94 corporate grant givers that might consider funding in areas related to the environment or animal welfare. The layout and design of the book will simplify any approach. The user can peruse profiles of the grant-making groups, locate potential funding sources by state (and city), identify grant makers by their interests (e.g., environment, wildlife), or confirm restricted support (e.g., in-kind, individuals). The consecutively numbered entries are alphabetical by state and city; the various indexes point to entries by number. For novices, there is a glossary, but more instructive are the profiles. For example, even though the James and Mary Ida Compton Foundation is listed, it accepts no applications—that is, the initial approach requires ingenuity. Some profiles include lists of recent grants made; they suggest the scope and size of future awards. The New England BioLabs Foundation, for example, supported environmental education projects at the Wau Ecology Institute (Papua New Guinea) and the Conservation Law Foundation (Boston) in 1989. Introductory pages describe other publications of the Foundation Center. A bibliography (1989-1991); locations for the Foundation Center cooperating collections network; and an index to donors, officers, and trustees complete the volume. The book is printed on recycled paper.— **Diane M. Calabrese**

SEX STUDIES

882. Bullough, Vern L., and others, eds. **Prostitution: A Guide to Sources, 1960-1990.** Hamden, Conn., Garland, 1992. 369p. index. (Garland Reference Library of Social Science, v.670). $56.00. Z7164.P95P76. 016.30674. LC 92-5112. ISBN 0-8240-7101-8.

Because of increased feminist research on prostitution, the willingness of scholars to investigate homosexuality and homosexual prostitution, and concern with the transmission of AIDS, the literature on prostitution has burgeoned during the last 20 years. This volume attempts to keep pace with the growth in the literature from 1960 through 1990 by adding sources to complement materials in *A Bibliography of Prostitution* (see ARBA 78, entry 643). Combined with that bibliography, this volume will provide "the most complete and comprehensive guide to prostitution available" (preface).

The bibliography includes books and articles in English, European languages (usually without abstracts), and non-European languages when English abstracts were available. The 1,965 entries are organized according to broad, alphabetically arranged headings that span a wide range of perspectives on, and facets of, prostitution. These categories include general sources (e.g., bibliographies, studies on feminism), area studies, biographies, economics, history, males and prostitution, medicine, pornography, sociology, and war and the military. In most categories, entries are arranged alphabetically, without further subdivision into subcategories. Given the current emphasis on multiculturalism in society as a whole, it is particularly noteworthy that the editors have segmented much of the material according to geographical area and historical period; their attention to social and cultural variation in prostitution implies a sensitivity to cross-cultural variation and recognition that prostitution has very different meanings according to context. While the compilation concentrates on English and European sources, it does attempt to be comprehensive within its limits. Many sources are merely listed without annotation, while others are briefly annotated, usually providing information on the content of the source rather than summarizing methods and conclusions. Two lengthy indexes of personal names and subjects guide the user to more specific topics.

Professionals interested in this complex topic will benefit from such a centralized source. Given the scope of coverage, brief summaries of the types of materials in each section would give the user a better idea of the volume's contents. — **Suzanne G. Frayser**

883. Carrera, Michael A. **The Language of Sex: An A to Z Guide.** New York, Facts on File, 1992. 180p. index. $22.95. HQ9.C35. 306.7'03. LC 91-2031. ISBN 0-8160-2397-2.

Carrera, a distinguished sex educator, believes that "sexual ignorance is not bliss." Therefore, he endeavors to provide a reference work that goes beyond description to present sexuality in a "comprehensive, multidimensional fashion." Intended for laypeople, the book includes such basic information as descriptions of sexual and reproductive anatomy and physiology, "normal" sexual and reproductive events in the life cycle, physical problems, sexually transmitted diseases, medical interventions and medications, variations in sexual behavior, and birth control. Resources for information on family planning, AIDS, gender, sexual abuse, and national sexuality organizations follow the alphabetized entries, as does a bibliography, primarily of trade books, on some of the basic topics covered in the text (e.g., sexual orientation, gender identity, sexual assault, sexuality in illness and disability).

Because the book is geared to laypeople, it is not clear why such technical terms as *lymphogranuloma venereum* and *hysterosalpingography* are included, unless they are given to provide patients with a translation of physicians' terms. Why are subjects of broad interest such as sexual addiction left out? A rationale for selection of topics would clarify this. Also, the selection and rendering of some illustrations, such as the many drawings of circumcised and uncircumcised penises, seems curious. Finally, there are details omitted that are sure to be bothersome to the specialist (e.g., specifications of different types of incestuous relationships, a mention of the benefits of RU 486 beyond pregnancy termination).

Nevertheless, the book succeeds in presenting succinct, easy-to-understand descriptions of many terms and concepts central to an understanding of human sexuality. The shortness of the book, the alphabetization of topics, and an index enhance its use. It is appropriate for laypeople but not for professionals, as Carrera intended. [R: RBB, 15 June 92, p. 1884; WLB, June 92, pp. 112-14]
— **Suzanne G. Frayser**

884. Kahn, Ada P., and Linda Hughey Holt. **The A-to-Z of Women's Sexuality: A Concise Encyclopedia.** rev. ed. Alameda, Calif., Hunter House, 1992. 362p. illus. index. $14.95pa. HQ30.K34. 306.7'082. LC 92-2852. ISBN 0-89793-095-9.

Labeled a "revised and expanded edition" of the 1990 hardbound version (see ARBA 91, entry 1661), this paperback differs little in form or content from the original. The title is slightly different, the cost is lower, and there are a few updates at the end of each alphabetical section (e.g., RU 486, endometriosis). However, there are no substantial revisions. The number of pages and location of information remain the same as in the 1990 edition. Given the swift changes in information about AIDS, the book would benefit from the inclusion of updated references in the bibliographic section on that subject.

As with the original version, laypeople and professionals will benefit from the broad range of alphabetically arranged entries that relate to women's sexuality. Included is information on sexual and reproductive anatomy and physiology, gender identity, developmental stages, diseases and health problems, birth control, organizations, significant figures in the field, and therapeutic techniques. Some entries are quite lengthy (e.g., menstruation, breast) and summarize a good deal of diagnostic and practical information. Extensive cross-references, an index, and a lengthy bibliography of books arranged by topic aid the use of the volume. A brief introduction that described the criteria for selecting topics and a statement of the authors' goals would enhance this work. — **Suzanne G. Frayser**

885. Phillips, Gillian. **Reproduction: A Guide to Materials in the Women's Educational Resources Centre.** Toronto, Ontario Institute for Studies in Education, 1991. 396p. index. (WERC Bibliography Series, 1; Resource Series, 3). $40.00 spiralbound. 016.6126'2. ISBN 0-7744-0373-X.

This work is a veritable treasure trove of information for feminist researchers. It provides access to more than 3,400 file items, books, periodical articles, and pamphlets about reproduction available in the Women's Educational Resources Centre (WERC). The WERC Library was established in 1976 to make available a collection of women's studies materials to students, scholars, researchers, and educators. The collection includes between 40,000 and 50,000 items. Its major focus is the women's movement in Canada and the involvement of Canadian women in the international movement. In addition to this bibliography, direct online access to the WERC database is available. The collection may be searched by author, title, subject, date, document type, or geographic area. A simple system of designated numerical box codes allows numerical access to items in the WERC Library.

This guide contains a bibliographic citation with key index terms for every item in the collection pertaining to issues of female sexuality and reproductive health. Subjects covered include abortion, reproductive rights, surrogacy, teenage pregnancy, birth control, reproductive technologies, reproductive health, midwifery, family planning, genetic engineering, childbirth and pregnancy, fertility and infertility, fetal rights, and sex education. There are more than 280 entries on abortion and more than 170 entries on birth control. Bibliographic control for this type of literature has always presented a problem for librarians, and it has resulted in inadequate subject access for users. The extensive indexing of this collection helps to alleviate this problem.

One glaring omission from this work is a list of abbreviations to help the reader identify periodical sources. Despite this flaw, it is a valuable source for feminist researchers and a useful finding aid. Recommended for Canadian and United States academic libraries. — **Marilynn Green**

886. Preston, John, ed. **The Big Gay Book: A Man's Survival Guide for the 90's.** New York, Plume/Penguin Books, 1991. 534p. illus. index. $14.95pa. HQ76.2.U5P74. 306.76'62. LC 91-10375. ISBN 0-452-26621-1.

Preston, a prominent writer and editor in the gay community, has compiled this handsome illustrated guide to issues, opportunities, and resources of special interest to gay men. Included are political, legal, special interest (e.g., ethnic groups, hobbies, personal characteristics), professional, and community organizations; switchboards and hotlines; a broad range of print, electronic, and broadcast media; bookstores; gay studies and college-related organizations; religious groups; and entertainment opportunities. Individual entries range from address and telephone number or brief citation to extended narrative descriptions. In addition to directory information, well-grounded advice is offered on just about every aspect of gay life: how and why to organize, confronting discrimination and violence, political action, jobs, creating relationships, relating to families, coming out, supporting gay youth, finances, health, safe sex, and recovery from addictions and abuse.

The index is disappointing. All subject, name, and title headings are listed only under state and city names. The only direct subject access is provided by a comprehensive table of contents. The next edition will need a real subject index in addition to the geographic one.

All libraries that serve people interested in the gay experience need this book. Those libraries with few gay-oriented materials can use its media recommendations to strengthen their collections.

— **James D. Anderson**

SOCIAL WELFARE

887. **Assistance & Benefits Information Directory: A Guide to Programs and Printed Material....** Kay Gill, ed. Detroit, Omnigraphics, 1992. 2v. index. $155.00/set. HC110.P63A77. 361'.0025'73. LC 92-7645. ISBN 1-55888-423-8.

The past quarter century has witnessed the proliferation of a wide variety of programs that offer financial and other types of assistance to individuals rather than businesses. Until now, there has not been a reference work that described most of these varied benefit programs. This very useful set fills this information void.

Volume 1 covers more than 2,000 programs administered by federal or state governments and national and regional organizations. These entries are divided into six broad categories: health and social services, cultural affairs, housing and home energy, employment training, justice and legal services, and education. Each entry provides, when available, the type and amount of assistance, eligibility, requirements for aid, and contact person. A particularly helpful section contains a series of appendixes that give the names, addresses, and telephone numbers of the federal, state, and regional agencies that administer these assistance programs.

Volume 2 contains an annotated list of 1,200-plus publications that pertain to the benefit programs covered in volume 1. The publications include monographs, reports, journal articles, and pamphlets that discuss available assistance resources and are organized within the same six subject fields. Both volumes contain useful indexes that provide readers easy access to the information in this valuable reference tool. — **Jonathon Erlen**

SUBSTANCE ABUSE

888. Clements, Bonnie L., comp. **Drug Abuse Bibliography for 1988.** Troy, N.Y., Whitston Publishing, 1991. 790p. index. $85.00. LC 79-116588. ISBN 0-87875-412-1.

This is the 18th annual supplement to Joseph Menditto's *Drugs of Addiction and Non-Addiction*. It is nearly comprehensive for periodical literature for 1988 and also includes several 1987 entries that were omitted in the previous supplement. Fifty-five primary indexes have been checked for articles; 1,272 periodicals are covered. The arrangement for the periodical literature section is alphabetical under 440 different subjects, from abortion to women. Included are popular magazines (e.g., *Sports Illustrated, TV Guide*) as well as scientific journals (e.g., *Brain Research*) and several foreign scholarly periodicals. These entries are not annotated. There is an author index for the periodical literature, but a sample check of page 166 indicates that of 15 entries, 8 authors listed on that page were not cited for those particular entries in the author index. The coverage of books, monographs, and pamphlets is limited to 95 entries, of which 44 are government documents. There are 27 doctoral dissertations listed. It is hoped that future bibliographies will include more consistent author indexing to enhance rapid and complete citation retrieval. However, the list of subject headings and the list of journals cited help the user obtain a quick overview. This lengthy review of drug abuse will be useful to researchers.

— **Karen Y. Stabler**

889. Miletich, John J., comp. **Treatment of Cocaine Abuse: An Annotated Bibliography.** Westport, Conn., Greenwood Press, 1992. 234p. index. (Bibliographies and Indexes in Medical Studies, no.9). $49.95. RC568.C6M55. 016.61686'4706. LC 91-35403. ISBN 0-313-27839-3.

The well-publicized abuse of cocaine and crack in the United States raises a host of public policy and public health questions, not the least of which concern the physiological correlates, effects, and treatment of cocaine abuse. This bibliography annotates more than 600 books, book chapters, articles, dissertations, government documents, and other items on these and related aspects of cocaine abuse. Its scholarly and popular entries, which span the late nineteenth and twentieth centuries, are intended to be of use to psychologists, nurses, lawyers, sociologists, chemists, librarians, and interested laypeople.

Entries are arranged in four large chapters: "Definitions, Identification, Diagnosis"; "Treatment"; "Specific Occupations"; and "Women and Children." Within these sections, arrangement is alphabetical by author or title. The annotations are descriptive and range in length from a sentence to a paragraph; they often indicate the number of tables, figures, and footnotes or references in articles. The book also includes a list of acronyms and appendixes that provide common names for cocaine, relevant videocassettes, and a chronology of events in the history of cocaine. Author and subject indexes are supplied.

This is a good bibliography with strong coverage of literature drawn from a variety of health care and popular sources. However, the title is a bit misleading in that much more than treatment issues are addressed. There are entries on the causes and etiology of abuse; the incidence of abuse among various occupational groups; and an entire chapter on women and children that addresses, among other things, cocaine babies. Clearly, the book's title does not do justice to the content. Furthermore, the subject index does not fully access the entries. For example, while there is a whole chapter devoted to occupations, there is no specific access to these in the index. Consequently, finding all of the entries on baseball players, medical students, or lawyers would require scanning the entire chapter. These criticisms aside, this is a valuable resource on an important topic, and both public and academic libraries should find it useful. [R: Choice, Oct 92, p. 276] — **Stephen H. Aby**

890. O'Brien, Robert, and others. **The Encyclopedia of Drug Abuse.** 2d ed. New York, Facts on File, 1992. 500p. index. $45.00. HV5804.E94. 362.29'03. LC 89-71531. ISBN 0-8160-1956-8.

In 1984, the first edition of this book (see ARBA 85, entry 1580) was selected by both *Choice* and *Library Journal* as one of the outstanding reference books of the year. The number of entries in this new edition has doubled to more than 1,000. There are 40 additional pages in the entries section; the other sections remain about the same length in both editions. "The History of Drugs and Man" is an excellent background, but "A Glance at the Future" from the previous edition has unfortunately been omitted.

Designed for both lay and professional readers, the book is international in scope and covers a wide range of terms including medical, physical, psychological, and political topics. Entries range from one sentence to several pages. Some entries, such as *moonshine* and *quinine*, remain unchanged, while *prisoners and drug abuse* and *trafficking* have been significantly updated. Topics such as crack cocaine, ice, and role models have been added. The entry on heroin is more than four pages long and includes the alarming statistic that heroin use in the United States has possibly quadrupled in the last 10 years.

Although there are several dictionaries on drug abuse, this volume remains among the best. Recommended for all libraries. [R: BR, Nov/Dec 92, p. 53; RBB, 15 Feb 92, p. 1130]
— **Karen Y. Stabler**

891. Rebach, Howard M., and others. **Substance Abuse among Ethnic Minorities in America: A Critical Annotated Bibliography.** Hamden, Conn., Garland, 1992. 469p. index. (Garland Library of Sociology, v.20; Garland Reference Library of Social Science, v.737). $72.00. Z7164.D78S8. 016.36229'08693. LC 91-45032. ISBN 0-8153-0066-2.

This timely annotated bibliography contains articles from 65 different journals that cover ethnic minorities' abuse of alcohol and drugs. The authors state that substance abuse among groups that vary from the dominant culture need more careful and intensive study because members are especially high risk abusers due to poverty, substandard housing, and other anomie-producing conditions. In addition, alcohol and drugs of abuse are more readily available to minorities, and research has not kept up with the increased demographic trend among minorities. Some 168 articles published between 1973 and 1989 have been selected; however, the majority of entries are from 1985-1988. Entries range from two to five pages each and generally include type of article, purpose, method, results, discussion, and (the most useful section) the authors' evaluation. The evaluations tend to be critical. The majority (90) of the articles use Blacks as one of their population groups, while more than 40 include Hispanics, 28 include Native Americans, and 13 include Asian-Americans. There are more studies on alcohol than drug abuse. Particularly useful is a bibliographic guide that lists the articles by ethnic groups, age groups, topical approach, and substance abused. The reference list somewhat duplicates the guide to bibliography. There is no entry for 133 and two entries for 134. This bibliography is recommended for academic and large public libraries. — **Karen Y. Stabler**

892. Tullis, LaMond. **Handbook of Research on the Illicit Drug Trade.** Westport, Conn., Greenwood Press, 1991. 641p. index. $75.00. HV5801.T78. 363.4'5. LC 90-25218. ISBN 0-313-27846-6.

Produced in cooperation with the United Nations Research Institute for Social Development, this handbook is intended to provide researchers and interested laypeople with a guide to the literature on the socioeconomic and political consequences — and to some extent the causes — of the international drug trade. It addresses the complex web of factors that affect the production, distribution, and consumption of illicit drugs, factors that, in a sense, make up the infrastructure of the problem.

The handbook is divided into two major parts. The first part contains literature reviews on the production and consumption of cocaine, heroin, and cannabis; the consequences of these illegal behaviors; and the proffered new solutions for dealing with the problem. The second part has a selective, annotated bibliography of 2,058 books, articles, and press reports on illicit drugs. The bibliography is arranged alphabetically by author, with descriptive annotations ranging from a sentence to a paragraph in length. Coverage of the illicit drug trade is international in scope and includes some citations to sources in Spanish. Most of the entries were published after 1980.

The only drawback to this thorough and informative guide is the subject index. The subject headings, specifically those that refer to the annotated bibliography, are far too broad and make little use of subheadings. This results in numerous subject headings with large numbers of cited entries. For example, there are over 200 entry numbers listed under "cannabis." Clearly, subheadings are needed and would enhance subject searching; this is especially important given the author arrangement of the bibliography. Nevertheless, this is a useful source and is appropriate for college and university reference collections. [R: Choice, Feb 92, p. 880] — **Stephen H. Aby**

YOUTH AND CHILD DEVELOPMENT

893. **Guide to Federal Funding for Child Care and Early Childhood Development.** Pamela B. Silverman and others, eds. Arlington, Va., Government Information Services, 1992. 1v. (various paging). index. $128.00 looseleaf w/binder. ISBN 0-933544-50-2.

Anyone who has waded through the *Federal Register* (Office of the Federal Register, daily) for funding information will appreciate the clarity of this work, which is published by a private research firm. More than 40 programs worth more than $15 billion in grants, loans, tax credits, and contracts are included. Arrangement is by broad topics, such as aid for children with disabilities. A subject index provides quicker access to specific interests, such as foster grandparents, literacy programs, and child nutrition. Each chapter includes information for eligibility, procedures for applications, funding levels, and funding restrictions. Contacts at the federal and state levels are also included, along with citations to relevant legislation or regulations.

This source is complementary to the equally expensive *National Guide to Funding for Children, Youth and Families* (see ARBA 92, entry 827), which contains 2,500-plus listings of private and community foundations and corporate giving programs that support children. It is unfortunate that the personnel who need this data the most (e.g., directors of Head Start programs) are the least able to afford this book. Because the information will be dated soon, libraries will need to purchase cautiously and share it with interested parties so that federal dollars can be put to good use. — **Ilene F. Rockman**

894. Honig, Alice Sterling, and Donna Sasse Wittmer. **Prosocial Development in Children: Caring, Helping, and Cooperating: A Bibliographic Resource Guide.** Hamden, Conn., Garland, 1992. 384p. index. (Reference Books on Family Issues, v.19; Garland Reference Library of Social Science, v.538). $49.00. Z7164.C5H66. 016.305'23'1. LC 91-36676. ISBN 0-8240-7846-2.

This annotated bibliography is a comprehensive effort by the authors. It contains 584 references that cover theories, research, assessments, and strategies in the field of prosocial development, or altruism, in children and adolescents over the last 20 years. It begins with a preface that is highly informative, offering the reader a substantial taste of what is to come.

The references are divided into two sections. The first contains research references about variables, such as empathy, loyalty, cooperation, and sharing. Theoretical articles address such issues as how children learn and develop prosocial behaviors and moral judgment. The second section, for the most part, contains strategies and applications to help parents, teachers, counselors, and other caregivers, in school and at home, to promote social behaviors and interactions. Entries are listed alphabetically by author in both sections, making it fairly easy to track down an author by name.

Overall, the annotations are very good. They are often lengthy and give readers a good idea of the content and thrust of the resources. However, the writing style can be cumbersome and confusing, both in the annotations and in the preface. Also, the typeface has problems. Throughout the book, lowercase "i's" are almost indistinguishable from lowercase "l's." In general, the book has the appearance of a rough draft.

A more serious problem concerns the subject index. First, it refers to page numbers rather than entry numbers, but this fact is not explained. Second, the page numbers under the subject headings often do not lead to those subjects. For example, under *shyness*, references are given to pages 279 and 324, but neither page includes the word *shyness* nor anything specifically related to the topic. Finally, the index is not comprehensive; for example, the term *cooperative learning* appears on page 287, but the index does not list that page under the subject heading.

Without a usable subject index, this work loses much of its value as a reference book, which is unfortunate. The excellent annotations and obvious hard work of the authors deserve much better treatment. [R: Choice, Oct 92, p. 275]—**Marilyn Rothschild**

895. Weiss, Irving, and Anne D. Weiss. **Reflections on Childhood: A Quotations Dictionary.** Santa Barbara, Calif., ABC-Clio, 1991. 398p. index. $50.00. PN6084.C49R44. 305.23. LC 91-24746. ISBN 0-87436-646-1.

This nicely printed book is aptly titled because it does indeed reflect on the state of childhood. The text is divided by subject matter, usually allocating about two pages per subject. The alphabetically arranged subjects begin with adaptability and include memories of childhood, discipline, education, family, habits, intelligence, love, manners, play, respect, shame, talking back, and willfulness. The authors whose works are quoted include well-known individuals in the fields of literature (e.g., Agatha Christie, C. Day Lewis), biological sciences (e.g., Charles Darwin), education (e.g., John Dewey), philosophy (e.g., Immanual Kant, Bertrand Russell), and psychoanalysis (e.g., Sigmund Freud, Ernest Jones). Not only are the subjects and authors diverse, but dates range from Ancient Greece through the late twentieth century. This dictionary is a gentle yet realistic treatment of childhood. [R: RBB, 1 Jan 92, p. 852]—**Celia J. Wintz**

896. Wilson, Miriam J. Williams. **Help for Children from Infancy to Adulthood: A National Directory....** 5th ed. Shepherdstown, W.Va., Rocky River, 1991. 251p. index. $10.95pa. LC 91-062711. ISBN 0-944576-07-9.

Compiled by a registered nurse and mother of eight, this source lists crisis hotlines, helplines, organizations, clearinghouses, and support services for families. Close to 500 organizations are listed to help with problems or emergencies, but no criteria for inclusion or sources consulted are noted. Arrangement is by broad subject category (e.g., child safety, parental support), with entries reflecting such groups as the National PTA, the Consumer Product Safety Commission, and the American Allergy Association. Each entry provides a brief statement of purpose, followed by an address and a telephone number. A subject index concludes the work; it is especially useful for ready-reference, as it lists not only the page number of the entry but also the name of the organization and its telephone number. Users can easily find education enhancers (e.g., Science-By-Mail), toys for special children, hotlines for missing children, regional poison control centers, and alcohol abuse services. In addition, the inside front cover conveniently lists 24-hour national hotlines.

Libraries that already own the slightly less expensive *Directory of National Helplines* (see ARBA 91, entry 849) may find some duplicate information. This work is suitable for school or public libraries, caregivers, social workers, law enforcement officials, medical professionals, education personnel, and parents. [R: RBB, 1 Mar 92, p. 1306-07]—**Ilene F. Rockman**

17 Statistics, Demography, and Urban Studies

DEMOGRAPHY

897. **Demographic Statistics 1991. Bevolkerungsstatistik. Statistiques Demographiques.** Brussels, Statistical Office of the European Communities; distr., Lanham, Md., UNIPUB, 1991. 189p. $13.00pa. ISBN 92-826-2758-6.

This publication will aid the study of demographic trends within the European Community and enable country-to-country comparisons. Interesting phenomena, such as where infant mortality rates are falling and when the number of legal abortions was highest, are illustrated. The tables, with accompanying graphs, are arranged in 10 sections. Nine topical areas (e.g., population, fertility, marriage, and divorce) are followed by a section on the Federal Republic of Germany as constituted in October 1990. The 1980s are emphasized, with selected coverage of the 1960s and 1970s, some historical data back to 1949, and projections for 2000 and 2010. These figures show a total population that is expected to peak at 334 million in 2010 and then fall.

Access to the tables and graphs is accomplished through the detailed table of contents, which is given in French, German, and English. Any limitations (e.g., to EUR 12) or additions (e.g., Yugoslavia, Turkey) are so designated in the contents. Section C has population (e.g., age, sex, density) data for cities and areas within member nations, an area of interest to persons investigating business opportunities in Europe. There is no topical index; however, the table of contents should suffice. Any inconsistencies in the data will disappear as member general population censuses are synchronized. This volume is recommended for academic libraries and libraries with international business collections.
—**Sandra E. Belanger**

898. Goyer, Doreen S., and Gera E. Draaijer. **The Handbook of National Population Censuses: Europe.** Westport, Conn., Greenwood Press, 1992. 544p. maps. index. $95.00. HA37.E93G69. 304.6'0723. LC 91-39111. ISBN 0-313-28426-1.

This is a compilation of censuses and population counts made in Europe over the last two centuries. Although the handbook contains a bit of population data, it is not intended to be a record of population and its changes over the years. In this it is very different from a number of such sources, the most extensive of which is probably *Four Thousand Years of Urban Growth* by Tertius Chandler (St. David's University Press, 1987). Instead, this book lists and describes enumeration methods made in all sovereign nations in Europe and certain other territories that fulfill specified criteria. It is the last-published of three volumes that cover the world. An introduction defines and describes the various methods used and the conditions that differentiate between them. The entries for each country give the kinds of data obtained and the conditions under which the census or population count was held.

This book will be of interest to students of demography and is not likely to attract a wider readership. Overall, it is a valuable reference for those with an interest in how demographical data have been obtained and how the methods and results differ from one epoch or country to another.
—**Arthur R. Upgren**

899. Lainhart, Ann S. **State Census Records.** Baltimore, Md., Genealogical Publishing, 1992. 116p. $17.95. LC 92-72944. ISBN 0-8063-1362-5.

State censuses are often ignored or overlooked as resources by genealogists. However, Lainhart points out in a brief, informative introduction that they serve to fill in gaps for missing federal censuses; they may provide different data; and they are not bound by the 72-year federal waiting period for release of census information. This work is a significant contribution to genealogical research because it provides the first comprehensive list of state census records ever published. Lainhart challenges the accuracy of five of the standard sources that discuss state censuses, and she reports on the availability of state census data in individual state summaries that range from less than a page to several pages in length. Included are locations of original state censuses and identification of published material. Lainhart possesses an impressive background in genealogy that lends authority to the book. *State Census Records* should be added to any collection with an interest in genealogy. [R: LJ, 1 Sept 92, pp. 168-70; RBB, 15 Oct 92, p. 460]—**Donald E. Collins**

900. Moffat, Riley. **Population History of Eastern U.S. Cities and Towns, 1790-1870.** Metuchen, N.J., Scarecrow, 1992. 227p. $42.50. HA218.M64. 304.6'0974. LC 92-6364. ISBN 0-8108-2553-8.

This historical gazetteer fills a lacuna in the available bibliography of populations of U.S. communities. Its coverage is chronological from 1790 to 1870 and geographically eastward from the states that form the west side of the Mississippi River, from Minnesota to Louisiana. Except for a very brief introduction and bibliography, the work is made up of tables arranged alphabetically by state (but with West Virginia combined with Virginia as the two did not separate until 1863). Each table consists of communities with at least one viable census within the period covered; the year of each census is given.

The book would be more convenient to use if the state in question were labeled on every page; as it is, one must frequently consult the index. It also avoids the question of changing corporate limits. For example, New York and Brooklyn are given as separate communities, as they should be, because they did not merge until 1898, long after the period covered here. Many less famous examples of this kind occur, and a knowledge of changing corporate limits is essential for scholarly use. Also, a column for remarks would be useful to clarify special cases. For example, Alexandria, Virginia, was in the District of Columbia until its return by an act of retrocession in 1846. Here it is incorrectly listed under both D.C. and Virginia with identical populations. Annotations that could clarify such confusion are not given.—**Arthur R. Upgren**

901. **The 1920 Federal Population Census: Catalog of Microfilm Available. [Supplement to Volume I,** *AGLL Catalog***].** Bountiful, Utah, American Genealogical Lending Library; distr., Bountiful, Utah, Historic Resources, 1991. 79p. $5.00pa.

This catalog was created to assist those who wish to order microfilm of the 1920 census enumerations and the 1920 soundex index to the census records. It is arranged alphabetically by state and then by county, and gives series and roll numbers for each of the 10,661 rolls of microfilm. It also contains information on the enumeration districts, research hints, and an explanation of the soundex coding. The catalog is identical to the 1991 National Archives publication of the same title (but subtitled *Catalog of National Archives Microfilm*), with the exception that the prices of the microfilm are less than the film sold by the National Archives. Recommended.—**Carol Willsey Bell**

STATISTICS

Bibliography

902. Harter, H. Leon. **The Chronological Annotated Bibliography of Order Statistics. Volume IV: 1962-1963.** Columbus, Ohio, American Sciences Press, 1991. 173p. (American Sciences Press Series in Mathematical and Management Sciences). $95.00pa. LC 81-66077. ISBN 0-935950-22-2.

This is a continuation of the series that briefly summarizes virtually all papers on order statistics. Materials summarized include books, journal articles, dissertations, theses, technical reports, and notes from a wide variety of sources (including some not in English). The work is encapsulated in around 10 to 20 lines of text, with all references (by last name and year). Volumes 5 to 7 (to be completed in the next few years) will form a closed set with respect to references and will cover papers up to 1970. For those with a research interest in order statistics, this series will be extremely valuable.

—Robert A. Campbell

Dictionaries and Encyclopedias

903. Garwood, Alfred N., and Louise L. Hornor, eds. **Dictionary of U.S. Government Statistical Terms.** Palo Alto, Calif., Information Publications, 1991. 247p. $50.00; $45.00pa. ISBN 0-931845-25-4; 0-931845-24-6pa.

Nonspecialist users of U.S. government publications, such as Census Bureau products, often need to know the precise definitions of federal statistical terms, such as the difference between *money income* and *personal income*. This dictionary provides convenient access to more than 1,000 terms with specialized meanings used extensively in federal publications. Each alphabetical entry includes the term, the defining agency or agencies, brief collection methodology, and related terms connected by *see* and *see also* references. Highly specialized statistical and technical terms, ratios, and indexes are not included. A few definitions come from private sector data reprinted by the government. In addition to definitions, a bibliography of source publications from which definitions were taken (many verbatim) and a list of abbreviations are included.

While the term *zip code* is defined, the meaning of the acronym is not. Also, while *Gross National Product* (GNP) is defined, the term *Gross Domestic Product* (GDP) is omitted. However, the dictionary is very useful, accurate, and reasonably complete within its scope. Recommended for public and academic library documents and reference collections. [R: Choice, Sept 92, p. 76; WLB, June 92, pp. 108-110] – **Jeanette C. Smith**

904. **The HarperCollins Dictionary of Statistics.** By Roger Porkess. New York, HarperPerennial/HarperCollins, 1991. 267p. $25.00; $12.95pa. LC 90-56000. ISBN 0-06-271527-5; 0-06-461020-9pa.

This dictionary provides an in-depth explanation of terms found in the study of statistics, with more than 450 entries and extensive diagrams and charts. It includes lists of symbols (4 pages) and formulas (6 pages) and 22 statistical tables. Definitions are well written, understandable, and quite complete. As an example, the term *coefficient of determination* is explained in two and one-half pages and includes a figure and an example. The term *confidence interval* (CI) is given three pages and has an example for calculating a CI for a mean as well as a proportion. It also lists a cross-reference to *Fisher's Z transform*. Occasionally, some difficulty in understanding a definition is encountered. In the definition of the *Buffon's Needle*, a probability of 2l/(a*pi) is given. It is difficult to distinguish between 2l and 21; it would have been better to use 2L or 2*l.

Overall, the book is very readable and accurate. It will prove a useful companion for a quick review of terminology or for understanding new words or concepts. – **Robert A. Campbell**

905. Theriault, Yves, with Estelle Beauregard and Michel Charuést. **Statistics and Surveys Vocabulary. Vocabulaire de la Statistique et des Enquetes.** Ottawa, Department of the Secretary of State of Canada, 1992. 555p. (Terminology Bulletin, 208). $35.95pa. (U.S.). 310'.3. ISBN 0-660-57072-6.

This specialized dictionary was developed by staff in the Translation Bureau and Statistics Canada in the Department of the Secretary of State of Canada. It includes about 4,300 entries and 730 definitions. Arranged in a very readable two-column format, it has two sections. The first is alphabetized by English terms, the second by French terms. A broad range of terms may be found, including those concerned with testing and measurement, sampling terminology, mathematical terms, and experimental design. Because not all of the terms are defined, the use of this dictionary by those who are not familiar with statistics and experimental design is necessarily limited. The book will, however, be very useful to English speakers who are trying to read and understand the results of studies written in French and vice versa. This work will be most useful in university or research libraries and could be an essential tool for some researchers and students. – **Margaret McKinley**

Handbooks and Yearbooks

906. Ambry, Margaret, and Cheryl Russell. **The Official Guide to the American Marketplace: The Real Facts about How Well-Educated, Healthy, Family-Oriented, Rich, Productive, Demanding, and Opinionated We Are.** Ithaca, N.Y., New Strategist, 1992. 477p. maps. index. $69.95. ISBN 0-9628092-1-7.

This ready-reference work draws information from U.S. government sources such as the 1990 Census, the Bureau of Labor Statistics, and the Federal Reserve Board. Tables and graphs provide information on what the authors consider the eight major factors that drive consumer markets: population characteristics, household characteristics, income, spending and wealth, labor force, education, health, and attitudes. The last chapter in the book lists 15 federal agencies and their addresses and telephone numbers, along with the type and cost of information available from each. The book concludes with a glossary and index. Although the latter is only two pages long, it seems to be comprehensive, especially when used in conjunction with the list of tables and maps.

The title makes it appear that the book is only meant for businesses that seek information about consumers, but this is not its sole use. It also provides data for talks and research papers, and sometimes (like a book of lists) the information is very interesting to read. Librarians, however, will not like the skimpy citations provided with each table, as it will be tedious to check the original information source. Despite this limitation, the book is recommended. [R: LJ, Aug 92, p. 86; RBB, Aug 92, p. 2040]
—**Nathan M. Smith**

907. **Comecon Data 1990.** edited by the Vienna Institute for Comparative Economic Studies. Westport, Conn., Greenwood Press, 1991. 449p. index. $85.00. ISBN 0-313-28392-3. ISSN 0263-3701.

This is a comprehensive statistical assessment of population, national income accounts, production, consumption, foreign trade and debt, domestic prices and finance, energy, currency, and the standard of living in the formerly socialist countries of Eastern and Central Europe in 1990. Data are included for Bulgaria, the Czech and Slovak Federal Republic, the German Democratic Republic, Hungary, Poland, Romania, the Soviet Union, and Yugoslavia. There are lists of references and sources and a useful index.

This is a most useful statistical guide both because its many tables and graphs are consistent and well organized and (more significantly) because it makes a good deal of quantitative information more accessible than would otherwise be the case. Not only is it a compilation of insightful economic and social indicators from a diverse array of local, regional, and international sources but it is also a collection of data from sources previously available only in the languages of the Comecon countries.

This is the final edition of this handbook in its present form, because 1990 was the last year of existence of Comecon and even the final year of existence for a few of its member states. However, the dramatic economic and political events of the recent past only intensify the importance of having and analyzing useful quantitative information. In order to comprehend the profound transition of this region, it must first be placed in its proper historical context.—**Timothy E. Sullivan**

908. **County and City Extra, 1992: Annual Metro, City and County Data Book.** Courtenay M. Slater and George E. Hall, eds. Lanham, Md., Bernan Press, 1992. 1101p. maps. $79.95. ISBN 0-89059-004-4. ISSN 1059-9096.

Slater, former chief economist for the U.S. Department of Commerce, and Hall, former associate director of the Census Bureau, have edited this massive reference book on all the states, counties, and metropolitan areas in the United States. Able to stand without bookends, this sturdy large volume is the first publication of Bernan Press, a private distributor of U.S. government publications. The work is intended to be an annual update to the *County and City Data Book* (Bureau of the Census, 1988), a popular library reference tool that is marred only by its infrequent publication.

This book, drawn primarily from the 1990 Census and data from other federal agencies, includes statistics on land areas, population, crime, health services, education, housing, employment, climate, trade, income, and other areas of social and economic activity. The opening section offers selected population and economic comparisons (with rank orders) of the 75 largest counties, the 75 largest metropolitan areas, and the 50 states (plus the District of Columbia). The remainder of the volume presents selected data on geographic areas listed in alphabetical order. Tables A and B, for instance, include 202 statistics for each state and each of the 3,143 counties and 337 metropolitan areas within the states. Tables C and D present 134 statistics for the 951 cities with 1980 populations greater than 25,000, and 12 statistics for the 11,000-plus geographic areas with 1980 populations greater than 2,500. Concluding the book are several useful appendixes that define the geographic concepts and codes used in the volume, list and locate on state maps the various geographic areas, and provide sources for the data included in the tables. This easy-to-read data book, complete with maps and explanatory appendixes, will benefit researchers interested in finding the latest information about our metropolitan centers. [R: LJ, Aug 92, p. 88; WLB, Sept 92, p. 111]—**Terry D. Bilhartz**

909. Hornor, Edith R., ed. **Almanac of the 50 States: Basic Data Profiles with Comparative Tables.** 1992 ed. Palo Alto, Calif., Information Publications, 1992. 447p. $50.00; $42.50pa. ISBN 0-931845-28-9; 0-931845-27-0pa. ISSN 0887-0519.

This handy, annual ready-reference source has not changed its format since last reviewed (see ARBA 86, entry 95). It is still in two parts. The first profiles every state, the District of Columbia, and the whole United States. Information given for each profile consists of 13 subject categories: state summary; geography and environment; demographics and characteristics of the population; vital statistics and health; education; social insurance and welfare programs; housing and construction; government and elections; governmental finance; crime, law enforcement, and courts; labor and income; economy, business, industry, and agriculture; and communication, energy, and transportation. The comparative tables in the second part of the book give rankings for each of 54 selected characteristics chosen from the state profiles (e.g., households, average cost per hospital stay, high school graduates, crime rate, personal income per capita). The 1992 edition includes 1990 census data, and the publishers claim that every state's data have been revised and updated. As a first source for basic information on the states, this is a valuable tool for most libraries.—**Nathan M. Smith**

910. **A Matter of Fact: Statements Containing Statistics on Current Social, Economic, and Political Issues. [Volume] 14-15 1991.** C. Edward Wall, ed. Ann Arbor, Mich., Pierian Press, 1992. 583p. $74.50pa./yr. ISBN 0-87650-305-9.

This reference book consists of abstracts of current statistics and facts on socioeconomic, political, cultural, and environmental topics of interest to the general public. Abstracts are from more than 200 newspapers and periodicals published or received in 1991. The sources of information are generally available in libraries. The *Congressional Record* and Congressional hearings are included. Library of Congress subject headings are followed, and abundant cross-references refer to this volume as well as to volume 12.

This book is not comprehensive in coverage, nor are sources of statistics cited in the newspapers and periodicals mentioned. However, the work will be helpful to school, public, and undergraduate libraries. It is available online on both FirstSearch and EPIC.—**Karen Y. Stabler**

911. Mitchell, B. R. **International Historical Statistics: Europe 1750-1988.** 3d ed. New York, Stockton Press, 1992. 942p. $250.00. ISBN 1-56159-038-X.

This book lists, as its title implies, historical data for the constituent countries of Europe from 1750 through 1988. Population, labor force, agriculture, industry, trade, transport, finance, and education constitute most of the major categories. A serious attempt is made to subdivide the continent into autonomous regions in order to cope with national boundary changes while providing as much continuity as possible. Definitions of terms and limitations to the data are carefully explained in the introductory remarks.

This is the kind of reference work that is very limited in appeal but very necessary and valuable to those in need of firm historical facts about Europe and its individual states. It belongs in any reference library because its material is easily understood by the layperson.—**Arthur R. Upgren**

912. Morgan, Kathleen O'Leary, Scott Morgan, and Neal Quitno, eds. **State Rankings, 1991: A Statistical View of the 50 United States.** Lawrence, Kans., Morgan Quitno, 1991. 347p. index. $39.95pa. ISBN 0-9625531-1-5. ISSN 1057-3623.

This work contains data that comes directly from original sources (noted where possible). It is useful for comparing and contrasting statistics such as state government debt per capita, total, and percent of national total. Comparisons can be made on agriculture, crime and law enforcement, defense, economy, education, employment and labor, energy and environment, geography, government finance, health, housing, population, social welfare, and transportation.

This edition is 25 percent larger than the 1990 one (see ARBA 91, entry 901). It also relies less on the *Statistical Abstract of the United States* (Bureau of the Census, annual) and more on original sources, such as the 1990 census, for populations and households. The volume is entertaining, educational, and easy to read and understand. It would be nice to have the information on a floppy disk for inclusion in reports and papers and for extended analysis on correlations and modeling.

—**Robert A. Campbell**

913. **Statistics Sources 1993: A Subject Guide to Data....** 16th ed. Jacqueline Wasserman O'Brien and Steven R. Wasserman, eds. Detroit, Gale, 1992. 2v. $345.00/set. LC 84-82356. ISBN 0-8103-7665-2. ISSN 0585-198X.

This ready-reference tool has been reviewed in ARBA six times (see ARBA 87, entry 838 for the most recent one). Since the 1987 review (of the 10th edition) its price has increased 38 percent, but citations have also increased from 48,000 to 95,000, and sections have been added for federal statistical telephone contacts and federal statistical databases. The 16th edition seems little changed, however, from the 15th. The prefaces are identical except for a note in this new edition that says names used for Eastern European countries and Yugoslavia are unchanged from the previous one. But some changes have been made. A quick check of the first three sections (seven pages) of the selected bibliography of key statistical sources shows that two entries have been removed from the 16th edition, seven have been added, and one source has been updated from a 1988 edition to a 1990 edition.—**Nathan M. Smith**

914. Wood, Elizabeth J., and Floris W. Wood. **She Said, He Said: What Men and Women** *Really* **Think about Money, Sex, Politics and Other Issues of Essence.** Detroit, Visible Ink Press/Gale, 1992. 284p. $9.95pa. ISBN 0-8103-9411-1.

The statistical data offered in this book are derived from a very much larger work, *An American Profile—Opinions and Behavior, 1972-1989* (see ARBA 92, entry 79). This book focuses on male and female opinions on many important issues connected with family, money, work, politics, sex, and religion. Despite the respectable polling system by which the original material was collected (the General Social Survey conducted by the National Opinion Research Center of the University of Chicago), *She Said, He Said* touts itself chiefly for its entertainment value and its ability to provoke lively conversation. Its serious import is undercut by the curiously flippant attitude of the Woods. Their preface, for instance, quotes Thomas Jefferson as postulating three kinds of lies: "lies, damned lies and statistics." And the racy comments that accompany the various sections and specific questions often seem dismissive of what is revealed. It seems as if the Woods' mild but persistent amusement at the differences in the outlook of the two genders proceeds from an attitude that amusement is appropriate because the differences need not be taken seriously.—**John B. Beston**

Indexes

915. **IIS: Index to International Statistics 1990: A Guide to the Statistical Publications of International Intergovernmental Organizations.** Bethesda, Md., Congressional Information Service, 1991. 2v. $580.00/set. ISBN 0-88692-204-6.

This is a master guide and index to current English-language statistical publications of about 100 major intergovernmental organizations, including the United Nations, the European Community, the Organization of American States, commodity organizations, and development banks. The annual editions of IIS, of which this is the eighth, cumulate and supersede quarterly issues of the abstracts and indexes, which are also cumulative. Quarterly issues, in turn, cumulate and supersede monthly issues. One five-year cumulation, covering 1983-1987, has been published.

Data indexed include economic, demographic, industrial, and social statistics. In the index volume the largest index is arranged by subjects, names, and geographic areas, and subarranged by major geographical areas. There are also indexes by categories, such as industry, and by issuing sources.

Finally, there is a title index and an index of publication numbers. Indexed items include issuing agency, title, publication type, and abstract number. There are also lists of selected standard classifications of commodities and industries and members of selected intergovernmental organizations. Many of the publications indexed are available in the IIS Microfiche Library. All are abstracted in a separate volume, arranged by issuing agency. Abstracts of periodicals are especially thorough and include data sources, format and data presentation, and amount of statistical data provided.

While this publication is clearly not one that every library can afford, every librarian should be aware of its existence. It provides ready access to statistical data that would be difficult and time-consuming to obtain otherwise. Meticulously compiled and easy to use, IIS will be demanded by the clienteles of college, university, research, and corporate libraries. — **Margaret McKinley**

916. Skapura, Robert, ed. **Charts, Graphs & Stats Index 1988-1991.** Fort Atkinson, Wis., Highsmith Press, 1992. 285p. $42.00. ISBN 0-917846-09-5. ISSN 1060-1465.

This is an index to the graphically illustrated statistics found in nine popular, widely available magazines: *U.S. News and World Report, Business Week, Newsweek, Time, Black Enterprise, Scholastic Update, FDA Consumer, Bulletin of the Atomic Scientists*, and *Ms.* The editor states that these magazines contain the largest number of graphically illustrated statistics in all subject areas. The index lists 3,300 unique entries and approximately 5,300 total entries for the period covered.

Traditional graphs, charts, diagrams, and maps are indexed, but excluded are what the editor considers trivial subjects, public opinion surveys, and projections (e.g., the budget impact of the Democratic proposal on taxes). The main part of the index is an alphabetical/topical list of citations. Enough information is listed under a topic to clarify the content of the chart or graph and to find it in the appropriate magazine. The last part of the index is a helpful alphabetical list of subject headings.

Libraries, including school libraries, will have most of the magazines that are indexed, and this work should be helpful to the researching student for whom it was designed. Recommended. [R: RBB, 1 Sept 92, pp. 82-85] — **Nathan M. Smith**

URBAN STUDIES

917. Barlow, Diane, and Steven Wasserman, comps. **Moving and Relocation Sourcebook: A Reference Guide to the 100 Largest Metropolitan Areas in the United States.** Detroit, Omnigraphics, 1992. 1v. (various paging). maps. index. $140.00. HT334.U5M5. 307.76'4'0973. LC 91-43714. ISBN 1-55888-309-6.

An average of one out of every five families moves each year. This relocation sourcebook will meet their destination needs with its detailed information on the 100 most populated U.S. metropolitan areas and their components. Preliminary pages explain the book's coverage and organization and offer detailed tips on the moving process. In the major section of the directory, users will easily find facts in the straightforward A to Z arrangement by principal city, even if they are unfamiliar with the U.S. Bureau of the Census jargon used in dividing the country into metropolitan statistical areas (a system the compilers have adapted for their use). Triple access aids to identify these city entries include an opening chart that notes city and county components under their metropolitan areas, a compilation by state of metropolitan areas within its borders, and a general index that locates all entities that appear in the text. No attempt is made to rank the areas according to desirability, as is done in *Places Rated Almanac* (see ARBA 91, entry 908). Details within each entry do present an indication of that location's demographics, economic factors, government, quality of life, and cultural advantages. Readers familiar with specific areas may quibble about the inclusion or omission of specific data. For instance, components of the Phoenix, Arizona, entry fail to include the fast-growing city of Chandler and the retirement communities of Sun City and Sun City West, destinations of increasing numbers of movers. Appendixes include Census Bureau maps of each state with the statistical areas defined; a ranking of the entities by land area, population, and population density; and a 1990-1991 housing costs survey by city. Librarians will find this well-organized, legible sourcebook to be a user-friendly, one-stop compilation of pertinent area information and an unqualified boon to their mobile citizenry. [R: RBB, July 92, p. 1962; RQ, Fall 92, pp. 117-18; WLB, June 92, pp. 114-16] — **Eleanor Ferrall**

918. Carpenter, Allan, with Carl Provose, comps. **Facts about the Cities.** Bronx, N.Y., H. W. Wilson, 1992. 473p. $50.00. HT123.C385. 307.76'0973. LC 91-19057. ISBN 0-9242-0800-5.

This is the initial edition of a book that features data of many kinds for 331 American cities. The list includes almost all cities with a population greater than 75,000 and a selection of smaller places. The cities are ordered alphabetically by state and similarly within each state. Following a descriptive paragraph, the facts for each city are grouped by climate, population, work force, cost of living, taxes, housing, education, library facilities, government, crime, health, cultural resources, and a few other categories.

The book brings together information drawn from a variety of governmental and other sources. However, it lacks a clear distinction between a central city and its metropolitan area. Information contained in many of the subgroups (e.g., housing, education, cultural resources) applies sometimes to the central city only and sometimes to the larger region. Thus, for example, the cities of the greater Boston area—Boston, Brockton, Cambridge, Lowell, Lynn, Newton, and Quincy—are each listed as having a metropolitan population of almost four million, although the breakdown by age and race differs among them. The division between these cities of the cultural, communications, and sports facilities that serve the entire area strikes an artificial note; such division among core cities and suburbs reduces the usefulness of the data in some cases.

The climate data is useful, but it is marred by an error. The figures given for the highest and lowest monthly temperatures are not averages as stated. The temperature given for the highest monthly average is in fact the mean daily high temperature for the hottest month, and the lowest monthly average is the average nighttime low for the coldest month. Because the spread between the mean diurnal high and low temperatures varies between seasons and between cities, this information is of little value as given. [R: Choice, June 92, p. 1516; LJ, Aug 92, p. 88; RBB, 15 May 92, p. 1716; SLJ, May 92, p. 31; WLB, May 92, p. 124]—**Arthur R. Upgren**

919. Giese, Lester J., L. Anne Thornton, and William Kinnaman. **The 99 Best Residential and Recreational Communities in America for Vacation, Retirement & Investment Planning.** New York, John Wiley, 1992. 274p. maps. index. $34.95; $17.95pa. MT169.57.U6G54. 307.76'8. LC 91-4756. ISBN 0-471-54577-5; 0-471-54578-3pa.

This is one of a class of books that makes a list from a self-contained set of principles—accept the guidelines and the conclusions follow. In this case, 99 residential and recreational communities are featured out of the thousands in existence. The greatest value of the book for many readers is likely to be its first 36 pages. Within these is a valuable discussion of the definition and the legal and social characteristics of such communities, criteria for the choices made by the authors, and points to consider for prospective buyers.

The book has a shortcoming: the choices and criteria are very strong on sports but rarely consider cultural opportunities. This may be why so many of the favorites are Sunbelt properties. For example, skiing facilities are well featured (despite the Sunbelt tilt), but theaters, concerts, library facilities, and other cultural amenities are ignored. With the graying of America, this imbalance will be in need of review in the future.

This book is not highly recommended for libraries on a tight budget because it will quickly become dated. Even if they remain unchanged, the criteria are likely to lead to a partially different set of choices next year, as new or improved communities come into being. The useful introductory information is probably available in other sources.—**Arthur R. Upgren**

920. Marlin, John Tepper, with others. **The Livable Cities Almanac.** New York, HarperPerennial/HarperCollins, 1992. 416p. $30.00; $14.00pa. HN60.M36. 306'.0973'021. LC 91-16666. ISBN 0-06-270035-9; 0-06-273134-3pa.

Although the title implies that this book merely rates cities for a casually curious reader, this volume is a much more valuable resource. It is a well-rounded discussion of the environmental factors—both natural and social—that contribute to the quality of life in one's home and community. Much of the volume contains city-by-city reports on seven issues that help to determine a city's "livability": mortality rates, crime (more positively known in this book as "public safety"), economy, environmental conditions and weather, health resources availability, publicly sponsored recreational services, and school health services. Another category, called "disclosure," is a rating of the level of cooperation the data collectors received in trying to elicit information from city agencies and officials. More than 100 cities or urban areas are listed in alphabetical order by city name. Each entry includes a summary pictograph that serves as an easily read report card for every city. Many of the entries include the names of city officials to contact for further information.

The first eight chapters of the book are thoughtful, well-documented remarks about the factors considered in the cities' evaluations and about the impact of an individual's specific habits or practices on the health of the environment. The contents of these chapters range from recipes for safe household cleaning solutions to explanations of pollutant categories to a discussion of the success of health education programs in public schools. Also included are lists of organizations (addresses, telephone numbers, and purposes) that are good sources of information about health issues.

This volume is an excellent resource for all libraries. The paperback edition will be a worthwhile investment for personal reference collections because of its content, Marlin's broad approach to the idea of a healthy environment, and the source information embedded in the text. [R: LJ, 15 May 92, p. 86; RBB, 1 June 92, p. 1777; WLB, June 92, pp. 114-16] — **Linda A. Naru**

921. Rosenberg, Lee, and Saralee Rosenberg. **50 Fabulous Places to Retire in America.** Hawthorne, N.J., Career Press, 1991. 251p. maps. $14.95pa. ISBN 0-934829-29-2.

This volume is an armchair tour and shopping expedition for people who are dreaming of a particular retirement lifestyle but are not sure where (or if) it exists. Among the selected locations are college towns, military towns, state capitals, and golf and ski meccas, with climates that vary from tropical, semitropical, desert, and semiarid to year-round mild. The book provides relevant facts, inside information, and a feel for what it is like to live in each area.

For each location there is a profile that examines 17 categories of interest and more than 40 different factors within those categories, such as fabulous features, possible drawbacks, recreation, culture, local real estate, what things cost, "the tax ax," medical care, continuing education, services for seniors, crime and safety, earning a living, and getting around town. Sources for more information are also given. Area profiles are presented in alphabetical order by state, then city. A "Fast Facts" section lists all 50 locations with key facts and the best reasons to move there; it serves as a quick guide if one particular factor, such as size, climate, or housing cost, is paramount in the selection of a retirement location. The Rosenbergs give helpful information on getting ready for retirement. A particularly useful chapter details the variables and charges that can be factored into moving costs; it also provides tips for a smooth moving day and for filing and handling claims. Easy to use, the book can be a helpful comparative guide not only to those planning retirement but also to people who may want to relocate for other reasons. [R: LJ, 1 Mar 92, pp. 80-82] — **Roslyn Attinson**

922. Schaad, Evelyn, comp. **Rural Development: An Annotated Bibliography of ILO Publications and Documents, 1983-1990.** Washington, D.C., International Labor Office, 1991. 338p. index. (International Labour Bibliography, no.7). $28.00pa. ISBN 92-2-106451-4.

This bibliography of books, working papers, conference reports, and journal articles published by the International Labor Office (ILO) focuses on rural poverty issues in developing countries. Rural economies experienced the effects of significant changes in international capital expenditures during the time period covered. The publications abstracted cover strategies for rural development, including employment, education, health care, and other social programs. The more than 750 entries are arranged in seven chapters by type of publication (e.g., book, research and working papers). Each entry includes complete bibliographic information and a brief abstract with highlighted subject descriptors. The volume has an excellent and extensive subject index, a personal name author index, and a corporate author index. All of the publications cited in this bibliography are available for free or for a cost that is quoted in the entry from the ILO Publications Office. *Rural Development* is appropriate for research library reference collections or for specialized collections in international labor or economics. [R: Choice, June 92, p. 1528] — **Linda A. Naru**

18 Women's Studies

BIBLIOGRAPHY

923. Carson, Anne. **Goddesses & Wise Women: The Literature of Feminist Spirituality.** Freedom, Calif., Crossing Press, 1992. 247p. index. $39.95. Z7963.R45C37. LC 91-47603. ISBN 0-89594-536-3.

A compilation of books, articles, periodicals, and audiovisual materials, this book serves as a companion volume to the author's *Feminist Spirituality and the Feminine Divine* (see ARBA 87, entry 848). Topics in the 1,190 entries include feminism and women's spirituality, the goddess through time and space, witchcraft, traditional Europe and feminist wicca, Christianity and Judaism, woman-centered re-visioning, fiction and fantasy literature, and children's literature. Included among the references are healing, menstruation, archaeological research, witchcraft, Third World spiritualities, and eco-feminism. The inclusion of some works critical of or hostile towards feminist theology and the Goddess movement suggests the seriousness with which these writings are being taken by modern mainstream thinking.

Given the profusion of materials published during the years under consideration, a brief discussion of the parameters used in selecting and excluding materials, especially considering the "Wise Women" in the title, would help explain the omission of some significant works, particularly in the Christianity and Judaism section. Why, for instance, are there no materials from the Gnostic tradition? In addition, the index could benefit, as noted in an earlier review, from considerable expansion, perhaps including authors' names for cross-reference. These shortcomings merely suggest that this volume should not be a sole resource; they do not imply that it is not useful. Indeed, paired with its companion, it belongs in every public and academic library and in private libraries if finances allow. [R: Choice, Oct 92, pp. 268-70; LJ, 15 Feb 92, p. 156] — **Susan Tower Hollis**

924. Hallgarth, Susan, and Tina Kraskow, eds. **WIP: A Directory of Work-in-Progress & Recent Publications.** New York, National Council for Research on Women, 1992. 439p. index. $30.00pa. ISBN 1-880547-10-6.

This is one of a series of recent directories published by the National Council for Research on Women. The Council is a coalition of more than 70 member organizations that has the purpose of promoting, supporting, and conducting feminist research, policy analysis, and education programs. The WIP directory is a print version of 1,000-plus women-specific records in the Research-in-Progress Database available in Research Libraries Information Network (RLIN). Books, journal articles, book chapters, dissertations, survey/data collections, bibliographies, videotapes, curriculum guides, policy guidelines, and photograph sets are among the many different types of works compiled.

Arranged alphabetically by principal author, each citation is numbered and provides the name, address, and telephone number of the submitter; the title and type of work; the source of publication and publication date; a three- to five-sentence abstract; funding information; and key words. Several indexes enhance access: a name index of all primary and secondary authors, a geographical index that lists contributors by state (in the United States) or country, a type of work index, an index of funding sources, an index of publishers and distributors, and a keyword index. The keyword index is quite thorough and has generous cross-references. Keyword terms have been edited to conform to *A Women's Thesaurus* (see ARBA 88, entry 905). Several terms, such as *feminist theory, gender, images of women*, and *women's history*, have long strings of citation numbers and could have been subdivided. A list of member centers completes the directory.

The directory succeeds admirably in revealing the depth and diversity of current feminist research, policy, and educational resources from all over the world. It will be highly useful to women's studies scholars, students, and librarians. Projected to be published annually, this source is recommended for all academic libraries that support research on women. —**Linda A. Krikos**

925. Huber, Kristina Ruth. **Women in Japanese Society: An Annotated Bibliography of Selected English Language Materials.** Westport, Conn., Greenwood Press, 1992. 484p. index. (Bibliographies and Indexes in Women's Studies, no.16). $65.00. Z7964.J3H82. 016.30542'0952. LC 92-15371. ISBN 0-313-25296-3.

Huber, a reference and bibliographic instruction librarian and an assistant professor at St. Olaf College, has greatly facilitated future studies on Japanese women. The volume contains references to articles (excluding those from newspapers) and books published between 1841 and 1990. It has more than 2,300 entries and reflects the history and development of the scholarship on women in Japan. The useful annotations include a synopsis and evaluation, an evaluation of the English translation (where appropriate), and a brief biographical sketch of the main personalities. The entries are arranged into five broad categories (women's place, women in the private sphere, women in the public sphere, women as artists, and others), and each category consists of one to six chapters (e.g., women at home; legal status of women; modern prose writers; non-Japanese women in Japan). The chapters on women writers and on women's spoken language were compiled by Kathryn Sparling, a professor of Japanese language and literature at Carlton College. The indexes to the volume are arranged by author, editor, translator, and interviewee; by title, phrases, series, and proceedings; and by subject. This source is strongly recommended for libraries on Japanese studies and on women's issues. —**Seiko Mieczkowski**

926. McClelland, Averil Evans. **The Education of Women in the United States: A Guide to Theory, Teaching, and Research.** Hamden, Conn., Garland, 1992. 227p. index. (Source Books on Education, v.23; Garland Reference Library of Social Science, v.551). $35.00. LC1752.M34. 376'.973. LC 91-14495. ISBN 0-8240-4842-3.

The major objective of this bibliography is to introduce the reader to the general subject of the education of girls and women in the United States, with some reference to historical antecedents in Western civilization (beginning with the ancient Greeks). It is intended as a guide to further research on the subject and is meant for use primarily by scholars in education and other social sciences, scholars in women's studies, classroom teachers, and anyone interested in the consequences of gender for females in schools and other educational settings.

The subject of the education of women is defined in terms of major themes that weave together the diverse elements of women's educational experiences. In general, items in the bibliography include books, journal articles, essay and other reviews, chapters and essays in collected works, and dissertations and some other unpublished work. Bibliographical material is organized by theme and then by chronology. The bibliography is selective; one criterion is the availability of the sources. It is believed that all of the cited works can be found in or through public library systems. The bibliography is also selective because the literature on women's education is selective. For example, there is not much on the education of lower-class working women or on women of color. In addition, only material in English is included. —**Janet Mongan**

927. Mehaffey, Karen Rae. **Victorian American Women 1840-1880: An Annotated Bibliography.** Hamden, Conn., Garland, 1992. 180p. (Garland Reference Library of the Humanities, v.1181). $25.00. Z7964.U49M43. 016.30542'0973. LC 91-22206. ISBN 0-8240-7142-5.

This highly selective annotated bibliography focuses on "everyday" Caucasian, middle-class women who lived in the northeast region of the United States during the Victorian period. The works listed deal primarily with the general topics of social and family life; few sources reflect the lives of specific women.

The bibliography is arranged in general sections, such as "The Victorian Woman," "The Genteel State," and "The Cult of Domesticity," that are then divided into narrower categories. Each section begins with a brief but well-written introduction that gives an overview of the topic and research tips. This is followed by an annotated list of references, usually subdivided into primary and secondary sources. Oddly, Mehaffey seems to define "primary" sources as only those *published* during the period of 1840 to 1880; the few entries for letters, diaries, and the like are treated as secondary sources. An unannotated list of other sources of interest closes each section.

The bibliography has one major weakness aside from its extremely narrow focus: the absolute lack of any indexing. The only access to the material is through the table of contents, which is insufficient for precise access to specific subjects. Because of these problems, this bibliography can be recommended only for research collections in American history and women's studies. [R: Choice, June 92, p. 1524] — **Susan Davis Herring**

928. Mori, Monica, and Janet McNern. **Women and Aging: An Annotated Bibliography, 1986-1991.** Vancouver, B.C., Gerontology Research Centre, Simon Fraser University, 1991. 223p. index. $20.00 spiralbound. ISBN 0-86491-112-2.

This bibliography contains 378 references to journal articles on women and aging that cover the period from 1985 to mid-1991. They have been selected from searches of such databases as Ageline, Index Medicus, Nursing and Allied Health, PsycINFO, and Sociological Abstracts. It is designed to supplement *Women and Aging: A Comprehensive Bibliography* by Donna Lee Hawley (Gerontology Research Centre, 1985). Selections are limited to items available at the Gerontology Research Centre.

The bibliography is arranged in subject sections that deal with such topics as attitudes toward elderly women, economic status, health care, psychosocial aspects, and social relationships. Entries provide author, article title, journal title, date, volume, issue, and page numbers. They also include abstracts, almost 90 percent of which have been taken from the articles, and key words that may be used to locate related articles through keyword and related keyword indexes. An author index is also supplied. The book has a spiral binding, which may affect its durability. *Women and Aging* will be useful to students and to those seeking a general introduction to recent research on various aspects of women and aging. — **Gari-Anne Patzwald**

929. Nordquist, Joan, comp. **The Feminist Movement: A Bibliography.** Santa Cruz, Calif., Reference and Research Services, 1992. 68p. (Contemporary Social Issues: A Bibliographic Series, no.24). $15.00pa. ISBN 0-937855-46-4.

This unannotated bibliography lists approximately 500 books, journal articles, pamphlets, dissertations, and book chapters about the feminist movement. Sources were gathered from a wide variety of social, political, general, feminist, and alternative indexes and directories. Most material dates from the 1980s and 1990s although earlier materials are included.

The bibliography is divided into seven main sections that are further subdivided into categories. The first two sections deal with materials about the history of the feminist movement. The third section concentrates on the contemporary movement, with an emphasis on the United States. Issues of race, the women's movement around the world, and the sexuality/sadomasochism and pornography/censorship debates are the focus of the next three sections. The final resource section lists bibliographies, directories, and organizations. Within each section and subcategory, entries are arranged alphabetically by author or title (if there is no author). Books and articles are listed separately.

Not meant to be comprehensive, this title still presents a basic list of sources on the subject. A variety of viewpoints are represented, and there is a nice mix of scholarly and general materials. The international coverage is important, and sexuality and race are among the most sensitive issues facing the women's movement today. Emphasis is on the most recent sources available, particularly in sections on the present movement. The resource section provides a good path to more in-depth study.

Although the table of contents is fairly specific and none of the sections or subcategories is very long, an index would still be helpful. Some subjects, such as Asian-American women, are not included in the table of contents. The criteria for inclusion also needs to be explained. At least one book published in 1992 is included, but Susan Faludi's *Backlash: The Undeclared War against Women* (Crown, 1991) is not. The first edition of *Women: A Bibliography of Bibliographies* (see ARBA 81, entry 801) is listed although a second edition was published in 1986. Other recent appropriate bibliographies, such as *Latinas of the Americas* (see ARBA 90, entry 863) and *Women, Race, and Ethnicity* (University of Wisconsin System, 1991) are also not listed. Finally, it might have been prudent to list the books about sexuality separately from the books about sadomasochism. As it stands, most of the materials about lesbianism are listed in this subdivision, which creates an unfortunate juxtaposition. In spite of these drawbacks, *The Feminist Movement* still provides decent coverage of an important topic and will be useful in academic libraries that support women's studies courses, undergraduate collections, and selected large public libraries. — **Linda A. Krikos**

930. Nordquist, Joan, comp. **Simone de Beauvoir: A Bibliography.** Santa Cruz, Calif., Reference and Research Services, 1991. 64p. index. (Social Theory: A Bibliographic Series, no.23). $15.00pa. ISBN 0-937855-45-6.

This bibliography offers a comprehensive list, through 1991, of all works by or about Simone de Beauvoir. The collection is impressive and quite helpful. The first of four sections contains de Beauvoir's works that have been translated into English as well as all books originally written in French. Citations for reviews and commentaries about those books appear here as well. Section 2 lists de Beauvoir's essays, interviews, and excerpts from books. Section 3 identifies books in English that discuss her work. Included in this section, but contained under subheadings (e.g., Feminism and Literature), are books that address de Beauvoir's writings directly or indirectly. Dissertations are listed as a separate category. Section 4 lists articles or critical commentary in English on de Beauvoir's works that cover the period 1950 to 1991.

For those who wish to read more by or about de Beauvoir, this is the place to begin. Research on her will be aided immensely by this offering. — **Michael A. Foley**

931. Shult, Linda, Susan Searing, and Elli Lester-Massman, eds. **Women, Race, and Ethnicity: A Bibliography.** Madison, Wis., University of Wisconsin System Women's Studies Librarian, 1991. 202p. index. $7.00pa.

This volume is a bibliographic listing of college-level print and audiovisual resources about women of non-WASP backgrounds in the United States. Focusing primarily upon recently published scholarship, it is intended by its editors to be a "starting point for research" and should not be considered a comprehensive bibliography. More than 60 percent of the nearly 2,500 sources cited in the volume were written or produced within the last decade. Most of these references are described with brief annotations. The entries are classified under 28 disciplines and topics, such as anthropology, education, history, law, and sports. Within each discipline, the references are organized into the following subsections: Asian and Pacific American women, Black women, Euro-American women, Indian women, Jewish women, Latinas, and general and cross-cultural studies. To help the investigator, the volume also includes a 30-page subject index and the current addresses of the distributors of the nonprint resources. Recommended for university and research libraries. [R: RQ, Spring 92, pp. 432-33]

— **Terry D. Bilhartz**

BIOGRAPHY

932. Barker-Benfield, G. J., and Catherine Clinton. **Portraits of American Women: From Settlement to the Present.** New York, St. Martin's Press, 1991. 622p. illus. $17.53pa. LC 89-62776. ISBN 0-312-03687-6.

Twenty-five women from all periods of U.S. history — 2 Native Americans, 4 African-Americans, and 19 European-Americans — are covered in this collected biography. The book is divided into eight periods, from the colonial era through contemporary times. Each section begins with a 10- to 12-page essay that places the subjects within their times and reviews the gender roles and expectations of the particular period. The portrait for each woman includes an artistic rendering of the subject (usually a painting or photograph), a short paragraph with highlights of her life and accomplishments, a more detailed account of the highlights, and a list of notes and sources. According to the preface, the subjects have been chosen on the basis of "significant contributions to the public realm" and accessibility to materials. Included are a religious martyr (Anne Hutchinson), a "war woman" (Nancy Ward), an abolitionist (Maria Weston Chapman), political wives (e.g., Mary Todd Lincoln), a variety of activists and reformers (e.g., Elizabeth Cady Stanton, Alice Paul, Ella Baker, Betty Friedan), an anthropologist (Margaret Mead), and an artist (Georgia O'Keeffe).

Most of the portraits are based on primary sources and have been written specifically for this book by specialists conducting ongoing biographical research, but a few are reprinted from sources published in the 1960s, 1970s, and 1980s. Gender roles and expectations are traced in each section only for Caucasians and African-Americans. Native Americans are hardly mentioned after the first two historical periods. Coverage of Asian women and Hispanic women is limited to quotations from Cherrie Moraga and Maxine Hong Kingston in the final section's introductory essay. The vast majority of the women are covered in *Notable American Women* (see ARBA 82, entry 771), *Women in Particular* (see ARBA 86, entry 869), and *Index to Women in the World* (see ARBA 91, entry 878).

This title might make a good supplementary or introductory text. Lack of indexing and the limited number of women included hinder its usefulness as a reference tool. Recommended for circulating collections in public and academic libraries. — **Linda A. Krikos**

933. Echols, Anne, and Marty Williams. **An Annotated Index of Medieval Women.** New York, Markus Wiener, 1992. 635p. $69.95. CT3220.A56. 920.72'094. LC 90-39810. ISBN 0-910129-27-4.

One of the more valuable spinoffs of the women's movement has been the attempt to revise previously male-centered history and to accommodate the growing interest in women from earlier time periods. Medieval women have recently received so much attention that an index of their names is now possible. This work is the first to make use of the recent outpouring of historical scholarship on the lives and accomplishments of women who lived between A.D. 800 and 1500.

Following an introductory section that explains how to use the book, the main listings are arranged alphabetically by first name, with variant spellings cross-indexed. Each contains a brief biographical sketch, including dates and native country, the categories (e.g., insanity, queens, politics) under which the woman might be mentioned, and an abbreviated list of sources. The biographical sketch may be too brief for many needs; many women get just a line or two, and even Joan of Arc receives only half a page.

The main listing is followed by cross-reference listings according to dates, countries, biographical categories, last names, titles, regions, and cities, and by a complete bibliography of sources with and without authors. The cross-referencing makes it possible to look for women in very specific categories, such as English women dramatists (one—Katherine of Sutton) or Italian murder victims (many). Some of the categories are too wide and should have been further subdivided. It is, for example, unnecessarily confusing to put murderers and victims in the same general category. The list of sources is extensive but not exhaustive—a situation to be expected in such a rapidly evolving field.

The serious historical researcher will find this index a handy guide. Recommended for libraries with collections on women's studies and on medieval history. — **Lynn F. Williams**

934. Golemba, Beverly E. **Lesser-Known Women: A Biographical Dictionary.** Boulder, Colo., Lynne Rienner, 1992. 380p. index. $65.00. CT3203.G57. 920.72. LC 91-41182. ISBN 1-55587-301-4.

Golemba, a professor of sociology at Saint Leo College, has produced a dictionary that includes biographical sketches on more than 800 accomplished but lesser-known women of the seventeenth through the twentieth centuries. According to Golemba, the women are individuals who not only have made outstanding contributions within their fields of endeavor but also are representative of other women whose accomplishments have been ignored by history. The biographical entries are well written but brief, varying in length from about 100 to 250 words. The entries are arranged chronologically according to the year of the woman's most noteworthy accomplishment. The dictionary also includes several indexes that place the women by name, country, ethnicity, and profession.

While the volume contains some interesting information, the chronological (rather than alphabetical) arrangement of the entries mars its usefulness as a quick ready-reference source. Another limitation is its Anglo-American orientation: more than 6 in 10 of the women are from the United States; 3 in 4 are of either British or North American heritage. Also, while the work cites 783 sources used to produce the volume, this number includes 173 references to entries in the *Encyclopaedia Britannica* and scores of other citations from uncritical secondary sources of dubious credibility. For information on U.S. subjects, *Handbook of American Women's History* (see ARBA 91, entry 929) remains the more user-friendly and dependable reference source on lesser-known (as well as well-known) women of distinction. [R: WLB, Nov 92, p. 93] — **Terry D. Bilhartz**

935. Griffin, Lynne, and Kelly McCann. **The Book of Women: 300 Notable Women History Passed By.** Holbrook, Mass., Bob Adams, 1992. 160p. illus. index. $10.95. ISBN 1-55850-106-1.

In *The Book of Women*, Griffin and McCann profile the lives and accomplishments of women who have largely been ignored throughout the centuries. The table of contents provides a subject list of 69 categories with 3 to 6 women listed under each. Some of the unusual topics included are rodeo stars, sting artists, daredevils, founding mothers, women who took male identities, agricultural pioneers, women who wore what they pleased, and spies. The brief biographical sketches in each category are listed chronologically. A black-and-white pen-and-ink portrait highlights one of the women from each category. The index provides an alphabetical list of those in the book, while a bibliography gives additional sources for further reading.

Readers interested in lesser-known women will find this a fascinating book. Although the authors concede they did not write this book for scholars and researchers, this concise work will be a useful addition to school and public library collections.

— **Jennie S. Johnson**

936. Shelnutt, Eve, ed. **The Confidence Woman: 26 Women Writers at Work.** Atlanta, Ga., Longstreet Press, 1991. 392p. illus. $17.95. LC 90-063897. ISBN 0-929264-91-6.

The editor of *The Confidence Woman* chose women whose work she admires and invited each "to write an essay about your career, shaping it in any manner you like." The writers whose responses are collected here have been, with a few exceptions, born in the United States and almost exclusively Caucasian. In this sense the book is considerably more limited than it might have been. But the women are not, on the whole, well known, and this fact, plus their diverse manners of responding to the editor's invitation, makes the book a refreshing change from the predictability of many such collections. The essays tend to focus on such influences on the writers' careers as family, education, early reading, and the developing sense of self as a writer. Some — Patricia Goedicke is a good example — use their lives and excerpts from their poetry or prose to illuminate each other. The quality of the essays is somewhat uneven, ranging from the rather ordinary and sometimes cliched to the passionate, vibrant, and even humorous. (Debora Gregor's essay is a series of drawings.) A bibliography is included for each writer. As many of the writers featured here have not been included in other such works, this book should be a useful addition, especially to libraries with interests in creative writing, contemporary American literature, or women's studies. — **Robin Riley Fast**

937. **Who's Who of Women in World Politics.** Munich, New Providence, N.J., Bowker-Saur, 1991. 311p. index. $95.00. 323.34. ISBN 0-86291-627-5.

This reference work contains more than 1,500 alphabetized, single-paragraph biographies of women in positions of political influence in 115 countries. Biographees are heads of state, members of governments or national legislatures, leaders of parties or trade union federations, and regional leaders. The volume includes a map, a preface by U.S. political scientist Ruth Mandel, a five-language key to the biographies, a list of abbreviations, and a very useful set of statistical appendixes based on a compilation of data from the biographies. The volume concludes with an index of names by country.

There are many uses for this fascinating compendium of information about women's occupancy of political leadership roles. There are some spelling errors in the book, however. Shulamit Aloni, for example, is listed as Shumalit both in her biographical entry and in the index. Although problems such as this are likely when reference works are based on many languages, users must be sure, nevertheless, to double-check the information in this volume before considering it definitive. [R: Choice, June 92, pp. 1530-31; RBB, 1 May 92, p. 1637; RQ, Fall, pp. 123-25; WLB, Mar 92, pp. 122-23]

— **Shulamit Reinharz**

DICTIONARIES AND ENCYCLOPEDIAS

938. Mills, Jane. **Womanwords: A Dictionary of Words about Women.** New York, Free Press/Macmillan, c1989, 1992. 291p. $22.95. HQ1115.M546. 305.4'03. LC 91-46687. ISBN 0-02-921495-5.

As have philosophers and linguists, feminists have long recognized that words have a life and power of their own and that meaning is often quite different from definition. In this tradition, Mills has gathered nearly 300 words that have been applied to women over the centuries, giving their etymology, history, changing meanings, and connotations. The words are carefully selected "to explore the history of changing (and sometimes relentlessly unchanging) attitudes toward women." Each is accompanied by an essay—from a few lines to several pages—that bounds through mythology, history, popular culture, and feminist theory while pointing out stereotypes and lexicological prejudice.

Usually negative in her opinions, and with an unfortunate tendency to draw unsupported conclusions, Mills makes no attempt to write with the objectivity normally expected from the author of a reference book. She also neglects to provide an index or cross-references for the many words discussed and defined under the entries for other words. Despite these major failings, however, this is a lively and interesting sourcebook that would be a good addition for larger libraries or for those serving women's studies scholars. [R: LJ, 1 Apr 92, p. 112]—**Susan Davis Herring**

939. Tierney, Helen, ed. **Women's Studies Encyclopedia. Volume III: History, Philosophy, and Religion.** Westport, Conn., Greenwood Press, 1991. 531p. index. $65.00. HQ1115.W645. 305.4'03. LC 88-32806. ISBN 0-313-27358-8.

Read cover-to-cover as a fine introduction to the recorded history of women in the West (including special sections on African-American women) and Asia, this volume offers novices a departure point for more study (about half the entries include suggestions for further reading). Contributors pick up the strands of medieval abbesses, vestals, and seventeenth-century adolescent females who accused older women of witchcraft, ultimately weaving a rich outline of the social history of women. The philosophy (largely French feminist) and religion are secondary themes to the main one, which remains implicit: biology has more often than not determined the courses of women's lives. There are exceptions: burial grounds in northeast China suggest women attained higher status than men until about 2500 B.C.; Spartan women co-opted others and escaped the constraints of caring for offspring; and women periodically embraced asceticism as a way to pursue activities not dictated by reproduction.

There are discrepancies in the depth of coverage. For example, a discussion of the twentieth-century development of the antiabortion movement in the United States includes attention to nativist sentiment, but the account of the connection of nursing to the Civil War misses many nuances, including the proscription that caregivers be physically unattractive or elderly women. These are minor inconveniences in an otherwise strong volume. [R: Choice, July/Aug 92, p. 1662; LJ, 15 Mar 92, p. 80; RBB, 1 Jan 92, p. 847]—**Diane M. Calabrese**

DIRECTORIES

940. Tulloch, Paulette P., comp., and Susan A. Hallgarth, ed. **NWO: A Directory of National Women's Organizations.** New York, National Council for Research on Women, 1992. 664p. index. $40.00pa. ISBN 1-880547-10-5.

This comprehensive work lists national nonprofit organizations whose primary focus is women. It also includes professional organizations for traditionally women-intensive occupations (e.g., nursing), reproductive rights coalitions, and family planning organizations. The member centers of the National Council for Research on Women, a 70-member coalition that supports and conducts research, policy analysis, and educational programs, are described.

The organizations are arranged alphabetically by name. Each entry, on a separate page, includes address, telephone number, name of contact person, description, area of focus, services offered, publications, user access, target population, and organization meeting. To enhance access to this information, a rotated list of all organizations indexed is provided, arranged by each main word in the organization's name. There are, in addition, a detailed keyword index with cross-references and an index by state. Both of these features enhance the directory's usefulness. There are also 10 pages of unindexed organizations that have only name, address, contact person, and telephone number (further information was unavailable).

There are five appendixes: listings of women's funds, women's PACs (Political Action Committees), federal agencies and offices, state commissions on women, and Council member centers. These supply name, address, contact person, and telephone number. The introduction provides a good orientation to the directory and its use, scope, and organization. It also has information about women's organizations in general and the National Council for Research on Women. There is a selected bibliography of directories/organizational resources and books and articles about women's organizations.

Both negative and positive aspects of the physical format of the book can be noted. Although the margins are wide, making photocopying easier, the cover and binding are not strong, and with use it will probably need to be reinforced or rebound. Although the paper appears heavy, the type on the reverse side of the page is visible. The typeface, although clear, is small. A greater variety in type styles and sizes would have made the information stand out better and easier to read. However, considering the scope and content of the directory, the price is reasonable.

The directory brings together a wide range of women's organizations in a convenient multi-indexed volume that will do much to improve access to, and increase understanding and knowledge of, the efforts and activities undertaken by these organizations. The book represents an important contribution to women's studies and is a valuable resource for public, academic, and special library collections.
—Susan J. Freiband

HANDBOOKS AND YEARBOOKS

941. Armitage, Susan, and others, eds. **Women in the West: A Guide to Manuscript Sources.** Hamden, Conn., Garland, 1991. 422p. (Women's History and Culture, v.5; Garland Reference Library of the Humanities, v.1086). $59.00. Z7964.U49W6. 016.3054'0978. LC 91-24898. ISBN 0-8240-4298-0.

Focusing on primary source materials that chronicle the multicultural experience of women in the American West, this useful guide provides access to a great deal of information that has previously been overlooked or ignored by researchers. Much of this material is held by small archives or has been hidden within existing collections and includes diaries, photographs, letters, oral histories, census data, and other documents that shed a long overdue light on the lives of western women from 1610 to 1910. The repositories included are limited to the 20 states west of the Mississippi that received statehood after 1850 (Texas is, nevertheless, included).

Preceded by a foreword by Lillian Schlissel and an introduction that clearly defines the parameters of the guide, the archival entries are arranged alphabetically by state with further subdivisions. Each entry includes the name, address, and telephone number of the archive; the name of the person in charge; and the hours and services provided (e.g., photocopying). Collection information varies among entries but usually includes general holdings data (e.g., size and focus of collection, types of materials), specialized multicultural materials, items of note, and guides or finding tools specific to the collection. An alphabetical list of archives arranged by state concludes this work.

Women in the West is a well done, highly accessible, specialized guide that will be a welcome supplement to Andrea Hinding's more general and inclusive *Women's History Sources* (R. R. Bowker, 1979). It includes much information not found elsewhere and deserves a place in the reference collections of most academic libraries, particularly those that support programs in American history or women's studies. [R: C&RL, Sept 92, p. 424; Choice, May 92, p. 1378]—**Kristin Ramsdell**

942. **The Bloomsbury Guide to Women's Literature.** Claire Buck, ed. New York, Prentice Hall General Reference, 1992. 1171p. illus. $40.00; $20.00pa. PN471.B57. 809'.89287'03. LC 92-10415. ISBN 0-13-689621-9; 0-13-089665-9pa.

This outstanding work should become a standard in any reference collection. Amazingly comprehensive, it covers women's literature of all times and languages, from early Greece to the modern world, including the often underrepresented countries of the Far East, Middle East, and Africa. It is divided into two parts: an opening section of essays and the main body of encyclopedic entries. Points of emphasis throughout the book include the interrelationships between language and literature, the inadequacies of scholarship and translation in women's literature, and the difficulties of applying traditional definitions to women's literature.

The essays are brief overviews of the literatures of various countries or regions, covering the literary history and highlighting the major authors of each period and concluding with a brief discussion of the history of feminist criticism. The biases of traditional scholarship are reflected in these essays, despite the best efforts of the editor and writers. Great Britain is covered in four essays, for example, while all of Eastern European literature is lumped into one. Still, these are valuable summaries that provide good launching points for further research. The encyclopedic entries, which give brief discussions of authors, works, genres, styles, and movements, provide sufficient information for quick answers to specific questions, or just enough to whet the appetite of the curious student. There are plentiful cross-references, both in the essays and the short entries, but an unfortunate lack of references to secondary sources. This exemplary reference book should be on the "must have" list for almost every library. — **Susan Davis Herring**

INDEXES

943. *Journal of Women's History* **Guide to Periodical Literature.** Gayle V. Fischer, comp. Bloomington, Ind., Indiana University Press, 1992. 501p. $39.95; $18.95pa. Z7962.F57. 016.3054'05. LC 91-28470. ISBN 0-253-32219-7; 0-253-20720-7pa.

The major objective of this work is to provide a compilation of periodical literature in the field of women's history in the United States and abroad from 1980 to 1990. Its purpose is to facilitate the work of scholars, teachers, and general readers in women's history, to help readers keep up with the latest scholarship, and to assess those areas in which more research needs to be done. The articles are drawn from more than 750 journals. There are 40 subject entries arranged alphabetically and divided into subcategories, which include over 5,500 individual articles that have been extensively cross-listed in order to enhance use. Twenty-three percent of all entries are about countries other than the United States. Each entry gives author, title, periodical, volume, date, and pages. In the foreword Fischer outlines the transformation of the history profession by the feminist movement; in the introduction she discusses the development of women's history as a discipline. These accounts of the beginnings and present status of the discipline chart the course to current positions and provide a guide to future paths.

The particular strength of this book lies in its coverage of a large number of journals, including not only women's and women's studies journals but many of the basic disciplinary and interdisciplinary journals as well. For this reason the work would be a good addition to libraries whose users seek a systematic source for periodical articles on women's history in the period covered. [R: RBB, 15 Apr 92, p. 1552] — **Janet Mongan**

QUOTATION BOOKS

944. Sumrall, Amber Coverdale, ed. **Write to the Heart: Wit & Wisdom of Women Writers.** Freedom, Calif., Crossing Press, 1992. 194p. illus. $19.95; $8.95pa. PN6081.5.W74. 081'.082. LC 92-11268. ISBN 0-89594-566-5; 0-89594-550-9pa.

When one looks at the usual quotation books from a feminist perspective, it is easy to be appalled both by the overall lack of quotations by women and by the stereotypical few that are included. In *Write to the Heart*, Sumrall has given us a partial solution to this problem. All of the quotations included in this book are by women, and the vast majority are not found in any other reference source. The subjects covered are diverse: fame and fortune, transformation, time, politics, childhood, books, courage, love, domestic life, education, men, resistance, silence, and truth, among others. Two themes are woven through all the topics: women's lives and the act of writing.

This is essentially a book for browsing. The selection of quotations comes from years of collecting by Sumrall and is highly personal. Perhaps because of her method of collection, the book suffers from a total lack of references: quotations are identified only by author, with no sources given. The subject arrangement is fluid and rather arbitrary, and there is no index, either by author or subject, to make access easier. But despite these failings, *Write to the Heart* is an inspiring collection that adds significantly to the body of quotations available to the general public. It is suitable for any library. [R: BL, Aug 92, p. 1975; LJ, 15 Oct 92, p. 60]—**Susan Davis Herring**

Part III
HUMANITIES

19 Humanities in General

GENERAL WORKS

945. **The American Humanities Index for 1991. Volume XVII.** Troy, N.Y., Whitston Publishing, 1992. 2v. $210.00/set. ISBN 0-87875-417-2. ISSN 0361-0144.

Source material for this index derives from more than 500 creative, critical, and scholarly journals held in the little magazine collection of the College of William and Mary. As most of these journals are indexed exclusively by *American Humanities Index* (AHI), bibliographic access is provided to thousands of articles that would otherwise remain unknown.

A subject/author index that will prove valuable to many students and researchers, AHI does have a few shortcomings that must be overcome if it is to be used effectively. Not the least of these is the problem of vocabulary control; the editors incorporate standard terminology in the humanities (e.g., poetry, drama, theater, stories) with no clear thesaurus to define the scope of these concepts. Furthermore, it is indicated that periods of history within a subject are filed alphabetically, yet one witnesses variations to this rule throughout the index. Some entries receive multiple-access indexing, while others do not. Omitted from the index are editorials; reprints; letters to the editor; and short (less than 500 words) book reviews, news items, and editor's notes. In spite of these deficiencies, AHI remains an important tool for bibliographic access to primary and secondary source material in humanities research.
— **Edmund F. SantaVicca**

946. **Directory of Grants in the Humanities 1992/93.** 6th ed. Phoenix, Ariz., Oryx Press, 1992. 696p. index. $84.50pa. ISBN 0-89774-695-3. ISSN 0887-0551.

This directory of humanities grants (as opposed to grants in the social sciences) contains 3,808 listings on grants related to languages, literature, art, philosophy, and so forth. Now in its 6th edition, the text is also available online through DIALOG and on CD-ROM. The electronic database is updated monthly, while the CD-ROM format is updated bimonthly, but they are also quite expensive. This directory is comparatively inexpensive, and it is likely more affordable for smaller libraries and institutions with limited funds for reference materials.

The heart of the text is an alphabetical list of grant programs. Each program is assigned an accession number and includes grant title, description, restrictions, requirements, amount of grant funding, application procedure and renewal dates, catalog of federal domestic assistance number (where available), sponsor information, and contact person. The text concludes with an excellent subject index and a list of sponsoring agencies and grants arranged under the types of sponsors.

Readers should be cautioned that this may not be the sole source for grant information in the humanities in the United States and Canada, although it appears quite exhaustive. Additional resources on this subject may also be available, for example, through the Foundation Center and its various publications. — **James M. Murray**

947. **Guide to Albert Schweitzer Collections.** 2d ed. New York, Albert Schweitzer Fellowship, 1991. 60p. $7.50pa.

Albert Schweitzer (1875-1965) was an internationally known figure: a humanistic missionary physician in Africa; a world-class organist; and a leading advocate for world peace, for which he received the 1952 Nobel Peace Prize. This partial guide to collections of published and unpublished material by or about Schweitzer updates the 1981 edition and is intended to stimulate further research into the careers and accomplishments of this fascinating, diverse individual.

This brief volume is divided into three sections: institutional and governmental repositories, papers and other items in the hands of private collectors, and materials located outside the United States. The size of these various collections ranges from one letter to extensive correspondence, manuscript, and photographic holdings. The following information is provided for each entry: location, contact person, telephone number, rules of usage, and a very short description of the resources housed in the collection. Because the information was gathered only through the use of questionnaires, the compilers make no claims to comprehensive coverage.

While Schweitzer was one of the twentieth century's leading figures, the inclusion of a brief biographical sketch would have been worthwhile. Still, this reference tool is a good starting point for anyone wanting to research the careers and impact of this amazing man.

—**Jonathon Erlen**

948. **Humanities Index.** (Indexing coverage: 2/84-6/25/92). [CD-ROM]. Bronx, N.Y., H. W. Wilson, 1992. Hardware requirements: WILSONLINE Workstation, IBM PC, or compatible; 640K; hard disk drive. $1,295.00.

Humanities databases on CD-ROM are few and far between; many of those that do exist are available from H. W. Wilson. Examples include the MLA International Bibliography. The WILSONDISC system is well known to most librarians because H. W. Wilson has donated hardware and software to all accredited library schools. Although the interface is not much different than before, this new version has several enhancements, notably in the easier installation and setup phases. The search commands have been simplified; the user now has the ability to substitute the "$" and "?" truncation for the traditional WILSONLINE ":" for multiple characters.

However, the large memory requirements (a minimum of 487K of free conventional memory) have not changed. Because of all the memory-resident programs necessary for other programs, using a WILSONDISC with other CD-ROM software is difficult. A Windows version of the software or an ability to use extended memory would alleviate these problems.—**Johan Koren**

949. **Index to Reviews of Bibliographical Publications: An International Annual. Volume X: 1985.** Thomas R. Liszka and Barbara L. Berman, eds. Troy, N.Y., Whitston Publishing, 1991. 243p. $40.00. LC 78-645642. ISBN 0-87875-405-9.

This index has been completely reorganized since it was last reviewed (see ARBA 83, entry 28). The scope of coverage is still roughly the same: "international and general bibliographical subjects or those related specifically to British or American literature or language...." Reviews must still be at least 100 words long, and although reviews and reviewed publications may be in any language, the editors have attempted to be exhaustive only in English, and nearly so in French and German. The number of items reviewed has remained about 900 per year.

The fundamental change in volume 10 concerns the organization of the main section. Instead of listing all reviewed publications alphabetically by author or editor, the *Index* now arranges the entries under seven broad categories: general studies; textual criticism; facsimiles; concordances and indexes; enumerative and descriptive bibliography; collecting and exhibiting; and production, trade, and impact. Most of these categories are further subdivided into actual studies and discussions of theory or history. This is a much more sensible approach as it allows users to turn directly to their area of interest and find the relevant publications instead of bouncing back and forth between the indexes and the main section. The indexes themselves have been streamlined and improved. The current scholar index combines the former editor and reviewer indexes. The new subject index is now more specific and useful than before and employs ample cross-references. One thing appears not to have improved, however: the gap between the year covered and the date of publication of the *Index*. Ten years ago that gap was three years; it has now doubled to six.—**Jeffrey R. Luttrell**

950. McGreal, Ian P., ed. **Great Thinkers of the Western World: The Major Ideas and Classic Works of More Than 100 Outstanding Western Philosophers....** New York, HarperCollins, 1992. 572p. index. $40.00. B72.G74. 190. LC 91-38362. ISBN 0-06-270026-X.

Great Thinkers of the Western World introduces the novice to the major works and ideas of 116 dominant minds in philosophy, theology, and science. Chronologically arranged by thinker, each entry, four to eight pages long, begins with several declarative sentences that summarize the thinker's principal ideas. The main part of the entry provides biographical information and discusses the subject's writings and ideas. An annotated list of recommended readings concludes each piece. Articles are signed by one of the 35 scholars who contributed to this effort. A bibliography of the thinkers' classic works and an index, alphabetically arranged by thinker, are supplied.

As an introductory tool, *Great Thinkers* competes with other sources already in the field, such as Frank N. Magill's fleet of literary digests. The writings of more than half of the "great thinkers" are also reviewed in Magill's *World Philosophy* (see ARBA 84, entry 1012). The major publications of another quarter are found in other Magill sources, such as *Masterplots 2* (see ARBA 92, entry 1128). The inclusion of great scientific minds, such as Hippocrates, Ptolemy, Isaac Newton, Max Planck, and Heisenberg, makes this source more versatile than others in the market.

The contributors hold or held positions at colleges, universities, and seminaries in the United States and generally succeed at making complex ideas understandable. At one point this reviewer was surprised to read in the opening paragraph on Saint Augustine that the author of *The City of God* was "the most influential figure in Western history." One hopes that beginners will recognize an overstatement when they see it.

Although this work duplicates some of the information already available in the reference room, this does not make *Great Thinkers* useless. Students of complex ideas appreciate all the help they can get. *Great Thinkers*, similar to the Magill sources, provides a valuable service: it introduces students to the major Western ideas that shaped our world. [R: RBB, 15 Dec 92, p. 762] – **John P. Stierman**

20 Communication and Mass Media

GENERAL WORKS

951. Bennett, James R. **Control of the Media in the United States: An Annotated Bibliography.** Hamden, Conn., Garland, 1992. 819p. index. (Garland Reference Library of Social Science, v.456). $125.00. Z5634.U6B46. 016.3633'1'0973. LC 91-26064. ISBN 0-8240-4438-X.

This extensive bibliography presents mass-media research with emphasis on the relation between mass communication and the U.S. corporate state. The collection's introduction emphasizes the conflict between the corporate elite's dominate power and its dissenters over the influence on decision making and control in the United States. The author strives to present a balance, with the assumption that diversity and competition of ideas are essential to democracy.

The bibliography's nearly 5,000 entries are arranged in three parts. Part 1 cites 545 books on the structure of the corporate state, grouped by "Master Institutions" (e.g., corporation, government, military, anticommunism) and "Secondary Institutions" (e.g., law, education, religion, sports). Part 2, the majority of the bibliography, contains more than 3,500 books and articles that address "the role of all discourses and media in big business/big government's symbiotic relationship"; the arrangement covers the media, advertising and public relations, electronic media, print media, and art and music. Part 3 counteracts and balances the first two parts by offering more than 600 works on alternatives to the dominant institutions in the media, advertising, broadcasting, print, and the arts. Each citation is briefly annotated. Extensive author and subject indexes conclude the compilation.

The method of compiling this bibliography included surveying more than 20 standard bibliographies and examining more than 450 periodicals. The latter examination was chosen by the author because of the lack of reliable and consistent coverage of magazines that are "seriously skeptical and systematically investigative of the nexus of power" (with cited exception of *The Alternative Press*). Coverage is primarily post-World War II, with emphasis on publications of the decade prior to 1991. The author acknowledges omission of a separate section on "education, discourse and media" although more than 40 annotations are included to describe education as a "secondary institution" within the control of the corporate state, and entries are identified elsewhere through the index under "education" headings. Under the library-related headings, nine entries link librarianship to defense of freedom of speech and access to information, but there is only one citation from the growing literature about the FBI library surveillance program.

This work offers a source for identifying research and opinions for those interested in exploring the viewpoint that political-economic-media relations dominate and control the United States and also challenge the First Amendment rights. Recommended for academic and research library collections supporting programs in public policy and mass communications/journalism and for those interested in understanding this view of power and influence in contemporary America. [R: Choice, Dec 92, p. 597]
— **Danuta A. Nitecki**

952. **The Canadian Media List 1992/1993: A Comprehensive Guide to Television, Radio and Print Media in Canada.** Toronto, Canadian Book Information Centre, 1992. 390p. $300.00 looseleaf. ISBN 1-895080-04-5.

This annual comes out every July. Available for half price to nonprofit groups (including libraries), it is meant mainly for publishers and advertisers. It is expensive in comparison to other works in the field, such as *Matthews List* (see ARBA 91, entry 937). Indexes are in the front of this work, and listings are nominally by cities or by periodical categories (e.g., law, journalism, women's studies). Section 1 covers radio, television, and newspapers, arranged by city. Section 2 covers news wire services, radio and television networks, and publications at colleges and universities. Section 3 arranges the periodicals by subject and includes a press gallery directory (for those journalists who cover politics in Canada) and a fax directory. Each entry contains full address, telephone and fax numbers, and network affiliation when applicable. Circulation or audience figures are presented. Next come the names of important personnel, such as news directors, book review editors, advertising managers, areas of interest for books to be reviewed, "reported frequency of reviews," and whether there are in-house reviews. This work is useful for all those who want a list of the relevant media in Canada or for those in Canada who need to pinpoint criteria on marketing books (for sending review copies or for targeting advertising). – **Dean Tudor**

953. Drost, Harry, ed. **The World's News Media: A Comprehensive Reference Guide.** Harlow, England, Longman; distr., Detroit, Gale, 1991. 604p. $198.00. ISBN 0-582-08554-3.

This new title covers 198 countries, from Afghanistan to Zimbabwe. For each entry some political background is given, along with statistics on literacy, daily newspaper circulation, and the number of radio receivers and television sets owned. Brief background information is provided for news sources, the press, and broadcasting. This narrative section is followed by a directory of mass-media services and related associations. Brief information is given about each media source along with addresses and telephone numbers, including international dialing codes. Three appendixes list primary sources of official information (names only), associations for newspaper publishers, and journalists' associations. A subsection is devoted to regional and world media sources. Much of the data provided can also be found in *Europa World Year Book* (see ARBA 90, entry 91), but there is an advantage to having the information together. [R: Choice, Dec 92, p. 606; WLB, Nov 92, p. 97] – **Helen M. Gothberg**

954. **Index to Journals in Communication Studies through 1990.** Ronald J. Matlon and Sylvia P. Ortiz, eds. Annandale, Va., Speech Communication Association, 1992. 2v. $60.00pa./set. LC 87-061400. ISBN 0-944811-08-6.

Now in its 4th edition, this index to major scholarly journals that pertain to speech and journalism has been expanded to include four additional communication periodicals. All 19 of the titles indexed are covered from their inception through 1990. Due to its extended coverage, the index has been split into two volumes. Volume 1 contains the tables of contents for primary articles in the journals indexed. Volume 2 consists of a contributor index, a classified index of subjects based on a system developed for the National Center for Education Statistics, and a keyword index to terms used for subcategories in the classification scheme.

A significant improvement in this edition is the provision of direct access from the keyword index to the articles cited in the tables of contents. Previously, this index referred users to codes in the classified subject index, thus necessitating an inefficient two-step process to identify pertinent articles. Unfortunately, the value of the keyword index is diminished by the omission of a number of important subcategories, including those for politics and advertising, public service announcements, and film ratings. Locating index references, which consist of a letter that represents the journal title and a number that denotes the article within the journal continues to be a frustrating procedure, as the tables of contents are not arranged in alphabetical order by the journal symbols. Indeed, the arrangement of journal titles in the table of contents follows no discernible logic. All but four of the journals indexed in this source are also covered in *Communication Abstracts*. However, this work's importance lies in its cumulative and retrospective coverage (the earliest journal indexed began in 1915) and an indexing system that provides both broad and precise subject access. For example, the classified index brings together all the articles that relate to public address, whereas the keyword index provides references to specific speakers, places, movements, and the like.

Although this edition is a notable improvement over its predecessors, it is still somewhat cumbersome to use. In spite of its flaws, it remains a valuable source for academic libraries that support programs in speech communication, journalism, or mass media.

—Marie Ellis

955. **The Instant National Locator Guide.** San Francisco, Calif., Creighton-Morgan, 1991. 1v. (various paging). maps. $15.95pa. HE8721. 384.6'025'73. ISBN 0-9620096-5-2.

This guide enables the user to quickly find ZIP codes and area codes, and conversely, to learn which areas they represent. The first of five individually paged sections provides ZIP and area codes for all cities and towns with a population of more than 2,500 and all county seats. It does not provide individual ZIP codes by street for cities that have more than one ZIP code, however. Cities are listed alphabetically on a nationwide basis, with columns for state, area code, ZIP code, county, population, and the page number of the state map on which the city can be located. Symbols and type changes direct the user to additional information located at the bottom of the page (e.g., "Bold = Over 15,000").

State maps are found in the second section, with the first three digits of ZIP codes for different areas prominently displayed. Cities, counties, county seats, and state capitals are clearly indicated, and even crowded maps are easy to read. A third section lists counties by state with the name of the county seat, and the fourth section lists ZIP codes in numerical order with their corresponding cities. The final section lists states alphabetically with their area codes and then reverses the procedure, listing ZIP codes numerically with their appropriate state. Except for a few typographical errors, *The Instant National Locator Guide* seems to be an accurate (and reasonable) purchase for all public libraries and for anyone who is in need of this type of information. [R: RBB, 1 Jan 92, pp. 849-50]

—Jo Anne H. Ricca

956. Phillips, Donald E., with Marcia K. Malott. **Human Communication Behavior and Information Processing: An Interdisciplinary Sourcebook.** Hamden, Conn., Garland, 1992. 938p. index. (Garland Reference Library of Social Science, v.620). $128.00. P90.P46. 302.2. LC 91-37399. ISBN 0-8240-3531-3.

This extensive bibliography contains 5,766 entries that range from the purely theoretical to applied works. The rationale for the bibliography is to provide a sourcebook that brings together the disciplines that contribute to an understanding of human communication and information processing. Seven principles, or perhaps assumptions, that support the rationale for the book are stated and discussed in the introduction. Examples include "Communication behavior and information processing are basic life processes"; "Communication is a means of expressing love, views of truth, and beauty"; and "Communication is relational, our basic way of relating to the world, and to each other." These principles appear to form the criteria for selecting works for the bibliography.

The entries have been compiled from library catalogs, databases, periodicals, special bibliographies, and the like. Specific resources are not listed. The "more important" entries are annotated. When present, the annotations range from a single, general, and sometimes vague sentence to a short paragraph. The bibliography is difficult to use because of the lack of well-developed author and subject indexes. (The index provided is similar to a table of contents.) The book's format provides another distraction. Much of the text is difficult to read because the computer program used to justify the text placed too much space between some words. Nevertheless, the bibliography provides a wealth of information unavailable elsewhere and will make a valuable contribution to the reference collection of academic, public, and special libraries. [R: Choice, Oct 92, p. 178]

—William E. Hug

AUTHORSHIP

957. **Children's Writer's & Illustrator's Market, 1992.** Lisa Carpenter and Roseann Shaughnessy, eds. Cincinnati, Ohio, Writer's Digest Books, 1992. 311p. index. $17.95pa. ISBN 0-89879-487-0. ISSN 0897-9790.

Writer's Digest has been publishing annual editions of this guide for several years, just as it has many other aids for writers of all stripes. The present volume gives sound, hard-headed advice to prospective authors on all aspects of the writing of children's books, from the initial sale of a manuscript to dealing with agents and editors to reviewing proofs. The heart of the book is, of course, the entries on individual publishers, including not only directory information but also topics published, method of contact preferred, and other essential data that budding authors ignore at their peril. Interrupting this march of data are thumbnail sketches of successful writers of children's material.—**Philip A. Metzger**

958. Day, Robert A. **Scientific English: A Guide for Scientists and Other Professionals.** Phoenix, Ariz., Oryx Press, 1992. 125p. illus. index. $15.95pa. PE1475.D38. 808'.0665. LC 92-9672. ISBN 0-89774-722-4.

This sprightly tome exemplifies the author's thesis—that English, simply taught, is a simple language. The didactic portion of the text is organized around the basic parts of speech, with additional chapters dealing with punctuation, prefixes and suffixes, sentence structure, redundancies, jargon, and the like. The book is full of little gems of information, such as the rule for the use of numbers (whether to spell them out or to use numerals). Further, the generous use of humorous examples and cartoons make this treatment of a rather arid subject almost enjoyable to read. The author has drawn on his lengthy experience as an editor and publisher of scientific journals to provide numerous examples of horrible prose.

The title is too modest in defining the subject as "scientific English"—this book can be read with profit by anyone attempting to convey information by the use of the written language. Highly recommended for all types of libraries and for personal purchase.—**Edwin D. Posey**

959. Furberg, Jon, and Richard Hopkins. **College Style Sheet.** 3d ed. Vancouver, B.C., Vancouver Community College Press, 1992. 66p. index. $4.95pa. 808'.02. ISBN 0-921218-43-5.

This book has been widely used in colleges in British Columbia and in other schools in Canada. Last issued in 1988, this new edition incorporates the American Psychological Association's (APA) style (to also cover sociology and biology), nondiscriminatory language, paraphrase, summary, proofreading marks, and the use of word processors. It also now has an index and more examples in general. The source material for the manner of style is taken from the *MLA Handbook for Writers of Research Papers* (see ARBA 89, entry 832); Kate Turabian's *A Manual for Writers of Term Papers, Theses, and Dissertations* (see ARBA 88, entry 924)—which is itself derived from *The Chicago Manual of Style* (see ARBA 83, entry 85); the APA; the American Library Association style manual for citing microforms and nonprint media (1978); and the University of Toronto's bibliographical form for Canadian government publications (1985-1986). The book is extremely useful for Canadians.—**Dean Tudor**

960. **Grants and Awards Available to American Writers.** New York, PEN American Center, 1992. 163p. index. $8.00pa.; $12.50pa. (libraries and institutions). ISBN 0-934638-11-X.

Writers wish that the large advances that make headlines in *Publishers Weekly* were the rule rather than the exception. However, save for those few who crash the best-seller lists, the monetary rewards for writing are small, and the opportunities for support for writers while they create their works are few and far between. Through this edition of its directory of grants and awards, the PEN American Center gives the struggling writer a chance to secure needed resources to keep working or to recognize completed work in a tangible way. It lists awards available for use in the United States, Canada, and other countries and, with a few exceptions based on an award's prestige, limits itself to "those grants and awards carrying a cash stipend of $500 or more, or involving publication of a manuscript or production of a dramatic or performance work." It also includes residence programs that offer writers a peaceful place to work and room and board rather than cash.

The awards are listed alphabetically by key words based on the granting organizations' names, with country-specific awards listed under those countries' names. Symbols in the margin that correlate to the categories in the subject index promote serendipitous discoveries and make it easy to scan the listings to identify awards for fiction, poetry, drama, and other categories. Each entry describes the purpose of the program and the nature of its award, eligibility and application requirements, deadlines, and contact person. The lack of telephone and fax numbers in the listings means that prospective applicants must either obtain them from another source or write for application information. An appendix lists state and provincial arts councils, and award and organization indexes supplement the directory's organization.

Writers of more than modest ability will appreciate the convenience of having information on these 500-plus programs gathered in one book. Libraries that experience heavy demand for *Writer's Market* (see ARBA 91, entry 945) ought to have this and make sure that the users of one are also aware of the other. —**James Rettig**

961. **Guide to Literary Agents & Art/Photo Reps, 1992.** Robin Gee, ed. Cincinnati, Ohio, Writer's Digest Books, 1991. 250p. index. $15.95. ISBN 0-89879-485-4. ISSN 1055-6087.

Although Writer's Digest Books has included agent information in its various subject-specific guides, this new work is the first to concentrate solely on these creative brokers. It is formatted in the familiar Writer's Digest manner, beginning with 10 essays about literary agents—what they do, how to choose one, when to change, and so on. The entries that follow are divided into sections on nonfee and fee-charging literary agents, script agents, commercial art and photography representatives, and fine art representatives. Entries are dense with data; up to 20 pieces of information may be given for each (e.g., date of agency establishment, member agents, areas of interest, conferences attended). There is also a section of resources that lists recommended publications and professional organizations for writers and artists. A glossary and various indexes round out the book.

Comparison with *Literary Agents of North America* (see ARBA 92, entry 896) is inevitable. That publication lists more than 1,000 literary agents to *Guide*'s 500, in part because it covers the West Coast more thoroughly. (Of course, *Guide* also lists art representatives.) Both have some fairly "empty" entries, but *Literary Agents* seems to have the most. *Literary Agents* has much more detailed and readable indexes (those in *Guide* are in paragraph form rather than in a list down the page). Each book starts with handy information about the agent scene, but *Guide* goes into more depth in specific areas and also discusses art/photography representatives. Each book has agencies that the other lacks, although *Literary Agents* lists more of those in *Guide* than vice versa. Finally, *Literary Agents* is published every few years, whereas *Guide* will most likely become an annual.

Both of these highly informative books are worthwhile purchases. Ideally, a library should have both, especially at their reasonable prices (*Literary Agents* is nearly twice the price of *Guide*, which is still not expensive). If a choice must be made, *Literary Agents* would be better for a writing-oriented clientele, and *Guide* would be better for a varied audience. [R: RBB, 15 Jan 92, pp. 972-74]
—**D. A. Rothschild**

962. Lester, Meera. **Writing for the Ethnic Markets.** Cupertino, Calif., Writers Connection, 1991. 259p. index. $14.95pa. PN165.L4. 808.02. ISBN 0-9622592-4-1.

This publication is intended "for writers interested in learning how to evaluate, write, target, and sell their materials to markets that accept manuscripts dealing with ethnic themes, issues, and elements" (introduction). It consists of two major parts. The first includes chapters called "Cultural Diversity: A Theme for Writers"; "Sizing Up the Market"; "Putting Power in Your Prose"; "Writing Short, Ethnic Oriented Nonfiction"; and "Ethnicity in Film." The second part includes information sources pertaining to book publishers, periodicals, film and television markets, multicultural resources, and other relevant markets. A comprehensive subject index concludes the work. Probably the weakest part of this publication is the section on periodical publishers, which includes few ethnic-oriented serials. Also, the section on multicultural resources does not include such important centers as the Center for the Study of Ethnic Publications and Cultural Institutions at Kent State University, Ohio. Regardless, Lester's guide is an important addition to ethnic reference literature. [R: RBB, 1 Mar 92, p. 1309]

—Lubomyr R. Wynar

963. Mandell, Judy, comp. and ed. **Fiction Writers Guidelines: Over 260 Periodical Editors' Instructions Reproduced and Indexed.** 2d ed. Jefferson, N.C., McFarland, 1992. 337p. illus. index. $28.50pa. PN3355.M26. 808.3. LC 92-53504. ISBN 0-89950-673-9.

Submitting material to publishers is more complicated than it may seem. What sort of stories are they looking (and *not* looking) for? Do they accept material on disk? Do they want the author to format the piece in a special way? *Fiction Writers Guidelines* reproduces a number of periodical publishers' rules for submitting fiction (and poetry in many cases). The selection of periodicals—obviously not comprehensive—is a good mix of small and large, secular and religious, genre and general magazines that range from *Aboriginal Science Fiction* to *Lutheran Woman Today* to *ZYZZYVA*. Children's publications are listed, as are some literary magazines. Even pornographic markets appear. A section at the end lists 10 magazines with no guidelines. The index is very thorough, listing everything that appears in the guidelines (e.g., abstract mind trips).

There are some minor quibbles with the entries. More Jewish-themed magazines could have been included. As each entry consists solely of the reprinted guidelines, some of the periodicals would benefit from a little explanation as to their content (e.g., *ZYZZYVA* gives no clue as to the type of material in which it specializes, save that it only wants West Coast writers). At least one entry (for the *Signal*) appears to have been copied from *Writer's Market* (see ARBA 91, entry 945), but it was submitted by *Signal* and, therefore, is not the fault of Mandell. While most of the entries have reproduced well, that for *Home Life* is fuzzy and hard to read. Most of the children's magazines are religiously oriented.

Overall, this is an excellent and useful work. It will save writers time and postage and expose them to a number of markets they may not have considered. While everyone will miss a favorite publisher, there should be enough here to satisfy specific tastes. And it is fascinating to see how differently each set of guidelines is formatted! Highly recommended for public, college, and personal libraries.

—**D. A. Rothschild**

964. **The Merriam-Webster Concise Handbook for Writers.** Springfield, Mass., Merriam-Webster, 1991. 310p. index. $8.95pa. PE1408.M517. 428.2. LC 91-27326. ISBN 0-87779-602-5.

This practical handbook for writers was written by the publisher's editorial staff, drawing on a database of 14 million examples of English words used in context from books, newspapers, magazines, newsletters, annual reports, and institutional mailings. Intended for home, school, and office use, it offers treatment of the mechanics of writing and the basics of composition and grammar. The chapter on numbers is extensive and goes into more detail than does the *Chicago Manual of Style* (see ARBA 83, entry 85), explaining many fine points that *Chicago* sidesteps or ignores. There is a chapter on notes and bibliography as well as a chapter on copyediting and proofreading. The organization is practical, with a table of contents preceding each chapter and numbered paragraphs that allow readers to easily find their way to cross-referenced material.

This is a good usage manual, but, as are other handbooks on the English language, it is limited in its coverage of the topic by the need to remain reasonable in length and price. It lacks, for instance, definitions of restrictive and nonrestrictive clauses in the context of using "which" and "that." However, it offers contemporary opinions on usage, reflecting the ever-changing form of the English language, and will be helpful when used in conjunction with old standbys such as *Chicago* and handbooks written specifically for a writer's interest area. The book is a worthwhile purchase for school, public, and academic libraries and will be of use to all editors and writers.—**Louis R. Ruybal**

965. Naylor, Lynne, comp. and ed. **Television Writers Guide.** 2d ed. Los Angeles, Calif., Lone Eagle, 1991. 442p. index. $49.95. ISBN 0-943728-37-1.

This edition updates and adds to the entries that appeared in the first edition (see ARBA 90, entry 919). It covers the 1978-1990 television seasons. The first section consists of two parts—an Emmy Awards and nominations list followed by the main section on writers. The latter is arranged alphabetically by writer with the television credits for each person. An asterisk denotes Writers Guild of

America membership, while alternate names and cowriters are noted when appropriate. In most cases either an agency or a contact with telephone number is provided.

The second section is the genre list—comedy series, daytime shows, drama series, movies of the week, specials, and variety shows. For each genre there is an alphabetical arrangement of shows with their corresponding production companies and networks. There are indexes of television titles, agents and managers, and advertisers.

This useful book contains indispensable information for a limited clientele. Large academic libraries with specialized mass media/communication/film departments or programs will find it valuable.—**R. Errol Lam**

966. **Novel & Short Story Writer's Market, 1992.** Robin Gee and Christine Martin, eds. Cincinnati, Ohio, Writer's Digest Books, 1992. 638p. illus. index. $19.95pa. ISBN 0-89879-486-2. ISSN 0897-9812.

The format of this work has not changed significantly in quite a while (see ARBA 90, entry 902 for an earlier review). It is still one of the best and most thorough—if not the most comprehensive—guides to writers' markets available. Entries contain just about everything the hopeful prose writer needs in order to submit material in the correct format to the proper place. Some 300 new markets have been added, and 90 percent of the entries have been updated (although, as does any directory, this one already has out-of-date information). There are four new lists under "Resources": conferences and workshops, retreats and colonies, organizations and other resources for writers (e.g., "rooms"), and periodicals of interest. The essays that begin the book are entirely new, as are the author and publisher profiles scattered throughout. It is still easy to take exception with the paragraph-style indexes, and writers should be aware that the markets listed are by no means the only places to submit their stories; but in general, this book should be routinely purchased by nearly all libraries.—**D. A. Rothschild**

967. **The Oxford Dictionary for Scientific Writers and Editors.** New York, Clarendon Press/Oxford University Press, 1991. 389p. $45.00. T11.094. 808'.0666. LC 91-350. ISBN 0-19-853920-7.

Scientific writers and editors have a particularly difficult time in the preparation of material for publication. Because of the progressive and international nature of science, such things as spelling, punctuation, abbreviations, symbols, nomenclatures, prefixes, and suffixes used by scientists can vary from country to country and field to field, or even era to era. This is particularly true where a distinction exists between the usage and spelling common in the United States and the United Kingdom. This loosely titled "dictionary" is primarily a style guide for over 9,500 terms, acronyms, and names of scientists in the fields of physics, chemistry, botany, zoology, biochemistry, genetics, immunology, microbiology, astronomy, mathematics, and computer science. It is designed as a companion volume to the *Oxford Dictionary for Writers and Editors* (see ARBA 82, entry 1239). A unique feature of the book is its advocacy of the Harvard (author-date) system for references, although Oxford University Press also uses the numbered system. An entire appendix describes the systems and their advantages in detail, while a shorter explanation appears in the body of the book. This is a handy little volume for quick reference when writing or editing, but a scientific writer will still need a full scientific dictionary for fuller definitions of most of the terms.—**Robert J. Havlik**

968. **The Penguin Dictionary for Writers and Editors.** By Bill Bryson. New York, Viking Penguin, 1991. 403p. $20.00. LC 91-65576. ISBN 0-670-83767-9.

This small format book is something of a curiosity. The author's aim is to address a variety of "problems of spelling and usage" although the prefatory material does not define these problems. Scanning the pages reveals them to be confusion over proper usage (e.g., *farther* vs. *further*), spelling of proper names (and location of place-names), frequently misspelled words (e.g., *numskull, scary, foreword*), British and United States variations in spelling (e.g., *analyse* vs. *analyze*), words often confused for each other (e.g., *breach* vs. *breech*), and common errors of grammar. Selection criteria are not explained. The author has included quite a wide variety of terms, from the truly general (e.g., *a, an*) to the questionably specific (e.g., *Aberystwyth*, a place-name in Wales). No explanation is given as to why some words are defined (briefly) while others are not; it is left to the reader to conclude that undefined terms are there merely because they are often spelled incorrectly.

Many features of this book would be of use to an author or editor, such as the short but handy table of "able" versus "ible" words, the currency table, and the conversion tables. On the other hand, it is hard to imagine what real use the European Vehicle Identification Code and list of major airports would be to anyone other than a traveler. An author or editor who needs information on British monarchs would do better to refer to the *Cambridge Biographical Dictionary* (see ARBA 92, entry 25) or another standard biographical work rather than to the list in this book. All in all, this is an interesting book but not an essential reference. [R: LJ, Jan 92, p. 104] – **Sharon Langworthy**

969.   Perdue, Lewis. **The High-Technology Editorial Guide and Stylebook.** PC ed. Homewood, Ill., Business One Irwin, 1991. 194p. $39.95pa. (with disk). QA76.165.P47. 808'.066004. LC 91-27524. ISBN 1-55623-531-3.

Anyone who has written or read much in the computer field has probably noticed the lack of consistency between publications in their use of computer terms and the difficulty of determining such matters as spelling and capitalization of software or business names. *The High Technology Editorial Guide and Stylebook* fills a need for a definitive stylebook of high-tech terminology. Modeled on *The Associated Press Stylebook and Libel Manual* (Addison-Wesley, 1987), it is an alphabetical list of high-tech terminology, trademarks, and business and corporate names; it is also useful as a general editorial guide. Perdue should be applauded for deriding the jargon, redundancies, and misuses common in the high-tech world (e.g., *Impact*: "Not a verb. Not a verb. Not a verb").

Unfortunately, this work is not without its problems. Perdue contradicts his own style in several instances. He specifically says to spell *U.S.* without a space, then uses *U. S.*; *Mandelbrot Set* is used on one occasion and *Mandelbrot set* on another; and he has a half-page entry on the difference between *that* and *which* but misuses *which* several times. The disk that accompanies the book comes with no more instruction or explanation than that it is "in ASCII format which can be imported into most spell checkers," assuming computer knowledge on the part of users. Also, Perdue lists *Word For Windows*, when Microsoft Corporation's own literature specifies *Word for Windows*.

Despite these minor problems and the relatively high price, this book deserves to become the accepted source of style for high-technology publishing. It is easy to use and comprehensive and should provide much-needed consistency in this burgeoning field. As is so much of the technology it deals with, it is young and will no doubt improve with age. [R: RBB, 1 Mar 92, p. 1307]

– **Stephen Haenel**

970.   Rubens, Philip, ed. **Science and Technical Writing: A Manual of Style.** New York, Henry Holt, 1992. 513p. illus. index. $40.00. T11.S378. 808'.0666. LC 91-36422. ISBN 0-8050-1831-X.

In addition to the more traditional content of style manuals for scientific and technical writing, this book provides information on creating useful illustrations and usable data displays. The key words here are "useful" and "usable." With the easy availability of desktop publishing software, scientific and technical writers are often tempted to include visual material that is poorly conceived and executed. One of the most valuable sections of this manual shows the same information in unacceptable and then acceptable format. For example, the unacceptable bar chart is more difficult to understand because it uses complex shading and other unnecessary graphic effects.

This book also provides chapters on solving paragraph and sentence problems, punctuating scientific and technical text, handling specialized terminology, and addressing nonnative readers. Another important section covers indexing and includes such topics as planning and organizing the index, index page design, and indexing procedure. The author's own index is a model of clarity and readability. This manual is a valuable reference work for library acquisition, and anyone who does scientific or technical writing will want a copy. [R: RBB, 15 Oct 92, pp. 458-60]

– **Renee B. Horowitz**

971.   Shuman, R. Baird. **Resources for Writers: An Annotated Bibliography.** Pasadena, Calif., Salem Press, 1992. 167p. index. (Magill Bibliographies). $40.00. Z5165.S55. 016.808'02. LC 91-36214. ISBN 0-89356-673-X.

The premise underlying this book is worth a round of applause! Rather than take the easy route to compiling a bibliography that will offer advice to the aspiring writer—a route that would weave in and out of the stacks in a large research library—Shuman has instead focused on his audience. In other words, because a majority of people in this country live in small towns, he has concentrated on the resources available in the local public library. This approach will make this book an extremely important addition to the collections of those small public libraries.

The book is organized around the following categories: short fiction, novels, nonfiction, drama, poetry, film and television, juvenile literature, autobiography/biography/family history, magazines and journals, and preparing/marketing/promoting manuscripts and books. Some general titles that do not fit neatly into these categories are given in the author's introduction. Each entry has a brief annotation. The final chapter provides additional resources: the names of postsecondary writing programs (arranged by state), writers' conferences and workshops (also arranged by state), writers' colonies, and additional print sources.

While this book is important to the collections of small public libraries, it can also be a welcome addition to large libraries of any type. Definitely recommended. [R: RBB, 1 June 92, p. 1776]

—**Darlene E. Weingand**

972. Tarutz, Judith A. **Technical Editing: The Practical Guide for Editors and Writers.** Reading, Mass., Addison-Wesley, 1992. 454p. index. $25.95pa. T11.4.T37. 808'.0666. LC 92-11644. ISBN 0-201-56356-8.

The job of technical editors is different from that of other editors because they deal with specialized subjects written for specific clientele. Most technical editors work for companies or corporations and are involved in the production of manuals, data sheets, specification sheets, technical reports, and proposals. To be successful in all these areas, the technical editor must act as a writer, proofreader, production editor, copy editor, literary editor, and development editor, all under the pressure of deadlines and technical accuracy. The goal of this book is to present a practical guide to the tricks of the trade to get the job done. It is organized into three sections: "The Editor's Role," "The Editor's Job," and the "Editor's Career." Besides its use as a handbook to current editorial practice, it has value as a career guide for new entrants or persons already working in the field. The appendixes include case studies, sample style guides, answers to exercises, a glossary, a bibliography, and an index.

—**Robert J. Havlik**

973. van Leunen, Mary-Claire. **A Handbook for Scholars.** rev. ed. New York, Oxford University Press, 1992. 348p. index. $29.95; $12.95pa. PN146.V36. 808'.027. LC 91-19230. ISBN 0-19-506953-6; 0-19-506954-4pa.

Written by an editor of scholarly books, this revised handbook features new chapters on preparing manuscripts using computers. While van Leunen does not delineate the sections with major revisions, her introduction points out her revised thinking about the muddle of "he/she" and "him/her" pronoun usage—the style of which she has changed to the feminine in this edition.

Generally, the book offers scholars guidance in preparing writing projects to avoid the woodenness, pedantry, and crypticness of typical scholarly writing. Van Leunen makes no excuses for the formality and allusiveness of scholarly writing but emphasizes—in her own clear and crisp writing style—clarity, force, and grace. She takes the reader through four major areas of manuscript preparation: text, references, reference lists, and the mechanical aspects of putting together a project. One excellent section is a discussion of the uses of *which* and *that*. Her advice is practical, to the point, and clever. In a lengthy chapter on using quotations, she writes, "Quote only the quotable. Quote for color; quote for evidence. Otherwise, don't quote. When you are writing well, your sentences should join each other like rows of knitting, each sentence pulling up what went before it, each sentence supporting what comes after (that's how I think knitting works). Quotation introduces alien patterns—someone else's diction, someone else's voice, someone else's links before and afterward."

The book is rounded out with an appendix on vita preparation and another on federal documents—what they are and how to access them. An index provides reasonable access but contains a puzzling entry—"job for vistas"—that is probably a typographical error. The typeface is clear and very readable. The line leading is generous, and the interior book design is as lean as a scholarly text, with examples set off in typescript font. Overall, this is a good book for academic and public libraries and for editors in scholarly publishing companies. It would also make a good general reference for other editors and nonacademic writers. — **Louis R. Ruybal**

974. **Who's Who in Writers, Editors & Poets: United States and Canada 1992-1993.** 4th ed. Curt Johnson and Frank Nipp, eds. Highland Park, Ill., December Press, 1992. 547p. index. $97.00. LC 87-648220. ISBN 0-913204-25-0. ISSN 1049-8621.

This directory was first published in 1987. With the 3d edition Canadians were added; the present and rather awkward title was adopted at that time. Individual entries continue to be brief, providing standard biographical information (e.g., education, birth date and place, family, awards, current address). Information on an author's publications is, perforce, brief. Many of the individuals included are not well known and this, perhaps, is the directory's major contribution. However, many of the individuals can be found in other sources. Since 1988, the directory has been indexed in *Biography and Genealogy Master Index* (see ARBA 87, entry 420).

This edition does not include the present editor of the *New Yorker* magazine, Robert Gottlieb, or the editor of Time-Life Books, Tom Flaherty. A random check of university press editors indicates that most — if not all — are not included in this edition. For information on Canadians, librarians will prefer *Who's Who in the Writers' Union of Canada* (Writers' Union, 1988), *Who's Who in Canadian Literature* (Reference Press, 1992), and *Profiles in Canadian Literature* (Dundurn Press, 1980-). Information on creative authors is provided by sources such as *Directory of American Poets and Fiction Writers* (see ARBA 91, entry 946) and the well-known *International Authors and Writers Who's Who* (see ARBA 87, entry 1075). — **Milton H. Crouch**

NEWSPAPERS AND MAGAZINES

975. Bjorner, Susan N., comp. and ed. **Newspapers Online: A Directory to North American Daily Newspapers Whose Articles are Online in Full Text.** Needham Heights, Mass., BiblioData, 1992. 179p. index. $80.00pa. ISBN 1-879258-04-8.

Newspapers are useful current sources of regional information and information on people, events, businesses, industries, and so forth that are of particular local interest. This directory provides data on more than 125 American and Canadian daily general-interest newspapers available online within (at most) 72 hours of original publication.

Availability information given for each newspaper includes online system vendors, file names, start date for full coverage, and lag time; if the paper is also available on CD-ROM, that fact and vendor names are given. Each entry also has a short description of the region covered and publication data on the newspaper, including frequency, time of day, and various editions and special features. The directory lists parts of the newspaper that are included or excluded from the online edition. A useful feature is the "newsmakers" section, which lists some people, places, and things important in that region and about which one might expect good coverage in the local papers. There is also a newsmakers index, but this listing is not comprehensive and uses no controlled vocabulary.

The main listing is alphabetical by title; titles that contain no place of publication are alphabetized under the city of publication added in parentheses. Thus, *Deseret News* is listed under *(Salt Lake City) Deseret News*. Sometimes one entry covers two closely affiliated papers in the same city. An alternative title index gives access to the actual names. There is also a geographic locator that has both political and geographic terms. An appendix gives names and addresses for the 14 online and CD-ROM vendors included in the directory, and another section provides information on alternative vendors, service agreements, and gateways. A helpful feature is a short bibliographical guide to sources for help in how to search newspapers online. [R: Choice, Oct 92, p. 277; LJ, 15 Mar 92, p. 80] — **Marit S. MacArthur**

976. Connery, Thomas B., ed. **A Sourcebook of American Literary Journalism: Representative Writers in an Emerging Genre.** Westport, Conn., Greenwood Press, 1992. 408p. index. $69.50. PS366.R44S68. 818'.08. LC 91-17127. ISBN 0-313-26594-1.

Truman Capote's *In Cold Blood* and Tracy Kidder's *House* are widely divergent works. However, both are examples of literary journalism, a form of nonfiction that combines elements of conventional reporting with narrative techniques characteristic of fiction. This useful guide provides the most comprehensive coverage to date of this particular literary realm. It features essays on 35 nineteenth- and twentieth-century American writers whose works are representative of this prose style. In addition to Capote and Kidder, individuals treated include Mark Twain, Stephen Crane, Ernest Hemingway, Lillian Ross, Tom Wolfe, and Joan Didion. Contributed by scholars in the fields of journalism and communication, the chronologically arranged essays average nine pages. Each analyzes the writer's journalistic prose and illustrates narrative technique through the generous use of quotations from selected works. A selective bibliography of primary and secondary sources follows each essay.

In his lengthy introduction Connery offers various definitions of literary journalism, traces its history, and provides a review of the literature pertaining to literary journalism and the new journalists. He also briefly profiles 19 literary journalists not accorded separate essays. The well-conceived index, which includes references to writers, topics, and titles, could serve as a model for sources of this type. This excellent compilation is particularly appropriate for academic libraries that support communication, journalism, mass media, or writing programs. [R: Choice, Sept 92, p. 92; LJ, Jan 92, p. 110; RBB, 1 Feb 92, pp. 1057-58; WLB, June 92, p. 158]—**Marie Ellis**

977. Lane, Susan, and Elizabeth Hasten. **The 1992-1993 Guide to Newspaper Syndication, 1992-1993.** Irvine, Calif., Newspaper Syndication Specialists, 1992. 179p. index. $19.95pa. LC 91-066481. ISBN 0-9615800-4-6.

For those interested in newspaper syndication—from cartoonists wanting to market their products through a syndicate to students or scholars who need information about syndicates or the products of syndicates—this guide will be invaluable. The first and longest section is a directory that provides basic information for more than 250 U.S. newspaper syndicates: name, address, telephone number, key contact person, recently begun features, and what sorts of materials are of interest. The next section, "Syndicate Profiles," contains interviews with 10 syndicate executives, providing advice and suggestions for those hoping to syndicate their work. Shorter sections contain a variety of information about the world of syndication: trends, best-selling features, and the 100 largest circulation newspapers. Finally, there are guidelines for submitting material along with sample cover letters. This specialized but useful work is appropriate for reference collections that serve schools of journalism or large public libraries. [R: LJ, July 92, p. 78; RBB, Aug 92, p. 2038]—**Evan Ira Farber**

978. **Newsletters in Print 1993-94: A Descriptive Guide to More Than 11,000 Subscription, Membership, and Free Newsletters....** 6th ed. John Krol and Terri Kessler, eds. Detroit, Gale, 1992. 1483p. index. $175.00. ISBN 0-8103-7520-6. ISSN 0899-0425.

This volume is a treasure trove of information about newsletters, those ubiquitous members of the media family. There are thousands—some 11,000 are listed here, with 1,700 more new entries than in the previous edition. Krol and Kessler have managed to list this astonishing array in a useful manner with six indexes for access—online, free, those that carry advertising, publisher, subject, and title. To find a given newsletter takes some tracking—ethics, for example, is divided into several subsections—but almost every one of consequence is listed. Readers are invited to inform the editors of omissions. The lifetime of a newsletter, alas, is often as short-lived as a snowfall in April, and some of the casualties are still listed. This is, nonetheless, a handy book that can be put to use by anyone in communication, advertising, or public relations. Descriptions, addresses, telephone numbers, and brief precis of content make this a valuable addition for writers as well.—**S. L. Harrison**

979. Schulze, Suzanne. **Horace Greeley: A Bio-Bibliography.** Westport, Conn., Greenwood Press, 1992. 212p. index. (Bibliographies and Indexes in American History, no.22). $45.00. E415.9.G8S38. 016.07092. LC 91-46697. ISBN 0-313-26736-7.

Works cited in this bio-bibliography are arranged in two principal sections: works by Horace Greeley and works by other authors in which Greeley or his writings are featured. The portion of the book devoted to Greeley's writings includes separate subsections on books, periodical articles, other published materials (e.g., lectures, speeches), and contributions to other published works. A separate subsection itemizes newspapers and printers for whom Greeley worked or that he established. The biographical section has separate subsections for complete biographies, biographical and historical works, citations in reference sources, periodical articles, theses, manuscript collections, and government documents. There are author and subject indexes and a chronology of Greeley's life.

Schulze has examined most of the works included and has prepared detailed annotations. She has also included a remarkably thorough biographical sketch. The care and close attention to accuracy and detail that she has devoted to this book are evident in every paragraph. The organization of citations and their annotations are models of clarity and bibliographic and literary style. Libraries with an interest in American history, politics, newspaper history, or Horace Greeley should give serious consideration to acquiring this work. — **Margaret McKinley**

980. **A Select Index to** *Svoboda*, **Official Publication of the Ukrainian National Association, Inc.... Volume One: 1893-1899.** Walter Anastas and Maria Woroby, comps. Saint Paul, Minn., Immigration History Research Center, University of Minnesota, 1990. 387p. $25.00pa. LC 89-82654. ISBN 0-932833-10-1.

981. **A Select Index to** *Svoboda*, **Official Publication of the Ukrainian National Association, Inc.... Volume Two: 1900 to 1907.** Walter Anastaziovsky, with Roman Stepchuk, comps. Saint Paul, Minn., Immigration History Research Center, 1991. 410p. $25.00pa. LC 89-82654. ISBN 0-932833-11-X.

Svoboda, the Ukrainian daily published by the Ukrainian National Association, is the oldest and most important Ukrainian newspaper in America. The publication of two initial volumes that index the daily from 1893 to 1907 is a welcome event not only for the scholarly community interested in immigration trends but also for the Ukrainian community at large. This index was compiled at the Immigration History Research Center of the University of Minnesota, an important repository of manuscript holdings of many ethnic groups. The first volume contains an informative introduction by Leonid Rudnytzky about the importance of *Svoboda* for studies of immigration pattern as well as the daily life of the Ukrainian-American community. A lengthy preface provides information on how to use this index; subject and geographical headings, personal names, cross-references, alphabetization, and information on terminology conclude the volume. Several useful changes have been introduced in the second volume. Subject headings are now more concise; there are numerous abstracts in English that describe the contents of more important articles; and the overall scope of the index has been reduced somewhat, eliminating nonessential articles.

Probably the weakest part of this useful compilation is the brief bibliography titled "List of References and Background Materials." There is quite a difference between the works of Halich and Swyripa versus an older edition of the Bartholomew atlas or even Tronko's Soviet encyclopedic work on Ukrainian regions. For so-called background information one can cite an endless number of titles, and such a brief bibliography can be confusing for the uninitiated. There are some other shortcomings, but in general these are well-executed works that should be found in most academic and larger public libraries. — **Bohdan S. Wynar**

982. Sova, Harry W., and Patricia L. Sova. **Communication Serials "An International Guide to Periodicals in Communication, Popular Culture, and the Performing Arts."** 1992/1993 ed. Virginia Beach, Va., SovaComm, 1992. 1041p. index. $129.00pa. ISBN 0-929976-00-2. ISSN 1041-7893.

The most inclusive guide now available to journals in the wide-ranging fields that comprise communication, *Communication Serials* is remarkable for the number of titles covered, the quantity of information given for each title, and the specificity of its indexes. The Sovas include journals from "40 areas of communication," listed on the back cover—from advertising to vaudeville. Emphasis is on mass communication; the field of cultural or intercultural studies is unlisted although several of its journals are recorded. Solid annotations describe the contents of typical issues and provide critical guidance about a title's importance in the field. Details about title changes help to document the complicated publication histories of such titles as *Broadcasting* and *Screen International*. Indexes cross-reference the titles by subjects, indexing and abstracting sources, ISSNs, publishers, variant titles, and other features.

Communication Serials certainly merits the praise it has received from communication scholars and librarians alike. Its journal coverage surpasses all other previous guides, such as Rebecca B. Rubin,

Alan M. Rubin, and Linda J. Piele's *Communication Research*, 2d ed. (Wadsworth, 1990), and Jean Ward and Kathleen Hansen's *Search Strategies in Mass Communication* (Longman, 1987). On the other hand, as a reference work that aims to set the standard in its field, *Communication Serials* has shortcomings. The most serious deficiencies concern its approximation of comprehensiveness. Granted, the Sovas nowhere claim comprehensiveness; however, the work does not list all of the journals in *Communication Abstracts*—something one might expect of a guide that includes more than 2,700 titles. An immediately obvious limitation is that "international" coverage here means English-language titles. (In fairness to the Sovas, neither the other guides in the field nor *Communication Abstracts* covers non-English-language serials.) As a result, the many non-U.S. titles covered are not their nations' most important communication journals. In general, however, far too many important, readily available, and well-indexed titles have been omitted. In the field of telecommunication, for example, omitted titles include the scholarly journals *Information Economics and Policy* and *Space Communication*, the trade journal *Telephony*, and the expensive newsletter *Communications Daily*.

In light of the coverage of drama and theater in a standard resource such as the biannual *MLA Directory of Periodicals* (Modern Language Association of America), the coverage of journals in these fields seems both redundant and perhaps even eccentric. At the same time, an interest in historicism seems to motivate inclusion of the obscure; it is difficult otherwise to explain the inclusion of such journals as *The Dramatic Censor*, published in London from 1800 to 1801.

The most serious omissions, however, concern journals in the field of interpersonal communication and access to them via the indexes: both are nonexistent in *Communication Serials*. Such titles as *Journal of Social Psychology, Journal of Educational Psychology,* and *American Behavioral Scientist* are not recorded. No subject index heading is provided for interpersonal communication, nor is interpersonal communication used as a subheading under other subjects.

Because of this uncomprehensiveness—bordering on imbalance in some areas—this work is not as useful as one might expect it to be. It is certainly not a vade mecum of communication journals, nor will all users find it equally helpful. The Sovas, who have put substantial effort into this work, will doubtless amend such shortcomings in their updates and subsequent editions.—**James K. Bracken**

RADIO, TELEVISION, AUDIO, AND VIDEO

Bibliography

983. Kraeuter, David W. **Radio and Television Pioneers: A Patent Bibliography.** Metuchen, N.J., Scarecrow, 1992. 319p. index. $35.00. Z7224.U6K7. 016.621384'027273. LC 92-8879. ISBN 0-8108-2556-2.

If one needs a list of radio and television inventors and a handy compendium of their patents, then this is the book to have. For each inventor (e.g., Marconi, De Forest, Pupin, Armstrong) Kraeuter has provided a chronological list of patents awarded, together with a brief citation (name of device, patent number, date, volume, and page) sufficient to locate the patent in the *Official Gazette of the Patent Office*. Only U.S. patents are listed. Most patents can be consulted via their patent number in patent depository libraries. At the end of the volume Kraeuter has provided a handy list of multiple patent holders by personal name. The style, typography, and layout of the work is similar to other Scarecrow Press products. This volume is recommended for libraries whose clients are interested in the development of U.S. radio and television. [R: Choice, Dec 92, p. 602]—**Ralph Lee Scott**

984. **Words on Cassette 1992.** New Providence, N.J., R. R. Bowker, 1992. 1603p. index. $124.95pa. ISBN 0-8352-3175-5.

Previously established as the definitive source for spoken-word audiocassettes, *On Cassette* (see ARBA 89, entry 849) has merged with Meckler's *Words on Tape* (see ARBA 90, entry 921); the result is an annotated list of more than 49,000 recordings of literary, business, historical, political, biographical, and humorous works. The expanded content and format will prove invaluable for librarians building cassette collections, for meeting patrons' needs, and for satisfying the equal access requirements of the 1990 Americans With Disabilities Act.

Arranged by title, entries identify reader, price, running time, date, contents, live or studio recording, number of cassettes, rental status (a concern of previous reviews), and price. The author and reader indexes facilitate the location of such recordings as Pablo Neruda reading his own poetry and Vincent Price reading ghost stories. The index, for more than 124 subjects, repeats all data except content description. Foreign-language instruction and literature tapes are available for 30 languages. Unfortunately, not all languages and all materials in a language, regardless of subject, are clearly represented. For example, Vietnamese materials appear under "Afro-Asiatic" or "English as a Second Language," but not under Vietnamese. Future additions should correct such difficulties because many libraries face growing demand from a multicultural clientele for materials in native languages. This work continues to be a necessary acquisition for all libraries. – **Sandra E. Belanger**

Biography

985. Watson, Elena M. **Television Horror Movie Hosts: 68 Vampires, Mad Scientists and Other Denizens of the Late-Night Airwaves....** Jefferson, N.C., McFarland, 1991. 242p. illus. index. $29.95. PN1992.8.F5W37. 791.45'616. LC 91-52642. ISBN 0-89950-570-8.

Thirty-one hosts of television horror movies are portrayed in this book. They range from 1954's Vampira (Maila Nurmi), who was reportedly the first such host, to Grampa Munster (Al Lewis), a recent addition to cable television. Factual information is provided, but the material is largely anecdotal. Much of the text is written somewhat tongue in cheek. Most of these hosts have had movie careers, and their film achievements are noted. The many black-and-white photographs will no doubt delight fans. Quite a few are full page and awash in ghoulishness. There is a reasonably good index to names and titles, although not everyone mentioned is indexed. A filmography-discography of the hosts is appended, as is a brief bibliography.

This work will help answer many of the questions asked about this genre. It is a must for public and school libraries, but academic libraries may want to pass on it. – **Helen M. Gothberg**

Dictionaries and Encyclopedias

986. Brown, Les. **Les Brown's Encyclopedia of Television.** 3d ed. Detroit, Gale, 1992. 723p. illus. index. $39.95. PN1992.18.B7. 791.45'03. LC 91-48157. ISBN 0-8103-8871-5.

This is the 3d edition of a work that began in 1977 as *The New York Times Encyclopedia of Television*. A helpful introduction provides an overview of what has happened in the television industry in the 10 years since the 2d edition was published. This edition has added new entries for a total of more than 800, has revised entries from the 2d edition, and has included a general subject index. It sports a new, international scope and an expanded bibliography. Appendixes include many valuable lists, such as top-rated network programs, commissioners of the Federal Communications Commission (FCC), and worldwide television advertising expenditures. Photographs, mainly of personalities, help break up the text.

On the down side, entries are uneven, some more appropriate to a dictionary than an encyclopedia. Entries of a historic or regulatory nature tend to be lengthier and more detailed – a single entry for acquisitions and mergers takes up five and one-half pages. Some program and people entries give only short plot capsules or biographical sketches, raising more questions than they answer. The expanded bibliography does not include many titles one might expect to find. *The Television Industry* (see ARBA 92, entry 914) comes to mind, especially as the present volume is reminiscent of it. Short bibliographies or references at the end of each entry would be very helpful in addition to a more thoroughly researched general bibliography. The index fails to cross-reference many entries adequately. For example, there is no index entry for mergers and acquisitions; those used to hearing that phrase must look for "acquisitions and mergers." In spite of these shortcomings, this work belongs in all comprehensive television collections. [R: Choice, Oct 92, p. ;268; RBB, 1 Sept 92, p. 86] – **Glynys R. Thomas**

987. **The Facts on File Dictionary of Film and Broadcast Terms.** By Edmund F. Penney. New York, Facts on File, 1991. 251p. $29.95. P87.5.P43. 001.51'03. LC 88-7023. ISBN 0-8160-1923-1.

Written by a screenwriter and director, this dictionary of 2,500 short definitions for trade words is intended as a utilitarian manual to be used by anyone with "an active interest" in film and television. Entries emphasize production, covering hardware (including brand-name equipment), technology, and practices and industry structures (some history). Twelve appendixes—script forms, budget forms, releases, and other tools—also increase the book's practical value. The intended audience, however, is unclear; the author assumes a users' familiarity with classic films and television shows but includes definitions in general circulation that are not at all exclusive to film and broadcasting. The reader will find other stylistic inconsistencies in the structure of entries (e.g., capitalization, alternate terms, abbreviations). The casual tone of the entries reflects Penney's stated anti-intellectual bias. This leads to the main problem with the dictionary: because Penney does not give historical background of usage, the dictionary lacks the detail to extend its relevance beyond the present. In a field where words and usage evolve quickly, it would have been helpful to know the context of that evolution.

This volume is not as well executed as some previous Facts on File dictionaries and encyclopedias. It lacks the precision and depth of *The Facts on File Dictionary of Personnel Management and Labor Relations* (see ARBA 87, entry 275), which includes such details as addresses of organizations mentioned, and *The Facts on File Dictionary of Telecommunications* (see ARBA 84, entry 1084), with its highly technical appendixes. *Film and Broadcast Terms* is important to a media reference library as a captured moment in media oral history, but it will have a limited shelf life as a working manual. [R: Choice, May 92, pp. 1372-73; RBB, 1 Feb 92, pp. 1054-57; SLJ, June 92, p. 155]—**Lori Elaine Taylor**

988. Inman, David. **The TV Encyclopedia.** New York, Perigee Books/Putnam, 1991. 800p. $35.00; $18.95pa. PN1992.4.A2I66. 791.45'092273. LC 90-24917. ISBN 0-399-51718-9; 0-399-51704-9pa.

There have been other compilations of performers' roles in regular television series, but this collection expands on those by noting the appearances of celebrities in guest roles, or as writers or directors, in television episodes. Arrangement is by name of celebrity, with the person's birth name, birth and death dates, a quick identification of the best-known role, title and year of each specific episode as a guest cast member, television movies and miniseries roles, and stints as a director or writer. Animated cartoon voices and news personalities are included, but appearances on most talk shows and the Academy Award telecasts are not. The year of any Emmy awards is noted at the end of the entry, but there is no indication of what role netted the award. A few programs that may have extra appeal for trivia fans, such as "All in the Family" and "Gilligan's Island," have a separate entry in addition to the casts' credits.

It is fascinating for television fans to scan the long list of appearances logged by many stars of all media before becoming famous overnight. However, this work would serve reference librarians more effectively if it was not so uneven. The entries vary widely in content; some celebrities are given the full treatment, while others have practically no information or dates, or any comment of their significance. Some of Inman's comments border on the cruel and have no place in a reference book with serious intent. Yet there are other entries where the comments are informative and interesting. There are also some surprising omissions. Raquel Welch is not noted as having been a regular on "Hollywood Palace," nor is Marlo Thomas given credit for her lead role in the television movie "It Happened One Christmas." Mark Lenard is not noted as Sarek (the father of Mr. Spock) on "Star Trek" (nor is the episode included under his name), yet Jane Wyatt is noted as Spock's mother in the same episode. The availability of birth dates is most erratic and should have been easy to verify through standard tools. There is no index nor other points of access to this work. Sidebars with information such as "TV's Top Ten 1952-53" can only be found by flipping through the book. There are 13 trivia quizzes mixed in, with answers in the back.

With its careless design and erratic contents, this book is a disappointment for the reference department. Its best use might be for trivia questions or as a general-interest item for public libraries. It is also acceptable for school and academic libraries where there is a strong interest in popular culture. [R: WLB, Mar 92, p. 119]—**Gary R. Cocozzoli**

Directories

989. **Bowker's Complete Video Directory 1992.** New Providence, N.J., R. R. Bowker, 1992. 2v. index. $189.95/set. ISBN 0-8352-3043-0.

R. R. Bowker, which has been publishing essential trade bibliographies since 1872, published the first edition of this much-needed reference tool in 1990. It is a *Books in Print* for videos. Rather cumbersomely divided into two volumes, each of which can be purchased separately, the 1992 edition lists, describes, and gives current source and price information for 87,000 programs from more than 1,500 manufacturers and distributors. Volume 1 ($99.00) lists 35,000 entertainment and performance videos (e.g., movies, cartoons, sports events, concerts, operas), up from 28,000 in 1990. Volume 2 ($129.00) lists 52,000 educational and special-interest videos, which represents an enormous increase over the 34,000 listed in the earlier edition. Entries vary in completeness and detail, but they typically include a good annotation, full ordering information, and an indication of formats in which the program is available. Volume 1 entries often contain MPAA (Motion Picture Association of America) ratings and important credits. All of its listings are on home video. Volume 2 often gives information on public performance rights and on the availability of the video for rental or preview.

There are many indexes. Volume 1 has indexes for cast and director, genre, awards, and Spanish language (videos in Spanish or with Spanish subtitles). Volume 2 has a subject index that lists titles under 500 broad subject headings. Both volumes have indexes for series, format (e.g., laserdisc, 8mm, Pal/Secam), and closed caption. There is an excellent directory of manufacturers and distributors and one for video services and suppliers. There are also toll-free and fax number indexes.

In a 1990 study (*Public Libraries* v.30 [March/April 1991]: 106-111) this reviewer compared the first edition of the Bowker publication with its closest competitor, Gale Research's *Video Source Book* (see ARBA 92, entry 909). It was concluded that, although each tool contained listings and valuable information not found in the other, *Bowker's Complete Video Directory* was by far the superior source for current listings. The 1992 edition of *Bowker's* gives no indication of how frequently new editions will be published, nor does it suggest there will be any supplements issued between editions. Libraries that need very current video information may want to consider subscribing to *Variety's Video Directory Plus*, the CD-ROM version of *Bowker's*. The CD-ROM is updated quarterly and offers many advantages including keyword searching and the ability to download to create videographies and order forms. In addition, the CD-ROM contains the full text of more than 2,000 movie reviews from *Variety*, the entertainment industry trade journals.

—Joseph W. Palmer

990. Brewer, Annie M., and Donald E. Brewer. **Talk Shows and Hosts on Radio: A Directory Including Show Titles and Formats, Brief Biographical Sketches of Hosts, and Locators.** Dearborn, Mich., Whiteford Press, 1992. 199p. index. $24.95pa. ISBN 0-9632341-0-2.

Radio talk shows have expanded their toehold to establish a firm footing in popular culture. Overturned legislation, countless lovelorn problems solved (or at least shared), murder, and the inevitable Hollywood film all attest to the phenomenal impact of so-called talk radio. For those who want to share the action, this directory lists 651 radio talk shows, both network- and nonnetwork-produced, broadcast in the United States and Puerto Rico. Section 1 has a geographical list of nonnetwork shows with address, frequency, market, station format, ownership information, whether guests are featured, and telephone/fax numbers for each entry. Section 2 contains a similar list for network programs. Section 3 supplies brief biographies of 97 radio talk show hosts. Section 4 provides indexing by station hosts; show formats by subject, such as cooking or careers; and a copy of the questionnaire used to collect the information for this volume. Bolder lines or headings between state listings would make its use easier.

In addition to listeners, radio time buyers, public relations directors, and job and talent seekers may also find this directory useful. A similar volume for television talk shows would be welcome. Recommended for public libraries and academic libraries with a broadcasting concentration. [R: RBB, 15 Nov 92, pp. 628; WLB, Oct 92, pp. 113-15]—**Glynys R. Thomas**

Handbooks and Yearbooks

991. **AV Market Place 1992.** New Providence, N.J., R. R. Bowker, 1992. 1389p. index. $119.95pa. LC 69-17201. ISBN 0-8352-3155-0. ISSN 1044-0445.

The AV industry, now reasonably mature, still seems to be growing by leaps and bounds. The current edition of this work is larger than many urban telephone books. This comprehensive directory covers products, manufacturers and services, and suppliers in North America. Contact data is given for almost 7,000 companies that furnish more than 1,300 products. Film, audio, and visual references and resources are all listed. But while computer systems is a category, there is little about the "information" industry and hardly any mention of software producers.

Special sections list related trade associations, film commissions, awards and festivals, a 1992-1993 calendar of meetings, trade serials, and books. Organization names and personnel are in one alphabetical index. Considering this work's price and size, perhaps a computer database or CD-ROM would be better, cheaper, and more efficient to search. — **Dean Tudor**

992. **Broadcasting & Cable Market Place 1992.** New Providence, N.J., R. R. Bowker, 1992. 1v. (various paging). index. $159.95pa. LC 71-649524. ISBN 0-8352-3178-X. ISSN 0000-1384.

This massive publication is the new and improved incarnation of the media industry standard, *Broadcasting Yearbook*, formerly published by *Broadcasting* magazine. In addition to including cable television in its listings, Bowker's editors have completely reorganized the material with an eye to enhanced access and ease of use. They have met their goals and in many cases exceeded them.

The work encompasses nearly every type of radio and television industry information imaginable. Its 10 sections cover radio; broadcast television; cable television; satellites and other carriers; market statistics, advertising, and marketing services; programming services; general services and suppliers (technology and professional services); associations, events, education, and awards; books, periodicals, and videos; and law and regulation, government agencies, and ownership. The index section includes nearly 600 pages of "yellow-pages" listings for the radio, television, and cable industries; an index to radio and television by state/possession/province; and indexes to sections and advertisers. The directory-type listings for radio, broadcast, cable, and satellite identify such things as ownership, location, and format as well as quite a bit of other interesting and useful information. For example, under the section for television, in addition to the listing of stations in the United States and Canada, there are listings for low-power, Spanish-language, experimental, and independent television stations; college, university, and school-owned stations; and stations that broadcast in stereo.

The supplementary materials are especially useful because many of the items would be difficult to track down at best. These include a calendar of trade shows; excellent annotated bibliographies of books and periodicals by Chris Sterling; a glossary; an extremely useful history of the evolution and development of radio, television, cable, satellite, and other mass communication media; a brief survey of the current state of affairs in broadcast and cable television; and a chronology that describes the landmark events in broadcast radio and television and cable from 1931 to 1991. The last three items alone make this book extremely valuable to anyone who has tried to pull together this information from disparate sources.

The editors have made a couple of decisions in this edition that they may want to rethink with the next. For some reason Sterling's bibliographies are each followed by "second" bibliographies. In the case of the book bibliography, Sterling's section is followed by another listing with the note that the materials (unannotated for the most part) have been taken from the *Books in Print* database. This list is largely limited to books published in 1990, 1991, and 1992 and is meant to complement the annotated book listing; it may or may not include those titles. Was this included simply to mention another Bowker product? The same has been done with the periodicals bibliography. These "additions" only serve to distract from Sterling's work. In a similar vein, why include the 40 "industry-related" home videos taken from Bowker's *Complete Home Video Directory* database in a publication so clearly geared toward professionals and industry interests?

These caveats aside, Bowker has done an admirable job of producing an outstanding reference that will be useful for large public libraries and in many academic settings. It is likely to give the other "industry standard," the expensive, multivolume *Television & Cable Factbook* (Warren Publishing), some serious competition. [R: RBB, 1 Sept 92, p. 81] — **G. Kim Dority**

993. Gianakos, Larry James. **Television Drama Series Programming: A Comprehensive Chronicle, 1984-1986.** Metuchen, N.J., Scarecrow, 1992. 705p. index. $69.50. PN1992.3.U5G533. 791.45'0236'0973. LC 92-27808. ISBN 0-8108-2601-1.

With the publication of volume 6 in his ongoing historical guide to dramatic television programming, Gianakos has now provided a continuous chronicle from 1947 through summer 1986. As did its predecessors, this volume presents a historical and sociological overview of the television seasons covered, followed by a section that details the prime-time television schedules for each day of the week. Also listed in this section are dramatic programs offered off the major networks and on cable. As this volume supplements the previous five, Gianakos documents the ongoing television series begun prior to 1984 by providing vital information (e.g., title, key personnel, air date) for each episode. The 1984-1986 seasons receive the same treatment, but programs that premiered during this time also include information on series regulars and a brief synopsis. Other appendixes that appeared in previous volumes (e.g., "Shakespeare Representative Teleplays, 1947-1990") have been updated. A cumulative index for the entire series is included.

A past reviewer of a volume in this series (see ARBA 84, entry 1088) has noted many of the organizational deficiencies inherent in the set. It is messy, not particularly easy to use, and filled with addenda not adequately noted in the index; moreover, a library is required to own all the previous volumes. Still, it has become a standard reference source that contains a tremendous amount of information not found elsewhere. It is absolutely essential for large research institutions with a strong subject collection in television. — **David K. Frasier**

994. Godfrey, Donald G., comp. **Reruns on File: A Guide to Electronic Media Archives.** Hillsdale, N.J., Lawrence Erlbaum, 1992. 322p. index. $65.95; $29.95pa. P96.A722U54. 302.23'02573. LC 91-35707. ISBN 0-8058-1146-X; 0-8058-1147-8pa.

This is a list of primary broadcast sources located in 39 states, the District of Columbia, Canada, and the United Kingdom. Locations listed include libraries and archives as well as commercial distributors. A number of pages are devoted to the Library of Congress collections. Formats included range widely, from wax cylinders to compact discs, with all types of audio and video recordings in between. Interesting prefatory material provides a brief history of recorded sound; a four-page section explains how to locate broadcast archive materials.

Organization of the book is alphabetical by state, with Canada and the United Kingdom at the end. Each entry contains location and contact information in addition to a description of program types and subject areas covered, special interests, and accessibility. Accessibility notes are detailed when necessary. There are indexes for subjects and for programs. Many classic titles from the 1930s and 1940s are indexed, such as *Fibber McGee and Molly*. Gary Cooper, Jackie Gleason, and Jacqueline Kennedy are among the persons indexed under their first names, which may be a problem for reference work.

This book will be a useful resource for historians and media scholars in this underresearched area. Academic libraries, archives, large public libraries, and appropriate special libraries will want to own it. [R: Choice, May 92, p. 1368] — **Helen M. Gothberg**

995. Lovece, Frank. **The Television Yearbook: Complete, Detailed Listings for the 1990-1991 Season.** New York, Perigee Books/Putnam, 1992. 271p. $16.95pa. PN1992.3.U5L68. 791.45'75'0973. LC 91-27977. ISBN 0-399-51702-2.

This new television reference book fills a gap for devoted fans and students of television. Although many genre-specific reference works have appeared as labors of love, there are few general, comprehensive works that give detailed program information. *The Television Yearbook* is the start of an ambitious effort to provide information on prime-time television programs for each season. (Television seasons run from September to September.) Each episode of every 1990-1991 prime-time network television comedy, drama, or variety series, plus selected cable station and syndicated programs, appears in this volume. For television programming information for earlier years, *Television Drama Series Programming* (see ARBA 89, entry 856) is useful.

Entries are alphabetical by series title and list network, series description, and regular cast. Each episode within a series follows with episode title, a plot synopsis, cast, writers and directors, and air date (including preemptions). Data was verified by viewing credits from each program, and last-minute cast changes, original telecast dates, and other "inside" information are included. Two sections in the back of the volume list unsold programs, both those aired and those unscheduled for air time.

This is a useful source of data for anyone who wishes to reconstruct episodes, recall actors, or verify characters and writers. Its real potential lies in whether it will indeed be an annual volume. A comprehensive index would double the work's size but make it more useful as a reference work, and an alphabetical guide on the top margin would help in negotiating the mass of fine print that confronts the user. This is a good addition to comprehensive television and mass media collections.

—**Glynys R. Thomas**

996. Perry, Jeb H. **Screen Gems: A History of Columbia Pictures Television from Cohn to Coke, 1948-1983.** Metuchen, N.J., Scarecrow, 1991. 371p. index. $42.50. PN1992.92.C65P47. 791.45'75'0973. LC 91-33388. ISBN 0-8108-2487-6.

Screen Gems covers the first 35 years of Columbia Pictures's television studio offerings. Only about the first 35 pages of this book deal with corporate history. The balance of the book consists of lists of series for television (with dates, brief descriptions, cast notes, credits, and sponsors), telefeatures (a polite term for "made-for-TV movies"), pilots (usually unsold), and specials (usually musical shows built around a celebrity). Thus, this book only covers television production materials, not the distribution of Columbia Pictures films and other products. At the back there is a program chronology of premieres and cancellation dates, plus a list of Emmy Awards (both nominees and winners for Columbia's Screen Gems).

The cast listings are for 246 shows, and while the regulars are included, not every performer appears. Nor are there plot summaries and the like for each show, just general highlights for each series, such as the more important milestones in the life of "Route 66," "The Naked City," "Bewitched," "The Monkees," "Father Knows Best," and "The Donna Reed Show." This is a good reference listing for the television buff. —**Dean Tudor**

997. Pratt, Douglas. **The Laser Video Disc Companion: A Guide to *the* High-End Delivery System for Home Video.** updated ed. New York, New York Zoetrope, 1992. 472p. $24.95pa. LC 91-67114. ISBN 0-918432-89-8.

This book was first published in 1988. It now has about 5,000 title listings (both domestic and foreign) that cover 1981 through 1990. Pratt reviews almost 4,000 of these, both critically and technically (quality of transfer and of sound). Included are features (by far the largest category), documentaries, animation, and television shows. Entry is by title only, and there is no other bibliographic data (e.g., label, price, cast). The comments are basically technical, as in the description of *Above the Law*: "a bit on the orange side, particularly where flesh is involved."

Additional materials in the book include Pratt's nominations for the 100 best laser discs (judged on entertainment value and visual nature, plus disc clarity), which includes *Airport, Ben Hur* (letterboxed), *Doctor Zhivago* (letterboxed), and *La Dolce Vita*. Another section is devoted to listings of out-of-print titles, Japanese discs, X-rated titles, karaoke sing-along discs, and CD-videos. There are a mail-order source listing, with appropriate addresses, and a list of video disc producers. The bibliography is mainly composed of periodicals. An oversized book packed with data in a three-column format of tiny print, it is unfortunately marred by sloppy proofreading, but it is a great guide to a neglected area.

—**Dean Tudor**

998. Terrace, Vincent. **Fifty Years of Television: A Guide to Series and Pilots, 1937-1988.** Cranbury, N.J., Cornwall Books/Associated University Presses, 1991. 864p. index. $29.95. PN1992.3.U5T47. 791.45'75'0973. LC 87-47835. ISBN 0-8453-4811-6.

According to the most recent estimates, most adolescents watch about six hours of television a day. It behooves us, then, to know what is on television. *Fifty Years of Television* adequately fills that need,

not only by synopsizing what has been on television over the last 50 years but also by covering unaired series pilots. It is the only guide available with such complete coverage. Included in the 4,800 alphabetically arranged titles are brief story lines, complete cast lists, producers, air dates, running time, and network (including cable stations). The volume does not include 90-minute and 2-hour pilot made-for-television movies, miniseries, daytime serials, specials, sports, or news programs. Television aficionados and communication majors will benefit from this impressive book.
—**Mark Y. Herring**

999. **Traveler's Guide to World Radio.** 1992 ed. Andy Sennitt and Bart Kuperus, eds. New York, Billboard Books/Watson-Guptill, 1991. 199p. illus. $9.95pa. ISBN 0-8230-7767-5.

This is a handy guide for individuals who carry a shortwave radio with them on their international travels. Arranged by major city, each entry begins with the GMT (Greenwich Mean Time) difference, voltage used, main languages spoken, currency, and international dialing prefix and area code. A chart gives the hours of operation for each radio station listed. Times of listening are provided for both local and international shortwave stations. For each city, major AM and FM stations are listed together with their frequency and format type (e.g., sports, news, classical music). Local hours of listening are given for the following international shortwave services: the BBC (British Broadcasting Centre) World Service, Christian Science Monitor World Service, Deutsche Welle (the Voice of Germany), HCJB (Quito, Ecuador), Radio Australia, Radio Canada International, Radio France International (RDTF), Radio Japan, Radio Netherlands, Swiss Radio International, the Voice of America, and the Voice of Free China. Not all services are listed for every city, but the major ones are. In the beginning of the book are a description of some of the international services, a survey of portable radios (highly selective), and excellent worldwide plug and socket standards charts that show the local type of power plug needed.

While this is a useful and handy volume, there seem to be some inaccuracies. For instance, the BBC World Service is available daily for three hours later than indicated, and the Radio Japan schedule is not accurate. One can only assume that other cities suffer from similar inaccuracies. This volume is a handy paperback that fits easily into carry-on luggage. Readers who need more than this compact format would be better served by the *World Radio TV Handbook* (Watson-Guptill, 1992).
—**Ralph Lee Scott**

1000. **World Radio TV Handbook. Volume 46.** 1992 ed. Andrew G. Sennitt, ed. New York, Billboard Books/Watson-Guptill, 1992. 590p. illus. maps. $27.95pa. ISBN 0-8230-5923-5.

The shortwave listeners' bible, *World Radio TV Handbook* is a comprehensive country-by-country list of radio, television, and satellite stations. A typical country entry lists the medium, long, and shortwave stations together with addresses, frequencies and times of operation, program identification (international signal), and method of verification of signal reception. (Most radio listeners send in reception reports to stations and receive a certificate or QSL card from the station.) A large table lists each radio and television frequency in use and the stations likely to be found broadcasting on that frequency.

Another section of the handbook is devoted to projected reception conditions, solar activity, and recommended listening frequencies for 1992. Other sections cover English-language broadcasts, international broadcasting organizations, DX-clubs, and religious organizations that operate broadcast stations. Increasingly, a portion of the handbook is devoted to the growing use of satellite reception dishes. A listing is provided of the type of channel programming for most satellites now in Earth orbit. The volume ends with a section called "Listen to the World," which has tips, antennas, and radio product reviews that are eagerly awaited each year by the shortwave listening community. Because this work has an international focus, most domestic (United States) television and radio stations are better referenced by the *Broadcasting Yearbook*. This volume serves a distinctive need on the reference shelf. Suggested for all libraries. —**Ralph Lee Scott**

Indexes

1001. **Transcript/Video Index, 1991: A Comprehensive Guide to Television News and Public Affairs Programming.** Denver, Colo., Journal Graphics, 1992. 418p. $24.95pa. ISBN 1-879762-02-1.

The rapid expansion of cable television has generated a proliferation of syndicated news and information programs that were formerly the sole province of network and public television. For librarians, more channels mean more patron requests for information on topics covered by programs as diverse as PBS's *Frontline* and *The Maury Povich Show*. Since 1980, Journal Graphics has acted as the librarian's savior by transcribing selected network, syndicated, and public television programs and selling them at reasonable prices. Their current index accesses transcriptions for almost 7,000 shows that appeared in 1991 on some 84 "hard news" and "tabloid television" programs, such as *Wall Street Report, Nightline, Geraldo*, and all the CNN programs.

Entries are chronologically arranged by air date under 251 broad subject headings, including abortion, pornography, weather, and women. Only a few personal name subject headings (e.g., George Bush, Elvis Presley, Boris Yeltsin) are offered. Information contained under each entry includes abbreviated show title (e.g., GR = *Geraldo*), episode number, broadcast date, a brief episode summary, and availability on video. Titles of show episodes are boldfaced.

The lack of a general or name index is a major flaw in this source and necessitates that the user ponderously scan for information within overly broad subject headings. Despite this drawback, Journal Graphics has produced a useful tool for tracking down highly ephemeral, timely information from a previously "fugitive" source. Three earlier indexes for 1968-1986, 1986-1989, and 1990 are also available. Recommended for public and academic libraries. – **David K. Frasier**

21 Decorative Arts

COLLECTING

Coins

1002. Bowers, Q. David. **Commemorative Coins of the United States: A Complete Encyclopedia.** Wolfeboro, N.H., Bowers and Merena Galleries, 1991. 768p. illus. index. $49.95; $39.95pa. ISBN 0-943161-35-5; 0-943161-34-7pa.

This encyclopedia contains a great deal of historical information about the 15 gold and 64 silver commemorative coins issued by the U.S. Mint between 1848 and 1991. It also covers such related issues as their grading, pricing, and market history. On every topic Bowers presents fascinating background information, such as when he traces the market history of commemorative coins as a whole at five-year intervals. The seven initial chapters containing this general information set the stage for a series of lengthy essays on each individual coin that describe their origins and history, initial distribution, and information of value to collectors. Each essay opens with a black-and-white drawing of both sides of the coin and closes with a concise summary of its characteristics and a detailed market index for five intervals since its issuance. An appendix that contains brief biographical sketches for artists connected with the design of these coins is especially useful because information about many of them is not readily available elsewhere. Another appendix that contains an index of motifs and items mentioned in the legends and inscriptions on the coins is useful to those who collect coins on a topical basis. The text concludes with a brief bibliography and a standard index. *Commemorative Coins of the United States* is an informative and entertaining supplement to the many standard coin books that typically provide only brief descriptive information. — **Norman D. Stevens**

1003. Highfill, John W. **The Comprehensive U.S. Silver Dollar Encyclopedia.** Broken Arrow, Okla., Highfill Press, 1992. 1233p. illus. index. $100.00. LC 91-65854. ISBN 0-9629900-0-0.

U.S. silver dollars have long been a favorite collector's item, as these coins have a rich and varied history. This book attempts to cover all aspects of the numerous types, including patterns, counterfeits, and the recent nonsilver issues, from both the collector's and dealer's point of view. The book is a collection of 81 chapters written by 52 "guest authors" and Highfill. Each chapter is preceded by a photograph and a brief biography (including credentials) of the author. A glossary is located at the beginning of the book. At the end of the glossary, obverse and reverse features are labeled, using a Morgan dollar as an example. This is very helpful when these terms are used in the chapters that follow.

Highfill admits that this book is more an anthology than an encyclopedia. There is no obvious sequence of chapters, such as an alphabetical rendering of subjects, nor is there a date- or series-based arrangement. The chapters devoted to specific aspects of silver dollars, such as die varieties, mints, grading, errors, special series (e.g., Gobrecht dollars), or sets (e.g., the King of Siam proof set), are what one would expect in a book that claims exhaustive coverage of these coins. A significant number of chapters are devoted to the investment side of coin collecting. There are contributions on retailing and merchandising, and the regulation of professional numismatics, the investment aspects of U.S. silver dollar ownership, and the related precious metals arena are discussed. The last two chapters are date-by-date analyses of Morgan and Peace dollars. Two pages of data are given for each date and mint mark, including a high-quality photograph of such things as the obverse and reverse, mintages, strike quality, and die varieties, as well as graphical data that covers pricing histories and populations of the higher grade coins, as determined by the Professional Coin Grading Service (PCGS) and the Numismatic Guaranty Corporation of America (NGC). These chapters would make an extremely useful handbook by themselves. However, the chapters of personal stories and anecdotes, convention reports with silly photographs, and a pictorial chapter devoted to "family and friends" hardly seem appropriate; they detract from the scholarly chapters.

The size of the book allows for large-scale, detailed photographs, which are very useful. However, text is provided in a single-column, single-spaced format that is difficult to read. The targeted audience is not readily obvious, but some chapters will appeal to both the serious silver dollar collector and the more general coin enthusiast (although the price may be daunting for the average collector). This work is recommended for public libraries. [R: LJ, July 92, p. 76] — **Margaret F. Dominy**

Firearms

1004. **Standard Catalog of Firearms.** 2d ed. By Ned Schwing, Herbert Houze, and M. Howard Madaus. Iola, Wis., Krause Publications, 1992. 704p. illus. $24.95pa. LC 90-62405. ISBN 0-87341-178-1.

For the firearms collector, the serious shooting sportsperson, or those who look at guns as investments, this is a vital work. Covering 10,000-plus makes of guns from more than 1,000 manufacturers, the work offers prices for 6 grades of condition. It would have been strengthened by a fuller introduction and more details on how prices were determined, but the "guts" of the work — the actual prices — are what will interest most users. Quite simply, this is the most comprehensive, credible volume of its sort available at a reasonable price, although serious collectors will want to own some of the more specialized catalogs as well. This work belongs in public libraries where there is a substantial population of hunters or gun enthusiasts (virtually everywhere in the rural United States), and it is highly recommended for private individuals. — **James A. Casada**

CRAFTS

1005. **Crafts Index for Young People.** By Mary Anne Pilger. Englewood, Colo., Libraries Unlimited, 1992. 286p. $32.50. TT157.P533. 016.7455. LC 92-12996. ISBN 1-56308-002-8.

Parents, teachers, librarians, and community center staff often request ideas contained in books for educational craft projects that children can do, such as a craft related to a holiday, culture, medium, or part of nature. This index will easily provide that service. More than 1,000 books have been consulted, and they are listed in numerical sequence in the back of the index. Subjects are listed in alphabetical order in the main portion of the work. Thus, under "C" a teacher may look for projects relating to cacti, calendars, carnivals, cats, China, Christmas, clay, and costumes, among many others. Each item contains the number of the book and the page number of the project. While the index contains thousands of entries and extends 257 pages, the introduction consists of only two brief paragraphs. In these the user learns that "craft" has been interpreted broadly to include various activities, including foods, to represent a particular culture or event. However, there is no mention of the criteria for choosing these books, nor an indication as to whether the books are recommended or if the projects are illustrated or described in the text. — **Simon J. Bronner**

1006. Gallivan, Marion F. **Fun for Kids II: An Index to Children's Craft Books.** Metuchen, N.J., Scarecrow, 1992. 482p. $42.50. TT160.G34. 016.7455. LC 92-16667. ISBN 0-8108-2546-5.

Teachers, parents, and librarians who want to help children from preschool through eighth grade fashion crafts of almost any type and form are well served by Gallivan's updated companion to her 1981

Fun for Kids (see ARBA 82, entry 1007). All materials referenced in this index were published after 1981. The book has three separate indexes. First, more than 300 books, with complete bibliographic data, are alphabetically indexed by author or title. The heart of the book, nearly 300 pages, is devoted to indexing craft books by the kinds of crafts they describe. This index is extremely thorough and easy to use. For example, 5 pages devoted to dolls are subdivided and indexed into more than 30 categories, including Peruvian dolls and dolls made from spools, newspaper, and pipe cleaners. The final index lists crafts by types of construction material, such as clay, aluminum foil, chalk, and shells. This work is easy to use and will save teachers and parents many hours of work in locating fine craft activities for young people. [R: RBB, 1 Dec 92, pp. 687-88] – **Jerry D. Flack**

1007. Jerde, Judith. **Encyclopedia of Textiles.** New York, Facts on File, 1992. 260p. illus. index. $45.00. TS1309.J47. 677'.003. LC 91-20756. ISBN 0-8160-2105-8.

Jerde, for six years the conservator of costume at the Metropolitan Museum of Art and currently a consultant in clothing and textiles, presents the general reader with a comprehensive overview of all aspects of textile design, manufacture, care, and use. She gives definitions and descriptions of fiber types, dyes, printing techniques, and weaving processes accompanied by illustrations, many in color, that show the differences among various weaves, fiber types, and patterns. Longer entries are provided for cotton, linen, wool, silk, and synthetic fibers, explaining how they are manufactured and their properties, uses, and care. The entry on dyes describes the history of the use of dyes, the preparation of natural dyes, and the development and use of synthetic dyes. In addition, brief biographies of noted individuals in the textile business are included.

This encyclopedia is intended to be used regularly by anyone interested in working with textiles, from the beginning craftsperson to the professional designer. Its particular strength is in describing and illustrating the many textures and patterns of textiles. Although a handsome book fit for the coffee table, it is also suitable for use at the workbench. [R: BR, Nov/Dec 92, p. 54; Choice, Dec 92, p. 602; LJ, 15 Mar 92, p. 76; RBB, 1 June 92, p. 1774; SLJ, Oct 92, p. 155] – **Ann E. Prentice**

1008. McCreight, Tim. **The Complete Metalsmith: An Illustrated Handbook.** rev. ed. Worcester, Mass., Davis; distr., New York, Sterling Publishing, 1991. 189p. illus. index. $14.95 spiralbound. LC 81-66573. ISBN 0-87192-240-1.

Here is an excellent introduction and working guide to metalworking and related processes. Chapter topics include materials, surfaces, shaping and joining, and casting. Within chapters, topics are succinct, clearly written, and illustrated. The melting point, specific gravity, and atomic weight are provided for materials, and enough historical information is given to whet readers' appetites. The reading list at the end of the book will lead to more specialized works.

Other useful charts, lists, and formulas are provided, along with a list of materials suppliers. The book is spiralbound for easy use in the studio. It is also well suited to the reference departments of public libraries and art collections with information needs on artistic processes. – **Maureen A. Beck**

1009. Strickler, Carol, ed. **A Weaver's Book of 8-Shaft Patterns: From the Friends of** *Handwoven.* Loveland, Colo., Interweave Press; distr., Chicago, Contemporary Books, 1991. 240p. illus. index. $36.95. TT848.W365. 746.1'4041. LC 91-28618. ISBN 0-934026-67-X.

In an age dominated by computers, it is refreshing to see a work such as this one. Strickler has gathered together weaving patterns and drafts from more than 250 weavers from the United States, Canada, and Australia, and assembled them in a loving tribute to the continuance of a traditional weaving heritage. For most weavers, *A Weaver's Book* is like coming home to an old familiar friend, as it is an 8-shaft version of the classic *A Book of Patterns for Hand-Weaving* by Mary Meigs Atwater (Shuttle-Craft Guild, 1925-). Each individual pattern is shown in a small black-and-white photograph. Tie-up and treadling instructions accompany each pattern, and a brief introduction in chapter 1 explains how the drafts are read. The volume is divided into 25 chapters that arrange the patterns into families. Some of the major groups include twills, shadow weaves, overshot and crackle, double weave, and Bronson weave. A brief bibliography of sources for weaving patterns is included, and there is an index to the named patterns. – **Steven J. Schmidt**

FASHION AND COSTUME

1010. Peacock, John. **The Chronicle of Western Fashion: From Ancient Times to the Present Day.** New York, Harry Abrams, 1991. 224p. illus. $29.95. GT511.P42. 391'.009. LC 90-1053. ISBN 0-8103-3953-3.

    Peabody's work provides a good representation of the development of dress through recorded Western history. It contains examples of costumes from all major historical periods. Beginning in ancient Egypt around 2000 B.C., it covers ancient civilizations, the Middle Ages, the Renaissance, and the sixteenth through twentieth centuries (through A.D. 1980). The book is made up of color plates that are divided into periods, with detailed descriptions accompanying each plate. Although most of the costumes are from upper-class fashion, the book does show the dress of people from a variety of social levels and occupations, such as clergy, shepherds, maids, workers, and military personnel. It also gives examples of various types of dress, such as formal wear, swimwear, and sleepwear. The illustrated glossary of fashion terms is quite helpful for defining many obscure or archaic terms.

    This book is an excellent reference tool for school and academic libraries. It is of particular value to theater students; historians; and anyone interested in costume, fashion, and social history.
—**Stephen Haenel**

1011. Yarwood, Doreen. **Fashion in the Western World 1500-1990.** New York, Drama Book, 1992. 176p. illus. index. $29.95. ISBN 0-89676-118-5.

    Yarwood's purpose in this book is "to present, as clearly as possible, the characteristics of (primarily) fashionable dress worn in the western world during the last five hundred years." She presents the trends and relates them to the historical, social, and technological developments mirrored in the dress of the day and the nation. Clothes of men, women, and children are described, along with footwear, head coverings, hairstyles, cosmetics, accessories, and ornamentation. Yarwood also discusses the manufacture of textiles; the designing, making, and taking care of clothes; and the marketing and presentation of fashion. The costume of the last 200 years is stressed. The volume is divided into 12 chapters that cover such styles and influences as "Elegance and Naturalism," "Baroque Richness," "Rococo Delicacy," and the dress of today. The volume concludes with a glossary, bibliography, and index. This is an excellent reference title for anyone interested in the history of fashion.—**Kathleen J. Voigt**

PHOTOGRAPHY

1012. **Holography Market Place: The Reference Text and Directory of the Holography Industry.** 3d ed. Brian Kluepfel and Franz Ross, eds. Berkeley, Calif., Ross Books, 1991. 170p. index. $35.00pa.

    This work is packed with a wide variety of information about the holography industry. The cover and several insert pages illustrate different types of holograms covered in the text. Librarians will find the topical chapters, which explain and illustrate most areas in holography, very worthwhile. Chapter 10 provides conventional marketplace information, such as copyright holder, manufacturer, chain of distribution, distributor, wholesaler, and retailer. It also covers the year in review. Chapters 11 through 13 deal with holography businesses, businesses by category, and individuals in the industry. The volume concludes with a bibliography and a glossary, which explains such terms as *cross talk, embossed hologram, rainbow hologram,* and *shadowgram.*—**Ronald L. Buchan**

1013. Lambrechts, Eric, and Luc Salu. **Photography and Literature: An International Bibliography of Monographs.** New York, Mansell/Cassell, 1992. 296p. index. $100.00. Z1023.L33. 016.096'1. LC 91-34752. ISBN 0-7201-2113-2.

    This work provides an introduction to the relationship of photography and literature. Salu has coauthored a related work, *History of Photography* (see ARBA 90, entry 943). In this work he and Lambrechts have compiled approximately 3,900 titles in 20 languages. Included in the list are books, exhibition catalogs, dissertations, and special issues of magazines. The authors list the criteria for a bibliographic entry in the introduction. Books range from those that explore the relationship of photography and literature to works where the literary text is complemented by photographs. The bibliography is arranged alphabetically by author or photographer with numerous cross-references. Each complete entry gives the necessary bibliographic data and language of the text. A subject index completes the volume.

As with any bibliography, certain works have been overlooked in this one. This is not an indictment of the work, but rather a comment on the general nature of bibliographies, especially true in emerging research areas such as this. As noted in the foreword, this bibliography "will enjoy broad appreciation among researchers, photohistorians, critics, literary scholars, semiologists, and iconographic experts." Any academic or large public library will also find it a worthy purchase.

—**Gregory Curtis**

1014. Rudisill, Richard, and others. **Photographers: A Sourcebook for Historical Research.** Brownsville, Calif., Carl Mautz, 1991. 103p. illus. index. $25.00pa. ISBN 0-96219-402-6.

With the increasing interest in historical photographs and photographers, this volume will find considerable use on the shelves. The first section consists of six essays on researching and writing about regional photographers. Each essay covers a different aspect of the search, recording, and reporting technique of history. The first two provide thoughtful insights into the collection of names, addresses, and other biographical data. Others discuss the outcomes of the collected data beyond alphabetically arranged lists of names and dates.

Section 2 is an annotated list of directories of photographers. International in scope, this section is divided geographically by country, or by region and state in the case of the United States. The annotations range from one to three sentences in length. An index of authors completes the volume. This work will be especially useful for collections that support courses in photography, art, or cultural and social history. —**Gregory Curtis**

22 Fine Arts

GENERAL WORKS

Bibliography

1015. **Annual Bibliography of Modern Art, 1990: The Museum of Modern Art Library, New York.** New York, G. K. Hall, 1991. 472p. $225.00. ISBN 0-8161-0517-0.

The Museum of Modern Art Library was founded in 1929 and became a special member of the Research Libraries Group in 1980. The main strengths of the library include predominantly European and United States painting, drawing, sculpture, prints, and contemporary art in all its forms. Since 1981, its cataloging records have been entered into the RLIN database. This alphabetical bibliography lists the acquisitions of the library; it has been compiled from RLIN records of both old and new publications acquired by purchase, gift, or exchange and cataloged during 1990.

The format of this title is by main entry, added entries, titles, series titles, and subject headings. The main entry gives full bibliographic information including tracings. Subject headings appear in capital letters and boldface type. Entries provide author, short or main title, subtitle and other title page information, place and date of publication, publisher, pagination, illustration statement, size, notes, ISBN, LC Card Number, Dewey Decimal Number, subject headings, LC Call Number, and MOMA Call Number. *See* references have been taken from the New York Public Library authority file. This title will be very useful to public libraries and special art libraries.—**Kathleen J. Voigt**

1016. **Art on Screen: A Directory of Films and Videos about the Visual Arts.** By the Program for Art on Film. Nadine Covert, ed. New York, G. K. Hall, 1991. 283p. illus. index. $65.00; $35.00pa. N366.A78. 016.7. LC 91-34548. ISBN 0-8161-7294-3; 0-8161-0538-3pa.

Preceded by *Films and Videos on Photography* (see ARBA 91, entry 999), this is a fascinating directory to films that deal with art in some way. Subjects cover the spectrum, with famous artists, art forgery, Japanese painting, and puppets just a few of the hundreds of topics explored. The criteria for inclusion are many; 914 titles have been gleaned from a database of more than 17,000. Notably, the films must have been favorably reviewed by Program for Art on Film staff or other respected reviewing mediums. Also, works generally had to have been produced between 1975 and 1990.

The main part of the book is divided into two sections: documentaries and shorts, and feature films, with entries arranged alphabetically by title in each section. Every entry can include title (usually English), series title, running time, color or black-and-white, format, year of release and rerelease, country of producing agency, language, edition or version, producing agency, credits, distributor, a synopsis, an evaluation, comments, citations of reviews, and awards. The section on documentaries and shorts is considerably longer than that on feature films and is much better annotated, with interesting evaluations and comments appended to many of the films. Feature film annotations are merely descriptive. Also, some of the feature films deal with art only peripherally (e.g., *History of the World: Part 1, Raiders of the Lost Ark*).

The book opens with six well-written essays on such topics as filmography and evaluating films on art. A list of subject headings and excellent subject, director, name, series title, and source indexes provide access to the text through every possible element. (The latter index has directory information for the distributors in the book.) The design of the book is very nice, with a crisp, eye-pleasing typeface and appropriate use of white space. Beautiful black-and-white photographs highlight the work.

All in all, this work is highly recommended for any collection that deals with art or film. School, college, and public libraries should also consider it. [R: Choice, Sept 92, p. 71]—**D. A. Rothschild**

1017. Harnsberger, R. Scott, comp. **Ten Precisionist Artists: Annotated Bibliographies.** Westport, Conn., Greenwood Press, 1992. 348p. index. (Art Reference Collection, no.14). $55.00. Z5961.U5H38. 016.75913'09'041. LC 92-14511. ISBN 0-313-27664-1.

The aim of this volume is to serve as a research guide to scholars. The Precisionists (sometimes called Cubist-Realists or Immaculates) selected are 10 American artists, leading practitioners of the movement: George Ault, Peter Blume, Ralston Crawford, Charles Demuth, Preston Dickinson, O. Louis Guglielmi, Louis Lozowick, Morton L. Schamberg, Charles Sheeler, and Niles Spencer. Following a thorough introduction to Precisionism, the artists are introduced, each with a biographical sketch and a section devoted to writings, statements, interviews, monographs, exhibition catalogs, articles, essays, exhibition reviews, book reviews, dissertations, theses, reference sources, archival sources in general, and sources for annotated reproductions. Indexes include a keyword index to source volumes, an author index, a short-title index to exhibition catalogs, and a subject index. The book contains just one black-and-white illustration, a reproduction of Lozowick's lithograph *Minneapolis* (1925). This thorough guide is an invaluable resource for anyone researching either Precisionism in general or its adherents in particular.—**Koraljka Lockhart**

1018. McWilliam, Neil, and others, eds. **A Bibliography of Salon Criticism in Paris from the Ancien Regime to the Restoration, 1699-1827.** New York, Cambridge University Press, 1991. 263p. index. (Cambridge Studies in the History of Art). $49.95. Z5961.F7M38. 016.7'011'8094409033. LC 90-37988. ISBN 0-521-34634-7.

1019. McWilliam, Neil. **A Bibliography of Salon Criticism in Paris from the July Monarchy to the Second Empire, 1831-1851.** New York, Cambridge University Press, 1991. 302p. index. (Cambridge Studies in the History of Art). $49.50. Z5961.F7B54. 016.7'011'8094409034. LC 90-2169. ISBN 0-521-40091-0.

During its two-hundred-year history (1699-1899), the series of art exhibitions collectively known as the Paris Salons was the most important art event in the world. Begun initially as a way to court aristocratic commissions for the members of the Royal Academy during the period of Louis XIV, the Salons evolved into nineteenth-century art "blockbusters" that displayed some 30 rooms of new art to nearly one-half million viewers annually.

The two volumes under consideration are important new tools in the study of the Paris Salons and their impact, because despite the critical importance of the Salons, the long history of exhibitions, and the large number of works shown each year have proven daunting to scholarly history and analysis. These books collect the wide range of critical reaction to the Salons, from an initial 2 citations in 1699 to 72 articles that discuss the works shown at the end of the Second Republic in 1851. The format is simple in each volume, but the systematic survey and listing make known 3,239 opinions that had been only partially published in what are now obscure and out-of-print sources. Indexes to authors and periodicals complete each volume. Together with *Bibliography of Salon Criticism in Second Empire Paris* (see ARBA 87, entry 976), these valuable works provide almost complete coverage of press reaction to French art during the history of the Salons.—**Stephanie C. Sigala**

1020. **The Worldwide Bibliography of Art Exhibition Catalogues 1963-1987.** Millwood, N.Y., Kraus International, 1992. 3v. index. $375.00/set. Z5939.W675. 016.7'074. LC 91-58780. ISBN 0-527-98004-8.

Included in this magnificent set are citations to more than 17,500 exhibition catalogs from galleries and museums around the world. Highly selective in scope, this compilation is derived from catalogs listed and reviewed in *Worldwide Art Catalogue Bulletin* (WACB), a quarterly publication. Consequently, the set also serves as an index to WACB, volumes 1 (1963) through 23 (1987).

Five major sections comprise this classed bibliography. The first volume coincides with the first major section—"Geographical"—which in turn is subdivided into Western art (11 chapters) and non-Western art (8 chapters). This arrangement is repeated in volume 2—"Media"—with 19 chapters subdividing the major category. Volume 3 includes topical, monograph, and title sections, each with its own classed arrangement. A useful classification schedule and "Note to the User" preface the volumes, explaining content and idiosyncrasies.

Each entry is keyed to the classification schedule by an alphanumeric designator, and entries are numbered consecutively throughout a chapter. Each presents the following information: full title and English translation, author or editor, first exhibiting institution and year, organizer of the exhibition, publisher or distributor of the catalog, pagination, number of illustrations, dimensions, LC card number, ISBN, language of text, Worldwide Books stock number, and citation to volume and issue of WACB in which the catalog was reviewed. A masterful and impressive bibliography, index, and finding tool, this monumental work should be in the collection of every serious academic, museum, and gallery library. [R: Choice, July/Aug 92, pp. 1662-63; WLB, June 92, p. 158]—**Edmund F. SantaVicca**

Biography

1021. Cummings, Pat, comp. and ed. **Talking with Artists.** New York, Bradbury Press/Macmillan, 1992. 96p. illus. $18.95. NC975.T34. 741.6'42'092273. LC 91-9982. ISBN 0-02-724245-5.

Cummings has illustrated several popular picture books. Because of her interest, she has traveled around the country meeting school children and adults who are interested in art. These people tend to ask her similar questions, such as how an artist works, how an illustrator was first assigned a book, and what were some of their childhood influences. Interest from these groups led her to write this book. She has conversed with 14 favorite children's book illustrators, including Leo and Diane Dillon, Stephen Kellogg, and Chris Van Allsburg, asking them the same 8 questions but getting many different answers. The questions asked are: Where do you get your ideas? What is a normal day like for you? Where do you work? Do you have any children or pets? What do you enjoy drawing the most? Do you ever put people you know in your pictures? What do you use to make your pictures? How did you get to do your first book?

A childhood photograph and a current photograph are included for each illustrator, along with artwork from both eras. A glossary and a bibliography of five favorite books illustrated by each artist conclude the volume. The large print and simple language of these personal stories will have appeal to both children and adults.—**Kathleen J. Voigt**

1022. Marantz, Sylvia, and Kenneth Marantz. **Artists of the Page: Interviews with Children's Book Illustrators.** Jefferson, N.C., McFarland, 1992. 255p. index. $29.95. NC965.M34. 741.6'42'0922. LC 91-50951. ISBN 0-89950-701-8.

Warm and inviting in its conversational tone, this work is filled with insights into the careers and lives of 30 children's book illustrators. Through interviews with the artists we learn of their backgrounds, training (both formal and informal), working styles, influences, and philosophies. Some of the most talented members of an exclusive fraternity appear in this volume, so this work is a significant contribution to a field that has had slight coverage in existing reference works. Arranged alphabetically, each chapter has a sampling of works in print by the artist, a brief background sketch, and several pages devoted to the actual interview—a distillation of conversations with the artists. The articles have been reviewed and occasionally edited for greater clarity by the artists themselves. An update appears at the end of the chapter for many individuals. A brief bibliography and an index to names and books completes the work, which will complement what little information there is on the topic of children's artists and authors. Highly recommended for any public, school, or academic setting. [R: BL, July 92, p. 1948; SLJ, Aug 92, p. 91]—**Gregory Curtis**

Dictionaries and Encyclopedias

1023. **The Bulfinch Pocket Dictionary of Art Terms** 3d ed. David Diamond, ed. New York, Little, Brown, 1992. 1v. (unpaged). illus. $8.95pa. N33.D468. 703. LC 91-58791. ISBN 0-8212-1905-7.

This title replaces *Pocket Dictionary of Art Terms* (New York Graphic Society, 1979), a standard reference work in many libraries. Designed to be a portable guide to art and architecture terms, this work specializes in short, current definitions in an easy-to-read format. Unlike most other term dictionaries, no biographies of artists are included. Although much of the introductory matter and the bibliographic entries are unchanged from the earlier edition, Diamond has taken pains to update older subject entries and to add up-to-the-minute topics. In the "A" section alone, there are seven new subjects, from Afrocentrism to azulejos. The currency of the entries is welcome in a subject area where most of the reference tools date from the 1960s and 1970s and contemporary art movements get little attention. Because of its currency, this title will get a lot of use; however, a pronunciation guide to foreign-language terms is suggested for future editions.

—Stephanie C. Sigala

1024. **Encyclopedia of Living Artists in America: A Catalog of Works by Artists in America....** 6th ed. Renaissance, Calif., Art Network Press/Directors Guild, 1991. 87p. illus. index. $17.95pa. ISBN 0-940899-18-3.

Purchasing this volume based solely on its title would lead to major disappointment. The word *encyclopedia* usually conveys a work of great magnitude and depth. That is not the case here, as only 70 artists are represented. Furthermore, "American" without the delineation of "North," "South," or "Central" is often used to include all three. The vast majority of artists listed are from the United States, with one from Argentina and two from Canada. There are a smattering from the rest of the world.

It is claimed that the selection of artists for this volume has been made through careful screening, yet there is no mention of who did the screening or on what basis selection was made. According to the publisher, the intent of this volume is to provide an advertising platform for the artists. Selection for inclusion was subjective; those making the selections did so based on what they thought would sell.

To the selectors' credit, the artists represented cover a number of different media: painting, sculpture, mixed media, and photography, in both abstract and more traditional representations. Full-color reproductions of the works are included on good quality paper, showing the works to full advantage. A profile of each artist is given, along with address, telephone number, and agent. Three indexes (artists' names, media of the works, and locations of the artists) conclude the work.

The next edition of the encyclopedia is due out in 1993. In fairness to those considering the work for purchase, this reviewer feels that the title should be modified to describe its true content or the scope of the work should be enlarged. The title and the concept have considerable potential; it would be nice to see this realized.—**Marjorie E. Bloss**

1025. **The HarperCollins Dictionary of Art Terms and Techniques.** 2d ed. By Ralph Mayer. New York, HarperPerennial/HarperCollins, 1991. 474p. illus. $13.00pa. ISBN 0-06-461012-8.

Artist and educator Mayer died in 1979, 10 years after having published the initial edition of this book. Now the 2d edition, still bearing his name, keeps his work alive. The two editions are essentially the same. Steven Sheehan, director of the Ralph Mayer Center at Yale University School of Art, has made some minor revisions. Only a handful of new terms appear, such as *batik, mixed media,* and *post-painterly abstraction.* From the illustrations found in the original edition, only the line drawings have been retained; the reproductions of paintings and photographs of art works and techniques have not. This is no great loss except in a few instances; for example, two illustrations that depict foreshortening will be missed. A more noticeable editorial decision that does detract greatly from the utility of the dictionary is the outdated bibliography at the end. No new books have been included, so the bibliography stagnates in the late 1960s.

Mayer's original definitions were carefully crafted for precise communication; they remain untouched. Moreover, his succinctness has been followed by Sheehan in the few new definitions. To clarify the content of the dictionary, a more exact title would be "Art Supplies, Techniques, and

Terms," since a good part of the dictionary concerns that which a well-equipped artist's studio contains. Highly recommended as a classic in the field; libraries that do not own the original edition should purchase this one. [R: Choice, June 92, p. 1522]—**Bill Bailey**

Handbooks and Yearbooks

1026. **Black Arts Annual 1989/90.** Donald Bogle, ed. Hamden, Conn., Garland, 1992. 170p. illus. $59.95. ISBN 0-8240-6099-7. ISSN 1042-7104.

The third anthology in the series, this work offers a summary of the year's activities in photography (by Deborah Willis), literature (by Tonya Bolden), popular music (by Michael Erik Ross), jazz and classical music (by Herb Boyd), dance (by William Moore), theater (by Niamani Mutima), and movies and television (by Bogle, who has already made major contributions in these areas). Other graphic arts are not included. When the information in the annuals is reasonably current, ephemera and milestones are registered. (In years to come, they will provide cause for intensified nostalgia.) Major contributions, conferences, festivals, concerts, publications, recordings, and exhibitions are cited with commentary; the illustrations from dance and photography are especially important. Fads and stylistic innovations are traced (e.g., rap, "bup art" versus mainstream) as well as such issues as censorship and copyright. It is pleasant to see that new figures who have been tested in the arts are not ignored, such as baritone Herbert Perry, tenor Gregory Hopkins, and authors Tina Ansa and Melvin Dixon. The obituaries have entries on Ben Holt; Sammy Davis, Jr.; Alvin Ailey; William Dawson; and Dexter Gordon. Critical, social, and editorial commentaries are provocatively provided.

Sources for the information are not overtly acknowledged, suggesting that the contributors' role included heavy reliance on journalists and uncited artists' word of mouth. However, while some events that could be thought of major importance may not be included, coverage is not limited to one or two cities nor to the United States. This work will be of particular interest to the casual reader but will prove a handy reference for the arts enthusiast as well.—**Dominique-Rene de Lerma**

1027. Katlan, Alexander W. **American Artists' Materials. Vol.II: A Guide to Stretchers, Panels, Millboards, and Stencil Marks.** Madison, Conn., Sound View Press, 1992. 544p. illus. $64.00. LC 91-67376. ISBN 0-932087-19-1.

With this series Katlan seeks to help art dealers, collectors, and researchers identify and authenticate unsigned and undated nineteenth-century American paintings. Volume 1 was published in 1987 and concentrated on the suppliers of artists' materials; volume 2 focuses on the actual art materials. Katlan emphasizes the analysis of stretchers, panels, artist boards, and canvas with nearly 300 illustrations and text. Stretcher patents issued by the U.S. Patent Office from 1849 to 1949 are documented. Included is a chapter containing 39 pertinent sections of original trade catalogs of major American and English artists' materials supply firms.

Volume 1 provided a directory of art supply firms active in New York and Boston during the nineteenth century. Katlan continues this feature in volume 2 by providing checklists of suppliers in Philadelphia and Baltimore. A checklist of eighteenth-century New York City carvers, gilders, and related craftspeople is also included, as well as information on the English art supply firms that exported to the United States from the eighteenth through the twentieth centuries. The volume concludes with three case histories—the art materials of Thomas Cole, Jasper Cropsey, and Albert Bierstadt—that illustrate how this information can support the art historians' research process. A selection bibliography is supplied. This is an excellent tool for art researchers.—**Kathleen J. Voigt**

1028. Naylor, Colin, ed. **Contemporary Masterworks.** Chicago, St. James Press, 1991. 933p. illus. index. $135.00. 709. ISBN 1-55862-083-4.

More than 450 works of art, architecture, photography, and design are included in this work. According to the editor, they have achieved the status of "masterpiece" or "classic" and have made a significant contribution to twentieth-century culture. Twenty distinguished critics, curators, historians, and scholars made up the Advisory Board that made the recommendations for selection. Most of the works were produced after 1945, but if a design originated earlier in the century and made its most profound cultural impact after 1945, it has been included.

Each entry includes a signed, critical essay contributed by one of 160 specialists. The essays assess the importance of the works in their artistic and cultural contexts. A full-page black-and-white illustration accompanies each work, together with catalog data that includes the artist's life dates, title of work and date, media, size, and location. The entry concludes with a short bibliography. Biographical notes on the advisors and contributors, and an index to artists, architects, photographers, designers, engineers, design studios, and manufacturers are given.

The choice of contributors and works is commendable. This title will be a good reference source for art and general reference librarians. [R: RBB, 15 Apr 92, p. 1548; RQ, Fall 92, pp. 109-110; WLB. Apr 92, p. 121] — **Kathleen J. Voigt**

1029. Van Keuren, Frances. **Guide to Research in Classical Art and Mythology.** Chicago, American Library Association, 1991. 307p. index. $35.00. N7760.V3. 709'.38. LC 91-11122. ISBN 0-8389-0564-1.

This compact and important volume contains a wealth of information valuable to scholar and student alike. It definitely fulfills its purpose of helping the researcher make use of the various works that classify classical art and mythology. For scholars it illuminates initial library materials, while for students (including secondary school students) it provides a varied number of works that can help them research a piece of art or a myth for a project and can also give them a guided introduction on how to go about conducting a research project.

The 17 chapters are arranged in 3 main sections: general research, mythology, and media studies. Under general research are Greek, Etruscan, and Roman art and architecture, each represented by one major work. The author begins each chapter by discussing the major work (or the several works in the sections on mythology and media studies), describing its main purpose and themes under "Art Form." This is followed by a discussion of the kinds of research possible when using the particular reference, which is in turn followed by a description of the work's organization. Then the author provides annotated discussions of complementary sources, handbooks, and supplementary sources, the latter including a list, without annotation, of additional supplementary sources. After each of the annotated discussions is a list of bibliographic entries mentioned previously. Further enhancing the use of this volume is the author-title index.

The author is most thorough in her discussions, noting both the positive and the negative features of her references. The materials represent contemporary scholarship and are not limited to English, although where possible, English sources are given (and all foreign titles and virtually all foreign words are translated into English). The book belongs in every college, university, and museum library as well as in larger public and high school libraries. [R: C&RL, Sept 92, p. 421; RBB, 1 Jan 92, p. 849; WLB, Apr 92, p. 124] — **Susan Tower Hollis**

Indexes

1030. **Art Index.** (Indexing coverage: 9/84-6/25/92). [CD-ROM]. Bronx, N.Y., H. W. Wilson, 1992. Hardware requirements: WILSONLINE Workstation, IBM PC, or compatible; 640K; hard disk drive. $1,495.00.

Since 1929, *Art Index* has been a comprehensive and easy-to-use reference tool. Currently it covers 222 periodicals in 5 languages, representing the fields of studio art, art history, architectural history, interior design, and other related topics. Its CD-ROM counterpart was first issued in 1987. This version, which is updated quarterly, can hardly be called equivalent to the print index because it is capable of so much more. Although the data remains the same, both access to it and manipulation of it have been enhanced considerably.

Like the other WILSONDISC CD-ROMS, *Art Index* is searchable by three modes: BROWSE for simple subject searches, WILSEARCH for multiterm searches, and WILSONLINE for command-driven searches. The first two are straightforward and, unlike the third option, do not require knowledge of a command language. However, the third option offers the most freedom when searching with Boolean operators, while the WILSEARCH mode is less flexible in this area. The WILSEARCH mode does allow for searching by many different fields. Additionally, an online connect mode, for citations added since the CD-ROM was produced, is an option available on terminals equipped with a modem.

In its simplest mode (BROWSE), *Art Index* does a keyword search of assigned subject headings. Users are aided by an on-screen thesaurus, and all assigned subject headings appear when records are displayed. The on-screen thesaurus gives *see* and *see also* references, but these need to be approached cautiously. Generally they are helpful, but some are too broad to be of use, others are blind, and a few are absent. Subjects include personal names, titles of art works and films, and names of buildings and movements. Indexing under the initial article of foreign names and titles is annoying in that it is done frequently and without consistency.

The WILSEARCH mode searches subjects and personal names in the subject and title fields of the database records. It can limit by organization, journal, and year of publication. The "personal name" field leads to some confusion because it searches names as both subjects and article authors. This mode easily allows for multiterm searches, but it does not tell the user whether it is "anding" or "oring" (it is "anding"). The third mode, the command-driven WILSONLINE, searches all indexed fields. Nine words are reserved as commands and should not be used as search terms.

When compared to the CD-ROM periodical indexes produced by SilverPlatter and UMI, Wilson's *Art Index* is user-friendly and affordable, offering coverage from 1984 to 1992. Although two indexes that cover periodicals and other resources (e.g., books, exhibition catalogs, festschriften) are available online through DIALOG, no CD-ROM index comparable to *Art Index* is on the market.

—**Megan S. Farrell**

1031. **The Fine Art Index.** 1992 North American ed. Chicago, International Art Reference; distr., New York, Distributed Art Publishers, 1991. 666p. illus. maps. index. $69.95. ISBN 0-9629816-0-5. ISSN 1057-8269.

Created for both the sophisticated collector and the new art enthusiast, *The Fine Art Index* surveys contemporary art by 350 artists in North America. Showcased are more than 1,000 stunning full-color reproductions of artwork from both established and emerging artists, arranged alphabetically by artist name. Each artist is profiled in a biography (averaging 150 words) that selectively provides information on birthplace (but not date), education, exhibitions, permanent collections, and early career. Categories covered are paintings, drawings and prints, conceptual and installed artwork, sculpture, and photographs. Biographies are cross-referenced to pages in the text where gallery affiliation and color photographs are available.

Each artist is represented by a single page with up to three photographs of art, names of the pieces shown, solo and group exhibitions, gallery information (e.g., address, telephone and fax numbers), gallery focus (e.g., contemporary American, European, drawings, sculpture), techniques and materials used, date of composition, and size. The inclusion of many women artists is a testament to their perseverance and success in the art market. No price information is provided. The tabbed directories support the artwork with entries for galleries, museums, business services (some Canadian and Mexican), exhibition schedules through 1992, and 21 maps of prominent gallery communities by city. Indexes to galleries, artists, appraisers, art associations, expositions/fairs, auction houses, and conservators are provided. A bibliography of periodicals, newspapers with art sections, and transporters concludes the book.

Inevitably, one can quibble with some items. No criteria are given for inclusion other than being actively represented by the galleries listed. Information about each artist is slight and uneven. For example, the entry for Eddie Arning recounts his repeated bouts of severe depression and institutionalization, and subsequent decline at age 75. No exhibition or collection information is provided on his long career. However, many entries, such as the one for Judy Coleman, highlight *only* professional exhibitions and provide no personal information whatsoever. An essay of the contemporary art scene would be welcome and would help set the tone of the book. Also, the type size chosen for the text is very small and crowded, making for tedious reading.

While the volume has popular and commercial appeal, it may have limited scholarly use. *American Art Directory* (see ARBA 92, entry 983) provides comprehensive coverage of the art world in the United States and Canada, and lists more than 5,000 artists' profiles and directories of major departments of art, museums, magazines, critics, open exhibitions, and booking agencies. On the whole, however, the sumptuous photographs and usable format of *The Fine Art Index* are impressive. A handsome volume, it is ideal for artists, students, librarians, and others involved in information exchange on art. Recommended for all academic, large public, and museum libraries. [R: Choice, May 92, p. 1366; LJ, 1 Mar 92, p. 82]—**Judy Gay Matthews**

1032. **Print Price Index '93: 1991-1992 Auction Season.** Peter Hastings Falk and others, eds. Madison, Conn., Sound View Press, 1992. 1470p. $149.00. ISSN 1058-2339.

This title gives a record of prints sold at 443 auctions in North American and Europe during the 1991-1992 auction season. Although this edition is 50 percent larger than the previous one, the price has remained the same. Three basic media are included: etchings, engravings, and lithographs. Aquatints, drypoints, wood engravings, woodblock prints, and screenprints are also listed among the 70 different types of printmaking media. Both high- and low-priced prints are noted.

Each entry consists of the artist's name, nationality, and birth and death dates; three prices (in United States dollars, British pounds, and German deutchmarks [unless the auction took place in a different country]); title; medium; date; edition number; cross-reference information; extra notes; margins; dimensions; presence of signature; whether stamped; whether annotated; auction house and date; lot number; and whether illustrated. Additionally, many artists are given a gallery price range, which will help users evaluate the works of lesser-known or young, contemporary printmakers whose materials are infrequently sold through auctions. The main index is by artist, but there are eight additional indexes by print categories: botanical, sporting, topographical, natural history, Japanese and oriental, books, portfolios, and posters. The volume also provides a directory of print dealers, catalogues raisonnes by artist, a bibliography, and a glossary that translates important terms (e.g., *ansikte* [face]) that often appear in titles.

This index will be used by collectors, dealers, scholars, curators, and auctioneers. It should be included in all library art collections. [R: Choice, May 92, p. 1374]

—**Kathleen J. Voigt**

1033. Thomison, Dennis, comp. **The Black Artist in America: An Index to Reproductions.** Metuchen, N.J., Scarecrow, 1991. 396p. index. $47.50. N6538.N5T46. 016.704'0396073. LC 91-33050. ISBN 0-8108-2503-1.

Thomison's index fills a number of previously unaddressed needs. First, it lists nearly all prominent Black artists—those who have achieved recognition from having their work reproduced in books, periodicals, and exhibition catalogs. Second, it provides a history of recognition of Black artists from colonial times to the present. Third, it catalogs each artist's most important works, telling where to find them. Fourth, it suggests biographical and portrait sources to consult for each artist. And fifth, it offers excellent bibliographies—albeit selective—that chronicle a growing interest in the Black artist in America.

Thomison's job was not easy. Since Black artists have not been well represented in traditional art surveys, he first had to collect names and then search for reproductions, instead of the other way around. Recent publications are beginning to redress this oversight, such as the Dallas Museum of Art's *Black Art: Ancestral Legacy* (1989). Thomison notes that Theresa Cederholm's *Afro-American Artists* (see ARBA 74, entry 912) makes a good companion volume to use with this index. Often in an art survey a Black artist is not identified as such, or a Caucasian artist who employs Black subject matter may be mistaken as Black. There is no such confusion in Thomison's book. Highly recommended for all art libraries and Black studies collections. [R: C&RL, Sept 92, pp. 423-424; Choice, July/Aug 92, p. 1662]—**Bill Bailey**

Periodicals

1034. Robinson, Doris. **Fine Arts Periodicals: An International Directory of the Visual Arts.** Voorheesville, N.Y., Peri Press, 1991. 570p. index. $89.00pa. ISBN 1-879796-03-1.

This ambitious new periodical directory will win a place of honor on the desk of art librarians and bibliographers. It brings together 2,790 periodicals, newsletters, and newspapers in a subject arrangement that features reference serials, visual arts, museums and galleries, decorative arts and crafts, commercial art, buildings and interiors, and photography. Both the famous and the ephemeral in international art serial publishing are represented. Entries in most cases give current directory information, subscription details, audience, a summary of the contents, and information of interest to authors or advertisers. Strengths of this work are its coverage, easy-to-read large-print format, and browsability—features that will make it a handy tool for someone who wants a quick and easy checklist on, for example, conservation and restoration. There are indexes to titles, publishers, organizations, ISSNs, and subjects. The price of this thick paperback may limit its purchase to those without access to *Ulrich's International Periodicals Directory* (see ARBA 92, entry 65) or to those desiring a deeper look at the art periodical universe than *Ulrich's* provides. [R: Choice, July/Aug 92, p. 1660; LJ, 15 Apr 92, p. 86]—**Stephanie C. Sigala**

ARCHITECTURE

1035. **Directory of Building and Equipment Grants: An Innovative Reference Directory....** 2d ed. Loxahatchee, Fla., Research Grant Guides, 1992. 216p. index. $49.50pa. ISBN 0-945078-04-8.

Grants for buildings and equipment used to be easier to obtain than grants for salaries or research, because it was more prestigious to place an individual's name on a large edifice or piece of equipment. No longer is this the case; money is in short supply, and fund-raisers must now work hard to find new building or equipment grants. This updated 2d edition will go a long way in aiding the search. In addition to advice on the philosophy of grantsmanship, foundation and corporate grants, gifts-in-kind, and federal programs, it has appendixes that provide lists of foundations by state; federal programs, including their eligibility requirements and application and award procedures; and services of the Foundation Center. Any agency involved in seeking funds to aid a broad range of interests, from health and educational programs through religion and social welfare, will find valuable information in this volume.—**Robert J. Havlik**

1036. Gretes, Frances C. **Directory of International Periodicals and Newsletters on the Built Environment.** 2d ed. New York, Van Nostrand Reinhold, 1992. 442p. index. $79.95. NA1.G7. 016.72'05. LC 91-43506. ISBN 0-442-00792-2.

This directory, which locates international periodical sources in the built environment, has been updated and expanded to include more than 500 new periodicals and newsletters that were not covered in the original edition (see ARBA 87, entry 992). More than 1,600 titles from 57 countries are arranged alphabetically under 14 major subject categories such as architecture, office practice, building types, interior design, and job leads. Each entry includes complete bibliographic information, and in most cases a brief editorial description is given. The alphabetical, geographical, and subject indexes help the user find information quickly. A separate section that lists indexes, abstracts, and online services is helpful to researchers. Attractively bound, nicely formatted, and easy to use, this comprehensive directory will be of great value to acquisition librarians, faculty, and researchers in architecture and engineering libraries.—**Diane J. Turner**

1037. **Means Illustrated Construction Dictionary.** new ed. Kingston, Mass., R. S. Means, 1991. 691p. illus. $99.95. ISBN 0-87629-218-X.

Since its first appearance in 1985, *Means Illustrated Construction Dictionary* has won awards as an outstanding reference source and has earned a space on the shelves of many architecture libraries, architecture firms, and construction companies. It contains nearly 14,000 definitions of words, terms, and concepts on all aspects of the construction business (2,000 more terms than in the original edition). Almost every page has several line drawings that illustrate various terms. Each alphabet is preceded by a list of standard and nonstandard abbreviations. A six-part reference section at the end of the volume presents practical tables of weights, measures, conversions, size determinations, and symbols, along with a useful list of professional associations concerned with the construction industry. An unusual feature is the inclusion and definition of slang terms used in the industry.

While some cross-references to similar terms are provided, the book would benefit from more of them. Also, some of the illustrations are repeated throughout the book with only arrows to point out the different features being defined. All in all, this is an excellent reference book; the purchase of the new edition will be a good decision.—**Robert J. Havlik**

1038. **The Penguin Dictionary of Architecture.** 4th ed. By John Fleming, Hugh Honour, and Nikolaus Pevsner. New York, Penguin Books, 1991. 497p. illus. $12.00pa. ISBN 0-14-051241-1.

The first three editions of this work were written and coordinated by Pevsner, a distinguished British architect. This is the first edition to be published since his death in 1983. The dictionary covers architecture in general but is especially strong in history and biography. Most of the articles are short, and the new editors have added articles on community architecture, neorationalism, postmodernism, and vernacular, as well as biographies of many new architects who have come into style or prominence since the early editions. Most biographies or discussions on style cite one or two recent works on the topic. Further information on the citations is found in the list of biographical abbreviations at the end of the volume. There are also 88 line drawings of plans and details. The pocket size of this volume makes it a handy reference, not only for libraries and architectural offices but also for the shelves of students or informed readers.—**Robert J. Havlik**

1039. **The RAIC Directory of Scholarships and Awards for Architecture.** Timothy Kehoe, ed. Ottawa, Royal Architectural Institute of Canada, 1991. 95p. $15.00pa. 730'.079'71. ISBN 0-919424-14-7.

Canada has a long but little-recognized reputation for excellent architecture education and solid contributions to the profession. This work is a directory of scholarships and awards currently available to Canadian architecture and engineering students. Section 1 gives the names and addresses of 13 Canadian architecture schools and the various scholarships and awards available at each. Most are awarded annually and range from $5,000 to book awards or recognition by faculty. Part 2 lists 15 private Canadian organizations and their awards. Most of these organizations are architectural associations, and these awards are more general than the specific awards from individual colleges in part 1. In its effort to encourage more excellence in architectural education, the Canadian government also has several substantial awards and scholarships that range as high as $32,000; these are listed in part 3. Also included are some United States-sponsored awards for which Canadians are eligible. Because travel is so important in architecture education, 16 sources for travel money have been listed. Although this directory is primarily for Canadians, other architecture school libraries may find it of interest.

—**Robert J. Havlik**

1040. Sharp, Dennis, ed. **The Illustrated Encyclopedia of Architects and Architecture.** New York, Whitney Library of Design/Watson-Guptill, 1991. 256p. illus. index. $39.95. NA40.I45. 720.3. LC 91-710. ISBN 0-8230-2539-X.

A notable feature of this reference volume is its two-part format. Part 1 is a biographical dictionary of over 350 historical and contemporary architects. Short biographies, evaluations, bibliographies, and occasional photographs of outstanding work are given. Part 2, "Architecture and the History of Ideas," is a collection of visual essays on the history of architecture from the ancient world to the present. The black-and-white and color photographs have been well selected to illustrate short statements on architectural styles, movements, and influences on both Western and non-Western culture throughout the ages. Important architects mentioned in part 2 are cross-referenced to their biographies in part 1. There are also an index and a glossary of terms, movements, and abbreviations.

The editor is executive editor of the international journal *World Architecture*, and the credentials of the various contributors are impressive. However, the essays and biographies are too short to be satisfying. The architects selected are mostly European or British; some well-known United States architects have been lumped under firm names rather than having entries of their own.

—**Robert J. Havlik**

GRAPHIC ARTS

1041. Liungman, Carl G. **Dictionary of Symbols.** Santa Barbara, Calif., ABC-Clio, 1991. 596p. illus. index. $65.00. BL603.L5413. 302.2'22. LC 91-36657. ISBN 0-87436-610-0.

Liungman is a Swedish scholar who has published well-received books on linguistics and semiotics. The work in hand is a translation of his *Symboler-Vasterlandska Ideogram* published in 1974. It is arranged in five sections. Part 1 is an introduction that consists of 20 brief chapters that are in essence scholarly essays. The initial chapter explores the differences between signs, symbols, and ideograms. "The Ideographic Struggle in Europe during the 1930s" explores the Nazi use of the swastika. The final chapter is a five-page annotated bibliography.

Part 2, "Ideographic Dictionary," the major portion of this work, covers more than 450 pages. It is further subdivided into 54 groups of signs that are identified by the makeup of the signs (e.g., single-axis, symmetric, soft open signs with crossing lines; asymmetric, both soft and straight-lined, open signs with crossing lines). The ideogram itself is clearly presented along with a paragraph or two that explains its origin and meaning. Part 3 is a word index that refers back to the dictionary. Part 4 is a 34-page graphic index where one may search for a particular symbol and locate the place in the dictionary where it is discussed. Part 5 is a "Graphic Search Index" which includes definitions and hints on using the book. Ranging from prehistoric symbols to signs used in computer flowcharting, this book should be of interest to a wide audience. [R: BR, Sept/Oct 92, p. 67; Choice, June 92, pp. 1520-22; LJ, 15 Apr 92, p. 45; RBB, 1 Jan 92, p. 849; RQ, Fall 92, p. 110; WLB, May 92, pp. 122-23]

—**Frank J. Anderson**

1042. Stevenson, George A. **Graphic Arts Encyclopedia.** 3d ed. Revised by William A. Pakan. New York, Design Press; distr., Blue Ridge Summit, Pa., TAB Books, 1992. 582p. illus. $57.95. Z118.S82. 686.2'03. LC 91-10685. ISBN 0-8306-2530-5.

Excellent for quick reference, this work lists hundreds of terms and procedures used in producing art and printed pieces in the graphic arts industry. In this edition Pakan revises and updates entries to keep in step with new systems, materials, and technologies. He includes electronic and computer applications along with the more standard and familiar processes. However, as Pakan admits in the preface, "Graphic arts terms often take on the flavor of the local area in which they are used and understood; the same usage could cause misunderstanding if applied in other areas of the country." Thus, if one wants to look up a term offered by an instructor or client, it may not be found here because of the difference in perceived definition. Were it possible to note these differences after the introduction of the term (e.g., Crop Marks [*also known as cut marks or trim marks*]), that would make this a graphic arts encyclopedia and reference book to reckon with!

Cross-referencing terms with their related appendix pieces would have also been helpful. To complete the definition of the term *Neugebauer equation*, for example, a simple notation (*See Appendix 10 for a breakdown of the equation*) could have been added. In addition, the important element of color could have been demonstrated with color visuals as well as with text. Still, this encyclopedia is a remarkable accomplishment considering the complexity and extensiveness of the topic. It should prove a valuable source for students and artists starting out in the field while serving as a quick refresher tool for the professional.—**Joan Garner**

PAINTING

1043. Merritt, Helen, and Nanako Yamada. **Guide to Modern Japanese Woodblock Prints: 1900-1975.** Honolulu, University of Hawaii Press, 1992. 365p. illus. index. $90.00. NE1323.M46. 769.952'09'04. LC 91-40576. ISBN 0-8248-1286-7.

A companion to the authors' earlier volume, *Guide to Modern Japanese Woodblock Prints: The Early Years*, the current work surveys artists born primarily after 1900 but before World War II. Arranged into selected chapters, the work includes biographical notes; art schools, organizations, and exhibitions; Dojin magazines; publishers; print series; and artists' signatures and seals. The biographical notes are arranged in the traditional Japanese manner, with surname appearing first. A cross-reference index appears at the end of the volume for artists working in the Western tradition; in this, the given name usually appears first on the print. Each entry in the biographical section includes the Japanese characters for the artists' name, birth and death dates when known, schools of study, exhibitions, associations, and other significant data. Two sections are worth further mention from a collector's and historical standpoint: those on series and on signatures and symbols. Individual works in series by selected artists appear with dates and dimensions in centimeters whenever possible, thus providing a starting point for analysis of a given work. Likewise, the signature and symbols chapter will be of great importance in interpreting the provenance of a given print.

This work, as did its earlier counterpart, will fill a significant gap in the understanding of Japanese printmaking during the nineteenth and twentieth centuries and Japanese art in general. (Many of the printmakers listed in this volume also had interests in other artistic areas as well.) The work will be a useful addition to any academic library or public library with a strong interest in Japanese culture or the arts in general. [R: Choice, Nov 92, p. 446] — **Gregory Curtis**

1044. Windsor, Alan, ed. **Handbook of Modern British Painting 1900-1980.** Brookfield, Vt., Scolar Press/Gower Publishing, 1992. 287p. $49.95; $29.95pa. ISBN 0-85967-823-7; 0-85967-887-3pa.

This book provides an alphabetical guide to modern British painters (artists working after 1900, or those who had established themselves no later than 1980). Some naturalized or foreign-born artists who spent most of their lives in Great Britain are also included as long as their work was influential in British circles. In all cases, painting or "coloured graphic work" must have played a significant part in an artist's work to merit an entry here, although minimal references to artists who also worked as sculptors, printmakers, and the like are sometimes included. In addition to artists, major schools, groups, societies, and galleries are covered if they had a significant influence on the development of British art. A few leading patrons of the arts, art critics, institutions, and special arts organizations are also given brief entries. In most cases, one or two bibliographical sources are suggested for further reading or reference.

The major shortcoming of this book is a sometimes irritating lack of cross-references. For example, the entry on Situationists explains that this was a group of "former COBRA artists led by Asger Jorn." But neither COBRA or Jorn are included elsewhere in the book, which reduces the value of the explanation for any but the already informed. However, as a quick reference for brief biographical data and thumbnail descriptions of an artist or an entry's significance (e.g., the Courtauld Institute), this is a convenient, if limited, reference work. The lack of any illustrations means that no graphic sense of an artist's work is conveyed in any of the descriptions offered here. [R: LJ, 15 June 92, p. 70]

— **Joseph W. Dauben**

1045. Wright, Christopher, comp. **The World's Master Paintings from the Early Renaissance to the Present Day: A Comprehensive Listing of Works by 1,300 Painters and a Complete Guide to Their Locations Worldwide.** New York, Routledge, Chapman & Hall, 1992. 2v. index. $399.00/set. 750. ISBN 0-415-02240-1.

Words such as *ambitious* and *mammoth* come to mind about this compendium on European painters since the thirteenth century. In one hefty set are a biographical dictionary of artists, a museum collection guide, and a painting locator for major works, particularly those of the Renaissance and Baroque periods. Users seeking biographical information will find a biographical dictionary of 1,300 artists arranged chronologically by century and nationality. Each entry gives a short career summary, a reference to a catalog raisonne (if one exists), and a list of titles of works and their locations. Worldwide museums with old master painting collections are covered in another long chapter; there are a short summary of institutional collection strengths and a list of artists represented in each museum. The third major component is a title register, so that one can find an artist when only the title of an indexed work is known.

The Achilles heel of this otherwise useful publication is the fact that most of the institutional information was gathered from museum handbooks of varying currency. For example, the Nelson Gallery in Kansas City has become the Nelson-Atkins Museum with very different collecting strengths since that institution's cited handbook was published (1959). Other handbooks are more current, yet the deaccessioning of artworks that has become typical in the United States has undoubtedly affected the location of some paintings. With that caveat in mind, librarians and researchers should welcome the magnitude and usefulness of this new art reference tool. [R: Choice, Nov 92, p. 451; RBB, 15 Oct 92, pp. 460-61; WLB, Sept 92, pp. 122-23]—**Stephanie C. Sigala**

23 Language and Linguistics

GENERAL WORKS

Bibliography

1046. Baer, E. Kristina, and Daisy E. Shenholm. **Leo Spitzer on Language and Literature: A Descriptive Bibliography.** New York, Modern Language Association of America, 1991. 172p. index. $49.50. Z8831.18.B34. 016.41. LC 91-9845. ISBN 0-87352-195-1.

After the Austrian-born Romance philologist Leo Spitzer (1887-1960) settled in the United States in 1936, he established a formidable reputation for himself in the fields of literary criticism, critical practice, and linguistic theory. As the authors of this excellent bibliography demonstrate, Spitzer's achievements in these areas, plus his contentious approach to scholarship, have long overshadowed his lifelong contributions in etymology, lexicology, grammar, morphology, and syntax. Baer and Shenholm have assembled a comprehensive bibliography of Spitzer's works, including 1,006 books, articles, and book reviews. These types of publication are arranged separately, with book and review citations being unannotated and all entries for articles having detailed summaries. The entries for book-length anthologies list the volume contents and give cross-references to the original appearances of each article. Article entries are arranged chronologically in general subject categories, which are etymology and lexicology; grammar, morphology, and syntax; semantics; literary criticism and theory; and stylistics. These are further divided by language. Indexes of persons, titles, and words or phrases provide additional access. Baer's introductory essay gives a thorough overview of Spitzer's career and the development of his ideas. This well-executed work will be an aid to scholars in any of the areas that Spitzer wrote for so actively.—**John R. M. Lawrence**

1047. Gordon, W. Terrence. **Semantics: A Bibliography, 1986-1991.** Metuchen, N.J., Scarecrow, 1992. 280p. index. $29.50. Z7004.S4G69. 016.401'43. LC 92-27597. ISBN 0-8108-2598-8.

This is the third in a continuing series; the author previously published comparable volumes for the periods 1965-1978 and 1979-1985. The book begins with an introduction that describes the subfields of semantics; this is followed by a glossary of technical terms. The heart of the volume is the annotated bibliography. Section 1 is devoted to book-length publications; after this, articles and conference papers are listed in 22 sections that cover such topics as reference, ambiguity, synonymy, antonymy, homonymy, polysemy, semantic fields, kinship terms, color terms, negation, modals, idioms, child language, and semantic universals. The authors listed include philosophers, linguists, anthropologists, and psychologists. The book ends with two indexes, one of words discussed and one of authors' names. The coverage area is North America and Western Europe.

The growing importance of semantics as a field of study is indicated by the increasing number of items listed in Gordon's volumes. In organization, accuracy, and scholarship, this bibliography is exemplary. With its two predecessors, the work is definitive for its subject matter.

—**William Bright**

1048. Kister, Kenneth F. **Kister's Best Dictionaries for Adults & Young People: A Comparative Guide.** Phoenix, Ariz., Oryx Press, 1992. 438p. index. $39.50. PE1611.K57. 423. LC 91-40679. ISBN 0-89774-191-9.

Useful for both librarians and the general public, this book is a consumer guide to a wide variety of English-language dictionaries. Included are descriptive and evaluative reviews of 303 United States, Canadian, and British dictionaries in both print and electronic formats. Reviews are arranged in separate categories for adult and young people's dictionaries (132 adult and 168 young people's dictionaries are reviewed). Subdivisions include, for the adult category, unabridged, college desk, family and office, and pocket and paperback dictionaries; for young people the categories are high school, junior high, upper elementary, primary school, and preschool dictionaries, as well as alphabet books.

Each review, in addition to standard bibliographic information, assesses the merits of the work, sometimes including quotations from other reviews. Very significant dictionaries, such as *The Oxford English Dictionary* (see ARBA 90, entry 1006), receive longer reviews than less important works. Kister writes clearly, without pedantry but also with a contagious enthusiasm. His long introductory essay should be required reading for library school students in general reference classes, although it is accessible to the general reader as well. It discusses the many different uses of dictionaries, their history, how they are compiled, the debate about whether they should prescribe or describe how the language is used, whether offensive words should be included, major publishers, how dictionaries are bought and sold, and selection criteria. This essay is worth the price of the book even for libraries that own most of the titles reviewed. Kister's guide should be especially useful in public, school, or small academic libraries. [R: LJ, 15 Oct 92, p. 62; RBB, 1 June 92, pp. 1776-77; WLB, May 92, p. 128] – **David Isaacson**

1049. Ostler, Rosemarie. **Theoretical Syntax 1980-1990: An Annotated and Classified Bibliography.** Philadelphia, John Benjamins, 1992. 192p. index. (Amsterdam Studies in the Theory and History of Linguistic Science. Series V: Library & Information Sources in Linguistics, v.21). $49.00. Z7004.S94O88. 016.415. LC 91-42086. ISBN 1-55619-251-7.

Intended both for the scholar and for students just beginning in linguistics, this bibliography has 914 monographs and articles that deal with theoretical syntax. Each item has a brief descriptive annotation that indicates the subject coverage. Ostler has tried to include all of the major trends as well as some minor ones. She neither attempts to be comprehensive nor evaluative. Many scholars will be grateful for the even-handed treatment, but undergraduates may well wish for more guidance about the most important works in an area. Materials in languages other than English and all unpublished materials are excluded. Periodical articles are taken only from the 14 most influential, widely available, and often cited journals. The book is arranged under 10 subject headings, and author and topic indexes provide additional access. There is also a helpful index by language studied or used as example. This volume will be useful primarily in large academic collections with strong holdings in linguistics.
– **Adele M. Fasick**

Dictionaries and Encyclopedias

1050. **International Encyclopedia of Linguistics.** William Bright, ed. New York, Oxford University Press, 1992. 4v. maps. index. $395.00/set. P29.I58. 410'.3. LC 91-7349. ISBN 0-19-505196-3.

Probably the most outstanding component of this encyclopedia is its treatment of languages; no other encyclopedia offers such detailed information, and so much of it, on so many languages. In the case of the most important languages (e.g., Sanskrit or Arabic on the upper part of the scale, Czech on the lowest part), there are a few columns (or even pages) in which the history of the language and a sketch of its structure are given. The rest of the languages are treated in a well-organized way. There are general entries on such things as African languages; these entries give a general survey with maps and similar material. Then there are entries for the single families of African languages and their subfamilies; in the latter, the single languages are enumerated and, if possible, briefly described. All these entries are interconnected by frequent cross-references. The degree of finesse with which this is done can be gathered from the fact that the entry on Adelbert Range languages (a small group in New Guinea) enumerates no less than 44 languages spoken by approximately 46,156 people. The amount of information offered in these cases varies, sometimes because there is not much to say. Such is the treatment of Ndai, one of the Adamawa branch of the Adamawa-Ubangi subgroup of the Niger-Congo languages: "only a few speakers left, in Tchollire, Mayo-Rey District, North Province, Cameroon; also called Galke." At the end of the fourth volume there is a general survey of languages of the world by families and by areas.

Apart from the single languages, linguistics is mostly treated in large, comprehensive entries. Some of these are written by several authors; "History of Linguistics" is authored by sections (e.g., ancient, medieval, Renaissance). This system is very good because it allows the selection of the best specialist for a given topic. The consequence of this, however, is that "Lexicostatistics" is one of the sections of the entry "Historical Linguistics," and "Language Planning" is a section of the entry "Applied Linguistics." Cross-references help with the location of information sought, and an index lists all the terms, names of languages and persons, and more. There are also entries on historically important linguists (e.g., Bopp, Schleicher, Bloomfield). A particularly useful feature is the full treatment of such recent theories as lexical-functional grammar.

The discussion and the references are invariably good and fairly exhaustive; the editing has been done with equal care. Only occasionally are things omitted; for example, the entry "Analogy" does not mention W. Manczak; the entry "Semiotics" mentions Bakhtin several times, but no reference is given; and the text on the New Guinea languages puts Timor to the east of the Salomon Islands and the islands to the west of Timor, not the other way round. Overall, this is an excellent work for reference and browsing. [R: LJ, 1 Apr 92, p. 112; 15 Apr 92, pp. 44-45; RBB, 1 Feb 92, p. 1057; WLB, Mar 92, pp. 115-16]—L. Zgusta

1051. Lauther, Howard. **Lauther's Complete Punctuation Thesaurus of the English Language.** Brookline Village, Mass., Branden Publishing, 1991. 341p. index. $19.95. PE1450.C74. 428. LC 91-14703. ISBN 0-8283-1945-6.

This reference book will be useful to writers baffled by where to place punctuation and the most appropriate uses for the different types of marks. Lauther presents punctuation the way it should be presented—as an integral part of the way we communicate through writing. Consequently, the first of two ways provided to use this book, "Punctuation Categories," might be more accurately referred to as "Word Categories." Rules for and examples of how to use punctuation are categorized under such topics as phrases and adverbial clauses, sentences, and quotations. Subsections of these topics are further divided into rules, which comprise the thesaurus.

The alphabetized general index is the second mode provided for finding rules. It may be more helpful for users because it lists in boldface type some of the more specific key words for locating the rules, which are not emphasized in the list of punctuation categories. At the same time, these boldface entries may also be confusing because they appear to be major entries followed by subentries, when, in fact, most are individual entries in their own right. An introduction that covered the book's organization and style would better serve the reader than the one-page "How to Use This Book," which does no more than tell readers of the two ways to find the rules and that the rules are numbered.

Users are cautioned that this thesaurus is not the preemptive reference guide to punctuation. For example, Lauther relies on the antiquated guidance of placing a comma in a sentence according to where one would be expected to pause; he also overlooks the distinction between restrictive and nonrestrictive clauses.—**Heidi Ann Olinger**

1052. Malmkjaer, Kirsten, ed. **The Linguistics Encyclopedia.** New York, Routledge, Chapman & Hall, 1991. 575p. illus. index. $99.00. P29.L52. 410'.3. LC 90-38466. ISBN 0-415-02942-2.

This encyclopedia is designed to guide its readers, educated laypeople as well as students and scholars of linguistics, through the complex world and history of the study of language. The articles of this one-volume work have been written by an international group of linguists, who succeed in striking just the right balance between detail and brevity on the one hand and depth and clarity on the other. Each article covers a single topic of linguistics; well-defined segments, such as acoustic phonetics, glossematics, and case grammar, are treated in detail; and broader areas, such as sociolinguistics and syntax, are broken up into several subareas to assure adequate coverage. Each section ends with a list of suggested readings for further information. Numerous cross-references, illustrations, an extensive index, and a 40-page bibliography complete the volume. Given the fact that many nonlinguists will use this reference book, a glossary would have been a welcome addition for definitions of unfamiliar terms.

In 1992 a similar title was published by Oxford University Press: the four-volume *International Encyclopedia of Linguistics*, edited by William Bright. Libraries and individuals who do not need (or cannot afford) the more extensive coverage of the larger encyclopedia will find a good, dependable substitute in *The Linguistics Encyclopedia*. [R: LAR, May 92, p. 334]

—Zsuzsa Koltay

Handbooks and Yearbooks

1053. DeAngelis, Carl, and Ed Battle, eds. **Eng'lish Lan'guage and O'ri-en-ta'tion Pro'grams in the United States.** 10th ed. New York, Institute of International Education, 1992. 307p. index. $42.95pa. ISBN 0-87206-194-9.

When compared with the version published in 1988 (see ARBA 90, entry 994), the new edition shows several substantial improvements and additions. It is now based on an extensive survey and the results of questionnaires sent in 1991 and 1992 to more than 3,000 U.S. colleges and universities. Thus, this edition offers comprehensive and representative information about important areas of teaching English as a Second Language (ESL) in the United States. The first section lists 481 intensive ESL programs arranged alphabetically by state and program name. The second section covers 459 colleges, universities, and institutes that offer standard courses or semi-intensive programs of English for foreign students. Some 87 secondary school programs are described in the third section. The final section, which is new, provides information on 21 specialized summer programs for foreign teachers of English (with intermediate or advanced English proficiency). Typical program entries include addresses; telephone, fax, and telex numbers; proficiency levels; admission requirements; and basic information about tuition and fees. Several instructive introductory chapters, indexes, and appendixes contribute to the general usefulness of this directory.—**Lev I. Soudek**

1054. **The Oxford Companion to the English Language.** Tom McArthur and Feri McArthur, eds. New York, Oxford University Press, 1992. 1184p. index. $45.00. ISBN 0-19-214183-X.

Oxford bills this new work as "everything you always wanted to know about the English language but were afraid to ask," because it is the first major one-volume reference devoted to the English language. It contains more than 3,500 signed entries from nearly 100 scholars on almost 1,200 pages. Coverage ranges over all aspects of our changing and influential language, including grammar, history, pronunciation, usage, education, literature, culture, linguistics, politics, and technology, with numerous related articles on tangential subjects. Additional features cover notable people, word games, media, sexist language, political correctness, place-names, jargon, dialects, sign language, biblical English, Black English, transitional phrases, and much more. Extensive cross-referencing allows the reader to follow a trail of information from general to increasingly specific articles and vice versa.

Those fascinated with language and its relationship to culture will relish the range of topics covered, such as bilingual education, child language acquisition, and biographies of shapers of English (e.g., William Shakespeare, Noah Webster, Noam Chomsky, James Joyce). Arrangement is alphabetical, with people, places, and things interfiled; there are bibliographies for many topics. Because English is an eclectic language, readers should not be surprised to learn where now-familiar borrowed words (e.g., ketchup, chipmunk, commando, banjo, shampoo, galore, cookie, albino, molasses) came from, but they still may be in for surprises.

The only drawbacks are the numerous and frequent abbreviations and the crowded pages of small print, lacking illustrations. Be forewarned that an intended brief foray to research a specific item can lead to a daisy chain of fascinating browsing and flipping back and forth, so the reader will need discipline and focus. Perhaps the best thing about this authoritative and substantial volume is that it is an encyclopedia, a dictionary, and a compendium of language-related trivia all rolled into one. Enthusiastically recommended! [R: LJ, 1 Nov 92, p. 81; RBB, 15 Oct 92, p. 457; WLB, Nov 92, pp. 94-95]—**Bruce A. Shuman**

ENGLISH-LANGUAGE DICTIONARIES

Abridged

1055. **The American Heritage Dictionary.** Boston, Houghton Mifflin, 1991. 1568p. illus. maps. index. $16.95. PE1625.A54. 423. LC 82-9346. ISBN 0-395-32943-4.

The first edition of *The American Heritage Dictionary* appeared in 1969. Its aim was to be a reference that would not only list words in English but also guide its users toward "grace and precision" in the use of that language. The introduction of this edition states that this goal continues to be pursued.

While all dictionaries are basically alphabetically arranged lists of words with information about each word, the *American Heritage Dictionary* also uses many illustrations and has separate sections for geographic and biographic entries. This edition uses a simplified pronunciation system with the schwa(g) as its only nonalphabetical symbol. More than 3,000 entries contain illustrative examples. Etymologies are presented in the standard form after the definitions. A listing may also contain usage notes and a list of synonyms. The volume has highly readable articles on language and usage, a style manual, and lists of abbreviations and two- and four-year colleges.

This edition has added more than 10,000 new vocabulary words and meanings; 5,000 new scientific and technical terms; 400 new usage notes; 5,000 more entries in the geographical and biographical sections; and more than 3,000 new photographs. The format has the usual small print necessary when more than 200,000 definitions and 3,000-plus illustrations fill only 1,568 pages, but it is still attractive and easy to read. New words are not listed separately, as in some dictionaries, and current meanings are listed first, with the older ones last, contrary to traditional lexicography. For its price, *The American Heritage Dictionary* has much to offer the general school or office user. [R: RBB, 1 Oct 92, p. 350]
– **Kay O. Cornelius**

1056. **The American Heritage Dictionary of the English Language.** 3d ed. Boston, Houghton Mifflin, 1992. 2184p. illus. maps. $39.95. PE1628.A623. 423. LC 92-851. ISBN 0-395-44895-6.

Representing 4 years of work by 175 contributors, this new edition of a popular dictionary has 200,000 boldface headwords that generate more than 350,000 meanings, including 16,000 new words and meanings. Biographical and geographical entries are interfiled with others, as are abbreviations. Within entries, the usual arrangement is headword (syllabicated), pronunciation, part of speech, inflections, definitions (in order of frequency of use), and a brief etymology. The definitions, many with examples, are generally clear, with no specialized lexicographic terms or abbreviations to stand between the reader and the meaning. The entries are supplemented by about 4,000 well-chosen black-and-white photographs and line drawings that appear in the margins near the words they depict. Graphic aids include drawings of the Heimlich maneuver and tables of Morse code, Braille, and the manual alphabet. Near the appropriate headwords are such bonus features as currency tables; Gregorian, Jewish, and Moslem calendars; the periodic table (placed a page or two after *element*); a list and description of subatomic particles; symbols and signs; a measurement table; and proofreaders' marks.

A distinctive feature of this dictionary is its Usage Panel, now composed of 173 writers, editors, scholars, and distinguished members of various professions. Its function is to rule, via periodic ballots, on questions of current English usage. This democratic approach to grammar and syntax will disturb prescriptivists, but the panel's deliberations have resulted in more than 500 helpful notes and comments, including a discussion of *hopefully* as a sentence adverb (of which most panel members disapprove), lengthy and sensitive treatments of the generic use of *he/him/his* and the word *man*, and a note on the use of singular verbs with the subject *data*. It is clear that this dictionary's editors see their work as a guide rather than as a set of rules, and in the absence of an English equivalent of the French Academy, this does not seem to be an unreasonable approach. There are also more than 900 cross-referenced synonym paragraphs, many of which discuss connotations and varying shades of meaning. Another highlight is the inclusion of 400-plus special word histories, revised and expanded etymological discussions of particularly interesting words, such as *Hoosier, posh, OK, pickle,* and *alligator*. A unique feature of this edition is a set of more than 100 regional notes that treat dialect words and expressions.

In addition to an apologia for the existence of the Usage Panel, a helpful guide to the dictionary, and a pronunciation key, the front matter includes some well-written, authoritative articles on the history of English, with emphasis on its Indo-European (I-E) origins and on the particular development of American English. The end matter consists of more detailed information on the Indo-Europeans by Calvert Watkins, including an appendix that seems to be a revision of his book *The American Heritage Dictionary of Indo-European Roots* (Houghton Mifflin, 1985). The endpapers consist of a fascinating diagram of the I-E family of languages.

No dictionary is immune from criticism. For example, a reader may find the statement that AIDS is "transmitted primarily by venereal routes" a bit quaint. Also, it is surprising that the expansion of *ZIP code* does not acknowledge that ZIP is an acronym for *Zone Improvement Program*. In general, the geographic entries are disappointing. A spot-check of entries for major U.S. cities reveals that the population figures given (with no dates) come from the 1980 census and not the most recent enumeration. Maps are simple, two-tone line drawings that typically indicate only a country's location relative to other countries and its capital city. No doubt experts in various specialized areas will complain about other definitions and illustrations.

However, no quibbling should obscure the fact that *The American Heritage Dictionary of the English Language* is an attractive, easy-to-read, authoritative dictionary with an up-to-date word list and a strong emphasis on etymology, regionalisms, and usage. This is an excellent dictionary that is strongly recommended for both home and library purchase. It may be more expensive than most desk or college dictionaries, but it is worth the extra cost. [R: LJ, Aug 92, p. 86; WLB, Nov 92, p. 91]—**Henry J. Ricardo**

1057. **Chambers Concise Dictionary.** Catherine Schwarz and others, eds. New York, Chambers Kingfisher Graham, 1991. 1296p. $20.00. ISBN 0-550-10570-0.

Compiled from the Chambers English Language database, the *Chambers Concise Dictionary* attempts to be not only a dictionary for general use but also a reflection of the language and culture of the last decade of the twentieth century. New terms from technology, such as *earcon*, *NICAM*, and *motherboard*, are defined in concise, clear language. Another characteristic of this descriptive dictionary is the attention given to slang and colloquial language. Indeed, the spoken language of the 1990s is clearly the focus of this dictionary. The work defines 130,000 terms, and there are about 50 pages of appendixes on grammar, spelling, and general information. For a general dictionary or a more prescriptive approach to the English language, one should perhaps look elsewhere; but for a snapshot look at English (both American and British) at the end of the century, this work does the job admirably.—**Valerie R. Hotchkiss**

1058. **The Merriam-Webster Concise School and Office Dictionary.** Springfield, Mass., Merriam-Webster, 1991. 674p. illus. $7.95pa. PE1628.M35. 423. LC 91-9382. ISBN 0-87779-600-9.

This dictionary contains a core vocabulary of 60,000 words and phrases and is based on *Webster's Ninth New Collegiate Dictionary* (see ARBA 91, entry 1050). Each entry is hyphenated and provides pronunciation, part of speech, and a brief definition. Some entries contain adverbs and adjectives, and a few black-and-white illustrations appear. Some terms, such as *numbers* and *planets*, have useful tables. Other sections of the book give foreign words and phrases, nations of the world and selected U.S. cities with populations, signs and symbols, and a style guide. Introductory material contains notes of explanation and identification of abbreviations.

This dictionary appears to be an updated and expanded version of *The Merriam-Webster Dictionary* (see ARBA 77, entry 1077), which contained 57,000 entries. The dictionary under review has many recent terms such as *AIDS, acid rain, affirmative action*, and *air bag*, but some newer terms are missing, such as *CD-ROM, cellular phone*, and *closed caption*. Overall, it is a reliable, authoritative source for the home and high school library. Larger public and academic libraries will need a larger vocabulary.—**O. Gene Norman**

1059. **Random House Webster's College Dictionary.** New York, Random House, 1991. 1568p. illus. index. $18.00; $20.00 (thumb indexed). PE1628.W55185. 423. LC 90-21963. ISBN 0-679-40110-5; 0-679-41410-X (thumb indexed).

The database for this work was created from the *Random House Dictionary of the English Language*, 2d ed. (see ARBA 88, entry 1095). It is notable for being the first developed from the Random House Living Dictionary Project, a merger of traditional lexicography and the ability to instantly add and edit new terms online. This project has helped the Random House lexicographers meet their goal of providing a "reliable, up-to-date guide to information about our vigorous, constantly evolving language." Among the more than 180,000 vocabulary words that comprise the dictionary are those that reflect contemporary U.S. life. The inclusion of terms such as *mommy track*, *love handles*, and *Soweto* lend permanency and validity to what otherwise would be mere fads of language and lifestyle. The dictionary also presents 2,500 idioms, 450 synonym studies, thousands of sentences and phrases that demonstrate word use, 32,000 etymologies, 4,000-plus biographical entries, more than 7,000 geographical entries, and entries specific to Native American peoples and languages. It contains nearly 20,000 more entries than its closest competitor, and 800 entries are accompanied by clear and useful illustrations.

Important features of the entries include the organization of definitions from the most frequently used to the archaic and cross-references to other main entries and their variants. Dates that indicate when the words entered the language are given, and words of U.S. origin are noted. All entries, including abbreviations, acronyms, and biographical and geographical listings, are organized into one alphabetical guide. Foreign terms, book titles, and names of ships are italicized, reflecting the way they usually appear in print. In addition, terms that begin with *St.* or *Mc* are listed alphabetically as *St.* or *Mc* to complement the way everyday dictionary users—not editors—think about words. Usage notes delineate clearly between generally accepted, formal, and hypercorrect uses of words in context, including explanations of the standards for use in spoken and written forms.

Preceding the dictionary is a section that describes its features in detail and how it can be used as more than a spelling guide. Unlike similar sections in other reference works, this one is accessible due to a generous point size, the leading, and a page layout in which explanatory matter has been set on the inner half and sample entries on the outer half of each page. An annotated pronunciation guide follows, and a key to abbreviations used within the dictionary concludes the front matter.

The sections following the dictionary make up something of a style guide. A basic but good guide for writers explains the use of capitalization, italics, and basic and specialized punctuation. A list of reference styles shows how to prepare author-page and author-date citations for 18 different types of publications. The last section of the style guide deals with avoiding sexist language. Ironically, this part is undercut by definitions in the dictionary that enforce the notion that *man* is the standard and *woman* something other. For example, a congressman is "a member of a congress," while a congresswoman is "a woman who is a member of a congress." A key to locating correct spellings based on how words sound and a one-page index end the book; the latter is of questionable utility because of its random list of diagrams and illustrations. Overall, users looking for a desk companion for home, school, or office will find this dictionary indispensable.—**Heidi Ann Olinger**

Etymology

1060. Kohl, Herbert. **From Archetype to Zeitgeist: Powerful Ideas for Powerful Thinking.** Boston, Little, Brown, 1992. 246p. illus. index. $19.95. AB105.K64. 031. LC 91-37658. ISBN 0-316-50138-7.

The carelessness with which speakers use words and then hide behind inexactness, as if every word required Talmudic genius, baffles the mind and confuses audiences. Kohl's slim volume provides readers with meanings to ideological words. Many words are compared or contrasted here, such as *iconography*, *iconoly*, *a posteriori*, *digitalize*, *geist*, *phylogeny*, and *apartheid*. The words are taken from literature, arts, philosophy, religion, sociology, economics, anthropology, logic, and other disciplines. Kohl has used definitions that are well drawn but facile in interpretation, a definite drawback. A brief bibliography is included. The index, the main access point unless the subject area is known, covers both words in the list and words defined but not given specific entries.

This volume is a godsend for incoming freshmen who need to know these words but have never seen them. It will also help readers in other areas who may think they know certain words but use them incorrectly. [R: RBB, 15 Oct 92, pp. 452-53; SLJ, Nov 92, p. 137]—**Mark Y. Herring**

Grammar

1061. Johnson, Edward D. **The Handbook of Good English.** New York, Facts on File, 1991. 427p. $21.95. LC 91-21872. ISBN 0-8160-2711-0.

Writer's guides should be comprehensive; they should cover minor points of grammar and punctuation (the bane of copyeditors and proofreaders); and they should be authoritative, presenting rules with a confidence born of experience and practice. All of these criteria have been met in *The Handbook of Good English*.

Johnson brings to his work more than 30 years of editing experience at such major publishing houses as Simon & Schuster and Alfred A. Knopf. He writes with wit, style, and a love of English, the combination of which has been rarely seen since the classic *Elements of Style*. His book is divided into four main sections that cover grammar, punctuation, styling written English (e.g., numbers, generic terms), and diction and composition. (The latter sections are fairly short.) A glossary/index of more than 100 pages provides lengthy definitions of terms and discussions of such controversies as *bring* versus *take*, cross-referenced to numbered sections in the text.

Perhaps Johnson's greatest strength is his provision for each rule of many sample sentences and a substantial explanation for its rationale. For example, in the discussion of the diagonal, he questions whether *and/or* is a word or "just a convenient device to save writers trouble and suggest that they have gone to the trouble of considering every possibility." He never fails to note if a rule is controversial and why, or when he prefers one usage over another. Because of the abundance of text and the lack of a more detailed index separate from the glossary, the book is less useful as a ready-reference than as a tome for careful study. However, Johnson covers so much so well that his book often solves problems that other guides gloss over or omit (e.g., *more importantly* versus *more important*) and is therefore appropriate for even the smallest collection. [R: BR, Jan/Feb 92, p. 58]—**D. A. Rothschild**

Idioms, Colloquialisms, and Special Usage

1062. **Dictionary of American Regional English. Volume II: D-H.** Frederic G. Cassidy and Joan Houston Hall, eds. Cambridge, Mass., Belknap Press/Harvard University Press, 1991. 1175p. maps. $70.00. PE2843.D52. 427'.973. LC 84-29025. ISBN 0-674-20512-X.

Volume 1 of the *Dictionary of American Regional English* (DARE) (see ARBA 86, entry 1050) was published in 1985 after decades of preparation. DARE represents the first effort to study the language of an entire country. Its purpose is to document and record the regional folk words, expressions, metaphors, and similes of English as it is spoken in the United States. The project's primary tool is a carefully worded survey of 1,847 questions that touch on most aspects of everyday life. Over a 5-year period, natives of 1,002 communities throughout the country were interviewed to form a database of more than 2,500,000 items. Also used were 7,000 private and public written sources.

The DARE editors list entries alphabetically. Variant pronunciations are shown through the use of the International Phonetic Alphabet. After the definitions, examples and sources are listed in chronological order, with the oldest references listed first. For some items, computer-generated maps illustrate the regional distribution of words and phrases. Along with a great deal of other front matter, these maps were explained in volume 1. To understand them, readers of volume 2 must refer to the first volume, a potential drawback when the first volume is missing or in use, and time-consuming at best.

The content of the DARE volumes is both enlightening and entertaining. Those who believe that years of hearing "standard American" speech through radio, movies, and television has produced a single American English will find that many regional differences in language still exist. In addition, many expressions that have died out in today's usage are now recorded for posterity. (Linguists and writers should especially welcome that aspect of DARE's work.) Anyone with an interest in American history and life in general will enjoy browsing through this volume.

—Kay O. Cornelius

Juvenile

1063. **Troll Young People's Dictionary.** By David Smith and Derek Newton. Mahwah, N.J., Troll Associates, 1991. 128p. illus. $14.89; $9.95pa. PE1628.5.S6. 423. LC 89-27331. ISBN 0-8167-2255-2; 0-8167-2256-0pa.

Around 1,200 words are defined in this dictionary for primary-age children. Approximately one-fourth of the entries give multiple definitions, usually 2, with more than 40 words receiving 3 or more. Clear pronunciation guides are provided following each word, but no key is given. There are an average of two illustrations per page. Most that involve people are essentially Caucasian males (72 percent), with some white females and only 2 that represent other cultures or races. The illustration of tools includes an electric drill; that of a telephone shows a traditional desk model; the dress illustrated has a short skirt and an unusually low back, and is worn with very high heels.

Many words that could have been defined do not appear. *Church* is defined but not *temple, synagogue, mosque, Christian, religion, Jew* or *Hebrew, pastor, priest, preacher,* or *rabbi*. As usual in children's dictionaries, no definitions are given for elimination or sex-related words. Other definitions are incomplete or confusing. For example, *love* does not include the sense of liking, as in "I love food," and *pen* does not include a definition of an enclosure. *Attack* is defined as "to start a fight. Cats attack mice." *Grape* is defined as growing in bunches, but the illustration is of a single grape growing on a vine. The *American Heritage First Dictionary* (see ARBA 88, entry 1087), *Macmillan First Dictionary* (see ARBA 92, entry 1046), and *My First Dictionary* (Scott, Foresman, 1990) offer more entries and more illustrations for comparable prices.—**Betty Jo Buckingham**

New Words

1064. Algeo, John, with Adele S. Algeo, eds. **Fifty Years "Among the New Words": A Dictionary of Neologisms, 1941-1991.** New York, Cambridge University Press, 1991. 257p. $60.00. PE1630.F5. 423'.1. LC 91-26694. ISBN 0-521-41377-X.

The heart of this book is a photographically reduced but still legible reproduction of 113 columns of "Among the New Words," a feature of the journal *American Speech* since 1941. For this collection, John Algeo, former editor of *American Speech* and the cocompiler of "Among the New Words," has prepared a complete index and glossary to all the words cited in this column from April 1941 through the winter of 1990. He has also written a marvelous introduction that describes the formation of new words and some of the reasons for devising them. "Like the growth rings of a tree, our vocabulary bears witness to our past," Algeo states. Although one can use the alphabetical index to search for specific words, it is more fun to browse through the columns and let 50 years of our British and American linguistic history pass by. At the time of their original discussion in the column, with full citations of usage, few of these words appeared in standard dictionaries. Many have since found reasonably permanent places in English, while others have merely achieved the linguistic version of Andy Warhol's 15 minutes of fame. Thus we find *landing strip* and *lumberjill, OPEC* and *Olliemania, scuba* and *suppie* (Southern yuppie).

Similar to the various Barnhart dictionaries of new English (see, for example, ARBA 91, entry 1059), the articles in this collection have been a major source of linguistic information to generations of commercial dictionaries. All those interested in the development of the English language owe John Algeo and the Cambridge University Press a debt of gratitude for providing such a valuable resource. [R: RBB, 1 Apr 92, pp. 1472-73; WLB, Mar 92, p. 115]

—Henry J. Ricardo

1065. **The Oxford Dictionary of New Words: A Popular Guide to Words in the News.** Sara Tulloch, comp. New York, Oxford University Press, 1991. 322p. $19.95. PE1630.O94. 423. LC 91-18814. ISBN 0-19-869170-X.

In 750 entertaining, informative articles, *The Oxford Dictionary of New Words* presents more than 2,000 words, phrases, and new meanings that became popular in the 1980s and 1990s. Drawing on the vast resources of the Oxford Dictionary Department, this book provides a cultural history of the last 15 years or so. The words come from many areas of modern life and represent different registers. There is heavy emphasis on neologisms from the United Kingdom and the United States, with sparser contributions from Canada, Australia, and other English-speaking countries.

Each article has a headword in large boldface type that is followed by its pronunciation in International Phonetic Alphabet symbols; its part of speech or grammatical category (in italics); alternative spellings; the subject area (indicated by one or more of 11 icons); a definition section; the word or phrase's etymology, history, and usage; and recent illustrative quotations taken from journalism and fiction. Multiple meanings of the same word are indicated by superscripts. There is extensive cross-referencing.

This is a much more ambitious and satisfying undertaking than *Neo-Words* (see ARBA 92, entry 1058) and is closer in content to *The Third Barnhart Dictionary of New English* (see ARBA 91, entry 1059) or to *Fifty Years "Among the New Words,"* edited by John Algeo (Cambridge University Press, 1991). Although not as comprehensive as these last two books, the Oxford dictionary gives its chosen word-hoard a more extensive and more captivating treatment. A reader may find a favorite word or two missing, but there is much to delight in here. This *awesome* (p. 21) dictionary is heartily recommended for individual, school, and library purchase wherever English is spoken. [R: Choice, May 92, p. 1372; CLJ, Oct 92, p. 403; LJ, 1 Feb 92, pp. 80-82; RBB, 15 Feb 92, p. 1132; WLB, Feb 92, p. 111]
—**Henry J. Ricardo**

1066. **Tuttle Dictionary of New Words: Since 1960.** By Jonathon Green. Rutland, Vt., Charles E. Tuttle, 1992. 339p. $16.95pa. PE1630.G74. 423'.1. LC 92-20737. ISBN 0-8048-1803-7.

Originally published in England under the title *Neologisms* (1991), this book describes nearly 2,700 new words and phrases that have entered the mainstream of the English language since 1960. In particular, British English is the standard for inclusion.

The entries are displayed alphabetically in two columns, with each headword in boldface type, followed by the part of speech, a date in square brackets, a definition or discussion, and illustrative quotations that are marked off by boldfaced asterisks. No pronunciations are given. The entries are informative and well written. Although no explanation of the bracketed date is given, it is clearly meant to approximate the entrance of the word into the general (British) public consciousness. The words cover a wide range of human activity, with particular attention paid to slang and jargon. In his introductory comments Green declares his intention to avoid esoteric scientific terminology, but computer terms (e.g., *floppy disk, OOPS*) are well represented.

Neologisms of the past 30 years have been covered pretty thoroughly by the three Barnhart dictionaries, the most recent of which is *Third Barnhart Dictionary of New English* (see ARBA 91, entry 1059), and by John Algeo's *Fifty Years among the New Words* (see index for entry number). Sara Tulloch has concentrated on the last decade's crop of words in *The Oxford Dictionary of New Words* (see index for entry number). Nevertheless, there should be room for Green's inexpensive, interestingly written book in individual, school, and public libraries.—**Henry J. Ricardo**

Other English-Speaking Countries

1067. Fischer, Andreas, and Daniel Ammann. **An Index to Dialect Maps of Great Britain.** Philadelphia, John Benjamins, 1991. 150p. (Varieties of English around the World. General Series, v.10). $45.00pa. PE1705.F57. 427'.941'0223. LC 91-7244. ISBN 1-55619-439-0.

Designed for linguistics scholars, this volume will prove highly useful to its specialized audience. It indexes the maps in various atlases of English dialects based on surveys, some of which overlap and even duplicate each other. Its chief virtue is that it enables a researcher to easily locate specific information from these surveys.

The introduction traces the history of English, Scottish, Anglo-Welsh, and Anglo-Irish dialectology, followed by a brief description of each survey indexed. Because these studies were fragmented, the organization of the index, although straightforward, requires a lengthy explanation of the conventions for citing the surveys. The index appears in columnar form. The first lists the Standard English, or, in some cases, dialect word usually given in response to the standard questions that appear in column 2. The third column identifies, with an abbreviated reference, the linguistic surveys, citing specific maps. The *Survey of Anglo-Welsh Dialects* by David Parry (Swansea: University College, 1977, 1979), for example, contains vocalic, consonantal, syntactic, morphological, and lexical maps. The volume concludes with 12 pages of references.

Because only large research institutions are likely to hold the linguistic sources indexed in this book, it will have limited use. This may account in part for the high price of this slender, poorly bound work. Nevertheless, scholars in the field will find it invaluable.—**Bernice Bergup**

1068. Grote, David. **British English for American Readers: A Dictionary of the Language, Customs, and Places of British Life and Literature.** Westport, Conn., Greenwood Press, 1992. 709p. $85.00. PE1704.G76. 423. LC 91-45575. ISBN 0-313-27851-2.

1069. Moss, Norman. **British/American Language Dictionary for More Effective Communication between Americans and Britons.** Lincolnwood, Ill., National Textbook, 1991. 191p. $8.95pa. LC 90-63159. ISBN 0-8442-9116-1.

Yet another entry in the increasingly crowded British English dictionary field, *British English for American Readers* (BEFAR) is the most expensive; the next most costly book, *British English A to Zed* (BEATZ) (see ARBA 88, entry 1082), is less than half the price. As the subtitle indicates, BEFAR is more than just a list of words and their meanings; also included are cultural and geographical terms, such as *Desert Island Discs* (a radio program) and *Greenwich* (the city). An unusual and welcome feature of the book is that British attitudes toward certain things (e.g., abortions) are outlined. Appendixes include an explanation of money and values, with lists of British coins and their values, compositions, dates of use, and nicknames; reigns of monarchs and historic dates; class structure; a calendar of holidays and festivals; military ranks; and honors and initials. The selected bibliography is quite extensive (although it lists few British/American English dictionaries and neglects BEATZ); it ranges from reference books to travel guides to history. Cross-references are numerous and useful. The book is admittedly not exhaustive, Grote having "selected only those entries that seem to me to have the potential to confuse a reader who knows only American English." A check of BEATZ shows that both books have unique entries, with BEFAR having more geographical terms and BEATZ having more slang. Still, Grote has largely met his goal. The work contains few typographical errors; it is also less humorous than books of this ilk are wont to be. It could use more examples of actual usage.

British/American Language Dictionary (BALD) is an updated version of one published several years ago (see ARBA 86, entry 1048). It is intended more for travelers than reference shelves, having been compiled expressly for communication between Britons and Americans. It contains two main parts: an American-language section followed by a British-language one. Moss enlivens entries in both sides with usage examples from literature and television. Neither side is exhaustive, of course, but a fair number of the common expressions from both countries are included. Notable omissions include *O-level* (*A-level* appears) and *Green Party*. As before, a useful section at the end arranges words by subject (e.g., accommodations, business and finance).

Changes from the previous edition are not extensive. The enjoyable introduction has been lengthened; unfortunately, an entire paragraph is duplicated on page 2. The book is about 10 pages longer and the typeface is more prominent, but most of the definitions remain the same, with new ones inserted here and there. The majority of new entries are on the American-language side. A few outdated terms, such as *batman*, have been removed. In general, the lack of significant change is disappointing and does not justify the 50 percent increase in price.

Neither of these books is a first choice for libraries that want a British English dictionary. Moss's work is not comprehensive enough on either side, and Grote's work, while containing much convenient information, is overpriced. *British English A to Zed* is still the best purchase for material of this nature. [R: LJ, Aug 92, p. 88; RBB, 15 Sept 92, pp. 186-88]—**D. A. Rothschild**

1070. Lewis, Ivor. **Sahibs, Nabobs and Boxwallahs: A Dictionary of the Words of Anglo-India.** New York, Oxford University Press, 1991. 266p. $29.95. ISBN 0-19-562582-X.

The British came to India in 1600 to conduct business and eventually became rulers of the country, governing from 1757 to 1947. During their stay as "Masters" (*sahibs*), they had to deal with royal families (*nabobs*), tradespeople (*boxwallahs*), and others in a land where English was not spoken. Therefore, *sahibs* created a language of their own called Anglo-Indian for daily speech and record keeping. It is, in fact, a mixture of words from English and a few Indian languages, including Hindi and Urdu.

This is not the first dictionary of its kind. Several were published in the past, including *Hobson-Jobson* by Henry Yule and A. C. Burnell (Humanities Press, c1903, 1968) and *Indian Words in English* by G. Subba Rao (Oxford University Press, 1954). But all were limited in many respects. The present comprehensive work has 4,000 words in the dictionary that have been compiled on historical principles. All words introduced from 1600 to 1947 have been included, some for the first time. Each word has a full history of its origin and how its meaning has changed. The source of each entry has also been included, and there are many cross-references.

An attractive feature of this dictionary is an excellent historical introduction by Lewis. He deals with the historical development of the new language, including how and when many British authors used Anglo-Indian words in their writings. The last chapter contains an extensive but selective bibliography of primary and secondary sources arranged alphabetically under various subject headings. The book also has a list of principal abbreviations. This dictionary is a rich harvest of Anglo-Indian vocabulary and is highly recommended for all researchers, scholars, and libraries interested in British and Indian history and literature. [R: Choice, Sept 92, pp. 82-84] – **Ravindra Nath Sharma**

Rhetoric

1071. Lanham, Richard A. **A Handlist of Rhetorical Terms.** 2d ed. Berkeley, Calif., University of California Press, 1991. 205p. $35.00; $14.00pa. PE1445.A2L3. 428.1. LC 91-27410. ISBN 0-520-07668-0; 0-520-07669-9pa.

The first edition of this one-of-a-kind dictionary appeared in 1968 to good reviews and quickly became a standard. Lanham's revisions enhance its usefulness by expanding the contents, adding more cross-references, and extending the entries. The dictionary is the most scholarly of its kind. (Nearly 1,000 formal rhetorical terms are defined.) For example, *solecism* can be found in nearly every language dictionary; here it is referred to as "Solecismus," named for Greek colonists at Soloi in Cilicia who spoke bad Greek. Lanham shows how *Solecismus* differs from *Barbarismus*, which means misspeaking a single word, not butchering the language consistently. He also cites Quintilian for an in-depth discussion of the term and adds a passage from a Portuguese-English phrasebook to show modern usage. Many of the terms are explored at even greater length, *dissoi logoi* (double arguments), *enallage* (interchange of grammatical elements), and *period* (a theory of prose rhythm). The additional cross-references are important because of the interrelatedness of the terms beyond that of nonrhetorical terms, and because they take notice of opposites. Lanham ends with a classified bibliography of works cited and appendixes on the divisions of rhetoric, terms by type, and important dates (when influential books were published).

Even though this is a technical directory, it will assist undergraduates and be invaluable to graduate students. Because most of these terms aid logical discourse, philosophers, elocutionists, and writers will benefit from understanding their meanings and developments. The divisions of rhetoric section distills a college semester's work into an attractive primer. Recommended. [R: Choice, July/Aug 92, p. 1658]

– **Bill Bailey**

Synonyms and Antonyms

1072. McCutcheon, Marc. **Descriptionary: A Thematic Dictionary.** New York, Facts on File, 1992. 476p. $40.00. PE1591.M415. 423'.1. LC 91-12986. ISBN 0-8160-2487-1.

Neither scholarly nor exhaustive, McCutcheon's thematically arranged dictionary is both practical and entertaining, providing specialized terminology in nontechnical language. Broad categories such as architecture, transportation, and the military are subdivided into more specific topics. For example, under the category on the human body and mind are subsections for muscular system, heart and circulatory system, and psychology and psychiatry, among others. Someone needing information about golfing terms could consult that section in the sports category.

The definitions are descriptive, the language clear and easily understood. Similar to the usual dictionary, this one has no index, so the user cannot identify words with variable meanings based on context. For example, most people may know that the word *pancake* refers to a kind of makeup used by film actors, but fewer will know that it also is a code for landing in certain military parlance.

McCutcheon makes no claim to comprehensiveness. As a result, coverage within some categories is rather eclectic and arbitrary. Under food and drink, for example, only French cooking terms are described, along with bottles and glasses, wines and wine terms, and liqueurs. On the other hand, the section on hair identifies 34 terms related to beards and 19 for mustaches. This work will delight the general reader as well as serve the would-be writer needing easy access to specialized terminology for some everyday topics. [R: BR, Sept/Oct 92, p. 68; Choice, Sept 92, p. 84; LJ, Jan 92, p. 108; RBB, 1 May 92, p. 1620; SLJ, July 92, p. 98; WLB, June 92, p. 108]—**Bernice Bergup**

Terms and Phrases

1073. Dickson, Paul. **Dickson's Word Treasury: A Connoisseur's Collection of Old and New, Weird and Wonderful, Useful and Outlandish Words.** New York, John Wiley, 1992. 378p. illus. index. $14.95pa. PE1449.D52. 428.1. LC 91-25819. ISBN 0-471-55168-6.

This is one of those books where page after page is packed with the curious and the amusing. Dickson, who has compiled previous works on such subjects as baseball, jokes, names, ice cream, and slang, has made a lifetime hobby out of collecting words and phrases—not just ordinary words, but the offbeat, the bizarre, the ludicrous, and the obscure. Dickson provides 58 separate chapters—he calls them "museum style displays"—with captions such as "Outdoors Words," "Curses," "Junk Words," and "Soused Words." In the chapter on "Outdoors Words," for example, we learn that "hill nutty" is the outdoor equivalent of cabin fever; that a "rock jock" is, not surprisingly, a climbing enthusiast; and that "Sanibel stoop" is the near-permanent stance adopted by people who go to Sanibel Island, Florida, to look for shells. A chapter on "Fighting Words" includes "megacorpse," a nuclear-age word for a million dead people, and "rug rank," a higher-ranking officer who rates a rug on the floor of an office. For those searching for a new way to express the term *drunk*, there are 35 closely packed pages of ways to say it. Only rarely does Dickson provide information on where the words or phrases originated or from what time period they came. In the chapter on monsters, we learn that "Champ" is Lake Champlain's gigantic serpent, but we are not told anything about the history of sightings, the estimated size of the beast, or (for that matter) the location of Lake Champlain. But this is not a book to be taken seriously, and one should not quibble about such fine points. This is a book for fun.

There is absolutely no reason to include *Dickson's Word Treasury* in a library reference collection. It would, however, be a delightful addition to a home library where the owner is—to borrow a term from Dickson's own list—a grammatologist (a worshiper of words) or where the reader practices *paronomasia* (the punning or playing with words). For that person the treasury would be *eellogofusciouhipoppokunurious* (very good, very fine). [R: LJ, 15 June 92, p. 68]

—**Donald C. Dickinson**

Thesauri

1074. **The Merriam-Webster Concise School and Office Thesaurus.** Springfield, Mass., Merriam-Webster, 1991. 690p. $7.95pa. PE1591.M477. 423'.1. LC 91-11462. ISBN 0-87779-601-7.

Essentially the *Webster's Collegiate Thesaurus* (see ARBA 77, entry 1082), this shorter version differs little from its parent except in size—690 pages compared to 944. Its economy in cost and format has been achieved by using poorer paper; reducing the page and print size; eliminating the introduction;

placing the key to symbols at the bottom of the right-hand pages only; and following the pattern adopted by *Roget's II: The New Thesaurus* (see ARBA 90, entry 1032) of making the secondary entries *see* references to the main entry in whose synonym list the secondary entry appears. For example, "**gravestone** *n* **syn** see tombstone" in the *Concise* appears as "**gravestone** *n* **syn** tombstone, footstone, grave marker, headstone, ledger, monument" in the *Collegiate*, making it unnecessary for the user to turn to the main entry, *tombstone*, to find its synonyms. The preface also notes that some "specialized or abstruse entries were eliminated and a few synonyms not likely to be of general interest were dropped." The explanatory notes on how to use the book have been made much more readable in the *Concise* edition by typographic and layout changes that show up each section distinctly.

Every library needs a Webster's thesaurus, and this one is a bargain. But if your library already owns the *Collegiate*, you will not need this one.—**Blaine H. Hall**

1075. **Roget's International Thesaurus.** 5th ed. Robert L. Chapman, ed. New York, HarperCollins, 1992. 1141p. index. $18.95. PE1591.R73. 423'.1. LC 92-7615. ISBN 0-06-270014-6.

This new edition of a popular reference work, following the principles of Roget's original thesaurus (1852), contains approximately 350,000 words and phrases grouped into 15 newly rearranged large classes (e.g., "The Body and the Senses," "Feelings," "Place and Change of Place") with 1,073 subcategories, 31 of which are new. Within each section, words are grouped by part of speech in the following order: nouns, verbs, adjectives, adverbs, prepositions, conjunctions, and interjections. Boldface type is used for the words that are most commonly chosen for the idea at hand. There is also an extensive alphabetical index with the familiar pinpoint reference system that directs the user quickly from the index to numbered paragraphs of the right words. Included in the front matter are an informative biography of Roget, a helpful description of the book's features and use, a synopsis of categories, and a list of abbreviations.

Two especially attractive features of this book are the thousands of descriptive quotations provided and the dozens of specialized word lists. These alphabetically arranged lists catalog names of specific things, such as legislatures of different countries, musical instruments, types of glass, and computer words. A reader browsing through the subcategory "Knowledge" will find extensive lists of "-ologies" arranged both by name and by subject. As might be expected, because Chapman also edited *The New Dictionary of American Slang* (see ARBA 88, entry 1076), this thesaurus is particularly strong in capturing the language of the 1980s and 1990s, giving plenty of examples of "the special sense and force given by non-formal words and phrases."

Only extended use of a thesaurus can indicate whether a particular selection and arrangement of words is more conducive to verbal creativity than another. Still, it can be stated that this new edition is an attractively printed, up-to-date, easy-to-use treasury of words that should be helpful to anyone who wishes to use the English language creatively. Highly recommended for purchase by individuals and libraries. [R: LJ, 1 Nov 92, p. 76; RBB, 1 Oct 92, pp. 350-51; WLB, Nov 92, p. 96]—**Henry J. Ricardo**

1076. **Roget's 21st Century Thesaurus in Dictionary Form.** By Barbara Ann Kipfer. New York, Dell, 1992. 978p. index. $18.00. PE1591.K54. 423'.1. LC 91-37916. ISBN 0-440-50386-8.

Compiled electronically, *Roget's 21st Century Thesaurus* presents 17,000 main entries in alphabetical order with a total of 450,000 synonyms. Each headword is followed by its part of speech, a brief definition, and an alphabetically arranged list of its synonyms or related words and phrases. An asterisk marks nonstandard usage. Cross-referencing these main entries are 837 concepts, which are subclasses of 10 major headings that make up the concept index. This index is a "semantic hierarchy of the most common concepts we use in American English": actions, causes, fields of human activity, life forms, objects, the planet, qualities, senses, states, and weights and measures. For example, the headword *omnipotent* cross-references a list of words related to the concept *superiority* under the subheading "Comparative" of the major heading "Qualities."

This book's classification scheme provides a unique guide to the relationships of words and their meanings; but despite its overall readability and usefulness, there are some cavils. For example, in an allegedly modern book, there is a paucity of computer terms. In general, the book's approach to sexual terms, especially slang terms, is very prudish compared to *Roget's International Thesaurus* (see index for entry number). Finally, the indexing system in the "Quick Reference Guide to Concepts" is erroneous, beginning with the index range for the concepts related to motion.

Although recommended for purchase by high school and college students, office workers, and libraries as a solid, attractively priced reference work, this thesaurus is, in the final analysis, rather bloodless (colorless, dull, characterless). If only one thesaurus is to be bought, comparisons should be made with the recently published 5th edition of *Roget's International Thesaurus*. [R: LJ, 1 Sept 92, p. 168; RBB, 15 Oct 92, p. 449] — **Henry J. Ricardo**

Visual

1077. **The Macmillan Visual Dictionary.** Jean-Claude Corbeil, ed. New York, Macmillan, 1992. 862p. illus. maps. index. $45.00. PE1629.C64. 423'.1. LC 91-34460. ISBN 0-02-528160-7.

When *What's What: A Visual Glossary of the Physical World* (see ARBA 83, entry 58) appeared in 1981, it got rave reviews for its easy-to-follow illustrative format. Such a good idea for a reference work — diagrammatic labeling of everything from the human body to nuclear reactors — was bound to spawn imitators. The *Facts on File Visual Dictionary* (see ARBA 87, entry 1033) covered some of the same subjects as *What's What* but added new visuals. Both works used black-and-white drawings and photographs to display and dissect.

In *The Macmillan Visual Dictionary* the pictures are larger and in full color. The computer-produced illustrations are so brightly hued and precise they look artificial — which is no fault, as they leap off the page and are of a size to ensure identification of parts. The terminology used throughout the dictionary has been verified in technical sources. The 25,000 terms, the 3,500 color illustrations, and the 600 subjects encompass almost all of the physical world. The scope includes historical objects such as the parts of a castle, the elements of ancient costumes, types of sailboats, and ancient weapons.

As good as *What's What* and *Facts on File* are, this work is superior. Macmillan has created a pedagogical reference source of unsurpassed beauty and utility. Children will be fascinated by, and adults amazed at, the extraordinary illustrations. It is hard to imagine a 2d edition more complete than this one. Recommended for all libraries. [R: RBB, 1 Dec 92, p. 688]

— **Bill Bailey**

1078. **The Visual Dictionary of Everyday Things.** New York, Dorling Kindersley; distr., Boston, Houghton Mifflin, 1991. 64p. illus. index. (Eyewitness Visual Dictionaries). $14.95. LC 91-060898. ISBN 1-879431-17-3.

The subjects depicted in this fascinating visual dictionary range from saddles and espresso machines to chainsaws and trench coats. Similar to other volumes in this series, *Everyday Things* features exquisitely reproduced photographs that first show each item in its familiar "together" state, then with all of its component parts laid out and identified. The single-paragraph introduction that accompanies each entry's two-page spread often provides a rudimentary explanation of the item's workings. The reader learns, for example, that as a lawnmower's engine rotates the blades, it also turns the rear wheels, thus propelling the machine forward. However, the focus of this dictionary is to identify — rather than define or place in context — the components of the 27 subjects it covers. Roughly 1,500 terms are included, as reflected in the index that concludes the work.

The publisher has taken a simple idea — a visual dictionary — and from it produced a thematically interesting, visually stunning reference work sure to engage any reader, regardless of age or education level. Given its reasonable price, *Everyday Things* should find a welcome home in all public and school libraries. [R: BR, May/June 92, p. 60; RBB, 1 Feb 92, p. 1058; WLB, Jan 92, p. 132]

— **G. Kim Dority**

NON-ENGLISH-LANGUAGE DICTIONARIES

Byelorussian

1079. Ushkevich, Alexander, and Alexandra Zezulin. **Byelorussian-English; English-Byelorussian Dictionary with Complete Phonetics.** New York, Hippocrene Books, 1992. 290p. $9.95pa. ISBN 0-87052-114-4.

Byelorussian is the language of what is now called Belarus, whose capital is Minsk. It gained recognition as an independent language of its own, not a dialect of Russian, only after 1917. Between 1977 and 1984, a monolingual dictionary of Byelorussian in five volumes was published in Minsk. The dictionary under review is a remote reflection of that dictionary, because it accurately follows that work's orthography in all the spellings. It is a minimal dictionary that, besides the sequence of entries, offers only information about the sequence of the English variety of the Roman script and of the Byelorussian variety of Cyrillic, with a table of the phonetic values of the Cyrillic letters. In addition, each Byelorussian headword is followed by the indication of its pronunciation in approximative English spellings, and of each English headword in approximative Byelorussian Cyrillic spellings.

Obviously, each part of the dictionary is supposed to have another audience. For instance, the English headword *gift* is followed by three Byelorussian equivalents, two of them divided by a comma, the third by a semicolon. The first two equivalents belong to the sense *donation*, the third to *talent*, but there is no discrimination. Clearly, this is intended only for a speaker of Byelorussian. Conversely, Byelorussian *svedchanne* has two English equivalents, namely *evidence* and *certificate*, without discrimination; this is obviously meant for an English speaker only. This latter policy can be defended; whether Byelorussian speakers will buy this dictionary may, however, remain moot. The selection of the vocabulary is good, so this can be used as what can be called the "first-help dictionary" of the traveler. — **L. Zgusta**

Carolinian

1080. Jackson, Frederick H., and Jeffrey C. Marck, with others, comps. **Carolinian-English Dictionary.** Honolulu, University of Hawaii Press, 1991. 453p. (PALI Language Texts. Micronesia). $24.00pa. PL6228.Z5J33. 499'.5. LC 91-3220. ISBN 0-8248-1411-8.

The publication of the first dictionary of the three dialects of Saipan is an important event. Saipan is an island in the Northern Mariana Islands to which some people from the Central Caroline Islands, probably speakers of what is today Trukese, migrated long ago. The three (Trukic) dialects spoken by their 2,000-3,000 descendants are called "Carolinian" as a cover term.

The *Carolinian-English Dictionary* comprises the first 195 pages of this work. Clearly, it is a linguist's dictionary, and it is constructed as such with much care; it has penetrating analyses of the lexicon, etymologies, and more. A typical headword is followed by such information as "haam HAMA [POC *tama*] (TAN)." This means that the headword's underlying form (which is useful for the derivation of other forms) is *hama*, that the Proto-Oceanic etymon is reconstructed as *tama*, and that the headword belongs to the Tanapag dialect. Most of the entry describes the entry word's meaning, distributes its polysemy, gives illustrative examples, and contains derivations from the entry word as subentries. All this is carefully done with explanatory glosses and Latin terms for the designations of plants and fishes, but it is not too encyclopedic or ethnographic. In this respect, the present dictionary compares favorably with other linguistic dictionaries of good quality. Its outstanding feature is that the lexical relations are indicated. Whenever possible, the entry contains a reference to the entry word's (or a derivation's) synonym and antonym, a word with a related meaning, a synonym from another dialect, a synonym from another dialect in whose entry some further information can be found, and other entry words that belong to the same etymological root. It is this network of cross-references that makes a systematic study of the Carolinian lexicon easier.

The majority of this work contains the "English-Carolinian Finder List," a reasonable title, as it is not an English-Carolinian dictionary or a glossary. The cultural component in Carolinian is so strong that the designata have distinctive features that no simple English equivalent could have; hence, while an explanatory equivalent is frequently chosen in the Carolinian-English part and serves its function there well, it would be a formidable task to determine under which English headwords the Carolinian glosses should be listed. A simple example is found under *spasms*: *torota* 'to have spasms in the throat from food that is lodged there, to gag.' Few entries are as simple as this one; in some cases, an entry contains a whole onomasiological field. Probably the longest entries of this type are *fish* and *fishing*, which stretch from page 277 to page 280.

There are three weaknesses in the dictionary. First, the polysemy of the English headwords in the finder is not discriminated, so that the Carolinian expressions are not distributed by the English senses, which seems preferable. Second, in the Carolinian-English dictionary, there are occasional entries of words with particularly broad meanings formulations, such as *liye* 'woman, girl, daughter, sister, etc., in discourse and as a term of address.' Who can tell how far down the list of female relatives does the "etc." stretch? Third, there is a problem with the alphabetical sequence. The language has both geminate consonants and vocals (at least graphically); the alphabetization does not fully respect this, although it seems to take into consideration the diacriticized letters. As this is a linguist's dictionary, the compilers' opinion that this alphabetization keeps related words together carries much weight. Still, one must wonder.

The book is well printed; the only significant misprints occur on page xxv, where the computer mixed up the phonetic values of Carolinian letters in the respective list. (The reasonable thing to do would be to glue a list of errata to this page.) The University of Hawaii Press has already published many excellent dictionaries from the Pacific area; this dictionary continues the tradition.—**L. Zgusta**

Chinese

1081. Creamer, Thomas, ed. **A Chinese-English Dictionary of the Wu Dialect (Featuring the Dialect of the City of Shanghai).** Kensington, Md., Dunwoody Press, 1991. 192p. $38.00. LC 91-70271. ISBN 0-931745-81-0.

Although many dictionaries that deal with the Wu dialect of the Chinese language have been published in China in recent years, nearly all are in Chinese. This dictionary is therefore useful for English-speaking readers who are interested in this dialect, which is spoken by an estimated 70 million people in the central coastal region of China, including the provinces of Jiangsu, Zhejiang, and Jiangxi. Containing some 7,200 basic Wu words and phrases, the dictionary is arranged by the number of strokes in the head character of each entry. To facilitate use, an entry index and a pinyin head-character index are provided. A scholarly work, this reference tool will be useful to collections of materials on East Asia and to a select group of users.—**Hwa-Wei Lee**

Estonian

1082. Kyiv, Ksana, and Oleg Benyuch. **Estonian-English, English-Estonian Dictionary.** New York, Hippocrene Books, 1992. 180p. $11.95pa. ISBN 0-87052-081-4.

This is yet another dictionary in the Hippocrene series of what this reviewer calls first aid, or traveler's, dictionaries. The introduction promises that the book will be useful for both Estonian and English speakers, but the real intention seems primarily to help the former. This is clearly shown in that only English polysemy and English synonyms are at least partly discriminated and some syntactic patterns of English verbs are given. Also, the English-Estonian part is twice as long as the Estonian-English. The vocabulary of both parts is modern and well selected. The Estonian front matter gives a useful index of Estonian place-names, and the English part has an English gazetteer with pronunciation. The English-speaking traveler may also find useful a descriptive index of the Estonian national cuisine. The inclusion of the Estonian national anthem with an English rhymed translation is a moving feature, but users will probably miss an index of English irregular verbs and some grammatical information on each of the languages. The dictionary is printed in very small type, so the traveler may have difficulty reading the text. On the other hand, misprints are rare.

The serious reference library will want the *Estonian-English Dictionary* by P. Saagpakk (French & European Publications, 1982), which the English-speaking traveler will not have room to carry. For Estonians, this dictionary will be the first choice.

—L. Zgusta

French

1083. **The Oxford Guide to the French Language.** By William Rowlinson and Michael Janes. New York, Oxford University Press, 1992. 523p. index. $12.95pa. PC2105.R64. 448.2'421. LC 91-45898. ISBN 0-19-282957-2.

This title is actually two books in one, bound together. Rowlinson leads off with a detailed guide to French grammar. Somewhat jarringly, the book just begins; there is no introduction, foreword, or preface. There are, however, easy-to-understand rules and plenty of examples (taken from everyday speech, newspapers, and magazines) for every assertion made. In the case of nouns, there is help in resolving the problem of gender for those whose native tongue considers things to be inherently neuter. Separate subheads treat parts of speech, word order, and the like. Two interesting short chapters that deal with translation problems and pronunciation traps are designed to prevent the English speaker from blundering into embarrassment in social discourse. Commendably, Rowlinson provides phonetic pronunciation without using the complicated symbology of lexicographers (e.g., *boeuf* (beef) is rendered phonetically as "berf"; *cuiller* (spoon) is given as "kwee-yair"). This makes it easy for Anglophones to get their mouths around the unfamiliar sounds of spoken French. Verb tables are provided at the end.

The book is then handed off to Janes, who provides a good 45,000-word bilingual dictionary. Pronunciation is given here as well, but this time standard phonetic symbols are employed to denote sounds. The dictionary is not very prescriptive, but usage notes (nonstandard usage denoted by the appellation "argot") abound. The emphasis on French-to-English translation is to British English.

This is a handy paperback, although its principal value will be for the traveler rather than for the library user seeking reference material. Highly recommended for either use.—**Bruce A. Shuman**

Georgian

1084. Torikashvili, John J. **Georgian-English, English-Georgian Dictionary.** New York, Hippocrene Books, 1992. 347p. $8.95pa. ISBN 0-87052-121-7.

This is yet another small dictionary in the format typical of the Hippocrene Concise Dictionary series. It gives a basic Georgian-English glossary on the first 190 pages and its English-Georgian counterpart on the remaining 150 pages. Each of the two parts is intended for a different readership; hence, the Georgian-English section gives the pronunciation of the Georgian words in Roman transcription that approximates the "normal" pronunciation in English, whereas the English-Georgian part indicates the pronunciation of English words by (highly approximative) transcriptions into the Georgian script (without any indication of the stress). (Mkhedruli, the Georgian script, is not particularly difficult because it is alphabetical. However, a table that gives the sequence of letters would be useful because the position of the letters for *kh, sh, ch, ts, pf*, and so forth is not predictable.)

In any case, this is a minimal glossary. Beyond the pronunciation, the only information given is the word class of the headwords (e.g., noun, verb). The Georgian user does not get any information about English irregular verbs, let alone about syntactic patterns or other grammatical indications. As far as the English user is concerned, Georgian is a language with a terribly difficult morphology, in which distinctions such as to write/to write for oneself/to write for somebody, and many more are expressed by changes of the root and frequently by prefixes. If English users know this grammar, they probably will not need a dictionary as small as this and will prefer E. Cherkesi's *Georgian-English Dictionary* (Oxford University Press, 1950). No collocations or idioms are given in either part. Thus, this is a "first aid dictionary" for the tourist who wishes to say isolated words accompanied by pointing (and who has had the patience to learn Mkhedruli using some other help), or for the individual who has just arrived in the United States. The vocabulary selected is generally good, with only occasional lapses (e.g., why *erotica*, particularly since the Georgian equivalent [in transcription] is *erotika*?).

For dictionaries in which foreign scripts are used, the publisher should invest in better paper. In the review copy Mkhedruli can be read in the English-Georgian part, but in the Georgian-English section the finer distinctions of the Mkhedruli letters are occasionally blurred.—**L. Zgusta**

German

1085. **NTC's Dictionary of German False Cognates.** By Geoff Parkes and Alan Cornell. Lincolnwood, Ill., National Textbook, 1992. 226p. $16.95. ISBN 0-8442-2495-2.

A dictionary of German words that sound or look like English words but are not related may strike many as an odd reference work. Indeed, rather than a dictionary, it should perhaps be described as a word list meant for browsing or studying systematically. The intended audience is probably not linguists, because false cognates usually have no etymological link. German language pedagogues might use this work as a teaching aid, but it is primarily intended for the student of German.

The authors suggest that students should browse the list in an attempt to learn about these "false friends" before they make a mistake (e.g., *Praservativ* is not a preservative but a condom). A goal in language instruction, however, is to overcome the desire to translate the foreign language into one's mother tongue in order to understand or communicate. This word list undermines the process by emphasizing connections that many students (and bilingual speakers, for that matter) would not ordinarily make. Moreover, many of the words are not false cognates but related words with slight differences in meaning in English and German (e.g., *Kontrolle, Schal, Weg*). Most entries include examples of proper usage, but there is no indication of pronunciation, part of speech, or true etymology. Although some of the entries might help one steer clear of mistakes, others will confuse the student. Recommended, with reservations, for libraries with extensive holdings in German language pedagogy.—**Valerie R. Hotchkiss**

Hawaiian

1086. Pukui, Mary Kawena, with others. **New Pocket Hawaiian Dictionary with a Concise Grammar and Given Names in Hawaiian.** Honolulu, University of Hawaii Press, 1992. 256p. $4.95pa. PL6446.P84. 899'.4. LC 91-25854. ISBN 0-8248-1392-8.

Two authors of this dictionary, Pukui and Samuel H. Elbert, published a large Hawaiian-English dictionary in 1957; it quickly needed several new editions. Apart from this, both authors have published, together and independently, several important works on Hawaiian grammar, Hawaiian place-names, poetic sayings and expressions, and other such topics. This dictionary is a reduction of its predecessors; however, it has been enriched by some additional terms. For instance, if hula dancing is looked up in the English-Hawaiian part, under English is found "*Hula*, Kinds: *'olapa, 'uli'uli, pa'i umauma, 'ili'ili, 'auana, kahiko.*" There are no explanatory glosses here, but in the Hawaiian-English part is found "*'olapa*.....2. Dancer, as contrasted with the chanter or *ho'opa'* (memorizer); now, any dance accompanied by chanting and drumming on a gourd drum. *'uli'uli*: a gourd rattle containing seeds and fitted with colored feathers at the top, used in certain hulas..... *pa'i umauma*: chest clapping hula."

In this way, the user ultimately finds much information in this small format, but it is sometimes necessary to search for it. In the next edition of this dictionary, usual and more frequent definitions might be highlighted. For instance, if one seeks the so frequent (and sometimes mysterious) expression *mauka*, one is sent to *uka* "Inland, upland, toward the mountain; shore, uplands; shoreward (from at sea) (often preceded by the particles *i, ma-*, or *o* and often written *mauka*)." The common meaning is hidden in the third equivalent. On the other hand, entries such as the English *rare* are well discriminated: "1. Infrequent *kaka'ikahi*. 2. Underdone *mo'a iki, mo'a kolekole* (as of meats)." Most interesting, traces of the missionary tradition of the islands can be found in the dictionary. For instance, "*rash* 1. Bold *'a'a makehewa*. 2. Of sin *'ohune*."

There is a grammatical sketch in the appendix, minimal but good, with charming traces of American structuralism at its best (e.g., p. 228, para. 4.1.: "Verbs may be defined as content words that may be preceded by verb-marking particles"). Another appendix contains a useful index of Hawaiian names and of names adapted to Hawaiian phonology; a missionary trace can be found here again, in the Hawaiian form of many names from the Bible.

The printing is good, with few misprints. On the whole this is a small, but valuable, and competently (if somewhat unevenly) compiled dictionary.—L. Zgusta

Hebrew

1087. **Webster's New World Hebrew Dictionary: Hebrew/English, English/Hebrew.** By Hayim Baltsan. New York, Prentice Hall General Reference, 1992. 827p. $35.00. PJ4833.B26. 492.4'321. LC 91-32079. ISBN 0-13-944547-1.

Several transliterated Yiddish dictionaries have recently appeared, such as David Mendel Harduf's *Transliterated English-Yiddish; Yiddish-English Dictionary* (see index for entry number), but *Webster's* is a first for Hebrew. The purpose of this dictionary is "to render Hebrew ... accessible to all ... even ... beginners not acquainted with the Hebrew alphabet" (p. vii). The work includes two main sequences with a total of 60,000 entries: a Hebrew-English section in which headwords or proper names are Romanized, and an English-Hebrew section in which definitions are given in Roman characters. In both sections, the term is also given in Hebrew characters, but without vowel points. Besides the guide to the dictionary, there is a 13-page introduction to Hebrew that contains basic information about the alphabet and the structure of the language. To use the dictionary effectively, the non-Hebrew speaker must be able to isolate a word from Hebrew speech and master the idiosyncratic transcription scheme it employs. There are double entries for variant pronunciations.

The major editorial flaw in this work is the failure to print the transliteration key on the inside front cover, despite repeated references to it. Additionally, the contents of the two main sections are not entirely parallel. For example, the guide provides a model entry: the definition of *villa*. No one in Israel is likely to use the word *khaveelah*, however. The English-Hebrew section notes the colloquial term *veelah*, but the Hebrew-English section does not include this as a headword. Also, the filing of digraphs is inconsistent. Words that begin with *kh*, for example, are in a separate section of the alphabet, but medial *kh* precedes *kl*. The work will be of little help to librarians looking for assistance in the Romanization of Hebrew because it does not use the ALA/LC scheme and it ignores grammatical fine points of Hebrew that catalogers need to know. In addition, the section on the Jewish calendar does not provide the formula for converting Hebrew dates to Gregorian ones, which catalogers must often do.

The typefaces, designed by the compiler's son, are attractive, and the paper and binding are of good quality. The major advantage of the dictionary is the currency of its vocabulary. It thus supplements Reuben Alcalay's classic bilingual dictionary, *The Complete English-Hebrew Dictionary*.
—**Bella Hass Weinberg**

Irish

1088. **Irish/English; English/Irish Dictionary and Phrasebook.** New York, Hippocrene Books, 1992. 1v. (various paging). $7.95pa. ISBN 0-87052-110-1.

This is one of the minimal books for the traveler in which Hippocrene specializes. There are 36 pages of English-Irish glossary, 28 pages of Irish-English glossary, and more than 70 pages of miscellaneous information and conversational phrases. That little can be done in this space goes without saying. However, the vocabulary included in the glossaries is quite reasonable. Probably the best features of the book are the consistent indication of the Irish pronunciation of each word and sentence and the detailed explanation of the difficult Irish orthography. There are even some sandhi rules given in the conversational part. This part is organized like a thesaurus, by topics; single pertinent words, phrases, and occasional whole sentences are provided. Probably the best of them is given in the section that deals with "the art of conversation" (which is said to be "a popular pastime in Ireland"). The sentence is *ta tu ag glagaireacht*, which means "you are talking nonsense"—undoubtedly a felicitous way to enliven a conversation. The last page gives the reader a map showing the few small areas of Ireland where Irish is yet spoken, in case the traveler wishes to put the book to the test.—**L. Zgusta**

Mahican

1089. **Schmick's Mahican Dictionary.** Carl Masthay, ed. Philadelphia, Pa., American Philosophical Society, 1991. 188p. maps. (Memoirs of the American Philosophical Society, v.197). $30.00. LC 86-90530. ISBN 0-87169-197-3.

The term "Mahican" refers to an Algonkian tribe and language native to the upper Hudson Valley in eastern New York state, western Massachusetts, and northwestern Connecticut. It was made famous (in a variant spelling) by James Fenimore Cooper's novel *The Last of the Mohicans*. (The Mahicans/Mohicans should not be confused with the Mohegans, also an Algonkian group, of southeastern Connecticut.) The Mahican language died out in the 1930s.

Johann Jacob Schmick (1714-1778) was a German missionary of the Moravian Church who spent years among the Mahicans. Between 1753 and 1755 he compiled a handwritten dictionary in two sections, English-Mahican-German followed by Mahican-English. The manuscript is preserved in the library of the American Philosophical Society, Philadelphia. In the present volume, Carl Masthay has transcribed, translated, and rearranged the entire work to produce a usable dictionary. Several introductory sections provide information about Schmick and about the historical and geographical relationships of the Mahicans. Schmick's relatively nonsystematic orthography for Mahican is retained throughout; however, the prefatory material includes an essay on Mahican historical phonology by David H. Pentland that will enable scholars to interpret the data in both descriptive and comparative terms. Such a dictionary will obviously not be useful to a large readership but will be valued highly by students of Algonkian linguistics and history.—**William Bright**

Persian

1090. Kasraie, Asadollah, and Hassan Kasraie. **A Persian and English Glossary for Humanities and Social Sciences.** Burnsville, N.C., Celo Valley Books, 1991. 346p. $65.00. H40.K37. 300'.3. LC 91-6483. ISBN 0-923687-09-2.

This work provides an extensive resource of Persian and English terms used in the humanities and social science fields. As indicated in both the Persian and English prefaces, this glossary has been compiled from 35 sources, which include translations from English as well as works written originally in Persian. The primary source of this book is a glossary published in Tehran in 1976 under the name *Vazhegan-e Falsafe va Olum-e Ejtema'i*. A complete list of sources is found as part of the Persian introduction. The glossary is divided into two parts and arranged alphabetically, first in English, then in Persian. The print is clear, and each page has only one column of Persian and English equivalents.

This work is a welcome addition to Persian-English reference books. Attention in the past has been paid more to glossaries of a very general nature or with a scientific focus. A slight limitation of this book might be that the majority of the sources of vocabulary (31 out of 35) are more than 15 years old. A newer usage or very recently coined phrase may not appear. This, however, does not detract from the book's value to those scholars, professionals, translators, and students interested in the humanities and social sciences, as the majority of the entries would be considered standard. Not only does this glossary serve as a good reference, but its easy-to-read format also makes it interesting to browse.

—**Martha Miller Yazhari**

Portuguese

1091. **The Random House Portuguese Dictionary: Portuguese-English, English-Portuguese.** Bobby J. Chamberlain, ed. New York, Random House, 1991. 396p. $6.00pa. PC5333.R36. 469.3'21. LC 90-8886. ISBN 0-679-40060-5.

This concise dictionary of 38,000 entries, which stresses Brazilian Portuguese rather than that spoken in Portugal, includes Portuguese/English-English/Portuguese equivalents, the part of speech of each word, and the gender for Portuguese words. It also provides other information in tabular format for easy reference, such as numerals; weights and measures; names of days of the week, the months, and the seasons; useful phrases; common signs; and verb conjugations. It is a good choice for travel or other personal use because of its small size, but its physical dimensions will make it prone to theft in a library setting.—**Ann Hartness**

Russian

1092. Apresjan, Yuri D. **Lexical Semantics: User's Guide to Contemporary Russian.** Ann Arbor, Mich., Karoma, 1992. 633p. index. $185.00. ISBN 0-89720-039-X.

1093. **RELEX for Russian.** [Machine-readable Data File]. Ann Arbor, Mich., Karoma, 1992. Hardware requirements: MS-DOS/IBM PC compatible; DOS 3.0 or higher. $175.00.

Lexical Semantics: User's Guide is a translation of the author's 1974 Russian volume, *Lexical Semantics: Synonymic Devices of Language.* The original was a scholarly, theoretical investigation of Russian's semantic system. Apresjan's theory posits a small number of abstract semantic units that are (re-)combined into the near infinity of complex units that make up any real language. Most of these derived complex units are synonymic—albeit often in some very extended sense—and are related to each other by lexical or syntactic transformations. Apresjan offers the first large-scale, systematic survey of these synonymic relationships and provides a multitude of categorized examples.

Individual examples presented by Apresjan in his original book were, due to that work's organization and format, essentially inaccessible to most users. The new English version attempts to make this body of information available to a much wider audience in two ways: first, by the translation of text and, even more crucially, the presentation of parallel Russian and English synonymic structures side-by-side; and second, by the addition of three exhaustive indexes that for the first time make it possible to locate the discussion of any Russian and English word usage. Thus, Apresjan's work has been, after a fashion, converted into a reference volume. In particular, the new RELEX for Russian computerized bilingual dictionary is page referenced to Apresjan's work so that the RELEX user can find further information on word usage. In general, linguistic specialists will be the chief users of Apresjan's monograph.

RELEX is a Russian-English/English-Russian dictionary and translation-aid computer program that interfaces with most standard word processing programs. RELEX has several advantages over a printed dictionary. One, of course, is sheer convenience. Another is that the user can look up several words at once (300 characters maximum). The dictionary gives supplementary information that helps the user pick the correct word for a particular context from several offerings, as well as information on appropriate syntactic patterns. Those who want still more detailed guidance are referred to Yuri Apresjan's *Lexical Semantics*, which may be ordered as a companion volume.

After a gloss has been chosen, the program then sends the translated word back to the word processor screen. RELEX has its own Cyrillic driver that converts from one alphabet to the other in both the dictionary and the word processor, and it can also be used independently. Although it is not a full translation program, RELEX is a 25,000-word automated bilingual dictionary that requires 2.2 MB of hard drive space. Its output is in raw form (i.e., it does not put the translated words into appropriate grammatical forms). Likewise, entries for dictionary lookup and translation must be in their exact dictionary form, and the user must apply the rules of Russian or English grammar. Still, the program performs a major service in providing possible equivalencies and guiding the user to the best choice. It can facilitate the translation process and help users improve their Russian (or English). The on-screen cross-references to the Apresjan book, while potentially useful, will generally be of little value, for the book's exposition is far too technical for nonspecialists. The publisher promises a 39,000-word upgrade that features science and business vocabulary and more specialized upgrades for the computer and petroleum industries.—**D. Barton Johnson**

1094. Beniukh, Oleg, and Ksana Beniukh. **English-Russian Dictionary with Phonetics.** New York, Hippocrene Books, 1992. 209p. $11.95pa. ISBN 0-87052-100-4.

The intent of this book is to provide "phonetic" transcriptions of English words by use of the Russian alphabet. The authors' prefatory note, written only in Russian, announces that this dictionary is designed for Russian-speakers "who do not know English well enough and who have difficulty in reading transcriptions." In that statement the two main weaknesses of the book are inherent. The first is the authors' failure to clearly define the nature and educational background of their audience. What is meant by "not knowing English well enough"? And for how long does difficulty in reading the English alphabet persist? (It is surely a very temporary difficulty.)

The second weakness is to attempt to use the Russian alphabet to render the English sound system, an idea which is misconceived rather than novel. The Russian alphabet represents a very special sound system, and transliteration between Russian and English presents difficulties either way. The authors do acknowledge certain difficulties, such as rendering the English *th* and the schwa(g) (which they call the "neutral vowel"), but they do not acknowledge their failure to render the English *w* or *ae* or to distinguish between the *o* sounds in *pot* and *pour*. And they use the Russian *E* to render three quite distinct vowels in English: *ae*, *e*, and *a*. Sometimes American pronunciation is recorded, sometimes British English, but neither one clearly prevails.

What remains puzzling is that the authors did not use the International Phonetic Alphabet, a practice that has become standard in English-Russian dictionaries because it is essential. True, it is one more alphabet, but it is easily learned and gives a precise frame of reference.—**John B. Beston**

1095. Corten, Irina H. **Vocabulary of Soviet Society and Culture: A Selected Guide to Russian Words, Idioms, and Expressions of the Post-Stalin Era, 1953-1991.** Durham, N.C., Duke University Press, 1992. 176p. index. $24.95. PG2691.C6. 491.73'21. LC 91-31876. ISBN 0-8223-1213-1.

The post-Stalin years have seen a vocabulary explosion on the Soviet (and now post-Soviet) scene. Many of these terms, widely used in Russian newspapers and magazines, have not yet found their way into Russian, much less Russian-English dictionaries. Moreover, their definitions often require extensive contextual commentary. Corten (University of Minnesota) has compiled about 400 mostly recent words, acronyms, and phrases that cover much of the often unsavory past and the new reality of modern Russian life. Many are effectively illustrated by anecdotes. Each entry is defined and accompanied by a brief discussion of its history and social context. Some terms are cross-referenced. The glossary focuses on six broad categories: ideology, the economy, education, culture, social problems, and everyday life. Corten intentionally avoids Russian's rich "unprintable" vocabulary and terms from specialized, professional argots. The terms chosen for elucidation are initially listed by subject category, first in English transcription and then in Cyrillic. The lexicon is alphabetical with the headwords in English transcription. Separate English and Cyrillic indexes list both the major and secondary references to each word.

Corten's work will be most useful to students reading recent Russian-language publications, although its historical and cultural commentary on many terms also makes it useful to readers interested in the changes in Russian society over the last 40 years. All libraries with Russian holdings should own this book, as should students of the Russian scene.—**D. Barton Johnson**

1096. Marder, Stephen. **A Supplementary Russian-English Dictionary.** Columbus, Ohio, Slavica, 1992. 522p. $27.95pa. ISBN 0-89357-228-4.

Dictionaries date rapidly, especially in times of intense social flux. Readers of current Russian prose who rely on the standard *Russian-English Dictionary* by A. Smirnitsky (see ARBA 75, entry 1275) or M. Wheeler's *The Oxford Russian-English Dictionary* (see ARBA 85, entry 975) are well aware of their numerous lacunae. Marder's *Supplementary Russian-English Dictionary* (SRED) sets out to fill in these gaps with 29,000 entries not found in Smirnitsky or Wheeler. Most are neologisms that consist of both new coinages and older words with new meanings. The remaining third of the work consists of extant words that are not in the standard dictionaries. One of SRED's great virtues is the number of multiword or phrasal subentries—often of an idiomatic nature. Most are conveniently listed under each of their component terms. Both these and single lexical items are generously cross-referenced and supplied with synonyms. Also praiseworthy are the concise, colloquial English translations that show a good sense of equivalent stylistic levels. In addition, Marder serves up a bountiful helping of slang, obscenities, abbreviations, and technical terms that have gained wide currency.

SRED is well designed and handsomely printed in a large, easily legible format. All Russian words are stress-marked, and each headword is accompanied by basic grammatical information. While aimed primarily at a student audience, SRED is equally useful for Russian-reading professionals who already command the standard vocabulary of Smirnitsky and Wheeler. With its 29,000 entries, SRED far surpasses Irina Corten's *Vocabulary of Soviet Society and Culture* (Duke University Press, 1992), which, however, provides in-depth accounts of 400 words that are central to Soviet and post-Soviet life. The two volumes complement each other nicely. — **D. Barton Johnson**

1097. Zalucky, Henry K. **Compressed Russian: Russian-English Dictionary of Acronyms, Semiacronyms and Other Abbreviations Used in Contemporary Standard Russian....** New York, Elsevier Science Publishing, 1991. 890p. $185.50. PG2693.Z28. 491.73'21. LC 90-42785. ISBN 0-444-98728-2.

Shortcuts and abridgments have a long history in English, but the Russians "opened their gates" for abbreviations at the threshold of the twentieth century. In specialized fields of numerous expanding disciplines, students are bewildered by breathtaking changes and the proliferation of the newly formed abbreviations. Some of the latter are suffering from inadequately identified designations and overuse. More than a quarter of Russian vocabulary in print, speech, and audiovisual media consists of specialized words and expressions. Not only foreign students but also the most educated native speakers encounter difficulties in comprehending contemporary Russian utterances. This outstanding dictionary contains about 40,000 abbreviations with their pronunciations, stress, Russian meaning, and English equivalents. They cover every aspect of life in the former Soviet Union with its urban and rural components. The list of terms is preceded by an introduction and an outline of Russian abbreviology and followed by tables that compare Russian and American terms. The work is highly recommended for all readers of Russian books—economic, technical, military, or scientific—magazines, and daily newspapers as an indispensable tool for clarifying the meaning of difficult terms and concepts. [R: C&RL, Sept 92, p. 416]— **Oleg Zinam**

Sign Language

1098. **The Perigee Visual Dictionary of Signing: An A-to-Z Guide....** rev. ed. By Rod R. Butterworth and Mickey Flodin. New York, Perigee Books/Putnam, 1991. 480p. illus. index. $11.95pa. HV2475.B87. 419'.03. LC 91-13007. ISBN 0-399-51695-6.

Not much has changed since publication of the first edition of this work in 1983 (see ARBA 85, entry 941). The audience is still students and others who need rudimentary sign language vocabulary. Prefatory material includes tips for signing, illustrations of basic hand shapes, and the manual alphabet and numbers. A brief history of sign language has been added. Within the dictionary's alphabetical arrangement, words and concepts are represented by well-drawn illustrations, clear descriptions of positioning and movement, a memory aid, and an example of usage. Almost all entries are reproduced from the 1983 edition, with the same pagination. A few additional entries have been squeezed in; a few have been changed to accommodate current usage. Several illustrations have been redrawn to make hand positions or movement clearer. A supplemental signs section includes 48 new signs, about one-third of which represent geographic proper names. Entries for these signs are integrated into the main entry and synonym index. Illustrations of inflections (e.g., *-ment, -er, -ing*) have been expanded and moved to the supplementary section.

For most libraries that own the 1983 publication, the changes are not significant enough to warrant purchase of this edition. However, for specialized collections, heavily used sign language collections, and those who need to replace a tattered copy of the previous edition, this volume remains a bargain. Certainly, those who missed buying the first edition should acquire this one.

— **Pam M. Baxter**

Somali

1099. Zorc, R. David, with Madina M. Osman and Virginia Luling. **Somali-English Dictionary.** 2d ed. Kensington, Md., Dunwoody Press, 1991. 530p. $65.00. LC 91-70497. ISBN 0-931745-71-3.

This edition of the dictionary, published only four years after the first, offers more than one-third more entries, and it is a work of great lexicographic sophistication. The English equivalents of the Somali entry words are well chosen and are as translational as possible. In addition to that, there are explanatory glosses in many entries. Some of these explanations give important pragmatic information; some pertain to semantic features of the entry word that are not captured by the equivalent, and some are semantic but verging on the encyclopedic. Naturally, many glosses are purely encyclopedic and culture-bound. Quite frequently there are notes on synonymic variation, important in a language not yet fully stabilized. Various alternative forms are given either in parentheses after the headword or in the explanatory notes. A similar function is performed by the examples; they illustrate either the usage or the formation of words when the entry deals with a bound morpheme. Somali is a language with strong morphophonemic phenomena; the internal sandhi particularly seems to produce quite a lot of surface irregularities in many forms. Hence, it is a laudable feature that the dictionary gives many difficult forms as headwords. One of the complex features of the language is that particles and clitic pronouns coalesce into clusters; again, many of these are given as headwords.

The dictionary is based on a grammatical description of Somali; a short version of this is given in the front matter. The description is a detailed one; for example, the verb is divided into 11 morphological classes and the noun into 12. Each headword is classified as to the category in which it belongs in this degree of finesse. The front matter also contains a section on sound changes and spelling variations; this is important because it is stated that "since Somali spelling is not yet fully standardized, most people write as they pronounce, and consequently you may encounter a word in a rather different form from that which is given here." Given this, it would be good to tell the user more about the pronunciation of the Roman script. Overall, this dictionary will be most useful for both practical and linguistic purposes.
—L. Zgusta

Spanish

1100. **Collins Spanish-English/English-Spanish Dictionary. Collins Diccionario Espanol-Ingles/Ingles-Espanol.** 3d ed. By Colin Smith and others. New York, HarperCollins, 1992. 908p. $27.50. PC4640.S595. 463'.21. LC 91-36013. ISBN 0-06-275504-8.

Because living languages are ongoing cultural complexes, no dictionary can ever claim to be complete. Rather, each represents a record of common modern usage compiled to the best of the ability of its authors at a given point in time. An accelerated pace of neologistic creation has been met in this edition of a work first published in 1971 by the addition of 30,000 references and 50,000 translations, which has raised the total number of entries to 230,000. Moreover, great efforts have been made to improve coverage of usage in the United States and Latin America. Preceding the Spanish-English and English-Spanish dictionaries are useful notes on using the dictionary, pronunciation, and orthography. The main body of the book contains up-to-date word lists that cover main areas of modern life, including regional usages and slang items. Many illustrative expressions show how particular words are used in context, and style labels indicate whether a word is literary or vulgar, formal or informal, and dated or euphemistic.

The value of the dictionary is greatly enhanced by the "Language in Use" section that concludes the volume. It contains 72 pages of functional idiomatic expressions to provide a bridge between the passive and active knowledge of a foreign language. In this part the approach is monolingual rather than bilingual. It is designed as a tool for nonnative speakers to avoid the framing of thought in their native tongues with possible distortion of meaning in the subsequent literal translation. On the whole, this is a masterpiece of a dictionary that will be cherished by users on all levels of proficiency. [R: Choice, Oct 92, p. 281]—**Oleg Zinam**

1101. **The Facts on File English/Spanish Visual Dictionary.** By Jean-Claude Corbeil and Ariane Archambault. New York, Facts on File, 1992. 924p. illus. index. $39.95. AG250.C65. 036'.1. LC 90-37183. ISBN 0-8160-1546-5.

The main value of this English/Spanish visual dictionary is in helping the general reader identify a wide range of technical terms from various areas by providing graphic representations of essential features and noting their English and Spanish names. More than 3,000 illustrations and 25,000 words in a wide range of areas, such as food, furniture, clothing, communication, sports, and energy, are included, as well as useful indexes and tables. It is important to note that this dictionary favors words used by the average person as opposed to terms used by specialists. Also, when various Spanish regionalisms are used, the authors have selected words used in Mexico. In the case of English, the dictionary provides British usage in italics and American usage in roman type. Inexplicably, the English introduction does not mention the Spanish language at all but insists on the French language—this introduction was previously used in the French version of this dictionary (see ARBA 88, entry 1098). This is a useful dictionary; it is unfortunate that the editors did not use the correct introduction or correct a few typographical errors in the Spanish preface. [R: Choice, Dec 92, p. 598; RBB, 1 Dec 92, p. 693]—**Isabel Schon**

Tagalog

1102. Chua, Romulo L., and Rodolfo L. Nazareno. **Ang Mahalaga sa Buhay (A Handbook of Filipino Values).** Quezon City, Philippines, New Day; distr., Detroit, Cellar Book Shop, 1992. 177p. $10.75pa. ISBN 971-10-0474-7.

This work is indeed about Filipino values, but it has an unusual arrangement. It is divided into nine sections, each indicating a major value: family, nation, character, fate, emotion, humanity, appearance, thought, and matter. Then in each section, root words in Pilipino, the national language of the Philippines, concerned with this value are listed in alphabetical order. All other entries are arranged under the words from which they are derived.

It is important to note the book's intended audience: Filipinos in the Philippines, especially youths in the schools. The authors wish to convey to this audience "a more profound understanding of our own language, the various meanings or shades of meaning of its words and their metaphorical usages" (preface). The definitions of Pilipino value words are quite enlightening to non-Filipinos, and one can learn quite a lot about Filipino culture by browsing through the book's various entries. The appendix acts as a glossary, matching English words with their Pilipino equivalents. It would have been helpful here to indicate page numbers for entries to these words, because there is no index.

In the final analysis, this book suffers from an identity crisis. Is it a handbook of Filipino values or a Pilipino-language dictionary? This confusion is reflected in its organization and the lack of an index.—**Marshall E. Nunn**

1103. Zorc, R. David, and Rachel San Miguel, comps. **Tagalog Slang Dictionary.** Kensington, Md., Dunwoody Press, 1991. 128p. $20.00. LC 90-86224. ISBN 0-931745-56-X.

Tagalog is a major Philippine language spoken by residents of the Manila area and of the South Luzon Island region of the Philippines. It is also the basis of Pilipino, the national language of the Philippines. "This [title] represents the first printing of a Tagalog Slang database" (preface). It is the compilers' intention to define words that cannot be found in already existing sources and to capture the language of such diverse groups as students, jeepney drivers, movie stars, members of the armed forces, and homosexuals. The result is a fascinating record of a vibrant and ever-changing language and its vital slang components. The prefatory notes on Tagalog slang and its role in Philippine society are brief but quite enlightening. In the dictionary, the structure of each entry includes the Tagalog slang expression, its pronunciation, its part of speech, its English equivalent, cross-references to related words, the derivation, and its equivalent in modern standard Tagalog. This is a "one-way" dictionary; there is no English-Tagalog section. Nevertheless, it is a valuable and unique source.—**Marshall E. Nunn**

Vietnamese

1104. Dihn-Hoa, Ngyuen. **Vietnamese-English Dictionary.** Rutland, Vt., Charles E. Tuttle, c1966, 1991. 568p. $19.95pa. LC 66-17773. ISBN 0-8048-1712-X.

This dictionary is a reprint of the 1966 edition. No visible changes have been made between that one and this one. Entries are well chosen, and the glossary is excellent. Explanations, equivalents, and synonyms are given for ambiguous entries. Also included is a guide to Vietnamese regional pronunciation, which can be helpful for non-Vietnamese-speaking persons. Although this work was originally intended for students of Vietnamese, it has proven extremely useful for Vietnamese-speaking users who need help understanding and expressing themselves well in English. In fact, more Vietnamese, both in the United States and Vietnam, use this dictionary than do English-speaking persons. Thus, it would be helpful to include English pronunciation in the next edition. This reasonably priced book should prove useful for libraries serving Vietnamese individuals.—**Binh P. Le**

Yiddish

1105. Gross, David C. **English-Yiddish, Yiddish-English Dictionary.** New York, Hippocrene Books, 1992. 117p. $7.95pa. ISBN 0-87052-969-2.

This "practical dictionary," as the cover announces, responds to a revival of interest in Yiddish, associated primarily with pre-World War II East European, Argentinian, and American Jewry. It is a practical guide because of its compact size and "the hope of the author that mastery of the words in this slim book will enable the reader to carry on a conversation in Yiddish, to understand Yiddish, and to help preserve a wonderfully rich source of human knowledge" (p. vii). It will not be practical for researching most written Yiddish because this book only uses transliterated spellings. Written Yiddish uses Hebrew letters, and the major dictionaries of Yiddish respect this literary arrangement (e.g., *Modern English-Yiddish/Yiddish-English Dictionary* by Uriel Weinreich [see ARBA 79, entry 1156], *Yiddish-English-Hebrew Dictionary* by Alexander Harkavy [Schocken Books, c1928, 1988]). At least two other dictionaries have appeared in the last six years with transliterated spellings in addition to the Hebrew renderings to aid English speakers and editors: *The Yiddish Dictionary Sourcebook* (see ARBA 87, entry 1057) and *Transliterated English-Yiddish; Yiddish-English* by D. M. Harduf (Harduf Books, 1991). Even Weinreich's weighty dictionary, the standard by which others are judged, employs transliterated spellings to an extent. Purely transliterated word and idiom guides, such as the popular titles *The Joys of Yiddish* by Leo Rosten (Pocket Books, 1968) and *A Dictionary of Yiddish Slang & Idioms* by Fred Kogos (Citadel Press, 1967) claim as their purpose appreciation and entertainment rather than linguistic usage. Gross's guide lacks the anecdotal features of such popular titles, and it equally lacks the linguistic aids to usage and form that distinguish reference works with both Hebrew and transliterated spellings. As a guide to words heard in conversation, Gross's list is problematic, because, as he himself recognizes, "there are various ways of speaking Yiddish" (p. viii). He offers, perhaps misleadingly, "the accent spoken by most Jews" (without identifying this accent, Gross employs "Litvak" pronunciations). Gross's dictionary (actually a glossary) has limited value for the reference shelf.—**Simon J. Bronner**

1106. Harduf, David Mendel. **Transliterated English-Yiddish; Yiddish-English Dictionary.** Willowdale, Ont., Harduf Books, 1991. 1v. (various paging). $25.00pa. ISBN 0-920243-22-3.

An independent scholar from Toronto, Harduf has produced many useful reference works for Jewish biblical and language studies. This self-published reference expands upon his *English-Yiddish; Yiddish-English Dictionary* published in 1983. Although the number of entries has not appeared to increase, the latest version has two significant changes. First, it has added English transliterated versions of Yiddish words traditionally rendered in Hebrew letters. Second, the dimensions of the work have been enlarged, and the print size has increased for easier reading. Another consequence of this expansion is increased thickness. One needed addition that is absent, however, is an introduction to explain the selection and definition of words. This would have been helpful for Yiddish, prone as it is to differences in dialect. Harduf appears to use the "standard" pronunciation and vocabulary associated with

"Litvak" usage, although his unusual reliance on "ei" (as in "weigh"; usually rendered as "ey" as in "hey") and "ai" (as in "fine"; usually rendered as "ay" as in "stein") lend themselves to alternate readings. Unlike the transliterated dictionary *Yiddish Dictionary Sourcebook* (see ARBA 87, entry 1057), Harduf has not arranged the dictionary by the transliterated English equivalents; keeping with tradition, he has alphabetized following the sequence of Hebrew letters. Although not approaching the extensive detail and scope of Uriel Weinreich's classic reference *Modern English-Yiddish, Yiddish-English Dictionary* (Schocken Books, 1968, repr. 1977), Harduf's volume is easier to use and may thus be particularly appealing to students of Yiddish. It may also be useful to editors and writers seeking transliterated English equivalents for their texts. — **Simon J. Bronner**

24 Literature

GENERAL WORKS

Bibliography

1107. **MLA International Bibliography.** (Indexing coverage: 1/81 - 6/25/92). [CD-ROM]. Bronx, N.Y., H. W. Wilson, 1992. Hardware requirements: WILSONLINE Workstation, IBM PC, or compatible; 640K; hard disk drive. $1,495.00.

The *MLA International Bibliography* is without question the premier source in its field. The WILSONDISC CD-ROM version of it provides access to an important reference work that in its print format has long been daunting to patrons and librarians. The Wilson CD-ROM retrieval system offers coverage from 1981 to the present for books, periodical articles, essays, festschriften, and dissertations published throughout the world on topics relating to literature, linguistics, and folklore. Updated monthly, the system currently provides access to over 450,000 citations.

Installation of the WILSONDISC program is extremely easy, and a toll-free number for technical support is provided. The program asks whether or not instructions are needed and requires little else to complete installation. Although this disc was tested on a machine with a CD-ROM system already in place, the reviewers removed all the related commands from the AUTOEXEC and CONFIG.SYS files and rebooted the computer prior to installation. WILSONDISC had to make all the connections by itself. The program created a subdirectory, WILSONPC, and installed the program with no problems. Accessing the CD-ROM drive does require a Wilson product in the drive. The only oddity is that in order to completely remove the program from a computer, the installation program must be used. The DOS commands delete and erase result in an ACCESS DENIED message.

There are many good things to say about the Wilson CD-ROM version of the MLA bibliography. Unfortunately, some fairly major problems override the positive aspects of the product. The main one is the schizophrenic nature of the generic Wilson search program. While some aspects of the program are obvious and usable by the novice some features can only be understood by librarians familiar with Boolean logic. For example, the approach in the BROWSE mode is the same as that applied to the printed index, but the BROWSE mode will not fully plumb the depths of the bibliography, a fact not made plain to the searcher. For instance, entering the term "Harlem Renaissance" in the BROWSE mode produces 68 entries. Using either WILSEARCH or WILSONLINE and the Boolean approach "(Harlem or Black or Negro) and Renaissance" produces 91 entries.

WILSEARCH and WILSONLINE, however, are not without their drawbacks, as accomplishing the search noted above is not straightforward in either mode. WILSEARCH presents the user with a boiler-plate menu that provides for searches by three subject terms ("subject" is specified, although key words are meant), personal name, title key words, journal name, organization name, and year. The explanation of the search offered on the screen is inadequate at best and assumes that the user knows what "Boolean" means. A default "and" connects all the terms on the screen, but a user wishing to employ "or" is forced into the convoluted construction "or Harlem or Black or Negro." Further, the "not" operator is unavailable.

WILSONLINE, the command-driven mode, is the most powerful search tool, yet requires either extensive previous knowledge or considerable use of help screens. In this mode all Boolean operators, as well as truncation, are finally available. While the help screens do provide an explanation of Boolean searching and truncation, they do not help in constructing more than two-term searches. Because of the way the program parses searches, complex queries require the use of ellipses, a technique that is explained in neither the documentation nor the help screens.

Considering these difficulties and the disc's cost, libraries may wish to consider other approaches to the MLA bibliography. The SilverPlatter CD-ROM version is an option, as is OCLC's First Search database ($1,350 buys 1,500 searches), which goes back to 1966 and provides 15 more years of citations than are available on either of the two CD-ROM versions. In the end, libraries will have to make decisions based on local needs and users.

—Donald C. Dickinson and Charlie Seavey

Biography

1108. **Contemporary Authors: A Bio-Bibliographical Guide to Current Writers.... Volume 133.** Susan M. Trotsky, ed. Detroit, Gale, 1992. 443p. $104.00. LC 62-52046. ISBN 0-8103-1958-6. ISSN 0010-7468.

1109. **Contemporary Authors: A Bio-Bibliographical Guide to Current Writers.... Volume 134.** Susan M. Trotsky, ed. Detroit, Gale, 1992. 506p. $104.00. LC 62-52046. ISBN 0-8103-1965-9. ISSN 0010-7468.

More than 98,000 authors have been represented in the Contemporary Authors series since its beginning. Writers in almost all genres—fiction, nonfiction, drama, poetry, and so forth—have been included, and prominent people in areas such as newspaper and television reporting, editing, screenwriting, and other media also appear. Among those listed in volumes 133 and 134 are L. Frank Baum, Roald Dahl (obituary notice), Patti Davis, Albert Einstein, Anne Frank, Peter Jennings, Otto Preminger, and Casper Weinberger, representing a wide field of coverage.

Information is generally gathered from the writers through questionnaires and correspondence. If authors fail to respond to requests, material is obtained from other reliable sources. Data on living authors is sent to biographees for verification. Essays may contain personal and career information, addresses, organizational memberships, awards and honors, publications (e.g., books, articles, periodical articles), and biographical sidelights. These last may consist of critical analyses of the individual's works, interviews, or other material. Several other titles in related Contemporary Author series have updated older volumes from this particular series. A volume update chart that follows the preface shows which of the earlier volumes may be discarded. Academic and large public libraries will want to purchase these volumes to have the most current information available on contemporary authors.

—Anna Grace Patterson

1110. Lindfors, Bernth, and Reinhard Sander, eds. **Twentieth-Century Caribbean and Black African Writers. First Series.** Detroit, Gale, 1992. 406p. illus. index. (Dictionary of Literary Biography, v.117). $112.00. LC 92-8972. ISBN 0-8103-7594-X.

This work adheres strictly to the format established in previous volumes of the Dictionary of Literary Biography (DLB) series. Individually authored chapters on 31 writers (19 African and 12 Circum-Caribbean) are arranged alphabetically by writer's name. All authors featured in this volume are of the twentieth century, with the exception of Olaudah Equiano, and all are from former British colonies and write in English. Individual chapters begin with a bibliography of the writer's publications and end with a bibliography of published interviews with the writer and critical and biographical works about the person. They are also illustrated with photographs of the authors and of dust jackets from their books. The lengths of chapters vary from slightly more than 4 pages on Jamaican John Hearne to 22 pages on St. Lucian Nobel laureate Derek Walcott. The chapters vary in quality; some of the longer ones tend to be uneven and rambling. As do all volumes in the DLB, this one contains a cumulative index to this and related series. This book complements another recent Gale publication, the three-volume *Black Literature Criticism* (see index for entry number). That set presents a succinct and balanced critical overview of the authors' work while DLB's coverage is a more in-depth view.

—Fred J. Hay

Dictionaries and Encyclopedias

1111. Harris, Wendell V. **Dictionary of Concepts in Literary Criticism and Theory.** Westport, Conn., Greenwood Press, 1992. 444p. index. (Reference Sources for the Social Sciences and Humanities, no.12). $75.00. PN41.H36. 801. LC 91-20040. ISBN 0-313-25932-1.

The key word in the title is "Concepts." After a hasty look one might think this dictionary is in direct competition with J. A. Cuddon's *A Dictionary of Literary Terms and Literary Theory*, 3d ed. (see ARBA 92, entry 1101) or C. Hugh Holman and William Harmon's continuation of the classic *A Handbook to Literature*, 5th ed. (see ARBA 87, entry 1076). Harris differs in that he defines and analyzes only the most basic concepts in more depth than has previously been available in a reference source. For example, Harris devotes five full pages to the concept *imagination*; Cuddon allows four pages, and Holman and Harmon provide two. In addition, Harris includes a full page of bibliography and notes for further study; Cuddon provides none, and Holman and Harmon give just a sampling. And under keener focus, Harris's references for *imagination* offer a historical viewpoint, whereas Holman and Harmon opt for more current studies. To differentiate Harris even more, he does not include the term *imagery*—surely a basic literary concept—which received almost as much attention as *imagination* in the comparative works. Finally, Harris's list of concepts stops at 70; many times that number appear in the other works. Because Harris is an able scholar and a lucid writer, his essays on particular terms are superior to the others. He is certainly adept at incorporating every essential critical remark on a term, thereby imbuing each term with the utmost meaning. However, unless the term sought is of the most general kind, the other two works will be needed. Strongly recommended for all literature collections. [R: Choice, Oct 92, pp. 272-74; LJ, 15 Mar 92, p. 76]

—Bill Bailey

1112. Hawthorn, Jeremy. **A Concise Glossary of Contemporary Literary Theory.** New York, Routledge, Chapman & Hall, 1992. 210p. $15.95pa. PN44.5.H365. 801'.95'014. LC 91-33911. ISBN 0-340-53911-9.

1113. Hawthorn, Jeremy. **A Glossary of Contemporary Literary Theory.** London, Edward Arnold/ Hodder & Stoughton; distr., New York, Routledge, Chapman & Hall, 1992. 282p. $49.95. PN44.5.H37. 801'.95'014. LC 91-32095. ISBN 0-340-53912-7.

The increased importance of theory in current literary studies is reflected in titles of some of the most recent dictionaries of literature. Not only did J. A. Cuddon see fit to amend the 3d edition of his long-revered compilation to *A Dictionary of Literary Terms and Literary Theory* (see ARBA 92, entry 1011), but also during the first few months of 1992 alone, two more works have appeared that focus on this aspect of a field that has already been glossed in countless reference works. *Dictionary of Concepts in Literary Criticism and Theory* by Wendell V. Harris (Greenwood Press, 1992) is one; Hawthorn's *Glossary of Contemporary Literary Theory* is the other.

Emphasis here is on "contemporary." Hawthorn has concentrated primarily on terms used by critics since 1970 that are not found in more general lists of literary definitions. Some entries are very short, such as that on transgressive strategy; others, such as that on modernism and postmodernism, cover several pages. Supporting sources are mentioned briefly within entries and cited in full in an extensive bibliography at the back of the book. Unfortunately, no index is included, but cross-references are numerous, and the introduction provides a grouping of entries by school or subject field, allowing the reader to see at a glance terms relevant to a broader concept such as discourse analysis or feminism. Hawthorn's inclusiveness at times leads to overspecialization and trendiness. Will terms such as *wet-diaper writing* or *genotext* be remembered 10 years from now? Also, explanations of more difficult concepts, such as deconstructionism, are abstract and unwieldy. Harris's work includes fewer terms but is considerably more readable and has indexing as well.

Hawthorn's glossary is definitely for the initiated. Only large collections that serve scholars and graduate students concentrating on literary theory should consider it; others will do fine with Harris's book and more general works, such as Cuddon's. Or they might consider the abridged paperback version of Hawthorn's work, *A Concise Glossary of Contemporary Literary Theory*. Seventy-two pages shorter and less than one-third the cost of the hardback edition, it contains much the same information. The introduction has been shortened and is aimed at students instead of seasoned scholars, and numerous entries have been pared down. Some have been left out altogether, but these tend to be general or peripheral terms, such as *agenda setting*; those that are no longer really contemporary, such as *New Criticism*; and those of dubious value, such as the aforementioned *genotext* and *wet-diaper writing*. As the most useful material has been kept intact, it seems safe to say that most libraries could get by with the less-expensive version. [R; C&RL, Sept 92, p. 422; Choice, Oct 92, pp. 272-74; WLB, Sept 92, pp. 112-15] — **Willa Schmidt**

1114. Orr, Leonard. **A Dictionary of Critical Theory.** Westport, Conn., Greenwood Press, 1991. 464p. index. $75.00. PN98.S6077. 801'.95'03. LC 90-22816. ISBN 0-313-23527-9.

Numerous other dictionaries of literary terms exist, some of which define critical terms, but this is the first dictionary in English exclusively devoted to critical terminology. Thus, this source defines *feminist criticism* and *deconstruction* but not *metaphor* and *sonnet*. Orr has also published a related work, *Research in Critical Theory since 1965* (see ARBA 90, entry 1067). As he notes in his preface, there has recently been a renewed interest in the study of critical theory that this dictionary may aid. Included are both general and specific terms frequently used in anthologies of critical theory or standard histories of criticism, as well as terms associated with schools of criticism and key terms in foreign languages. Excluded are biographical entries; terms associated with genres, rhetoric, verse forms, or historical periods; terms taken from other disciplines (unless, as in *psychoanalytical criticism*, a specific literary use has developed); and terms in general use, such as *Darwinism*. Bibliographical references follow the most significant entries. There are an appendix of foreign terms and an index of theorists mentioned in the main entries. Some of the definitions are very concise, but key terms are discussed at considerable length (e.g., *hermeneutics* takes up 23 pages, with another 10 pages of bibliography).

Although Orr suggests that this book may be useful to undergraduate and general readers, its most obvious audience is professors and advanced graduate students. This is only occasionally a dictionary for quick reference; its more probable use is for extended reading by researchers interested in making fine distinctions between abstract, esoteric terms. [R: Choice, May 92, p. 1372] — **David Isaacson**

Handbooks and Yearbooks

1115. **Black Literature Criticism: Excerpts from Criticism of the Most Significant Works of Black Authors over the Past 200 Years.** James P. Draper, ed. Detroit, Gale, 1992. 3v. illus. $250.00/set. ISBN 0-8103-7929-5.

Produced in the same format as, and partially derived from, Gale's *Literary Criticism* series, *Black Literature Criticism* has entries for 125 Black writers from around the world. Authors covered were all born in the nineteenth and twentieth centuries, with the exception of Jupiter Hammon (1711?-1800?) and Phillis Wheatley (1753?-1784). Most of the entries are for twentieth-century writers. Entries are arranged alphabetically and have a general biographical overview, a list of principal works, excerpts from critical essays by recognized authorities, and suggestions for further reading. Excerpts are arranged chronologically, and an attempt has been made to select criticism addressing each author's early and later work and, if deceased, retrospective criticism. Most entries have selections from an interview with the author. At least one photograph is included in each entry. Author, nationality, and title indexes are provided.

This essential reference work serves as a very good introduction to the authors covered. The excerpts from critical essays are well chosen and, taken together, present a comprehensible, intellectual portrait of the writers and their critical receptions. However, it remains a mystery as to how the subjects of this anthology were chosen, since many outstanding Black authors, such as Pulitzer prize-winner James Alan McPherson and Georgia novelist Raymond Andrews, have been omitted. [R: Choice, Sept 92, p. 72; RQ, Summer 92, p. 564] — **Fred J. Hay**

1116. Coyle, Martin, and others, eds. **Encyclopedia of Literature and Criticism.** Detroit, Gale, c1990, 1991. 1299p. index. $125.00. 801.95. ISBN 0-8103-8331-4.

This comprehensive reference work is no mere dictionary of literary and critical terms; it is instead a collection of 91 lengthy and substantive essays. The editors have organized the topics in a way that both reinforces and challenges the traditional concepts and demarcations often used when we speak of English literature.

The essays are grouped under 10 broad categories. After an introduction in which the concepts of literature and criticism are defined and their histories delineated, there are four sections organized along conventional lines: literature and history, poetry, drama, and the novel. In these sections essays cover literary movements, periods, and genres. Section 6 covers criticism in all its manifold "schools" (e.g., Marxist, feminist, Romantic, psychoanalytic). The presence of a section on production and reception marks this work as truly (post)modern. Here the cultural conditions that affect literature are explored: literacy, censorship, publishing, libraries, and universities. The section on contexts discusses literature in relation to other arts and to the history of ideas. Other "English" literatures (e.g., Australian, Canadian, African) are described in section 9. The book concludes with a turgid but thought-provoking afterword.

In addition to comprehensiveness and a narrative format, what distinguishes this work is the fact that the editors encouraged the authors of the essays to be provocative and challenging, rather than to strive for a more definitive, more "objective" approach. Some essays are jargon-laden, but most rise to the challenge and take a fresh look at their subjects. The result is a work that is very much a product of its time, but candidly so, and one that will inform and stimulate the serious student of literature.
—**Jeffrey R. Luttrell**

1117. **In the Beginning: Great First Lines from Your Favorite Books.** By Hans Bauer. San Francisco, Calif., Chronicle Books, 1991. 204p. index. $8.95pa. ISBN 0-8118-0011-3.

The major question concerning this work is whether it is a reference book at all. Bauer has collected the first lines of some 500 novels, arranged them alphabetically by the title of the book, and provided an index by author. There is no prefatory material, nothing that explains how these books were chosen or why they are characterized as "your favorite books." There is no index beyond the one by author, hence no way to locate a particular book by a theme or a character. The brief blurb on the back of the book states that it is "informative, entertaining, and satisfying." It is entertaining and satisfying as a book to pick up and explore in an idle moment, but it is not especially informative. Recommended for home use but not for library purchase.—**Terry Ann Mood**

1118. **World Literature Criticism 1500 to the Present: A Selection of Major Authors from Gale's Literary Criticism Series.** James P. Draper, ed. Detroit, Gale, 1992. 6v. illus. index. $360.00/set. ISBN 0-8103-8361-6.

In keeping with its title, this set focuses on the critical response to 231 major writers of the last 500 years. Although Gale characterizes it as a "one-stop, authoritative guide to the whole spectrum of world literature" (introduction), its emphasis is on European and American writers. Japan, Algeria, Chile, Argentina, New Zealand, and Colombia are each represented by one author; Mexico, Nigeria, and South Africa, by two. Among the older writers are Rabelais and Miguel Cervantes, while contemporary authors include William S. Burroughs, Joyce Carol Oates, and Tom Stoppard. With the help of an advisory board made up largely of high school teachers and high school and public librarians, authors have been selected based on a review of curricula and textbooks. Material has been extracted from other Gale Literary Criticism series and updated for this set.

Each entry introduces an author's work, framing it in a biographical context; the discussion concludes with reference to the other Gale literary series. Next follows the section of critical commentary, which usually consists of three to six excerpts, in some cases complete essays, arranged chronologically by date of publication. These purportedly are selected because they reflect the initial or changing responses to the author's work or a particular critical approach. Thus, for example, Thomas Hardy's work is discussed in a 1928 essay by Virginia Woolf, an excerpt from a 1949 critical work by Albert J. Guerard, a 1966 piece by Irving Howe, and a 1990 study by F. B. Pinion. To place the criticism in context, a caption that prefaces the selection identifies either the critic or the focus of the piece. Following the critical selections is a list of sources for further study, usually no more than six, each briefly annotated.

A list of principal works appears in each article. Some also include a list of media adaptations (motion picture and television) of an author's works. The works of Sinclair Lewis, Dylan Thomas, and Tennessee Williams are highlighted in this manner, but Truman Capote's are not. Also, the motion pictures of Emily Bronte's *Wuthering Heights* are noted, but Charlotte Bronte's *Jane Eyre* is not.

A portrait of the author—photograph, etching, or drawing—appears at the beginning of the article. Occasionally, other illustrations and photographs, also in black-and-white, are interspersed with the text. The author index, which conveniently cross-references 26 other Gale series, is supplemented by a nationality index, and a title index provides quick identification of a work as well as access to the section where it is discussed.

Given the work's composite nature and broad scope, the treatment of individual authors allows for wide variation. The approach, however, is sound and, given its intended audience, has merit. The critical commentary is sufficient to stimulate interest without overwhelming the beginning student or general reader, and more advanced students are directed to further sources. The set will be welcomed by high school and smaller academic and public libraries, especially those whose limited resources preclude extensive collections of secondary literary criticism. [R: RBB, 1 Dec 92, p. 692]—**Bernice Bergup**

1119. **The Writers Directory 1992-94.** 10th ed. Chicago, St. James Press, 1991. 1088p. $125.00. PN12.808'.02'05. ISBN 1-55862-093-1.

Libraries that own the Gale set of *Contemporary Authors* (CA) (see ARBA 92, entry 1096) already have the best source available for locating names and addresses of writers and noting their literary accomplishments. That set covers 99,000-plus writers as compared to 17,000 in this one-volume directory. *Contemporary Authors* offers ample biographical and anecdotal information for each writer, whereas this directory contains only the bare minimum of personal data and works cited. Both sources are international for English-language writers. An index to writing categories in a separate section helps the directory user find the genre and subject interests for each writer. Cross-references for pseudonyms appear throughout. The reader should keep in mind that this directory includes all of the 6,000 entrants featured in other St. James publications (e.g., *Contemporary Poets* [see ARBA 92, entry 1244]). Of course, CA is much more expensive and voluminous, but it is also a library staple. For reference purposes CA is definitely superior. (Brief essays can be written from its text—a plus for undergraduate assignments.) As a desktop referral for a quick check on a writer, *The Writers Directory* will suffice. Recommended.—**Bill Bailey**

CHILDREN'S LITERATURE

Bibliography

1120. Brown, Muriel W., Rita Schoch Foudray, and Jim Roginski, comps. **Newbery and Caldecott Medalists and Honor Book Winners: Bibliographies and Resource Materials Through 1991.** 2d ed. New York, Neal-Schuman, 1992. 511p. index. $59.95. Z1037.A2B76. 011'.62'079. LC 92-14324. ISBN 1-55570-118-3.

1121. Sharkey, Paulette Bochnig, and Jim Roginski, comps. **Newbery and Caldecott Medal and Honor Books in Other Media.** New York, Neal-Schuman, 1992. 142p. index. $29.95. Z1037.A2S4. 028.1'62. LC 92-15391. ISBN 1-55570-119-1.

Assembling the vast amount of information offered in this set of reference books is an awe-inspiring task. In the first title the compilers have provided an alphabetical list of all authors and illustrators who have received the Newbery or Caldecott awards, with a complete bibliography of their other works, information on collections of original materials, and sources for information about the authors and illustrators. Although the compilers include a caveat in the introduction that describes their wide-ranging efforts to determine accuracy of information, three glaring typographical errors in the table of contents are disconcerting: "Frances" for Francis Kalnay, "Rawlines" for Marjorie Rawlings, and "Raith" for Faith Ringgold. In spite of such errors, having all this information in one resource will be useful to anyone working with children's books. The background sections will be particularly helpful for librarians or teachers developing author studies.

The companion title, *Newbery and Caldecott Medal and Honor Books in Other Media*, provides information on media materials related to the winning books: audio, braille, large-print, film, filmstrip, book/audio combinations, software, television, and video. Information on items such as postcards, posters, and calendars is also included. Useful appendixes include a bibliography of resources, a directory of media producers and distributors, and a list of titles by media formats. Together, these indispensable volumes provide a wealth of information for librarians and teachers who want to quickly locate a variety of resources on Caldecott and Newbery winners. [R: LJ, 1 Oct 92, p. 78; RBB, 1 Nov 92, p. 552; WLB, Oct 92, p. 111]—**Suzanne I. Barchers**

1122. Carroll, Frances Laverne, and Mary Meacham, eds. **More Exciting, Funny, Scary, Short, Different, and Sad Books Kids Like....** Chicago, American Library Association, 1992. 192p. index. $15.00pa. Z1037.C294. 011.62. LC 92-11588. ISBN 0-8389-0585-4.

Similar to its 1984 predecessor (see ARBA 86, entry 1104), this annotated bibliography of books children actually read was assembled by polling librarians across the United States. Its 54 lists, 9 with subdivisions, are headed by the kind of questions that book-seeking children ask (e.g., "Do you have any books about aliens?"). Each list includes 5 to 15 recommended fiction and nonfiction titles, most published between 1984 and 1990. The book also contains author/title and subject indexes.

This edition of *Books Kids Like* complements, not replaces, the earlier bibliography. Its headings are different, and, where it repeats titles from the earlier work, its annotations are longer. As with the previous edition, annotations are designed to be read by children in the second to fifth grades. One possible weakness is that many are such complete synopses that they may spoil the plot instead of luring children to the books. A major improvement is the addition of a subject index that makes the lists useful when children's questions differ from those in the chapter headings. In spite of a title that defies memorization, this is a bibliography that many librarians will remember when faced with curious children or with problems of developing a collection that children will really use. [R: RBB, 15 Sept 92, pp. 188-89; SLMQ, Fall 92, p. 73]—**Raymond E. Jones**

1123. Dreyer, Sharon Spredemann. **The Best of *Bookfinder*: A Guide to Children's Literature about Interests and Concerns of Youth Aged 2-18.** Circle Pines, Minn., American Guidance Service, 1992. 451p. index. $75.00; $40.00pa. LC 91-076898. ISBN 0-88671-440-0; 0-88671-439-7pa.

Drawing from the well-received and highly respected first three volumes, this work describes "676 children's books according to more than 450 psychological, behavioral, and developmental topics of concern to children and adolescents, aged 2 and up" (p. xiii). Criteria for inclusion of a title are that it is in print (some that are too important to omit are noted by "o.p." for out-of-print), is timely, has a universal theme, is the only book on a particular subject, and presents a topic in a "particularly enduring and outstanding way" (p. xvii). The introductory section describes the use of children's literature by parents, librarians, teachers, and school counselors in a variety of situations.

Users familiar with the earlier volumes will recognize the format for each entry: bibliographic information; main subject headings or primary themes; a synopsis of the book; a commentary and the book's message; reading level; and whether the book is available in braille, in paperback or large-print format, or on film, filmstrip, tape, cassette, disk, or record. The subject index (with numerous cross-references), an author index, and a title index provide easy access to the numbered entries. A publishers/producers directory is included. Recommended for school and public libraries and others that serve adults concerned with the mental health of youth. [R: RBB, Aug 92, p. 2034]—**Phyllis J. Van Orden**

1124. Friedberg, Joan Brest, June B. Mullins, and Adelaide Weir Sukiennik. **Portraying Persons with Disabilities: An Annotated Bibliography of Nonfiction for Children and Teenagers.** 2d ed. New Providence, N.J., R. R. Bowker, 1992. 385p. index. (Serving Special Needs Series). $34.95. Z1037.9.F735. 011.62'083. LC 92-15047. ISBN 0-8352-3022-8.

This first-rate bibliotherapeutic guide provides access to more than 300 titles published between 1980 and 1991 that are suitable for preschool through high school readers. It is an excellent companion to the similarly titled fiction volume reviewed elsewhere in this volume, and it extends the contents of *Accept Me As I Am* (see ARBA 86, entry 797). The first 35 pages set the stage by providing 4 well-written and well-documented chapters on selection criteria, social and historical perspectives, reference books, and patterns and trends of disability portrayal. The bibliography is divided into broad topics of physical problems (e.g., AIDS, cancer, organ transplants), sensory problems, cognitive/behavioral problems, and multiple/severe disabilities. Biographies, case histories, and other forms of nonfiction are included. Entries are alphabetical by author and subdivided by title. Each entry contains a standard citation, a suggested reading level, citations to previous reviews, the specific disability, one to three pages of plot summary, an objective analysis (noting strengths and weaknesses of the book), and suggested uses. Author, title, and subject indexes round out the work.

The authors have succeeded admirably in their goal to present interesting, informative, and well-written nonfiction books that promote positive attitudes toward differences. They have identified works that are distinguished in their literary style, that are appropriate for their intended audiences, that portray "real" people, that provide accurate information about multiple disabilities, and that include a diversity of illustrations. The analyses are direct, honest, and compassionate. This is a terrific guide for parents, special education teachers, librarians, health professionals, and others who care about children and teenagers. These books should be read by those with and without disabilities to decrease stereotypes and gain insight and understanding. [R: SLMQ, Fall 92, p. 74] – **Ilene F. Rockman**

1125. Hobson, Margaret, Jennifer Madden, and Ray Prytherch. **Children's Fiction Sourcebook: A Survey of Children's Books for 6-13 Year Olds.** Brookfield, Vt., Ashgate/Gower Publishing, 1992. 285p. index. $43.95. ISBN 1-85742-022-5.

This survey of work by "the best and most popular" authors of fiction for 6- to 13-year-olds contains 131 alphabetically arranged author entries. Each provides annotated lists of selected titles. A separate section briefly lists 22 authors of "classic" texts and 4 anthologists. The remaining sections are not annotated and recommend titles from British publishers' series, list books featured on British television since 1985, and list all winners for 19 major children's fiction awards. The book concludes with author, title, and genre (actually genre and subject) indexes. Lack of page references makes the latter index awkward to use.

The authors profess to offer "thorough guidance," but the book has a number of weaknesses. First, biographical material is inconsistent; 2 entries contain no information, 10 lack birth dates, 6 do not begin (as the rest do) with the author's nationality, 22 omit contact addresses, and 34 lack the overview paragraph that introduces the annotated lists. Second, although the authors admit "a U.K. bias," their claim to "good coverage" of others does not withstand scrutiny – only 14 United States, 2 Canadian, 4 Australian, and 3 New Zealand authors are listed. Third, principles of selection are unclear. Age-appropriate books, such as Paula Fox's *The Slave Dancer*, are mentioned as award winners but are not included in the annotated lists. The most serious weakness, however, is the unevenness of the annotations. Some, such as that for Betsy Byars, are informative; others contain mostly hollow phrases, especially "delightful story." Some assess literary merit; some focus on physical presentation; some state the fact of popularity. This work's inadequate treatment of North American books, its exclusively British bibliographical data, and its uneven quality make it ineffective as a guide for North Americans. – **Raymond E. Jones**

1126. Khorana, Meena. **The Indian Subcontinent in Literature for Children and Young Adults: An Annotated Bibliography of English-Language Books.** Westport, Conn., Greenwood Press, 1991. 350p. index. (Bibliographies and Indexes in World Literature, no.32). $49.95. Z1037.K475. 015.54062. LC 91-31867. ISBN 0-313-25489-3.

A labor of love, 5 years in the making, this work has more than 900 annotated entries for books written in or translated into English about the countries and peoples of Bangladesh, Bhutan, India, Nepal, Pakistan, Sikkim, Sri Lanka, and Tibet. Arrangement is first by country (with the "Himalayan Kingdoms" of Bhutan, Nepal, Sikkim, and Tibet grouped together), then by genre (traditional literature, fiction, poetry, biography, and informational books). Books on more than one country are cross-listed, with different annotations for each country. Indexes by author, illustrator, title, and subject provide thorough access. Khorana also includes an essay on the history and current status of children's literature in each of the countries covered and on the literature of the countries published in the West.

As might be expected, most of the material is on India, with the other countries receiving fewer than 30 pages each. Khorana has listed titles that are "available," although she had to resort to embassies, private collections, and interlibrary loan to view most of them, and she actually purchased some 400 others. Even with the list of distributors she provides, libraries may have trouble obtaining some of the books, although an increase in demand for the titles might encourage dealers to stock them. Khorana's efforts will certainly increase awareness of this material, but a lower price would have helped to distribute her work more widely. Highly recommended for all school and public libraries. [R: Choice, July/Aug 92, p. 1658; RBB, 15 Apr 92, pp. 1551-52]—**Marilyn R. Pukkila**

1127. Miller-Lachmann, Lyn. **Our Family, Our Friends, Our World: An Annotated Guide to Significant Multicultural Books for Children and Teenagers.** New Providence, N.J., R. R. Bowker, 1992. 710p. index. $44.95. Z1037.M654. 011.62. LC 92-24549. ISBN 0-8352-3025-2.

At last! An intelligent, sensitive, and meticulous reference work on culturally conscious books for teenagers and children written by experts. *Our Family, Our Friends, Our World* is a compendium that all libraries will want. It is also affordable for classroom teachers and faculty members interested in this timely topic.

The 21 contributors represent a variety of ethnic groups and professional expertise so critical to a work of this caliber. The entries, for fiction and nonfiction, cover some 1,000 books published between 1970 and 1990. The book reflects its international and multicultural focus and also highlights the four primary minority groups in the United States: African-Americans, Asian-Americans, Hispanic-Americans, and Native Americans. Care and detail can be seen in each entry; for example, in the entry for *The Education of Little Tree* is the late-breaking news about Forrest Carter being a pseudonym for the racist Asa Earl Carter. Yet the balanced view shows that the book's origins do not diminish its importance. Chapters on the regions of the world give the cultural diversity present in these areas. An introduction places this work in context, delineating the publishing of multicultural books since the 1960s and highlighting the small presses that have pioneered this field. The introduction also provides detailed reasons for the criteria used in the evaluations. The annotations are all full paragraphs, giving weight to each entry. Each chapter contains a preliminary essay that sets the stage for the entries to follow. The appendix contains extensive lists of professional sources, series titles, and publishers. There is an inclusive author/title/series/subject index. This book is a rare treat, one that will be a landmark reference. [R: Choice, July/Aug 92, p. 1658; EL, Nov/Dec 92, pp. 45-46; RBB, 1 May 92, pp. 1633-34; RQ, Fall 92, pp. 137-38; SLJ, May 92, p. 50; SLMQ, Summer 92, p. 242; WLB, Apr 92, p. 126]
—**Anne F. Roberts**

1128. **The Newbery and Caldecott Awards: A Guide to the Medal and Honor Books.** 1992 ed. By Association for Library Service to Children. Chicago, American Library Association, 1992. 139p. index. $13.00pa. Z1037.A2N474. 011'.62. LC 92-9250. ISBN 0-8389-3411-0.

Although a number of books have been published that list and discuss the Newbery and Caldecott award books, this latest compilation is an excellent, concise, well-annotated example. The ALA has been publishing the lists for many years, but the format changed in 1991 (see ARBA 92, entry 1120). The list has been augmented with annotations and a pertinent article on the development of the awards. In this edition, Belle J. Peltola describes the "Newbery and Caldecott Medals: Authorization and Terms." Another useful addition is a list of the media used in each of the Caldecott winners and honor books. The entries are arranged by descending date and give author (and illustrator for Caldecott books), title, publisher, and a brief annotation, not only for the winners but also for each honor book. The work concludes with author/illustrator and title indexes.

This is an excellent work to use in selection and in the development of young readers. At its modest price, teachers and school and public librarians will want to purchase it as a reader's advisory tool. [R: SLJ, Sept 92, p. 152; SLMQ, Fall 92, p. 74]—**Joann H. Lee**

1129. Peterson, Carolyn Sue, and Ann D. Fenton. **Reference Books for Children.** 4th ed. Metuchen, N.J., Scarecrow, 1992. 399p. index. $39.50. Z1037.1.P4. 028.1'62. LC 92-14234. ISBN 0-8108-2543-0.

More than 1,000 reference books and reviewing tools published before June 1990 that are of value to children (through middle school age) are annotated and arranged in broad subject categories. Both a buying list and a guide for library science classes that deal with selection and reference, the volume covers recent titles and valuable older ones. It is arranged by discipline (e.g., humanities, recreation, social science) and then subarranged by category. Each entry is numbered and includes a complete bibliographic citation and a brief quasi-critical annotation.

This book is about half the size of *Guide to Reference Books for School Media Centers* by Margaret Irby Nichols (see index for entry number), but Nichols covers grades K-12. A comparison of the two shows that they are different not only in scope but also in the definition of what constitutes a reference book. This volume includes many children's single-volume fact books that may be deemed nonfiction in Nichols. Annotations in both volumes are comparable, but Nichols includes references to reviews in ARBA, making the latter a superior purchasing tool.

Comparing *Reference Books for Children* to *Elementary School Library Collection* (ESLC) (see index for entry number) finds many more reference titles included in the former. Thus, both it and *Guide to Reference Books for School Media Centers* are good supplementary tools for ESLC. Libraries that cannot afford both books should consider *Guide to Reference Books* if a larger span of years is of interest. For elementary school or young children, either volume will be a welcome addition. [R: RBB, 15 Oct 92, p. 458; SLJ, Dec 92, p. 38; WLB, Nov 92, p. 95]—**David V. Loertscher**

1130. Rasinski, Timothy V., and Cindy S. Gillespie. **Sensitive Issues: An Annotated Guide to Children's Literature K-6.** Phoenix, Ariz., Oryx Press, 1992. 277p. index. $29.95pa. Z1037.R23. 011.62. LC 92-18682. ISBN 0-89774-777-1.

Designed to help whole language teachers and librarians, this work identifies juvenile titles published since 1975 and suggests activities to help children explore the issues portrayed. The entries include bibliographic information, suggested grade levels for independent reading, suggested grade levels for reading aloud, a descriptive annotation, and suggested activities. The issues covered are divorce, substance abuse, death, nontraditional home environments, child abuse, prejudice, cultural differences, moving, illness, and disability. The index provides access to authors, titles, and subjects.

The authors do not state any criteria, beyond the coverage of the issues, for including a specific title. A wide range of literary quality is found in the works listed. Other bibliographies, such as *The Best of Bookfinder* (see index for entry number), provide more extensive and selective listings.

—**Phyllis J. Van Orden**

1131. Richey, Virginia H., and Katharyn E. Puckett. **Wordless/Almost Wordless Picture Books: A Guide.** Englewood, Colo., Libraries Unlimited, 1992. 223p. index. $27.50. Z1037.R47. 011'.62. LC 91-29364. ISBN 0-87287-878-3.

Filling a unique bibliographic niche, this work provides an alphabetically arranged author list of 685 picture books with little or no text. The sheer number of such works amazed this reviewer who, while aware of the format, simply did not know that so many existed.

An 80-page subject index with specific topics (e.g., acrobats, anger, autumn) is an extremely helpful feature for teachers, librarians, and others seeking such books for particular uses. Due to the nature of this format, there are some adult books included, but the majority appear to be children's works. No age designations are given, as these books can be used in a wide variety of ways. English as a second language classes, adult education, children's story hours, and regular classrooms all come to mind.

Five additional indexes further increase the book's usefulness: title, series, illustrator, format, and use of print. The format index identifies books with unusual forms, such as accordion fold, back-to-back (backwards), pop-up, or pull-tab. The index to use of print identifies the degree to which a particular title contains print, thus increasing its utility for language acquisition and the teaching of reading.

Entries provide complete bibliographic information. Some out-of-print works are included. Besides a brief annotation, each listing gives one or more format designations. The authors appear to have been all-inclusive within their designated format; however, the work does not contain entries that were not personally examined, although Richey and Puckett apparently made extensive use of interlibrary loan in gathering appropriate titles.

From its interesting foreword by Caldecott Award winner David Wiesner to its final subject index entry, this is an excellent bibliography. Given its reasonable price, it should be considered a first purchase for either personal or professional collections and for all children's libraries. [R: RBB, July 92, p. 1966; SLJ, Oct 92, p. 48; SLMQ, Fall 92, p. 74]—**Carol Truett**

1132. Robertson, Debra E. J. **Portraying Persons with Disabilities: An Annotated Bibliography of Fiction for Children and Teenagers.** 3d ed. New Providence, N.J., R. R. Bowker, 1992. 482p. index. (Serving Special Needs Series). $39.95. Z1037.9.R63. 016.80883'93520816'083. LC 91-39177. ISBN 0-8352-3023-6.

Looking for fiction books to help K-12 readers cope with cancer, asthma, or emotionally dysfunctional parents? Then this source is the one to consult. It covers more than 450 books and serves as an excellent companion to the earlier titles *Notes from a Different Drummer* (see ARBA 78, entry 179) and *More Notes from a Different Drummer* (see ARBA 83, entry 1018). Not only does it sensitively select positive titles that accurately portray disabled characters, but it includes thoughtful, insightful essays for overcoming stereotyping and understanding trends in fiction published in the last decade.

Fiction is defined in the broadest sense to include picture books, suspense novels, mysteries, junior novels, and historical fiction. Folklore is excluded. Disabilities are also broadly viewed and encompass physical, sensory, cognitive, behavioral, and other severe problems. Titles are grouped under each major category, and entries include an enhanced bibliographic citation (reading levels, page numbers, and references to earlier reviews are provided), followed by an extensive annotation. It is not uncommon for annotations to cover more than a page, as plot summaries are followed by critical analyses of thematic elements. Rounding out the work are a five-page, unannotated list of professional books and separate indexes for author, title, and subject that include references to *Notes* and *More Notes*. The detailed subject index also covers plot elements.

Librarians, parents, teachers, university faculty, and special education administrators will appreciate the timeliness and solid content of this work. It is easy to use, well conceived, and well executed. In addition, the strong binding should stand up to frequent use. [R: SLMQ, Fall 92, p. 74]

—**Ilene F. Rockman**

1133. Rosenberg, Judith K., with C. Allen Nichols. **Young People's Books in Series: Fiction and Non-Fiction, 1975-1991.** Englewood, Colo., Libraries Unlimited, 1992. 424p. index. $27.50. Z1037.R688. 011.62. LC 91-36646. ISBN 0-87287-882-1.

Rosenberg's bibliography of series books for children in grades 3-12 updates and improves her *Young People's Literature in Series* (see ARBA 78, entry 1122), a combined updating of separate lists of fiction (1972) and nonfiction (1973). The fiction bibliography, which conveniently numbers titles within each series, is arranged alphabetically by author; the nonfiction, by series title. Both provide brief assessments and age-level recommendations. There are indexes of series titles for both fiction and nonfiction, nonfiction subjects, and authors and titles.

The nonfiction section now includes in-print books for K-2 "if they are truly informational," but it is of limited utility because it does not evaluate individual titles. In contrast, despite significant flaws, the fiction section is very useful. Whereas earlier editions ignored works "of consistently low quality," this one covers all series published during the period, even providing complete title lists for those previously excluded. Although more current and comprehensive than either *Sequences* (see ARBA 86, entry 1112) or *Fiction Sequels for Readers 10 to 16* (see ARBA 92, entry 1115), it has weaker annotations; many merely summarize plots, and those for long series are too brief. Furthermore, patches of awkward, vague, or ungrammatical writing undermine confidence in Rosenberg's judgment. Finally, asterisks that indicate inclusion of prior titles in an earlier bibliography and numbers for third volumes are inconsistently placed. Nevertheless, the fiction bibliography justifies this book's purchase: it will help many librarians acquire and recommend popular fiction. [R: WLB, Sept 92, p. 123]

—**Raymond E. Jones**

1134. Sutherland, Zena, Betsy Hearne, and Roger Sutton. **The Best in Children's Books: The University of Chicago Guide to Children's Literature 1985-1990.** Chicago, University of Chicago Press, 1991. 492p. index. $37.50. Z1037.S96. LC 91-23100. ISBN 0-226-78064-3.

As in earlier volumes in the series, this is a selection of reviews of recommended fiction and nonfiction from the *Bulletin of the Center for Children's Books*. Arranged alphabetically by author of the reviewed work, the 1,146 numbered entries are approximately 75 to 225 words in length, ample enough to provide both a lucid summary and meaningful criticism. Reviews are laid out cleanly, with full bibliographic details in the heading and age or grade recommendations in the margin, where, along with asterisks that signal works of "special distinction," they are clearly visible to browsers.

Few would seriously quarrel with the selection or quality of the reviews, but deficiencies in the apparatus make this book fall short of excellence as a reference work. It includes six indexes, but only those for title and reading level are inclusive; unaccountably, some titles do not appear in the others. The first sentence of the review of Lloyd Alexander's *The El Dorado Adventure*, for example, calls it a sequel, but it is not listed under sequels in the types of literature index. In fact, it does not appear at all in that or the developmental values, curricular uses, or subject indexes. Fiction titles generally are not indexed under enough headings to suggest their richness and usefulness in a variety of curriculum situations. This work's closest rival, *Best Books for Children* (see ARBA 91, entry 1111), includes more titles but limits summaries to a single sentence. *The Best in Children's Books* can be frustrating, but it provides more substantial information and will ultimately be of greater use to those willing to browse through it patiently. [R: RBB, 1 Jan 92, p. 846]—**Raymond E. Jones**

1135. Watson, Benjamin. **English Schoolboy Stories: An Annotated Bibliography of Hardcover Fiction.** Metuchen, N.J., Scarecrow, 1992. 198p. index. $25.00. Z1037.W338. 016.823008'0352054. LC 92-12388. ISBN 0-8108-2572-4.

"I say, you chaps, this could be useful" might be the reaction of Billy Bunter, the fat owl of Greyfriars School and hero of some 30 books. Stories of boys and youths in the privately financed public schools of England began about 1800 and carry on today, although they flourished from the 1850s to 1920. Nostalgia buffs or student/critics occasionally pursue this entertaining, moralistic, and sometimes perverse genre, and they need reference support such as this bibliography. This work is restricted to stories not only of schoolboys but also of boys in school settings in England, Scotland, or Wales. Watson, a librarian, made the subject a focus for an alphabetical list of authors presented with their pertinent titles. Sources are given for the bibliographical information and for the biographical paragraph on the author. Cross-references lead from pseudonyms to real names, but no list of pseudonyms appears under the real name. There is no critical comment on the author, and the short content note on a book yields little about its flavor, style, or issues. Many of the 700 titles lack annotations because the authors were prolific and the formula stories were no doubt repetitive. There are a title index and a delightful index of actual schools represented in fiction. Schoolboy fiction is not unappreciated by social and literary critics, and this bibliography does a service for them by gathering these titles together.—**Claire England**

1136. **Young Adult 1991 Annual Booklist.** Los Angeles, Calif., Adult Services, Los Angeles Public Library, 1991. 73p. index. $10.00pa.

The Los Angeles Public Library's annual booklist includes about 250 books reviewed by young adult staff members during the year. Originating in 1983, the list is a useful selection tool for public and school librarians, and more than just a "booklist." It is well organized by general subject categories (e.g., science, art and music, literature, business and economics) and fiction. Each entry gives author, title, publisher, date, and price, and each book is annotated, evaluated, and rated by librarians as to its success with young adults.

The evaluation designations, which are especially useful to librarians in small libraries with limited selection tools, indicate usability, popularity, first purchase recommendation, suitability for booktalks, and high interest/easy reading. Other categories include suggestions that a title should be more widely purchased, that it should not be replaced in the young adult collection in the future, that it should be "shelved adult" because it has not appealed to young adults, or that it should be "sent to children's collection." Titles that are included on other selection lists—YASD (Young Adult Services Division of the

American Library Association) "Best Books," "Quick Picks," and *Booklist*'s "Editor's Choice" lists—are noted. There are a list of series regularly selected and author and title indexes.

The Los Angeles young adult list comes off well in a comparison with the New York Public Library's *Books for the Teen Age* (see ARBA 91, entry 362), which has been published for a number of years. The latter has more titles (1,250 as compared to about 250 a year); however, it continues many items from year to year, noting new ones with an asterisk but omitting publication dates. While the subject headings are much more specific in the New York list, the Los Angeles list describes and evaluates books much more thoroughly. It is well worth the modest price for libraries selecting books for young adults.—**Joann H. Lee**

1137. **The Young Adult Reader's Adviser.** Myra Immell, ed. New Providence, N.J., R. R. Bowker, 1992. 2v. index. $79.95/set. Z1037.Y674. 011.62. LC 92-3232. ISBN 0-8352-3068-6.

Those familiar with *The Reader's Adviser* (see ARBA 89, entries 7-9) will welcome the arrival of this new work. The stated purpose of these two hefty volumes is "to help students, teachers, and librarians find recommended reading material on subjects and authors currently included in the middle, junior high, and high school curricula." Four major topical areas are covered: literature and language arts, mathematics and computer science, social science and history, and science and health. Within each curricular area, individuals important to that area are featured. For example, in nuclear chemistry Marie Curie is profiled. Her entry (and all others) includes a biographical sketch and books by and about her. Books are starred if readable by younger readers (ages 12-14), and all have been selected with the high school student in mind. The value of the bibliographies is that specific editions of literary works are recommended for the teen audience.

While the main approach to curriculum is through people, the set also includes annotated bibliographies of topical interest, such as adolescence, pregnancy and parenthood, and aging. Titles listed in nonfiction topics have primarily been published in the 1980s, with a few 1990 and 1991 titles.

For the senior high school *The Young Adult Reader's Adviser* joins two other major bibliographies: *Best Books for Senior High Readers* (see ARBA 92, entry 1117) and *Senior High School Library Catalog* (see ARBA 88, entry 640). The arrangement of these titles is, of course, different, but cross-checking titles reveals insignificant overlap except for very standard titles. Examining each carefully reveals that *The Young Adult Reader's Adviser* is aimed at a more sophisticated audience than the other two. None of the three covers audiovisual or electronic sources.

All three bibliographies are excellent and should be owned by every school library that is building in-depth collections. *The Young Adult Reader's Adviser*, however, is a first choice because it is an education in itself. It introduces curricular topics and the important people and works of each field. It is fascinating background reading for librarians, teachers, and students. For the home schooler who is pursuing an education through reading, this book is an ideal tool. At its price and size, it is also a bargain. [R: BR, Nov/Dec 92, p. 55; RBB, 1 June 92, p. 1780; SLJ, Nov 92, p. 140; SLMQ, Fall 92, p. 74; WLB, Sept 92, p. 123]—**David V. Loertscher**

Biography

1138. **Author Profile Collection.** Worthington, Ohio, Linworth Publishing, 1992. 106p. illus. $24.95pa. ISBN 0-938865-12-9.

Twenty-one children's and young adult authors and illustrators are presented here, ranging from Arnold Adoff to Jane Yolen and from David Wiesner to Daniel and Susan Cohen. The three- to six-page accounts include some biographical information and noncritical discussions about the author or illustrator's work. Final sections include two articles on author visits, one article about whole language, a chronological list of birthdays for authors and illustrators, and a short section of instant art.

Overall, these sketches are quite readable and are appropriately illustrated with pictures of the people and their books. Bookmark bibliographies, ready to photocopy, are an added bonus. The three-ring notebook format does facilitate the use of the material. The problems with this collection primarily arise from the fact that the profiles included have been lifted directly from the pages of the *Book Report* and *Library Talk*, and citations to those profiles are not given. Comparisons between this collection of reprints and the originals show no changes or updating. An address is given for those who wish to write John Steptoe, who died in 1989, and David Wiesner's Caldecott book *Tuesday* is not mentioned. The quality of the photographs in the original material is much better than in these reproductions, which look like poor photocopies. The birthday list in the back does not include all of the people profiled in the book.

There are many useful bibliographic tools for librarians, media specialists, teachers, and young readers to use. This collection of author and illustrator sketches needs some revision and rewriting before it can be recommended. [R: BL, July 92, p. 1946] – **Carol A. Doll**

1139. Rollock, Barbara. **Black Authors & Illustrators of Children's Books: A Biographical Dictionary.** 2d ed. Hamden, Conn., Garland, 1992. 234p. illus. index. (Garland Reference Library of the Humanities, v.1316). $35.00. Z1037.R63. 809'.89282. LC 91-37402. ISBN 0-8240-7078-X.

Adding some 35 new authors and illustrators to the lineup of African-American writers included in the initial edition, this work contains short biographical sketches of some 150 personalities, both living and dead, in the field of children's literature. While any biographical work related to a field in such popular demand as multicultural literature is useful, a few limitations of this work need to be pointed out.

Coverage of biographees is not always even, with birth dates sometimes left out. Many include quoted introductory material, but in the majority of articles this has been omitted. Also, article length does not appear proportional to the importance of the author or illustrator discussed. For example, while Glennette Turner, who has only done a handful of books, is certainly an up-and-coming author, her biography is almost two and a half pages long, while John Steptoe, who illustrated 16 works, including a 1985 Caldecott Honor Book, has slightly more than a page devoted to him.

Noteworthy features of the work, however, are numerous: a simple-to-use dictionary arrangement; a clean, readable format; more than 85 pictures of the authors and illustrators as well as some of their better-known works; and an index of 500 book titles. Appendixes contain a list of children's award and honor books for the authors and illustrators included, with all Coretta Scott King Award recipients given, and a useful list of Black children's publishers' series. School districts, school and public libraries, and children's literature collections should all have this useful biography reference tool. [R: Choice, Sept 92, p. 90] – **Carol Truett**

Handbooks and Yearbooks

1140. Ammon, Bette D., and Gale W. Sherman. **Handbook for the Newbery Medal and Honor Books, 1980-1989.** Hagerstown, Md., Alleyside Press/Freline, 1991. 274p. index. $19.95pa. ISBN 0-913853-15-1.

Intended to assist "librarians, teachers, and other readers who are involved in children's literature and interested in promoting lifelong reading habits" (p. xi), this handbook briefly describes information to guide such efforts. Part 1 covers Newbery's life and contributions, a history of the Medal, the voting process, and strategies for promoting reading. In part 2, terms used by the authors are defined.

The guides to 36 Medal and Honor books includes bibliographic information, paperback editions, genre, theme, readability and interest level, excerpts from reviews, author/illustrator information, plot summary, read-aloud guide for two selections from the book, booktalk ideas, curriculum implementation ideas, books of similar interest, and other books by author/illustrator. This brief information can serve as a starting point for presenting the titles. The appendixes include works used by the authors; a complete list of Newbery and Honor books, 1922-1989; and addresses for additional resource materials (audiovisual materials). The indexes are by author/illustrator/title and subject.

Users unfamiliar with the books will want to read them before implementing these ideas. Individuals who want to refer to related titles ("of interest" or "by author/illustrator") will need to turn to other sources for information about those works. – **Phyllis J. Van Orden**

1141. **Children's Literature Review: Excerpts from Reviews, Criticism, and Commentary on Books for Children and Young People. Volume 25.** Gerard J. Senick and Sharon R. Gunton, eds. Detroit, Gale, 1991. 277p. illus. index. $95.00. LC 76-643301. ISBN 0-8103-4649-4. ISSN 0362-4145.

The latest volume of this standard children's literature reference source competently continues the series aim of providing permanent access to the growing body of critical material on children's literature and its authors and illustrators. International in scope, the series includes authors and illustrators, both living and dead, who have created in a variety of children's literature genres; the current volume highlights 16 individuals in 15 entries. (The husband-and-wife writing team of Alvin and Virginia Silverstein is covered in a single entry.)

Entries are arranged alphabetically by author and include the author's dates; a portrait (if available); genres; major works; and an introductory discussion of the author's themes, style, and other relevant information. References to pertinent entries in Gale's other literary series are also listed. This prefatory section is followed by the criticism. The critical material is of three types: author commentary (when available), general commentary (when available), and individual title commentary. The author commentary features material written by the author or an interviewer; the general commentary consists of critical excerpts from articles that discuss more than one work by the author; and the single title commentary includes excerpts from critical reviews of individual works. Items within each title section are arranged chronologically by publication date. A complete bibliographic citation is given for each excerpt. Illustrations, when available and appropriate, are scattered throughout the entry.

Introduced by an explanatory preface and acknowledgments section, this work is concluded by cumulative indexes to authors, nationalities, and titles. The author index includes references to relevant articles in Gale's other literary series. Well arranged, readable, and filled with useful (often scattered) information, this series will be helpful in public libraries with a large juvenile clientele. It should be standard in all academic library reference collections that support programs in children's literature.

—**Kristin Ramsdell**

1142. McElmeel, Sharron L. **Bookpeople: A Multicultural Album.** Englewood, Colo., Libraries Unlimited, 1992. 170p. illus. index. $23.50pa. PN497.M34. 809'.89282. LC 92-13252. ISBN 0-87287-953-4.

Spotlighting 15 children's book authors and illustrators who deal with multicultural concerns, this work offers suggestions to teachers and media specialists who want to develop a multicultural focus in their schools. Biographical sketches and photographs of authors or illustrators are given, and their works are introduced. Discussion questions to be used with the books are suggested, and related titles by other authors are listed and annotated. Among the artists included are Mitsumasa Anno, Donald Crews, Mem Fox, Paul Goble, Jamake Highwater, Nicholasa Mohr, and Laurence Yep. Individuals selected are either members of a minority culture (whether or not their books are about that culture) or have written or illustrated books about such a culture. This broad scope has enabled McElmeel to include artists who will appeal to children at various grade levels. The suggestions for further reading and the discussion questions are appropriate for a wide range of children and should spark interest in the books. To accompany a reading of Ashley Bryan's *All Night, All Day*, for example, children are encouraged to illustrate one of the spirituals included; for Mem Fox's *Night Noises*, children are asked to interview their grandmother or grandfather and write down some of the memories shared. Imaginative teachers and media specialists will be able to build on the suggestions presented here. *Bookpeople* will be a valuable addition to both classrooms and media centers.—**Adele M. Fasick**

1143. Snodgrass, Mary Ellen. **Characters from Young Adult Literature.** Englewood, Colo., Libraries Unlimited, 1991. 229p. index. $27.00. Z1037.A1S6. 028.5'5. LC 90-20844. ISBN 0-87287-883-X.

Seventy-one titles in English are described in this work; they are mostly fiction, but some plays, biographies, novels, and nonfiction are included. The selection is fairly standard fare, although some attempt has been made to represent more than just male Caucasian voices and to cover time from the sixteenth to the late twentieth centuries. Each entry gives the date of the work, the name and dates of the author, the genre, the settings, and a plot synopsis. Major and minor characters are then described, both in appearance and behavior. Some of the descriptions are easier to follow if one already knows the story, but that is in keeping with the intent of the work as an aid to memory rather than as a substitute for reading the book. Author and character indexes are included, the latter showing some of the usual difficulties of indexing (e.g., all the aunts appear under "Aunt" instead of under their names; Frodo Baggins is under "Frodo," while Bilbo Baggins is under "Baggins"). Snodgrass means to be prescriptive as well as descriptive; she views her selection of titles as "a detailed listing of what young people are reading or should be reading." While some might take issue with a few of her omissions, this could nonetheless be a useful work for librarians and teachers of junior and senior high school students. [R: BL, 1 Jan 92, p. 839; RBB, 1 Jan 92, p. 847; SLJ, May 92, p. 30; SLMQ. Fall 92, p. 74]

—**Marilyn R. Pukkila**

Indexes

1144. **Biographical Index to Children's and Young Adult Authors and Illustrators.** March 1992 ed. By David V. Loertscher. Castle Rock, Colo., Hi Willow Research and Publishing; distr., Englewood, Colo., Libraries Unlimited, 1992. 277p. $45.00 looseleaf w/binder. ISBN 0-931510-40-6.

This work represents one of the best core reference purchases of the year. It furnishes academic, school, and public librarians with a treasure trove of biographical information on not only children's and young adult authors and illustrators but also authors of adult material read by secondary school students. In addition, the work includes cartoonists and combination print and media professionals such as Walt Disney and Jim Henson.

The index is easy to use. Beginning with an integrated alphabetical index of individuals, each entry contains at least one reference to a particular biographical source. The user simply records the titles by each number and retrieves those sources within a local library or library network.

Of the many positive features of this index, the first is the large number of individuals cited. More than 6,930 writers, illustrators, and others are listed and linked to at least one of 1,577 autobiographical, collective biographical, biographical, or nonprint biographical sources. Created as a spinoff from *State-by-State Guide to Children's and Young Adult Authors and Illustrators* (see ARBA 92, entry 1130), this work has expanded its scope to cover international authors. Librarians who desire biographical information for multicultural projects will find this facet of the index an excellent resource. A second positive aspect of this work concerns its broad series coverage. The contents of such standard biographical series as Gale's Something about the Author and H. W. Wilson's Current Biography are cited.

The last and most important feature of this work relates to continuous updating. Produced by computer, the index is easily revised. Loertscher promises that updating will be completed more frequently than annual and that a library's local holdings data, if recorded in their biographical index, can be incorporated into each succeeding update. A toll-free call is all that is needed to confirm the edition currently for sale. Librarians who need this type of information should consider this flexible, outstanding reference a mandatory acquisition.—**Kathleen W. Craver**

1145. **Children's Book Review Index: Volume 16, 1990.** Neil E. Walker and Beverly Baer, eds. Detroit, Gale, 1991. 694p. $99.00. LC 75-27408. ISBN 0-8103-6899-4. ISSN 0147-5681.

This reference book is efficient and functional. It provides the user with sources for a multitude of reviews about children's books, drawn from *Book Review Index* (BRI) (see ARBA 90, entry 70). It uses a mere 13 pages to introduce and explain the use of the book and provide basic information for the various publications indexed. The heart of this book consists of author, illustrator, and title indexes. It is curious that the author section is neither marked visually, as are the other sections, nor identified in the table of contents; the first-time user may not assume that "Children's Book Review Index" is the author section. But this is a minor point. The index is invaluable for anyone interested in discovering what the critics have to say about children's books.—**Suzanne I. Barchers**

DRAMA

1146. Davis, Gwenn, and Beverly A. Joyce, comps. **Drama by Women to 1900: A Bibliography of American and British Writers.** Toronto and Buffalo, N.Y., University of Toronto Press, 1992. 189p. index. (Bibliographies of Writings by American and British Women to 1900, v.3). $100.00. 016.822008'09287. ISBN 0-8020-2797-0.

This volume is the third in a series of bibliographies covering literary writings by British and American women prior to the twentieth century. Volume 1 covered diaries, travel logs, and other personal writings (see ARBA 90, entry 855), while volume 2 was devoted to poetry (see ARBA 92, entry 1245). Defining drama broadly to encompass such forms as dramatic poems, recitations, pageants, and tableaux, the compilers identify plays by women that were published, produced, or written before 1900. In her excellent introduction, Davis provides a historical overview of women dramatists during this period and discusses various patterns that emerge from a statistical analysis of these playwrights and their works.

Based on citations culled from national bibliographies, specialized bibliographies of drama, and the OCLC (Online Computer Library Center) database, the 2,828 numbered entries are arranged alphabetically by author, each identified by nationality and dates or century. In addition to standard bibliographic information, entries note the sources in which each play was cited and frequently provide additional information, such as type of drama, alternate titles, and place and date of the first production. A subject index includes entries for dramatic or musical forms (e.g., masque, operetta) and for topics (e.g., French Revolution, temperance). Other useful features include an appendix that categorizes playwrights by broad chronological periods, a list of dramatists who were also actresses or theater managers, and an index of writers whose works were adapted or translated by the women in this bibliography. Unfortunately, there is no title index.

The amazing number and diversity of literary writings by women between 1475 and 1900 becomes increasingly evident with the appearance of each volume in this series. Both collectively and individually these bibliographies make an invaluable contribution to the study of women and literature; they are particularly appropriate for large academic or research libraries. [R: Choice, Nov 92, p. 440]

—Marie Ellis

FICTION

General Works

1147. Rosenberg, Betty, and Diana Tixier Herald. **Genreflecting: A Guide to Reading Interests in Genre Fiction.** 3d ed. Englewood, Colo., Libraries Unlimited, 1991. 345p. index. $35.00. PS374. P63R67. 016.813009. LC 91-28074. ISBN 0-87287-930-5.

The 3d edition of this outstanding guide to genre fiction is an indispensable tool to any high school or public librarian whose responsibilities include reading guidance or acquisitions. Despite a hodgepodge appearance, it contains a wealth of information about authors, titles, themes, and topics related to the western, thriller, romance, science fiction, fantasy, and horror genres.

The introduction provides an intellectual defense of genre fiction, a description of its essential characteristics, and annotations of various journals that regularly review this fiction. It also includes a general organizational structure for the book and a caveat that the guide is not a comprehensive bibliography of either authors or titles. The criteria for citing a particular author's works include their quantity, popularity, and availability in print. Chapter 1, entitled "The Common Reader, Libraries, and Publishing," is a fascinating account of the historical necessity for genre fiction and its soothing effects on the reader's humdrum existence. Included is a bibliographical essay that cites various histories and justifications for purchasing genre fiction by public libraries. The remaining chapters are devoted to describing the themes, types, and topics of westerns, thrillers, romances, science fiction, fantasy, and horror. Within thrillers, for example, are types of detective stories and various detectives classed by geographic area and occupation. The latter might be a doctor or lawyer and, within that class, one who solves crimes primarily in the Orient. This section is further subdivided into stories that feature a specific locale or topic, such as locked-room, English-country-house, or sports mysteries. Under the topic category are lists of biographies of fictional detectives, stories, anthologies, additional bibliographies, criticism, encyclopedias, films, magazines, writers' manuals, associations and conventions, publishers, and book clubs.

Such specialized access is the best aspect of this guide. It leads the user to additional areas of genre fiction and caters to a genre fiction fan's narrow field of interest. Public and secondary school librarians who are unfamiliar with certain types of genre fiction, such as westerns and romances, can provide a reader with a tailor-made list of similar "Wagons West and Early Settlement" books or period romances or use this guide for acquiring titles in a requested genre. This guide is a recommended purchase even if a library owns the previous two editions. [R: RBB, July 92, p. 1960]—**Kathleen W. Craver**

1148. Seymour-Smith, Martin. **Dictionary of Fictional Characters.** rev. ed. Boston, The Writer, 1991. 598p. $17.95pa. PN56.4.S49. 820'.3. LC 92-5025. ISBN 0-87116-166-4.

Some 50,000 characters appear in this book. Listed with each character's name are the author, the title of the work from which it came, and the names and relationships of other characters in the book. Seymour-Smith also provides an index by author and title of the works included.

This edition is an update of two earlier ones: William Freeman's original 1963 edition, and its 1973 revision by Fred Urquhart (see ARBA 75, entry 1326). Seymour-Smith has extensively revised both, restoring some of the material that Urquhart deleted and dropping some of Freeman's entries and some of Urquhart's additions. He has also added new works, more works by women and Commonwealth authors, and more American fiction, thus making this book a useful companion to the earlier editions.

Some inconsistency is found in the appendix. Seymour-Smith offers explanations of terms he says he uses in his annotations, such as *realism, naturalism*, and *saved character*. A fairly thorough examination of the text found no uses of these terms outside the appendix. Even those characters or authors used in the appendix as examples of a particular term are not so characterized in the annotations. For example, Mrs. Moore of E. M. Forster's *A Passage to India* is described as a "saved character" in the appendix's discussion of that term, but the annotation to Mrs. Moore does not include this term. Nor are various Thomas Hardy characters (an author mentioned in the appendix as being a "provincial" or regional author) labeled as such. The appendix descriptions are interesting but do not seem to relate to the main body of the work. [R: RBB, Aug 92, pp. 2035-36]—**Terry Ann Mood**

1149. Whissen, Thomas Reed. **Classic Cult Fiction: A Companion to Popular Cult Literature.** Westport, Conn., Greenwood Press, 1992. 319p. index. $65.00. PN3340.W48. 809.3. LC 91-25723. ISBN 0-313-26550-X.

The 50 novels that comprise this study are works that have achieved a cult following, not trivial writing devoid of literary merit that somehow achieved success. Whissen clearly distinguishes between his subject—good to great literature—and what cult or occult literature can signify to some readers. Those novels included have been judiciously selected and cover a wide spectrum of genres. *The Great Gatsby* follows *Frankenstein* and precedes *The Hitchhiker's Guide to the Galaxy*. These are mainstream books, not simply offbeat or dissident literature. Of the 50, just 4 were written before 1900 (e.g., Goethe's *The Sorrows of Young Werther*). The critiques are not of the Magill type (long on plot and characterization, short on meaning and societal impact). In fact, the reader must be fairly familiar with each fictional work to keep up with Whissen. The critiques average five pages in length with a brief bibliography appended. Whissen is a thorough critic who knows the material and can find new interest in the classics. As insightful as the critiques are, the best part of the study appears in the introduction when Whissen sets forth the components of cult literature. After digesting this, the reader has a firmer grasp of what has enshrined a particular book and what made possible the enshrinement. Not a plot summary source, this work is more appropriate for the stacks. Highly recommended for all literary history and U.S. history collections. [R: RBB, 1 June 92, p. 1773]—**Bill Bailey**

Crime and Mystery

1150. Adey, Robert. **Locked Room Murders and Other Impossible Crimes: A Comprehensive Bibliography.** rev. ed. Minneapolis, Minn., Crossover Press, 1991. 411p. $45.00. ISBN 0-9628870-0-5.

The main part of this work gives basic information about each of 2,019 stories, arranged alphabetically by author (or pseudonym). Included in every entry are title; type (novel, novelette, or short story); first publication in the United States, United Kingdom, or other country; variant title; publisher; date; reference to source; name of detective; and a terse description of the nature of the problem (e.g., "Death by fright in a locked room"). Another section gives for each title a brief description of the solution (e.g., "Fear caused by deadly snake"). Introducing these works is a 32-page, well-written bibliographic essay that is generally chronological. There is no index; one by title would be useful. A check of a sample of the information suggests accuracy, except for one of the solutions. Adey obviously loved his task, and 73 other people are given credit for providing "information and encouragement." This interesting presentation is recommended for collections where any of the users are addicted to mysteries. [R: Choice, May 92, p. 1363; WLB, Jan 92, p. 113]—**Robert N. Broadus**

1151. Bailey, Frankie Y. **Out of the Woodpile: Black Characters in Crime and Detective Fiction.** Westport, Conn., Greenwood Press, 1991. 188p. index. (Contributions to the Study of Popular Culture, no.27). $42.95. PS374.D4B34. 813'.0872093520396073. LC 90-45804. ISBN 0-313-26671-9.

Bailey presents a well-written, sometimes uncomfortable, honest look at the Black character in British and American mystery and detective fiction. These characters are often embarrassingly stereotypical. Bailey has researched her topic thoroughly and brings insights and perceptions from her background in criminal justice, an aspect that makes this work even more valuable as a reliable source of information.

Covering several different approaches to the mystery genre, the book is divided into three chapters. The first explores the characterizations found in the fiction of Edgar Allan Poe's era and ends with the pre-World War II era of Rex Stout. Chapter 2, titled "Urban Blues," explores the Black character in the urban environment through stories from authors such as Dashiell Hammett and Richard Wright. The last chapter explores the assimilation of Black women and detectives into the mainstream of modern detective fiction. Sara Paretsky and John D. Ball are among those examined in this section.

The book is rounded out by the proceedings of a symposium conducted by Bailey in which she contacted 14 mystery and detective fiction writers, asking them each the same set of questions concerning their views on creating Black characters. Their comments are included in the book. Also provided is an extensive bibliography on the image of Blacks in books, films, and television. This work is highly recommended.—**Christine E. Thompson**

1152. Mackler, Tasha. **Murder ... by Category: A Subject Guide to Mystery Fiction.** Metuchen, N.J., Scarecrow, 1991. 470p. index. $52.50. Z2014.F4M34. 016.823'087208. LC 91-37638. ISBN 0-8108-2463-9.

This is a compilation of annotated mysteries written between 1985 and 1991 and arranged according to their subject matter (e.g., academics, accidents). For each subject category there is a generalized description of what it entails. For example, under academics is an annotation which explains that a few of the "newer mystery writers" are university professors. Each book includes author, title, date, place of publication, and any other category that is assigned to it. The best part of this work is the synopsis of the crime or mystery listed. It mentions the main character (usually the detective) and some of the other players. British women mystery writers and female detectives (their names, professions, and the authors who created them) are also given. A thorough list of reference books on murder and mystery includes a few bibliographies on crime that cover 1749-1980. The last part of this book is the author index.

Murder is well organized, well documented, and unusual for its synopses of the mysteries and crimes. Highly recommended to all libraries and individuals. [R: Choice, June 92, p. 1522; LJ, 1 Feb 92, p. 80; RBB, 1 Mar 92, p. 1308; RQ, Fall 92, p. 118; WLB, May 92, p. 128]—**Lise Rasmussen**

1153. **Twentieth-century Crime and Mystery Writers.** 3d ed. Lesley Henderson, ed. Chicago, St. James; distr., Detroit, Gale, 1991. 1294p. $115.00. 823.0872. LC 90-63662. ISBN 1-55862-031-1.

This edition is bigger and longer (by 200 pages) than its predecessor (see ARBA 86, entry 1123), and sports a larger, bolder typeface, sturdier binding, and a new editor and publisher. As in the previous edition, the format remains the same: brief biographies of more than 700 writers, followed by a bibliography of books, short stories, plays, screenplays, manuscript collections, theatrical and recording activities, and works about the author. Many of the signed critical essays are quite extensive, and, whenever possible, entries include comments by the author. Where appropriate, entries have been revised and updated through 1990. Nineteenth-century and foreign-language authors are still separated from the main section. The title index also includes serious characters. While more than 100 new authors, such as Tom Clancy, Sara Paretsky, and Scott Turow, have been added, some 117 writers, among them Kingsly Amis, Ray Bradbury, and Bram Stoker, have been dropped.

The larger size and wider columns make this edition easy to use and read. The commentaries by and about the authors and their works remain a strong point. Libraries that need thorough, up-to-date coverage of this widely read genre should consider purchase.—**Joy Hastings**

Science Fiction, Fantasy, and Horror

1154. Aldiss, Margaret. **The Work of Brian W. Aldiss: An Annotated Bibliography & Guide.** San Bernardino, Calif., Borgo Press, 1992. 360p. illus. index. (Bibliographies of Modern Authors, no.9). $39.00; $29.00pa. Z8025.45.A4. 016.823'914. ISBN 0-89370-388-5; 0-89370-488-1pa.

Brian Aldiss is one of the most influential and prolific writers in the science fiction field. He has written many novels and stories, including *Barefoot in the Head*, *Helliconia Spring*, and *Frankenstein Unbound*, as well as *Billion Year Spree*, a history of science fiction (later revised as *Trillion Year Spree*). He has won the Hugo, Nebula, and Campbell awards and has also been important as an editor and a critic. Because this bibliography of his work was prepared by his wife and annotated by him, it can safely be called authoritative. An update of two earlier guides edited by Margaret Aldiss, it is the latest in the Borgo Press series of Bibliographies of Modern Authors. Although Margaret Aldiss believes she may have missed some foreign-language translations or reviews—and has, in fact, omitted some minor dramatic performances at conventions—she has produced a detailed listing of her husband's novels, stories, and nonfiction articles, including such trivia as his Library of Congress number. Entries in each category are listed chronologically, and book entries include a brief description of the contents and a list of secondary sources and reviews. Other chapters contain critical quotations (mostly favorable), an autobiographical essay, and indexes. There are fewer typographical errors, and the print is better than in earlier Borgo Press editions. Recommended for libraries with substantial science fiction collections.

—**Lynn F. Williams**

1155. Burgess, Michael. **Reference Guide to Science Fiction, Fantasy, and Horror.** Englewood, Colo., Libraries Unlimited, 1992. 403p. index. (Reference Sources in the Humanities Series). $45.00. Z5917.S36B87. 016.8093'876. LC 91-44853. ISBN 0-87287-611-X.

Fans and scholars alike will find this guide to science fiction, fantasy, and horror literature extremely useful. Burgess has attempted to include all major, and most of the minor, reference books for these three related genres published through early 1992. The 551 entries include complete bibliographical data for every work cited; a description of the organization, content, and purpose of each work; and an evaluation of how well authors have met their stated objectives. Burgess's evaluations will especially help reference and collection development librarians, as he usually comments on a title's appropriateness to specific types of libraries. He is also careful to balance negative with positive comments wherever possible and to compare each title to similar ones.

The volume is arranged by types of tools: encyclopedias and dictionaries; atlases and gazetteers; yearbooks, annuals, and almanacs; biographical and literary directories; magazine and anthology indexes; and bibliographies, among others. A scope note at the head of each section explains what is included. Bibliographies are subdivided into six categories: general, national, subject, publisher, author, and artist. Among the subject bibliographies are topics such as alternate histories, Atlantis, drugs, future war fiction, sexuality, Star Wars fiction, vampire fiction, and women writers. Individual author bibliographies comprise about 30 percent of the entire volume and range from Brian Aldiss to Roger Zelazny. General author bibliographies are also cited. Miscellaneous categories include character dictionaries, film/television catalogs, and price lists for collectors. As an added feature, Burgess offers lists of core reference collections for academic, public, and personal research libraries.

It would seem that Burgess has achieved his primary goal of providing an evenhanded, fair, and consistent guide for the uninitiated. His closest rival is Neil Barron, who has edited three separate guides: *Anatomy of Wonder* (see ARBA 89, entry 1042), *Fantasy Literature* (see ARBA 90, entry 1137), and *Horror Literature* (see ARBA 90, entry 1138). While Barron's compilations remain essential for most libraries, Burgess's work, being a one-person effort, is more consistent in its language and commentary than Barron's separate titles, which use multiple contributors.

This guide should serve for quite a while as the standard one-volume source to reference books on this complementary literature. Frequent revisions would certainly be welcome. [R: Choice, Dec 92, pp. 597-98; RBB, 15 Nov 92, p. 628] — **Gary D. Barber**

1156. Kies, Cosette. **Supernatural Fiction for Teens: More Than 1300 Good Paperbacks to Read for Wondermet, Fear, and Fun.** 2d ed. Englewood, Colo., Libraries Unlimited, 1992. 267p. index. $25.00pa. Z1037.K485. 016.80883'937. LC 91-45469. ISBN 0-87287-940-2.

Updating and expanding *Supernatural Fiction for Teens: 500 Good Paperbacks to Read for Wonderment, Fear, and Fun* (see ARBA 88, entry 1130), this nicely done 2d edition includes more than twice as many books that focus on the supernatural. They have been chosen on the basis of their probable appeal to young adults and their current availability in paperback. As in the first edition, selected works must fall into three broad categories: parapsychology and psychic phenomena, tales and legends with strong magical and occult elements, or horror in the supernatural gothic tradition. Pure fantasy (unless strongly based on traditional mythological or occult themes) and science fiction are not included, nor are stories that employ animal personification, alternative worlds, swords and sorcery, or futuristic scenarios.

Prefaced by an introductory section that also includes a brief list of additional reference sources to the genre, the bibliography is divided into two parts: one lists individual titles, the other, anthologies. Each section is arranged alphabetically by author or editor, with entries numbered consecutively throughout the bibliography. In addition to basic citation information, each entry includes pagination; ISBN; a brief annotation; subject headings; and when applicable, original publication information, other works by the author, and movie version information. Each entry also has a letter code that indicates whether the work was written originally for teens, for younger teens, or for adults, or is now considered a classic. The work is concluded by a list of books in series; a glossary of subject headings; and indexes of movies, titles, and subjects.

Clearly organized, attractively formatted, and containing a nicely eclectic listing of titles in a genre that has long been a favorite of young adults, this bibliography will be used (and enjoyed) by librarians, teachers, parents, and readers. It should be both a collection development tool and a reference source in any library that serves a young adult clientele. [R: RBB, 1 Sept 92. p. 91] — **Kristin Ramsdell**

1157. **Reginald's Science Fiction and Fantasy Awards: A Comprehensive Guide to the Awards and Their Winners.** 2d ed. By Daryl F. Mallett and Robert Reginald. San Bernadino, Calif., Borgo Press, 1991. 248p. index. (Borgo Literary Guides, no.1). $30.00; $20.00pa. P96.S34R4. 808.83'876'079. LC 90-15074. ISBN 0-89370-826-7; 0-89370-926-3pa.

This very complete work covers major and minor science fiction, fantasy, and horror awards, both English-language and foreign. The authors start at the inception of each award and list the works that have received each one in chronological order. They include all the categories of the award, such as professional editors, movies, and best fanzine.

The awards are arranged into two categories — English and foreign — and then alphabetically by name. There is a brief description of the award before the winners are listed, providing a little of the award's history. The appendixes include major conventions, an author index, and statistical tables on the most outstanding winners of each award. (Unfortunately, the tables are rather hard to read and use.) There is also an index of awards. This is a useful work for libraries that need a good bibliography of major science fiction, fantasy, and horror works, especially for those trying to complete their collection of classic works. [R: Choice, Sept 92, p. 90; LJ, 1 Mar 92, p. 84; RBB, 1 May 92, p. 1637; WLB, May 92, p. 129] — **Deborah D. Hollis**

1158. **Science Fiction & Fantasy Book Review Annual 1990.** Robert A. Collins, Robert Latham, and Catherine Fischer, eds. Westport, Conn., Greenwood Press, 1991. 711p. index. $75.00. LC 89-642022. ISBN 0-313-28150-5. ISSN 1040-192X.

It has never been easy to define or distinguish the literary domains of "science fiction" (SF), "fantasy," and "horror fiction." Despite the hazy boundaries, however, this literary genre (if one permits the inclusive singular) attracts new readers every year. This reviewing annual, first published in 1988, treats SF, horror, and fantasy together, not only evaluating and reviewing but even rank ordering the year's contributions. Despite the conspicuous 1990 in the title, be advised that this 1991 work takes for its scope the combined output of the year 1989. The editors, together with 6 contributing colleagues, analyze 1989's work in SF, fantasy, and horror and come forth with more than 500 reviews by appropriate subject specialists, beginning with a survey of the year in fiction in each of the three areas (with understandable blurring and overlapping among categories). The reviews are considerably longer, more dissertative, and more emotional than those of such traditional reviewing sources as *Library Journal, School Library Journal,* and *Booklist.*

Arrangement is alphabetical, with separate listings for adult and young adult fiction and nonfiction. Recommended reading lists in each category and a comprehensive title index round out the work. The editors and their contributors are not shy or reticent about expressing their views. When a reviewer thinks a book poorly written, exploitive, or cliche-ridden, the reader is flatly told to give it a miss, and there may even be criticism of author and publisher for foisting an inferior product off on the reading public. This series is highly recommended because of the ongoing popularity of the three types of literature and the fine, strong, opinionated writing of experts in the literary fields. — **Bruce A. Shuman**

1159. Watson, Noelle, and Paul E. Schellinger. **Twentieth-Century Science-Fiction Writers.** 3d ed. Chicago, St. James Press, 1991. 1016p. $123.00. 823.087609. ISBN 1-55862-111-3.

This massive tome is the 3d edition of a reference book previously edited by Curtis C. Smith (whose work goes unaccountably unmentioned in the introduction). Covering more than 600 English-language science fiction writers, with an appendix on another 38 foreign-language writers, this is by far the most inclusive biocritical guide to the field. It should not be confused with the much less useful *Twentieth-Century American Science-Fiction Writers* (see ARBA 82, entry 1301) or *Reader's Guide to Twentieth-Century Science Fiction* (see ARBA 90, entry 1108). It includes not only well-known writers but also minor figures who have written only one or two science fiction books.

Each entry begins with a brief biography that is followed by chronological lists of science fiction novels and short stories, other publications, bibliographies, and critical studies. Pseudonyms are included, as are non-science fiction works. The most substantial section contains a critical discussion of the author's work, often introduced by a brief commentary supplied by living authors. The length varies greatly and is not always in proportion to the importance of the writer. There is also a reading list of critical works, a list of the writers, and an index of book titles.

Many of the 166 contributors to this volume are well-known professionals in the science fiction field. As is inevitable with so many different critics, the entries are uneven and sometimes unreasonably laudatory, but are on the whole well written and authoritative. However, while the book is more carefully edited than the previous editions, there are many errors in the bibliographical material. For example, two of C. J. Cherryh's short story collections are mislabeled. Despite its faults, this is still the most useful and up-to-date guide to science fiction writers and their work. Most large and medium-sized libraries will want it. — **Lynn F. Williams**

Short Story

1160. Hooper, Brad. **Short Story Writers and Their Work: A Guide to the Best.** 2d ed. Chicago, American Library Association, 1992. 70p. index. $15.00pa. PN3373.H6. 809.3'1. LC 92-11944. ISBN 0-8389-0587-0.

Much as a short story tries to capture the essence of a relationship or an event in its brief space, the entries in this book try to convey the essence of each author's work. The entries are not the specific critiques of stories found in a work such as *Contemporary Authors*. Rather, they are Hooper's overall encapsulated assessment of the stories and of the author's influence on literature. Nor is the coverage as broad as in the more conventional sources, with only some 100 authors listed.

This updated edition of the earlier *Short Story Writers* (see ARBA 88, entry 1045) is divided into four sections: classic authors, writers working today, various genres of short story (mystery, science fiction, and ghost), and anthologies (an extremely short list). The 2d edition does reflect more cultural diversity than did the first, including more women authors and more authors from non-United States and European traditions. However, objections made about the first edition still hold true here: the choice of authors strikes one as arbitrary, and the number included and the annotations are too sparse to be of use to researchers. This is an interesting work to dip into, but it is not valuable as a reference work.—**Terry Ann Mood**

1161. **Twentieth-Century Short Story Explication: An Index to the Third Edition and Its Five Supplements 1961-1991.** Warren S. Walker and Barbara K. Walker, eds. Hamden, Conn., Shoe String Press, 1992. 254p. $47.50. Z5917.S5W332. 016.8093'1. LC 91-9856. ISBN 0-208-02320-8.

This index is intended to simplify the use of the entire run of *Twentieth-Century Short Story Explication*, from 1961 to 1991. The volumes covered are the 3d edition (1977), which was cumulative, and its five supplements (1980, 1984, 1987, 1989, and 1991). Thus, the index lists all citations compiled during the last 30 years for any given short story published between 1800 and 1988; the explications included are those published since 1900. While there is no restriction on the language of the short story, the explications are limited to those that appeared in major Western European languages. Drawn from books, essays, and journal articles, they cover 16,691 stories by 2,304 authors. The preface lists the top 20 authors by number of short stories explicated (Rudyard Kipling takes top honors) and the 20 short stories that received the greatest number of explications (Joseph Conrad's "Heart of Darkness" wins handily).

The format is simplicity itself. Authors are listed alphabetically (although they appear, irksomely, in forename/surname order). Under each author appears an alphabetical list of short stories, with citations to the appropriate volume and page numbers in the main volumes, where a full list of the actual bibliographical citations is found. In addition to being a useful and timesaving index to *Twentieth-Century Short Story Explication*, this volume is a reference tool in its own right: the reader can see at a glance which authors and stories have received the most critical attention over the length of this century.
—**Jeffrey R. Luttrell**

NATIONAL LITERATURE

American Literature

General Works

1162. **Bibliography of American Literature. Volume 9: Edward Noyes Westcott to Elinor Wylie.** Jacob Blank, comp. New Haven, Conn., Yale University Press, 1991. 496p. $80.00. LC 54-5283. ISBN 0-300-05141-7.

After volume 8 of this notable reference work was published (see ARBA 91, entry 1144) and 37 years after volume 1 appeared, volume 9 concludes the set. As is outlined in the preface in volume 1, the series is a bibliography of some 300 writers from the beginning of the Federal period to the end of 1930, who were popular in their own time but are not necessarily recognized today as major writers.

Among the 14 authors covered in volume 9 (beginning with Edward Noyes Westcott and ending with Elinor Wylie) are James Abbott McNeill Whistler, Walt Whitman, and John Greenleaf Whittier. Material for each author is listed chronologically within the following categories: first editions of books, pamphlets, and any other book that contains the first appearance of a work; revised editions; and selected biographical and bibliographical references. Later editions, translations, periodical and newspaper publications, and nonliterary works are generally excluded. Bibliographical references for each primary work include title, imprint, pagination, signature collation, information on the binding, and copyright date. Many of the entries include library location symbols.

A work of meticulous literary scholarship, this noted bibliography belongs in any library that owns the first eight volumes. Although it is not an essential purchase, other libraries with major literature holdings may wish to purchase the entire set.—**Jack Bales**

1163. Chielens, Edward E., ed. **American Literary Magazines: The Twentieth Century.** Westport, Conn., Greenwood Press, 1992. 474p. index. (Historical Guides to the World's Periodicals and Newspapers). $89.50. Z1231.P45A44. 016.8108'005. LC 91-30603. ISBN 0-313-23986-X.

This is the second of a two-volume set that covers the history of prominent literary magazines in the United States. The first volume, which dealt with the eighteenth and nineteenth centuries, was published in 1986 (see ARBA 87, entry 1126). As did the first volume, this one focuses on the most famous of the "little" literary magazines, so-called because they began with small budgets and circulation and may have been short-lived. Some of these magazines, however, such as the *New Yorker*, have continued for many years and have become well known to many people. Others, including the *Smart Set* and the *Kenyon Review*, are no longer published but were the first to showcase authors who later became world famous.

Most of this volume is devoted to 76 alphabetically arranged profiles of these magazines. Each entry, written by various literary scholars, librarians, and editors, is a critical and historical essay that discusses major events in the magazine's history, the editors, and prominent authors published. Entries end with a list of information sources that indicate bibliographies of the magazines, separate indexes (if available), reprint editions, and major library locations. Also included is a capsule publication history of each magazine. Three very useful appendixes include a briefly annotated list of minor literary magazines that are not significant enough to warrant a full profile but are still important enough to be listed in this history; a chronology of social and literary events between 1900 and 1991, which lists these events in one column and important literary magazine events in the adjoining column; and a detailed analysis of 28 major and minor repositories of little magazines in the United States and Canada. This appendix alone is worth the price of the book to scholars who need precise information about the locations of runs of these magazines. Also included is a detailed author, name, and subject index, as well as notes on the 43 contributors. — **David Isaacson**

1164. Magill, Frank N., ed. **Masterpieces of African-American Literature.** New York, HarperCollins, 1992. 593p. index. $40.00. PS163.N5M264. 810.9'896073. LC 92-52542. ISBN 0-06-270066-9.

Magill's latest book features critical summaries of 149 literary works by 96 African-American authors from the eighteenth century to the present. Works include novels, plays, poetry, short stories, biographies, autobiographies, and essays. Among the authors surveyed are Maya Angelou, James Baldwin, Gwendolyn Brooks, Charles Chesnutt, Eldridge Cleaver, W. E. B. Du Bois, Alex Haley, Lorraine Hansberry, Malcolm X, Toni Morrison, Alice Walker, and Richard Wright. The formula seldom varies. The signed summaries feature brief analyses of such stylistic devices as themes, characters, and settings, and each contributor places the studied work in its literary and historical context. Each critical essay is approximately 2,500 words in length. The volume includes author and title indexes.

For many librarians and educators, Magill and his various series of digested literary works are synonymous with *Cliff Notes* and similar study aids on which students rely. Still, if Magill's volumes are used as supplementary research rather than primary reading, they are no worse than similar works that are found in virtually all public and academic libraries. Also, if they introduce students and casual readers to the vitality of world literature, they will have proved useful. — **Jack Bales**

1165. Maxwell, Donald W. **Literature of the Great Lakes Region: An Annotated Bibliography.** Hamden, Conn., Garland, 1991. 485p. index. (Garland Reference Library of the Humanities, v.1252). $34.00. Z1251.G8M39. 016.8108'0977. LC 91-14663. ISBN 0-8240-7027-5.

This bibliography includes citations to 1,707 novels, plays, short story collections, and poetry collections that are set in, or that describe life in, the Great Lakes region. Maxwell has applied the geographic definition of the "Old Northwest," so the work's regional scope is Ohio, Indiana, Illinois, Michigan, Wisconsin, and Minnesota. The citations cover works from the nineteenth century to 1990. Maxwell has used general literature and regional bibliographies, regional-interest publications, and current book review journals to compile this volume. Included are both classics and many so-called minor works that are the literary voice of the Great Lakes region. The entries are arranged by author and include adequate bibliographic information and brief annotations. The author and title indexes are very helpful.

This bibliography is recommended for academic libraries that support programs in social history and regional literature. It will also be of interest to large public libraries that serve the Great Lakes area. [R: RQ, Spring 92, p. 420-21]—**Linda A. Naru**

1166. Zimmerman, Marc. **U.S. Latino Literature: An Essay and Annotated Bibliography.** Chicago, MARCH/Abrazo Press, 1992. 156p. $10.95pa. ISBN 1-877636-01-0.

Zimmerman's book, now in a 2d edition, attempts to bring to the new reader or researcher of U.S. Latino literature an "initial orientation" to the subject. The book takes the form of a critical-historical study of this literature and has lengthy bibliographical annotations distributed among seven categories. Zimmerman opens the volume with a polemical essay that touches on U.S. Latino culture, the current debate on an appropriately inclusive term for this ethnic group, the history and development of Latino literature in the United States, and a review of the models and theories that inform present-day critical approaches to Latino literature. This informative study is followed by bibliographic entries grouped under Chicano literature, U.S. Puerto Rican literature, U.S. Cuban literature, Latino-tending U.S. Latin American writing, Latino children and young adult books, Chicanesque literature, and secondary materials. The entries, annotated with an attention to detail and thoroughness rarely seen in this kind of work, guide the reader in a useful, direct way.

Because U.S. Latino literature has become a prolific, rich, and popular area of interest, Zimmerman's book is particularly welcome as it meets a recognized need. Up-to-date and comprehensive, it provides readers with a sound, authoritative view of this important subject. [R: RBB, 15 June 92, p. 1891]—**Bart Lewis**

Drama

1167. Bzowski, Frances Diodato, comp. **American Women Playwrights, 1900-1930: A Checklist.** Westport, Conn., Greenwood Press, 1992. 420p. (Bibliographies and Indexes in Women's Studies, no.15). $59.50. Z1231.D7B95. 016.812'52099287. LC 92-12301. ISBN 0-313-24238-0.

The reasons for Bzowski's choice of the period surveyed are interesting. The beginning of the twentieth century, she points out, offered women playwrights a unique opportunity: it accepted their right to express themselves at a time when there was a concurrent strong little-theater movement across the country. However, the depression brought women's social freedoms to an end until the women's movement reemerged in the 1970s. (The plays written by women in that period will be the subject of another bibliography.) Given the output of some 12,000 plays by American women during the period, the fact that this bibliography was compiled by one person represents an impressive achievement. Limitations of time and energy, however, have led Bzowski to skimp on certain aspects, notably biographical data on the writers. Also, her vague information that certain plays were "probably published, but not located" is not really helpful without any indication of the evidence on which that judgment was made. Overall, this bibliography maintains the high standard of scholarly thoroughness of the earlier volumes in the series. [R: Choice, Dec 92, p. 598]—**John B. Beston**

1168. Eddleman, Floyd Eugene, comp. **American Drama Criticism. Supplement III to the Second Edition.** Hamden, Conn., Shoe String Press, 1992. 436p. index. (Drama Explication Series). $55.00. Z1231.D7P3. 016.812009. LC 92-3977. ISBN 0-208-02270-8.

In content and format this supplement follows that of its two predecessors (see ARBA 90, entry 1129 and ARBA 85, entry 1066). The scope is limited to United States and Canadian playwrights, although a few European dramatists who lived and worked in the United States or Canada are also included. Under the name of the playwright, articles of a general nature precede articles on specific plays. When known, the year of the premiere is cited. Coverage is neither exhaustive nor critical, and with few exceptions the same sources are surveyed here as in the earlier works. Access is enhanced by convenient indexes of playwrights, titles, and critics and a list of adapted authors and works.

Eddleman notes that this supplement, covering 1988 through 1990, is larger than previous supplements, primarily because of the burgeoning of feminist criticism and multiculturalism. Although the earlier works noted coverage of plays by and about African-, Asian-, and Hispanic-Americans, this one calls attention to Jews, Native Americans, immigrants, gays and lesbians, and women. Users will need to consult the introductory information in the 2d edition and each of its supplements to determine specific differences or changes.

Much of the material on drama as literature can now be retrieved easily on the CD-ROM version of the Modern Language Association (MLA) international bibliography. However, the merit of Eddleman's work is that it combines citations to the drama as a literary work with performance reviews as well as critical works on the playwrights. Libraries holding the 2d edition will want this update.—**Bernice Bergup**

Fiction

1169. Carter, Susanne. **War and Peace through Women's Eyes: A Selective Bibliography of Twentieth-Century American Women's Fiction.** Westport, Conn., Greenwood Press, 1992. 293p. index. (Bibliographies and Indexes in Women's Studies, no.14). $55.00. Z1231.F4C37. 016.813'5080358. LC 91-33399. ISBN 0-313-27771-0.

This is a very thorough bibliography and analysis of novels and short stories with war themes written by U.S. women or women living in this country. Its declared selectivity is presumably explained by the omission of fiction "of a more popular than literary nature" (p. vii). An introduction composed of a scholarly essay on war literature is followed by five chapters, with annotations on World War I, World War II, Vietnam, nuclear war, and war and peace. Each chapter has an analysis of the literature it covers and a bibliography of relevant criticism. Annotations include a critical summary and often excerpts from the work and partial reviews or criticism about the piece or author. Separate author, title, and subject indexes refer to entry numbers.

Every aspect of this bibliography is praiseworthy: it is attractively laid out, easy to use, and excellently annotated. Moreover, while other bibliographies exist on women's war-related writings, this one has the widest scope to date. [R: Choice, July/Aug 92, p. 1652]—**Cathy Seitz Whitaker**

1170. O'Connor, Leo F. **The Protestant Sensibility in the American Novel: An Annotated Bibliography.** Hamden, Conn., Garland, 1992. 201p. index. (Garland Reference Library of the Humanities, v.1082). $28.00. Z1231.F4O28. 016.813009'382. LC 91-38034. ISBN 0-8240-4605-6.

O'Connor has selected 701 American novels from the late eighteenth century to the present that he believes reveal Protestant sensibility. The novels have been rather arbitrarily assigned to seven different classifications: sermon novels (interpreted to mean any message novel, from children's books such as the *Five Little Peppers* to romances such as *Ramona*), historical religious novels, the New England novel, portraits of sects and denominations, social gospel, the Black religious experience, and a sort of catchall entitled "Protestant Sensibility Novels." Although authors are listed alphabetically under each heading, one must frequently look through each section to find where a particular person has been placed. While there is a topical index of almost 350 categories, from abolition to Brigham Young, there is a serious need for an index by author or title.

Many of the novels listed are little known, so the brief annotations are particularly helpful. Practically all major novels are listed, including secular works such as John Updike's *Rabbit Redux* and Ernest Hemingway's *The Sun Also Rises*. A few British writers (e.g., George Whyte-Melville) have also slipped in. There is a valuable list of secondary sources consulted.

O'Connor acknowledges that this volume does not attempt to be definitive, and certainly other compilers might have created a different list. Nevertheless, this bibliography will be helpful to anyone tracing the historical influence of Protestantism on the American novel. [R: Choice, June 92, p. 1526]—**Charlotte Lindgren**

Individual Authors

James Fenimore Cooper

1171. Dyer, Alan Frank, comp. **James Fenimore Cooper: An Annotated Bibliography of Criticism.** Westport, Conn., Greenwood Press, 1991. 293p. index. (Bibliographies and Indexes in American Literature, no.16). $45.00. Z8191.7.D9. 016.813'2. LC 91-27084. ISBN 0-313-27919-5.

Dyer is a librarian "with a special interest in colonial American history." This well-thought-out reference work on an important literary figure deserves space on most academic library shelves. It contains references to works on Cooper published between 1820 and 1990, with a total of 1,943 items, among them reviews, journal articles, newspaper articles and editorials, dissertations, and books. Annotations are descriptive rather than critical.

The arrangement of these items is conducive to ready-reference. Dyer has created broad subject categories subdivided by individual works, and he further distinguishes material contemporary with the author's life from that published after his death. Categories include bibliography, biography, general studies, frontier and Indian novels, literature of the sea, social and political writings, and miscellaneous publications. There are indexes for authors and editors, as well as a subject index. [R: Choice, Apr 92, p. 1206]—**Maureen A. Beck**

Stephen Crane

1172. Dooley, Patrick K. **Stephen Crane: An Annotated Bibliography of Secondary Scholarship.** New York, G. K. Hall, 1992. 321p. index. $40.00. Z8198.2.D66. 813'.4. LC 91-38132. ISBN 0-8161-7265-X.

This bibliography lists and annotates almost 1,900 books, book chapters, and newspaper and magazine articles on the life and work of Stephen Crane. The bibliographical entries cite materials published from 1901 (one year after Crane's death) to 1991. The material is arranged in chapters on biography and general criticism, then subarranged by Crane's major works (*The Red Badge of Courage* and *Tales of Whilomville*) or kinds of writing (e.g., poetry; the "Journalism, Tales and Reports" chapter). Dooley's annotations are generally insightful and authoritative, although some seem ingenuously conversational and a few are cryptic. His philosophical perspective lends depth to the comments on Crane's work and critical analyses of it. He has written introductory remarks to each chapter that are intended as general overviews for "students and beginning scholars." The cited journals and books are readily available in academic or research libraries or through interlibrary loan; they should be accessible to undergraduates as well as to more sophisticated researchers. The volume includes a chronology of Crane's brief life (1871-1900); a list of indexes, bibliographies, and databases searched; journals surveyed; and an author index. Dooley has produced a skillful and thorough bibliographic work that should be acquired by all academic libraries. [R: Choice, Oct 92, p. 271]

—**Linda A. Naru**

William Faulkner

1173. Bassett, John E. **Faulkner in the Eighties: An Annotated Critical Bibliography.** Metuchen, N.J., Scarecrow, 1991. 322p. index. (Scarecrow Author Bibliographies, no.88). $35.00. Z8288.B39. 813'.52. LC 91-31218. ISBN 0-8108-2485-X.

Bringing up to date the listings of Faulkner criticism and scholarship in Bassett's two earlier books, *William Faulkner: An Annotated Checklist of Criticism* (see ARBA 74, entry 1330) and *Faulkner: An Annotated Checklist of Recent Criticism* (see ARBA 85, entry 1071), *Faulkner in the Eighties* charts the course of Faulkner studies in the 1980s by listing more than 100 books and scores of articles and reviews, theses, and dissertations that have appeared during the decade. As Bassett explains, the basic format remains the same, with sections for books; items on individual novels or stories; more general critical, biographical, and bibliographical articles; and other materials, such as reviews of books about Faulkner. Although not included for every citation, the annotations given are very helpful in locating specific sources of information.

More diverse in the 1980s than in any other decade and filled with traditional formalist, thematic, bibliographic, and psychoanalytic studies as well as the newer rhetorical, semiotic, Marxist, deconstructionist, poststructuralist, and even proto-poststructuralist approaches to Faulkner and his world, this bibliographic project is particularly useful to anyone interested in studying William Faulkner, Jefferson and Yoknapatawpha County, and Southern culture. With foreign interest in Faulkner growing every decade, this study also takes on a welcome international significance.

—**Colby H. Kullman**

Ernest Hemingway

1174. Reynolds, Michael. **Hemingway: An Annotated Chronology: An Outline of the Author's Life and Career....** Detroit, Omnigraphics, 1991. 155p. index. (Omni Chronology Series, 1). $48.00. PS3515.E37Z7546. 813'.52. LC 90-24608. ISBN 1-55888-427-0.

   Prepared by the author of an ongoing, multivolume biography of Ernest Hemingway, this work lists and occasionally comments on such events as Hemingway's marriages and divorces, his literary successes and failures, his personal triumphs, and his suicide. As a subject of biography, Hemingway was a movable feast who rarely stayed in one place for very long; in fact, according to Reynolds, Hemingway did some of his best writing on the road. This work reflects well his worldwide movements. Reynolds concentrates on the pre 1940 period of Hemingway's life for the simple reason that he knows that period best, as do most biographers.

   In addition to the introduction, this book also includes a brief bibliography of works by Hemingway and secondary sources used in compiling the chronology. It features a detailed index as well as sketchy maps of Italy, France, Spain and Portugal, and Switzerland (but not Cuba), with no reference to their relation to Hemingway's life.

   "Legendary lives," says Reynolds in his introduction, "are most legendary when they are least encumbered by specific information." But Hemingway's life, even when seen in detail, is as interesting as the myth that the writer created of himself. Libraries with limited biographical resources on Hemingway should find this little volume useful, informative, and even entertaining. But libraries with limited financial resources will probably find the price intimidating. [R: Choice, Sept 92, p. 90]

— Edwin S. Gleaves

Jerzy Kosinski

1175. Cronin, Gloria L., and Blaine H. Hall. **Jerzy Kosinski: An Annotated Bibliography.** Westport, Conn., Greenwood Press, 1991. 104p. index. (Bibliographies and Indexes in American Literature, no.15). $35.00. Z8467.523.C76. 016.813'54. LC 91-21555. ISBN 0-313-27442-8.

   Controversial because of his shocking accounts of depraved human nature, nihilistic critique of American politics and culture, and experimental strategies probing "the fictionality of fiction" and language as "the prison house of perception," Jerzy Kosinski used the avant-garde to underscore the disruption of the bourgeois mentality. Cronin and Hall's annotated bibliography documents the extent of this gifted writer's career and shows that he is just now beginning to receive recognition; the majority of the more than 400 critical articles and reviews about Kosinski and his world in English have been written within the past 10 years.

   Listing primary and secondary sources by and about Kosinski through 1990, this work is a timely tribute to the troubled genius who survived the Holocaust only to commit suicide in 1991. The first section categorizes Kosinski's works under novels, short stories, miscellaneous writings, interviews, articles, books, recordings, and reviews. The second section focuses on secondary sources under headings such as bibliographies and checklists, books and monographs, biographical sources, criticism and reviews, and dissertations. Except for the interviews, the primary sources appear without annotations. Concise and descriptive, the annotations for the secondary sources skillfully present the critical thesis of each work and a brief summary of the argument. This reference tool will be useful to scholars interested in such varied subject areas as post-World War II fiction, the psychology of deviance, modern American politics and culture, black humor, cinematic techniques, the gothic grotesque, and media responsibility. [R: Choice, Jan 92, p. 718] — **Colby H. Kullman**

Louis L'Amour

1176. Hall, Hal W. **The Work of Louis L'Amour: An Annotated Bibliography & Guide.** San Bernadino, Calif., Borgo Press, 1991. 192p. index. (Bibliographies of Modern Authors, no.15). $26.95; $16.95pa. Z8476.5.H34. 016.813'52. LC 88-34678. ISBN 0-8095-0510-X; 0-8095-1510-5pa.

   When Louis L'Amour died in 1988 he had two distinctions as a Western fiction writer: an enormous published output and an inversely puny amount of critical attention. He published 101 books during his lifetime, and all were in print at his death. More than 200 million copies had been sold around the world. Yet most literary reference books are hard-pressed to list 10 studies of his work.

This annotated, descriptive bibliography mostly lists works by L'Amour but includes more secondary sources than this reviewer has found elsewhere. Hall's list of 130 books by L'Amour, which stretches through 1991, includes reprints and foreign editions of the novels as well as autobiographies and other pieces of nonfiction. He includes plot synopses and reviews and indicates if there were any adaptations. Similar detail is brought to the other categories of L'Amour's writings: short fiction (191 items), nonfiction, poetry, audio recordings, and film adaptations. A bibliography of 200 secondary sources includes articles, book chapters, essays, newspaper articles, and ephemera. The book is enhanced by a 1985 interview with L'Amour, a series list of the novels that form the various family sagas, and a subject index. A clean layout adds to this work, which will be of interest to collections of Western fiction and popular culture. — **John P. Schmitt**

Mary McCarthy

1177. Bennett, Joy, and Gabriella Hochmann. **Mary McCarthy: An Annotated Bibliography.** Hamden, Conn., Garland, 1992. 442p. index. (Garland Reference Library of the Humanities, v.1251). $70.00. Z8531.8.B46. 016.8185'209. LC 91-47702. ISBN 0-8240-7028-3.

This is the first bibliography of works by McCarthy since Sherli Evens Goldman's *Mary McCarthy: A Bibliography* (Harcourt, Brace, 1968). Goldman is still useful as a descriptive primary bibliography of first editions in English, but while the Bennett volume does not provide detailed physical descriptions of McCarthy's books, it does include citations to paperback and British editions as well as translations of each of McCarthy's books. In addition, Bennett includes a bibliography of works about McCarthy, while Goldman is restricted to works by her.

Section 1 of Bennett includes separate lists of McCarthy's books, essays, short stories, book reviews, theater and film reviews, translations, letters to the editor, miscellanea, and interviews. Republications are noted, as are revisions. Essay collections include contents notes. Section 2 includes general criticism, book reviews, theses (both master's and Ph.D. dissertations), biographies, and obituaries. General criticism includes major studies confined to McCarthy's work and other substantial studies that include her. Some significant letters to the editor commenting on her work also appear in this section. All named persons and titles are indexed. A separate index lists authors of all secondary works. Annotations are objective rather than evaluative. This book will be essential to scholars and beginning students of McCarthy, both for the comprehensiveness of its primary bibliography and for the usefulness of its selective, briefly annotated secondary bibliography. [R: Choice, Oct 92, p. 268]
— **David Isaacson**

Herman Melville

1178. Hayes, Kevin J., and Hershel Parker. **Checklist of Melville Reviews.** Evanston, Ill., Northwestern University Press, 1991. 157p. index. $34.95. Z8562.58.H394. 813'.3. LC 91-40709. ISBN 0-8101-1028-8.

This new checklist is a revision of the 1975 checklist by Steven Mailloux and Hershel Parker. The compilers have attempted to list "every published study of Melville's contemporary reception," recognizing that some remain undiscovered and others are irretrievably lost. First issues in London and New York of Melville's writings appear in the section on primary works, followed by reviews (written between 1846 and 1876) of each work listed in order of publication. Two 1889 reviews of "John Marr" are also included. Interestingly, *Typee*, also published in Holland, Germany, Denmark, and Sweden, has 278 reviews compared to only 148 for *Moby-Dick* (64 for *Typee* and 45 for *Moby-Dick* have been added since the 1975 edition).

Reviews are identified and indexed by the initial letter of the work and numbered (e.g., *Typee* reviews are T1 to T278). Some are briefly annotated, with contemporary reviews cross-indexed. New to this edition are Melville's public lectures on "Statues in Rome," "The South Seas," and "Travelling," with contemporary reports on them. Books written before 1876 that mention Melville are recorded under a section called "General Reputation." "Sources" gives a bibliographic listing of 121 modern critical works on Melville. The index is organized primarily by city and then by periodical titles. The appendix reproduces "The Leyda Wand," a quick reference of publication dates of Melville's writings.

Serious study of reviews contemporary with Herman Melville and their effect on his career is just beginning. This checklist provides an invaluable aid to both review hunters and interpreters. [R: Choice, Oct 92, p. 274]—**Charlotte Lindgren**

Walter M. Miller, Jr.

1179. Roberson, William H., and Robert L. Battenfeld. **Walter M. Miller, Jr.: A Bio-Bibliography.** Westport, Conn., Greenwood Press, 1992. 149p. illus. index. (Bio-bibliographies in American Literature, no.3). $39.95. Z8575.56.R6. 016.813'54. LC 92-7335. ISBN 0-313 27651-X.

Walter M. Miller, Jr., is known primarily for his highly regarded science fiction novel *A Canticle for Liebowitz*, although he also wrote short stories and television scripts for "Captain Video and the Video Rangers." Roberson and Battenfeld begin with a brief biographical and critical essay and follow it in part 1 with a chronologically arranged list of Miller's books, short fiction in periodicals, short fiction in anthologies, nonfiction, and so forth. Each entry gives a synopsis of the story and a list of characters. Writings about Miller (part 2), both articles and book reviews, are in similar order and annotated. Addenda include glossaries of characters and terms as well as allusions, references, and associations in *A Canticle for Liebowitz*. Indexes cover names/titles/characters from part 1 and names/titles and subjects from part 2. This title is essential for those interested in Miller and the history of science fiction.—**Deborah Hammer**

Frank Norris

1180. McElrath, Joseph R., Jr. **Frank Norris: A Descriptive Bibliography.** Pittsburgh, Pa., University of Pittsburgh Press; distr., Ithaca, N.Y., CUP Services, 1992. 355p. illus. index. (Pittsburgh Series in Bibliography). $120.00. Z8633.M33. 016.813'4. LC 92-7198. ISBN 0-8229-3712-3.

This analytical bibliography provides a technical description of the physical format of every Frank Norris work in English published from 1899 to 1990. Its frontispiece is the frontispiece portrait of Norris that was printed in *The Pit*. Also reproduced are facsimiles of title pages, front covers, and front wrappers or dust jackets of his first editions. Section A is a chronological list of all books and pamphlets by Norris, with printings, issues, and states. Leaf dimension, pagination, collation of gatherings, contents, typography, paper, textual variants, binding, end papers, and advertisements added during binding are described. The date and printer of first bound copy and any prior periodical publication are given as are the locations of libraries and collections that hold the copies described. Briefly annotated are early reprintings in Great Britain, Canada, and Australia. Supplement AA discusses collected editions.

Section B chronologically presents first appearances of Norris's writings in books and pamphlets not wholly or substantially written by him. Section C has first appearances in magazines or newspapers subsequently published in books or pamphlets. Section D details "Keepsake Writings" with prior or subsequent publication dates. Section E lists 519 writings misattributed to Norris in scholarly studies of his life and work. Appendixes include a revision of *McTeague* required for English publication, a revision of *A Man's Woman* done between the first and second American printings, and an alphabetical list of 34 books about Norris. The index is followed by the titles of the other volumes in the Pittsburgh Series in Bibliography, all of which are essential to scholarly libraries and specialized bibliophiles.
—**Charlotte Lindgren**

Edward Taylor

1181. Craig, Raymond A., ed. **A Concordance to the Minor Poetry of Edward Taylor (1642?-1729): American Colonial Poet.** Lewiston, N.Y., Edwin Mellen Press, 1992. 2v. index. $99.95(v.1); $109.95(v.2). PS850.T2Z49. 811'.1. LC 92-3910. ISBN 0-7734-9632-7(v.1); 0-7734-9633-5(v.2).

This concordance can be most profitably used in combination with Gene Russell's *A Concordance to the Poems of Edward Taylor* (Microcard Editions, 1973), which is based on the texts of Taylor's major works as found in Donald E. Stanford's standard edition of *The Poems of Edward Taylor* (Yale University Press, 1960). Craig concords some 145 poems based on the text of *Edward Taylor's Minor Poetry*, edited by Thomas M. Davis and Virginia L. David (Twayne, 1981). This edition collects Taylor's minor poetry, which was preserved in six manuscripts, fully described in Stanford and in Constance J. Gefvert's *Edward Taylor: An Annotated Bibliography, 1668-1970* (Kent State University Press, 1971). The Davis edition's major exclusion is Taylor's more than 20,000-line "Metrical History of Christianity"; this text is excerpted in Stanford's edition. Additionally, Craig excludes two poems not by Taylor that are appended in the Davis edition. To facilitate linguistic analysis, Craig notes that "every effort was made to reproduce the base text exactly" (p. xv); that is, from the Davis edition. Researchers should consult the Davis's discussion of modernizations, regularizations, and expansions as well as Craig's preface. Context lines in Craig's concordance, for example, not only record Taylor's uses of capitalization, apostrophes, and hyphens but also attempt to typographically represent drawn Hebrew and Arabic characters. Extensive cross-references identify orthographic and homographic variants, such as "again," "againe," "'gain," "'gaine," and "ag'en". The concordance integrates Taylor's Latin vocabulary; his Greek words are appended. A frequency index and a list and verbal index of articles, conjunctions, prepositions, and pronouns omitted from the concordance conclude the set. Craig's concordance should promote advanced scholarship on Taylor's poetical canon. – **James K. Bracken**

Henry David Thoreau

1182. Scharnhorst, Gary. **Henry David Thoreau: An Annotated Bibliography of Comment and Criticism before 1900.** Hamden, Conn., Garland, 1992. 386p. index. (Garland Reference Library of the Humanities, v.1218). $60.00. Z8873.S3. 818'.309. LC 92-15648. ISBN 0-8240-5349-4.

This comprehensive annotated bibliography records all lectures, essays, and books by Henry David Thoreau and reviews, biographical memoirs, and commentaries about him that were published between 1840 and 1900. The entries show the growth of his reputation from one of failure to recognition as an important seminal figure in U.S. thought. There are only two items for 1840, his first year of publication, when he wrote a poem for *Dial* and was mentioned in Ralph Waldo Emerson's "Woodnotes." By 1862, the year of his death, there were 80 items, although many of these are obituaries and personal tributes by friends. Each year thereafter his works were increasingly appreciated and included in most collections of major U.S. writers.

This work corrects errors that appeared in previous bibliographies and has nearly doubled the number of entries. Each of the 2,087 items is numbered for easy reference. Whenever possible, the place and date of the original publication is followed by any accessible modern reprints. The annotations are a delight to read, with apt quotations that show the reactions of his contemporaries to his lifestyle and ideas. The index not only lists names but also cross-references works by topics such as abolitionism, anarchism, Transcendentalism, and vegetarianism. Under "Thoreau, Henry David" the numbered entries are listed under lectures, poems, and prose, as well as such topics as humor, music, and mysticism. This is bibliography at its best and a necessary tool for scholarly research.

– **Charlotte Lindgren**

Mark Twain

1183. Machlis, Paul, with Deborah Ann Turner. **Union Catalog of Letters to Clemens.** Berkeley, Calif., University of California Press, 1992. 407p. (University of California Publications. Catalogs and Bibliographies, v.8). $60.00. Z6616.T926M3. 016.818'409. LC 92-1225. ISBN 0-520-09743-2.

Clemens, otherwise known as Mark Twain, was the quintessential American writer. It is refreshing to see Twain's correspondence collected in this *Union Catalog of Letters to Clemens* (UCLC).

The work was born of the Mark Twain Project (Bancroft Library at the University of California at Berkeley), which edited and published an authoritative edition of the works and papers of the famed humorist. The alphabetical entries reveal the correspondent, date of correspondence, entry numbers, and a symbol of annotation for the type of response the correspondence generated. More than 18,000 letters (used in the most liberal of senses) are included here. To be included, a document must have been written to Twain, his wife, or their daughters; to Clara Clemens (Gabrilowitsch, later Samossoud) after the death of Twain on April 21, 1910; or to nonmembers of the Clemens family who have "significant" relevance to the study of Clemens's work or life. The last criteria is admittedly arbitrary and has been adjudicated by the Mark Twain Project editors. This reference volume should be in the largest of libraries and in the hands of scholars doing significant research or teaching in Twain studies.

—Mark Y. Herring

Richard Wilbur

1184. Bixler, Frances. **Richard Wilbur: A Reference Guide.** New York, G. K. Hall, 1991. 266p. index. (Reference Guide to Literature). $60.00. Z8974.15.B59. 016.811'52. LC 91-11042. ISBN 0-8161-7262-5.

This volume lists and annotates all books, critical articles, book reviews, and biographical notes on Richard Wilbur. Wilbur has written an interesting foreword in which he states that the main function of criticism is to mediate between books and readers, not to instruct authors, adding that there are types of essays and reviews that may prove unprofitable for poets to read. He takes great pains to acknowledge his gratitude to the best of those critics carefully summarized in this valuable reference tool.

In her preface Bixler explains the need for this updated guide and details various matters included in her study. Next she provides a detailed chronology, a 26-page introduction that traces Wilbur's career and the writings about Wilbur from 1935 to 1991. A detailed index enhances this work and allows the reader access to virtually everything included in the almost 1,000 entries and the highly favorable critical reception of most of Wilbur's work.—**G. A. Cevasco**

Tennessee Williams

1185. Gunn, Drewey Wayne. **Tennessee Williams: A Bibliography.** 2d ed. Metuchen, N.J., Scarecrow, 1991. 434p. index. (Scarecrow Author Bibliographies, no.89). $49.50. Z8976.424.G85. 016.812'54. LC 91-34939. ISBN 0-8108-2495-7.

Critical articles on Tennessee Williams's *Cat on a Hot Tin Roof*; Scandinavian productions of Williams's plays; December 26, 1944, opening night reviews of Williams's literary classic *The Glass Menagerie*; Williams's revised New Directions text of *Clothes for a Summer Hotel* (first performed in 1980 at Washington's Kennedy Center)—information about such subjects is only seconds away with Gunn's 2d edition of *Tennessee Williams: A Bibliography* in hand. This carefully researched, elaborately detailed, and seemingly exhaustive reference tool is an essential guide for the study of Williams and his significance to world drama and American culture.

Much more than an expansion and updating of the 1980 edition, Gunn's bibliography presents a virtually new book that brings together invaluable information about each of Williams's works. The works are arranged alphabetically by title under various broad headings: plays and screenplays; short stories and novels; poems and lyrics; occasional pieces, autobiography, and letters; miscellaneous materials (recorded readings, paintings and sketches, and productions based on words or ideas); bibliographical sources; manuscripts; translations and foreign language productions; and prior bibliographies. With more than one-third of the information new to this edition, Gunn includes more than 40 new works by Williams, 24 works published under his birth name (Thomas Lanier Williams), and primary and secondary publications through 1991. An introductory overview of Williams's literary career, a chronology of his life, a chronological list of his publications, and three concluding indexes are extremely helpful for the curious generalist as well as for the serious Williams scholar.

—Colby H. Kullman

Poetry

1186. Gwynn, R. S., ed. **American Poets since World War II. Third Series.** Detroit, Gale, 1992. 425p. illus. index. (Dictionary of Literary Biography, v.120). $112.00. LC 92-25459. ISBN 0-8103-7597-4.

With the publication of volume 120 in the Dictionary of Literary Biography (DLB), Gale establishes itself once again as the north star of literary reference. *American Poets since World War II* follows the usual modus operandi of volumes: short biographical sketches are followed by a small dose of literary criticism and reputation assessment. The poets surveyed number 67 and include Dana Gioia,

Rachel Hadas, Heather Miller, Bin Ramke, and Lisa Zeidner. In a way, this volume chronicles the deterioration of American poetry. None of these individuals approaches the stature of such classic poets as Robert Frost, Walt Whitman, and Emily Dickinson. Nevertheless, the volume is excellent reading for just about any level of literary sophistication, and will provide invaluable information for first-year English teachers and professors. Small and medium-sized libraries will probably want to purchase volumes that meet a wider need. — **Mark Y. Herring**

1187. **Index of American Periodical Verse: 1990.** By Rafael Catala and James D. Anderson. Metuchen, N.J., Scarecrow, 1992. 656p. $59.50. LC 73-3060. ISBN 0-8108-2587-2.

This 20th annual volume indexes the poems published by 289 participating periodicals from Canada, the United States, and Puerto Rico. Poems are indexed by author, with more than 7,000 entries for individual poets and translators, and by title or first line, with 20,000-plus entries. The 1990 edition has dropped 9 periodicals from the previous edition and has added 29 new ones. These are listed at the front of the volume, along with abbreviations used and complete information on each indexed periodical. The body of the work also follows the same format as its predecessors, listing entries alphabetically by surnames of the indexed authors, from "Aafjes, Bertus" to "Zydek, Frederick." Under each poet's name, poems are arranged alphabetically by title or by first line if there is no title. The periodical citation includes title, volume, issue numbers, date, and pages, all in brackets.

This index is a valuable addition to any collection used by poets and other persons who want to know what is being written by whom and in which periodicals. A glance through the pages of this work reveals some extremely prolific poets who have written for many periodicals, as well as hundreds of others who are accorded one line. As a possible market source, the detailed publishing information on each indexed periodical is invaluable. From *Abraxas* to *Zyzzyva*, they are all here. From scholars interested in studying literary trends to readers looking for work by a favorite author, the *Index of American Periodical Verse* remains the premier choice in its field. — **Kay O. Cornelius**

Wit and Humor

1188. Ellenbogen, Glenn C., ed. **The Directory of Humor Magazines and Humor Organizations in America (and Canada).** 3d ed. New York, Wry-Bred Press, 1992. 282p. illus. index. $34.95. LC 91-68398. ISBN 0-9606190-5-4.

Humor in all forms has experienced a renaissance over the last decade. This entertaining and informative directory lists some 85 magazines (including college), newspapers, periodicals, and organizations devoted to humor. The first edition (see ARBA 87, entry 881) contained 154 pages; this work is nearly double in size. From the American Association for Therapeutic Humor to the Society for the Preservation and Enhancement of the Recognition of Millard Fillmore, Last of the Whigs (SPERMFLOW) to Norman Stevens's Workshop Library on World Humour, the reader will be struck by the variety and extremes of humor that exist in print today.

Individuals who wish to publish jokes, satire, cartoons, and the like will find detailed directions for submission. Each entry also provides lengthy and lively examples of the publication or organization's type of humor. The typography and illustrations are first-rate.

This work is recommended for college and public libraries where there is interest in humor. As a result of budget cuts and other constraints on libraries in the 1990s, it may be considered a luxury item by other institutions. [R: LJ, 15 Oct 92, p. 60] — **Bill Bailey and Anne F. Roberts**

1189. Nilsen, Don L. F. **Humor in American Literature: A Selected Annotated Bibliography.** Hamden, Conn., Garland, 1992. 580p. index. (Garland Reference Library of the Humanities, v.1049). $78.00. Z1231.W8N55. 016.817009. LC 91-42821. ISBN 0-8240-8395-4.

This bibliography is an unusual compendium of works primarily on U.S. humor and humorists. The 1,293 annotations, averaging 250 words each, are based on books, articles, or reviews, often from the Dictionary of Literary Biography (DLB) series and the magazine *Thalia*. Citations refer users to the sources.

The material is organized in chapters that cover the seventeenth through the twentieth centuries and categories such as parody, satire, Southwestern, ethnic, and sex-role humor. An author/subject index facilitates access to personal names and subjects such as Jewish humor that one might not think to look up under "Ethnic."

Some major authors are slighted while some minor ones are given considerable space. Nilsen has included works according to the overall significance of the author's writing to the field of humor as well as the availability of recent criticism—material written specifically about the author's humor within the past two decades. So one finds nothing about Thorne Smith, on whose comic fantasies many classic films and television shows have been based.

Occasional minor errors in such a massive work are to be expected, whether due to Nilsen's lack of familiarity with all the works mentioned or a typesetter's slip. For instance, referring to a character named Houston in Faulkner's *The Hamlet*, Nilsen says that Houston lived in the village, when in fact he lived on his prosperous farm. This useful-in-many-ways volume should not be allowed to languish hidden in reference stacks while librarians automatically run to the DLB or Contemporary Literary Criticism. [R: Choice, Oct 92, p. 277]—**Mary Jo Walker**

British Literature

General Works

Dictionaries and Encyclopedias

1190. Coghlan, Ronan. **The Encyclopaedia of Arthurian Legends.** Rockport, Mass., Element; distr., Lanham, Md., National Book Network, 1991. 234p. illus. maps. $18.95. 398.352. ISBN 1-85230-199-6.

This small volume is not an encyclopedia in the ordinary sense and should not be confused with the far more compendious *The New Arthurian Encyclopedia* (see ARBA 92, entry 1190). It would have been better to call this work a dictionary of Arthurian names and places. Coghlan begins with a brief and readable summary of the Arthurian legend, from Gildas to Tennyson and Tolkien. He is particularly well grounded in the Welsh material. The body of the book contains a list of Arthurian names, places, and a few objects (e.g., the Grail) and actions (e.g., the Dolorous Stroke). There are no listings for authors, works, manuscripts, films, themes, or theories, although these are occasionally mentioned in the text. Most entries are brief. The biography of Lancelot, for example, runs to approximately four columns and includes a genealogical chart, whereas Eneuavc, daughter of Bedivere, gets a single line. Entries usually have footnotes that tie the names to an appended list of core texts, but this is not done consistently. There are useful genealogical charts and maps along with attractive but irrelevant illustrations. Appended are a list of the chief Arthurian sources, core texts, and further works.

Despite the author's claim that this is a work of scholarship, it will not be useful to most serious students or to anyone interested in sources, themes, authors, or modern versions. The list of "core texts" contains only modern translations, ignoring all editions in foreign languages or even in Middle English, and is far from complete. However, the book will be handy for someone searching for an obscure name and is suitable for a high school or town library. It is handsomely printed.

—**Lynn F. Williams**

Handbooks and Yearbooks

1191. **British Writers. Supplement II: Kingsley Amis to J. R. R. Tolkien.** George Stade, ed. New York, Scribner's, 1992. 626p. index. $90.00. PR85.B688 Suppl. 820'.9. LC 87-16648. ISBN 0-684-19214-4.

This is the second update to the highly regarded *British Writers*, which has become a standard reference source in most academic and many public libraries. As with the first supplement (see ARBA 88, entry 1199), this volume is not intended to acknowledge new, young British writers, but rather to fill in some significant gaps in the coverage. Therefore, some well-established names are included among the 26 chosen writers: Max Beerbohm, Agatha Christie, Noel Coward, Arthur Conan Doyle, T. E. Lawrence, Stephen Spender, Lytton Strachey, and J. R. R. Tolkien. The emphasis is on twentieth-century writers, so important contemporary names are also covered: Kingsley Amis (but not his son

Martin), Elizabeth Bowen, John Le Carre, Barbara Pym, and Jean Rhys. Following the *British Writers* tradition of broadly interpreting what is considered "British," Irish writers (Brendan Behan and Seamus Heaney) and South Africans (Alan Paton and Nadine Gordimer) are also included.

The entries in this volume were specifically commissioned by the publisher, unlike those in the previous volumes, which were based on the British Council's Writers and Their Work series. However, the intent of the essays remains the same: to provide a concise introduction to the life and work of important writers for a general, educated audience. The entries range in length from 10,000 to 13,000 words, contain liberal excerpts from the authors' writings, and include selected bibliographies. A cumulative index to the entire set completes this volume.

Although there is sufficient reference material available on modern British writers (almost all of these writers are, for example, included in the multivolume Dictionary of Literary Biography series), this and the other British Writers volumes are highly recommended as a major resource for most libraries. It is hoped that a third supplement will include such neglected names as V. S. Pritchett, Alan Sillitoe, John Wain, David Lodge, Cyril Connolly, Fay Weldon, and Anita Brookner. [R: BR, May/June 92, p. 57; WLB, Apr 92, p. 120]—**Thomas A. Karel**

1192. **Contemporary Writers, 1960 to the Present.** Detroit, Gale, 1992. 582p. illus. index. (Concise Dictionary of British Literary Biography, v.8). $65.00. ISBN 0-8103-7988-0.

This is the last of the eight-volume Concise Dictionary of British Literary Biography set. Entries have been selected from the Dictionary of Literary Biography (DLB) series to meet the needs of libraries that do not have the budget to purchase the more than 100 volumes in the DLB. Each of these eight volumes spans a different chronological period, beginning with a volume covering the Middle Ages and the Renaissance. The series is directed toward high school and beginning college students. Every volume consists of alphabetically arranged biographical entries devoted to major authors. Each entry, which is essentially the same as the essay on which it is modeled in the DLB, has the same format: a chronological list of the author's works, a biography focusing on major events in the author's career, a discussion of major works reflecting the most important critical interpretations of these works, and a selected list of interviews and critical works. Each entry includes photographs of the author, reproductions of typescript or manuscript pages of key works, and at least one dust jacket of a representative book.

Few scholars or general readers could quarrel with the 27 authors selected for this 582-page volume. The adjective *contemporary* in the title reflects the fact that the authors (with the exception of the poet/librarian Philip Larkin and the playwright Joe Orton) are alive and writing. Genres include detective and mystery fiction (e.g., P. D. James, John le Carre, Len Deighton, John Mortimer), fantasy (e.g., Doris Lessing), fiction (e.g., Anthony Burgess, Iris Murdoch, V. S. Naipaul), poetry (e.g., Seamus Heaney), and drama (e.g., Harold Pinter, Arnold Wesker, Peter Shaffer).

Entries in this volume, as in others of the set and in the parent volumes of the DLB, may serve the general reader as an introduction to an author, or they may be consulted by a more advanced reader for basic biographical facts. This reviewer's experience as Humanities Librarian confirms that this set is very popular with both beginning college students and high school students, although the level of writing is occasionally beyond that which some of these students can appreciate.—**David Isaacson**

1193. Greenfield, John R., ed. **British Romantic Prose Writers, 1789-1832: Second Series.** Detroit, Gale, 1991. 431p. illus. index. (Dictionary of Literary Biography, v.110). $108.00. LC 91-27535. ISBN 0-8103-4590-0.

This volume of the Dictionary of Literary Biography lives up to its predecessors. In a second series of British Romantic prose writers, it focuses on those writers born after 1775 and whose major works were written between 1810 and 1845. To create a sense of the intellectual climate and concerns of that age, it includes prose essayists, journalists, polemicists and political writers, writers known for works in other genres but who have significant prose works, writers known for their friendships with other writers, and popular or important writers now forgotten. Each entry provides biographical information in conjunction with the history of that author's writing and reputation. In the appendix, articles discuss the treatment of literature in some of the important quarterlies and magazines of the age. Each author's entry is copiously (and often amusingly) illustrated and includes a primary bibliography and bibliographies of letters, of bibliographies, and of secondary sources, as well as the location of the writer's papers. The journal articles include secondary sources. The volume ends with "Books for Further Reading" and a cumulative index to the series. Each entry, be it author or journal, is well written and informative, and the book is satisfying to mind and hand. It provides plenty of helpful information without the aura of unimaginative scholarship.—**Rebecca Jordan**

1194. **Late Victorian and Edwardian Writers, 1890-1914.** Detroit, Gale, 1991. 434p. illus. index. (Concise Dictionary of British Literary Biography, v.5). $65.00. ISBN 0-8103-7985-6.

This volume of selected entries from Gale's Dictionary of Literary Biography (DLB) series is part of a series of eight, each devoted to a particular historical period. It is designed for libraries that need a smaller, less expensive alternative to the complete DLB. The entries on the 21 British late Victorian and Edwardian writers have been updated by the same scholars who prepared the originals.

Arranged alphabetically from Barrie to Yeats, the volume is easy to use. Names are followed by dates of birth and death; brief notes on each contributor; extensive lists of selected works by the authors; and cogent essays, varying in length from 5 pages on H. H. Munro (Saki) to 54 pages on Yeats, that summarize major events in the authors' lives, the reception of their works, and some critical evaluation. These are followed by bibliographies of works about the authors and the places where their papers are archived. No women are included. While Lady Gregory is mentioned in several of the essays, her own work is not discussed. Illustrations include portraits of the authors; pictures of their homes, wives, and friends; manuscript pages that show handwriting and corrections; and dust jackets of selected editions.

The index has all people, places, and works mentioned in this volume. A cumulative index of author entries lists the authors featured in all eight volumes. A complete list of Gale books on literary biography, British and American, is given on the end pages. The Concise Dictionary of British Literary Biography series is a useful addition to any library. [R: VOYA, Dec 92, p. 318]—**Charlotte Lindgren**

1195. **Modern Writers, 1914-1945.** Detroit, Gale, 1991. 480p. illus. index. (Concise Dictionary of British Literary Biography, v.6). $65.00. ISBN 0-8103-7986-4.

Similar to its companion series, the Concise Dictionary of American Literary Biography, this eight-volume series on prominent British writers is intended primarily for use in small academic, public, and secondary school libraries (those libraries that are unlikely to own the more comprehensive corresponding volumes of the Dictionary of Literary Biography [DLB] series). As an alternative reference source to the DLB, the concise series scores high marks for its selectivity and the quality of its biographical essays. Most of these are updated versions of essays originally published in the DLB, although some have simply been reprinted without revision. A complete list of the writer's works and a selected bibliography are included, as are several relevant photographs and illustrations.

The eight volumes of this series are arranged chronologically and trace the development of British literature from the Middle Ages to the present. The individual volumes, however, are not being published chronologically. Volumes 4, 5, 6, and 7 appeared in 1991, with the remainder scheduled for publication in 1992. Most volumes contain 20 to 25 biographical entries; the two volumes that cover 1945 to the present have the most entries. This particular volume, which covers a transitional period in British literature and spans World War I, the Great Depression, and World War II, features a number of truly major writers: W. H. Auden, H. M. Forster, Robert Graves, Aldous Huxley, James Joyce, T. H. Lawrence, Somerset Maugham, G. B. Shaw, Evelyn Waugh, H. G. Wells, and Virginia Woolf. Of somewhat lesser stature, but nonetheless representative of the period, are Rupert Brooke, Joyce Cary, Agatha Christie, Noel Coward, Sean O'Casey, Wilfred Owen, J. B. Priestley, Dorothy Sayers, and P. G. Wodehouse.

With compilations such as this series, one can always quibble about the selection criteria and wish that the volumes or the series were longer and more inclusive. Many writers could have been placed in more than one volume. In volume 6, for example, one looks in vain for George Orwell, who wrote most of his work prior to 1945; he is found in volume 7. Among the names completely missing from the series are V. S. Pritchett, David Storey, Salman Rushdie, and David Lodge. Still, this is a useful series and is highly recommended for any library that lacks the resources to invest in the complete DLB. [R: LJ, Jan 92, p. 110; VOYA, Dec 92, p. 318]—**Thomas A. Karel**

1196. Mudge, Bradford K., ed. **British Romantic Novelists, 1789-1832.** Detroit, Gale, 1992. 438p. illus. index. (Dictionary of Literary Biography, v.116). $112.00. LC 92-9153. ISBN 0-8103-7593-1.

It is interesting to note that 17 of the 33 major and minor novelists included in this volume are female. Mudge points out in the introduction that when circulating libraries made books available to the middle classes, increasing numbers of popular novels were written by and for women and were condemned as dangerous to cultural standards.

The entries, which appear alphabetically from Jane Austen to Edward Trelawny, vary considerably in length, from 40 pages on Sir Walter Scott to 5 pages for little-known Irish writer John Banim, but they are nearly always informative and entertaining. Each literary biography appears under the author's name with dates of birth and death and full bibliographic information on novels and editions. At the end of each essay are listed letters, biographies of the writer, and reference works. Locations of the papers and manuscripts are also given. The iconography is exceptional, with illustrations of the writers, their families and homes, manuscript pages, frontispiece drawings, and title pages of first editions. A checklist of further reading suggests 45 useful reference works on the Romantic novel. A list of the contributing scholars and the colleges with which they are associated concludes the volume.

Each volume in the series contains a cumulative index that lists the names to be found in all volumes of the Dictionary of Literary Biography and its related series, citing the appropriate volume and page number. Each volume provides a treasury of information within its special framework.
—**Charlotte Lindgren**

1197. **Victorian Writers, 1832-1890.** Detroit, Gale, 1991. 516p. illus. index. (Concise Dictionary of British Literary Biography, v.4). $65.00. ISBN 0-8103-7984-8.

Anyone curious about the collective quality of the 21 biocritical essays in this book need look no further than the pages of past volumes of ARBA, for all of the essays have been reprinted in full with updates to the bibliographies of secondary works from various volumes of the Dictionary of Literary Biography (DLB) series. The borrowings from *Victorian Novelists before 1885* (see ARBA 84, entry 1187); *Victorian Novelists after 1885* (see ARBA 85, entry 1130); *Victorian Poets before 1850* (see ARBA 86, entry 1096); *Victorian Poets after 1850* (see ARBA 86, entry 1097); *Victorian Prose Writers before 1876* (see ARBA 88, entry 1201); *Victorian Prose Writers after 1867* (see ARBA 88, entry 1202); and *British Mystery Writers, 1860-1919* (see ARBA 89, entry 1097), naturally carry the strengths and weaknesses identical to the originals. As literary biographies and career summaries, they provide excellent introductory overviews of these writers' lives and works. As biocritical essays they are less successful, providing less critical than biographical insight, particularly because critical comments tend to come from the authors' contemporaries rather than latter-day readers. Numerous illustrations, many of them portraits of the writers and people closely associated with them, strengthen the biographical element. Where an author has been treated in more than one volume of the DLB, this volume reprints the essay from the volume covering that author's principal genre (e.g., the essay on Matthew Arnold as prose essayist rather than as poet). A volume-specific index made up mostly of proper names and titles of literary works adds value to the essays.

The intent of this volume and the set of which it is a part is analogous to that of the Concise Dictionary of American Literary Biography—to make available to libraries that cannot afford the entire DLB those essays that cover the principal, most frequently studied authors of a nation's literary heritage. The eight volumes of this set, when complete, will span English literature from the Middle Ages to the present. Among the writers covered, one can question only the inclusion of Wilkie Collins, whose contributions to mystery fiction, while indisputably significant, have been eclipsed by more artful masters of the genre.

With their emphasis on biography and their generous use of illustrations, these volumes will serve a wider audience than the more analytical essays in *British Writers* (see ARBA 80, entry 1268) and its supplements (see ARBA 88, entry 1199). Although libraries that have the DLB source volumes have no need of *Victorian Writers, 1832-1890*, other libraries can now obtain a sample of its most important essays at a price designed to meet the needs of smaller budgets. [R: LAR, Aug 92, p. 533]—**James Rettig**

1198. **Writers after World War II, 1945-1960.** Detroit, Gale, 1991. 420p. illus. index. (Concise Dictionary of British Literary Biography, v.7). $65.00. ISBN 0-8103-7987-2.

This eight-volume series is designed primarily for high school and junior college students, for use especially in small or medium-sized libraries. It takes its origins in a reduction of the multivolumed Dictionary of Literary Biography (DLB) (now composed of more than 100 volumes), which covers literary biographies in many languages. The focus in the Concise Dictionary of British Literary Biography is, as indicated in the title, specifically on British literature.

The eight volumes are organized, the editors maintain, in chronological sequence, but their chronological divisions work best prior to this century. The three volumes dealing with this century cover, respectively, 1914-1945 (volume 6), 1945-1960 (the volume under review), and 1960-present (volume 8). No rationale is offered for the division of the twentieth century into these periods, which are curiously uneven; the bounds of this present volume, only 15 years, seem oddest of all. What do these 15 years represent in the long lives of the writers included here: their early publications or the years of their most important productions? No clear answer emerges. And on what principle is Muriel Spark included in this volume while her contemporary, Iris Murdoch, is deferred until the next volume?

The entries are taken complete from the DLB, without abridgment, and all entries are accompanied by a bibliography of the author and a list of critical references. The selection of author entries is traditional and patriarchal; few women are included in any of the volumes. Only 3 of the 25 entries in this volume are of women. And in the three volumes that cover this century, the most glaring omissions are of women: Katharine Mansfield in volume 6, Stevie Smith in this volume, and Barbara Pym in volume 8.—**John B. Beston**

1199. **Writers of the Middle Ages and Renaissance before 1660.** Detroit, Gale, 1992. 436p. illus. index. (Concise Dictionary of British Literary Biography, v.1). $65.00. ISBN 0-8103-7981-3.

Designed for school and small public libraries, this is the first in an eight-volume selective version of Gale's expensive and massive Dictionary of Literary Biography (DLB) series. The entries chosen for inclusion are identical to those in the DLB. The series concentrates on British literature in chronological sequence from the Middle Ages to the present. As in the DLB, this series provides illustrated biographies and bibliographies of major authors in 10- to 20-page signed articles that focus on the author's literary development and influence without ignoring biographical detail. A list of secondary sources follows each article, and references to editions of personal correspondence, bibliographies, and biographies are provided when possible.

This particular volume contains essays on the anonymous poem *Beowulf* and 17 well-known male writers, such as Geoffrey Chaucer, Thomas Malory, Ben Johnson, William Shakespeare, and Edmund Spencer. Conspicuously absent are Julian of Norwich, Margery Kempe, Elisabeth Cary, and other notable women writers who have finally found their way into the literary canon. In the 8 volumes in this series, there are fewer than 20 women out of almost 200 authors. Nonetheless, the figures included certainly number among the most illustrious in British literature and the most often read in American schools.—**Valerie R. Hotchkiss**

1200. **Writers of the Restoration and Eighteenth Century, 1660-1789.** Detroit, Gale, 1992. 580p. illus. index. (Concise Dictionary of British Literary Biography, v.2). $65.00. ISBN 0-8103-7982-1.

As are the seven other volumes in the series, volume 2 of the Concise Dictionary of British Literary Biography is an abbreviated version of part of the monumental Dictionary of Literary Biography (DLB) series. It is intended for high school and small community libraries unequipped with the more than 100 volumes of the longer version.

As in the rest of the series, the entries are essentially the same as those in the DLB and have the same format: a list of works in recommended editions; an account of the author's life; summaries of major works; and an updated list of material on the author, including letters, bibliographies, biographies, and critical works. The entries are profusely illustrated in rather muddy black and white. All the major male writers of the period from 1660 to 1789, including John Milton, are included, but minor writers such as James Thomson and William Cowper are not; and there are no women authors at all, an unfortunate omission for a work published in 1992.

The intended readers of the Concise Dictionary are high school and undergraduate students, who will find this material useful and informative. Recommended for libraries without the complete DLB.
—**Lynn F. Williams**

1201. **Writers of the Romantic Period, 1789-1832.** Detroit, Gale, 1992. 468p. illus. index. (Concise Dictionary of British Literary Biography, v.3). $65.00. ISBN 0-8103-7983-X.

The eight volumes of the Concise Dictionary of British Literary Biography, of which this is the third, are an attempt to make some of the material in the Dictionary of Literary Biography (DLB), the standard reference work for large libraries, available to a wider audience. An emphasis on biography is still current in high school teaching, so this abridgment is an appropriate choice for high school, college, and small public libraries that cannot afford (and may not need) the more than 100 volumes of the parent work.

The entries are essentially unabridged from DLB but have been updated through 1990. As in DLB, they are arranged alphabetically within the volume. Each article begins with a list of works in recommended editions, then continues with the author's life and fairly detailed summaries of major works. Although some account is given of a work's reception at publication, critical judgments are kept to a minimum. The articles are generously illustrated, but the black-and-white reproductions are often muddy, a particularly annoying fault when an important manuscript is too out of focus to be readable. An extensive bibliography of secondary works completes the entry.

The volume covers all the major romantic writers who lived long enough to be considered a Victorian, from Robert Burns and William Blake to Thomas Carlyle. It includes Mary Wollstonecraft and Jane Austen but omits Anne Radcliffe, Dorothy Wordsworth, Robert Southey, and John Clare, among others. The decision to reprint the DLB entries unabridged retains the original scholarship but means that this short version is limited to major authors, omitting less well known ones whose lives might have interested some readers. Nevertheless, within its limitations this series will provide a valuable resource for smaller libraries and is recommended for those without the complete DLB. [R: RBB, 1 Feb 92, p. 1058; VOYA, Dec 92, p. 318] — **Lynn F. Williams**

Drama

1202. Fordyce, Rachel. **Caroline Drama: A Bibliographic History of Criticism.** 2d ed. New York, G. K. Hall, 1992. 332p. index. (Reference Publication in Literature). $40.00. Z2014.D7F67. 016.822'509. LC 91-39346. ISBN 0-8161-1835-3.

This edition almost doubles the number of entries in Fordyce's original work (see ARBA 79, entry 1008) — an indication that, in her view, Caroline drama has come into its own. (As Fordyce notes in the introduction, some of the lesser Caroline dramatists have begun receiving greater attention from scholars.) More than 1,600 entries are arranged into 4 sections: general reference and bibliographies, textual considerations, Caroline drama, and stage history. English- and foreign-language books, articles, and dissertations are annotated in a way that emphasizes their historical, critical, or bibliographic importance. Notes often identify a single aspect of the work, with suggestions for use in research. Entries from the first edition are included; their annotations have been modified only slightly, if at all. Key words from the annotations, identifying topics and the names of playwrights, serve as the basis for the subject index, which can also be used for cross-references. Authors of secondary works appear in a separate index, as does a list of play titles and early sources. Research libraries will want this edition for their collections, not only because it tracks the substantial increase of work in this area but also because it is a valuable contribution to the scholarship in the field. — **Bernice Bergup**

Fiction

1203. Harner, James L. **English Renaissance Prose Fiction, 1500-1660: An Annotated Bibliography of Criticism (1984-1990).** New York, G. K. Hall, 1992. 185p. index. $35.00. Z2014.F4H372. 016.823'009. LC 92-10036. ISBN 0-8161-9088-7.

A continuation of Harner's *English Renaissance Prose Fiction, 1500-1660: An Annotated Bibliography of Criticism* (see ARBA 86, entry 1158) and its supplement for 1978-1983, this volume annotates criticism in books and articles published from 1984 through 1990. As did its predecessors, this book includes editions and studies of English prose fiction, both original works and translations, written or printed in England from 1500 to 1600. Harner restricts his 745 entries to concise and informative treatments of works generally classified as romances, novellas, histories, anatomies, or jest books (or

combinations thereof). Entries are divided into four sections: bibliographies, anthologies, general studies, and authors/translators/titles—all alphabetically arranged. Harner also includes doctoral dissertations and publications unavailable earlier or overlooked. Recommended for libraries that house collections on the English Renaissance, sixteenth-century collections, and early British prose fiction.
—**C. B. (Bob) Darrell**

1204. Ruddick, Nicholas. **British Science Fiction: A Chronology, 1478-1990.** Westport, Conn., Greenwood Press, 1992. 250p. index. (Bibliographies and Indexes in World Literature, no.35). $55.00. PR830.S35R84. 016.823'08762. LC 92-6409. ISBN 0-313-28002-9.

According to Ruddick, British science fiction, as an entity distinct from American, has received short shrift from critics, and this chronology, along with the author's forthcoming companion study *Ultimate Island* (Greenwood Press, 1993), sets out to redress the situation. Although arranged chronologically, this is more than a typical chronology. There are four sections that may appear under any given year. Under BIO are listed biographical details about British science fiction writers, arranged by dates of birth or death; FIC gives information about British science fiction published that year, arranged by author; FTV has information about British science fiction on film, radio, and television; and GEN includes general material, such as information about anthologies, comics, or fandom. The listings begin with 1478, the year Sir Thomas More (author of *Utopia*) was born, and conclude with 1990. The chronology is divided into five periods, each with a brief introduction: "The Descent of Scientific Romance" (1478-1894), "The Wellsian Synthesis" (1895-1936), "British Science Fiction" (1937-1961), "New Wave S(peculative) F(iction)" (1962-1978), and "The British Fantastic" (1979-1990). The entries are cross-referenced; there are author, title, and FTV indexes; and Ruddick provides an illuminating general introduction.

Ruddick is quite candid about his biases regarding the inclusion or exclusion of material (e.g., he prefers novels to magazine stories), but the reader must consult *Ultimate Island* for a complete discussion of what exactly constitutes British science fiction. Suffice it to say, however, that he uses the term *science fiction* broadly to include fantasy (e.g., Tolkien) and utopian/dystopian fiction (e.g., *Utopia, Brave New World*). The usefulness of this work is further enhanced by the inclusion of nonbook media, such as films, television, radio, and comic books. This comprehensive and detailed chronology should become a standard reference work in the field. [R: Choice, Nov 92, p. 448]—**Jeffrey R. Luttrell**

Individual Authors

Robert Bridges

1205. Hamilton, Lee Templin. **Robert Bridges: An Annotated Bibliography, 1873-1988.** Cranbury, N.J., University of Delaware Press/Associated University Presses, 1991. 243p. index. $39.50. Z8119.2.H36. 016.821'8. LC 88-40577. ISBN 0-87413-364-5.

Scholars interested in Robert Bridges will find this annotated bibliography useful although they may be disappointed by some of its errors and omissions. The 13-page introduction gives good biographical information about the poet but is marred by such editorializing as the suggestion that education at Eton and Oxford seems "terribly middle class" or that Bridges's interests and skills may exceed that of any man in this century, or perhaps in any age since the Renaissance.

Annotation in chapters 1 and 2 is sketchy. Chapter 1 lists all the editions of poems, dramas, and hymns by Bridges but does not attempt to trace the first publication of poems in magazines or journals. Chapter 2 lists Bridges's prose including critical essays, introductions, memoirs, and letters. Chapter 3, on reviews, criticisms, and anthologies, has fuller annotations but more omissions. In all three sections, works are numbered and arranged alphabetically under each year. Index A lists alphabetically all of Bridges's prose and poetry found in chapters 1 and 2. Index B lists anthologies, and index C, by far the most extensive, cites secondary source material.

Much has been written about the Poet Laureate since *A Bibliography of Robert Bridges* by George McKay was published in 1933. The lack of a definitive biography of Bridges makes this bibliography, which covers the whole period from the first publication of *Poems* in 1873 to 1988, a necessary resource. [R: Choice, Jan 92, p. 722]—**Charlotte Lindgren**

George Mackay Brown

1206. Yamada, Osamu, Hilda D. Spear, and David S. Robb. **The Contribution to Literature of Orcadian Writer George Mackay Brown: An Introduction and a Bibliography.** Lewiston, N.Y., Edwin Mellen Press, 1992. 105p. (Studies in British Literature, v.16). $39.95. Z8123.6.Y35. 016.821'914. LC 91-33423. ISBN 0-7734-9651-3.

To understand the work of George Mackay Brown, the introduction to this well-organized study maintains, it is necessary to appreciate the spirit of the islands—the Orkneys—from which he hails. Accordingly, several pages detail the wind, the storms, and the extremes of weather that affect existence on the 65 islands that lie some 10 miles north of the Scottish mainland, across the Pentland Firth. Here the poet and storyteller Brown was born some 70 years ago, and it is here that he has lived and created literature all of his life. Although his reputation is somewhat limited, critics familiar with his work agree that he excels within a remarkably narrow range: the inherently restrictive setting of the Orkneys and a tendency to denounce the modern world and its materialistic values. His observations on life and human behavior are so finely responsive, nevertheless, that even the depopulated Orkneys provide him with a wealth of creative material. What Dickens discovered in London, Brown, remarkably, finds in his own microcosm. His narrow range conceals an immense scope of human sympathy and energetic artfulness.

Appropriately, this bibliography is divided into primary and secondary sources. It lists all his books of poetry, fiction, essays, and drama and provides a complete record of his hundreds of contributions to periodicals and newspapers. And it catalogs all the articles, books, and theses—more than 100—written about his life and work.—**G. A. Cevasco**

Joseph Conrad

1207. Knowles, Owen. **An Annotated Critical Bibliography of Joseph Conrad.** New York, St. Martin's Press, 1992. 255p. index. (Annotated Critical Bibliographies). $39.95. 28189.7.K58. 016.823'912. LC 91-37610. ISBN 0-312-07556-1.

A selective bibliography on the scholarship and criticism of the works of English novelist Joseph Conrad, this book ranges from 1914 to 1990. For convenience, the materials in each chapter are arranged chronologically and include the principal modern editions of Conrad (from 1963), bibliographies, anthologies, reference works, and "full-length" books that deal with criticism. Separate chapters cover major novels, such as *Heart of Darkness, Lord Jim*, and *Nostromo*, as well as shorter fiction, such as *Youth*. In the chapter "Aspects of Conrad" there are articles on the wider philosophical and linguistic influence of the writer. Many of the journals from which the articles on Conrad have been selected are not specialized. Most of the larger academic libraries will have such serials as the *Times Literary Supplement, Modern Language Review*, and *Critical Quarterly*, therefore making this bibliography useful for most patrons. A complete list of the journals is included, and there are author and subject indexes. Recommended for most academic libraries. [R: Choice, Sept 92, p. 82]—**J. C. Jurgens**

John Fowles

1208. Aubrey, James R. **John Fowles: A Reference Companion.** Westport, Conn., Greenwood Press, 1991. 333p. illus. index. $49.95. PR6056.085Z52. 823'.914. LC 91-9553. ISBN 0-313-26399-X.

This book, about the English novelist famous for *The French Lieutenant's Woman*, is both a comprehensive bibliographic aid to scholars and a useful guide to general readers of Fowles's works. The first section is a detailed biography, including photographs, divided into chronological periods and focusing on the close relationship between his life and works. The next section is an extensive expository essay on Fowles's nonfiction, divided into genres (e.g., autobiography, biography, literary criticism, history, nature writing). This is followed by analyses of each of Fowles's novels, including discussions of their compositions, plot summaries, interpretations of major themes, critical and popular receptions, and stage and film adaptations. (Many of his novels have been adapted into movies.) The next section provides a succinct overview of biographical, psychological, deconstructive, historicist, feminist, reader-response, and formalist critical perspectives on the fiction. An extensive "Notes to the Fiction" section provides a glossary of name and place allusions likely to be unfamiliar to general (especially U.S.) readers. (This section will probably not be useful to most scholars.) The next section is an alphabetical list of all the characters—even the unnamed ones—in Fowles's fiction, including their nicknames and functions in the stories. The final section is an unannotated bibliography (divided by genre) of his works, followed by a selected secondary bibliography of works about him. [R: Choice, May 92, p. 1363]—**David Isaacson**

Barbara Pym

1209. Salwak, Dale. **Barbara Pym: A Reference Guide.** New York, G. K. Hall, 1991. 162p. index. (Reference Guide to Literature). $37.50. Z8721.4.S25. 016.823'914. LC 90-13044. ISBN 0-8161-9076-3.

The novels of Barbara Pym were almost ignored until 1977, when poet Philip Larkin and Lord David Cecil both submitted her name in response to a *Times Literary Supplement* request for a list of the most underrated novelists of the century. Since then there has been a spate of reviews and articles. This increasing recognition is clearly seen in this bibliography, for in 1950 there were only five reviews of her first published novel, *Some Tame Gazelle*. By the year 1984 there were 109 reviews, articles, and even a doctoral dissertation. While the number of entries dropped by 1990, the list now includes two book-length works about her. Salwak, author of *The Life and Work of Barbara Pym* (University of Iowa Press, 1987), praises her in his preface for her realistic and comic portrayal of middle-aged spinsters, anthropologists, and men, all of whose lives are bound by the Anglican Church.

Following the preface is a list of the 12 novels and other posthumous works by Pym with dates of publication, including reprints. "Writings about Barbara Pym 1950-1990" contains over 600 entries with items listed alphabetically and numbered consecutively under each year. Every reference gives the critic's name (if known), title, date of publication, and pertinent pages. Annotations are descriptive, not evaluative. The index is comprehensive with authors, titles of works by and about Pym, and general topics interfiled. Each alphabetized item lists the years and reference numbers. Under a title such as *A Few Green Leaves* there are over 100 citations. Barbara Pym fans and scholars will find this reference guide extremely useful.—**Charlotte Lindgren**

Sir Walter Scott

1210. Bolton, H. Philip. **Scott Dramatized.** New York, Mansell/Cassell, 1992. 579p. index. $160.00. 016.8237. ISBN 0-7201-2060-8.

Sir Walter Scott was very popular in his time, and his novels, tales, and narrative poems, which are highly dramatic in nature, lent themselves easily to the stage. Thus it should come as no surprise that dramatic adaptations of his works flourished both during his lifetime and well after his death in 1832. What is astonishing is that Bolton, author of the similar *Dickens Dramatized* (see ARBA 88, entry 1369), has been able to catalog more than 4,500 such productions, from 1810 to the present.

Scott Dramatized is "both a calendar of dramatic performances and a bibliography of published texts and unpublished manuscripts" based on Scott's works. The works are arranged in chronological order of publication. Each chapter begins with an introductory essay that, among other things, compares the number of dramatizations of that work with others; notes the proportions of London, Edinburgh, and American productions; mentions operatic versions; lists the actors and actresses who played some of the major roles; notes music and scenery; and lists burlesque, radio, television, and film versions. After this essay comes the "Calendar of Performance," which lists, in chronological order, all productions of the work that Bolton has been able to unearth. Each entry gives the title, playwright, dates of production, cast list, and other details.

Bolton has scoured an impressive number of sources, both national and local. He has searched systematically through playbill collections through 1900, and less thoroughly in the twentieth century, when Scott's reputation had declined. The remarkably comprehensive index is especially valuable, listing everyone associated with the productions, as well as theater names and locations. This superb piece of research provides documentary evidence of the vagaries of Scott's popularity and should prove invaluable to its specialized audience.—**Jeffrey R. Luttrell**

William Shakespeare

1211. Dietrich, Julia. *Hamlet* in the 1960s: An Annotated Bibliography. Hamden, Conn., Garland, 1992. 771p. index. (Garland Shakespeare Bibliographies, no.18; Garland Reference Library of the Humanities, v.477). $115.00. Z8812.H2D54. 016.8223'3. LC 91-29683. ISBN 0-8240-8990-1.

That Shakespeare's *Hamlet* generated worldwide scholarly and popular interest in the 1960s is ably documented in Dietrich's excellent bibliographic guide. Including about 2,500 entries for books, articles, parts of books, dissertations, and stage and film reviews published in an extraordinary range of languages, Dietrich's coverage more than doubles that of Randal Robinson's *Hamlet in the 1950s* (see ARBA 85, entry 1122). Consciously following Robinson's guide in both organization and indexing, Dietrich chronologically subarranges entries in topical sections that cover criticism; source, dating, and textual studies; enumerative bibliographies; editions; stage histories; and adaptations, influence studies, and synopses. For many items, annotation is quite cursory: "Includes discussion of *HAMLET*," for example, is repeated in several entries. About 400 items are reported "unseen" and, therefore, unannotated (except for indicating language). Aside from these, however, the majority of entries provide full and detailed paragraphs. Notable English-language studies, such as Morris Weitz's *Hamlet and the Philosophy of Literary Criticism* (University of Chicago Press, 1964), are accorded full pages. Additionally, Dietrich describes works in foreign languages "not widely available to scholars" (p. xxvii) at length. Annotations for one article in Russian and another in Dutch extend to three pages. Although Dietrich indicates that "length of annotation" suggests a work's importance, it is unfortunate—given the guide's scope and comprehensiveness—that annotation is otherwise nonevaluative. Indeed, she seldom notes the relative significance of particular works.

Advanced researchers will applaud Dietrich's achievement. Identifying, assembling, and describing criticism in such languages as Arabic, Armenian, Serbian, and Ukrainian; editions in Gujarati, Icelandic, Tamil, and Urdu; and reviews of performances in Budapest and Tashkent provide a valuable service to scholarship. On the other hand, less sophisticated students or those interested in learning something about the play will struggle to discover just where to start research on the ghost's meaning. For guidance of this variety, David Daniell's chapter on *Hamlet* in the new edition of *Shakespeare: A Bibliographical Guide* (see ARBA 92, entry 1210) is perhaps a more helpful starting point.

—**James K. Bracken**

1212. Kolin, Philip C. **Shakespeare and Feminist Criticism: An Annotated Bibliography and Commentary.** Hamden, Conn., Garland, 1991. 420p. index. (Garland Reference Library of the Humanities, v.1345). $55.00. Z8811.K76. 822.3'3. LC 91-27900. ISBN 0-8240-7386-X.

This annotated bibliography of feminist criticism in English on Shakespeare covers the period between 1975, when Juliet Dusinberre published her ground-breaking *Shakespeare and the Nature of Women*, and 1988. During this time, as Kolin notes, feminist criticism grew from studies of "Shakespeare's women" to important new readings of both female and male sexuality. The extensive introduction summarizes the relationship of feminist studies to other critical approaches, such as deconstructionism, Marxism, and linguistics, and deals with important areas such as Shakespeare as a feminist, differing views on marriage and Renaissance ideology, cultural and sexual stereotypes, and boy actors and androgynous heroines. There are three indexes.

Unfortunately, the introduction does not explain exactly what Kolin considers "feminist" criticism. The list of books and articles, arranged by year and then alphabetically, seems to be selective rather than inclusive, omitting some articles mentioned in earlier bibliographies. It is not clear whether Kolin missed them or excluded them as not relevant. In any case, no important work has been left out.

The strength of the bibliography lies in its annotations. Unlike the skimpy one-line summaries typical of most "annotated" bibliographies, these run to at least half a page for articles and four or five pages for books, followed by a list of reviews. (Dissertations, although included, are not annotated because DAI supplies abstracts.) This space allows Kolin to give his reader a reasonably accurate summary of the content and critical stance of his items. Any reader interested in feminist issues will find these summaries useful and timesaving. Highly recommended for university libraries and readers interested in either feminism or Shakespeare. [R: Choice, Apr 92, p. 1210]—**Lynn F. Williams**

1213. Miner, Margaret, and Hugh Rawson. **A Dictionary of Quotations from Shakespeare: A Topical Guide to Over 3,000 Great Passages....** New York, E. P. Dutton, 1992. 368p. index. $23.00. PR2892.S4177. 822.3'3. LC 92-1354. ISBN 0-525-93451-0.

With all the reference works on Shakespeare, including 10 concordances listed in *Subject Guide to Books in Print* (see ARBA 92, entry 15), 13 entries under SHAKESPEARE – QUOTATIONS, and other large volumes of quotations in which the bard is heavily represented, it seems scarcely necessary to consider adding to the collection a work such as this. However, this small, pleasant book deserves attention. It presents quotations under subject headings, with a keyword index that itself constitutes a kind of brief concordance. The main body of the work is generous with cross-references, and nearly half the entries include concise, useful notes, such as explanation of meaning and identification of speaker or situation. The authors have attempted to choose quotations "that are relevant to modern times and present-day problems" (introduction); the subject headings also reflect this aim. Recommended for libraries that serve the general reader. [R: LJ, Aug 92, p. 86; RBB, 15 Nov 92, p. 628]

—**Robert N. Broadus**

1214. Rosenblum, Joseph. **Shakespeare: An Annotated Bibliography.** Pasadena, Calif., Salem Press, 1992. 307p. index. (Magill Bibliographies). $40.00. Z8811.R68. 016.8223'3. LC 92-4863. ISBN 0-89356-676-4.

Rosenblum's work examines the major twentieth-century criticism of Shakespeare's plays and poems, focusing on books but also including seminal articles. Rosenblum annotates studies essential to Shakespeare and evaluates their significance in the ongoing stream of Shakespearean criticism. Viewed together, these entries illustrate the varied, rich, and sometimes controversial literary viewpoints characteristic of approaches to understanding the master dramatist. This volume also includes a helpful introduction; good lists of bibliographies, reference works, editions, biographies, and Shakespearean stage studies; and a less-than-adequate list of studies of Shakespeare on stage. Then follows a solid selection of general studies and annotations of studies by individual play; these are alphabetically arranged. Undergraduates (and a few graduates) will be the principal beneficiaries of these annotations. Frequently, the annotations include references to reviews, also likely to assist the beginning Shakespeare student. The typeface is highly readable. Strongly recommended for collections on liberal arts studies, drama and theater libraries, and graduate libraries that collect dramatic literature.

—**C. B. (Bob) Darrell**

1215. Sajdak, Bruce T., ed. **Shakespeare Index: An Annotated Bibliography of Critical Articles on the Plays 1959-1983.** Millwood, N.Y., Kraus International, 1992. 2v. $295.00/set. Z8811.S25. 822.3'3. LC 91-28335. ISBN 0-527-78932-1.

Shakespeare Index is a monumental work that indexes the contents of more than 7,000 articles on Shakespeare written between 1959 and 1983. Each entry in volume 1 is placed in one of 48 categories, which include such areas as general textual studies, Shakespeare's life, language, studies of plays by genre, each play, and the apocrypha. Within each category, entries are arranged by date and alphabetical order, and contain complete bibliographical data plus a brief summary of their contents. Sajdak has drawn from a large list of bibliographical sources and has examined both well-known and obscure journals and books.

The importance of the work lies in the indexes that follow the bibliography; these are arranged by author, character, scene, and subject. One can therefore search not just for general subjects, but also for all the commentaries on the character of Cleopatra, or on *Hamlet* II:1, or on a combination of subjects such as sexuality and death (this combination produced articles on six plays, *not* including Othello, interestingly enough). As one might expect, even in such a large undertaking there are limitations in subject matter; excluded, for example, are the nondramatic poems; the authorship controversy; translations; and all editions, adaptations, and productions after Shakespeare's death. But there is still a great deal here for the literary researcher.

A far more important limitation of this index is the terminal date. Although the volumes were published in 1992, the citations end in 1983. The bibliographical sources do not go beyond 1988, thus omitting a large number of important works, including the new edition of *Shakespeare: A Bibliographical Guide* (see ARBA 92, entry 1210). Whether this time lag is due to the extensive work needed to track down articles or to delay by the publisher, it is a serious problem, because the past 10 years have been active ones in Shakespearean scholarship. Nevertheless, any university or research library where serious study of Shakespeare takes place will want this major work on its shelves. [R: Choice, Oct 92, pp. 280-81; WLB, June 92, pp. 116-58] — **Lynn F. Williams**

Bernard Shaw

1216. Weintraub, Stanley. **Bernard Shaw: A Guide to Research.** University Park, Pa., Pennsylvania State University Press, 1992. 154p. index. $35.00. Z8814.5.W44. 016.822'912. LC 91-41779. ISBN 0-271-00831-8.

Students of Shaw have been fortunate to have eminent scholars of the Irish playwright serve as bibliographers, sorting through the vast body of primary and secondary writings. Weintraub is a prolific Shaw critic, biographer, and editor who here applies his talent to writing descriptive essays on selected Shavian criticism and bibliography. While Shaw's dramatic productions date back 100 years, Weintraub reports mainly on the secondary literature of the last 3 or 4 decades. His intent is to describe the most useful research, especially that which makes use of more recently available primary source material.

Weintraub arranges the book into brief chapters on editions, bibliographies, autobiographical material, early and general criticism, criticism of individual plays, short sections on Shaw's fiction and Shaw in fiction, and an excellent section of Shaw's influence and reputation. By way of example, the section on *Heartbreak House* runs 5 pages and discusses 30 articles and essays. Along the way Weintraub highlights critical trends and areas of research deserving further attention. Indexes of authors, works, and subjects are provided.

Other bibliographies have been far more exhaustive. The two-volume *Bernard Shaw: A Critical Bibliography* (see ARBA 85, entry 1124) contains more than 3,900 primary source citations, and more than 8,000 entries fill the three volumes of *G. B. Shaw: An Annotated Bibliography of Writings about Him* (see ARBA 88, entry 1225). Weintraub brings a more selective focus to the enormous volume of literature and succeeds in putting it into a meaningful perspective for students and scholars. [R: Choice, Dec 92, pp. 605-06] — **John P. Schmitt**

Poetry

1217. Stainsby, Meg. *Sir Gawain and the Green Knight:* **An Annotated Bibliography, 1978-1989.** Hamden, Conn., Garland, 1992. 197p. index. (Garland Medieval Bibliographies, v.13; Garland Reference Library of the Humanities, v.1495). $33.00. Z6521.G38S73. 016.821'1. LC 91-36810. ISBN 0-8153-0504-4.

This volume, which covers the period from 1978 to 1989 (with some items up to 1991), is intended as an update of Malcom Andrew's *The Gawain Poet* (see ARBA 81, entry 1317). It more or less follows Andrew's format, being divided into sections on editions, translations, adaptations and performances, reference works, general criticism, and so forth. It omits dissertations, which are indexed in *Dissertation Abstracts*. The annotations are brief but will be helpful to the scholar and general reader. Stainsby has included a good selection of non-English-language criticism. There are a few omissions, possibly intentional. One might have expected a reference to the rewritten version of *Sir Gawain and the Green Knight* (SGGK) in Thomas Berger's *Arthur Rex* (Dell, 1979) and also to the extensive article on SGGK in *The Arthurian Encyclopedia* (see ARBA 87, entry 1161), which was also published by Garland.

Although this volume is extensive and up-to-date, much of its material is available in other works, including bibliographies by Michael Foley (in *Chaucer Review* 23 [1989]), Joanne A. Rice (in *Middle English Romance* [see ARBA 88, entry 1211]), and William Vantuono (in his translation of the poem which includes a bibliography), and the annual bibliographies of the International Arthurian Society and the Modern Language Association. Only large research libraries or those that do not already have other bibliographies will find it a necessary purchase.

— **Lynn F. Williams**

Canadian Literature

1218. **Canadian Literature Index: A Guide to Periodicals and Newspapers: Cumulative Index to 1986 Publications.** Janet Fraser, ed. Toronto, ECW Press, 1991. 480p. $195.00. 016.81. ISBN 1-55022-078-0.

1219. **Canadian Literature Index: A Guide to Periodicals and Newspapers: Cumulative Index to 1987 Publications.** Janet Fraser, ed. Toronto, ECW Press, 1991. 530p. $195.00. 016.81. ISBN 1-55022-084-5.

First issued for the year 1985 (see ARBA 88, entry 1236), the 1986 and 1987 editions of the *Canadian Literature Index* were published in 1991. Following the same basic format as the original volume, this reference source improves access to Canadian primary and secondary materials in the field of Canadian literature. Carefully edited to accomplish dual objectives, the volumes include indexing of Canadian authors writing in any language. Indexing, however, is not bilingual; only the actual literature is presented in the original language, with English indexing. Each volume consists of two major index sections—the first by author, which lists works by Canadians, and the second by subject, which includes topic headings as well as authors and titles. Cross-references in the original language from translated title subject headings have been added in these volumes. Another change is the adaption of international style for French-language information, with only the first significant letter of a title capitalized. Four periodical titles were added for indexing in the 1986 volume and are in both cumulative volumes. The editor anticipates periodical additions in subsequent volumes. Useful appendixes that give subscription and interlibrary loan information have once again been provided. Supplying general readers, students, and researchers with a periodical guide that has an exclusively Canadian literature focus, this index does an admirable job of covering both Canadian and international sources. [R: Choice, June 92, p. 1514]—**Virginia S. Fischer**

1220. Ripley, Gordon, and Anne Mercer. **Who's Who in Canadian Literature 1992-93.** Teeswater, Ont., Reference Press, 1992. 369p. $35.00pa. 810'.9'005. ISBN 0-919981-26-7. ISSN 0715-9366.

Now in its 4th edition, this biennial was originally published in 1983. It includes information about living Canadian poets, playwrights, story writers, novelists, children's writers, critics, editors, and translators. The majority of data came from questionnaires sent to more than 1,200 writers. Secondary sources were also used. All in all, more than 1,100 individuals are described briefly as to birth date and place, parents, education, spouse, children, memberships, awards, publications, works in progress, anthologies, mailing addresses, sources of critical information, and the like. Not included are writers who died before November 1983, journalists, and historians (unless they have written "letters"). Unfortunately, a glaring omission is perhaps the top critic in Canada: Bob Fulford.—**Dean Tudor**

French Literature

1221. Levi, Anthony. **Guide to French Literature: 1789 to the Present.** Chicago, St. James Press; distr., Detroit, Gale, 1992. 884p. index. $115.00. 840.9. ISBN 1-55862-086-9.

This encyclopedic guide apparently is the first of an intended two-volume set, although it chronologically covers a later time period. Levi promises that the introduction to that "first" volume will explain in detail the editorial criteria of the whole work. The introduction in this volume, however, does provide a great deal of this information, as well as an explanation of the links between literary and social histories. The main body of the work consists of well-written, often lengthy entries for individuals and literary movements. Personal entries also include lists of publications and critical and biographical studies. The lengthier personal entries are divided into sections on the individual's life and works. A title index lists the entries in the publications lists, and the detailed general index allows the user to find references to subjects and individuals contained within the main entries.

Subheadings under the index entries are listed in page-number order rather than alphabetically, which means that the user must browse through these lists in order to locate the desired entry. The index also is inconsistent in the treatment of pseudonyms. Entries in only the main body of the work are given to the most commonly known form of an author's name, although an author's real name is included as part of the entry. Unfortunately, not all of these real names are included in the index, which means that a user who knows only a real name may have difficulty in locating the entry for an individual. These minor flaws aside, this impressive work will be an essential addition to any library with an interest in French literature. —**Barbara E. Kemp**

1222. Sartori, Eva Martin, and Dorothy Wynne Zimmerman, eds. **French Women Writers: A Bio-Bibliographical Source Book.** Westport, Conn., Greenwood Press, 1991. 632p. index. $85.00. PQ149.F73. 840.9'9287. LC 91-2519. ISBN 0-313-26548-8.

This well-written collection of essays provides a solid introduction to the works of French women authors. The preface clearly states the criteria for inclusion. Women "who have written in French and identified themselves with French culture and intellectual life" are eligible to be listed. Another major criterion for inclusion is the creation of a substantial body of work. Most of those selected have written novels, letters, memoirs, plays, and poetry. The result is a core list of 51 individual authors and a composite entry for the women troubadours of the twelfth and thirteenth centuries.

Each of the signed essays is about 10 pages long and follows the same format: a biography, a discussion of the author's major themes, a survey of criticism and a bibliography of primary works, English translations, and selected critical studies. The essays are in alphabetical order by writers' names. One appendix is a chronology that situates women writers in French history; a second lists the authors by date of birth. Together, they help the reader place the authors in a historical context. Detailed title and subject indexes provide excellent access to the contents. Intended for general readers, students, and scholars, this volume should be in any collection of French literature. [R: Choice, May 92, p. 1368]
—**Barbara E. Kemp**

German Literature

1223. Furness, Raymond, and Malcolm Humble. **A Companion to Twentieth-Century German Literature.** New York, Routledge, Chapman & Hall, 1991. 305p. $49.95. Z2230.C65. 830.9'0091. LC 90-35826. ISBN 0-415-01987-7.

This informative, well-written guide offers 414 alphabetically arranged entries that focus chiefly on authors of imaginative texts in traditional high-culture genres, with a few crossovers from other art forms (e.g., cabaret) as well. Cinema, well covered elsewhere, seems to have been excluded. Also absent are entries on editors, publishers, producers, and critics, unless they are also poets or writers of prose fiction or drama. It appears that a necessary precondition for inclusion was the establishment of a literary reputation prior to the early 1980s.

That said, the authors (both Germanists at the University of St. Andrews) have chosen generously and well within their restricted purview. Most of the contemporary canon of university teaching and repeated scholarly attention is present, as is a broad scattering of other representative figures. Jewish writers, women writers, and writers of the former German Democratic Republic fare well. Usually ranging from a half dozen sentences to a page or so (few literary giants get longer entries), the entries give essential biographical information, highlight key elements of a writer's oeuvre, and situate the latter in historical and literary contexts. Critical judgments—personal, of course, but not idiosyncratic—flesh out these readable sketches.

One grave flaw is the lack of an index (hardly compensated for by some uneven internal cross-referencing). The volume is rich in titles of literary works, in names of persons not given entries of their own, and in references to places and to literary and other intellectual groups and movements. Making these accessible to specific searches would have enhanced the value of this still very useful book. [R: Choice, Jan 92, p. 716]—**John B. Dillon**

Italian Literature

1224. Consoli, Joseph P. **Giovanni Boccaccio: An Annotated Bibliography.** Hamden, Conn., Garland, 1992. 484p. index. (Garland Medieval Bibliographies, v.9; Garland Reference Library of the Humanities, v.971). $65.00. Z8106.C66. 016.858'109. LC 91-39513. ISBN 0-8240-3147-4.

Whether Giovanni Boccaccio (1313-1375) is regarded as the last great writer of the Middle Ages or the first great writer of the Renaissance, his importance can hardly be overstated. While *The Decameron* has always been his best-known and most admired work, he wrote many other works in all the important literary genres of his time (e.g., prose and verse, Italian and Latin). The magnitude of this bibliography clearly indicates that interest in the man and his works remains high today.

Covering works in English, Italian, French, Spanish, Portuguese, and German published from 1939 through 1986, the 1,348 entries provide comprehensive coverage of monographs and scholarly papers in journals, festschriften, and proceedings of conferences, plus selective coverage of review articles, newspaper items, and minor studies. All titles listed have been examined by Consoli. Excluded are editions of Boccaccio's works (and accompanying critical introductions) and material in general works on Italian literature or textbooks. Entries are arranged by 11 broad topics and subarranged alphabetically by author. Each includes author, title, brief bibliographic data, and a descriptive annotation that ranges from a few lines to a full page in length. There are comprehensive author and subject indexes.—**Paul B. Cors**

Latin American and Caribbean Literature

1225. Balderston, Daniel, comp. **The Latin American Short Story: An Annotated Guide to Anthologies and Criticism.** Westport, Conn., Greenwood Press, 1992. 529p. index. (Bibliographies and Indexes in World Literature, no.34). $65.00. Z1609.F4B35. 016.863'010898. LC 92-7336. ISBN 0-313-27360-X.

This is the first attempt at a bibliography of the Latin American short story and general criticism of it. The work is divided into two parts: anthologies and criticism. The first part is divided into general anthologies, general anthologies in English translation, regional anthologies, and sections on the anthologies of each country. The criticism section is divided into short story theory, general criticism, literary history, bibliography, regions of Latin America, secondary literature, and critical studies of the short story of each country.

For the anthologies, Balderston usually includes the author and title of the story in the collection along with a brief critical comment. Unannotated items are marked "Unable to locate." It is doubtful if the collections of short stories by Chicano authors should be included under Mexico, and one will not always agree with the compiler's value judgments.

The second section annotates critical studies of a general nature on the Latin American short story. The extremely brief annotations are usually quite useful. The section of criticism of Brazilian short stories contains 28 items, 16 of which are unannotated.

One notes that the title page is no longer sacred to bibliographers, for Balderston gives Mexico City for Mexico, Guatemala City for Guatemala, and Havana for La Habana. It is puzzling that he has been unable to annotate items that have been published in such U.S. journals as *Chasqui, Studies in Short Fiction*, and *Southwest Review* and such important Latin American journals as *Atenea, Plural*, and *Asomante*.

The introduction should be carefully read. The indexes of authors, critics, and titles should render this reference even more valuable to the user. It will be an essential addition to all Latin American collections. [R: Choice, Dec 92, p. 597]—**Hensley C. Woodbridge**

1226. Fenwick, M. J. **Writers of the Caribbean and Central America: A Bibliography.** Hamden, Conn., Garland, 1992. 2v. index. (Garland Reference Library of the Humanities, v.1244). $200.00/set. Z1595.F46. 016.8088'99729. LC 91-35701. ISBN 0-8240-4010-4.

This is a monumental bibliography of the belles lettres of 43 geographical areas that are in or that touch the Caribbean. Writers are listed by nation of birth and colisted under nations of other significant residence. The writer's original works are given in chronological order, followed by magazines and anthologies in which the author's work appears.

A discussion of a bibliographical nature would have been helpful. What does a date like 1873-(1879-)1950(1952) for Mariano Azuela mean? Why are dates provided for some books and not for others? What percentage of the works listed have been personally examined? (*La cordillera*, listed under Juan Rulfo, was never published.) How did Fenwick decide what to list in the "Works appear in ..." section? How did he decide on an author's nationality? Juan Larrea (born in Spain) is listed under Venezuela; why is he not under Mexico (if he must be included) since he spent many years in exile there? It is doubtful if Isabel Allende should be listed under Venezuela. Fenwick may have good reasons for everything he has done, but he does not share them with the user. A number of anthologies are mentioned many times. It would have been helpful had a section been devoted to providing full bibliographical data on them instead of just author, title, and date.

There are numerous examples of Fenwick's incompleteness. For example, under Rodrigo Re Rosa (which he hyphenates) he lists only a dateless *The Beggar's Knife*. Yet, as of 1990, there are three book-length translations of this author: *The Beggar's Knife* (1985), *The Path Doubles Back* (1982), and *Dust on Her Tongue* (1989). Also, his works have appeared in *El Imparcial, City Lights Review, Threepenny Review, Boston Review,* and *Frank Magazine* (Paris).

This work, while extremely valuable, especially for lesser-known areas, must be used with a degree of caution. As this set deals with areas not covered before by publications in the United States, libraries will find it an important addition to their reference collections. For areas of greater importance (e.g., Mexico, Cuba, Venezuela, Colombia), they would do well to purchase literary dictionaries of these countries published there or in Spain. [R: C&RL, Sept 92, p. 422; Choice, July/Aug 92, p. 1655; LJ, 1 Apr 92, p. 110]—**Hensley C. Woodbridge**

1227. Foster, David William. **Mexican Literature: A Bibliography of Secondary Sources.** 2d ed. Metuchen, N.J., Scarecrow, 1992. 686p. index. $67.50. Z1421.F63. 016.8609'972. LC 92-4630. ISBN 0-8108-2548-1.

This work, by the foremost U.S. bibliographer of Hispanic literature, is divided into 28 sections of general references and 82 sections on authors. The author section has more than two dozen new authors, and all sections have been updated from the 1981 edition. The work includes books and monographs, papers in academic periodicals, and articles and notes in cultural and literary reviews. Doctoral dissertations have been excluded. Misprints are extremely few.

As one who has used the first edition and who has recommended it to graduate students, this reviewer has nothing but high praise for the volume's coverage. The inclusion of doctoral dissertations and literary supplements would have been desirable, but because Foster clearly spells out the perimeters of this bibliography, he can hardly be faulted.

There are some small problems. Item 15.12 is reprinted in Mario Benedetti's *El ejercicio del criterio* (Mexico: Nueva Imagen, 1981). One wonders at the omission of Margaret Sayers Peden as the translator of item 37.303, and the imprint data on item 15.31 seems to make no sense.

This volume should be in the reference collection of all libraries where there is an interest in Mexican and Latin American literature. Specialists in Mexican literature will want their own copies. [R: LJ, July 92, p. 76]—**Hensley C. Woodbridge**

1228. Sefami, Jacobo, comp. **Contemporary Spanish American Poets: A Bibliography of Primary and Secondary Sources.** Westport, Conn., Greenwood Press, 1992. 245p. index. (Bibliographies and Indexes in World Literature, no.33). $45.00. Z1609.P6S4. 016.861. LC 91-40413. ISBN 0-313-27880-6.

This is a guide to 86 poets born between 1910 and 1952. The data about each poet is divided into works and critical studies about them. Sefami has included poetic works, compilations and anthologies, and other works (e.g., fiction, essays). Translations of the poets' work are not generally included, although *A Rosario Castellanos Reader*, an anthology of Castellanos's work in English translation, is listed. The secondary sources consist of bibliographies and critical studies. In the latter, Sefami has selected items that deal mainly with the poetry of the corresponding writer. The section of general works at the end complements the main body of the bibliography; it does not include anthologies and refers mostly to Spanish-American poetry of the last 50 years. English reviews of English translations are provided.

As Sefami notes that this compilation is not exhaustive, there is little point in quibbling over what he has included or excluded. Users who need more data can search other bibliographies on the authors that Sefami lists. Overall, this is an excellent guide for the authors that are dealt with and should be in any library interested in Latin American culture and literature. It seems to be extremely accurate and has few typographical errors. [R: Choice, June 92, p. 1528]

—Hensley C. Woodbridge

Oceanian Literature

1229. Simms, Norman. **Writers from the South Pacific: A Bio-Bibliographical Critical Encyclopedia.** Washington, D.C., Three Continents Press, 1991. 184p. illus. maps. index. $35.00; $17.50pa. Z4501.S57. 016.809'8995. LC 91-24535. ISBN 0-89410-594-9; 0-89410-595-7pa.

Despite being mistitled and often poorly executed, this volume does have merits. Simms inexplicably includes the Southeast Asian nations of Malaysia and Singapore in the "South Pacific" but excludes the more southern and Pacific nations of the Philippines and Indonesia. Had the book been restricted to the geocultural area of its title, this reviewer's complaints would have been far fewer. Authors from Singapore and Malaysia (comprising about one-third of the alphabetical entries) suffer from minimal entries, as if their contributions consisted only of having been included in an anthology rather than major works. If Malay, authors are sometimes entered under their fathers' names (e.g., Muhammad Haji Salleh and Shanon Ahmad). Important reference sources—even in English—for correct information on these authors (e.g., *A Biography of Malaysian Writers* [Kuala Lumpur: Dewan Bahasa dan Pustaka, 1985]) are omitted from the minimal bibliography.

The strength of the volume lies in its treatment of the South Pacific, including non-European authors from Australia and New Zealand. Moreover, with a number of these authors (and a few from Singapore), Simms engages in a dialog that attempts to present their thinking on the relationship of writers to their societies. These lengthier entries somewhat compensate for Simms's lamentable decision "to work as much as possible *not* from pre-existing information or 'dead data'" (p. 7, emphasis added), despite the general unavailability of the latter. Although this work is seriously flawed, the paucity of information on South Pacific writers makes it a useful addition to larger or literary reference collections.—**K. Mulliner**

Russian Literature

1230. Ignashev, Diane M. Nemec, and Sarah Krive. **Women and Writing in Russia and the USSR: A Bibliography of English-Language Sources.** Hamden, Conn., Garland, 1992. 328p. index. (Garland Reference Library of the Humanities, v.1280). $51.00. Z2503.5.W6N45. 016.891709'9287. LC 92-9246. ISBN 0-8240-3647-6.

This volume fills a long-standing need on the part of two audiences. Its primary readership includes those seeking guidance on belletristic writing by women and on those writing about women and their literary work. Although limited to materials available in English, it includes works by and about women not only from Russia but also from many of the numerous languages and cultures of the former Russian and Soviet empires. The volume's secondary audience consists of researchers interested in the larger social context of the area's women, including such categories as education, health and medicine, religion and spirituality, work, and national and ethnic identities. This secondary subject matter, which is less fully treated, is intended to provide background for studies of the women covered in the earlier (and much more substantial) sections.

The needs of the first audience are well met, given the English-only limitation. The volume serves as an excellent starting point for research on women writers in a huge and culturally diverse area. Users interested in nonliterary aspects of women's studies will need more specialized bibliographic assistance. Serious researchers with either interest will soon have to go beyond the English to sources in the original languages, German, and French. Expansion of the very brief bibliographies section to include a few basic foreign-language reference materials would have made the volume useful to a still wider audience. Current through 1990, this volume will be the basic bibliographic handbook for any initial orientation in women's cultural history of the former Russian Empire.

—**D. Barton Johnson**

Scottish Literature

1231. Brown, Anthony E. **Boswellian Studies: A Bibliography.** 3d ed. Edinburgh, Edinburgh University Press; distr., New York, Columbia University Press, 1991. 176p. index. $42.50. 820.016. ISBN 0-7486-0303-4.

For students and researchers involved with the life and writings of Boswell, this new edition of a standard specialized reference tool will be invaluable. Brown has updated the bibliography through 1989, with a total of slightly more than 1,500 entries, including addenda. This edition also has three new sections. The arrangement includes a beginning section that lists editions of Boswell's works from 1760 to 1989, including both published (1760-1989) and unpublished (1857-1989) works, with notices, reviews, extracts, and commentaries; trade editions of Boswell's journal, 1950-1989; research editions of Boswell's papers and letters, 1966-1988; and translations of Boswell's works. Sections that follow include "Memorabilia," a listing of obituaries and early memoirs published from 1795 to 1803, and biographies of Boswell published from 1891 through 1984; general studies, the largest of the eight sections, with selectively annotated entries; newspaper and magazine paragraphs; theses and dissertations; bibliographies; an addenda; and a subject index.

Useful for its scope and detail, this bibliography will likely continue to serve as a keystone in Boswell studies for some time. It is a valuable addition to scholarly and research collections of English literature. — **Edmund F. SantaVicca**

1232. Cochrane, Hamilton E. **Boswell's Literary Art: An Annotated Bibliography of Critical Studies, 1900-1985.** Hamden, Conn., Garland, 1992. 162p. index. (Garland Reference Library of the Humanities, v.969). $22.00. Z8110.2.C63. 016.828'609. LC 91-30751. ISBN 0-8240-1516-9.

This bibliography of 685 books, scholarly articles, and dissertations about James Boswell is well annotated and easy to use. Although it is subtitled "An Annotated Bibliography of Critical Studies, 1900-1985," it also includes biographies of Boswell and discussions of his legal career. The titles have been numbered consecutively throughout the volume and arranged chronologically under six sections according to topic: biographical studies; bibliographical studies; accounts of the Boswell Papers; studies of particular works by Boswell, subdivided under *Life of Johnson, Journal of a Tour to the Hebrides, An Account of Corsica*, journals, correspondence, and miscellaneous writings; general studies about Boswell; and miscellaneous topics, such as religion, politics, and law. The listing does not, for the most part, include reviews, articles in newspapers and popular magazines, dramatizations, or works that deal with Boswell peripherally (e.g., the major biography on Samuel Johnson by W. Jackson Bate). Although the critical introductions to various editions have generally been omitted, the important essays from the Yale Editions of the Private Papers of James Boswell are included. Dissertations that do not circulate and are not on microfilm are listed but not annotated.

There are author and subject indexes, the latter very useful. For example, under the heading "Boswell, James" there are six columns of topics divided into four sections: "Character," "Life," "Other Topics," and "Writings." This well-organized book not only presents an excellent survey of Boswell scholarship but also provides perceptive annotations. [R: Choice, July/Aug 92, p. 1652]
— **Charlotte Lindgren**

Spanish Literature

1233. Zubatsky, David S. **Spanish, Catalan, and Galician Literary Authors of the Twentieth Century: An Annotated Guide to Bibliographies.** Metuchen, N.J., Scarecrow, 1992. 184p. $27.50. Z2691.A1Z83. 016.016849'509. LC 92-4041. ISBN 0-8108-2518-X.

Zubatsky's interest in author bibliographies goes back more than 15 years. His previous volume along these lines was the outstanding *Latin American Literary Authors* (see ARBA 88, entry 1255). This volume provides data on twentieth-century authors of Spain who have published in Spanish, Galician, and Catalan. He has sought his bibliographies in parts of books, journals, and festschriften; a few entries are book-length bibliographies of the most important authors of the century.

The annotations are extremely useful. They usually are an outline of the bibliography's organization, often including an indication of the number of entries and occasionally a note concerning the strengths and the weaknesses of the bibliography. More critical comments would add to the strength of this work, such as the note on H. Hernandez Pelayo's *Bibliografia critica de Miguel de Unamuno (1888-1975)*, which states that "Because of bibliographical inconsistencies, the work must be used with caution." There is no indication, for instance, in the annotation of Anton Donoso and Harold C. Raley's *Jose Ortega y Gasset: A Bibliography of Secondary Sources* that it contains numerous incomplete bibliographical citations.

This excellent bibliography will save scholars and students of twentieth-century Spanish literature countless hours of searching. It is unique; no one else has ever tried to compile such a volume. It is to be hoped that Zubatsky will provide similar works on other phases of the literatures of Spain. This book should be in the libraries of all colleges and universities where Spanish literature is taught. [R: Choice, Nov 92, p. 452]—**Hensley C. Woodbridge**

Yugoslav Literature

1234. Mihailovich, Vasa D. **Second Supplement to** *A Comprehensive Bibliography of Yugoslav Literature in English* **1986-1990.** Columbus, Ohio, Slavica, 1992. 301p. index. $19.95pa. ISBN 0-89357-230-6.

This supplement is the continuation of a project started in 1976 by Mihailovich, a project that has thus far yielded a preliminary volume (see ARBA 86, entry 1225) and the *First Supplement* (see ARBA 90, entry 1212). The present volume lists translations and critical essays published between 1986 and 1990, and it also includes additions to the previous bibliographies. The book is divided into three sections: an alphabetical list of translations of folk literature; translations of poetry, fiction, drama, and literary essays by individual authors; and indexes to English titles or first lines of anonymous works, titles or first lines in the original, titles of newspapers and periodicals, and subjects and names. The latter index does not include all authors and names listed in the book. Because the individual chapters feature authors in alphabetical order, one is advised to search for them without relying on the index. Preceding the main body of the book is a comprehensive list of abbreviations. Because Yugoslavia has recently splintered into several countries, this overview will have to be the last under the heading of "Yugoslav," which gives it added historical significance. This work will be useful to university libraries and scholars involved with literature of the South Slavs.—**Koraljka Lockhart**

POETRY

1235. **The Columbia Granger's Dictionary of Poetry Quotations.** Edith P. Hazen, ed. New York, Columbia University Press, 1992. 1132p. index. $99.00. PN6082.C57. 808.881. LC 91-42240. ISBN 0-231-07546-4.

Most indexes to poetry provide access by title and first line. The sine qua non of these is *Granger's*, first published in 1904 and known in its 9th and latest incarnation as *The Columbia Granger's Index to Poetry* (see ARBA 91, entry 1250). With the publication of *Last Lines* (see ARBA 92, entry 1246), poetry quotation seekers received additional help, and the present volume seeks to bridge the remaining gap by unlocking interior lines as well. Quotations included have been selected by 8 Columbia University specialists from the 4,000 most-anthologized poems, as shown by *The Columbia Granger's Index*. Indeed, the list of approximately 400 anthologies perused for this task is identical to that of the aforementioned 9th edition.

Arrangement is alphabetical by poet, beginning with a 20-page section by "Unknown," and alphabetical by title under each name. Almost 700 poets (plus a few other sources, such as the Bible and Mother Goose) of all centuries and origins are included, although English-language writers predominate. Subject and keyword indexes occupy more than half the volume and seem generally effective, although a test using Gerard Manley Hopkins's "Summer and Fall" found it to be indexed only under the key word "Goldengrove" and not "Margaret" or "unleaving," words equally crucial to the lines quoted. The same poem was not located under the subject "Mortality," a puzzling oversight. Given the ambitious task this volume undertakes, however, it has made a good beginning. Libraries of all types will find it useful, particularly for access to contemporary poetry, which is not yet widely indexed in books of general quotations. [R: Choice, Dec 92, p. 598; WLB, Nov 92, p. 92]

—Willa Schmidt

1236. Magill, Frank N., ed. **Critical Survey of Poetry: English Language Series.** rev. ed. Pasadena, Calif., Salem Press, 1992. 8v. index. $475.00/set. PR502.C85. 821.009'03. LC 92-3727. ISBN 0-89356-834-1.

This set is an update of the 1982 edition. It covers 390 authors arranged in alphabetical order. There is no direct statement of intended audience, but examination of the entries indicates that the writing style and level of difficulty are appropriate for high school through undergraduate collections. Of particular note is the readability and sense of closure of the entries. There is no "rush to finish" in any examined.

Compared to the 1982 edition, 27 of the 390 entries are completely new, and, according to the publisher's note, all entries have been revised. Entries contain approximately five pages per poet. Each has birth and death dates and locations (when known), principal poetry, other literary forms, achievements, a brief biography, an analysis, other major works, and a bibliography. The major elements of interest are the principal poetry produced, the achievements, and the analysis. In the entries examined, each of these elements is consistent with the mainstream of English literature criticism. In short, there are no unpleasant surprises; but neither does this work break any new critical ground. What it does (and does well) is to pull together a wide variety of material on a wide range of poets. The trade-off is "plain vanilla" criticism, although the material is challenging. An example is the entry on William Blake. Blake's life and poetry are presented from a variety of different perspectives: philosophical, psychological, and political. The results are mixed. The reader comes away with a sense that there are a number of ways of viewing Blake's work but little sense of the strengths and shortcomings of the individual approaches.

However, this work is not intended to be used at the forefront of poetical criticism; it is designed to be an entry to the world of English-language poetry. To his credit, Magill has used a considerable number of experts in the field. They were apparently responsibly for the bibliographies at the end of the entries. This is the only area where greater editorial control would have improved the work, as the bibliographies range from strictly descriptive to mildly critical. Depending on the use to which the work is put, this makes some entries much more useful than others.

Overall, this is a reasonable work. It is recommended for collections where a primary concern is to introduce readers to English-language poetry. [R: LJ, 1 Oct 92, p. 78; RBB, 1 Nov 92, pp. 540-42]

—C. D. Hurt

1237. Magill, Frank N., ed. **Masterplots II: Poetry Series.** Pasadena, Calif., Salem Press, 1992. 6v. index. $425.00/set. PN1110.5.M37. 809.1. LC 91-44341. ISBN 0-89356-584-9.

This is an interesting collection of material. The six-volume set is impressive for its breadth of poets but is unremarkable for the poetry covered. Although it appears that the most popular poetry is included, the introduction gives no clue as to the criteria for selection. The overall work corresponds to an anthology one would expect in a high school English literature class.

The work is arranged by title of poem (or by translation, if foreign). Included in each annotation are the author's name and dates, a delineation of the type of poem, and where the poem first appeared in published form. There appears to be no controlled list of types of poetry used by the contributors or any editorial control exerted for this information. Fortunately, the types used are index items. The results are mixed, however, with a single entry under "Mock Epic" and approximately 500 under "Lyric."

Following some ready-reference information, each narrative is subdivided into three sections: the poem, forms and devices, and themes and meanings. The narratives, which generally run three pages each, are not critiques; they are decidedly descriptive. Written by a large number of reviewers, each is signed. There is certainly nothing in them that cannot be found elsewhere in one of the works in the bibliographies listed in the back of volume 6.

This is a good, solid reference work for the junior high school through community college level. It is not a substitute for critical works of greater depth, and the work does not make that claim. (Part of the difficulty with the work is that it makes *no* claims.) It would have been preferable to see this portion of the Masterplots series move the watermark of the entire series higher, although it certainly does not lower it. Given the difficulty of handling poetry, that is reasonable praise in itself. [R: LJ, July 92, p. 78; RBB, 1 Nov 92, p. 549; SLJ, Nov 92, pp. 137-38; WLB, Sept 92, p. 115]—**C. D. Hurt**

1238. **Poetry Index Annual 1990: An Author, Title, First Line and Keyword Subject Index to Poetry in Anthologies.** By the Editorial Board. Great Neck, N.Y., Poetry Index Press/Roth Publishing, 1991. 258p. $54.99. ISBN 0-89609-311-5. ISSN 0736-3966.

This work indexes 38 anthologies published in 1989. The criteria for selecting the anthologies are not indicated, beyond the fact that the poems were all written in or translated into English. Several of the books collect contemporary poetry; others concentrate on topics (e.g., religion), regions or countries, or poetry written by members of various ethnic groups.

Each poem is indexed by author, title, and first line (if the first line differs significantly from the title). Each anthology is given an alphanumerical symbol, and page numbers appear to be provided for each listed poem, but this detail is not explained. For example, in "P212/88," the "P212" refers to the anthology, and presumably the cited poem is on page 88. A separate keyword index lists significant words from the poems' titles.—**Robin Riley Fast**

25 Music

GENERAL WORKS

Bibliography

1239. Haroon, Mohammed. **Indian Music Literature.** Delhi, India, Indian Bibliographies Bureau; distr., Columbia, Mo., South Asia Books, 1991. 144p. index. $37.50. ISBN 81-85004-28-5.

According to Haroon, the bibliographic control of information on Indian music is very poor. To address this deficiency he has compiled a bibliography of concert reviews, newspaper and journal articles, books, and dissertations published between 1970 and 1989. He has indexed the contents of approximately 150 newspapers and journals and included 450 books and 200 dissertations in this volume. About 2,500 unannotated entries are provided that cover all aspects of Indian music. The arrangement of the bibliography is classified, offering some subject access, and an author index is included. Although citations are provided in English, there is no indication as to whether the documents are in English or Hindi.

This book will be of most value to libraries that actively collect in the areas of Indian or world music. General music collections and collections without this emphasis may find this volume less useful, as the publications indexed here are primarily Indian and may be difficult to acquire. [R: Choice, Mar 92, p. 1046]—**Allie Wise Goudy**

1240. Heller, George N. **Historical Research in Music Education: A Bibliography.** 2d ed. Lawrence, Kans., Department of Art and Music Education and Music Therapy, University of Kansas, 1992. 122p. $15.00 spiralbound. ISBN 1-879818-05-1.

This work brings together various kinds of research related to the history of music education. It is divided into three sections. The first consists of biographies; the second pertains to music education in specific geographic areas; and the third covers a multitude of topics, from "Jesuits and Music: The European Tradition, 1547-1622" to "A History of the College Band Directors National Association." The referenced research represents books, periodicals, reviews, dissertations, and theses. It is drawn from research as recent as 1991, and also from that done in the last 50 years, with the oldest entry dating back to 1885. Dissertations and theses account for a significant portion of the referenced material.

This compilation has no preface. It would be of interest to know how the work was compiled and for whom Heller intends it; as it stands, it is difficult to determine how complete it is. However, assuming that this work is aimed at the academic or student interested in music education and its history, it most definitely provides examples of a wide range of topics. To that extent, it could be useful for those looking to do research in this field.—**Martha Miller Yazhari**

1241. Lems-Dworkin, Carol. **African Music: A Pan-African Annotated Bibliography.** Munich, New Providence, N.J., Hans Zell/K. G. Saur, 1991. 382p. illus. index. $78.00. ML120.A35L4. 018.78'098. LC 91-33581. ISBN 0-905450-91-4.

Access to information on African music has become increasingly important, the subject being so imperfectly considered in so many of the sources issued prior to the last few decades, as Lems-Dworkin's introduction acknowledges. The 1,703 entries in this handsomely produced bibliography are the latest in the chain of such surveys, including Douglas Varley's *African Native Music* (London: Royal Commonwealth Society, 1936); Alan Merriam's "An Annotated Bibliography of African and African-derived Music since 1936" (which appeared in the October 1951 issue [vol. 21] of *Africa*); and John Gray's *African Music: A Bibliographical Guide to the Traditional, Popular, Art, and Liturgical Musics of Sub-Saharan Africa* (Greenwood Press, 1991).

Lems-Dworkin now securely joins the field. Her annotations are very useful, being at times abstracts, at times reviews. She has examined the literature without concern for language restrictions, unhesitatingly including items in Arabic as well as Yoruba and European languages, dropping no diacriticals enroute. The entries are offered in one alphabet, which gives focus to the productivity and subject expertise of the investigators and importance to the subject index. This work merits acquisition by all collections with an African component and those interested in the many interdisciplinary implications of its subject. [R: Choice, Oct 92, p. 275] – **Dominique-Rene de Lerma**

1242. Schuursma, Ann Briegleb. **Ethnomusicology Research: A Select Annotated Bibliography.** Hamden, Conn., Garland, 1992. 173p. index. (Garland Library of Music Ethnology, v.1; Garland Reference Library of the Humanities, v.1136). $24.00. ML128.E8S4. 780'.89. LC 90-3736. ISBN 0-8240-5735-X.

Given the explosion in the field of ethnomusicology over the past 30 years, it is surprising that this resource is the first general bibliography to appear since Jaap Kunst's *Ethnomusicology* (Nijhof, 1959) and Bruno Nettl's more selective resource, *Reference Materials in Ethnomusicology* (Information Coordinators, 1973). Schuursma's bibliography includes important and representative English-language resources published after 1960. Due to the existence of specialized bibliographies on popular music and dance, materials concerning these areas have usually been omitted.

The 468 entries are divided into 5 major sections covering the history of the field, ethnomusicological theory and method, fieldwork methods and techniques, musical analysis, and resources from the related social sciences – anthropology, folklore, linguistics, sociology, and psychology. Within each section, entries are arranged alphabetically by author. Cross-references are made when a resource fits into more than one section. Name and subject indexes are provided. Besides including ethnographic cultural groups and geographical areas, the subject index also supplies titles of monographs when those titles do not mention either a cultural group or a geographic area. The subject index is cross-referenced.

Written to address the needs of both scholar and lay reader, this bibliography is an excellent basic resource. The introductory overview of research and developments is well written, as are the annotations. Every library should have this resource among their music reference materials. [R: Choice, July/Aug 92, pp. 1660-61] – **Renee J. LaPerriere**

1243. Thompson, Donald, and Annie F. Thompson. **Music and Dance in Puerto Rico from the Age of Columbus to Modern Times: An Annotated Bibliography.** Metuchen, N.J., Scarecrow, 1991. 339p. index. (Studies in Latin American Music, no.1). $37.50. ML125.P8T55. 016.78'097295. LC 91-40519. ISBN 0-8108-2515-5.

This scholarly work identifies books, chapters and sections of books, theses and dissertations, and journal articles on music, musicians, musical life, and dance in Puerto Rico. It does not attempt to cover the subject of Puerto Rican music and dance on the United States mainland, so it includes few references to off-island careers of noted Puerto Rican performers. Only publications whose actual existence could be verified by the Thompsons are included. Titles rumored or reported but unseen have been excluded. An attempt has been made to locate articles in island publications not regularly indexed abroad, whereas articles in publications easily located through the *Music Index* are deemphasized.

The immediate precursor of the bibliography is Annie F. Thompson's *An Annotated Bibliography of Writings about Music in Puerto Rico* (Music Library Association, 1975). The scope of the present work is greatly expanded, covering 995 consecutively numbered items. The references are grouped into categories: bibliography; reference, histories, and essays; biography, interviews, and eulogy; panoramic surveys; and chroniclers, travelers, and historians. The next six chapters present types of music and dance, including concert and church music, lyric theater and ballet, traditional folk music and dance, urban music and dance, the "danza Puertorriquena," and "La Borinquena." The final chapter presents miscellaneous sources. Within each chapter, references are arranged alphabetically by author or title. There is a separate subject index and an index of authors, compilers, and editors. The annotations are generally short and descriptive. However, critical comments are sometimes included. Specific relevant pages or sections are noted in the annotations as well as cross-references to other items. This improves the book's usefulness. The style is clear and concise.

Donald Thompson is a retired university professor and former chair of the Music Department at the University of Puerto Rico, Rio Piedras. He is a music historian and a well-known music critic and conductor. Annie F. Thompson, a former music librarian, is active in the Music Library Association and is director of the Graduate School of Library and Information Science, University of Puerto Rico, Rio Piedras. Their combined knowledge and expertise are clearly reflected in the bibliography, enhancing its credibility. The potential audience for the bibliography is broad, including not only scholars, researchers, and students but also teachers, musicians, performers, and laypeople interested in Puerto Rican music and dance, musicians, and performers. For this reason the book serves as a valuable resource for university, college, community college, and public library reference collections. [R: Choice, June 92, p. 1529]—**Susan J. Freiband**

Biography

1244. **Baker's Biographical Dictionary of Musicians.** 8th ed. Revised by Nicolas Slonimsky. New York, Schirmer Books/Macmillan, 1992. 2115p. $125.00. ML105.B16. 780'.92'2. LC 91-24591. ISBN 0-02-872415-1.

This work contains information on musicians of all genres, times, and places. At the age of 97, the Russian-American musicologist Slonimsky continues to entertain with his sharp wit and inform through his detailed research in music. In this edition he has added 1,100 new entries and has revised 1,300 others. The additional entries include a wider coverage of popular music, women composers, and ethnomusicologists than did the 7th edition (see ARBA 86, entry 1232). Most entries contain brief biographical information, a list of works and writings, and a bibliography. Items in the bibliography are arranged in chronological order; some are as recent as 1990. Although the information about each person is brief, it serves as an excellent starting point for further research. This work remains one of the core resources for music reference collections. [R: LJ, Jan 92, p. 104; RBB, 1 Feb 92, p. 1052; SLJ, May 92, p. 32; WLB, Mar 92, pp. 113-14]—**Margaret A. Grift**

1245. **Contemporary Musicians: Profiles of the People in Music. Volume 6.** Michael L. LaBlanc, ed. Detroit, Gale, 1992. 286p. illus. index. $52.95. ISBN 0-8103-2216-1. ISSN 1044-2197.

Eighty-seven musical artists from all genres have been profiled in this volume. Following the format of the previous volumes, a clearly marked box briefly summarizes personal statistics and career information, and biographical essays of varying length outline the artists' personal and professional lives. Photographs appear in each entry. Several examples of critical response to each artist's work are provided as well as lists of major recorded works. Sources for additional information direct the reader to book and periodical articles. All entries are signed. Two cumulative indexes, by subject and musician, provide easy access to data by indicating in which volume of the set an artist or topic can be found. Although information on these performers may be available in other sources, the value of this series is that it provides comprehensive data on a wide range of artists in one easy-to-use reference set. It will find much use in all types of libraries.—**Marilyn Strong Noronha**

Dictionaries and Encyclopedias

1246. Cary, Tristram. **Dictionary of Musical Technology.** Westport, Conn., Greenwood Press, 1992. 542p. illus. $79.95. ML102.E4C37. 780'.3. LC 92-14583. ISBN 0-313-28694-9.

While it is not uncommon for a composer to write a book, a dictionary is another matter. Cary, who founded the Royal College of Music electronic music studio in 1967, has not only done it but also has managed to incorporate many of his interesting perspectives on the subject while retaining the factual integrity expected of a reference work. In addition to electronic and computer music technology, there is considerable information on audio topics. Most of the some 800 entries are under half a page in length, but there are multipage treatments of subjects such as computer music composition. A number of line drawings, primarily related to acoustics and system flow charts, are provided. Cary offers the most comprehensive treatment of this subject available, although Richard Dobson's recent *Dictionary of Electronic and Computer Music Terminology* (see index for entry number) should not be ignored. It offers a tutorial approach that may appeal to some and also has more information about individual electronic instruments and pieces of software. —**Robert Skinner**

1247. Dobson, Richard. **A Dictionary of Electronic and Computer Music Terminology: Instruments, Terms, Techniques.** New York, Oxford University Press, 1992. 224p. index. $39.95. ISBN 0-19-311344-9.

The rapidly evolving electronic and computer music technologies have not spawned much in the way of traditional reference resources. In addition to being timely, Dobson's dictionary is also interestingly conceived. The majority of its information is conveyed in multipage, overarching entries, such as *acoustics* or *components, electronic*. While this can be frustrating for those wanting quick definitions and who must constantly cope with *see* references (e.g., "Resistor, Resistance: *See* COMPONENTS 1"), the "big picture" approach has merit and makes this dictionary more readable than most. It also allows the work to be used as a tutorial. Most of the topics one would expect to find are present; music notation software, such as *Finale* and *Score*, is an important exception (although software sequencers, for example, are represented). Explanations are clear and not overly technical. There are separate indexes for names and products/manufactures, the latter including more than 350 products.

Ironically, another book on this topic, *Illustrated Compendium of Musical Technology* by Tristram Cary (Faber and Faber, 1992), also appeared this year. Cary's volume is more than twice the length of Dobson's, and its arrangement and entries are more traditionally conceived. Part of the reason for the disparity in length is that Cary has considerable material related to audio technology; Dobson, on the other hand, is still stronger on individual instruments and products. Both volumes would be good additions to libraries, with Cary, because of its size, probably being of more value to a wider audience. —**Robert Skinner**

1248. Leuchtmann, Horst, ed. **Dictionary of Terms in Music: English-German; German-English. Worterbuch Musik.** 4th ed. Munich, New Providence, N.J., K. G. Saur, 1992. 411p. $55.00. ISBN 3-598-10913-X.

This work reads like a standard bilingual dictionary. The terms include some phrases, arranged letter-by-letter. The preface and the directions for the user, in both languages, are given before the body of the work; English is presented first. In back is a brief list of titles of musical works in both languages, with references to the form in the other language (some titles are in a third language).

Not much has changed since the 3d edition (1981). Comparing the two, one finds about a 10 percent increase in the book's height and a commensurate increase in the number of entries. The text is now arranged in columns. The prefaces to the two editions are virtually identical, which is unfortunate; Leuchtmann states in both that "the diagrams of musical instruments from the 1st edition have been reintroduced." In fact, they are nowhere to be found; moreover, other elements of music that were in the 3d edition's appendix have also been dropped. The English preface appears to have been translated from the German, as do the directions for the user. The orientation of this work is towards a German readership, as is appropriate for one of German authorship and publication. English readers will find the language stilted and would be better served by a statement written especially for them about what purposes the work can serve. Knowledge of grammar is a prerequisite in many cases for interpretation of such things as verb tenses. Four compound German words beginning with "Nicht-" are included; but not the phrase "Nicht schleppen!" which is found as a tempo characterization in scores. Also regrettable is the decision not to cite acknowledgments, which in the 2d edition (1977) amounted to a page. If acknowledgments and sources were included, they would enhance the work considerably by providing authority beyond that of Leuchtmann and the publisher.

Regrettably, this work does not attain its potential. It cannot be evaluated in terms of goals, as none are stated. With proper attention the author and publishers could have provided the scholarly community with an authoritative tool. Not recommended. — **Ian Fairclough**

1249. **The New American Dictionary of Music.** By Philip D. Morehead with Anne MacNeil. New York, E. P. Dutton, 1991. 608p. illus. $24.95. ML100.M857. 780'.3. LC 91-16198. ISBN 0-525-93345-X.

The British tabloid *News of the World* says "All human life is here"; this book could almost say, "All musical life is here!" Intentionally and unabashedly brief in its definitions, this dictionary crams an incredible breadth and quantity of musical information into its pages. Instruments, terms, and people (composers, impresarios, and performers) from music history and classical, folk, and popular music can be found here in 10 lines or less, for the most part. Longer entries are provided only for some important concepts, names, or instruments (e.g., fugue, Haydn, Handel, Benny Goodman, pianoforte). Unfortunately, Madonna is not here, nor is the current Engelbert Humperdinck, although the Engelbert Humperdinck who composed *Hansel und Gretel* is, as are Andrew Lloyd Webber, John Blow, the Esterhazy family, Eartha Kitt, and Muzak. Similarly, look for folk rock, hard rock, punk rock, acid rock, and psychedelic rock. Folk instruments such as the Norwegian Hardanger fiddle, the Swedish *nyckelharpa*, the Welsh *clwd*, and the West African *kora* are also found. Translations are provided for non-English terms; thus, we learn that *ukelele* is Hawaiian for "leaping flea." Except for the Guidonian Hand, the only illustrations are of musical instruments or musical examples of intervals, ornaments, and the like. A glossary of musical terms in English, French, Italian, and German completes the volume. The brief nature of the entries makes this dictionary useful for ready-reference or as a first stop on the way to more detailed information. [R: WLB, Jan 92, p. 128] — **Johan Koren**

Handbooks and Yearbooks

1250. Gottesman, Roberta, and Catherine Sentman, eds. **The Music Lover's Guide to Europe: A Compendium of Festivals, Concerts, and Opera.** New York, John Wiley, 1992. 434p. illus. maps. index. $14.95pa. ML12.M87. 780.78'4. LC 91-14409. ISBN 0-471-53310-6.

This volume aims to provide a guide for Europe-bound music lovers, those in search of information about various concerts, music festivals, and opera seasons. It does not include any specific listings of what is happening at each particular site, because that would be impossible in a book of this kind. However, average music lovers, particularly the opera-oriented ones, already know where they want to be and when, so this guide will provide them with addresses and telephone numbers of most organizations they may want to contact. (Fax numbers are not plentiful, a strange omission, as they could have easily been found in many basic sources.) As a resource for travel agents, the book could be a handy reference source, providing them with help for "what's going on in the area" questions.

Each entry includes a brief, intelligently written paragraph about a particular festival (or concert series, or opera company), along with a short list of recent performers to give the reader an idea of the general caliber of performing artists to be expected. Listings to Eastern European festivals and opera companies are barely adequate, something the authors point out in the introduction. Still, one wonders whether a little additional effort would have yielded at least a bit of information on Prague, for instance, which is one of Europe's major cultural centers, home of the Czech Philharmonic, and site of one of Europe's loveliest old opera houses. Hungary, Poland, and Yugoslavia fare similarly, which is too bad, because the book is quite thorough in listing the rest of the European musical sites.

— **Koraljka Lockhart**

1251. Haggin, B. H. **The Listener's Musical Companion.** new ed. Compiled and edited by Thomas Hathaway. New York, Oxford University Press, 1991. 499p. index. $39.95. MT6.L14L6. 781.1'7. LC 90-40982. ISBN 0-19-506374-0.

First published in 1956, the 8th edition of this volume purports to be written for persons who "wish to select a few out of hundreds of works available on records, [and] want to know which of these works are the greatest...." This goal is achieved if (and it is a very large "if") one shares Haggin's likes and dislikes. In his distaste for Wagner, for example, he not only allows that composer a mere 4 pages (Mussorgsky gets 14) but also manages to reduce one of the giants of the operatic stage, Hans Hotter, to a mere mention of his Lieder singing. Brahms "produced bad music in the attempt to write greater than he felt." Charles Ives gets short shrift ("fitful and eccentric"), and Aaron Copland is hailed as the outstanding American composer of serious music. Mussorgsky and Berlioz are acclaimed as the only two originals in nineteenth-century music. These are thought-provoking opinions, to be sure, but unexpected in a volume whose title makes one think it will be long on facts and short on opinions. The discussion on singers and their recordings is fairly thorough as far as older performers are concerned (e.g., Caruso, Chaliapin, Bjoerling, Rethberg) but fairly cursory on more recent ones. As for the recommended recordings, these are introduced with so many disclaimers that one might as well pick selections straight from the *Opus* catalog (see ARBA 91, entry 1293). A search through the recommended recordings revealed at least one oddity: the list of selected Mahler symphonies does not include a single one conducted by Leonard Bernstein! The bibliographic section is less than basic and omits some major composers (e.g., Handel, Mahler). The book provides an interesting insight into the thought processes of a music critic (the author spent a number of years reviewing music for *The Nation* and other publications), and that may very well be its chief value. – **Koraljka Lockhart**

1252. **Handbook of Research on Music Teaching and Learning.** Richard Colwell, ed. New York, Schirmer Books/Macmillan, 1992. 832p. index. $95.00. MT1.H138. 780'.7. LC 91-29363. ISBN 0-02-870501-7.

This work is the result of a project of the Music Educators National Conference. A primary reference source for music education in the United States, with contributions from Great Britain, Canada, and Australia, it consists of 55 reviewed essays by scholars, which are organized into 8 broad sections. Each essay addresses a specific research topic in considerable depth. For example, in the section called "Conceptual Framework" there are essays on philosophical foundations and model building. Other sections cover such information as perception and cognition, teaching and learning strategies, and schools/curriculum.

Colwell's preface describes the project from the time the need for it was perceived through the mechanics of its execution. Chapters end with a reference list; in some cases endnotes are also provided. Within the essays, subheadings set in a variety of fonts help break up the text. Scattered throughout are charts, diagrams, and other figures; usually, however, two columns of text dominate the page. Brief biographies of contributors, a name index, and a subject index conclude the work.

The content pages make excellent use of typefaces, layout, and white space to guide the eye to needed information; however, data presented are limited to section headings, titles of chapters, and authors. In contrast, the indexes are dense and more difficult to use than necessary. The name index merely lists page references; topical subdivisions would help. The subject index serves as a memory aid to one thoroughly familiar with the material, rather than as an access tool for someone preparing a strategy for searching the book. It is highly detailed, but these details are rendered inaccessible by the alphabetical arrangement and small typeface. Many entries are far more specific than necessary; the result is a preponderance of lengthy phrases, such as "Logical questions, in music education research" – hardly an entry that a user would seek. An arrangement that listed topics that a researcher would be likely to seek when commencing preparation for a project would vastly improve access.

A daunting tome to consult, the work nevertheless is the fruit of excellent scholarship. It is destined to become the seminal work in music education. All libraries that specialize in education or music should acquire it. – **Ian Fairclough**

COMPOSERS

1253. Canning, Nancy, comp. **A Glenn Gould Catalog.** Westport, Conn., Greenwood Press, 1992. 230p. index. (Discographies, no.50). $47.95. ML156.7.G68C3. 016.7862'092. LC 92-24263. ISBN 0-313-27412-6.

In her opening chapter, Canning presents an interesting profile of Glenn Gould that points out the many talents of the pianist, especially noting his interest and skill in radio broadcasting techniques. The main section of the volume is a Gould discography, which is arranged by composer's name (Anhalt to Webern) and offers such data as composer, composition, source, catalog number, matrix number, program or album, and pertinent notes. Other sections cover Gould's musical repertoire (arranged by composer), a recording chronicle (1940-1982), CBC (Canadian Broadcasting Corporation) archives (radio or video presentations), Sony catalog (1956-1990), other commercial releases (1953-1991), unreleased recordings (1950-1982), and Gould's published writings. A person involved in Gould research should be armed with Canning's volume and the two-volume *Descriptive Catalogue of the Glenn Gould Papers* (see index for entry number), published by the National Library of Canada. *The Glenn Gould Papers* offers more supplementary data in the area of unreleased recordings, the CBC archives, and Gould's writings. However, *A Glenn Gould Catalog* has much more information on Gould's recording career, chronicling in detail his multiple recordings of compositions. It is an important contribution to the understanding of this complex artist and should be useful to pianists, Gould fans, discographers, and researchers. Highly recommended for music reference divisions and schools of music.

—**Robert Palmieri**

1254. **Contemporary Composers.** Brian Morton and Pamela Collins, eds. Chicago, St. James Press; distr., Detroit, Gale, 1992. 1019p. $125.00. 780.922. ISBN 1-55862-085-0.

As described in the editors' foreword, this is a summary of almost 500 living composers, not necessarily the most prominent. All were living at the start of this project, around 1989, although a few have died since that time. Following a who's who-style biography, the works of each composer are listed along with the dates of composition and first performance. The third portion of the listing is a description of the entrant's style and manner of composition and place in the vast spectrum of contemporary classical composition. This appears to be the justification for the project, and it succeeds in achieving this goal, although it may possibly suffer from the omission of some prominent names from the list. It is hoped that future revisions will rectify the omission.

No close parallel to this work is apparent. Only among living composers listed in Grove's standard work; in the most recent edition of *Baker's Biographical Dictionary of Musicians*, edited by Nicholas Slonimsky (Schirmer Books/Macmillan, 1992); or in *Greene's Biographical Encyclopedia of Composers* (see ARBA 87, entry 1223) can one find a list of current composers even close to this one. Only one typographical error was found and that in the necrology, probably the most difficult part to keep up-to-date in a work of this kind. Recommended for any extensive reference library. [R: Choice, Dec 92, p. 598; RBB, 1 Dec 92, pp. 686-87; WLB, Oct 92, p. 104]—**Arthur R. Upgren**

1255. **Descriptive Catalogue of the Glenn Gould Papers. Catalogue Raisonne du Fonds Glenn Gould.** Ottawa, National Library of Canada, 1992. 2v. illus. index. $51.95/set (U.S.). 016.7862'092. ISBN 0-660-57327-X.

It is a joy to see that Canada's most gifted pianist, Glenn Gould, is being honored with an archive in the National Library of Canada. Gould was a musical genius, and this catalog clearly demonstrates his multifaceted gifts. With text in both English and French, it covers a wide range of material on the man. Volume 1 describes the materials that relate to Gould's professional output; volume 2 lists items that are more concerned with his private life. An index to the whole set appears in volume 2, and some 35 illustrations are dispersed throughout the two volumes. Volume 1 contains a chronology (1932-1982), bibliographic data on writings by Gould, musical compositions and arrangements by Gould that are part of the National Library's Glenn Gould Papers, a list of Gould's programs, noncommercial sound recordings and videocassettes, promotional papers, and a list of honors (1940-1984). Volume 2 contains a list of incoming and outgoing correspondence, both business and personal (although Gould preferred the telephone for communicating with his friends and colleagues); a list of photographs (more than 2,000 are in the collection); lists of official papers and financial and medical records; "keepers" (so labeled by Gould), which were items important enough for him to retain; a list of printed materials (e.g., Gould's own books, annotated published scores); "realia," some 70 items that include furniture, clothing, and equipment; "collections elsewhere," which indicates materials found in other places; a listing of selected bibliographies (about Gould, not by him); and a Gould discography. Volume 2 concludes with the index.

The *Descriptive Catalogue of the Glenn Gould Papers* is an important compilation that displays the totality of this remarkable person. It will help musicians and researchers locate specific items on Gould. The volumes are a must for musical institutions and reference libraries.—**Robert Palmieri**

1256. Dixon, Joan DeVee. **George Rochberg: A Bio-Bibliographic Guide to His Life and Works.** Stuyvesant, N.Y., Pendragon Press, 1992. 684p. illus. $44.00. ML134.R575D6. 016.78'092. LC 92-3452. ISBN 0-945193-12-2.

Those researching the works of this extraordinary composer will have their work half done once they start using this volume. In meticulous detail it outlines the chronology of Rochberg's life, from his birth to 1988, followed by a list of his works. The latter chronicles his compositions, giving for each the date, publisher, number of pages in score, timing, commission, date and site of premiere, dedication, recordings, and detailed instrumentation. A separate section features complete texts used in works with voice and even includes a complete libretto to Rochberg's *The Confidence Man*. The second part of the book contains articles and essays written by Rochberg; letters housed in public collections; a discography (including a list of authors of liner notes); a list of Rochberg-related manuscripts and documents housed at the Library of Congress, the New York Public Library, Harvard University, and the Theodore Presser Company; and an extensive bibliography. The last section is a list of dissertations (and one thesis) dealing with Rochberg.

Thoroughly researched, the book contains minimal typographical errors (with the exception of the consistent misspelling of Maestro Maazel's first name). The only cavil is that the book stops in the year 1988, but George Rochberg is still alive, and it is therefore incomplete. [R: Choice, Nov 92, p. 440]
—**Koraljka Lockhart**

1257. Evans, Joan. **Hans Rosbaud: A Bio-Bibliography.** Westport, Conn., Greenwood Press, 1992. 298p. index. (Bio-bibliographies in Music, no.43). $59.50. ML134.5.R68E9. 016.7842'092. LC 91-34620. ISBN 0-313-27413-4.

This book is devoted to the life and accomplishments of the Austrian conductor Hans Rosbaud (1895-1962). Rosbaud held a variety of positions, from Kapellmeister in Frankfurt to music director of the Tonhalle Orchestra in Zurich, and was a pioneer in the use of radio in symphonic performances. He particularly distinguished himself as a conductor of modern works, but his concerts spanned almost the entire repertoire of concert music.

The preface describes this as the first work in any language devoted to Rosbaud and his achievements. After a foreword that consists of personal reminiscences by Pierre Boulez, a short laudatory and well-annotated biography describes Rosbaud's life and works, highlighted by his conflict with Hitler's government. The major portion includes an impressive list of first performances and some other significant premieres, a complete discography, and a list of recordings made for radio broadcasts to which Rosbaud contributed extensively. Each entry includes the work and composer, orchestra, soloist (if any), recording, date, and cross-reference to other sections as appropriate. This material is well organized and appears free of printing errors. A complete, descriptive bibliography and indexes conclude the work. This volume is focused upon a narrow subject but is likely to remain definitive within its purview and is thus appropriate for libraries in which music plays a significant role.—**Arthur R. Upgren**

1258. Harris, Steve. **Film and Television Composers: An International Discography, 1920-1989.** Jefferson, N.C., McFarland, 1992. 302p. index. $55.00. ML156.4.M6H28. 016.7815'42'0266. LC 91-52637. ISBN 0-89950-553-8.

Harris's previous *Film, Television and Stage Music on Phonograph Records* (see ARBA 89, entry 1187) contained listings by title of original and adapted music specifically for film or television productions. His new book is largely the same material from those sections, rearranged by composer. Admittedly, there are three years' worth of later films not in the original (December 1989 is now the cut-off date), and some composers and earlier films have been added. Unfortunately, a major category of information that was in the original volume—date of release—has for some reason been omitted here. While Harris may have compiled the most comprehensive list of films that have been recorded, it would be more useful to have a single reference book that contained a list of composers with all of their films (whether recorded or not); the studio that released the film; the film's year of release; and basic discographical information on at least the most important recordings, including reissues (e.g., format, size, speed, performers, record label and number, date released, date withdrawn). Also helpful would be some hint of the existence of video recordings, particularly if there was never a soundtrack (this could be done with superscript symbols to indicate that a commercial videotape or videodisc exists). [R: RBB, 15 June 92, pp. 1880-82; RQ, Fall 92, p. 113]—**Robert Skinner**

1259. Hess, Carol A. **Enrique Granados: A Bio-Bibliography.** Westport, Conn., Greenwood Press, 1991. 192p. index. (Bio-bibliographies in Music, no.42). $45.00. ML134.G79H5. 016.78'092. LC 91-32585. ISBN 0-313-27384-7.

Enrique Granados has always been in the unfortunate position of being compared with his more famous contemporary compatriots Manuel de Falla and Isaac Albeniz. The comparison usually leaves Granados being considered the least important of the three. However, Hess's work makes one look more closely and reevaluate the importance and historical significance of this musician.

The volume first contains a biography that surveys Granados's career as pianist and composer. (His professional life was not an easy one, as there seem to have been financial difficulties from the beginning [he often performed as a cafe pianist to help offset this problem].) Hess also includes a list of compositions with data on first performances; a selective discography (currently available or of historical interest); a list of original works by scoring; a Granados chronology; and a main corpus of 408 bibliographic entries that identify books, articles, theses and dissertations, program notes, and newspaper articles/reviews. It is interesting to read reviews of concerts that Granados performed and to see what literature he used. Pianists are certainly familiar with his suite *Goyescas*, but they may not be aware of his transcriptions of 26 Scarlatti sonatas, or of his arrangement of Clementi's *Sonatina* Op. 36, Nos. 1-4 for string trio.

Enrique Granados is highly recommended; it will be of special interest to pianists, composers, musicologists, lovers of Spanish music, and library reference divisions. It is a well-compiled and well-written survey of this important Spanish composer.—**Robert Palmieri**

1260. Horne, Aaron, comp. **String Music of Black Composers: A Bibliography.** Westport, Conn., Greenwood Press, 1991. 327p. index. (Music Reference Collection, no.33). $55.00. ML128.B45H7. 016.787'08996. LC 91-26742. ISBN 0-313-27938-1.

In addition to the entries one would expect to find for African-American composers, there are separate, useful sections for African, Afro-European, and Afro-Latino composers. And beyond the expected coverage of the chamber music repertory, music for larger groups has also been included. Coverage extends through solo voices with strings and other instruments, choir music, works for chamber orchestra, and even opera and ballet. Also unexpected in a work of this kind is the biographical information about each composer with additional sources included. The book, therefore, exceeds in value the restrictions of its title by providing more than a list of chamber works by Afro-American composers. In fact, some of the secondary virtues compete in importance with the book's implied purpose.

The discography is useful as far as it goes. It does contain entries for obscure works issued by small record companies, but it is far from complete, as is plainly shown by a sample of entries under the famous arrangers of spirituals. Under Burleigh, for example, it is surprising to find the violin arrangement of "Deep River" by Jascha Heifetz listed but none of the famous sung versions. [R: Choice, Mar 92, p. 1046]—**George Louis Mayer**

1261. Lewis, Thomas P., ed. **A Source Guide to the Music of Percy Grainger.** White Plains, N.Y., Pro/Am Music Resources, 1991. 339p. illus. $35.00pa. ISBN 0-912483-56-3.

Lewis presents an interesting collection of material on the Australian pianist and composer Percy Grainger. The book consists of biographical sketches (or, as the author puts it, "Artistic Vignettes"), a catalog of Grainger's works, the location of scores, program notes, discographies, and a Grainger bibliography. The biographical section of the *Source Guide* quotes material by Grainger, Margaret Hee-Leng Tan ("Free Music of Percy Grainger"), Harriette Bower ("Percy Grainger"), and Dana Perna (Chicago Symphony Orchestra Program Notes), to name a few. The catalog of Grainger's music is based on Teresa Balough's important work *A Complete Catalogue of the Works of Percy Grainger*

(University of Western Australia Department of Music, 1975). The section of the volume titled "Program Notes," which is the most extended chapter, contains descriptive miniarticles obtained from record jackets, scores, books, concert programs, and journals. This section proves to be the most interesting, especially for those who are unfamiliar with Grainger or who want to know more personal details about this fascinating and energetic man. There are two major sections in the discography unit: recordings of Grainger's music performed by others and recordings by Percy Grainger. The last chapter consists of a bibliography of books, articles, catalogs, and dissertations that deal with Grainger. All sources for the entries are listed at the end of each chapter. *A Source Guide to the Music of Percy Grainger* will be useful to pianists and composers and should be included in reference divisions of university music libraries.—**Robert Palmieri**

1262. Yoell, John H., comp. **Antonin Dvorak on Records.** Westport, Conn., Greenwood Press, 1991. 152p. index. (Discographies, no.46). $39.95. ML156.5.D9Y6. 016.78'092. LC 91-24038. ISBN 0-313-27367-7.

This discography of Dvorak, prepared for the 150th anniversary of his birth, is intended to complement the revised edition of Jarmil Burghauser's *Antonin Dvorak: Thematic Catalogue* (Prague: Export Artia, 1960). The first discography of any scope in over 30 years, it incorporates material contributed by Czech scholars in a number of countries, including Australia. A knowledge of Czech and German was, in fact, a prerequisite for this undertaking. However, Yoell's English is not always pristine; Germanicisms that occur can be distracting. Notably, he seems unaware of pejorative undertones in certain words and phrases, as when he writes "*For all his tinkering with* the 'Slavonic Dances' and other items, the failure of Fritz Kreisler to record the Violin Concerto seems strange," or "*If nothing else*, 'Armida' offers a juicy title role" (italics reviewers).

The entries are annotated in somewhat arbitrary ways. Operas are summarized as well as evaluated; influences on Dvorak's compositions are suggested at whim; works are variously characterized or evaluated or both. But the annotations are always interesting and are frequently informative, especially on the subject of American influences on Dvorak's music during his three-year residence in the United States. They attest, too, to a deep love of the Czech master. Yoell repeatedly stresses Dvorak's carefulness as a composer, but surprisingly stops short of making high claims for him: "Whether or not ... Dvorak eventually will be considered an important—as opposed to merely likable—composer only time will tell." This timidity does justice neither to Dvorak nor to the value of Yoell's own undertaking.

—**John B. Beston**

INSTRUMENTS

Oboe

1263. Haynes, Bruce. **Music for Oboe, 1650-1800: A Bibliography.** 2d ed. Berkeley, Calif., Fallen Leaf Press, 1992. 432p. illus. index. (Fallen Leaf Reference Books in Music, 16). $49.50. ML128. O2H55. 016.7885'2. LC 91-34794. ISBN 0-914913-15-8.

Many bibliographies of music composed for specific instruments are designed merely to lead the user to repertory for the instrument alone or in various chamber music combinations. This bibliography, with the limitations imposed by the dates of coverage, takes the user back into music history and demands a scholarly and musicological approach to the contents. Commanding attention are such issues as national origin and style of the music, the various types of oboes in use during the period covered, and the identification of compositions when the composer is not clearly stated. Arrangement is by composer with entries coded by instrumentation. Important information about manuscripts, original publications, library locations, and modern editions is provided in each entry. The format is opulent for a book of this kind. Wide margins and space between entries guarantee that each entry stands out clearly on the page. There are seven attractive illustrations, mostly eighteenth-century engravings. More than 10,000 works are listed. The relatively short period between the 1986 edition and this one is less a matter of expansion, however, than of refinement of the information provided in the citations. Many of the works listed have now been examined in greater detail than was originally possible. Those who found the original work useful will need to replace it with this edition. [R: Choice, Oct 92, p. 274] — **George Louis Mayer**

Piano

1264. Walker-Hill, Helen. **Piano Music by Black Women Composers: A Catalog of Solo and Ensemble Works.** Westport, Conn., Greenwood Press, 1992. 143p. index. (Music Reference Collection, no.35). $42.95. ML128.P3W3. 016.7862'089'96073. LC 91-38146. ISBN 0-313-28141-6.

Carefully researched and fluently written, Walker-Hill's new book is destined to be of great help to anyone interested in locating piano music by women. Walker-Hill concentrates on African-American women of the twentieth century but includes some nineteenth-century figures and some British women of color. These composers, listed in alphabetical order, are given biographical sketches and annotated lists of their works for piano. The biographies are thorough, authoritative, and very readable. Because most of the composers Walker-Hill deals with do not appear in many of the standard biographical dictionaries, her biographies are valuable indeed. In many cases she has acquired much of her information directly from the composer or from close relatives; hence, she provides much information that is not available elsewhere.

The lists of works could serve as models for anyone engaged in preparing similar material for publication. Information given for most pieces includes the dates of composition and publication; key signatures; tempo and meter markings; and information on dedications, premieres, available recordings, and where to obtain a score. In addition, Walker-Hill includes a concise description of each piece, conveying in a few well-chosen phrases the essence of the music. The works lists include both music for solo piano and for piano with other instruments, but no music for piano and voice or vocal ensemble. Of general interest is Walker-Hill's introduction to the volume, a historical sketch of the contributions African-American women have made to music, especially to that of twentieth-century America.

Although there are some disagreements between Walker-Hill and some of the standard biographical references on such information as birth dates or debuts, these are infrequent and minor. Also minor are the few stylistic inconsistencies and errors the proofreader overlooked. All in all, Walker-Hill has done pianists and scholars a great service in producing such an informative and useful bibliography. [R: Choice, June 92, p. 1530] — **Karin Pendle**

Voice

1265. Ackelson, Richard W. **Frank Sinatra: A Complete Recording History of Techniques, Songs, Composers, Lyricists, Arrangers, Sessions and First-Issue Albums 1939-1984.** Jefferson, N.C., McFarland, 1992. 466p. index. $55.00. ML156.7.S56A25. 016.78242'163'092. LC 91-52629. ISBN 0-89950-554-6.

Frank Sinatra has enjoyed a lengthy career as an actor and live entertainer. This discography of his approximately 1,250 recordings provides the researcher with virtually the entire body of his recorded legacy. Because several general biographies about Sinatra have already been published, only one chapter is devoted to his personal life. Here, the emphasis is on his Italian-American background in New Jersey, and the cultural effects that shaped his later musical talent. The recording information is contained in the subsequent chapters, beginning with a master song list that is followed by a variety of additional lists and indexes. The master song list is alphabetical by song title. Also given are alternate and subordinate titles, dates of recording sessions, publication dates, music composers, lyricists, arrangers, conductors/bands, and record labels.

Historically interesting is a chronological list by the date a song was first published (beginning with the melody commonly known as "Greensleeves" in 1580). Also helpful are profiles of those composers represented by 12 or more songs recorded by Sinatra. This is followed by biographical sketches of 20 additional composers whose songs were important in his career. Subsequent chapters provide similar information about the lyricists and arrangers. As an additional help in studying the singer and his place in time, this book contains a catalog of Sinatra's recording sessions from his first on February 3, 1939.

Albums are discussed in the order in which they were released. There is also a list of World War II "Victory" discs. Even bootleg albums are included.

Altogether, this is a thorough, well-arranged discography. Only when seeing a compilation such as this does one really begin to appreciate Frank Sinatra's prolific 45 years as a recording artist.

—**Louis G. Zelenka**

MUSICAL FORMS

General Works

1266. Goodfellow, William D. **Wedding Music: An Index to Collections.** Metuchen, N.J., Scarecrow, 1992. 197p. $25.00. ML128.W4G6. 016.7815'87'0263. LC 92-13745. ISBN 0-8108-2575-9.

Certain to be welcomed by musicians in search of appropriate music for their wedding repertoires, this slim index provides access to more than 3,400 vocal and instrumental compositions in 191 widely diverse collections. Materials range from the traditional to the popular and include both secular and sacred (primarily Christian and Jewish) selections. The collections focus specifically on wedding music; anthologies of general music that contain only a limited number of appropriate wedding selections are omitted.

Introduced by a preface and concluded by a brief biographical sketch of Goodfellow, this source consists largely of a series of indexes and a section that details the collections included. The "Collections Indexed" section is alphabetically arranged by author/editor or title, and each entry includes complete bibliographic information, performance medium (e.g., piano/guitar/vocal, organ/vocal), and, interestingly, the OCLC (Online Computer Library Center) number. Access is provided by three separate indexes, one each for title/first line, composer, and type of instrument.

The emphasis of this concise, straightforward, and easily used source is on materials that are readily available at local libraries or bookstores or that can be obtained through interlibrary loan (hence the OCLC number). As a result, while not necessarily the means for locating the unusual or the arcane, this index is highly practical and will be an invaluable aid to musicians and librarians alike. It should find a place in the reference collections of most church and music libraries and those public and academic libraries that have large music collections. [R: WLB, Oct 92, p. 115]—**Kristin Ramsdell**

Choral

1267. Tiemstra, Suzanne Spicer. **The Choral Music of Latin America: A Guide to Compositions and Research.** Westport, Conn., Greenwood Press, 1992. 317p. (Music Reference Collection, no.36). $49.95. ML128.C48T5. 016.7825'098. LC 91-46317. ISBN 0-313-28208-0.

This reference tool is the product of a choral conductor's need for a resource on Hispanic choral music. The lack of such a work prompted Tiemstra to publish her research—despite the fact that she is not fluent in Spanish. Her motivation is admirable; her product, unfortunately uneven.

The body of the work is devoted to cataloging the choral works of Latin American composers of art music; folk music is included only when it is the basis for a choral setting. The catalog is arranged alphabetically by composer, with most entries providing name, dates, nationality, biography, publishers, locations of manuscripts, compositional style, and general or biographical references. Tiemstra freely admits that some entries have insufficient data due to her biases, but she considers this work to be the first step in an ongoing process.

The weakest part of the work is the brief history of art music in Latin America, which contains generalizations, oversimplifications, and poor writing. Terms such as "Baroque period" and "Romanticism" are used when a brief mention of specific stylistic traits would prove more illuminating. Other sections provide lists of music publishers, recording companies, music archives, periodicals, biographical and general bibliographies, a discography, and a list of scholars with interests in Latin American music. Noticeably absent is an index to composers' nationalities.

Tiemstra has gathered a great deal of information on Latin American music, and some of it will prove useful to those starting an investigation in the field. Few resources in Latin American music exist to compete with this one. However, the work lacks authority; the way has been opened for ethnomusicologists fluent in Spanish to follow Tiemstra's first step with more comprehensive and better-written reference tools. [R: Choice, Nov 92, p. 451] – **Gregg S. Geary**

Church

1268. Baker, Paul. **Paul Baker's Topical Index of Contemporary Christian Music.** Cincinnati, Ohio, Standard Publishing, 1991. 223p. $14.99pa. ML128.C54B34. 016.78225. LC 91-14782. ISBN 0-87403-720-4.

The purpose of this index is to promote the wider and better use of contemporary Christian music (CCM). The topic list and Bible reference sections index 1,070 songs from 101 recordings that have been chosen with several criteria in mind: they had to have been on the top of the charts from the late 1980s to early 1991, or they had to have a strong theme. Also, Baker sought to include a wide range of styles and record labels, so there is a degree of subjectivity in the selection of the 101 albums.

The topic list is quite detailed. Some songs are indexed by as many as eight subject terms. The introduction contains a thorough explanation of how the indexing works, including cross-references. The Scripture index is arranged according to the order of books in the Bible. If readers want additional information about a particular song (e.g., writer, publisher, performing rights, recording label, release date, recording length, general music style) they would refer to the song list. Unfortunately, there is no list of the 101 recordings indexed. This would be helpful for those who want entire CCM recordings rather than individual songs. In spite of this shortcoming, this work will help those seeking wider access and exposure to CCM. Baker suggests several groups of people who could use this index: church groups, songwriters, radio deejays, and bookstore/music store clerks. – **Margaret A. Grift**

1269. Poultney, David. **Dictionary of Western Church Music.** Chicago, American Library Association, 1991. 234p. index. $40.00. ML102.C5P77. 782.32'03. LC 91-12325. ISBN 0-8389-0569-2.

Although "intended for the use of those who provide music for worship services, including both professional and nonprofessional church musicians" (preface) and thus especially suitable for church and seminary libraries, this work will also answer questions about Christian sacred music in general libraries as well. The alphabetically arranged entries include musical and religious terms (e.g., *a cappella, Hosanna, Office, schola cantorum*), genres (e.g., Baptist church music, hymn, mass, oratorio, Stabat Mater), and 80 composers of church music from the Middle Ages to the present. There is an explicit emphasis on Roman Catholic, Anglican, Episcopalian, Lutheran, Methodist, and Baptist traditions and an implicit but distinct emphasis on liturgical music, with less complete treatment of hymnody, popular and ethnic sacred music, and concert music on sacred themes. The articles range in length from one line to several pages; they are clearly written for the nonspecialist and avoid technical language as far as possible. When musical examples are included, they are well chosen and can be understood by anyone with a basic knowledge of reading music. Sources are not indicated. The appendixes include directories of American church music publishers and of church music societies in the United States, and a selective bibliography of sacred music periodicals (all but one from the United States). There is an index of "compositions discussed and/or exemplified"; extensive cross-references in the text make a subject index unnecessary. [R: Choice, May 92, p. 1374; RBB, 15 Feb 92, p. 1128]
– **Paul B. Cors**

Classical

1270. Brown, Jonathan, comp. ***Parsifal* on Record: A Discography of Complete Recordings, Selections, and Excerpts of Wagner's Music Drama.** Westport, Conn., Greenwood Press, 1992. 152p. index. (Discographies, no.48). $45.00. ML156.5.W2B7. 016.7821'026'6. LC 92-12292. ISBN 0-313-28541-1.

This work is a must for diehard Wagnerians, music librarians, classical music stations, and performing arts organizations. It contains a record of all complete *Parsifal* recordings and major and minor excerpts from the opera. The compiler has excluded a large group of recordings: those of radio broadcasts, many of which exist on legal or illegal tapes. (This omission is completely understandable, as compiling a record of all worldwide *Parsifal* broadcasts would be next to impossible.) The volume also includes a section devoted to *Parsifal* arrangements and excerpts found in various Wagner anthologies. Principal singers and conductors are featured in the index.

Some minor inconsistencies and typographical errors have crept into an otherwise meticulously researched book. For example, on page 5 Brown says that the Knappertsbusch 1958 Bayreuth Festival recording is "crammed unhappily onto nine sides." In the next paragraph he deals with the same conductor's 1960 Bayreuth version, which happens to be on eight sides, but that fact is not mentioned at all. The most notable mistakes have to do with German quotations of the most familiar phrases from the opera. It is not "Deiner Mutter is tot" (an ungrammatical way of saying "Your mother is dead"), but "Seine Mutter is tot" ("His mother is dead"), and "Schlafe, schlafe" ("Sleep ...") should be "Schlafen, schlafen" ("To sleep"). Parsifal does not say "ah diesen Küss" (the case is misplaced, and the umlaut makes the word for "kiss" into a German nonword) but "ah, dieser Kuss." Otherwise, the book makes for intriguing reading, even if one is just moderately interested in the subject matter. For research purposes it is more than intriguing; it is valuable. — **Koraljka Lockhart**

Motion Picture

1271. Limbacher, James L., and H. Stephen Wright. **Keeping Score: Film and Television Music, 1980-1988 (with Additional Coverage of 1921-1979).** Metuchen, N.J., Scarecrow, 1991. 916p. index. $92.50. ML128.M7L5. 016.7815'42. LC 91-21180. ISBN 0-8108-2453-1.

This book is the third by Limbacher on this topic; it follows the format of his previous works, *Film Music* (see ARBA 75, entry 1147) and *Keeping Score: Film and Television Music, 1972-1979* (see ARBA 82, entry 1052). New to this volume is the participation of Wright, who prepared the section called "Recorded Musical Scores, a Discography" and a necrology that lists the birth and death dates of 45 composers.

Primary data (date, title, and composer) is presented in both of the first two sections. The section on films and their composers/adapters arranges the data by year, title, and composer, together with a code that indicates the publisher or (for foreign films) country. The section on composers and their films lists the titles by year under the composer's name. (Listing these by title would be easier to use.) The index is from title to year, so it is a two-step process to discover the composer of a film's music: one needs to find the year and then look under the year in the first section. Or, to find a recording, one can look up the title directly in the third section.

The discography is preceded by a short explanation; it lists both 33-1/3 rpm and compact discs (the latter marked CD) and covers 1980-1987. Publisher name and numbers are given, as is the date of release or first broadcast of the film for recordings of individual films. Anthologies of both film and television music have a list of contents (in which the phrase "and other themes" can appear). It is regrettable that no indexing to these selections is provided. Thus, although Ron Grainer's *Dr. Who* is recorded on *The Exciting Television Music of Ron Grainer* and is listed in the second section under Grainer's name, one can only discover the recording by perusing the pages of the "TV Anthologies" section.

This work belongs in any library that specializes in twentieth-century music, as well as film and television collections. Limbacher's two earlier works are available; for proper collection development, it is desirable to own all three. [R: RBB, 15 June 92, pp. 1880-82] — **Ian Fairclough**

1272. Stubblebine, Donald J. **Cinema Sheet Music: A Comprehensive Listing of Published Film Music....** Jefferson, N.C., McFarland, 1991. 628p. index. $65.00. ML128.M7S88. 016.7821'4'0263. LC 91-52514. ISBN 0-89950-569-4.

This book grew out of Stubblebine's fascination with songs from movies. It provides a list of published film music and songwriters from the past 75 years. The arrangement of the book is alphabetical by movie title; each entry includes studio, year of release, the two leading stars, songs sung during the film, composers and lyricists, publisher, and a brief description of the album cover. The number of films listed is 6,200; the number of songs is 15,000. A bibliography of books about films is included, and three appendixes provide special information. The two major indexes are by composer and song title.

The work is well researched, and the information is easy to access. It will be of value to music collectors, film historians, and libraries with extensive film and music collections. [R: Choice, May 92, p. 1376]—**Marilyn Strong Noronha**

Operatic

1273. Croissant, Charles R. **Opera Performances in Video Format: A Checklist of Commercially Released Recordings.** Canton, Mass., Music Library Association, 1991. 121p. index. (MLA Index and Bibliography Series, no.26). $15.00pa. ML1700.C8. 016.7821'026'7. LC 91-32737. ISBN 0-914954-43-1.

Croissant's lists of operas and opera-related materials in video format serves as a valuable guide in an area where one might otherwise have to consult at least a half dozen other sources to find far less information. Limited to videos that have been released commercially in the United States before April 1991, *Opera Performances in Video Format* is a practical volume that should appeal especially to teachers and to opera lovers residing outside areas where live performances are readily available.

The book is organized into three main sections: a list, alphabetical by composer, of complete operas on video; appendix A, videos that feature individual artists in excerpts from various operas; and appendix B, collections of operatic excerpts not focused on the performances of a single artist. All three lists include information on the participants in the performances, where and when recorded (if known), language, whether subtitles in another language are included, timing, format (e.g., Beta, VHS, laserdisc), name of U.S. distributor, and locations of reviews of the recorded performance. When documentary or biographical material forms part of the video, this fact is mentioned. A final appendix lists names and addresses of distributors. Indexes of titles, performers, and ensembles and performance sites close the volume.

Croissant presents his information with a clarity that makes the book a pleasure to consult. However, there are infrequent and usually minor errors. For example, parts of *Les Troyens* were recorded before the main production of October 1983, not after; Malcolm Donnelly, not Norman Bailey, should be listed in the cast of *Gloriana*; and Ingmar Bergman's *Magic Flute* was recorded in 1973, not 1975. More confusing than serious are the errors mentioning Massenet's (it should be Mascagni's) *Cavalleria Rusticana* on page 42; the listing of Galina Vishnevskaya (really Oleinichenko) in the cast of *The Tsar's Bride* (which was filmed in 1966, not 1963); and the strange name of Walker Kraft in the Chicago cast of *Eugene Onegin* (in actuality, Sandra Walker and Jean Kraft—two singers, not one). Appendixes A and B have more typographical errors than does the main list, and some of these are carried over into the index. Finally, one wonders why the video dealing with Philip Glass's *Akhnaten*, which is at least half documentary and includes only excerpts of the opera, appears in the first list rather than in appendix B. All in all, however, Croissant's videography is a valuable reference tool that will be used widely and gratefully.—**Karin Pendle**

1274. Dillard, Philip H. **How Quaint the Ways of Paradox! An Annotated Gilbert & Sullivan Bibliography.** Metuchen, N.J., Scarecrow, 1991. 208p. index. $25.00. ML134.S97D5. 016.7821'4'0922. LC 91-3763. ISBN 0-8108-2445-0.

Dillard has identified nearly 1,000 articles, monographs, and dissertations by and about William S. Gilbert and Arthur S. Sullivan. Categories include histories about Gilbert and Sullivan, their works, biographies, analyses, criticisms, concordances, handbooks, dictionaries, and musical scores. Also included are a chapter listing, an assortment of material for juvenile use, and a chapter devoted to bibliographies and discographies.

Several chapters are specifically of value to those engaged in productions and performances or musical research in those areas. The section that covers production lists those works that would likely be of value in staging, the training of choruses, designing, and conducting. There are separate chapters devoted to librettos, plays, and poems. Completing coverage in the performance/research area is a chapter on musical scores. A final chapter contains unclassified and unresearched material. A brief chronology of the composers features their works and milestones in their lives. Indexing is very thorough, with a title index as well as a name index. This is a valuable reference for music libraries, researchers, and students. [R: Choice, June 92, p. 1516; RQ, Fall 92, pp. 115-16]—**Louis G. Zelenka**

Popular

General Works

1275. **Best Rated CDs 1992: Jazz, Popular, Etc.** Voorheesville, N.Y., Peri Press, 1992. $19.95pa. ISBN 1-879796-06-6.

CD Review Digest, published quarterly as well as in annual compilations (see ARBA 92, entries 1288 and 1308), provides pertinent information on all compact discs reviewed in 50 major music magazines. *Best Rated CDs* presents the top 10 percent of CDs included in the first five volumes of the aforementioned work, which encompass virtually the entire history of CD recording. Criteria for selection in *Best Rated CDs* include notice by at least two reviewers and an award for excellence from at least one. Along with excerpts from reviews and a list of honors and awards, a rating of 1 to 5 stars is assigned to each recording as a general indication of its level of recognition. As with the parent work, *Best Rated CDs* is published in two parts (the other covers classical music). "Jazz, Popular, Etc." is further subdivided into sections on blues, jazz, pop/rock/roots, and show music. Clearly and logically organized, and containing a wealth of relevant information, this is a useful guide to jazz and popular music on compact disc. [R: RBB, 1 Oct 92, pp. 351-364]—**A. David Franklin**

1276. **Billboard's Hottest Hot 100 Hits.** By Fred Bronson. New York, Billboard Books/Watson-Guptill, 1991. 406p. illus. index. $19.95pa. ML156.4.P6B77. 016.78242164'026'6. LC 91-26029. ISBN 0-8230-7570-2.

According to the *Billboard* charts, the number one pop single in the United States on July 9, 1955, was "Rock around the Clock" by Bill Haley and the Comets. That date, for the purposes of this book, is considered the beginning of the rock era. Thus, the 35 years of hits included in this book reached their chart peaks between that 1955 date and December 29, 1990.

The work is well arranged. Artists are listed first (e.g., the top 100 songs of the Beatles), followed by writers (e.g., the top 50 songs written by Carole King). The top producers of the rock era are also ranked; there is a brief sketch of each. A major section lists the most successful chart singles of 43 different labels. Not all top songs of the rock era were, in fact, rock. For example, the number one song on the Dot label was Pat Boone's "Love Letters in the Sand," which dates from the 1930s. Of interest to an assortment of users are the lists in the section "The Years." Individual years have their top 100 songs, and the decades are also thusly summarized.

Small sections offer specialty information (e.g., the top 100 songs about places, animals, colors, or days of the week). Other rankings include the top 100 songs by male solo artists, by female solo artists, duets, instrumentals, and by teenagers and preteens. The top 3,000 hits of the entire rock era are listed in order (Chubby Checker's "The Twist" ranks number one, with Elvis Presley's "Don't Be Cruel/Hound Dog" in the second spot). A final list gives the ranking of all 3,000 hits in alphabetical order by title. The inclusion of a modest number of photographs of some of the artists, composers, and producers lends the work added interest. Well organized and well researched, this book should be in the popular music section of libraries.—**Louis G. Zelenka**

1277. Kiner, Larry F. **Nelson Eddy: A Bio-Discography.** Metuchen, N.J., Scarecrow, 1992. 683p. illus. $79.50. ML156.7.E2K5. 016.782'.0092. LC 92-1232. ISBN 0-8108-2544-9.

Containing a great deal of information gathered from a wide variety of sources, this is the first work to list all the performances, recording sessions, motion pictures, and television appearances of Nelson Eddy. Sharon Rich, president of the Jeanette MacDonald/Nelson Eddy Friendship Club, has provided a brief biography of Eddy as a foreword. Eddy's professional career from 1929 until his death in 1967 is then covered. Dates and geographical locations of performances and recording sessions are given along with such details as announcers, sponsors, and orchestra conductors. The work is arranged chronologically, with access provided by a song title index. The book contains numerous photographs, both studio formals and on-the-scene shots from Eddy's radio days. There are also reproductions of labels from phonograph records, sheet music covers, and even the covers of videocassettes that are currently available to collectors.

Appendixes list 78 RPM, 45 RPM, LP records, and compact discs by label and catalog number. There are also indexes of opera performances and motion picture titles. Not just a significant reference source, this attractively bound book is also a fitting tribute to one of the greatest American baritones of the century. – **Louis G. Zelenka**

1278. O'Brien, Robert F., comp. and ed. **School Songs of America's Colleges and Universities: A Directory.** Westport, Conn., Greenwood Press, 1991. 197p. index. $39.95. ML128.S7502. 782.42'159. LC 91-11337. ISBN 0-313-27890-3.

College and university band directors would welcome a directory to school songs, but this book will probably disappoint them. The stated objective is to provide access to titles, composers, arrangers, and publishers of school alma mater and fight songs. Entries are arranged alphabetically by state and then by name of institution. Also included is a list of song sources, a list of school names, a bibliography, a publishers index, and a school song (title) index. The data was gleaned from four questionnaire mailings to colleges and universities listed in *Lovejoy's College Guide* (see ARBA 91, entry 335). O'Brien does not state which edition of *Lovejoy's* was used, what exactly was asked, or to whom the questionnaires were directed. These questions come to mind when one notices the numerous citations that lack indications of composer, lyricist, or copyright date. It seems that most of the data has come from people with only the band arrangement at their disposal rather than a copy of the original song with text. For example, the citation for Baylor University makes no mention that the tune to their alma mater was borrowed from "In the Good Old Summertime," even though the song sources index was designed for just such a purpose. Another problem with the list of song sources is that it does not provide any reference back to the school songs that use the tunes. Finally, the entry for the University of North Texas places the institution in the wrong town (it is in Denton, not Denison). Such errors do little to lend credibility to this directory. What the compiler really provides is a list of school songs with occasional bits of information scattered in some entries. For the price, one deserves more. [R: WLB, Mar 92, p. 117] – **Gregg S. Geary**

1279. **Popular Music: An Annotated Guide to American Popular Songs.... Volume 15: 1990.** Bruce Pollock, ed. Detroit, Gale, 1991. 153p. index. $58.00. LC 85-653754. ISBN 0-8103-4947-7. ISSN 0886-442X.

This is the most recent volume in a series that helps scholars identify songs published since 1900. The series is composed of annual volumes that date back to 1985, a single volume for the years 1980-1984, a revised cumulation for 1920-1979, and a companion volume for 1900-1919. The set was initiated by Nat Shapiro and the Adrian Press in 1964; Pollock has edited many of the recent volumes. Pollock's review-of-the-year essays in each of the volumes he has edited should not be overlooked by librarians seeking information on U.S. popular culture; they delight and inform the reader.

The set has an established format. Song titles are listed alphabetically, and there are separate indexes of lyricists and composers, important performances, and awards. A list of current publishers completes the volume. The index to performances has become an essential feature of the book, organizing song titles by performance medium: album, movie, musical, performer, revue, and television show. The title listing includes information on alternate titles, country of origin if not the United States, author, composer, current publisher (they change frequently), copyright date, and performance history. The bibliography is not intended to lead users directly to words or music published in anthologies; that function is ably performed by the *Popular Song Index* (see ARBA 90, entry 1276).

– **Milton H. Crouch**

1280. Spencer, Peter. **World Beat: A Listener's Guide to Contemporary World Music on CD.** Chicago, A Cappella Books/Chicago Review Press; distr., Chicago, Independent Publishers Group, 1992. 160p. illus. $12.95pa. ML156.4.P6S7. 016.78163'0266. LC 91-45607. ISBN 1-55652-140-5.

This handbook is designed to assist the contemporary music listener who seeks to explore beyond what is well known in the music scene. Intended for beginners in world music and not as a scholarly work, the book surveys many styles of music, such as salsa, Cajun, Afro-pop, and samba. Coverage of world music is selective based on Spencer's judgment and is restricted to 250 CDs released in the United States. Descriptions range from a half page to two pages and include backgrounds of the music and reviews. Approximately one out of every five descriptions has a photograph of the artist. Artists are grouped into chapters that cover the music of the following regions: southern Africa, western Africa, northern and eastern Africa, eastern Europe, western Europe, the Caribbean Islands, North America, South America, and India and Australasia. Each chapter includes a discography of highly recommended CDs.

In addition to providing information about world music, Spencer helps the reader acquire it by providing a list of mail-order addresses and retail record stores where the CDs may be available. (However, an average of only two or three stores are listed for each state.) At the back of the book is a brief bibliography of books and periodicals for further information. This work is a welcome response to the rise in world music and will serve as a catalyst to increase its popularity.—**Margaret A. Grift**

1281. **The Trouser Press Record Guide.** 4th ed. Ira A. Robbins, ed. New York, Collier Books/Macmillan, 1991. 763p. $18.95pa. ML156.4.P6T76. 016.78164'026'6. LC 91-18564. ISBN 0-02-036361-3.

Since the 3d edition of this book (see ARBA 90, entry 1235), the price has increased by $2; the number of bands has increased from 1,900 to 2,500; the number of records has climbed from 6,200 to 9,500 (and these are now mostly CDs and cassettes, with very few LPs); and the number of pages has increased by 70. In addition, the typeface has been reduced in size and a cheaper grade of paper has been used. Checking through the "Z" section reveals that Frank Zappa is now included but the Zasu Pitts Memorial Orchestra has disappeared (there is no index to the book, but there are plenty of internal cross-references). The Reivers are now known as Zeitgeist. Zerra One is gone, as are Z'Ev, Zippers, and Zodiac Mind Warp and the Love Reaction. Newcomers include Zero Boys, Zoviet France, Zulus, and Zvuki M. A description about the Zantees in the 3d edition—"aren't too serious"—has been replaced by "aren't overly serious." Why? The current album listings run through March 1991. The entries are arranged alphabetically by artist, with appropriate cross-references (Robbins has an immense explanation of the principles of alphabetization) and year of release. The reviews are signed by 46 critics. Robbins lists eight magazines (some British, some trade) plus two stores for mail orders.

This is a rapidly changing field (as can be seen by the increased coverage), so by the time this review appears it may be appropriate to place an order for the 5th edition in 1993 or 1994. This is a standard work in the field; every library that deals with popular music for young listeners should have it by now. [R: RBB, 1 Feb 92, pp. 1053-54]—**Dean Tudor**

1282. Whitburn, Joel, comp. **Billboard Top 1000 Singles 1955-1990.** Milwaukee, Wis., Hal Leonard Publishing, 1991. 135p. illus. $8.95pa. ML156.4.P6W454. 016.78242164'026'6. LC 91-10286. ISBN 0-7935-0347-7.

Whitburn has a substantial database of chart information from which he generates lists from time to time. This volume is a revised edition of a 1988 publication (for the years 1955-1987), which was itself a revised edition; it is composed of a list of the top 1,000 hits, followed by a ranking of top 40 hits year by year, color photographs of the covers of the top 100 albums, lists of artists and song titles in alphabetical order, and miscellaneous data (e.g., a list of songs recorded by two different artists). Scattered throughout the text are black-and-white reproductions of advertisements for hit songs from the 1960s. Ranking is based on highest position at which a record peaks, total weeks in top position, total weeks in the top 10, total weeks in the top 40, and total weeks charted. All of this is based on *Billboard* lists, but nowhere is it explained how *Billboard* determines these listings. However it is done, popularity of this type makes some strange bedfellows—number 3 is "Physical" (Olivia Newton-John), while number 4 is "You Light up My Life" (Debbie Boone)—the first refers in slightly veiled terms to the physical side of love, while the second is (according to the singer) about God. As this work is frequently revised, libraries may choose to buy a copy every 5 or 10 years, depending on user needs.

—**Mary Larsgaard**

Band

1283. Rehrig, William H. **The Heritage Encyclopedia of Band Music: Composers and Their Music.** Westerville, Ohio, Integrity Press, 1991. 2v. index. $110.00/set. LC 91-73637. ISBN 0-918048-08-7.

The backbone of the research for this work is Robert Hoe's series of LP band records, described in appendix 9. In contrast to the American scope of the LPs, the encyclopedia's goal is international—to document all music for concert and military bands, with biographies of composers, source references, and work lists. Certain limits apply: brass band music is excluded on the laudable grounds that this genre is sufficiently specialized to merit a work of its own; South America and Africa are not represented as it was too hard to find information from those areas; and some materials are not included because publishers declined to be of assistance. Bands themselves do not fall within the work's scope.

Rehrig has created an impressive tool. Biographies for composers not likely to be in other sources are given to the extent of information available; better-known composers are treated more briefly. Appendixes include histories of American band music and publishing practices, with instructions for substituting modern instruments for historical ones; lists of publishers, distributors, and band journals; special instructions for performing foreign band music in America; a list of marches; notes on possible repositories of band music (a section that could well be expanded in a subsequent edition); and research journals. The title index refers to composers and gives some indication of genre; it has running titles, which partially mitigate the tiny typeface in use throughout the work.

With its superior physical production, this work could become the tool of first recourse for information on band music. But it does not displace other publications. Users will still wish to consult, among others, *Band Music Notes* by Norman Smith and Albert Stoutamire (Kjos West, 1979) for program descriptions of specific pieces and David Whitwell's *The History and Literature of the Wind Band and Wind Ensemble* (Winds, 1984) for primary sources, as well as for many other composers and works. Any library that holds these titles should acquire *Heritage Encyclopedia*. It is appropriate for all libraries that collect in music and popular culture. [R: Choice, Apr 92, p. 1212; LJ, Jan 92, p. 110; WLB, Jan 92, p. 127]—**Ian Fairclough**

1284. Renshaw, Jeffrey H. **The American Wind Symphony Commissioning Project: A Descriptive Catalog of Published Editions, 1957-1991.** Westport, Conn., Greenwood Press, 1991. 383p. index. (Music Reference Collection, no.34). $55.00. ML128.B23R46. 016.7848. LC 91-30220. ISBN 0-313-28146-7.

This work describes 159 of more than 350 works commissioned by Robert Boudreau for use by the American Wind Symphony Orchestra (also called the American Waterways Wind Orchestra), published by C. F. Peters. Two facing pages are devoted to each work; on the left is a description, with number of performers, any soloists, dates of composition and publications, publisher's number, duration, availability of score, nationality of composer, and full instrumentation listing. Also included is a biographical sketch of the composer (most taken from secondary sources) and brief characterizations of such compositional features as harmony, melody, and rhythm. The facing page contains, when available, a reproduction of a page of the score (usually the first). Following the catalog are several brief essays on the publisher (including an interview with its president, Stephen Fisher); the orchestra; its sailing vessel, *Point Counterpoint II*; and Boudreau. Of the nine appendixes, seven list works by nationality of composer, soloists, number of performers, date of composition or publication, duration, programming category, and publisher's number. The eighth lists scores available for purchase, and the ninth is a discography. Composer and title indexes are provided.

The work attains its objective of providing a reference source and basis for study of these works, individually or as a unit. Some questions remain. For example, why is the orchestra referred to by two different names? Only briefly, in the introduction, is reference made to the remainder of the repertory; what has happened to these works? Are any published elsewhere? How can one find out about them? Most works have not been performed by other orchestras: which are these?

The physical arrangement of the book might be improved in several ways. Since arrangement of the work is by author, the author index is not necessary; rather, this information should be presented as part of the table of contents. The contents page is poorly laid out, with excessive space at the head, yet with the indexes as orphans on the verso. The essays should be at the front, not the back. Discographical information is in two separate places in back; for the works described, it belongs in the description with the score. The list of recordings by the American Waterways Wind Orchestra confuses Bading's *Pittsburgh Concerto* with Penderecki's *Pittsburgh Overture*. The abbreviations for instrumentation in appendix 3 are explained in the preface.

Despite these shortcomings, this work is a valuable tool for access to this repertory. Directors of wind orchestras and composers will welcome it.—**Ian Fairclough**

Jazz

1285. Brown, Denis, comp. **Sarah Vaughan: A Discography.** Westport, Conn., Greenwood Press, 1991. 166p. index. (Discographies, no.47). $39.95. ML156.7.V4B7. 016.78242164'092. LC 91-27632. ISBN 0-313-28005-3.

Although there is some controversy as to what constitutes jazz singing, a handful of vocalists have been enthusiastically embraced by the jazz community. Sarah Vaughan was one of the greatest among those few. From the time she started out with the Billy Eckstine band in the mid-1940s until her death in 1990, her sophisticated ear for harmonies, extraordinary vocal range, impeccable sense of time, and intensely expressive voice quality had a significant impact on jazz singing. That she was also appreciated by the general public is confirmed by her having had several hit records over the years.

The present work, compiled by an experienced English discographer, lists all known American and British issues of Sarah Vaughan's hundreds of 78 RPM, 45 RPM, and LP releases. Recordings from other countries are included when they are the only versions. CDs, except for four that Brown considers especially important, have been excluded. The book's four sections are devoted to chronologically listed information about each song recorded, including date and location, accompanying musicians, matrix number, and record company catalog numbers; a cross-referenced, alphabetized list of song titles with their composers; individual record releases alphabetized by record company and numerically ordered; and indexes of musicians and orchestras present on the recordings. A short list of bibliographic sources and references is also provided.

Although Brown acknowledges the possibility that a few recordings could have been overlooked, this extensive discography is more than likely complete. Its information is pertinent and comprehensive and presented in a clear and orderly fashion.—**A. David Franklin**

1286. Gray, John, comp. **Fire Music: A Bibliography of the New Jazz, 1959-1990.** Westport, Conn., Greenwood Press, 1991. 515p. index. (Music Reference Collection, no.31). $75.00. ML128.J3G7. 016.78165'5. LC 91-20601. ISBN 0-313-27892-X.

During the 1960s and the early 1970s, a style of jazz variously called "the avant garde," "the new thing," or (more often) "free jazz" attracted a large number of practitioners. Indeed, the free style—so called because of its emancipation from predetermined rules of harmony, rhythm, melody, form, and tone color—was a powerful force in the music until traditional jazz values reasserted their primacy in the 1970s.

This work serves as a reference to books, articles, dissertations, films, videos, and audiotapes about free jazz that appeared in the major Western languages from 1959 to early 1990. The main body of the book includes a chronology of free jazz along with citations of sources that deal with its historical and cultural context and with the actual music and its exponents. Four appendixes contain guides to reference works and research centers along with lists of performers by country and by instrument. Additionally, there are artist, subject, and author indexes.

Gray is director of the Black Arts Research Center in Nyack, New York and has previously published several other works on African or African-American culture. Although there have been other jazz bibliographies, this is the first to specialize in a particular style. Derived from an extensive list of reference sources, it is comprehensive and meticulously detailed. As with any achievement of this kind, there are a few inevitable controversial inclusions and omissions. Nonetheless, this informative work is an important addition to the jazz reference literature. [R: Choice, Mar 92, p. 1040; LJ, 1 Mar 92, p. 82]—**A. David Franklin**

1287. Lord, Tom. **The Jazz Discography. Volume 1.** Redwood, N.Y., Cadence Jazz Books; distr., Redwood, N.Y., North Country, 1992. 1v. (various paging). $45.00pa. ISBN 1-881993-00-0.

1288. Lord, Tom. **The Jazz Discography. Volume 2.** Redwood, N.Y., Cadence Jazz Books; distr., Redwood, N.Y., North Country, 1992. 1v. (various paging). index. $45.00pa. ISBN 1-881993-01-9.

1289. Lord, Tom. **The Jazz Discography. Volume 3.** Redwood, N.Y., Cadence Jazz Books; distr., Redwood, N.Y., North Country, 1992. 1v. (various paging). $45.00pa. ISBN 1-881993-02-7.

Contemporary jazz discographies have until now either covered the various jazz styles individually (e.g., early jazz, swing, modern jazz, fusion) or have surveyed the entire field within the limits of a restricted time period. In contrast, the present work includes every type of jazz recorded from 1898 until the publication of each volume. The completed set of around 20 volumes—scheduled for publication over a 4-year period—is expected to contain approximately 100,000 listings. Volume 1 ends with "Bankhead," volume 2 with "Boustedt," and volume 3 with "Cathcart." Periodical updates, as well as a musicians index and a tunes index, are planned.

The following information is given for each recording session: name of leader; title of album; name of group; names and instruments of performers; location and date of recording; and names of selections performed, along with matrix and album numbers. Entries are alphabetized by leader, with individual recording sessions listed chronologically under the leader's name. A number is assigned to each session for cross-reference with the upcoming musicians and tunes indexes.

Lord is an experienced discographer who has generated a special computer database for this project. In spite of the inevitable minor errors (e.g., the misspelling of an obscure name), the presentation of so much essential information in such a clear, succinct, and easy-to-use form is an extraordinary accomplishment. The complete set will make a major contribution to music scholarship.—**A. David Franklin**

Rock

1290. Gribin, Anthony J., and Matthew M. Schiff. **Doo-Wop: The Forgotten Third of Rock 'n Roll.** Iola, Wis., Krause Publications, 1992. 613p. illus. $19.95pa. LC 91-77560. ISBN 0-87341-197-8.

The distinctive vocal music of such 1950s groups as the Flamingos (e.g., "I Only Have Eyes for You") and the Rays (e.g., "Silhouettes") are examples of the style that has come to be known as "doo-wop." The characteristics of doo-wop are well described in a sequence of incisive essays in the beginning of this work. Typically, there is vocal group harmony, a wide range of voices that often includes a falsetto (e.g., in the Penguins' "Earth Angel"), simple music and lyrics, strings of nonsense syllables (e.g., "rama-lama-ding-dong"), and a simple beat with light instrumentation. Following this excellent introductory material, most of the work is composed of a "songography" of doo-wop artists and their songs, with year and record label specified for each. Many of the groups are obscure one-hit wonders, which makes this directory an especially valuable resource. Numerous old black-and-white publicity stills help evoke this bygone musical era.

The authors are not professional musicians. These "Doctors of Doo-Wop" (one a psychiatrist, the other a psychologist) both grew up during this period, attended college in New York City, and developed an abiding affection for doo-wop music. They bring an erudite enthusiasm to the subject that makes for fascinating reading. They identify specific periods and subcategories in the genre's history (e.g., "classical doo-wop," "Italo doo-wop") and provide detailed charts that explain the distinctive qualities of each. Highly recommended for academic and general collections.—**Richard W. Grefrath**

1291. Paraire, Philippe. **50 Years of Rock Music.** New York, Chambers Kingfisher Graham, c1990, 1992. 243p. illus. index. $9.95pa. ISBN 0-550-17011-1.

Translated from the French *50 Ans de Musique Rock*, the goal of this encyclopedic guide is to show which people, inventions, trends, and events have played a part in the development of rock since 1935. The 200 short entries are arranged in rough chronological order and cover major bands, performers, and developments (e.g., the introduction of the Gibson Les Paul guitar). Also included are medium-length general essays about the evolution of rock music, blues, adolescent rock, commercial rock, rock on film, Black pop music, English pop music, and United States countercultures; a list of significant bands that the author could not include in the main body of the work; a good table of contents; and an index. The entries are short, critical, and biographical and include name of artist, type of music, a useful (but sometimes simplistic) one-line description of the artist (e.g., "Born to be wild" for Steppenwolf), a one-sentence summary of what is distinctive about the artist, and a discography of notable recordings. Scattered through the book are highlighted rectangles that contain bits of trivia or updated information and many excellent photographs. Generally, coverage of bands ends with their accomplishments through the late 1980s, although from time to time a very current reference is included.

Criteria for inclusion are slanted toward those who have made a mark on the European music charts, although the introduction states that Paraire intends to cover the most important contributors to the development of rock. Much attention is given to American blues (very popular in England), British Invasion bands, the mods, European punk, and European new wave. Less attention is paid to U.S. contributions from country music, the post-new-wave guitar band revival, the hardcore punk movement, and rap.

This work is not comprehensive and makes no attempt to be, but it accomplishes the goals it set for itself. The European bias of the coverage is not so much a detraction as a different perspective on what people often mistake as a uniquely American music form. Because of its easy-to-read, brief format, it should be a useful addition to a library's general interest collection.—**Daphne Fallieros Potter**

Soul

1292. Bartlette, Reginald J. **Off the Record: Motown by Master Number, 1959-1989. Volume 1: Singles.** Ann Arbor, Mich., Popular Culture, Ink., 1991. 508p. illus. index. $55.00. LC 89-92326. ISBN 1-56075-004-9.

Founded by Berry Gordy, Jr., in 1959, the legendary Motown Record Corporation prospered for 30 years and headlined truly great performers. In 1988 Gordy sold Motown to MCA/Boston Ventures Group for $61 million, ending an era.

The present volume provides entries for the more than 6,400 singles released by Motown from 1959 to 1989. (Volume 2, in preparation, will cover commercial and promotional albums.) Each entry specifies master number, song title, running time, performers, catalog number, record size, date of release, and entry number. The entries are arranged sequentially by master number—the system of master numbers, matrix numbers, delta numbers, and the like are explained in the introduction. Dozens of record companies associated with Motown are described, such as the "Anna" label, owned by Gordy's sister. Throughout the work there are reproductions of more than 200 actual record labels, of interest to the audience of record collectors and music historians for whom this comprehensive discography is intended. [R: Choice, Apr 92, p. 1203]—**Richard W. Grefrath**

1293. Gregory, Hugh. **Soul Music A-Z.** London, Blandford/Cassell; distr., New York, Sterling Publishing, 1991. 266p. illus. $24.95. 782.4216440922. ISBN 0-7137-2179-0.

Many initial and significant studies on Black American music have been published by British writers (e.g., Paul Oliver on the blues, Viv Broughton on gospel music, Jeffrey Green on concert life). Such orientations have also cast light on idiomatic manifestations in the United Kingdom, providing American readers with a richer perspective than they might have expected. In this biographical encyclopedia of just fewer than 600 entries, "soul music" (a term in pop music that lost favor in the 1970s) refers to figures from these years but expands the application to non-Black performers without designation of race, a decision more readily justified (as it is in the front material) than would have been popular in the past. The term is defined as a synthesis of rhythm and blues and gospel, thus accounting for the many individuals who were active in both idioms, with the liberal inclusion policy providing biographies of others even more acculturated. Not all entries are of performers; many are of those active in the industry, either in record production or broadcasting. Performer entries include discographic reference by album title, with label and year of issue. The single bibliography offers no surprises and is of little value by itself. The success of the handbook rests in the facile coverage of its subjects, which will readily satisfy the interests of those not seeking a critical study. [R: Choice, Oct 92, p. 272; RBB, 1 Sept 92, p. 91]—**Dominique-Rene de Lerma**

26 Mythology, Folklore, and Popular Culture

FOLKLORE

1294. **Brewer's Dictionary of 20th-Century Phrase and Fable.** Boston, Houghton Mifflin, 1992. 662p. $30.00. LC 91-29299. ISBN 0-395-61649-2.

When Ebenezer Cobham Brewer's *Dictionary of Phrase and Fable* appeared in 1870, it reflected the fascination of the Victorian era with the accumulation of facts and fantasies. Brewer's volume has been updated many times since, always with the intention of entertaining as well as informing its intelligent and curious audience. Using Brewer's vision for a useful and compelling reference, this modern volume concentrates on "the most evocative and interesting words and phrases" introduced during the twentieth century. Admitting that the number of these words and phrases is immense, the editors have made selections that focus on those "about which there is something worthwhile to say." Another editorial decision had to be made about Brewer's fondness for fable, for "the 20th century is not especially known for its fables." The editors therefore interpret fables in the broad sense of "myths" (to use their word), ranging from famous murders and military disasters to political scandals and legendary film stars. Although folklorists will probably quarrel with this usage, a reader does get a sense of the cultural consciousness among English speakers produced by the events and figures of the twentieth century.

The volume documents in a popular fashion many phrases that evade explanation in standard dictionaries. Checking under *Black*, for example, the *American Heritage Dictionary of the English Language* (Houghton Mifflin, 1992) (a bellwether for modern usage) includes contemporary phrases such as *Black Hand, Black Market, Black Power,* and *Black Shirt. Brewer's Dictionary* defines these terms more extensively than *American Heritage* does, and it additionally includes phrases such as *Black Hole, Black Monday, Black Panther, Black September,* and *Black Sox.* Also, *Brewer's* British origins (and British spelling) result in many references to phrases in use in the British Commonwealth, such as *Black Friday* and *Blackpool Illuminations.* Not quite a comprehensive guide to modern English idioms, not quite a dictionary of slang, Brewer's volume is nonetheless a useful reference to English terms and phrases arising out of the events and movements of the twentieth century. [R: LJ, 1 Mar 92, p. 80; RBB, 15 May 92, p. 1712; WLB, June 92, p. 107]—**Simon J. Bronner**

1295. **The Cassell Book of Proverbs.** By Patricia Houghton. New York, Sterling Publishing, c1981, 1992. 152p. illus. index. $14.95. ISBN 0-304-34165-7.

1296. **The Concise Oxford Dictionary of Proverbs.** 2d ed. John Simpson with Jennifer Speake, eds. New York, Oxford University Press, 1992. 316p. index. $22.95. PN6421.C64. 398.9'2103. LC 91-39366. ISBN 0-19-866177-0.

"You can't tell a book by its cover" is an apt proverb for any review and one that is especially pertinent to at least one, if not both, of these titles. *The Cassell Book of Proverbs* is simply a reprint, under a different title, of the 1981 *A World Book of Proverbs.* It is a very brief assortment of favorite proverbs arranged in 10 topical groupings (e.g., "From the Cradle to the Grave"). About 1,500 proverbs are provided with, in some cases, a simple attribution to author or country of origin.

The first edition of *The Concise Oxford Dictionary of Proverbs* (see ARBA 84, entry 51) provided a general history of all proverbs in common use in Great Britain in the twentieth century. This new edition has been expanded to include some new background material, a few proverbs known principally in North America, and a thematic index. In total, approximately 1,000 proverbs are included, with about 100 of them being new to this edition, along with a considerable number of dated citations. Because it contains attributions and citations, it is perhaps the best of the small proverb dictionaries available, but its brevity works against it. For most purposes *The Penguin Dictionary of Proverbs* (see ARBA 85, entry 62) or *The Facts on File Dictionary of Proverbs* (see ARBA 84, entry 52), both of which include about 6,000 proverbs, are better choices as compact sources of proverbial information. The chances of locating a particular proverb, which is, after all, the main use of such dictionaries, increase substantially with the number of entries. To that end, either *The Oxford Dictionary of English Proverbs* (see ARBA 72, entry 1330); *The Prentice-Hall Encyclopedia of World Proverbs* (see ARBA 87, entry 95); or *The Macmillan Book of Proverbs, Maxims and Familiar Quotations* (see ARBA 89, entry 1245), each of which contains around 20,000 proverbs, is a better first choice for libraries that need extensive access to this information. – **Norman D. Stevens**

1297. **The Folklore of American Holidays: A Compilation of More Than 500 Beliefs, Legends, Superstitions, Proverbs, Riddles, Poems, Songs, Dances, Games, Play, Pageants, Fairs, Foods, and Processions....** 2d ed. Hennig Cohen and Tristram Potter Coffin, eds. Detroit, Gale, 1991. 509p. index. $85.00. GT4803.F65. 394.2'6973. LC 91-14994. ISBN 0-8103-7602-4.

The first edition of this reference was a lively and useful guide to customs, rituals, stories, and beliefs – the folklore – associated with America's varied set of holidays. The guide began with New Year's Day and covered holidays sequentially through the calendar. The editors introduced each holiday's historical and cultural background with a headnote and then presented excerpts from newspapers, collections, books, or articles to illustrate practices. After many of the excerpts, the editors provided comments in addition to listing the sources. The reference included indexes to subjects; to ethnic groups and geographic locations; to collectors, informants, and translators; to song titles and first significant lines; and to motifs and tale-types.

The expanded 2d edition retains the organization and appearance of the previous one while containing 78 more pages. The editors have inserted additional material under entries for previously listed holidays, particularly Halloween, Christmas, St. Patrick's Day, and Valentine's Day. They have also added new entries to represent the cultural diversity of the United States, such as Persian New Year (March 21), Greek Independence Day (March 25), the Feast of Our Lady of Mount Carmel and St. Paulinus (July), and Kwanzaa (December 26-31). There are also more "booster" festivals in this edition, including the Iowa Girls State Basketball Tournament, Cheyenne Frontier Days, and the anniversary of Elvis Presley's death. Perhaps the largest addition is in the area of "spring rites of college students" to complement collegiate celebrations previously listed. These additions are welcome and make this reference even more useful as the primary contemporary guide to American holiday customs. Still, there remains a problem of representative coverage among the holidays because of the scrapbook format; for example, Jewish holidays are abundant in folk customs and scholarship devoted to them, but the coverage in the reference may not give a good indication of this compared to other traditions. The door remains open for a different kind of reference that will be valued by scholars and the public.
—**Simon J. Bronner**

1298. MacDonald, Margaret Read, ed. **The Folklore of World Holidays.** Detroit, Gale, 1992. 739p. index. $80.00. GT3930.F65. 394.2'6. LC 91-38032. ISBN 0-8103-7577-X.

This source provides information on more than 340 festivals and holidays from over 150 countries and many diverse ethnic groups. It is arranged chronologically according to the Gregorian calendar, with an introduction that explains a number of other calendrical systems. Topics covered range from recipes (e.g., sticky millet from China) to games (e.g., *yoot* from Korea) and religious celebrations of all kinds. Wherever possible, the entries are taken from firsthand accounts of the participants themselves, with additional information supplied by folklorists and anthropologists.

The contents listing at the beginning of the book shows entries by date, then alphabetically by country. Each text entry is followed by a bibliographical notation of its source, and a detailed subject index at the end of the book includes ethnic, geographic, and subject entries. Some entries are several pages long (e.g., Christmas, harvest festivals), while other entries consist of only a few sentences. Each date is accorded a separate page, resulting in many pages that are largely blank.

The book can be used to find information about a specific feast or holiday or to learn what is being celebrated on any particular day of the year. For example, one can learn how Easter is observed in 39 countries, or that March 5 is the Feast of Excited Insects in China and Korea. A lack of illustrations and the level of language used throughout the book make it more suitable for older students and adults than for children. [R: BR, Sept/Oct 92, p. 62; Choice, June 92, p. 1518; SLJ, May 92, p. 27; WLB, May 92, p. 124] – **Kay O. Cornelius**

1299. Mieder, Wolfgang, Stewart A. Kingsbury, and Kelsie B. Harder, eds. **A Dictionary of American Proverbs.** New York, Oxford University Press, 1992. 710p. $49.95. PN6426.D53. 398.9'21'0973. LC 91-15508. ISBN 0-19-505399-0.

This work contains about 15,000 proverbs and variants culled from approximately 150,000 citation slips gathered in the United States and parts of Canada over a 30-year period by the American Dialect Society. Focusing on those in use between the mid-1940s and the end of the 1970s, the emphasis is on traditional proverbs and genuinely new American proverbs. The present work differs from such references as *The Concise Oxford Dictionary of Proverbs* (see ARBA 84, entry 51) in relying on oral rather than written sources. Another feature of this book is its indication of geographical distribution. The entries, arranged in two columns, are in alphabetical order according to the most significant key word, which is in boldface print. As is usual in such extensive collections, the meanings of the proverbs are not given. There are many cross-references.

As an example of content, consider the headword *picture*. Under the headword the entry for the proverb "One picture is worth ten thousand words" contains the variant "A picture is worth a thousand words" and information indicating that the proverb was recorded in California, Colorado, New York, Ontario, and Utah; the earliest known written source is the December 8, 1921, issue of *Printer's Ink*; and the proverb is also registered in two standard Anglo-American proverb collections.

An informative introduction; a list of abbreviations; and an extensive, multisection bibliography add to the usefulness of this work. The book should please the general reader and be a useful reference for scholars in such fields as linguistics, literature, sociology, and cultural history. [R: Choice, May 92, p. 1364; RBB, 1 Feb 92, p. 1052; WLB, Apr 92, p. 121] – **Henry J. Ricardo**

1300. Steinfirst, Susan. **Folklore and Folklife: A Guide to English-Language Reference Sources.** Hamden, Conn., Garland, 1992. 2v. index. (Garland Folklore Bibliographies, v.16; Garland Reference Library of the Humanities, v.1429). $120.00/set. Z5981.S74. 016.398. LC 92-13594. ISBN 0-8153-0068-9.

As the discipline of folklore and folklife studies has grown, tracking its essential reference works has become more difficult. The discipline has expanded its scope to cover more material genres, such as folk art and architecture, and the rise of doctoral programs in folklore and folklife since the 1950s has resulted in an impressive scholarly output of new contributions. The most ambitious bibliography that tracks international studies on this topic is the *Internationale Volkskundliche Bibliographie* (Rudolph Habelt GmbH, 1954-), published biennially. Its listings are unfortunately not annotated, and there is a lag of four to five years between the years covered and the publication date. The *MLA International Bibliography* is not as comprehensive and is also not annotated, but it is more timely. It has a separate annual bibliography (published one year after the year it covers) and is available on CD-ROM. *Folklore and Folklife* differs from these ongoing projects by annotating English-language reference sources in a two-volume set. The bibliography is aimed at "students and 'beginning' folklorists rather than folklore scholars," according to Steinfirst. The contents are arranged by subjects: introduction to folklore and folklife, history and study, folk literature, ethnomusicology and folk music, folk belief systems, folk ritual and rites, material culture, folklife and folklife societies, and journals. Indexes for author, title, and subject are provided.

Although any folklore scholar can point out a number of omissions (especially for books published since 1987) in this work, the set is a valuable first stop for the serious student or the scholar crossing disciplines. As an artifact, it represents the rise and change of folklore and folklife studies, particularly in the last 30 years. As a reference, it should stand well as a useful foundation for research.

—Simon J. Bronner

MYTHOLOGY

1301. Accardi, Bernard, and others, comps. **Recent Studies in Myths and Literature, 1970-1990: An Annotated Bibliography.** Westport, Conn., Greenwood Press, 1991. 251p. index. (Bibliographies and Indexes in World Literature, no.29). $45.00. Z2014.M985R4. 016.82'0915. LC 91-18070. ISBN 0-313-27545-9.

Modern mythic criticism began with James C. Frazer's monumental *The Golden Bough* and may have attained its high-water mark with Northrop Frye's archetypal criticism that began in the late 1950s. This volume, however, clearly signals that myth criticism continues to flourish; more than 1,000 entries appeared within the designated 20-year period. The opening chapter surveys studies of the mythic figures in literature, such as Orpheus, Oedipus, Cain, and Faust. The second chapter annotates entries on myth in classical literature. The next five chapters parallel major periods in British and American literatures, including general studies and those focused on particular authors, such as William Shakespeare, John Milton, Herman Melville, James Joyce, William Faulkner, Toni Morrison, and John Updike. An excellent subject index provides speedy access to mythical figures, major theories, theorists, topics, and themes. An author index accesses the critical studies. This excellent volume for undergraduate and graduate academic libraries will also be useful to larger public libraries. [R: C&RL, Sept 92, pp. 420-21; Choice, Mar 92, p. 1054]—**C. B. (Bob) Darrell**

1302. Comte, Fernand. **Mythology.** New York, Chambers Kingfisher Graham, c1988, 1991. 244p. illus. index. $9.95pa. ISBN 0-550-17000-6.

This is a dictionary of the principal personae from mythologies worldwide. As such, it presents accounts of the feats and adventures of various gods and heroes as they have been transmitted to us through literature, the visual arts, and rites revealed by archaeology. Equivalents or analogies between Greek and Latin myths are indicated, and gods and heroes are placed alphabetically under their Greek names. The volume is organized according to universal myths, gods and heroes, the pantheons, and civilizations with their gods and heroes. The latter category includes Greece and Rome, Mesopotamia (e.g., Babylon, Sumer, Akkad), Egypt, India, Gaul, the Celts, the Nordics, the Slavs, Pre-Columbian America, China, Japan, the Pacific Islands, Africa and Madagascar, the Judeo-Christian world, and mythical creatures from different civilizations.

While many versions of the myths exist, this volume focuses on those that have proved enduring and are most widely known. It is a handy reference tool if the reader keeps in mind that the editor has drawn together literary renditions of matter that is most relevant when viewed in its living context. That is to say, the rendition of selected versions of myth on the static page will always be a pale reflection of the moving, changing, shifting matter of belief and custom found in the living traditions of people.

—**Arthur Gribben**

1303. Elkhadem, Saad. **The Concise Dictionary of Greek, Roman, Norse, and Egyptian Mythology.** Fredericton, N.B., York Press, 1991. 50p. $6.95pa. 291.1'3'03. ISBN 0-919966-83-7.

The task implied by the title of this book is well accomplished. Entries are brief (about 75 words average) and informative; they provide an excellent, concise list of relevant gods, people, animals, plants, and places for students of Western mythology. Probably three-fourths of the entries relate to Greek mythology. After hearing the scholar Robert Graves (in *The Greek Myths* [Penguin Books, 1955]) cite one variation after another for any element in a myth, it is easy to fault this work for leaving out elements (e.g., the account of Osiris's body shipped off in a chest, the early labors of Theseus) or alternative telling of elements (e.g., the geographical origin of Apollo). However, given the size and stated purpose of this work, that would be picky.—**Robert T. Anderson**

1304. Ellis, Peter Berresford. **Dictionary of Celtic Mythology.** Santa Barbara, Calif., ABC-Clio, 1992. 232p. $52.00. BL900.E45. 299'.16. LC 92-872. ISBN 0-87436-609-7.

  This dictionary is designed as an introduction to Celtic mythology for the lay reader. A composite, alphabetically arranged work, the dictionary presents the general sweep of Celtic mythology and makes comparisons between the various branches of the myths from country to country (e.g., Ireland and Wales). No attempt is made to split the work into subsections, but where entries derive from the two major culture groups, abbreviations are used for identification: [I] for Irish and [W] for Welsh. The most popular form of spelling for names in the native language—the work is a virtual who's who and what's what of sagas and tales—is used in cases where variant spellings abound.

  The introduction to the volume is an excellent survey of the cultural history and the scholarship pertaining to the Celts and their descendants, the Bretons, the Irish, the Cornish, the Manx, the Scots, and the Welsh. Combined with this and the excellent bibliography, the entries offer a fine introduction to the most important *dramatis personae*, events, and places in the Celtic realms. Where appropriate, connections are made to more popular literature (e.g., the Arthurian legend and the romance of Tristan and Iseult) and to history. On the theoretical level, however, it seems problematic to equate Celtic culture with Celtic language, specifically with Irish or Scottish Gaelic. If this is indeed valid, then these very languages, which themselves have long since departed from whatever the original Celtic tongue was, are themselves highly suspect. In the final analysis, this volume will be a welcome aid to lay readers and students of Celtic culture faced with the task of keeping tabs on the elements of Celtic mythology. [R: Choice, Dec 92, p. 600; LJ, July 92, p. 74; RBB, Aug 92, p. 2035; SLJ, Nov 92, pp. 136-37; WLB, Oct 92, pp. 104-06]—**Arthur Gribben**

1305. Leach, Marjorie. **Guide to the Gods.** Santa Barbara, Calif., ABC-Clio, 1992. 995p. index. $150.00. BL473.L43. 291.2'11. LC 91-35820. ISBN 0-87436-591-0.

  The breadth of coverage in this work is impressive. More than 20,000 entries list the gods, goddesses, and lesser deities of numerous cultures and time periods, ranging from Egyptian and classical Greek and Roman gods to Native American and contemporary African deities. The arrangement is classified according to realm of influence (e.g., Solar, Fire, Fertility). Within each of the 53 categories, names are listed in alphabetical order (without pronunciation), with brief descriptions of the deity's functions, attributes, and cultural context. In addition, bibliographic references lead the user to English-language secondary material for further information.

  Although the preface states that the "determining factor for inclusion has been—are they or have they been worshipped," Leach excludes Jewish, Christian, and Muslim traditions. These faiths, admittedly, tend toward monotheism and are the subject of numerous individual reference works, but the absence of Allah, Jahweh, and Jesus Christ imposes, to this reviewer's mind, a double standard that relegates religions of other periods or less powerful cultures to mere "mythology." There is an index of names but no subject or geographical indexes. The classified arrangement, with its sometimes vague headings, such as "Gods of the Cardinal Points" and "Gods of Religious Activities," is not always useful. Browsing through various sections can be fascinating, but the user should not view this as a "quick" reference source due to the lack of good indexes. While some of the figures listed would not be found easily in standard works on mythology and religion, this is not a definitive or highly useful resource for the price. [R: BR, Sept/Oct 92, p. 66; Choice, July/Aug 92, p. 1658; RBB, 15 Mar 92, pp. 1402-03; WLB, May 92, pp. 124-26]—**Valerie R. Hotchkiss**

POPULAR CULTURE

1306. **The Books of the Fairs: Material about World's Fairs, 1834-1916, in the Smithsonian Institution Libraries.** Chicago, American Library Association, 1992. 268p. illus. index. (Smithsonian Institution Libraries Research Guide, no.6). $99.00. Z5883.S63. 016.9074. LC 91-26804. ISBN 0-8389-0556-0.

  This handsome volume contains an annotated bibliography of almost 1,700 items held by Smithsonian Institution Libraries as well as microfilm numbers for the identically named set of microfiche issued by Research Publications. It also contains a superb introductory essay of more than 60 pages by Robert W. Rydell, professor of history at Montana State University-Bozeman.

The work is meant as a guide for serious researchers and as an introduction to the literature of international fairs, expositions, and exhibits. Rydell's essay covers the various kinds of publications associated with these events and includes a brief description of major collections of international exposition materials outside the Smithsonian Institution. There are numerous black-and-white illustrations taken from exposition publications and eight pages of color plates. An appendix lists by year the fairs and expositions represented in Smithsonian collections, and there is an index of titles as well as a good general index. This well-planned, well-produced, and well-illustrated volume will be of use to anyone interested in the history of society and technology. [R: Choice, Nov 92, p. 450]

—Richard H. Swain

1307. **Emily Post's Etiquette.** 15th ed. By Elizabeth L. Post. New York, HarperCollins, 1992. 783p. illus. index. $28.00. BJ1853.P6. 395. LC 91-58284. ISBN 0-06-270047-2.

This edition of a classic guide to etiquette continues to maintain the readability and accessibility of earlier editions. Major reorganization is evident. The old "good conversationalist" and "correspondence" segments have been moved to a new section on "communications," which includes guidelines for the proper use of telephone answering machines, cellular telephones, fax machines, and electronic mail. The tone of the advice is less rigid than in the previous edition. For example, in the treatment of "shaking hands with the handicapped," the handicapped person now has the option of replying "Please forgive me if I don't shake hands, but I'm very glad to meet you" (p. 21). A major coverage change is the expansion of business manners and business travel. "Interrelationships" covers many contemporary lifestyles, including the etiquette of sexual intimacy. Other writers address such situations more directly. Readers interested in how to socially interact with individuals who have AIDS will need to turn to *Letitia Baldrige's Complete Guide to the New Manners for the '90s* (see ARBA 91, entry 1335).

The comprehensive information on entertaining, invitations, and weddings remains. The range of entertainment stretches from the traditional formal dinner served by servants to the informal BYOB (Bring Your Own Bottle) and BYOF (Bring Your Own Food) party. Some advice, such as handling the inebriated guest, appears in more than one section. The quotations from the 1922 edition, found in the 14th edition, have been dropped. As in previous editions, there are many examples of ways to word invitations and illustrations to help those planning weddings and dinner parties. The work continues to address both the questions of the novice and those of the more socially sophisticated. [R: WLB, Oct 92, pp. 106-07]—**Phyllis J. Van Orden**

1308. **Holidays and Special Days Project Index for Young People.** By Mary Anne Pilger. Englewood, Colo., Libraries Unlimited, 1992. 160p. $29.50. GT3933.P54. 394.2'6. LC 92-12977. ISBN 0-87287-998-4.

This index is designed to provide quick reference to books that contain ideas for celebrating a variety of holidays and other special occasions. From well-known days, such as Christmas and Halloween that have pages of listings, to truly unique occasions, such as a "Miss Piggy" class-day celebration, just about everything that can be observed is alphabetically noted. Ethnic or place celebrations are also included, and the list is well cross-indexed.

Subjects are listed in capital letters, followed by a brief description of the nature of the project or observance, then the number of the indexed book (in brackets) in which the material appears. This list, containing 1,161 books, is a valuable bibliography for anyone who chooses books for young people. While at least one of the indexed volumes dates back as far as 1954 (the classic *Games of Many Nations* from Abingdon Press), most are more recent, with many from 1990 and 1991. Even the most spartan library should contain many of these books.

This index will help the reader find activities, games, foods, crafts, costumes, decorations, recipes, and instructions for creating successful occasions. The classroom teacher, youth leader, or student who must plan everything from calendars and bulletin boards to plays and hands-on crafts will find this book a source of delightful information and unusual ideas that cannot be found in any other single work.—**Kay O. Cornelius**

1309. Johnson, Linda Carlson. **Our National Symbols.** Brookfield, Conn., Millbrook Press, 1992. 48p. illus. index. (I Know America). $12.90. JC346.Z3J65. 929.9'2'0973. LC 91-38893. ISBN 1-56294-108-9.

Lessons on patriotism and the meaning of symbols will be enhanced by the use of this colorfully illustrated work. Johnson's clearly written text will help readers in grades 3 through 6 understand such U.S. symbols as the flag, the Liberty Bell, the bald eagle, the great seal, Uncle Sam, the bison, the Statue of Liberty, and the yellow ribbon that is commonly used today. The chronology, bibliography, index, and sturdy binding enhance the value of this attractive work.

Although it is less colorfully illustrated, James Giblin's *Fireworks, Picnics, and Flags* (Clarion, 1983) is similar in its coverage. Johnson's book might lead young readers to other books on symbols of the United States, such as Jim Hargrove's *Gateway to Freedom* (Childrens Press, 1986) and W. G. Crampton's *Flag* (Alfred A. Knopf, 1989).—**Vandelia L. VanMeter**

1310. **Limca Book of Records 1991.** 2d ed. Vijaya Ghose and Thomas Abraham, eds. Bombay, Bisleri Beverages; distr., Columbia, Mo., South Asia Books, 1991. 237p. illus. index. $8.00. ISBN 81-900115-1-0.

In its second year of publication, *The Limca Book of Records* parallels the *Guinness Book of Records* (see ARBA 91, entry 1337), but *Limca* is devoted to records only for the state of India. As such, it lists the great, the exceptional, and the infamous achievements of India and Indians, including many world records that deserve to be included in *Guinness*, if they are not already. The book is divided into 13 sections that include humans, agriculture, government, the armed forces, structures (architecture), transport, communications, culture, the sciences, economy and business, the natural world, sports (the largest section by far), and an addendum. A one-page preamble introduces each section, and each section is further divided into topics. The book contains more than 250 color pictures, and many charts expand the material. An index is provided.

There is a wealth of interesting factual data for both scholars and the general public. For instance, India has the world's largest population of cattle (92,453,000), had the world's first all-woman air crew, was the first country to send mail by airplane, has the only "Rat" temple in the world, is the world's largest sugar producer, and has lost 80 percent of its forests since 1900. Some sections will be of interest primarily to scholars, especially the section on agriculture, and the section on sports will interest the general public. However, due to the format, scholars will not find this volume easy to use. Consequently, it will be used mostly by the general public who are interested in knowing unusual facts about India and her people (e.g., an Indian who has grown his little fingernail to a length of 33½ inches).
—**David L. White**

1311. Olderr, Steven, comp. **Reverse Symbolism Dictionary: Symbols Listed by Subject.** Jefferson, N.C., McFarland, 1992. 181p. $29.95. CB475.O37. 302.2'22. LC 90-53517. ISBN 0-89950-561-9.

This slim volume functions as a complement to Olderr's *Symbolism: A Comprehensive Dictionary* (see ARBA 87, entry 866). In fact, it is based on that work. The previous volume presented entries on symbols, explaining the subject matter. In contrast, this volume is arranged alphabetically by subject or thing, with each entry listing the symbols that might be used to represent the subject. In a brief foreword Olderr attempts to clarify the scope of symbols as encompassed by this work—allusions, associations, attributes, emblems, and symbols. Also included is a brief list of further sources for consultation.

Entries are short and to the point but sometimes frustrating in their brevity. Readers might benefit from a lengthier explanation of the qualifiers attached to certain symbolic representations, to assure proper use. Although Olderr claims the work can be used independently from *Symbolism*, one may need to consult a variety of other works on the subject to assure correct usage and representation of an idea. The primary audience for this work will likely be those involved in creative aspects of fine arts or literature, students and researchers working in these fields, and reference librarians.
—**Edmund F. SantaVicca**

1312. Pilger, Mary Anne. **Multicultural Projects Index: Things to Make and Do to Celebrate Festivals, Cultures, and Holidays around the World.** Englewood, Colo., Libraries Unlimited, 1992. 200p. $35.00. LC1099.P55. 016.37019'6. LC 92-13731. ISBN 0-87287-867-8.

For the many school and public librarians who have for years pulled their hair out trying to locate information on how-to crafts from the world's cultures, Pilger has come to the rescue with this handy index. Dedicated to the notion that world peace and harmony rest on an understanding of another's culture, this index covers food, shelter, clothing, games, and expressions of creativity from every continent in the world. It is arranged alphabetically by subject (in boldface type) with qualifiers in small print. For example, a listing might read: "AFRICA - COOKERY lemon grass drink, recipe, making." Thus, the user can select what is needed among the many entries under AFRICA - COOKERY. Each entry also contains a page number and a source number. A "Key to Index" in the beginning pages furnishes detailed instructions on how the index is structured and how to use it. More than 1,100 numbered titles are listed in the back of the volume. These represent a massive database of titles that is used as the basis for this and two other Libraries Unlimited published indexes: *Crafts Index for Young People* (1992) and *Holidays and Special Days Project Index for Young People* (1992). A major concern is that some of the titles are currently out of print (some titles date back to the 1960s), thus limiting the volume's usefulness in newer library collections.

The possibilities for using this index are limitless. Classroom teachers and school children will find it extremely useful in enriching learning experiences in all areas of the curriculum (e.g., language, social studies, art, music). In addition, church groups, community festival planners, and others who work with celebrations should find this index invaluable. Individuals who have interests in unique crafts, hobbies, and cooking may also find it helpful. [R: RBB, 15 Nov 92, p. 628; WLB, Nov 92, p. 94]

—**Melvin M. Bowie**

1313. Spies, Karen. **Our National Holidays.** Brookfield, Conn., Millbrook Press, 1992. 48p. illus. index. (I Know America). $12.90. GT2703.S66. 394.2'6'0973. LC 91-38894. ISBN 1-56294-109-7.

This colorfully illustrated work clearly explains the purpose of national holidays. The work is suitable for readers in grades 3 through 6; it will meet the need for reports and will attract browsers. Chapters divide the holidays by purpose: celebrating our nation's roots (Independence, Flag, Labor, and Citizenship days), honoring famous people (Martin Luther King, Jr., George Washington, Abraham Lincoln, and Christopher Columbus), honoring the armed forces (Memorial and Veteran's days), celebrating our heritage (Thanksgiving, Chinese New Year, Cinco de Mayo, Kwanzaa, and Native American Day), and celebrating our Earth (Arbor, Bird, and Earth days).

The illustrations, chronology, bibliography, index, and sturdy binding add to the value of this attractive work. Other titles on this topic suitable for this audience include Valorie Grigoli's *Patriotic Holidays and Celebrations* (Franklin Watts, 1985).—**Vandelia L. VanMeter**

1314. **World of Winners: A Current and Historical Perspective on Awards and Their Winners.** 2d ed. By Gita Siegman. Detroit, Gale, 1992. 1315p. index. $80.00. ISBN 0-8103-6981-8. ISSN 1041-3529.

Derived in large part from Gale's more extensive *Awards, Honors, and Prizes* (see ARBA 90, entry 66), this 2d edition of *World of Winners* follows the same general selection criteria as the previous edition. It covers worldwide awards of interest to the general public or those reported in the national media (e.g., television, newspapers, magazines), as well as awards issued by leading professional, trade, and governmental organizations.

This volume updates the 1989 edition in many ways, first by adding some 500 new listings and identifying more than 100,000 winners of approximately 2,500 awards granted between 1844 and 1991. Entries have been arranged under five indexes, making it easier to access the listings. The main list of awards is arranged alphabetically by award name, followed by a chronological list of winners. The organization index lists agencies that issue awards, and the awards index lists all awards given, including subcategories as appropriate (e.g., Academy Awards—Best Supporting Actress). The expanded subject index classifies these awards under some 460 topical headings and cross-references, making it somewhat easier to identify winners and awards than in the previous edition. The winners index gives an alphabetical list of honorees and provides the year in which each award was given. As with the initial edition, variant name forms (e.g., Land, Edwin H.; Land, Edwin Herbert) still present some problems for the user; a bit of detective work may be required to identify all awards given to a particular individual. Minor quibbles aside, this work should prove a useful, if not quick, reference tool.

—**Elizabeth Patterson**

27 Performing Arts

GENERAL WORKS

Bio-bibliography

1315. Barranger, Milly S. **Jessica Tandy: A Bio-Bibliography.** Westport, Conn., Greenwood Press, 1991. 150p. illus. index. (Bio-bibliographies in the Performing Arts, no.22). $39.95. PN2287.T16B37. 792'.028'092. LC 91-25094. ISBN 0-313-27716-8.

Critics and theater lovers recognized Jessica Tandy as a major star in 1947 when she played Blanche DuBois in the first Broadway production of *A Streetcar Named Desire*. She capped her career in 1989 by winning an Oscar for playing Miss Daisy in the film *Driving Miss Daisy* 42 years later. Barranger expertly lists the events and facts about Tandy's long acting career in this continuation of Greenwood's series of performing arts bio-bibliographies. Following a brief biography and a separate chronology of the high points in Tandy's career through June 1991, Barranger gives details about Tandy's work on the stage, in films, on television, and in spoken-word recordings. There are a list of awards and award nominations and a bibliography of reviews, articles, and professional notices. The book concludes with a subject index.

Tandy is best known as a stage actress, and Barranger itemizes 101 separate appearances, including a few repeat roles. The entries for major plays provide production date, detailed production credits, full cast list, a paragraph on the play's history, a synopsis of the story, a commentary by Barranger, and excerpts from reviews. The filmography follows the same format for Tandy's 24 motion pictures. This is an excellent, no-frills summary of a distinguished professional life. [R: Choice, Mar 92, p. 1038]
— **Berniece M. Owen**

1316. Billips, Connie. **Janet Gaynor: A Bio-Bibliography.** Westport, Conn., Greenwood Press, 1992. 155p. illus. index. (Bio-bibliographies in the Performing Arts, no.23). $42.95. PN2287.G4B55. 791.43'028'092. LC 91-36239. ISBN 0-313-27574-2.

Janet Gaynor lived from 1906 through 1984, years that spanned a long, successful career on the stage and in films, radio, and television. She won Academy Awards for her performances in *Seventh Heaven, Sunrise,* and *Street Angel* early in her professional life (1927-1928), and film buffs remember her as the young heroine in *Daddy Long Legs* (1931) and in *A Star Is Born* (1937).

Billips follows the pattern set in previous Greenwood bio-bibliographies and gives details of Gaynor's life and career in a short introductory biography. Following this is a chronology of significant events, a filmography; listings of radio, stage, and television appearances; a discography; a bibliography; and an index. Each listing for performances includes full credits and a brief story outline. The bibliography has both reviews and interviews and a special section on fan magazine coverage of Gaynor's career, but Billips has not tried to be comprehensive. Eighteen black-and-white photographs illustrate the text. — **Berniece M. Owen**

1317. Bryan, George B. **Ethel Merman: A Bio-Bibliography.** Westport, Conn., Greenwood Press, 1992. 298p. index. (Bio-bibliographies in the Performing Arts, no.27). $45.00. ML134.5.M47B8. 782.1'4'092. LC 92-6428. ISBN 0-313-27975-6.

For more than half a century the distinctive voice of Ethel Merman (1912-1984) could be heard on radio or television and in such films as *The Big Broadcast of 1936, Alexander's Ragtime Band, It's a Mad, Mad, Mad, Mad World*, and *Airplane!* However, she will be best remembered for her roles in Broadway musicals, particularly *Anything Goes, DuBarry Was a Lady, Panama Hattie, Call Me Madam, Gypsy*, and *Annie Get Your Gun*. Bryan has endowed this valuable reference with substantial details on these facets of her career; a bibliographic introduction and chronology; and a discography and bibliography, both significant and annotated. The index is exemplary. For research on Merman, her colleagues, and their immediate environments, this volume will prove helpful.

—**Dominique-Rene de Lerma**

1318. Fowler, Karin J. **Anne Baxter: A Bio-Bibliography.** Westport, Conn., Greenwood Press, 1991. 296p. index. (Bio-bibliographies in the Performing Arts, no.20). $42.95. PN2287.B39F6. 791.43'028'092. LC 91-22264. ISBN 0-313-27543-2.

Although Anne Baxter was not a superstar, she had a long, solid career. This work brings together a great deal of information on her in a convenient format for students and scholars of film. Following the arrangement of earlier volumes in the series, it starts with a concise biography and chronology of Baxter's life and career, followed by extensive listings of her work on stage and in film, television, radio, and music. Entries for film and stage performances also include references to critical reviews. An extensive bibliography has more than 500 annotated entries and 100 unannotated listings. A list of Baxter's awards and a detailed index round out the volume.

The indexing and abundant cross-references increase the book's usefulness. Unfortunately, the printing detracts from the whole. In particular, the lack of right-side justification may create serious problems if rebinding becomes necessary.—**Barbara E. Kemp**

1319. Molyneaux, Gerard. **James Stewart: A Bio-Bibliography.** Westport, Conn., Greenwood Press, 1992. 289p. illus. index. (Bio-bibliographies in the Performing Arts, no.24). $45.00. PN2287.S68M65. 791.43'028'092. LC 91-36134. ISBN 0-313-27352-9.

This bio-bibliography continues the high level of scholarly excellence established by its predecessors. Each is a painstakingly researched reference tool that provides a concise biography, annotated lists of credits in various media, and a bibliography of sources (special collections and publications), all thoroughly cross-referenced. The Stewart biography traces the actor's life from his roots in Indiana County, Pennsylvania, where he was born in 1908, through childhood, student productions at Princeton University, Broadway, and a long Hollywood career, up to July 1991. In addition to 14 stage credits (1929-1975) and a 108-item filmography (1934-1990), the book lists and annotates 141 radio appearances (1934-1990), 75 television appearances (1953-1991), 39 sound recordings (1931-1990), 2 commercials, and 83 honors (1939-1991). The sound recordings, for instance, begin with a 78 rpm of Stewart crooning "Day after Day" and conclude with cassettes of the actor reading from the book of poems he published in 1989. Annotations typically include full production details, a synopsis, commentary, review citations, and selected review quotations. Other sections describe 24 collections of relevant primary source materials and cite 643 books and articles that deal with Stewart.

This reference book is both a researcher's joy and great fun to browse. Molyneaux is to be commended for assembling this marvelous resource and for his vigorous, lucid writing style.

—**Joseph W. Palmer**

1320. Riggin, Judith M. **John Wayne: A Bio-Bibliography.** Westport, Conn., Greenwood Press, 1992. 154p. index. (Popular Culture Bio-bibliographies). $39.95. PN2287.W454R54. 791.43'082'092. LC 91-35218. ISBN 0-313-22308-4.

As another in a series that combines biography with bibliography, this work has two purposes: to indicate the intertwining and consequent blurring of man and myth, and to provide sources of further information on John Wayne's life, career, and character for those wishing to pursue topics Riggin only touches on. The first two chapters discuss biography and image; the third includes a well-known 1971

Playboy interview to suggest the inner man; the last two are devoted to a bibliography and additional sources of information. Two appendixes provide a filmography and chronology.

Given the abundance of material available on Wayne, ranging from fan magazines to scholarly articles, Riggin makes no attempt to include every article or book on Wayne that has appeared. Instead, the third chapter discusses the most significant books and articles, while the fourth lists, without comment, those sources used in preparing the biography, articles in popular and fan magazines, and information on archives and nonprint sources. An unannotated bibliography of articles in fan magazines held by the Library of Congress suggests both the development of Wayne's career and the difficulty in tracking a star: such magazines generally remain unindexed, and library holdings are often incomplete. Because private papers remain inaccessible, Riggin draws largely from published information and does not convincingly separate man from myth, but she does provide ample information for those who wish to pursue the issue further. — **Rebecca Jordan**

1321. Royce, Brenda Scott. **Lauren Bacall: A Bio-Bibliography.** Westport, Conn., Greenwood Press, 1992. 283p. index. (Bio-bibliographies in the Performing Arts, no.30). $45.00. PN2287.B115R69. 791.43'028'092. LC 92-12500. ISBN 0-313-27831-8.

Once in a while a library receives a book that patrons cannot wait to have processed. This book was such a one for students at this reviewer's college, where students frequently research a single performer. It is intended as a comprehensive reference for information about Bacall's work. A detailed biographical sketch provides a good background and includes references to Bacall's biographies and autobiography for those needing more in-depth information.

The biography is followed by a chronology, then a separate chapter for each facet of her work, including films, television and radio appearances, and characterizations. Section entries are very detailed. Film and stage entries include credits, producers, cast of characters, plot summary and review excerpts, notes and *see also* references, and awards received. The filmography even includes roles Bacall refused. An extensive, annotated bibliography; appendixes for advertisements and for the fan club; and an index are included.

Each reference in the index includes a code letter that leads the user to the appropriate chapters of the book. For example, "*Key Largo*, 10-11, F6" means that film is mentioned on pages 10 and 11 of the biography and can be found listed as entry number 6 in the filmography. This makes it very clear where to go within the book to find information. This thorough, well-organized, well-documented reference could be improved by a more readable typeface, but it is a good purchase for public and academic libraries with film collections. — **Glynys R. Thomas**

1322. Steverson, Tyrone. **Richard Burton: A Bio-Bibliography.** Westport, Conn., Greenwood Press, 1992. 324p. index. (Bio-bibliographies in the Performing Arts, no.31). $45.00. PN2598.B795S74. 792'.028'092. LC 92-14592. ISBN 0-313-27650-1.

This title chronicles the career of one of the best-known actors of this century. Following the format of others in the series, it includes a short, informative biography; a chronology of significant events in Burton's life; chapters that outline his stage, film, television, and radio performances; a discography; a selected bibliography of books and articles; and an index. Each entry in the lengthy chapters on stage and film performances provides production credits; cast; awards and nominations; a synopsis of the story; excerpts from selected reviews; and comments that give background information on the work, its author, and Burton's participation.

For some reason, bibliographic citations for reviews omit volume and issue numbers. This may have been a deliberate decision, as the information is easy to find in standard film reference sources. Also, several entries in the bibliography for newspaper articles omit page and column numbers; clip files were used by the author, who states that "indices, hard copies, microfilm, or microfiche were not available for verification." Despite these flaws, any library with a strong film collection will want to consider acquiring this reference work. — **Deborah V. Rollins**

1323. Sweeney, Kevin. **Henry Fonda: A Bio-Bibliography.** Westport, Conn., Greenwood Press, 1992. 278p. index. (Bio-bibliographies in the Performing Arts, no.25). $45.00. PN2287.F558S92. 791.43'028'092. LC 91-47057. ISBN 0-313-26571-2.

Sweeney, an entertainment reporter for Lerner newspapers in Chicago, begins this biobibliography with a 37-page chronicle that traces Fonda's life and career, from his birth in 1905 through amateur theatrics in his native Nebraska, early struggles, ultimate success on Broadway and in Hollywood, a Best Actor Oscar in April 1982 for *On Golden Pond*, and his death four months later. This short biography is followed by a well-annotated, 110-item bibliography; a detailed filmography (1935-1981); and a list of theatrical performances (1925-1981). Most entries give full production credits, a brief synopsis, and two or three relevant quotations from contemporary reviews or standard reference books. Subsequent sections include television and radio credits, awards and honors, and several minor lists of miscellaneous information (e.g., true life portrayals, films of Jane and Peter Fonda).

While not on a level with the best titles in this series (e.g., Gerard Molyneaux's *James Stewart* [Greenwood Press, 1992]), which are more detailed, analytical, and anecdotal and which have examined more primary source materials, this is a competent effort that collects a great deal of valuable information in an easy-to-use format. This will be a good first source for those seeking information on Fonda.—**Joseph W. Palmer**

Biography

1324. **Contemporary Theatre, Film, and Television: A Biographical Guide.... Volume 9.** Emily J. McMurray and Owen O'Donnell, eds. Detroit, Gale, 1992. 491p. index. $115.00. LC 84-649371. ISBN 0-8103-2072-X. ISSN 0749-064X.

The ninth volume of *Contemporary Theatre, Film, and Television* (CTFT) continues its comprehensive coverage of the lives and work of performing arts professionals. Almost 450 entries encompass performers, directors, writers, producers, and other specialists in film, theater, and television from the United States and Great Britain, bringing the total number of the references in CTFT to more than 5,500. Its focus is on individuals currently active in these fields, although obituaries are included, as well as revisions of previous entries. Students, educators, researchers, librarians, and general readers comprise the audience for this volume.

Individual entries list name, biographical facts, addresses, career focus, memberships, awards, title-by-title credits and work information, recordings, writings, and sources for further information. The last feature is especially important, as such a comprehensive work cannot go into great detail on any single person. Entries vary from one column to several pages.

A cumulative index provides access to the entire nine-volume series and also to Gale's *Who's Who in the Theatre* (the former title of this work) and *Who Was Who in the Theatre* (see ARBA 80, entry 1022). Thus, information on a wide range of entertainment figures is made available and will be supplemented by future volumes of this ongoing publication.—**Anita Zutis**

1325. Smith, Ronald L. **Who's Who in Comedy: Comedians, Comics and Clowns from Vaudeville to Today's Stand-Ups.** New York, Facts on File, 1992. 528p. illus. $50.00. PN1583.S6. 792.7'028'0922. LC 91-42881. ISBN 0-8160-2338-7.

A series of approximately single-page, alphabetically arranged biographical sketches of 450 comedy performers comprises the heart of this work. The comedians have been drawn from vaudeville, the stage, film, television, radio, and nightclubs. They are mostly from the United States and worked (or are still performing) during this century. Most are well known to the public, but some are obscure and only of historical interest. Each biography is preceded by a birth name and date (and date of death if applicable) and is followed by film, television, stage, publication, and recording credits. Three appendixes are supplied: nicknames or character names, catch phrases, and types of comedians. There are no indexes.

This work is neither exhaustive nor scholarly, but it is fun to read. Its charm is partly due to its ability to evoke nostalgia as well as to deliver interesting information in a charming style. Readers will be surprised by particular inclusions and exclusions; selection of the comedians was based purely on Smith's preferences. The book is handsomely produced and should provide many hours of delightful reading. [R: LJ, 15 Sept 92, p. 62; RBB, 15 Nov 92, p. 629]—**Charles Neuringer**

Handbooks and Yearbooks

1326. Niemeyer, Suzanne, ed. **Money for Performing Artists.** New York, ACA Books/American Council for the Arts, 1991. 268p. index. $14.95pa. PN2293.E5M66. 791'.079. LC 91-29393. ISBN 0-915400-96-0.

    The American Council for the Arts (ACA) advocates artistic expression in all its forms with a publishing program; information services to artists; and active promotion of the arts before all kinds of public forums, including legislative bodies. This directory is a guide to 223 organizations that support professional, individual performing artists (dancers, choreographers, musicians, composers, actors, playwrights, directors, and performance artists) in the United States and Canada. Each entry has details about how to contact the organization, what sort of support it offers, and what its requirements may be for successful applicants. The guide is in alphabetical order by the agency's full name. Following are indexes by name (including shortened or popular names), discipline, geographic area, and type of support (e.g., grants, awards, fellowships, residencies, competitions, technical assistance).

    Claiming to be unique and comprehensive, the directory is easy to use and to read. However, editorial accuracy may be slightly suspect because the running head for the indexes appears to be from a different ACA Books publication. (The index entries are accurate, however.) [R: Choice, Sept 92, p. 86; RBB, 1 Apr 92, p. 1474] – **Berniece M. Owen**

1327. Pruett, Barbara J. **Popular Entertainment Research: How to Do It and How to Use It.** Metuchen, N.J., Scarecrow, 1992. 581p. index. $62.50. PN1576.P78. 791'.072. LC 92-3800. ISBN 0-8108-2501-5.

    The heart of this reference work is a compilation of resources that can be useful to the individual involved in entertainment (theater, music, film, radio, and television) research. The resources include original document archives, research centers, fan collections, public and private library collections, commercial databases, scholarly journals, popular print media, book collections, memoirs, and existing resource compilations. The annotated citations vary from primary through secondary to tertiary source materials. The annotations describe the resources and provide hints as to how to best make contact with private or restricted resources and how to best use the materials. There are general hints about how to conduct research, do interviews with performers, and fully use local resources if the researcher cannot travel to large population centers. In the future, Pruett might give more emphasis to the use of the computer-based Internet, which allows users to access the catalogs of distant libraries. A useful chapter on conducting research in Great Britain is provided, along with an exhaustive index. This wide-ranging reference tool will assist writers, journalists, scholars, fans, and all others interested in researching materials in the areas of entertainment. [R: Choice, Dec 92, p. 604] – **Charles Neuringer**

DANCE

1328. Towers, Deirdre, comp. **Dance Film and Video Guide.** Princeton, N.J., Princeton Book, 1991. 233p. illus. index. $24.95pa. GV1595.D32. 792.8'0216. LC 91-25015. ISBN 0-87127-171-0.

    Although guides and directories of videocassettes and films have proliferated in recent times, those dealing with dance alone are rare. *Guide to Opera and Dance on Videocassette* (see ARBA 91, entry 1342) was quite limited (only 175 titles were included), and it emphasized opera rather than dance. *Dance Film and Video Guide* fills this void. It lists approximately 2,000 commercially available dance performances of various types, such as ballet, folk, ballroom, jazz, and instructional. The titles are given in alphabetical order. Each entry includes length, format, distributor, date of production, producer, director, choreographer, dance company, principal dancers, and a brief description of the content. Excellent indexes make it easy for a user to select a performance according to the style of dance (e.g., ballet, tap, flamenco), purpose (e.g., anthropological, experimental, documentary), or geographical location (e.g., Africa, Asia, Europe, Oceania). Indexes of choreographers, composers, dance companies, and directors are also provided.

This is a good, comprehensive, handy guide. Any institution that has a collection of dance videos and films, or that is planning to have one, will find it of invaluable help.

—Natalia Sonevytsky

FILM

Bibliography

1329. Catchpole, Terry, and Catherine Catchpole. **The Family Video Guide.** Charlotte, Vt., Williamson Publishing, 1992. 188p. index. $12.95pa. PN1998.C34. 016.79143'75. LC 91-46899. ISBN 0-913589-64-0.

The authors have produced a video guide to help parents select and share movies with their children. Their compendium of more than 300 movies is based on the sound principle that "Quality is timeless." Firm in the belief that movies can provide a basis for family discussions regardless of their rating, the Catchpoles even include 10 R-rated films, such as *Network* (1976) and *Apocalypse Now* (1979), that they feel provide valuable insights into the world. By viewing these types of "controversial" films with their children, parents can explain sensitive material and enrich family time.

Each of the entries contains enough information to identify the film and to place it in a thematic context. Fifteen popular film themes are identified (e.g., rebellious youth, race relations), and movies from various decades are offered to demonstrate the evolution of thematic concerns over time. Each review is cross-referenced to the themed sections for easy use. The introductory list of 100 "non-objectionable" films suitable for viewing by the entire family is nicely complemented by an appendix that includes selected films for older children. While several good parenting tools for the video age are available (*A Parent's Guide to Video and Audio Cassettes for Children* [see ARBA 88, entry 951] and *The Family Guide to Movies on Video* [see ARBA 89, entry 857]), this guide is noteworthy for its obvious love of movies and its earnest desire to share that love in a family environment in a supremely sane and nonthreatening manner. Recommended for public libraries.—**David K. Frasier**

1330. **Film & Video Finder.** 3d ed. Medford, N.J., Plexus Publishing, 1991. 3v. index. $295.00/set. ISBN 0-937548-20-0.

Since 1964 the National Information Center for Educational Media (NICEM) has attempted to bring bibliographic control to the nonprint media market in education. NICEM keeps a 300,000-plus item database of all types of educational media, out of which it produces a number of medium-specific print products, a complete online DIALOG file, and a complete CD-ROM product titled AV Online from SilverPlatter. The *Film & Video Finder* is a subset of this massive database. The current edition is a remarkable achievement considering the continued roller-coaster health and sickness of the educational film and video industry.

Entry into the main two-volume index is through titles. Each entry includes title, series title, format, content summary, length, subject headings, producer, distributor, and date. Entries are formatted for ease of reading and scanning—no mean feat, considering the tiny typeface. The first volume is a massive subject index that uses a thesaurus developed by NICEM. Subject headings are too broad; many have hundreds of titles listed. Because film titles are not often indicative of content, users must spend a great deal of time looking up entries in the alphabetical section to select possible films for purchase or preview. However, a level indication (from elementary through adult) is some help. Producers and distributors are coded for subject and title indexes, and a separate producer and distributor address directory is provided.

While missing details and some errors were noted, the *Finder* serves a vital function for media centers, schools, and libraries that need to track down films for purchase, preview, or rental. All libraries seeking information about educational films and videos and that can afford the cost will need this edition.—**David V. Loertscher**

1331. Gibberman, Susan R. *Star Trek*: **An Annotated Guide to Resources....** Jefferson, N.C., McFarland, 1991. 434p. index. $39.95. Z7711.G5. 016.79145'72. LC 91-52502. ISBN 0-89950-547-3.

This work covers every aspect of *Star Trek*, from the television shows (original, new, and animated) and the movies to the people (actors, writers, and directors) and the novels. There is also a discography and a guide to videos. The book provides a balanced picture of the *Star Trek* phenomenon. Not only does Gibberman present the positive aspects of the show but she also discusses some of the less favorable moments, such as off-screen tension between actors.

The book has two minor flaws. First, Gibberman does not explain that articles quoted may be excerpts rather than complete pieces. Second, the organization of the material seems somewhat random; for instance, multiple entries about the same topic do not always appear in chronological order. Regardless, *Star Trek* fans are in for a treat when they read through the more than 1,300 entries in this work. [R: Choice, May 92, p. 1368; RQ, Summer 92, p. 579; VOYA, June 92, p. 141]

—**Lisha E. Goldberg**

1332. Rimmer, Robert H. **The X-Rated Videotape Guide II.** Buffalo, N.Y., Prometheus Books, 1991. 625p. illus. $17.95pa. PN1995.9.S45R56. 016.79143'09'093538. LC 85-27062. ISBN 0-87975-673-X.

The first edition of this guide was published in 1984 (see ARBA 85, entry 799). Intended as a buyers' guide for purchasers and renters, it contained 600 reviews of heterosexual and bisexual adult videos. In 1986 a much enlarged 2d edition was published that included 1,350 reviews and 4,000 supplementary listings that covered films and videos produced between 1970 and 1986. The present volume is a supplement to the 2d edition. It reviews 1,520 additional titles that were released between 1986 and mid-1990. (Prometheus Books has purchased unsold copies of the 1986 edition and can provide the two volumes as a set.) Entries are listed alphabetically by title and begin with a coded legend that indicates the types of sexual activity depicted. This is followed by information concerning year of release, production company, producer, director, and featured cast members. Finally, a fairly lengthy annotation enthusiastically and explicitly describes plot and sexual action. Sometimes there are evaluative comments, but the objectives of the guide are not scholarly, and the commentaries provide little, if any, serious analysis or criticism.

The intended audience for this publication should find it useful. It would be even more useful if there were cast and director indexes and a directory of sources. Very large cinema collections will want to acquire this publication because the adult film genre is certain to be of interest to researchers in the future.—**Joseph W. Palmer**

1333. Steadman, Susan M. **Dramatic Re-Visions: An Annotated Bibliography of Feminism and Theatre 1972-1988.** Chicago, American Library Association, 1991. 367p. index. $50.00. Z5784.F45S73. 016.792'09. LC 91-16333. ISBN 0-8389-0577-3.

This work annotates 850 books, monographs, and articles that discuss the relationship between women and society as well as the political realities and goals of both as evinced by plays, performances, and theaters. Rather than focusing solely on texts, it outlines the connection between feminism and the total dramatic experience while providing a full range of feminist views. Intended for scholars, people affiliated with the theater, students, and teachers—and without being exhaustive—it includes everything written in English that is accessible to someone using the resources of a scholarly library in this country. However, it is restricted to those works that approach issues from a feminist perspective or those whose discussion reveals such a perspective. The 50-page introduction provides a 40-page history of feminist criticism in general (as well as its development in the theater) and a 10-page explanation of Steadman's methods, scope, organization, and purpose. The eight chapters, each grouped thematically by theory, chronology, or topic, provide an overview of the relationship between feminist criticism and all aspects of theater and drama. Each chapter is divided into a section on books and monographs and one on periodicals, serials, and annuals. Within each chapter, entries are lettered and numbered. Each annotation is descriptive rather than evaluative and reflects the thesis of each entry. Three appendixes list resources, special periodicals, and selected works published after 1988. Four indexes, arranged by letter and number, provide access to the entries by title, name, category, and subject. Within its limits, the book provides a great deal of information on feminist dramatic criticism. [R: Choice, Apr 92, p. 1214]—**Rebecca Jordan**

1334. **Viewers' Choice Guide to Movies on Video.** By Joe Blades and the editors of Consumer Reports Books. Yonkers, N.Y., Consumer Reports Books, 1991. 351p. index. $16.95pa. PN1992.95.B52. 016.79143'75. ISBN 0-89043-476-X.

With the advent of the videocassette and the VCR came the convenience of viewing films at home. However, selecting appropriate movies from the abundance displayed at the video store is not so convenient. This guide attempts to ease the situation by providing the viewer with a directory of films available on video and guidance as to their content.

The 3,500-plus movies included are taken from the *Consumer Reports* Movie Poll, which began in 1947. Those that have earned ratings of "excellent" or "very good" in the poll, and are also available on video, are listed alphabetically in the main section of the book within 10 categories (biographies, comedies, dramas, family viewing/children's, foreign language, horror and science fiction, musicals, suspense and mystery, war, and westerns). Lower-rated films are included in the appendix. A helpful index lists all films in the book.

Each main entry contains title, rating, release year, distributor, running time, whether the film is in black-and-white or color, director, and cast. This is followed by a brief synopsis of the plot and any other pertinent information, such as awards or production details. Appendix entries omit the second paragraph.

This collection of "people's choice" recommendations is useful in assisting consumers in selecting movies for home viewing. Because new titles become available each week, it is hoped that supplemental editions will be forthcoming. — **Anita Zutis**

Biography

1335. **International Dictionary of Films and Filmmakers. [Volume] 3: Actors and Actresses.** 2d ed. Nicholas Thomas, ed. Detroit, St. James Press/Gale, 1992. 1080p. illus. $115.00. 791.43. ISBN 1-55862-039-7.

This work lists 635 international actors and actresses of the cinema, giving for each a brief biography, a complete filmography, a selected bibliography of works on and by entrants, and an expository essay by a specialist in the field. The volume is best defined by a few excerpts from the Editor's Note: "The selection of entrants ... is based on the recommendations of the advisors.... It was not thought necessary to provide criteria for selection.... The book is intended to represent the wide range of interests within North American, British, and West European film scholarship and criticism. The eclecticism in both the entrants and critical stance of the different writers emphasises the multifarious notions of the cinema."

Interesting in its scope but perplexing for its inclusions and omissions, the book walks a line between reference and critique. In doing so, it falls short of completely satisfying either side. It is difficult to regard it as reference because of the exclusion of several veteran and contemporary actors. And it is more difficult to consider the book as critique because the expository essays are quite broad, lacking in-depth, academic-like explorations of performance, consistency, and contribution. Compared to other books of this nature, this dictionary does well as an informative source, but its price might restrict its acquisition only to libraries with abundant funding and to the serious film connoisseur. [R: RBB, 1 Dec 92, p. 687] — **Joan Garner**

1336. Katchmer, George A. **Eighty Silent Film Stars: Biographies and Filmographies of the Obscure to the Well Known.** Jefferson, N.C., McFarland, 1991. 1067p. illus. index. $75.00. PN2285.K34. 791.43'028'092273. LC 90-28262. ISBN 0-89950-494-9.

This work provides information on actors and actresses who might otherwise be no more than footnotes in the history of the cinema. It focuses not on those whose names remain known, such as Mary Pickford, Douglas Fairbanks, and Rudolph Valentino, but on those whose faces may only be barely remembered from the many films they appeared in. The entries are arranged alphabetically, from Art Acord to Guinn "Big Boy" Williams, and numbered. Despite the passage of time, the frequent dearth of reliable information, and the contradictory stories created by publicity, self-promotion, or scandal, every entry provides the most accurate and complete biography and list of films possible for each actor. The biographies range in length from two to several pages and include date and place of birth if known; original name; family background; reason for becoming an actor; key events and films; anecdotes and favorite sayings; personal and professional problems; and information about deaths, funerals, and survivors. The filmographies are arranged chronologically and list studio, director, writer, length, and cast. The sources for this information are included in the section of notes on the filmographies. The index lists other actors and actresses mentioned in the main biographies and references to the main entries elsewhere in the text. For fans of silent films, this volume will recall a vanished world, and the biographies are generally interesting, if somewhat informal. [R: Choice, May 92, p. 1370; RBB, 1 Mar 92, p. 1305]—**Rebecca Jordan**

1337. Peary, Danny. **Cult Movie Stars.** New York, Simon & Schuster, 1991. 608p. illus. index. $17.00pa. ISBN 0-671-71103-2.

Peary sets the tone of this work by dedicating it not to a loved one, friend, or family member but to "Young women who do John Wayne impressions." Readers are then treated to an impressive cast of characters (750 names or so) who have in common appearances in feature-length movies and being considered cult figures. "Cult," Peary explains (if never quite defines), refers to "only those [actors] who have had strong emotional impact on at least a fair-sized number of movie fans." This may or may not explain why there are entries for Greta Garbo, Humphrey Bogart, James Dean, Fatty Arbuckle, Natalie Wood, Bud Abbot and Lou Costello, John Cleese, Brigitte Bardot, and four members of the Carradine family, while not one of the (unrelated) Keatons (Diane, Michael, or Buster) is included. Why did Peary choose Randy Quaid but not brother Dennis and Peter Fonda but not Jane or Henry? His introduction does admit that strong, emotional fanship breeds controversy.

There is very little biographical information on the stars; to learn where they were born or whom they married, the reader must look someplace else. What *is* provided is a witty and concise treatment of what gave each person a fanatical following, whether it was beauty, brawn, good acting, charisma, wit, *Grand Guignol*, or willingness to romp nude. Approximately one black-and-white photograph per page salts the text. Peary is not afraid to interject his own biases, naming, for example, his favorite actress (Natalie Wood) and stating that someone "can't act a lick" (Jean-Claude van Damme). He also divulges gossip such as who hated who. He evaluates the careers of his subjects, providing each with a selective filmography broken down into unique categories (e.g., cult favorites, other key films, sleepers, also recommended, and also of interest).

While Peary provides director and year for each film, and there is an index of titles, this work is not for serious students of film research. Weekend movie buffs and late-night television watchers will enjoy it for looking up favorites or just browsing. [R: RBB, 1 Jan 92, pp. 848-49]—**Bruce A. Shuman**

1338. Quinlan, David. **Quinlan's Illustrated Directory of Film Comedy Actors.** New York, Henry Holt, 1992. 302p. illus. $35.00. PN2285.Q56. 792'.28'092273. LC 92-12512. ISBN 0-8050-2394-1.

Film journalist Quinlan has given us a pithy treatment of almost 300 film comedians, from the days of Ben Turpin (1868-1940) to Whoopie Goldberg. He states his intention "to inform and to entertain," an aim he reaches with succinct analyses of acting careers and talents. He profiles mainly American and British comics, although an occasional figure such as Jacques Tati shows up too. The articles range from a half-column (e.g., John Belushi) to three pages (e.g., Charlie Chaplin, Buster Keaton), with women accounting for about one-sixth of the subjects. Each entry concludes with a fairly extensive filmography, usually more complete for contemporary actors than for those of the silent era. The work is well illustrated with promotional shots, stills, and portraits.

Because many of these actors had overlapping careers on stage and in television, Quinlan devotes space to describing these other areas. Occasionally, as with Chaplin, the discussion of the London music hall days is very informative. At other times the subject's television career considerably outweighs film achievements, as in the case of Sid Caesar. Selectivity means making choices, and Quinlan has done a commendable job; but one wonders whether he really intended to omit Michael J. Fox and Madeline Kahn. Occasional Britishisms crop up, as in the author's description of Mickey Rooney as "a human catherine-wheel." Quinlan does not hesitate to make judgment calls, but readers will find them balanced and perceptive.—**John P. Schmitt**

1339. Ragan, David. **Who's Who in Hollywood: The Largest Cast of International Film Personalities Ever Assembled.** New York, Facts on File, 1992. 2v. $135.00/set. PN1998.2.R34. 791.43'028'0922. LC 90-2980. ISBN 0-8160-2011-6.

The cast referred to is indeed large—more than 35,000 entries reflect the history of the motion picture industry from 1893 to 1991. Anyone who ever appeared on the silver screen—stars, legends, international figures, and bit players—may be included. Film scholars, students, and movie buffs are the book's intended audience.

Living performers' birth dates, places, and current residences are noted, along with a selection of their motion picture credits. For deceased players the year and age at death and titles of significant films are listed. It is stated that movie credits are not complete but constitute a "telescoped sampling" of the person's work. Winners of Academy Awards and of special Oscars are noted. Scattered throughout the volumes are short biographies and insights into the lives of the players. A brief bibliography lists other compendiums of film history.

Of course, the sheer volume of coverage precludes detailed profiles of all the performers. Entries range in length from one word to almost a page. Although the work would be even better if some of the individual entries were more informative, it can serve as a starting point for further research. A more complete edition with expanded coverage is promised for the future. [R: BR, Nov/Dec 92, p. 38; Choice, June 92, p. 1526; RBB, 15 Apr 92, pp. 1555-56; WLB, Apr 92, p. 128]—**Anita Zutis**

1340. Slater, Thomas J., ed. **Handbook of Soviet and East European Films and Filmmakers.** Westport, Conn., Greenwood Press, 1992. 443p. index. $69.50. PN1993.5.R9H28. 791.43'0947. LC 91-9255. ISBN 0-313-26239-X.

This is an exhaustive survey of filmmaking in the Soviet Union, Poland, Czechoslovakia, Yugoslavia, Hungary, East Germany, Romania, and Bulgaria. Aimed primarily at the scholar, it covers all of the major movies (accent on "major"; not every film ever made in these countries is listed) and movie makers from the Eastern bloc in the past 100 years. In addition, a historical essay puts the film industry of each country into proper perspective, providing a geographical and political overview as well as an accurate appraisal of the origins and development of the film industry. The appendix features a chronological list of major historical, cultural, and film events in the former Soviet Union and Eastern Europe between 1890 and 1990. The volume is rounded out by a subject index and a film index. The titles in the latter are given in English translations, followed by original (mostly transliterated) titles. Strangely enough, no indications are given as to whether the films are in black-and-white or color. Spelling is mostly accurate, no mean feat in a book with a myriad of foreign titles and names that feature just about every diacritical mark known in Europe.

The book is not for the casual browser or movie buff; persons seeking brief movie synopses will not find them here, and some categories, such as music, are given short shrift. For instance, Shostakovich and Dunayevski made it into the book, but one of the most prolific and talented contemporary composers who wrote a number of Soviet film scores, Alfred Schnittke, did not, except for one dry listing in a Klimov film. Sergei Prokofiev (Eisenstein's *Alexander Nevsky* and *Ivan the Terrible*) does not rate a separate entry either. Still, students and scholars of the genre will find this volume a valuable resource. [R: Choice, June 92, p. 1520]—**Koraljka Lockhart**

1341. **Who's Who in Canadian Film and Television 1991-92. Qui est Qui au Cinema et a la Television au Canada.** Waterloo, Ont., Wilfrid Laurier University Press; distr., Atlantic Highlands, N.J., Humanities Press, 1991. 616p. $49.95pa. 791.43'025'71. ISBN 0-88920-210-9. ISSN 0831-6309.

First published in 1986, this comprehensive directory of the Canadian production community provides information on more than 2,500 film and television directors, picture editors, writers, producers, cinematographers, art directors, composers, production managers, costume designers, sound personnel, and publicists. Professional and biographical information in the entries is based on data supplied by those responding to a form sent to them by the Academy of Canadian Cinema and Television. Entries appear in English or French depending upon the language used by the respondent to answer the form. Explanatory texts are in both English and French.

Personnel entries are grouped under 14 alphabetically arranged job designations, from art directors to writers. Each entry contains union, guide, or association membership; home or work address;

and telephone number. The subsections titled "Types of Production and Credits," "Genres," "Biography," and "Selected Filmography" complete the entry and identify the individual's principal areas of professional endeavor. Entries are rife with abbreviations that some users may find cumbersome, but a complete list of these is offered, and their use is uniform. A name index provides access to entries alphabetically listed under the 14 job designation sections. Also included is the text of the Canadian government's "Canadians First Employment Policy." Recommended for academic libraries with strong television and film collections. [R: Choice, June 92, p. 1530]—**David K. Frasier**

Catalogs and Collections

1342. Bidd, Donald W., ed. **The NFB Film Guide: The Productions of the National Film Board of Canada from 1939 to 1989. Repertoire des Films de l'ONF.** Montreal, National Film Board of Canada, 1991. 2v. illus. index. $240.00/set. 015.7'037. ISBN 0-660-56485-8.

Created by an Act of Parliament in 1939, Canada's National Film Board (NFB) was mandated "to interpret Canada to Canadians and other nations" through the medium of the moving image. Since its inception, the NFB has produced over 8,000 documentaries, feature films, and animated productions that chronicle and reflect the social realities of Canadian life. The $78 million parliamentary allocation received by the NFB in 1991-1992 supports the training of filmmakers, audiovisual centers, and the main research facility in Montreal. It is a unique institution that, unfortunately, has no U.S. counterpart.

The two volumes comprising this guide to NFB films produced from 1939 to 1989 are divided into separate filmographies of 4,475 English-language films and of 3,355 French-language films (text entirely in French). Entries are alphabetically listed; each contains information on release dates, series title, date of production, running time, credits, format, and a short synopsis. Ordering information for an item's rental or purchase is also supplied. Titles of French-language films are translated and included in the English-language volume. A series of indexes (subject, series, director, producer, and production year) provide more than 40,000 access points to the filmographies. Also of note are an NFB and Canadian film industry timeline of historical events, signed essays on the scope of the NFB, sets of photographic montages, a 437-item bibliography on the NFB, and a guide to research resources for the study of this venerable institution. The English-language volume of the set is not available individually. Highly recommended for any type of library that supports a large audiovisual department.

—**David K. Frasier**

1343. Darby, William. **Masters of Lens and Light: A Checklist of Major Cinematographers and Their Feature Films.** Metuchen, N.J., Scarecrow, 1991. 1043p. index. $99.95. PN1998.D285. 011'.37. LC 91-20656. ISBN 0-8108-2454-X.

Although most critical and audience attention focuses on a movie's actors, director, or writers, the technical skill and art of the cinematographer contribute significantly to the effect of the film. Darby's checklist is the most extensive work available, with filmographies for 708 cinematographers (those who are credited on at least 5 works) and miscellaneous listings for notable films. The work covers cinema from its beginnings in the 1910s to 1990. Most entries are for U.S. cinematographers, although there are several from other countries. The list includes only feature-length films (at least 45 minutes). The entries are arranged alphabetically by photographer and consist of an alphabetical list of films with their dates of issue and studio or country of origin. There is an index to film titles. Darby provides a list of films that were nominated for and won United States Academy Awards for cinematography from 1927 through 1990; British Academy Award winners are listed for 1963 through 1989. This work is an essential addition to any extensive collection that supports research in the history and art of cinema. [R: Choice, May 92, p. 1364; WLB, Apr 92, p. 125]—**Linda A. Naru**

1344. Gifford, Denis. **Books and Plays in Films 1896-1915: Literary, Theatrical and Artistic Sources of the First Twenty Years of Motion Pictures.** London, Mansell and Jefferson, N.C., McFarland, 1991. 206p. index. $35.00. PN1997.85.G54. 016.79143'75. LC 91-14174. ISBN 0-89950-650-X.

Approximately 3,000 film adaptations of literary and artistic works are listed in this guide, which covers the first two decades of the silent film era. Thus, it complements A. G. S. Enser's *Filmed Books and Plays* (see ARBA 88, entry 1335), which begins with the talkies. Yet to be analyzed from the aspect of their literary sources are the classic feature films produced from 1916 to 1927, the heyday of silent cinema.

Gifford, a prolific compiler of works that pertain to film and popular culture, identifies films based on operas, songs, comic strips, and cartoons, as well as those adapted from novels, plays, short stories, poems, and nonfiction. Although most of the films included were produced in the United States, Great Britain, or France, other countries are also represented. Entries are arranged alphabetically by author or creator, with film adaptations of the individual's works then listed chronologically by the date of their first showing. Following the film title is the film production company, the number of reels, and a symbol denoting the genre of the source material (e.g., "Bio" for biography, "Pm" for poem). When it differs from the film title, the title of the original work is also noted. Other features include an index to titles of films and original works and an appendix that lists film production companies by country.

Unfortunately, this work is marred by some notable omissions, such as *Le Voyage dans la lune*, based in part on works by Jules Verne and H. G. Wells, and the Famous Players production of *The Count of Monte Cristo*. In addition, a number of inconsistencies and errors occur. For example, Gifford gives the release date for *Regeneration* as September 1915 in one entry and as October 1915 in another, and he neglects to note that this film was based on the book *My Mamie Rose*. Also, he lists *Salomy Jane* as five reels in one entry and six in another and incorrectly identifies *Tess of the Storm Country* as four reels instead of five.

In spite of its flaws, however, this compilation is valuable because it is the only work of its type on the silent film period. It is most appropriate for academic libraries that support the study of film history. [R: Choice, May 92, p. 1368] — **Marie Ellis**

Dictionaries and Encyclopedias

1345. Browne, Steven E. **Film-Video Terms and Concepts.** Stoneham, Mass., Focal Press/Butterworths, 1992. 181p. illus. $24.95pa. TR847.B76. 778.5. LC 91-33264. ISBN 0-240-80111-3.

This work is a practical guide to specific terms and to some more general concepts that define the technical similarities and differences between the two visual media of film and video. The terms are arranged in alphabetical order and clearly defined. Browne uses a convenient key of five symbols, which appear in the margins, to indicate a term that applies to film only, to video only, or to both media; that is used in both media with different meanings; or that indicates the equivalent definition of a term in the alternate medium. There are *see* and *see also* references within the definitions and some useful illustrations and photographs.

This handbook is intended for users that have some background in either film or video; therefore, terms are sometimes defined by technical words or phrases that might be unfamiliar to the layperson. This work is recommended for reference collections that support work or scholarship in film or video. — **Linda A. Naru**

1346. **Chambers Concise Encyclopedia of Film and Television.** Allan Hunter, ed. New York, Chambers Kingfisher Graham, 1991. 401p. illus. $14.95pa. ISBN 0-550-17253-X.

Chambers is known to most libraries as a long-respected British publisher of encyclopedias and reference books. The preface acknowledges that television and the film industry, once implacable rivals, are now symbiotic companions in the entertainment business, each feeding (and feeding off) the other. This concise encyclopedia presents a single alphabet of some 700 technical terms, people, and key films and television programs, all selected for their significance by Hunter, who has admittedly used for criteria his own knowledge, critical judgment, and preferences. That is not all bad, however, as this compact paperback contains some wonderfully incisive and perceptive annotations on its subjects, and a lot of information is packed into its pages.

Hunter acknowledges a bias toward the contemporary but provides biographical entries and film write-ups for silent-screen stars and directors of pioneer films and television shows on both sides of the Atlantic. He admits that many readers may experience disappointment or irritation at the omission of their favorite film, director, or actor, but he promises successive editions that will consider neglected favorites. Entries include biographical sketches that have human interest tidbits; films or television shows, with a brief history of each project, a soupcon of plot, and its critical reception; equipment; and occupational titles (e.g., best boy, focus puller, gaffer). Foreign-language titles are listed both ways, with cross-references to the English version. All told, there are 400-plus biographical sketches and appraisals and discussions of about 200 films and television shows; the rest are explanations and definitions of specialist terms and concepts. In lieu of an index, a supplement lists winning entries in various film festivals and awards through the years.

Chambers is to be commended for erasing the no-longer-germane distinction between film and television. While this is a subjective work, it will be a welcome addition to any library's performing arts reference section.—**Bruce A. Shuman**

1347. Lenburg, Jeff. **The Encyclopedia of Animated Cartoons.** rev. ed. New York, Facts on File, 1991. 466p. illus. index. $40.00. NC1766.U5L46. 791.43'75'0973. LC 90-21182. ISBN 0-8160-2252-6.

A considerable body of nostalgia revolves around the classic animated films and shorts of the past, a nostalgia that *The Encyclopedia of Animated Cartoons* attempts to mine. The first part of the book consists of a foreword by Gary Owens, whose voice is well known in announcements and cartoons; a lengthy section of acknowledgments; and a nutshell history of American animated cartoons. Animated features are then divided into silent cartoon series, theatrical sound cartoon series, full-length animated features, animated television specials, and television cartoon series. For each series the title, background and story information, directors, type of color (e.g., Technicolor) when appropriate, studio, major voice providers, and titles of individual cartoons (in chronological order) are given. Features also include the identification of the actors for all voices, place and date of premier, and any rebroadcast dates. A section on awards and honors, a bibliography, and an index complete the book. The latter has some problems, such as a blind reference to "Lucky Luke" and an indication that Alan Hale, Jr., appears on pages "338-378."

It is sheer bad luck that this book came out before the advent of original cartoons on Fox and Nickelodeon (e.g., *Taz-Mania, Ren & Stimpy*) and Disney's milestone *Beauty and the Beast*. Otherwise, coverage appears complete, with Japanese and European cartoons syndicated in the United States included. The European *Asterix the Gaul* movies, which have aired in North America on cable, are not listed; they may be outside the book's scope, however. (The aforementioned "Lucky Luke," also European, was briefly aired here; was this entry dropped for some reason?)

Comparison of the section on television specials with George Woolery's *Animated TV Specials* (see ARBA 91, entry 974) shows complete agreement through 1987 (the year that Woolery's work ends); in fact, it sometimes seems as if Lenberg's annotations have been condensed from Woolery's. (Another of Woolery's books appears in the bibliography, but *Animated TV Specials* does not.) Woolery provides much more complete information about each special; in general, his books should be the first choices of libraries that want material about animation on television. However, those works are showing their age; Lenberg is up-to-date through 1990 and makes a good supplement to them. His book is also more accessible to the casual animation fan (although the use of black-and-white illustrations is disappointing). Recommended for public and school libraries, and for other collections where there is interest. [R: Choice, May 92, p. 1370; LAR, June 92, p. 412; RBB, 1 Jan 92, pp. 847-48; SLJ, Nov 92, p. 137]

—**D. A. Rothschild**

Directories

1348. Balski, Grzegorz, comp. and ed. **Directory of Eastern European Film-Makers and Films 1945-1991.** Westport, Conn., Greenwood Press, 1992. 546p. index. $79.50. PN1998.2.D55. 791.43'0233'092247. LC 91-22023. ISBN 0-313-28278-1.

Eastern Europe has undergone such sweeping changes in recent years that all the maps of the area have had to be redrawn. From a bibliographic standpoint, this turn of events has made the assignment of nationalities to persons a nightmare. Balski does his best, organizing more than 350 major postwar Eastern European filmmakers by country, but some disputes about nationality are obvious; one filmmaker is identified as Polish but was born in Vilnius (now Lithuania), while another, born in Vilnius, is identified as Ukrainian.

The scope is chronological, from the end of World War II through 1991. Having made at least three feature-length films since 1945 is Balski's primary criterion for inclusion, with a few exceptions made for directors working mainly in animation and documentaries. Arrangement is alphabetical by director's name, giving for each the date and place of birth (and death, where relevant), with disappointingly scant biographical information. Film lists are chronological, consisting only of year and title (in the original language, then translated into English). Short films and features are listed separately. Cyrillic titles are transliterated, where necessary, into the roman alphabet, but the book provides no help in pronunciation for the English-speaking reader. A 14,500-entry index of titles (all languages in one alphabet) concludes the work, along with a general index and selected bibliographic references (by nationality) for further reading.

Oversized, this book uses print large enough for the partially sighted, with abundant white space around everything (half of many pages are blank). It is hard to understand why a large, unwieldy, and expensive format was chosen for such scant material. For its subject and scope, this work may be of value to libraries that support curricula in which Eastern European film is studied, but because of the negligible biographical information presented about the filmmakers, most film collections can pass on this one. — **Bruce A. Shuman**

Filmography

1349. Broderick, Mick. **Nuclear Movies: A Critical Analysis and Filmography of International Feature Length Films....** Jefferson, N.C., McFarland, 1991. 219p. illus. index. $35.00. PN1995.9.N9B76. 791.43'658. LC 91-52631. ISBN 0-89950-543-0.

This volume abounds with global cinematic responses to the demonstrable and hypothetical effects of artificially induced nuclear and thermonuclear reactions. Casting a very large methodological net has yielded a surprisingly diverse catch of the most remotely nuclear-related titles. Beginning with the 1914 U.S. film *Radium Rays* and ending with the 1989 comedy *Zadar! Cows from Hell*, this compilation includes 850 movies from 36 countries (exclusive of the perhaps equally large number of documentaries). Each category (pre-1950, 1960s, 1970s, and 1980s) is prefaced with a useful literary and scientific timeline. Broderick's abbreviations for the national origin of films and their major production studios and distributors are generally useful. This volume contains the most comprehensive list available of the nuclear-related film and its subgenre and is a good reference work for public and college libraries. [R: WLB, Apr 92, p. 126] — **Eric H. Christianson**

1350. Cocchiarelli, Joseph J. **Screen Sleuths: A Filmography.** Hamden, Conn., Garland, 1992. 231p. illus. index. (Garland Filmographies, 3; Garland Reference Library of the Humanities, v.1322). $37.00. PN1995.9.D4C63. 791.43'655. LC 91-28737. ISBN 0-8240-5427-X.

Focusing on films in which the central theme revolves around the solution of a mystery or crime rather than the criminal, this book surveys detective or sleuthing films from 1928 to 1991. A filmography of approximately 200 entries gives basic acting and production credits, a brief plot summary, an equally brief critical assessment, and (occasionally) so-called memorable scenes or quotations. Twelve films chosen for their overall relevance to detective films are the subjects of individual analytical essays. A chronology lists approximately 500 films by year of release, and a brief bibliography on crime film and an index complete the work.

The analytical essays provide some interesting insights and, as they are arranged chronologically by film date, they also give a sense of the development of this particular style of film. However, the book has some drawbacks. As one might expect, readers may quarrel with the inclusion or omission of titles. For instance, it might reasonably be argued that *Klute* should have been included in the chronology, if nowhere else. Similarly, *Famous Movie Detectives* (see ARBA 80, entry 1027), *Famous Movie Detectives II* (see ARBA 92, entry 1365), and *The Great Detective Pictures* (see ARBA 91, entry 1381) have been omitted from the bibliography. More serious, though, are the problems caused by the arrangement and indexing. Criteria for inclusion are not well elucidated, and there is no indication of what is included in the index. The majority of the latter's entries appear to refer to the prefatory matter and the analytical essays, but a few isolated references to the material in the filmography also appear. Anyone trying to find a reference to a specific film, therefore, may have to check three separate sections, one of which is only in chronological order. These deficiencies make the book harder to use and decrease its value as a reference tool. —**Barbara E. Kemp**

1351. Erickson, Hal. **Baseball in the Movies: A Comprehensive Reference, 1915-1991.** Jefferson, N.C., McFarland, 1992. 402p. illus. index. $39.95. PN1995.9.B28E7. 791.43'655. LC 91-42875. ISBN 0-89950-657-7.

Three cheers and five stars for *Baseball in the Movies*, a meticulously researched and joyfully written overview of the movies (up to 1991) in which baseball is the chief subject. The films are listed alphabetically by title. Erickson gives a quick plot summary and then goes into detail as to why the movie does or does not work, first as an accurate depiction of baseball, then as entertainment. Separate sections cover baseball short subjects and movies with a baseball tie-in but in which the sport is not the main subject.

Erickson's introduction discusses the myths about baseball movies, including "they all have the same plot" and "they are box office poison." His strengths are his obvious knowledge, not only about baseball but also about the movie business; his ability to explain *why* a particular movie works instead of just rhapsodizing about it; and his not being afraid to call trash, trash. Another plus is his sense of humor. Of a thinly disguised parody of a famous team owner in *Blue Skies Again*, he says the movie leaves "no Turner unstoned." All in all, this is a marvelous book, valuable both to the film student and the baseball fan. Very highly recommended. [R: RBB, 15 Oct 92, p. 450]

—**R. S. Lehmann**

1352. Fetrow, Alan G. **Sound Films, 1927-1939: A United States Filmography.** Jefferson, N.C., McFarland, 1992. 954p. index. $75.00. PN1993.5.U6F46. 016.79143'75'0973. LC 91-52635. ISBN 0-89950-546-5.

Cable television and videotapes have revolutionized viewers' access to the early sound films of Hollywood, making it possible for them to see many forgotten and neglected movies. As a result, guides to films have grown dramatically in size as they add both the endless crop of new films and many long-buried older films. Fetrow's new filmography is a list of the 5,000-plus feature-length sound films made in the United States from 1927 through 1939, Hollywood's greatest year. Films are listed alphabetically by title with individual entries providing information on production company; year of release; cast, sometimes including the name of the character each person played; producer, director, and writer; whether the film was an adaptation of a play or book; running time; alternate titles in Great Britain; awards and nominations; availability on video; a brief plot synopsis; and other films that used the same story, even before 1927 and after 1939. A detailed index of personal names allows the tracing of individuals' careers. There is also a separate list of award-winning films and a brief bibliography.

Because Fetrow covers a much narrower time period and geographical area, his filmography lists many films not included in *Halliwell's Film Guide* (see ARBA 90, entry 1332) and often supplies more detailed information on the cast. As a result, his work is a welcome addition to the reference library of film history and prompts eager anticipation of companion volumes on the films of the 1940s, the 1950s, and beyond. —**Ronald H. Fritze**

1353. Flynn, John L. **Cinematic Vampires: The Living Dead on Film and Television....** Jefferson, N.C., McFarland, 1992. 320p. illus. index. $39.95. PN1995.9.V3F58. 016.79143'675. LC 92-53578. ISBN 0-89950-659-3.

Intended for media students, film critics, filmgoers, and historians of popular culture, this study takes a serious and comprehensive look at the vampire film genre. At the same time Flynn briefly traces the worldwide origins of vampire mythology. He provides a filmography of vampire films from 1896 through 1992 and lists projects planned for 1993. He also examines the role of the vampire genre in film history and attempts to explain its continuing popularity in our culture. Some 372 vampire films, both

English-language and foreign titles, are described, including *Bram Stoker's Dracula*, which was released in late 1992. The book's 10 chapters are arranged in chronological order and provide an introductory essay, followed by lengthy descriptions of the films. Each entry includes year of general release, production credits, actors, story synopsis, and Flynn's assessment of the film's importance to the genre. Alternate titles and original foreign-language titles are noted in the descriptions and appear in the film index (which does not include subjects or names). Following the text is a list of the 10 best and worst films, films never made, a list of vampire film trivia questions, and a selected bibliography. Illustrations are numerous and well chosen, including stills and poster art that accompanied the films.

—**Berniece M. Owen**

1354. Hanke, Ken. **A Critical Guide to Horror Film Series.** Hamden, Conn., Garland, 1991. 341p. illus. index. (Garland Reference Library of the Humanities, v.1214). $51.00. PN1995.9.H6H36. 791.43'616. LC 91-19952. ISBN 0-8240-5545-4.

Hanke, author of *Charlie Chan at the Movies* (see ARBA 90, entry 1339), again shows himself to be an articulate movie historian with a vast knowledge of genre films. The present volume critiques 30 American and British horror series, both the famous and the obscure. They range from Lon Chaney/Tod Browning collaborations of the late silent era to such thrillers of the 1980s as the *Halloween* and *Nightmare on Elm Street* films. Each chapter provides detailed evaluations with an abundance of fascinating movie lore and commentary and a complete filmography.

Hanke writes with such authority and conviction, and his judgments seem so astute and well reasoned, that it is only when he deals with familiar films that the reader is likely to suspect that some of his preferences are idiosyncratic. For instance, was *The Exorcist*, a movie that mesmerized audiences and critics, really a poor film? Was *The Exorcist II*, widely regarded as the worst sequel of all time, a work of genius? Hanke argues persuasively. Only those who have actually seen the films are likely to be unconvinced. Clearly, other opinions are needed. Unfortunately, not a footnote nor a scrap of bibliography is to be found. This total lack of bibliographic documentation, a failing common to too many books by movie historians, is this intriguing reference's greatest deficiency. [R: Choice, Apr 92, p. 1209]—**Joseph W. Palmer**

1355. Hiatt, Sky. **Picture This! A Guide to Over 300 Environmentally, Socially, and Politically Relevant Films and Videos.** Chicago, Noble Press, 1992. 389p. $12.95pa. PN1995.9.S62H5. 016.79143'75. LC 91-50642. ISBN 1-879360-05-5.

Hiatt, self-styled film critic and social activist, explains the rationale for this work in the introduction. Movie-making is not just about telling a story well or dazzling audiences with special effects; it is only worthwhile when it makes a socially relevant statement, even if that statement is unpopular or objectionable. The book is intended both to promote a selection of 300 or so films that Hiatt deems socially relevant and to serve as homage to the artists who have dedicated their careers (entirely or in part) to socially relevant film work. Some of these films have been banned, blacklisted, or pulled from theaters for political reasons. Others have been unfairly denigrated by moralistic critics. A prominent, recurrent theme is intolerance (e.g., prejudice against Blacks and Japanese). Other films ponder the death penalty, revolution, environmental polluters, and the morality of war. Most of the films cited will be familiar to the unschooled but frequent moviegoer, but a few are bound to open new vistas to any reader. Examples of socially relevant films are such classics as *All Quiet on the Western Front* (1930), *All the President's Men* (1976), *Animal Farm* (1955), *Apocalypse Now* (1980), *Au Revoir Les Enfants* (1987), and *The Autobiography of Miss Jane Pittman* (1973). But Hiatt, no snob, also includes such films as *Above the Law* (1988) (featuring the violent Stephen Seagal) and *Air America* (1990) (played largely for laughs by Mel Gibson and Robert Downey, Jr.). Hiatt unstintingly opposes censorship, whatever the reason and whomever the censor, and similarly excoriates critics who judge films primarily on technical brilliance, paying little attention to their messages. A minor problem with the book is that proofreading standards seem a bit lax.

This book fills an important niche in writings about film, especially film as propaganda. Hiatt writes powerfully, preferring to get right to the social impact of a film rather than dwelling on plot or characterization. Recommended for all film collections. [R: LJ, 1 June 92, p. 112]—**Bruce A. Shuman**

1356. Hunter, Allan, ed. **Movie Classics.** New York, Chambers Kingfisher Graham, 1992. illus. index. $9.95pa. ISBN 0-550-17008-1.

While conceding that a movie classic "can only be measured on an unscientific scale of public affection and esteem" (p. 1), Hunter presents essential information on 188 films that arguably rank among some of the finest and most enduring movies ever made. International in scope, the films range chronologically from *The Great Train Robbery* (1903) to *The Silence of the Lambs* (1991). Each one-page entry contains a short plot synopsis, selected technical credits and cast list, and a brief but informative commentary on the film's cinematic significance. Box office grosses and discussions of noteworthy directors are often included in these well-written essays. Twenty essays on the historical development of the movies and genres and themes (e.g., horror, Westerns, neorealism, epics) are interspersed throughout the alphabetically arranged film titles and offer accurate overviews of these topics. A serviceable index provides access to the text but omits references to cast and crew members cited in credits. The work is adequately illustrated.

This affordable paperback is a good general introduction to some of the world's most outstanding, beloved, and honored films. While much of the information can be found in myriad other film sources, this title serves as an attractively packaged, concise, and accurate encyclopedic guide for the lay reader. It is a good purchase for public libraries and interested individuals.
—**David K. Frasier**

1357. **Jewish Film Directory: A Guide to More Than 1200 Films of Jewish Interest from 32 Countries over 85 Years.** Westport, Conn., Greenwood Press, 1992. 298p. index. $65.00. PN1995.9.J46J48. 791.43'65203924. LC 91-22024. ISBN 0-313-28279-X.

This directory is an alphabetical listing (by English title) and description of major films about various aspects of Jewish history or culture that were produced from 1907 to 1992. Theatrical releases, documentaries, short features, Yiddish films, educational films, and made-for-television miniseries from all over the world are included. Each entry provides the following information: film title in English, titles in other languages, subtitles, country and date of production, running time, classification (e.g., feature, documentary), producer, director, scriptwriter, source material, cinematographer, music credits, main cast, description of contents, and citations to reviews in *Variety* or the *Monthly Film Bulletin*. The volume includes director, subject, and source material indexes; a list of Jewish film festivals; and a very brief bibliography.

The chief strength of this work is that information has been collected both from film archives and libraries and from individuals who have worked on the films in this subject area. The range of films included thus has been expanded to include more titles and types of films from a broader geographic scope. Recommended for collections that support research or academic programs in film studies or the history of cinema. [R: RBB, 1 June 92, p. 1776]—**Linda A. Naru**

1358. Limbacher, James L. **Haven't I Seen You Somewhere Before? Remakes, Sequels, and Series in Motion Pictures, Videos, and Television, 1896-1990.** Ann Arbor, Mich., Pierian Press, 1991. 438p. $65.00. ISBN 0-87650-244-3.

Most of this compilation is devoted to a list of films and television programs that are remakes of films featuring ideas, stories, or events that have a timeless appeal. Limbacher identifies his audience as those who research the sources of films: librarians, teachers, film, radio and television personnel, and film historians.

The main heading for an entry is the title of the film's original manifestation. Information about the first version includes production company (or country of origin), year of release, source of idea (e.g., book, play, legend, an individual's life and work), and a list of subsequent versions in order of production. Cross-references from titles of remakes direct users to the original film. Both international and U.S. works are included.

Next is a brief section of sequels—one or two films that specifically follow the events and characters in the original film. Finally, there is a longer section of series titles. A series must include three or more films that feature the same characters, ideas, authors, or actors. The series list is in alphabetical order by the name of the key character or idea (e.g., Krazy Kat, King Kong, Roy Rogers), and the titles are in date order under the name. There is no apparent repetition of titles between the lists. A general index to names and titles would have been helpful. [R: RBB, July 92, p. 1961]

—Berniece M. Owen

1359. Moss, Joyce, and George Wilson, eds. **From Page to Screen: Children's and Young Adult Books on Film and Video.** Detroit, Gale, 1992. 443p. index. $35.00. ISBN 0-8103-7893-0.

Librarians appreciate help in encouraging children to read the book after viewing the film, and this source makes it possible for the reverse to occur as well. It assembles several hundred books that have been made into films, with ordering and rental information. The stated focus is young audiences, with films that are meant to be motivational for young, reluctant, or nonreaders. Organization is alphabetical by title. A typical entry has a brief synopsis, citations to reviews, and a list of cinematic adaptations. If more than one film has been made from a book, that is so noted. Appendixes include lists of films for the hearing-impaired and film and video distributors. There are indexes by award, age level, subject, and author/film title. Some evaluations are from reviewing media, while others are the subjective viewpoints of Wilson and Moss. Cute cartoon icons are used to denote a subjective film rating and the degree to which the film adheres to the book.

Included are more than 750 literary works and information on almost twice as many 16mm films, videos, and laserdiscs adapted from them. The editors explain their selection criteria as being "state education recommendations, as well as librarians and educators." The age range of the intended audience is K-12. Experts have been consulted to make the distinctions that divide children's, young adult, and adult films.

While this is a useful work, and its lapses are not fatal, there are many gratuitous errors. A boy is called "Alexander" on one line and "Anthony" on the next; there is confusion as to who is dying in *Bang the Drum Slowly*; and two classics are misspelled as "*Billy Bud*" and "*Cask of Amontialldo, The.*" One might wish for longer and more thoughtful synopses, and some of the inclusions are questionable (e.g., *Portnoy's Complaint*). *Huckleberry Finn* and *Tom Sawyer*, however, have spawned, respectively, four and five movies; it is nice to have help in making selections. While this is a valuable reference source for teachers, its consistent lack of basic proofreading bespeaks a puzzling lack of pride.[R: RBB, 1 Oct 92, pp. 368-69; SLJ, Sept 92, p. 152; SLMQ, Fall 92, p. 74; WLB, Oct 92, pp. 107-10]—**Bruce A. Shuman**

1360. Parish, James Robert, and Michael R. Pitts. **The Great Hollywood Musical Pictures.** Metuchen, N.J., Scarecrow, 1992. 806p. illus. $79.50. PN1995.9.M86P37. 791.43'6. LC 92-7483. ISBN 0-8108-2529-5.

In a format already tested by at least a dozen previous topical film listings, the authors provide detailed data on works they term "great." Each of the more than 300 films is initially provided with issuing studio identification, date, and duration, followed by the names of those involved in the production: text and script authors, costume designer, choreographer, editor, set and art directors, music director and arranger, makeup artists, and those responsible for sound and camera. Songs and instrumental works used in the film are cited with composer and lyricist (although these are not distinguished), with a cast list and the roles of the individuals. The plot is then summarized, followed by a brief history of the film's reception and any additional notes thought relevant. Photographs enhance the coverage.

This is, then, a splendid source for the curious film lover and can serve the preliminary interests of the scholar, but the only back material is a chronology (indicating a range from 1927's *The Jazz Singer* through 1988's *School Daze*) and biographical sketches of the authors. Several indexes would have endowed the publication with important advantages (but would also have required at least a second volume). As for the authors' definition of "great," this is overt evidence of subjective selectivity and seems to have been indirectly influenced by a movie's financial success. [R: RBB, 1 Nov 92, p. 547]

—**Dominique-Rene de Lerma**

1361. Rainey, Buck. **Sweethearts of the Sage: Biographies and Filmographies of 258 Actresses Appearing in Western Movies.** Jefferson, N.C., McFarland, 1992. 632p. illus. index. $95.00. PN2285.R35. 791.43'028'0922. LC 91-52639. ISBN 0-89950-565-1.

In a work similar in format and theme to *Those Fabulous Serial Heroines* (see ARBA 91, entry 1394), Western film authority Rainey pays tribute to the lives and careers of 258 leading ladies of the Hollywood Western. Certainly this was among the most enduring of all Hollywood genres (more than 2,000 "B" programs were produced during the 1930s and 1940s alone), but literature on the Western has tended to ignore the contributions made by its nearly anonymous female stars and instead to focus on the more glamorous cowboy. Rainey, who definitively covered many of the male stars in his *Saddle Aces of the Cinema* (see ARBA 82, entry 1122) and the genre itself in *Shoot-Em-Ups* (see ARBA 79, entry 1031) and its supplement (see ARBA 92, entry 1367), rectifies this oversight in a reference volume that combines a true fan's affection with impressive scholarship.

Biographical entries are arranged in one of four categories determined by the time period and type of Western made: "Pathfinders" (actresses in pre-1920 westerns), "Trailblazers" (actresses of the 1920s), "The Pioneers" (actresses of the 1930s and 1940s), and "Homesteaders" (actresses in "A" type or post-1940s films). Inclusion is based on either an actress's popularity, the uniqueness of her roles, her appearances in at least eight Westerns, or Rainey's interest in her career. Each entry combines an informative essay with a small bibliography of selected readings usually cited from specialist publications, such as *Classic Images*. A complete filmography that chronicles the entirety of an actress's career concludes each entry. The work is liberally illustrated and has a general bibliography and title index.

Once again Rainey has beautifully documented the lives and careers of several players who would certainly have suffered undeserved professional obscurity had he not noted their contribution to the most American of all movie genres. Highly recommended for academic libraries that support film and popular culture collections.

—David K. Frasier

1362. Reimer, Robert C., and Carol J. Reimer. **Nazi-retro Film: How German Narrative Cinema Remembers the Past.** New York, Twayne/Macmillan, 1992. 256p. illus. index. (Twayne's Filmmakers Series). $23.95; $13.95pa. PN1995.9.N36R45. 791.43'658. LC 92-18054. ISBN 0-8057-9316-X; 0-8057-9322-4pa.

Hitler's Third Reich ended in 1945, yet even half a century later, German filmmakers continue to explore the actions and feelings of a Germany at war. The expression "Nazi-retro" has been coined to refer to narrative films made by Germans about their nation's involvement in the war, and it reflects a great variety of attitudes towards the subject. Since the end of World War II, more than 100 major films (and even more minor ones) have dwelt on the wartime years—some unapologetic, others seeking to expiate collective guilt or simply to explain or understand. The Reimers explore numerous fascinating aspects of wartime Germany as they analyze and explain the ideas in the films they discuss.

More than 100 films are analyzed, some of them well known (e.g., *Das Boot, The Tin Drum, The Nasty Girl*) to international audiences, while others are, to U.S. audiences, obscure. Among the most ubiquitous subjects are Hitler's megalomania; the formulation of Nazi policies; the reaction of ordinary citizens to events; resistance movements; and the persecution and murder of Jews, including life (and death) in the camps. In these films wartime Germans are seen variously as cartoon characters; men and women without conscience; brave citizen-warriors; fanatical zealots; or world-weary, resigned victims of forces they cannot control. Each title discussed is listed both under its name in German and its name translated into English. The Reimers write with style, wit, and perception; for example, they are critical of *Das Boot*, which gives a gritty picture of daily life on a Nazi submarine in wartime, as a whitewash of the cause for which such men fought. The brave sailors of the film, they say, are exonerated from their Nazihood through heroism in defense of their homeland and by their repulsion by the excesses of National Socialism; they often resemble "laborers, victimized by unfair management practices." Overall, however, the films tend to indict, seeing clearly their homeland's criminal madness.

The overall effect of this book is much more than mere filmography or film criticism. One can almost see the German filmmakers trying desperately to make sense of a period of madness within their own country. The writing is crisp, and the text is salted with black-and-white half-page illustrations from the films. For its unique perspective on both German national psychology and film, this work is a "don't miss" title for all film collections.

—Bruce A. Shuman

1363. Richard, Alfred Charles, Jr. **The Hispanic Image on the Silver Screen: An Interpretive Filmography from Silents into Sound, 1898-1935.** Westport, Conn., Greenwood Press, 1992. 571p. index. (Bibliographies and Indexes in the Performing Arts, no.12). $65.00. PN1998.R54. 016.79143'6520368. LC 92-8917. ISBN 0-313-27832-6.

The film genre is a vivid and powerful vehicle that conveys images that become embedded in the national consciousness. Hispanics, as well as other members of racial and ethnic groups, have historically been portrayed in demeaning roles. A key determinant of the salience of race and ethnicity reproduced on the screen are the somatic and linguistic attributes that are real and identifiable. For example, the Cisco Kid says to Carmencita, "Oh no no. My Spanish she is not so good. You see, my-my-my father she was born in San Luis Obispo...." Other stereotypical images of Hispanics are those of the "Senorita vamp" and the "cantina cutie."

Richard has compiled a first-rate reference work, the first of a projected multivolume filmography. The lucid introductory essay explores the numerous themes that are associated with these negative images; it will be of great interest to those interested in the topic. The volume covers 1,800 films. The citations are listed chronologically, and each entry provides the reader with an in-depth annotation and cross-references. The book includes numerous indexes that simplify locating information: feature films, subjects, actors and actresses, and countries and place-names. This is a highly readable and important book that should be a welcome addition to all academic and large public libraries. [R: Choice, Dec 92, p. 604] — **Dario J. Villa**

1364. Schutz, Wayne. **The Motion Picture Serial: An Annotated Bibliography.** Metuchen, N.J., Scarecrow, 1992. 375p. index. $42.50. Z5784.M9S36. 016.79143'05. LC 91-41833. ISBN 0-8108-2484-1.

This bibliography is a compilation of motion picture serials, actors, and production personnel (e.g., writers, directors, editors, music composers) with citations to books and magazine articles on various aspects of the serial genre. The information is arranged in four parts: "The Silent Era (1912-1929)," "The Sound Era (1930-1956)," "Serial Production Personnel," and "Serial Players." The parts are further subdivided into more specific categories; there is an introductory essay for each segment and brief annotations for many of the citations. Schutz consulted books and more than 130 magazines for the list of compilations and citations. The work includes an index of personal names and film titles, and the main body of the book contains numerous cross-references. This bibliography should be acquired by academic libraries supporting film or cinema history programs. — **Linda A. Naru**

1365. Schwartz, Ronald. **The Great Spanish Films: 1950-1990.** Metuchen, N.J., Scarecrow, 1991. 134p. illus. index. $32.50. PN1993.5.S7S29. 791.43'0946'09045. LC 91-38947. ISBN 0-8108-2488-4.

In a sequel to his excellent *Spanish Film Directors (1950-1985)* (see ARBA 87, entry 1311), Schwartz discusses 70 significant films made in Spain over the 4 decades generally recognized as the "modern" period of Spanish cinema. Selected from thousands of productions, each film reflects some aspect of the Spanish mentality during the reign of General Francisco Franco. Following the dictator's death in 1975, a lessening of censorship resulted in a plethora of bold films by directors such as Pedro Almodovar and Vicente Aranda that dealt with formerly taboo topics such as the sexual revolution, feminism, and crime. By focusing on the films of a handful of directors, Schwartz cogently elucidates their evolving thematic concerns.

A brief chronology that traces the major events and films in the development of Spanish cinema from 1896 to 1990 introduces the book's decade-by-decade format. Each decade from the 1950s through the 1980s is individually discussed, with films chosen from the period chronologically listed. For each film the Spanish and English titles are provided, as well as the director, major credits, cast, background, a plot synopsis, and critical commentary. Background information places the work in the historical evolution of Spanish cinema. Forty films receive this expanded treatment, with another thirty lesser "great" films included in an appendix that follows a similar format minus the discussion of background or plot. Liberally illustrated, the volume includes a select bibliography and an index that provides access only to major film titles (no English translations) and directors discussed in the text. Recommended for large academic libraries and those institutions that already own Schwartz's earlier study. — **David K. Frasier**

1366. Walker, Mark. **Vietnam Veteran Films.** Metuchen, N.J., Scarecrow, 1991. 226p. index. $25.00. PN1995.9.V44W35. 791.43'658. LC 91-28813. ISBN 0-8108-2475-2.

This book joins a number of recent studies of Vietnam War films, most notably Lawrence Suid's *Science of Conflict* (University Press of America, 1990); *From Hanoi to Hollywood*, edited by Linda Dittmar and Gene Michaud (Rutgers University Press, 1991); and *America Rediscovered*, edited by Owen W. Gilman, Jr., and Lorris Smith (Garland, 1990), as well as several fine bibliographic essays and doctoral dissertations. However, the focus of this volume is different. Walker, a freelance writer and teacher, notes films that include a Vietnam veteran in some capacity. He offers a brief essay, with copious film references, on each of ten genres: biker, vigilante, caper, detective, police, war, horror, comedy, melodrama, and art. A concluding filmography provides the major credits, Vietnam veteran characters, availability in video, and a brief plot summary for 215 films. A separate filmography lists credits for 28 films set in Vietnam during the war.

The synopses of so many films has obvious value, and the essays are interesting reading. However, Walker's efforts at "genre analysis" are weak and his conclusions rather facile—for example, that major studios were leery about representing Vietnam veterans in certain genres or that independent studios often represented veterans while major ones did not. His primary judgments—that the veteran image fits within clearly recognizable mythic archetypes and that the image of the Vietnam veteran in film is overwhelmingly a heroic one—are more proclaimed than proven. If not all that it professes to be, the volume is still a useful reference tool for most libraries.—**Joe P. Dunn**

1367. Weisser, Thomas. **Spaghetti Westerns—the Good, the Bad and the Violent: A Comprehensive, Illustrated Filmography of 558 Eurowesterns and Their Personnel, 1961-1977.** Jefferson, N.C., McFarland, 1992. 502p. illus. index. $45.00. PN1995.9.W4W32. 016.79143'6278. LC 92-50002. ISBN 0-89950-688-7.

The spaghetti Westerns under consideration are more accurately described by the author as European Westerns. These are films set in the Old West of the United States but produced and directed by Europeans with international casts of performers, often including United States actors to increase North American box office potential. The majority were filmed in Spain, which has a landscape that resembles the Mexican border regions of the Old West. Weisser details 558 films that were lensed between 1961 and 1977. The films are arranged alphabetically by their best-known English titles. Each entry lists other English-language and foreign names that identify the film—sometimes as many as four titles—and there are cross-references in the main list from each of these alternate titles to the main entry. As actual release dates vary widely by country, date of filming is used, not date of release. Credits of the cast and those who produced, directed, wrote, photographed, and scored the film are included. Weisser then evaluates the film in a descriptive and critical annotation that describes the notable (or ignoble) aspects of the film. The range and sheer number of films included is surprising. Avid film fans will likely recognize about half of these titles (e.g., *Hannie Caulder, Shalako, They Call Me Trinity*), which received popular North American release or television play, while others (e.g., *Have a Good Funeral, My Friend ... Sartana Will Pay; My Horse, My Gun, Your Widow; Seven Nuns in Kansas City*) will have had limited exposure.

The special features at the end of the work are outstanding. There is a list of performers with all their included films and the directors who directed them, followed by a list of directors (with pseudonyms) and their films. The music composers, scriptwriters, and cinematographers each have their own lists as well. Other sections chronicle the films about the screen characters "Django" and "Sartana." There is a list of American-made films that attempted to copy the style of the European Western, as well as lists of best and worst films. The work is capped by a bibliography and an extensive index that locates any mention of a film or personality throughout the book. There are numerous photographs and movie posters, but these are not indexed or noted in the text.

This extremely well designed, informative work is a pleasure to read. Weisser's knowledge gives the subject an aura of importance, and his gentle sense of humor helps keep things in perspective. The book can be recommended without reservation for film, television, or popular culture collections and on a selective basis to general collections with clients who have a strong interest in film.—**Gary R. Cocozzoli**

Handbooks and Yearbooks

1368. Avallone, Susan, comp. and ed. **Film Writers Guide.** 3d ed. Los Angeles, Calif., Lone Eagle, 1991. 414p. index. $49.95. ISBN 0-943728-48-7.

This is the eighth film trade directory published by Lone Eagle; others cover such individuals as directors, editors, and television writers. The intent of this guide is primarily to serve as an industry contact book, not to provide biographical information. Because this is a profession subject to change, there have been three editions in three years.

Avallone lists current film writers alphabetically, along with their agents; produced scripts; and unproduced "screenplays," which may or may not be "in development." The writers appear to be largely North American, but there are a few Western European and Australian writers, among others. Academy Awards and nominations are indicated in the name list and in a separate appendix. There are indexes of titles and of agents and managers. No further biographical information is provided. Libraries interested in biographical and critical information on major American film writers of the past and present will be better served by the Dictionary of Literary Biography volumes *American Screenwriters* (see ARBA 85, entry 1239) and *American Screenwriters, Second Series* (see ARBA 87, entry 1285). — **John P. Schmitt**

1369. Fredrickson, Jim, and Steve Stewart. **Film Annual 1992.** Aliso Viejo, Calif., Companion, 1992. 336p. illus. index. $14.95pa. ISBN 0-9625277-2-6. ISSN 1061-4214.

This affordable trade paperback covers 392 significant American and foreign feature, independent, and documentary films released in the United States during 1991. Each alphabetically arranged title entry contains a brief plot synopsis, detailed cast and credits, the MPAA (Motion Picture Association of America) rating and an averaged critical rating based on the reviews of at least 10 unnamed critics. A "Film Facts" subsection in each entry categorizes the film by genre (e.g., action, drama), gives its running time, and notes if a soundtrack is available. Academy Award nominees and winners in major categories for 1991 are offered, as is a chronology of top winners from 1927 to 1990. Numerous other 1992 awards (e.g., People's Choice) for films released in 1991 are also included. Of particular note is an illustrated, chronologically arranged obituaries section. Three indexes cover critics ratings, genre type, and individuals cited in the cast and credits. Embarrassing misspellings abound in the text, and the cast and credits index is suspect. For example, actress Carrie Snodgress's name is spelled "Snodgrass," while the corresponding index entry refers to the wrong page.

Serious film researchers will want to look elsewhere. However, while not as ambitious or detailed as the annual updates of *The Motion Picture Guide* (see ARBA 90, entry 1352), its attraction lies in its low cost, currency, and detailed lists of cast and credits for 1991 films. Recommended for public libraries. — **David K. Frasier**

1370. **The Guinness Book of Movie Facts & Feats.** By Patrick Robertson. New York, Abbeville Press, 1991. 236p. illus. index. $19.95pa. ISBN 1-55859-236-9.

If there ever is a question as to what movie has the most kisses or who was the first U.S. woman film director, *The Guinness Book of Movie Facts & Feats* is the place to find the answer. It is a useful reference book that will also provide hours of entertainment for film fans and trivia buffs. Profusely illustrated with well-chosen stills, publicity shots, posters, and magazine advertisements, it has 16 chapters that cover broad categories such as character and themes, music, censorship, and shorts and documentaries. It is indexed by name, subject, and movie title.

In addition to the usual Guinness categories of first, oldest, longest, most expensive, and the like, there are a number of interesting lists not found elsewhere. Examples include a look at age and the leading lady over the years and "Top Jobs," an analysis of film role occupations for men and women from 1920 to 1990. Tables and graphs present statistics on such things as the number of movie screens in the United States from 1945 to 1990, weekly cinema attendance, and Hollywood and sport. Most entries are annotated with fascinating background information and anecdotes.

No documentation is provided to support the facts contained in this book, but the information that can be verified in other sources seems to be accurate, and Robertson has made corrections to the text of this edition when necessary. The title remains current and interesting with the inclusion of illustrations from recent movies, updated tables, and the addition of new lists and the deletion of others. Recommended for most public and academic libraries. [R: SLJ, Jan 92, p. 146] — **Deborah V. Rollins**

1371. Pecchia, David, comp. and ed. **Cinematographers, Production Designers, Costume Designers and Film Editors Guide.** 3d ed. Los Angeles, Calif., Lone Eagle, 1991. 480p. index. $49.95. ISBN 0-943728-43-6.

This is one of nine directories published by Lone Eagle that list people currently active in film and television. Other guides focus on directors, writers, actors, composers, special effects people, and several other categories of professionals. The present volume lists cinematographers, production designers, costume designers, and film editors in separate sections. Name and selected credits are given, with an emphasis on feature films produced in the past 10 years. Sometimes an agent, affiliation, or telephone number is given; otherwise, users are advised to contact listees through the appropriate guild. A single film title index to the entire volume is an improvement over the 2d edition (see ARBA 92, entry 1375), which indexed each section separately. Entertainment industry professionals and libraries that serve them should welcome this update. A computerized version of the Lone Eagle directories is reportedly in the development stage. — **Joseph W. Palmer**

1372. Singer, Michael, comp. and ed. **Michael Singer's Film Directors: A Complete Guide.** 9th ed. Los Angeles, Calif., Lone Eagle, 1992. 560p. illus. index. $65.00. ISBN 0-943728-46-0. ISSN 0740-2872.

The latest edition of this guide is not so much a scholar's reference book as an industry rolodex. Its intent is to provide access to a director's credits and agent for interested parties such as film writers and producers. Telephone and fax numbers are more in evidence than addresses. Singer claims his guide is selective, but he still manages 260 pages of double columns on active U.S. and foreign film directors and their works. Directors' credits include feature films, documentaries, television miniseries, concert films, animations, and features for home video and cable. Usually the production must run a minimum of 90 minutes to qualify for inclusion. The second half of the guide is devoted to notable directors of the past. Singer lists their credits in the same unelaborated directory style. There are indexes of film titles and foreign-based directors; also appearing are brief lists of managers, agents, and state and international film commissions.

To be useful, an industry contact book must be current; this one meets that goal. It does not attempt to be a reference book that enhances one's knowledge of directors or their work, except perhaps in its indications of who is active at this time. [R: LJ, Aug 92, p. 90] — **John P. Schmitt**

Indexes

1373. **The International Film Index 1895-1990.** Alan Goble, ed. Munich, New Providence, N.J., K. G. Saur, 1991. 2v. $325.00/set. 791.430321. ISBN 0-86291-623-2.

In one of the most ambitious projects ever undertaken in film studies, Goble has amassed an impressive two-volume title and director index to more than 177,000 international films made between 1895 and 1990. The index covers 90 percent of all mainstream films made in the United States and Europe as well as significant numbers of films produced in more than 120 other countries. "Films" include features, documentaries, shorts, serials, made-for-television movies, art and animated films, and alternative cinema.

Goble has compiled the title list and directors' filmography from more than 400 reference works included as a bibliography in volume 2. The accuracy of this index is dependent on the quality of these sources. For mainstream films, where scholarship abounds, Goble's index is highly accurate and comprehensive. For lesser known "cult" directors, it is suspect. For example, "sexploitation" director Russ Meyer never made two films Goble attributes to him (*Steam Heat* and *Kiss Me Quick!*) although they are often cited in sources consulted by the author. With this caveat, Goble's work is destined to become a standard source.

For each film listed in volume 1, which covers film titles, information is provided on a film's original title, year of release, director, country of origin, type, and alternative titles. Of the 232,000 entries listed, 177,000 are master titles, and the remainder are fully cross-referenced alternative titles. Volume 2, the directors' filmography and indexes, offers a chronological filmography of the work of some 25,000 filmmakers. Each entry contains biographical data on their country of origin, dates, occupation (e.g., producer, director), and pseudonyms (also cross-referenced). Indexes include directors by country and directors of animated films. In keeping with the work's international scope, introductory material is offered in English, German, French, and Italian. This work is absolutely essential for large academic and public libraries. [R: LJ, 15 Mar 92, p. 76]—**David K. Frasier**

Quotation Books

1374. **Chambers Film Quotes.** Tony Crawley, comp. and ed. New York, Chambers Kingfisher Graham, 1991. 296p. index. $9.95pa. ISBN 0-550-21024-5.

Quotable quotations have long been in demand as anecdotes, gossip, biographical insights, and one-liners. This book makes fascinating reading because, for some reason, if a famous person said it, it is imbued by the rest of us with extra meaning. Crawley offers more than 2,000 celebrity quotations from Hollywood movie makers, stars, directors, and producers: some perceptive, some cutting and abrasive, and some highly amusing.

Unlike other books of quotations that are arranged by personal name, Chambers's compilation is commendably arranged by topic, with an index that provides access to quotations by named person. Therefore, several quotations are grouped together on a single topical theme, and, in the back, quotations are grouped together by speaker. Each quotation is furnished with a printed source, but source details leave something to be desired. All that is usually provided is the journal name and year. For a few quotations, however, Crawley unaccountably gets specific (although page numbers, absent throughout, would be nice). But the point of this book is to present distilled wisdom from the rich and famous and not so much to give accurate references for those nuggets of wisdom. A few of the quotations will sound familiar to anyone who has kept up with the performing arts, but any reader is sure to find something new, revealing, insightful, or even profound in these pithy remarks of the great and near-great. Highly recommended.—**Bruce A. Shuman**

THEATER

Bibliography

1375. Duffy, Susan, comp. **The Political Left in the American Theatre of the 1930's: A Bibliographic Sourcebook.** Metuchen, N.J., Scarecrow, 1992. 213p. index. $27.50. Z1231.D7D84. 016.812'5209358. LC 92-10822. ISBN 0-8108-2577-5.

The broad field of American political theater has many facets that have not been studied in depth. In her own studies Duffy has located many sources that should be of vital importance to those who wish to explore these new fields. While the emphasis is on the 1930s, many sources go back into the 1920s or forward into the 1940s. The section on books and book chapters contains about 300 entries, most annotated. Articles number about 800 and are arranged by periodical or newspaper title, following a practical system borrowed from another bibliographer, Hallie Flanagan. This is very useful even though it is at odds with standard MLA form. The part of the book that covers plays includes both individual scripts and anthologies. Other sections are devoted to dissertations, archival collections, and funding sources for research projects. The index covers all important entries but intentionally excludes play titles, which are easily found in the section of the book devoted to plays.

The introduction and the prefatory remarks for each chapter reveal Duffy to be a practical researcher who has succeeded in bringing these materials together in a way that will be as helpful as possible to those who work with them. Her suggestions for doing what she calls "long distance" research offers helpful ideas about what is reasonable to expect and how to go about this type of research. She even points out the cost savings of hiring a researcher in a distant city versus the price of travel and lodging. Archivists and librarians can only hope that these guidelines will be followed, thus providing them the pleasure of helping researchers with reasonable and well-planned requests. This is a first-rate sourcebook and should be useful to all who use it.—George Louis Mayer

1376. Gildzen, Alex, and Dimitris Karageorgiou. **Joseph Chaikin: A Bio-Bibliography.** Westport, Conn., Greenwood Press, 1992. 285p. index. (Bio-bibliographies in the Performing Arts, no.29). $49.95. PN2287.C46G55. 792'.028'092. LC 92-10617. ISBN 0-313-26273-X.

A concise and comprehensive guide to the life and professional achievements of Joseph Chaikin, monument of the twentieth-century theater world, this volume provides an array of information and citations pertinent to the subject, up-to-date through mid-1991. An opening biographical essay of some 20 pages chronicles Chaikin from birth (1935) to the present, detailing and highlighting his developing relationship with the world of theater. This is followed by documentation about productions—live and recorded performances and directorial and recorded directorial credits. A comprehensive bibliography follows, with works by Chaikin as well as works about him (books, parts of books, dissertations, theses, articles, and reviews). Entries include complete bibliographic information and brief annotations. A final section of the work is a listing of the manuscript catalog of the Joseph Chaikin Papers, housed at the Department of Special Collections and Archives at Kent State University Libraries. Supplementing this is a short appendix that reproduces a letter written by Chaikin to the Open Theater Company in 1971. An author/title/subject index is keyed to the coded, numbered entries of the volume. This work is a worthwhile addition for academic library collections and special collections focused on theater history and biography.—Edmund F. SantaVicca

1377. Horn, Barbara Lee. **David Merrick: A Bio-Bibliography.** Westport, Conn., Greenwood Press, 1992. 260p. index. (Bio-bibliographies in the Performing Arts, no.33). $45.00. PN2287.M618H6. 792'.0232'092. LC 92-19789. ISBN 0-313-28520-9.

David Merrick was a very successful Broadway producer and probably the last of the great independent impresarios. An opening chronology gives an overview of his career. There is a serious error in it, however; it incorrectly states that Merrick produced the 1975 film *One Flew Over the Cuckoo's Nest*, when he actually produced the 1963 stage version.

Although this work is called a bio-bibliography, the biography is really only a lengthy introduction. Nearly half the book is composed of a chronological productions list with detailed information about each show, including a plot summary and reviews. This is followed by a list of the films Merrick produced; for some reason the movie reviews are not included here, but in the bibliographical section instead. The second half of the book contains the bibliography, which is divided into three parts: writings by Merrick, books and periodicals, and (by far the largest section) newspaper articles. The work concludes with a chronological list of awards won by Merrick productions and those shows later produced as films. Finally, there is a single author, name, and production title index. Subject access would have been a helpful addition.

This work is not recommended because of its limited use to researchers. Horn has omitted all page numbers from newspaper entries and from the magazine reviews in the productions list. This will make it very difficult to obtain copies of the articles, particularly as many of them are from New York newspapers only available through interlibrary loan.—Christine E. King

1378. Horn, Barbara Lee. **Joseph Papp: A Bio-Bibliography.** Westport, Conn., Greenwood Press, 1992. 409p. index. (Bio-bibliographies in the Performing Arts, no.26). $49.95. PN2287.P23H67. 792'.0232'092. LC 91-46308. ISBN 0-313-28021-5.

Joseph Papp was a major force in modern American theater, and future theater historians will need to evaluate his impact. This volume contains a chronology of Papp's life, a short biography, and a chronological list of 429 Papp productions from 1952 to 1990. Each listing gives the name of the production, the venue if known, run dates, production crew and cast, and selected review citations. The production list is followed by annotated lists of writings by Papp and those about him and his productions. A set of appendixes deals with Papp's awards, television and film credits, and nontheatrical activities. Author, playwright, play title, production crew, and cast indexes are supplied.

The citations are admittedly incomplete because Papp's Public Theatre files were not available at the time of compilation. (They are now available in New York's Performing Arts Library.) The annotated comments for writings by and about Papp are somewhat sparse and sometimes uninformative. But Horn has done an important service by gathering together the available bibliographical references on Papp that researchers can use as a starting point. – **Charles Neuringer**

1379. Oggel, L. Terry. **Edwin Booth: A Bio-Bibliography.** Westport, Conn., Greenwood Press, 1992. 294p. illus. index. (Bio-bibliographies in the Performing Arts, no.28). $49.95. PN2287.B488O34. 792'.028092. LC 92-8910. ISBN 0-313-26195-4.

This text provides a starting place for anyone interested in Edwin Booth, whom Oggel regards as an exemplum of nineteenth-century American values and culture. As with others in this series, the volume combines a brief biography with an extensive bibliography. The introduction describes the structure of the book and lists the organizational principles Oggel has employed; each section of the bibliography begins with a brief statement of rationale and explanation of method. In the inclusion of dissertations and nineteenth-century articles (what Oggel terms "ephemera"), he has provided an invaluable resource for people without access to research libraries or nineteenth-century journals. The inclusion of Booth's own writings, both published and unpublished, justifies Oggel's belief in Booth's significance. Perhaps the greatest drawback of the text is the need for compression created by the wealth of materials included. For instance, although Oggel explains the abbreviations he uses at the beginning of the section on unpublished primary sources, a separate page that listed abbreviations would probably simplify the reader's task. Visually, setting the item number above the bibliographic entry separates the two. Whereas annotations for primary sources are generally lengthy, those for secondary sources are treated parenthetically and are therefore less helpful than they might otherwise be. Finally, if one does not read the introductory material, one may not understand the logic behind the annotations. – **Rebecca Jordan**

1380. Shuman, R. Baird. **American Drama 1918-1960: An Annotated Bibliography.** Pasadena, Calif., Salem Press, 1992. 177p. index. (Magill Bibliographies). $40.00. Z1231.D7S55. 016.822'508. LC 91-44643. ISBN 0-89356-682-9.

The materials found in this work are those that the author feels would be available in a typical small community public library. The citations serve as a source for those interested in theater research who do not have access to large research libraries. Accordingly, only books are cited. The volume is divided into sections on general reference works and resources, regional theater, theater groups, and little theater. The heart of the volume is annotated comments and criticism on 27 American playwrights whom the author has selected as having had an impact on American drama between 1918 and 1960. An index, largely of names, is also supplied.

The author visited 38 small community libraries to evaluate their shelf and reference department holdings. Thus, there is some validity to the selectivity of the citations. But the result is a sparse reference work. Too many playwrights and reference works have been ignored to make this work anything more than minimally useful. Also, the author's premise that small community libraries are bibliographically impoverished is questionable. The smallest library for even a single individual can, through computer networks such as the Internet, access the catalogs of major United States, Canadian, and British research libraries. Interlibrary loan is available, as are computerized databases. (See Barbara J. Pruett's *Popular Entertainment Research* [Scarecrow, 1992] for information about the wide variety of theater research resources available to anybody at any time.) – **Charles Neuringer**

1381. Taylor, Thomas J. **American Theatre History: An Annotated Bibliography.** Pasadena, Calif., Salem Press, 1992. 162p. index. (Magill Bibliographies). $40.00. Z5781.T25. 016.792'0973. LC 91-43961. ISBN 0-89356-672-1.

This volume contains about 500 unnumbered listings of books and dissertations on American theater history. The entries are divided into five sections: "Beginnings to 1914"; "1914 to 1945"; "New York: 1945 to the Present"; "Regional Theatre"; and "Experimental, Ethnic, Community, Academic, and Children's Theatre." Each entry is followed with a brief annotation that covers the book's content, style, range, and critical apparatus and illustration. Entries that span more than one period are placed in the first period or the period in which the subject did the best work. (This arrangement is confusing at best.) Taylor has chosen only book-length studies and sources and has omitted books that deal with textual approaches as opposed to theatrically oriented studies. He does not specify a cutoff date, and some of the newer studies are not included. Only a very few of the many major dissertation studies that should have been included appear. There is a section on periodicals in the area, followed by an index. Taylor indicates that one of the values of this bibliography is for browsing; that is the best use for this volume. —**Jackson Kesler**

Biography

1382. Mikotowicz, Thomas J., ed. **Theatrical Designers: An International Biographical Dictionary.** Westport, Conn., Greenwood Press, 1992. 365p. index. $65.00. PN2096.A1AM54. 792'.025'03. LC 91-28086. ISBN 0-313-26270-5.

This volume presents biographical and analytical data on the editor's selection of the 270 most important set, costume, and lighting designers and theater architects from the fifteenth century to the present. The entrants are international in scope, but an emphasis is placed on United States and Western European subjects. Entrants are designated as to the particular fields of design in which they excelled and their dates, countries of birth, biographical sketches (including professional experience), and awards, plus suggestions for further reading when available. The author of each entry is identified. An entry's length reflects the designer's importance and available data. The alphabetically arranged listing is preceded by a historical survey on the evolution of theatrical design. There are three appendixes: a list of the designers chronologically by birth date; a list by country of birth; and periodicals and theater collections. There are an index and an annotated general bibliography on theatrical design and designers.

The value of this volume is found in the wide scope of its entrants, the concise presentation of vital data, and its unique subject. Researchers will undoubtedly find it useful as a quick reference and guide to sources for more in-depth investigation. —**Jackson Kesler**

1383. Owen, Bobbi. **Lighting Design on Broadway: Designers and Their Credits, 1915-1990.** Westport, Conn., Greenwood Press, 1991. 159p. index. (Bibliographies and Indexes in the Performing Arts, no.11). $39.95. PN2091.E4094. 792'.025'09227471. LC 91-24007. ISBN 0-313-26533-X.

This publication is Owen's third volume in an attempt to list all Broadway designers and their credits from 1915 to 1990. The focus of the book is on lighting designers; more than 400 are listed alphabetically and profiled with a biographical sketch. Also given is a chronological list of Broadway credits for lighting and for scenic and costume design when relevant. An introduction briefly surveys the development of the professional Broadway lighting designer since the earliest attempts at illumination in indoor theaters. Appendixes list winners of the three major awards in the field: Tony, Maharam, and American Theatre Wing Design. There is a selective bibliography on lighting design. The index provides access from play title to designer's name and, in doing so, indicates every play for which a lighting designer was credited. This is a comprehensive volume that enhances the author's other volumes on theater. It will be valuable to researchers and professionals in lighting design, related design areas, and theater history in general. —**Jackson Kesler**

1384. Owen, Bobbi. **Scenic Design on Broadway: Designers and Their Credits, 1915-1990.** Westport, Conn., Greenwood Press, 1991. 286p. illus. index. (Bibliographies and Indexes in the Performing Arts, no.10). $55.00. PN2096.A1094. 792'.025'09227471. LC 91-25254. ISBN 0-313-26534-8.

This volume continues the author's valuable and extensive project of profiling the designers who have worked on Broadway between the 1915-1916 and 1989-1990 seasons. This book follows the first volume, which was devoted to costume designers. There are more than 900 biographies of scenic designers arranged alphabetically, each of which contains a chronological list of credits in scenic design. Also listed are credits in lighting and costume design. An introduction surveys professional scenic design in the twentieth century, with attention devoted to the development of American design from the "New Stagecraft." The four appendixes list winners of the Tony, Maharam, American Theatre Wing

Design, and Donaldson awards. There are a selected bibliography, an index of plays, and a section of 12 original renderings that span the period of the study.

This book is significant for its unique subject, careful research, and concise presentation of extensive data. Unquestionably, it will be a valuable source for those researching this period of American scenography. [R: Choice, Apr 92, p. 1212]—**Jackson Kesler**

Chronology

1385. Bordman, Gerald. **American Musical Theatre: A Chronicle.** 2d ed. New York, Oxford University Press, 1992. 832p. index. $49.95. ML1711.B67. 782.1'4'0973. LC 91-15671. ISBN 0-19-507242-1.

Chronicle is too tame a subtitle for this epic book on the American musical. Bordman's aim is to tell the story and make it entertaining. He does it well, and the book is satisfying whether consulted for information or read for pleasure. Bordman gets his facts straight, and his opinions are trustworthy.

The original edition of this book covered the history of American musical theater to the mid-1970s. An expanded paperback edition went forward to the 1984-1985 season, and this new one reaches through the 1989-1990 season. Coverage is basically season-by-season with detours for brief biographies (easily accessible through the index), special topics, and discussions of trends (e.g., British invasions of Broadway). A special and important feature of the new edition is an appendix that covers turn-of-the-century musicals that toured from city to city and from neighborhood to neighborhood in large cities such as New York without ever playing in a major house. They are considered as a separate genre here and were omitted from earlier editions.

Those looking for more facts, exact statistics about runs, full cast listings, complete information about a musical's songs and other musical numbers, recordings, and the like will have to go to other sources. In some discussions the composer and lyricist are mentioned, but in others they are not identified and do not show up in the index, which only indexes information given in the text. For example, Henry Krieger appears as the composer of *Dreamgirls* but not of *The Tap Dance Kid* even though both are discussed in the text. This is a characteristic of the book, not a weakness. This is an essential book for anyone interested in the subject. [R: RBB, July 92, p. 1956]—**George Louis Mayer**

1386. Wearing, J. P. **The London Stage 1940-1949: A Calendar of Plays and Players.** Metuchen, N.J., Scarecrow, 1991. 2v. index. $115.00/set. PN2596.L6W3846. 792'.09421'09041. LC 91-36206. ISBN 0-8108-2500-7.

Wearing's day-by-day calendar of plays produced by major and minor London theaters continues the tradition of scrupulous scholarship already established in his series. As before, this calendar includes full cast lists, production credits, and review information for each entry. His net is flung wide; the 2,409 listed productions include the expected plays (both new and revived), musicals, ballets, and operas, as well as lesser productions such as pantomimes, opera bouffes, and variety reviews. The second volume of this set is an extremely useful index volume.

This particular set may have value for scholars not usually inclined to theater research. The 1940s were, of course, a tumultuous decade, and the war in Europe (not to mention nightly bombing raids that interrupted theatrical performances at home!) could never be far from the theater-goer's mind. A social historian concerned with the British homefront, for example, may find this calendar an unexpected source of inspiration. For a library that supports theater research or British social history, this is an essential purchase. [R: Choice, June 92, p. 1530]—**James Edgar Stephenson**

Directories

1387. Charles, Jill, Anne Graham, and Gene Sirotof, comps. and eds. **Summer Theatre Directory 1992: A National Guide to Summer Employment for Professionals and Students....** Dorset, Vt., Theatre Directories, 1992. 149p. index. $13.95pa. ISBN 0-933919-20-4. ISSN 0884-5840.

The main body of this employment guide is a geographic list of theater companies and theme parks that hire for the summer in both the United States and Canada. Entries include addresses, telephone numbers and who to contact, whether the company hires equity or nonequity actors, the year the company was formed, facilities, season, hiring and salary information, and transportation and housing information. A description of each playhouse and its recent productions is included in each entry. The main section is followed by a list of training programs and apprenticeships, with a few in the United Kingdom. The volume's appendixes are particularly useful. They provide tips on finding the "right" summer theater and on preparing for combined and musical auditions, including a list of (in the compilers' opinion) overdone audition pieces that should be avoided. Other appendixes cover union information and a bibliography of sources of hiring information.

The many advertisements that probably pay for the annual production of the directory are informative in themselves, and the guide is sparsely but nicely illustrated. Along with good, useful information, the writing in such things as the introduction and the list of 10 good reasons to do summer theater lends an informed, friendly, and supportive voice to all budding, as well as blossomed, actors and actresses. — **Glynys R. Thomas**

1388. Charles, Jill, with Debra J. Bromley and Gene Sirotof, comps. and eds. **Regional Theatre Directory 1992-93: A National Guide to Employment in Regional & Dinner Theatres....** Dorset, Vt., Theatre Directories, 1992. 177p. illus. index. $14.95pa. ISBN 0-933919-21-2. ISSN 1041-9411.

A key directory for performers, directors, designers, technicians, and other theater staff, this annual employment guide provides specific information on hiring and casting procedures at 439 theaters around the country that run fall-winter-spring seasons. Included are Equity, non-Equity, and dinner theaters.

Arranged alphabetically by state (and region, as appropriate), then by name of theater, each entry contains the following information: contact names and addresses; a listing of the known productions for the 1992-1993 season; recommended procedures for interviews and auditions; projected hiring and casting needs for the upcoming seasons; indication of internship opportunities for students and younger professionals; and a brief description of the company, usually including aesthetic philosophy. Supplementing the major text are a number of appendixes that provide information on unions, service organizations, combined auditions, trade periodicals, casting aids, drama specialty bookstores around the country, and reviews of recent how-to books.

Recommended for theater reference collections in large public and academic libraries. School libraries and young thespians are also likely to benefit from the information provided.
— **Edmund F. SantaVicca**

Handbooks and Yearbooks

1389. **The Back Stage Theater Guide.** By Trevor R. Griffiths and Carole Woddis. New York, Back Stage Books/Watson-Guptill, 1991. 466p. illus. index. $18.95pa. PN1625.B3. 792'.03. LC 91-29166. ISBN 0-8230-7573-7.

Concentrating on the contemporary theater scene in Great Britain and the United States, this revised edition of the *Bloomsbury Theatre Guide* (Bloomsbury, 1988) not only updates entries to include plays first produced between 1988 and 1991 but also modifies the decidedly British slant of its predecessor. Most of the entries on British theater companies have been dropped, while coverage of United States playwrights has been significantly expanded, and a number of articles specifically relating to United States theater have been added.

More than 90 percent of the approximately 500 entries treat playwrights whose works are currently being produced on the British and United States stage. Because the contemporary theatrical repertory spans the ages and the continents, writers such as Aeschylus, Beaumarchais, and Sheridan appear along with modern dramatists such as Athol Fugard, Sam Shepard, and Caryl Churchill. Generally ranging in length from one-half to three pages, entries for playwrights include a chronological list of major plays, a discussion of significant works and themes, and a section that provides cross-references to other dramatists who deal with similar or contrasting themes or who have similar styles. The remaining entries concern such topics as African-American theater, British theaters and companies, off- and off-off-Broadway, one-person shows, and women dramatists. Black-and-white photographs of scenes from recent productions complement the text. The commendably detailed index includes titles of plays, theater companies, topics, playwrights, actors, and other individuals mentioned in the entries. Unfortunately, page references to main entries are no longer indicated in boldface type as they were in the earlier edition.

One of this guide's principal strengths is its coverage of a number of emerging playwrights who are not yet established enough to appear in such standard sources as *Contemporary Dramatists* (see ARBA 89, entry 1255), *The Oxford Companion to the American Theatre*, 2d ed. (Oxford University Press, 1992), or *The Cambridge Guide to Theatre* (Cambridge University Press, 1992). Due to its currency and the perspective offered by its cross-references, this work will be a useful addition to collections that serve active theater practitioners or avid theatergoers. — **Marie Ellis**

1390. Charles, Jill, and others, comps. and eds. **Directory of Theatre Training Programs: Profiles of College and Conservatory Programs Throughout the United States.** 3d ed. Dorset, Vt., Theatre Directories, 1991. 176p. index. $19.95pa. ISBN 0-933919-19-0. ISSN 1041-5211.

This reference work is a useful guide for those who wish to receive training for a career in the theater. Details of 333 different theater training programs (college and conservatory) are found here, listed alphabetically by state. Each entry contains contact and scholarship information, enrollment statistics, admission, and tuition. The types of degrees offered and profiles of the faculty and their interests are also detailed. In addition, there are lists of courses that are taught, descriptions of theater facilities, connections with professional companies, and recent guest artists. Each entry contains a statement of the school's philosophy of training. Three articles on theater training offer advice to the reader on what to look for in the various programs, what questions to ask, and what to realistically expect from the training. An alphabetical index of training programs details the type of degree granted.

This book should be consulted by students who wish to start or continue theater training, and it will be a valuable resource for high school and college counselors. However, the reader should be cautious about the entry data, as it appears that each entry was generated by the named training program. Because entries may be out of date and may possibly exaggerate the schools' facilities and faculty, this work should be used as a starting point for further investigations of training programs of interest. — **Charles Neuringer**

1391. **International Dictionary of Theatre. [Volume] 1: Plays.** Mark Hawkins-Dady, ed. Chicago, St. James Press; distr., Detroit, Gale, 1992. 954p. illus. $120.00. 792.0321. ISBN 1-55862-095-8.

The first of a three-volume set that will include playwrights (volume 2) and actors, directors, and designers (volume 3), this lengthy and full volume includes critical summaries of some 620 notable plays. Inclusions have been selected by a team of advisers and written by a large group of contributors. Plays are arranged alphabetically by title (popular English title if originally foreign), with cross-references as necessary and appropriate. Information provided for each play includes place and date of first publication; place and date of first production; citations to books and articles of criticism (10-20 on average); and a critical summary of the play, including its historical significance. Some entries also include a photograph of a particular stage production of the work.

Although the format is pleasant, the photographs are interesting, and the critical evaluations of the plays are sound, there is little here that might not be found in similar works (among them the Magill series that addresses notable plays from the ancient Greeks to the present) and other summary anthologies. No criteria are presented for inclusion or exclusion of criticism cited, save that in most cases the criticism has appeared in the recent past. Foreign-language material in modern European languages is included. Separate lists of plays by title and by author preface the main text, which is supplemented by brief paragraphs that identify the advisers and contributors and their qualifications. Perhaps better labeled a "digest" than a "dictionary," this volume could find use in library collections that have no comparable title or reference tool. — **Edmund F. SantaVicca**

28 Philosophy and Religion

PHILOSOPHY

Bibliography

1392. Barth, Else M. **Women Philosophers: A Bibliography of Books through 1990.** Bowling Green, Ohio, Philosophy Documentation Center, Bowling Green State University, 1992. 213p. index. $39.00. ISBN 0-912632-91-7.

Users should carefully study Barth's preface before consulting this bibliography, for the title could be misinterpreted. "Women philosophers" means books by and about women philosophers, *philosophy* being interpreted very broadly. Barth, a philosopher at the University of Groningen, organizes the work according to a classification used in the Netherlands. Works are included if they are identified in a review or publisher's brochure as a philosophical work, if they are written by a member of a university department of philosophy, or if their content can be considered philosophical rather than scientific. Thus, Diane Collinson's *Fifty Major Philosophers* (see ARBA 88, entry 1381) is included because Collinson is an academic philosopher, even though all of the philosophers in her study are male.

Users should note that works have not been critically evaluated for content and that their inclusion in the classification is based largely on title. Barth uses the Dutch system to bring order to a large and varied body of material; the assignment of items to a particular category may appear somewhat arbitrary, although there are cross-references to related categories, with a name index appended. In general, works from the countries of Eastern Europe are not included, nor those from non-English-speaking countries outside Europe. The majority of works are from the twentieth century, with a cutoff date of 1990.

With this bibliography Barth hopes to incorporate the work of women philosophers into the corpus of the discipline, showing the variety of women's contributions as well as promoting their use. This work is a first step in that direction. While it is an impressive collection of material, the entries need to be critically evaluated in greater depth if the book is to achieve its purpose. – **Bernice Bergup**

1393. Bell, Albert A., Jr., and James B. Allis. **Resources in Ancient Philosophy: An Annotated Bibliography of Scholarship in English, 1965-1989.** Metuchen, N.J., Scarecrow, 1991. 799p. index. $79.50. Z7125.B39. 016.18. LC 91-39912. ISBN 0-8108-2520-1.

Bell and Allis have put together an annotated guide book to sources on ancient philosophy (from Thales to Augustine). Unlike in most bibliographies, however, the authors have not simply listed items but have prepared thoughtful critical introductions to each of the philosophers. The introductions also include mention of especially important items within each chapter. For example, each of Plato's dialogs are listed with a short introduction. Following each dialog are the listed works from 1965 to 1989. The subject index, while brief, is still useful since it lists items as they would have been used by ancient philosophers.

Bell and Allis have produced what will become the philosopher's or philosophy instructor's vade mecum. Students, lay readers, and those pursuing serious philosophical research will want this volume nearby, and academic libraries of any size will want to acquire it. Because the source lists general as well as specific topics, public libraries may also want to investigate the usefulness of this remarkable reference work. [R: Choice, Oct 92, pp. 267-68; RQ, Fall 92, p. 122]—**Mark Y. Herring**

1394. Boucher, Wayne I. **Spinoza in English: A Bibliography from the Seventeenth Century to the Present.** Kinderhook, N.Y., E. J. Brill, 1991. 226p. (Brill's Studies in Intellectual History, v.28). $68.75. Z8831.B68. 016.199'492. LC 91-24542. ISBN 90-04-09499-7.

Although Boucher has written a number of government-related publications, this is his first book on Spinoza. The intent is to update and supplement earlier bibliographic treatments of the man. The 2,100-plus annotated citations are presented in two parts: those by Spinoza and those about him (the latter presented in alphabetical order by author). The annotations are neither abstracts nor critiques but refer users to citations in A. S. Oko's *The Spinoza Bibliography* (G. K. Hall, 1964) or to other bibliographies or databases used by Boucher. They do give a variety of other important bibliographical information (e.g., earlier forms of the publication). In the case of collections of essays, all those related to Spinoza are listed twice—once under the name of the editor of the volume, and again by the names of the authors of the articles—and when only a small part of a book deals with Spinoza, pertinent chapter or page numbers are supplied. Fictional works, newspaper articles, and minor book reviews are omitted.

Aside from occasional errors (e.g., "Preus, Samuel J." for "Preus, James S." on page 162) and omissions (e.g., R. David Freedman, "The father of modern biblical scholarship," *The Journal of the Ancient Near Eastern Society* 19 [1989] 31-38), the volume seems well written, carefully edited, and thorough. The type is clear and the margins are adequate. Although the work would have been improved by a subject index and the inclusion of non-English-language materials, Boucher has produced an important tool for Spinoza research. It is recommended for libraries that support humanities research. [R: Choice, Feb 92, p. 870]—**M. Patrick Graham**

Dictionaries and Encyclopedias

1395. Becker, Lawrence C., and Charlotte B. Becker, eds. **Encyclopedia of Ethics.** Hamden, Conn., Garland, 1992. 2v. index. (Garland Reference Library of the Humanities, v.925). $150.00/set. BJ63.E45. 170'.3. LC 91-4978. ISBN 0-8153-0403-X.

Any list of core reference titles in philosophy must henceforth include this work. Advertised as the first comprehensive reference work on philosophical ethics in more than 50 years, it not only fills a definite need but fills it very well indeed. A team of more than 250 contributing and consulting editors includes most of the prominent names in philosophical ethics (among those writing in English) of the past four decades (e.g., Kurt Baier, Sissela Bok, Richard Brandt, R. M. Hare, Alasdair MacIntyre). Even those authors who are less well known have usually made substantial contributions to the subjects on which they write here. Some 435 articles, typically 2 to 5 pages in length, address a fascinating diversity of topics. Predictable entries include the standard schools and theories (e.g., utilitarianism, emotivism, virtue ethics), key thinkers (e.g., Immanuel Kant, Jean-Paul Sartre, Martin Luther King), specific ethical concepts (e.g., duty and obligation, teleological ethics, universalizability), and significant areas of moral decision making and controversy (e.g., business ethics, homosexuality, punishment). Among the less predictable, even surprising, articles are those on academic freedom, forgiveness, land ethics, moral luck, racism and related issues, and women moral philosophers, as well as several on the professional ethics of specific fields, including library and information professions. Unusual also is a sequence of 12 essays under the entry "History of Western Ethics" that survey the major periods, from pre-Socratic Greek to twentieth-century Anglo-American. Inevitably, many articles, however well done, only scratch the surface of their subject matter; but excellent bibliographies, some quite extensive, always point to sources for further reading.

On the whole, the encyclopedia provides solid coverage of the long history of Western, and to a small degree non-Western, philosophical thought about ethics. At the same time, it offers an outstanding representation of contemporary philosophical ethics "as it is practiced among English-speaking academics" (introduction). To the extent that the latter domain of ethical inquiry is perceived as deficient, this encyclopedia will undoubtedly be found to share some of that deficiency—for instance, by those who regard as misconceived any moral reasoning not founded on religious premises. (It must be stressed that the focus here is philosophical, not religious, ethics, although there are articles on the ethics of the world's major religions, Christian ethics included.) And certainly, anyone who may turn to this work for a solution to a concrete moral dilemma is as likely as not to learn more questions than answers. Within its limits, however, this work makes a distinguished contribution, useful not just to academics but to anyone with a serious interest in ethical issues. [R: Choice, Nov 92, p. 440; LJ, 15 June 92, p. 68; RBB, 1 Oct 92, pp. 366-67; WLB, June 92, p. 110]

—Hans E. Bynagle

1396. Dent, N. J. H. **A Rousseau Dictionary.** Cambridge, Mass., Basil Blackwell, 1992. 279p. index. (Blackwell Philosopher Dictionaries). $49.95; $19.95pa. Z2042.D46. 848'.509. LC 92-17607. ISBN 0-631-17568-7; 0-631-17569-5pa.

Dictionaries on individual philosophers have not been a staple of philosophy's reference literature. A handful of works ostensibly representing the genre were published by Philosophical Library from 1951 to 1972, but these are merely quotation dictionaries—and poor to mediocre at that. The Blackwell Philosopher Dictionaries series promises a new approach, and, judging by this work on Jean-Jacques Rousseau, it is a welcome one.

About 100 alphabetically arranged entries cover key ideas, concepts, and themes in Rousseau's thought or summarize his major writings and identify their historical settings. Biographical matters are primarily handled in an introductory essay, which is followed by a chronology. The articles are all substantial; there are no short definitions, although a number of terms are handled through cross-references to more comprehensive articles. Dent demonstrates a firm grasp of the Rousseau corpus, and while some of his explanations must be deemed interpretations, these are responsible and not idiosyncratic. He also takes due note of those elements in his subject's thought that have been controversial or widely criticized. On balance, perhaps, he could be accused of being too defensive for Rousseau, but this is at worst a mild criticism.

Rousseau's own writings are cited extensively throughout. Secondary literature is not cited directly, but references for further reading at the end of every article are keyed to a secondary bibliography of 349 books and articles. The dictionary will be useful for Rousseau students at virtually any level.

—Hans E. Bynagle

1397. Lineback, Richard H., and Lynn Walkiewicz, eds. *The Philosopher's Index* **Thesaurus.** Bowling Green, Ohio, Philosophy Documentation Center, Bowling Green State University, 1992. 112p. $19.00pa. ISBN 0-912632-20-8.

This work is meant to simplify searching the Philosopher's Index Database in its CD-ROM and DIALOG incarnations. It provides a succinct account of the database: subjects included; scope; audience; indexing policies; and lists of general and periodical abbreviations, philosophers, and descriptors. The latter is much less detailed than that provided by such similar works as *The Thesaurus of ERIC Descriptors* (see ARBA 91, entry 302) or *The Thesaurus of Psychological Index Terms* (American Psychological Association, 1991). Descriptors used five or more times are in boldface type, and there are a few *see also* references, but there are no *see* references and no indications of broader or narrower terms. There is also a short section of searching hints particularly aimed at the DIALOG version of the database; this section includes a key with examples of how to search for Greek terms and operators and expressions common in symbolic logic. This highly specialized work will be of interest largely to libraries that do extensive searching of the database.—**Richard H. Swain**

RELIGION

General Works

Bibliography

1398. Brown, Kenneth O. **Holy Ground: A Study of the American Camp Meeting.** Hamden, Conn., Garland, 1992. 254p. index. (Religious Information Systems, v.5; Garland Reference Library of Social Science, v.717). $44.00. BV3798.B76. 269'.24'0973. LC 92-9742. ISBN 0-8240-4837-7.

This is an outstanding overview of a social and religious phenomenon in U.S. culture and life—the camp meeting. Camp meetings originated on the southern frontier during the Protestant revival between 1787 and 1805. The concept has many terms; Brown lists Bible conferences, chautauquas, assembly grounds, and Christian retreat centers as aspects of these religious meetings, which attracted tens of thousands of participants. He credits the Methodists as being the founders of the meetings. A comprehensive history and bibliographical review of the literature on camp meeting organizations, with the list of more than 2,000 of these bodies, fill a niche in religious culture information. Today the camp meeting is an international institution.

The history of such meetings is controversial, and Brown does not definitively establish the first one, but he points to the first encampments. The working list of camp meetings is by state, Canadian province, and other countries. No omissions were found from the United States, but the international list is incomplete. Photographs of influential camps are helpful. This work will be most useful to university and liberal arts college collections, seminaries, Bible colleges, and public libraries within areas where camp meetings are located.—**Gerald D. Moran**

1399. Daniels, Ted. **Millennialism: An International Bibliography.** Hamden, Conn., Garland, 1992. 657p. index. (Garland Reference Library of Social Science, v.667). $90.00. Z7835.M54D36. 016.2919. LC 91-39298. ISBN 0-8240-7102-6.

The compiler of these 7,500 bibliographic citations describes himself as trained in social science and folklore but not in theology. He explains that his research for the present volume consisted primarily of working through bibliographies and reference works, because he found online searching "worse than useless" (p. ix). He sought to include important, published works on all aspects of the millennium but resolved to give little attention to theology. The book is introduced by a 20-page essay on millennialism and presents its bibliographic citations in 2 parts. The first consists of 340 pages of annotated entries, verified by Daniels and indexed by subjects and authors, and 10 pages of references cited. The second has 232 pages of bibliographic entries only, unverified by Daniels but indexed by groups/movements, and 2 brief lists of bibliographies and reference works.

Two critical aspects of this work merit comment: works selected for inclusion, and the annotations. As for the first, it appears that many works that deal specifically with the millennium and that are listed in the CD-ROM version of *Religion Indexes* (377 entries under "Millennialism" and 214 under "Millennium") have been omitted, while other works that are less specific to the topic are included (e.g., entries 146, 533, and 550). As for the annotations, they vary from two lines to three pages and not only describe the contents of publications but often critique them. While this surely enhances the value of the bibliography, it also presents some problems. Many items in the "Annotations" section of the work have no annotation (e.g., entries 535-538, 761-766). Some sharply criticize an author whose work is known to Daniels only through a review (e.g., entry 441). Some seem to show that he misunderstands the issue treated in the work (e.g., entry 47). In some it is difficult to sort out what should be attributed to the author of a publication, its reviewer, or to Daniels himself (e.g., entry 178). Finally, some reflect poorly on Daniels's sophistication (e.g., in entry 550 he points out that the author of a book overlooked the fact that God was "purely imaginary, at least from a scientific point of view"). Therefore, while this work should prove useful to researchers, it is by no means comprehensive, and the annotations leave something to be desired. [R: Choice, Dec 92, p. 598]—**M. Patrick Graham**

1400. Kepple, Robert J., and John R. Muether. **Reference Works for Theological Research.** 3d ed. Lanham, Md., University Press of America, 1992. 250p. index. $49.50; $24.50pa. Z7751.K46. 016.2. LC 91-42222. ISBN 0-8191-8564-7; 0-8191-8565-5pa.

This new edition of a highly regarded work (see ARBA 83, entry 1015) contains a number of changes and new features. It now has a coauthor and a newly added chapter on computer assisted research; and it now annotates more than 800 works (more than 25 percent are new to this edition). The majority of the selections are wisely chosen; relatively few are questionable. Some chapters have been renumbered, and two others have been merged into one, but the work itself is still divided into 2 parts: general and general religious/theological lists (19 chapters that cover bibliographical guides, encyclopedias, book review indexes, and the like) and subject area lists (20 chapters, including biblical studies, philosophy of religion, Christian education, and worship). Entries have sometimes been shifted within chapters from the way they appeared in the 2d edition, but more significantly, bibliographic data is now uniformly presented in a title-first format. The work has also now been typeset rather than photocopied from typescript. The table of contents serves as a handy outline; the annotations are clear and succinct; and the index, in one alphabet, contains entries for authors, editors, titles, and alternative titles.

Kepple and Muether have produced an invaluable and still relatively compact guide to religious and theological reference material. This is an important work for any library with a sizable religion collection. — **Glenn R. Wittig**

1401. Melton, J. Gordon, and Michael A. Koszegi. **Religious Information Sources: A Worldwide Guide.** Hamden, Conn., Garland, 1992. 569p. index. (Religious Information Systems, v.2; Garland Reference Library of the Humanities, v.1593). $75.00. Z7751.M45. 016.2. LC 91-47697. ISBN 0-8153-0859-0.

Melton and Koszegi have put together what amounts to a printed version of the Bible and Religion reference librarian. The book does not have the depth of coverage of John Graves Barrow's *A Bibliography of Bibliographies in Religion* (Edward Brothers, 1955). Neither, however, did Barrow attempt to supply anything more than a bibliography. Melton and Koszegi have attempted to identify worldwide sources on any given subject area in religion, in whatever its form. Thus, sources on Shinto, Taoism, the philosophy of religion, science and religion, church history, Christianity, women and religion, and much, much more are included. What makes this book so important a contribution to the field is not only its apparent exhaustive coverage of print sources but also the meticulous care given to nonprint and unconventional sources of information in religion. Ancillary concerns to religion, such as Christianity and the arts, denominations, New Age, and interfaith dialogs, are also covered. Computer databases are annotated, along with oral histories, CD-ROMs, and professional religious associations. Ample author (including translator and compiler), title, subject, and organizations indexes are included.

For future editions, some thought might be given to defining the word *religion* more closely. The definition here appears to be anything that people are apt to worship, and thus Judaism appears in the same volume as magic. Under so loose a definition, at least one hundred other obsessions to which flesh is heir could have been added. Conservative outlets of religious information should also be given closer scrutiny.

Plans are in the works to update this volume periodically, if demand warrants it. Every library remotely concerned with religious studies or involved in disseminating religious information will need this volume. [R: RBB, 1 Dec 92, p. 691] — **Mark Y. Herring**

1402. Parry, Donald W., Stephen D. Ricks, and John W. Welch, comps. **A Bibliography on Temples of the Ancient Near East and Mediterranean World.** Lewiston, N.Y., Edwin Mellen Press, 1991. 311p. (Ancient Near Eastern Texts and Studies, v.9). $79.95. ISBN 0-7734-9775-7.

The compilers of this small volume have attempted to accomplish a Herculean task: to provide a bibliography about temples in the ancient Near East and Mediterranean worlds, although they do warn it is not meant to be comprehensive. The first half of the book is arranged into two major divisions: general studies of templates according to geographic areas, and rituals and symbols of temples by subject (e.g., kingship and coronation, priesthood). The last half of the volume provides an author index that identifies in which section of the volume each entry appears.

The compilers' short introduction explains their use of John Lundquist's typology of the temple as presented in several short articles and (presumably) his unpublished dissertation. However, this discussion omits the major typology of the Egyptian temple as a representation of the cosmos, presented very clearly in R. R. Finnestad's *Image of the World and Symbol of the Creator* (1985). Another key resource omitted is Richard Clifford's *The Cosmic Mountain in Canaan and the Old Testament* (1972). Both omissions are surprising because other materials by these authors appear. Also disturbing is the use of E. A. Wallis Budge's work on Osiris from 1911 when J. Owyn Griffiths's authoritative work on Osiris and his cult from 1980 is lacking. In fact, when moving outside the sphere of Canaan and Israel, the compilers' major interest, one finds many very old volumes included, perhaps at the expense of more recent books and articles. Thus, the book appears directed toward the biblical scholar, while those from the other disciplines will find it of limited use. Correspondingly, biblical scholars must take into account the limited nature of the sources from nonbiblical fields. —**Susan Tower Hollis**

Biography

1403. Brosse, Jacques. **Religious Leaders.** New York, Chambers Kingfisher Graham, c1988, 1991. 234p. illus. index. $9.95pa. ISBN 0-550-17006-5.

Guided by strict criteria, Jacques Brosse has sifted through antiquity, Judaism, Christianity, Islam, Hinduism, and Buddhism for entrants in this compact reference to the world's religious leaders. The traits he looked for were absolute selflessness, a lack of concern for worldly status, association with a major religious tradition, and an awareness that one's own path was not necessarily the only avenue to God. (According to Brosse, genuine leaders are concerned only with guiding others to the truth and are uninterested in material rewards.) Given this volume's enormity of scope and brevity of space, Brosse has had to be highly selective. Even so, some of his choices are puzzling. Should Socrates, Plato, and Epicurus be regarded as religious leaders? And if Joseph Smith of the Church of Jesus Christ of Latter-day Saints and George Whitefield are included, why not Alexander Campbell of the Church of Christ and Billy Graham? The study is far from exhaustive.

Such questions notwithstanding, this is a useful paperback reference. Most of its 163 entries, which average one to two pages of relatively small print, are on individuals, but several deal with groups, such as the Sikhs and Neoplatonists, and some describe sacred writings, such as the Vedas and the Book of the Dead. Enhanced by illustrations, a brief glossary, and an adequate index, this work will be helpful to people seeking general information about major religions and their principal leaders. [R: LJ, 1 Nov 92, p. 76]—**John W. Storey**

1404. Hinnells, John R., ed. **Who's Who of World Religions.** New York, Simon & Schuster Academic Reference Division, 1992. 560p. maps. index. $75.00. BL72.W54. 291'.092'2. LC 91-36866. ISBN 0-13-952946-2.

Biographical dictionaries abound for biblical and Christian notables but are hard to find for other religions. That palpable gap is filled to some extent by this volume, with its coverage from African religions to Zoroastrianism, and people from the mists of legend (e.g., Gilgamesh) to such contemporary religious leaders as the Maharishi, Sun Myung Moon, and Pope John Paul II. Not surprisingly, Christians take up most of the work, but an attempt has explicitly been made to provide balance by emphasizing non-Western Christians, and the terms C.E. and B.C.E. are used in place of B.C. and A.D.

Each entry provides full name, dates, indication of religious subject group, references to the extensive bibliographies, and a biographical sketch. Initials indicate the author of the entry, who can be found among the list of scholarly contributors in the front. Cross-references are somewhat haphazard. For example, Children of God's Moses David is found under his real name, David Berg, but there is no cross-reference, while there is from Khomeini, Ayatollah to Khumayni, Ayat Allah Ruh Allah (but not from Ayatollah Khomeini). Altogether, a nice balance is provided, not only among religions but also between teachers or founders of religions (e.g., Buddha, L. Ron Hubbard); the poets, artists, or singers of religions (e.g., J. S. Bach, Giotto); and between men and women (e.g., Sarah as well as Abraham; Nefertiti as well as Akhenaten). [R: Choice, June 92, p. 1531; LJ, 1 Feb 92, p. 82; RBB, 15 Mar 92, p. 1406; RQ, Summer 92, pp. 583-84]—**Johan Koren**

Dictionaries and Encyclopedias

1405. Cohn-Sherbok, Dan. **A Dictionary of Judaism and Christianity.** Philadelphia, Trinity Press International, 1991. 181p. $15.95pa. BM50.C62. 296'.03. LC 91-22076. ISBN 1-56338-030-7.

In recent years constructive dialog between Christians and Jews has increased significantly. This is due in part to the efforts of scholars from both traditions. The number of scholarly volumes on the shared heritage of the two faiths has grown steadily. However, there are few reliable resources for laypeople to turn to for basic information on the elements common to Judaism and Christianity. Granted, much (if not all) of the information contained in this dictionary can be found in other sources. But there are two strengths that still recommend Cohn-Sherbok's work. First, he has brought the material together into a concise (and affordable) volume. Second, he presents not only the distinctive importance of the concepts for Christians and Jews separately, but he compares and contrasts them as well.

The entries are arranged alphabetically from abortion to Zohar. About 200 cross-references direct readers from possible access points to the appropriate entries. A very few mistakes in these cross-references escaped proofreading ("Preaching" refers users to "Sermon," which then refers them to "Homiletics"). None of the entries includes cross-references to related items. For example, a person reading the entry on festivals finds no indication about which of the festivals are treated individually. The addition of *see also* references would be a welcome improvement in a 2d edition.

Some may object that the author overlooks or ignores the finer points at issue in topics such as law and Hellenism. But those who would raise these criticisms must keep in mind the intended audience. Cohn-Sherbok knows his subject and his audience. He has chosen to initiate readers rather than overwhelm them (which would be easy to do given the amount and complexity of current scholarly research on early Jewish-Christian relations). The entries are written on a level that will appeal to nonspecialists and be intelligible to them. This will prove to be a useful addition to public and academic reference collections. – **Craig W. Beard**

1406. **Encyclopedia of the Early Church.** By the Institutum Patristicum Augustinianum. Angelo Di Berardino, ed. New York, Oxford University Press, 1992. 2v. illus. maps. index. $175.00/set. BR66.5. D5813. 270.1'03. LC 91-23934. ISBN 0-19-520892-7.

W. H. C. Frend, author of *Archaeology and History in the Study of the Early Church* (Valorium Reprints, 1988), has written the foreword and updated the bibliography for this work, which was translated from the Italian by Adrian Walford. These volumes consolidate and facilitate access to the results of the vast research related to the Early Church in the past few decades. The time parameters have been set at 735 C.E. in the West and 759 C.E. in the East, with special focus on church personalities and the interaction between Christianity and pagan religions. The result is a multitude of short articles on a very wide spectrum of early church leaders and extended articles on Aristotelianism, Hellenism, Platonism, Neoplatonism, and major Christian figures.

An extended synoptic table or dateline of 38 pages correlates secular and ecclesiastical events with cultural and doctrinal matters. There are also 30 pages of minimally detailed two-color maps of various parts of the Mediterranean world, chiefly indicating city locations at different time periods. Almost 150 pages of illustrations, mostly black-and-white, depict and well annotate art and architecture from many sites.

Some searches were disappointing. Thecla, the legendary companion of Paul, is hidden and unassociated with Paul among others of the same name in a very brief article. The Samaritans are briefly described in time periods before and after the early church but basically ignored in the relevant period; works by Montgomery and Crown are not cited. Commentary on women's dress codes in the early church are elusive in this work despite relevant material in the New Testament, Tertullian, and elsewhere. The timeline suggests surprisingly early dates for most of the gospels and Catholic letters. Mark, 1 Peter, 1 Timothy, and Titus are dated in 64, and Matthew, Luke, Hebrews, 2 Timothy, Jude, and 2 Peter are dated in 65. Otherwise, the dates are quite conventional. English references are relatively rare, and despite the claim of updating, references after the 70s are scant in most entries. Overall, this work is attractive in format, solidly bound, comprehensive and rich in content, and highly recommended for libraries. [R: Choice, Sept 92, p. 76; LJ, 1 June 92, p. 110; WLB, June 92, pp. 110-11]

– **Robert T. Anderson**

1407. Williamson, William B., ed. **An Encyclopedia of Religions in the United States: One Hundred Religious Groups Speak for Themselves.** New York, Crossroad Publishing, 1992. 359p. $29.95. BL2520.E53. 291'.0973. LC 91-14252. ISBN 0-8245-1094-1.

This work provides general information on contemporary Judeo-Christian groups of 100,000 adherents or more, ranging from Adventists to the Society of Natural Science to the Unification Church. Other bodies, such as Buddhists, Hindus, Muslims, and Shintoists, are also included, albeit in an appendix. The denominational summaries, supplied for the most part by the religious bodies themselves, follow a standard format. Each contains information on the founders and major leaders, unique doctrines, forms of worship, organization, significant terms, contributions to U.S. culture, and suggested readings. Such current themes as civil religion, televangelism, the decline of mainline Protestantism, changes within Catholicism, and pluralism are dealt with in the editor's introduction.

Although too general for serious scholars, this hardback will nevertheless be helpful to anyone looking for a quick overview of today's religions. Alphabetized by denomination, the material is readily accessible, although there are a few minor problems. The Assemblies of God should have been subsumed under Pentecostals, and the Nazarenes will be hard to find by anyone unfamiliar with Methodism. The absence of an index is also unfortunate. Such flaws notwithstanding, all high school and university libraries should add this volume to their reference collections. [R: LJ, 1 Feb 92, pp. 78-80; RBB, 1 Mar 92, pp. 1305-06] – **John W. Storey**

Directories

1408. Melton, J. Gordon. **Religious Bodies in the United States: A Directory.** Hamden, Conn., Garland, 1992. 313p. index. (Religious Information Systems Series, v.1; Garland Reference Library of the Humanities, v.1568). $55.00. BL2525.M452. 200'.25'73. LC 91-41564. ISBN 0-8153-0806-X.

Melton is well known for his bibliographies and other publications on American religion. The present work is a revision of his *Directory of Religious Bodies in the United States* (see ARBA 78, entry 984) and includes all religious groups operating in the United States as of summer 1991. The heart of the directory consists of chapters that treat interfaith organizations, Christianity, Buddhism, Hinduism, Islam, Judaism, Latter-day Saints, metaphysical/ancient wisdom/New Age groups, Shinto, Sikhism/Sant Mat, Taoism, and various unclassified religious groups. Each chapter begins with a brief introduction to the larger religious category and includes a list of intrafaith organizations and the other groups that fall within it. In each case a brief description of the organization and the address and telephone number of its headquarters are provided. A list of periodicals that serve the bodies concludes each chapter. An introduction, a brief bibliography of sources consulted, and a general index round out the volume.

The present work differs significantly in both structure and content from the 1977 edition. It omits the earlier edition's attempt to describe and classify the primary religious groups but has added descriptions of individual religious organizations and supplied additional periodical titles. The result is a much improved and badly needed revision of this important reference work. While similar directory information is available in the latest issue of *Yearbook of American & Canadian Churches* (see ARBA 90, entry 1384), Melton's work includes an additional 1,300 religious groups and many more periodical titles. The volume would be enhanced by an index or table that grouped the organizations under each major religious group (e.g., all groups with Methodist affiliation). Nevertheless, the book is a gold mine of information and is indispensable for any general reference collection. [R: C&RL, Sept 92, p. 426; LJ, 1 May 92, p. 76; WLB, June 92, p. 116] – **M. Patrick Graham**

Handbooks and Yearbooks

1409. Eliade, Mircea, and Ioan P. Couliano, with Hillary S. Wiesner. **The Eliade Guide to World Religions.** San Francisco, Calif., HarperSanFrancisco, 1991. 301p. index. $22.95. BL80.2.E415. 291. LC 90-56452. ISBN 0-06-062145-1.

The name Mircea Eliade is synonymous with the modern study of religion and religions. This volume was the last major project of his distinguished career, and, although most of the writing was done after Eliade's death in 1986, it is fitting that the guide bears his name. It opens with a brief introduction to religion and its study, followed by 33 alphabetically arranged chapters on major religious traditions, from African religions to Zoroastrianism. More than one-half of these traditions are "living religions" (that is, those that are actively and somewhat widely practiced today). Although the chapters do not follow a predefined uniform arrangement, most of them include some history and the essential distinctive features of the particular tradition. Buddhism, Christianity, Islam, and Judaism receive the most extensive treatment. The chapters are concluded with bibliographies that vary in length from one item on dualistic religions to two full pages on Christianity. An annotated subject index and glossary, which functions like the earlier version of the *Encyclopaedia Britannia* (see ARBA 92, entry 41) "Micropaedia," rounds out the volume.

Each of the chapters has been written based in part on information gathered from Eliade's *History of Religious Ideas* (University of Chicago Press, 1981-1988) and the *Encyclopedia of Religion* (see ARBA 88, entry 1392), which he edited. Within the space constraints of a single compact volume, the articles are fairly thorough and informative. On a few occasions, though, the reduction of complex concepts has been accomplished at the expense of clarity. Not surprisingly, the influence of the history of religions is evident throughout the book. This approach draws attention to common elements among religious traditions, which is appropriate to a point. However, it can, and sometimes does, lean far enough in that direction that unique features of a tradition are overshadowed.

The Eliade Guide to World Religions will serve well those libraries looking for a concise, authoritative handbook. Libraries that already hold the 16-volume *Encyclopedia of Religion* may be able to do without it. [R: RBB, 15 May 92, p. 1715]—**Craig W. Beard**

1410. Melton, J. Gordon. **Encyclopedic Handbook of Cults in America.** rev. ed. Hamden, Conn., Garland, 1992. 407p. index. (Religious Information Systems, v.7). $65.00; $18.95pa. BL2525.M45. 291'.0973. LC 92-11540. ISBN 0-8153-0502-8; 0-8153-1140-0pa.

Interest in cult groups and alternative religions has not waned since the first edition of Melton's well-received handbook (see ARBA 87, entry 1354). Perhaps, though, it is now motivated less by fear than by curiosity (both popular and scholarly). According to Melton, the past decade has witnessed numerous changes within the cults and among those on the outside looking in. This new edition presents the current state of affairs of 33 alternative religious groups and movements (including the somewhat amorphous new age movement).

The work has been revised throughout. Melton has updated the chapters on the cults, the general essays—"What Is a Cult?" "Counter-Cult Groups," and "Violence and the Cults"—and most of the bibliographies. In addition, he has added chapters on four groups not included in the first edition: the Reorganized Church of Jesus Christ of Latter-day Saints, the Unity School of Christianity, the International Society for Krishna Consciousness of West Virginia, and the Movement of Spiritual Inner Awareness. James H. Sweetland's evaluation of the strengths (currency, thoroughness, and evenhanded treatment of the cults) and weaknesses (apparent bias against anticult groups and lack of subject indexing) of the 1986 edition are still valid for this update.

Libraries that have the 3d edition of Melton's *Encyclopedia of American Religions* (see ARBA 91, entry 1415) may want to add this title for the essays mentioned above. Those that have found the earlier edition of the handbook useful will likely want this one because of the updated information it provides. Recommended for all libraries where there is interest in alternative religions.—**Craig W. Beard**

1411. Olson, Stan, Ruth Kovacs, and Suzanne Haile, eds. **National Guide to Funding in Religion.** New York, Foundation Center, 1991. 530p. index. $125.00pa. ISBN 0-87954-380-9.

Similar in appearance and quality to other well-respected Foundation Center publications, this specialized guide is intended "as a starting point for grantseekers looking for foundation and corporate support for religious organizations." There are entries for 2,824 programs and foundations, including company-sponsored foundations, direct corporate giving programs, community foundations, operating foundations, and independent foundations. Three Foundation Center publications were used to identify the grantmakers included in this resource: *The Foundation Directory* (see ARBA 91, entry 866), the *National Directory of Corporate Giving* (see ARBA 91, entry 144), and the Grants Index database. The guide does not claim to represent all possible funding sources for programs for religion and includes a two-page essay on "Researching Foundations and Grantseeking from Corporations," which has suggestions to help the reader identify the best funding sources within the guide and also to identify other sources not included. The 11-page annotated list, "Publications and Services of The Foundation Center," can also lead the reader to other grant sources.

The guide is arranged alphabetically by state and then by foundation name under each state. Entries include the name, address, telephone number, and officers of the foundation, plus financial data, purposes and activities of the foundation, types and limitations of support given, and application information. Indexes are to donors, officers, and trustees; places; types of support; subjects; and foundations and corporate giving programs.

Because it brings together information from several other reference books, this thorough guide to funding in the field of religion should be a welcome timesaver for grantseekers. It would be an excellent addition to any public or academic library reference collection. — **Dorothy E. Jones**

Quotation Books

1412. Tomlinson, Gerald, comp. and ed. **Treasury of Religious Quotations.** Englewood Cliffs, N.J., Prentice-Hall, 1991. 341p. index. $39.95; $14.95pa. PN6084.R3E53. 291. LC 91-18940. ISBN 0-13-276429-6; 0-13-276411-3pa.

Including stanzas from hymns and poems, quotations from philosophers, great and not-so-great religious leaders, the Bible, the Book of Mormon, the Koran, and many other sources, this book is exactly described by its title. Tomlinson is a writer and editor who specializes in religion and business. He explains his research and criteria for selection in the introduction, establishing credibility and trust. All the world's religions are covered. There are more than 2,000 quotations organized alphabetically by subject from achievement to zeal. An interesting and valuable feature is a section of brief biographies, selected from the many source authors. This is followed by a section entitled "Thirty Religions and Philosophies in Microcosm." A list of the 250 basic sources and an index complete the publication.

This book will be of use to ministers, public speakers, speechwriters, and anybody else wishing to add to their message. It will never replace the standard compilations of quotations, but it will be useful to public and church libraries. Smaller libraries may find the paperback edition more within their budgets. — **Edward P. Miller**

Buddhism

1413. Murthy, K. Krishna. **A Dictionary of Buddhist Terms and Terminologies.** Delhi, India, Sundeep Prakashan; distr., Columbia, Mo., South Asia Books, 1991. 181p. $28.50. ISBN 81-85067-67-8.

This work contains the germs of a valuable reference work but is itself almost useless. Entries are most often merely foreign technical terms given in Roman letters, but they are sometimes given in the original script. For example, the 80 minor marks of a Buddha are listed only under the term *Asityanuvyanjanani*. Minor mark 74 (similar to the other minor marks) is set forth in the original Asian script, and then an English equivalent that is often unintelligible is given without explanation (e.g., "having hair like a bee"). Some entries cite sacred texts and secondary sources, but the references are given in highly shortened form (an abbreviation, one word from the title of a text, or the name of an author), and there is no bibliography or other explanation of the citations.

The work is divided into three sections: religion, theology, and philosophy; art, architecture, and iconography; material culture. Some sections have subsections, but there is no explanation of the overall organization of the work. There seems to be some attempt at using standard alphabetical order, but there are strange unexplained deviations. The terms defined on pages 4-8 in order of their appearance are *Ajivo, Anagamin, Anatta, Anicca, Arhat, Arupa, Triratna, Three Yanani, Dhyani Buddhas, Chathvaryarya Satyani, Dosa, Dukkha, Arya Shtangikamargah, Asavas,* and *Asceticism.* Additionally, there is no index. Furthermore, although the work purports to be a general dictionary of Buddhist terminology, it contains no references to East Asian Buddhist terms, such as *Zen* or *Chan*, and only incidental reference to Central Asian terms.

Only the most sophisticated user, one already possessing a high degree of technical and linguistic knowledge, could begin to make sense of the information presented in this book. Not recommended.
— **Richard H. Swain**

1414. Powers, John. **The Yogacara School of Buddhism: A Bibliography.** Metuchen, N.J., Scarecrow, 1991. 257p. index. (ATLA Bibliography Series, no.27). $29.50. Z7864.Y64P69. 016.2943'92. LC 91-37139. ISBN 0-8108-2502-3.

Yogacara (along with Madhyamika) is one of the two major schools of Indian Buddhism. The name *Yogacara* means "one whose practice is yoga," and its alternate name *Vijnanavada* (doctrine [vada] that phenomena are created by consciousness [vijnana]) indicates its philosophical and psychological stance. Yogacara spread northward and then eastward from India, and hence its canonical languages include Sanskrit, Tibetan, Chinese, and Japanese. There is a large body of secondary sources in Japanese as well as Western languages. Powers's goal is "to list every work in every language"; this is, therefore, a wide-ranging, highly technical, and scholarly work.

Powers has provided a good introduction describing the organization and aims of the bibliography. The work is divided into two major sections: primary sources, including sutras and commentaries, historical and philosophical texts, Tibetan works, and Indian works; and secondary sources. There are indexes for modern authors and technical terms, traditional Indian authors, Sanskrit titles, Tibetan authors and titles, and traditional Chinese and Japanese authors and titles. The bibliography locates primary sources within collections or libraries and by standard citation where possible. Translations of primary sources are listed under the transliterated title of the original work. Scholars should be forewarned that all authors and titles are given in romanized form—that is, all words are written using the Latin alphabet instead of the symbols of their original language. This will make the bibliography difficult for Japanese or Chinese scholars to use. In addition, Powers uses the old Wade Giles romanization rather than the pinyin system made official by the People's Republic of China.

This is by far the most comprehensive bibliography available on Yogacara, and the author can be justly proud of it. The extensive listing of Tibetan works is particularly notable. A work of remarkable scholarship and thoroughness, it should prove invaluable to scholars. Highly recommended to libraries serving serious students of Buddhism. [R: Choice, Sept 92, pp. 88-90]—**Richard H. Swain**

Christianity

General Works

Almanacs

1415. Draper, Edythe, ed. **The Almanac of the Christian World.** Wheaton, Ill., Tyndale House, 1992. 865p. illus. index. $14.95pa. ISBN 0-8423-1687-6. ISSN 1052-2670.

The purpose of this work "is to provide the Christian public with a resource book that covers all facets of the Christian world" and that contains "historical and contemporary information, products and services of interest to evangelical Christians" (copyright page). While this clarifying definition is elastic enough to include some mainstream Protestants, Roman Catholics, and Orthodox interests, the work is generally taut on theological, social, and political issues. Nineteen chapters divide material into the year in review, "Declarations," the world in review, countries of the world, calendars and special events, the arts, the Bible, church history, church life, education, evangelicalism, the family, leisure time, the media, missions, organizations and foundations, social and political concerns, sports, and a writer's guide.

This edition covers July 1, 1990, to December 31, 1991; the only information for current or future use is in the calendar section and the list of Christian cruises under leisure time coverage. The balance of the work—consisting of tables, pie charts, lists, chronologies, handbook information, ratings, and bibliographical recommendations—has primarily been excerpted from a variety of evangelical publications. Some material, such as popularity ratings and awards, is not easily found elsewhere. Thus, the work is a cross between a standard almanac, a Christian pop chart guide, and a Christian trivia book. Although it will be of use for some individuals and evangelical institutions that need one-stop quick information (particularly at its attractive price), it will not replace general tools for most libraries. However, for students of popular culture, the work provides an index of what interests the kind of evangelical Christian the publishers have identified.—**Donald G. Davis, Jr.**

Bibliography

1416. Donnelly, Dorothy F., and Mark A. Sherman. **Augustine's *De Civitate Dei*: An Annotated Bibliography of Modern Criticism, 1960-1990.** New York, Peter Lang, 1991. 109p. $29.95. Z8047.7.D66. 016.239'4. LC 91-26511. ISBN 0-8204-1607-X.

Since Augustine wrote *De Civitate Dei* more than one and one-half millennia ago, a myriad of philosophers, theologians, political theorists, and other scholars have reflected upon and attempted to explain the thought of the brilliant Bishop of Hippo. This handy reference guide is an annotated bibliography of 95 modern works devoted to the study of *De Civitate Dei*. Roughly two-thirds of the text discusses the 64 monographs, articles, and dissertations, arranged alphabetically by author, that appeared in North America between 1960 and 1990. The remainder of the volume covers 13 pre-1960 American publications and 18 foreign studies that the authors considered major contributions. Each entry consists of a bibliographical citation and a 200- to 500-word annotation. The annotations are descriptive summarizations of often complex arguments that are written in an engaging, straightforward style without excessive philosophic jargon. The volume also includes a chronologically arranged bibliography of the writings by Augustine, a nonannotated bibliography of selected general studies on Augustine and his works, and a brief chronology of the highlights of his life.

Although the authors insist in the preface that "the growing scholarly interest in Augustine, and especially the significant increase in studies on *De Civitate Dei*" has created the need for this comprehensive bibliography, the work itself seems to suggest that interest in the subject may be waning. Over the last decade, for instance, roughly two studies per year on *De Civitate Dei* have appeared, as opposed to an average of five per year during the early 1970s. But if the authors have perhaps overstated the timeliness and critical importance of the volume, they nonetheless have produced an informative and readable reference guide that will be appreciated by specialists in the field. Recommended for university libraries. — **Terry D. Bilhartz**

1417. Sheldon, Joseph K. **Rediscovery of Creation: A Bibliographical Study of the Church's Response to the Environmental Crisis.** Metuchen, N.J., American Theological Library Association and Scarecrow, 1992. 282p. (ATLA Bibliography Series, no.29). $35.00. Z7799.S44. 016.2618'362. LC 92-104. ISBN 0-8108-2539-2.

This work, copublished with the American Theological Library Association, hopes to ensure that "the church is theologically prepared to respond intelligently to ecological issues." The book tries to include all "major players in the theological discussion about the environment." Actually, the book surveys popular, scientific, and theological literature (including theses and dissertations) that "address humanity's relationship with Creation." It admittedly limits itself to Judeo-Christian works, emphasizing almost exclusively those of Christian perspective. Only works in English are included. Some of the entries are annotated; most fall in the post-1970 period.

Following a variety of prefaces and introductions, there is a historical overview of the church's response to environmental subjects. Most of the book (more than 200 pages) is devoted to the bibliography. Topics covered range from agriculture and biodiversity to ecofeminism, genetic engineering, animal rights, and the wilderness. Also included are works related to conservation biology, the pro-life movement, Earth Day 1990, and end-times theologies, as well as new age and creation spirituality. A list with addresses of Christian organizations that focus on creation is also provided, including curriculum materials on "creation care." — **Joseph W. Dauben**

Biography

1418. Holte, James Craig. **The Conversion Experience in America: A Sourcebook on Religious Conversion Autobiography.** Westport, Conn., Greenwood Press, 1992. 228p. index. $59.95. BV4930.H65. 291.4'2. LC 91-32173. ISBN 0-313-26680-8.

Holte, an Associate Professor of English at East Carolina University, has produced a concise, eloquently written, and scholarly volume that deserves a much wider readership than its price is likely to allow. His work contains 5- to 10-page, alphabetically arranged entries on 30 American religious autobiographers who have written about their conversion experiences. Each entry is subdivided into 4 sections: "Biography" (a 200-600 word introduction to the life and times of the autobiographer), "The Autobiography" (a 1,000-2,000 word discussion of the narrative), "Criticism" (a 200-500 word summation of how scholars have interpreted and assessed the significance of the piece), and "Bibliography" (an unannotated listing of related sources about the subject). The volume concludes with a brief bibliographic essay and index.

While the volume covers 350 years of conversion narratives, it is weighted in favor of twentieth-century writers. Seventeen of the thirty subjects published their works this century, and 11 were born in the quarter-century between 1915 and 1940. This modern focus gives the volume a mass market appeal but limits its usefulness for readers interested primarily in American religious autobiography during the seventeenth through nineteenth centuries. The work includes entries on men and women from a wide variety of ethnic and religious backgrounds. Seven of the subjects are female; nine are minority voices. Twenty-two belong to a Protestant denomination; four are Roman Catholic; the remaining four represent the Black Muslim, Shaker, Native American, and Buddhist religious traditions. Taken together, the entries demonstrate the great diversity of American conversion experiences. Recommended for college, university, and community libraries. [R: Choice, Nov 92, p. 444]—**Terry D. Bilhartz**

Dictionaries and Encyclopedias

1419. Harrison, R. K., ed. **Encyclopedia of Biblical and Christian Ethics.** rev. ed. Nashville, Tenn., Thomas Nelson, 1992. 472p. index. $14.95pa. BJ1199.E53. 241'.03. LC 92-3120. ISBN 0-8407-3391-7.

This volume is a "modest revision" of the 1987 first edition (see ARBA 88, entry 1393) and differs little from it. Of the more than 540 entries in this edition, only two are new ("Acquired Immune Deficiency Syndrome [AIDS]" and "Homelessness"), and only nine have been updated ("Abortion," "Addiction," "Civil Rights," "Contraception," "Euthanasia," "Fetal Rights," "Kinsey Report," "Nuclear Warfare," and "Population Control"). The publisher does not offer any explanation for the choice of entries updated. Thus, it is not clear why, for example, "Kinsey Report" was among the articles chosen for revision and "Apartheid" was not (especially in light of the changes that have taken place in South Africa). Additionally, some of these updated entries do not differ markedly in substance from those in the 1987 edition (the article on "Euthanasia" does, however, mention Jack Kevorkian), although there are some more recent books in the bibliographies.

The remainder of the revision, according to the publisher, consists of "corrections and an increase in the number of cross-references throughout the book" (preface). That being the case, more effort should have been invested in these aspects of the revision. Many entries that lacked either a signature or a bibliography (sometimes both) were apparently overlooked when other corrections were made. Also, spot-checking revealed significant weaknesses in the cross-referencing that were not remedied in the revision. For example, there is no reference from "Venereal Disease" (retained from the first edition) to the new entry on AIDS, and there are no cross-references under "Discrimination" although the volume contains entries on "Racism" and other related topics (all from the first edition).

Most people who have the first edition will not find enough new material in this book to merit its purchase. However, those who are looking for a solid, helpful reference work on the subject should consider this one in spite of the publisher's decision to release it as a paperback.—**Craig W. Beard**

1420. Ludlow, Daniel H., ed. **Encyclopedia of Mormonism: The History, Scripture, Doctrine, and Procedure of the Church of Jesus Christ of Latter-day Saints.** New York, Macmillan, 1992. 4v. illus. maps. index. $340.00/set. BX8605.5.E62. 289.3'03. LC 91-34255. ISBN 0-02-879605-5.

1421. **Encyclopedia of Mormonism.** [CD-ROM]. Orem, Utah, Infobases, 1992. Hardware requirements: IBM PC or compatible; 512K RAM; DOS 3.0 or higher; hard disk, with at least 7 MB free. $195.00.

Encyclopedia of Mormonism is the most comprehensive overview of the Church of Jesus Christ of Latter-day Saints (commonly known as the Mormon Church) that has been assembled to date. Ludlow, noted professor of religion at Brigham Young University, has assembled a cadre of Mormon and non-Mormon scholars to write hundreds of articles about the Church. The basic encyclopedia is in four volumes; a fifth volume (an optional purchase) contains the sacred scriptures of Mormonism (*The*

Book of Mormon, The Doctrine and Covenants, and *The Pearl of Great Price*). The main encyclopedia consists of short and moderately long signed articles in five main areas of interest: history of the Church, scriptures of the Church, doctrines of Mormonism, organization of the Church, and practices of Church members in society. Articles are arranged alphabetically but are linked through a thorough and useful synoptic outline that allows exploration of themes. Volume 4 contains a fairly detailed index that permits specific access. Individual articles are written in a scholarly tone, have numerous bibliographical references, and are illustrated with many rare photographs and very readable maps that show the rise of Mormonism from Vermont to Utah and its expansion worldwide.

The tone of the encyclopedia is apologetic, but no more so than other comparable encyclopedias, such as *The Catholic Encyclopedia* (see ARBA 89, entry 1339). While not an official publication of the Mormon Church, the encyclopedia contains the closest-to-official statements about doctrine and policy available to the general public. Controversial topics (e.g., Mormons and Blacks, polygamy, the Mountain Meadows Massacre, feminism, abortion, the Mark Hoffman forgeries of Mormon documents, the Church's role in business) discussed regularly by anti-Mormon sources are dealt with frankly by the various authors. The tone of these articles is fair without undue apology for the positions taken over the 150-plus-year history of the Church. Historical articles are particularly good, with biographical sketches of church leaders past and present. Some doctrinal articles are written in such Mormon-specific terminology that non-Mormons will have a difficult time understanding them.

The CD-ROM version of the encyclopedia contains all the words and illustrations (but not the sample Mormon hymns) on a single disc using Folio search software. The Folio engine allows the searching of any word, preassigned phrase headings, and main topical sections. Boolean searches are incredibly fast compared to other CD-ROM products. The entire encyclopedia can be read screen by screen, and the text is sprinkled generously with electronic links that act as cross-references to illustrations and to other sections of the encyclopedia on the same topic. The Folio engine is so easy to use that novices will readily get in and out and search for and print sections with little instruction or supervision.

Encyclopedia of Mormonism is recommended for all types of libraries that want an authoritative but apologetic source on Mormonism. No other publication comes close to its exhaustive nature and scholarly excellence. [R: BR, Nov/Dec 92, p. 56; Choice, July/Aug 92, p. 1654; LJ, 15 Feb 92, pp. 156-58; RQ, Fall 92, pp. 111-12; WLB, Apr 92, pp. 121-22] – **David V. Loertscher**

1422. McKim, Donald K., ed. **Encyclopedia of the Reformed Faith.** Louisville, Ky., Westminster/John Knox Press, 1992. 414p. $36.95. BX9406.E56. 284'2.'03. LC 91-37540. ISBN 0-664-21882-2.

The Reformed faith of the title refers to that stream of Protestant thought and practice that flowed out of the Swiss Reformation, led chiefly by Calvin but also by Zwingli and others less well known. Spreading through Europe, it reached high-water marks (outside Switzerland itself) in Scottish Presbyterianism, the Dutch Reformed churches, and (more ambiguously) English Puritanism. Channeled through these various branches onto American soil, it produced major currents running through the history of American Protestantism. These European and North American developments are the primary focus of McKim's encyclopedia. Streams branching off to other continents are, as he acknowledges, minimally represented, although there are articles on Africa and Australasia, several that relate to South Africa, and one that describes Presbyterianism's prominence in Korea.

About 40 percent of all entries are biographical. Others cover noteworthy events, organizations, creedal statements, distinctive doctrines and practices, and Reformed perspectives on key theological issues and concepts. One regrettable lack is the absence of entries for specific Reformed denominations, although more general articles, such as that on Presbyterianism in America, cover some of this territory. And, at least for American church bodies, alternative sources for such information are somewhat common.

Easily more than half of the material in this work is not covered by more general encyclopedic works, such as the ubiquitous *Oxford Dictionary of the Christian Church* (see ARBA 75, entry 1220). Even where there is overlap, differences of emphasis and perspective tend to make this volume a worthwhile supplement. It is definitely a welcome addition to the small number of encyclopedic works devoted to one major Protestant tradition, comparable to (although not as comprehensive and detailed as) J. Bodensieck's three-volume *Encyclopedia of the Lutheran Church* (Augsburg, 1965) or N. Harmon's two-volume *Encyclopedia of World Methodism* (Abingdon, 1974). [R: Choice, July/Aug 92, p. 1655; LJ, 1 Mar 92, p. 82; RBB, 1 June 92, p. 1775] – **Hans E. Bynagle**

1423. Stake, Donald Wilson. **The ABCs of Worship: A Concise Dictionary.** Louisville, Ky., Westminster/John Knox Press, 1992. 196p. $9.95pa. BV15.S69. 264'.003. LC 91-45294. ISBN 0-664-25246-X.

"Worship defines who we are as the Church of Jesus Christ in this world and is not to be taken lightly." So says Stake in his introduction to this concise dictionary. Writing from the perspective of the Reformed tradition, Stake, pastor of the Union Presbyterian Church in Schenectady, New York, attempts to provide for the layperson some basic answers as to what worship expressions and activities mean. What is an agape meal and when is it observed? What is the difference between infant and believer baptism? What is Maundy Thursday? Some 176 terms are defined, from *acclamation* and *Advent* to *worship, worship committee*, and *X. Baptism, gesture and posture, hymn, symbols*, and *time* receive extended treatment. On the other hand, *affirmation of faith, Christ the King, good news, homily, Pascha, recessional, Trinity Sunday*, and *X* are defined in 10 lines or less. The average definition seems to be just less than one page. Cross-references are heavily used; it is supposedly possible to start with any given word and be led by the references to most aspects of worship (but not always; there is a reference from *response* to *antiphon*, but not the reverse). Stake has written simple definitions in down-to-earth, pastoral terms, but he sometimes provides less than adequate explanation, such as regarding the function of dance in worship.

This work is recommended for undergraduate or church libraries. A more authoritative, exhaustive work for larger collections is *The New Westminster Dictionary of Liturgy and Worship* (see ARBA 88, entry 1426). [R: LJ, 15 Mar 92, p. 80] – **Glenn R. Wittig**

Handbooks and Yearbooks

1424. Codignola, Luca. **Guide to Documents Relating to French and British North America in the Archives of the Sacred Congregation "de Propaganda Fide" in Rome, 1622-1799.** Ottawa, National Archives of Canada, 1991. 250p. index. $29.95pa.; $35.95pa. (U.S.). 282'.71. ISBN 0-660-13758-5.

The impact of the Holy See on North American development cannot be answered in general terms, but only with reference to areas, individuals, and times found in specific materials. Accordingly, the Research Centre in Religious History of Canada at St. Paul University, in conjunction with the National Archives of Canada, has produced a systematic calendar of documents that relate to French and British North America in the Archives of the Sacred Congregation "de Propaganda Fide" in Rome. Chronologically, 1622 seemed the logical starting point, as it was in that year that Propaganda was established; and 1799 is the terminal date, because it was the end of the eighteenth century and the beginning of another era for the church in Europe. Encompassing 177 years, the calendar contains descriptions of 2,441 documents conserved in different series of the Propaganda Fide archives. Entries in this volume summarize the contents of the documents with respect to facts and individuals in French and British North America within the time frame.

A long introduction sets forth an interpretative schema in regard to the series and subseries under which the entries have been subsumed. An elaborate index allows for retrieval of all sorts of information. Because the full calendar could not be rendered in a single volume, it is available on microfiche from the National Academy of Canada. Research scholars working with such documents will find this volume invaluable. – **G. A. Cevasco**

1425. **Fund Raiser's Guide to Religious Philanthropy.** 5th ed. Bernard Jankowski, ed. Rockville, Md., Taft Group; distr., Detroit, Gale, 1992. 309p. index. $129.00pa. ISBN 1-879784-17-3. ISSN 1042-0053.

Religious organizations and agencies are by far the principal beneficiaries of charitable donations in the United States. In 1990, for instance, such groups garnered more than half of all such contributions, whereas health organizations, educational institutions, and human service agencies obtained only 8 to 10 percent each. Who are these contributors to religious enterprises? *Fund Raiser's Guide* addresses this question by profiling 396 philanthropic sources of support for religion. While a minimum gift of

$50,000 was required for inclusion, some 80 percent of the foundations and trusts summarized actually gave $100,000 or more. Collectively they awarded more than $400 million during their last reporting period. With grants that totaled more than $46 million to Protestant and Catholic causes, the Lilly Foundation was the most generous, followed by the Duke Endowment, whose $24.8 million went to North Carolina churches and religious agencies, and the Weinberg Foundation, whose $21.4 million favored Jewish and Christian ventures.

For any religiously affiliated entity searching for charitable funds, this volume is a must. The alphabetized profiles make for easy use, and the indexes provide information on current officers and directors, the denominational and geographic preferences of the foundations, types of grants usually awarded, and recent recipients.—**John W. Storey**

Bible Studies

1426. Balz, Horst, and Gerhard Schneider, eds. **Exegetical Dictionary of the New Testament. Volume 2.** Grand Rapids, Mich., William B. Eerdmans, 1991. 555p. $44.95. BS2312.E913. 225.4'8'03. LC 90-35682. ISBN 0-8028-2410-2.

This is the second volume of the *Exegetical Dictionary of the New Testament* (EDNT); only the third volume of the *Exegetisches Worterbuch zum Neuen Testament* (EWNT) (Stuttgart: W. Kohlhammer, 1978-1980) remains to be translated. (A review of the first volume of EDNT may be found in ARBA 91, entry 1423.) The editors and most of the other 112 contributors are from Germany and include some of the most prominent names in current New Testament (NT) scholarship.

The EDNT provides the dictionary form of each word in the Greek NT, along with its English transliteration and definition and a brief explanation of its use in the NT. Occasionally, cognate words are treated together. In the case of more important theological terms, a brief bibliography concludes the article, and when there are English translations of works cited in EWNT bibliographies, the editors have substituted the English version of the publication.

Although some errors in the German edition have been corrected (e.g., punctuation in the bibliography of the "Jericho" article, p. 175), others remain (e.g., two instances of the wrong accentuation on plural forms of *megistan*, p. 401). Nevertheless, the EDNT is an excellent reference work that fills a void in the body of resources available for the study of the NT and is another outstanding achievement for Eerdmans. It should be popular among students, pastors, and others involved in the study of the Greek NT.—**M. Patrick Graham**

1427. Chamberlin, William J. **Catalogue of English Bible Translations: A Classified Bibliography of Versions and Editions....** Westport, Conn., Greenwood Press, 1991. 898p. index. (Bibliographies and Indexes in Religious Studies, no.21). $125.00. Z7771.E5C43. 016.2205'2. LC 91-27497. ISBN 0-313-28041-X.

The basic catalog in this work is a very helpful list of thousands of English Bible translations, including complete Bibles, Hebrew Scriptures (Old Testaments), New Testaments, individual biblical books, partial translations (e.g., David Rosenberg's poetic J tradition in Harold Bloom's *Book of J*), paraphrases, children's Bibles, and Apocryphal Books (understandably, since most of the latter are or have been part of various sectarian canons). Less understandable is the extension of the lists to include the Dead Sea Scrolls, the Church Fathers, Josephus, and the Koran. The criteria for inclusion are not obvious, and the introduction is of little help in focusing the nature, rationale, and value of this volume. It contains miscellaneous citations (e.g., Isaac Asimov, Eric Fromm, Joseph Lewis of the American Atheist Association, an article in a popular archaeological magazine), most in defense of the value of the Bible. A list of Bibles with notorious typographical errors is entertaining.

The major fault with the catalog is that undated and broadly dated volumes (some of which could be more closely dated) are placed at the beginning of each section before the earliest datable volumes. Thus, works by modern writers may be found both at the beginning and end of a chronological list. Also, the appropriate designation of the Old Testament as Hebrew Scripture can lead to problems, such as unraveling English translations of Greek translations of the Hebrew Scripture. Finally, it is sometimes not clear whether an unfamiliar book contains any biblical material. [R: WLB, May 92, pp. 121-22]—**Robert T. Anderson**

1428. Green, Joel B., and Scot McKnight, eds. **Dictionary of Jesus and the Gospels.** Downers Grove, Ill., InterVarsity Press, 1992. 933p. index. $34.95. BS2555.2.D53. 226'.03. LC 91-32382. ISBN 0-8308-1777-8.

The last work comparable to this one was Hastings's multivolume *Dictionary of Christ and the Gospels* (Scribner's, 1906-1908). With the developments in research on the Gospels and on the historical Jesus that have taken place in the intervening decades, the time is ripe for the appearance of *Dictionary of Jesus and the Gospels* (DJG). While DJG does not supplant the Hastings work, it is a worthy supplement to it.

As DJG is published by InterVarsity Press, it is not surprising that its tenor is evangelical. However, it is not only evangelical, it is also critical, in the best sense of both terms. It is critical because the writers know and use, where they feel it is appropriate, modern scholarly approaches to biblical and theological study. It is evangelical because these scholars are committed to the authority of Scripture as divine revelation and to the Gospels as a trustworthy witness to the life and teaching of Jesus Christ. The list of contributors is impressive—a virtual who's who of New Testament scholars. Many of the writers have contributed articles on topics they have researched and written about, often extensively (e.g., "Targums" by Bruce Chilton, "Literary Criticism" by Edgar McKnight, "Synoptic Problem" by Robert Stein, "Rhetorical Criticism" by Duane Watson, "Miracles and Miracle Workers" by Barry Blackburn, "Son of Man" by Howard Marshall).

Scholarship is evident in the articles. Thus, the work will serve those whose interest in Jesus and the Gospels is, at least in part, academic (that is, students and scholars). But it is not written on such a level that will render it inaccessible to pastors and laypeople. In fact, part of DJG's appeal is that it makes the fruits of critical biblical scholarship available to a wider audience. The book is well laid out, easy to use, and sturdily bound. Cross-references are plentiful, and the bibliographies that accompany the articles are current and (for a work of this size) rather full, directing readers to essential sources for further reading. This work is appropriate for the reference collections of seminary, academic, and some public libraries, and is highly recommended.—**Craig W. Beard**

1429. McLean, Bradley H. **Citations and Allusions to Jewish Scripture in Early Christian and Jewish Writings through 180 C.E.** Lewiston, N.Y., Edwin Mellen Press, 1992. 138p. index. $49.95. BS1160.M35. 221'.09'015. LC 91-38309. ISBN 0-7734-9430-8.

The Hebrew Bible is scripture not only for Jews but also for Christians, as it is the Christian Old Testament. For Jesus and his early followers it was their only "Bible," as the New Testament canon as we know it was not solidified until the middle of the fourth century. Thus, it is not surprising that traces of it are found in many early Christian and Jewish writings. This slim volume indexes quotations of, and allusions to, the Hebrew Bible (and the Apocryphal/Deuterocanonical books) that are found in the Old Testament pseudepigrapha, the Dead Sea Scrolls, Josephus, Philo, the New Testament, apocryphal Gospels and Acts, gnostic writings, the Early Church Fathers, and Eusebius. There are other tools, including indexes, that make it possible to locate these citations and allusions in certain of the above sources, but McLean brings it all together in one volume.

The index is arranged according to the traditional Protestant canonical order: Genesis through Malachi followed by the Apocrypha. Under the heading for each verse or passage listed are citations to the passages in the early Jewish or Christian sources where the quotation or allusion is found. The text of neither the scripture nor the quoting/alluding source is given, only the citation. Next comes a 195-item bibliography of publications that contain texts, translations, or both of the cited Christian and Jewish writings. The following collections of translations of the primary sources are missing from the bibliography: Bentley Layton's *The Gnostic Scriptures* (1987), Geza Vermes's *The Dead Sea Scrolls in English* (1987), and the new editions of James M. Robinson's *The Nag Hammadi Library* (1988) and Edgar Hennecke's *The New Testament Apocrypha, Volume One. Gospels and Related Writings* (1991). The earlier editions of the latter two are included. Because McLean does not specify his inclusion criteria, it is not clear whether these omissions are intentional or accidental.

Physically, the typeface is easy on the eyes and the binding is sturdy. The work's focus limits its audience to academic and seminary library users involved in biblical studies and in early Jewish and Christian studies. For them it will be a handy tool.—**Craig W. Beard**

1430. Minor, Mark. **Literary-Critical Approaches to the Bible: An Annotated Bibliography.** West Cornwall, Conn., Locust Hill Press, 1992. 520p. index. $50.00. Z7770.M66. 016.2206'6. LC 92-7469. ISBN 0-933951-48-5.

Containing 2,254 annotated and cross-indexed entries of books, edited collections, and articles, this is an outstanding reference. Although extensive, it is not exhaustive. It includes only materials published in English, and it excludes book reviews, most Bible commentaries, and works of historical criticism. Minor's concern is strictly literary criticism. Admittedly, historical and literary criticism sometimes overlap, but Minor nevertheless makes a clear distinction. Whereas historical criticism seeks to get "behind" the written biblical text to piece together the oral traditions and other sources of the written word, literary criticism focuses on the final text itself, seeking to understand how its parts interact to produce the whole. To the historical critic, the biblical text is merely a depository of earlier records; to the literary critic, the text is a finished product.

A literary approach to the Bible, as Minor states, is hardly new. Even so, studies of this nature have proliferated enormously since the 1960s, and Minor's is the first extensive effort at referencing this body of material. It is sensibly organized; works dealing broadly with the Bible in general and the Hebrew Bible in particular are followed by more specific studies of each individual book of the Hebrew Bible and the New Testament, from Genesis to Revelation. An author index enhances the usability of this material. Serious scholars of biblical studies will be interested in this volume, and university libraries should have a copy for research purposes. [R: Choice, Dec 92, p. 604] – **John W. Storey**

1431. **Nelson's Concordance of Bible Phrases.** Nashville, Tenn., Thomas Nelson, 1992. 685p. index. $19.99. BS425.P47. 220.5'2033. LC 92-28531. ISBN 0-8407-4262-2.

Hundreds of biblical phrases and their locations are listed in alphabetical order in this work, which refers to the King James Version. Key words are also listed in a separate index, with an indication of the phrases that contain them. An introduction argues that it is much easier to find the 48 occurrences of the phrase "Word of God" in this "new kind of concordance" than to look under either "word" or "God" in a regular concordance, as there would be several hundred listings under each word. That point was more relevant in 1986 when this work was first published as *The Phrase Concordance of the Bible*. In 1991 two significant concordances to the New Revised Version were published, *The NRSV Concordance Unabridged* (see ARBA 92, entry 1442) and *NRSV Exhaustive Concordance* (see ARBA 92, entry 1443). Both code a phrase such as "word of God" before the multiple listing of all occurrences of "word," so that the user can spot "word of God" without noting other listings under "word." Because a general concordance offers many other features and includes the function of this work, *Nelson's* utility is less obvious. Many of the included phrases occur few times anyway, and several, such as "perilous pestilence" and "gates are desolate," are so obscure that it is unlikely that anyone would look for them at all. – **Robert T. Anderson**

1432. Powell, Mark Allan, with Cecile G. Gray and Melissa C. Curtis, comps. **The Bible and Modern Literary Criticism: A Critical Assessment and Annotated Bibliography.** Westport, Conn., Greenwood Press, 1992. 469p. index. (Bibliographies and Indexes in Religious Studies, no.22). $65.00. Z7770.P68. 016.2206'6. LC 91-38128. ISBN 0-313-27546-7.

Powell divides this annotated list of almost 1,000 books, articles, and reviews into 6 categories: "Basis," the seminal works in philosophy, sociology/anthropology, and linguistics that led to modern literary criticism; "Theory," representatives of different schools of literary theory; "Method," scholars developing methods of applying literary theory to the Bible; "Criticism," works that apply the methods to biblical texts; "Evaluation," critiques of critical studies; and "Implications," studies that suggest how literary theory can affect kindred fields like theology and homiletics. An excellent 16-page introductory essay, following the same outline, provides a clear, comprehensive, and well-organized introduction, not only to the book but also to the discipline of modern literary criticism. The emphasis is on objective and pragmatic critiques as opposed to mimetic or expressive foci of literary criticism because the former command current primary interest. There are indexes of authors, titles, and subjects with no serious omissions apparent.

There is a tendency in the foreword, preface, and introductory essay to imply that the major quarrel generated by literary criticism is between secular and religious approaches to scripture. Certainly, biblical literalists are concerned about literary criticism, as they are with any form of criticism, but the more relevant focus of debate is within scholarly circles distinct from religious affiliations. Indeed, the works listed under "Evaluation" do focus on the academic quarrels. [R: Choice, Oct 92, pp. 178-80]—**Robert T. Anderson**

1433. **The Revell Concise Bible Dictionary.** By Laurence O. Richards. Tarrytown, N.Y., Fleming H. Revell, 1991. 695p. illus. maps. $14.95. BS440.R4845. 220.3. LC 91-21230. ISBN 0-8007-1658-2.

In an earlier review (see ARBA 91, entry 1432) *The Revell Bible Dictionary*, in its "deluxe color edition," was welcomed as an attractive, theologically conservative entry into a Bible market (translations, dictionaries, and assorted other resources) that showed no signs of shrinking. Attractively produced, containing 6,750 entries, and priced at less than $30, the "deluxe" edition was recommended, presumably to take its place on the reference shelves of many libraries.

The new, "concise" edition contains almost the entire text of the earlier edition (6,500 versus 6,750 entries). Compression is achieved through the use of smaller type, which is bound to put a strain on many users' eyes, and especially (and regrettably) through the omission of color illustrations and a variety of eye-catching, multicolor charts. It is unlikely that even the most cash-strapped institution would wish to forego acquisition of the larger edition simply to save a few dollars. However, libraries might consider purchasing several copies of the concise version for general circulation. This work might also be an attractive gift to graduates and budding theologians.—**Leonard J. Greenspoon**

1434. Smith, Jerome H., ed. **The New Treasury of Scripture Knowledge.** Nashville, Tenn., Thomas Nelson, 1992. 1659p. index. $29.95. BS430.N48. 220.5'2033. LC 91-45487. ISBN 0-8407-7694-2.

This volume is a new edition of *The Treasury of Scripture Knowledge*, which first appeared about 1836 and has been reprinted several times. It is essentially a compendium of cross-references based on the King James Version of the Bible with some limited commentary. It presents for virtually every verse a selection of other verses that Smith believes are clarifying or explanatory. He has added more than 100,000 new references in this edition. The stated intention is to allow the Bible to comment on and explain itself. The principle flaw that significantly limits the utility of this volume is the extent to which it is based on the interpretative strategies of a much older generation of scholars. With few exceptions the bibliographical resources on which Smith relies consist of outdated works (some go back to the mid-eighteenth and mid-nineteenth centuries and informed the original compilation) that are not conversant with contemporary critical scholarship. This work will be useful primarily to conservative and fundamentalist ministers and religious educators who are unable to work with concordances to the Hebrew and Greek and who, for religious reasons, are uncomfortable with contemporary critical scholarship.
—**Harold O. Forshey**

1435. Wigoder, Geoffrey, Shalom M. Paul, and Benedict T. Viviano. **Almanac of the Bible.** New York, Prentice Hall General Reference, 1991. 448p. illus. index. $40.00. BS417.W48. 220'.02'02. LC 91-13229. ISBN 0-13-026899-2.

This almanac is basically a series of annotated, alphabetical lists of peoples, places, and other items related to the Bible. Separate listings of "The Matriarchs" and "The Apostles" are particularly notable. A tally of U.S. towns with biblical names is interesting, although many names (e.g., Jordan, Lebanon, Samaria) are more popular than this list would indicate. There are brief general articles on topics such as religions, languages, geography, everyday life, "The Intertestamental Period," the early Church, Bible translations, and the reflection of the Bible in various art forms. Several of the cited literary works are in German. Charts itemize biblical miracles, Israelite tribes, judges, and kings. Many black-and-white photographs and eight pages of color plates illustrate relevant sites, art works, and artifacts.

This is a coffee-table book for the casual browser rather than a research tool. Bible dictionaries or encyclopedias would be a better source for the latter. Even the browser may be discomforted by some of the shortcomings of the volume. Much of the same material is duplicated in the sections on canon and books of the Bible. Some of the material is of questionable value—the total entry for Shepharad is that it is a "Place to which the Jews of Jerusalem were exiled (Obad 20)." Some material is erroneous. For example, the structure found on Mount Gerizim in the 1980s was not the Samaritan Temple but a platform built in Roman times. Much of the text is spent describing biblical stories without illuminating them with literary or historical information. [R: RBB, 1 Apr 92, p. 1468]—**Robert T. Anderson**

Sikkism

1436. Tatla, Darshan Singh. **Sikhs in North America: An Annotated Bibliography.** Westport, Conn., Greenwood Press, 1991. 180p. index. (Bibliographies and Indexes in Sociology, no.19). $39.95. Z1361.S47T37. 016.973'0882946. LC 90-13998. ISBN 0-313-27336-7.

Tatla, lecturer at Hall Green College in Birmingham, England, has provided an invaluable tool for those interested in any aspect of the Sikh experience in North America during the twentieth century. The bibliography is extensive and usefully organized into sections arranged by subject, including general sources, migration and settlement, employment, education, family and social life, language/literature/media, politics, and religion. The subject sections contain books, official and semiofficial reports, dissertations and theses, scholarly articles, audiovisual materials, and newspaper articles. A majority of the entries are briefly described (without, however, critical statements). Especially noteworthy are sections that locate and describe special libraries/archives that contain relevant material; the extensive section that covers newspaper, journal, and literary material in Punjabi as well as English; and the inclusion throughout the bibliography of unpublished material, such as papers delivered at scholarly conferences. An appendix contains a handlist of Punjabi-language periodicals published in North America.

Given the Sikhs' historical involvement in the North American continent and the contemporary ongoing struggle in India's Punjab Province, North America's Sikhs are of considerable interest. This bibliography is a thorough and useful tool for any library's reference collection. [R: Choice, May 92, p. 1376]—**David L. White**

Part IV
SCIENCE AND TECHNOLOGY

29 Science and Technology in General

BIBLIOGRAPHY

1437. Miller, Gordon L. **The History of Science: An Annotated Bibliography.** Pasadena, Calif., Salem Press, 1992. 193p. index. (Magill Bibliographies). $40.00. Z7405.H6M5. 016.509. LC 92-6433. ISBN 0-89356-675-6.

This bibliography contains approximately 550 brief descriptions of important works in the history of science. Most of the items discussed have been published since 1950, with the latest dating from 1991. The subject areas include the physical, biological, medical, and human sciences as well as mathematics. Basic resources, reference books, and general works are treated as are a number of special topics, such as the philosophy of science, science and religion, and scientific institutions. While most of the entries are books, significant journal articles are also represented. The emphasis is upon Western science, although some works from other cultural traditions are included. According to Miller's introduction, the selected items range from high school level to advanced treatises; however, no specific indication of difficulty is given in the individual descriptions. These, averaging about 100 words in length, are generally well written and reflect a considerable amount of research and selectivity. A complete author index is provided; subject and topical indexes would have been useful as well. Overall, this appears to be a carefully constructed reference work of use to anyone wishing to study in this field. – **John U. Trefny**

BIOGRAPHY

1438. **American Men & Women of Science 1992-93: A Biographical Directory of Today's Leaders in Physical, Biological and Related Sciences.** 18th ed. New Providence, N.J., R. R. Bowker, 1992. 8v. index. $750.00/set. LC 6-7326. ISBN 0-8352-3074-0. ISSN 0192-8570.

This standard biographical sourcebook on leading United States and Canadian scientists follows the same format and guidelines used in earlier editions (see ARBA 90, entry 1420). A few enhancements have been introduced, including state subdivisions within the discipline index and a list of recipients of major scientific honors and awards.

Approximately 122,000 living scientists in the fields of physical and biological sciences, public health, engineering, mathematics, statistics, and computer science are listed. Entrants have been selected based on distinguished achievement, research activity, or attainment of a position of responsibility. Each entry includes basic biographical and educational background, professional experience, membership in professional organizations, research interests, and mailing address. The addition of state subdivisions to the discipline index directly addresses the lack of geographic indexing in earlier editions. The 7 new specialties added to the index increase the number of scientific disciplines to 171 but still leave many of them too broad for really useful indexing.

This remains a standard reference source for academic and larger public libraries. Libraries expanding their CD-ROM capability might prefer to spend slightly more and acquire this work as part of Bowker's SciTech Reference Plus CD-ROM. [R: C&RL, Sept 92, p. 426] – **Susan Davis Herring**

1439. Noonan, Jon. **Nineteenth-Century Inventors.** New York, Facts on File, 1992. 114p. illus. index. (American Profiles). $16.95. T39.N66. 609'.2'273. LC 91-13584. ISBN 0-8160-2480-4.

This slim volume provides brief biographies on eight important nineteenth-century inventors of the United States. Although no criteria for inclusion are given, all eight created important devices still valuable today (e.g., the computer, the telephone, the telegraph). The book, written for young adults, gives generally serviceable biographies, introductions to the importance of the inventions, life chronologies, and lists of further readings (which usually consist of other young adult-oriented titles).

The text of the biographies is somewhat uneven and at times convoluted, especially considering the intended audience. However, most of the entries are sufficiently clear, if not particularly engaging. The inventions are explained in a nontechnical manner that should be accessible to students. Noonan successfully elucidates the implications of the inventions for the larger social context in which they occurred. The chronologies may have some use, but they are quite brief and could have been expanded without risking unnecessary detail.

Each of the eight figures is Caucasian and male. The publisher includes volumes on Black and women scientists in this series to offset this bias. Overall, this work may be of some use to school or public libraries wishing to supplement general encyclopedias' basic biographical data on the history of technology. [R: BR, Jan/Feb 92, p. 51] — **Christopher W. Nolan**

1440. Stankus, Tony, ed. **Biographies of Scientists for Sci-Tech Libraries: Adding Faces to the Facts.** Binghamton, N.Y., Haworth Press, 1992. 228p. (*Science & Technology Libraries*, vol.11, no.4). $29.95. Q141.B535. 509.2. LC 91-31241. ISBN 1-56024-214-0.

This volume contains a variety of essays that identify sources of biographical information on scientists. The editor's intent is that the listed titles will go beyond the merely scientific contributions of the scientists to explore some of the drama of their lives, thereby making science look more appealing to those considering such a career. Consequently, consistency of approach and comprehensiveness of coverage are not goals. The scientists represent both U.S. and foreign figures, almost all from the nineteenth and twentieth centuries. The essays, each covering one discipline, vary considerably in style. Some are lists of key figures with brief biographies and lists of references included; some are general bibliographic essays; and one is a mixture of the history of the discipline with a hodgepodge of tables, including Library of Congress subject headings and classification numbers, as well as lists of periodical indexes and monographic series.

This work succeeds only so far as each essay does. Some, such as that on animal scientists and the editor's introduction, provide their biographees with lively annotations that emphasize the excitement of science. Others, such as those on computer science and physics, are less selective in their sources and fail to indicate which titles might be especially engaging.

This is a monographic reprint of a volume of the serial *Science & Technology Libraries*, and the publishers have elected to include several articles unrelated to the title and purpose of the book. Additionally, no index is provided, so reference use of the work is severely limited. Most of the scientists covered are sufficiently famous to appear in other reference works, such as the classic *Dictionary of Scientific Biography* (see ARBA 91, entries 1461-62), which also contains extensive bibliographies. The volume under review might be useful in circulating collections to pique student interest in science, but it does not offer much to a reference collection that owns other biographical sources in the sciences. [R: LJ, July 92, p. 133] — **Christopher W. Nolan**

1441. Veglahn, Nancy J. **Women Scientists.** New York, Facts on File, 1991. 134p. illus. index. (American Profiles). $16.95. Q130.V44. 509.2'2. LC 90-26995. ISBN 0-8160-2482-0.

Finding biographical information on women scientists written at an appropriate level for middle and high school students can be difficult. With this volume the American Profiles series takes a major step toward improving that situation. Eleven American women, from botanist Alice Eastwood (1859-1953) to physicist Mildred Dresselhaus (born 1939), are introduced in 7- to 10-page essays, each with a bibliography for further exploration. The essays stress the ways these women faced and overcame the many barriers to their work, including social and family pressures to conform, limits to education and research opportunities, and discrimination within their fields. This decidedly feminist approach provides active encouragement for female students, who often still experience pressure to choose a career outside of science, math, or engineering.

Veglahn selected the 11 women based on the importance of their work and the variety of time periods and scientific fields they represent. It is always easy to argue with such a limited list, but Veglahn's choices are diverse and inspiring. Her writing is clear, and the more specialized terms have been defined within the text. Like the earlier volumes in this series, *Women Scientists* is an outstanding source for any school or public library. — **Susan Davis Herring**

1442. **Who's Who in Science in Europe: A Biographical Guide in Science, Technology, Agriculture, and Medicine.** 7th ed. Harlow, England, Longman Group; distr., Detroit, Gale, 1991. 4v. index. $885.00/set. ISBN 0-582-08659-0.

In a multidisciplinary world, extracting the essence of a research scientist's work challenges the most determined biographer. Here the anonymous compiler succeeds thousands of times. The reader benefits from an indexed pathway, which is marked by 62 categories, to the top-tier scientists based in Europe (but excluding those in the former Soviet Union). Perhaps because of existing companion volumes that cover the fields, entries related to agriculture and natural sciences are much sparser than those in disciplines such as medicine and engineering. Because the compilation is based on a degree of self-selection — 30,000 solicitations for information were mailed — the user cannot know why some individuals are omitted. But many prominent scientists anchored at museums are missing (e.g., Nils Andersen in Denmark, Richard Pankhurst in Scotland, Richard Vane-Wright in England). Moreover, although the introduction notes the omission of social scientists, at least some are included among the biographical entries. As a source of addresses and telephone numbers, the volumes will hasten the connection to the author of a "reference cited" and the person who penned a book but did not include an address. (Electronic mail addresses would make the next edition even stronger.) Both novice and established researchers will benefit from perusing the volumes to answer the question, "Do I know my European counterparts and potential collaborators?" — **Diane M. Calabrese**

1443. Yount, Lisa. **Black Scientists.** New York, Facts on File, 1991. 111p. illus. index. (American Profiles). $16.95. Q141.Y68. 500'.89'96073. LC 90-19159. ISBN 0-8160-2549-5.

Eight Black scientists are profiled here, including three physicians, an agriculturalist, a cell biologist, two chemists, and an engineer. Three were alive at the time of publication. The author does not describe how the eight were chosen. A separate chapter is devoted to each scientist, beginning with a useful introduction that places the individual's work in context within the scientific field. Each biography includes a life history, education, and the significance of the individual's work. In addition, the author describes obstacles and challenges that are unique to the Black experience. Bibliographies are found at the end of each chapter.

This work is suitable for junior high and high school libraries and perhaps freshman level college students. In a college library it would be more appropriate on the circulating shelves than in the reference collection. — **T. McKimmie**

DICTIONARIES AND ENCYCLOPEDIAS

1444. **Academic Press Dictionary of Science and Technology.** Christopher Morris, ed. San Diego, Calif., Academic Press, 1992. 2432p. illus. $115.00. Q123.A33. 503. LC 90-29032. ISBN 0-12-200400-0.

Users of this new work, which is reported to be the largest scientific dictionary ever published in English, will be impressed. More than 133,000 entries are contained in its pages. There are 124 scientific fields covered, ranging from chemistry to crystallography to chaotic dynamics. A short article about each field, written by such distinguished authors as Stephen Jay Gould, Gilbert Grosvenor, and Glenn T. Seaborg, gives its history, scope, and interesting notes about current developments. The articles are located alphabetically within the main text. The layout includes excellent drawings and striking photographs; the 24 color plates contain nearly 100 photographs and images that range from computer graphics to scanning electron and light micrographs of computer chips to images of a human fetus at different stages of development. They add a great deal to the aesthetics of this book.

Each entry includes the name of the scientific field within which the definition is placed. Some entries include several variations, each defined within a specific field. For example, the term *filament* is defined separately within the fields of astronomy, botany, biology, electricity, electronics, and metallurgy. Organisms are defined to the family level, with occasional inclusion of genus and species names. The line drawings and black-and-white photographs that accompany many entries provide variation as well as visual information. Many molecular structure drawings, such as those for caffeine and carotene, will also prove useful. The definitions for chemical compounds and minerals contain molecular formulas, and many mathematical definitions provide equations for clarification. In general, terms are well defined, although some definitions are weak or awkward. Appendixes include physical constants, international units and conversions, the periodic table, a geologic timetable, a five-kingdom organism classification, and a chronology of scientific events from 1403 to 1992. This work is comparable to the *McGraw-Hill Dictionary of Scientific and Technical Terms* (see ARBA 90, entry 1428) in its quality. It is timely, well produced, and attractive. — **T. McKimmie**

1445. Brennan, Richard P. **Dictionary of Scientific Literacy.** New York, John Wiley, 1992. 334p. illus. $22.95. Q123.B68. 503. LC 91-4307. ISBN 0-471-53214-2.

Science and technology are filtering into almost every aspect of modern life; therefore the average citizen should be familiar with the terminology that exists today. Since scientific literacy has emerged as a central goal of education as recommended by the National Council on Science and Technology Education, this source fills a definite need.

Over 650 scientific and technical terms, concepts, and principles are listed, with many cross-referenced to avoid confusion. The text has been written in language the average person can understand and covers terms commonly encountered in everyday life. Illustrations enhance this work, as do the clear format and reasonable price. For more comprehensive works on scientific terms, *Van Nostrand Reinhold's Scientific Encyclopedia* (see ARBA 90, entry 1430) or *McGraw-Hill Concise Encyclopedia of Science and Technology* (see ARBA 85, entry 1331) are desirable. Brennan's dictionary of scientific definitions for everyday applications will be welcomed by school and public librarians, undergraduates, and inquisitive laypeople. [R: LJ, 1 Mar 92, p. 42; SBF, Mar 92, p. 43] — **Diane J. Turner**

1446. **McGraw-Hill Encyclopedia of Science & Technology.** 7th ed. Sybil P. Parker, ed. in chief. New York, McGraw-Hill, 1992. 20v. illus. maps. index. $1,900.00/set. Q121.M3. 503. LC 91-36349. ISBN 0-07-909206-3.

This encyclopedia has been substantially revised since its last edition of five years ago. The 7,500 articles attempt to cover all areas of the physical and natural sciences, as well as engineering and technology. Authors of the signed articles are recognized experts in their respective fields and include 21 Nobel prize winners. Their articles follow the pyramid model of explanation, beginning with a definition, then a basic overview, and then the finer details. No explicit audience is given in the work's introduction, and the articles vary considerably in their level of writing. The article on anorthosite, for example, contains both basic and technical information that makes the piece suitable for high school students up to those with substantial familiarity with geology. On the other hand, a much smaller article on anorthoclase is highly technical and fairly useless to the geologically uninitiated. Fortunately, the majority of the articles seem accessible and useful to a wider audience. Article length typically is proportional to either the perceived popularity of the topic or its generality; average length is probably two pages. This usually works well, although some inconsistencies are puzzling. For example, aging receives about one-and-one-half pages and aggression is given one-half page. Agricultural aircraft, however, covers nearly four pages.

As always, this encyclopedia can be rated highly for its attention to detail and accuracy. A spot-check of articles found a strong level of correspondence to facts published in other sources and a lack of notable bias. One unfortunate exception is the article on AIDS, which implies — largely through omission — that homosexual men and drug abusers are the only groups at significant risk. No mention is made of heterosexual transmission of the AIDS virus. Furthermore, the short bibliography contains no citations more recent than 1988. While many articles show revision since the last edition, more attention could have been paid to currency. It is surprising to find no entry under global warming, a highly publicized issue in the past few years. The article on the greenhouse effect, a logical place for such discussion, was substantially the same as in the 1987 edition, and more appropriate information (although not necessarily more current) could be found only by skimming several articles on climatology and ozone. On the positive side, the massive eruption of Mount Pinatubo in mid-1991 is noted under the entry on volcanoes.

Beyond the text itself, a few bibliographies are not current, and some articles (e.g., Alzheimer's disease) need a bibliography; typically, however, the cited references are up-to-date and useful. Many list both technical and popular sources, a good decision in light of the varied audience. An entire volume is given over to an excellent and detailed index. Finally, the profuse use of illustrations (more than 13,000) is laudable. Although few color photographs are included, the two- and three-color drawings and diagrams serve well in clarifying the accompanying text.

As was mentioned in an earlier review (see ARBA 88, entry 1448), this set has few competitors in scope or quality. The *Encyclopedia of Physical Science and Technology* (see ARBA 88, entry 1445), another high-quality work, is more technical, has much longer articles, and omits the biological sciences. The McGraw-Hill set remains an excellent resource for school, college, and public libraries that can afford it. [R: RBB, 1 Sept 92, pp. 80-81; WLB, Sept 92, p. 116]—**Christopher W. Nolan**

1447. Messadie, Gerald. **Great Inventions through History.** New York, Chambers Kingfisher Graham, c1988, 1991. 237p. illus. index. $9.95pa. ISBN 0-550-17005-7.

1448. Messadie, Gerald. **Great Modern Inventions.** New York, Chambers Kingfisher Graham, c1988, 1991. 236p. illus. index. $9.95pa. ISBN 0-550-17001-4.

Companion pieces, these volumes are English translations of French works published in 1988. The first volume, *Great Inventions through History* (GIH), discusses inventions from ancient times to around 1850, although some topics are also addressed in the second volume, *Great Modern Inventions* (GMI), which covers 1850 to the present. The introduction to GIH states that its purpose is to contribute to a new history of technology, one that acknowledges technological advances before the Industrial Revolution. However, topics are not limited to technology in the strict sense of the word. For example, there are entries on trade unions and insurance, which make this work an eclectic, interesting overview of inventions as both physical and intellectual tools. For a more detailed, technological approach, one may prefer to consult sources such as the *Oxford Illustrated Encyclopedia of Inventions and Technology* (see index for entry number). The introduction to GMI is a bit more philosophical, emphasizing that a history of technology in the twentieth century must include a study of both its revolutionary benefits and its devastating consequences. Similar to the first volume, its content ranges from the highly technical (e.g., monocrystalline superconductors) to the everyday useful (e.g., milk chocolate).

Each volume contains more than 300 entries arranged within broad alphabetical categories. These categories differ only slightly between the two works and include agriculture and food; chemistry and physics; communication, culture, and the media; daily life; electronics and math; energy and mechanics; medicine and health; transportation; and warfare. Each section is prefaced by a brief introduction to the history of that particular category and the impact that its development has had on civilization. Individual entries vary in length but tend to be brief, well-written introductions to the history of a topic. They are preceded by the creator of the invention (many of whom in GIH are "anonymous"), a country or region, and a year or period in time. Entries contain terms highlighted in boldface type, which, according to GMI, indicate the principal stages that contributed to the invention. Unfortunately, GIH does not offer this explanatory note. In addition, these highlighted terms are not included in either index. Both volumes contain about 33 historical illustrations and photographs. However, in a work such as this, additional illustrations to complement the descriptive text would be particularly helpful. A list of references for further reading, which is not included, would also be valuable.

In general, these companion volumes offer a readable and interesting introduction to the history of inventions and, by extension, civilization. Recommended for all types of libraries that serve users with science needs. [R: LJ, 1 Nov 92, p. 76]—**Janice M. Griggs**

1449. Messadie, Gerald. **Great Scientific Discoveries.** New York, Chambers Kingfisher Graham, c1988, 1991. 237p. illus. index. $9.95pa. ISBN 0-550-17002-2.

This title is a translation of the original French edition published by Bordas in 1988. The selection of what discoveries to include in an encyclopedic guide for everyone is obviously a difficult task. The criterion in this book, which covers 120 discoveries, is that these important discoveries must affect not only pure science but also our collective knowledge and everyday life to some extent.

The discoveries cover scientific fields such as anthropology, astronomy, biology, chemistry, mathematics, medicine, and physics. Some examples are anesthesia, heavy water, and quasars. Each discovery description starts with the discovery topic, discoverer names and dates, and a brief descriptive phrase. This is followed by a short, detailed, narrative description of the circumstances that lead to, and the implications of, the discovery. Photographs and diagrams supplement the descriptions. A combined subject and discoverer index in the back help the reader locate the scientific items in the descriptions.

This is a useful little reference book for the general reader. It introduces users to the long, exciting, and circuitous route of scientific discoveries and gives them an appreciation of how these discoveries have improved our lives. [R: LJ, 1 Nov 92, p. 76] – **Anne C. Roess**

1450. **The New Book of Popular Science.** Lisa Holland, ed. Danbury, Conn., Grolier, 1992. 7v. illus. maps. index. $219.00/set. Q162.N437. 500. LC 91-38365. ISBN 0-7172-1218-1.

This set has undergone significant revision since the last edition (see ARBA 92, entry 1457). The editors have taken various criticisms into account and have completely updated the section on astronomy. Most articles have been heavily revamped or are completely new. There are now individual articles on all the planets, not just the first six, and they – as does the rest of the section – sport some lovely new photographs and illustrations. New entries in the section include one on collapsed and failed stars, three pieces on astronauts, and one titled "The Early Sky Watchers." Several articles, such as those on black holes and quasars, replace their outdated predecessors.

The rest of the set, which had fewer noticeable problems in the previous edition, has seen updating of some 65 articles. For example, information on 1991 volcanic eruptions in the Philippines and Japan has been incorporated into the article on such phenomena; all the statistics in the energy section have been made current, and the Kuwaiti oil fires are now covered; cold fusion is mentioned; and dental sealants, flossing, and dental implants are discussed in detail. Again, responding to reviewers' criticisms, the selected readings for each volume have been overhauled. While some older titles still appear, the majority now date from the mid-1980s to 1991 (although there must be some newer books on earthquakes than the two mentioned; they date from 1974 and 1975). Finally, the index (a separate paperback volume) has been reworked and is much more useful.

The editors of *The New Book of Popular Science* are to be commended for recognizing this set's problems and working so vigorously to correct them; they have made a merely excellent product outstanding. The changes are substantial enough that libraries with an earlier version, even the previous one, will want to seriously consider its purchase. The set can be recommended with confidence to school, public, and community college libraries. [R: RBB, 1 Oct 92, p. 370] – **D. A. Rothschild**

1451. **Oxford Illustrated Encyclopedia of Invention and Technology.** Monty Finniston and Christopher Bissell, eds. New York, Oxford University Press, 1992. 391p. illus. $49.95. ISBN 0-19-869138-6.

This work is the sixth volume of a proposed eight-volume set (see ARBA 91, entry 932; ARBA 90, entries 535-36; and ARBA 86, entries 58-59). Each volume is thematic, as noted in its title, and is meant to be self-contained. However, a separate index and ready-reference volume will eventually complete and unify the set, making terms much more accessible. (The *Invention and Technology* volume does not contain an index.) As stated in the foreword, the purpose of this volume is to present a broad conspectus of modern technology, although elements of primitive technologies, such as spears, are also represented. The number of entries on space technology is limited because a separate volume devoted to this topic is in publication and should appear shortly. Entries are brief, about 50 to 1,000 words, and are arranged alphabetically letter by letter, ignoring spaces, which can be disorienting. For example, the entry for electronic mail falls between the entries for electron beam and electron microscope. In addition to topical entries, approximately 150 extremely brief biographies of eminent technologists are included. The foreword notes that very few are women.

Cross-references and alternative names are noted with asterisks. However, boldface type would have made these terms easier to identify. In addition, cross-references are not given automatically, so the user's guide at the front of the volume advises readers to check for separate entries on topics of interest even if not marked with an asterisk—an annoying omission. Readers must also remember that this volume is a British publication and that entries are listed under British terms, such as "lift" and "aeroplane." There are no entries or cross-references for "elevator" and "airplane."

The volume is handsome and of first quality. The print is easy to read, and the color illustrations nicely complement the text, particularly in describing complicated processes or topics, such as integrated circuits. The intended audience does not need previous detailed knowledge on a subject, but the work appears to be most appropriate for secondary students and adults. As a single-volume source of brief information on technology topics, this work fulfills its purpose. For more detailed, in-depth coverage and lengthier entries, readers should consult works such as the *McGraw-Hill Encyclopedia of Science and Technology*, 7th ed. (McGraw-Hill, 1992), which also offer bibliographic references, a feature that the *Oxford Illustrated* omits. [R: RBB, 1 Dec 92, p. 690]—**Janice M. Griggs**

DIRECTORIES

1452. **Science Sources 1991**. Compiled by Office of Communications, American Association for the Advancement of Science, 1991. 162p. index. $12.00pa. ISBN 0-87168-399-7.

This directory is an updated version of the *Public Information Contact Directory, 1988-89* (see ARBA 90, entry 1433). According to the introduction, the new name reflects a broadening in scope (it would, however, have been better to retain the word *directory* in the title). Entries, which include addresses, telephone and fax numbers, and contact persons, are arranged by type of institution, such as federal agencies and laboratories or colleges and universities. Contacts listed at the institutions vary, but most are public relations or communications staff. Alphabetical and geographical indexes and a computer diskette (not seen) that replicates the content of the book in ASCII are included.

As was its predecessor, this edition is selective (*eclectic* might be more descriptive) in its content. Some areas are better represented than others; the list of museums is especially short and thus not very useful. This volume will be useful mainly to those in the communications fields, especially reporters and editors, who need to contact scientific institutions.—**Joseph Hannibal**

HANDBOOKS AND YEARBOOKS

1453. **Encyclopedia of Physical Science and Technology 1991 Yearbook**. Robert A. Meyers, ed. San Diego, Calif., Academic Press, 1991. 617p. index. $185.00. ISBN 0-12-226918-7. ISSN 0898-9842.

This is the third yearbook since the first (see ARBA 90, entry 1425) was published as a supplement to the *Encyclopedia of Physical Science and Technology* (see ARBA 88, entry 1445). The 1991 volume continues to report on important recent advances in the physical sciences and technology, with 39 signed articles by 45 scientists and engineers from universities, research institutes, and technical firms throughout the world. Each article covers a rapidly advancing field and follows the format of the parent encyclopedia: a glossary of terms, a table of contents, an introductory definition of the subject, a detailed discussion of the subject, and a bibliography.

Five of the articles appear in a featured article section based on their importance to the physical sciences and technology as well as their impact on related disciplines or recent exceptional expansion of theoretical data or engineering content. These articles cover cometary physics, parallel computing, microprocessor systems, electro-optics and computers in defense, and free-electron lasers. The remainder of the articles cover computer science and technology, computer-related electronics, military science, physics, chemistry, communications, gas turbine combustion, astronomy, and mathematics. A table of contents helps the reader select a specific topic. An added value is the cumulative subject index, which refers the reader to subjects covered in all three yearbooks. The yearbook's format is very appealing due to boldface headings and many diagrams, illustrations, and photographs.

This yearbook continues to reflect the high standards of scholarship set by the Executive and Editorial Advisory Boards. It is an excellent, useful addition to the literature of the physical sciences and technology. — **Anne C. Roess**

1454. Glover, Thomas J., comp. **Pocket Ref.** Morrison, Colo., Sequoia Publishing, c1989, 1992. 480p. index. $9.95pa. LC 89-90848. ISBN 0-9622359-0-3.

As the name indicates, this is a pocket-sized book. The contents lean toward the applied sciences and industrial trades, although there is a general information section. There are numerous conversion tables and broader sections that cover areas such as electrical, chemical, geological, plumbing, and surveying and mapping. One can also refer to the book for information on such topics as computer ASCII codes, minerals sorted by hardness, windchill factors, element properties, and other information that can be presented in a table format. There are an index, a page in the beginning to record personal information, and four blank pages in the back for notes.

Given the work's small size and personal orientation, it is not an ideal acquisition for libraries unless there is a specific need for this information and provision is made to keep the book at the reference desk. For trade specialists, it will prove both handy and valuable. — **Byron P. Anderson**

1455. **The Henry Holt Handbook of Current Science & Technology: A Sourcebook of Facts and Analysis....** By Bryan Bunch. New York, Henry Holt, 1992. 689p. index. $50.00. Q158.5.B86. 500. LC 92-6119. ISBN 0-8050-1829-8.

The effort needed by scientists and the scientifically literate to keep up with current advances in science and technology is prodigious. This book provides a comprehensive review and analysis of the current state of research and discovery in the fields of astronomy and space, chemistry, earth science, environmental issues, life science, mathematics, physics, and technology. For each topic there is a short essay on the overall state of the science through the early 1990s. This is followed by a timetable of the major developments in the field. The main body of the book has topics, articles, and subtopics that summarize recent advances as reported in the popular scientific press, with appropriate references. For the newer and more complex developments, a short background essay is frequently given. There are also tables and charts. Appendixes list some selected books for further reference, 1990-1991 obituaries of scientists, and various units of measurement. An extensive index rounds out the book. For its sheer volume and information content, this book may prove to be one of the outstanding science reference books of the year. Scientists, science writers, reference librarians, and anyone interested in current science and technology will find it a valuable addition to their work shelf. [R: RBB, 15 Dec 92, pp. 762-63] — **Robert J. Havlik**

1456. Tanford, Charles, and Jacqueline Reynolds. **The Scientific Traveler: A Guide to the People, Places, and Institutions of Europe.** New York, John Wiley, 1992. 335p. illus. maps. index. $16.95pa. Q127.E8T36. 509.4. LC 92-5489. ISBN 0-471-55566-5.

This is a traveler's guide to sites of scientific interest across Europe, from England to Poland and Russia. It is not a guide in the "quick look-up" sense; it has a chatty, narrative style. The authors are both well-known scientists who love travel and scientific history.

The book is divided into sections, each one devoted to a country. A section starts with a brief map and an overview of the scientific highlights for the whole country, some quite lengthy and interesting. Following the overview is a section of principal places to visit, which can be towns, regions, or institutions. Descriptions of these are also in a narrative style and are very educational. Countries can be found in the contents pages, and there are indexes for names, places, and subjects. Some black-and-white photographs are scattered throughout the book.

This easy-to-use guide will be useful in general collections where people who are new to the sciences can get brief historical information. It will also make excellent reading for armchair travelers. Because it deals with only the highlights of scientific achievements and is not an in-depth book, it probably will not serve well in a historical collection. — **Lillian R. Mesner**

INDEXES

1457. **Applied Science & Technology Index.** (Indexing coverage: 10/83-8/27/92). [CD-ROM]. Bronx, N.Y., H. W. Wilson, 1992. Hardware requirements: WILSONLINE Workstation, IBM PC, or compatible; 640K; hard disk drive. $1,495.00.

This CD-ROM index includes about 400 periodicals in most engineering disciplines and the applied science portions of such fields as chemistry, geology, mathematics, physics, and food science. The selection of periodicals for inclusion is accomplished by a vote of subscribers to the service. In addition, the index attempts to be "balanced" in its coverage of all applied science fields. Language coverage is English only. The disc may be searched in three modes: BROWSE, WILSEARCH, and WILSONLINE.

Installation of the software was uneventful and consisted of largely following a series of screen prompts. The software requires an IBM-compatible machine that runs DOS 3.1 (or higher), a minimum of 640K installed (more would be nice) with 487K free memory, at least 2 MB of free hard disk storage space, and a CD-ROM player (MS-DOS CD-ROM Extensions is not required for a Hitachi, Sony, or Philips player). If users run out of machine memory during installation, they can check the CONFIG.SYS file to see if additional space can be freed up (the memory stack should be set to 0,0). Installation documentation is good (but not exhaustive), with a number of online diagnostics to aid in troubleshooting a system. A toll-free technical support help desk is available. This reviewer's experience with the support desk was very favorable; questions were answered promptly and material needed was sent quickly. Inexperienced CD-ROM installers should find a helping hand here.

When the Wilson search engine was first introduced, it was greeted by a large groan from a number of librarians who were reluctant to learn yet another searching system. As CD-ROM search systems have become more prevalent, the various differences between the search engines have become more accepted in the reference community. Each engine has librarians that feel it is the best and the brightest search system around; however, every system has its drawbacks. The Wilson subject BROWSE mode is fast, easy to learn, and lets one look at the online thesaurus. The patron, however, will miss some entries in this mode. For example, in a search for the word "Sputnik," the BROWSE mode turned up no entries, while there are, in fact, three subject and three title entries under this heading on the disc. The WILSEARCH mode takes a little more time to learn and is basically a proprietary search engine that enables one to look at extended search fields, such as SIC (Standard Industrial Classification) code, journal name, title, and personal name. Using this method to search for "Agent Orange," some 36 entries were retrieved. Looking for the same term in the BROWSE mode retrieved 159 entries (with cross-references to Dioxin). Searching in the WILSEARCH mode for "Agent Orange" or "Dioxin" produced only 31 entries, a reduction of five. (Boolean logic is not used in the WILSEARCH mode.)

The final mode available for the Wilson CD-ROM indexes is the WILSONLINE search engine. It is similar to some other well-known online search service commands. Here one can do commands such as truncation, neighboring, expanding, and Boolean logic. This is also the mode one would use to search the online versions of the Wilson indexes by modem dialup to Wilson in New York. Wilson also provides what they call their "Journal Holdings Manager," which enables librarians to insert on the display screen fixed holdings information for their library. Typical screens include the name of the Wilson index, the dates the disc covers, and the search term used (when in the BROWSE mode). The screens are well designed and well thought out.

The quality of the Wilson database is excellent, and cross-references are frequent, enabling searchers to locate references with a minimum of applied vocabulary, always a help for reference librarians working in the sciences. Most libraries will benefit from patron use of this CD-ROM index as it is faster and easier to use than the printed versions. Highly recommended. – **Ralph Lee Scott**

1458. **Biological & Agricultural Index.** (Indexing coverage: 7/83-6/25/92). [CD-ROM]. Bronx, N.Y., H. W. Wilson, 1992. Hardware requirements: WILSONLINE Workstation, IBM PC, or compatible; 640K; hard disk drive. $1,495.00.

The Biological and Agricultural Index (BAI) is a useful CD-ROM index for general purposes. Its intended audience ranges from undergraduates to experienced researchers. The index covers all agricultural and biological topics, including veterinary medicine, but it indexes only 225 of the major biological and agricultural journals, about one-third of them strictly agricultural. None are popular, so that topics such as the Gaia hypothesis are better searched in the General Science Index (GSI), also published by Wilson (see index for entry number), as GSI covers popular science magazines. It is a good idea to search GSI for other biological topics as well because BAI does not cover general science journals such as *Science* and *Nature*. It and the other Wilson indexes do cover book reviews as well as articles, which can be useful for helping patrons find books about a subject in the absence of other online resources. However, this feature can be bothersome when looking for articles alone. It is possible, but not easy, to eliminate the book reviews.

The WILSONDISC Version 2.4 search software is designed for novice end-users. It is easily installed and has no unusual hardware requirements, although a modem and telephone line are required to do online searching of updates. These updates are available to subscribers to BAI on CD-ROM and the other Wilson databases (although the disc is updated monthly, so the online updates may not be needed by the typical user). The CD-ROM screens are uncluttered and easy to read. There are three search levels: BROWSE (browse subject headings), WILSEARCH (fill in screen with key words), and WILSONLINE (command mode); these are explained in the review of GSI. There are some interesting assumptions underlying the software. For instance, the print default in the install program only allows printing in blocks of 10 citations, up to a limit of 100 (of course, this can be changed). Most other CD-ROM printing defaults are much more liberal. Other WILSONDISC software quirks include implicit "anding" of all terms unless specifically told otherwise and the rather simplistic rule of always truncating any word ending in *s*. All of these tactics make sense for novice end-users but may be less welcome to more experienced searchers.

The indexing of BAI is rather minimal. Each article is given no more than three or four subject headings, some rather broad. There are no abstracts, which further limits retrieval. The lack of true phrase searching can be troublesome when trying to search by genus and species, although in most cases "anding" the names will lead to only a few false hits.

All in all, the BAI is just what the doctor ordered for novice end-users up to the undergraduate level. The limited indexing and coverage make it less useful for graduate students and researchers. For most topics, it is a good idea to search both the GSI and BAI as there is very little overlap and many excellent articles in general periodicals may be missed by searching BAI only. **– Diane Schmidt**

1459. **General Science Index: Vol. 14, No.7.** Bronx, N.Y., H. W. Wilson, 1992. 503p. sold on service basis. ISSN 0162-1963.

This venerable reference tool has changed little since it was last extensively reviewed (see ARBA 88, entry 1453). The number of periodicals monitored has dropped from 113 to 107, but the indexing features have remained constant. Although sold on a service basis, there is a minimum annual subscription cost of $160.

While the layperson will find a surprising amount of information, it is recommended that other scientific and technical indexing sources should also be consulted for thorough coverage. These would include, but not be limited to, the other Wilson technical indexes, as well as more specialized ones such as *Chemical Abstracts, Science Citation Index*, and those covering foreign-language materials.

– Andrew G. Torok

1460. **General Science Index.** (Indexing coverage: 5/84-6/25/92). [CD-ROM]. Bronx, N.Y., H. W. Wilson, 1992. Hardware requirements: WILSONLINE Workstation, IBM PC, or compatible; 640K; hard disk drive. $1,295.00.

Wilson's *General Science Index* (GSI) is well known in its paper incarnation. According to the publisher, GSI covers all scientific areas, including medicine, chemistry, astronomy, physics, and biology. It is designed for use by nonspecialists at all levels, from high school students on up. It indexes only 140 periodicals (up from 102 prior to 1992), but the selection is very good. The materials range from popular science magazines, such as *Science News*, to major journals, such as *Bulletin of the Atomic Scientists*. Coverage of topics of general interest, such as the effects of Mount Pinatubo's eruption, is generally good. It is possible to locate more esoteric topics, but the small number of journals indexed limits GSI's usefulness for such searches.

The search software used by the GSI is Wilson's WILSONDISC version 2.4, which is easily installed. The installation guide is reasonably clear and useful, although the helpline number is not included in it. The system requirements are quite normal. The WILSONDISC search software has three search levels: BROWSE (browse subject headings), WILSEARCH (fill in screen with key words), and WILSONLINE (command mode). The BROWSE mode is the simplest and least flexible. WILSEARCH allows the most flexibility while still providing structure, as it allows Boolean logic within a field structure. The command mode is reasonably flexible and easy to use as well, although the WILSEARCH mode is best for most users. There are a few oddities in the software, most due to a simplification of the search process. In the WILSEARCH mode, all terms or fields are combined with *and* unless otherwise indicated, and in order to combine terms with *or*, the line must begin with either *any* or *or*, such as "or cat kitten felis." Another search quirk is that the system automatically truncates any word ending in S, so *felis* also retrieves *felig* and *felix*. Also, phrase searches can only be done on subject headings. A plus for the database is the Quick Reference Guide booklet provided with the GSI. It is clear and easy to understand and includes most of the information that a user needs. WILSONDISC also has a Journal Holdings Manager component, which allows a library to note those journals that are held locally. The holdings were simple but tedious to mark, and considerable flexibility is allowed in creating messages. This feature is very useful and timesaving for patrons at all levels.

Aside from a few quirks in the software, the biggest problem with the database is its indexing. Each article has no more than three or four subject headings, which are not standard across Wilson's databases. In some cases, the headings are so general that they are almost useless. There are no abstracts, which also limits retrieval.

All caveats aside, there is no question that the *General Science Index* has its place in most libraries. The broad coverage of subjects and the mix of general interest and technical periodicals make it a natural for libraries up to the undergraduate level. Libraries catering to advanced researchers will find the database less useful, simply because of the small number of journals covered and the unsophisticated indexing. – **Diane Schmidt**

1461. Pilger, Mary Anne. **Science Experiments Index for Young People Update 91.** Englewood, Colo., Libraries Unlimited, 1992. 133p. (Libraries Unlimited Data Book). $21.00. ISBN 0-87287-858-9.

Complementing the original volume, this book updates and expands *Science Experiments Index for Young People* (see ARBA 89, entry 1359) by indexing 328 additional titles from 1964 to 1991. Intended as a companion publication, the entry numbers continue where the original volume left off. The basic format remains essentially the same, with two welcome additions: cross-references in the experiment subject index have been added, and in the book index a space has been provided for the insertion of local call numbers. Although not specifically noted, cross-references are intended to lead to entries in the original volume as well. Both volumes are recommended as welcome titles for reference collections. [R: WLB, May 92, p. 129] – **Sarah A. Freegard**

1462. **Science Fair Project Index 1985-1989: For Grades K-8.** Cynthia Bishop, Katherine Ertle, and Karen Zeleznik, eds. Metuchen, N.J., Scarecrow, 1992. 555p. $47.50. Q182.3.S34. 016.5078. LC 92-22221. ISBN 0-8108-2555-4.

Suppose a student wants to undertake an exploration of fog for a science fair project. A parent or teacher could show the student how to search through the numerous books about such projects and experiments. Or the adult could begin with this index. Using Library of Congress subject headings, the editors have prepared a topical guide to science fair projects and experiments. For example, a user who looks up *volcano* will find a cross-reference to *rocks—igneous*. Ample cross-indexing helps the user make connections (e.g., compost to humus and the reverse). This is the third supplement in a series of indexes. The original volume spanned 1960-1972. All except 10 of the books included were published between 1985 and 1989. For the most part, the entries point to projects in science and technology; experiments in psychology, investigations in sociology and behavior, and activities deemed crafts are not included. Young readers will need assistance with the guide for two reasons: projects are not indexed according to suitability by grade level, and some of the materials that serve as integral parts of projects (e.g., acetone, acetic acid, naphthalene) should be used with caution. Stretching from abacus to yo-yo, and including Lotus 1-2-3, the volume will serve not only those who seek a project to replicate or amplify but also those who would like to make a quick assessment of what has not been done recently or often. — **Diane M. Calabrese**

PERIODICALS AND SERIALS

1463. Kronick, David A., comp. **Scientific and Technical Periodicals of the Seventeenth and Eighteenth Centuries: A Guide.** Metuchen, N.J., Scarecrow, 1991. 332p. index. $39.50. Z7403.K76. 016.505. LC 91-32012. ISBN 0-8108-2492-2.

This book contains a list of 1,858 scientific and technical periodicals extant in the seventeenth and eighteenth centuries. The majority of these were published in Europe, although entries from other parts of the world are included as well. The selections represent a broad range of scientific disciplines, from agriculture and anatomy to zoology, including such fields as commerce, economics, and the military. In addition to the listings, which occupy 252 pages, there are useful indexes of subjects, titles, and personal and institutional names. The compiler has been careful to indicate where each periodical can currently be found. In this way the book may be especially helpful to those interested in this important period of scientific and technological development. [R: WLB, Apr 92, p. 126] — **John U. Trefny**

30 Agricultural Sciences

GENERAL WORKS

1464. Axtell, B. L. **Minor Oil Crops.** Rome, FAO of the United Nations; distr., Lanham, Md., UNIPUB, 1992. 241p. illus. (FAO Agricultural Services Bulletin, 94). $25.00pa. ISBN 92-5-103128-2.

Minor Oil Crops covers approximately 50 minor food and nonfood oil crops. Information furnished for the crops includes scientific and common names; description; main uses; cultivation; harvesting; oil composition; and postharvest handling, including oil extraction methods if known. The length of the entry for each crop varies considerably as little scientific and technical information is readily available for some of the crops. For example, the entry for macadamia nuts is seven pages long, while the tonka bean is covered in scarcely more than one page. A short bibliography is included at the end of each entry. Some of the bibliographies do not have complete citations, which could make a few of the cited sources difficult to find. There is no subject index, but a table of contents appears at the front of the volume.

The preface indicates that minor crops such as the ones included in this publication could provide new market opportunities for developing countries. Due to the interest in alternative crops in the United States, *Minor Oil Crops* may also be of value to agriculture and food researchers in that country.
—**William H. Wiese**

1465. Bourke, D. O'D. **French-English Agricultural Dictionary with English-French Index.** Wallingford, England, C. A. B. International; distr., Tucson, Arizona, University of Arizona Press, 1992. 293p. $85.50. ISBN 0-85198-767-2.

This dictionary contains more than 20,000 entries that emanate from France and other francophone countries. The term *agriculture* has been interpreted in its widest sense to include agronomy, animal husbandry, agricultural engineering, animal and plant diseases, agricultural economics, soil science, statistics, parasites, weeds, and horticulture. Its scope has been broadened to include current developments in computerization, farm forestry, rural recreation and tourism, ecology, and such activities as fish farming and snail farming.

The simple style of the *French-English Agricultural Dictionary* is clear and easy to use. Gender of words is given throughout. Indications have been inserted mostly where there is a risk of confusion. Nouns are not usually indicated, except where a distinction has to be made between singular and plural or when identical words can be used as both adjectives and nouns (e.g., bovine). Recommended for reference collections in public, academic, or agricultural libraries and for agronomists, researchers, administrators, farmers, and those concerned with overseas aid.—**Marilynn Green**

1466. **Commodity Review and Outlook 1990-91.** Rome, FAO of the United Nations; distr., Lanham, Md., UNIPUB, 1991. 150p. (FAO Economic and Social Development Series, no.49). $45.00pa. ISBN 92-5-103011-1.

The Food and Agriculture Organization of the United Nations is concerned with all aspects of food and fiber production throughout the world. The periodic compilation and publication of statistical summaries of commodities, as in this work, help assess the recent past and provide a basis for decisions. National and international policy-makers judge progress and formulate new policies from such data based on their independent determinations as to the causes that drive the data and the effects that changes are expected to make. This text provides an overview and an outlook by commodity, which consists primarily of production, price, export, and import data on products that range from bananas to wine and animal hides to saw logs. Commodity data is typically summarized over the past five years. Weather, fertilizers, and prices are briefly discussed, but other major factors, such as the rice integrated pest management program in Indonesia, are not. The compilation appears thorough and useful.

— **Marvin K. Harris**

1467. **Elsevier's Dictionary of Aquaculture: In Six Languages: English, French, Spanish, German, Italian and Latin.** Cheryl E. Marx, comp. New York, Elsevier Science Publishing, 1991. 454p. $157.00. SH201.E46. 639'.8'03. LC 91-25973. ISBN 0-444-88663-X.

After a succinct explanation of how the 4,553 terms were selected for this volume, Marx leaps ahead to provide their French, Spanish, German, and Italian equivalents. Latin binomials, or scientific names, are given for most species; the Latin names for most higher taxa are also included. The body of the dictionary offers English access. Entries in separate indexes for the other languages are cross-referenced to the English words by numbers. Cognates abound, of course. Who would not recognize *Gallenstein* as gallstone? But one can imagine a user with little facility in Italian trying to quickly interpret table headings: *larghezza* could be translated easily to width or breadth and *lunghezza* to length. Even so, entry selection might have been explained more fully. For example, *octopus* is included; *jellyfish* is not. *Worm, polyp*, and cnidospores are included; *medusa* and *starfish* are not. And, perhaps because birds have only minimal interactions at aquaculture sites, *egret* is one of the few such creatures included. In general, however, aquaculturists will have in a single and visually pleasing volume information they could only find with several scientific dictionaries at hand. — **Diane M. Calabrese**

1468. Herren, Ray V., and Roy L. Donahue. **The Agriculture Dictionary.** Albany, N.Y., Delmar, 1991. 553p. illus. $24.95; $17.95pa. S411.H47. 630'.3. LC 90-45709. ISBN 0-8273-4095-8; 0-8273-4097-4pa.

This work has more than 10,000 words with relatively succinct definitions but no aids to pronunciation. The terms have been drawn from 18 disciplines. The definition of *British Thermal Unit* includes a thoughtful conversion to calories; *square* is also defined as an "unopened flower bud of cotton" in addition to flooring, roofing, and tool usages. Abundant illustrations appear in the margins.

Criticisms of commission and omission are inevitable. "Specie," used in the preface, is properly spelled in the dictionary. *Abaxial* is defined, but *adaxial* is not included. *Pyrene* appears in defining *nut* but not as a separate entry. *Tolerance* is poorly defined as an "acquired ability of an animal or insect to take poison without ill effects." (The ability is innate, rather than acquired, and not exclusive to animals; it includes plants exposed to herbicides, for example.) *Pesticide resistance* is not defined, nor is *placebo, biomagnification, lifter*, or *diamondback moth*; however, *harlequin bug* is presented as "the most important enemy of cabbage" in the southern United States. (Maybe this was true 40 years ago.) Still, while pedants from the 18 disciplines certainly will find shortcomings in their specialty areas, this work has a wealth of useful information and is a good starting place for definitions of agricultural terms. — **Marvin K. Harris**

1469. Rehm, Sigmund, and Gustav Espig. **The Cultivated Plants of the Tropics and Subtropics: Cultivation, Economic Value, Utilization.** Weikersheim, Germany, Margraf; distr., Lanham, Md., UNIPUB, 1991. 552p. illus. index. $38.00. ISBN 3-8236-1169-0.

The increased demand and interest in plants for food, spice, medicine, and commodities for export has contributed to a proliferation of books dealing with tropical crops. This source includes more than 1,000 cultivated plants arranged by usage (e.g., starch, oil, vegetables, beverages and stimulants, dyes, spices, fibers, resins, waxes). Each chapter begins with a review of the specific uses, production, and economics of the plant group. Oil plants, for example, are compared for nutritional value, fatty acid composition, methods of extraction, and human usage. Individual plants are then described in one to several pages. Their botany and morphology, breeding, and ecophysiology are discussed. Cultivation, diseases, harvest, processing, and production are also treated. Although brief, the descriptions are well written. The bibliography contains more than 2,000 references for more in-depth description. Minor crops are treated with tables and shorter descriptions. Excellent illustrations and a comprehensive index add to the book's usefulness.

Comparison with J. W. Purseglove's excellent two-volume *Tropical Crops* (John Wiley, 1986) is natural. These volumes, arranged by family, provide more extensive treatment of individual crops. The arrangement by plant usage of Rehm and Espig's work makes for convenient and easy access to plants as products. It will be useful for both academic and public libraries. — **T. McKimmie**

FOOD SCIENCES AND TECHNOLOGY

Bibliography

1470. Ostroff, Harriet, and Tom Nichols. **Specialty Cookbooks: A Subject Guide. Volume I.** Hamden, Conn., Garland, 1992. 659p. index. (Garland Reference Library of the Humanities, v.1297). $90.00. Z5776.G2.O84. 016.6415. LC 91-37398. ISBN 0-8240-6947-1.

The increased number of specialty cookbooks published over the last decade reflects the interest our diverse society has in food and cooking. In this guide the authors provide a comprehensive index to 4,500 English-language books published between 1980 and 1990 in the United States, Canada, the United Kingdom, and other English-speaking countries. The subject index is divided into four sections: specific ingredients (e.g., apples), type of dish or courses (e.g., appetizers), specific meals (e.g., bag lunches), and special cooking techniques (e.g., stir-fry). In each section is an alphabetical list of subjects. Listed under each subject by entry number are citations in chronological order by publication date, then alphabetically by title within the specified year. The full citations are given, and in some cases a brief description is included with the entry. Children's cookbooks are entered at the end of the particular topic. Cookbooks that cover more than one topic are listed in only one category but are cross-referenced by entry number to the other pertinent categories. Broader and narrower topics are also cross-referenced at the end of a specific topic. Users will find the author and title indexes for all the citations an added plus. Although the quality of the titles was not a consideration for inclusion in the index — thus limiting its use for collection development — an attempt was made to include books currently in print. Ostroff and Nichols, both librarians, give complete user instructions and professional advice in obtaining the cookbooks via libraries, bookstores, various literary sources, publishers, and authors.

General, ethnic, and regional cookbooks, along with some specialized categories, are not included. Works on special diets, equipment, and other such needs are also not in this volume but are planned for inclusion in volume 2. The serious researcher, collector, or culinary novice will find this source useful and fun to browse. [R: Choice, Nov 92, p. 448; RBB, 1 Dec 92, p. 692; WLB, Nov 92, p. 96]
— **Jennie S. Johnson**

1471. Shih, Tian-Chu. **Health-Related Cookbooks: A Bibliography.** Metuchen, N.J., Scarecrow, 1991. 401p. index. $42.50. Z6665.D53S54. 016.6158'54. LC 91-38133. ISBN 0-8108-2513-9.

This unusual bibliography includes a wide range of health-related cookbooks instead of a list of cookbooks devoted to a single subject (e.g., diabetes). The list is also eclectic, as it contains "authoritative" books as well as vanity press books and government publications. Shih, who is a librarian, has an amazing number of entries (1,092) for the time periods covered. She has limited popular topics, such as low-fat cooking, to the years 1980-1991. More uncommon topics cover the years from 1970 to the present. Subject coverage is divided into two sections. The first covers specific diseases or disorders (e.g., cancer, hypertension, obesity), and the second deals with diets for general health and the life stages. Each section begins with comments on a particular disease condition and the nutritional ramifications. These are all documented in a bibliography of references at the end of the book. At the end of each chapter there is a list of selected associations and foundations for each category. The table of contents directs the reader to the main sections, and detailed chapter outlines take readers to specific topics of cookbooks. Author, title, and keyword indexes conclude the book, along with a directory of selected cookbook publishers.

Shih mentions in her foreword that comprehensiveness was not her main focus, which explains omissions such as Mollie Katzen's books or the classic *Laura's Kitchen*. However, the bibliography will be a good addition to public libraries or any library that supports a dietary or food service program. [R: Choice, July/Aug 92, p. 1661; RBB, 1 June 92, p. 1775; RQ, Fall 92, pp. 114-15] — **Lillian R. Mesner**

1472. Vassilian, Hamo B., ed. **Ethnic Cookbooks and Food Marketplace: A Complete Bibliographic Guide & Directory to Armenian, Iranian, Afghan, Israeli Middle Eastern, North African and Greek Foods in the U.S.A. & Canada.** 3d ed. Glendale, Calif., Armenian Reference Books, 1992. 144p. illus. $29.95pa. TX725.M628V37. 380.1'456415956'025. LC 92-16356. ISBN 0-931539-06-4.

A combination bibliography and directory, this book offers broad coverage of English-language cookbooks and United States and Canadian businesses that specialize in Armenian, Persian, Middle Eastern, Israeli, Afghan, and Greek foods. Part 1 is a bibliography that includes entries for about 275 cookbooks with author, title, and subject access. Copyright dates range from 1948 to 1992. Part 2, "Ethnic Food Marketplaces in the U.S. and Canada," lists 2,300 businesses and is subdivided by categories such as bakers, caterers, grocers, nightclubs, and restaurants. The directory information is reorganized by company name in part 3 and by geographic location in part 4.

All types of libraries serving the food industry, gourmet cooks, and ethnic food enthusiasts will find the information both useful and extensive. Perhaps in the next edition, the editor will take the bibliography a step further and provide brief annotations for book entries and an index.

— **Ahmad Gamaluddin**

Dictionaries and Encyclopedias

1473. Hui, Y. H., ed. **Encyclopedia of Food Science and Technology.** New York, John Wiley, 1992. 4v. illus. index. $495.00/set. TP368.2.E62. 664'.003. LC 91-22434. ISBN 0-471-50541-2.

This impressive set brings together a wide range of data on foods and food processing. As noted in the foreword, this information has previously been scattered and written only for the scientist. This set is usable by any level of student or practitioner.

An editorial board of scientists have chosen the subjects for inclusion and directed the projects. The encyclopedia is made up of more than 380 articles, some quite lengthy, written by experts. Each article is signed and has its own bibliography. The topics are divided into three main groups: basic and applied sciences, such as chemistry or biology; processing technology, engineering, and 23-unit operations (e.g., extrusion of snack foods); and food laws and regulations. Within these areas is a lot of information. The set can be used as a regular encyclopedia by looking up topics alphabetically. This works for broader topics, but an extensive and excellent index at the end of the fourth volume is really the key to finding information in the articles.

This is an important work in the field of food technology. Its audience will range from the scientist to the layperson. It would be an important addition to laboratories and offices as well as to academic or public libraries. [R: Choice, Sept 92, p. 76] — **Lillian R. Mesner**

1474. Johnson, Hugh. **Hugh Johnson's Pocket Encyclopedia of Wine 1992.** New York, Fireside Books/Simon & Schuster, 1991. 207p. maps. $11.95. ISBN 0-671-73841-0.

This perennial favorite just seems to get better and better each year (it was first published in 1977). There are thumbnail sketches of more than 5,000 wines from around the world. Also provided are informative overviews on each wine-producing country, wine type, chateau (in France), and vintage. There are comments on the 1990 vintage (a good year in each country), a series of maps, a current guide to wine labeling, and an updated chart for what to drink in 1992. Wine and food accompaniments are given as well.

Unfortunately, there are two difficulties for readers in North America. Johnson goes out of his way to criticize the "100-point-system" as used by Robert Parker and *Wine Spectator* magazine. There is nothing better, and there is nothing more computer-oriented, if one was to do a search, than to rank a wine out of 100 points. Using stars or adjectives (e.g., excellent, good, ordinary) just does not work. The other difficulty relates to wines of the Northeast. Johnson claims that the book has been fully revised, with new material on East Europe, South America, and Texas. If so, then why is there not an update on the Niagara/Finger Lake regions of Canada and New York State? The one and a half pages supplied contain misinformation and are outdated, and wineries are given short shrift. Where are the eisweins, the chardonnays, and the rieslings? It is hoped that the book will improve such coverage with the 1993 edition. Still, it is a good bargain for the price. — **Dean Tudor**

1475. Kurmann, Joseph A., Jeremija Lj. Rasic, and Manfred Kroger. **Encyclopedia of Fermented Fresh Milk Products: An International Inventory of Fermented Milk, Cream, Buttermilk, Whey, and Related Products.** New York, Van Nostrand Reinhold, 1992. 368p. $94.95. SF275.C84K87. 637'.1. LC 91-30210. ISBN 0-442-00869-4.

This book is a modern, worldwide view of milk fermentation. Four hundred entries on both traditional and nontraditional fermented milk products and by-products are listed by their English names or translations; their French and German equivalents, including different spellings and regional synonyms; and trade names. Important characteristics of these edibles are listed, such as country or area of origin, types of production (including both nondefined cultures and defined microflora), types of milk utilized, preparation, how the product is used, organoleptic properties, details of product description, history, manufacturing, food value, chemical composition, significance to health, related products, and references. The manuscript is well written and easy to read; it is amazing how much information is packed into this document. The appendixes include conversion tables, products by region, products by milk type and by starter culture, products by food value and health claims, general subjects, and a glossary of technical terms. No other comprehensive work in this area is available. It should be interesting to food scientists, dairy technologists, nutritionists, public health personnel, regulatory officials, educators, physicians, students, historians, and anyone concerned with fermentation or milk products.
— **Herbert W. Ockerman**

1476. Netzer, Corinne T. **The Corinne T. Netzer Encyclopedia of Food Values.** New York, Dell Publishing, 1992. 903p. $25.00. TX551.N42. 641.1. LC 91-36727. ISBN 0-440-50367-1.

This reviewer's first question about this book concerns the author's authority in the field of nutrition. The only mention found is on the book jacket, where Netzer is called "America's most trusted authority on the nutrient content of food." Further examination shows that she has written seven other "counter" books, such as calorie counters. She may not need any credentials in nutrition, however, because her "source list" at the end of the book lists the USDA Handbook No. 8 (the classic in this field); Agriculture Handbook No. 456, which was written in 1975; two government documents from Japan and the Caribbean; and a statement that "data for all brand-name foods were obtained from manufacturers, producers, and suppliers." Essentially, what Netzer has done is repackage free government information with some data from the private sector.

The book has three basic sections after the requisite introduction about what the basic nutrients are. The first section is called "food values" and covers calories, protein, carbohydrates, total fat, saturated fat, cholesterol, sodium, and fiber. The second section, much smaller, covers the most well-known vitamins (A, six of the B complexes, and C; no D or E). The third section, also small, details eight minerals.

The foreword says that the book contains "all the information currently available." Her list of sources, however, gives dates from the 1970s on a number of her sections of Agriculture Handbook No. 8. There are much more recent revisions of the handbooks (a few of her handbooks are from the middle and late 1980s), as the USDA is constantly revising them. As far as the nutrient values provided by the private sector go, be aware that the food industry has a reputation for being less than candid about what is in their foods.

This is a good nutrient guide book for consumers. Its advantages lie in the commercial and non-U.S. foods that have been added to the lists. Netzer has also used portions that are easily understood (not the 100-gram portions used by the USDA). The book is designed in an easy alphabetical list with good cross-references. This encyclopedia is appropriate for public libraries and some

two-year programs that include food curricula. The book is not recommended for professionals, however. Handbook No. 8 is much more complete and particular in the nutrients covered.
—**Lillian R. Mesner**

Directories

1477. **North American Brewers Resource Directory 1992-93.** Compiled by the Institute for Brewing Studies. David Edgar, ed. Boulder, Colo., Brewers, 1992. 345p. index. $80.00pa. ISBN 0-937381-30-6.

This is a great resource tool, well worth the price for anyone seriously interested in beer and for all libraries that serve such clientele (including food and hospitality academic programs). It reviews the beer-related events of 1991, covering regional and large breweries, imported beer, microbreweries, and brewpubs (micro-microbreweries that sell draft beer through a tavern operation). The beer and brewery statistics cover new and closed operations, taxable production (subdivided by type of establishment and by United States or Canada), and world beer production. The regulatory agencies are listed with all relevant names and addresses. Other topics in this tool include lists of continuing education courses; a bibliography; a section on libraries; a lexicon of beer styles; lists of associations and consultants; equipment manufacturers; a beer brand chart (which company makes what beer); and a suppliers' directory for malt, hops, yeast, packaging, and marketing.

There are indexes to microbreweries and brewpubs in both Canada and the United States, as well as indexes to regional and large brewers. Here are names and addresses, dates of founding, capacity, names of important technical personnel, and the like. The Canadian material is separate from, but adjacent to, the United States counterparts. A quick check of the Canadian facts and figures shows that this material is indeed up-to-date and correct. —**Dean Tudor**

Handbooks and Yearbooks

1478. Bencini, Marina Carcea. **Post-harvest and Processing Technologies of African Staple Foods: A Technical Compendium.** Rome, FAO of the United Nations; distr., Lanham, Md., UNIPUB, 1991. 354p. (FAO Agricultural Services Bulletin, 89). $40.00pa. ISBN 92-5-103076-6.

This compendium summarizes statistical agricultural information available on traditional African staple food crops and evaluates the preservation and reduction of postharvest losses in each commodity. It also evaluates pest control and gives an overview of commerce and trading in the commodities listed. Crops are categorized under the headings of cereal, food legumes (pulses), fruits and vegetables, roots and tubers, and oil seed. Each section is subdivided into an introduction, statistical aspects, agricultural aspects, postharvest treatment, primary processing, and secondary processing. The appendixes give a collection of African recipes and statistical information for different crops. The book is well written, well referenced, and full of factual information that is available from no other source. The author is an African food expert. The book should be of interest to anyone who is a student of Africa or food. —**Herbert W. Ockerman**

1479. **Codex Alimentarius. Volume One: General Requirements.** Rome, FAO of the United Nations and World Health Organization; distr., Lanham, Md., UNIPUB, 1992. 337p. $60.00pa. ISBN 92-5-103120-7.

The *Codex Alimentarius* establishes world food standards aimed at protecting the health of consumers and facilitating international trade in foods. This collection of standards includes those for all principal foods, whether processed, semiprocessed, or raw. It also provides information on hygiene and nutritional quality, including microbiological norms, provision for food additives, pesticides, residues, contaminants, labeling, and methods of analysis and sampling. There is advisory information on codes of practice, guidelines, and recommended procedures. Volume 1 of 14, this work covers general requirements divided into general principles of the *Codex Alimentarius*, definitions of purposes, code of ethics, food labeling, food additives, contaminants in food, food hygiene, and irradiated foods.

This book is a must for anyone interested in food regulations or international trade in foods. As in all FAO books, the contributors are experts from many areas of the world. —**Herbert W. Ockerman**

This book is a must for anyone interested in food regulations or international trade in foods. As in all FAO books, the contributors are experts from many areas of the world. — **Herbert W. Ockerman**

1480. **Food Aid in Figures. Vol. 8/2: 1990. L'Aide Alimentaire en Chiffres. La Ayuda Alimentaria en Cifras.** Lanham, Md., UNIPUB, 1991. 135p. $40.00pa. ISBN 92-5-003103-3.

This book traces the transfer, from donor to recipient country, of food commodities. The commodities are arranged into 13 categories and are listed in tables by country of origin or through multilateral organizations. Commodities include wheat, rice, coarse grains, skim milk powder, cheese, vegetable oil, and butter oil. The manuscript is primarily tables divided by years from the late 1970s to the early 1990s and then subdivided into commodity categories and countries. Both donor and recipient countries are listed, and the commodities are often converted into grain equivalence. A glossary translates table headings into the three languages used (English, French, and Spanish).

Easy to use, the work is essentially the only source of this type of information. The editors have assembled the best (although not always the most complete) information available. The book will be indispensable to anyone interested in foreign aid. — **Herbert W. Ockerman**

1481. **How Many Calories? How Much Fat? Guide to Calculating the Nutritional Content of the Foods You Eat.** By Rosemary Baskin and the editors of Consumer Reports Books. Yonkers, N.Y., Consumer Reports Books; distr., New York, St. Martin's Press, 1991. 372p. $14.95pa. TX551.B27. 641.1'4. LC 91-34719. ISBN 0-89043-421-2.

Composed of data from a variety of reputable, well-known sources, nutritional information for thousands of foods (including brand-name and restaurant items) is presented in this useful reference. This volume compares more than calories and fats; also noted are sodium, potassium, dietary fiber, calcium, iron, protein, carbohydrates, and vitamin content. This book differs from others of its type, such as *Nutrients in Foods* by Gilbert A. Leveille (Nutrition Guild, 1983), in the information found in the introduction. In *How Many Calories?* there is a discussion of recommended daily allowances and U.S. recommended daily allowances and how they differ; labels and how to read an ingredient listing; and fat intake, cholesterol, and other nutritional aspects as an aid in comparing the content of foods. There is no index as the book is divided by food sections. It is easier to read than *Bowes and Church's Food Values of Portions Commonly Used*, 15th ed., by Jean A. T. Pennington (Harper & Row, 1989).

What is disappointing, although no fault of this book or those responsible for it, is the lack of information available for saturated and polyunsaturated fat for many of the entries. Much of this information has not been available or is just beginning to be revealed by the manufacturers or the USDA. The completeness of this book and its affordable price make it a practical addition to any collection.
— **Joy Hastings**

FORESTRY

1482. Boross, P. A., and M. H. Mitchell. **Bibliography, 1988-1990.** Chalk River, Ont., Petawawa National Forestry Institute, 1991. 125p. index. (Information Report, PI-X-106E). free pa. 016.6349. ISBN 0-662-58651-4.

This is the third bibliography, in both English and French, of all of the publications produced by the Petawawa National Forestry Institute. Materials were published in 1988, 1989, and 1990. The work is arranged by author's name, and each entry is assigned a number that is referred to in the indexes. Each entry is well annotated so that the user knows exactly what the publication is about. There are indexes of authors, titles, species and key words, information report lists, and technical report lists. This will be a valuable addition to collections in forestry. — **Lillian R. Mesner**

1483. **FAO Yearbook: Forest Products 1979-1990. FAO Annuaire: Produits Forestiers. FAO Anuario: Productos Forestales.** By the Statistics and Economic Analysis Staff of the Forestry Department, FAO. Rome, FAO of the United Nations; distr., Lanham, Md., UNIPUB, 1992. 332p. (FAO Forestry Series, no.25; FAO Statistics Series, no.103). $50.00pa. ISBN 92-5-003111-4.

This yearbook provides statistics on the worldwide production, import, and export of forest products: roundwood, fuelwood, logs, pulpwood and pulp, plywood, particle board, and many other products for 1979 to 1990. Approximately 160 countries are included.

Introductory material consists of a list of regions and countries covered and definitions of the terms used for forest products. In the first of three sections, each commodity has a set of tables with data grouped by world regions and then alphabetically by country within each region. There is a column for each of the 12 years covered. For every commodity there is a table for production, two for imports (quantity of trade and monetary value of trade), and two for exports (quantity and value also). The second section has matrix charts that show the direction of trade between selected countries for 1989 and 1990. The final section consists of tables that provide the unit value of some of the commodities traded, computed by dividing the total value of the trade by the total volume traded.

The world trade in forest products is covered here in a massive amount of detail. This yearbook should be in the libraries of all academic institutions with forestry programs. —**John Laurence Kelland**

1484. Sayer, Jeffrey A., Caroline S. Harcourt, and N. Mark Collins, eds. **The Conservation Atlas of Tropical Forests: Africa.** New York, Simon & Schuster Academic Reference Division, 1992. 288p. illus. maps. index. $95.00. G2446.K3C6. 333.75'096022. LC 91-39120. ISBN 0-13-175332-0.

This work is the second in a series and follows *Conservation Atlas of Tropical Forests: Asia and the Pacific* (see ARBA 92, entry 1764). The atlas was produced under the Forest Conservation Programme of the IUCN (International Union for Conservation of Nature and Natural Resources), the World Conservation Union. The general objective of the atlas is to address deforestation in Africa, where forests are being depleted faster than on any other continent.

The book is organized into two major parts. Part 1, containing 10 chapters, concerns major issues such as the history of forests and climate, biodiversity, the people, timber trade, and the future. Topics are covered in a broad sense and provide groundwork for later detail. Part 2 consists of country studies, with 22 chapters that are each devoted to a country or region. Every country survey is organized similarly, which helps the reader compare data among countries. Subsections on the forests, forest resources and management, deforestation, biodiversity, conservation areas, and initiatives for conservation are common to each country chapter.

The volume is produced in large format, which enhances the four-color maps and photographs. Illustrations are plentiful and well done; satellite and radar imagery and aerial photography have been used to produce reliable, detailed maps. The atlas also contains a list of acronyms, a glossary, an index of species (flora and fauna), and a general index.

The atlas does not state as its purpose the resolution of difficult interdisciplinary problems concerning African deforestation. However, it contains in one volume a plethora of information vitally important to anyone studying this continental problem of worldwide implications. [R: LJ, 15 Sept 92, pp. 58-60; RBB, 1 Sept 92, p. 81] —**Michael G. Messina**

HORTICULTURE

1485. **Garden Literature: An Index to Periodical Articles and Book Reviews. Volume 1, Number 2.** By Sally Williams. Boston, Garden Literature Press, 1992. 153p. $50.00/yr.; $75.00/yr. (institutions). ISSN 1061-3722.

For the burgeoning numbers of curious "individuals who appreciate plants in any setting" (p. v), here is an index to periodicals and books about gardening. It exudes excellence, as it is easily maneuvered by author or topic, amply cross-referenced, and nicely arranged to satisfy voracious users. Addresses for offices of publications cited are given, as is a guide to abbreviations. Book reviews merit a separate section.

This work would benefit from a bit of pruning as it grows. For example, the citation of a *New York Times* article that reports conflict between the Bush Administration and the biodiversity pact is out of place. So too is an entry under "Garden Parties," which points to the pitfalls of serving alcohol at parties in general but that happened to appear in *American Nurseryman*. Conversely, a February 1992 article in the *Wall Street Journal* – "Valentines for Gardeners" – should have been picked up in this volume. Gardeners ought to clamor for their public libraries to subscribe to this index; communities will benefit. [R: RBB, 15 Oct 92, p. 453] — **Diane M. Calabrese**

1486. Kramer, Jack. **The New Gardener's Handbook and Dictionary.** New York, John Wiley, 1992. 555p. illus. index. $28.50. SB453.K719. 635. LC 91-17159. ISBN 0-471-52090-X.

This book provides all the information a new or experienced gardener needs to start a garden. Growing plants, garden design, deciding what to plant, and plant protection are all covered. Charts and tables deal with soil and climatic conditions, sowing and flowering times, and other such information. A major part of this work is the gardening dictionary, which is really a compendium of information about more than 700 plants rather than a dictionary in the strict sense. There are brief references to other species and varieties for a total of more than 2,000 listings. Each entry presents the common and scientific names of the plant, a description, the best conditions for growth, and planting advice. The coverage of plants is selective, largely those the author is familiar with and that are easy to grow. Some are illustrated with vivid color photographs, and there are also line drawings and black-and-white photographs.

This handbook is a good one for the beginning gardener; it has a lot of basic how-to information not found in most garden books. The material on plant diseases and pests is limited, but there are all levels of books on that topic. — **John Laurence Kelland**

1487. **North American Horticulture: A Reference Guide.** Compiled by the American Horticultural Society. Thomas M. Barrett, ed. New York, Macmillan, 1992. 427p. index. $75.00. SB317.56.U6N67. 635'.02573. LC 90-20435. ISBN 0-02-897001-2.

Although this is the 2d edition of *North American Horticulture* (Scribner's, 1982), this is actually the 4th edition of what was originally titled *Directory of American Horticulture* (American Horticultural Society, 1971). As with past editions, the goal of this book is to be as inclusive as possible in listing horticultural institutions. The American Horticultural Society has done this exceedingly well, taking into account the interests of both amateurs and professionals.

Because gardening is dependent on local conditions, more regional information is included, such as state organizations. Many of the chapters are arranged first by state and then alphabetically, to aid finding something close to home. To meet the ever-growing interest in native plants and seed preservation, chapters have been added for each of these areas. Another expanding area of interest is horticultural therapy, so this chapter has been correspondingly expanded. Besides these specialized areas, there is information about libraries, herbaria, gardens, periodicals, and educational programs, as well as the garden clubs one would expect to find. In an attempt to keep current, a sample registration form is included as well as a toll-free number so readers can add favorite horticultural organizations to the database. Full entries include standard directory information, purpose of the organization, gardens operated, publications, scholarships, and other services offered. Cross-references are also included.

The index by organization name is useful if one knows the group being sought. A subject index, or at least a key-word-in-context index, would be more useful to help identify specialized groups, such as those dealing with the American Chestnut. The index of states is relatively useless, being simply a list of pages where referrals for each state occur. Except for this slight shortcoming, this volume is an excellent addition to a reference collection. [R: Choice, Sept 92, p. 86; LJ, 1 June 92, p. 116; RBB, 1 Sept 92, p. 90] — **Angela Marie Thor**

1488. **Prentice-Hall Pocket Encyclopedia [of] Organic Gardening.** Geoff Hamilton, ed. Scarborough, Ont., Prentice-Hall Canada, 1991. 224p. illus. index. $14.95pa. 635.9'87. ISBN 0-13-722091-X.

While not as comprehensive as the *Encyclopedia of Organic Gardening* (see ARBA 79, entry 1539), this is a useful little encyclopedia. Chapter 1 lists plants that can be grown organically and groups them as flowering plants, herbs, vegetables (salad, shoot, bulb, pod, seed, fruiting, squash, root, and leaf), and fruits (tree, citrus, and soft). For each plant, a helpful high-quality color photograph is included. The remaining 10 chapters cover planning a garden; improving the soil; setting up an organic framework; creating ornamental borders; growing herbs, vegetables, and fruits; tools and techniques; pests and diseases; and organic weed control. In the chapters on growing, plants are listed alphabetically,

with subsections on soil and site, sowing and planting, maintaining, harvesting, and pests and diseases. The book concludes with a seven-page index that lists common and scientific plant names. Although not exhaustive, the encyclopedia is a good value and is recommended, particularly for public libraries.
— **Nathan M. Smith**

1489. **Rodale's All-New Encyclopedia of Organic Gardening: The Indispensable Resource for Every Gardener.** Fern Marshall Bradley and Barbara W. Ellis, eds. Emmaus, Pa., Rodale Press, 1992. 690p. illus. index. $29.95. SB452.4.R633. 635.0484. LC 91-32088. ISBN 0-87857-999-0.

This volume, from America's voice on organic gardening for the past 30-plus years, has been eagerly awaited. It contains all the up-to-date information one needs to garden using the organic method. Covering everything from abelia to zucchini, this resource has information on plant varieties, insect and disease control, fertilizers, propagation, and much more. The information is based on the experience and research the public has come to expect from *Organic Gardening Magazine*.

Organized in an A-Z format, the book is simple to use and useful for all sizes of gardens, from potted plants to an acre or more of crops. Side notes give everything from additional references on a variety of topics to sources for certain plants. The 420 entries are completely cross-referenced. Included are an extensive index, a large number of plant illustrations, step-by-step instructions for planting and plant maintenance, and garden diagrams from the simple to the sensational. [R: BL, 15 Mar 92, p. 1326] — **Linda Sue Smith**

VETERINARY SCIENCE

1490. **Black's Veterinary Dictionary.** 17th ed. Geoffrey P. West, ed. Lanham, Md., Barnes & Noble Books; distr., Savage, Md., Rowman & Littlefield, 1992. 660p. illus. $67.50. ISBN 0-389-20994-5.

In this edition some entries have been increased in length (e.g., U.K. law and health hazards for those involved in animal and related industries), while others have been rearranged into another section (e.g., abdomen is cross-referenced to other appropriate headings; cattle plague, *see* rinderpest). All but two diagrams in the bandages and bandaging entry has been eliminated. Newer entries include the European Community, identichip, and the surgical procedures gastropexy and stents. In spite of these changes, this edition is not significantly different from the previous one (see ARBA 90, entry 1476). Unless one has a much older *Black's* or needs to purchase a comprehensive veterinary dictionary, it is not necessary to buy this edition. — **Joy Hastings**

1491. Porter, Valerie. **Cattle: A Handbook to the Breeds of the World.** New York, Facts on File, 1991. 400p. illus. maps. index. $45.00. SF198.P67. 636.2. LC 90-47367. ISBN 0-8160-2640-8.

An online literature search reveals that this book is unique in its effort to trace the development of cattle breeds and close relatives (e.g., buffalo) of the world. The focus of the book is the history of the breeds related to their progenitors and subsequent migration, evolution, adaptation, role change brought on by humans, and selective breeding by humans. The underlying theses of this work encourages the retention of diversity of breeds.

The book is divided into sections related to geographic areas and breeds specific to those areas. Each section deals with the development of breeds and selection of desired traits specific to the needs of humans and the ability of the land to support the breeds. For example, the Aberdeen Angus was bred to mature rapidly despite less than optimal forage availability. Information regarding weight gain, butterfat percentage, and milk yield are provided for many breeds.

The book is liberally illustrated with color plates of cattle from the various geographic areas. It also has a number of supplementary tables and is well illustrated with maps that show the distribution of the cattle varieties indigenous to those areas. There are six appendixes, including a metrication table; a glossary of common terms; and four separate lists of cattle breeds with synonyms, endangered European cattle breeds, extinct breeds, and useful addresses. Bibliographic documentation and a comprehensive index complete the volume. This book would be a valuable addition to academic and public library collections. [R: Choice, Sept 92, p. 88] — **Patricia S. Wilson**

31 Biological Sciences

BIOLOGY

1492. **The Visual Dictionary of the Human Body.** New York, Dorling Kindersley; distr., Boston, Houghton Mifflin, 1991. 64p. illus. index. (Eyewitness Visual Dictionaries). $14.95. LC 91-060899. ISBN 0-879431-18-1.

The amazing complexity of the human body is beautifully captured in this visual dictionary of human anatomy. Using illustrations, cut-away models, photographs, and photomicrographs, this book identifies not only all of the body's internal and external parts but also the systems (e.g., circulatory, skeletal, reproductive) of which they are a part.

Twenty-five topics are covered, including the head, body organs, skull, bones and joints, muscles, hands, feet, skin and hair, the digestive and respiratory systems, and the developmental stages of a fetus. A brief narrative introduces the subject explored in each two-page spread. This text somewhat supplements the photographs and illustrations with their identifying labels, none of which is defined beyond its name. Approximately 1,400 terms are identified; all appear in the dictionary's concluding index.

An example of the outstanding quality of this slim volume is the entry for body cells, which offers the clearest and most easily understood graphic of a human cell this reviewer has ever seen. The same entry also presents full-color photomicrographs of various cell types: bone-forming cells, spinal-cord nerve cells, sperm cells in semen, secretory thyroid gland cells, and several others. In addition, there is a diagram of the DNA double helix, accompanied by a concise explanation of DNA's pivotal role in genetic coding.

Although basically an introductory and fairly cursory treatment of human anatomy, *Visual Dictionary* is also an informative and graphically stunning resource. Its reasonable price should make it a welcome addition to public, school, and family libraries. [R: BR, May/June 92, p. 60; RBB, 1 Feb 92, p. 1059; WLB, Jan 92, p. 132]—**G. Kim Dority**

BOTANY

General Works

Bibliography

1493. Johnston, Stanley H., Jr., comp. **The Cleveland Herbal, Botanical, and Horticultural Collections: A Descriptive Bibliography of Pre-1830 Works from the Libraries of the Holden Arboretum, the Cleveland Medical Library Association, and the Garden Center of Greater Cleveland.** Kent, Ohio, Kent State University Press, 1992. 1012p. illus. index. $85.00. Z5352.J64. 016.581. LC 90-5383. ISBN 0-87338-433-4.

A chronological listing of little-known resources from the libraries mentioned in the title, this work provides extensive, descriptive bibliographic cataloging of items concerned with vegetable, medicinal, botanical, or horticultural topics that began publication before 1830. Certain items have been excluded, but pharmacopoeias and dispensatories that emphasize vegetable simples or that are arranged by drug or vegetable (rather than disease) are included. Entries are arranged alphabetically by the surname of the author or the first word of the title. Users will need to read the introductory notes to decipher the descriptive bibliographic elements as they are presented in this text. Any deviations of the Cleveland copies from the ideal are noted, and citations to the comparison copies are referenced. No contents are given, and the notes section varies according to the information available for a particular book. Readers will be limited to inferring content from the transcription of the incipit, cover title, engraved title, or title page. However, a brief biography of the author, information on the relationship to other editions, and statements that note the importance of the work are given. An extensive bibliography of reference materials used in the compilation and separate indexes for authors and titles; printers, publisher, and booksellers (arranged alphabetically by place-name); illustrators; portraits; and nonbotanical illustrations are included.

Although this catalog records the existence of rare and historically valuable works, it will unfortunately join many other union lists on the reference shelves, underused and unknown except to librarians and a few researchers. Those who will be attracted to it will probably be limited to libraries or institutions that support research in pharmacognosy, botany, or horticulture, or individuals with personal collections of herbals or interest in medicinal plants. Another very select group of readers may benefit from the index of printers, publishers, and booksellers and the index of illustrators, which includes all artists, engravers, woodcutters, and lithographers. A greater audience would use this work if it and similar works were published on microcomputer or CD-ROM disks or if efforts were made to enter the data into OCLC (Online Computer Library Center). — **Vicki J. Killion**

Catalogs and Collections

1494. Browne, Edward T., Jr., and Raymond Athey. **Vascular Plants of Kentucky: An Annotated Checklist.** Lexington, Ky., University Press of Kentucky, 1992. 180p. maps. index. $20.00. QK162.B76. 582.09769. LC 91-2499. ISBN 0-8131-1675-9.

This is a straightforward list of Kentucky plant species. It is an updating of a list done in 1942 and contains 3,142 species, varieties, subspecies, and hybrids. The new list is derived from the authors' own collections as well as exhaustive review of floristic literature and studies in major herbaria in the Northeast. The checklist is preceded by four brief sections: a preface, an introduction, an essay on plants and Kentucky physiography, and a section on how to use the book.

There are many more entries than in the last list because the authors have been able to resolve numerous problems of synonymy in names. However, they acknowledge that the work is still not exhaustive and the area needs more study.

Listings in the main part of the book are by family, then by genus and species, variety, and subspecies. Plants not native to Kentucky are marked and proper synonyms are given. Also, entries are coded for the geographic area of distribution and as to which herbarium has the plant in its collection. A well-formatted index lists plants by genus and species as well as family. This is an important addition to the floristic literature of Kentucky and needs to be in any collection that deals with botany.

— **Lillian R. Mesner**

Dictionaries and Encyclopedias

1495. Bojnansky, V., and A. Fargasova. **Dictionary of Plant Virology: In Five Languages: English, Russian, German, French and Spanish.** New York, Elsevier Science Publishing, 1991. 472p. $157.00. QR351.B64. 576'.6483'03. LC 91-6391. ISBN 0-444-98740-1.

This is a multilingual technical dictionary designed for researchers interested in the literature of viral, mycoplasmic, and rickettsial infections of plants. It is divided into two parts. In the first, technical terms and phrases common to the study of these plant infections are listed in alphabetical order in English and given sequential numbers. Each term or phrase is followed by its equivalent in Russian,

German, French, and Spanish, and a short definition is given in Russian and English. This is followed by four alphabetical indexes of the equivalent terms in Russian, German, French, and Spanish, each keyed by number back to the basic entry and definition in the English section.

In the second part, common viral-like diseases of plants (mostly vascular seed plants) are listed alphabetically by the names of the genera and species of plants that they infect. Thus, the main index goes from *Forsythia* (entry 801) to *Fragraria* (strawberry, entries 802-839 for several species), and on to *Fraxinus* (ash, 841-849), listing in each case the names of the various infections. Again, where appropriate, each entry is followed by the name of the disease in Russian, German, French, and Spanish, and the following four alphabetical indexes allow one to trace the disease's name in each language back to the generic index and its English name.

The lists of terms and diseases are by no means exhaustive (although there are more than 2,000 terms and 2,500 disease names treated), but the work covers the most commonly encountered terms and infections. The definitions of the terms in the first part are generally lucid and brief. This is definitely a tome for technical collections. — **Bruce H. Tiffney**

1496. **Elsevier's Dictionary of Plant Genetic Resources.** Compiled by International Board for Plant Genetic Resources. New York, Elsevier Science Publishing, 1991. 187p. $85.50. SB123.3.E45. 631. 5'23'03. LC 90-26707. ISBN 0-444-88959-0.

A dictionary such as this one reflects rapidly expanding interest in conserving plant genetic resources on an international scale. Articles on this topic have appeared in general scientific journals, such as *Bioscience, Nature, Science,* and *Scientific American*, for most of the last decade. Additionally, at least two newsletters present and discuss issues relevant to the worldwide plant genetic resources community: *Plant Genetic Resources Newsletter* and *Diversity.* The International Board for Plant Genetic Resources (IBPGR), an autonomous international scientific organization under the aegis of the Consultative Group on International Agricultural Research, has compiled the present glossary to define more than 1,800 terms distinctive to plant genetic resources, from such diverse areas as plant taxonomy and molecular genetics. Consultants include numerous experts in the field. In the future the dictionary will be issued in a multilingual version translated into Arabic, Chinese, French, and Spanish. The arrangement of the volume is alphabetical, with most definitions contained in two to three sentences, although some more complicated concepts require several paragraphs.

This dictionary will be useful for students, teachers, and staff involved in programs concerned with plant genetic resources. It is appropriate for libraries that hold materials pertinent to agriculture, food and animal sciences, horticulture, molecular genetics, and plant biochemistry and physiology.
— **Elisabeth B. Davis**

1497. **Elsevier's Dictionary of Terrestrial Plant Ecology: English-Spanish and Spanish-English.** By H. Resinger and J. M. Gomez-Gutierrez. New York, Elsevier Science Publishing, 1992. 664p. $157.00. QK900.4.R47. 581.5'264'03. LC 92-3699. ISBN 0-444-88977-9.

This dictionary covers plant ecology and related fields such as plant physiology, climatology, and biostatistics. It is divided into two sections: English-Spanish and Spanish-English. Within each section, definitions run down the middle of the page and corresponding terms are on the right and left of the page. This format makes the information very accessible. Definitions are brief but generally adequate and make the work useful as a dictionary in its own right as well as an aid to translation. Entries also contain synonymous terms that may be useful as key words for searching subject indexes; for example, under iteroparous, one will also find the terms *anabiotic, polycarpic,* and *polycarpous.* Not all terms are cross-referenced, however; nothing is listed under polycarpic or polycarpous, but there is a *see* reference under anabiotic.

This work will be useful for biology programs that serve Spanish-speaking students and for those who need to translate English or Spanish technical terms in plant ecology. Unfortunately, the work is not typeset and is aesthetically lacking. One does not expect such a lack of quality from Elsevier, especially in such an expensive book. — **T. McKimmie**

Handbooks and Yearbooks

1498. Bell, Peter R. **Green Plants: Their Origin and Diversity.** Portland, Oreg., Dioscorides Press/Timber Press, 1992. 315p. illus. index. $39.95; $24.95pa. QK45.2.B46. 581.3'8. LC 91-18615. ISBN 0-931146-20-8.

This is a revised edition of *The Diversity of Green Plant*, 3d edition (London: Edward Arnold, 1983), an undergraduate plant morphology text written by Bell and Christopher L. F. Woodcock. Bell, sole author of this latest revision, is professor emeritus of botany, University of London. Photosynthetic plants are covered from the simplest to the most complex: algae, mosses and liverworts, ferns and fern allies, gymnosperms, and angiosperms (the flowering plants). Many black-and-white drawings and photographs accompany the text. The beginning chapter discusses the plant kingdom in general; subsequent chapters deal with reproduction, life histories, evolution, fossil records, and general features within each of the broad categories of plants mentioned above. A glossary is provided, as well as suggested further reading lists for each of the chapters. A subject index completes the volume.

Green Plants is most suitable for college undergraduates and advanced high school students. It could also be profitably read by nonstudents interested in botany, provided they have had previous exposure to biological principles. – **William H. Wiese**

1499. Daughtrey, Margery, and A. R. Chase. **Ball Field Guide to Diseases of Greenhouse Ornamentals: Includes Certain Problems Often Misdiagnosed as Contagious Diseases.** Geneva, Ill., Ball Publishing, 1992. 218p. illus. index. $65.00pa. SB608.G82D38. 635.9'2. LC 91-35939. ISBN 0-9626796-3-1.

With more than 500 photographs of sick plants, this is an unexpectedly delightful book. The photographs are good to excellent and carefully selected to allow the reader to rapidly identify common greenhouse plant diseases and problems. The book is organized by plant name (alphabetically), with photographs that show the diseases and a short statement about their distinguishing features. The table of contents lists the plant names used in the book, but the reader may need to know common names and genera. While plant diseases are the central theme, other conditions are included, such as nutrient deficiencies, environmental problems, mechanical damage, mites, and nematodes. No control measures or life cycles are mentioned. A short glossary and reference list are very useful.

This book fits nicely in a hip pocket, right where it will be useful on many occasions. Recommended as a quick identification aid to diseases of greenhouse plants. – **John A. Jackman**

1500. Gleason, Henry A., and Arthur Cronquist. **Manual of Vascular Plants of Northeastern United States and Adjacent Canada.** 2d ed. Bronx, N.Y., New York Botanical Garden, 1991. 910p. index. $74.60. QK117.049. 582.0974. LC 91-23110. ISBN 0-89327-365-1.

The Englerian arrangement followed by Gleason in his *New Britton and Brown Illustrated Flora of the Northeastern United States and Adjacent Canada* (Hafner, 1952) and in the 1963 edition of this manual has been abandoned in this work. Instead, the more modern arrangement elucidated in the 2d edition of Cronquist's *Evolution and Classification of Flowering Plants* (New York Botanical Garden, 1988) has been followed. The general keys, based on the most easily observed characters, lead students and interested laypeople directly to 5 groups or refer to 17 other sections, such as vascular cryptograms or gymnosperms. Using so many sections reduces the left-margin dichotomous indentation and heightens the contrast between alternative or contrasting choices by bringing them into closer proximity. Because families often contain both widely differing members and those with only superficial differences, the keys are constructed so the same family may be reached by two or more routes. Following the general keys, synoptical keys to the subclasses of Magnoliopsida (Dicotyledons) and Liliopsida (Monocotyledons) provide further conceptual aids. This constant concern for assisting the learning user permeates the entire unillustrated text. (Users with access to *New Britton and Brown* will easily use those illustrations to confirm their Cronquist-keyed identifications.) Finally, the index combines both scientific and common names into one alphabet. Lighter in weight and more lucid in explanation than the unrevised 8th edition of *Gray's Manual of Botany* by Merritt L. Feruald (Dioscorides Press, c1950, 1987), this manual is highly recommended for undergraduates or graduate students and science divisions of large public libraries. [R: Choice, Apr 92, p. 1208] – **Helen M. Barber**

1501. Nelson, Ruth Ashton. **Handbook of Rocky Mountain Plants.** 4th ed. Revised by Roger L. Williams. Niwot, Colo., Roberts Rinehart, 1992. 444p. illus. index. $19.95pa. LC 91-66684. ISBN 0-911797-96-3.

This is a new and substantially revised edition of a classic field guide first published 25 years ago. Numerous additional species have been included, and in contrast to previous editions that emphasized common names, this edition uses scientific names in all keys.

The *Handbook of Rocky Mountain Plants* is not a picture guide for the casual hiker or tourist. Several excellent guides of this nature exist, including *Rocky Mountain Wildflowers* (see ARBA 87, entry 1476) and *Alpine Wildflowers of the Rocky Mountains* (see ARBA 91, entry 1525). Rather, this is a much more complete source, including not only showy wildflowers but also trees, ferns, and grasses. Instead of photographs or color paintings, species are pictured in simple but accurate line drawings. All identification is based on botanical keys, although unlike many keys, these employ a minimum of technical language and are relatively easy to follow.

The text is extensive and full of fascinating details about plant ecology, anatomy, and history. There is excellent introductory material on the Rocky Mountain region and on botanical terminology. While this book may prove too much for those interested in the simple, quick identification of a few wildflowers, students and amateur botanists will treasure it.—**Carol L. Noll**

1502. **The Visual Dictionary of Plants.** New York, Dorling Kindersley; distr., Boston, Houghton Mifflin, 1992. 64p. illus. index. (Eyewitness Visual Dictionaries). $14.95. QK49.E94. 581. LC 91-58208. ISBN 1-56458-016-4.

This is one in a series of visual dictionaries that try to do with photography and graphics what most reference books do with words. Such an approach works well for botany, which relies heavily on terminology and classification according to physical characteristics. Although termed a dictionary, this book is arranged more like a textbook. There are 25 topics, each of which is treated in a lavish 2-page picture essay. (A detailed and complete index gives dictionary-like access.) Topics range from specific parts of the plant (e.g., leaves, flowers) to plant types (e.g., carnivorous plants) to physiological topics (e.g., photosynthesis). Each topic receives only about one paragraph of textual explanation, giving a basic overview of the subject with a minimum of specialized terminology. Details are given in a series of gorgeous color close-up photographs, micrographs, and color diagrams. Most of the book's information lies in the precise labeling of every part of each illustration. The overall effect is visually stunning and should be inviting to students and adults just being introduced to botany. However, it is difficult to portray subtle concepts and scientific principles without more sophisticated text. Thus, as a reference work this is no substitute for a good botanical dictionary, but it makes a wonderful supplement to one. [R: SBF, June 92, p. 142; SLJ, Sept 92, p. 288]—**Carol L. Noll**

Flowering Plants

1503. Crittenden, Mabel, and Dorothy Telfer. **Wildflowers of the West.** Blaine, Wash., Hancock House, 1992. 206p. illus. index. $14.95pa. QK133.C75. 582.13'0978. ISBN 0-88839-270-2.

This selective guide provides descriptions of the most common wildflowers in the continental United States west of the Rockies. Included are descriptions of 246 of the most commonly encountered flowering species, representing 37 botanical families. With few exceptions, coverage is limited to annual and perennial plants; most flowering shrubs, trees, and succulents are excluded. The authors, both elementary school teachers, have developed a simplified botanical key as a means of introducing third to fifth grade students to the vocabulary and methodology of botanists.

The first chapter provides an overview of the parts of the flower and other clues for flower identification. The second chapter consists of the botanical key, and the remaining chapters divide the entries according to petal arrangements. The entries for individual species give plant and flower characteristics, blooming season, habitat, range, and background comments. Black-and-white line drawings detail the flower and leaf structures for every entry, and frowning or smiling faces are used to highlight poisonous or edible plants. A brief glossary and an index of common and scientific names complete the volume. There are many guides to wildflowers of this region that provide more

comprehensive coverage, but the authors' simple approach, thorough descriptions, and excellent drawings make this volume a useful introduction to wildflower identification for novices of all ages.
—**John R. M. Lawrence**

1504. Davidian, H. H. **The Rhododendron Species. Volume III: Elepidotes Continued: Neriiflorum-Thomsonii, Azaleastrum and Camtschaticum.** Portland, Oreg., Timber Press, 1992. 381p. illus. maps. index. $54.95. SB413.R47D258. 583'.62. LC 81-23232. ISBN 0-88192-168-8.

Rhododendrons are among the showiest of temperate to subtropical flowering shrubs, embracing more than 800 species and countless horticultural varieties. This combination of features makes them of great interest and simultaneously difficult to keep track of. The last complete systematic treatment of the genus was published in 1947. Subsequent activities of plant hunters, breeders, and taxonomists dictate that this comprehensive, three-volume revision is overdue. The first volume treats the "lepidote" (hairy) *Rhododendron* species, while volume 2 and this volume deal with the "elepidote," or hairless species. The author of this treatise is a recognized expert on the genus.

The introduction includes political and climatic maps of East Asia, Europe, and the United States, followed by a glossary of both terms and drawings of various important morphological structures. Next is a key to the elepidote series and subseries of *Rhododendrons*, which covers groups treated in volumes 2 and 3. This key leads to other keys scattered throughout the work that identify species within the series and subseries. The keys appear to be straightforward. Individual descriptions are extensive, direct, and clear and include information on the discovery, natural setting and ecology, and cultivational history of the species. The descriptions are occasionally accompanied by a good line drawing, and the center of the book features 161 magnificent color pictures of the native habitats, floral characteristics, and cultivational settings of many of the species. The work is concluded by a variety of lists, indexes, and synopses, including a synonymy and Latin descriptions of new taxa. This treatment will probably become the standard reference for *Rhododendron* systematics for the next generation and will interest horticulturists and scientists alike.—**Bruce H. Tiffney**

1505. Pesman, M. Walter. **Meet the Natives: The Amateur's Field Guide to Rocky Mountain Wildflowers, Trees and Shrubs.** 9th ed. Denver, Colo., Denver Botanic Gardens and Niwot, Colo., Roberts Rinehart, 1992. 237p. illus. index. $12.95pa. QK139.P47. 582.0978. LC 88-6009. ISBN 1-879373-31-9.

This work was first written by Pesman and illustrated by Emma Ervin in 1942. This edition was revised by a group of volunteer professional botanists at the Denver Botanic Gardens. Plants are grouped by climatic zone (e.g., subalpine, foothills, plains) and then within plant types (e.g., trees, shrubs, herbs), by color, and alphabetically. Thus, if one is in the foothills, one can quickly find a blue herb. The current "authors" have retained Pesman's original technique of line-drawing illustrations. There are no color illustrations (except for the cover), and the only black-and-white photograph is on the verso of the title page. General material in the book includes a list of town, peak, pass, and park elevations; "Botanical Terms Explained"; "About Plant Families"; and "What Do These Scientific Terms Mean?" The bibliography ("Useful References") is up-to-date as of 1990.

The perfect binding of this work will not stand up to much field use. Narrow margins will prevent much rebinding of the material, but the volume's low cost will enable the purchase of another copy for little more than the cost of binding. A few errors were spotted in the "Botanical Terms Explained" section. "Panicle" is illustrated on page 211, but no explanation of the term is given in the text; likewise, "Filament" is illustrated on pages 213 and 214, but is unexplained; and there appears to have been a cancellation of the illustration on the top of page 212 (perhaps the likeness of a pod). On a more positive note, the volume has a handy edge index. This volume will be of interest to libraries in the Rockies and elsewhere that have clients with a need for a good field guide to Rocky Mountain plants. Overall, it is very well done.—**Ralph Lee Scott**

1506. van Gelderen, D. M., and J. R. P. van Hoey Smith. **Rhododendron Portraits.** Portland, Oreg., Timber Press, 1992. 424p. illus. index. $75.00. SB413.R47G4513. 635.9'3362. LC 91-23264. ISBN 0-88192-194-7.

The genus *Rhododendron* (literally "rose tree") is one of the showiest of temperate to subtropical shrubs commonly grown in gardens. In its natural state the genus occurs in limited numbers in the Mediterranean and Europe, in greater numbers in North America, and with extreme diversity in eastern Asia. The variety of wild material, together with the spectacular flowers of many species, has led to the artificial breeding of hybrids during the last 200 years and the appearance of a devoted band of "rhodie" enthusiasts. This volume is a graphic testament to the delight of these enthusiasts, as it is a color catalog of more than 1,000 species of the large, flowered, evergreen *Rhododendrons* (excluding the segregate genus *Azalea*).

A short introduction details the organization, conventions, and scope of the book. This is followed by an equally brief (13-page) summary of the major groups of evergreen *Rhododendrons*. The remainder of the book (nearly 400 pages) is given to 1,144 color photographs, organized by the taxonomic system described in the introduction and systematic summary. Each photograph is accompanied by a shorthand report of the species' breeding history, awards, height, flowering time, and hardiness zone. The photographs are generally clear, but they do not necessarily depict all the distinguishing characters of the species. They are occasionally affected by the difficulty of rendering some colors (especially those involving blue) in color pictures. A spectacular book for the aficionado, this is probably of greatest interest for libraries associated with horticultural collections.—**Bruce H. Tiffney**

1507. Waddick, James W., and Yu-tang Zhao. **Iris of China.** Portland, Oreg., Timber Press, 1992. 192p. illus. maps. index. $27.95. SB413.I8I845. 635.9'3424. LC 91-19496. ISBN 0-88192-207-2.

The genus *Iris* (300-plus species) provides some of the most popular and prolific of temperate garden flowers and has developed a large and avid cult of fanciers. While the greatest diversity of wild species is found in the Near and Middle East, China hosts more than 60 species, including many of the species commonly referred to as the Siberian irises. The present book is a two-part summary of the irises of China.

The first part, by Waddick, contains three chapters from a horticultural perspective that describe Chinese *Iris* species in the wild and their transfer into cultivation. Particularly useful are the descriptions of the natural ecological situations of the species or species groups and the corresponding suggestions for horticultural practice. Various anecdotes creep into the text along the way, making this interesting reading.

The second portion of the book is a translation of Zhao's systematic treatment of the genus *Iris* in China, as originally published in 1985 in Chinese as volume 16 of the *Flora Reipublicae Popularis Sinicae* (Beijing). This is a professional botanical summary of the genus and includes a key to the Chinese species of *Iris*, followed by technical descriptions of the individual species with line drawings from the original publication. The translation is terse but clear. The volume ends with a series of appendixes full of useful geographical, climatological, and horticultural data; a glossary; a topical bibliography; and an index. Professional botanists or serious iris-lovers, particularly those fond of irises of the Siberian type, will find this work a treasure trove of useful systematic and horticultural data.
—**Bruce H. Tiffney**

1508. Woods, Christopher. **Encyclopedia of Perennials: A Gardener's Guide.** New York, Facts on File, 1992. 350p. illus. index. $50.00. SB434.W66. 635.9'32. LC 91-15280. ISBN 0-8160-2092-2.

The premise of this book is an illustrated summary of perennial herbs for gardens of temperate regions. Its outward appearance is that of a coffee-table special, and the glossy color photographs are in keeping with this image. However, the text is direct and clear and often has good insights for the gardener. After a brief introduction to the logic of the work and to some aspects of gardening (soil, bugs, fertilizer, and a recognition that gardening means some serious labor!), the body of the book is given to an alphabetical-by-genus list of interesting perennial herbs. Each entry occupies about a half page; includes notes on cultivation, propagation, and pests; and is generally accompanied by a photograph. Some of these display the flower, others the habit or habitat of the plant. Of note is the inclusion of several uncommon plants that ought to be more popular in the garden, such as the eastern and western North American "skunk cabbages" (*Symplocarpus, Lysichiton*).

While the world is full of glossy "don't-you-wish-you-had-this-garden" books, most are without much useful content. The serious gardener seeks out the professional literature, which is likely to scare off the beginner. This book offers a nice level of encouragement and sound (if uncomplicated and generalized) advice paired with nice (if rather small) pictures. It is marred by too much unused white space, occasional typographical errors, and at least one instance where photographs have been inverted. [R: Choice, Oct 92, p. 282; LJ, 15 May 92, p.90; RBB, 1 June 92, p. 1774; SLJ, Aug 92, p. 195; WLB, Sept 92, p. 118]—**Bruce H. Tiffney**

Fungi

1509. Metzler, Susan, and Van Metzler. **Texas Mushrooms: A Field Guide.** Austin, Tex., University of Texas Press, 1992. 350p. illus. index. (Corrie Herring Hooks Series, no.18). $39.95; $17.95pa. QK617.M49. 589.2'22'09764. LC 91-2239. ISBN 0-292-75125-7; 0-292-75126-5pa.

That mushroom guides are now being published for areas such as Texas and the American Southwest is an indication of the increased popularity of mushroom hunting. There have always been guides for the more traditional mushroom-hunting areas of the Northwest and Northeast, and even guides that nominally cover all of North America really concentrate on these sections of the United States. However, as the authors of this exceptionally fine field guide point out, mushrooms can be found everywhere, and hundreds of species flourish all over Texas. And unlike in the North, mushroom hunting in Texas can be a year-round activity, due to the absence of a hard winter.

Most mushroom guides use one of two methods of identification: either the dichotomous key, a sure system that is very difficult for the beginner, or simple "picture matching," equally frustrating for all but the most distinctive specimens. The authors of this guide have come up with a remarkably usable combination of the two. Initially, readers are asked to place their unknown mushroom in a broad group according to a picture chart. Then, after determining spore color with a spore print, a series of tables of characteristics places the sample in a family and genus. Only then is the reader referred to the text to match the fungus with the color pictures of species. At this point, identification should be possible, using the outstanding color photographs and descriptions.

In addition to pictures and description, for each of about 200 species the authors include comments on habitat, season of occurrence, distribution throughout Texas, and edibility. The authors are quite careful in this last respect, cautioning the reader on mushrooms that are edible but easily confused with poisonous ones. There is also an interesting section of recipes with a Texas flair—including pickled mushrooms with jalapeno peppers and chanterelle enchiladas.—**Carol L. Noll**

Grasses and Weeds

1510. Hu, Shing Tsung (Peter), David B. Hannaway, and Harold W. Youngberg. **Forage Resources of China.** Wageningen, Netherlands, PUDOC; distr., Lanham, Md., UNIPUB, 1992. 327p. illus. maps. index. $80.00. ISBN 90-220-1063-5.

This book provides a detailed account of China's forage resources. There is a chapter for each major region: northeast China, Inner Mongolia, northwestern China (including Sinkiang), Tibet, and the tropical and subtropical southeastern regions. Within each chapter, major terrains (e.g., grasslands mixed with farmlands, those mixed with wooded areas) are treated, as well as smaller subregions. In the latter, various types of grasslands and meadows are described. Plant associations are covered and grass species inventories are provided. Soil and climatic conditions are discussed along with the geology of each subregion. Tables of the nutritional values of the grasses for forage animals are included. Each chapter has a map of the region and black-and-white photographs for many of the grasslands and other surface features. The photographs lack some contrast and clarity, but they serve their purpose in this book. Each chapter has references, and there is an extensive bibliography at the end of the book. There are indexes for geographic names and scientific names.

This excellent book provides extensive and thorough coverage of its subject and will be valuable in libraries of institutions with programs in agriculture, plant science, and natural resource science.

—**John Laurence Kelland**

1511. Mulligan, Gerald A. **Common and Botanical Names of Weeds in Canada. Noms Populaires et Scientifiques des Plantes Nuisibles de Canada.** 1992 ed. Ottawa, Agriculture Canada, 1992. 131p. (Publication, 1397/B). $12.00pa.; $14.40pa. (U.S.). 581.6'52014. ISBN 0-660-56484-X.

This list of weed names is intended to provide authoritative common names for Canadian weeds. *Weed* is broadly defined to include any plant that might be undesirable. Because the book is an official Canadian document, common names are given in both English and French. The main body of the book consists of three tables of approved names in alphabetical order by scientific, English, and French names. Each table includes all three official names, and the scientific table also has the family name of the weed. The arrangement of English common names may be slightly confusing to nonbotanists, as taxonomically correct and incorrect terms are treated differently. Quack grass is listed as "grass, quack," for instance, while bear-grass, which is not a true grass, is listed as bear-grass, with a cross-reference leading to the correct heading. Aside from a few common exceptions, unapproved names are not included in the tables. Thus, the book is useful for official purposes such as labeling herbicides but is less helpful for someone who only knows a weed by an unofficial name.

The book is also good for areas outside Canada, as weeds ignore political boundaries, and Mulligan has adopted the names suggested by the Weed Science Society of America for weeds found in both countries. The volume is most useful for agriculture or biological libraries, but public libraries that serve farmers or gardeners will also find it helpful. Its modest price will not strain the budget.

— **Diane Schmidt**

Liverworts

1512. Hicks, Marie L. **Guide to the Liverworts of North Carolina.** Durham, N.C., Duke University Press, 1992. 239p. illus. maps. index. $34.95. QK556.5.N8H53. 588'.3309756. LC 91-12055. ISBN 0-8223-1175-5.

Among the small delights of the plant world lie a diminutive, often unfamiliar, but not uncommon group of plants called liverworts. Related to the more familiar mosses, liverworts are similarly without conducting tissue, and thus generally grow low to the ground. To understand and become familiar with these plants, one generally has two types of reference. In the Picture Key series of books is H. S. Conard's *How to Know the Mosses and Liverworts* (Wm. C. Brown, 1956). At the other end of the spectrum lie the great professional tomes, capped by R. Schuster's sweeping four-volume *Hepaticae and Anthocerotae of North America* (Columbia University Press, 1966-1980). The present book (one of several "regional" floras) lies in between these extremes and describes the liverworts of North Carolina. (It will have varying degrees of use throughout eastern North America, as many of the species are fairly widespread.) It begins with a brief introduction to the biology and collection of liverworts. This is followed by a dichotomous key to the genera, leading to the systematic descriptions. These generally start with a key to the species. Each species entry contains a short paragraph describing the species, its distribution and habitat, and occasionally additional comments. Individual descriptions are accompanied by line drawings of important characters. A standard bibliography, a glossary, a list of taxa, and an index complete the work, along with an excellent set of distribution maps of 154 of the described species. — **Bruce H. Tiffney**

Marine Flora

1513. Schneider, Craig W., and Richard B. Searles. **Seaweeds of the Southeastern United States: Cape Hatteras to Cape Canaveral.** Durham, N.C., Duke University Press, 1991. 553p. illus. index. $49.95. QK571.5.S68S36. 589.4'5. LC 90-42415. ISBN 0-8223-1101-1.

This manual is the first comprehensive account of the seaweeds of the southeastern United States since W. D. Hoyt published "The Marine Algae of Beaufort, N.C., and Adjacent Regions" in the 1920 volume of the *U.S. Bulletin of the Bureau of Fisheries*. The authors of the current work are longtime diving companions and scholars whose aim was to produce a field guide and laboratory handbook for professional and amateur biologists interested in the identification of marine plants. Although emphasis is placed on keys, descriptions, and illustrations, which take up most of the book, Schneider and

Searles devote approximately 20 pages of text to introductory material that summarizes the history of phycology along the southeastern coast of the United States; the geological and hydrographic environment; biogeography and ecology; and methods for collection, preservation, and microscopic examination of seaweed specimens.

Arrangement of the flora is taxonomic and includes more than 300 species of seaweed living in deep offshore waters and along the coast from North Carolina to northern Florida. Natural keys are provided for all taxa, with a supplemental, artificial key to the genera included at the end of the taxonomic arrangement. Information for each species consists of the accepted name accompanied by the basionym; detailed description of the species; literature citations under the accepted name, synonyms, and misapplied names; habitat and seasonal data; and distribution. There are 560 illustrations to aid in differentiation and identification of the more distinctive seaweeds. The book concludes with an 11-page glossary, a list of collection sites with latitude and longitude, species distribution tables, a list of literature cited, and an index to scientific names.

The authors succeed admirably in writing a field guide that is a valuable addition to the literature. It is a definitive, trustworthy account of the subject matter and will serve as an important verification and research tool for scientists, students, and the informed layperson. It is appropriate for academic, special, and large public libraries. – **Elisabeth B. Davis**

Medicinal and Edible Plants

1514. Kindscher, Kelly. **Medicinal Wild Plants of the Prairie: An Ethnobotanical Guide.** Lawrence, Kans., University Press of Kansas, 1992. 340p. illus. maps. index. $25.00; $9.95pa. E78.G73K56. 581.6'34'097. LC 91-38471. ISBN 0-7006-0526-6; 0-7006-0527-4pa.

Documenting the use of 203 native prairie plant species used as medicines by Native Americans, settlers, and doctors, this book is primarily historical, as the natives of the region made the greatest use of the plants and only a few have recently been studied to determine their biologically active compounds. Each entry for the 43 plants that have had the widest use includes common, native, and scientific names; a description; a line drawing; approximate geographic distribution; habitat; parts used; native and Anglo folk use; medical history; scientific research; and harvesting and cultivation information. The remaining plants of secondary importance, and for which limited information is available, are covered in a separate section. The sections on use, medical history, and scientific research constitute the main portion of each entry and are fully referenced. A brief glossary of medical terms used in the descriptions is found at the end of the book. The index contains both scientific and common names.

The intended audience is stated as being broad; the author hopes to promote a greater understanding of prairie plants and their uses and to encourage the conservation, protection, and reestablishment of prairie plants and prairies throughout the region. While the book represents the first study of medicinal plants of the entire "Prairie Bioregion," as the author calls the North American Prairie, some readers will be disappointed in the limited information on medicinal uses. But the purpose of the book is not to promote experimental use of these plants. The entries are descriptions, not prescriptions, and are intended to establish the plants' value as a vital part of American folk culture and potential sources of future medicines. Anthropologists, ethnobotanists, historians, and the local gardener will find this book surprisingly readable and scientifically sound. – **Vicki J. Killion**

Trees and Shrubs

1515. Blouin, Glen. **Weeds of the Woods: Small Trees and Shrubs of the Eastern Forest.** Fredericton, N.B., Goose Lane Editions, c1984, 1992. 125p. illus. $14.95pa. 582.1'7'09715. ISBN 0-86492-127-6.

The "weeds" of the title are the small trees and shrubs that a logger might consider worthless. This is a field guide to such plants of New Brunswick, Canada, and is designed to show loggers and others how important they are. Only about 20 species are included, but more data is provided about each than in most field guides. Information includes a detailed, nontechnical description of the various parts of each plant, as well as facts about its habitat and use by wildlife, local Native Americans, and the early settlers. Blouin also supplies the scientific name and several common names for each plant in English,

French, Micmac, and Maliseet (two local Native American tribes). There are even a few recipes, including one for elderberry wine. The photographs are numerous; most plants are illustrated by pictures of their twigs, bark, leaves, flowers, and fruits or nuts, which makes the guide useful in any season.

This guide would be useful for areas outside of New Brunswick as well as within, as all of the listed plants are found across much of Canada and the United States. Unfortunately, the range of the plants is rarely given for areas outside of New Brunswick. Still, this guide is highly recommended for any library in eastern Canada and the northeastern United States and for others where there is an interest in the use of forest plants. — **Diane Schmidt**

1516. Coe, Malcolm, and Henk Beentje. **A Field Guide to the Acacias of Kenya.** New York, Oxford University Press, 1991. 148p. illus. index. $49.95; $29.95pa. QK495.L52C63. 583'.321. LC 91-16673. ISBN 0-19-858410-5; 0-19-858411-3pa.

Acacias are a dominant visual element in the flora of Africa and an important source of food for grazing mammals and insects. This guide covers the 43 species of Acacia that occur in Kenya (out of 129 known from Africa). A brief introduction to their ecology and distribution is followed by a description of their most important characters. These are summarized in tables that list species that may be recognized by specific characters. Three keys follow, one to flowering plants without leaves, one to plants without flowers or leaves, and one to plants with leaves but without flowers. This largess allows the identification of a tree in virtually any season. Each species is succinctly summarized in a single page list of its characters, faced by a very clear line drawing of foliage, fruit, twigs, and shape of the inflorescence. A brief bibliography, glossary, and index complete the book. The work will be of some interest to professional botanists, largely for its succinct ecological data (a few words) on each species. It will be of great interest to wildlife biologists and botanically oriented individuals of all kinds as a very succinct guide to the identity of these common trees in Kenya and adjacent countries.

— **Bruce H. Tiffney**

1517. Crittenden, Mabel. **Trees of the West.** Blaine, Wash., Hancock House, 1992. 220p. illus. index. $14.95pa. QK133.C752. 582.16'0978. ISBN 0-88839-269-9.

This guide has illustrations of trees on the West Coast of the United States. Conifers, palms, broadleaf trees, and introduced species are included. A useful introductory chapter covers the major characteristics to look for, such as leaf shapes and seed and fruit types. In chapter 2 there is a fairly extensive key to the species, and smaller keys for some of the families appear in later chapters. The entry for each species contains the common name, alternate common names, scientific name, descriptions of leaves and other parts, growth characteristics, habitat, economic use, and any edible or poisonous parts. Growing trees from seeds is also covered. The guide is well written, with good descriptions that will be understandable by the general public. There are a glossary, a bibliography, and an index.

The illustrations are line drawings. While the whole tree illustrations are good, some of the leaf and needle drawings are too small, and they do not compare well with the color illustrations in many other tree guides. While the range of each species is covered in the text, there are no range maps. Supposedly the key "can be used to identify the majority of trees anywhere in North America." This is doubtful. *A Field Guide to Eastern Trees* (see ARBA 89, entry 1437) covers 455 species in the east, while this guide covers no more than 160 West Coast species. — **John Laurence Kelland**

1518. Eastman, John. **The Book of Forest and Thicket: Trees, Shrubs, and Wildflowers of Eastern North America.** Harrisburg, Pa., Stackpole Books, 1992. 212p. illus. $14.95pa. QK115.E28. 581.974. LC 91-28395. ISBN 0-8117-3046-8.

The purpose of this book is to foster an understanding of each species in relation to other species and the habitat. It is written for the general public. Woodlands and brushy edges in northeastern and north central North America are covered. Some associations and species are excluded: lichens, mosses, many fungi, and those plants and insects that do not have a specific relationship to another species. Each plant species entry includes common and scientific names, family, close relatives, a lifestyle section (covering growth, development, and the life cycle), associated species (including other plants or trees associated with it and the animals — mainly insects — that feed on it), and lore. There are numerous line drawings with descriptive captions. While there is no index, the table of contents lists each plant species entry. A three-page glossary is included.

This book covers only 101 tree and plant species, but the author has personally inspected all of them in the wild. It introduces the reader to these species and their associations very nicely. It is well written, and the educated layperson will find it easy to use. The illustrations are excellent, and the figure captions are very informative. — **John Laurence Kelland**

1519. Perry, Jesse P., Jr. **The Pines of Mexico and Central America.** Portland, Oreg., Timber Press, 1991. 231p. illus. maps. index. $35.95. QK494.5.P66P45. 585'.2. LC 90-10774. ISBN 0-88192-174-2.

Pines are the most important trees in Mexico and Central America, and Mexico has the largest number of pine species in the world. This work is a scholarly but readable and up-to-date guide to these trees; it is meant for botanists, taxonomists, foresters, and people "just interested in pine trees" (preface).

The origin of pines in North America, the migration of these trees to Mexico and Central America, and the climate and rainfall in these areas are covered in the introduction. The chapter on classification and identification of pine trees is enhanced by highly detailed line drawings of pine leaf anatomy, decurrent and nondecurrent leaf bracts, pine cones, and the like.

Most of the book describes the individual species, with a key to the subgenera, sections, and subsections immediately preceding the species descriptions. Each entry provides the tree's Latin and common names, description, bark, branchlets, leaves, conelets, cones, cone scales, seeds, wood, distribution, habitat, specific directions to the location of a specimen (e.g., "look for a dirt road on the left leading to the village of San Telmo"), and notes and comments. Black-and-white pictures and a small distribution map are a part of every entry.

The final chapters cover the present status of the pine forests in each country (generally threatened), rare and endangered pines, and Perry's plea for the preservation of these vanishing "natural ... genetics laborator[ies]." An extensive selected bibliography will lead interested readers to books and articles in both English and Spanish. Libraries that support programs in botany, forestry, and land management and libraries in Mexico, Central America, and states along the United States-Mexico border will find this volume useful. — **D. A. Rothschild**

1520. Walters, James E., and Balbir Backhaus. **Shade and Color with Water-Conserving Plants.** Portland, Oreg., Timber Press, 1992. 165p. illus. maps. index. $39.95. SB439.8.W35. 712. LC 91-26607. ISBN 0-88192-214-5.

Walters is writer of a national gardening column, and Backhaus is a horticulture writer, photographer, and consultant. *Shade and Color with Water-Conserving Plants* should be a great help to home gardeners, landscapers, and nursery owners who want to select and grow attractive shrubs and trees that are adapted to the warm-arid U.S. southwest. The region includes parts of five states: Arizona, California, Nevada, New Mexico, and Texas. A few brief chapters that deal with climate, soils, landscape planning, and culture precede the main part of this book, which contains the individual plant descriptions. The plants are arranged in alphabetical order by their botanical names. Each entry includes a basic description, the common name, pronunciation, landscape uses, climate requirements, culture, and possible problems that may be encountered. More than 200 attractive color photographs, most supplied by Backhaus, are grouped together in the middle of the volume. A table of contents and an index are included, as well as a common name/botanical name list, a short glossary, and several other reader aids. — **William H. Wiese**

1521. Young, James A., and Cheryl G. Young. **Seeds of Woody Plants in North America.** rev. ed. Portland, Oreg., Dioscorides Press/Timber Press, 1992. 407p. illus. $49.95. SB170.Y68. 634.9'562. LC 91-21710. ISBN 0-931146-21-6.

This volume is an enlarged and revised edition of the U.S. Forest Service's *Agriculture Handbook 450*, first published by the Government Printing Office (GPO) in 1948. Listed are almost 400 genera of woody plants, about double the number covered in the 1948 edition. Long out of print through the GPO, this new edition drops some of the readily available taxonomic information that was in the previous edition. The main use of the handbook will be for seedling propagation, but some additional

culture notes are given for each genera. Seed collecting, storage, testing for germination, and planting notes are accompanied by photographs and line drawings of seeds, pods, and young plants. For most genera, paragraphs also cover growth habit, occurrence, and use; collection, extraction, and storage of seed; pregermination treatment; and nursery and field practice. An extensive bibliography appears to be current up to the late 1980s. Appendixes include a glossary and a chapter that cover the common and scientific names of plants and germination characteristics by genera. The volume has an attractive format and a sturdy library binding. Foresters, nursery professionals, horticulturists, seed producers, and researchers in forestry will find the volume a handy compendium of useful information. Serious gardeners will also find some material of interest. Recommended for all forestry and agricultural libraries.
—Ralph Lee Scott

NATURAL HISTORY

1522. Andrews, Jean. **A Field Guide to Shells of the Texas Coast.** Houston, Tex., Gulf Publishing, 1992. 176p. illus. index. (Texas Monthly Field Guide Series). $23.95; $16.95pa. QL415.T4A63. 594'.0471'09764. LC 91-37622. ISBN 0-87719-211-1; 0-87719-210-3pa.

Many casual collectors of marine shells along the Gulf Coast can get by with standard, general guidebooks to the shells of that region. However, the specialist and the dedicated collector need more detailed works, such as this one, which was originally published as *Texas Shells: A Field Guide* (University of Texas Press, 1981). This edition is basically similar to that earlier version, but there have been emendations, including changes in species assignments, and a section of color plates has been added. As was its predecessor, this book is derived from the author's *Shells and Shores of Texas* (see ARBA 78, entry 1334), a more comprehensive work. However, *A Field Guide to Shells of the Texas Coast* is more up-to-date than that parent work.

The lay user will probably find the book a bit difficult to work with, as some technical terms are not identified on the diagrams included in the introduction. A glossary would have been helpful. However, the illustrations alone should enable one to come close to the correct identification of a particular shell.—**Joseph Hannibal**

1523. Arnold, Tim. **Natural History from A to Z: A Terrestrial Sampler.** New York, Macmillan, 1991. 58p. illus. index. $15.95. QL49.A76. 591. LC 88-26879. ISBN 0-689-50467-5.

This children's book is a volume that can be easily read and understood by almost any intermediate school youngster. It will also serve parents who enjoy reading to their even younger children. The author uses the alphabet to present a lettered series of 26 two-page narratives on a few plants, animals, and concepts. Natural history and terrestrial organisms are the stated unifying themes, but each lettered story is focused on a topic that might be of interest to a youthful readership. Topics from A through Z range from anteaters (and aardvarks) through the zebra finch, with subjects such as basenjis, coatimundis, dragonflies, ivy, jaguars, kiwis, ladybugs, xylem, and yaks discussed in between. Each chapter is designed for easy comprehension. The presentations are entertaining and minimally informative. The information tendered is reasonably accurate. Brighter children will be disappointed by the oversimplifications and absence of depth. The print is large and bold, and line spacing is wide for easy reading. All narratives are supplemented by relevant illustrations (also by the author), both color and monochrome.

This book offers little that will set it apart from hundreds of other children's natural history books. It is simply an adequate reader for young people at the intended level of readership. Recommended for purchase by school libraries serving grades 3 through 6.—**Edmund D. Keiser, Jr.**

1524. Bates, G. W., comp. and ed. **Natural History Museums, Vol. 1: An Illustrated Guide to Over 350 Museums in the Eastern United States.** Fort Lauderdale, Fla., Batax Museum Publishing, 1992. 109p. illus. index. $12.95pa. QH70.U6B38. 508'.074'73. LC 91-31840. ISBN 0-9629759-5-8.

Bates, a member of the National Taxidermist Association, the Florida Paleontological Society, and the American Association of Museums, has prepared an up-to-date list of 358 natural history museums found in the District of Columbia and the 25 states east of the Mississippi River. Natural history museums are defined as permanent institutions that conserve and display objects of cultural or scientific interest, with at least a portion of their collections dedicated to natural history. All efforts to evaluate the size and quality of included institutions have been avoided beyond the addition of a star to indicate museums that refer to themselves specifically as natural history museums. All the states, their cities, and (if applicable) the several institutions therein are arranged alphabetically. Because exhibits are constantly changing, each entry includes only the institution's name, street address, and telephone number. Users are urged to call for visiting hours, admission prices, and accessibility. A list of ideas to enhance museum visits, 26 photographs of museum buildings and displays, an essay urging museum membership, and a short reading list about museums concludes this brief, affordable book. However, teachers planning first-time field trips or families planning visits to unfamiliar localities should probably also consult their academic or public library's *Official Museum Directory* (National Register Publishing, 1991) for further details about collections, facilities, and activities. Recommended as a supplemental purchase for public and undergraduate libraries. [R: RBB, 1 Apr 92, p. 1475]—**Helen M. Barber**

1525. Clewis, Beth. **Index to Illustrations of Animals and Plants.** New York, Neal-Schuman, 1991. 217p. $49.95. QH46.5.C54. 574'.022'2. LC 90-23816. ISBN 1-55570-072-1.

Provided as a supplement to *Index to Illustrations of the Natural World* (see ARBA 78, entry 1277) and *Index to Illustrations of Living Things outside of North America* (see ARBA 83, entry 1310), this work enables one to find pictures of a variety of plants and animals. In all, 142 books have been indexed. Arranged by common name (scientific name is listed as well), the information includes the book or books (by codes) where the illustration can be found and whether it is a black-and-white picture or an illustration presented on either a black-and-white or colored plate. In addition, a scientific name index gives the corresponding common name. There are two lists of the books that are indexed: one arranged by the code given to the book, and the other arranged alphabetically by title. The former can be found on the opening pages, while the latter concludes the book.

This is an extremely useful work as illustrations such as these are not always easy to find. Its usefulness diminishes, however, depending on the number of indexed books one has available. In addition, it should be noted that the majority of the books indexed deal with animals (a number of arthropods and the vertebrates). Recommended for public and high school libraries; highly recommended for college and university libraries. (Recommendations are based on the number of indexed books these libraries are likely to have in their collections.) [R: RQ, Fall 92, p. 116]—**George H. Bell**

1526. **Nature in America.** Pleasantville, N.Y., Reader's Digest Books, 1991. 456p. illus. index. $32.50. QH104.N26. 508.73'03. LC 90-46146. ISBN 0-89577-376-7.

Containing more than 1,200 entries and abounding with excellent color photographs, this volume considers the more familiar terms that deal with animals, plants, landforms, and other natural features found in the United States. Arranged alphabetically, the majority of the terms are defined in easy-to-understand language and relate basic information to the reader. The length of the definitions varies from one paragraph to several pages. In addition, two-page spreads are given for certain ecological niches, such as cypress swamps, deciduous forests, and deserts. Along with a brief description of the niche, a variety of photographs depict certain animals and plants endemic to the region. Colored letter tabs make looking up topics easy. A combined subject and common name index concludes this mini-encyclopedia. Recommended for public and elementary and secondary school libraries. [R: BR, May/June 92, p. 60; RBB, 15 Jan 92, p. 978]—**George H. Bell**

1527. **Nature Projects on File: Experiments, Demonstrations, and Projects....** By the Diagram Group. New York, Facts on File, 1992. 1v. (various paging). illus. index. $145.00 looseleaf w/binder. QH55.N38. 508. LC 91-40846. ISBN 0-8160-2705-6.

Learning science need not be boring and complicated. This work presents some 69 projects in 8 categories (Earth, weather, animal, plant, ecology, pollution, energy, and environment) for students to perform. Each project is self-contained and copyright-free, allowing copying for nonprofit educational use. The looseleaf notebook form facilitates use for teaching. Experiments are well presented, and results can be compared (or anticipated) with a section of expected findings in a separate chapter. Among the projects are those that simulate tectonic plates, pitfall traps, anemometers, seismographs, and calorimeters using discarded jars, cans, modeling clay, felt pens and paper, and other simple materials. Also included are ways of looking at our world through graphs and models that should stimulate any student. The majority of experiments are for grades 6-12 with a minimum of supervision. Safety precautions are provided. These projects are superb, but the text would benefit by adding suggested readings for captivated students; teachers would find them useful as well. [R: RBB, 1 Sept 92, p. 89; WLB, Sept 92, pp. 116-18]—**Marvin K. Harris**

1528. O'Clair, Rita M., Robert H. Armstrong, and Richard Carstensen. **The Nature of Southeast Alaska: A Guide to Plants, Animals, and Habitats.** Bothell, Wash., Alaska Northwest Books/GTE Discovery, 1992. 254p. illus. maps. index. $17.95pa. QH105.A4035. 508.798'2. LC 91-41861. ISBN 0-88240-419-9.

This book on the natural history of southeast Alaska or, as it is commonly called, the Alaskan Panhandle, will be welcomed not only by local residents but also by thousands of tourists who annually visit this beautiful and interesting area. The three authors represent various fields of science, with their expertise mainly in botany and zoology. They have studied the available scientific literature and have researched the ecosystems of the area through travel and interviews and consultations with local experts. In this book they focus on 21 wilderness areas that encompass about 43 percent of southeast Alaska, including 2 national parks, 3 national wildlife refuges, and a national monument wilderness. The book opens with a map that shows the wilderness areas, followed by descriptions of various types of natural habitats, such as old-growth forests, high country, streams, rivers and lakes, fresh water marshes and meadows, and salt marshes. This is the most important chapter in terms of emphasis and space allotted. Other chapters treat the material topically: mammals, birds, fish, invertebrates, fungi and lichens, and plants. Appended are 16 pages of color photographs of the spectacular landscapes and interesting animals and plants of southeast Alaska. Additionally, a list of common and scientific names of plants and animals is provided. The book closes with a bibliography and an index. The text is written clearly and will be easily understood by nonprofessionals.—**Ludmila N. Ilyina**

ZOOLOGY

General Works

1529. Allaby, Michael, ed. **The Concise Oxford Dictionary of Zoology.** New York, Oxford University Press, 1991. 508p. $39.95. QL9.C66. 591.03. LC 90-21596. ISBN 0-19-866162-2.

One of the problems with studying a discipline such as zoology is understanding its terminology. With the rising interest in conservation of wildlife, there is even more demand for such information. This dictionary has definitions for more than 6,000 entries from *aardvark* to *zymogenous*, written in a straightforward, understandable style. Many of the entries are from another publication of Allaby's, *Oxford Dictionary of Natural History* (see ARBA 87, entry 1460), but have been revised or rewritten to reflect current information. The length of each definition varies from a few words to more than a column.

The terms are primarily taxonomic (i.e., phylums, classes, orders, families, and some species). The animal groups covered are the invertebrates, especially the arthropods; fish; reptiles; amphibians; birds; and mammals. Common names are listed with a cross-reference to the scientific name where the full definition is found. Information on each group includes a description of the organism, number of species, and geographic distribution. In addition, subject terms in ecology, behavior, cell structure and function, physiology, zoogeography, and genetics are covered. Short biographical information is given for a few important people in zoology (e.g., Konrad Lorenz, Charles Darwin).

This is the only current dictionary that covers the entire field of zoology. It may be used to update Robert Pennak's *Collegiate Dictionary of Zoology* (Ronald Press, 1964), which is still in print and covers more terms (19,000 entries) than are found in this source. Another recent dictionary that may be used to supplement terms is Michael Stachowitsch's excellent *The Invertebrates: An Illustrated Glossary* (Wiley-Liss, 1991). For amateur naturalists, students, and zoologists who need an up-to-date source on unfamiliar zoological names or terms, this dictionary should prove useful. Recommended for high school, public, academic, and specialized zoological libraries. [R: Choice, June 92, p. 1516]

— Diane B. Rhodes

1530. Kerrod, Robin. **Animals around the World.** New York, Prentice Hall General Reference, 1992. 96p. illus. maps. index. $15.00. LC 91-66997. ISBN 0-13-033382-4.

The environment is of interest to both young and old, but each group has different informational needs. Prentice Hall has targeted junior high school students with the Prentice Hall World of Nature Series. This particular volume deals with ecology, how animals and plants differ from place to place, and how they interact.

The book starts with a geography lesson, introducing the concepts of zoogeographic regions and biomes and giving a good overview of the wildlife habitats discussed. From there readers travel through the various forest types to the hot dry regions, the cold regions, and the full range of aquatic habitats. Within a habitat readers learn about the climate and the plant life, major factors in determining the types of animals that live in the area. Some of the common animals are introduced within the discussion so that the interrelationship is emphasized.

Only representative species are depicted, but the coverage is well rounded. Insect life is included, although the photographs and drawings lean toward birds and mammals. Maps and diagrams further the readers' understanding of the habitat by depicting worldwide locations and climate information. A glossary and index of species increase the usefulness of this volume. If the rest of the series is as nicely done, the books will make a fine addition to any library with a junior high clientele. [R: SLJ, Nov 92, p. 135] — **Angela Marie Thor**

1531. Lambert, David. **The Children's Animal Atlas: How Animals Have Evolved, Where They Live Today, Why So Many Are in Danger.** Brookfield, Conn., Millbrook Press, 1991. 95p. illus. maps. index. $18.90. G1046.D4L3. 591.9'022'3. LC 91-30147. ISBN 1-56294-167-4.

A geographic review of the remarkable diversity of the world's animals is the central theme of this richly illustrated book. It uses the large global units that are major ecological regions known as biomes (e.g., savannas, deserts, salt marshes, temperate forests, coral reefs). The diversity of biomes is reviewed with regional maps and collections of representative animal photographs, all in extra-large, full-color format. Artwork is also used to illustrate simple ecological themes such as food chains and layering in a rain forest. Throughout, the text is brief but adequate for children (a glossary helps youngsters with biological terms). In addition to the review of the world's biomes, there are shorter sections on animal migration and the evolution of animals (including domestication). Conservation concerns, such as habitat loss, are mentioned throughout the text; a few pages dedicated to endangered species and saving wildlife are welcome reminders of people's responsibilities and a fitting conclusion to this attractive book. [R: RBB, 15 May 92, pp. 1710-11] — **Charles Leck**

1532. **Macmillan Animal Encyclopedia for Children.** By Roger Few. New York, Macmillan, 1991. 120p. illus. maps. index. $16.95. ISBN 0-02-762425-0.

This encyclopedia gives children a chance to learn about animals and the kinds of places in which they live. Nine of the Earth's major habitats are profiled, along with a sample of the species that live in each. Habitat background includes the geography of the region, its climate, and the plant life. A selected group of animals that are well adapted to the habitat is introduced by common name, and a brief description of why they are suited to that area is given. Next is a "catalog of the more spectacular species" that inhabit the region. Scientific name, size, and a few sentences about the animal's habits are given. The "Focus On" section outlines a few more details about a particular region within a habitat, such as the Siberian tundra within the "Ice Caps and Tundra" section.

Not just the cute and cuddly are included. Birds, reptiles, amphibians, and fish appear along with the mammals. The index will help locate specific animals, but the glossary is a single page with only 20 entries. However, this beautifully illustrated volume with its sound bites of information should serve its young audience well. [R: RBB, 1 Jan 92, p. 851] — **Angela Marie Thor**

1533. Van Tighem, Kevin. **Wild Animals of Western Canada.** Banff, Alta., Altitude Publishing, 1992. 96p. illus. $9.95pa. 591.9712. ISBN 0-919381-97-9.

More than 40 of Western Canada's wild mammals are described and pictured in this easy-to-read guide. It serves as an introduction to wildlife in all of North America, as it covers the most commonly known animals, such as the wolf, cougar, river otter, bison, weasel, red fox, woodchuck, and elk. Each mammal is introduced with a story from an experience Van Tighem, who works for the Canadian Parks Service, has had with each. For example, his escape from a raging cow moose introduces the two-page article on that animal. Each article is illustrated with a full-color photograph of the animal and a drawing of the track the animal makes. Conservation issues are addressed for protecting the environment these animals inhabit. A brief bibliography and a list of agencies and organizations where further information can be found is included at the end of the text. There is no index.

Entertaining reading and striking color photographs make this an easy way to discover the common mammals of Western Canada. Those wanting a more comprehensive source may choose *Mammals of Canada* by A. F. Banfield (University of Toronto Press, 1974). Another source is *The Handbook of Canadian Mammals* (National Museum of Natural Sciences, 1978-), but only volumes 1 and 2 of a projected multivolume work have been completed, and so far covers only the marsupials, insectivores, and bats. Van Tighem's book is suitable for upper elementary, junior high, or high school libraries as well as public libraries. – **George H. Bell**

1534. **The Visual Dictionary of Animals.** New York, Dorling Kindersley; distr., Boston, Houghton Mifflin, 1991. 64p. illus. index. (Eyewitness Visual Dictionaries). $14.95. LC 91-060901. ISBN 1-879431-19-X.

This visual dictionary identifies roughly 2,000 terms, pieces, and parts affiliated with zoological classification and animal anatomy. As in other works in the series, it does so in two-page spreads with more than 200 photographs and illustrations that are masterpieces of visual clarity and photographic rendering. Young children and the faint-of-heart may be somewhat unnerved by the graphic nature of the photographs, especially those showing body parts in dissected or detached stages. For the intrepid or curious, however, *Animals* presents fascinating information clearly and understandably. It covers 26 topics, including animal bodies, animal heads, arachnids, worms, flukes and leeches, mollusks, crocodilians and turtles, eggs, carnivores, ungulates (e.g., horses, cattle), primates, marsupials and monotremes, animal tracks, and animal classification. For each animal entry there is a brief introductory paragraph, then photographs of the subject and illustrations depicting its internal anatomy. Every body part is identified with both its general and scientific name where appropriate. The section on animal tracks is well done and informative, and the two-page spread on animal classification is especially noteworthy for its concise explanation of the animal classification systems and its graphic layout of the "*Kingdom Animalia.*" An index concludes the dictionary.

Certainly this is an introductory work. But what it does, it does beautifully, and at a price that makes it a reasonable purchase for all school and public libraries. [R: BR, May/June 92, p. 60; RBB, 1 Feb 92, p. 1059; WLB, Jan 92, p. 132] – **G. Kim Dority**

1535. **World Wildlife Habitats.** North Bellmore, N.Y., Marshall Cavendish, 1992. 3v. illus. maps. index. $139.95/set. OH541.W635. 591.5. LC 91-35958. ISBN 1-85435-433-7.

With worldwide concern for preserving and protecting our wildlife habitats, more readers are requesting books on these habitats to help understand the delicate balance that keeps them intact. This set covers 23 of the major ones, including caves, deserts, marshes, mountains, coral reefs, tropical rain forests, and even cities and towns. Each habitat is treated globally, so that the section on tropical rain forests includes all such habitats, whether they are in South America, Africa, or East Asia. The habitat is introduced with a world map shaded in green that shows where it is found throughout the world. The text covers the geography and climate of the habitat and a description of the animals that live there, showing how the close relationships between the habitat and animals make survival outside of it usually impossible. A feature of the set is the use of striking full-color photographs on almost every page. Volume 3 contains a 16-page index that includes the common and scientific names of animals (few plants), place-names, major geographical features, and some subject headings (e.g., canopy layer).

This set is a companion to the *Marshall Cavendish International Wildlife Encyclopedia* (see ARBA 91, entry 1555), and its emphasis is on the animal wildlife in each habitat. Those looking for detailed information on the plant life will be disappointed. Two points that lessen the authority of this set are the lack of identification of the author and the omission of a bibliography of sources. The coverage of world habitats is good, however, and provides easy, informative reading on a vital topic of the day. Recommended for public libraries and those that serve upper elementary through high school students. [R: RBB, Aug 92, p. 2041; SLJ, Nov 92, p. 140] — **Diane B. Rhodes**

Birds

1536. Alderton, David. **The Atlas of Quails.** Neptune, N.J., T. F. H. Publications, 1992. 144p. illus. maps. index. $39.95. ISBN 0-86622-145-X.

This magnificent work considers all the quail species found throughout the world. A two-page spread is devoted to each quail mentioned, one page for the description and the other for colored paintings of the birds.

Generally given for each species are the common and scientific names, namer, date of naming, a large geographical range map, bird's length, geographical distribution, coloration (young and adult), breeding success in captivity, nest building, number of eggs in a clutch, incubation period, and other interesting facts. Colored paintings of the male and female accompany the descriptions, which are usually no more than one to four paragraphs in length (coverage differs considerably depending upon what is known about each quail).

Other sections, illustrated with color photographs, consider such subjects as the keeping, housing, feeding, breeding, and health care of quails. There is also a checklist of the genera and species of quail that uses both scientific and common names. A combined subject/common/scientific name index concludes the volume.

This work is highly recommended for all college and university libraries that support programs in zoology. Large public libraries will also wish to purchase a copy. — **George H. Bell**

1537. **The Audubon Society Encyclopedia of North American Birds.** By John K. Terres. New York, Wings Books/Outlet Book, 1991. 1109p. illus. index. $39.99. QL681.T43. 598.297. LC 91-21877. ISBN 0-517-03288-0.

This beautifully illustrated and fact-filled encyclopedia is a reprint of the 1980 edition published by Alfred A. Knopf (see ARBA 82, entry 1484). If one already has the 1980 edition, there is no need to purchase this one. — **George H. Bell**

1538. Brazil, Mark A. **The Birds of Japan.** Washington, D.C., Smithsonian Institution Press, 1991. 466p. illus. maps. index. $55.00. LC 90-62321. ISBN 1-56098-030-3.

This work considers 583 species of birds found in Japan. Introductory chapters deal with climate, ocean currents, avifauna, distribution, migration, and bird watching in that country. Species are arranged under their respective family. For each bird mentioned, the common, scientific, and Japanese names are given, followed by a brief description that considers habitat, geographic range, and breeding characteristics. The length of the accounts varies from a quarter to a full page. In addition to line drawings, colored plates of many of the birds can be found throughout the source. Except for those in the drawings and plates, no identifying anatomical characteristics are considered in the text. Range maps for each species mentioned appear in the appendix. A 1,286-entry bibliography, a Japanese name index, and a combined common/scientific name index conclude the work.

Recommended for those college and university libraries with strong programs in zoology, especially ornithology. Large public libraries with client interest also may wish to purchase a copy.

— **George H. Bell**

1539. Brewer, Richard, Gail A. McPeek, and Raymond J. Adams, Jr. **The Atlas of Breeding Birds of Michigan.** East Lansing, Mich., Michigan State University Press, 1991. 594p. illus. maps. index. $39.95. QL684.M5B74. 598.29774. LC 91-53206. ISBN 0-87013-291-1.

Including all birds known to breed in the state of Michigan, this work represents 215 species. Each account takes up two full pages; one consists of descriptive information, the other includes a geographical range map of Michigan. The birds are entered by their common name, followed by their scientific name. Information on each species consists of breeding range, habitat, diet, feeding behavior, nesting sites, seasonal occurrences, and status of their breeding patterns now and in the past. In some cases conservation information is present. The geographical range map indicates by means of colored circles the possible, probable, and confirmed breeding sites throughout the state. Each descriptive account is accompanied by a drawing of the bird. The introductory chapters consist of methods and procedures used in compiling the information found within the geographical range maps; the land, climate, and vegetation of Michigan; original avifauna and postsettlement changes; biogeography and ecology; and priorities and prospectives in conservation.

A 27-page bibliography appears near the end of the volume. References here represent those cited throughout the descriptive information in the text. Appendix 1 consists of a taxonomic list of species (birds and other animals and plants) found in the work and arranged by common name with scientific name equivalents. Appendix 2 lists numerical information in a tabular format that shows distribution patterns within blocks that represent divisions of the state. A list of contributors and a combined common/scientific name index complete the volume.

This is a first-class publication whose main focus represents breeding patterns and habits of birds in Michigan. Interesting and informative, it takes a scholarly approach based on the breeding distribution surveys as well as the references cited to the literature. The amount of statistical information on breeding distribution numbers is commendable. Highly recommended for colleges and universities that have substantial programs in zoology. [R: Choice, June 92, p. 1569]—**George H. Bell**

1540. **The Cambridge Encyclopedia of Ornithology.** Michael Brooke and Tim Birkhead, eds. New York, Cambridge University Press, 1991. 362p. illus. maps. index. $37.50. ISBN 0-521-36205-9.

Arranged by broad categories that cover the form, function, and behavior of birds, this source is a first-rate publication. It is not typical of other bird encyclopedias, which, for the most part, list and describe particular species of birds. Rather, its focus is on the biological principles endemic to the bird group. It covers migration, flight, food and feeding, geographical distribution, nests, eggs, courtship displays, anatomy and physiology of systems, and much more. Bird groups and species are introduced in these sections to illustrate biological principles. In addition, a section on modern birds lists and describes families and presents the number of species within each family. Line drawings, geographical range maps, graphs, and colored photographs illustrate these informative sections. A list of ornithological organizations; a brief glossary; a list of references for each of the 11 chapters; and subject, common name, and scientific name indexes complete the source.

This work could easily serve as a supplement to a text in ornithology. Highly recommended for large public, college, and university libraries. [R: BR, Mar/Apr 92, p. 53; LJ, 15 Apr 92, p. 42; RBB, 1 Mar 92, pp. 1304-05; RBB, 15 June 92, p. 1870; SLJ, May 92, p. 152; WLB, Jan 92, p. 125]
—**George H. Bell**

1541. Ehrlich, Paul R., David S. Dobkin, and Darryl Wheye. **Birds in Jeopardy: The Imperiled and Extinct Birds of the United States and Canada, Including Hawaii and Puerto Rico.** Stanford, Calif., Stanford University Press, 1992. 259p. illus. index. $45.00; $17.95pa. QL676.55.E38. 333.95'8137'097. LC 91-29555. ISBN 0-8047-1967-5; 0-8047-1981-0pa.

Employing the USFWS (United States Fish and Wildlife Service) and the National Audubon Society lists as well as other information, this source provides data on those birds throughout most of North America (including Hawaii) that are endangered, threatened, or extinct. The birds are arranged under threatened or endangered continental species/subspecies, Puerto Rican species/subspecies, and species that are candidates for the threatened or endangered list. A full page of data, including common and scientific names, nesting information, diet, geographical range, conservation status, and recovery plans, is given for each bird. A colored drawing of the head of the bird being described accompanies each entry.

There are also entries for birds not on the official lists but that exhibit vulnerability and for birds that have become extinct since 1776. Some general information on the conservation of birds and environment threats is provided, and a seven-page bibliography and a name index conclude the work. Highly recommended for college, university, and public libraries. — **George H. Bell**

1542. Gray, Mary Taylor. **Watchable Birds of the Rocky Mountains.** Missoula, Mont., Mountain Press, 1992. 155p. illus. index. $12.00pa. QL683.R63G73. 589'.0723478. LC 92-10101. ISBN 0-87842-281-1.

This work provides general biological information on 69 species of birds. It is divided into three parts: birds of the plains (22 species), birds of the wetlands (27 species), and birds of the mountains (20 species). Given for each of the species are the common, alternative common, and scientific names; family; coloration; habitat; behavioral antics; vocalization patterns; and when and where to see them. In addition, a series of bird silhouettes alerts the reader to the approximate size of the bird under discussion. A color photograph of the bird accompanies the page-long descriptive account. Some general information on bird-watching and a map that depicts the geographical areas covered appear in the introduction. A common and scientific name index closes the field guide.

This is a handy source for public and school libraries as it covers the more familiar bird species found in the Rockies and discusses their behavioral patterns in an entertaining way. The novice bird-watcher may also find it of interest. However, because it is not comprehensive, its usefulness for the serious ornithologist is limited. — **George H. Bell**

1543. Inskipp, Carol, and Tim Inskipp. **A Guide to the Birds of Nepal.** Washington, D.C., Smithsonian Institution Press, c1985, 1991. 400p. illus. maps. index. $55.00. LC 91-60470. ISBN 1-56098-097-4.

The 836 species contained herein are arranged by common group-names, such as grebes, game birds, ducks, kingfishers, and parrots. For each species listed, its common and scientific names, the name of the person who first recorded it, other common names, subspecies, geographical range, and habitat are given. Each description is usually no more than a quarter of a column. Geographical range maps of Nepal and line drawings of the species accompany the descriptive information. The range maps contain symbols that are used to represent where the specimen has been recorded, as well as where it was recorded in the breeding season. In addition, possible and proven breeding locales are considered. Eight pages of colored plates can be found in the middle of the source.

The opening section of this work, which encompasses about 80 pages, considers typography, climate, vegetation, bird distribution and conservation, protected areas, migration, ornithological history, bird-watching areas, identification section, and key to the maps. The identification section covers some of the more difficult groups of species and is illustrated with line drawings. Species are arranged under common name groups. Information given in this section includes common and scientific name, length, coloration, and (in many cases) wing length and span. A bibliography that contains 819 entries and a separate common name/scientific name index concludes the book. Material cited in the text can be found in the bibliography. Highly recommended for those colleges and universities having strong programs in zoology. — **George H. Bell**

1544. Lodge, Walter. **Birds Alternative Names: A World Checklist.** London, Cassell; distr., New York, Sterling Publishing, 1991. 208p. index. $19.95. 598.014. ISBN 0-7137-2267-3.

Yellow-fronted Canary, Green Singing Finch, Yellow-eyed Canary, Icterine Canary, Mozambique Serin, and Shelley are all alternative names for the same canary. Conversely, the single common name Cape Canary has been used for two different canaries. Lodge's book attempts to help bird-watchers solve these name problems. The checklist is arranged by the scientific name for the family and then the genus, with species names listed alphabetically under the genus. The common or English names for the species are given in a column to the right of the species name. For example, beside the family Strigidae (owls) and the genus and species *Ninox connivens*, the two common names Barking Owl and Winking Owl are listed. No indication of which name is the more common or preferred name is given. An indication of which country uses a particular name would also have been helpful. An appendix deals with the second problem of a single English name that is used for more than one species of bird. For example, the common name Painted Finch has been used for both *Emblema picta* and *Chloebia gouldiae*. The appendix is arranged alphabetically by the first word of the common name.

There are two indexes: one for English names, the other for genus names. The English name index is frustrating to use since it is alphabetical by the base name, such as finch or grackle, not the full alternative name. To find the name Rothschild's Grackle one must look under grackle in the index, which lists three different pages in the text that must be scanned. Although Lodge says in the introduction that names were found in "many sources, including numerous field guides and other ornithological literature, avicultural books, journals, magazines and society newsletters, CITES lists ...," these are not reflected in the bibliography. Also, many old titles are included when newer ones are available, and very few titles (40) are listed in comparison with the enormous amount of literature in ornithology.

In spite of the aforementioned problems, this checklist generally succeeds in its purpose. Useful for academic and large public libraries and in communities with active bird-watchers.

—Diane B. Rhodes

1545. Simpson, Marcus B., Jr. **Birds of the Blue Ridge Mountains: A Guide for the Blue Ridge Parkway, Great Smoky Mountains, Shenandoah National Park, and Neighboring Areas.** Chapel Hill, N.C., University of North Carolina Press, 1992. 354p. illus. maps. index. $29.95; $14.95pa. QL683.B57S56. 598.29755. LC 91-24620. ISBN 0-8078-2018-0; 0-8078-4363-6pa.

From southern Pennsylvania to the northern expanses of Georgia, this source provides information on the geographic areas and types of birds found throughout the Blue Ridge Mountain range. The various parks and location sites are arranged mainly by state, such as those along the Blue Ridge Parkway in Virginia (e.g., Skyline Drive) and North Carolina. Another section of the book considers sites away from the Parkway. For each of the sites and geographical locations are presented seasonal considerations, access to the area, name of location maps, types of facilities (e.g., housing, food, gas), geographical considerations, history and vegetation of the area, a description of the trails, and the names of the birds most likely to be encountered in the area (rare birds are also considered). A number of excellent black-and-white drawings depict a few of the birds mentioned in the text. Some road maps for the different regions are also given. A compilation of the common bird names along with geographical locations, relative abundance of the birds, and seasonal considerations appear in an annotated checklist. Other sections include a list of Parkway district information names and numbers and a four-page bibliography. Common name and subject indexes conclude the source.

For those interested in birds that are likely to be encountered in a locality, park, or trail in or near the Blue Ridge Mountains, this work provides ample information in a readable and interesting manner. However, if an identification guide is needed, the work will be disappointing. There are no colored plates of the birds, nor are there any that identify anatomical features. Recommended for public, college, and university libraries.

—George H. Bell

1546. Thompson, Max C., and Charles Ely. **Birds in Kansas. Volume 2.** Lawrence, Kans., University Press of Kansas, 1992. 424p. illus. maps. index. $25.00; $14.95pa. QL684.K2T47. 598.29781. LC 89-5017. ISBN 0-89338-039-3; 0-89338-040-7pa.

Covering 207 of the 424 birds found in Kansas, this work concludes the biological information on these vertebrates that began with volume 1. That book considered nonsongbirds (nonpasserines) while this one concludes with song birds (passerines). The species are arranged under their respective family. Each species entry gives its scientific name, common name, status, dates when birds are observed, habits, habitat, external anatomical identifying characteristics, breeding information, and diet. Most of the descriptions average two pages in length. Not all of the biological parameters can be found in every account. A black-and-white photograph illustrates 177 of the descriptive accounts, and each has a geographical range map of Kansas that depicts species sightings within the counties. A five-page bibliography and a combined common scientific name index complete the volume. Recommended for colleges and universities with strong programs in zoology, large public libraries throughout the country, and public libraries in Kansas.

—George H. Bell

Butterflies

1547. Carter, David. **Butterflies and Moths.** New York, Dorling Kindersley; distr., Boston, Houghton Mifflin, 1992. 304p. illus. maps. index. (Eyewitness Handbooks). $29.95; $17.95pa. QL544.2.C37. 595.78. LC 91-58221. ISBN 1-56458-034-2; 1-56458-062-8pa.

More than 500 species of butterflies and moths from around the world are described and illustrated in this informative and colorful guide. Carter is senior scientific officer in the entomology department of the London Natural History Museum; he has authored several other guides to butterflies. This one includes all 5 butterfly families and 22 of the major moth families.

The introductory material covers 26 pages and includes such information as life cycle, early stages, conservation, survival, rearing, and geographical distribution. The arrangement of the main part of the guide is by family, first butterfly, then moth. Every family is introduced with a short paragraph on its basic characteristics, followed by descriptions of selected species. Each species is described with brief general information as well as notes on early stages and distribution; a map highlights the general area where it may be found.

A feature of this guide is the use of full-color photographs next to each description, rather than separating the color plates from the text. The photographs are annotated with brief notes that point out distinguishing characteristics, such as "red eyespot in the corner of each hind-wing" or "characteristic white antennae." The photograph and text describing each species take up one-half page and are enclosed by color-coded headers for family (pink), species (green), and author (beige). A color-coded band borders the end of the description with information on time of flight and habitat, plus wingspan dimensions.

This new manual provides a visually pleasing and easy-to-read guide to the more common butterfly and moth species. It can be used by amateur and specialist alike. Recommended especially for public and school libraries from junior high on up, it can also prove useful to academic libraries as an introduction to this beautiful and fascinating group. [R: LJ, 1 Sept 92, p. 170; SLJ, Nov 92, p. 136]
— **Diane B. Rhodes**

1548. Miller, Jacqueline Y., ed. **The Common Names of North American Butterflies.** Washington, D.C., Smithsonian Institution Press, 1992. 177p. index. $14.95pa. QL548.C66. 595.78'9097'014. LC 91-21343. ISBN 1-56098-122-9.

Access to common names for butterflies in North America north of Mexico has just become much easier. Butterfly watchers and lepidopterists can reach for this single volume to match a common name with a taxonomic one; the index provides an entryway via the familiar or the scientific. The utility of the book extends beyond the subsorting accomplished. A tidy bibliography makes simple the work of finding important references, particularly state guides, from Comstock in California to Stiling in Florida. Species are tied to their broad geographical ranges. Endangered and possibly extinct species are noted, and common names used in standard references are cited. A foreword provides a context for naming things in the natural world, a sphere where curiosity and concern for the environment require consistent communication.

There is fun in just reading varied common names applied to the same species: voracious caterpillars such as the parsleyworm (or celeryworm) have captured as much attention as the adult black swallowtail, and the "wanderer" habit and food preference of the monarch (or milkweed butterfly) have long been known. Suggested improvements for the next edition are amplified criteria for selection of the "preferred common names," the addition of authors for the binomial nomenclature, and the use of standard definitions (e.g., "teemed," not "teamed"). That wish-list written, this work stands as an excellent beginning and an absolutely useful tool. — **Diane M. Calabrese**

1549. Opler, Paul A. **A Field Guide to Eastern Butterflies.** Boston, Houghton Mifflin, 1992. 396p. illus. maps. index. $24.95; $16.95pa. (Peterson Field Guide Series, 4). QL551.E16065. 595.78'9'097. LC 91-44477. ISBN 0-306-36452-3; 0-395-63279-Xpa.

This new edition of a 40-year-old classic by Alexander Klots, *A Field Guide to the Butterflies of Eastern North America* (Houghton Mifflin, 1951), promises to be a classic itself. Opler's excellent text and Vichai Malikul's beautiful color paintings make a winning combination not only for accurate identification of eastern butterflies but also for a true appreciation of them. Introductory chapters on butterfly study, gardening, conservation, and habitats lead into sections on identification of true butterflies (swallowtails, whites and sulphurs, harvesters, coppers, hairstreaks and blues, metalmarks, and brushfoots) and the skippers. In all, 524 known species found east of the 100th meridian are described. Each account covers size range (in inches and millimeters), color and outward appearance of males and females, a description of the early stages (caterpillar), food plants, flight dates, geographic range, habitat, and remarks on other distinguishing features. Clear, easy-to-read range maps are provided for most species and are usually found on the same pages as the species accounts. Supplementary material includes a life list, a glossary of terms used in the descriptions, references for further reading, a directory of butterfly societies, and butterfly collecting tips. Indexes to the host and nectar plants and to butterfly names finish this comprehensive guide.

A feature of this guide is 541 fine color paintings by Malikul. These and 104 color photographs of live specimens (including some caterpillars and chrysalids) are found on 48 plates in the center of the text. The paintings illustrate the species resident in the eastern United States and a few with five or more occurrences in this area.

This excellent work will soon be found in the hands of many amateur and professional lepidopterists enjoying a day in the field. Highly recommended for all libraries.—**Diane B. Rhodes**

1550. Riotte, J. C. E. **Annotated List of Ontario Lepidoptera.** Toronto, Royal Ontario Museum, 1992. 208p. maps. index. (Life Sciences Miscellaneous Publication). $19.95pa. 595.78'09713. ISBN 0-88854-397-2.

This checklist of butterflies and moths is annotated with information on their geographical distribution in Ontario. It not only provides information on which butterflies and moths are in Ontario but also where they are found. It is, however, strictly a checklist. It has no pictures, and because it makes little use of common names, it is an information source only for the specialist or the dedicated amateur.

The checklist is arranged by family name, with species names listed in alphabetical order under each genus. It follows the nomenclature and classification of the *Checklist of the Lepidoptera of America North of Mexico* by R. W. Hodges and others (E. W. Classey, 1983). After each species name Riotte has added a number that represents one of the four main faunal regions of Ontario: the Tundra, northern Ontario, central Ontario, and southern Ontario. In many cases districts, counties, regional municipalities, and other selected localities from the region are included after the name. These localities are shown on three black-and-white maps at the beginning of the text. Occasionally information on flight period, food plant preferences, and other remarks is included after the geographical data. The work concludes with a seven-page bibliography of the literature cited in the checklist and a lengthy, detailed index to scientific names. Although this is a very useful and needed checklist, it is very specific to Ontario; as such, it will be of best use in Canadian collections and those in the United States that strongly collect entomological works.—**Diane B. Rhodes**

1551. Stokes, Donald, Lillian Stokes, and Ernest Williams. **The Butterfly Book: An Easy Guide to Butterfly Gardening, Identification, and Behavior.** Boston, Little, Brown, 1991. 95p. illus. maps. $10.95pa. QL548.S76. 595.78'9097. LC 91-15323. ISBN 0-316-81780-5.

This economical compendium gently guides anyone in the continental United States who would welcome and identify butterflies. Writing from the premise that one cannot have too many flowers, the authors outline a direct approach for aspiring butterfly gardeners. Identified are the top 10 flowers for tempting butterflies, common food plants for caterpillars, and 2 simple garden plans. The essentials are complemented by glorious photographs of common caterpillars and butterflies, distribution maps, descriptions, taxonomic placement, and tips for rearing and attracting particular species. History and natural history are nicely meshed. For example, introduced fennel and citrus enabled the anise swallowtail to expand its western range and increase its yearly generations. Tantalizing biological notes—the mutualism between ants and caterpillars of blues, and 10-month life of the mourning cloak adult, and the attractiveness of ultraviolet range colors—invite more study. The layout makes the book stand well without an index. A resource guide includes suggested reading (*Wings in the Meadow* by

Jo Brewer ought to have appeared), societies, and butterfly house locations. A Nabokov quotation opens the book; it might have closed with Yeats: " ... But every butterfly to a friend."

—Diane M. Calabrese

Domestic Animals

1552. **The Complete Dog Book: The Photograph, History and Official Standard of Every Breed Admitted to AKC Registration....** 18th ed. New York, Howell Book House/Macmillan, 1992. 724p. illus. index. $27.50. SF427.C69. 636.7'088'8. LC 91-42714. ISBN 0-87605-464-5.

This standard work follows the format of earlier versions. It is still an official publication of the American Kennel Club (AKC) and is the primary source for information on all breeds recognized by the AKC. This edition has been updated and extensively revised. Of the 134 breeds listed, two-thirds have new, revised, or reformatted standards.

A general chapter discusses all breeds. The next sections are divided into the seven standard groups, with a separate entry for each animal classed in the group. Provided for each breed are a brief history; a photograph; and the official AKC standards on appearance, size, proportions, coat, color, gait, and temperament. The last major section deals with owning, caring for, and training dogs. The healthcare portion has been updated by the faculty of the University of Pennsylvania School of Veterinary Medicine. The photographs that accompany the listing for each dog are in black-and-white and do not greatly assist in defining the required color of the coat. However, there are two nice sections of color photographs, many of which show the dogs in action. An extensive glossary of 500-plus terms, samples of the forms needed to register a dog with the AKC, and descriptions of the club's activities add to the work's value, particularly for the novice owner. This title is a useful reference source for every public library and many school and university collections. [R: RBB, 15 Oct 92, pp. 450-52]

—Susan Ebershoff-Coles

Fishes

1553. Axelrod, Herbert R., and others. **Dr. Axelrod's Atlas of Freshwater Aquarium Fishes.** 6th ed. Neptune City, N.J., T. F. H. Publications, 1991. 1151p. illus. index. $79.95. ISBN 0-86622-217-0.

In this edition (for a review of the previous one see ARBA 90, entry 1548) the photographs have been increased to more than 7,000 and, unfortunately, most descriptive text has been eliminated. Photograph captions to scientific names and symbols represent sex, feeding habits, reproduction, aquarium lighting, temperament, swimming habits, desirable pH of the water, temperature tolerance, maximum size, and the capacity of the tank that suits the fishes best. A symbol chart is reproduced on page 12 and on the back cover. The book attempts to standardize common names applied to fishes that cannot be distinguished readily by an ichthyologist (e.g., tank-raised varieties of swordtails, platies, mollies, guppies, angelfish, and discus) because of small size, shape, and form.

The book is laid out zoogeographically in six regions: North American, Eurasian, Neotropical, African, Southeast Asian, and Australasian. Use of the 62-page index of common and scientific names is critical but does not guarantee identification. Only the scientific name is given under photographs, so if identification cannot be made by sight alone, the novice is sure to be confused. Endangered and threatened species are not identified. Many pages have a distinct cut-and-paste feel, with scattered species and a lack of page numbers. Also, page numbers do not appear in the same place on all pages, making a reference point more difficult to identify.

There are several concerns about the lack of balance between the technical index and species names and the very brief introduction in lay language. While this book may recruit people to the wonders of freshwater aquariums and the lovely fish that can be raised with success and minimum effort, hobbyists would be better served by *Dr. Axelrod's Mini-Atlas of Freshwater Aquarium Fishes* (see ARBA 89, entry 1456), which includes 250 pages of information on the aquarium environment and more than 1,800 color photographs. Reference and public libraries holding the 5th edition of the work under review may wish to wait for a future update.—**Judy Gay Matthews**

1554. Burgess, Warren E., Herbert R. Axelrod, and Ray Hunziker. **Dr. Burgess's Mini-Atlas of Marine Aquarium Fishes.** Neptune City, N.J., T. F. H. Publications, 1991. 1023p. illus. index. $29.95. ISBN 0-86622-404-1.

Designed for the identification of marine fishes, this pictorial aid will delight novice and seasoned enthusiasts with 1,900 full-color photographs and outline drawings. Arranged in systematic sequence, each illustration has symbols that indicate feeding preferences, light requirements, temperament, and preferred water temperature. Symbols are printed on the front and back flaps of the book jacket and on pages 23-24. The front matter provides information on the sex of fishes, reproduction, swimming habits, and how large individual species grow. The photographs have been lifted from *Dr. Burgess's Atlas of Marine Aquarium Fishes* (see ARBA 90, entry 1549) and are printed in reverse from the original volume, giving the appearance of unique shots.

The aquarium section includes the most up-to-date methods of maintaining a tank, tank construction, auxiliary equipment, salt water requirements, handling fishes, diseases and parasites, the importance of algae, and breeding characteristics. This section does not appear in the parent volume. The information is presented clearly, concisely, and logically. Indexes combine both scientific and common names for all fishes illustrated. Thick glossy paper allows the fish colors to dazzle the eye.

The body of data provided in this condensed atlas is recommended for ichthyologists, biologists, naturalists, students, and teachers. However, if one already owns the parent volume, this work would be an optional purchase unless specific information on tank set-up and maintenance is needed.
—Judy Gay Matthews

1555. Coad, Brian W. **Guide to the Marine Sport Fishes of Atlantic Canada and New England.** Toronto, Canadian Museum of Nature and Toronto and Buffalo, N.Y., University of Toronto Press, 1992. 307p. illus. index. $50.00; $19.95pa. 597.092'145. ISBN 0-8020-5875-2; 0-8020-6798-0pa.

Covering 70 species of fish that have been classified as either fish used for bait, fish caught for sport, or fish that make good eating, this source provides general information on the identification of these vertebrates. The introductory material consists of 55 pages devoted to the various aspects of fish biology, including (but not limited to) such topics as how to identify fish, preserving fish for identification, commercial fisheries, and fish farming. The species of fish, arranged phylogenetically, are presented under their respective families. The common name of each family is given along with the number of species within the group and general information on the group's external anatomy. For each species presented, the common and scientific names, namer, date of naming, and other names are considered. In addition, basic external anatomical features, coloration, geographical distribution, size and weight, behavioral patterns, diet, and commercial value are given. Citations to the literature and a black-and-white drawing that shows gross morphology accompany the descriptive account. In some cases, geographical range maps are also present. Besides the drawings, a number of black-and-white photographs of fish can be found interspersed among the species accounts.

A number of appendixes deal with such information as taxidermy; fish prints; knot tying; recipes; and tides, charts, and weather reports. The bibliography contains books useful for the angler. An illustrated glossary, an English to French lexicon that contains fish terms, metric conversions, and an index complete the volume. Recommended for sports enthusiasts fishing in these waters and for regional public libraries.—George H. Bell

1556. Eccles, David H. **Field Guide to the Freshwater Fishes of Tanzania.** Rome, FAO of the United Nations; distr., Lanham, Md., UNIPUB, 1992. 145p. illus. maps. index. (FAO Species Identification Sheets for Fishery Purposes). $25.00pa. ISBN 92-5-103186-X.

Supported by the United Nations Development Programme and executed by the Food and Agriculture Organization of the United Nations, this source provides information that will enable users to identify those freshwater fish found throughout Tanzania. The species are arranged under their respective genera. The scientific name, person who first named it, date of naming, alternative scientific name, local name (if any), geographical distribution, and habitat are given for each organism. A line drawing of the fish and its family name accompany the description. Basic external anatomical characteristics are pointed out in the line drawings. Each description is no more than a third of a page in length. A pictorial index to the families found near the beginning of the guide aids in the identification process; a guide to the orders and families precedes it. The book also has a generalized map of Tanzania, a table that lists the species and their distribution, a short bibliography, and an index.

Because this work is very specific, it is recommended for those college and university libraries with strong programs in zoology, especially ichthyology. Individuals doing field work in Tanzania will definitely want a copy. — **George H. Bell**

1557. **FAO Species Catalogue. Vol.13: Marine Lobsters of the World: An Annotated and Illustrated Catalogue of Species of Interest to Fisheries....** By L. B. Holthuis. Rome, FAO of the United Nations; distr., Lanham, Md., UNIPUB, 1991. 292p. illus. maps. index. (FAO Fisheries Synopsis, no.125, v.13). $55.00pa. ISBN 92-5-103027-8.

This series focuses on commercially important marine animals. Volume 13 identifies lobster species and provides factual information on each. It covers 149 species of lobster in 3 infraorders, 10 families, and 33 genera. These species are used for food, sold for bait or other products, or have potential value.

After introductory material on lobster anatomy and a very good illustrated glossary of terms, the systematic catalog begins. It is arranged by order, then suborder to family, with detailed species entries under family. Species information includes an FAO designated common name (in English, French, and Spanish), type locality, geographical distribution (with range map), habitat and biology, size, interest to fisheries, and citations to the literature for further reading. Excellent, detailed black-and-white drawings of each species are provided, with some additional anatomical details also featured. Illustrated dichotomous keys to family and subfamily are found throughout the text. Following the catalog is a section, with map, that shows what species are found in various major fishing areas of the world. A 13-page bibliography and an index of scientific and common names finish the volume.

This specialized source is meant for use by commercial fisheries personnel, students, serious amateurs, and scholars interested in crustaceans. Very thorough and scholarly, it is recommended for specialized or academic libraries that support programs in commercial fisheries, marine science, or invertebrate studies. — **Diane B. Rhodes**

1558. Rojo, Alfonso L. **Dictionary of Evolutionary Fish Osteology.** Boca Raton, Fla., CRC Press, 1991. 273p. illus. $69.95. QL639.R54. 597'.0471. LC 91-16508. ISBN 0-8493-4214-7.

Some 375 English-language terms dealing with fish osteology (mainly the names of the bones of fish) are arranged alphabetically in this work. Under each the name is then translated into French, German, Latin, Russian, and Spanish. Definitions (in English) are also provided, the lengths of which vary from a paragraph to several pages. In some cases, references to the literature are given.

The introduction has information on the skeleton plan of a fish along with techniques and chemicals that are useful in preparing fish skeletons. Preceding the list of terms is an analogical section that arranges the words under broad subject categories. Therefore, if one is interested in terms that deal with the integumentary system, one will find a listing of these with corresponding page numbers in this section. Other headings are basic terms, morphology, appendicular system, skeletal system, digestive system, reproductive system, and organ of equilibrium.

An 18-page bibliography precedes the alphabetical list of terms. In addition, separate indexes of the entries in English, French, German, Latin, Russian, and Spanish appear near the end of the work. Concluding the book are a large number of labeled line drawings that depict the various skeletal parts of fish. Highly recommended for those colleges and universities with strong programs in vertebrate zoology, especially ichthyology. — **George H. Bell**

1559. **World Fishes Important to North Americans: Exclusive of Species from the Continental Waters of the United States and Canada.** Bethesda, Md., American Fisheries Society, 1991. 243p. index. (American Fisheries Society Special Publication, 21). $38.00; $30.00pa. LC 91-71562. ISBN 0-913235-54-7; 0-913235-53-9pa.

The species within this checklist are arranged under their respective families, which in turn are entered under order and class. Brief information on the order and class is provided, such as diet, number of genera and species, and identifying characteristics of the group as a whole. For each of the fish are given the scientific name, person who first named it, date of naming, common name, alternative scientific names (if any), importance codes, and geographical distribution. The importance codes correspond to the terms *aquarium, bait, aquaculture, endangered or threatened, food, industrial, poisonous, sport, textbook* (species that are used in textbooks to exemplify a group), and *experimental research*. An index to the families is at the beginning of the work, and a combined common/scientific name index completes the source.

It should be noted that the species listed in this volume have no geographic or bathymetric limitation (other than what is suggested in the title), as do the fish listed in the publisher's *A List of Common and Scientific Names of Fishes from the United States and Canada* (5th ed.). In that work, only North American freshwater and marine species north of Mexico that occur in waters shallower than 200 meters are included. Therefore, there is very little overlap in coverage of species between the two publications. Recommended for those universities having strong programs in zoology, especially in ichthyology. —**George H. Bell**

Insects

1560. Bousquet, Yves, ed. **Checklist of Beetles of Canada and Alaska.** Ottawa, Research Branch, Agriculture Canada, 1991. 430p. index. (Publication, 1861/E). $29.95pa.; $35.95pa. (U.S.). 595.76. ISBN 0-660-13767-4.

Beetles account for close to one-third of all known animals on Earth and are found in almost all the Earth's environments. This checklist provides the correct names and synonyms of the 24,000 species of beetles that occur in Canada and Alaska and indicates in what areas they may be found. It is arranged by suborder, then by family, and so on down to genus and species. Classification and basic information for each family group is written by one of the 10 contributors to this checklist. This family information also includes references to key publications on the taxonomy of the group where further information on identification may be found. These references are included in a 29-page bibliography. An index to taxa, including synonyms, above species level is included at the end of the text.

A comparable work is *A Catalog of the Coleoptera of America North of Mexico* (U.S. Department of Agriculture, 1979-), which covers the geographic ranges of Canada and Alaska. This catalog is published irregularly in 124 fascicles, each with information on a particular family.

This scholarly work was produced primarily by the Biosystematics Research Centre of Agriculture Canada, with other contributors from universities in Canada and one from the University of Wisconsin, Madison. It is an indispensable list of the beetles for this area and should be a standard source for years to come. Primarily for the professional entomologist and serious student, it is recommended for academic and large public libraries and those with strong collections in zoological sciences.

—**Diane B. Rhodes**

1561. Christiansen, Kenneth, and Peter Bellinger. **Insects of Hawaii: A Manual of the Insects of the Hawaiian Islands.... Volume 15: Collembola.** Honolulu, University of Hawaii Press, 1992. 445p. illus. maps. index. $48.00pa. QL489.H3Z5. 595.700969. LC 48-45482. ISBN 0-8248-1300-6.

This book is a comprehensive regional taxonomic work on the springtails, or Collembola. This fascinating order of insects is poorly understood and too often overlooked. The approach is basically a species-by-species technical summary of the knowledge of Collembola in Hawaii. The text is well written and carefully edited, and the keys to species and tables of characters make the book very useful. The illustrations are nicely done, concentrating as they do on important taxonomic features. Distribution maps support the text where appropriate.

Taxonomic works of this type are invaluable to scientists for decades after they appear. This one is certain to be important thanks to its inclusion of 63 new species descriptions. Serious students of springtails will want a copy of this book.

—**John A. Jackman**

1562. Goulet, Henri. **The Genera and Subgenera of the Sawflies of Canada and Alaska. Hymenoptera: Symphyta.** Ottawa, Agriculture Canada, 1992. 235p. illus. index. (Insects and Arachnids of Canada, pt.20). $24.95pa.; $29.95pa. (U.S.). 595.79. ISBN 0-660-14249-X.

1563. Platnick, Norman I., and Charles D. Dondale. **The Ground Spiders of Canada and Alaska. Araneae: Gnaphosidae.** Ottawa, Agriculture Canada, 1992. 297p. illus. maps. index. (Insects and Arachnids of Canada, pt.19). $25.95pa.; $31.15pa. (U.S.). 595.4'4. ISBN 0-660-14222-8.

1564. Vockeroth, J. R. **The Flower Flies of the Subfamily Syrphinae of Canada, Alaska, and Greenland. Diptera: Syrphidae.** Ottawa, Agriculture Canada, 1992. 456p. illus. maps. index. (Insects and Arachnids of Canada, pt.18). $22.95pa.; $27.55pa. (U.S.). 595.7'5. ISBN 0-660-13830-1.

These titles are the latest in a series of 20 excellent monographs published so far on the insects, spiders, mites, and ticks of Canada. Examples of other volumes in this series are those on bark beetles, crab spiders, mosquitoes, spittlebugs, larval midges, grasshoppers, wolf spiders, and nurseryweb spiders and lynx spiders. Each volume is authored by a specialist in the field and describes and provides identification keys for the group. For example, in the volume on flower flies, Vockeroth provides introductory material on the distribution, economic importance, general biology, mimicry, anatomy, and collection and preservation of this group. The main part of the book covers classification and taxonomy, with illustrated keys to subfamilies, genera, subgenera, and species. Each species is then described in a page or more that covers the male and female, their distribution (with detailed maps), specimens identified, their biology, and some miscellaneous notes on remarkable features. Fine black-and-white drawings of selected species are found throughout the text. A glossary of terms used in the text, a complete set of references, and an index to scientific name are found at the conclusion of the work.

These are excellent books, written and illustrated with scholarly attention to accuracy and detail. Although focused on Canadian species, much of the information and many of the keys will be useful in other countries as well. Individual titles may be purchased, but it is best to collect all volumes of this comprehensive work. Intended primarily for the specialist, but useful to the serious amateur, they are recommended to academic and large public libraries and other libraries with strong entomology collections. — **Diane B. Rhodes**

1565. Howarth, Francis G., and William P. Mull. **Hawaiian Insects and Their Kin.** Honolulu, University of Hawaii Press, 1992. 160p. illus. maps. index. $19.95. QL489.H3H68. 595.709969. LC 91-48257. ISBN 0-8248-1469-X.

The interesting text and beautiful full-color photographs in this book provide an entertaining introduction to the native insects and related organisms of Hawaii. The authors' purpose is to describe the most common native species, show how their study improves understanding of evolution and ecology, and encourage the appreciation and study of these fascinating animals. Both authors are entomologists affiliated with the well-known Bernice P. Bishop Museum in Hawaii.

The first 40 pages cover general information on the Hawaiian Islands; a history of entomology studies there; and the origin of Hawaiian insects and their evolution, conservation, and use in educational programs. A chapter that covers the classifications of the insects and their kin in Hawaii precedes brief descriptions of 177 of the most common species. The species descriptions list the insect's family and common names, the name of the island where it is usually found, its habits, and interesting notes on behavior. Each species description has a striking full-color photograph (most taken by Mull) that covers one half to a full page. The photographs of three Happyface Spiders are especially arresting, as a perfect happyface on the back of the spider smiles up at the reader. A nice bibliography of sources on Hawaiian natural history and arthropods follows the text. An index only to scientific names is provided; it would have been helpful in this beginner's guide to have included some common names in the index as well.

This work provides a good introduction to insects and their relatives in Hawaii for the student, amateur entomologist, or anyone with an interest in Hawaii or the amazing diversity of insects. Advanced students may want to progress to *Insects of Hawaii* (University of Hawaii Press, 1948-), a comprehensive set still being added to that includes 15 volumes so far. Recommended for public, high school, and college and university libraries. — **Diane B. Rhodes**

1566. Rowell, C. H. F. **Locust Neurobiology: A Bibliography, 1871-1991.** New York, Springer-Verlag, 1992. 247p. $33.00pa. (with disk). ISBN 0-8176-2747-2.

Locusts (acridoids) are the most commonly studied creatures in insect neurobiology. The amount of data on these acridoid grasshoppers probably exceeds that on all other insects combined. This title includes hundreds of articles in English, German, and French specific to their nervous systems or muscles. According to Rowell, the selection of material on hormones and neuropeptides is arbitrary and eclectic.

Stretching back to the 1920s but mostly published in the last two decades, materials are listed alphabetically by author and include date, title, journal, and key word (for the database on disk). Citations have been spot-checked for accuracy and appropriateness and appear to be complete. A list of all the key words is supplied in the book. None of the citations is annotated. Unfortunately, there are no indexes; however, used in an appropriate program, the disk version makes it possible to search by key words and then order the results by date, author, or journal. Because the database is supplied in the form of an ASCII file, the information can be imported into almost any word processor or database program. This process may be tedious because the data fields are not delimited in any way, but the copy on diskette will likely be the most useful format of this bibliography. Although this is a specialized topic, the comprehensive nature of the work and the convenience of having it in a single volume make it useful.—**John A. Jackman**

1567. Soos, A., and L. Papp, eds. **Catalogue of Palaearctic Diptera. Volume 7: Dolichopodidae-Platypezidae.** New York, Elsevier Science Publishing, 1991. 291p. index. $214.50. OL534.C38. 595.77'091811. LC 84-13534. ISBN 0-444-98731-2.

This work lists the names and geographic distributions of approximately 1,900 flies. It is the seventh in a series of volumes that will eventually cover the 25,000 different species of flies known from the Palaearctic Region. This region covers Europe and most of Asia, with its southern border defined by the editors as extending along the Tropic of Cancer in Africa to the southwestern border of Pakistan, along the western border of Pakistan to the Himalayas (excluding Nepal), and through China and Japan at 30 degrees north latitude. This book covers five closely related families of flies, and, similar to others in the series, it is a concise guide to the names and more important literature describing these insects. It is intended for a relatively select audience of amateur and professional entomologists, but the price will almost certainly keep it from being used by all but the most ardent of dipterists and museum curators.

Entries are arranged by family, with all but one of the smaller families separately authored by an expert on the group. A brief introduction (one page or less) provides general details of adult and larval morphology, classification, and biology for each family. Citations for each species are limited to the original taxonomic description. An alphabetical index to all names, essential in a work of this nature, is included at the end of the volume. Cross-references within the volume are generally accurate, but the page heading and table of contents erroneously list the page number for Lonchopteridae. The list of references is extensive, and occasional commentaries on dates of publication increase the value of the work. More references to biology and to recent compilations of larval forms under the introduction to each family would have increased the usefulness of this volume for entomologists.

—**Robert A. Wharton**

1568. Ward, James V., and B. C. Kondratieff. **An Illustrated Guide to the Mountain Stream Insects of Colorado.** Niwot, Colo., University Press of Colorado, 1992. 191p. illus. index. $19.95; $9.95pa. QL475.C6W37. 595.709788. LC 92-17076. ISBN 0-87081-253-X; 0-87081-260-2pa.

Comprehensive information on the systematics, ecology, and biology of the mountain stream aquatic insects of Colorado is provided in this extensively illustrated text. Because this work deals with a very specific geographic range, it provides a simple identification scheme to the aquatic insects of the area that can be used by specialists or individuals who enjoy stream fishing.

The book first surveys the ecology of mountain streams and their controlling factors, such as temperature, discharge, substrate, and chemical condition, as well as human impact on the streams. The main part of the book provides illustrated keys to order, family, and common genus of the underwater stages of the aquatic insects. References are given to other keys for further identification. Brief textual descriptions are also provided. The book covers the orders of Plecoptera (stoneflies),

Ephemeroptera (mayflies), Trichoptera (caddisflies), Coleoptera (beetles), and Diptera (true flies and mosquitoes). The other orders are not found as extensively in Colorado.

The selected species are beautifully illustrated in almost 100 black-and-white drawings that usually cover an entire page. Three appendixes show the geographical distribution of mountain stream mayflies, stoneflies, and caddisflies in major drainage basins in the area. A two-page glossary is included, but it is not complete enough to help the amateur understand the terminology of the keys (a good entomology dictionary would help in using them). An extensive list of references alerts the reader to more sources of information. The work concludes with scientific name and subject indexes.

This excellent guide to aquatic insects in Colorado's mountain streams is written primarily for the aquatic entomologist but is presented in a form that can be used by many groups, student and amateur alike. The limited geographic range makes it small enough for readers to grasp the information, and the current bibliography can lead to further study for the specialist. Recommended for large public and academic libraries and all specialized entomology collections.—**Diane B. Rhodes**

Mammals

1569. Forrester, Donald J. **Parasites and Diseases of Wild Mammals in Florida.** Gainesville, Fla., University Press of Florida, 1992. 459p. illus. index. $59.95. SF996.4.F65. 639.9'6'09759. LC 91-536. ISBN 0-8130-1072-1.

One of the most beautifully produced scientific monographs of the year, this work has a pleasing format, excellent tables and line drawings, attractive drawings of wildlife by David S. Maehr, and good maps. Even the halftone illustrations are good, considering that they are not on glossy paper. Ironically, the subject is grim; the purpose of the book is to provide data on the distribution, prevalence, and significance of parasites and diseases. Forrester makes clear the destructiveness of the diseases to wild mammal populations, the relationships of these diseases to domesticated animals, and their public health significance. If identified, environmental contaminants are discussed, a most important feature for the general reader. The book is organized by animal or host, not by the names of the various parasites and diseases. Information is provided for 61 indigenous and 8 nonnative species.

The discussion is replete with technical terms but so clearly and interestingly written that high school students will be able to use it for school projects. Bibliographic information is complete, but some journal abbreviations may cause minor problems for some users.

Forrester is professor of parasitology in the College of Veterinary Medicine, University of Florida and a well-known scholar. He and the University Press of Florida have produced an exemplary work.
—**Milton H. Crouch**

1570. Redford, Kent H., and John F. Eisenberg. **Mammals of the Neotropics: The Southern Cone. Volume 2: Chile, Argentina, Uruguay, Paraguay.** Chicago, University of Chicago Press, 1992. 430p. illus. maps. index. $95.00; $39.50pa. QL725.A1E38. 599.098. LC 88-27479. ISBN 0-226-70681-8; 0-226-70682-6pa.

This is the second volume of a planned three-volume set that makes a comprehensive survey of terrestrial and marine mammals of the neotropical region. The volume covers Chile, Argentina, Uruguay, and Paraguay. The first volume (see ARBA 90, entry 1555), prepared by Eisenberg, was met with high praise for its quality and scholarship. This second volume continues the tradition yet is not as complete. The authors have relied more on literature and museum records for accounts of species in this area as neither has had extensive field experience there. Fewer keys to identification, less detail on the distribution maps, and fewer drawings are given. The authors include 360 species to the 450 species covered in volume 1. However, this is still a unique work that provides the first comprehensive treatment of mammals for this region.

The arrangement is the same as in volume 1. An introductory chapter on the biogeography of this area is followed by individual chapters on 11 mammalian orders arranged in taxonomic order, from Marsupialia to Lagomorpha. Each family within the order is described, as well as each genus and species. The species description is the most thorough, with a complete table of measurements, a physical description, the geographical distribution, a life history, and the ecology. A large black-and-white map is provided next to each description; black dots indicate where the species were collected. Drawings of skulls for some species are also included. Eighteen plates of excellent color and black-and-white drawings by Fiona Reid, who was also the artist for volume 1, are inserted near the end of the text. A lengthy list of references appears at the end of each chapter. Two final chapters summarize mammalian community ecology and the effects of humans on the mammals of this region. Separate indexes to scientific and common names complete the text.

This set fills a gap for a current, comprehensive reference for mammals of this region and should prove to be a standard for years to come. Highly recommended for all academic and large public libraries. [R: SBF, Sept 92, p. 166]—**Diane B. Rhodes**

1571. **The Sierra Club Handbook of Seals and Sirenians.** By Randall R. Reeves, Brent S. Stewart, and Stephen Leatherwood. San Francisco, Calif., Sierra Club; distr., New York, Random House, 1992. 359p. illus. index. $18.00pa. QL737.P6R44. 599.74'5. LC 92-946. ISBN 0-87156-656-7.

This handbook is a companion to the *Sierra Club Handbook of Whales and Dolphins* (see ARBA 84, entry 1351) and describes 42 other marine mammals, including the pinnipeds (seals, sea lions, and walruses), the sirenians (manatees, dugongs, and sea cows), otters, and polar bears. After a general introduction to the four groups, the various species in each are described in 4 to 13 pages. Every species account has a note on the nomenclature, physical description, geographical distribution, natural history and, conservation status; a list of references for further reading; and a full-color painting by Pieter Folkens. Additionally, black-and-white photographs are found throughout the text. The three appendixes include a list of the common and scientific names of animals and plants mentioned in the book (besides the mammals in the text), a list of pinniped species and their dental formulas, and the principal breeding ranges in the major ocean areas.

This work and its companion volume provide concise, up-to-date information on these important species. A more thorough work is the four-volume *Handbook of Marine Mammals*, edited by S. H. Ridgway and R. J. Harrison (Academic Press, 1981-1989). However, for their price and portability in the field, the two Sierra Club books will serve well. Recommended for all public and academic libraries and school libraries from junior high school on up.—**Diane B. Rhodes**

1572. **Walker's Mammals of the World.** 5th ed. By Ronald M. Nowak. Baltimore, Md., Johns Hopkins University Press, 1991. 2v. illus. index. $89.95/set. QL703.N69. 599. LC 91-27011. ISBN 0-8018-3970-X.

It has been 8 years since the publication of the 4th edition of *Walker's Mammals of the World* (see ARBA 84, entry 1352) and 27 years since the publication of the initial edition of this classic work in mammalian systematics by Ernest P. Walker, then director of the National Zoological Park in Washington, D.C. This new edition has been revised and updated by Ronald N. Nowak, who served as senior author with John L. Paradiso on the 4th edition. In 1986 Nowak began the considerable task of examining the relevant literature on mammalian systematics published primarily between 1982 and 1988. The result of this work is a new edition with only moderate changes from the 4th edition, the set that included the most revision and updating since the original edition. Specifically, there are 106 new generic accounts, 300 new photographs that either replace or supplement older materials, separate accounts for each extinct genus known to have lived within the last 5,000 years, and textual revisions to reflect new information from the literature.

The arrangement of this two-volume work is the same systematic arrangement by order as was in the original edition. Each order is introduced with general information on the group, followed by descriptions of each family and genus in the order and including information on threatened or endangered status. Black-and-white photographs accompany most descriptions. Care has been taken to include photographs of live animals, with photographs of museum specimens or drawings used only for the rare or extinct genus. Each volume has a complete index to both volumes, with entries for the scientific names of orders, families, and genera in boldface type and common names in medium type. A 113-page bibliography completes volume 2.

Many libraries may purchase this new edition because it is the newest edition of a standard reference work. However, if the 4th edition is already owned, the library may consider purchase of comparable works on mammals since the revisions in this new edition are not critical. One such option is the five-volume *Grzimek's Encyclopedia of Mammals* (see ARBA 91, entry 1593). That set is almost as comprehensive as *Walker's* and includes more behavior, ecology, and conservation information plus color photographs and illustrations, but it carries a much higher price tag. The one-volume *Encyclopedia of Mammals* (see ARBA 85, entry 1465), although not as comprehensive, is a good choice for its overall treatment of the subject with authoritative sources, interesting reading, color photographs, and a bargain price. However, those looking for the most complete descriptions with photographs of the 21 orders, 135 families, 1,116 genera, and 4,444 species of mammals should choose this new edition of *Walker's*. Recommended for large public libraries, academic libraries, and others with complete collections in zoology. [R: Choice, Apr 92, pp. 1211-12; RBB, 15 Mar 92, pp. 1404-06; RBB, 15 June 92, pp. 1872-74; SBF, Apr 92, pp. 78-79; WLB, Mar 92, pp. 119-22] – **Diane B. Rhodes**

Marine Animals

1573. Behrens, David W. **Pacific Coast Nudibranchs: A Guide to the Opisthobranchs Alaska to Baja California.** 2d ed. Monterey, Calif., Sea Challengers, 1991. 107p. illus. index. $25.95pa. QL430.4.B43. 594'.30. LC 91-13522. ISBN 0-930118-17-0.

This is a field guide to the nudibranchs (along with four other orders of mollusks closely related to the nudibranchs) of the Pacific coast of North America from the Bering Strait to the tip of Baja California. In all, 217 species are described and illustrated. The extensive introduction covers the behavior, ecology, and anatomy of these mollusks, as well as their collection and preservation, biogeography, and nomenclature. There are a pictorial glossary and a pictorial key to the orders and suborders covered. Each species description gives identification, description of the radula, natural history, size, range, and (for some) etymology of the scientific name. The species descriptions are arranged according to biological classification. In addition, an appendix classifies all the species covered. A bibliography and an index to scientific names are included.

The species descriptions are well written and represent an excellent aid to distinguishing the mollusks. Each entry has a color photograph that reveals the great beauty of these animals and makes identification even easier. This work will be useful as a field guide and in the reference collections of academic libraries that serve zoology or marine biology programs. – **John Laurence Kelland**

1574. **Peterson First Guide to Seashores.** By John C. Kricher. Boston, Houghton Mifflin, 1992. 128p. illus. index. (Peterson First Guide Series). $4.95pa. QH95.7.K75. 574.909'46. LC 91-38829. ISBN 0-395-61901-7.

As are other little books in the Peterson First Guide Series, this one is designed as a beginner's introduction to nature, in this case the seashores of North America. The author is a well-known writer of educational natural history. Hundreds of the most common coastal animals and plants are illustrated in color (albeit many figures are quite small), with a short text for each. The novice will be aided by the simple organization of organisms by geography and habitat (e.g., eastern sandy beaches, rocky tidal pools). The major taxa include land plants and algae, the wide variety of marine invertebrates, and higher organisms (especially birds and fishes). Comments emphasize features of identification and interesting aspects of ecology and behavior. Children and others starting with this guide will probably graduate quickly to more advanced guides. [R: SLJ, Nov 92, p. 146 ; VOYA, Oct 92, p. 250]
– **Charles Leck**

Reptiles and Amphibians

1575. Cogger, Harold G. **Reptiles & Amphibians of Australia.** 5th ed. Chatswood, Austral., Reed Books and Ithaca, N.Y., Cornell University Press, 1992. 775p. illus. maps. index. $97.00. QL663. A1C63. 597.6'0994. LC 91-34103. ISBN 0-8014-2739-8.

Covering approximately 664 species, this volume is a first-class publication on the amphibians and reptiles found throughout the Australian continent. It is broader in scope and provides more information than *Australian Reptiles & Frogs* (see ARBA 91, entry 1602). The species are arranged under their respective genera, which in turn are entered under families, orders, and classes. General information is given for the class, order, family, and genus. For each of the genera listed, the person who first named it and the date of naming are also presented. Biological keys to the families, genera, and species precede the descriptive accounts.

The scientific and common names, person who first named it, date of naming, coloration, geographical distribution, and habitats are given for each species. The descriptive accounts are usually one-quarter to one-half column in length. A geographical range map and an excellent color photograph accompany most of the descriptions. In addition, line drawings enhance the biological keys.

Information such as conservation and protection, collecting methods, vegetation and climatic zones, and snakebite and treatment can be found in the introductory section, which is well illustrated by a large locality map and a vegetation and climatic zone map of Australia. An appendix that lists name changes of Australian reptiles and frogs is given. A glossary, a bibliography whose citations are arranged under families, and a common and scientific name index complete the volume.

This work is extremely well done and comprehensive in scope. Highly recommended for those college and universities with programs in the zoological sciences. Large public libraries may also wish to purchase a copy.—**George H. Bell**

1576. Ernst, Carl H. **Venomous Reptiles of North America.** Washington, D.C., Smithsonian Institution Press, 1992. 236p. illus. maps. index. $35.00. QL666.O6E77. 597.96'0469'0973. LC 91-3535. ISBN 1-56096-114-8.

This source considers 20 poisonous snakes found in the families Elapidae and Viperidae, along with the Gila monster. Each species has its own chapter. For each of the species listed, the scientific name, person who first identified it, date of identification, and common name are given. In addition, the descriptive account deals with size, coloration, anatomical measurements, differences between male and female, karyotype, fossil record, geographical distribution, geographical variation, similar species, habitat, behavior, reproduction, growth and longevity, food and feeding, venom and bites, predators and defense, populations, conservation status, and other interesting facts. These accounts are detailed but very readable and usually run from 4 to 10 pages. A general introduction is also presented for each of the families, and a range map accompanies each of the descriptions.

The introductory section consists of some general information on the external anatomy of snakes and on venom. Medical treatment for venomous bites is also discussed. Excellent color and black-and-white photographs of these reptiles are provided. A bibliography, a glossary of scientific terms, and an index conclude the work. Highly recommended for college, university, and public libraries. [R: RBB, 1 Oct 92, p. 372; SBF, Dec 92, p. 265]—**George H. Bell**

1577. **Peterson First Guide to Reptiles and Amphibians.** By Roger Conant, Robert C. Stebbins, and Joseph T. Collins. Boston, Houghton Mifflin, 1992. 128p. illus. index. $4.95pa. QL651.C66. 597.6'097. LC 91-33016. ISBN 0-395-62232-8.

Based upon Conant and Collins's *Field Guide to Reptiles and Amphibians* (see ARBA 92, entry 1587) and Stebbins's *Field Guide to Western Reptiles and Amphibians*, this novice-level work provides general information necessary to identify the more common species of amphibians and reptiles found throughout North America. The 350 species are arranged under broad common name groups, such as giant salamanders, mole salamanders, true frogs, chorus frogs, blind snakes, and water snakes. Each is provided with its common name, size, coloration, habitat, and brief behavioral characteristics, plus a color picture on the opposite page. A common name index is supplied. A very useful identifying tool for the beginner, this work is recommended for public and junior college libraries. [R: SLJ, Nov 92, p. 146; VOYA, Oct 92, p. 250]—**George H. Bell**

1578. **Poisonous Snakes of the World.** By U.S. Department of the Navy (Bureau of Medicine and Surgery). Washington, D.C., Government Printing Office; repr., Mineola, N.Y., Dover, 1991. 203p. illus. index. $14.95pa. QL666.O6P56. 597.96. LC 90-20200. ISBN 0-486-26629-X.

This is an unabridged republication of a U.S. Navy Bureau of Medicine and Surgery handbook: *Poisonous Snakes of the World: A Manual for Use by U.S. Amphibious Forces* (U.S. Government Printing Office, 1966). First issued by the Navy in 1962, the 1966 version was revised in its entirety by Sherman A. Minton, Jr.; Herndon G. Dowling; and Findlay E. Russell, all distinguished ophidian scientists. The edition now reissued by Dover has a time-enduring accuracy, consistency, and completeness that reflect the professional efforts of the revisers.

The text is organized into nine chapters. The first explains the purpose of the book. Chapters 2 through 5 focus on snakebite avoidance, recognition, first aid, and medical treatment. Chapter 6 relates attributes for recognition of venomous snakes and includes an identification key to world snake families. Chapter 7 is divided into 10 sections, each corresponding to a world land region and each with a table of contents. A typical section defines its land region and summarizes the families and species of snakes known within. Detailed species accounts and discussions of regional distributions follow. An identification key, an area map, and a regional distribution table complete each section. Chapter 8 is on the distribution and identification of the poisonous sea snakes. Included are a summary table, a key to genera, and species accounts. Chapter 9 is a list of antivenin sources. A glossary, a list of references, and an index complete the book. Numerous middling to high-quality monochrome and color photographs and line drawings complement the text.

Despite certain nomenclatural and classification changes and a few outdated statements, this book remains relevant for today's world. Recommended for general purchase by public, college, and university libraries. – **Edmund D. Keiser, Jr.**

1579. Schwartz, Albert, and Robert W. Henderson. **Amphibians and Reptiles of the West Indies: Descriptions, Distributions, and Natural History.** Gainesville, Fla., University of Florida Press/University Presses of Florida, 1991. 720p. maps. index. $75.00. QL656.5.A1S37. 597.6'09729. LC 90-48025. ISBN 0-8130-1049-7.

The 585 species in this work, 157 of which are amphibians and 428 of which are reptiles, are arranged under their respective orders. For each of the organisms listed are given the scientific name, namer, date of naming, holotype, size, identifying external anatomical features, coloration, references to publications that provide illustrations of the animals, geographical distribution, subspecies if any, and natural history (e.g., breeding, diet, vocalization, egg production). A systematic index and a general list of references can be found in the introductory section, and there are a bibliography and a scientific name index. A range map of the appropriate island accompanies each of the descriptive accounts, which average half a page in length; a few cover several pages. The references to illustrative publications allow access to line drawings and both black-and-white and color photographs. Unfortunately, the references do not indicate which type of illustration is present in the publication, and the volume itself does not contain any pictures.

Although this is a comprehensive source, the absence of illustrations reduces its utility. Recommended for college and university libraries with strong programs in zoology, especially herpetology.
– **George H. Bell**

1580. Sprackland, Robert George. **Giant Lizards.** Neptune, N.J., T. F. H. Publications, 1992. 288p. illus. index. $79.95. ISBN 0-86622-634-6.

This source covers all lizards of the world that are considered large (approaching one meter or more and having significant bulk). No legless species are included. Information given for each of the lizards includes common name, scientific name, person who first named it, date of naming, etymology of name, other common names, geographical distribution, habitat, size in centimeters and inches, and a variety of other facts. The length of the descriptions varies from a half page to several pages. Beautiful colored photographs accompany the text. A small section on the medical care of these animals is provided. The pages of the book are glossy, enhancing its value and adding even more interest to the subject matter. A brief glossary, a four-page bibliography, and a combined subject/common/scientific name index conclude this source. Highly recommended for high school, college, and public libraries.
– **George H. Bell**

32 Engineering

ASTRONAUTICAL ENGINEERING

1581. **Space Station Glossary. Lexique de la Station Spatiale.** By Spatial Terminology Standardization Committee. Ottawa, Department of the Secretary of State of Canada, 1992. 127p. (Terminology Bulletin, 213). $18.15pa. (U.S.). 629.44'2'03. ISBN 0-660-57414-4.

Every field has its own terminology. New fields such as space science tend to develop a lingo that can be confusing to individuals from other fields, even those closely aligned with the field itself. In such cases, glossaries are particularly useful. Lists of terms, even without meanings attached (as in a dictionary), can also be helpful to librarians and information specialists who are called upon to provide information in those fields. *Space Station Glossary* is an example of this type of reference, and it is a good one. Of particular interest is the bilingual approach. Although mandated by printing rules that govern Canadian government publications, the French-English and English-French columns in the text provide further value to this reference text. The first list is alphabetical by English terms, the second, by French terms. A bibliography and list of other Translation Bureau publications completes the text.

The work is restricted to 900 terms associated with the space station alone. The goal has been to include terms with "translation problems or vague, unusual or misleading concepts." The introduction promises other glossaries that will deal with satellites and other aspects of space technology. This book is recommended for libraries that emphasize space, particularly where there are writers, translators, editors, engineers, or other specialists who must communicate their work to the world.

—**Edward P. Miller**

CHEMICAL ENGINEERING

1582. Corish, Patrick J., ed. **Concise Encyclopedia of Polymer Processing & Applications.** Elmsford, N.Y., Pergamon Press, 1992. 771p. illus. index. (Advances in Materials Science and Engineering). $280.00. TP1087.C65. 668.9'03. LC 91-26436. ISBN 0-08-037064-0.

Most of the articles in this work have been derived from the *Encyclopedia of Materials Science and Engineering* (EMSE) (see ARBA 87, entry 1570) or its supplements. It appears to be intended for the engineer or engineering student. The processing and applications of polymers (consisting primarily of elastomers, plastics, fibers or textiles, and composite materials) are covered in 160 chapters. Other topics range from historical developments to adhesives, coatings, aging, recycling, and special uses of polymers.

The general treatment is good, but several drawbacks exist. To begin with, the index is selective rather than complete, and there is no glossary. While there are hundreds of references, not all of the authors mentioned are listed in the bibliographies. In many cases more recent references could have been included. The quality of the writing varies, as can be expected in a work with numerous authors. The introduction is arranged by subject, and although it does little more than list chapter titles, it is essential in determining how coverage is presented.

This work would probably be more useful if it were arranged by broad subject category rather than alphabetically and if each subject category were given a thorough introduction. It could be a valuable addition to a reference collection as information on polymer science is conveniently accessed in one volume. However, the information is mostly repackaged material and, therefore, is not essential to libraries that own the EMSE. – **T. McKimmie**

1583. Sewer, June, ed. **The Directory of Chemical Engineering Consultants.** 9th ed. New York, American Institute of Chemical Engineers, 1992. 49p. $25.00pa. TP12.D475. 660.2'025'73. LC 83-16268. ISBN 0-8169-0552-5.

This directory will be useful to government and community agencies, legal firms, corporations, and academic and other research units that require consultation expertise in chemical engineering. It is not comprehensive, however, but limited to those who have paid a fee for inclusion. Therefore, many prominent consultants do not appear. The value of the work would be greatly increased by additional listings.

Consultants, both individuals and firms, are listed alphabetically. Addresses, type of organization, and areas of specialization are provided. There are actually two listings, one for full-time and one for part-time consultants. This division is without explanation and seems unnecessary. Indexing is by state and by area of specialization. The latter index is extensive, providing good access into the many specialty areas of chemical engineering. Examples from it include construction management, energy technology, environmental regulation, petrochemical technology, plant design, and waste disposal. Recommended for academic libraries. – **T. McKimmie**

1584. Szostak, R. **Handbook of Molecular Sieves.** New York, Van Nostrand Reinhold, 1992. 584p. illus. index. $139.95. TP159.M6S96. 660'.2842. LC 91-45180. ISBN 0-442-31899-5.

This handbook is a convenient and quick source of information on more than 500 molecular sieve and zeolite materials. It is organized in alphabetical order by the names of materials. Following each name, detailed data and brief descriptions are provided on the material's structure, synthesis, thermal properties, spectroscopy, and adsorption and ion exchange properties. For synthetic materials, a patent number (if applicable) or a citation and historical information on the development of the material follows the name. Within the structure section, both compositional and X-ray powder diffraction data are provided. The synthesis section gives the methods of synthesis for molecular sieves; organic additives used in the process; and (when available) formulas or ratios used for, or common impurity phases from, the synthesis process. When information is available, reported thermal properties and stabilities are provided in the thermal properties section. Infrared spectroscopy information is given in the spectroscopy section, and the adsorption and ion exchange section provides information on these capacities. In addition, there are indexes to subjects, structure codes, and organic additives.

While this book provides a compilation of available data, it does not include a summary on the fundamentals of the subject matter or provide the necessary tools with which to interpret and use the data. However, within the introduction the author has identified several references that should aid readers' understanding of this book. There are no adequate definitions of acronyms, parameters, or notations within the text, making use of this handbook confusing for those first starting to research the topic. Overall, it should be of value for researchers, scientists, and engineers working with these materials. – **Gabriel P. Sabadell**

CIVIL ENGINEERING

1585. **Elsevier's Dictionary of Civil Engineering: In Four Languages: English, German, Spanish and French.** Marcos F. Gutierrez, comp. New York, Elsevier Science Publishing, 1991. 392p. index. $157.00. TA9.G87. 624'.03. LC 91-26688. ISBN 0-444-88987-6.

Designed as a "consulting work," this polyglot dictionary covers all aspects of civil engineering, including construction and construction equipment, foundation techniques, cost control, water resources, tunnels and tunneling, soil engineering, dams, and irrigation. It contains more than 6,000 terms, of which more than half are multiword phrases. As with other polyglot dictionaries, there are no definitions. While the book is arranged in alphabetical order by English word, words in German, Spanish, or French are accessible through word lists that are differentiated from the main text by means of a thumb index. This book is of particular interest to civil engineering collections with users who often work in Latin America or Europe and for those collections that serve translators.—**Susan B. Ardis**

1586. Fai, Stephen. **Construction Technology Information Sources.** Ottawa, Royal Architectural Institute of Canada, 1991. 1v. (unpaged). index. $15.00pa. 026'.69'002571. ISBN 0-919424-20-1.

   Developed for firms that need to maintain a competitive edge in the construction industry, this directory provides easy access to technical information in governmental, institutional, and private organizations. Including more than 500 organizations and companies, the vast majority located in Canada, the entries are limited to Canadian noncommercial entities that provide either technical information or services to the construction industry. When possible, each entry contains contact person, address, telephone and fax numbers, activities, funding and training programs, publications, and facilities. The subject index and easy-to-use format help the user quickly find information. Although the binding could be improved and yearly updates will be necessary, this directory is a good investment for special, academic, and large public libraries that have clientele who deal with the construction industry in Canada.—**Diane J. Turner**

ELECTRIC ENGINEERING AND ELECTRONICS

1587. **American Electricians' Handbook.** 12th ed. Wilford I. Summers, ed. New York, McGraw-Hill, 1992. 1v. (various paging). illus. index. $69.50. TK151.C8. 621.319'24. LC 91-18395. ISBN 0-07-013933-4.

   There are many handbooks for electrical engineering that have detailed formulas and mathematical principles for researchers but that lack crucial information for electricians. This handbook is specially written and compiled for that neglected audience, with detailed information to lead to the intelligent design, selection, installation, and maintenance of electrical equipment. A major effort has been made to ensure conformity to the 1990 edition of the National Electrical Code. In addition to comprehensive coverage of the basics of conductors, batteries, transformers, generators, wiring, lighting, and so forth, this edition also includes new information on current concerns such as energy-saving devices, new conductor and cable types, and surge protection devices. This handbook is a must for electricians as an up-to-date reference for the trade.—**John Y. Cheung**

1588. Benson, K. Blair, and Jerry C. Whitaker. **Television Engineering Handbook: Featuring HDTV Systems.** rev. ed. New York, McGraw-Hill, 1992. 1v. (various paging). illus. index. $99.95. TK6642.T437. 621.388'87. LC 91-35079. ISBN 0-07-004788-X.

   High definition television (HDTV) will not be commercially available in the United States until 1993 (optimistic view) or 1995 (pessimistic view), but it already represents one-third of the television-related entries in the 1990 *Engineering Index*. Hence, it occupies three important chapters in this broad-gauged handbook that ranges from audio to optics to digital effects to motion picture engineering. (Film in the future will only be used for prints distributed to theaters.) The handbook's target is the developer, operator, student, or evaluator of phenomena, equipment, management, or standards relating to the television function.

   The "state of the art survey" these 25 chapters represent can only be prepared by experts. A number of the authors are listed as "retired"; many also represent traditional institutions. However, the latter chapters are more venturesome and do include those from North American affiliates of Japanese and European organizations.

   Even though the publisher lists 23 other related handbooks, this one is a 2d edition and is certain to have a long life—even exceeding that of its impregnated paper binding, which probably will not stand up to use in large academic departmental libraries or metropolitan public libraries.—**Eugene B. Jackson**

1589. **EL&P U.S. Electric Utility Industry Directory, 1992.** Tulsa, Okla., PennWell Books, 1992. 663p. index. $195.00pa. ISSN 1058-2479.

This directory provides information on investor-owned, municipal, and publicly owned electric utilities as well as rural electric membership corporations, federal power agencies, systems or projects, and power pools in the United States and Canada. Regulatory agencies are also indexed. The book is far more limited than the expensive *Moody's Public Utilities Manual*, but it does provide access to information about publicly owned electric utility entities, giving addresses and telephone numbers for various regulatory agencies. There are type of utility, personnel, and geographic indexes. The publisher claims to provide extensive detail, but because the information was self-submitted, some listings have just utility name, address, and responsible person (with title). The information has not been edited or reviewed by the publisher. In the more extensive company listings, information on the utility includes assets; debt; equity; gross operating revenues; net income; number of employees; services provided; territory with square miles, size, and population; circuit miles; and the value of power purchased. Customer average rate for services is provided in such a manner that comparisons with other utilities can be conducted easily. This is an excellent choice for the small public, community college, and scientific and technical libraries. – **Gerald D. Moran**

1590. **Electric Utility Industry Software Directory, 1992.** 2d ed. By Wayne Beaty. Tulsa, Okla., PennWell Books, 1991. 171p. index. $165.00pa. ISSN 1051-3981.

This annual directory provides a list of computer software programs that are specifically related to the electric utility industry. The directory is divided into two sections. The first contains descriptions of available software according to the type of industry application, and the second is an alphabetical list of software vendors with contact data and complete information on their products and distributors. The directory is comprehensive, with 500-plus software programs in more than 50 applications areas. For each program a short description of the applicable functions is given along with the scope, language used, operating system, and hardware platform that the program is designed for. The price is also included when available. This directory provides a handy way for engineers and practitioners in the field to see what software is presently available, and it is an essential acquisition for professional libraries in this area. – **John Y. Cheung**

1591. Evetts, Jan, ed. **Concise Encyclopedia of Magnetic & Superconducting Materials.** Elmsford, N.Y., Pergamon Press, 1992. 703p. illus. index. (Advances in Materials Science and Engineering). $280.00. QC764.52.C66. 620.1'1297. LC 91-37830. ISBN 0-08-034722-3.

1592. Mahajan, S., and L. C. Kimerling, eds. **Concise Encyclopedia of Semiconducting Materials & Related Technologies.** Elmsford, N.Y., Pergamon Press, 1992. 582p. illus. index. (Advances in Materials Science and Engineering). $260.00. TK7871.85.C595. 621.381'52. LC 91-37828. ISBN 0-08-034724-X.

These titles represent 2 of the 11 entries in the series, which also includes works on materials economics, advanced ceramics, materials characterization, minerals, polymer processing, composites, building and construction materials, wood, and medical/dental material. The volumes are compilations from the *Encyclopedia of Materials Science and Engineering* (see ARBA 87, entry 1570) and its three supplements; there is also some new or updated material. Because each title represents a grouping of interest areas, each volume can stand alone as a reference work. Except for a few minor editing differences, many articles appear to be exactly the same as in the original encyclopedia; many others do not appear there at all or have been revised or combined into new articles. Each article is signed and has been prepared by an expert in the field; the level and quality of scholarship is even throughout. Most of the entries include tables, charts, graphs, or illustrations, and the *see* references within the text and the *see also* recommendations at the end of the majority of articles are helpful. It is unfortunate that the bibliographies for the entries examined show little or no updating from those in the parent encyclopedia. The index is comprehensive, which is fortunate as it is essential to consult it first to fully access the text. The contents, however, are not for the casual user; the sophisticated tone of the text assumes that the reader has familiarity with the technical and scientific aspects of the materials covered.

While the quality of the volumes examined is apparent, the need for these works in the reference department depends entirely on the depth of collection in these subject areas. Those with the original encyclopedia and supplements may wish to consider these for the circulating collection or acquire items from the series on a selective basis. Those with more narrowly focused collections may choose from these books with confidence. — **Gary R. Cocozzoli**

1593.   Finn, Bernard S. **The History of Electrical Technology: An Annotated Bibliography.** Hamden, Conn., Garland, 1991. 342p. illus. index. (Garland Reference Library of Science and Technology, v.18; Garland Reference Library of the Humanities, v.418). $48.00. Z5832.F56. 016.6213'09. LC 91-20644. ISBN 0-8240-9120-5.

The study of the history and development of a particular scientific field often reveals valuable insights to researchers, scientists, and historians. Throughout the course of development of any field, many review articles and historical reviews are usually published in fairly obscure places, particularly difficult to find for those who are not experts in the field. The present book is a comprehensive, thorough annotated bibliography of articles about electrical technology specifically written from historical perspectives. Not only are broad historical works and reviews included but a large section of the book also lists crucial publications by researchers, agencies, and companies categorized by their respective fields. More specifically, the development of communications (e.g., telephony, radio, television) and power (e.g., lighting, motors, transmission) is covered in detail. This text is a valuable asset to those interested in the history of science and is highly recommended for professional libraries. [R: Choice, May 92, p. 1368; RQ, Summer 92, pp. 509-10] — **John Y. Cheung**

1594.   Gibilisco, Stan. **International Encyclopedia of Integrated Circuits.** 2d ed. New York, McGraw-Hill, 1992. 1142p. illus. index. $84.95. TK7874.G5. 621.381'5. LC 91-697. ISBN 0-8306-3026-0.

This handbook presents information on integrated circuits (ICs) available from eight United States manufacturers and one manufacturer each from Canada and the United Kingdom. The ICs are grouped into one of seven primary-use categories: clocks/counters/timers, communications circuits, control circuits, data converters, logic circuits, microcomputer peripherals, and power supplies and test equipment. The master list groups items under one of these categories by manufacturer and device designation number. *See* references lead the user to other sections as needed.

Because the information has been supplied by the individual manufacturers, the available data varies slightly from section to section. Typically, there are tables with general specifications; safety maximum ratings; thermal, electrical, and other characteristics; performance data; pin or connection diagrams; schematics; logic diagrams; and other appropriate information. The index is extensive and lists each company's individual IC by its suggested use and by company designation number ("part number"). It is generally legible, but long lists of information under a general heading can be confusing for the user on some pages; alternating typefaces or using boldface print would have been helpful.

Overall, this work is well designed and contains extensive information in the areas it covers. It will be favorably received by anyone who is interested in electronics, from the hobbyist to the professional. [R: RBB, 1 May 92, p. 1629] — **Gary R. Cocozzoli**

1595.   **The HarperCollins Dictionary of Electronics.** By Ian R. Sinclair. New York, HarperPerennial/HarperCollins, 1991. 363p. $25.00; $12.95pa. LC 90-56001. ISBN 0-06-271528-3; 0-06-461022-5pa.

Sinclair is a prolific British writer with a number of books on audio, computers, and technology. The cover note reads "In-Depth Explanations and Examples Covering Over 2,000 Entries with Extensive Diagrams and Charts." There are at least 100 diagrams. No entry exceeds a half-page.

A prime objective of this work is to assist beginning students, active practitioners, and nonspecialists in the subject field. Hence, it seems reasonable to compare it with Oxford University Press's *Concise Science Dictionary* (see ARBA 86, entry 1425), which seeks a similar audience, costs nearly the same, and lists 15 degreed contributors. On comparable entries, neither book has objectionable Continental usage common a decade ago, and the HarperCollins volume has more diagrams. Excessive use of cross-references is avoided in both.

By reason of its handy size and low cost, the paperbound version of the HarperCollins title might find a niche as a circulating aid to those new to the subject field. However, for reference use in medium-to-large collections, either the Oxford volume or *The Illustrated Dictionary of Electronics*, 5th ed. (see ARBA 92, entry 1607) would be preferable. —**Eugene B. Jackson**

1596. Holdsworth, Brian, and Graham R. Martin, eds. **Digital Systems Reference Book.** Stoneham, Mass., Butterworths, 1991. 1v. (various paging). illus. index. $250.00. TK7868.D5D485. 621.381. LC 90-1951. ISBN 0-7506-1008-5.

The editors of this major undertaking invited 50 experts from the various fields of digital electronics to be the contributors of the 64 chapters. The chapters are grouped into five basic sections: fundamentals (e.g., logic, modulation theory), devices (e.g., semiconductors, architectures of computers and processors), software and hardware system design (e.g., programming languages, bus systems), software engineering and system development (e.g., simulation, CAD), and applications (e.g., digital signal processing, computer graphics, satellite communication). Each chapter is well illustrated with charts, graphs, formulas, and tables, and most have extensive references and suggestions for further reading. The chapter on expert systems alone has 365 bibliographic references, but the documentation level varies depending on the author and the nature of the individual chapter. Despite the number of different authors, the text is even and consistently well written. The index is extensive, with a design that is easy to read and to use, and there are *see* references. There is also a limited service glossary for quick identification of terms and acronyms, but it has no in-depth definitions. Because of the highly technical nature of this work, the reader must have a firm understanding of mathematics and electronics terms and principles to be able to use the contents. It will be a welcome addition to engineering collections that serve engineering professionals, upper-division academic libraries, and other sophisticated clientele. [R: Choice, Apr 92, p. 1205]—**Gary R. Cocozzoli**

1597. Junge, H.-D. **Dictionary of Measurement Engineering and Units. Worterbuch Messtechnik und Einheiten.** New York, VCH, 1991. 593p. $100.00. 620.0044. ISBN 0-89573-530-X.

In this age of international industrial collaboration, knowledge of technological terms in languages other than English is essential. This dictionary provides a translation of technical and engineering terms from English to German and from German to English. All terms are alphabetically listed for ease of use. However, in order to fully convey meanings, groups of terms are collected and translated together for comparison. In addition to the definitions of terms, half of the work is devoted to the difficult task of translating units, something that most dictionaries do not include. The translations in this dictionary are quite thorough. Highly recommended for professional libraries if there is much material written in German. —**John Y. Cheung**

1598. Kurtz, Edwin B., and Thomas M. Shoemaker. **The Lineman's and Cableman's Handbook.** 8th ed. New York, McGraw-Hill, 1992. 1v. (various paging). illus. index. $69.50. TK3221.K83. 621.319'22. LC 91-34745. ISBN 0-07-035695-5.

Planned as a handbook for the apprentice or professional line or cable worker, this edition also merits consideration for libraries. The scope of coverage is quite broad, ranging from the basics of electricity and electric delivery systems to pole structures (wooden and other types), transmission towers, underground systems, and types and uses of cable. Other affiliated areas of coverage include tree trimming, street lighting, manhole construction, laying conduit, protective equipment, and safety rules. The text is illustrated extensively with photographs, diagrams, and tables and is quite readable for those with a basic familiarity of the terminology. The many charts and tables cover a variety of subjects, such as specifications and comparison of rope, growth characteristics and types of trees, and safety charts for rescue and resuscitation of the injured. The tables are not included in the index or the table of contents. However, the index to the text is fairly extensive, and the various illustrative materials are properly keyed to the text. Other aspects of note for reference are the electrical drawing symbols, electrical formulas with examples of calculations, and illustrations of knots and splices for rope or cable. A portion of the OSHA (Occupational Safety and Health Administration) Safety Act of 1970 (part 1926, sections 950-960 and 550-551) is also reprinted. Suitable for libraries that support governmental or utility interests, this work is also appropriate for academic libraries with electrical technology curricula or for larger public libraries. – **Gary R. Cocozzoli**

1599. Lee, R. R. **Pocket Guide to Electrical Equipment and Instrumentation.** 2d ed. Houston, Tex., Gulf Publishing, 1992. 339p. illus. index. $26.00pa. TK151.L4. 621.3. LC 91-19670. ISBN 0-87201-234-4.

This is a curious book trying to fit a market that may not exist. It is intended, according to the publisher's notice, for those in chemical plants, refineries, manufacturing facilities, and utilities. It may find a home there, but most of these facilities will already have reasonable reference facilities available to them, albeit not in pocket form. ("Pocket guide" should not be taken literally – this work is smaller than the "normal" book, but the veracity of the claim depends on one's taste in clothing.)

The information found in the book is standard fare. So standard, in fact, that the illustrations and photographs resemble their lackluster counterparts in many technical reference tools. The two areas that the book claims difference in are also the two areas that are most problematic. First, a new chapter explains bar coding as a control procedure. The hardware and software described is ancient by most technical standards. Showing a schematic that purportedly specifies a 1200-baud modem for data transmission does not engender confidence in the technical level of the chapter. Second, the description of an "easy-to-remember" seven-digit code for identifying valves is interesting, and perhaps useful, but there is no real discussion about the benefits of this system over competing ones.

This book will find a reasonable market with its intended audience. Libraries and information centers are advised to avoid this book because the great majority of the material it contains is also available elsewhere, and the size of the book will cause problems on shelves. – **C. D. Hurt**

GENETIC ENGINEERING

1600. **Vocabulary of Cell Engineering. Volume 1: Cell Structure. Vocabulaire du Genie Cellulaire.** By Edgard Delvin and Gisele Pham. Ottawa, Medical Research Council of Canada and Department of the Secretary of State of Canada, 1992. 315p. (Terminology Bulletin, 211). $27.55pa. (U.S.). 574.87'2'03. ISBN 0-660-57091-2.

This bilingual dictionary (French/English) is the result of a project by the Medical Research Council of Canada to promote the use of correct terminology in both languages in the medical community. The Council felt this was necessary because most of the vocabulary in this area is undergoing rapid growth, and cell engineering is a major activity in industrialized countries. Further, because English is the dominant language, the Council felt it was necessary to promote the standardization of relevant French-language terms.

The dictionary defines terms from biotechnology, including genetic engineering, enzyme engineering, and cell engineering. Terms and definitions were found by scanning the literature and using bibliographic data banks such as Medline and Pascal. In most cases, main entry terms are accompanied by a definition or context. Three types of definitions are represented: those reproduced exactly from the source document, those written by combining elements of existing definitions, and those formulated or suggested by experts. In some rare cases, equivalent terms in either English or French could not be found; these cases are clearly indicated. At the end of the work is a bibliography of monographs and journals in both languages that were scanned for words, definitions, and the contexts in which the words are used. This is a specialized tool for a very specialized audience. – **Susan B. Ardis**

INDUSTRIAL ENGINEERING

1601. Guertin, Lucie, comp. **Vocabulary of Safety and Security Equipment. Vocabulaire du Materiel de Securite et de Protection.** Ottawa, Royal Canadian Mounted Police, 1991. 1v. (various paging). price not reported spiralbound. 620.8'6. ISBN 0-660-56542-0.

This vocabulary of safety and security equipment (including fire safety, first aid, building security, and protective clothing) is English-to-French when turned one way; turned upside-down, it is French-to-English. Every word and term has been verified in one of 49 vocabulary sources or dictionaries from both languages, and the source is noted in the entry. In each language section, there are three columns. The left column has the word in the first language; the second has the code for one or more of the 74 fields where the word is used; and the third column has the equivalent expression in the other language. Although French terms often have a definition, English terms rarely do. The introduction of the work is a dizzying explanation of all the codes, abbreviations, lexicographic data, linguistic parameters, and so forth; it may delight linguists but will confuse more casual users. Fortunately, the work is accessible on a simple level as well, as these codes are used only on a limited basis for most entries. The many cross-references and synonyms should be of help for the main audience of this book (outside of the Royal Canadian Mounted Police Translation Branch): technical writers working in French and English. The very narrow focus of this work will limit its value for most libraries. Although the book is spiralbound, there is adequate gutter space to allow for the rebinding that may be necessary in any high-use situation. — **Gary R. Cocozzoli**

1602. **Industrial Engineering Terminology.** rev. ed. New York, McGraw-Hill, 1991. 1v. (various paging). index. $80.95. T56.24.I53. 670.42'014. LC 91-36339. ISBN 0-07-031730-5.

The stated purpose of this compendium is to encourage standard terminology in the field of industrial engineering. It is, of course, also meant to be used as a dictionary. This intention is well carried out in the sections that deal with biomechanics, computer and information systems, human factors, and anthropometry. In other sections the dictionary function is occasionally forgotten. For example, the word *chip* is defined thusly: "the metal is removed from the workplace in the form of chips." *Laggards*, we are told, "prefer to do things the way they have been done in the past and are very suspicious of new ideas." The division of terminology into arbitrary fields has led to duplication; computer terminology is found in the section on computer systems, a subsection of materials processing, and the section on manufacturing systems. Several sections have bibliographies, and the index refers to all sections. [R: RBB, Aug 92, pp. 2038-40] — **Robert B. McKee**

1603. **Maynard's Industrial Engineering Handbook.** 4th ed. William K. Hodson, ed. New York, McGraw-Hill, 1992. 1v. (various paging). illus. index. $99.50. T56.M39. 658.5. LC 92-13512. ISBN 0-07-041086-0.

This edition of a valued reference source has taken more than 20 years to materialize. Due to the massive developments and technological changes in the field of industrial engineering, more than 90 percent of this book is entirely new. Still, the editor urges those who have the 3d edition (see ARBA 72, entry 1784) to keep it because it will be a useful companion to this new edition.

Computers have made the greatest impact on industrial engineering, but the human factor has also become significant. This new handbook reflects the importance of those changes. With contributions from more than 100 expert authors, it supplies the industrial engineer with information on all relevant topics. Divided into 15 sections, it provides case studies and real-life examples of the different concepts and techniques used in industrial engineering. The work has a clear format, an easy-to-use index, and informative bibliographies.

Although this work has some similarities to the 2d edition of Gavriel Salvendy's *Handbook of Industrial Engineering* (John Wiley, 1991), it still provides unique information. Recommended for academic libraries and large public libraries that serve management and industrial engineering clientele.
— **Diane J. Turner**

MATERIALS SCIENCE

1604. **ASM Handbook. Volume 18: Friction, Lubrication, and Wear Technology.** Prepared under the direction of the ASM International Handbook Committee. Scott D. Henry, ed. Metals Park, Ohio, ASM International, 1992. 942p. illus. index. price not reported. TA459.M43. 620.1'6. LC 90-115. ISBN 0-87170-380-7.

This, the first separate volume on tribology produced by the American Society for Metals, is more akin to an encyclopedia than a handbook. The basic divisions are friction, lubrication, and wear, with most of the book devoted to the latter. Each of the well-illustrated 98 sections has been produced by a different expert; thus, they are authoritative. The bibliographies, if gathered together, would create a substantial book.

The volume's use as a handbook is hampered by its diversity. For example, there are 12 sections that each deal with a different kind of wear, and 5 groups of sections that cover wear in a different environment. In the first of these, five articles examine wear in bearings, gears, and seals. Another five are concerned with wear in transportation system components and the like. Generality, in short, is not well served. However, as a reference, this is certainly the best single volume available.

—Robert B. McKee

1605. Brundle, C. Richard, Charles A. Evans, Jr., and Shaun Wilson, eds. **Encyclopedia of Materials Characterization: Surfaces, Interfaces, Thin Films.** Stoneham, Mass., Butterworths, 1992. 751p. illus. index. (Materials Characterization Series). $95.00. TA418.7.B73. 620'.44. LC 92-14999. ISBN 0-7506-9168-9.

This is the first of a projected 10-volume set intended to provide materials users with practical information. While this first volume deals with the specific techniques for finding information on surface, interface, and thin film microcharacterization, subsequent volumes will cover specific materials such as ceramics or composite materials. The aim is to provide information in a clear way that is easily accessible to engineers and students.

The first part consists of one-page technique (really instrument) summaries. Some examples include ultraviolet photoelectron spectroscopy, solid state nuclear magnetic resonance, neutron reflectivity, and scanning electron microscopy. Each summary includes a descriptive paragraph followed by a tabular presentation of specific properties, such as machine size and cost range, destructiveness, range of elements of materials, sample requirements, depth probed, accuracy, sensitivity, and major uses.

The second (and largest) part consists of 50 short signed articles. Each gives a more detailed description of the technique, covers the range of materials to which the technique is applicable, provides a few typical examples of uses, and compares the technique with related ones. A short list of references is found at the end of each article, and in several articles the references are evaluated. For example, a reference on page 239 says "best book on the subject. Especially relevant is the chapter by J. Stohr." This is a very nice touch; it is too bad more authors do not use this technique.

All in all, this is a nicely done book, with a lot of information presented in a clear and concise way. It is of interest to collections in chemistry, engineering, materials science, and geophysics.

—Susan B. Ardis

1606. Schwartz, Mel M., ed. **Composite Materials Handbook.** 2d ed. New York, McGraw-Hill, 1992. 1v. (various paging). illus. index. $79.50. TA418.9.C6S38. 620.1'18. LC 91-39341. ISBN 0-07-055819-1.

Handbooks are designed to convey to the user, usually an expert, useful information in a timely fashion. In this case, the textual material has considerable revisions and is up-to-date and well written. The entire work could be vastly improved, however, by revisions and updates to the graphic material and illustrations as well. For example, a Boeing 737 with clear tail markings is identified as a 747, an aircraft with a significantly different silhouette. The illustrations are mainly overexposed or grainy photographs reminiscent of handbooks of 25 years ago. In addition, the schematics and line drawings appear to have been drawn with a template. Given the variety of CAD/CAM software applications in existence, they are unacceptable. The best that can be said of the illustrations is that they do help convey the meaning of the text.

The book is full of interesting and germane information. It also contains some information that is slightly odd. As an example, on page 4.7, text and illustration make the point that the Maypole is an example of Braiding Theory. While true, the accompanying illustration, complete with what appears to be gender-balanced stick people, is of questionable necessity to make the point. Overall, this is a good but not essential handbook for academic or special collections that serve materials science.—**C. D. Hurt**

PLANT ENGINEERING

1607. Cubberly, W. H., ed. **Comprehensive Dictionary of Measurement and Control: Reference Guides for Measurement and Control.** 2d ed. Research Triangle Park, N.C., Instrument Society of America, 1991. 506p. illus. $69.95. TS156.8.C62. 670.42. LC 91-24460. ISBN 1-55617-320-2.

A dictionary of terms for a specific field is useful to those outside the field, not to mention those within. This one, prepared by the Instrument Society of America (ISA), is a comprehensive list of terms and their specific meanings for the field of measurement and control. More than 11,000 terms, abbreviations, acronyms, and phrases are included. The definitions, authenticated by several experts (members of ISA listed in the volume), provide primary meanings and other possible interpretations. References to applicable ISA Standards are given where needed. Many general engineering terms are included, as well as an expanded number of computer and data processing terms used in this field. Adding to the value of this volume are two sections in the back of the book: a 25-page list of abbreviations and acronyms, and a 50-plus-page section of 25 sets of symbols, detailed in the table of contents. This latter section includes basic engineering symbols, universally applied, and diagrams for flowcharting in various fields. For example, one set is a compilation of symbols for function blocks and function designations, complete with mathematical equations for derivation. Highly recommended for academic and special engineering libraries. — **Edward P. Miller**

1608. Snow, Dennis A., ed. **Plant Engineer's Reference Book.** Stoneham, Mass., Butterworths, 1991. 1v. (various paging). illus. index. $195.00. TS184.P58. 696. LC 90-2105. ISBN 0-7506-1015-8.

This is an excellent handbook for plant engineers, provided they are in the British Isles. The coverage is extensive to the point of having sections on making presentations to management on energy conservation, relationships between contractors and other parties, and landscaping on reclaimed land. The arrangement of the work is curious, beginning with a chapter on physical considerations and ending with a chapter on lubrication. The penultimate chapter describes education and training, making a very curious ending to the work.

The handbook is entirely British in outlook. The examples and units of measure are all geared to the British system. This will make the work of lesser importance in all but the broadest North American collections. Even at that, plant engineering is not an area of growth in most schools of engineering in the United States. The chemical engineer will probably have the most interest in this work, but only marginally.

This is an excellent reference book and highly recommended for purchase in British or British-influenced collections. The price of this work would be much better spent on other materials in a U.S. library. — **C. D. Hurt**

SOILS ENGINEERING

1609. Richard, Francois. **Glossary Geotextiles. Lexique Geotextiles.** Ottawa, Department of the Secretary of State of Canada, 1992. 74p. $10.75pa. (U.S.). 677'.4'03. ISBN 660-57069-6.

This slender glossary is one of a series of spin-offs from the Canadian English-French database known as Termium. Although designed to provide equivalencies between French and English, it coincidentally provides a nice list of geotextile terminology. The single alphabet highlights English terms in blue. The volume concludes with a bibliography and a list of other publications in the series. The subject specialist in soil mechanics or in geotextiles will find it a handy companion. *Soil Mechanics and Foundations* (see ARBA 92, entry 653), a related glossary in the series, should also be of interest.
— **Ronald L. Buchan**

TOOLS

1610. Blackburn, Graham. **The Illustrated Encyclopedia of Woodworking Handtools Instruments & Devices.** rev. ed. Chester, Conn., Globe Pequot Press, 1992. 147p. illus. $14.95pa. TT186.B52. 684'.082'028. LC 91-25510. ISBN 0-87106-168-6.

   Blackburn is a custom furniture maker, author of many books on carpentry and home repair, and editor of *Woodwork* (Ross Periodicals, 1989-). His stated objective for this work is to create a comprehensive index of woodworking tools common to Western civilization from the eighteenth century to the present. Two qualifications are used for a tool's inclusion. First, it must be a "handtool." No power tools, whether powered by water, gasoline, electricity or foot, are included. Second, the tool must have been used by a woodworker, which includes not only carpenters but also joiners, cabinetmakers, coopers, coach builders, wheelwrights, shipwrights, wainwrights, turners, pattern makers, and even whittlers.

   The revised edition includes additions, corrections, and a new typeset look, but it retains the basic alphabetical format of the 1974 edition. Although it is not a historical treatise, some historical background and etymologies are included with the definitions. More than 500 line drawings by the author depict each tool discussed, and a variety of historical illustrations provide a context for the subject matter. A short bibliography and a list of seven historical museums with collections of older tools conclude the book.

   This is a unique and useful reference work for those interested in collectible old tools, handwork, and custom-made furniture. However, if one has the first edition, this revision may not be an essential purchase. [R: LJ, 1 Mar 92, p. 80; RBB, 1 May 92, pp. 1623-1629] — **Jay Schafer**

1611. Philbin, Tom, and the editors of Consumer Reports Books. **The Illustrated Hardware Book.** Yonkers, N.Y., Consumer Reports Books, 1992. 210p. illus. index. $16.95pa. LC 91-48159. ISBN 0-89043-417-4.

   The selection of the right item for a particular job is often not an easy task for unskilled or semi-skilled homeowners. *The Illustrated Hardware Book* assists in that process by categorizing and describing several hundred common items and illustrating more than 200 of them with detailed line drawings. All kinds of general, electrical, and plumbing hardware and a miscellaneous assortment of other items, such as adhesives, lubricants, and tapes, are included. Each brief entry provides the name of an item and a practical description, explains what it is used for, and gives some tips on how it is used. A standard dictionary may define a nail and show one; this text describes the differences between 19 different kinds of nails and pictures 11 of them. One appendix describes metals and finishes; a second covers safety equipment; and a third provides ratings from *Consumer Reports* for 15 items, such as heat guns, that it has evaluated and ranked. A lengthy index provides ready access to specific items (provided, of course, that the name of the item is known). Although designed as a home reference tool, this simple-to-understand, well-illustrated handbook should be of special value to public libraries with a strong home repair collection. — **Norman D. Stevens**

1612. Wilbur, C. Keith. **Home Building and Woodworking in Colonial America.** Old Saybrook, Conn., Globe Pequot Press, 1992. 121p. illus. index. $12.95pa. TH4809.U6W55. 694'.0973'09031. LC 92-14213. ISBN 1-56440-019-0.

   The interest, especially in the northeastern United States, in colonial houses and in projects to build or restore them has created a demand for reference books that explain the tools needed and the techniques used to construct such houses. This text offers a detailed, step-by-step description of those techniques, from the felling of trees to the final completion of the house. A profusion of line drawings explain many aspects that the words cannot. Scattered throughout are accurate pictures of the wide variety of tools used in the process. All of this useful information is supplemented by an appendix that also uses many line drawings to describe advances in the development of woodworking tools since prehistoric times.

While intended primarily for the would-be home builder or restorer, the detailed text and the splendid drawings make this an equally valuable reference tool for historians, students, and others interested in learning how colonial houses were built or the historical development of hand tools. Although the index lacks adequate detail to guide the reader to every technique and tool mentioned, the detailed table of contents is a good guide, and the work is readily scanned. A brief bibliography cites most of the relevant works on the subject. — **Norman D. Stevens**

TRANSPORTATION ENGINEERING

1613. Papageorgiou, Markos, ed. **Concise Encyclopedia of Traffic & Transportation Systems.** Elmsford, N.Y., Pergamon Press, 1991. 658p. illus. index. (Advances in Systems, Control, and Information Engineering). $410.00. TA1145.C58. 388'.03. LC 90-22479. ISBN 0-08-036203-6.

Expectations have been high for this volume, the first of a series of seven intended to amplify the content of *Systems and Control Encyclopedia*, which was favorably reviewed in ARBA 88 (see entry 1449). The review noted a complex content arrangement that remains true for this first volume of the subset. In addition, efforts to continue a truly international work have been successful; the 123 entries have been authored (or coauthored) by 135 individuals from 16 countries, with most from France, Italy, and Germany.

The physical makeup of the volume is well done; it has a two-column format with a well-selected typeface and good paper. Illustrations are mostly well-labeled line drawings; there are a few halftones. When English units are better known and used, the International units are also given in equivalents. The recommendations of the Royal Society have been followed invariably. Cross-references to other entries in the volume use the author-year form in the body of the entries, while the bibliography at the end of each article uses the author-year-title-series-pages format. A reasonable proportion of 1980s references appear along with older government laboratory research reports and well-known classics. Self-citation is in evidence. Many of the mathematical expressions are in boldface type and very clear.

Particular attention is called to the editor's introduction in which he explains the subject areas into which the 126 articles fall: general aspects (e.g., social issues of transportation), road traffic measurements and communications, traffic modeling and simulation, road traffic control, freeway traffic control, general traffic networks, automated vehicle traffic, rail transport, air traffic control, sea transport, and other classifications (e.g., those that overlap). While it is the editor's prerogative to set the arrangement of his work as he chooses, the result in this case is an extra step for the reference librarian via the three-level subject index. This does reinforce the observation in the *Systems and Control Encyclopedia* review cited earlier that the reference staff need to work with this volume before routinely adding it to the collection. There are hints in the prefatory material that the Honorary Editorial Advisory Board may be considering adding supplementary volumes to the encyclopedia besides the seven listed in the present work. This might not be wise in view of the present budget crunch that major U.S. technical libraries are facing (the editor might find this true also with U.K. technical libraries). The present volume is recommended to those academic and public library collections with major emphasis on traffic-related subjects. [R: Choice, Mar 92, p. 1111] — **Eugene B. Jackson**

33 Health Sciences

GENERAL WORKS

1614. **Consumer Health & Nutrition Index. Volume 8, Number 1.** Alan M. Rees with Cynthia B. Strong, eds. Phoenix, Ariz., Oryx Press, 1992. 48p. $135.00/yr. ISSN 0883-1963.

This is a quarterly index to consumer literature; it cumulates at the year's end. It fills a very special niche as it covers publications that print articles about nutrition and medical issues that are geared to lay readers. Instead of journals in the hard sciences, it covers medical center newsletters (e.g., *Harvard Medical School Health Letter*), popular magazines (e.g., *Prevention*), general interest magazines (e.g., *Consumer Reports*), news magazines (e.g., *Time*), nutrition newsletters (e.g., *Nutrition Today*), pediatric newsletters (e.g., *Child Health Alert*), and major newspapers (e.g., *Wall Street Journal*). Starting with this volume, it also includes some of the major medical journals (e.g., *New England Journal of Medicine*). Subjects are indexed in depth, and coverage seems to be very good. MESH (National Library of Medicine Subject Headings) has been used as the thesaurus, but it has also been modified and expanded to include lay terminology. The format of the index is good, with aids such as topic headings in boldface type that make it easier to use. *See* and *see also* references are very common. This index will be important in any library that holds these titles, but it will be especially important in public libraries, where the general public can access this information. – **Lillian R. Mesner**

1615. **Glossary of Health Care Terms.** 2d ed. Compiled by the 1990 Health Care Services Committee of the International Foundation of Employee Benefit Plans. Bernard Handel, ed. Brookfield, Wis., International Foundation of Employee Benefit Plans, 1991. 37p. $10.00pa. LC 91-72186. ISBN 0-89154-420-8.

The health care environment constantly changes, and it is hard to provide a single definition of a term because the focus keeps shifting. This glossary, a handy reference tool, is intended to provide assistance and not to serve as a definitive source. It provides longer entries than a dictionary, and it includes almost 500 terms. The format is dictionary style and alphabetization is letter-by-letter. Antonyms, cross-references, and synonyms, if used, appear at the end of the dictionary. Following the glossary is a list of abbreviations and acronyms used in the glossary, alphabetized as if they were single words. There is no index.

Whereas a glossary can be more selective than a dictionary, the omission of some important terms from this work may cause some confusion. For example, the term *principal diagnosis* is defined, but there is no entry for the term *primary diagnosis*. The lack of any distinction drawn between these two terms may cause problems for medical record practitioners, physicians, and others involved with reports and surveys.

This glossary can be compared to the similarly titled *Glossary of Health Care Terms*, 3d ed. (American Medical Record Association [AMRA], 1986). The AMRA book is more helpful, particularly to practitioners, because it discusses the gray area surrounding primary diagnosis and principal diagnosis, among others. The glossary under review will be a useful tool for reference librarians, although it is not the most authoritative work on the subject. It will not be a helpful source for the layperson who wants a better understanding of what different types of health providers can offer. Recommended for special libraries in organizations that pertain to health law and health care policy, medical insurance, and employee benefits. —**Marilynn Green**

1616. **Glossary of Health Services. Lexique des Services de Sante.** Ottawa, Department of the Secretary of State of Canada, 1991. 133p. (Terminology Bulletin, 205). $17.95pa. (U.S.). 362.1'03. ISBN 0-660-56533-1.

A group of Canadian translators in the field of health care got together in 1983 to assist each other with translation and terminology. Eventually, ETS (Entraide Traduction Sante) decided to publish the terminology records so that all translators, terminologists, interpreters, and health professionals could profit from the work. The Terminology and Linguistic Services Directorate, charged with promotion of the two official Canadian languages (French and English), agreed to publish the resulting *Glossary of Health Services* as part of its terminology series. There are two main sections: English-French and French-English. Each page is arranged in parallel columns. Most of the terms are commonly used in hospital activities and administration and public health services, but there is a sprinkling of medical or scientific terms (e.g., *porphyrin, hypercalcemia*). Useful addenda are a bilingual list of health organizations in Canada, a bibliography, and a list of other publications of the Translation Bureau.

Many terms and expressions in the English listing, such as *servery, anamnesis, parapodium, social parent*, and *grade-aid,* are meaningless to most people in the United States working in health care. Often abbreviations prove confusing: for example, AIDS is SIDA. However, for the specified Canadian audience this seems to be an excellent bilingual compilation of basic health service terms. *Hospital Administration Terminology* (see ARBA 87, entry 1584) is a good choice for U.S. users.
—**Harriette M. Cluxton**

1617. **The Marshall Cavendish Encyclopedia of Family Health.** North Bellmore, N.Y., Marshall Cavendish, 1991. 12v. illus. index. $449.95/set. ISBN 1-85435-420-5.

This encyclopedia is addressed to the family, but few families are likely to spend so much for a 12-volume set of colored picture books, beautiful though they may be. Scarcely a page is without at least one picture, ranging from medical text reproductions to photographs or magazine-type illustrations; they often have little relevance to the text and are certainly a factor in pricing.

Most of the 900 individual subjects, arranged alphabetically, rate a single page. On the left of a page is a series of questions and answers. A headline statement is followed by clearly written text, frequently phrased as if a doctor is talking to the reader and often containing the "ask your doctor" advice common to consumer health literature written by professionals. It is not clear who wrote any of the articles; there is a long list of editors with only one, the chief editorial consultant (Trevor Weston of Family Health Publications), identified as an M.D. No sources or bibliographies are given. The goal of presenting the "hard facts" needed to cope with everyday health care while "dispelling myths and fallacies" is probably accomplished; however, the quality of the articles is far from uniform, and the often patronizing tone may offend some readers.

A minor problem with this set is its British English, not noticeably alleviated by a one-page United Kingdom/United States glossary. A major problem is that the bindings are so tight that the volumes will not lie flat; the inner columns are hard to read even when a book is hand held. This "reference" edition is a revision of an older 24-volume set, which may partially explain the narrow margins and crowded pages.

Volume 12 contains alphabetical and classified indexes, the United Kingdom-United States glossary, a first aid handbook, an illustrated medical glossary, a title listing by volume of all the articles, 20 reading lists of related articles, and forms for family medical records. Although the indexes are quite detailed, there are surprises; for example, the term *transplants* appears, but not *implants*. (Eventually, one can find silicone implants discussed under *prostheses.*)

School, hospital, and public libraries with strong interests in consumer health may find this encyclopedia useful. *Family Health and Medical Library* (see ARBA 86, entry 1603), an Australian set that is older and cheaper but at a somewhat more advanced level of medical coverage, may be more attuned to United States tastes. [R: BR, May/June 92, p. 54; LJ, 15 Mar 92, p. 78; RBB, 1 May 92, p. 1630]
—**Harriette M. Cluxton**

1618. **Minority Health Resources Directory.** Patricia A. President, ed. Rockville, Md., ANROW Publishing, 1991. 355p. index. $50.00.

Beginning with the premise that "special populations" within our society do not share equally in our generally improved health status, this directory gathers information on the government and private organizations that confront minority health issues, so as "to encourage use of these resources and thereby enhance their value." Organizations listed must either provide or fund cultural or ethnic minority health services on a national or regional level; local treatment centers or community-based organizations are excluded. Some 360 descriptive profiles are arranged alphabetically under federal government agencies and programs, private organizations, or foundations. Entries give contact information and an overview of the organization; point out activities specifically directed to minorities; and mention publications, databases, and meetings sponsored. Indexes are by special population focus, organization names, and subject areas. These sections are separated by reproductions of the cover, with appropriate titles.

Most of the government agencies and foundations are well covered in other directories. However, the proliferation of private groups with minority health care concerns is astounding; the editor has done an exceptional job of locating material on associations with as few as two or three staff members that are making a national contribution to minority health care (e.g., The National Council on Black Aging). Descriptions used have been provided by listees. No source is given for statistics used in the introduction. — **Harriette M. Cluxton**

1619. **National Health Directory, 1992.** Gaithersburg, Md., Aspen, 1992. 643p. maps. $89.00. RA7.5N37. 353.008'41'02573. LC 77-647206. ISBN 0-8342-0295-6. ISSN 0147-2771.

Tracing a piece of legislation or a health issue in the federal or state governments can be a frustrating experience. This book can potentially decrease that frustration by helping researchers learn who to contact and how to contact them. The book provides the customary directory information on members of Congress; the executive branch of the U.S. government; and other federal, state, and local officials and agencies that deal with health. Major congressional committees and subcommittees, their responsibilities related to health, and their memberships are also included.

The book is easy to use. Names of all officials are initially listed alphabetically by level of government and then cross-indexed by page number for further information. Each page has a corner heading, allowing for rapid location of the agency or level of government desired. State and local listings are alphabetized by state name. A particular asset of the book is the inclusion of names and telephone numbers for the health aides of each member of Congress and congressional committees. Maps, including Capitol Hill, congressional districts, and the National Institutes of Health, are helpful, but the print on some is too small to be visible.

The only major deterrent to the directory is its longevity. Personnel change, especially during a major election year, and this edition already carries outdated listings. The addresses and telephone numbers will most likely be stable, however. Perhaps the publishers could indicate elected officials, political appointments, and career officials in the next edition. Overall, the book meets its purpose and is recommended for all types of libraries and agencies who lobby the government.

— **Mary Ann Thompson**

1620. Romaine-Davis, Ada, Ayeliffe A. Lenihan, and Moira D. Shannon, comps. **Home Health Care: An Annotated Bibliography.** Westport, Conn., Greenwood Press, 1992. 145p. index. (Bibliographies and Indexes in Gerontology, no.16). $42.95. Z6675.H69R65. 016.3621'4. LC 91-46848. ISBN 0-313-28334-6.

Home health care continues to be a viable alternative to institutional care, particularly for the elderly. This book, one of a series of bibliographies and indexes on gerontology, lists and reviews books, journal articles, and government documents in the field. The resources are current; the majority were published in the 1980s or 1990s. The citations are organized by topical chapters, including system-wide issues, specifics to practice in the home, professional and lay caregiver issues, administration, research, and ethics. Within chapters, listings are presented alphabetically by author's last name and are also consecutively numbered. Cross-indexing by author and subject area is provided.

This bibliography provides a general, but not comprehensive, review of the literature in this field. The content is most appropriate for administrators or students of gerontology or home health. Unfortunately, the title implies a review of all home health care literature rather than specifying the elderly as the focus. The availability of computer databases limits the need for such indexes. However, this book would be an asset to college libraries without such access. [R: Choice, Oct 92, p. 280]

—**Mary Ann Thompson**

1621. Slee, Vergil N., and Debora A. Slee. **Health Care Terms.** 2d ed. St. Paul, Minn., Tringa Press, 1991. 456p. $25.00pa. RA423.S55. 613'.03. LC 90-28543. ISBN 0-9615255-1-7.

The U.S. health care system, and those persons who work in it, have their own language. Dealing with the various words, phrases, and abbreviations can lead to culture shock for people outside or new to the system. This book helps to ease the cultural transition. It does not focus on defining diseases, but rather on the terminology specific to the organization, administration, financing, and personnel of the system. The book includes more than 2,500 terms arranged alphabetically and cross-referenced by common abbreviation when applicable. Italicized words or phrases within a definition indicate that those terms are also defined within the reference. The definitions are concise and easy to read. A particular strength is the inclusion of court cases that have set precedents within the health care system.

The book would be easier to use if beginning and ending terms were highlighted at the top of each page, as in a traditional language dictionary, and if some definitions were more in-depth. Overall, however, the book meets its stated purpose. *Health Care Terms* will be helpful to the general public, health care professionals and administrators, and board members of health care institutions. Recommended for hospital, public, and college/university libraries.—**Mary Ann Thompson**

MEDICINE

General Works

Acronyms and Abbreviations

1622. **The Charles Press Handbook of Current Medical Abbreviations.** 3d ed. Philadelphia, Charles Press, 1991. 184p. $9.95pa. R123.C442. 610'.148. LC 90-15090. ISBN 0-914783-47-5.

About 6,000 abbreviations now commonly appearing on patient charts are included in this pocket-sized manual. Older and less-used forms have been dropped in favor of those that have evolved with changes in clinical medicine. Parenthetical explanations are added to abbreviations from Latin words and to those referring to specific doctor's orders, such as laboratory tests. Careful distinction is made when the same letters are used for several meanings; for example, of the four items under CVS, *chorionic villi sampling* is further defined as a procedure in gynecology. The clinically used form ADHD (attention deficit hyperactivity disorder) appears; the form A.D.D., used by patient support organizations, does not.

Compiled by 30 consultants, including doctors, nurses, and medical record administrators, this up-to-date handbook of clinically used abbreviations should be helpful to all health care workers involved with patient care, including nurses and house staff. For an exhaustive reference collection of abbreviations, see *The Davis Book of Medical Abbreviations* (see ARBA 92, entry 1644).—**Harriette M. Cluxton**

1623. **Stedman's Abbrev.: Abbreviations, Acronyms & Symbols.** William R. Hensyl, ed. Baltimore, Md., Williams & Wilkins, 1992. 664p. $21.95pa. R123.S69. 610'.148. LC 91-30701. ISBN 0-683-07926-3.

This unique directory is a companion work to *Stedman's Medical Dictionary* (see ARBA 91, entry 1664), enhancing Stedman's coverage with more than 20,000 clinically relevant and alphabetically arranged abbreviations, acronyms, and symbols used in the medical profession. Preferred or official usages have not been exclusively cited, as official nomenclature is often slow to be accepted. Rather, the editor logically includes all varied forms. The text is easy to understand, and each entry includes all possible meanings, but the reader would be wise to peruse the explanatory notes at the beginning in order to make the best use of the text. The book also has a breakdown of the Greek alphabet and concludes with an excellent definition of symbols used in the medical field. This specialized dictionary is highly recommended for medical libraries as well as special and public libraries that have *Stedman's Medical Dictionary*. — **James M. Murray**

Bibliography

1624. McKusick, Victor A., with Clair A. Francomano and Stylianos E. Antonarakis. **Mendelian Inheritance in Man: Catalogs of Autosomal Dominant, Autosomal Recessive, and X-Linked Phenotypes.** 10th ed. Baltimore, Md., Johns Hopkins University Press, 1992. 2v. index. $150.00/set. Z6675.M4M33. 016.5732'1. LC 92-13202. ISBN 0-8018-4411-8.

This book has been the vade mecum of geneticists since its first edition was published in 1966. Its wealth of information is organized into two sections. The catalog of Mendelian traits contains 5,710 entries organized alphabetically according to Mendelian classification as autosomal dominant, autosomal recessive, or X-linked. These are listed as phenotypes but represent genetic loci. As a list alone, this compilation would have enormous utility, but it goes far beyond being a list. Each entry describes the phenotype and reviews the literature. When the locus has been mapped to a specific chromosomal location, that and the evidence for the mapping information are noted. When the gene has been cloned, its name and location on the human gene map are noted, along with a summary of how the cloning was accomplished and appropriate citations. The listings are alphabetical by name within Mendelian class, and the index is helpful if the name of the phenotype or locus is unknown. There is also an author index to the citations. The first 214 pages are a small textbook of human genetics, with emphasis on gene mapping and description. Summaries of the Human Gene Mapping Workshops, idiographic representations of the human nuclear and mitochondrial genome, and listings by chromosome and of all mapped genes are part of this section.

The online version, OMIM, is part of the Genome DataBase, available by SprintNet from the Welch Medical Library at Johns Hopkins University. It is updated frequently, but it does not contain the first 214 pages, a distillation of some of McKusick's wisdom and knowledge. All geneticists must own this set. — **Margretta Reed Seashore**

1625. **Medical and Health Care Books and Serials in Print 1992: An Index to Literature in the Health Sciences.** New Providence, N.J., R. R. Bowker, 1992. 2v. index. $185.00/set. LC 77-94389. ISBN 0-8352-3198-4. ISSN 0000-085X.

One of the most frequently asked questions of librarians is "What books and journals are currently available for purchase on a particular subject?" This indispensable reference tool is the standard guide for answering this query when it concerns health-related materials. It contains a list of 61,219 monographic titles and 13,681 serial entries currently in print through July 1992. These entries are arranged alphabetically by author name and organized by main entry and by Library of Congress subject headings. The book titles are works published or distributed in the United States, while serial coverage is international in scope. Entries are drawn from the broad range of health care professions and biomedical sciences. Each main entry contains the following information: author, title, ISBN or ISSN, publisher, year of publication, and price. A particularly useful section for acquisitions work provides the names, addresses, and telephone numbers of publishing firms that work in the health arena. While this reference work is primarily intended for health-related information services, the inclusion of nontechnical works in certain areas also makes these volumes essential for public and high school libraries. — **Jonathon Erlen**

1626. Morton, L. T., and Shane Godbolt, eds. **Information Sources in the Medical Sciences.** 4th ed. Munich, New Providence, N.J., K. G. Saur, 1992. 608p. index. (Guides to Information Sources). $100.00. R118.I56. 610'.7. LC 91-40653. ISBN 0-86291-596-1.

The preface states that "this book is intended to serve as an evaluative guide to the most important sources of information that each contributor has recommended from experience of the subject, rather than as a directory of sources." Most of the 24 contributors are identified as qualified medical librarians in Great Britain; it is not always clear why they are considered specialists in the subject covered in their chapter. Generally, each reviewer considers books, journals, indexing and abstracting services, audiovisuals, and databases in the preclinical or clinical area addressed. A chapter on medical imaging has been added to this edition, as well as new material on subjects of current medical concern. Initial chapters cover medical libraries and standard indexes and reference sources, including online sources. Cross-referencing is adequate.

Although extensive coverage of international literature is claimed, the slant is definitely British. With the exception of major indexes, specialty journals, and the "old war horse" texts, coverage of U.S. medical literature is limited. European and WHO (World Health Organization) material is moderately represented. While British hospital librarians may find this book of practical value, in North America it will appeal to larger libraries with interests in medical bibliography. – **Harriette M. Cluxton**

1627. **Morton's Medical Bibliography: An Annotated Check-List of Texts Illustrating the History of Medicine (Garrison and Morton).** 5th ed. Jeremy M. Norman, ed. Brookfield, Vt., Scolar Press/Gower Publishing, 1991. 1243p. index. $145.00. ISBN 0-85967-897-0.

Nothing is more challenging than restructuring and updating a standard reference tool to meet current needs. This is the daunting task undertaken by Norman in this major revision of Garrison and Morton's classic bibliography of the history of medicine, which first appeared in 1943. Covering monographic and journal literature, this volume has been the main reference tool for bibliophiles, scholars, and librarians researching the history of medicine literature.

This edition contains 8,927 items, as compared to the 7,800 in the 4th edition. Besides the increased number of entries, 2,313 previous items have been rewritten or revised, while 119 have been deleted. Only a few entries are annotated, with annotations varying in length from a few words to a paragraph. The major changes in this edition are the new, improved organizational structure and the addition of several new subject headings (e.g., aviation medicine, paleopathology, acupuncture, sports medicine). Within each subject category, items are chronologically arranged and authors' dates are provided. Personal name and subject indexes provide easy access.

The main weakness of this volume is in the attempt to cover post-1950 medical literature. While claiming the need for selectivity, Norman fails to explain his criteria for the selection process. The exclusion of a number of major post-1950 publications raises serious concerns about the quality of this segment of the bibliography; for example, Beecher's 1966 landmark article on human experimentation should have been included under medical ethics, and the major reference works by Corsi and Erlen should have been included under medical bibliography.

Despite this significant weakness, Norman is to be congratulated for the revised organizational scheme, which enhances the use of this bibliography. As in the past, this work will be the mainstay for anyone seeking entrance into the history of medicine literature. – **Jonathon Erlen**

Catalogs and Collections

1628. Shepard, Thomas H. **Catalog of Teratogenic Agents.** 7th ed. Baltimore, Md., Johns Hopkins University Press, 1992. 534p. index. $95.00. QM691. LC 616'.043. LC 91-35396. ISBN 0-8018-4414-2.

This book is a catalog of data about teratogenic agents and the effects of more than 2,000 drugs, chemicals, alkaloids, biological and physical agents, and other potential teratogens. There is also a summary of experimental or observational data on the effects of fetal exposure to these agents in humans and animals. The book's format and size are very convenient. Entries are alphabetical by chemical or common name and have a brief summary and relevant literature citations. When there is information on related chemical compounds, these are noted. The entry discusses the data about the mixture and refers the reader to separate entries on the individual compounds that comprise it. Where there is little information, the entries are short, with one or two literature citations. Controversial or extensive information is found in entries that are longer (although not exhaustive), and there are 6 to 10 literature references. The entries are authoritative and concise; the literature references are both archival and recent, up to 1991; and the reader can find up-to-date and unbiased information and pertinent literature references. If one knows the chemical or common name of a compound, its listing can be located directly. An exhaustive index also contains many trade names of drugs whose chemical name may not be known to the reader. There is also an index by author of the cited references.

The book will be of great use to physicians and other health professionals who care for women during pregnancy. To geneticists and dysmorphologists caring for children with birth defects or congenital malformations, it will be useful in assessing the role of a chemical, biological, or physical agent in the cause of those birth defects. For experimental teratologists, it begins a review of the literature.

—Margretta Reed Seashore

Dictionaries and Encyclopedias

1629. **Black's Medical Dictionary.** 37th ed. Gordon Macpherson, ed. Lanham, Md., Barnes & Noble Books; distr., Savage, Md., Rowman & Littlefield, 1992. 645p. illus. $67.50. LC 59-167. ISBN 0-389-20989-9.

Published for nearly 90 years, *Black's* remains one of the easiest medical dictionaries to use, due to the clarity and conciseness of its definitions and descriptions and to its extensive cross-referencing. This edition covers more than 4,500 terms and concepts and has been carefully revised and updated by its new editor to reflect current medical practice. British spellings, expressions, and institutional referrals are only minimally disruptive to the U.S. reader. Specific drug names come from the *British Pharmacopoeia*. Text and diagrams are easy to understand. Biographical material, abbreviations, and the like are not included. The new appendix on basic first aid is too brief to represent much of an addition. Health care professionals, students, lawyers, and laypeople can profitably use this dictionary when simple explanations are sufficient.—**Harriette M. Cluxton**

1630. **Davies' Medical Terminology: A Guide to Current Usage.** 5th ed. By John Loveday. Stoneham, Mass., Butterworths, 1991. 350p. index. $34.95pa. R123.L88. 610'.14. LC 91-29477. ISBN 0-7506-0175-2.

This popular reference for allied health students and workers and medical secretaries has been updated and revised by Loveday, and some new tables have been added to the appendix. The most significant change that has occurred is that the text has been reorganized into chapters for quick reference, so that terms used, tests, diseases, treatments, and other features of a given body system are all in one place. Entries are explained clearly and simply in a readable style. This feature may make the book useful for consumer health education in the United States, despite occasional British English. (The work was developed at the Royal Surrey County Hospital, Guildford, England.) The references are almost all to standard British texts of the 1970s and early 1980s and are unlikely to be readily available here. This limits the guide's secondary purpose "for more systematic study," but it is still helpful for those wishing "to acquire a good working knowledge of medical terms in current use in medical practice." Real-life usage of medical words in health care, rather than a mere list of vocabulary, and the attempt to help allied health workers understand what is happening in hospital work distinguish this useful book from other terminology texts.—**Harriette M. Cluxton**

1631. De Lorenzo, Barbara, and Doris Fedun. **Medical Word Book A-Z.** Springhouse, Pa., Springhouse Publishing, 1992. 747p. $29.95pa. LC 87-43342. ISBN 0-87434-413-1.

This medical spelling reference contains thousands upon thousands of medical terms, commonly used phrases, combining forms, and some abbreviations, all arranged alphabetically, with two columns per page. The terms are largely Latin or the Latinized words found in standard medical dictionaries. Long lists are used for anatomical structures, diseases, tests, syndromes, and the like, but the items are also listed individually.

It seems strange not to find AIDS or any of its associated vocabulary in a work dated 1992, while words such as *pill* and *down* are considered important enough to be listed. *Chorionic villi* appears, but not the currently important CVS (chorionic villi sampling). However, coverage of accepted medical vocabulary is quite extensive. The book has lay-flat binding and space at the bottom of each page for additional entries. Authors, editors, transcriptionists, and medical secretaries should find the book valuable and easy to use. If word division or pronunciation is important, *Churchill-Livingstone's Medical Word Guide* (see ARBA 92, entry 1654) may be consulted.—**Harriette M. Cluxton**

1632. **Encyclopedia of Medical Organizations and Agencies 1992-93: A Subject Guide to Some 12,200....** 4th ed. Karen Backus, ed. Detroit, Gale, 1992. 1211p. index. $195.00. LC 84-640206. ISBN 0-8103-6910-9. ISSN 0743-4510.

One of the most common health-related questions encountered by reference librarians is how to contact a specific medical organization. This edition of a standard reference tool contains coverage of around 12,200 medically related organizations and agencies, which is an increase of nearly 1,000 entries since the 3d edition. These organizations are sponsored either by state or federal governments, foundations, academic institutions, or research centers.

Focusing on U.S. health-related institutions, organizations, and agencies, the guide is divided into 69 topical categories. Coverage spans a wide range of health care (e.g., surgery, pathology, public health, smoking, nutrition, social work). The following information is provided for each organization when available: address, telephone number, membership size, publications, contact person, and a brief description of major research interests and funding priorities. Entry cross-referencing, subject cross-indexing, and name and keyword indexes provide easy access to the material. This valuable reference work is an important resource for any large reference collection and is excellent for locating funding sources for the wide variety of biomedical science research projects. — **Jonathon Erlen**

1633. Inlander, Charles B., and Paula Brisco. **The Consumer's Guide to Medical Lingo.** Allentown, Pa., People's Medical Society, 1992. 95p. index. $5.95pa. ISBN 0-9627334-4-X.

This handy booklet of medical, health, and dental terms fills a need for definitions that can be understood by most laypeople. Within 15 brief chapters the authors provide word stems (prefixes, roots, and suffixes), abbreviations, types of medical specialists, nontraditional therapies, types of hospital health professionals and health care facilities, medical tools, diagnostic tests, frequent inpatient and outpatient procedures, dental terms, health insurance terms, medication families, and measurements and equivalents. All of these terms have concise and clear definitions. The index allows specific information to be found quickly. This compendium will be useful for individuals or general public libraries serving active consumer populations. — **John H. Hunter**

1634. Murray, Michael T., and Joseph E. Pizzorno. **An Encyclopedia of Natural Medicine.** Rocklin, Calif., Prima Publishing; distr., New York, St. Martin's Press, 1991. 622p. illus. index. $18.95pa. RZ433.M87. 615.5'35'03. LC 90-49007. ISBN 1-55958-091-7.

Two leaders in the field of naturopathic medicine (they are associated with Bastyr College of Seattle) have written an excellent encyclopedia on natural medicine. Part 1 explains the philosophy and principles of such medicine. Part 2 discusses the importance of mental attitude, diet, detoxification, immune system function, life extension substances, pain control, and stress. Part 3, the largest section, addresses 62 health problems ranging from acne to varicose veins. The section also covers conditions such as chronic fatigue syndrome, for which there is little treatment in traditional medicine. There is a thorough and clear discussion of symptoms and causes of the condition with recommendations of nutrients, vitamins, and herbs that offer relief. At the end of the volume is a glossary of terms and an extensive bibliography for each chapter. Many of the sources are from medical journals, with the latest publication date being 1989.

This is one of the best books on alternative, natural medicine. It will be a valuable addition to medical collections. — **Marilyn Strong Noronha**

1635. Payne, Peter A., ed. **Concise Encyclopedia of Biological & Biomedical Measurement Systems.** Elmsford, N.Y., Pergamon Press, 1991. 490p. illus. index. (Advances in Systems, Control, and Information Engineering). $280.00. RC71.C65. 610'.28'7. LC 91-19982. ISBN 0-08-036188-9.

The continuing rapid development of medical science has been accompanied by a bewildering growth of various medical and biological instrumentation and measurement systems. This encyclopedia has been created to assist the advanced researcher in keeping up with this information explosion. Payne's main goal is to present "a comprehensive survey of biological and biomedical measurement, covering both the measurement systems and the biological systems and subsystems on which the measurements are made." The book is composed of 85 major articles written by 81 experts. Each article provides up-to-date information and very useful bibliographies of current literature pertaining to that broad subject. Outstanding use is made of charts, graphs, and other illustrations. The alphabetically arranged topics cover the broad scope of medical and biological measurement, from absorption spectroscopy to x-ray imaging. Detailed subject indexing and cross-referencing make this volume's contents easy to access.

This reference tool is intended for physical scientists, medical and healthcare personnel, and researchers working in the biological sciences. The technical language and nature of the material presented put this encyclopedia beyond the scope of the general public. – **Jonathon Erlen**

1636. **The *Prevention* How-to Dictionary of Healing Remedies and Techniques: From Acupressure and Aspirin to Yoga and Yogurt....** By the editors of *Prevention* Magazine Health Books. John Feltman, ed. Emmaus, Pa., Rodale Press, 1992. 499p. illus. $26.95. RM36.P74. 615.5'03. LC 92-9053. ISBN 0-87596-114-2.

The word *dictionary* in the title of this book is somewhat misleading because it is not a dictionary in the usual sense. It is more of an alphabetized information source on a wide variety of healing options. Easy to understand, relatively balanced information is available on issues from drugs, surgical techniques, and herbal remedies to biofeedback and low-fat diets. A valuable component of this book is the "Master Chart of Complaints and Remedies," which allows the reader to focus on entries related to specific health problems. At the end of many of the dictionary entries, a *see also* suggestion directs the reader to additional headings that can provide more insight on a topic. Many of the listings have pronunciation aids; however, more liberal use of these aids would have strengthened the book. The editors have also included illustrations to help the reader understand complicated remedies and a chart that describes vitamins and minerals used in nutritional therapy.

The book is a reference text only, not a medical manual. The editors intend the information to be used to help readers make more informed decisions about their health. [R: LJ, July 92, p. 78]
– **Robert L. Jones**

1637. **Stedman's Medical Speller.** Harriet Felscher, ed. Baltimore, Md., Williams & Wilkins, 1992. 1150p. $24.95pa. R123.S7. 610'.14. LC 91-40215. ISBN 0-683-07938-7.

1638. **Stedman's Pathology Lab Medicine Words.** Baltimore, Md., Williams & Wilkins, 1992. 624p. $25.00pa. RB115.S73. 616.07'014. LC 92-224. ISBN 0-683-07939-5.

The compact *Stedman's Medical Speller* has been condensed from *Stedman's Medical Dictionary* (see ARBA 91, entry 1664). In an effort to avoid extensive duplication, the more obvious terms, abbreviations, and phrases have been culled. Within 1,150 pages there are more than 127,000 words and phrases, with 50,000 cross-references of adjectival and noun phrases. Within the organization the words are alphabetized letter-by-letter, with the main entries appearing in boldface type. These entries may be nouns or adjectives, such as *Foramen* or *abdominal*, with subentries that relate to the main entry appearing in lighter type and abbreviated (e.g., *aortic f.*). The reader is also instructed on the proper use of punctuation for eponymic entries (e.g., Down's Syndrome [John L. H. Down], Downs' Analysis [William B. Downs]).

The accompanying *Pathology Law Medicine Words* is composed of 55,000 words and cross-references and has a similar arrangement. However, this reviewer likes the *Medical Speller*'s practice of breaking the entries into their component syllables for ease of pronunciation. *Pathology* does list the full meaning of numerous laboratory medicine abbreviations (e.g., TTD [tissue tolerance dose], ALC [approximate lethal concentration]). That work has 50 pages of appendixes divided into four sections: laboratory reference range values, eponymic diseases and syndromes, laboratory test names, and culture media. Both of these volumes are comprehensive and would be useful to the practicing medical specialist or a library that supports a biomedical or allied medical curricula. – **John H. Hunter**

1639. Szycher, Michael. **Szycher's Dictionary of Biomaterials and Medical Devices.** Lancaster, Pa., Technomic Publishing, 1992. 259p. $85.00. LC 91-67901. ISBN 0-87762-882-3.

Researchers and manufacturers working in the broad area of biomaterials find themselves dealing with a number of scientific disciplines, each with its own unique terminology. Drawing on technical terms from pharmacology, medicine, and physiology, this dictionary is intended to negate the need for biomaterials scientists to consult several different dictionaries. The definitions are very brief, varying in length from a sentence to a short paragraph. Their brevity may force the user to seek out other sources for more detailed or complete explanations. While there are a few charts, it would have been helpful if Szycher had included more graphics and illustrations. The highly technical level of the definitions means that this volume is inappropriate for use by the general public.

Professionals from such diverse disciplines as biochemistry, organic chemistry, metallurgy, and polymer chemistry will find this book a useful starting point. However, they should not expect this dictionary to be a comprehensive, detailed guide to the terminology of biomaterials.—**Jonathon Erlen**

1640. Wade, Carlson. **The Home Encyclopedia of Symptoms, Ailments and Their Natural Remedies.** West Nyack, N.Y., Parker Publishing; distr., Englewood Cliffs, N.J., Prentice-Hall, 1991. 284p. index. $24.95; $9.95pa. RC81.A2W33. 616.02'4. LC 91-29632. ISBN 0-13-395492-7; 0-13-395484-6pa.

Written by a leading medical-nutrition reporter, this encyclopedia provides information that enables the reader to relieve pain and discomfort and promote the healing or alleviate the symptoms of more than 100 different ailments through the use of foods, nutrients, herbs, water, and lifestyle changes. The book covers topics such as AIDS, alcoholism, jet lag, varicose veins, and digestive disorders. Synopses of case histories are presented for some disorders, and documentation is provided from medical books, journals, and interviews. The information represents the author's collection of healing remedies from health practitioners around the world. For more serious afflictions, the information is somewhat skimpier than for minor conditions, such as corns or calluses, that may be easier to treat naturally. Some of the suggestions are simple common sense, while others present specific information. The reader must keep in mind that suggestions for healing are not a substitute for consultation with a duly licensed doctor.

The coverage is not as thorough as that in *The Encyclopedia of Natural Medicine* by Michael T. Murray and Joseph F. Pizzorno (St. Martin's Press, 1991); however, the book's concise presentation and easy-to-read language should make it a popular choice for the layperson who does not wish to wade through a lot of text. It has a definite place in holistic collections.—**Marilyn Strong Noronha**

1641. Willey, Joy. **Glossary of Medical Terminology.** Springhouse, Pa., Springhouse Publishing, 1992. 302p. $19.95pa. LC 88-42960. ISBN 0-87434-412-3.

Keeping pace with the ever-changing language of medicine is a problem for transcriptionists, secretaries, and many other health care workers. Much of the technical information needed is not available in regular medical dictionaries: new procedures, techniques, and instruments seem to come thick and fast. The terms included in this glossary are *not* readily found in standard works on terminology. In the alphabetical listing, terms are defined or spelled out in full if they are abbreviations, often with the medical specialty in which they are used indicated in parentheses. In the second portion of the book, the same words and phrases are listed under special categories, such as arthroscopy. All pages have a lined portion at the bottom for additional entries.

Willey states that spelling and capitalization have been carefully verified, and acknowledges the collaboration of cotranscriptionists at St. Vincent Hospital and Medical Center, Portland, Oregon. A special binding allows the volume to lie flat on the desk. Both as a reference and a training guide, this skillfully compiled and wide-ranging glossary should be useful to health care workers, not just to the designated audience of transcriptionists.—**Harriette M. Cluxton**

Directories

1642. **Canadian Medical Device Directory.** Ottawa, Chemicals and Bio-Industries Directorate with Industry, Science and Technology Canada, 1991. 282p. free pa.

This Canadian government publication uses a broad definition of the term *medical device*, including such mundane products as bandages and food service carts in addition to dialysis equipment and pacemakers. It includes only products manufactured in Canada and is meant to assist domestic purchasers and promote exports. Items are listed under key words and modifiers, such as "Prosthesis (Orthopedic)." Several indexes list product names and various alternate keyword headings. A more accurate title for this volume would be "Canadian Medical Manufacturers Directory," as the names, addresses, and telephone numbers of the manufacturers are the only data given for the products listed—there are no specifications, descriptions, or prices included. — **Carol L. Noll**

1643. **Directory of Pathology Training Programs in the United States and Canada 1993-94: Anatomic, Clinical, Specialized and Information about Pathology as a Career in Medicine.** 25th ed. Bethesda, Md., Intersociety Committee on Pathology Information, 1992. 617p. illus. index. $55.00pa. ISBN 0-937888-09-5.

The purpose of this directory is to describe the various options open to medical students who wish to specialize in pathology. The contents of the book include career information and certification in pathology, membership in pathological professional societies, United States and Canada residency training programs, postsophomore fellowships in pathology, and a training staff index. The training programs sections include detailed descriptions of programs, types and numbers of appointments, facilities, community demographics, stipends and maintenance, faculties, and application information. The information is timely, accurate, and well organized. This book should be purchased as a career guide by academic libraries and large public libraries. — **Theresa Maggio**

1644. Naifeh, Steven, and Gregory White Smith. **The Best Doctors in America 1992-93.** Aiken, S.C., Woodward/White, 1992. 712p. index. $60.00. R712.A1N25. 610'.25'73. LC 92-223. ISBN 0-913391-05-0.

Patients and their physicians are often confronted with the problem of finding the best specialist to consult for a particular medical problem. This volume, from the publishers of *The Best Lawyers in America* (1992), is meant to assist in that search. Doctors have been chosen by recommendation and review by their peers. Most of the initial contacts were made at major medical centers, such as the Mayo Clinic and Johns Hopkins, and, as can be expected, most of the physicians included are at universities and research centers throughout the country. All, however, are clinicians, not just engaged in research.

The book is arranged by general medical fields, then subspecialties. Information on physicians includes name and address, academic and hospital affiliations, telephone numbers, and sometimes further treatment specialization. Close to 4,000 doctors are listed, with representatives from all areas of the United States and a substantial number from Canada. However, one should not assume that only those doctors listed are fine physicians; the methodology used has given a definite preference to doctors who work in high-profile fields and in well-known institutions. [R: LJ, 15 Sept 92, p. 62] — **Carol L. Noll**

1645. **The National Directory of Chiropractic.** 3d ed. Olathe, Kans., One Directory of Chiropractic, 1992. 333p. $95.00pa.

This directory is divided into three sections. The first section is composed of advertisements for providers of equipment, supplies, and services to the chiropractic profession. The next section lists chiropractors by state and city. Entries provide the physician's name, address, telephone number, college attended, year of graduation, and chiropractic techniques used. Not all entries are complete. An alphabetical name index follows the geographical listings. The third section provides information on the practice of chiropractic in each state, including the scope of practice, licensure eligibility requirements, a general description of the licensing examination, and names and addresses of state chiropractic organizations.

While this last section may be useful in some libraries, the information in the directory is readily available elsewhere and at less cost. This work will primarily be of use to chiropractors in locating suppliers and in referring patients to other chiropractors who use specific therapeutic techniques.
— **Gari-Anne Patzwald**

Handbooks and Yearbooks

1646. Dorros, Gerald, and Darrell Seeley. **Understanding Lasers: A Basic Manual for Medical Practitioners Including an Extensive Bibliography of Medical Applications.** Mount Kisco, N.Y., Futura Publishing, 1991. 176p. illus. index. $24.50. R857.L37D667. 610'.28. LC 90-14068. ISBN 0-87993-398-4.

Designed for physicians who wish to explore the use of lasers in their practice yet are daunted by the mathematics involved, this work is about half manual and half bibliography. It is intended as a tool to help bridge the gap between laser physicists and laser-using medical practitioners. The first six chapters comprise the manual. Chapter 1 covers geometrical optics, explaining in basic language such phenomena as the index of refraction and thin lenses. The next three chapters discuss wave optics, the properties of laser light, and basic laser elements (the active medium, population inversion, and optical feedback). The types of lasers are listed in the lengthy chapter 5, and specifics are supplied for each of the three main laser elements plus their medical applications and, in some cases, their costs and power outputs. (These last two could be provided more consistently.) The final chapter in the manual deals with laser safety in medicine and surgery.

Nearly 100 pages long, the bibliography is arranged alphabetically by topic (e.g., cancer, gastroenterology) and then by author. (Running heads would help distinguish the topical sections.) Citations are largely to English-language journal articles published in the late 1980s, with a few earlier ones. A short appendix of technical and mathematical terms and an index to the manual and the appendix—but not to the bibliography—round out the text. This reasonably priced work should find an appreciative audience in medical libraries, and more general academic and large public libraries may wish to consider it for its clear discussion of laser basics.—**D. A. Rothschild**

1647. **The Essential Guide to Vitamins and Minerals.** By Health Media of America and Elizabeth Somer. New York, HarperPerennial/HarperCollins, 1992. 403p. index. $14.00pa. QP771.S66. 612.3'99. LC 91-55390. ISBN 0-06-273045-2.

This book provides nearly exhaustive information about vitamins and minerals, including such topics as deficiency symptoms and dietary sources, when supplements are needed, nutritional consequences of specific medicines, and the role of vitamins and minerals in diseases. The first section is divided into the basics of vitamins and minerals. The second section covers the treatment of diseases with specific vitamins and minerals. The last section is concerned with nutritional aspects, supplements, questions on vitamins and minerals, and body basics. It also has references, a glossary, and an index. Color photographs and diagrams would have been a nice addition to the text.

This book is comprehensive in its coverage of the subject. The layperson will find it easy to read, and it would be an excellent addition to any public library's collection. [R: Choice, June 92, pp. 1528-29]—**Theresa Maggio**

1648. Starck, Marcia. **The Complete Handbook of Natural Healing.** St. Paul, Minn., Llewellyn, 1991. 393p. illus. index. $12.95pa. R733.S834. 615.5. LC 91-14163. ISBN 0-87542-742-1.

This handbook provides a broad introduction to nontraditional ways of viewing health and disease. It is designed as a home reference guide to health products and services that are currently available. In 15 well-written chapters, all natural healing methods used today are presented. Among those discussed are dietary regimens, nutritional supplements, cleansing and detoxification, vitamins and minerals, herbology, homeopathic medicine, traditional Chinese medicine, ayurvedic medicine, and crystal healing. An important feature of the book is the section that describes 44 specific ailments. It gives information about their physical, mental, and emotional causes and recommendations for healing using natural treatments of diet, herbs, supplements, and body work (e.g., acupuncture, massage). Appendixes list addresses and directory information for consultation and herb sources; homeopathic remedies; flower essences; correspondence courses in ayurvedic medicine, crystals, and aromatherapy; and organizations that provide information about food irradiation. There is a bibliography at the end arranged by chapter.

Starck does not have any traditional healing degrees, but the material is well researched, accurately presented, and interesting to read. This work is an excellent resource for those seeking an overview of natural healing or an explanation of a particular healing system.—**Marilyn Strong Noronha**

Psychiatry

1649. Kaplan, Harold I., and Benjamin J. Sadock. **Comprehensive Glossary of Psychiatry and Psychology.** Baltimore, Md., Williams & Wilkins, 1991. 215p. $14.95pa. RC437.K36. 616.89'003. LC 90-22810. ISBN 0-683-04527-X.

    This glossary is part of a set aimed at mental health professionals and students. Two other titles in this set are *Comprehensive Textbook of Psychiatry* (Williams & Wilkins, 1989) and *Synopsis of Psychiatry* (Williams & Wilkins, 1991), both authored by Kaplan and Sadock. As noted in the preface, the related volumes are often the source of definitions for the glossary. Entries consist of brief definitions of terms and acronyms, sources of eponyms, short biographical entries, and descriptions of professional and health care organizations. Cross-references are used frequently to refer to acronyms and related terms. The four-page psychotherapeutic drug identification guide, providing color illustrations of medications, has been extracted from the *Synopsis*. Three appendixes of tables classify drugs often prescribed in psychiatric practice, commonly abused substances, and drugs considered by the U.S. Drug Enforcement Administration to have abuse potential. An outline of diagnostic categories from the *Diagnostic and Statistical Manual of Mental Disorders* (see ARBA 89, entry 1550) is reprinted on the inside front and back covers.

    As a source of quick definitions of terms needed by the intended audience, the glossary is passable. As a stand-alone reference tool, it pales beside *Psychiatric* (see ARBA 90, entry 1672), which Kaplan and Sadock acknowledge as the source of some definitions. Certainly, *A Student's Dictionary of Psychology* (see ARBA 90, entry 746), *The International Dictionary of Psychology* (see ARBA 90, entry 747), and *Dictionary of Behavioral Science* (see ARBA 90, entry 90) afford more comprehensive coverage of psychology as a discipline.—**Pam M. Baxter**

Specific Diseases

AIDS

1650. Anderson, John R., Christine P. Landry, and Jody L. Kerby, eds. **AIDS: Abstracts of the Psychological and Behavioral Literature 1983-1991.** 3d ed. Washington, D.C., American Psychological Association, 1991. 301p. index. (Bibliographies in Psychology, no.6). $27.50pa. RC607.A26A34529. 616.97'92. LC 91-22115. ISBN 1-55798-148-5.

    This edition of a title that has now become a valuable, key bibliography to the literature of AIDS contains 2,333 entries, a 240 percent increase since the previous edition (1989). Included among the entries are 1,757 abstracts and citations to serial and dissertation literature published between 1983 and 1991.

    The bibliography is arranged in five sections. The first section contains a literature review focused on three areas: epidemiology and prevention, counseling and ethical issues, and special populations. The second (and major) section subdivides into six areas: etiology epidemiology and diagnosis of AIDS; treatment and counseling for patients and at-risk populations; special or at-risk populations; public education and knowledge about AIDS; attitudes toward AIDS—fear, stress, and family adjustment; and professional, legal, ethical, and policy issues. Following this is a section on selected references to books on AIDS, supplemented by separate author and subject indexes. An appendix provides search strategies to update references on AIDS.

    Researchers, scholars, students, and professionals should all find this work to be a valuable compendium of information and citations. For those libraries not yet equipped with electronic reference tools such as PsycLIT on CD-ROM or PsycINFO online, the volume is especially useful for freeing patrons from hours of searching through printed indexes. Academic and large public library collections, as well as health care and social work collections, should consider this work for acquisition.

—**Edmund F. SantaVicca**

1651. **Directory of Current HIV/AIDS Research in Canada 1988-1991. Repertoire de la Recherche dans le Domaine du VIH et du SIDA au Canada.** Montreal, Centre for AIDS Studies, Department of Community Health, Montreal General Hospital, 1991. 1v. (various paging). index. free pa. 616.97'0072071. ISBN 2-9800406-9-X.

An excellent guide to HIV/AIDS research in Canada, this volume includes information on 259 projects selected for inclusion on the basis of information solicited via mail questionnaire. The editors note that all information received, whether included here or not, is maintained and updated on a computerized database. Criteria for inclusion are that the research must be independently funded, at least one component of the project must take place in Canada, funds must have been awarded between April 1988 and March 1991, and the researcher must be willing to reveal the funding amounts per year.

Entries are arranged according to an assigned nine-digit code. Each entry includes the name of the principal researcher; directory information; name of funding agency; budget; duration of project; location; key words assigned to the project; and project title, accompanied by a brief summary of the scope of the project. Supplementing this core text are indexes to investigators, institutions of principal investigators and coinvestigators, funding agencies, and key words. Also given are addresses of public and private agencies and lists of additional funded projects for which investigators did not provide all requested information. This bilingual directory will prove to be of both current and historical value for its ability to inform researchers of other research projects being conducted in areas pertaining to HIV/AIDS research. – **Edmund F. SantaVicca**

1652. Huber, Jeffrey T., ed. **How to Find Information about AIDS.** 2d ed. Binghamton, N.Y., Harrington Park Press/Haworth Press, 1992. 290p. index. $14.95pa. RC607.A26H9. 362.1'969792'02573. LC 91-2237. ISBN 0-918393-99-X.

Although the intended audiences of this work are health care professionals and the general public, the quality of information included may limit the work's usefulness. Nowhere in the volume does Huber actually discuss how to find information about AIDS – a flaw all too typical of many of the volumes now appearing as guides to information on the topic. Basic directory or bibliographic information is included for organizations, health departments, research institutions, grant-funding sources, federal agencies, education and training centers, AIDS hotlines, electronic and print sources of information, and audiovisual producers/distributors. Most of these are simple listings with little guidance to the reader as to what information can be gleaned from them. As a basic directory for those who are already familiar with the field and who know a variety of search strategies for locating information, this volume has value in its updated listings. However, it does not provide even a remote notion to the uninitiated as to how to effectively search for information, nor how to retrieve needed information from the included works. As a basic resource guide, it cannot compare with *AIDS Information Sourcebook* (see ARBA 92, entry 1678); as a bibliography, it falls short of David A. Tyckoson's annual *AIDS* bibliography (see ARBA 90, entry 1679); and as a how-to handbook, it does not live up to the concept. [R: SLMQ, Summer 92, p. 241] – **Edmund F. SantaVicca**

1653. Murphy, C. Edward, ed. **AIDS Funding: A Guide to Giving by Foundations & Charitable Organizations.** New York, Foundation Center, 1991. 175p. index. $60.00pa. ISBN 0-87954-382-5.

Similar in format and design to other titles from the publisher, this volume contains a great deal of information pertinent to funding for projects related to AIDS. The body of the work is arranged alphabetically by state and then by name of foundation. Every entry provides full directory information and a profile of the foundation and its funding interests. Indicated for each are total dollars expended for programs administered by the foundation, type and number of loans, types of support and limitations, relevant publications, application information, and a list of recent grants for AIDS. Although much of the same information is provided in *Foundation Directory* (see ARBA 91, entry 866), it is not provided as effectively as it is in this volume. Enhancing the work are brief introductory essays on foundation and corporate support for AIDS/HIV, AIDS funding, researching foundations, and grant seeking from corporations. A guide to using the volume and a glossary are provided, along with a bibliography of funding for AIDS/HIV. Multiple indexes to donors, officers, trustees, geographic areas, types of support, grants by subject, foundations, corporate giving programs, and public charities supplement

the main text. This is a useful tool for those seeking funding for AIDS/HIV programs, including community service agencies, health facilities, libraries, and educational institutions.
—Edmund F. SantaVicca

Birth Related Conditions

1654. Weaver, David D. **Catalog of Prenatally Diagnosed Conditions.** 2d ed. Baltimore, Md., Johns Hopkins University Press, 1992. 415p. index. $75.00. RG626.W35. 618.3'2075. LC 91-46746. ISBN 0-8018-4415-0.

In a remarkable introduction, Weaver summarizes the history of prenatal diagnosis as reflected in the literature and discusses the ethical issues connected with it; he also explains how to use this catalog. The substantial growth of this field is well demonstrated by the fact that the first edition of this book (1989) had 445 conditions with 1,221 references; this one has 601 conditions and 1,848 references. The text is divided into chapters by disease category, then arranged alphabetically by condition. Each entry begins with the letters PD (prenatal diagnosis); a six-digit reference number; and the preferred name of the condition, with alternates and abbreviations. This is followed by a "McKusick number," if available, from *Mendelian Inheritance in Man* (John Hopkins University Press, 1992). Next are the methods used for diagnosis and the fetal abnormalities discovered. Specific information on the disorder, differential diagnosis, and prenatal treatment (if it exists) are provided. References and occasional comments are inserted throughout the abstracted information. Superscript letters indicate trimester of diagnosis. The extensive reference section gives full bibliographic data for all references in the text and introductory material. The alphabetical subject index refers to PD numbers and contains many cross-references.

The goal of this catalog is to provide a single source of much of the information that doctors and other health care workers need in order to learn if a birth defect or genetic condition can be diagnosed prenatally. It is also an excellent reference source for researchers. In a time when gene research is rapidly progressing and abortion is a volatile political, social, and health issue, this catalog should be made widely available, regardless of institutional involvement in the scientific side of reproductive medicine.—**Harriette M. Cluxton**

Cancer

1655. Dollinger, Malin, Ernest H. Rosenbaum, and Greg Cable. **Everyone's Guide to Cancer Therapy.** Kansas City, Mo., Andrews and McMeel, 1991. 624p. illus. index. $29.95; $19.95pa. RC263.D59. 616.99'406. LC 91-8397. ISBN 0-8362-2418-3; 0-8362-2417-5pa.

This excellent guide to the diagnosis and treatment of cancer is intended primarily for people with the disease and their families. The contributors are top authorities in the field. Approximately one-third of the book is devoted to general information on diagnosis, treatments, supportive care, advances and developments, screening, and prevention. The remaining portion lists the various common cancers alphabetically and devotes several pages to a discussion of each. Topics covered include risk factors, screening, common signs and symptoms, diagnosis, staging, factors that affect prognosis and treatment decisions, treatment overview and follow-up, recurrent cancer, and important questions to ask. Also provided are a glossary of medical terms; a list of anticancer drugs and their side effects; a directory of cancer centers, associations, and support groups; and suggested readings.

A special feature of the book is a chapter on the computerized information system, Physicians Data Query (PDQ). The database contains up-to-date information on clinical trials that are testing new treatment approaches for cancer patients. Those trials show which therapies are most effective, and PDQ recommends those that are state-of-the-art. Also, with the information provided, doctors can help patients who want to participate in a clinical trial to become enrolled in one that is suitable.
—**Theodora Andrews**

Hearing Disorders

1656. Turkington, Carol, and Allen E. Sussman. **The Encyclopedia of Deafness and Hearing Disorders.** New York, Facts on File, 1992. 278p. index. $45.00. RF290.T93. 617.8'003. LC 91-16451. ISBN 0-8160-2267-4.

With 1 out of 10 Americans having some degree of hearing loss and 1 of 400 being profoundly deaf, this book appears to be a valuable resource for hard-of-hearing people, educators, health professionals, and others in related fields. The main portion of the book consists of alphabetical entries that include clinical terms, devices and equipment, diseases and disorders, experts in the field, famous deaf individuals, physiology of the ear, and state-of-the-art technology. Additionally, 13 appendixes list organizations and groups, community and federal programs, homes and housing for those with special needs, residential programs and summer camps for children, periodicals of interest, training centers for hearing ear dogs, and more. An extensive bibliography at the end of the book is an aid to those wishing to explore a specific topic in further depth. The authors include a caution in the preface concerning the rapid changes that may occur in medicine and technology. They recommend that up-to-date technical information on hearing aids and assistive and telecommunications devices should be obtained from specialists. [R: Choice, Sept 92, p. 94; LJ, 15 Feb 92, p. 162; RBB, 1 Apr 92, pp. 1470-72; WLB, May 92, p. 123] – **Edith M. Dorenfeld**

Heart Diseases

1657. Goldman, Martin E. **The Handbook of Heart Drugs: A Consumer's Guide to Safe and Effective Use.** New York, Henry Holt, 1992. 297p. index. $29.95; $12.95pa. RM345.G635. 615'.71. LC 91-39966. ISBN 0-8050-1720-8; 0-8050-1721-6pa.

Approximately one American in nine takes some form of heart medicine. Goldman's book is written for these people and those who care for them. It begins with an important – if somewhat preachy – chapter on physician-patient relationships that tells patients how to select and communicate with cardiologists (and *only* cardiologists). Common forms of heart disease and disease symptoms are described next, followed three chapters later by a discussion of risk factors for heart disease. Sandwiched in between is a general overview of how heart drugs work, including tolerance levels, drug schedules, and possible adverse reactions. There is also a chapter devoted to the importance of patient compliance and monitoring. The second half of the volume profiles more than 90 commonly used heart drugs categorized according to function: diuretics, beta blockers, calcium antagonists, vasodilators, potassium supplements, antiarrhythmics, blood-related drugs, and antihyperlipidemics. Each profile lists a specific drug by brand and generic names, explains how it works, its purpose, dosage, possible side effects and adverse reactions, what to do for an overdose, and other relevant commentary. The handbook is clear, concise, and accessible to the lay reader. [R: LJ, July 92, p. 76] – **Bruce Stuart**

Syndromes

1658. Gibson, J., and O. Potparic. **A Dictionary of Medical and Surgical Syndromes.** Park Ridge, N.J., Parthenon, 1992. 202p. $48.00. RC69.G53. 616'.047'03. LC 91-16973. ISBN 1-85070-338-8.

This handy dictionary is composed of syndromes whose origins are of a medical or surgical nature. Contained within are more than 1,000 alphabetically arranged definitions from A & V syndrome to Zondek syndrome. Each is fully defined and may have such information as complications associated with the syndrome, physical descriptions of those affected, location where the syndrome may have first occurred, and other names by which it may be called. If a syndrome is more commonly known by another name, the reader is referred to that particular name (e.g., Trisomy 21 syndrome, *see* Down syndrome). The inclusion of Sick Building syndrome is quite timely. Although many of the syndromes are specialized, this work will be a useful addition to a scientific collection and a necessary one for most medical collections. – **John H. Hunter**

NURSING

1659. Bullough, Vern L., Lilli Sentz, and Alice P. Stein, eds. **American Nursing: A Biographical Dictionary. Volume II.** Hamden, Conn., Garland, 1992. 389p. illus. (Garland Reference Library of Social Science, v.368-). $95.00. RT34.A44. 610.73'092'2. LC 87-29076. ISBN 0-8240-7201-4.

Biographies of significant American nurses, born in 1915 or before and mostly deceased, are included in this second volume of *American Nursing*. A few retirees are listed, but today's active professional leaders will have to wait until the third volume, due in 1997 or 1998. Considerable overlapping exists with volume 1, but both volumes are necessary for a comprehensive view of the development of nursing in this country, as seen through the contributions of those who lived it—391 individuals, only 9 of them men.

Entries follow the format of the initial volume: identification of the person in relation to the contribution to nursing or American history in general, known personal and career information, books and articles written by the individual, selected bibliography, and contributor's name. A collection of portraits appears in the middle of the book. Indexes by decade of birth, first nursing school attended, area of interest or accomplishment, and state or country of birth supplement the dictionary arrangement. Further research could well be done on all of these outstanding people. Both volumes represent important additions to the biographical reference field, especially of women in America. [R: Choice, July/Aug 92, p. 1651]—**Harriette M. Cluxton**

PHARMACY AND PHARMACEUTICAL SCIENCES

1660. **AARP Pharmacy Service Prescription Drug Handbook.** 2d ed. New York, HarperPerennial/HarperCollins, 1992. 1137p. illus. index. $17.95pa. RS51.A28. LC 91-58281. ISBN 0-06-277037-3.

1661. **The Canadian Medical Association Guide to Prescription and Over-the-Counter Drugs.** Mark S. Berner and Gerald N. Rotenburg, eds. Montreal, Reader's Digest Association (Canada), 1990. 592p. illus. index. $39.95. 615'.1. ISBN 0-88850-162-5.

These two volumes join a growing collection of consumer guides to prescription and over-the-counter drug use. The Canadian Medical Association (CMA) guide is designed for Canadians, *not* people from the United States. The two countries have similar—but by no means identical—laws regarding the approval and distribution of drug products. U.S. readers should choose the *AMA Guide to Prescription and Over-the-Counter Drugs* (Random House, 1988), which is identical in format to the CMA volume.

The CMA and AMA guides are each organized into five parts. Part 1 presents a general introduction to drugs, drug classification schemes (prescription and over-the-counter), a description of how drugs work, and key elements in drug therapy. Part 2 contains a color pill identification guide and an index of approximately 3,200 medications by drug and brand name. Part 3 describes major drug groups according to the human systems they influence. Each drug group is summarized in a single page format that lists common drugs in that group and explains why they are used, how they work, how they affect patients, and what risks they present. Useful drawings and charts complement the descriptions. Part 4 contains page-long individual drug profiles for 320 selected medications listed alphabetically by nonproprietary name, with edge-of-page indexing for quick reference. The standardized profiles include brand names under which the drug is sold, and brief sections provide general and user information, special precautions, possible adverse effects and interactions, and information about prolonged use. Following the drug profiles are short sections on vitamins, minerals, and food additives. Part 5 includes a glossary, a general index, and a drug poisoning emergency guide.

The CMA guide and its U.S. cousin deserve high marks for clarity of language, ease of use, and striking visuals—features notably missing from the *AARP Pharmacy Service Prescription Drug Handbook*. The AARP handbook contains a general introduction, 12 chapters organized around specific diseases and disorders, a color identification guide to pills, and separate indexes for drugs and medical conditions. Ostensibly designed for senior citizens, the handbook's organization of material, instructions on drug use, and possible side effects are confusing at best and possibly hazardous to health at worst. Each chapter is divided into several disease-specific sections that are introduced with a two- to three-page description of the condition. Following are "drug charts" that list the condition (e.g., hypertension), a category of drug (e.g., diuretics—thiazides and related drugs), and specific chemical agents (e.g., Chlorothiazide). Following the drug charts are three to five pages of instructions, lists of side effects, and considerations for the elderly. These sections blend one into another with no page breaks and no index marks or other device to warn the reader to which particular drug the instructions refer. The material provided is of questionable value. While the sections on special restrictions (food and drug interactions and effects on daily living) contain clear and useful information, sections on what to tell your doctor prior to using a drug and possible side effects are simply bulleted listings with no discussion. For example, readers contemplating use of Clonide—a combination drug for hypertension—are presented with 34 conditions problematical to use and 59 possible side effects. On the other hand, the AARP handbook contains a more complete list of drug products than either the AMA or CMA guides. [R: RBB, July 92, p. 1956]—**Bruce Stuart**

1662. **The Complete Drug Reference.** 1992 ed. Yonkers, N.Y., Consumer Reports Books, 1992. 1v. (various paging). illus. index. $39.95. LC 81-640842. ISBN 0-89043-479-4.

Including more than 5,500 drugs, this work presents drug information to the patient in clear and easy-to-read language. The drugs are listed by their generic names. The drug monographs make up the greatest portion of the source. Information provided for each drug includes brand names, general description, risks to be considered before taking the medicine (e.g., allergies, pregnancy, breast-feeding), proper use, precautions to be taken while using the medicine, and side effects. The informative description discusses drug classification, therapeutic use, and side effects. Brand names include those used in the United States and Canada. In addition, the names of the drugs have been divided into syllables to aid in proper pronunciation. Other sections consist of a glossary, drugs that deal with combination chemotherapy, a list of drugs under their respective groups (e.g., antidepressants), a series of pictograms that give directions for appropriate drug use, a pregnancy and a breast-feeding precaution list of drugs, and a medicine chart. This last shows, by means of photographs, the most frequently prescribed medicines (approximately 1,400) in the United States. The volume closes with a combined generic- and brand-name index, with the latter in italic typeface.

This work, with its concise and understandable language, will be a welcome companion to the *Physician's Desk Reference* (PDR) (see ARBA 88, entry 1693). It should be noted, however, that the PDR contains information directly from the drug companies and not from many different sources, as this monograph does. In addition, the PDR only covers prescription drugs. This source contains both prescription and over-the-counter medications. All public, college, university, and specialized libraries that deal with medical and pharmaceutical information should have a copy. However, if one has or will be receiving the 12th edition of *Drug Information for the Health Care Professional* (United States Pharmacopeial Convention, 1992), this source need not be purchased as it is volume 2 of that multivolume set.—**George H. Bell**

1663. **Drug Information for the Health Care Professional 1992.** 12th ed. Rockville, Md., United States Pharmacopeial Convention, 1992. 4v. index. $200.00/set. LC 81-640842. ISBN 0-913595-61-6. ISSN 0740-4174.

Arranged by chemical name, volume 1, which spans two books, contains monographs on prescription and over-the-counter drugs. For each drug listed, the VA classification, brand names, mode of administration, drug category, indications, pharmacology (e.g., mechanisms of action, protein binding, half-life, duration of action, elimination), precautions (e.g., carcinogenicity, mutagenicity, pregnancy), side or adverse effects, and general dosing information are given. A very brief bibliography is included at the end of each monographic section. The appendixes at the end of volume 1 consist of additional products and indications; a selected list of drug-induced effects; veterinary information (drug monographs arranged by chemical name); the VA medication classification system; an orphan drug and biological listing; and a number of precaution listings that deal with pregnancy, breast-feeding, pediatrics, geriatrics, and athletes. In addition, a medicine chart includes photographs of frequently prescribed medicines in the United States. An indications index (arranged by affliction, followed by drugs used to treat same) and a general index complete volume 1. (The same general index can also be found in part 1 of volume 1.)

Volume 2 discusses precautions and adverse effects of the drugs in language that a nonmedical professional would understand. The appendixes consist of combination chemotherapy, categories of use (affliction and list of drugs useful in treating same), a compilation of pictograms (directions for appropriate drug use), a pregnancy and breast-feeding precaution list, a medicine chart (photographs of frequently prescribed medicines), and a chemical/brand-name index.

Volume 3 includes *The Orange Book* (approved drug products with therapeutic equivalence evaluations), compiled by the Food and Drug Administration. In addition, there is a list of notices that apply to standards, tests, and assays of the USP and USP-NF requirements on the strength, quality, purity, packaging, labeling, and storage of drugs. The medicine chart and a chemical/brand-name index conclude the work. This latest edition has more than 80 new drugs or combinations and a number of new nutritional supplements. Examples are dezocine, propofol, olsalazine, pipercuronium, biotin, and copper and zinc supplements.

This classic work is highly recommended for all major public, college, and university libraries. All specialized libraries that hold medical and pharmaceutical information should have it. —**George H. Bell**

1664. Harkness, Richard. **Drug Interactions Guide Book.** Englewood Cliffs, N.J., Prentice-Hall, 1991. 288p. index. $24.95; $12.95pa. RM302.H366. 615'.7045. LC 91-3801. ISBN 0-13-219601-8; 0-13-219619-0pa.

With the increasing proliferation of prescription and nonprescription drugs, the general public faces more questions and potentially dangerous choices about appropriate drug use when they are required to take two or more medications simultaneously. This reference work is intended to help readers "become active partners in their own health care" by avoiding hazardous adverse effects caused by drug interactions. The author is a consultant pharmacist who has published a number of similar works.

This compilation is organized so that it is easy to locate specific drugs by either their generic or brand names. Harkness has taken the information for this volume from several standard pharmaceutical texts; however, he fails to list these books. The segment that covers basic drug interactions provides the following information for each of the 314 entries: severity, probability, uses for the drugs, possible adverse effects, and advice on how to handle these bad reactions. Supplemental chapters very briefly deal with potentially dangerous depressants and stimulants that can act as add-on drugs, medications prescribed for 18 common health disorders, and possible bad interactions between basic foods and specific drug groups. This easy-to-use reference guide will be quite useful to the general public and is an appropriate resource for public libraries. [R: Choice, Mar 92, p. 1046]—**Jonathon Erlen**

1665. Lance, Leonard L., and Charles Lacy. **Quick Look Drug Book with Indications Index.** Baltimore, Md., Williams & Wilkins, 1992. 597p. $24.95pa. ISBN 0-683-07050-9.

This is an easy-to-use, concise pocket guide to the most commonly prescribed drugs in hospitals. The main text of the book is an alphabetical list of generic names, brand names, and synonyms, with cross-references from the latter two to the generic names. Information on the 1,247 drugs (listed under the U.S. adopted generic name) includes all brand names, synonyms, pronunciation, use, restrictions, pregnancy risk factor, usual dosage, and dosage forms. The appendix covers 14 drug-related topics, including a list of controlled substances, weights and measurements, overdose/toxicology information, normal laboratory values for adults, conversion charts, immunization guidelines, and an extensive list of acronyms. The indications index lists a disease or illness and then identifies the most commonly used drugs for treatment. There is no patient/family teaching information as in *Davis's Drug Guide for Nurses* (see ARBA 92, entry 1692). This is a good purchase for health care individuals and their libraries.—**Betsy J. Kraus**

1666. Paterson, Ellen R., comp. **Anabolic Steroids and Sports: A Selective Bibliography with Annotations.** Troy, N.Y., Whitston Publishing, 1991. 66p. index. $10.00. LC 90-83684. ISBN 0-87875-389-3.

This slim volume is a bibliography based on searches of 13 indexing and abstracting services. It is aimed at coaches, teachers, and parents of athletes. Many references are from the popular press, and scientific animal studies of steroid effects are not included. Entries are arranged in topics, such as side effects, testing, and training alternatives. About 200 of the 600 references are annotated. There is a brief, entirely inadequate subject index.

It is hard to see much lasting value in such a bibliography. Many of the references are to news articles of ephemeral interest (e.g., an entire chapter is devoted to the Ben Johnson incident). There are some valuable overview articles listed, but, in general, a search of the indexing services appropriate to one's interest would yield more current and useful information. — Carol L. Noll

1667. Stark, Richard W., and others, eds. **The Drug File: A Comprehensive Bibliography on Drugs and Doping in Sport. Dossier Dopage.** Gloucester, Ont., Sport Information Resource Centre, 1991. 179p. index. $45.00pa. (U.S.). 016.3634'5'024769. ISBN 0-921817-10-X.

This extensive bibliography lists 4,000 references to information on all aspects of the use of drugs in sports. Most citations refer to works published between 1984 and 1991, with some historical and technical articles dating to 1980. Sections on all major drug categories and doping methods are included. There are references to doping control research and sport-by-sport information specific to more than 50 sports. Citations refer to very technical information on such specific drugs as anabolic steroids, beta blockers, and human growth hormones and to articles on human rights, ethical issues, and sociological and psychological concerns. There are listings for rules and regulations, testing, detection methods, and policy and position statements. Educators, students, coaches, administrators, and athletes will find information on their particular concerns.

The citations vary from just the bibliographic information to one- or two-line annotations to fairly lengthy ones. Each citation provides a research level rating that tells the user the appropriate audience for the document. Level B is basic, Level A is advanced or research material, and Level I is intermediate and falls between the two. A very useful work on a timely topic, it deserves a spot on the shelves of every large public, high school, college, and university library. [R: RQ, Summer 92, p. 567]

— Susan Ebershoff-Coles

34 High Technology

GENERAL WORKS

1668. **AIIM Speakers Directory 1992-1993: A Listing of Speakers Available for Presentations at AIIM Functions.** Silver Spring, Md., AIIM, 1992. 278p. index. $95.00pa.

This directory from the Association for Information and Image Management (AIIM) is designed to aid its chapters and other professionals who wish to locate speakers on AIIM-relevant subjects. It lists 222 AIIM members who responded to a 1992 invitation to be listed. The respondents were not screened prior to listing. For each speaker, standard directory information is given as well as presentation topics, background and affiliations, prior speaking engagements, and fee. The speakers are listed in alphabetical order, with three indexes: topic, geographic, and fee. A variety of topics are listed, among them CD-ROM, cost/benefits analysis, disaster recovery, electronic image management systems, micrographics, and records management. This specialized directory will probably be of greatest use in large special libraries and associations interested in these subjects.—**Richard D. Johnson**

1669. **Cumulative Index to** *ONLINE, DATABASE & CD-ROM Professional* **1986-1991.** Linda K. Fetters, comp. Wilton, Conn., Eight Bit Books/Online, 1992. 210p. $29.95pa. ISBN 0-910965-06-4.

This volume consists of author and subject indexes. Under each entry is a list of relevant articles from the three periodicals mentioned in the title. The author index includes authors of books reviewed, book review contributors, and individuals who wrote letters. The subject index lists the news pages. Each entry gives the month, year, and pages of the article. Volume and issue numbers are not provided but are given as part of the introduction, which succinctly explains how the index is organized. It is possible to order any article listed by using the Online/CD-ROM Fax Article Delivery Service form included with the volume. The work is extremely easy to use and is a useful quick reference tool.
—**Linda Main**

1670. **Directory of Portable Databases. Volume 3, Number 2.** Kathleen Young Marcaccio and others, eds. Detroit, Gale, 1992. 473p. index. $99.00pa. ISBN 0-8103-8435-3. ISSN 1045-8352.

First published in 1989 (see ARBA 91, entry 1729), this semiannual directory describes 1,909 publicly available, portable database products, 934 on CD-ROM, 545 on diskette, and 430 on magnetic tape. The directory displays excellent organization. It has five parts: database product descriptions, a producer list, a vendor list, a subject index, and a master index. Products are divided into the three format categories of CD-ROM, diskette, and magnetic tape; within each category they are arranged alphabetically by name and individually numbered. Information in the product descriptions has been supplied by the information producer or vendor and varies in completeness. All product descriptions include information producer, vendor, price, type of database (e.g., bibliographic, directory, numeric), subject heading assigned to the product, extensive details on contents (e.g., subject areas covered, types of materials, number of records, print and online counterparts), geographic coverage, time span of the records, and updating frequency. Former and alternate product names are given when appropriate.

CD-ROM and diskette descriptions include, in addition, system requirements (e.g., hardware, operating system, memory) and software information.

The database producers and vendors are arranged alphabetically in their respective lists and individually numbered. Each entry includes address, telephone and fax numbers, and the names and entry numbers of their products. The subject index groups products under 330 headings. The master index is quite comprehensive, containing nearly every name mentioned in the product descriptions, as well as producers and vendors—a quite helpful feature.

CD-ROMs in Print (see ARBA 88, entry 1698) has 50 percent more CD-ROM entries than this directory, but its contents descriptions are usually briefer, and it lacks a master index of names. *Computer-Readable Databases* (see ARBA 90, entry 1717) focuses upon the source database and describes its derivative products, regardless of format, within the database's entry. It has 40 percent more entries for the same three formats and lists online databases as well, but it lacks the crucial, detailed information on system requirements.

This directory would profit from greater inclusiveness; many products are missing. System requirements are not given for magnetic tape products and are not always sufficiently detailed for CD-ROMs and diskettes. The number of records is not always indicated. Overall, however, the amount of detail in the product descriptions, the coverage of three formats, the excellent organization, the comprehensive master index, and the pleasing graphic layout make this directory a necessary purchase for libraries considering acquisition of databases for end-user access. (Note: This directory is available online as part of the *Cuadra Directory of Databases* file on ORBIT, Data-Star, and Questel.)—**John Lewis Campbell**

ARTIFICIAL INTELLIGENCE

1671. Junge, Hans-Dieter. **Dictionary of Artificial Intelligence and Neuronal Networks: English/German; German/English. Worterbuch Kunstliche Intelligenz und Neuronale Netzwerke.** New York, VCH, 1991. 238p. $60.00. ISBN 0-89573-942-9. ISSN 0930-6862.

Terms that describe elements in the new and rapidly growing fields of artificial intelligence and neurocomputers are increasing apace. Because of the newness of the field, most of these terms have not found their way into either scientific or general dictionaries. This list of approximately 5,000 terms, first in English with German equivalents and then the other way around, therefore provides the translator with a useful tool. Because this is a list of equivalents rather than a dictionary of definitions, its use is limited. Although such a reference tool is an excellent candidate for online access, in its present form it is useful to researchers who read scientific literature in both these languages.—**Ann E. Prentice**

COMPUTING

General Works

Bibliography

1672. McLellan, Hilary. **Virtual Reality: A Selected Bibliography.** Englewood Cliffs, N.J., Educational Technology, 1992. 60p. (Educational Technology Selected Bibliography Series, v.6). $14.95. Z5643.I57M4. 006. LC 92-8488. ISBN 0-87778-246-6.

Virtual reality denotes the increasingly sophisticated interaction of computing, communication, and display interface technologies to create a dazzling and convincing simulation of actual presence and participation by the technology's user. The revolutionary implications of this development for education, business, and society has spawned a literature so extensive as to make a selected bibliography such as this volume an attractive prospect.

Divided into a long section of general articles and nearly 24 classed by specific subjects, some 500 citations cover the time period from 1963 to 1992, with the majority of articles dating from 1989 to 1991. In addition to traditional books and articles, theses, internal corporate memoranda, demonstration systems, and videotapes are included. Inevitably, a selected bibliography will miss items; for example, some important educational articles have been omitted, and the section on that topic is only two pages long. A selection of citations were tested and verified as accurate, and no errors of spelling or transcription were noted. However, the abbreviated form of bibliographic citation used (most annoyingly, the publication data for conference proceedings are not included) can hinder access to those items that are outside the standard publishing mainstream. Given that such a large number of items are internal to a specific company (in particular, the Human Interface Technology Laboratory), contact addresses for those bodies should be listed in an appendix.

Clearly printed on single sides of good quality paper (but with a visually confusing double-spaced layout), this work's cover and binding will make it difficult to shelve in the traditional manner. Also, the rapid progress being made in this field will quickly render this publication obsolete, but its short-term utility may prove attractive to a specific audience. — **John Howard Oxley**

Catalogs

1673. Klein, Barry, comp. and ed. **Computer Catalogs.** West Nyack, N.Y., Todd, 1992. 114p. index. $12.95pa. ISBN 0-915344-27-0.

Mail-order marketing has become an established fixture in the retail sales business. *Computer Catalogs* describes some 300 mail-order catalogs (most are free) that can be obtained from companies that sell computers, software, supplies, and accessories by mail. The catalog listings provide name, address, fax number, voice number, customer/technical support number (if different), contact person, types of credit cards accepted, shipping cost notes, type of guarantee available, company sales, and a brief narrative description of the types of products offered. Some of the telephone numbers listed are toll-free. Readers will find familiar companies such as Black Box Corporation, Radio Shack, and Inmac as well as smaller and lesser-known vendors. There is little in the way of narrative in the book, just in the introduction and on the back cover. The rest of the book consists of catalog entries. The publisher hopes to make this an annual publication.

Many corporations and consumers have been able to save substantial money by purchasing through mail-order houses such as the ones listed in this book. On the down side, mail-order sales can be a source of frustration when things do not go right. Returns, defective merchandise, hand-holding, and bait-and-switch techniques are much harder to deal with through the mail than in person. Computers and associated supplies are famous for not hopping out of the box and working correctly the first time. [R: RBB, 15 June 92, pp. 1878-80] — **Ralph Lee Scott**

Dictionaries and Encyclopedias

1674. Atherton, Derek P., and Pierre Borne, eds. **Concise Encyclopedia of Modelling & Simulation.** Elmsford, N.Y., Pergamon Press, 1992. 539p. index. (Advances in Systems, Control, and Information Engineering). $240.00. QA76.9.C65C657. 003'.3. LC 91-33278. ISBN 0-08-036201-X.

This book includes a surprising variety of technical information about modeling and simulation. It is well planned, carefully edited, and quite attractive. Individual topics are covered in a variety of ways, from single-sentence definitions to about 20 pages of discussion. The terse style is essential for the successful presentation of so much information in a single volume. Mathematical expressions are abundant. Graphics are appropriately used and of consistent quality throughout. Many of the longer sections include a bibliography that will be most useful in pursuing the topic.

While each topic seems well chosen, the emphasis is clearly on engineering applications. For example, aeronautics, mechanics, and power plants are well covered while population biology and environmental models are hardly mentioned. Mathematical modeling is emphasized over simulation. Topic selection may reflect the authors' interests but is not objectionable, and sacrifices have undoubtedly been made to keep the size of the book manageable.

The concise encyclopedia style definitely makes this book a reference rather than a textbook. Nevertheless, one can browse through it to get an overview of modeling approaches in other fields. This book is recommended for professionals who use modeling; it will be an excellent addition to library shelves. — **John A. Jackman**

1675. Covington, Michael, and Douglas Downing. **Dictionary of Computer Terms.** 3d ed. Hauppauge, N.Y., Barron's Educational Series, 1992. 364p. illus. $8.95pa. QA76.15.C68. 004'.03. LC 91-21529. ISBN 0-8120-4824-5.

This pocket dictionary is as useful for library staff struggling with the "computer revolution" as it is as a reference resource for patrons. The rapid changes in computer and computer-mediated communications terminology mean that a "comprehensive" dictionary is likely to be dated even as it is printed. The well-selected 1,000 entries in this edition (see ARBA 90, entry 1710 for a review of the previous edition) are far from comprehensive yet provide an excellent starting point for beginners, while also serving more experienced users who seek brief and only moderately technical definitions. Entries vary from the very general (e.g., a word-for-word definition of TCP/IP [Transmission Control Protocol and Internet Protocol]) to the concrete (e.g., how to set up a spreadsheet under Lotus 1-2-3). Cross-references are particularly helpful, as is a reader's guide to selected terms by category. The latter lists the terms included under broad divisions: communications, desktop publishing, electronics, firms, graphics, hardware, logic gates and computer design, machines, mathematics, operating systems and operating systems concepts, programming concepts, languages, software, and (inexplicably) Windows and Macintosh.

With its durable cover, this volume should be attractive to libraries of nearly any size that want a reasonably priced, concise guide to the terminology. Moreover, the publisher's evident three-year update cycle assures relative currency at a modest cost.—**K. Mulliner**

1676. Freedman, Alan. **The Computer Glossary: The Complete Illustrated Desk Reference.** 5th ed. New York, AMACOM; distr., Detroit, Gale, 1991. 670p. illus. $34.95; $24.95pa. QA76.15.F734. 004'.03. LC 90-1269. ISBN 0-8144-5020-2; 0-8144-7749-6pa.

This glossary began as a terminology sheet for Freedman's computer seminars for businesspeople. Over the years it has grown into a book of encyclopedic length geared to business managers, students, and personal computer owners. The result is an impressive work useful to both the seasoned computer professional and the novice. Its stated purpose is to "provide a meaningful definition of every important computer term ... for personal computers, minicomputers or mainframes." As ambitious as this goal seems, Freedman appears to have met it. It is hard to find a term related to computing that is not in this book. A wide range of topics appears, from the technical (e.g., specifications for different computer systems, examples of assembly language) to the humorous (e.g., bunny suits [worn by workers in clean rooms], nerd). Particularly fascinating is the coverage of the history and development of electronics and computer technology. Even ancillary topics such as typography and publishing and business terminology are covered. All terms used are also defined, making the book easily accessible to the nontechnical reader. The ample illustrations are elucidating, although at times simplistic or cartoonish. *The Computer Glossary* is recommended for anyone looking for a general computer terminology reference book that has a satisfying depth of coverage, that is clearly written, and that provides insight into the arcane workings of high technology.—**Stephen Haenel**

1677. Lazure, Noel. **Ada Language Vocabulary. Vocabulaire du Langage Ada.** Ottawa, Department of the Secretary of State of Canada, 1991. 217p. (Terminology Bulletin, 206). $21.55pa. (U.S.). 005.13'3'03. ISBN 0-660-56505-6.

This handbook contains an English/French vocabulary of terms commonly used in Ada programming. Ada, the official United States Department of Defense computer programming language, is large, complex, and comprehensive, and some technical computer language terms, when used in the context of Ada, have special meanings related to this language. Thus, it is useful to have the definition of terms relative to Ada.

The book contains three sections. First is the English/French vocabulary, which gives the French translation of the English term. The second section is a French/English glossary of Ada terms. The final section is a brief bibliography of Ada literature.

The work is primarily useful for translating between French and English terms, of which there are about 2,000. Only one-quarter of the terms contain definitions, some of which are only in English while others are only in French. The definitions for those terms that have both English and French definitions are often not the same. For example, the English definition of *general-purpose language* is "Like Ada,

LISP is a general-purpose language." The French definition is "Language which permits the resolution of problems in a great variety of domains." Finally, the quality of some of the definitions is questionable. —**Maya B. Gokhale**

1678. **Macmillan Encyclopedia of Computers.** Gary G. Bitter, ed. New York, Macmillan, 1992. 2v. index. $150.00/set. QA76.15.M33. 004'.03. LC 91-45339. ISBN 0-02-897045-4.

This ambitious collection of more than 200 articles aims to provide a comprehensive picture of the field of computers to students and nonprofessionals. Virtually all significant areas of hardware and software are covered, together with applications, the history of computing, and societal issues. The two-column format is pleasing to the eye, and there are many helpful figures and illustrations. There is extensive cross-referencing, and volume 2 contains an index as well as a useful list of computer associations and manufacturers. Most articles end with a list of references and suggestions for further reading.

Despite its noble intent and its many fine articles, this encyclopedia is disappointing. The most obvious problem is one of unevenness, as some articles are scholarly and rather technical while others resemble magazine articles. Whereas it is almost axiomatic that a work such as this will be outdated as soon as it is printed, some of the out-of-date material could have been spotted by editorial diligence. Also, various articles contain typographical errors, inaccuracies, or questionable interpretations. For example, the first paragraph on the Relational Data Model (p. 242) interchanges the notions of *candidate key* and *primary key*. In another article it is distressing to find an author promoting his own commercial software product. Finally, the biographies are interesting but tend to emphasize personal details rather than analysis.

The more knowledgeable reader will conclude that many of the experts recruited for the task have been asked to write on topics outside their particular fields of expertise. *Caveat lector*. However, there is enough valuable material for the nonprofessional to justify the purchase of these books for school and public libraries. [R: Choice, Oct 92, p. 276; LJ, 1 June 92, p. 112; RBB, 1 Sept 92, pp. 86-87; WLB, June 92, p. 114] —**Henry J. Ricardo**

1679. **McGraw-Hill Dictionary of Information Technology and Computer Acronyms, Initials, and Abbreviations.** By Jerry M. Rosenberg. New York, McGraw-Hill, 1992. 209p. $24.95; $12.95pa. QA76.15.R68. 004'.03. LC 91-24861. ISBN 0-07-053936-7; 0-07-053735-6pa.

Perhaps no other field is as enamored of alphabetical shortcuts as high technology. Along with the boom in this technology has come a profusion of abbreviations and acronyms. Making sense of it all is a challenge, especially for those whose work has changed due to new applications of computer technology. Rosenberg's goal is to make the mind-boggling array of abbreviations accessible to computer professionals, business managers, and the home computer user. He has largely succeeded. This book does not actually define any of the entries; it is meant to be used in conjunction with a computer dictionary. It does help users get a handle on more than 10,000 commonly used abbreviations in the high-tech lexicon.

This work would benefit from the inclusion of file extensions, particularly for common software programs. Also, it lacks many references to electronic publishing acronyms; VGA (Video Graphics Array) and WYSIWYG (What You See Is What You Get) are some surprising omissions. Still, the work is impressive in scope and very easy to use. It should live up to its goal of encouraging precise communication in a field known for its obfuscation. As it seems to be chiefly a desk reference, it may be underused in most libraries. [R: RBB, 1 Jan 92, p. 851; WLB, Jan 92, p. 128] —**Stephen Haenel**

1680. Raymond, Eric S., ed. **The New Hacker's Dictionary.** Cambridge, Mass., MIT Press, 1991. 433p. illus. $25.00; $10.95pa. PN6231.E4H3. 004'.014. LC 91-18745. ISBN 0-262-18145-2; 0-262-68069-6pa.

A *hacker* wants to be understood as "a person who enjoys exploring the details of programmable systems and how to stretch their capabilities, as opposed to most users, who prefer to learn only the minimum necessary." This is in contrast to the common public misperception that all hackers are computer criminals. The hacker "culture" that developed in places such as MIT in the early 1960s and 1970s is now an amalgam of mainframe and microcomputer milieus, characterized by intellectual playfulness and a disdain for large companies and formal working conditions. It has been spread worldwide via computer networks.

A revision of a 1983 work, this book provides eye-opening glimpses into a strange new world. The dictionary proper consists of about 1,000 terms that have been accumulating in the online Jargon File, updated by contributions from centers of computer expertise throughout the world. This process of compilation has ensured a degree of freshness and authenticity missing from many academic compendia. Where else can one find the definitions of *angry fruit salad, flarp, mouse droppings, quantum bogodynamics,* and *xyzzy*? Headwords are in boldface type, and pronunciations are given for entries that are not standard English or are not pronounced in an obvious way. Origins of terms and their proper usage are explained. Emphasizing hacker usage in American English, the dictionary contains some contributions from abroad, with a strong British/Commonwealth influence. There are several supplementary essays on hacker language and folklore and a bibliography of influential works.

This lexicon has little in common with a standard dictionary of computer terms. Countercultural, witty, and replete with sociotechnological insights, *The New Hacker's Dictionary* is a valuable addition to the documentation of the computer age and is highly recommended for individual and library purchase. [R: Choice, Jan 92, p. 724] — **Henry J. Ricardo**

1681. Spencer, Donald D. **Computer Dictionary.** 3d ed. Ormond Beach, Fla., Camelot Publishing, 1992. 457p. illus. $24.95pa. QA76.15.S64. 004'.03. LC 91-9355. ISBN 0-89218-209-1.

This book aims to present an up-to-date vocabulary of more than 5,800 terms, words, acronyms, and abbreviations to students, teachers, businesspeople, and computer professionals. Hardware and software topics span micros, minis, and mainframes and treat such important areas as desktop publishing, computer graphics, networking, artificial intelligence, and object-oriented programming. Included is a series of brief descriptions of important calculating machines and short biographies of some 70 calculating and computing pioneers whose portraits are lumped together at the end of the book. Except for proper names and acronyms, terms appear alphabetically in boldface lower-case characters. There is no attempt to give pronunciations or syllabications. Terms that are cross-referenced (usually by *see* or *contrast*) are not set off by a special typeface. In fact, except for headwords, there is an unattractive uniformity in the typesetting. There are no diagrams, pictures, or charts to illustrate the concepts discussed.

Despite the wide coverage and the overall accuracy of the concise, easy-to-understand definitions, some lapses occur. For example, although IBM's MicroChannel bus is described, neither Apple's NuBus nor the EISA bus standard is mentioned. Similarly, there is an entry for the user organization SHARE, but not for the related group GUIDE. The definition of the mathematical constant *e* incorrectly suggests that its decimal expansion terminates. The definition of *access time* in terms of seek time and transfer rate seems careless, as is the omission of the effect of rotational time.

Spencer's lexicon is a sound, no-frills reference. However, while containing about 25 percent fewer terms, the 5th edition of *The Computer Glossary* by Alan Freedman (Gale, 1991) supplements its definitions with nearly 400 photographs and drawings. That work should be considered if only one paperback computer dictionary is to be purchased. — **Henry J. Ricardo**

Directories

1682. **Directory of Online Databases. Volume 13, Number 2.** Kathleen Young Marcaccio and Gwen E. Turecki, eds. Detroit, Gale, 1992. 1144p. index. $199.00pa. ISBN 0-8103-8429-9. ISSN 0913-6840.

Originally published by Cuadra and now published by Gale, this comprehensive directory provides access to more than 5,300 online databases produced worldwide. The directory is arranged in three sections — product descriptions, database producers, and online services — and has three indexes: geographic, subject, and master. The detailed product descriptions include type, subject, producer, contents, languages, time span, and frequency of updating. In some cases, conditions of use (e.g., subscriptions to particular services) are included, as are alternative formats (e.g., diskette). The content descriptions provide in-depth looks at each product and are particularly helpful in selecting desired databases. The scope of coverage is impressive; small or obscure databases are included as well as the well-known ones. The database producers and online services sections provide contact and product information on the more than 2,200 organizations and 800 vendors and distributors listed in the product descriptions.

The 13th volume has numerous enhancements that have improved use of the directory and access to databases. Entries are now numbered, and index citations refer to entry numbers rather than page numbers. The database types have been expanded to include new categories such as bulletin boards, dictionaries, and directories. The subject index now lists more than 1,200 subject headings, and the master index provides access through alternate and former names, acronyms, key words, and related organizations. The *Directory of Online Databases* should be owned by every library committed to the dissemination of information via computer.—**Stephen Haenel**

1683. Motley, Lynne. **Modem USA: Low Cost and Free Online Sources for Information, Databases, and Electronic Bulletin Boards Via Computer and Modem in 50 States.** Takoma Park, Md., Allium Press, 1992. 190p. $16.95pa. LC 91-076711. ISBN 0-9631233-4-3.

This volume provides information to access a number of low-cost or free online reference systems run by federal, state, and local agencies as well as private groups and individuals. Motley's directory divides bulletin boards by subject and then by state. This allows the user to look up a subject and then choose the boards that are local or low-cost, in-state toll telephone calls. A few boards have toll-free numbers. Subjects covered are medical, libraries, government, the environment, safety, science, music, jobs, gardening, real estate, genealogy, writing, and computers. Following the broad listings, Motley has included a brief bibliography on boards and telecommunications and a short glossary. A chapter with notes for newcomers provides helpful insights for the first-time caller. Some are quite inventive and useful.

This reviewer tried a number of the toll-free boards listed. All those accessed operated as advertised by Motley. Most libraries that have patrons with modems will find this work valuable. Highly recommended for small to medium-sized libraries that do not have other sources of bulletin board information. [R: Choice, July/Aug 92, p. 1659; RBB, 15 June 92, p. 1886]—**Ralph Lee Scott**

Handbooks and Yearbooks

1684. Glover, Thomas J., and Millie M. Young. **Pocket PCRef.** Morrison, Colo., Sequoia Publishing, 1991. 320p. index. $14.95pa. LC 91-090581. ISBN 0-9622359-3-8.

In terms of sheer density of information per unit volume, this little book must be close to the top of anyone's list. Most things anyone would ever want to know about PC hardware and software can be found somewhere in its pages. The information ranges from low-level concerns, such as the pin designations for cable connections, scan codes for PC keyboards, and hard drive characteristics, through a description of interrupt addresses, MS-DOS commands, Epson printer codes, and many other things. There is also a large section with telephone numbers of commercial organizations that operate in the computer sector. It is easy to envision someone using this little book to repair a hardware break, make a software patch, and then call the manufacturer when it does not work. The software section is entirely DOS-oriented. There is nothing about Windows, OS/2, or Unix here. The hardware sections are less restrictive; a large number of disk drives and printers are covered.

This edge-keyed little paperback is well bound and easily stored in a pocket or briefcase. The small print may require the reader to don eyeglasses, but the amount of information per page makes it a very attractive purchase for those involved with MS-DOS computers.—**George M. White**

1685. Vassiliou, M. S., and J. A. Orenstein. **Computer Professional's Quick Reference.** New York, McGraw-Hill, 1992. 266p. index. $34.95; $24.95pa. QA76.76.063V37. 005.4'3. LC 91-34128. ISBN 0-07-067211-3; 0-07-067212-1pa.

A quick reference for computer professionals, this densely written, well-indexed work delivers all that the title promises. It contains far more than its length or price would suggest. It treats hardware and software aspects of computer systems that are of interest to the modern computer professional and amateur alike.

There are three main sections. The first section describes salient features of six operating systems: UNIX, VAX-VMS, MVS-TSO, VM-CMS, MS-DOS, and Macintosh. Nearly all the material deals with the system shell and concentrates on the user interaction with the shell. Succinct information is given that would allow a casual user to make the system perform in a rational way. The book is, of course, in no way a system manual—the expert user must still read the official system manuals. This book skims across the top, explaining the most important and most used commands.

The second section is dealt with in the same way. The difficult world of data communications and file transfer is treated with emphasis on modems, networks, and two software packages (Kermit and FTP). The final section is concerned with the world of standards. Some of these, such as character/bit encoding (e.g., ASCII) and floating point representation, are explained at some length, while others, such as the Transport Layer class 4 protocols and computer graphics, are barely mentioned. Still, one can determine that standards for the three-dimensional Graphical Kernel System can be found in ISO 8805 (1988). If the information sought is not in the book, a pointer to it is.

This well-crafted book has had a great deal of care placed on its contents and presentation. It appears to be as free from error as the first edition of a reference work can be. It is clearly destined for the shelves of those who call themselves computer professionals. [R: RBB, July 92, p. 1958]
—George M. White

Indexes

1686. **Microcomputer Index: A Comprehensive Abstracts Journal Covering Microcomputing and Related Subjects. Volume 12: Cumulated Index 1991.** Lisa R. Jasper, ed. Medford, N.J., Learned Information, 1991. 372p. $149.00/yr. ISSN 8756-7040.

During the past decade, a large number of new magazines and trade journals have been published. Each issue has a number of review or technical articles that are of interest to a variety of people. While most of the advertisements become outdated rather quickly, the technical and review articles are, in a sense, timeless. There is a great need, then, for an index that quickly points the user to the right articles on the desired information. *Microcomputer Index* fills that need. The index covers more than 10,000 articles, abstracts, reviews, and the like, arranged in 5 indexes for easy searching: authors, company names, product names, compatibility (both hardware and software), and subjects. Both computer novices and professionals will be able to locate material of interest. This index is highly recommended for both general and professional libraries.—**John Y. Cheung**

Computer Graphics

1687. Kay, David C., and John R. Levine. **Graphics File Formats.** Blue Ridge Summit, Pa., Windcrest Books/TAB Books, 1992. 278p. index. $36.95; $24.95pa. T385.K376. 006.6. LC 92-4532. ISBN 0-8306-3060-0; 0-8306-3059-7pa.

Anyone who monitors the graphics forums on the Internet or various national information services knows that a topic of perpetual interest is how the standard graphics files formats are constructed, usually as a means for translating from one format to another. Kay and Levine's book details 23 of the most important file formats, including ones for specific computers (e.g., PCX on the IBM, MacPaint and PICT on the Macintosh, Gem on the Amiga) and those that are more generic (e.g., TIFF, GIF, Postscript, JPEG). In addition to these, a number of other formats are briefly mentioned. Two useful introductory chapters cover graphics theory and choosing formats. While the volume as a whole is very good as far as it goes (and it has no competition, at least among commercially published books), its value could have been considerably enhanced by the inclusion of a few pages, or even a table, on format translation software (which is really what most users want to know). For the next edition, the authors should also consider chapters on animation and moving picture formats, such as QuickTime and MPEG (which are currently mentioned only in passing).—**Robert Skinner**

1688. Latham, Roy. **The Dictionary of Computer Graphics Technology and Applications.** New York, Springer-Verlag, 1991. 160p. illus. $24.95. T385.L38. 006.6'03. LC 91-7692. ISBN 0-387-97540-3.

This volume is intended for both novices and graphics professionals. A wide variety of terms are briefly defined, including many that are proper nouns or commercial products. Some of the more popular graphics computer file extensions, such as .gif and .pcx, are widely included. The book is reasonably current, although *Quicktime, Multimedia PC*, and all of the CD formats except for CD-ROM are omitted. One interesting feature is a word list that includes graphics terms that "have been omitted from the lists of at least one of the three spell-checking programs tried by the author." On the negative side, many of the definitions seem too technical for the intended audience. For example, the term *window* is described as "a collection of one or more rasters plus additional properties, and usually having borders and other graphics elements established by the conventions of the window system...." This and many other definitions would benefit from illustrations. (Why, incidentally, does a book devoted to graphics have only 19 illustrations, even if these are well chosen?) From that standpoint, *Graphics, Design and Printing Terms* (see ARBA 91, entry 1724) is superior, although many more graphics terms are defined in the volume under review. — **Robert Skinner**

Software

1689. **The PC-SIG Encyclopedia of Shareware.** 4th ed. Blue Ridge Summit, Pa., Windcrest/TAB Books, 1991. 690p. illus. index. $19.95pa. QA76.76.S46P33. 005.365. LC 91-25481. ISBN 0-8306-2669-7.

Shareware is software that may be freely copied, distributed, and tried before buying. If the user decides to keep the program, a registration fee that can range from $10 to $100 is paid directly to the software author.

This work, compiled by a shareware distributor called PC-SIG, is a compendium of more than 2,500 IBM-compatible shareware computer programs. For each is given the program name and author, a short annotation, disk order number, special hardware requirements, and registration fee. The programs are organized by broad category with an alphabetical subject/title index and a disk number index. The book includes eight articles about shareware (reprinted from *Shareware* magazine), a glossary, a list of dealers, and some advertising. It contains no specific ordering instructions or disk costs, except for a statement saying "Order from your local PC-SIG Dealer." The preface says that "virtually every shareware program ever released can be found in the PC-SIG Library of Shareware." Not quite. A random selection of 25 titles from the catalog of another distributor (The Software Labs) showed only 7 in common. The annotations range in length from one paragraph to one-half page. They are well organized and easy to read, and PC-SIG is to be commended for pulling together some of this vastly scattered software. Unfortunately, program quality cannot be determined from the annotations, although a symbol shows if the author is a member of the Association of Shareware Professionals. Although there are some real gems among shareware, much of it is junk. One is not obliged to pay the registration fee for junk, but it is aggravating to pay even the disk and shipping costs for an inadequate, amateurish program. — **A. Neil Yerkey**

OPTICAL STORAGE DEVICES

CAD/CAM

1690. **CAD/CAM Abstracts Annual 1991. Volume 8.** New Providence, N.J., R. R. Bowker, 1992. 570p. index. $250.00. ISBN 0-8352-3153-4. ISSN 0000-1236.

The 3,600 abstracts in this volume cover literature that deals with computer-integrated manufacturing, graphics, control systems, simulation, automated assembly, and manufacturing design. The book is a cumulation of the 1991 issues of a monthly journal published by Bowker. Besides the journal and this cumulation, the abstracts are available online, on microfiche, on magnetic tape, and quarterly on CD-ROM. The full text of most abstracted articles is available on microfiche. Most of the abstracted articles were published in 1989-1990 and were taken from 350 journals, conference proceedings, and reports. They are indexed by category, subject, country (of non-U.S. items), patent assignee, SIC

(Standard Industrial Classification) code, author, and bibliographic source. Each abstract is assigned to one of 16 broad categories and about 6 subject headings. The subject heading list consists of some 500 descriptors. There are no *see* or *see also* references or similar guidance, nor any subheadings. Index entries include only titles and accession numbers keyed to a "Review Section" that contains complete bibliographic citations and 100-word staff-written abstracts. The abstracts, although brief, are well written and informative. Unfortunately, they are set in such tiny type that it takes a magnifying glass to read them. — **A. Neil Yerkey**

CD-ROM

1691. **The CD-ROM Directory 1992.** 7th ed. Matthew Finlay and Joanne Mitchell, eds. London, TFPL Publishing; distr., Detroit, Omnigraphics, 1991. 868p. index. $150.00pa. ISBN 1-870889-26-6.

Keeping up with new CD-ROM discs has become increasingly difficult, if for no other reason than the proliferation of multimedia optical formats, such as CD-I and DVI. Fortunately, there are at least four major bibliographies of CD-ROMs that have found their way into many libraries: *CD-ROMS in Print* (see ARBA 92, entry 1719), *Directory of Portable Databases* (Gale, 1992), *The Optical Publishing Directory* (see ARBA 92, entry 1720), and the volume under review. *The CD-ROM Directory* was first published in December 1986 and is the longest running of the titles cited. It is deliberately international in scope, although *CD-ROMS in Print 1992* bears the subtitle "An International Guide" and is also strong in this area.

Because *CD-ROMS in Print* is *The CD-ROM Directory*'s main competition in the United States, it is useful to compare the two sources. *CD-ROMS in Print* contains approximately 800 more entries than *The CD-ROM Directory*. Both include much the same bibliographic and descriptive information for each CD-ROM. Because of different publishing schedules, *The CD-ROM Directory* is more up-to-date, but as both are annuals, presumably the situation will be reversed in a few months when the next edition of *CD-ROMS in Print* appears. *The CD-ROM Directory* is clearly the winner in some of the peripheral sections: listings of CD-ROM hardware, software (e.g., authoring/development, search and retrieval tools), a bibliography of books and journals, a glossary, a list of international conferences and exhibits, and several indexes (e.g., contacts at individual CD-ROM companies). For smaller libraries, *CD-ROMS in Print*, at one-third the price of *The CD-ROM Directory*, will be the most cost-effective choice, especially for domestic CD-ROMs. For information on similar types of data that happen to be on diskette or magnetic tape, one will need *Directory of Portable Databases* (which also has the advantage of being issued twice yearly but which covers fewer than half of the titles in the other two works). For libraries with a strong need for international coverage and those that would benefit from ready access to information on the production and marketing side of CD-ROMs, *The CD-ROM Directory* is an important resource. [R: LJ, 15 May 92, p. 84] — **Robert Skinner**

1692. **CD-ROMS in Print: An International Guide to CD-ROM, CD-I, CDTV & Electronic Book Products.** [CD-ROM]. Westport, Conn., Meckler, 1992. Hardware requirements: IBM PC, XT, PS/2, or compatible; 512K; DOS 3.0 or better; MSCDEX; CD-ROM drive. $95.00. ISBN 0-88736-812-3. ISSN 1052-2638.

This work provides information on CD-ROM products and producers worldwide and claims to be the most comprehensive listing of such producers and products available. The disc contains two databases of 2,975 CD-ROM titles and 3,040 companies. The company database contains company name, address, telephone, contact name, and activities; the title database lists title, description, subject areas, number of discs and disc size, date of issue, data provider and publisher, national and international distributors, language, price, and technical details. Each of these areas acts as an index and can be searched, giving users excellent access to the data. The technical details include information such as computer system, memory, and hardware requirements. Thus, users can find, for example, CD-ROM titles in the environment that can be run on a Macintosh. The results of a search can be sent directly to a printer or to a text file in ASCII format.

The information has been compiled by research teams in the United States and the United Kingdom, and the titles tend to come mainly from these countries (which may also reflect the predominance of CD-ROM technology in these areas). Also included are soon-to-be-released titles. The ROMWARE/ DBServe software with SimpleFace interface from Nimbus Information Systems is extremely easy to use. Librarians will take to it immediately, and novices with only a modicum of computer knowledge should have no problems using it. The accompanying booklet and on-screen menus are clear and simple.

This work is an excellent reference for anyone who must purchase CD products for libraries or schools. With the continued growth in CDs for research and educational purposes, CD-ROMs in Print and its subsequent editions will probably become the reference tool of choice for librarians and school media specialists looking to selectively upgrade their collections. [R: LAR, Oct 92, p. 669]

—Stephen Haenel

Imaging Systems

1693. **International Imaging Source Book, 1992: Including Micrographics and Optical Imaging.** Mitchell M. Badler, ed. Larchmont, N.Y., Microfilm Publishing, 1992. 436p. index. $97.50pa. LC 72-624065. ISBN 0-917414-08-X. ISSN 1053-8291.

Only two years ago, volumes in this series were called the *International Micrographics Source Book* (see ARBA 91, entry 1736). The growth of electronic imaging technology has been sufficient to cause the change in name of this as well as a number of other serials (although in the present volume, pages devoted to micrographics still outnumber imaging by two to one). Companies that sell products and services are listed in four separate sections: two for micrographics and electronic imaging sources, and two for service bureaus. All are arranged by country, then state where applicable, and finally alphabetically by company. Although these four sections are called indexes, the true indexes are a keyword index toward the front of the volume and a master index at the back (the "Index to Indexes") that provides access by company or organization. Other sections in the book are the same as in previous volumes. The usefulness of future volumes would be improved by removing the word "index" from the names of the products/services sections and adding running heads.

A similar publication is the *Information Management Sourcebook: The AIIM Buying Guide and Membership Directory* (see ARBA 88, entry 620). It contains company listings, detailed company profiles, a product and services directory, and an AIIM membership directory. The AIIM volume concentrates on identifying the categories of products or services in which a company specializes, while the *International Imaging Sourcebook* provides information on specific products. Libraries with comprehensive collections in these areas will probably want both. If one has to choose between the two, the "kitchen sink" approach of the *International Imaging Source Book* offers more for the dollar.

—Robert Skinner

Microforms

1694. **Guide to Microforms in Print 1991: Author-Title.** New Providence, N.J., K. G. Saur, 1991. 1651p. $225.00. LC 61-7082. ISBN 3-598-11047-2. ISSN 0164-0747.

1695. **Guide to Microforms in Print 1991: Subject.** New Providence, N.J., K. G. Saur, 1991. 1408p. $245.00. LC 61-7082. ISBN 3-598-11005-7. ISSN 0163-8386.

This monumental work provides author, title, and subject indexes to all works in microforms, such as books, journals, government articles, and newspapers. More than 17 types of microforms are incorporated, including microfilms, microcards, microfiches, and ultramicrofiches. The present edition has a number of important improvements. First, all authors and editors are now included in the index. Second, cross-references from variant authors and editors have been provided. Third, the subject index has been completely revised to conform to the 20th edition of the Dewey Decimal Classification system. This guide is a necessary purchase for any library, general or professional, so that patrons can be made aware of what information is available and where to find it.

—John Y. Cheung

TELECOMMUNICATION

1696. **International Satellite Directory, 1992.** 7th ed. Sonoma, Calif., Design, 1992. 1v. (various paging). maps. index. $240.00pa. ISBN 0-936361-07-7. ISSN 1041-4541.

This annual industry directory is also valuable for the aerospace academician. It is divided into front matter and 10 chapters. Tabs are provided for each of the chapters, making it a user-friendly reference book. Chapter topics include international agencies, satellite operators, manufacturers of space equipment (both satellites and launch vehicles), manufacturers of ground equipment, manufacturers of TVRO (a direct broadcast service), users of satellite services, providers of satellite services, general services, geosynchronous satellites, and a buyers' guide and index. The index is quite thorough and should be consulted first. For example, there are 22 entries for NASA, including some subentries such as 2 entries for the NASA Wallops Flight Center. Buried between the buyers' guide and the index is a useful glossary of words commonly used in the satellite communications industry.

This publication complements the older *World Satellite Directory* (see ARBA 90, entry 1741), which is now in its 14th edition. For information on satellites that is directed toward students, the *World Satellite Almanac* (see ARBA 88, entry 943) could be consulted. Note that all three of these books deal primarily with communications satellites and do not really cover scientific satellites.
— **Ronald L. Buchan**

1697. Kahn, Ahmed S. **The Telecommunications Fact Book and Illustrated Dictionary.** Albany, N.Y., Delmar, 1992. 301p. $22.95pa. TK5102.K47. 621.382. ISBN 0-8273-4615-8.

No dictionary of telecommunication terminology remains up to date very long, and Kahn's is no exception. Such current expressions and terms as *wireless cable*, *IBC* (integrated broadband communications), and *personal communications system* (or *personal communications network*) are not to be found in Kahn's glossary. Nor are they in the slightly older, more widely recognized dictionaries in the field, such as *Facts on File Dictionary of Telecommunications*, revised ed. (see ARBA 92, entry 1721), *Data and Computer Communications* (see ARBA 91, entry 1751), and *Communications Standard Dictionary* (see ARBA 90, entry 889). Any of these dictionaries defines a wider range of terms than Kahn's. On the other hand, Kahn offers two features that might be regarded as advantages. The first is an "illustrated approach" (p. viii). Tables, figures, formulas, and black-and-white illustrations accompany perhaps a tenth of the definitions. Nearly three full pages of figures, for example, graphically represent the term *modulation*. These illustrations generally render complex technical terms more readily understandable. The other even more valuable feature is an extensive section (nearly half of the book) of appendixes that give a wide variety of information related to telecommunication. Here Kahn appears to have tried to anticipate topics and issues of future interest. Coverage of HDTV (high-definition television), fiber optics communication, and ISDN (Integrated Services Digital Network) is notable; other dictionaries treat these topics much less extensively. Additionally, other appendixes describe such things as telecommunication formulas, codes for information and data transmission, and symbols for electronic devices, as well as international telecommunication agencies and organizations, member countries of INTELSAT (International Telecommunications Satellite Organization), geosynchronous satellites, trade and scholarly journals, and telecommunication acronyms.

Whether this unindexed potpourri of telecommunication information is successful as "a self-contained quick reference to telecommunications jargon and facts" (p. viii) remains to be determined. Kahn's dictionary might prove handy for the student or business professional who needs a bit more general information about a topic in the field. — **James K. Bracken**

1698. **Telecommunications Directory: An International Descriptive Guide to More Than 2,300 Telecommunications Organizations, Systems, and Services....** 5th ed. John Krol and Gwen E. Turecki, eds. Detroit, Gale, 1991. 1033p. index. $310.00. LC 83-646142. ISBN 0-8103-7747-0. ISSN 1055-8454.

Formerly *Telecommunications Systems and Services Directory*, this work is a comprehensive source of information that covers more than 2,300 products, services, and related activities in the field. As defined for this directory, telecommunications includes electronic mail, local area networks, satellite transmission, interactive television, voice mail, and similar areas. It does not include broadcast media or telephone-related equipment services.

Each entry is listed alphabetically by organization name and includes address, telephone number, date established, unit head, function/service type, related organizations, size of staff, description, applications, access, area served, and rate structures and projected new services. Major telecommunication changes, such as the connection between IBM and Novell and British Telecom's acquisition of Tymnet from McDonnell Douglas, are included in the appropriate entries. Because of its coverage and currency, this work has become a first place to look for current product and service information.

A master index and others to functions/services, geographic locations, and personal names allow one to search for types of services, services specific to a location, or individuals. The directory is available on diskette and magnetic tape as well as in hard copy. The alternative formats make access to the directory a model that should be followed by those who are responsible for maintaining directories whose content demands that they be kept up-to-date and that they be easily accessible.

—**Ann E. Prentice**

35 Physical Sciences and Mathematics

GENERAL WORKS

1699. Magill, Frank N., ed. **Magill's Survey of Science: Physical Science Series.** Pasadena, Calif., Salem Press, 1992. 6v. index. $475.00/set. Q158.5.M34. 500.2. LC 91-32962. ISBN 0-89356-618-7.

The fourth series of scientific articles issued under the general title *Magill's Survey of Science* is devoted to the physical sciences. Following this six-volume set, the *Survey* will be completed with series on applied science and medical science. The organization of each of the sets has been uniform. In this one, 380 general articles that cover the disciplines of astronomy/astrophysics, physical chemistry, computational science, mathematics, and physics are presented. Each article averages seven to eight pages, providing an introductory classification (e.g., bubble chambers is labeled "Elementary particle [high-energy] physics," and its field of study is "Techniques") that is followed by a two- to six-line definition, the principal terms associated with the topic, a descriptive overview, applications, context, bibliography, and cross-references. Each volume has a list of topics found in the full set and a category breakdown (e.g., cosmology, one category under astronomy and astrophysics, lists four relevant articles: "The Big Bang," "Cosmology," "The Evolution of the Universe," and "Large-Scale Structure in the Universe"). Volume 6 has a 30-page index to the entire set.

As with earlier series, the articles are signed and, in general, prepared by staff members from U.S. universities or colleges. The content is intended for the nonspecialist and is comparable to textbook explanations, although the specific sections on applications and context, which place "the topic in one or both of two perspectives: the history of science and/or the panorama of physical science as a discipline" (publisher's note, p. vi), add valuable dimensions to each discussion. The bibliographies (from 5 to 10 titles) typically cite book chapters or books, most published in the 1970s and 1980s. When fully published, the *Magill's Survey of Science* will constitute a miniencyclopedia of the sciences that is readable and informative (albeit this and other sets omit the key component of useful illustrations). [R: Choice, July/Aug 92, pp. 1658-59; LJ, 15 Sept 92, p. 62; WLB, May 92, p. 128]—**Laurel Grotzinger**

ASTRONOMY

1700. Couper, Heather, and Nigel Henbest. **The Space Atlas.** New York, Harcourt Brace Jovanovich, 1992. 64p. illus. index. $16.95. QB500.22.C68. 520. LC 91-24142. ISBN 0-15-200598-6.

Space Atlas is an excellent introduction to the world of astronomy and astronautics. Aimed at the novice astronomer and young adult, the volume is lavishly illustrated with maps, drawings, and astronomical charts. Included in the atlas are topics such as all the planets and their satellites, comets, galaxies, and space travel. Data in the volume appear to be from around late 1990 or early 1991. Some coverage in the volume is spotty; for instance, while a large portion of a page is devoted to a European spaceplane (sort of a combination space shuttle and Concorde) called "Sanger/Horus" that has yet to get off the drawing boards, the ill-fated (but functioning) Hubble Space Telescope is dismissed with a small illustration and three scant sentences. Other coverage is excellent, however. Of special note is the treatment of the outermost planets (Uranus, Neptune, and Pluto); the birth, life, and death of a star; "Our Star City"; the Local Group (of galaxies); and exploding galaxies. In fact, each chapter has new and useful information to offer the reader.

Although oriented toward the young reader, most libraries will find client interest in this volume high. Modestly priced, it is the best one-volume compendium on the subject available. Highly recommended for reference collections and a must for all beginning science collections. [R: RBB, 15 May 92, p. 1712]—**Ralph Lee Scott**

1701. Gibson, Bob. **The Astronomer's Sourcebook: The Complete Guide to Astronomical Equipment, Publications, Planetariums, Organizations, Events, and More.** Rockville, Md., Woodbine House, 1992. 302p. illus. index. $19.95pa. QB64.G43. 520. LC 91-45817. ISBN 0-933149-43-3.

This sourcebook is correctly named, as it lists information and its sources rather than constellations and star charts (as would be the case in a field guide). Gibson intends it to be a comprehensive reference that lists astronomical books, periodicals, optical dealers, star atlases, museums, prominent astronomers, and other information. It is not strictly comparable to other sourcebooks because each gives somewhat different information.

Some of the lists in the book are not complete. For example, the leading planetarium in Connecticut is not listed; nor is the Astronomical Society of Greater Hartford, probably the most active amateur society in the state. The biographical section of famous astronomers has some curious omissions, such as ancients Aristarchus and Hipparchus and the early twentieth-century astronomers J. C. Kapteyn and Simon Newcomb. Despite a few flaws turned up in a random search (e.g., astigmatism is poorly defined; J. H. Oort did not die in 1989 but is still living), this book is useful; the amateur astronomer will find much of value. [R: Choice, Oct 92, p. 272; LJ, 15 Apr 92, p. 86; RBB, July 1992, pp. 1956-57]—**Arthur R. Upgren**

1702. **The HarperCollins Dictionary of Astronomy and Space Science.** By Dianne F. Moore. New York, HarperPerennial/HarperCollins, 1992. 338p. illus. $25.00; $13.00pa. QB14.M59. 520'.3. LC 91-55394. ISBN 0-06-271542-9; 0-06-461023-3pa.

This dictionary is directed to the secondary school student or amateur enthusiast of astronomy and space science. Brief nontechnical, nonmathematical definitions are provided with occasional illustrations, and extensive cross-referencing is used. Acronyms and abbreviations are included as appropriate for the readership. Biographical sketches are supplied for a number of famous scientists; however, astronauts and cosmonauts are given limited attention. Whereas Valentina Tereshkova is listed in the main part of the dictionary, Sally Ride is found only in an appendix. Surprisingly, Wernher von Braun is not listed.

Colloquial terminology related to astronomical occurrences or objects is also included, such as the Hay Moon or St. Elmo's Fire. Although many visual phenomena of the Earth's atmosphere are listed, descriptions of the green flash and lunar halos are not included, a major omission. Older or common names for constellations and stars are listed with some historical background. There are 10 appendixes of tables that include solar system physical and orbital properties, solar and lunar eclipses, data on the nearest and brightest stars, constellations, chronologies of space science and astronomy, and nebulas. A list of astronauts and cosmonauts might have been useful. Recommended for school and public libraries.—**Margaret F. Dominy**

1703. Kerrod, Robin. **The Children's Space Atlas: A Voyage of Discovery for Young Astronauts.** Brookfield, Conn., Millbrook Press, 1992. 95p. illus. maps. index. $18.90. QB501.3.K47. 520. LC 91-30148. ISBN 1-56294-164-X.

As a child, this reviewer was profoundly influenced by *The Golden Book of Astronomy* by Rose Wyler (Western Publishing, 1959), a large volume of good information and page after page of color drawings of the Sun, stars, and planets. Now, more than three decades later, comes what might be considered the 1990s version of that magic book: *The Children's Space Atlas*. This, too, is an introduction to the heavens for children, probably from age 7 to 12. It is chock-full of beautiful color drawings and photographs in a "gee-whiz" format that today's computer-literate, video-game-oriented children will easily relate to. Emphasis is on what has been learned from the exploration of space and what can be seen with large telescopes. There are five sections: the introduction, the Solar System, the night sky (which includes constellation maps), stars and galaxies, and exploring space. A glossary and index add to the volume's usefulness.

The text is clear and to the point and does not overwhelm the reader with difficult vocabulary or long explanations of phenomena, thus making it ideal for the younger reader. On the other hand, the text is a little too brief for older children, who might want something more substantial. The book's strongest point is its illustrations, including drawings, maps, and photographs. All work together with the text to create a book that will immediately attract and hold the attention of all types of young readers. It is an appropriate selection for the elementary school library and for the public library children's section. [R: RBB, 15 May 92, p. 1712]—**Robert A. Seal**

1704. Maran, Stephen P., ed. **The Astronomy and Astrophysics Encyclopedia.** New York, Van Nostrand Reinhold, 1992. 1002p. illus. maps. index. $89.95. QB14.A873. 520'.3. LC 91-23241. ISBN 0-442-26364-3.

A compendium of 403 articles written by experts in the field, this comprehensive volume attempts to furnish an authoritative summary of current knowledge about astronomy and astrophysics. The book succeeds on a number of levels. Each piece is well written, clear, and to the point. Although an advanced work such as this relies fairly heavily on mathematics and scientific terminology, it is nevertheless highly readable and informative. It also succeeds in being comprehensive and up-to-date (although the latter, of course, is a fleeting concept).

Aimed at educated laypeople, teachers, science writers, editors, and scientists, the encyclopedia provides the latest theories and data on the heavens, from the Earth's atmosphere to the farthest reaches of the known universe. Included, for example, is current information on our solar system (e.g., satellites, planetary rings), nonvisible astronomy (e.g., x-ray, infrared, gamma ray, ultraviolet), and exotic celestial objects (e.g., Bok globules, binary pulsars, black holes). Thorough coverage of the astronomer's tools—telescopes and auxiliary equipment—is also provided.

Entries are generally two to four pages in length and are accompanied by black-and-white photographs or line drawings. Each concludes with a short bibliography. The only recent book to compare with this work is the *Encyclopedia of Astronomy and Astrophysics* (see ARBA 90, entry 1744), a shorter volume with fewer but more in-depth pieces. While both works are appropriate for university and observatory collections, *Astronomy and Astrophysics Encyclopedia* is preferred for reference work, both library and personal. [R: Choice, Mar 92, p. 1037; RBB, 15 Mar 92, pp. 1399-1400]
—**Robert A. Seal**

1705. **Messier's Nebulae and Star Clusters.** 2d ed. By Kenneth Glyn Jones. New York, Cambridge University Press, 1991. 427p. illus. index. $49.50. QB851.06. 523.1'125. LC 89-22199. ISBN 0-521-37079-5.

Any amateur astronomer with more than a passing interest in observing the heavens knows the name Charles Messier (1730-1817), a French astronomer who published a list of some 100 nonstellar objects that remain to this day of great interest to many with a backyard telescope. Messier was primarily interested in observing comets; he discovered so many, in fact, that Louis XV called him "The ferret of comets." Whether he liked it or not, his enduring fame is his now famous list of star clusters, nebulas, and other nonstellar celestial objects—the so-called Messier objects. They have been treated in countless volumes for years, ranging from mere checklists to details on how to observe each one. Jones, in his 2d edition, provides the most comprehensive treatment of this subject ever seen. He not only gives specific data on each object, from M1 (the Crab Nebula) to M110 (an elliptical galaxy), but also provides useful historical information, drawings, tables, a bibliography, and much more.

The heart of the book, not surprisingly, is the catalog of Messier objects, each entry occupying two to five pages. Included for each is popular name (if any); classification (e.g., gaseous nebula, galaxy); numerical data; detailed descriptions, including comments by Messier and other astronomers; recent astrophysical data (something not seen in other works); and descriptions and drawings by the author, including notes on how to locate and observe. If this were not enough, the book also includes a wealth of other information, such as historical data on the discovery of nonstellar objects; a short biography of the astronomer; detailed descriptions of each class of Messier object; techniques useful for any type of astronomical observation; and several appendixes, including star maps, tables and lists, and photographs of each Messier object.

The work is very well written and is up to the usual high standards of Cambridge University Press. It is regrettable that such an excellent book will be out of the reach of nearly every amateur astronomer due to its cost. Public and academic libraries alike will wish to purchase a copy, as will observatory libraries with historical materials in their collections.—**Robert A. Seal**

1706. Simon, Seymour. **Space Words: A Dictionary.** New York, HarperCollins, 1991. 48p. illus. $14.95. QB497.S55. 500.5'03. LC 90-37402. ISBN 0-06-022532-7.

This dictionary contains 76 terms or phrases related to astronomy and space exploration. The appropriate audience for this book is primary school students. The average entry is two to three sentences long, and the definitions or descriptions are kept simple, with minimal embellishment. Concepts involving the extremely large sizes, masses, or distances of space may be difficult for some young readers to grasp. Some definitions have been so simplified that the term is not so much defined as introduced. (This is a reasonable approach for the intended audience.) Cross-referencing is limited to three *see* references and one *see also* reference. Nearly every entry is accompanied by an illustration, some large enough to cover two pages. The illustrations are colorful and enhance the descriptions, especially when comparative sizes are discussed, as in planets or stars, or when describing day and night.

Defining complex scientific terms to an audience of young readers is a challenging task. The author and the illustrator have done an admirable job. Recommended for public and primary school libraries.
—**Margaret F. Dominy**

1707. Stewart, John. **Moons of the Solar System: An Illustrated Encyclopedia.** Jefferson, N.C., McFarland, 1991. 244p. illus. $45.00. QB401.S74. 523.9'8. LC 91-52641. ISBN 0-89950-568-6.

This compact reference book consists of two roughly equal parts addressing our Moon and the moons of the other planets. While a good portion of the information presented is available elsewhere, no other work presents it all in one place in such a well-organized way and in so much detail. Part 1, "Luna, Earth's Moon," provides descriptive data on our nearest celestial neighbor, followed by a detailed dictionary of lunar features (e.g., craters, seas, mountains), which includes related information such as manned and unmanned exploration, lunar mapping, and phenomena and discoveries. A selective bibliography on the Moon rounds out this useful section.

Part 2 addresses in great detail each of the 70 known moons circling all the planets (except Mercury and Venus, which have no satellites). Arranged alphabetically by the name of the moons, each entry is a cornucopia of data useful for the researcher or reference librarian. Included are other names, who or what the moon is named for, pronunciation, distance from planet, location relative to the planet and other satellites, orbital data, diameter and shape, surface, origin, discovery, and much more.

Appendixes list the moons by planet and in order of discovery, of size, and of visible magnitude. The book also contains 62 (mainly) black-and-white and color photographs, but no maps appear due to the difficulty of including them in a small-format volume. Aimed primarily at the lay reader, this work is also useful for scientists and university students, and is appropriate for academic, large public, and special libraries. [R: Choice, May 92, p. 1376; WLB, Apr 92, pp. 125-26]—**Robert A. Seal**

CHEMISTRY

Dictionaries and Encyclopedias

1708. Ockerman, Herbert W. **Illustrated Chemistry Laboratory Terminology.** Boca Raton, Fla., CRC Press, 1991. 211p. illus. index. $19.95pa. QD51.O25. 542'.1'014. LC 91-8591. ISBN 0-8493-0152-1.

This book is a reference for foreign chemists who are not very familiar with the English names of typical pieces of laboratory equipment. Names of common items are listed in Chinese, French, German, Polish, Spanish, and Turkish, along with a reference to the main body of the text for each item in each language. The main text provides the English name and a picture reproduced from the catalogs of two well-known scientific supply firms. Each listing also gives a few sentences that use the name in combination with related terms.

The book seems straightforward and convenient to use. The coverage is fairly broad, listing more than 350 terms, although it is mainly limited to equipment found in a general supply catalog; advanced instrumentation is usually omitted. Some modifications that could make the book more useful include indicating the relative size of the various pieces of equipment and incorporating an easy way for an English speaker to reverse the finding process and look up the name of a piece of apparatus in the other languages.

The intended audience for this book is rather limited: foreign students planning to teach or do technical writing in English and the libraries that serve these students. For these groups, however, the work could be very helpful, because it includes more terms and provides more equipment illustrations than most foreign-language scientific dictionaries.—**Harry E. Pence**

Handbooks and Yearbooks

1709. Ash, Michael, and Irene Ash, comps. **Handbook of Industrial Chemical Additives: An International Guide by Product, Trade Name, Function, and Supplier.** New York, VCH, 1991. 859p. $195.00. ISBN 1-56081-521-3.

Chemical additives, whether based on naturally occurring or synthetic compounds, are included in a wide range of materials. Gums may be used, for example, to thicken foods or to give extra weight to paper. This volume catalogs those additives that enhance the properties of products used in industry and by the public. It contains a main first section that gives chemical trade names of about 18,000 additives produced by more than 700 manufacturers. Each listing includes chemical composition and properties, plus applications. The second section is a cross-reference of the chemical names of the products listed in section 1. (Here are listed the BHA and BHT that appear on the list of contents of a breakfast cereal packet.) Each entry in this section includes synonyms (where possible) and Chemical Abstracts Service Registry numbers. The third section lists functional categories such as antioxidants or whitening agents, with the products that perform those functions. The final section provides manufacturers' names and addresses.

This handbook has been carefully prepared and will be especially useful to manufacturers and to those seeking clarification of the chemical composition of additives. Because it is the type of compilation that needs regular updates, it would be useful to have it available as a computer-readable database. [R: Choice, Apr 92, p. 1203]—**Harold Goldwhite**

1710. Ash, Michael, and Irene Ash, comps. **Handbook of Plastic Compounds, Elastomers, and Resins: An International Guide by Category, Tradename, Composition, and Supplier.** New York, VCH, 1992. 872p. $195.00. TP1130.A84. 668.4. LC 91-32215. ISBN 1-56081-553-1.

Users, manufacturers, and distributors of the several thousand organic products, compounds, and supplies essential to the international plastic and rubber "families" of products are the intended users of this excellent five-part reference tool. There are at least 15,000 entries, and they are generally complete enough so that would-be purchasers and suppliers can have absolute agreement on what is wanted and what the cost should be.

Part 1 covers 640 pages of items by their category names in a telegraphic abstract format that is dense with information but easy to follow. (Among the questions answered is the physical form in which the product is delivered and the best range of operating temperatures.) Trade names are always cited and are readily located through part 2, "Trade Name Cross Reference." "Mylar®" is one that stands out. Its category name—"Polyester, Thermoplastic"—makes finding equivalents easy. (Knowing a trade name makes answering questions much easier.) Part 3, "Chemical Component Cross Reference," intends to list every substance mentioned in all the preceding entries. Once again, the format and type size aid use, especially with the long entries; for example, "Epoxy Resin [CAS 325928-9403]" uses more than three pages for its listings. (An aid to searching is to look for one of the unusual ingredients in a compound.) Part 4 is the chemical manufacturers' directory and includes each of the subsidiaries separately, as they may use different names for the same product. (No ex-Soviet Union addresses are given, which dates the compilation.)—**Eugene B. Jackson**

1711. Edenbaum, Jesse, ed. **Plastics Additives and Modifiers Handbook.** New York, Van Nostrand Reinhold, 1992. 1113p. illus. index. $149.95. TP1142.P57. 668.4'11. LC 91-23854. ISBN 0-442-23450-3.

Plastics are a ubiquitous part of everyday life. From car bodies to tennis rackets, it is difficult to find a product that does not involve these manmade materials. Despite this, technical data about the formulation of these substances are not always readily available, even to those in the field. Edenbaum has sought to assemble a handbook that will answer all of the questions about the predominant additives for the principally compounded thermoplastics. Although he admits this ideal may be unattainable, he has prepared an excellent, comprehensive review.

The book consists of two major sections. The first concisely discusses the historical background, basic chemistry and technology, and main uses for each of the major types of plastics and has many helpful charts, graphs, and diagrams. Much of this information is available in standard texts on polymer chemistry, but the treatment here is unusually complete and practical, reflecting the extensive industrial experience of the contributors. Despite the large number of authors, the organization and writing style are consistent.

The second, and largest, section of the book examines the many possible additives. These essential components of modern plastics are used to adjust various properties, including improved stability or strength, special colors, decreased flammability, and enhanced processing ability. This is probably the heart of the book, as it brings together information that would otherwise be scattered through the technical literature or else only available to specialists. In fact, the overall effect of the discussion is as though a team of such specialists were offering comments and advice. The book will probably be most valuable to the reader who already has some basic knowledge about the production of polymers, but any reader with some background in organic chemistry should find the treatment to be both accessible and useful. – **Harry E. Pence**

1712. Emsley, John. **The Elements.** 2d ed. New York, Clarendon Press/Oxford University Press, 1991. 251p. index. $55.00; $22.50pa. QD466.E48. 546. LC 88-19011. ISBN 0-19-855238-6; 0-19-855568-7pa.

This should be the first source consulted when looking for information about chemical elements. Each element (the book recognizes 105) is treated in 2 pages filled with information that ranges from properties to occurrence to biological importance. Chemical properties described include reactivity, size, electronegativity, reduction potential, and oxidation states. Among the physical properties listed are melting and boiling points, density, thermodynamics, electrical resistivity, molar volume, and crystal structure. Nuclear information and electron shell properties are also given.

Most of the revisions for this edition have been made in the environmental properties section. Here can be found the biological role of the element and its level and toxicity in humans. Also given are the abundance in the Sun and in the Earth's crust and atmosphere, as well as geological data such as ores, annual production, and reserves. Data is in SI units (International System of Units), with conversion information available. Introductory comments cite references to the source of the data and calculations. Appendixes present much of the information in tabular form and include element discoveries (date and discoverer), melting and boiling points, densities, enthalpies, resistivities, and NMR (nuclear magnetic resonance) frequencies. The data is presented so clearly and concisely that this work is very easy to use. – **T. McKimmie**

1713. Flick, Ernest W. **Water-Soluble Resins: An Industrial Guide.** 2d ed. Park Ridge, N.J., Noyes, 1991. 436p. index. $64.00. TP978.F56. 668'.37. LC 91-8368. ISBN 0-8155-1274-0.

This book is intended for those interested in using water-soluble resins in the formulation of consumer products, including coatings, adhesives, and foods. It presents properties and applications of more than 1,100 such resins available at the time of compilation (early 1991) from 47 suppliers in the United States. The descriptions are from information provided by the manufacturers and include specifications and properties such as viscosity, density, color, solubilities, and flash point. The work is legibly reproduced direct from typewritten copy. It has indexes of suppliers' addresses, trade names, and resin types. Considering the intended users of this work, additional material on possible hazards of the resins other than flammability would have been useful. – **Harold Goldwhite**

1714. Harper, Charles A., ed. **Handbook of Plastics, Elastomers, and Composites.** 2d ed. New York, McGraw-Hill, 1992. 1v. (various paging). illus. index. $89.50. TP1130.H36. 668.4. LC 91-38803. ISBN 0-07-026686-7.

This publication follows the format of the first edition; it has well-referenced chapters written by subject experts on industrial applications for polymer and plastic technology. Thoroughly revised, this edition features increased coverage of elastomers, particularly thermoplastic elastomers. Detailed discussions deal with high-performance requirements for products with chemical, mechanical, and electrical applications and with plastic compositions and improvements in processing capabilities. In addition to the 11 chapters, appendixes include a glossary, abbreviations, electrical and design properties, and international sources for standards and specifications. Surprisingly, for a contributed volume, there is little redundancy among the chapters. A detailed index and a table of contents make the volume easy to use. — **Andrew G. Torok**

1715. Hunting, Anthony L. L., comp. and ed. **A Formulary of Cosmetic Preparations. Volume One: Decorative Cosmetics.** Cranford, N.J., Micelle Press, 1991. 284p. index. $49.00. 668.5. LC 91-62235. ISBN 0-9608752-2-0.

This is the first in a series of volumes on cosmetic preparations. The formulations are from United Kingdom suppliers and agents, but many American companies are represented by these companies as well. Specific topics covered in this volume include face, eye, lip, nail, and body cosmetics. Fragrances and cologne are also included, as well as ethnic preparations. Additional sections include a glossary that provides the legal status of a few ingredients, addresses of all suppliers, and a bibliography that has both recent and classical reference sources.

Chemists, business personnel, cosmetologists, and physicians (especially dermatologists) will find this a valuable reference source. Recommended for medical, academic, business, and research libraries.
— **Estelle A. Davis**

1716. **Lange's Handbook of Chemistry.** 14th ed. By John A. Dean. New York, McGraw-Hill, 1992. 1v. (various paging). index. $79.50. LC 84-643191. ISBN 0-07-016194-1. ISSN 0748-4585.

Most chemistry laboratories have a copy of one (or both) of two reference handbooks: *Lange's Handbook of Chemistry*, now in its 14th edition, and the *Handbook of Chemistry and Physics* (CRC Press, 1992), currently in its 73d edition. While the latter is updated annually, *Lange's Handbook* offers a new edition every six years or so. The present volume is full of information essential for any chemist. Physical and chemical properties of the elements, of 1,400 inorganic compounds, and of 4,000 organic compounds form the core of the work. Other major sections are devoted to mathematics; nomenclature; thermodynamics; spectroscopy, including nuclear magnetic resonance data not only for hydrogen but also for many other useful nuclei; electrochemistry; polymers; and practical laboratory work. The inclusion of a table of common reactive and incompatible chemicals in this last section is useful, but the coverage of laboratory hazards is sparse and inadequate. Otherwise, this is an extremely valuable collection of data that will be used constantly by any laboratory chemist. [R: Choice, Dec 92, p. 603]
— **Harold Goldwhite**

1717. McLafferty, Fred W., and Douglas B. Stauffer. **The Important Peak Index of the Registry of Mass Spectral Data.** New York, John Wiley, 1991. 3v. $750.00/set. QC454.M3M38. 543'.0873. ISBN 0-471-55270-4.

Mass spectrophotometry is already a widely used analytical tool in fields as diverse as environmental, agricultural, pharmaceutical, and clinical chemistry. Recent developments suggest it may soon be of comparable importance for cell biology and medicine. The GC/MS (gas chromatography/mass spectrophotometry) instruments are now sufficiently inexpensive that they are found not only in university science departments but also in a significant number of small colleges. Thus, the publication of this mass spectral index of more than 135,000 compounds has been published.

Several features make this compilation especially useful. Rather than being indexed by the compound names, the listing is based on the major observed peaks, making it easier to identify an unknown compound. The index peaks are not necessarily chosen from those of greatest abundance, but rather those that are most helpful in making an identification. Peaks that are found in relatively few compounds are given more weight than fragments, such as propyl or acetyl, that appear in many different compounds. It is also convenient that each compound is listed three times, indexed by the three most important peaks in the observed spectra. These books should be a beneficial acquisition for both large university libraries and smaller college libraries that support high-quality science departments.

—Harry E. Pence

Indexes

1718. **Current Chemical Reactions (CCR). Volume 14: Number 2.** Philadelphia, Institute for Scientific Information, 1992. 1v. (unpaged). index. $860.00pa. (12 issues + annual index). ISSN 0163-6278.

This database is for those who want to keep abreast of both new and recently changed reactions and methods in the syntheses of organic compounds. More than 100 journals are perused for *Current Chemical Reactions*, which is published monthly. Four indexes are provided for access to the database: new synthetic methods (words or phrases from title and article), journals, authors, and corporate. Entries are grouped under journal title to allow scanning of specific journals. Each entry gives complete bibliographic information, reaction descriptor, graphic representation of the reaction, product yields, key step indicator, explosive reaction indicator, and Institute for Scientific Information number (for ordering purposes). When available, an author's summary and comments are given. A review section of articles is also included. —Patricia S. Wilson

1719. **Index Chemicus (IC). Volume 125: Number 1.** Philadelphia, Institute for Scientific Information, 1992. 1v. (unpaged). $5,100.00pa. (52 issues + annual index). ISSN 0891-6055.

To create this publication, which focuses on new organic compounds and their chemistry, ISI (Institute for Scientific Information) has perused more than 100 chemical and pharmaceutical journals for new substances. The entries are grouped under journal titles, which will allow scanning of specific journals. Access to the database is by six indexes. A keyword index was added as an enhancement to the 1991 annual cumulated index (which also includes a corporate index) and has been continued with the 1992 weekly issues. The others are journal, author, biological activity, unisolated intermediate, and labeled compound. Each abstract contains complete bibliographic information, illustrations of the structures and their associated reactions, use profile, and an ISI accession number (for ordering purposes). When available, an author's summary is included, and where applicable, unisolated intermediate identification and indicators of labeled compounds and explosiveness appear. If the synthesis of the compound is included in *Current Chemical Reactions* (ISI, 1992), it is so indicated.

—Patricia S. Wilson

EARTH AND PLANETARY SCIENCES

General Works

1720. **Chambers Earth Sciences Dictionary.** P. M. B. Walker, ed. New York, Chambers Kingfisher Graham, 1991. 250p. illus. maps. $40.00. 550. ISBN 0-550-13244-9.

Science dictionaries are almost a *sine qua non* for the desks of scientists and writers on science. The *Chambers Science and Technology Dictionary* (see ARBA 89, entry 1348) is widely available in libraries. The volume under review is both a condensed and specialized section of the parent work. Similar to all abridged versions, it includes the basic terms of the field, here comprising geology, mineralogy, mineral extraction, crystallography, and some related areas. The majority of definitions seem to be related to mining and mineralogy. With space for terms at a premium, one wonders why many subjects defined in most ordinary dictionaries, such as *Avogadro's number* and *atomic weight*, are included. *Punctuated equilibrium* seems an orphan in the text because nothing else about evolution, speciation, phylogeny, or cladism is offered. Also, *Eocene* is defined as the oldest epoch of the Tertiary. What happened to the Paleocene? Several page-length "panels" provide expanded coverage of some words and concepts. For example, the geologic column is presented, but epochs unfortunately are included under the heading "Periods." A panel on the Quaternary lists British stages only. Other panels focus on certain fossils, including one on dinosaurs, while another covers microfossils (e.g., dinoflagellates and spores). Neither provides definitions, and nondinosaurs are included in the panel. But there are panels that are appropriate (e.g., those on sodium and plutonic rock classification).

Despite these criticisms, the dictionary is useful for a general reader who needs quick definitions. The coverage will be less useful for professionals who can consult subject-specific texts or the parent volume. — **David Bardack**

1721. **Encyclopedia of Earth System Science.** William A. Nierenberg, ed. San Diego, Calif., Academic Press, 1992. 4v. illus. maps. index. $950.00/set. QE5.5E514. 550'.3. LC 90-29045. ISBN 0-12-226722-2(v.1); 0-12-226723-0(v.2); 0-12-226724-9(v.3); 0-12-226725-7(v.4).

Because understanding human interaction with the environment and its effect on the earth system is of vital importance today, this scholarly encyclopedia is a welcome addition to the literature in this area. Its four volumes of authoritative articles, covering subjects that either comprise or affect the earth system, illustrate the complexity of the processes involved. It is intended for anyone seriously concerned with these issues, whether they be professional scientists and engineers, students, or the informed general public.

The encyclopedia was developed by an advisory panel of nine scientists and an editor in chief. Distinguished scientists and experts from around the world were asked to contribute articles within their areas of expertise. All are from universities, corporations, governmental agencies, or research institutes that represent the many scientific disciplines of earth system science. A list of these 257 contributing authors, along with their affiliations and titles of their articles, appears in volume 4. Members of the advisory board are listed in the front of volume 1.

The format of the encyclopedia is similar to that of the excellent and well-received *Encyclopedia of Physical Science and Technology* (see ARBA 88, entry 1445), which is also published by Academic Press. Each signed article gives the author's affiliation and begins with a brief roman numeral outline of the main topics, followed by an introductory definition of the primary subject. In the main text the outline is further expanded. A bibliography follows the main text of the article. A glossary with definitions of significant terms in the context of their use ends each article. The lengths of the articles vary from 7 to 27 pages, reflecting the diverse complexity of the topics. For instance, acoustical oceanography is covered in 7 pages; coverage of magmatic sulfide deposits takes 27. The 180 articles in the 4 volumes are arranged alphabetically by title on double-columned pages. Each volume begins with a table of contents in which article titles are arranged so that the main subject or most important word in the title is listed first, such as brines in sedimentary deposits or clastic sediments. The small print of the text may present a problem for some readers. Page formats, with wide white margins and boldface type for both outline headings and glossary terms, are pleasing to the eye and allow easy access to information. Illustrations, photographs, diagrams, graphs, and maps are generously used throughout the articles. Each volume contains a small set of color plates that are referred to in a few of the articles. A helpful one-page guide to using the encyclopedia appears in the front of each volume.

The user can locate subjects by a number of methods. Cross-references to related articles appear in capital letters within brackets at the ends of paragraphs in the text of the entries. A relational index in volume 4 supplements the cross-references. Arranged alphabetically by article title, it lists other entries that are closely related in subject matter. The user can find more detailed topics in the extensive subject index in the fourth volume. All terms defined in the glossaries also appear as main subject headings in this index.

This encyclopedia is a very useful reference tool for any researcher seriously interested in this field, as well as for interested laypeople and policymakers concerned with the environment. The in-depth, expertly written articles are clear and understandable. The topics selected represent the current status of, and reflect the present interests in, earth system science as defined by the panel. (The criteria used by the advisory panel in their selection of articles are not described in the preface.) As the editor states in the preface, this field does not have any final, everlasting form or content. Because of its changing and complex nature, future supplements will be needed to cover advances in scientific knowledge. [R: Choice, July/Aug 92, p. 1654; LJ, 15 Feb 92, p. 156; RBB, 15 Mar 92, pp. 1400-01]

— **Anne C. Roess**

Climatology

1722. **The Weather Almanac: A Reference Guide to Weather, Climate, and Air Quality in the United States....** 6th ed. Frank E. Bair, ed. Detroit, Gale, 1992. 855p. illus. maps. index. $120.00. LC 81-644322. ISBN 0-8103-2843-7. ISSN 0731-5627.

This updated edition of a worthwhile reference manual gives both climatic information and a good synopsis of weather and its changes. The most useful feature is several types of data for each month from 1961 through 1990 for 109 U.S. cities. Publishing data in such a timely fashion is commendable. However, the average monthly values for 550 worldwide locations are primarily from 1931 to 1960 and should have been updated. Many of the maps in the first part of the book are also based on old data and need to be updated and redrawn. The explanations include virtually every type of weather phenomena: severe storms, floods, drought, and heat and cold waves; environmental concerns such as acid rain, ozone depletion, and global warming; and related subjects such as earthquakes, volcanic activity, and tsunamis. The effects of changing climate on agriculture, health, and economics are discussed. The structure of the National Weather Service and its planned overhaul are included as well as its new, improved tools: radar, satellites, and computers. Some weather folklore is given. There are a good table of contents and an index. This is a good reference manual for every library. — **Allen E. Staver**

Geology

1723. **Elsevier's Dictionary of Geosciences: Russian-English.** K. P. Bhatnagar, comp., and S. K. Bhattacharya, ed. New York, Elsevier Science Publishing, 1991. 1023p. $225.50. ISBN 0-444-88425-4.

This work contains approximately 56,000 Russian terms used in geochemistry and physical chemistry, geology and tectonics, meteorology and climatography, mineralogy, oceanology, paleontology, petroleum engineering that pertains to oil deposits and their explorations, petrology, petrography and rock mechanics, and sedimentology. It does not claim exhaustive coverage, because dictionaries on subjects that are developing at a phenomenal rate can never be exhaustive. Periodical research publications in Russian and English up to 1989 have been scanned to compile the dictionary.

The entries are arranged in alphabetical order, and group words are bunched under nouns. When a Russian term is used in more than one field and the corresponding English terms are different, this difference is indicated by a semicolon; the subject fields are not mentioned in order to save space. A slant line is used to indicate synonyms. The book begins with a list of the reference sources used and ends with an appendix that contains a brief list of abbreviations related to the field and their definitions.

The dictionary is based on the experience of more than two decades. It will be useful to translators of Russian scientific and technological literature and to English-speaking scientists who wish to read Russian literature in the original language. — **Janet Mongan**

Hydrology

1724. **Elsevier's Dictionary of Hydrology and Water Quality Management: In Five Languages: English, French, Spanish, Dutch and German.** J. D. van der Tuin, comp. New York, Elsevier Science Publishing, 1991. 527p. index. $214.50. GB653.2.T85. 551.48'03. LC 90-26784. ISBN 0-444-88672-9.

This work lists 5,928 terms that describe the basic aspects of hydrology and water management for both surface and subsurface waters. It contains a reference table, which enumerates the terms in English alphabetical order, and cross-reference indexes for French, Spanish, Dutch, and German. The reference table consists of English terms followed by equivalent terms in each corresponding language. The indexes provide lists of terms in alphabetical order for the respective language. Each term is assigned one or more reference numbers that correspond to the basic terms listed in the reference table. The guide to the use of the dictionary clearly explains the structure and user-friendly format.

The scope of this work focuses on the relevant scientific and engineering topics for the freshwater environment, including water properties, hydraulics, water quality, hydrology, water management, water and wastewater treatment, water use, and experimental methods for determining water quantity or quality. Selected terms on ecology, limnology, potamology, sedimentology, and oceanography have been included based on how they may affect freshwater quantity or quality. Given the increasing awareness of the environment and our natural resources, this dictionary is a worthwhile addition to any research or scientific library.—**Gabriel P. Sabadell**

Mineralogy

1725. **The Larousse Encyclopedia of Precious Gems.** By Pierre Bariaud and Jean-Paul Poirot with Michel Duchamp. New York, Van Nostrand Reinhold, c1985, 1992. 248p. illus. $60.00. TS722.B3713. 553.8'03. LC 91-9256. ISBN 0-442-30289-4.

Each of the many excellent reference books devoted to gems has its own focus, and each tends to appeal to a particular interest. The authors have aimed this one at those interested in the history and use of gems as art and decoration. First published in France in 1985, this is an information-packed tour of how gems have been fashioned by artisans into works of art to be seen and admired. The introductory section on the properties of gemstones emphasizes those attributes that contribute to the ease with which gems can be fashioned, such as hardness and resistance to mechanical, thermal, and chemical shock. The variabilities of color are also discussed. Gems explored in their historical contexts as gifts, religious artifacts, treasures, and adornment provide the reader with an unusual perspective on the subject.

The authors then describe, at varying lengths, approximately 200 gems, giving for each the origin of the name, where found, how mined, how used, and a history of that use. Descriptions vary from a sentence to 20 pages (in the case of diamonds), depending upon the popularity of the gem. Also covered are a number of substances, such as nacre, bone, and elephant hair, not usually considered as gems but included because they are regularly made into jewelry. The unusually well written text and the superb photographs are a mine of information for the general reader interested in how gems become jewelry. A brief bibliography and a list of museums with noteworthy gem exhibits complete this well-crafted reference book. [R: Choice, Sept 92, p. 72]—**Ann E. Prentice**

1726. Mange, Maria A., and Heinz F. W. Maurer. **Heavy Minerals in Colour.** New York, Routledge, Chapman & Hall, 1992. 147p. illus. index. $79.95. QE364.2.H4M36. 549'.1. LC 89-9199. ISBN 0-412-43910-7.

Sandstone and other silicastic sedimentary rocks are composed of grains from parent rocks. Heavy minerals are high-density constituents of these silicate sediments that, through geologic processes, were broken off from larger mineral sources and became part of this more recent combination. Although they make up less than one percent of sedimentary rock, heavy minerals are important markers for the study of patterns of erosion throughout geologic time. The study of heavy minerals became popular at the turn of the twentieth century. This interest waned during the 1940s, but as new techniques were developed, several studies were conducted in later decades. The authors provide an overview of the field and discuss the value of the study of sediments. They also describe the several methods of analysis of heavy minerals, each of which requires that the sedimentary rock be ground up and the heavy minerals separated out for identification. New techniques for identification, photomicrography in particular, are described. Descriptions of 61 transparent heavy minerals, each with full-color photomicrographs, are provided. The minerals are organized by type (e.g., silicates, oxides, carbonates), and for each mineral, information on grain morphology and optical and physical properties is given. Combined with the photomicrographs, this provides considerable data to assist in identification.

The authors provide a general overview, with bibliography, of a less well known area of geology. They also provide an identification guide to the smallest of mineral specimens. Although not a tool for the beginning geologist or the mineral collector, this work fills an important niche in the geology reference collection.—**Ann E. Prentice**

1727. **Non-Ferrous Metal Data 1990.** Secaucus, N.J., American Bureau of Metal Statistics, 1991. 153p. $350.00. LC 21-15719. ISBN 0-910064-24-5. ISSN 0065-7611.

This annual compilation of statistical data on copper, lead, zinc, aluminum, and other nonferrous metals brings under a single cover a wealth of information to the user. The publisher has elicited a strong collaboration from other interested parties to undertake these efforts. Such inclusions as silver and gold production and consumption worldwide and import and export data by country are crucial to particular industries. In addition to tabular information, domestic production is arranged by company. Several features that enhance the work include the 50-year coverage of copper, lead, and zinc production of the United States and the world; a comparison of the historical and constant prices of a variety of nonferrous metals; foreign exchange rates for the last five years; and an inventory of selected stockpile metals of the U.S. government. The nature of the information in this publication warrants inclusion in a comprehensive science and technology collection. However, its price may well restrict its use to those specialized collections that serve an audience within a proprietary environment.

—John H. Hunter

1728. Pellant, Chris. **Rocks and Minerals.** New York, Dorling Kindersley; distr., Boston, Houghton Mifflin, 1992. 256p. illus. index. (Eyewitness Handbooks). $29.95; $17.95pa. QE431.2.P45. 549. LC 91-58222. ISBN 1-56458-033-4; 1-56458-061-Xpa.

Several new rock and mineral identification books appear each year. All cover essentially the same information but do so in slightly different ways. Some are coffee-table books while others focus less on illustration than on nearly complete description. This work combines something of both and will appeal to the active rock hound who wishes to identify specimens in the field.

The introductory section provides an excellent, basic how-to guide for locating likely collecting sites; identifies the basic field kit for the rock hound; lists the tools necessary at home for preparing specimens for display; and gives tips on how to display a collection. Also included is a general description of mineral characteristics such as crystal systems, hardness, transparency, and color. A chart lists the most common minerals by hardness, specific gravity, cleavage, and fracture. The mineral identification section provides information on more than 400 minerals organized into 8 sections according to chemical group. Each mineral is described briefly by information on its formation, composition, and hardness. Chemical identification tests are also provided. The illustrations that accompany each mineral are useful in initial identification. There is no information on common location or rarity of the mineral. Rocks are categorized as igneous, metamorphic, and sedimentary and are described by composition, texture, and origin. As with the minerals, illustrations are adequate for initial identification. The rock hound will find this a useful field guide but will want to complement it with one or more of the guides that have better illustrations and that are almost invariably too large to take into the field. [R: LJ, 1 Sept 92, p. 170; SLJ, Nov 92, p. 136]

—Ann E. Prentice

1729. Schumann, Walter. **Minerals of the World.** New York, Sterling Publishing, 1992. 224p. illus. index. $19.95. QE366.8.S3813. 549. LC 91-42362. ISBN 0-8069-8570-4.

Approximately 500 of the more common minerals have been selected for inclusion in this guide. A mineral identification system based on streak, hardness, and specific gravity is described, and the reader is given instructions on applying each of these measurable properties. Additional methods of identification, including luster, cleavage, transparency, and fracture, are discussed briefly. Although the system may appear cumbersome, it is actually quite easy to follow.

The guide is organized by this system, with color of the streak as the primary property. As one opens the book, a bar along the left margin lists the three properties, starting with streak first and followed by hardness and specific gravity. Next to the bar is a brief description of the mineral, including unique characteristics, where found, other minerals that occur near it, crystal structure, and chemical composition. On the facing page are high-quality photographs, each of which is keyed by number to the description. The index provides immediate access to a particular mineral description. In the field one can make a preliminary mineral identification by checking the color of the streak and referring to the appropriate section, by checking hardness and determining which minerals with a particular streak have the identified hardness, and finally by referring to the illustrations. A great deal of information is included in this guide and the illustrations are excellent, making it one of the best such guides available. And it is small enough to fit in one's pocket. [R: RBB, 1 Sept 92, pp. 87-89]

—Ann E. Prentice

Oceanography

1730. The Random House Atlas of the Oceans. Danny Elder and John Pernetta, eds. New York, Random House, 1991. 200p. illus. maps. index. $40.00. ISBN 0-679-40830-4.

This volume contains a lot of material on the world's oceans. Written under the auspices of the World Conservation Union (WCU), the work portrays the immense diversity of the world's oceans, which are collapsing under the strain of coastal human populations. Chronicled are the conversion of coral reefs, tropical mangroves, and tidelands into polluted beaches, broken reefs, and life-threatening red tides. The tragic fate awaiting marine animals, such as whales, dolphins, turtles, and countless other species, is well documented in the atlas.

The book, most of which is text and photographs, begins with several background chapters on the origin of and current environments present in the world's oceans. The actual atlas, which comprises about 30 of the volume's 200 pages, is divided into maps showing regional bodies of water such as the Caribbean, the Southern Ocean, the Southeast Pacific, and the Arabian Sea. Data for the maps were supplied by the WCU. Each map shows the localized areas of greatest pollution (a pie chart shows industrial/mining, domestic, and oil pollution), together with the location of known radioactive waste ocean dump sites. Also depicted are tourist areas, fishing centers, sea beds, protected marine areas, reefs, and mangroves. Specific threatened species are shown in each area, as are whale migration tracks. The maps also have a wealth of "factoid" information on global and local ocean environments. The volume concludes with a list of threatened marine species, a list of map sources, and an index.

This volume is an attractive and well-done treatment of the topic. The binding is sturdy and should stand up to library use. The work is written more in the nature of a handbook than an atlas, with only about 15 percent of the volume devoted to mapping. Recommended for all types of libraries with patrons who have general interests in conservation, ecology, and coastal/marine studies. [R: LJ, 1 Apr 92, pp. 112-14; RBB, 1 May 92, pp. 1634-37]—**Ralph Lee Scott**

Paleontology

1731. Fleury, Bruce Edward. **Dinosaurs: A Guide to Research.** Hamden, Conn., Garland, 1992. 468p. illus. index. (Garland Reference Library of the Humanities, v.1196). $73.00. Z6033.D55F54. 016.5679'7. LC 92-232. ISBN 0-8240-5344-3.

During the last 20 years there has been a resurgence in both popular and scholarly interest in dinosaurs. This book, a selective bibliography (the subtitle is somewhat misleading) of more than 1,100 articles and books that deal with dinosaurs and related topics, reflects this increased interest. Most of the works listed were published in the 1970s through August 1991, but a number of classic older works are also included. The book concentrates on works likely to be found in good academic libraries, such as articles published in *Paleobiology, Journal of Vertebrate Paleontology,* and *Scientific American.* Annotations are descriptive for the most part. The book includes several handy appendixes, including a brief glossary, an index of curricular materials, and author and title indexes.

Overall, this is a satisfactory book, although the price seems high. It will be most useful to interested neophytes, especially college students working on term papers. Dinosaur specialists will be more likely to turn to bibliographic databases and Daniel J. Chure and John S. McIntosh's *A Bibliography of the Dinosauria (Exclusive of the Aves), 1677-1986* (Museum of Western Colorado, 1989). [R: Choice, Dec 92, p. 601; LJ, Aug 92, p. 88]—**Joseph Hannibal**

1732. Macmillan Children's Guide to Dinosaurs and Other Prehistoric Animals. By Philip Whitfield. New York, Macmillan Children's Books, 1992. 96p. illus. index. $16.95pa. QE862.D5W446. 567.9'1'03. LC 91-45562. ISBN 0-02-762362-9.

Children have long had a love affair with dinosaurs, and this title will be popular with them. Arranged in chronological order, each of the five sections describes a different geological era. Entries for more than 125 types of creatures provide information on size, shape, classification, unusual features, and the latest theories about behavior. Each chapter begins with a two-page spread of an artist's conception of life at that particular period. These spreads provide a fascinating impression of how the prehistoric world may have looked and should stimulate a child's imagination. The following pages describe what is drawn, and useful maps show the positions of the continents at the time portrayed. Each creature is drawn in color, and a brief description gives the best available information. All chapters have a special "Focus On" feature that looks at one particular creature or aspect in more detail. The majority of the creatures pictured are dinosaurs and other reptiles, but a few mammals and amphibians are included to help recreate the flavor of the time. The illustrations are the book's strong point from a child's perspective. The book is indexed, and a short bibliography can direct children and parents to other interesting material.

While this work does have reference value, it will probably get more use in a circulating collection. Recommended for school and public libraries.—**Susan Ebershoff-Coles**

PHYSICS

1733. **Encyclopedia of Applied Physics. Volume 2: Artificial Intelligence to Bus Systems and Computer Interfacing.** George L. Trigg, Eduardo S. Vera, and Walter Greulich, eds. New York, VCH, 1991. 658p. illus. $295.00. QC5.E543. 530.05. LC 91-8738. ISBN 1-56081-061-0.

1734. **Encyclopedia of Applied Physics. Volume 3: Calibration and Maintenance of Test and Measuring Equipment to Collective Phenomena in Solids.** George L. Trigg, Eduardo S. Vera, and Walter Greulich, eds. New York, VCH, 1992. 616p. illus. $295.00. QC5.E543. 530'.05. LC 91-8738. ISBN 1-56081-062-9.

Volumes 2 and 3 of this series both display the high standards and quality so evident in the first volume (see ARBA 92, entry 1750). Much of volume 2 is devoted to topics in biophysics, such as biological effects of radiation, biomagnetism, biomass, and biomedical engineering. Similarly, a large portion of volume 3 treats chemical-physics subjects, including chemical kinetics, chemical analysis, and chemiluminescence. In addition to these, there are excellent discussions of topics that range from artificial intelligence, astronomy, and the atmosphere to circuits, coal, and collective phenomena in solids. The sections that deal with relatively recent work on catastrophe theory and chaos are both excellent. All of the 48 major entries, averaging nearly 25 pages apiece, are well written and well organized, with tables of contents, glossaries, textual references, and suggestions for further reading. The books are profusely illustrated with photographs, figures, and even color plates. Although there is some variation in the style of figures from one article to the next, all are clear, well labeled, and complementary to the text. Overall, if the high professional quality of the first three volumes continues, this series will be of great value for many years as a basic reference and as an authoritative introduction to the represented fields of study.—**John U. Trefny**

1735. **INIS: Thesaurus.** Vienna, International Atomic Energy Agency; distr., Lanham, Md., UNIPUB, 1992. 880p. $160.00pa. ISBN 92-0-100392-7. ISSN 1014-1561.

This thesaurus is a product of the International Nuclear Information System (INIS). It is typical of its genre, showing hierarchical and relational terminology in the area of nuclear research. There are 17,939 descriptors listed. As stated in the introduction, the subject areas covered include, among many others, general, high-energy, and nuclear physics; chemistry; materials; earth sciences; radioisotope effects and kinetics; radiation protection and environment; instrumentation; waste management; economics and sociology; and nuclear law, as well as the economic and environmental effects of nonnuclear energy sources. Despite this impressive list, not all subjects are equally treated in depth or extent. For example, the entry for *mandable* is adequate for a search in medicine but does not assist the ornithological search.

This work would be particularly useful in specialized sci-tech or bio-med collections where it would assist end-user or librarian-mediated electronic literature searching. It would also be useful in a general reference department to aid searchers unfamiliar with nuclear terminology.

—**Margaret F. Dominy**

MATHEMATICS

1736. **Biographical Dictionary of Mathematicians: Reference Biographies from the** *Dictionary of Scientific Biography*. New York, Scribner's, 1991. 4v. index. $175.00/set. QA28.B534. 510'.92'2. LC 90-52920. ISBN 0-684-19282-9.

This work is a subset of the *Dictionary of Scientific Biography* (see ARBA 91, entries 1461 and 1462). Each of the 1,023 biographies includes the name of the contributor; some are collaborative efforts. Biographies of well-known persons whose work crossed over disciplines are written by a team of contributors, each focusing on a specific aspect of their subject's work.

The mathematicians selected span history from ancient times to the mid-twentieth century. No living individual is included. In the selection of subjects, the editors not only focus on individuals whose work falls well within the disciplines of mathematics but also those better known in other fields, such as Plato, Omar Khayyam, and Leonardo da Vinci. Although it is interesting to read of the contributions to mathematics and related fields made by these scientists, this dictionary would not be the first source of data for some. On the other hand, their mathematical efforts are not usually given as thorough a treatment in more general encyclopedias. The cultural distribution of subjects seems uniform, with a significant number of Asian and Arab mathematicians. Also included is the nonperson Nicolas Bourbaki (the pseudonym of an influential group of French mathematicians).

The articles vary in length from a single column to as many as 20 pages. They present a comfortable blend of information about the early life of the subject and analysis of the scientific contribution, giving the latter considerably more emphasis. A list of the subject's major publications and secondary literature about the person concludes each article. The contributors of the articles are either mathematicians—typically in the same field as the subject—or scientific historians. These articles are written for an audience familiar with college-level mathematics and science. In many cases the original notation is provided accompanied by the modern equivalent or explanation.

Three indexes in the fourth volume cover all volumes. The first sorts the mathematicians into broad fields: algebra; analysis and differential equations; arithmetic, computing, and number theory; astronomy, geodesy, and trigonometry; foundations, logic, and set theory; geometry and topology; history, philosophy, and dissemination of knowledge; mechanics, physics, and technology; and probability and statistics. The second index is a selected chronology; the third is a subject/name index.

Although it appears that the editors determined to produce a culturally balanced work, there seems to be a gender bias. Despite the fact that their contributions to mathematics rival those of many of their male colleagues, the dictionary contains no entry for Nina Bari, a leader of early twentieth-century Soviet mathematics; Ada Lovelace, one of the earliest contributors in the field of programming; Grace Young, the first woman to receive a doctorate in Germany in any field, who (with her husband, William Young) produced over 200 mathematical articles and several books; or Charlotte Scott, an early organizer of the American Mathematical Society, an editor of the American Journal of Mathematics, and the instigator of the College Entrance Examination Board. The lives of these mathematicians fall well within the limits of this dictionary.

Biographical Dictionary of Mathematicians is highly recommended for mathematics collections that might be distantly located from a general collection. Even if the main library or general collection has the larger and inclusive set of the *Dictionary of Scientific Biography*, the duplication would be warranted. — **Margaret F. Dominy**

1737. **Combined Membership List 1992-1993: American Mathematical Association, Mathematical Association of America, [and] Society for Industrial and Applied Mathematics.** Providence, R.I., American Mathematical Society, 1992. 584p. $50.00pa. ISBN 0-8218-0178-3.

This edition of the *Combined Membership List* (CML) contains key information as of June 1, 1992, for more than 56,000 members of the three most important American mathematical organizations. The CML is divided into three sections: an alphabetical list of individual members; a geographical list of individual members; and a list of academic, institutional, and corporate members. Thus, one could look up a teacher or researcher by name and find that person's mailing address (preceded and followed by an asterisk), society affiliation, title/position, place of employment, telephone number, and address for electronic mail. Alternatively, one could look at the three geographical subdivisions— United States, Canadian provinces, and other countries—where names of members are arranged according to city within state, province, or country. The academic and institutional list includes addresses and telephone numbers of university switchboards and departments in the mathematical sciences, whereas the corporate list gives a main address and telephone number.

Despite computerization and the fact that members of the various societies have online access for searching and updating entries, a careful reader will spot inconsistencies and inaccuracies, possibly the result of individual members' carelessness. However, these are minor criticisms of a useful directory that should be found in any library with an emphasis on science and mathematics.—**Henry J. Ricardo**

1738. Grinstein, Louise S. **Mathematical Book Review Index 1800-1940.** Hamden, Conn., Garland, 1992. 448p. (Garland Reference Library of Social Science, v.527). $72.00. Z6651.G75. 016.51. LC 91-37397. ISBN 0-8240-4114-3.

This bibliography covers reviews, from a wide range of periodicals, of 3,283 works in mathematics, science, philosophy, and education, published between 1800 and 1940. The list is limited to books in English (and works in foreign languages translated into English) published in either the United States or Canada. In addition to purely mathematical works, others concerned with the physical sciences, history of science, or statistics or logic are also given if they contain a significant amount of material of mathematical interest. Textbooks (along with their intended grade levels), reference books, and supplementary works—yearbooks, workbooks, review and problem books, theses, and tables of interest to "educators and general readers" alike—are included. The bibliography is arranged alphabetically by author, and each entry is annotated with keyword descriptions that indicate the type of works and topics covered. Historians of mathematics, education, and the sciences in the nineteenth and early twentieth centuries will find this an especially useful reference work. [R: Choice, Nov 92, p. 442]—**Joseph W. Dauben**

1739. **The HarperCollins Dictionary of Mathematics.** By E. J. Borowski and J. M. Borwein. New York, HarperCollins, 1991. 659p. $25.00; $14.95pa. LC 90-55995. ISBN 0-06-271525-9; 0-06-461019-5pa.

The major objective of this work, as stated in the preface, is to provide a dictionary of mathematical terms for students of mathematics at all levels, from secondary school to master's degree, as well as a more general readership. It is intended to be complementary to authoritative textbooks. In-depth explanations and examples cover more than 4,000 entries and all the major subjects. More than 400 diagrams illustrate such concepts as four-color theorem, hyperbolic function, and correlation. Also included are biographies of major mathematicians with detailed descriptions of their contributions to the field. There are formal accounts of terms of elementary arithmetic and informal accounts of common logical paradoxes.

The authors have tried to include any term that an undergraduate might encounter, not only within any course but also in related reading, and they have tried to tailor the explanation of each term to the mathematical knowledge of the reader who is likely to look for it. They give some weight to the existence of the other HarperCollins dictionaries and cover little computing or economics, for example, but a considerable amount of logic. However, their prime consideration is the likelihood that a mathematics student will encounter a given term. This accounts for their inclusion of mechanics and statistics because of the prominence of these subjects in many undergraduate syllabi. This book covers a wide range of technical terms from both pure and applied mathematics, going beyond basic definitions to provide helpful explanations and examples for both students and professionals.—**Janet Mongan**

1740. Hopkins, Nigel J., John W. Mayne, and John R. Hudson. **The Numbers You Need.** Detroit, Gale, 1992. 349p. illus. index. $29.95. QA93.H65. 513'.0212. LC 92-4305. ISBN 0-8103-8373-X.

The major objective of this book, as stated clearly in the introduction, is to provide answers to a wide range of numerical questions encountered in everyday life. It is a practical handbook to the hundreds of formulas used at work, home, and play in many different areas, providing the tables, statistics, definitions, and examples that make everyday calculations more accessible. The book is arranged into chapters on common consumer money matters (e.g., cars, taxes); money decisions that are usually considered long term (e.g., investments, insurance); banking; health and fitness; weather and the environment; the numerical aspects of gambling, cards, and other games; understanding the statistics found in the sports pages of daily newspapers; the numbers needed for many activities around the home; and popular science calculations. In the three appendixes are some of the basic mathematical tools needed to solve common practical numerical problems, an expansion on units of measurement that come into most numerical problems, and financial mathematics. Laypeople are the work's intended audience, and the clarity of the writing and illustrations appear well suited to fulfill their needs for simple calculations. Recommended for the public library and the quick reference desk wherever such questions are likely to be asked. [R: LJ, July 92, p. 78; RBB, 1 Sept 92, p. 90] — **Janet Mongan**

1741. Liang, Diana F., comp. **Mathematical Journals: An Annotated Guide.** Metuchen, N.J., Scarecrow, 1992. 235p. index. $29.50. Z6653.L5. 016.51'05. LC 92-18459. ISBN 0-8108-2585-6.

The major objective of this work is to provide an annotated bibliography of English-language journals—including those printed in English but from non-English-speaking nations—in the field of mathematics. It assembles a group of approximately 350 active journals from thousands of titles currently in print. The purpose of this publication is threefold: to provide an overview of English-language publications in the field of mathematics, to provide mathematicians and other scientists with a choice of journals to use for reading or for the submission of manuscripts, and to raise librarians' awareness and assist them in selecting and evaluating their own collections. In addition to mathematical publications, statistical and mathematically related computer science journals are covered.

Titles are arranged alphabetically, with each entry having two parts. The first part provides bibliographic information for the title, and the second part is a descriptive annotation. The titles were selected through database searches, reviews of current publications, and titles covered in *Mathematical Review*. Other bibliographic tools, such as Ulrich's Plus and the databases of NOTIS (Northwestern Online Total Integrated System) and OCLC (Online Computer Library Center), were also consulted. Liang visited many large academic libraries and the Library of Congress to examine current issues and collect accurate and up-to-date bibliographic data. — **Janet Mongan**

36 Resource Sciences

ENERGY RESOURCES

Dictionaries and Encyclopedias

1742. **Chambers Nuclear Energy and Radiation Dictionary.** P. M. B. Walker, ed. New York, Chambers Kingfisher Graham, 1992. 260p. illus. $40.00. ISBN 0-550-13246-5.

It is difficult to think of a more controversial topic than nuclear energy. Its proponents claim, with some justice, that it may well yet be the only reliable power source to bridge the gap between the exhaustion of fossil fuels and the arrival (perhaps a half-century hence) of more sophisticated technologies. Its detractors cite the inordinate cost of nuclear power plants, their potential environmental risks, and the alarming accumulation of nuclear waste. Yet even environmentalists are divided: Are nuclear plants more damaging to the Earth's ecosystems than the greenhouse effect of fossil fuel combustion?

Rationality in these arguments is both vital and rare, and anyone concerned with this issue will welcome the appearance of this detailed and dispassionate dictionary, which also includes—in language accessible to the layperson—general discussions on a dozen specific nuclear topics (e.g., energy from both fission and fusion, nuclear safety, weapons, health and biological effects). Numerous helpful diagrams illustrate this part of the book, while the dictionary itself is comprehensive and includes references to the more general earlier discussions. The only significant omission is a bibliography of sources; all the more irritating as many useful works are cited in the text but not further identified. Otherwise, anyone interested in the nuclear debate will find this a most helpful addition to the bookshelf.—**James R. McDonald**

1743. **A Dictionary for the Petroleum Industry.** Austin, Tex., Petroleum Extension Service, Division of Continuing Education, University of Texas, 1991. 317p. illus. $24.95pa. TN865.D48. 665.5'03. LC 91-14265. ISBN 0-88698-152-2.

This new dictionary was prepared by the staff of the Petroleum Extension Service (PETEX) to familiarize new staff members with the terms used in the petroleum industry. Definitions of the 7,000 terms are succinct and easily understood. Illustrations supplement many of the definitions. Terms are in boldface type, and *see* references are in italics. Abbreviations are also defined in the dictionary section, while in the back of the book there is a shorter list of abbreviations of physical units that duplicates some of the abbreviations listed in the text. SI units (International System of Units), SI units for drilling, and metric equivalents are also given. The definitions selected reflect PETEX's extensive teaching experience in the petroleum industry. The definitions come from many sources, such as writers and editors, industry personnel, PETEX instructors and coordinators, and published works (e.g., other technical dictionaries). This is a very useful reference tool for the general reader as well as the petroleum professional.—**Anne C. Roess**

1744. **International Petroleum Encyclopedia.** Jim West, ed. Tulsa, Okla., PennWell Books, 1992. 358p. illus. maps. index. $115.00. LC 77-76966. ISBN 0-87814-376-9.

This 25th anniversary issue of a well-known reference book produced by the staff of the *Oil & Gas Journal* continues the tradition of quality coverage of global developments in the petroleum and natural gas industries. Featured in this edition is an article on events of the past 25 years (including a 25-year chronology of the petroleum industry), with a prediction for the next 25 years. The book continues with a chronology of events in 1991 and descriptions of developments in these industries for individual countries arranged by world regions—the IPE (*International Petroleum Encyclopedia*) atlas. Topic articles, which summarize main events or developments that occurred during the year, include Eastern Europe opportunities, the U.S. Clean Air Act, Kuwait recovery, the tanker industry outlook, and Texas petroleum history. Tables of data on reserves, production, prices, consumption, refining, and gas processing are the second main feature of the encyclopedia. The many detailed maps in the IPE atlas are quite useful. A subject index leads the reader to more specific items.

This encyclopedia continues to provide comprehensive coverage of the two industries and has had a long history of serving them well. It is an excellent way of obtaining an overall picture of new developments.—**Anne C. Roess**

Directories

1745. **U.S.A. Gulf Coast Oil & Gas Industry Directory, 1992.** Tulsa, Okla., PennWell Books, 1992. 409p. index. $65.00pa. ISSN 1056-795X.

This new directory covers the oil and gas industry in the states that border the Gulf Coast—Florida, Alabama, Louisiana, Mississippi, and Texas. Its arrangement follows that for other PennWell directories. Oil and gas companies are arranged by company types in sections that represent segments of the industry, then alphabetically within each state in each of the sections. Directory information includes company name; address, telephone, fax, telex, and cable information; a short company description; and a list of executives. Principal companies are in boldface type, while subsidiaries and branch offices are in smaller type when listed under the parent company.

The sections are broad and not well defined. They cannot be depended upon to include all companies of a certain type. For example, gas utilities are included in some of the sections but are not defined as a separate section. Alabama Gas Company is listed only in the drilling/exploration/production section as a subsidiary of Energen Corporation. Some pipeline companies are not listed in the pipeline operators section. United Texas Transmission Company is only listed as a subsidiary of Occidental Petroleum Corporation in the integrated section and by itself in the gas processor section. It appears that all subsidiaries, regardless of company types, are listed in the section that applies to the parent company, but not all the subsidiary companies are listed in their appropriate sections.

Entries are duplicated and not uniform in content, particularly for different section listings of the same company. Southern Natural Gas Company has three entries, two of which are in the same section on opposite pages and one in the section on pipeline operators. The information provided varies: one page has a full-page description of the company's operations along with a short list of executives, while the other has a complete list of executives and a short paragraph description. Arkansas Louisiana Gas Company is duplicated in the drilling/exploration/production section. Fortunately, the company index will lead the user to all entries for each company.

PennWell directories have long been useful reference tools for the oil and gas industry and will continue to be so. One hopes that PennWell will have more time to provide better quality control for their other directories.—**Anne C. Roess**

Handbooks and Yearbooks

1746. **Energy Balances of OECD Countries 1980-1989. Bilans Energetiques des Pays de L'OCDE.** Washington, D.C., OECD Publications and Information Center, 1991. 450p. $60.00pa. ISBN 92-64-03500-1.

This is a companion volume to the publisher's *Energy Statistics of OECD Countries* (1991). The compilations reflect data expressed in a common unit suitable for uses such as estimation of total energy supply, forecasting, and the study of substitution and conservation. The energy balance illustrates the basic supply-and-demand data for all fuels in a manner that shows the main fuels together but separately distinguished and expressed in a common physical unit. This arrangement allows for easy comparison of each fuel and its contribution to the economy, as well as interrelationships through the conversion of one fuel to another. The information is expressed in three-part tables. The work is recommended for libraries that collect such material.

– **John H. Hunter**

1747. **Energy Statistics of OECD Countries 1980-1989. Statistiques de l'Energie des Pays de l'OCDE.** Washington, D.C., OECD Publications and Information Center, 1991. 721p. $84.00pa. ISBN 92-64-03299-1.

This publication is a consolidation of data compiled from 4 annual questionnaires sent to 24 nations. (Thus, the information varies in comprehensiveness.) The data reflects energy supply and consumption in original units for coal, oil, gas and electricity; it covers the period 1980 to 1989. All of the information is reflected in tables that are divided into three parts: supply elements and total requirements; transformation and energy sectors; and final consumption, which breaks down into various end-use sectors. An additional category includes solid fuels such as peat, wood and wood paste, municipal, vegetal and industrial waste, and sulphite (a residual from the paper industry). This tool would be useful in an information center that supplies international analytical and policy material.

– **John H. Hunter**

1748. **Financial Times Oil and Gas International Year Book 1993.** Detroit, Gale, 1992. 504p. index. $150.00. ISBN 0-582-09276-0.

This well-known reference source has long been used by the oil and gas industry for company information. The 93d edition continues its coverage of the activities of the major oil and gas companies in the world (see ARBA 90, entry 1787 for a previous review). The number of main entry upstream companies (exploration and production) is 403, while the number of downstream companies (transportation, refining, storage, marketing, distribution, and slop disposal) is 425. The many subsidiaries of these companies are included in the narrative descriptions and can be located by means of company and geographical indexes. Production and financial data are provided (the most current year is 1991) as well as information on business activities.

As stated in the preface, the editor would be pleased to hear from companies and associations not now covered in this yearbook. One hopes that the user who knows of a company not located in this source will do likewise, as the quality of a reference source depends on the accuracy and completeness of its coverage. – **Anne C. Roess**

1749. **Nuclear Power Reactors in the World.** 1991 ed. Vienna, International Atomic Energy Agency; distr., Lanham, Md., UNIPUB, 1991. 67p. (Reference Data Series, no.2). $11.00pa. ISBN 92-0-159091-1.

This small booklet is crammed with 19 multipage tables and 5 single-page graphs. For the most part these tables and graphs report, as of December 30, 1990, the number of reactors on order, canceled, or shut down, and the 423 reactors (listed by reactor type) worldwide that are connected to the electrical grid. There are also tables and graphs that display the frequency and causes of reactor downtime, operating efficiency and output, construction time span, longevity, and the percentage of a nation's total electricity produced by nuclear power. However, by the International Atomic Energy Agency's own admission, the data are incomplete because the agency relies on voluntary processing of the questionnaires by member states. No doubt authors of future critical studies will quality the incomplete data. The work is of little value to any library.

– **Eric H. Christianson**

Indexes

1750. **Oil & Gas Journal Exploration Index.** By G. Alan Petzet. Tulsa, Okla., PennWell Books, 1992. 56p. $43.95pa. ISBN 0-87814-378-5.

This work indexes more than 2,500 exploration articles that were published in the weekly *Oil & Gas Journal* from 1960 through 1991. It is arranged in two sections: a geographic index and a general subject index. The geographic index deals with articles on the geology and the oil and gas potential of the 11 different geographic areas of the world. Under each of the areas the countries, provinces, or states are listed. The general subject index covers other exploration articles on topics such as computers, economics and finding costs, forecasts and statistics, and different methods and techniques (e.g., geophysical and geochemical methods, seismology, operations).

Articles are listed by title and provide authors under the geographic or subject terms, along with the journal issue date and starting page. Titles of the articles are arranged chronologically, starting from the most current journal issue to the earliest one so that the most recent information is listed first. The geographic index is supplemented with a straight alphabetical index that helps the reader locate offshore geographic areas that are indexed differently, such as the Mexican Gulf of Mexico, which is indexed under "Latin American, Mexico." An appendix lists methods for obtaining copies of these articles.

This is a very useful and convenient index for the retrieval of exploration articles from 32 years of the *Oil & Gas Journal*. It covers many exploration articles that are not included in the companion annual index to the journal. The reader has to depend on the wording of the titles for a more specific subject approach, but they are easy to read. — **Anne C. Roess**

ENVIRONMENTAL SCIENCE

Almanacs

1751. Maclachlan, Graham. **The Green Almanac.** Moffat, Scotland, Lochar Publishing; distr., Cincinnati, Ohio, Seven Hills Books, 1991. 144p. illus. $12.95. 333.7. ISBN 0-948403-72-1.

Intended for the general reader, this "global guide to environmental issues" provides a quick survey of about 85 topics of concern, most of them genuinely worldwide, although a few local issues have been included. Arranged in eight main categories (wildlife, energy, consumerism, animal welfare, world resources, water, disasters, the developing world), the entries include a note on geographic scope, a one- or two-page summary of the problem, suggestions on "what you can do," and a brief list of organizations concerned with the issue. Many entries also include a color photograph. A directory of organizations and a short bibliography are appended.

Reflecting the book's origin, there is an emphasis on Great Britain and some use of British terminology that may be unfamiliar to readers in the United States. Because so many topics are treated in so little space, no issue is analyzed in great depth; there is not much information here that will not be known to anyone who has been following environmental issues during the past decade. However, the treatment is balanced and reasonable and the suggested actions quite practicable, so libraries may find it useful (if perhaps also shocking) to have an international survey brought together in a single handbook.
— **Paul B. Cors**

Bibliography

1752. Sinclair, Patti K. **E for Environment: An Annotated Bibliography of Children's Books with Environmental Themes.** New Providence, N.J., R. R. Bowker, 1992. 292p. index. $39.95. Z0137.9.S57. 011.62. LC 91-39577. ISBN 0-8352-3028-7.

This timely monograph contains 517 titles with environmental themes that are targeted at children from preschool through age 14. Covering a wide variety of environmentally related topics, such as ecology, pollution, and recycling, Sinclair has done an admirable task of selecting some of the best treatments to date for inclusion in this work. The entries cover 1982 through mid-1991. They are arranged alphabetically by author within five sections. Each entry has author's name; title; other contributors, such as editor or illustrator; publisher; date of publication; number of pages (or unpaged); ISBN; library binding; whether out of print; series titles, if any; fiction or nonfiction indicator; interest or age level; and an annotation. Two special features are awards for notable children's trade books in the field of social studies and outstanding science trade books for children. For further reading, Sinclair has listed a number of titles that are considered environmental classics. The volume concludes with author, title, and subject indexes. The inclusion of prices with the titles would have been a big plus. The binding is sturdy, and the print is easy to read. For the price, this work will be very useful to any library with a children's collection and will also serve as a good resource guide for collection development. [R: Choice, Sept 92, p. 92; RBB, 15 May 92, pp. 1714-15; SLJ, Aug 92, p. 91; VOYA, Dec 92, p. 317; WLB, June 92, p. 110] – **John H. Hunter**

Dictionaries and Encyclopedias

1753. **The HarperCollins Dictionary of Environmental Science.** By Gareth Jones and others. New York, HarperPerennial/HarperCollins, 1992. 453p. illus. maps. $13.00pa. LC 91-55392. ISBN 0-06-461040-3.

Environmental science is a rather ambiguous field. It covers a multitude of disciplines in order to study how people and their environment interact. Of course, with a field so broad, there is always a need to define terms within the context of the field. *The HarperCollins Dictionary of Environmental Science* is a useful desktop aid for those in need of explanations.

Geared toward college-age students, the dictionary covers four major areas of study: the physical world, the biological world, the built environment, and the agro-economic infrastructure. The authors have done a good job of coverage, with more than 2,000 entries included. The definitions are thorough, giving complete explanations of the terms.

The study of environmental science cuts across political boundaries. The authors have tried to minimize problems caused by international variations in interpretations and, where possible, to place each term within an international context. There is, however, a U.S./U.K. slant to the entries. Some terms, such as *shopping mall*, relate to a single country (in this case, the United States; the nearest equivalent in Great Britain is the hypermarket). Environmental agencies such as the EPA and Friends of the Earth are listed with a description of their purpose. Also, major environmental legislation (e.g., the Clean Air Act) is listed. Both the organizations and the legislation tend to be either United States, United Kingdom, or European Community. This, however, does not limit the usefulness of the book.

A few diagrams and charts are included, but not to a great extent. For its size, this dictionary should prove to be a good place to look for a quick answer. [R: Choice, June 92, p. 1520]

– **Angela Marie Thor**

1754. Winter, Ruth. **A Consumer's Dictionary of Household, Yard and Office Chemicals.** New York, Crown, 1992. 329p. $12.00pa. RA770.5.W56. 615.9. LC 91-33189. ISBN 0-517-58722-X.

A companion volume to Winter's *A Consumer's Dictionary of Food Additives* (see ARBA 85, entry 1351) and *A Consumer's Dictionary of Cosmetic Ingredients* (see ARBA 85, entry 1682), this title covers chemicals found in such common products as building materials, fabrics, paper, cleaning materials, paints and varnishes, fertilizers, pesticides, fuel, and lubricants. Except for pesticides, regulated by the Environmental Protection Agency, the products are only loosely (if at all) controlled by the U.S. Consumer Product and Safety Commission, which has little real power and relies largely on voluntary cooperation from manufacturers. (Labels are only required to name "hazardous" ingredients, with the determination of what qualifies as hazardous left to industry.) Winter is objective, not an alarmist, but she does point out problems that most consumers are not likely to be aware of.

Following an introductory chapter that discusses general concerns and gives instructions on how to use the book, the alphabetically arranged entries include name, synonyms, a brief description of the chemical and its uses, information about possible harmful effects (including symptoms of poisoning, but not first aid), and references to related entries. In some cases less dangerous alternatives for toxic substances are recommended. Directories of organizations concerned with environmental health, of

regional EPA offices, and of regional poison control centers are appended. There is a brief bibliography. There is no index, but the extensive cross-references in the text provide an adequate substitute. Intended primarily for home use, this work is also suitable for public libraries. [R: LJ, July 92, p. 79]
– Paul B. Cors

Directories

1755. **Environmental Industries Marketplace: A Guide to U.S. Companies Providing Environmental Regulatory Compliance Products and Services.** Karin Napoleon Meech, ed. Detroit, Gale, 1992. 779p. $175.00. ISBN 0-8103-8569-4. ISSN 1061-2122.

This directory is intended for those who need information on complying with state and federal environmental regulations. More than 10,000 firms that provide services, expertise, or products are included. Arrangement is alphabetical with subject and geographical (state and city) indexes. Main entries are brief, including address and telephone numbers, products, branch offices, and a description of the business. The latter descriptions are short and often very general; for example, many entries simply say "Provides services to the environmental industry." The numerous subject index categories include asbestos, hazardous waste, recycling, site assessment, and transportation/storage.

The problem with this work is that access via the indexes is inconvenient, partly due to the large number of entries. The subject index is composed of long lists of company names (no locations) and a reference number to the main alphabetical list. The user has no basis from which to choose the most appropriate entries. The geographical index is somewhat more useful. It is arranged alphabetically by city within each state, but the user must browse each entry to determine the area of expertise. This work would be immensely improved if the two indexes were cross-referenced. The subject index needs to include geographic locations, and the geographic index needs to be arranged by subject within each state and need not repeat the contact information of the main entries. This would greatly increase ease of access and permit the user to search for expertise or service within a specific location (e.g., environmental consultants in New Mexico). As it stands, use of this directory is quite difficult unless one already knows a firm's name. [R: Choice, Nov 92, pp. 440-42; LJ, 1 Sept 92, p. 166; RBB, 1 Nov 92, p. 546] – T. McKimmie

1756. **Environmental Telephone Directory 1992-1993.** By the Editorial Staff of Government Institutes. Rockville, Md., Government Institutes, 1991. 235p. maps. $59.00pa. LC 88-652053. ISBN 0-86587-278-3.

This rich and convenient directory gives one the ability to rapidly get in touch with the right person for the right information about critically important regulations, environmental laws, policies, and court decisions. The contents include an introduction and five sections: U.S. senators/representatives/environmental aids; U.S. Senate and House committees and subcommittees; the U.S. Environmental Protection Agency (EPA); other federal executive, legislative, and independent agencies; and state environmental agencies. The first section contains 538 addresses and telephone numbers for the people responsible for making environmental decisions. The second section provides the meeting times of about 500 professional staff members of federal institutions. In the EPA section there are two subdirectories: the first gives the organizational breakdown with names and titles (almost 750 entries), and the second contains a map of 10 EPA regions and a complete list of names and titles for each of the regions (a total of 522 entries). Section 4 provides information on the federal and independent institutions outside of the EPA. The fifth section gives each state's organizational structure for handling environmental matters. Several handy general information numbers are included here: state locator; legislative reference; and emergency response commissions, state radon contacts, and underground storage tank notification agencies. This directory is highly recommended for libraries, scientists in both environmental and nonenvironmental fields, and anyone responsible for making environmental decisions (not only in the United States but also in Canada and other countries). – **Ludmila N. Ilyina**

1757. **EPA Headquarters Telephone Directory.** 1991 ed. Rockville, Md., Government Institutes, 1991. 365p. $21.00pa. ISBN 0-86587-896-X.

The publishers of this directory state that it is of interest to people outside the EPA, be they in other branches of the federal government, business, or the public sector. The Washington Interagency Tele-communications System changed most of the EPA telephone numbers in the Washington, D.C., area in August 1991. Conversion of FTS (Federal Telecommunications System) and DDD (Direct Distance Dialing) telephone numbers are provided because the publishers realize that many users outside the federal government will need direct-dial numbers. Mailing addresses, some E-mail addresses, and hours of operation are also included. Organizational, alphabetical, headquarters subject, regional, and hotline directories provide access to everything from individual employee numbers to the various divisions within the EPA.

A wealth of information is included in this directory, which would be of interest to many users if other sources did not exist. Since the format needs improvement and the type is hard to read in some areas, other directories available from the Government Printing Office (GPO) would be more useful. Most of the information in this directory is available from the GPO in their own *EPA Headquarters Telephone Directory* and the new, well-done *Access EPA.* — **Diane J. Turner**

1758. **The Indoor Air Quality Directory 1992-1993.** Bethesda, Md., IAQ, 1992. 362p. index. $75.00pa. ISBN 0-9633003-1-8. ISSN 1062-0621.

Indoor air is now recognized as an important environmental factor related to human health. Homes, schools, public buildings, and offices and other work places are at risk. Common pollutants include formaldehyde, asbestos, tobacco smoke, radon, and microorganisms. Research in this area is expanding, and Congress is considering an indoor air quality act.

This directory is the first comprehensive work of its kind. It covers hundreds of organizations that are involved with various aspects of indoor air quality, such as detection of contaminants, remediation, product manufacture, research, and training. The introduction adequately explains the scope of indoor air quality problems, testing, and abatement procedures. The first three sections provide information about firms dealing in air quality service (e.g., contractors, laboratories), support services (e.g., consultants, attorneys), and product manufacture and distribution. Entries include address, key personnel, number of employees, affiliations, types of service, products, expertise, and contaminants evaluated. The two service firm sections contain much overlapping information and should be combined. This would also improve access to entries, as only the first service section has a geographic index. A useful publications section lists hundreds of periodicals, monographs, and reports, as well as telephone hotline numbers. This is more than a business directory and lists state and federal agencies as well as professional and special interest associations. The latter include public health associations, environmental organizations, legal institutions, and engineering societies. A glossary is supplied. This directory will be a valuable addition to a reference collection. [R: RBB, 1 Oct 92, p. 369] — **T. McKimmie**

1759. Lanier-Graham, Susan D. **The Nature Directory: A Guide to Environmental Organizations.** New York, Walker, 1991. 190p. index. $22.95; $12.95pa. TD169.L36. 363.7'0025'7. LC 91-6649. ISBN 0-8027-1151-0; 0-8027-7348-6pa.

As the environmental movement in the United States continues to expand in both magnitude and diversity, reference guides to the proliferation of such subjects as toxic chemicals, legal decisions, and (in this case) relevant organizations become ever more necessary if appropriate materials are to be gathered and intelligent decisions made. This book, which presents detailed information on 120 American environmental groups (non-U.S. organizations are not specifically considered, although many entries concern those with international dimensions), is a welcome contribution to this literature.

The format is clear and consistent, containing for each group the address and contact person, history and goals, past achievements, ongoing projects, future plans, and membership/volunteer information. In a field not known for dispassionate assessments, coverage here is happily evenhanded; inclusions range from conservative (e.g., National Wildlife Federation) to radical (e.g., Earth First!), from mainstream (e.g., National Audubon Society) to fringe (e.g., Center for Holistic Resource Management), and they are generally free of value judgments. A brief introductory chapter that summarizes the nature of environmental problems and organizational strategies is useful, as are the few pages on methods of personal involvement. A solid bibliography (arranged by subject matter) and a basic index complete the book.

Unfortunately, entries are arranged in strictly alphabetical order, which makes it difficult—even using the index—to identify groups concerned with specific issues (e.g., birds, energy, water quality). A detailed cross-referencing system would make this a much more useful work. Nonetheless, its jargon-free style and practical data should ensure its popularity with an environmentally concerned general audience. [R: Choice, Mar 92, p. 1050]—**James R. McDonald**

1760. Levine, Michael. **The Environmental Address Book: How to Reach the Environment's Greatest Champions and Worst Offenders.** New York, Perigee/Putnam, 1991. 252p. $14.95pa. TD169.6.L48. 363.7'0025. LC 91-10985. ISBN 0-399-51660-3.

One person can make a difference. That is the premise behind *The Environmental Address Book*: providing addresses of companies and individuals so users can tell them what they are doing wrong—or doing right. For the most part the addresses listed here are easily found in other publications. Listings are accessible only by broad subject chapter headings (e.g., air, water); there is no index. Nor are there written criteria for why these particular listings were chosen, so one can only assume it was by Levine's whim. This leads to omissions and inconsistencies. For example, under the heading "Education," a few schools that offer graduate degrees in environmental science are listed; but why include Yale and not Rutgers? Under the heading "Air," automobile manufacturers are listed, and the absence of Toyota is accentuated by the inclusion of Honda and Mazda. The most subjective chapter is "Bad Guys/Good Guys." This small (50 entries) chapter lists those businesses that Levine feels fit into either or both of these categories. Bumble Bee Seafood is listed as a "bad/good guy" due to their old dolphin-harming fishing practices and their new commitment to dolphin-safe practices. Yet Starkist Seafood Company is just a good guy because they were the first to switch to the new methods, their former habits apparently forgiven. There are probably addresses that might not show up in standard reference sources, and some users might enjoy the "Media and Celebrities" section. However, this hodgepodge of information is best left alone.—**Angela Marie Thor**

1761. Lilienthal, Nancy, Michele Ascione, and Adam Flint. **Tackling Toxics in Everyday Products: A Directory of Organizations.** New York, INFORM, 1992. 179p. $19.95pa. RA770.L55. 615.9'02'06073. LC 91-29961. ISBN 0-918780-56-X.

Toxic chemicals are a matter of growing concern in the lives of Americans across the nation. From Love Canal onward, more and more people have come to know the risks on all too personal a basis. Yet much misunderstanding and uncertainty remains. This work is an attempt to familiarize the average person with toxic chemicals they are likely to encounter in products used as a part of everyday life. The work consists of two distinct sections. The first has seven short chapters that give an overview of the problem, while the second, the heart of the book, lists organizations involved in monitoring, controlling, or otherwise overseeing toxic chemicals and their risks. It is the latter section of the work that will be of the greatest use, for it gives average citizens precisely the sort of information they need to take action. This work belongs on the shelves of libraries serving the general public across the nation. [R: Choice, Oct 92, pp. 275-76]—**James A. Casada**

1762. **U.S.A. Oil Industry's Environmental Directory, 1993.** Tulsa, Okla., PennWell Books, 1992. 795p. index. $165.00pa. ISBN 1062-0605.

This directory is very timely and one of the more significant additions to PennWell's growing list of publications. It provides a fairly wide array of information for those involved in the environmental industry, containing lists of companies who provide products or services of an environmental nature. A well-defined table of contents lists broad sections by company name with domestic and international subdivisions. Within the domestic category, companies are listed alphabetically by name, and in the international section, alphabetically by country, with a further subdivision by company name. (The international subcategory is not listed in the table of contents.) Each company name contains address, communications information, key company officials, year of establishment, type of company, services or products provided, parent company, and branch or sales offices listings (if available). For ease of use, the next broad category is a cross-reference list of companies by products and services. The last two major sections include governmental agencies involved with environmental protection and an alphabetical list of petroleum companies. Included in this list are addresses, communication information, and key executives responsible for handling environmental issues. It is disappointing to see Oregon listed as the lone state governmental agency with this kind of responsibility. Finally, a company index is provided. Although this work may be somewhat expensive for many libraries, it is recommended to larger public libraries and those academic libraries that have strong environmental science and technology emphases. — **John H. Hunter**

1763. **Who Is Who at the Earth Summit, Rio de Janeiro, 1992.** Tucson, Ariz., Terra Christa Communications and Waynesville, N.C., VisionLink Education Foundation, 1992. 481p. illus. $30.00pa. ISBN 0-9628405-3-X.

In 1992, the United Nations Conference on Environment and Development, commonly called the Earth Summit, brought together in Rio De Janeiro more than 30,000 participants to discuss the future of our planet. The meeting of 100-plus heads of state and more than 1,400 nongovernmental organizations represented an unprecedented gathering of those who are concerned with the need to balance economic development against environmental costs. Thus, the roster of those who attended the conference is a unique directory of environmental leaders and policy-makers throughout the world.

The book is well organized, making the information easily accessible. The main register, by country, includes not only names and addresses but also some telephone and fax numbers. Alphabetical cross-indexing by individual names and organizations provides more resources for accessing the main list.

This document is a worthwhile resource for those who wish to conduct research involving the international environmental movement. Even though normal turnover may soon make the list of individual names outdated, this book will continue to be useful for some time as a source of addresses.

— **Harry E. Pence**

Handbooks and Yearbooks

1764. Darnay, Arsen J., comp. and ed. **Statistical Record of the Environment.** Detroit, Gale, 1992. 855p. index. $89.50. TD180.D37. 363.73'00973'021. LC 91-30214. ISBN 0-8103-8374-8.

This statistical book draws an impressive picture of the American and global environment. The book is divided into 10 chapters: the media—land, air, and water; pollutants and wastes; effects of pollution; costs, budgets, and expenditures; tools and solutions; the pollution control industry; general industry and government data; environmental facts at the community level; laws and regulations; and politics and opinions. Each chapter is subdivided into topics, and within each topic, 851 tables, maps, graphs, and diagrams are sorted alphabetically by title. The special section, "Guide to the Subject Matter," presents a brief introduction and explanation to chapters and topics, as well as to some tables and graphics. Every figure has a complete citation to the original source. Data for all figures were drawn from reports and articles of national and state government publications and databases, and from periodical literature. More than 200 sources were consulted; approximately 150 were used. All are presented in three appendixes with sufficient information to allow the reader to contact primary sources directly. Many abbreviations and acronyms are collected in appendix 4. All subjects, companies, institutions, agencies, and geographical entities are presented in appendix 5, the keyword index. These are followed by tables and page numbers, and cross-references are provided. *Statistical Record of the Environment* allows readers to find specific information quickly and efficiently. The market for such a book is wide: from libraries to individuals, from journalists to scientists, and from Americans to foreign specialists. [R: Choice, May 92, p. 1364; LJ, 1 May 92, p. 76; RBB, 1 Mar 92, p. 1308; RQ, Summer 92, p. 580; WLB, Mar 92, pp. 118-19] — **Ludmila N. Ilyina**

1765. **Earth Journal, 1992: Environmental Almanac and Resource Directory.** By the editors of *Buzzworm* magazine. Boulder, Colo., Buzzworm Books; distr., Emeryville, Calif., Publishers Group West, 1991. 447p. illus. maps. index. $7.95pa. ISBN 0-9603722-9-6. ISSN 1059-6488.

Usually reference books are not the sort that one just wants to read. However, almanacs often fall into this category. They frequently have snippets of information that make the reader stop and say "Wow! I didn't know that." The editors of *Buzzworm* magazine have produced an environmental almanac so that those in the "emerging ecoculture of the '90s" can have something to "Wow!" over.

As with all almanacs, a lot of information is packed into this book. On the bottom of each page is a question and its answer for those who like to pursue politically correct trivia. The diary section chronologically covers events from October 1990 through September 1991, giving a brief description of each event and expanding on those topics that seemed to crop up continually during the year (e.g., famine). There is a list of the 10 best and 10 worst "envirostories" of the year and indications of who received various green awards. The section called "Earth Issues" provides a who, what, where, and why for various big issues (e.g., global warming, air pollution), written by individuals well known in each area (e.g., Cleveland Amory on animal rights). There is also a regional breakdown of the world with reports on the environmental situation as influenced by the local economy and politics.

The most entertaining part of the volume is the cultural/lifestyle information. There are lists of green businesses; ecotravel; books, movies, and music with an environmental theme; and religious groups that have an environmental slant. Green products are listed along with resources for more information on these subjects. Also included are directory listings of environmental organizations for those that want to become more involved. The only problem with this work lies in the index, which lacks enough subheadings. Listing 47 page ranges under the heading "Agriculture" is not very helpful. Other than that, *Earth Journal* is a useful almanac to keep by the reference desk. [R: Choice, July/Aug 92, p. 1653; RBB, 15 Apr 92, p. 1549] – **Angela Marie Thor**

1766.   **Environment Abstracts Annual 1991. Volume 21.** New Providence, N.J., R. R. Bowker, 1992. 1694p. index. $495.00. ISBN 0-8352-3150-X. ISSN 0000-1198.

There is more in this hefty, comprehensive collection of abstracts for the 1991 primary literature on the environment than the title suggests. A 69-page introductory section gives for 1991 an environment chronology, a review of U.S. congressional actions, a review of hazardous site remediation, directories of agencies and conferences, and an article for librarians about information management on environmental topics. The abstracts, which average about 100 words, fill 500 pages, and the rest of the volume is taken up by comprehensive indexes to key terms, subjects, industries, authors, and sources.

This is a valuable guide to the environmental literature, and R. R. Bowker offers fulltext service for many of the abstracted articles. Its contents are also accessible by other means, including monthly updated online services and quarterly CD-ROMs. – **Harold Goldwhite**

1767.   **Environment on File.** By the Diagram Group. New York, Facts on File, 1991. 1v. (various paging). illus. maps. index. $145.00 looseleaf with binder. QH541.15.M64E58. 333.7'022'3. LC 91-27522. ISBN 0-8160-2695-5.

This publication represents an unusual type of resource for teachers and others who deal with environmental issues. It has more than 250 pages of environmental illustrations for lecture presentations, examinations, or personal use. Many of the drawings consist of several component figures, so the actual number of usable illustrations is greater than 250. The diagrams are very clear and are well chosen to represent a broad view of the topics.

The figures are grouped into seven sections based on major environmental topics, such as population; agriculture; energy; and pollution of the soil, air, and water. Each section includes an introductory summary of the problem, the plates, and a brief outline of possible solutions. The drawings are on heavy paper with reinforced margins, and the identifying labels can be easily omitted for examinations. The publisher provides unlimited permission to photocopy this material for nonprofit, educational, or private use but specifically prohibits any storage or reproduction by electronic retrieval systems. Those who are looking for a collection of environmental illustrations will find this thoughtfully designed set of figures will provide maximum utility. [R: Choice, June 92, p. 1518; RBB, 15 Apr 92, pp. 1549-50]
– **Harry E. Pence**

1768.   **Gale Environmental Sourcebook: A Guide to Organizations, Agencies, and Publications.** Karen Hill and Annette Piccirelli, eds. Detroit, Gale, 1992. 688p. index. $75.00. ISBN 0-8103-8403-5. ISSN 1059-0919.

This sourcebook is solidly packed with information on 8,634 directory entries, conveniently arranged into 25 sections and 6 chapters. Part 1, "Descriptive Listings," comprises 70 percent of the volume and provides "live" and print information on 25 environmental topics of current high interest. It reflects modern trends, from natural resources to radon and sustainable agriculture. (They could be selected and arranged more logically.) There are international, federal, governmental, independent, commercial, nonprofit, published, and videotaped sources of environmental information. All entries are cross-referenced, and full names and addresses of organizations or agencies, telephone numbers, contact names, and a brief summary of essential activities are provided. Part 2 presents a list of titles of sources in alphabetical and subject orders. Part 3 is diverse. The glossary contains more than 250 terms and phrases that are also arranged alphabetically. The appendixes include 2 lists of endangered flora and fauna (as of July 1991) and 3 lists of 1,189 toxic cleanup sites in the United States (as of February 1991).

This work can be recommended not only for all public and scientific libraries but also for various research and educational institutions, engineering and business agencies, common and private associations, and others that are interested in the most reliable and up-to-date environmental information. [R: BR, Sept/Oct 92, p. 59; Choice, June 92, p. 1520; LJ, 1 June 92, pp. 110-12; RBB, 15 Apr 92, pp. 1550-51; WLB, Apr 92, p. 124] — **Ludmila N. Ilyina**

1769. Harte, John, and others. **Toxics A to Z: A Guide to Everyday Pollution Hazards.** Berkeley, Calif., University of California Press, 1991. 479p. index. $75.00; $20.00pa. RA1213.T76. 615.9. LC 90-25860. ISBN 0-520-07223-5; 0-520-07224-3pa.

There is a high level of public concern about the effects of exposure to toxic substances, but most of the books on this subject are either written for a technical reader or else display a strong bias. Therefore, a book such as this, which accurately discusses the problem in terms that are understandable to the lay public, is especially welcome.

The presentation is excellent. The first half of the book covers the general background needed to understand the topic, and the second half lists specific information about more than 100 commonly encountered toxicants. The writing is clear and accurate, although a reader with no previous scientific training may find some sections to be rather difficult. A main theme is how individuals can make small changes in their everyday lives that will decrease the risk of exposure. In general, the authors have been careful to represent the spectrum of positions on controversial topics. This may not win them friends from either extreme, but it does give the reader a more realistic picture of the situation. The book also includes a good index, an extensive glossary, and suggestions for further reading.

This valuable and timely book deals constructively with a complex and controversial topic at a level that is accessible to the general public. Recommended. [R: Choice, Mar 92, p. 1058; LJ, 15 Apr 92]
— **Harry E. Pence**

1770. Miller, E. Willard, and Ruby M. Miller. **Environmental Hazards: Toxic Waste and Hazardous Material: A Reference Handbook.** Santa Barbara, Calif., ABC-Clio, 1991. 286p. index. (Contemporary World Issues). $39.50. TD1030.M56. 363.72'87. LC 91-14545. ISBN 0-87436-596-1.

If the amount of federal legislation dealing with a topic is any measure, hazardous materials are a high public priority. The reason for this may be extensive media coverage of places such as Love Canal and Bhopal, or the fact that cancer is a major health risk often related to this problem. Whatever the cause, the issue seems to contribute to the environmental anxiety of many communities. This handbook is intended to be a reference source for those who wish to learn more about toxic materials.

The book consists of two major sections. The first is a brief history of the attempts to deal with hazardous chemical problems, focusing mainly on legislation and regulations. Despite the controversial subject, the authors' approach is reasonably well balanced. The intended audience is not identified, but the absence of chemical formulas and mathematics suggests the work would be appropriate for those without much technical background.

The second section offers a variety of options for finding further information, including a bibliography of selected books, articles, and government documents; brief summaries of major U.S. laws on this subject; names of some pertinent agencies and private organizations; and a selection of films and videotapes. The listing will be useful to those interested in this topic.

There are some oversights. Toxicity is often mentioned but never given a systematic treatment. A brief discussion of how toxicity is measured and a clarification that under the proper conditions *any* chemical can be toxic would be quite helpful. Federal and state right-to-know laws are neglected in the

text (although included in the bibliography), even though this legislation is responsible for some of the most useful sources of chemical information, such as material safety data sheets (MSDS). This book could serve as a good starting place for readers who wish to explore this topic, especially if their main interest is legislative. [R: BR, Sept/Oct 92, p. 60; Choice, June 92, p. 1524; RQ, Summer 92, p. 570]
— **Harry E. Pence**

1771. Montgomery, John H. **Groundwater Chemicals Field Guide.** Chelsea, Mich., Lewis, 1991. 271p. index. $45.00pa. RA591.5.M66. 363.73'94. LC 91-23632. ISBN 0-87371-554-3.

This work has a great deal of information on organic chemicals found in groundwater. The entries (more than 400) are arranged alphabetically by the name commonly used by the U.S. Environmental Protection Agency. Synonyms are given but are not cross-referenced in an index. There is, however, an index arranged by CAS (Chemical Abstract Service) registry number, thereby providing a second access point. Department of Transportation (DOT) and Registry of Toxic Effects of Chemical Substances (RTECS) numbers are also included. Physical and chemical properties listed in entries include boiling point, melting point, appearance and odor, solubility, density, dissociation constant, transformation products, flash point, and explosive limits. Health hazard information includes exposure limits and symptoms. Common usages for compounds are also given. The introduction provides a good description of the properties included and the derivations of various constants. The accompanying references are useful for finding further information on regulations. A bibliography provides hundreds of additional references, but they are not referenced in the text, and their arrangement by author instead of subject makes them essentially useless. [R: Choice, Apr 92, p. 1211]—**T. McKimmie**

1772. Pankratz, Tom. **Dictionary of Water and Wastewater Treatment Trademarks and Brand Names.** Chelsea, Mich., Lewis, 1991. 139p. $39.95. LC 91-31219. ISBN 0-87371-673-6.

Growth of the water treatment industry has resulted from an expanding population and the accompanying laws and regulations designed to provide clean water supplies. This dictionary presents more than 1,200 trademark and brand names of products used in the industry. Entries include brief descriptions of the product's use and the name of the manufacturer. The second half of the book consists of a directory of manufacturers. Available products and contact information are listed. This work will be useful for those in the business of treating water.—**T. McKimmie**

1773. Trzyna, Thaddeus C., and Roberta Childers, eds. **World Directory of Environmental Organizations: A Handbook of National and International Organizations and Programs....** 4th ed. Sacramento, Calif., in cooperation with the Sierra Club and IUCN, the World Conservation Union by California Institute of Public Affairs, 1992. 231p. index. (Who's Doing What Series, no.2). $45.00pa. LC 75-38124. ISBN 0-912102-97-7.

This directory describes governmental and nongovernmental organizations in all parts of the world that deal with the environment and natural resources. The 4th edition has been revised to include more than 2,600 organizations in 200-plus countries. Entries consist of organization profiles, providing addresses and telephone, telex, cable, and fax numbers where available.

The book is arranged into seven parts, thereby enabling the user to search by topic of interest, world region, and type of organization. "Who's Doing What: Problems, Resources and Biomes" in part 2 will be especially useful for seeking organizations concerned with any of 50 specific environmental issues, such as quality, forests and forestry, and wetlands. Other listings include the U.N. system, other intergovernmental organizations, international nongovernmental organizations, and a country and area listing. Organizations involved with related disciplines appear because environmental problems overlap other fields of endeavor. The book contains an appendix on directories and databases that list organizations concerned with the environment to direct users to further information sources. Finally, a general selective index lists all international organizations but only selected national organizations. The selection process is unclear and appears to be random. For instance, the Wilderness Society is included, but the older and larger National Audubon Society is not.

The index is the only weakness in this otherwise complete work. *World Directory* should be part of every library's reference collection.—**Michael G. Messina**

1774. Wasik, John F. **The Green Company Resource Guide: A Reference for Any Organization Facing Environmental Concerns.** Wauconda, Ill., New Consumer Institute, 1992. 183p. $49.95pa. ISBN 0-9632532-1-2.

Many companies are working to develop environmentally sound business practices, and many consumers wish to support these efforts. Unfortunately, state and federal regulations are far more likely to specify what should not be done rather than to identify the positive steps that would be most beneficial for the environment. This book is intended as a resource for both companies and consumers who are looking for a more constructive approach.

Wasik has gathered together a great deal of information that is not otherwise readily available or that may be scattered in a variety of sources. This ranges from directory listings, such as the addresses of groups that offer guidance on environmental policies, to brief essays on such relevant topics as descriptions of good (and bad) environmental marketing plans implemented by U.S. companies, summaries of marketing surveys that measured consumer preferences in this area, and explanations of the meaning of commonly used marketing terms.

Anyone interested in environmental policy issues should enjoy browsing through this book. Its major shortcoming, however, is in a crucial area for a reference source: it is difficult to locate specific information. There is no index, and the table of contents is not always enough to guide the reader to an item of interest. It is regrettable that this oversight detracts from what is otherwise a book that deals with topics of considerable interest to many readers. [R: LJ, 1 May 92, p. 74; RBB, July 92, p. 1960]
– **Harry E. Pence**

1775. **Who Is Who in Service to the Earth: People, Projects, Organizations, Key Words.** Hans J. Keller and Daniel Maziarz, eds. Waynesville, N.C., VisionLink, 1991. 524p. $19.95pa. ISBN 0-9628405-1-3.

This is an unusual book. Part 1 consists of a set of "41 Visions of a Positive Future." The writers of these essays do indeed take a positive view, although they express alarm about what humans have done, are doing, and appear to be continuing to do to the environment. There seems to be no regular arrangement of these essays, but a detailed table of contents provides adequate access. The writers are all included in part 2, which provides directories of people, projects, and organizations, as well as a list of key words. The criterion for the inclusion of people is that their "sincere and effective efforts in Service to the Earth make them worth knowing." The list introduces environmentalists and others, both the well known and the obscure, from all over the world. There are no full biographies, just each person's name, address, organization, and projects. The next section lists organizations with a contact person (who appears in the list of individuals, along with the organization's address) and a statement of purpose. The projects section is arranged alphabetically, again requiring the user to look up the contact person in the people list for access to information on organization and address. The keyword section serves as an index. Six order forms and four forms for data on individuals, organizations, and projects not included in the volume are appended. The price of the book is a pleasant surprise. Recommended for any library that wants a positive treatment of the Earth's environment and future. [R: Choice, Mar 92, p. 1050] – **Edward P. Miller**

1776. **World Resources 1992-93.** By the World Resources Institute, the United Nations Environment Programme, and the United Nations Development Programme. New York, Oxford University Press, 1992. 385p. illus. maps. index. $17.95pa. LC 86-659504. ISBN 0-19-506231-0. ISSN 0887-0403.

The focus of this volume is sustainable development, a pressingly important concept, and its susceptibility to the growth of populations and economies. The importance of human resources and the relationship of human welfare to the sustainable development equation is explored. Complicating factors such as the differences in priorities of wealthy and poor nations are analyzed. Particularly important is the in-depth discussion of national and global policies and institutional frameworks. Policy formulation, motivation, and alternative strategies for both citizen and governmental organizations are examined. The difficult issues of resource pricing and access, economics, and incentives for change are well presented. There are chapters on water, energy, population, climate and atmosphere, food, and natural resources (e.g., forests, wildlife). These sections present up-to-date background information, numerical data, and hundreds of references. For example, one can learn which countries participate in global environmental conventions, or which are in debt for nature swaps.

This work will be used both for ready-reference and as an aid for delineation of environmental issues. Recommended for all academic and public libraries.—**T. McKimmie**

Quotation Books

1777. Rodes, Barbara K., and Rice Odell, comps. **A Dictionary of Environmental Quotations.** New York, Simon & Schuster Academic Reference, 1992. 335p. index. $35.00. PN6084.N2D53. 333.7. LC 92-3055. ISBN 0-13-210576-4.

Reflecting a vast range of human interest in the environment, this book of quotations has appeared at an opportune time. Containing more than 3,700 quotations on environmental issues and covering 143 categories from acid rain to zoos, this dictionary will be useful to teachers, speech writers, students, politicians, and anyone else concerned about the world. The quotations provide provocative, witty, and intellectual comments from ancient philosophers, presidents, poets, and even bumper stickers.

In each category the quotations are arranged in chronological order, which provides the user a history of environmental thought over the years. The author and subject indexes refer to quotations by category number and the number of the quotation within that category. These indexes, along with the table of contents, allow easy access to a quotation in a certain subject area or by a specific person. The interesting content and clear format make this source a valuable addition to any public or academic library. [R: Choice, Dec 92, p. 600; LJ, 15 June 92, p. 72; RBB, 15 Nov 92, p. 626; WLB, Oct 92, p. 106]—**Diane J. Turner**

37 Transportation

GENERAL WORKS

1778. Barnett, Le Roy, comp. **Shipping Literature of the Great Lakes: A Catalog of Company Publications 1852-1990.** East Lansing, Mich., Michigan State University Press, 1992. 165p. index. $24.95. Z7164.S55B37. 016.386'5'0977. ISBN 0-87013-317-9.

This reference book contains 3,000-plus entries to sources found in more than 150 libraries. Entries are listed by shipping companies (each with an abbreviated history), and they concern ships, timetables, and other promotional matter. The information has been compacted for maximum informational value, and much of it is found only in single copies in libraries, which Barnett carefully indicates. Additional information provides statistics on places of publication of the cited items, maps, and interesting historical statistics on passengers by ports and by carrier, on freight shipped by ports, on kinds of commodities, and on ships that have plied the Great Lakes. A bibliography and an index close the book. The potential users of this source include historians, librarians, business scholars, book dealers, maritime enthusiasts, travel specialists, and collectors. Recommended especially to regional transportation specialists.—**Bogdan Mieczkowski**

AIR

1779. Blaugher, Michael A. **Guide to: 475 Aircraft Museums, 224 City-Displayed Aircraft, 37 Restaurants with Aircraft, 6 WWI Landmarks.** 10th ed. Fort Wayne, Ind., Michael A. Blaugher, [1992]. 1v. (various paging). $7.00pa. (Publisher's address: 124 E. Foster Pkwy, Fort Wayne, IN 46808-1730).

Aviation history buffs are aware of the high attrition rate of old and obsolete models of aircraft. Except for old photographs and occasional copies of partial blueprints, a serious collector or researcher has a slim chance of a hands-on experience with a classic aircraft. Those few that are left are scattered in museums, some city displays, a few aviation clubs, and (surprisingly) a few restaurants. This self-published guide lists 742 locations in the United States and Canada where one or more aircraft are on display. For research, its biggest value is its index to the location of individual aircraft by model type. Reproductions are noted when known. There are undoubtedly a lot of aircraft parts that will never be listed, but this work is probably the best (and only) guide available for documenting these antiques.
—**Robert J. Havlik**

1780. **Jane's All the World's Aircraft 1992-93.** Mark Lambert, Kenneth Munson, and Michael J. H. Taylor, eds. Alexandria, Va., Jane's Information Group, 1992. 749p. illus. index. $225.00. ISBN 0-7106-0987-6.

"All the world's aircraft" seems a grandiose claim, but this standard reference, in its 83d year, with 749 large illustrated pages, comes very close to a literal justification for its name. It is also authoritative, containing, for example, the most complete description of the F117 Stealth fighter/bomber that this reviewer has ever seen. In addition to civil and military fixed-wing and helicopter aircraft, sections are provided for sailplanes, private aircraft (including kit planes), microlights ("ultra light"), lighter-than-air craft, and engines. The description usually includes a photograph, a three-view drawing, and specifications. The amount of additional discussion depends in a general way on the importance of the aircraft. For example, Boeing's 767 transport occupies the better part of three pages; the yet-to-fly 777, a page; and a one-man company that offers plans for three aircraft, a short paragraph. A complete index and glossary are included. – **Robert B. McKee**

GROUND

1781. Edmonston, Phil. **Lemon-Aid New Car Guide 1992.** Toronto, Stoddart Publishing, 1992. 374p. illus. $15.95pa. 629.2'222'05. ISBN 0-7737-5462-8. ISSN 0714-5861.

This guide provides a comprehensive look at buying a new car in Canada. Effective directions and warning strategies are outlined, along with summary ratings of quality across category type. The heart of the book is the analysis of each 1992 car and minivan, with an overall rating for every model (amplified by a general discussion with recommended alternative buys), detailed discussions of reliability/safety, road performance, and comfort/convenience, all topped off with statistical/pricing data.

The text is written in clear, hard-punching prose that unflinchingly exposes the weaknesses of each car examined (including manufacturer's after-sales reputation, secret warranties, and legal precedents for consumers). Two notable advantages distinguish this book. Written for the Canadian buying public, it takes careful note of distinctive regulatory and environmental conditions peculiar to this country; and Edmonston's evaluative biases are plain, so those with different criteria can make allowance for this. Prospective buyers will also value the two- through five-year residual cost (depreciation) data provided for the models examined.

The major drawback to the book lies in the fact that while detailed evaluations are divided into "pro" and "con" sections, confusion results from including negative comments in the former and positive comments in the latter. Moreover, the statistical tables have no performance data. Otherwise, beyond a few spelling errors, the only other drawback is the lack of any index or analytic table of contents, which makes it impossible to find a specific car model quickly.

Any library that deals with automotive matters will value the way this book fills a specific consumer need. Featuring clear printing and average pictures printed on good quality paper in a sturdy perfect binding, the volume should stand up to the heavy use it will undoubtedly receive.
– **John Howard Oxley**

1782. Edmonston, Phil. **Lemon-Aid Used Car Guide 1992.** Toronto, Stoddart Publishing, 1992. 294p. illus. $15.95pa. 629.2'222'05. ISBN 0-7737-6463-6. ISSN 0714-587X.

This guide provides the facts about buying a used vehicle in Canada. The reader receives detailed instructions on used car buying tactics, together with an extensive section on relevant Canadian legal aspects. The evaluative section of the book covers selected major car and minivan models from 1983 through 1990 (giving a summary recommendation in each case), backing these judgments with reasons and pertinent servicing data. The text clearly specifies the strengths and drawbacks of each car examined (including extensive detail on secret warranties).

This book's particular value is its Canadian content that carefully notes this country's specific conditions. As well, buyers have their bargaining positions strengthened by the inclusion of suggested costs for each year covered, with inspection pointers to ensure the model discussed is in good shape. The major drawback to this volume is the limited selection of vehicles included. While most low-cost names appear, such brands as Mercedes, Porsche, and Jaguar are omitted entirely, and only the lower end of the BMW spectrum is evaluated. Furthermore, the lack of an index or analytic table of contents makes rapid information access difficult, and some of the technical illustrations are poorly positioned or captioned. Despite these flaws, this ready-reference source will be useful in any library that deals with automotive matters. – **John Howard Oxley**

1783. Mallet, Catherine M., and Linda S. Rothbart. **Trucksource 1992: Sources of Trucking Industry Information.** Alexandria, Va., American Trucking Associations, 1991. 247p. index. $30.00pa. ISBN 0-88711-138-6.

This volume is a reliable guide to sources on every conceivable area of interest to people connected with or interested in the U.S. trucking industry. A section headed "Trucking Fundamentals" includes lists of bibliographies, databases, dictionaries, directories, magazines, and statistical sources. "Trucking Business" has 28 topical headings, from accounting/finance through drug testing and insurance to warehousing. The final sections are "Trucking and the Law," "Contacts" (e.g., associations, manufacturers, government agencies), and a detailed index. All directory entries have brief annotations, and the index is admirably wide spaced, with "contacts" in boldface type. This work is specialized but likely to be useful in transportation and business collections. [R: Choice, Sept 92, p. 84] – **Walter C. Allen**

1784. **New Car Buying Guide.** 1992-93 ed. By the editors of Consumer Reports Books with Bill Hartford. Yonkers, N.Y., Consumer Reports Books, 1992. 156p. illus. index. $8.95pa. ISBN 0-89043-547-2.

Consumer Reports is the standard source for unbiased, factual information on household purchasing throughout North America. The volume under review encapsulates the Consumer Union's expertise to assist anyone wishing to buy a new car. The reader is instructed in how to shop for a car as well as what to look for and look out for in the case of a specific vehicle. Also, the price spreads and reliability data provided improve one's negotiating chances when closing the deal.

In addition to covering the new car buying process, the work clearly and concisely deals with important supplemental information such as child safety and theftproofing. But the heart of the book is the section of summary judgments of 1992 cars. These allow the prospective purchaser to gain a clear impression of a particular model's important aspects without ever setting foot in it, radically simplifying effective comparison of numerous alternatives. The assessments are crisply explained in no-nonsense language (and seem to correspond well with the actual facts), greatly assisting in making a final shortlist. There are only minor problems in the presentation. Some cars are not covered fully (*see* references to sister models are used instead), the small photographs are sometimes rather oddly cropped, and the interpretation key for the frequency-of-repair records is misprinted (although easily understood by reference to the same symbols used elsewhere in the book).

While the book is well printed, the paper quality is not particularly high, and the perfect binding is unlikely to stand up to the heavy use it will undoubtedly receive. Nevertheless, the value of the contents and the inclusion of an index make this volume an effective ready-reference tool for any library that serves potential automobile buyers. – **John Howard Oxley**

1785. **Statistics of Road Traffic Accidents in Europe 1991: Volume XXXVI.** New York, United Nations; distr., Lanham, Md., UNIPUB, 1991. 89p. $25.00pa. ISBN 92-1-016261-7. ISSN 0497-9575. S/N E/F/R.91.II.E.16.

Reviewed previously (see ARBA 90, entry 1813), this volume has updated figures. The current year's figures principally represent statistics for 1988 and 1989. Certain characteristics, as usual for this publication, are documented in five-year intervals back to 1955. As noted in an earlier review, certain countries remain undocumented; there is still no data for Albania, Andorra, Holy See (Vatican City), Liechtenstein, Monaco, or San Marino. However, the former Soviet Union lists statistics for Byelorussia and Ukraine along with the Soviet Union totals. Once again, the United States is included for comparative purposes. The general arrangement remains the same. Presented in English, French, and Russian, the volume has two sections: accidents and casualties, and background statistics that include type of vehicles, vehicle kilometers run, and population estimates. The work remains an accurate and authoritative source of information on the subject for all libraries (and a thought-provoking document in general). – **Gregory Curtis**

1786. **Used Car Buying Guide.** 1992-93 ed. By the editors of Consumer Reports Books with Alex Markovich. Yonkers, N.Y., Consumer Reports Books, 1992. 253p. index. $8.95pa. LC 86-70586. ISSN 1042-9476.

This is the 8th edition of this guide, which has recently become an annual. It is a pity that the editors at *Consumer Reports* have not quite come to grips with the fact that styling plays the dominant role in the choice of cars for most people. If this book has the tiniest flaw, it is that styling is not mentioned. Still—and this is to the editors' credit—most other auto attributes, good and not so good, are given their full due. While not every make and model is reported on, nearly every buyer will find the guide useful, if only to learn what to avoid, as in the section on "Good and Bad Bets in Used Cars" for 1986-1990 models.

There is a decided air of objectivity about the book. This is a function of the brisk, businesslike writing style in *Consumer Reports*, from which many of these reports have been taken. There are highly detailed comparison tests for the model years 1989, 1990, and 1991 (usually involving four similar cars that had been purchased new before testing). In addition, this vade mecum offers the always useful, survey-based "Frequency-of-Repair Records, 1986-1991." Less useful charts show mechanical specifications and body dimensions for 1991 cars only.—**Randall Rafferty**

1787. **The Visual Dictionary of Cars.** New York, Dorling Kindersley; distr., Boston, Houghton Mifflin, 1992. 64p. illus. index. (Eyewitness Visual Dictionaries). $14.95. TL206.E84. 629.222'03. LC 91-58205. ISBN 1-56458-007-5.

With superb photographs and artwork taking precedence over a smattering of text, this dictionary is for the visually and mechanically oriented person who finds it bothersome to deal with a book that has more words than pictures. The editors at Dorling Kindersley explain their purpose this way: "a picture will always explain a subject more clearly than words." But can a picture, even one enhanced by high-resolution color printing, go all the way around an object, show all its sides? No, and it is here that words should come into play. This dictionary adopts the approach of the car repair manual. There is not much expansiveness—just the illustration and its label. But the illustrations and photographs are outstanding, even beautiful to behold (if a cutaway view of a diesel engine, for example, can be a delight to the eyes).

The Visual Dictionary of Cars can be useful in the reference department in at least two ways: if one knows what a car part looks like and wants to know what it is called, or if one knows a part's name and wishes to see its likeness. In the first case, the double truck spread is consulted, as it displays the many systems of an ordinary car: engine, ignition, transmission, and so on. In the second case, the index is used. It goes into such details as "door-hinge pillar," "semi-elliptic leaf spring," and "throttle butterfly," to name a few among hundreds. Not all cars are displayed here—that would result in needless duplication. The cars that appear are shown whole and in exploded or cutaway views.

The editors claim that they are presenting a book for all ages of readers. However, it will appeal in the main to youngsters and to people whose interest in the subject is just awakening. [R: SBF, Aug/Sept 92, p. 180; SLJ, Sept 92, p. 288]—**Randall Rafferty**

WATER

1788. Delgado, James P., and J. Candace Clifford. **Great American Ships.** Washington, D.C., Preservation Press, 1991. 311p. illus. index. (Great American Places Series). $19.95pa. VM23.D45. 387.2'0973. LC 91-16933. ISBN 0-89133-189-1.

This is a catalog of more than 225 vessels that have been preserved and are open to the public in the 50 states. Written by the executive director of the Vancouver Maritime Museum (Delgado) and the staff photographer and manager of the "computerized inventory of maritime resources" for the U.S. National Park Service (Clifford), the volume is an excellent guidebook for the traveler and the maritime history enthusiast. Ships covered include Confederate gunboats, submarines, battleships of World War I and World War II, private yachts, Mississippi riverboats, tugs, lightships, eighteenth- and nineteenth-century sailing vessels, and small fishing crafts. The well-illustrated volume is arranged in geographic regions (e.g., Great Lakes, New England) and then by state, with vessels listed alphabetically under the places they are berthed. Brief histories are given for each ship, together with details on the current state (or lack) of restoration on the vessel. The foreword to the book is written by Edward M. Kennedy. Supplemental chapters include "Lost Ship and Losing Battles" (a chronicle of our lost maritime heritage); vessels in the National Register of Historic Places, further reading (a very nice bibliography of

American maritime history and conservation); information sources (a list of maritime organizations and agencies that will supply the reader with more information); and an index.

This is an excellent volume. Patrons with a general interest in the United States as well as travelers and maritime specialists will glean much about the U.S. maritime history from a close examination of it. Young adult readers will find the illustrations and text of interest. Highly recommended for all libraries. – **Ralph Lee Scott**

1789. Goetzfridt, Nicholas J., comp. **Indigenous Navigation and Voyaging in the Pacific: A Reference Guide.** Westport, Conn., Greenwood Press, 1992. 294p. index. (Bibliographies and Indexes in Anthropology, no.6). $55.00. GN440.I53. 623.89'099. LC 91-34621. ISBN 0-313-27739-7.

This volume fills a gap in the maritime history of the Pacific. Western historians have long stressed the importance of the European explorers, but only recently has attention turned to the early navigators of the vast reaches of the Pacific Ocean. Goetzfridt's book covers journal articles and monographs on both early and recent voyagers of the Pacific. The volume begins with a general Pacific voyage section and then divides into specific voyaging sections in island chains such as Polynesia, Micronesia, and Melanesia. Indexing is by the authors of the work cited, subjects, and named places. The exceptionally well-written annotations are among the best this reviewer has ever seen.

Maritime history libraries and most general history collections will want to add this valuable work to their holdings. It is hoped that some of the works cited can be incorporated into the corpus of our historical knowledge on the college level, thereby introducing general students of civilizations to the vast societies of the Western Pacific. This book is well worth its cost. [R: Choice, July/Aug 92, p. 1655] – **Ralph Lee Scott**

1790. **Maritime Affairs: A World Handbook: A Reference Guide for Modern Ocean Policy and Management.** 2d ed. Compiled by the Oceans Institute of Canada. Harlow, England, Longman Group; distr., Detroit, Gale, 1991. 479p. index. $165.00. ISBN 0-582-08693-0.

Last reviewed in ARBA 87 (see entry 1747), the current edition updates and expands the coverage provided in the earlier one. Seven chapters and an appendix are new, with several of the chapters in the earlier work having been revised and divided into two. The intent of the present publication remains the same as before: to be a multipurpose sourcebook that has statistics, abstracts, bibliographies, a directory, a history, and legal information on oceans and maritime matters.

The coverage of law of the sea has been greatly expanded, with several chapters and an appendix – "Law of the Sea Lexicon" – devoted to the subject. In fact, it is noted in the introduction that this is one of the prime reasons for the new edition. Other areas that receive expanded coverage are ocean usage and marine environment protection. Also, this edition now includes contributors' names and credentials, which is helpful to the understanding of certain chapters.

The index is adequate in referencing specific agreements or disputes. The general subject entries are a bit weak, however. For instance, a reference to the Indian Ocean appears without any further division. The detailed table of contents provides excellent coverage of chapter information and thus mitigates some of the weaknesses of the index.

As with the first edition, this one gives information in a nonpolitical format without judgments as to the use of this natural resource. For this the compilers deserve praise. Despite the work's rather high price, academic, law, and large public libraries will find it a useful volume to add to their shelves. [R: Choice, July/Aug 92, p. 1659] – **Gregory Curtis**

1791. Neill, Peter, and Barbara Ehrenwald Krohn, eds. **Great Maritime Museums of the World.** New York, Harry Abrams, 1991. 304p. illus. maps. index. $60.00. V13.A1074. 387'.0074. LC 91-10432. ISBN 0-8109-3362-4.

This splendid volume, lavishly illustrated with outstanding color photographs, is an up-to-date look at 24 of the world's major maritime museums. The directors or curators tell what is special about their museums and provide each institution's history, focus, and future. Neill is president of the South Street Seaport Museum and has contributed the chapter on his museum as well as a thoughtful introduction. Some of these major museums have only been established recently; for example, Sydney's Australian National Maritime Museum opened in 1988, and Yokohama's Maritime Museum opened in 1989. Six United States museums are presented along with museums in Australia, Canada, Denmark, France, Germany, Japan, the Netherlands, Norway, Portugal, Spain, Sweden, and the United Kingdom. Scholars will appreciate the fact that research libraries and facilities are part of these museum complexes. The signatures are sewn, but the binding boards seem to be a bit light for this large-format, glossy paper volume. [R: LJ, 1 Mar 92, p. 82] – **Frank J. Anderson**

1792. **Visual Dictionary of Ships and Sailing.** New York, Dorling Kindersley; distr., Boston, Houghton Mifflin, 1991. 64p. illus. index. (Eyewitness Visual Dictionaries). $14.95. LC 91-060900. ISBN 1-879431-20-3.

This graphic dictionary presents information on ships and sailing, both historical and contemporary. However, it ranges far beyond a basic identification of parts. Instead, encompassed in this slim work are such topics as humankind's earliest navigational efforts; the development of different ship structures and how that development reflected the culture, circumstances, and civilization from whence it came; and special topics such as fishing boats and fighting at sea (with cutaway models of a gun turret and a Royal Navy "hunter-killer" submarine).

The materials fall into three groups. The first entries focus on the history and development of ships and sailing (e.g., the first boats, the expansion of sailing [eighteenth century], paddle wheels and propellers). The next group of entries focuses on attributes of contemporary boats and ships: rigging, sails, navigation, charts and piloting tools, flags, signals, mooring and anchoring, ropes and knots, and more. The last group explores such special topics as battleships and "under the sea" items (e.g., scuba and diving gear). An index of all terms identified concludes the dictionary.

Each two-page entry focuses on a single theme, such as the anatomy of a wooden ship. Within that theme are presented exquisite photographs of scale models (or, occasionally, beautifully rendered and detailed illustrations) for which nearly every visible part is identified. Cutaways and "exploded" sections are used frequently. Each entry is accompanied by a brief narrative that describes the items presented and explains why those items are important and how they fit into the general context of the history and development of ships and sailing.

Although the detailed and comprehensive nature of the material included in *Ships and Sailing* gives new meaning to the phrase "information overload," the book is a joy to peruse. Its graphic depictions are breathtaking in their clarity and beauty, and its narrative is informative and engaging. The work will be appropriate for library patrons of any age group, because children will be drawn to its entrancing pictures and adults to its detailed, highly specialized information (as well as its gorgeous graphics). It will also be useful in any academic setting that supports nautical studies. [R: BR, May/June 92, p. 60; RBB, 1 Feb 92, p. 1059; WLB, Jan 92, p. 132] – **G. Kim Dority**

Author/Title Index

Reference is to entry number.

AACJC membership dir 1992, 359
AACR2 decisions & rule interpretations, 5th ed, 639
AARP Pharmacy Serv prescription drug hndbk, 2d ed, 1660
ABCs of worship, 1423
Abortion: a ref hndbk, 851
Abortion & family planning bibliog for 1989-90, 850
Aboussafy, David, 852
Abraham, Thomas, 1310
Academic American ency, 57
Academic Press dict of sci & tech, 1444
Academic yr abroad, 392
Acadiensis index, 1971-91, 526
Accardi, Bernard, 1301
ACCC dir of Canadian colleges & insts, 362
Access to UK higher educ, 380
Ackelson, Richard W., 1265
Acronyms, initialisms & abbrevs dict 1992, v.1, 1
Ada lang vocabulary, 1677
Adamec, Christine, 866
Adamec, Ludwig W., 121
Adams, Raymond J., Jr., 1539
Address bk for Germanic genealogy, 4th ed, 454
Adey, Robert, 1150
Adler, Larry, 830
Adoption choices, 869
Adoption lit for children & young adults, 868
Advances in librarianship, v.15, 627
Adventuring in B.C., 503
Afghanistan, 122
African American biogs, 423
African music, 1241
AFVA evaluations 1991, 395
Agriculture dict, 1468
AIDS: abstracts of the psychological and behavioral lit 1983-91, 3d ed, 1650
AIDS funding, 1653
AIIM speakers dir 1992-93, 1668
Aiki News ency of aikido, 838
Albala, Leila, 227
Alberta bibliog, 135
Alcorn, Marianne Sidorski, 596
Alderton, David, 1536
Aldiss, Margaret, 1154
Alexander, Fran, 680
Alexander, Robert J., 777
Algeo, Adele S., 1064
Algeo, John, 1064
Ali, Sheikh R., 781
Alkin, Marvin C., 331
Alkire, Leland G., Jr., 86
Allaby, Michael, 1529
Allen, Thomas B., 556
Allis, James B., 1393

Allswang, John M., 793
Almanac of ...
 American presidents from 1789 to the present, 519
 Canadian pols, 764
 higher educ 1992, 355
 the Bible, 1435
 the Christian world, 1415
 the 50 states, 1992 ed, 909
Altbach, Philip G., 381
Ambry, Margaret, 906
America & the Indochina wars, 1945-90, 733
American artists' materials, v.2, 1027
American Banker's banking factbk 1991, 236
American bk publishing record cum 1991, 26
American dir of organized labor, 306
American drama criticism, suppl.3 to the 2d ed, 1168
American drama 1918-60, 1380
American educators' ency, 330
American electricians' hndbk, 12th ed, 1587
American export register 1992, 318
American Heritage dict, 2d college ed, 1055
American Heritage dict of the English lang, 3d ed, 1056
American Horticultural Society, 1487
American humanities index for 1991, v.27, 945
American intelligence, 1775-1990, 785
American Jewish yr bk 1992, 439
American lib dir 1992-93, 623
American literary biographers, 2d series, 50
American literary mags, 1163
American men & women of sci 1992-93, 1438
American military cemeteries, 706
American musical theatre: a chronicle, 2d ed, 1385
American nursing, v.2, 1659
American originals, 54
American peace movement, 791
American poets since WW II, 3d series, 1186
American pol prints 1766-1876, 735
American theatre hist, 1381
American univs & colleges, 14th ed, 363
American wholesalers & distrs dir, 245
American Wind Symphony commissioning project, 1284
American women & the US armed forces, 707
American women playwrights, 1900-30, 1167
America's new fndns 1992, 870
Ammann, Daniel, 1067
Ammon, Bette D., 1140
Amphibians & reptiles of the W Indies, 1579
Anabolic steroids & sports, 1666
Anarchist thinkers & thought, 778
Anastas, Walter, 980
Anastazievsky, Walter, 981
Ancestry's red bk, rev ed, 455

Anderson, James D., 1187
Anderson, James M., 506
Anderson, John R., 1650
Anderson, Patricia J., 689
Andrews, Jean, 1522
Ang mahalaga sa buhay, 1102
Angelo, Joseph A., Jr., 805
Animals around the world, 1530
Anne Baxter: a bio-bibliog, 1318
Annotated bibliog of aboriginal-controlled justice programs in Canada, 569
Annotated bibliog of faculty status in lib & info sci, 634
Annotated critical bibliog of Joseph Conrad, 1207
Annotated index of medieval women, 933
Annotated list of Ont. lepidoptera, 1550
Annual bibliog of modern art, 1990, 1015
Annual register 1991, 725
Annual review of info sci & tech, v.26, 628
Anthropology in use, 417
Antonarrakis, Stylianos E., 1624
Antonin Dvorak on records, 1262
APA membership register, 1991, 802
Applied sci & tech index, 1457
Apresjan, Yuri D., 1092
Archaeology hndbk, 507
Archambault, Ariane, 1101
Ardagh, John, 143
Arden, Lynie, 308
Arestis, Philip, 177
Argentina, 152
Argyle, Christopher, 551
Arizona legal research gd, 596
Armenian genocide, 530
Armitage, Susan, 941
Armstrong, Robert D., 678
Armstrong, Robert H., 1528
Army dict & desk ref, 717
Arnold, Tim, 1523
Aronoff, Craig E., 178
Art & architecture thesaurus, suppl.1, 635
Art index, 1030
Art on screen, 1016
Artists of the page, 1022
Ascione, Michele, 1761
Ash, Irene, 1709, 1710
Ash, Michael, 1709, 1710
Asian Americans info dir, 421
Asimov, Isaac, 549
Asimov's chronology of the world, 549
ASM hndbk, v.18, 1604
ASM International Handbook Committee, 1604
Assistance & benefits info dir, 887
Association for Library Service to Children, 1128
Associations Canada 1992, 65
Associations yellow bk, v.2, no.1, 319
Astronomer's sourcebk, 1701
Astronomy & astrophysics ency, 1704
Atherton, Derek P., 1674
Athey, Raymond, 1494
Atlas of ...
   breeding birds of Mich., 1539
   medieval Jewish hist, 440
   Nfld. & Lab., 473
   quails, 1536

   S America, 484
   world affairs, 9th ed, 720
A-to-Z of women's sexuality, rev ed, 884
Aubrey, James R., 1208
Audubon Society ency of N American birds, 1537
Auger, C. P., 587
Augustine's De Civitate Dei: an annot bibliog of modern criticism, 1960-90, 1416
Australian pers in print 1991, 81
Australian ref dict, 131
Author profile collection, 1138
AV market place 1992, 991
Avallone, Susan, 1368
Avalos, Francisco A., 563
Awards almanac 1992, 871
Awards, honors, & prizes, 9th ed, 66
Axelrod, Herbert R., 1553, 1554
Axtell, B. L., 1464
A-Z gd to tracing ancestors in Britain, 4th ed, 461
A-Z of sailing terms, 842
Azevedo, Mario, 116

B&T link module 2, world ed, 27
Back Stage theater gd, 1389
Backhaus, Balbir, 1520
Backus, Karen, 421, 1632
Badler, Mitchell M., 1693
Baer, Beverly, 1145
Baer, E. Kristina, 1046
Bailey, Frankie Y., 1151
Bair, Frank E., 1722
Baker, Daniel B., 730
Baker, Jennifer, 738
Baker, Paul, 1268
Baker's biographical dict of musicians, 8th ed, 1244
Balay, Robert, 12
Balder, A. P., 466
Balderston, Daniel, 1225
Ball field gd to diseases of greenhouse ornamentals, 1499
Balski, Grzegorz, 1348
Baltsan, Hayim, 1087
Balz, Horst, 1426
Barbara Pym: a ref gd, 1209
Bariaud, Pierre, 1725
Barker, Keith, 7
Barker-Benfield, G. J., 932
Barlow, Diane, 917
Barnes, Dorothy L., 620
Barnett, Le Roy, 1778
Barr, Catherine, 629
Barranger, Milly S., 1315
Barrett, Thomas M., 1487
Barron's best buys in college educ, 2d ed, 364
Barron's Educational Series, College Division, 365
Barron's profiles of American colleges, 19th ed, 365
Barron's top 50, 366
Barth, Else M., 1392
Bartlett, John, 89
Bartlette, Reginald J., 1292
Baseball file, 825
Baseball in the movies, 1351
Baseball nicknames, 826
Baskin, Rosemary, 1481

Bassett, John E., 1173
Bates, G. W., 1524
Battenfeld, Robert L., 1179
Battle, Ed, 1053
Battle of Jutland, 693
Battles of Coral Sea & Midway, 1942, 695
Bauer, Hans, 1117
Bavishi, Vinod B., 263
Baxter, Angus, 456
Baxter, Pam M., 804
BBC World Service, 542
BBC World Service Gulf Crisis chronology, 542
Beaty, Wayne, 1590
Beauregard, Estelle, 905
Becker, Charlotte B., 1395
Becker, Lawrence C., 1395
Beentje, Henk, 1516
Behrens, David W., 1573
Behzad, Marion S., 863
Beinart, Haim, 440
Beirne, Piers, 602
Bejermi, John, 763
Bell, Albert A., Jr., 1393
Bell, Peter R., 1498
Bellinger, Peter, 1561
Bencini, Marina Carcea, 1478
Beniukh, Ksana, 1094
Beniukh, Oleg, 1094
Bennett, George John, 146
Bennett, James R., 951
Bennett, Joy, 1177
Bennett, Pramila Ramgulam, 146
Benson, K. Blair, 1588
Benson, Morton, 463
Bentley, William K., 603
Benyuch, Oleg, 1082
Bergano's register of intl importers 1992/93, 256
Berger, James L., 396
Berger, Sidney E., 690
Berle, Gustav, 200
Berleant-Schiller, Riva, 156
Berman, Barbara L., 949
Bernard Shaw: a gd to research, 1216
Berner, Mark S., 1661
Bernstein, Jake, 201
Bessette, Peg, 822
Best doctors in America 1992-93, 1644
Best in children's bks, 1134
Best of Bkfinder, 1123
Best rated CDs 1992: jazz, popular, etc., 1275
Best ref bks 1986-90, 8
Bhatnagar, K. P., 1723
Bhattacharya, S. K., 1723
Bible & modern literary criticism, 1432
Bibliographic gd to Middle Eastern studies 1990, 159
Bibliography, 1988-90, 1482
Bibliography of ...
    American lit, v.9, 1162
    Bali, 123
    law & economics, 564
    salon criticism in Paris from the ancien regime to the Restoration, 1699-1827, 1018
    salon criticism in Paris from the July Monarchy to the Second Republic, 1831-51, 1019
    seniors & the family research 1980-91, 852
    Sun Yat-sen in China's Republican Revolution, 1885-1925, 521
Bibliography on temples of the ancient Near East & Mediterranean world, 1402
Bickers, Kenneth N., 745
Bidd, Donald W., 1342
Big gay bk, 886
Big Powers & the German question, 1941-90, 538
Biggins, Alan, 152
Billboard top 1000 singles 1955-90, 1282
Billboard's hottest hot 100 hits, 1276
Billips, Connie, 1316
Biographical dict of ...
    American sports, 1989-92 suppl, 817
    dissenting economists, 177
    Indians of the Americas, 430
    life peers, 462
    mathematicians, 1736
    the board of governors of the Fed Reserve, 240
    the Middle East, 161
Biographical index to children's & young adult authors & illustrators, 1144
Biographies of scientists for sci-tech libs, 1440
Biography index, 34
Biography index: Sept 1990-Aug 1991, 33
Biography today, v.1, issue 1, 35
Biological & agricultural index, 1458
Birds alternative names, 1544
Birds in jeopardy, 1541
Birds in Kans., v.2, 1546
Birds of Japan, 1538
Birds of the Blue Ridge Mountains, 1545
Birkenhead, Frederick Edwin Smith, Earl of, 604
Birkhead, Tim, 1540
Bishop, Arthur, 697
Bishop, Cynthia, 1462
Biskupic, Joan, 588
Bissell, Christopher, 1451
Bitter, Gary G., 1678
Bixler, Frances, 1184
Bjorling, Joel, 806
Bjorner, Susan N., 975
Black American women in Olympic track & field, 843
Black artist in America, 1033
Black arts annual 1989/90, 1026
Black authors & illustrators of children's bks, 2d ed, 1139
Black bk publishers in the US, 679
Black lit criticism, 1115
Black resource gd, 10th ed, 422
Black scientists, 1443
Blackburn, Graham, 1610
Black's medical dict, 37th ed, 1629
Black's vet dict, 17th ed, 1490
Blackwell companion to the enlightenment, 555
Blackwell dict of cognitive psychology, 798
Blades, Joe, 1334
Blank, Jacob, 1162
Blatherwick, Francis John, 36
Blaugher, Michael, 1779
Bleaney, C. H., 166
Blessing, Patrick J., 437
Bloomsbury gd to women's lit, 942
Blouin, Glen, 1515
Blumberg, Herbert H., 789

BNA Library Staff, 582
BNA's dir of state & fed courts, judges, & clerks, 4th ed, 582
Bogle, Donald, 1026
Bohlander, Richard E., 486
Bojnansky, V., 1495
Bollig, Laura E., 827, 831
Bolton, H. Philip, 1210
Bongard, David L., 698
Book of ...
  European forecasts, 282
  forest & thicket, 1518
  women, 935
Book Report & Library Talk dir of sources, 666
Book review digest, 76
Booklist's gd to the yr's best bks, 1992 ed, 9
Bookpeople: a multicultural album, 1142
Books & articles on S.C. hist, 2d ed, 510
Books & mags: a gd to publishing & bkselling courses in the US, 681
Books & pers online, 1992 ed, 187
Books & plays in films 1896-1915, 1344
Books in print 1991-92, 29
Books in print plus with bk reviews plus, 28
Books of the fairs, 1306
Boone, Louis E., 218
Borden murders, 605
Bordman, Gerald, 1385
Borgatta, Edgar F., 847
Borne, Pierre, 1674
Boross, P. A., 1482
Borowski, E. J., 1739
Borwein, J. M., 1739
Bosnich, Victor W., 746
Boswellian studies, 3d ed, 1231
Boswell's literary art, 1232
Boswick, Storm, 382
Boucher, Wayne I., 1394
Bouckaert, Boudewijn, 564
Boultbee, Paul G., 157
Bourke, D. O'D, 1465
Bousquet, Yves, 1560
Bowers, Q. David, 1002
Bowker annual lib & bk trade almanac, 37th ed, 629
Bowker's complete video dir 1992, 989
Bowker's law bks & serials in print 1991, 565
Boyd, Andrew, 720
Bradley, Fern Marshall, 1489
Bradnock, Robert, 502
Bradnock, Roma, 502
Brands & their cos 1992, 188
Brannan, Deborah, 585
Brawer, Moshe, 484
Brazil in ref bks, 1965-89, 153
Brazil, Mark A., 1538
Breaking down the walls, 568
Brelin, Christa, 373
Brennan, Richard P., 1445
Brennan, Shawn, 235
Brewer, Annie M., 990
Brewer, Donald E., 990
Brewer, Richard, 1539
Brewer's dict of 20th-century phrase & fable, 1294
Brickman, William W., 383
Briggs, Asa, 38

Bright, William, 1050
Brimble, Raymond J., 267
Brisco, Paula, 1633
British electorate, 1963-87, 772
British English for American readers, 1068
British literary publishing houses, 1881-1965, 689
British Romantic novelists, 1789-1832, 1196
British Romantic prose writers, 1789-1832, 2d series, 1193
British sci fiction, 1204
British writers, suppl.2, 1191
British/American lang dict, 1069
Broadcasting & cable market place 1992, 992
Broadhead, Susan H., 112
Broderick, Mick, 1349
Bromley, Debra J., 1388
Bronson, Fred, 1276
Brooke, Michael, 1540
Brooklin Public Library Business Library Staff, 202
Brosse, Jacques, 1403
Brown, Anthony E., 1231
Brown, Denis, 1285
Brown, Jonathan, 1270
Brown, Kenneth O., 1398
Brown, Les, 986
Brown, Linda, 333
Brown, Muriel W., 1120
Brown Publishing Network, 346, 347
Browne, Edward T., Jr., 1494
Browne, Steven E., 1345
Brown's dir of instructional programs, 1992: K-8, 346
Brown's dir of instructional programs, 1992: 7-12, 347
Brundle, C. Richard, 1605
Brune, Lester H., 733
Bruntjen, Scott, 32
Bryan, George B., 1317
Bryant, Brian R., 333
Bryson, Bill, 968
Buck, Claire, 942
Bulfinch pocket dict of art terms, 3d ed, 1023
Bullough, Vern L., 882, 1659
Bunch, Bryan, 1455
Burek, Deborah M., 245
Burgess, Michael, 1155
Burgess, Warren E., 1554
Burke, Georganne, 583
Burma, 124
Burns, Richard Dean, 733
Burton, William C., 574
Burwell dir of info brokers 1992, 654
Burwell, Helen P., 654
Business & the environment, 249
Business connexions 1992, 228
Business info: how to find it, how to use it, 2d ed, 209
Business info sourcebk, 200
Business One Irwin bus & investment almanac, 1992, 220
Business orgs, agencies, & pubs dir, 6th ed, 190
Business pers index, 216
Business pers index: Aug 1990-July 1991, 215
Business rankings annual, 1992, 202
Butler, Penny, 205
Butterflies & moths, 1547
Butterfly bk, 1551
Butterworth, Rod R., 1098

Buttress, F. A., 2
Buzzworm magazine, editors of, 1765
Byelorussian-English, English-Byelorussian dict with complete phonetics, 1079
Byrne, W. J., 575
Bzowski, Frances Diodato, 1167

Cable, Greg, 1655
CAD/CAM abstracts annual 1991, 1690
Caelli, William, 315
Calhoun, Milburn, 110
California initiatives & referendums 1912-90, 793
Calvert, Peter, 774
Cambridge ency of China, 2d ed, 125
Cambridge ency of ornithology, 1540
Camp, Roderic A., 775
Campbell, Alta, 208
Campbell, Malcolm, 832, 833
Campus-free college degrees, 5th ed, 378
Canada: a reader's gd, 19
Canada legal dir 1992, 583
Canadian bk review annual 1990, 10
Canadian law symposia index, 598
Canadian lit index: cum index to 1986 pubs, 1218
Canadian lit index: cum index to 1987 pubs, 1219
Canadian master tax gd, 1992, 229
Canadian media list 1992/93, 952
Canadian Medical Assn gd to prescription & over-the-counter drugs, 1661
Canadian medical device dir, 1642
Canadian parliamentary hndbk, 763
Canadian studies: foreign pubs & theses, 4th ed, 134
Canavan, Diane D., 402
Canning, Nancy, 1253
Canter, Laurence A., 589
Career Associates, 309
Career connection, rev ed, 410
Carlson, Eric G., 377
Caroline drama, 2d ed, 1202
Carolinian-English dict, 1080
Carpenter, Allan, 918
Carpenter, Clive, 4
Carpenter, Lisa, 957
Carr, Jennifer L., 281
Carrera, Michael A., 883
Carroll, Frances Laverne, 1122
Carson, Anne, 923
Carstensen, Richard, 1528
Carter, David, 1547
Carter, Susanne, 1169
Cary, Tristram, 1246
Cassell bk of proverbs, 1295
Cassidy, Frederic G., 1062
Castello-Cortes, Ian, 172
Catala, Rafael, 1187
Catalog of prenatally diagnosed conditions, 2d ed, 1654
Catalog of teratogenic agents, 7th ed, 1628
Catalogue of ...
   audio & video collections of Holocaust testimony, 2d ed, 528
   Canadian catalogues, 3d ed, 227
   English Bible translations, 1427
   palaearctic diptera, v.7, 1567

Catchpole, Catherine, 1329
Catchpole, Terry, 1329
Catholic school educ in the US, 348
Catterall, Peter, 144
Cattle: a hndbk to the breeds of the world, 1491
Caughman, Jennifer T., 67
CD-ROM dir 1992, 1691
CD-ROM per index, 82
CD-ROM research collections, 660
CD-ROM reviews 1987-90, 659
CD-ROMS in print, 1692
Cencig, Didier, 132
Central Intelligence Agency, 105
Centre de Terminologie de Bruxelles, Institute Libre Marie Haps, 323
Chadwick, Bruce A., 867
Chalcraft, Anthony, 20, 21
Chamberlain, Bobby J., 1091
Chamberlin, William J., 1427
Chambers concise dict, 1057
Chambers concise ency of film & TV, 1346
Chambers dict of pol biog, 721
Chambers earth scis dict, 1720
Chambers film quotes, 1374
Chambers nuclear energy & radiation dict, 1742
Chang, Sidney H., 521
Channeling: a bibliographic exploration, 806
Chant, Christopher, 700
Chapman, Robert L., 1075
Characters from young adult lit, 1143
Charitable orgs of the US 1992-92, 878
Charles James Fox 1749-1806: a bibliog, 773
Charles, Jill, 1387, 1388, 1390
Charles Press hndbk of current medical abbrevs, 3d ed, 1622
Charts, graphics & stats index 1988-91, 916
Charuest, Michel, 905
Chase, A. R., 1499
Checklist of ...
   American imprints for 1842, 32
   beetles of Canada & Alaska, 1560
   Melville reviews, 1178
Cheney, Walter J., 853
Chernofsky, Ellen, 441
Cherry, Virginia R., 794
Chielens, Edward E., 1163
Childcraft: the how & why lib, 58
Childers, Roberta, 1773
Children's animal atlas, 1531
Children's bk review index, v.16, 1145
Children's fiction sourcebk, 1125
Children's lit review, v.25, 1141
Children's ref plus, 11
Children's space atlas, 1703
Children's writer's & illustrator's market, 1992, 957
China business dir 1992, 278
Chinese-English dict of the Wu dialect, 1081
Choi, Patricia E., 249
Choral music of Latin America, 1267
Christiansen, Kenneth, 1561
Chronicle career index, 405
Chronicle financial aid gd for 1991-92 school yr, 367
Chronicle 4-yr college databk for 1991-92 school yr, 368

Chronicle of ...
    Higher Education, editors of, 355
    the 1st World War, v.2, 551
    W fashion, 1010
Chronicle 2-yr college databk for 1991-92 school yr, 369
Chronicle vocational school manual for 1991-92 school yr, 406
Chronological annot bibliog of order stats, v.4, 902
Chua, Romulo L., 1102
CIFAR's global co hndbk, 1992 ed, 263
Cinema sheet music, 1272
Cinematic vampires, 1353
Cinematographers, production designers, costume designers & film eds gd, 3d ed, 1371
CIS 4-yr cum index, 1987-90, 758
Citations & allusions to Jewish scripture in early Christian & Jewish writings through 180 CE, 1429
Clark, Bernadine, 682
Clark, Burton R., 358
Clark, Jerome, 807
Clark, Murtie June, 457, 459
Classic cult fiction, 1149
Cleaver, Joanne, 78
Clements, Bonnie L., 850, 888
Cleveland herbal, botanical, & horticultural collections, 1493
Clewis, Beth, 1525
Clifford, J. Candace, 1788
Clinton, Catherine, 932
Close, Arthur C., 744
Clout, Hugh, 534
CMG Information Services, 361
Coad, Brian W., 1555
Cocchiarelli, Joseph J., 1350
Cochrane, Hamilton E., 1232
Codex alimentarius, v.1, 1479
Codignola, Luca, 1424
Coe, Malcolm, 1516
Coffin, Tristram Potter, 1297
Cogger, Harold G., 1575
Coghlan, Ronan, 1190
Cohen, Hennig, 1297
Cohn, Mary, 747
Cohn-Sherbok, Dan, 1405
Coldham, Peter Wilson, 452
Cole, Don, 180
Coleman, J. Gordon, Jr., 672
Collection agency dir, 2d ed, 237
Collection evaluation in academic libs, 677
College admissions data hndbk 1992-93, 370
College admissions index of majors & sports 1992-93, 379
College style sheet, 3d ed, 959
Collins, David N., 139
Collins, Joseph T., 1577
Collins, N. Mark, 1484
Collins, Pamela, 1255
Collins, Robert A., 1158
Collins Spanish-English/English-Spanish dict, 3d ed, 1100
Colombo, John Robert, 90
Colorado bk gd, 683
Columbia dict of European pol hist since 1914, 529

Columbia Granger's dict of poetry quotations, 1235
Columbus' dict, 517
Colwell, Richard, 1252
Combined membership list 1992-93, 1737
Comecon data 1990, 907
Commemorative coins of the US, 1002
Commodity review & outlook 1990-91, 1466
Common & botanical names of weeds in Canada, 1992 ed, 1511
Common names of N American butterflies, 1548
Communication serials, 1992/1993 ed, 982
Companies & their brands 1992, 189
Companies that care, 312
Companion to Irish hist 1603-1921, 539
Companion to 20th-century German lit, 1223
Comparative criminology, 602
Compendium of ...
    the Confederate armies: Ala., 711
    the Confederate armies: Fla. & Ark., 712
    the Confederate armies: N.C., 713
    the Confederate armies: Tenn., 714
    the Confederate armies: Va., 715
Complete bk of ...
    emigrants 1700-50, 452
    the Olympics, 1992 ed, 841
    US presidents, 3d ed, 514
Complete college financing gd, 2d ed, 371
Complete dir for people with disabilities, 1992, 862
Complete dir of large print bks & serials 1992, 30
Complete dog bk, 18th ed, 1552
Complete drug ref, 1992 ed, 1662
Complete hndbk of natural healing, 1648
Complete metalsmith, rev ed, 1008
Composite materials hndbk, 2d ed, 1606
Comprehensive dict of measurement & control, 2d ed, 1607
Comprehensive glossary of psychiatry & psychology, 1649
Comprehensive US silver dollar ency, 1003
Compressed Russian, 1097
Computer catalogs, 1673
Computer dict, 3d ed, 1681
Computer glossary, 5th ed, 1676
Computer mediated communication, 345
Computer professional's quick ref, 1685
Computer publishers & pubs, 1992-93 ed, 684
Comte, Fernand, 1302
Conant, Roger, 1577
Concise dict of ...
    Greek, Roman, Norse, & Egyptian mythology, 1303
    mgmt, 317
    military biog, 699
Concise ency of ...
    biological & biomedical measurement systems, 1635
    magnetic & superconducting materials, 1591
    modelling & simulation, 1674
    polymer processing & applications, 1582
    semiconducting materials & related techs, 1592
    traffic & transportation systems, 1613
Concise glossary of contemporary literary theory, 1112
Concise Oxford dict of ...
    geography, 489
    proverbs, 2d ed, 1296
    zoology, 1529

Concordance to the minor poetry of Edward Taylor (1642?-1729), 1181
Condon, Robert J., 815
Confidence woman, 936
Conflict & culture, rev ed, 419
Congressional Quarterly's gd to Congress, 4th ed, 747
Congressional voting gd: a 10 yr compilation, 4th ed, 746
Connery, Thomas B., 976
Connolly, Thomas, 519
Connors, Martin, 840
Conoley, Jane Close, 803
Conservation atlas of tropical forests: Africa, 1484
Consoli, Joseph P., 1224
Consolidated treaties & intl agreements, 756
Construction tech info sources, 1586
Consumer E Europe 1992, 283
Consumer health & nutrition index, v.8, no.1, 1614
Consumer Reports Books, editors of, 1334, 1481, 1611, 1784, 1786
Consumer Reports 1992 buying gd issue, 234
Consumer sourcebk 1992-93, 235
Consumer's dict of household, yard & office chemicals, 1754
Consumer's gd to medical lingo, 1633
Consumer's gd to tests in print, 2d ed, 333
Contemporary authors, v.133, 1108
Contemporary authors, v.134, 1109
Contemporary black biog, v.1, 426
Contemporary Britain: an annual review 1992, 144
Contemporary composers, 1254
Contemporary entrepreneurs, 178
Contemporary heroes & heroines, bk 2, 45
Contemporary masterworks, 1028
Contemporary musicians, v.6, 1245
Contemporary Spanish American poets, 1228
Contemporary theatre, film, & TV, v.9, 1324
Contemporary writers, 1960 to the present, 1192
Contribution to lit of Orcadian writer George Mackay Brown, 1206
Control of the media in the US, 951
Conversion experience in America, 1418
Cook, Charles, 835
Cook, Chris, 559, 719, 766
Corbeil, Jean-Claude, 1077, 1101
Corbett, James M., 603
Cordell, Helen, 127
Corinne T. Netzer ency of food values, 1476
Corish, Patrick J., 1582
Cornell, Alan, 1085
Cornell, Charles R., 33
Corporate eponymy, 184
Corporate finance sourcebk 1991, 238
Corporate mags of the US, 217
Corporate tech dir 1992, 246
Corporate yellow bk, v.8, no.3, 191
CorpTech, 303
Corten, Irina H., 1095
Costa, Marie, 851
Costa Rica, 154
Couliano, Ioan P., 1409
County & city extra, 1992, 908
Couper, Heather, 1700
Courage in the air, 697
Cousins, Jill, 203

Covert, Nadine, 1016
Covington, Michael, 1675
Covington, Paula H., 148
Cowie, Leonard W., 771
Cox, Andrew, 767
Cox, Richard William, 814
Coyle, Jean M., 854
Coyle, Martin, 1116
Crafts index for young people, 1005
Cragg, Dan, 704
Craig, Raymond A., 1181
Craighead's intl bus, travel, & relocation gd to 71 countries 1992-93, 264
Craven, Wesley Frank, 356
Crawford, Mary G., 111
Crawley, Tony, 1374
Creamer, Thomas, 1081
Creative fingerplays & action rhymes, 340
Creativity in the later yrs, 856
Creeth, Terry, 108
Cresswell, Julia, 465
Crewe, Ivor, 772
Crimes & criminals, 614
Criminology: a reader's gd, 606
Critical gd to horror film series, 1354
Critical survey of poetry: English lang series, rev ed, 1236
Crittenden, Mabel, 1503, 1517
Croissant, Charles R., 1273
Cronin, Gloria L., 1175
Cronquist, Arthur, 1500
Croquet: an annot bibliog from the Rendell Rhoades croquet collection, 829
Cross, Wilbur, 855
Cross-currents of Jungian thought, 796
Crowther, Kelly, 68
Cuberly, W. H., 1607
Cult movie stars, 1337
Cultivated plants of the tropics & subtropics, 1469
Cultural anthropology of the Middle East, v.1, 416
Cultural atlas of France, 143
Cummings, Mark, 59
Cummings, Pat, 1021
Cumulative bk index [CD-ROM], 25
Cumulative bk index 1991, 23
Cumulative bk index, v.95, no.2, 24
Cumulative index to ONLINE, DATABASE & CD-ROM Professional 1986-91, 1669
Current biog yrbk 1991, 37
Current chemical reactions (CCR), v.14, no.2, 1718
Curtis, Melissa C., 1432

Dabundo, Laura, 531
Daly, Ronald C., 471
Dance film & video gd, 1328
Danesh, Abol Hassan, 173
Daniels, Ted, 1399
Darby, William, 1343
Darnay, Arsen J., 204, 247, 250, 1764
Daughtrey, Margery, 1499
David Merrick: a bio-bibliog, 1377
Davidian, H. H., 1504
Davies, Ann, 743
Davies' medical terminology, 5th ed, 1630

Davis, Gwenn, 1146
Davis, Michael D., 843
Day, Alan, 98
Day, Alan J., 725
Day, Glenn, 748
Day, Neil, 772
Day, Robert A., 958
de Geest, Gerrit, 564
De Lorenzo, Barbara, 1631
Dean, John A., 1716
Dean, Virgil W., 513
DeAngelis, Carl, 1053
Dear, Ian, 842
Deegan, Mary Jo, 844
Defty, Jeff, 340
DeGregorio, William A., 514
Delgado, James P., 1788
Delvin, Edgard, 1600
Demographic stats 1991, 897
Dempsey, Michael, 482
Dennis, Marguerite J., 371
Dent, N. J. H., 1396
DePew, John N., 663
Descriptionary, 1072
Descriptive cat of the Glenn Gould papers, 1255
Design of bibliogs, 690
Desmarais, Norman, 659
Dewey, Clive, 524
Di Berardino, Angelo, 1406
Diagram Group, 1527, 1767
Dial in 1992, 662
Diamond, David, 1023
Dickens, Linda, 297
Dickson, Paul, 1073
Dickson's word treasury, 1073
Dictionary for the petroleum industry, 1743
Dictionary of ...
   American proverbs, 1299
   American regional English, v.2, 1062
   artificial intelligence & neuronal networks, 1671
   Buddhist terms & terminologies, 1413
   Canadian quotations, 90
   Celtic mythology, 1304
   computer graphics tech & applications, 1688
   computer terms, 3d ed, 1675
   concepts in cultural anthropology, 418
   concepts in literary criticism & theory, 1111
   concepts in physical anthropology, 415
   crime, 608
   critical theory, 1114
   economics, 185
   electronic & computer music terminology, 1247
   English law, 575
   English place names, 493
   environmental quotations, 1777
   evolutionary fish osteology, 1558
   fictional characters, rev ed, 1148
   info sci & tech, 622
   intl & comparative law, 577
   Jesus & the Gospels, 1428
   Judaism & Christianity, 1405
   measurement engineering & units, 1597
   medical & surgical syndromes, 1658
   musical tech, 1246
   occupational titles, 4th ed, 301
   personal finance, 243
   plant virology, 1495
   pols, 7th ed, 722
   polling, 103
   quotations from Shakespeare, 1213
   Russian personal names, 463
   scientific literacy, 1445
   symbols, 1041
   terms in music, 4th ed, 1248
   the martial arts, 839
   Third World terms, 136
   20th century hist 1914-90, 557
   20th century world biog, 38
   US govt statl terms, 903
   water & wastewater treatment trademarks & brand names, 1772
   W church music, 1269
Didik, Frank X., 284
Diehm, William J., 853
Dietrich, Julia, 1211
Diffor, Elaine N., 397
Diffor, John C., 397
Digital systems ref bk, 1596
Dihn-Hoa, Ngyuen, 1104
Dillard, Philip H., 1274
Dinosaurs: a gd to research, 1731
Directory, 1991-92: Japanese-affiliated cos in USA & Canada, 279
Directory of ...
   arctic sci & tech research in Canada, 118
   building & equipment grants, 2d ed, 1035
   business info resources, 1992, 192
   business to business cats, 1991, 194
   chemical engineering consultants, 9th ed, 1583
   computer conferencing in libs, 656
   corporate & fndn givers 1992, 872
   current HIV/AIDS research in Canada 1988-91, 1651
   E European film-makers & films 1945-91, 1348
   electronic jls, newsletters & academic discussion lists, 2d ed, 72
   ethnic professionals in LIS (lib & info sci), 625
   European sports orgs, 821
   faculty contracts & bargaining agents in institutions of higher educ, v.18, 360
   govt doc collections & librarians, 6th ed, 676
   grants in the humanities 1992/93, 946
   humor mags & humor orgs in America (& Canada), 3d ed, 1188
   incentives for bus investment & dvlpmt in the US, 3d ed, 221
   intl pers & newsletters on the built environment, 2d ed, 1036
   Japanese technical resources in the US 1992, 655
   legislative leaders 1991-92, 739
   merger & acquisition firms & professionals 1992, 193
   online databases, v.13, no.2, 1682
   pan-European orgs 1992, 138
   pathology training programs in the US & Canada 1993-94, 1643
   portable databases, v.3, no.2, 1670
   pressure groups in the European Community, 768
   research grants 1992, 873

special collections of research value in Canadian libs, 646
theatre training programs, 3d ed, 1390
UN documentary & archival sources, 783
Directory to fulltext online resources 1992, 626
Directory to intl bus educ in Canada, 230
Disability, sexuality & abuse, 865
Discover Indian reservations USA, 434
Discrimination & prejudice, 845
Distinguished classics of ref publishing, 18
Distinguished shades, 49
Dixon, Joan DeVee, 1256
Dobkin, David S., 1541
Dobson, Richard, 1247
Doerr, Juergen C., 538
Doing children's museums, 78
Dollinger, Malin, 1655
Donahue, Roy L., 1468
Dondale, Charles D., 1563
Donnelly, Dorothy F., 1416
Dooley, Patrick K., 1172
Doo-wop: the forgotten 3d of rock 'n roll, 1290
Dore, Susan Cole, 110
Dorgan, Charity Anne, 310
Dority, G. Kim, 8
Dorros, Gerald, 1646
Douglas, Joel M., 360
Downing, Douglas, 1675
Downs, Buck J., 71
Dr. Axelrod's atlas of freshwater aquarium fishes, 6th ed, 1553
Dr. Burgess's mini-atlas of marine aquarium fishes, 1554
Draaijer, Gera E., 898
Drama by women to 1990, 1146
Dramatic re-visions, 1333
Draper, Edythe, 1415
Draper, James P., 1115, 1119
Drewes, Athena A., 808
Dreyer, Sharon Spredemann, 1123
Drost, Harry, 953
Drucker, Sally Ann, 808
Drug abuse bibliog for 1988, 888
Drug file, 1667
Drug info for the health care professional 1992, 1663
Drug interactions gd bk, 1664
Duchamp, Michel, 1725
Duffy, Susan, 1375
Dufour, Pierre, 485
Dumouchel, J. Robert, 874
Dunmore, John, 487
Dupuis, Diane L., 840
Dupuy, Trevor N., 698
Duryea, Michelle LeBaron, 419
Dutch Filipiniana, 169
Dworsky, Alan L., 590
Dyer, Alan Frank, 1171
Dyer, Donald R., 796

E for environment, 1752
Eagles, D. Munroe, 764
Earth jl, 1992, 1765
Eastern Europe: a dir & sourcebk 1992, 140
Eastern Europe & the Commonwealth of Independent States 1992, 141
Eastern European business dir, 284
Eastman, John, 1518
Easy access to natl parks, 499
Eatwell, John, 242
Eccles, David H., 1556
Echols, Anne, 933
Eckhart, Mary Lawrence, 517
Economic indicators hndbk, 204
Economist atlas, 172
Economist desk companion, 205
Eddleman, Floyd Eugene, 1168
Edelheit, Abraham, 550
Edelheit, Abraham J., 535
Edelheit, Hershel, 535, 550
Edenbaum, Jesse, 1711
Edgar, David, 1477
Editorial Board, 1238
Edmonston, Phil, 1781, 1782
Education in the Arab Gulf states & the Arab world, 384
Education index, 341
Education of women in the US, 926
Educational media & tech yrbk, v.18, 398
Educators gd to ...
  free films, 52d ed, 397
  free guidance materials, 30th ed, 400
  free videotapes, 39th ed, 396
Educators index of free materials, 101st ed, 328
Edwin Booth: a bio-bibliog, 1379
Eggenberger, David, 39
Ehr, Catherine M., 190
EHR dir of awards: fiscal yr 1990, 875
Ehrens, Cheryl, 96
Ehrlich, Paul R., 1541
Eichholz, Alice, 455
Eighty silent film stars, 1336
Eis, Arlene L., 591
Eisenberg, John F., 1570
EL&P US electric utility industry dir, 1992, 1589
Elazar, Daniel J., 726
Elder, Danny, 1730
Electric utility industry sftwr dir, 1992, 1590
Elementary school lib collection, 18th ed, 667
Elements, 2d ed, 1712
Eleventh mental measurements yrbk, 803
Eley, Stephen, 828
Eliade gd to world religions, 1409
Eliade, Mircea, 1409
Elkhadem, Saad, 1303
Ellenbogen, Glenn C., 1188
Eller, William, 404
Ellis, Barbara W., 1489
Ellis, Peter Berresford, 1304
Elrod, J. McRee, 598
El-Sanabary, Nagat, 384
Elsevier's dict of ...
  aquaculture, 1467
  civil engineering, 1585
  geoscis, 1723
  hydrology & water quality mgmt, 1724
  office automation, 323
  plant genetic resources, 1496
  terrestrial plant ecology, 1497

Ely, Charles, 1546
Ely, Donald P., 398
Emerging techs & instruction, 344
Emily Post's etiquette, 15th ed, 1307
Emsley, John, 1712
Encyclopaedia of Arthurian legends, 1190
Encyclopedia Americana, intl ed, 59
Encyclopedia of ...
   adoption, 866
   African-American civil rights, 616
   aging & the elderly, 858
   American bus hist & biog: the airline industry, 248
   animated cartoons, 1347
   applied physics, v.2, 1733
   applied physics, v.3, 1734
   biblical & Christian ethics, rev ed, 1419
   bus info sources, 9th ed, 206
   career change & work issues, 409
   career choices for the 1990s, 309
   deafness & hearing disorders, 1656
   drug abuse, 2d ed, 890
   early childhood educ, 332
   earth system sci, 1721
   educl research, 6th ed, 331
   ethics, 1395
   fermented fresh milk products, 1475
   field trips & educl destinations, 352
   food sci & tech, 1473
   ghosts & spirits, 810
   golf, 832
   higher educ, 358
   Jewish symbols, 443
   lit & criticism, 1116
   living artists in America, 6th ed, 1024
   materials characterization, 1605
   medical orgs & agencies 1992-93, 1632
   Mormonism, 1420
   Mormonism [CD-ROM], 1421
   Native American religions, 432
   natural medicine, 1634
   Nfld. & Lab., v.3, 133
   N American sports hist, 819
   perennials, 1508
   physical sci & tech 1991 yrbk, 1453
   religions in the US, 1407
   romanticism, 531
   schizophrenia & the psychotic disorders, 799
   sociology, 847
   textiles, 1007
   the American Constitution, suppl.1, 576
   the early church, 1406
   the reformed faith, 1422
   the Third World, 4th ed, 137
   W lawmen & outlaws, 609
   world biog, 20th century suppl, v.17, 39
   world cultures, 413
Encyclopedic dict of ...
   American govt, 4th ed, 737
   economics, 4th ed, 180
   psychology, 4th ed, 800
   sociology, 4th ed, 849
Encyclopedic hndbk of cults in America, rev ed, 1410
Energy balances of OECD countries 1980-89, 1746
Energy stats of OECD countries 1980-89, 1747

English lang & orientation programs in the US, 10th ed, 1053
English Renaissance prose fiction, 1500-1660, 1203
English schoolboy stories, 1135
English-Russian dict with phonetics, 1094
English-Yiddish, Yiddish-English dict, 1105
Enrique Granados: a bio-bibliog, 1259
Ensor, Pat, 82, 660
Environment abstracts annual 1991, 1766
Environment on File, 1767
Environmental address bk, 1760
Environmental hazards: toxic waste & hazardous material, 1770
Environmental industries marketplace, 1755
Environmental telephone dir 1992-93, 1756
EPA headquarters telephone dir, 1991 ed, 1757
Epstein, Lee, 566
Equatorial Guinea, 114
ERIC identifier authority list (IAL) 1992, 636
Erickson, Hal, 1351
Ericson, Richard V., 606
Ernst, Carl H., 1576
Ertle, Katherine, 1462
Esanu, Warren H., 326
Esenwein, George, 790
Espig, Gustav, 1469
Essay & general lit index, rev ed, 77
Essential gd to hiking in the US, 835
Essential gd to vitamins & minerals, 1647
Estell, Kenneth, 190, 199, 265
Estonian-English, English-Estonian dict, 1082
Ethel Merman: a bio-bibliog, 1317
Ethnic cookbks & food marketplace, 3d ed, 1472
Ethnomusicology research, 1242
ETS test collection cat, v.6, 329
European accountancy yrbk 1992/93, 271
European advertising mktg & media data 1992, 285
European business rankings, 291
European compendium of mktg info, 286
European consultants dir, 287
European dir of consumer brands & their owners 1992, 288
European educ thesaurus, 1991 ed, 385
European employment & industrial relations glossary: Spain, 295
European employment & industrial relations glossary: UK, 297
European markets: a gd to co & industry info sources, 4th ed, 289
European wholesalers & distrs dir, 257
Evaluation thesaurus, 4th ed, 642
Evans, Charles A., Jr., 1605
Evans, Joan, 1257
Everyone's gd to cancer therapy, 1655
Evetts, Jan, 1591
Exegetical dict of the N.T., v.2, 1426
Extraordinary Hispanic Americans, 51
Extraterrestrial ency, rev ed, 805
Eynon, Derry, 491
Eysenck, Michael W., 798

Faces in the news, 40
Facts about the cities, 918
Facts on File dict of film & broadcast terms, 987

Facts on File English/Spanish visual dict, 1101
Facts on File world pol almanac, 2d ed, 719
Faculty white pages 1991, 361
Fai, Stephen, 1586
Fairchild, Halford H., 845
Falk, Peter Hastings, 1032
Falklands/Malvinas campaign, 694
Familiar quotations, 16th ed, 89
Families & aging, 854
Family video gd, 1329
Famous trials, 604
Fanfare for words: bkfairs & bk festivals in N America, 682
FAO species cat, v.13: marine lobsters of the world, 1557
FAO yrbk: forest products 1979-90, 1483
Fargasova, A., 1495
Fashion in the W world 1500-1990, 1011
Faulkner in the 80s, 1173
Federal domestic outlays 1983-90, 745
Federal systems of the world, 726
Fedun, Doris, 1631
Fegley, Randall, 114
Felscher, Harriet, 1637
Feltman, John, 1636
Female psychology, 797
Feminism & psychoanalysis, 801
Feminist movement: a bibliog, 929
Fenton, Ann D., 1129
Fenwick, M. J., 1226
Fernandez-Shaw, Carlos M., 427
Fetrow, Alan G., 1352
Fetters, Linda K., 1669
Fetzer, Mary, 73
Few, Roger, 1532
FIAF cataloguing rules for film archives, 638
Fiction writers gdlines, 2d ed, 963
FID dir 1991-92, 624
Field gd to ...
   E butterflies, 1549
   rock art symbols of the greater southwest, 508
   shells of the Tex. coast, 1522
   the acacias of Kenya, 1516
   the freshwater fishes of Tanzania, 1556
50 fabulous places to retire in America, 921
Fifty yrs "Among the New Words," 1064
50 yrs of rock music, 1291
Fifty yrs of TV, 998
Fighting men of the Indian wars, 515
Filby, P. William, 460
Filler, Louis, 49
Film & TV composers, 1258
Film & video finder, 3d ed, 1330
Film annual 1992, 1369
Film writers gd, 3d ed, 1368
Films for learning, thinking, & doing, 399
Film-video terms & concepts, 1345
Financial Times oil & gas intl yr bk 1993, 1748
Financial yellow bk, v.5, no.2, 239
Fine art index, 1992 N American ed, 1031
Fine arts pers, 1034
Finlay, Matthew, 1691
Finn, Bernard S., 1593
Finn, Edwin A., Jr., 236
Finniston, Monty, 1451

Fire music, 1286
First American Jewish families, 3d ed, 458
First-person accounts of genocidal acts in the 20th century, 548
Fischel, Jack, 442
Fischer, Andreas, 1067
Fischer, Catherine, 1158
Fischer, Gayle V., 943
Fischgrund, Tom, 366
Fitzherbert, Andrew, 809
Fleming, John, 1038
Fleury, Bruce Edward, 1731
Flick, Ernest W., 1713
Flint, Adam, 1761
Flodin, Mickey, 1098
Florida almanac 1992-93, 106
Florida statistical abstract 1991, 107
Flower flies of the subfamily syrphinae of Canada, Alaska, & Greenland, 1564
Floyd, Dale E., 692
Fly patterns, 2d ed, 837
Flynn, John L., 1353
Flynn, Robert A., 605
Focus on careers, 408
Folklore & folklife, 1300
Folklore of American holidays, 2d ed, 1297
Folklore of world holidays, 1298
Food aid in figures, v.8/2, 1480
Football coach quotes, 830
Forage resources of China, 1510
Fordyce, Rachel, 1202
Forgay, Beryl, 568
Formulary of cosmetic preparations, v.1, 1715
Forrester, Donald J., 1569
Forrester, Mary Flanigan, 741
Foster, Allan, 291
Foster, David William, 1227
Foudray, Rita Schoch, 1120
Foundation Center, 879
Fournier, Marion, 825
Fowler, Karin J., 1318
Fox, Anthony, 772
Fox, James R., 577
Francis, June, 498
Francomano, Clair A., 1624
Frank, David, 526
Frank Norris: a descriptive bibliog, 1180
Frank Sinatra: a complete recording hist, 1265
Frankel, Ellen, 443
Fraser, Janet, 1218, 1219
Fraser, Robert, 266, 290
Frazier, Nancy, 444
Frederic, Louis, 839
Frederick, Richard G., 509
Fredrickson, Jim, 1369
Free resource builder for librarians & teachers, 2d ed, 70
Freedman, Alan, 1676
French, Christopher C., 789
French women writers, 1222
French-English agricultural dict, 1465
Friedberg, Joan Brest, 1124
Fritz, Sara, 749
Fritze, Ronald H., 532
From archetype to zeitgeist, 1060

From page to screen, 1359
From the past to the future, 527
Fromberg, Doris Pronin, 332
Frome, Michael, 496
Fun for kids 2, 1006
Fund raiser's gd to religious philanthropy, 5th ed, 1425
Fund your way through college, 373
Furberg, Jon, 959
Furlong, Paul, 767
Furness, Raymond, 1223
Furtaw, Julia C., 421, 428

Gale environmental sourcebk, 1768
Gale, Robert L, 518
Gallivan, Marion F., 1006
Gamal Abdel Nasser: a bibliog, 543
Garden lit, v.1, no.2, 1485
Garwood, Alfred N., 903
Gattuso, John, 431
Gay 90s in America, 518
Gee, Robin, 961, 966
Gelbert, Doug, 820
Genera & subgenera of the sawflies of Canada & Alaska, 1562
General sci index [CD-ROM], 1460
General sci index, v.14, no.7, 1459
Genreflecting, 3d ed, 1147
George Rochberg: a bio-bibliographic gd to his life & works, 1256
George, Tracey E., 566
Georgian-English, English-Georgian dict, 1084
German-English genealogical dict, 453
Gerolemou, Chris, 215
Gettysburg: a battlefield atlas, 691
Ghose, Vijaya, 1310
Gianakos, Larry James, 993
Giant lizards, 1580
Gibberman, Susan R., 1331
Gibbons, Laura, 191
Gibilisco, Stan, 1594
Gibson, Bob, 1701
Gibson, J., 1658
Giese, Lester J., 919
Gifford, Charles S., 330
Gifford, Denis, 1344
Gifted & talented info resources, 339
Gilbar, Steven, 403
Gildzen, Alex, 1376
Gill, Kay, 887
Gillespie, Cindy S., 1130
Giovanni Boccaccio: an annot bibliog, 1224
Gladstone, Jane, 606
Glanville, Martyn P., 821
Gleason, Henry A., 1500
Glenn Gould cat, 1253
Global Tex.: intl trade info sourcebk, 267
Global trade white pages 1992, 268
Glossary geotextiles, 1609
Glossary of ...
    contemporary literary theory, 1113
    finance & debt, 231
    health care terms, 2d ed, 1615
    health servs, 1616

    Jewish life, 449
    medical terminology, 1641
Glover, Thomas J., 1454, 1684
Goble, Alan, 1373
Godbolt, Shane, 1626
Godden, Irene P., 627
Goddesses & wise women, 923
Godfrey, Donald G., 994
Godfrey-Smith, Anne, 131
Goedan, Juergen Christoph, 567
Goehlert, Robert U., 571
Goetzfridt, Nicholas J., 1789
Gold bk: a gd to commonly traded gold bullion coins & bars, 226
Goldman, Martin E., 1657
Golemba, Beverly E., 934
Golfers almanac, 833
Gomez-Gutierrez, J. M., 1497
Goodfellow, William D., 1266
Gordon, Leonard H. D., 521
Gordon, W. Terrence, 1047
Gorman, G. E., 652
Gottesman, Roberta, 1250
Goulet, Henri, 1562
Gousha new deluxe rd atlas, 467
Government assistance almanac 1992-93, 874
Government contracts ref bk, 580
Government dir of addresses & telephone nos, 740
Government giveaways for entrepreneurs, 3d ed, 210
Government Institutes, editorial staff of, 1756
Government ref bks 90/91, 74
Goyer, Doreen S., 898
Graham, Anne, 1387
Grant, George C., 625
Grant, Mary A., 348
Grant, Todd W., 592
Grants & awards available to American writers, 17th ed, 960
GRANTS subject authority gd, 637
Graphic arts ency, 1042
Graphics file formats, 1687
Gray, Cecile G., 1432
Gray, John, 1286
Gray, Mary Taylor, 1542
Gray, Randal, 551
Great American ships, 1788
Great athletes, 816
Great events from hist 2: human rights series, 617
Great Hollywood musical pictures, 1360
Great inventions through hist, 1447
Great maritime museums of the world, 1791
Great modern inventions, 1448
Great scientific discoveries, 1449
Great Spanish films: 1950-90, 1365
Great thinkers of the W world, 950
Great women athletes of the 20th century, 815
Green almanac, 1751
Green co resource gd, 1774
Green, Joel B., 1428
Green, Jonathon, 1066
Green plants, 1498
Greene, Thurston, 593
Greenfield, John R., 1193
Greenfield, Stanley R., 782
Greenland, 119

Gregory, Hugh, 1293
Greulich, Walter, 1733, 1734
Gribin, Anthony J., 1290
Griffin, Lynne, 935
Griffiths, Peter, 828
Griffiths, Trevor R., 1389
Grinstein, Louise S., 1738
Gross, David C., 445, 1105
Gross, Esther R., 445
Grote, David, 1068
Ground spiders of Canada & Alaska, 1563
Groundwater chemicals field gd, 1771
Grover-Lizardi, Judith, 197
Grow, Michael, 149
Grun, Bernard, 560
Gubser, Peter, 164
Guertin, Lucie, 1601
Guide to ...
   academic travel, 2d ed, 407
   Albert Schweitzer collections, 2d ed, 947
   campus & non-profit meeting facilities 93, 207
   collections relating to S.D. Norwegian-Americans, 451
   current indexing & abstracting servs in the Third World, 652
   docs relating to French & British N America in the archives of the sacred congregation "de Propaganda Fide," 1424
   E Asian collections in N America, 120
   fed funding for child care & early childhood dvlpmt, 893
   fed funding for volunteer programs, 876
   475 aircraft museums, 224 city-displayed aircraft, 37 restaurants with aircraft, 6 WWI landmarks, 10th ed, 1779
   free computer materials, 10th ed, 401
   French lit: 1789 to the present, 1221
   funding for intl & foreign programs, 880
   golf schools & camps, 834
   income tax preparation, 326
   literary agents & art/photo reps, 1992, 961
   MBA programs in Canada, 376
   microforms in print 1991: author-title, 1694
   microforms in print 1991: subject, 1695
   military installations, 3d ed, 704
   modern Japanese woodblock prints, 1900-75, 1043
   ref bks for school media centers, 4th ed, 670
   ref bks, suppl to the 10th ed, 12
   ref materials for Canadian libs, 8th ed, 16
   research in classical art & mythology, 1029
   the birds of Nepal, 1543
   the Canadian financial servs industry 1991, 232
   the gods, 1305
   the info activities of European dvlpmt networks, 630
   the John D. Crummey peace collection in the Hoover Inst, 790
   the liverworts of N.C., 1512
   the marine sport fishes of Atlantic Canada & New England, 1555
   the univs of Europe, 382
Guiley, Rosemary Ellen, 810
Guinness bk of ...
   answers, 8th ed, 4
   movie facts & feats, 1370
   records 1492, 558

Guitard, Michelle, 485
Gunn, Drewey Wayne, 1185
Gunton, Sharon R., 1141
Gupta, B. M., 647, 648
Gutierrez, Marcos F., 1585
Gwynn, R. S., 1186

Haas, Lawrence J., 731
Hadjor, Kori Buenor, 136
Haggin, B. H., 1251
Haile, Suzanne, 880, 881, 1411
Hajnal, Peter I., 783
Hall, Blaine H., 1175
Hall, George E., 908
Hall, Hal W., 1176
Hall, Joan Houston, 1062
Hallgarth, Susan, 924
Hallgarth, Susan A., 940
Hamilton, Geoff, 1488
Hamilton, Lee Templin, 1205
Hamlet in the 1960s, 1211
Hammill, Donald D., 333
Hammond gold medallion world atlas, 474
Handbook for scholars, rev ed, 973
Handbook for the Newbery medal & honor bks, 1980-89, 1140
Handbook of ...
   campaign spending, 749
   economic cycles, 201
   good English, rev ed, 1061
   heart drugs, 1657
   industrial chemical additives, 1709
   libs, archives & info centres in India, v.9, 647
   libs, archives & info centres in India, v.11, pt.1, 648
   modern British painting 1900-80, 1044
   molecular sieves, 1584
   natl population censuses: Europe, 898
   plastic compounds, elastomers, & resins, 1710
   plastics, elastomers, & composites, 2d ed, 1714
   private schools, 73d ed, 349
   real estate terms, rev ed, 325
   reconstruction in E Europe & the Soviet Union, 536
   research on curriculum, 334
   research on music teaching & learning, 1252
   research on social studies teaching & learning, 336
   research on the illicit drug trade, 892
   Rocky Mountain plants, 1501
   Soviet & E European films & filmmakers, 1340
   world stock & commodity exchanges, 1992, 222
Handbook on Japanese military forces, 705
Handel, Bernard, 1615
Handler, Jerome S., 541
Handlist of rhetorical terms, 2d ed, 1071
Hanke, Ken, 1354
Hannaway, David B., 1510
Hans Rosbaud: a bio-bibliog, 1257
Hanson, Robert P., 223, 224
Harcourt, Caroline S., 1484
Harder, Kelsie B., 1299
Hardin, Steve, 82
Harding, Jim, 568, 569
Harduf, David Mendel, 1106
Harkness, Richard, 1664
Harner, James L., 686, 1203
Harnsberger, R. Scott, 1017

Haroon, Mohammed, 1239
Harper, Charles A., 1714
Harper ency of military biog, 698
HarperCollins dict of ...
　American govt & pols, 736
　art terms & techniques, 2d ed, 1025
　astronomy & space sci, 1702
　electronics, 1595
　environmental sci, 1753
　mathematics, 1739
　sociology, 848
　stats, 904
Harris, Laurie Lanzen, 35
Harris, Merle, 135
Harris, Steve, 1258
Harris, Wendell V., 1111
Harrison, Charles, 350
Harrison, Harriet W., 638
Harrison, R. K., 1419
Harte, John, 1769
Harter, H. Leon, 902
Hartford, Bill, 1784
Hartman, Stephen, 243
Hartman, Stephen W., 241
Hartness, Ann, 153
Harvey, Joan M., 98
Hast, Adele, 260
Hasten, Elizabeth, 977
Hathaway, Thomas, 1251
Haven't I seen you somewhere before?, 1358
Hawaiian insects & their kin, 1565
Hawkins, Walter L., 423
Hawkins-Dady, Mark, 1391
Hawthorn, Jeremy, 1112, 1113
Hayes, Kevin J., 1178
Haynes, Bruce, 1263
Hazen, Edith P., 1235
Health care terms, 2d ed, 1621
Health Media of America, 1647
Health-related cookbks, 1471
Heaney, H. J., 2
Hearne, Betsy, 1134
Heaton, Tim B., 867
Heavy minerals in colour, 1726
Heck, Cheva, 876
Hein's cum index to interim precedent decisions of the Board of Immigration Appeals, 599
Helleburst, Lynn, 734, 750
Heller, George N., 1240
Help for children from infancy to adulthood, 5th ed, 896
Hemingway: an annot chronology, 1174
Henbest, Nigel, 1700
Henderson, Lesley, 1153
Henderson, Robert W., 1579
Henry David Thoreau: an annot bibliog of comment & criticism before 1900, 1182
Henry Fonda: a bio-bibliog, 1323
Henry Holt hndbk of current sci & tech, 1455
Henry Holt intl desk ref, 269
Henry Holt retirement sourcebk, 855
Henry, Marcia Klinger, 661
Henry, Scott D., 1604
Hensyl, William R., 1623
Herald, Diana Tixier, 1147

Herbert, Patricia M., 124
Herbsman, Yael, 446
Heritage ency of band music, 1283
Herman, Gerald, 552
Herren, Ray V., 1468
Hess, Carol A., 1259
Hiatt, Sky, 1355
Hickok, Ralph, 819
Hicks, Marie L., 1512
Hidden job market, 303
Higher educ in India, 391
Higher educ in the UK 1992-93, 386
Highfill, John W., 1003
High-technology editorial gd & stylebk, PC ed, 969
Hill, Carolyn N., 654
Hill, Joan, 602
Hill, Karen, 412, 1768
Hinnells, John R., 1404
Hippocrene insider's gd to Hungary, 505
Hippocrene insiders' gd to Nepal, 9th ed, 501
Hippocrene USA gd to black America, 424
Hirschfelder, Arlene, 432
Hispanic Americans info dir 1992-93, 428
Hispanic heritage, series 4, 150
Hispanic image on the silver screen, 1363
Hispanic presence in N America from 1492 to today, 427
Hispanic resource dir 1992-94, 429
Historic docs on presidential elections 1787-1988, 753
Historic US court cases 1690-1990, 578
Historical dict of ...
　Afghanistan, 121
　Angola, 2d ed, 112
　Laos, 128
　Libya, 2d ed, 115
　Mauritius, 2d ed, 147
　Mozambique, 116
　revolutionary China, 1839-1976, 523
　Singapore, 129
　the Central African Republic, 2d ed, 113
　the French 4th & 5th Republics, 1946-91, 537
　the Hashemite kingdom of Jordan, 164
　the Spanish empire, 1402-1975, 540
　Tudor England, 1485-1603, 532
Historical research in music educ, 2d ed, 1240
History of electrical tech, 1593
History of sci, 1437
Hitt, William D., 316
Hitzges, Norm, 812
Hladczuk, John, 404
Hobbie, Margaret, 438
Hobson, Margaret, 1125
Hochmann, Gabriella, 1177
Hockings, Paul, 413
Hodgkinson, Virginia Ann, 877
Hodgson, Godfrey, 520
Hodson, William K., 1603
Hoffman, Herbert H., 40
Hoffman, Louise J., 96
Hoffman, Verena, 725
Holdsworth, Brian, 1596
Holidays & special days project index for young people, 1308
Holland, Lisa, 1450
Holloway, Karen L., 268

Holography market place, 3d ed, 1012
Holt, Dean W., 706
Holt, Linda Hughey, 884
Holte, James Craig, 1418
Holthuis, L. B., 1557
Holy ground: a study of the American camp meeting, 1398
Holzer, Marc, 794
Home building & woodworking in colonial America, 1612
Home ency of symptoms, ailments & their natural remedies, 1640
Home health care, 1620
Honduras, 155
Honig, Alice Sterling, 894
Honour, Hugh, 1038
Hook, Brian, 125
Hooper, Brad, 1160
Hoover, Gary, 208
Hoover's hndbk of American bus 1992, 208
Hopkins, Nigel J., 1740
Hopkins, Richard, 959
Horace Greeley: a bio-bibliog, 979
Horn, Barbara Lee, 1377, 1378
Horn, Judy, 676
Horne, Aaron, 1260
Hornor, Edith R., 909
Hornor, Louise L., 903
Houghton, Patricia, 1295
Houston, James E., 636
Houze, Herbert, 1004
How many calories? how much fat?, 1481
How quaint the ways of paradox!, 1274
How to find info about AIDS, 1652
How to research the Supreme Court, 571
Howard-Reguindin, Pamela F., 155
Howarth, Francis G., 1565
Howarth, Lynne C., 639
Howlett, Charles F., 791
Hoyle, Gary D., 667
Hu, Shing Tsung (Peter), 1510
Hubbard, Linda S., 687
Huber, Jeffrey T., 1652
Huber, Kristina Ruth, 925
Hudson, John R., 1740
Hugh Johnson's pocket ency of wine 1992, 1474
Hui, Y. H., 1473
Human communication behavior & info processing, 956
Human resources glossary, 302
Human rights: 60 major global instruments, 615
Humanities index, 948
Humble, Malcolm, 1223
Humor in American lit, 1189
Hunt, Thomas C., 348
Hunter, Allan, 1346, 1356
Hunting, Anthony L. L., 1715
Hunting quotations, 836
Hunziker, Ray, 1554
Hutcheson, Helen, 233

Icons, 42
IEG dir of sponsorship mktg, 1991, 258
Iglitzin, Lynne B., 408

Ignashev, Diane M. Nemec, 1230
Illustrated almanac of histl facts, 553
Illustrated chemistry lab terminology, 1708
Illustrated dir of handicapped products 1991-92, 863
Illustrated ency of architects & architecture, 1040
Illustrated ency of woodworking handtools instruments & devices, rev ed, 1610
Illustrated gd to the mountain stream insects of Colo., 1568
Illustrated hrdwr bk, 1611
IMF glossary, 254
Immell, Myra, 1137
Immigrant experience, 420
Important peak index of the registry of mass spectral data, 1717
In search of your roots: a gd for Canadians, rev ed, 456
In the beginning: great 1st lines from your favorite bks, 1117
Index chemicus, v.125, no.1, 1719
Index of American per verse: 1990, 1187
Index to ...
 Commonwealth little mags 1987-89, 83
 dialect maps of Great Britain, 1067
 Fla. Jewish hist in the American Israelite 1854-1900, 446
 illus of animals & plants, 1525
 intl stats 1990, 915
 jls in communication studies through 1990, 954
 legal pers [CD-ROM], 601
 legal pers: Sept 1990-Aug 1991, 600
 reviews of bibliographical pubs, v.10, 949
 the Sporting News, 823
 US invalid pension records 1801-15, 459
Indexing from A to Z, 653
Indian music lit, 1239
Indian subcontinent in lit for children & young adults, 1126
Indiana factbk 1992, 108
Indians along the Oregon Trail, expanded ed, 436
Indigenous navigation & voyaging in the Pacific, 1789
Individuals with disabilities educ act 1980-91, 394
Indoor air quality dir 1992-93, 1758
Industrial engineering terminology, rev ed, 1602
Industrial group index, 649
Industrial research in the UK, 14th ed, 296
Informal economy, 173
Information bks for children, 7
Information marketplace dir, 1993, 685
Information security hndbk, 315
Information sources in patents, 587
Information sources in the medical scis, 4th ed, 1626
INIS: thesaurus, 1735
Inlander, Charles B., 1633
Inman, David, 988
Insects of Hawaii, v.15, 1561
Inside Japanese support 1992, 280
Inside the legislative process, 1991 ed, 751
Insider's gd to successful US immigration, 589
Insider's gd to the colleges 1993, 372
Inskipp, Carol, 1543
Inskipp, Tim, 1543
Instant natl locator gd, 955
Institute for Brewing Studies, 1477
Institutum Patristicum Augustinianum, 1406

Interlibrary loan policies dir, 4th ed, 657
International Board for Plant Genetic Resources, 1496
International business dict & ref, 255
International corporate yellow bk, v.5, no.1, 259
International defense electronic systems hndbk, 718
International dict of films & filmmakers, v.3, 2d ed, 1335
International dict of theatre, v.1, 1391
International dir of Canadian studies, 132
International dir of co hists, v.4, 260
International ency of integrated circuits, 2d ed, 1594
International ency of linguistics, 1050
International exchange locator, 387
International film index 1895-1990, 1373
International GIS sourcebk, 1993, 491
International gd to legal deposit, 651
International hndbk of reading educ, 404
International higher educ, 381
International histl stats: Europe 1750-1988, 3d ed, 911
International illus vocabulary of English-French fingerprint terminology..., 607
International imaging source bk 1992, 1693
International legal bibliogs, 567
International military ency, v.1, 702
International orgs & world order dict, 781
International petroleum ency, 1744
International research centers dir 1992-93, 68
International satellite dir, 1992, 1696
International trade, 270
International Trotskyism 1929-85, 777
Intner, Sheila S., 640
Introduction to US govt info sources, 4th ed, 73
Inventory of longitudinal studies in the social scis, 102
Iris of China, 1507
Irish in America, 437
Irish/English, English/Irish dict & phrasebk, 1088
Irvin, Linda, 257
Isaacs, Alan, 680
Isaacs, Ronald H., 449
Italian American material culture, 438
Izady, Mehrdad R., 165

J. K. Lasser Institute, 327
J. K. Lasser's your income tax 1993, 327
Jackson, Frederick H., 1080
Jackson, Philip W., 334
Jaderstrom, Susan, 324
James Fenimore Cooper: an annot bibliog of criticism, 1171
James Stewart: a bio-bibliog, 1319
Jane's all the world's aircraft 1992-93, 1780
Janes, Michael, 1083
Janet Gaynor: a bio-bibliog, 1316
Jankowski, Bernard, 1425
Jankowski, Katherine E., 280, 872
Japanese studies from pre-hist to 1990, 126
Jary, David, 848
Jary, Julia, 848
Jasion, Jan T., 651
Jasper, Lisa R., 1686
Jazz discography, v.1, 1287
Jazz discography, v.2, 1288
Jazz discography, v.3, 1289

Jenkins, Jon C., 784
Jerde, Judith, 1007
Jerusalem Center for Public Affairs, staff of, 726
Jerusalem, the holy city, v.2, 544
Jerzy Kosinski: an annot bibliog, 1175
Jessica Tandy: a bio-bibliog, 1315
Jewish film dir, 1357
Jewish museums of N America, 444
Jewish profiles, 450
Jewish wisdom, 445
Jewish-American hist & culture, 442
Job hunter's gd to 100 great American cities, 304
Job seeker's gd to private & public cos, 310
John Dewey: the collected works, 1882-1953: index, 342
John Fowles: a ref companion, 1208
John Wayne: a bio-bibliog, 1320
Johnson, Curt, 698, 974
Johnson, Edward D., 1061
Johnson, Hugh, 1474
Johnson, John W., 578
Johnson, Karl E., 634
Johnson, Linda Carlson, 1309
Johnson, Stanley H., Jr., 1493
Johnston-Des Rochers, Janeen, 252
Jolma, Dena Jones, 836
Jones, C. Lee, 663
Jones, Colin, 143
Jones, Gareth, 1753
Jones, John Oliver, 497
Jones, Kenneth Glyn, 1705
Jones, Lawrence K., 409
Jones, Lewis P., 510
Jones, Linda M., 134
Jones, Schuyler, 122
Jose, Jim, 778
Joseph Chaikin: a bio-bibliog, 1376
Joseph Papp: a bio-bibliog, 1378
Journal of Women's Hist gd to per lit, 943
Joyce, Beverly A., 1146
Joyce, Donald Franklin, 679
Junge, Hans-Dieter, 1671
Junge, H.-D., 1597

Kahn, Ada P., 884
Kahn, Ahmed S., 1697
Kaiser index to black resources, 1948-86, 425
Kalck, Pierre, 113
Kalfatovic, Martin R., 163
Kalnay, Alanna, 16
Kansas hist, 513
Kapel, David E., 330
Kapel, Marilyn B., 330
Kaplan, Harold I., 1649
Kaplan, Justin, 89
Karageorgiou, Dimitris, 1376
Karamitsanis, Aphrodite, 492
Karst, Kenneth L., 576
Kasic, Christopher, 68
Kasraie, Asadollah, 1090
Kasraie, Hassan, 1090
Katchmer, George A., 1336
Katlan, Alexander W., 1027
Katz, Bernard S., 240

Katz, Bill, 84, 85
Katz, Linda Sternberg, 84, 85
Kavass, Igor I., 562, 759
Kay, David C., 1687
Keenan, Linda, 661
Keeping score: film & TV music, 1980-88, 1271
Kehde, Ned, 823
Kehoe, Timothy, 1039
Keller, Hans J., 1775
Kelly, Melody S., 668
Kemp, Peter, 842
Kentucky ency, 109
Kepple, Robert J., 1400
Kerby, Jody L., 1650
Kerrod, Robin, 1530, 1703
Kessler, Jack, 626
Kessler, Terri, 978
Keyser, Daniel J., 337, 338
Khorana, Meena, 1126
Kidron, Michael, 475
Kies, Cosette, 1156
Kimerling, L. C., 1592
Kindscher, Kelly, 1514
Kiner, Larry F., 1277
King, Kamla J., 582
King, Martha P., 594
Kingsbury, Stewart A., 1299
Kingston, Mike, 111
Kinnaman, William, 919
Kipfer, Barbara Ann, 1076
Kirby, Debra M., 373, 377
Kirk, Mary E., 388
Kirk, Tim, 766
Kissane, Sharon F. Mrotek, 44
Kister, Kenneth F., 1048
Kister's best dicts for adults & young people, 1048
Kleber, John E., 109
Kleiman, Carol, 311
Klein, Barry, 1673
Kluepfel, Brian, 1012
Knopf, Kenyon A., 181
Knowles, Owen, 1207
Kobylka, Joseph F., 566
Koek, Karin E., 287
Kohl, Herbert, 1060
Kokernak, Jane, 675
Kolin, Philip C., 1212
Kondratieff, B. C., 1568
Kooyman, Mary, 128
Koszegi, Michael A., 1401
Kovacs, Diane, 72
Kovacs, Ruth, 880, 881, 1411
Kraeuter, David W., 983
Kramer, Jack, 1486
Kramer, Jack J., 803
Kraskow, Tina, 924
Kricher, John C., 1574
Krive, Sarah, 1230
Kroger, Manfred, 1475
Krogh, Suzanne Lowell, 351
Krohn, Barbara Ehrenwald, 1791
Krol, John, 978, 1698
Kronick, David A., 1463
Kruk, Leonard, 324
Kuman, Arthur Jr., 304

Kuperus, Bart, 999
Kurds: a concise hndbk, 165
Kurian, George Thomas, 137
Kurmann, Joseph A., 1475
Kurtz, Edwin B., 1598
Kyiv, Ksana, 1082

LaBlanc, Michael L., 426, 1245
Labour & population programme, 299
Lachmann, Richard, 849
Lacy, Charles, 1665
Lainhart, Ann S., 899
Lamb, Annette C., 344
Lambert, David, 1531
Lambert, Jean L. F., 607
Lambert, Mark, 1780
Lambrechts, Eric, 1013
Lamme, Linda Leonard, 351
Lance, Leonard L., 1665
Landry, Christine P., 1650
Lane, Jan-Erik, 727
Lane, Susan, 977
Lang, Jovian P., 17
Lange's hndbk of chemistry, 14th ed, 1716
Langley, Winston E., 615
Langlois, Denise, 252
Language of sex, 883
Language of the Constitution, 593
Lanham, Richard A., 1071
Lanier-Graham, Susan D., 1759
Lankford, Mary D., 399
Lantzy, M. Louise, 394
Laos, 127
Larousse ency of precious gems, 1725
Larson, Olaf F., 846
Laser video disc companion, updated ed, 997
Late achievers, 43
Late Victorian & Edwardian writers, 1890-1914, 1194
Latham, Robert, 1158
Latham, Roy, 1688
Latin America & the Caribbean: a critical gd to research sources, 148
Latin American serial pubs available by exchange, 633
Latin American short story, 1225
Latrobe, Kathy Howard, 669
Laudati, Despina, 319
Laughlin, Mildred Knight, 669
Lauren Bacall: a bio-bibliog, 1321
Lauther, Howard, 1051
Lauther's complete punctuation thesaurus of the English lang, 1051
Lavin, Michael R., 209
Law bks in print 1990, 570
Law firms yellow bk, v.2, no.1, 584
Law lib ref shelf, 2d ed, 572
Lawrance, Alan, 522
Lazure, Noel, 1677
Leach, Marjorie, 1305
Leary, William M., 248
Leatherwood, Stephen, 1571
Lebanon, rev ed, 166
Lee, Lauren K., 667
Lee, R. R., 1599
Lee, Thomas H., 120

Legal asst's notebk, 595
Legal desk bk 1992, 597
Legal researcher's desk ref 1992, 591
Legal thesaurus, 2d ed, 573
Lemon-aid new car gd 1992, 1781
Lemon-aid used car gd 1992, 1782
Lems-Dworkin, Carol, 1241
Lenburg, Jeff, 1347
Lenihan, Ayeliffe A., 1620
Leo Spitzer on lang & lit, 1046
Les Brown's ency of TV, 3d ed, 986
Lesko, Matthew, 210
Leslie, John, 271
Lesser-known women, 934
Lester, DeeGee, 516
Lester, Meera, 962
Lester-Massman, Elli, 931
Leuchtmann, Horst, 1248
Leung, Edwin Pak-wah, 523
Levi, Anthony, 1221
Levine, Barbara, 342
Levine, Caroline, 220
Levine, John R., 1687
Levine, Michael, 1760
Levine, Sumner N., 220
Levinson, Nadine A., 797
Levy, Leonard W., 576
Lewis, Audrey, 13
Lewis, Ivor, 1070
Lewis, Thomas P., 1261
Lexical semantics, 1092
Lexicon of economics, 181
Liang, Diana F., 1741
Librarianship & info work worldwide 1991, 631
Library lit, 632
Library, media, & archival preservation glossary, 663
Library serv to children, 665
Library use, 2d ed, 804
Lieutenant-governors of the NW territories & Alta. 1876-1991, 765
Lighthall, Lynne, 643
Lighting design on Broadway, 1383
Lignor, Amy, 194, 862
Lilienthal, Nancy, 1761
Limbacher, James L., 1271, 1358
Limca bk of records 1991, 1310
Lindfors, Bernth, 1110
Lineback, Richard H., 1397
Lineman's & cableman's hndbk, 8th ed, 1598
Linguistics ency, 1052
Listener's musical companion, new ed, 1251
Liszka, Thomas R., 949
Literary-critical approaches to the Bible, 1430
Literature of the Great Lakes region, 1165
Literature-based moral educ, 351
Little black bk of business words, 186
Liungman, Carl G., 1041
Livable cities almanac, 920
Locked room murders & other impossible crimes, 1150
Locust neurobiology, 1566
Loertscher, David V., 1144
London, Joy, 600
London stage 1940-49, 1386
Long, Kim, 352

Longley, Dennis, 315
Longman hndbk of world hist since 1914, 559
Looney, J. Jefferson, 357
Lord, Tom, 1287, 1288, 1289
Louisiana almanac 1992-93, 110
Lovece, Frank, 995
Loveday, John, 1630
Lower, Dorothy M., 460
Lowery, Charles D., 616
Luckert, Yelena, 447
Ludlow, Daniel H., 1420
Luling, Virginia, 1099
Lung, Rita Gaston, 861

MacDonald, Margaret Read, 1298
Macey, Samuel L., 14
Machlis, Paul, 1183
Mackenzie, Graham, 631
Mackenzie, Leslie, 192, 862
Mackler, Tasha, 1152
Macksey, Kenneth, 701
Maclachlan, Graham, 1751
Macmillan animal ency for children, 1532
Macmillan children's gd to dinosaurs & other prehistoric animals, 1732
Macmillan ency of computers, 1678
Macmillan 1st atlas, 476
Macmillan school atlas, 3d ed, 471
Macmillan visual dict, 1077
MacNeil, Anne, 1249
Macpherson, Gordon, 1629
Macrothesaurus for info processing in the field of economic & social dvlpmt, 641
Madaus, M. Howard, 1004
Madden, Jennifer, 1125
Magazines for ...
  children, 2d ed, 87
  libs, 7th ed, 85
  young people, 2d ed, 84
Mageli, Paul D., 420
Magic, witchcraft, & paganism in America, 2d ed, 811
Magill, Frank N., 617, 1164, 1236, 1237, 1699
Magill's survey of sci: physical sci series, 1699
Mahajan, S., 1592
Mahar, Mary, 353
Mahoney, Jim, 359
Major cos of the Far East & Australasia 1991/92, 8th ed, v.1, 281
Maki, Kathleen E., 213
Makinson, Larry, 752
Malbin, Michael J., 754
Malhotra, Nirmal, 391
Mallet, Catherine M., 1783
Mallett, Daryl F., 1157
Malmkjaer, Kirsten, 1052
Malott, Marcia K., 956
Mammals of the neotropics: the S cone, v.2, 1570
Mandell, Judy, 963
Mange, Maria A., 1726
Manley, Deborah, 558
Mann, Thomas E., 754
Manual of vascular plants of NE US and adjacent Canada, 2d ed, 1500
Manufacturing USA, 2d ed, 247

Mao Zedong: a bibliog, 522
Maran, Stephen P., 1704
Marantz, Kenneth, 1022
Marantz, Sylvia, 1022
Marcaccio, Kathleen Young, 1670, 1682
March, Andrew L., 15
Marcheteau, Michel, 182
Marck, Jeffrey C., 1080
Marcus, James L., Jr., 239
Marder, Stephen, 1096
Margetts, Juliet, 298
Marine atlas of the Hawaiian Islands, 466
Maritime affairs: a world hndbk, 2d ed, 1790
Maritime provinces atlas, new ed, 472
Markovich, Alex, 1786
Marlin, John Tepper, 920
Marsh, Arthur, 305
Marshall Cavendish ency of family health, 1617
Marszalek, John F., 616
Marth, Del, 106
Marth, Martha J., 106
Martin, Christine, 966
Martin, Elizabeth, 680
Martin, Fenton S., 571
Martin, Graham R., 1596
Marx, Cheryl E., 1467
Mary McCarthy: an annot bibliog, 1177
Mason, Francis K., 699
Masterpieces of African-American lit, 1164
Masterplots 2: poetry series, 1237
Masters of lens & light, 1343
Masthay, Carl, 1089
Maternal & child health legislation: 1991, 594
Mathematical bk review index 1800-1940, 1738
Mathematical jls, 1741
Matlon, Ronald J., 954
Matter of fact: statements containing stats on current social, economic & pol issues, v.14-15, 910
Mattera, Philip, 272
Matthews, Alison, 226
Matthews, Elizabeth W., 572
Maurer, Heinz F. W., 1726
Mauritius, 146
Maxfield, Doris Morris, 878
Maxwell, Donald W., 1165
Maxwell, F. C., 461
Mayer, Ralph, 1025
Mayhew, Susan, 489
Maynard's industrial engineering hndbk, 4th ed, 1603
Mayne, John W., 1740
Maziarz, Daniel, 1775
McArthur, Feri, 1054
McArthur, Tom, 1054
McCalla, Robert J., 472
McCann, Kelly, 935
McClain, Gary, 269
McClelland, Averil Evans, 926
McCormick, Curtis W., 744
McCreight, Tim, 1008
McCutcheon, Marc, 1072
McDonald, Ben, 525
McDonough, John E., 765
McDougall, D. Blake, 765
McElmeel, Sharron L., 1142
McElrath, Joseph R., Jr., 1180

McGraw-Hill dict of ...
   bus acronyms, initials, & abbrevs, 170
   info tech & computer acronyms, initials, & abbrevs, 1679
   Wall St acronyms, initials, & abbrevs, 171
McGraw-Hill ency of sci & tech, 7th ed, 1446
McGraw-Hill pocket gd to bus finance, 241
McGreal, Ian P., 950
McGuire, Paula, 41
McKay, David, 727
McKim, Donald K., 1422
McKnight, Scot, 1428
McKusick, Victor A., 1624
McLafferty, Fred W., 1717
McLean, Bradley H., 1429
McLean, Janice, 307
McLeish, John A. B., 856
McLellan, Hilary, 1672
McManus, Gary E., 473
McMillon, Bill, 335, 507
McMurray, Emily J., 1324
McNeill, Allison K., 188, 189
McNern, Janet, 928
McPeek, Gail A., 1539
McPhail, Martha E., 155
McWilliam, Neil, 1018, 1019
Meacham, Mary, 1122
Means illus construction dict, new ed, 1037
Measuring global values, 729
Medical & health care bks & serials in print 1992, 1625
Medical word bk A-Z, 1631
Medicinal wild plants of the prairie, 1514
Meech, Karin Napoleon, 1755
Meet the natives: the amateur's field gd to Rocky Mountain wildflowers, trees & shrubs, 9th ed, 1505
Mehaffey, Karen Rae, 927
Mellinkoff, David, 579
Mellinkoff's dict of American legal usages, 579
Melton, J. Gordon, 811, 1401, 1408, 1410
Mendelian inheritance in man, 10th ed, 1624
Mercer, Anne, 1220
Merriam-Webster concise hndbk for writers, 964
Merriam-Webster concise school & office dict, 1058
Merriam-Webster concise school & office thesaurus, 1074
Merriam-Webster dict of quotations, 91
Merritt, Helen, 1043
Messadie, Gerald, 1447, 1448, 1449
Messier's nebulae & star clusters, 2d ed, 1705
Metzler, Susan, 1509
Metzler, Van, 1509
Mexican legal system, 563
Mexican lit, 2d ed, 1227
Mexican pol biogs, 1884-1935, 775
Meyer, Jimmy Elaine Wilkinson, 860
Meyers, Robert A., 1453
Michael Singer's film directors, 9th ed, 1372
Microcomputer index, v.12, 1686
Middle East: a pol dict, 776
Middle East bibliog, 162
Mieder, Wolfgang, 1299
Mihailovich, Vasa D., 1234
Mikdadi, Faysal, 543
Mikotowicz, Thomas J., 1382

Miles, Susan G., 868
Miletich, John J., 889
Milgate, Murray, 242
Military fortifications, 692
Military hist of the US, 700
Millennialism: an intl bibliog, 1399
Miller, E. Willard, 1770
Miller, Gordon L., 1437
Miller, Jacqueline Y., 1548
Miller, Joanne, 324
Miller, Kenneth E., 119
Miller, Oscar J., 573
Miller, Ruby M., 1770
Miller, Shelley, 633
Miller-Lachmann, Lyn, 1127
Mills, J. J., 652
Mills, Jane, 938
Miner, Margaret, 1213
Minerals of the world, 1729
Minor, Barbara B., 398
Minor, Mark, 1430
Minor oil crops, 1464
Minor presidential candidates & parties of 1992, 748
Minority health resources dir, 1618
Misner, Amy J., 71
MIT dict of modern economics, 4th ed, 183
Mitchell, B. R., 911
Mitchell, Joanne, 1691
Mitchell, M. H., 1482
MLA dir of scholarly presses in lang & lit, 686
MLA intl bibliog, 1107
Modem USA, 1683
Modern companion to the European Community, 767
Modern writers, 1914-45, 1195
Moe, Edward O., 846
Moffat, Riley, 900
Mokotoff, Gary, 494
Molin, Paulette, 432
Molinaro, Lawrence, Jr., 249
Moll, Verna Penn, 158
Molyneaux, Gerard, 1319
Money for performing artists, 1326
Montgomery, John H., 1771
Montserrat, 156
Moody's hndbk of common stocks, spring 1992, 223
Moody's hndbk of dividend achievers 1992, 224
Moons of the solar system, 1707
Moore, Bob, 766
Moore, Dianne F., 1702
Moore, R. I., 545
More creative uses of children's lit, v.1, 671
More exciting, funny, scary, short, different, & sad bks kids like, 1122
Morehead, Joe, 73
Morehead, Philip D., 1249
Morgan, Brad, 840
Morgan, Bradley J., 822
Morgan, Hal, 312
Morgan, Kathleen O'Leary, 912
Morgan, Scott, 912
Mori, Monica, 857, 928
Moritz, Charles, 37
Morris, Christopher, 1444
Morris, Dwight, 749
Morris, Leslie R., 657

Morris, Sandra Chass, 657
Morton, Brian, 1255
Morton, L. T., 1626
Morton's medical bibliog, 5th ed, 1627
Moss, Joyce, 117, 160, 1359
Moss, Norman, 1069
Mossman, Jennifer, 1
Motion picture serial, 1364
Motley, Lynne, 1683
Movie classics, 1356
Moving & relocation sourcebk, 917
Mudge, Bradford K., 1196
Muether, John R., 1400
Mull, William P., 1565
Mulligan, Gerald A., 1511
Mulliner, K., 129
Mullins, June B., 1124
Multicultural aspects of lib media programs, 669
Multicultural projects index, 1312
Multilingual dict of publishing, printing & bkselling, 680
Municipal yellow bk, v.2, no.1, 741
Munson, Kenneth, 1780
Murder ... by category, 1152
Murphy, C. Edward, 879, 1653
Murray, Michael T., 1634
Murthy, K. Krishna, 1413
Music & dance in Puerto Rico from the age of Columbus to modern times, 1243
Music for oboe, 1650-1800, 2d ed, 1263
Music in British libs, 650
Music lover's gd to Europe, 1250
Mythology, 1302

Naifeh, Steven, 1644
Names of countries & their capital cities, 104
Nanton, Isabel, 503
NASDAQ yellow bk, v.4, no.1, 225
Nash, Jay Robert, 608, 609, 610, 611
Nash, Ralph C., Jr., 580
Nasrallah, Wahib, 174
National Association of State Development Agencies, 221
National bk of lists 1992, 211
National data bk of fndns, 16th ed, 879
National dir of ...
    addresses & telephone nos, 69
    chiropractic, 3d ed, 1645
    courts of law 1991, 586
    nonprofit orgs 1992, v.1, 195
National gd to funding for the environment & animal welfare, 881
National gd to funding in religion, 1411
National health dir, 1992, 1619
National park gd 1992, 496
National parks, 498
National trade policies, 320
Native America, 431
Natural hist from A to Z, 1523
Natural hist museums, v.1, 1524
Nature dir, 1759
Nature in America, 1526
Nature of SE Alaska, 1528
Nature projects on file, 1527

Naughton, Renee, 666
Naylor, Colin, 1028
Naylor, Lynne, 965
Nazareno, Rodolfo L., 1102
Nazi-retro film, 1362
NCAA basketball's finest, 827
NCAA football's finest, 831
NCEA/Ganley's Catholic schools in America 1992, 353
Neal-Schuman index to sports figures in collective biogs, 824
Neave, Guy R., 358
Nehmer, Kathleen Suttles, 401
Neill, Peter, 1791
Nelson Eddy: a bio-discography, 1277
Nelson, Michael, 753
Nelson, Ruth Ashton, 1501
Nelson's concordance of Bible phrases, 1431
Netzer, Corinne T., 1476
Nevada printing hist, 678
New American dict of music, 1249
New bk of knowledge, 60
New bk of popular sci, 1450
New car buying gd, 1992-93 ed, 1784
New, completely rev, greatly expanded, Madam Audrey's mostly cheap, all good, useful list of bks for speedy ref, 5th ed, 13
New cosmopolitan world atlas, census/environmental ed, 477
New gardener's hndbk & dict, 1486
New Grolier student ency, 61
New hacker's dict, 1680
New intl dict of acronyms in lib & info sci, 2d ed, 621
New Palgrave dict of money & finance, 242
New per title abbrevs, 86
New pocket Hawaiian dict, 1086
New pol parties of E Europe & the Soviet Union, 770
New standard ency, 62
New standard Jewish ency, 7th ed, 448
New state of the world atlas, 4th ed, 475
New treasury of Scripture knowledge, 1434
Newbery & Caldecott awards, 1992 ed, 1128
Newbery & Caldecott medal & honor bks in other media, 1121
Newbery & Caldecott medalists & honor bk winners, 2d ed, 1120
Newman, Oksana, 291
Newman, Peter, 242
Newman, Peter R., 539
Newsletters in print 1993-94, 978
Newspapers online, 975
Newton, Derek, 1063
Newton, Kenneth, 727
NFB film gd, 1342
Nichols, C. Allen, 1133
Nichols, Margaret Irby, 670
Nichols, Tom, 1470
Niemeyer, Suzanne, 1326
Nierenberg, William A., 1721
Nile notes of a howadji, 163
Nilsen, Don L. F., 1189
Nilsen, Kirsti, 16
1990 Health Care Services Committee of the International Foundation of Employee Benefit Plans, 1615
1992-1993 gd to newspaper syndication, 977
Nineteenth-century inventors, 1439
1920 fed population census: cat of microfilm available, 901
99 best residential & recreational communities in America for vacation, retirement & investment planning, 919
Nipp, Frank, 974
Nisonger, Thomas E., 677
Nixon, Judith M., 212
Nobari, Nuchine, 187
Nobel prize winners: suppl 1987-91, 41
Noll, Richard, 799
Non-ferrous metal data 1990, 1727
Nonprofit almanac 1992-93, 877
Noonan, Jon, 1439
Nordquist, Joan, 929, 930
Norm Hitzges histl sports almanac, 812
Norman, Jeremy M., 1627
North American brewers resource dir 1992-93, 1477
North American horticulture, 2d ed, 1487
Northcutt, Wayne, 537
Northern Ireland, 145
Notable black American women, 52
Novallo, Annette, 411
Novel & short story writer's market, 1992, 966
Nowak, Ronald M., 1572
NTC's dict of German false cognates, 1085
NTC's French & English bus dict, 182
Nuclear movies, 1349
Nuclear power reactors in the world, 1991 ed, 1749
Numbers you need, 1740
Nunn, Hilary, 649
Nursey-Bray, Paul, 778
NWO: a dir of natl women's orgs, 940

O'Brien, Jacqueline Wasserman, 913
O'Brien, Robert, 890
O'Brien, Robert F., 1278
Oceans Institute of Canada, 1790
Ockerman, Herbert W., 1708
O'Clair, Rita M., 1528
O'Connor, Leo F., 1170
Odell, Rice, 1777
O'Donnell, Owen, 1324
O'Donnell, Timothy S., 95, 273
Off the record, v.1, 1292
Office of Communications, American Association for the Advancement of Science, 1452
Official gd to the American marketplace, 906
Official museum dir 1992, 79
Official museum products & servs dir 1992, 80
Oggel, L. Terry, 1379
Oil & Gas Jl exploration index, 1750
Olderr, Steven, 1311
Olitzky, Kerry M., 449
Olsen, M. A., 226
Olson, James S., 540
Olson, Stan, 880, 881, 1411
Olympics factbk, 840
O'Meara, Meghan A., 261
Omni gazetteer of the USA, 495
100 best job$ for the 1990s & beyond, 311
1000 brave Canadians, 36

1001 quips & quotes for bus speeches, 219
O'Neal, Bill, 515
Online manual, 203
Open doors 1990/91, 389
Open secrets, 2d ed, 752
Opera performances in video format, 1273
Opler, Paul A., 1549
Orenstein, J. A., 1685
Organization charts, 212
Ornstein, Norman J., 754
Orr, Leonard, 1114
Ortiz, Sylvia P., 954
Osman, Madina M., 1099
Ostler, Rosemarie, 1049
Ostroff, Harriet, 1470
Ott, Bill, 9
Our family, our friends, our world, 1127
Our natl holidays, 1313
Our natl symbols, 1309
Out of the woodpile, 1151
Outstanding women athletes, 818
Owen, Bobbi, 1383, 1384
Owners & officers of private cos, 1992, 196
Oxford companion to the English lang, 1054
Oxford dict for scientific writers & eds, 967
Oxford dict of ...
  abbrevs, 3
  new words, 1065
  quotations, 4th ed, 92
Oxford gd to the French lang, 1083
Oxford illus ency of invention & tech, 1451

Pacific coast nudibranchs, 1573
Padwick's bibliog of cricket, v.2, 828
Palliative care of the elderly, 857
Palmisano, Joseph M., 411, 412, 878
Palmist's companion, 809
Pankratz, Tom, 1772
Papageorgiou, Markos, 1613
Paperbound bks in print, spring 1992, 31
Papp, L., 1567
Paraire, Philippe, 1291
Parapsychological research with children, 808
Parasites & diseases of wild mammals in Fla., 1569
Parent, Mary P., 328
Parish, James Robert, 1360
Park, James, 42
Parker, Hershel, 1178
Parker, Sybil P., 1446
Parkes, Geoff, 1085
Parks dir of the US, 500
Parrish, Michael, 769
Parry, Donald W., 1402
Parsifal on record, 1270
Parsons, Nicholas T., 505
Partington, Angela, 92
Passages: a treasure trove of N American exploration, 485
Passenger & immigration lists index, 1992 suppl., 460
Pastoral responses to older adults & their families, 859
Paterson, Ellen R., 1666
Patterson, Alex, 508
Patterson, Anna Grace, 22

Paul Baker's topical index of contemporary Christian music, 1268
Paul, Ellen, 869
Paul, Shalom M., 1435
Paulin, Mary Ann, 671
Paxton, John, 464
Payne, Peter A., 1635
Payton, Geoffrey, 464
PC-SIG ency of shareware, 4th ed, 1689
Peace: abstracts of the psychological & behavioral lit 1967-90, 789
Peacock, John, 1010
Pearce, David W., 183
Pearl Harbor, 1941, 696
Peary, Danny, 1337
Pecchia, David, 1371
Pellant, Chris, 1728
Penguin dict for writers & eds, 968
Penguin dict of architecture, 4th ed, 1038
Penguin dict of proper names, 464
Penguin ency of modern warfare, 701
Pennell, Allison A., 249
Penney, Barbara, 650
Penney, Edmund F., 987
Penny, Anne, 489
Pension lists of 1792-95, 457
People atlas, 414
People's chronology, rev ed, 554
Peoples of the world: Africans south of the Sahara, 117
Peoples of the world: the Middle East & N Africa, 160
Perdue, Lewis, 969
Perigee visual dict of signing, rev ed, 1098
Pernetta, John, 1730
Perren, Richard, 126
Perry, Jeb H., 996
Perry, Jesse P., Jr., 1519
Persaud, Tina, 4
Persian & English glossary for humanities & social scis, 1090
Pesman, M. Walter, 1505
Petersen, Neal H., 785
Peterson, Carolyn Sue, 1129
Peterson 1st gd to reptiles & amphibians, 1577
Peterson 1st gd to seashores, 1574
Peterson, Kimberley A., 261
Peterson's grants for grad study, 3d ed, 374
Peterson's grants for postdoctoral study, 375
Pettijohn, Terry F., 800
Petzet, G. Alan, 1750
Pevsner, Nikolaus, 1038
Pham, Gisele, 1600
Phelps, Erin, 102
Philbin, Tom, 1611
Philip, Alan Butt, 768
Phillips, Donald E., 956
Phillips, Gillian, 885
Philosopher's index thesaurus, 1397
Photographers: a sourcebk for histl research, 1014
Photography & lit, 1013
Piano music by black women, 1264
Piccirelli, Annette, 68, 1768
Picture this! a gd to over 300 environmentally, socially, & politically relevant films & videos, 1355

Pidgeon, Alice, 570
Pierce, Vivienne S., 859
Pierce, William L., 866
Pilger, Mary Anne, 1005, 1308, 1312, 1461
Pines of Mexico & Central America, 1519
Pinfold, John, 130
Pinkoski, Karen, 135
Pinsker, Sanford, 442
Pitts, Michael R., 1360
Pivotal conflict: a comprehensive chronology of the 1st world war, 1914-19, 552
Pizzorno, Joseph E., 1634
Place names of Alta., v.2, 492
Plant closings, 300
Plant engineer's ref bk, 1608
Plastics additives & modifiers hndbk, 1711
Platnick, Norman I., 1563
Pocket gd to electrical equipment & instrumentation, 2d ed, 1599
Pocket PCref, 1684
Pocket ref, 1454
Pockney, B. P., 142
Poetry index annual 1990, 1238
Poggi, Isotta, 811
Poirot, Jean-Paul, 1725
Poisonous snakes of the world, 1578
Pok, Attila, 546
Polish biographical dict, 44
Political & economic ency of S America & the Caribbean, 774
Political data hndbk: OECD countries, 727
Political leaders in Black Africa, 761
Political left in the American theatre of the 30's, 1375
Pollock, Bruce, 1279
Polmar, Norman, 556
Polner, Murray, 450
Popular entertainment research, 1327
Popular music, v.15, 1279
Population hist of E US cities & towns, 1790-1870, 900
Porkess, Roger, 904
Porter, David L., 817
Porter, Valerie, 1491
Portraits of American women, 932
Portraying persons with disabilities: an annot bibliog of fiction, 3d ed, 1132
Portraying persons with disabilities: an annot bibliog of nonfiction, 2d ed, 1124
Post, Elizabeth L., 1307
Post-harvest & processing techs of African staple foods, 1478
Potparic, O., 1658
Poultney, David, 1269
Pouyez, Christian, 132
Powell, Mark Allan, 1432
Power quotes, 730
Powers, John, 1414
Pranin, Stanley A., 838
Pratt, Douglas, 997
Pratt's gd to venture capital sources, 1992 ed, 197
Pravda, Alex, 788
Prentice-Hall pocket ency [of] organic gardening, 1488
President, Patricia A., 1618
Presner, Lewis A., 255

Preston, John, 886
Preston, Virginia, 144
Prevention how-to dict of healing remedies & techniques, 1636
Prevention Magazine Health Books, editors of, 1636
Price, Taff, 837
Prickett, Robert L., 343
Prime sources of Calif. & Nev. local hist, 511
Prince, Mary Miles, 562
Princetonians 1784-90, 356
Princetonians 1791-94, 357
Print price index '93, 1032
Prison slang, 603
Professional careers sourcebk, 2d ed, 411
Professional Secretaries Intl complete office hndbk, 324
Profiles 1989-90, 390
Program for Art on Film, 1016
Propas, Sharon W., 533
Prosocial dvlpmt in children, 894
Prospect researcher's gd to biographical research collections, 675
Prostitution: a gd to sources, 1960-90, 882
Protestant sensibility in the American novel, 1170
Provose, Carl, 918
Pruett, Barbara J., 1327
Prune bk: the 60 toughest sci & tech jobs in Washington, 757
Prytherch, Ray, 21, 631, 1125
Public admin research gd, 794
Public interest law, 566
Public interest profiles 1992-93, 795
Public schooling in America, 354
Public schools USA, 2d ed, 350
Publication sources in educl leadership, 343
Publishers dir, 1992, 687
Publishers, distrs & wholesalers of the US 1991-92, 688
Puckett, Katharyn E., 1131
Pukui, Mary Kawena, 1086
Purcell, Catherine, 376
Purvis, James D., 544

Quarles, Sandra L., 595
Quebedeaux, Richard, 511
Quick look drug bk with indications index, 1665
Quinlan, David, 1338
Quinlan's illus dir of film comedy actors, 1338
Quitno, Neal, 912
Quotable business, 218

Radio & TV pioneers: a patent bibliog, 983
Ragan, David, 1339
RAIC dir of scholarships & awards for architecture, 1039
Rainey, Buck, 1361
Raj, Prakash A., 501
Rake, Alan, 760
Rand McNally atlas of world hist, 1992 ed, 545
Rand McNally road atlas, 67th ed, 468
Rand McNally world atlas, 478
Random House atlas of the oceans, 1730
Random House compact world atlas, rev ed, 479

Random House Portuguese dict, 1091
Random House Webster's college dict, 1059
Ransley, John, 721
Rape: a bibliog 1976-88, 620
Rasic, Jeremija Lj., 1475
Rasinski, Timothy V., 1130
Rasor, Eugene L., 693, 694
Rawson, Hugh, 1213
Raymond, Eric S., 1680
Raymond, Walter John, 722
Raza, Moonis, 391
Reader's Digest children's world atlas, 480
Reader's gd to rational expectations, 175
Reader's quotation bk, 403
Reagan, Michael, 661
Rebach, Howard M., 891
Recent studies in myths & lit, 1970-90, 1301
Recommended pubs for legal research 1990, 574
Recommended ref bks in paperback, 2d ed, 15
Recommended ref bks 1992, 22
Redford, Kent H., 1570
Rediscovery of creation, 1417
Redman, Deborah A., 175
Reed, Jeffrey G., 804
Rees, Alan M., 1614
Rees, Mary Noel, 738
Reeves, Randall R., 1571
Reference and Adult Services Division, American Library Association, 17
Reference bks for children, 4th ed, 1129
Reference gd to sci fiction, fantasy, & horror, 1155
Reference sources for small & medium-sized libs, 5th ed, 17
Reference works for theological research, 3d ed, 1400
Reflections on childhood, 895
Reginald, Robert, 1157
Reginald's sci fiction & fantasy awards, 2d ed, 1157
Regional theatre dir 1992-93, 1388
Rehm, Sigmund, 1469
Rehrig, William H., 1283
Reilly, Bernard F., Jr., 735
Reimer, Carol J., 1362
Reimer, Robert C., 1362
RELEX for Russian, 1093
Religious bodies in the US, 1408
Religious info sources, 1401
Religious leaders, 1403
Renshaw, Jeffrey H., 1284
Reproduction: a gd to materials in the Women's Educl Resource Centre, 885
Reptiles & amphibians of Austr., 5th ed, 1575
Reruns on file, 994
Resinger, H., 1497
Resource dir for the disabled, 864
Resources for research in legal ethics, 592
Resources for writers, 971
Resources in ancient philosophy, 1393
Rettig, James, 18
Revell concise Bible dict, 1433
Reverse symbolism dict, 1311
Revolutionary & dissident movements, 3d ed, 728
Revolutionary orgs & revolutionaries in interbellum Poland, 779
Reynolds, Jacqueline, 1456
Reynolds, Michael, 1174

Rhoades, Nancy L., 829
Rhododendron portraits, 1506
Rhododendron species, v.3, 1504
Richard, Alfred Charles, Jr., 1363
Richard Burton: a bio-bibliog, 1322
Richard, Francois, 1609
Richard Wilbur: a ref gd, 1184
Richards, Laurence O., 1433
Richardson, Michael D., 343
Richardson, Selma K., 87
Richey, Virginia H., 1131
Ricks, Stephen D., 167, 1402
Riggin, Judith M., 1320
Riley, Sam G., 217
Rimmer, Robert H., 1332
Rinderknecht, Carol, 32
Ringelheim, Joan, 528
Riotte, J. C. E., 1550
Ripley, Gordon, 1220
Rise & fall of the Soviet Union, 535
Robb, David S., 1206
Robbins, Ira A., 1281
Roberson, William H., 1179
Robert Bridges: an annot bibliog, 1873-1988, 1205
Robertson, Dave, 498
Robertson, Debra E. J., 1132
Robertson, Patrick, 1370
Robinson, Doris, 1034
Robinson, Lesley, 203
Rocks & minerals, 1728
Rodale's all-new ency of organic gardening, 1489
Rodes, Barbara K., 1777
Roget's intl thesaurus, 5th ed, 1075
Roget's 21st century thesaurus, 1076
Roginski, Jim, 1120, 1121
Rojo, Alfonso L., 1558
Rollins, Alden, 547
Rollock, Barbara, 1139
Romaine-Davis, Ada, 1620
Romaniuk, Bohdan R., 870
Rome in the 4th century AD, 547
Romiszowski, Alexander J., 345
Room, Adrian, 184
Roosevelt research, 516
Rose, Jonathan, 689
Rosen, Stephen, 600
Rosenbaum, Ernest H., 1655
Rosenberg, Betty, 1147
Rosenberg, Jerry M., 170, 171, 1679
Rosenberg, Judith K., 1133
Rosenberg, Lee, 921
Rosenberg, Saralee, 921
Rosenblum, Joseph, 1214
Ross, Franz, 1012
Rotenburg, Gerald N., 1661
Roth, Wendy, 499
Rothbart, Linda S., 1783
Rousseau dict, 1396
Rowe, Fred A., 410
Rowell, C. H. F., 1566
Rowlinson, William, 1083
Roy, F. Hampton, 858
Royce, Brenda Scott, 1321
Rubens, Philip, 970
Rubinstein, W. D., 462

Ruddick, Nicholas, 1204
Rudisill, Richard, 1014
Rural dvlpmt, 922
Russell, Charles, 858
Russell, Cheryl, 906
Russian & Soviet educ 1731-1989, 383
Rutherford, Donald, 185

Sack, Sallyann Amdur, 494
Sadock, Benjamin J., 1649
Sahibs, nabobs & boxwallahs, 1070
Sajdak, Bruce T., 1215
Sallis, Lela, 359
Salmon, Richard D., 304
Salu, Luc, 1013
Salvatore, Dominick, 320
Salwak, Dale, 1209
San Miguel, Rachel, 1103
Sanborn, Lavonne Hayes, 402
Sander, Reinhard, 1110
Sandorfy, Michael, 360
Sarah Vaughan: a discography, 1285
Sartori, Eva Martin, 1222
Saterstrom, Mary H., 400
Saul, Pauline, 461
Savage, Kathleen M., 411, 412
Savola, Kristen L., 102
Sawoniak, Henryk, 621
Sawyer, Malcolm, 177
Sayer, Jeffrey A., 1484
Scenic design on Broadway, 1384
Schaad, Evelyn, 922
Scharnhorst, Gary, 1182
Schellinger, Paul E., 1159
Schiff, Matthew M., 1290
Schmick's Mahican dict, 1089
Schneider, Craig W., 1513
Schneider, Gerhard, 1426
Scholars' gd to Washington, DC for Latin American & Caribbean studies, 2d ed, 149
Scholarships, fellowships & loans 1992-93, 377
Schon, Isabel, 150
School lib media annual, v.10, 672
School songs of America's colleges & univs, 1278
Schooner, Steven L., 580
Schorr, Alan Edward, 429
Schuker, Eleanor, 797
Schulman, Martin, 223
Schulze, Suzanne, 979
Schumann, Walter, 1729
Schutt, David, 197
Schutz, Wayne, 1364
Schuursma, Ann Briegleb, 1242
Schuyler, Michael, 662
Schwartz, Albert, 1579
Schwartz, Carol A., 213
Schwartz, Mel M., 1606
Schwartz, Mortimer D., 573
Schwartz, Ronald, 1365
Schwarz, Catherine, 1057
Schwarzkopf, LeRoy C., 74
Schweitzer, David, 773
Schwing, Ned, 1004
Science & technical writing: a manual of style, 970

Science experiments index for young people update 91, 1461
Science fair project index 1985-89, 1462
Science fiction & fantasy bk review annual 1990, 1158
Science sources 1991, 1452
Scientific & technical pers of the 17th & 18th centuries, 1463
Scientific English, 958
Scientific traveler, 1456
Scott dramatized, 1210
Screen gems: a hist of Columbia Pictures TV from Cohn to coke, 1948-83, 996
Screen sleuths, 1350
Scriven, Michael, 642
Seabourne, Joan, 879
Seale, Doris, 433
Search sheets for OPACs on the Internet, 661
Searing, Susan, 931
Searles, Richard B., 1513
Sears list of subject headings: Canadian companion, 4th ed, 643
Seaweeds of the SE US, 1513
Second 50 yrs: a ref manual for sr citizens, 853
Second suppl to a comp bibliog of Yugoslav lit in English 1986-90, 1234
Seeds of woody plants in N America, rev ed, 1521
Seeley, Charlotte Palmer, 707
Seeley, Darrell, 1646
Seeley, Frank E., 853
Sefami, Jacobo, 1228
Segal, Ronald, 475
Segrave, Kerry, 612
Selden, Holly M., 245
Select index to Svoboda, v.1, 980
Select index to Svoboda, v.2, 981
Selected bibliog of modern historiography, 546
Selvon, Sydney, 147
Semantics: a bibliog, 1986-91, 1047
Senecal, A. J., 19
Senecal, Michael D., 519
Senick, Gerard J., 1141
Senior high school lib cat, 14th ed, 673
Senior movement, 861
Sennitt, Andrew G., 1000
Sennitt, Andy, 999
Sensitive issues: an annot gd to children's lit K-6, 1130
Sentman, Catherine, 1250
Sentz, Lilli, 1659
Serafin, Steven, 50
Serio, Joseph, 613
Service industries USA, 250
Settlement lit of the Greater Punjab, 524
Sewer, June, 1583
Seymour-Smith, Martin, 1148
Shade & color with water-conserving plants, 1520
Shafritz, Jay M., 736
Shain, Michael, 315
Shakespeare: an annot bibliog, 1214
Shakespeare & feminist criticism, 1212
Shakespeare index, 1215
Shannon, Michael Owen, 145
Shannon, Moira D., 1620
Sharkey, Paulette Bochnig, 824, 1121
Sharp, Dennis, 1040
Sharpe, Anne S., 342

Shaughnessy, Roseann, 957
Shaver, James P., 336
Shavit, David, 786
She said, he said, 914
Shearing, Clifford D., 606
Shedding the veil: mapping the European discovery of America & the world, 470
Sheldon, Joseph K., 1417
Shelnutt, Eve, 936
Shenhom, Daisy E., 1046
Shepard, Thomas H., 1628
Sherman, Gale W., 1140
Sherman, Mark A., 1416
Shermyen, Anne H., 107
Shields-West, Eileen, 732
Shih, Catherine, 225, 259
Shih, Tian-Chu, 1471
Shim, Jae K., 241, 243
Shimoni, Yaacov, 161
Shimpock-Vieweg, Kathy, 596
Shipping lit of the Great Lakes, 1778
Shoemaker, Thomas M., 1598
Short story writers & their work, 2d ed, 1160
Short-term economic stats: Central & E Europe, 292
Shrader, Charles R., 710
Shrout, Richard Neil, 864
Shuffelton, Frank, 512
Shult, Linda, 931
Shuman, R. Baird, 971, 1380
SIBD 92-93, 293
Siberia & the Soviet Far East, 139
Siegel, Joel G., 241, 243
Siegel, Martha S., 589
Siegman, Gita, 66, 1314
Sierra Club hndbk of seals & sirenians, 1571
Sifakis, Stewart, 711, 712, 713, 714, 715
Sigler, David Burns, 716
Sikhs in N America, 1436
Silverburg, Sanford R., 162
Silverman, Pamela B., 893
Simmons, Henry C., 859
Simms, Norman, 1229
Simon, Harriet Furst, 342
Simon, Seymour, 1706
Simoncini, Gabriele, 779
Simone de Beauvoir: a bibliog, 930
Simpson, James B., 94
Simpson, John, 1296
Simpson, Marcus B., Jr., 1545
Simpson, Mary, 503
Sinclair, Ian R., 1595
Sinclair, Patti K., 1752
Singer, David, 439
Singer, Michael, 1372
Singson, Karen P., 871
Sinnott, Susan, 51
Sir Gawain & the Green Knight: an annot bibliog, 1978-89, 1217
Sirotof, Gene, 1387, 1388
Skapura, Robert, 916
Skipper, James K., Jr., 826
Slapin, Beverly, 433
Slater, Courtenay M., 908
Slater, Thomas J., 1340
Slee, Debora A., 1621

Slee, Vergil N., 1621
Slonimsky, Nicolas, 1244
Small business sourcebk, 5th ed, 213
Smallwood, Carol, 70
Smith, Brenda, 673
Smith, Colin, 1100
Smith, Darren L., 500
Smith, David, 1063
Smith, Gregory White, 1644
Smith, Jane Bandy, 672
Smith, Jerome H., 1434
Smith, Jessie Carney, 52
Smith, Kathie Billingslea, 469
Smith, Myron J., Jr., 695, 696
Smith, Robert Selles, 581
Smith, Ronald L., 1325
Snodgrass, Mary Ellen, 43, 1143
Snow, Dennis A., 1608
Sobsey, Dick, 865
Social scis: an intl bibliog of serial lit, 1830-1985, 100
Social scis index [CD-ROM], 97
Social scis index: April 1990-March 1991, 96
Sociology in govt, 846
Socolofsky, Homer E., 513
Sokol, Stanley S., 44
Solorzano, Lucia, 364
Somali-English dict, 2d ed, 1099
Somer, Elizabeth, 1647
Soos, A., 1567
Soul music A-Z, 1293
Sound films, 1927-39, 1352
Source gd to the music of Percy Grainger, 1261
Sourcebook of American literary journalism, 976
Sources in European pol hist, v.3, 766
South Asian hndbk, 1992, 502
Sova, Harry W., 982
Sova, Patricia L., 982
Soviet Jewish hist, 1917-91, 447
Soviet security & intelligence orgs 1917-90, 769
Soviet stats since 1950, 142
Space atlas, 1700
Space station glossary, 1581
Space words, 1706
Spaghetti westerns, 1367
Spain: 1001 sights, 506
Spain, Patrick J., 208
Spanish, Catalan, & Galician literary authors of the 20th century, 1233
Spatial Terminology Standardization Committee, 1581
Speake, Jennifer, 1296
Spear, Hilda D., 1206
Specialty cookbks, v.1, 1470
Spence, Bruce, 569
Spencer, Donald D., 1681
Spencer, Peter, 1280
Spies, Karen, 1313
Spinoza in English, 1394
Spomer, Cynthia Russell, 306
Sport in Britain, 814
Sports fan's connection, 822
Sports halls of fame, 820
Sports Illustrated, editors of, 813
Sports Illustrated 1992 sports almanac, 813
Sprackland, Robert George, 1580

Springberg, Judith, 582
Spycatcher's ency of espionage, 787
St John, Ronald Bruce, 115
Staar, Richard F., 780
Stade, George, 1191
Stainsby, Meg, 1217
Stake, Donald Wilson, 1423
Standard cat of firearms, 2d ed, 1004
Stankus, Tony, 1440
Stansifer, Charles L., 154
Star Trek: an annot gd to resources, 1331
Starck, Marcia, 1648
Stark, Richard W., 1667
State & regional assns of the US, 1992 ed, 71
State census records, 899
State issues 1992, 755
State legislative sourcebk 1992, 750
State legislative staff dir 1991, 738
State rankings, 1991, 912
State ref pubns 1991-92, 734
Statistical hndbk on the American family, 867
Statistical record of the environment, 1764
Statistical yrbk for Latin America & the Caribbean, 1991 ed, 151
Statistics and Economic Analysis Staff of the Forestry Department, FAO, 1483
Statistics & surveys vocabulary, 905
Statistics of road traffic accidents in Europe 1991, 1785
Statistics sources 1993, 913
Statt, David A., 317
Stauffer, Douglas B., 1717
Steadman, Susan M., 1333
Stebbins, Robert C., 1577
Stedman's abbrev., 1623
Stedman's medical speller, 1637
Stedman's pathology lab medicine words, 1638
Steele, J. Valerie, 744
Steele, Philip, 414
Steen, Sarah J., 392, 393
Stein, Alice P., 1659
Stein, Robert M., 745
Steinfirst, Susan, 1300
Stelbecker-Pountney, Barbro E., 597
Stepchuk, Roman, 981
Stephen Crane: an annot bibliog of secondary scholarship, 1172
Stephen, Marg, 135
Stern, Malcolm H., 458
Stetler, Susan L., 188, 189
Steven A. Miles, 69
Stevenson, George A., 1042
Stevenson, Joan C., 415
Stevenson, John, 529, 559
Steverson, Tyrone, 1322
Stewart, Brent S., 1571
Stewart, John, 1707
Stewart, Robert, 553
Stewart, Steve, 1369
Stokes, Donald, 1551
Stokes, Lillian, 1551
Strangelove, Michael, 72
Straub, Deborah Gillan, 45
Strickler, Carol, 1009
Strijp, Ruud, 416

String music of black composers, 1260
Strong, Cynthia B., 1614
Stuart-Fox, David J., 123
Stuart-Fox, Martin, 128
Stubblebine, Donald J., 1272
Studwell, William E., 640
Suarez, Thomas, 470
Subject access to films & videos, 640
Substance abuse among ethnic minorities in America, 891
Sukiennik, Adelaide Weir, 1124
Sullivan, Michael J., III, 729
Summer theatre dir 1992, 1387
Summers, Wilford I., 1587
Sumrall, Amber Coverdale, 944
Supernatural fiction for teens, 2d ed, 1156
$upertrader's almanac, 2d ed, 321
Supplement to a gd to source materials for the study of Barbados hist, 1627-1834, 541
Supplement to Who's Who in America 1991-92, 53
Supplementary Russian-English dict, 1096
Supreme Court yrbk 1990-91, 588
Surrency, Erwin C., 756
Sussman, Allen E., 1656
Sutherland, Zena, 1134
Sutton, Elizabeth, 389
Sutton, Roger, 1134
Swanick, Eric L., 526
Sweeney, Kevin, 1323
Sweethearts of the sage, 1361
Sweetland, Richard C., 337, 338
Symonds, Craig L., 691
Szajkowski, Bogdan, 770
Szostak, R., 1584
Szycher, Michael, 1639
Szycher's dict of biomaterials & medical devices, 1639

Tabler, Judith, 71
Tackling toxics in everyday products, 1761
Tagalog slang dict, 1103
Talk shows & hosts on radio, 990
Talking with artists, 1021
Tanford, Charles, 1456
Tarutz, Judith A., 972
Tatla, Darshan Singh, 1436
Taucher, Frank A., 321
Taylor, Jane, 674
Taylor, Michael J. H., 1780
Taylor, Thomas J., 1381
Technical editing, 972
Teed, Peter, 557
Telecommunications dir, 5th ed, 1698
Telecommunications fact bk & illus dict, 1697
Television drama series programming, 993
Television engineering hndbk, rev ed, 1588
Television horror movie hosts, 985
Television writers gd, 2d ed, 965
Television yrbk, 995
Telfer, Dorothy, 1503
Ten precisionist artists, 1017
Tennessee attorneys dir, 1992, 585
Tennessee govt officials dir, 1991, 742
Tennessee Williams: a bibliog, 2d ed, 1185
Terrace, Vincent, 998

Terres, John K., 1537
Terry, Michael, 297
Test Collection, Educational Testing Service, 329
Test critiques, v.9, 337
Tests: a comprehensive ref for assessments in psychology, educ, & bus, 3d ed, 338
Teutsch, Betsy Platin, 443
Texas almanac & state industrial gd, 1992-93, 111
Texas mushrooms, 1509
Theatrical designers, 1382
The-Mulliner, Lian, 129
Theoretical syntax 1980-90, 1049
Theriault, Yves, 905
Thesaurus of psychological index terms, 6th ed, 645
Theuns, Leo, 504
Third World tourism research 1950-84, 504
Thode, Ernest, 453, 454
Thomas Jefferson, 1981-90: an annot bibliog, 512
Thomas, Nicholas, 1335
Thomison, Dennis, 1033
Thompson, Alice K., 584
Thompson, Annie F., 1243
Thompson, Donald, 1243
Thompson, Harry F., 451
Thompson, Max C., 1546
Thomsett, Michael C., 186
Thornton, L. Anne, 919
Thorson, Marcie Kisner, 378
Thoughts on leadership, 316
Through Indian eyes, 433
Thum, Marcella, 424
Tibet, 130
Tiemstra, Suzanne Spicer, 1267
Tierney, Helen, 939
Tiller, Veronica E., 434
Time: a bibliographic gd, 14
Times London hist atlas, 534
Timetables of hist, 3d ed, 560
Tingley, Kenneth W., 765
Tobias, Norman, 702
Today's world: a new world atlas, 481
Tomlinson, Gerald, 1412
Tompane, Michael, 499
Tools of the profession, 2d ed, 674
Torikashvili, John J., 1084
Tosh, Dennis S., Jr., 325
Totten, Samuel, 548
Towers, Deirdre, 1328
Toxics A to Z, 1769
Tracey, William R., 302
Trade & professional assns in Calif., 5th ed, 67
Trade union hndbk, 5th ed, 305
Trade unions of the world 1992-93, 313
Tradeshow week data bk, 1992, 322
Trafzer, Clifford E., 435
Trager, James, 554
Training & dvlpmt orgs dir, 5th ed, 307
Transcript/video index, 1991, 1001
Transliterated English-Yiddish, Yiddish-English dict, 1106
Transnational corps in S Africa, 276
Trattner, John H., 757
Traveler's gd to world radio, 1992 ed, 999
Traveling Jewish in America, 3d ed, 441
Treasury of religious quotations, 1412

Treatment of cocaine abuse, 889
Trees of the west, 1517
Triffin, Nicholas, 570
Trigg, George L., 1733, 1734
Troll student atlas, 482
Troll young people's dict, 1063
Trotsky, Susan M., 1108, 1109
Trouser Press record gd, 4th ed, 1281
Trucksource 1992, 1783
Trzyna, Thaddeus C., 1773
Tucker, Kerry, 312
Tudor, Dean, 10
Tullis, LaMond, 892
Tulloch, Paulette P., 940
Tulloch, Sara, 1065
Turecki, Gwen E., 1682, 1698
Turkington, Carol, 1656
Turks & Caicos Islands, 157
Turner, Deborah Ann, 1183
Tuttle dict of ...
   1st names, 465
   new words: since 1960, 1066
   quotations for speeches, 93
TV ency, 988
Twentieth-century Caribbean & black African writers, 1st series, 1110
Twentieth-century crime & mystery writers, 3d ed, 1153
Twentieth-century sci-fiction writers, 3d ed, 1159
Twentieth-century short story explication: an index, 1161
Twitchett, Denis, 125

UFO ency, v.2, 807
Ukman, Lesa, 258
Ukraine top 100 exporters, 294
Ulrich's intl pers dir 1992-93, 88
Understanding lasers, 1646
Unemployment insurance glossary, 252
Union cat of letters to Clemens, 1183
Union of International Associations, 75
United Nations Development Programme, 1776
United Nations Environment Programme, 1776
United States, 520
United States air force, 709
United States atlas for young people, 469
United States corporation hists, 2d ed, 174
United States in Latin America, 786
United States treaty index: 1776-1990 consolidation, 759
University pr bks for public & secondary school libs 1991, 664
Unreal! Hennepin County lib subject headings for fictional characters & places, 2d ed, 644
Upham, Martin, 313
Urban informal sector in Africa in retrospect & prospect, 277
U.S. aging policy interest groups, 860
U.S. Department of Commerce, National Technical Information Service, Office of International Affairs, 655
U.S. Department of Labor Employment and Training Administration, 301

U.S. Department of the Navy (Bureau of Medicine and Surgery), 1578
U.S. Latino lit, 1166
U.S. military logistics, 1607-1991, 710
U.S. outdoor atlas & recreation gd, 497
U.S. War Department, 705
U.S.A. Gulf Coast oil & gas industry dir, 1992, 1745
U.S.A. oil industry's environmental dir, 1993, 1762
Used car buying gd, 1992-93 ed, 1786
User's gd to the Bluebk, 590
Ushkevich, Alexander, 1079
Using children's bks in reading/lang arts programs, 402
Using govt docs, 668
USSR crime stats & summaries, 613

Vacation study abroad, 42d ed, 393
Valverde, Antonio Martin, 295
Van de Sande, Wendy S., 687
van den Muijzenberg, Otto, 169
van der Tuin, J. D., 1724
van Gelderen, D. M., 1506
van Hoey Smith, J. R. P., 1506
Van Keuren, Frances, 1029
van Leunen, Mary-Claire, 973
Van Orden, Phyllis, 665
Van Scotter, Richard D., 354
Van Tassel, David D., 860
Van Tighem, Kevin, 1533
Van Willigen, John, 417
Vanden Bloock, Cecile, 784
Vandome, Nick, 614
VanGrasstek, Craig, 149
Vanicky, Donna, 194
VanMeter, Vandelia, 561
Vascular plants of Ky., 1494
Vassilian, Hamo B., 530, 1472
Vassiliou, M. S., 1685
Veglahn, Nancy J., 1441
Venomous reptiles of N America, 1576
Vera, Eduardo S., 1733, 1734
Veterans benefits manual, 708
Victorian American women 1840-80, 927
Victorian studies, 533
Victorian writers, 1832-1890, 1197
Vienna Institute for Comparative Economic Studies, 907
Vietnam battle chronology, 716
Vietnam bk list, 525
Vietnam vet films, 1366
Vietnamese-English dict, 1104
Viewers' choice gd to movies on video, 1334
Virgin Islands, 158
Virtual reality: a selected bibliog, 1672
Visual dict of ...
    animals, 1534
    cars, 1787
    everyday things, 1078
    military uniforms, 703
    plants, 1502
    ships & sailing, 1792
    the human body, 1492
Vital stats on congress, 1991-92, 754
Viviano, Benedict T., 1435

Vocabulary of ...
    cell engineering, v.1, 1600
    free trade, 233
    safety & security equipment, 1601
    Soviet society & culture, 1095
Vocational careers sourcebk, 412
Vockeroth, J. R., 1564

Waddick, James W., 1507
Wade, Carlson, 1640
Waldman, Carl, 488
Walford's concise gd to ref material, 2d ed, 20
Walford's gd to ref material, 5th ed, v.2: social & histl scis, 98
Walford's gd to ref material, 5th ed, v.3: generalia, 21
Walker, Alvin, Jr., 645
Walker, Barbara K., 1161
Walker, Mark, 1366
Walker, Neil E., 1145
Walker, P. M. B., 1720, 1742
Walker, Warren S., 1161
Walker-Hill, Helen, 1264
Walker's mammals of the world, 5th ed, 1572
Walker's manual of W corps 1992, 214
Walkiewicz, Lynn, 1397
Wall, C. Edward, 910
Wall, Elizabeth J., 223
Wallace, Steven P., 861
Wallechinsky, David, 841
Walter M. Miller, Jr.: a bio-bibliog, 1179
Walters, James E., 1520
War & peace through women's eyes, 1169
Ward, Geoffrey C., 54
Ward, James V., 1568
Ward, John L., 178
Ward's bus dir of US private & public cos 1992, 198
Ward's sales prospector, 199
Warren G. Harding: a bibliog, 509
Washington almanac, 731
Washington info dir 1992-93, 743
Washington representatives 1992, 744
Washington Researchers Publishing, 251, 274, 289
Wasik, John F., 1774
Wasserman, Steven, 917
Wasserman, Steven R., 913
Watchable birds of the Rocky Mountains, 1542
Water-soluble resins, 2d ed, 1713
Watson, Benjamin, 1135
Watson, Bruce W., 709
Watson, Elena M., 985
Watson, Noelle, 1159
Watson, Susan M., 709
Watters, Carolyn, 622
Wearing, J. P., 1386
Weather almanac, 6th ed, 1722
Weaver, David D., 1654
Weaver's bk of 8-shaft patterns, 1009
Webb, Walter, 215
Webber, Bert, 436
Weber, Mary K., 585, 742
Webster's new world ency, 63
Webster's new world Hebrew dict, 1087
Webster's 2 New Riverside desk quotations, 94

Webster's 2 New Riverside desk ref, home & office ed, 5
Wedding music, 1266
Weeds of the woods, 1515
Weinberg, Meyer, 99, 618
Weintraub, Stanley, 1216
Weiss, Anne D., 895
Weiss, Carla M., 300
Weiss, Irving, 895
Weisser, Thomas, 1367
Welch, John W., 1402
Wellek, Alex, 737
Weller, Carolyn R., 636
Wellisch, Hans H., 653
Wepsiec, Jan, 100
West, Geoffrey P., 1490
West, Jim, 1744
West, John G., Jr., 576
Westerman-Alkire, Cheryl, 86
Western European economic orgs, 290
Western lang lit on pre-Islamic central Arabia, 167
West's tax law dict, 1992 ed, 581
Wexler, Alan, 488
Where once we walked: a gd to the Jewish communities destroyed in the Holocaust, 494
Where walls once stood, 388
Wheye, Darryl, 1541
Whissen, Thomas Reed, 1149
Whitaker, Jerry C., 1588
Whitaker, Joseph, 6
Whitaker's almanac 1992, 6
Whitburn, Joel, 1282
White, Joseph L., 585, 742
White, Stephen, 536
Whitfield, Philip, 1732
Whittaker, William, 502
Who is who at the Earth Summit, Rio de Janeiro, 1992, 1763
Who is who in serv to the earth, 1775
Who knows about foreign industries & markets, 13th ed, 274
Who knows about industries & markets, 13th ed, 251
Who was who: a cum index 1897-1990, 47
Who was who in world exploration, 488
Who was who 1981-90, 46
Who's who in ...
   Africa, 760
   America: jr & sr high school version, v.5-v.8, 55
   Asian & Australasian pols, 762
   bus & industry in the UK 1991, 298
   Canadian film & TV 1991-92, 1341
   Canadian lit 1992-93, 1220
   comedy, 1325
   finance & industry 1992-93, 179
   Hollywood, 1339
   intl orgs, 784
   Japan 1991-92, 48
   Pacific navigation, 487
   sci in Europe, 7th ed, 1442
   the UN & related agencies, 2d ed, 782
   world insurance, 253
   writers, eds & poets, 1992-93, 974
Who's who of ...
   American women 1991-92, 56
   the Asian Pacific Rim, 1992 ed, 168

women in world pols, 937
world religions, 1404
Wicker, Gerald L., 339
Wiesner, Hillary S., 1409
Wigoder, Geoffrey, 448, 1435
Wilbur, C. Keith, 1612
Wild animals of W Canada, 1533
Wilderness U: opportunities for outdoor educ in the US & abroad, 335
Wildflowers of the west, 1503
Wildhaber, Michael E., 708
Willey, Joy, 1641
William Wilberforce 1759-1833: a bibliog, 771
Williams, Brian, 656
Williams, Ernest, 1551
Williams, Leslie R., 332
Williams, Martha E., 628
Williams, Marty, 933
Williams, Robyn, 778
Williams, Roger L., 1501
Williams, Sally, 1485
Williamson, John B., 861
Williamson, William B., 1407
Willis, Stephen, 21
Wilson bus abstracts, 176
Wilson, George, 117, 160, 1359
Wilson, Joyce M., 10
Wilson, Miriam J. Williams, 896
Wilson, Shaun, 1605
Windrow, Martin, 699
Windsor, Alan, 1044
Winter, Ruth, 1754
Winthrop, Robert H., 418
WIP: a dir of work-in-progress & recent pubs, 924
Wiseman, John A., 761
Witt, Maria, 621
Wittmer, Donna Sasse, 894
WLN interlib loan policies dir, 658
Woddis, Carole, 1389
Womanwords, 938
Women & aging, 928
Women & writing in Russian & the USSR, 1230
Women in ...
   Japanese society, 925
   sociology, 844
   the west, 941
Women philosophers, 1392
Women, race, & ethnicity, 931
Women scientists, 1441
Women serial & mass murderers, 612
Women's studies ency, v.3, 939
Wong, Nancy C., 23
Wood, Clifford H., 473
Wood, Elizabeth J., 914
Wood, Floris W., 914
Woodhouse, William, 701
Woods, Christopher, 1508
Woodward, Ruth L., 356, 357
Woolum, Janet, 818
Wordless/almost wordless picture bks, 1131
Words on cassette 1992, 984
Work of Brian W. Aldiss, 1154
Work of Louis L'Amour, 1176
Work-at-home sourcebk, 4th ed, 308
World almanac of presidential campaigns, 732

World beat: a listener's gd to contemporary world music on CD, 1280
World Bk atlas, 483
World Bk ency, 64
World Bk ency of people & places, 490
World business dir, 261
World class business, 272
World debt tables 1991-92, 244
World dict of legal abbrevs, 562
World dir of ...
   diplomatic representation, 723
   environmental orgs, 4th ed, 1773
   human rights research & training insts, 2d ed, 619
   peace research & training insts, 7th ed, 792
World economic data, 3d ed, 273
World ency of organized crime, 610
World ency of 20th century murder, 611
World explorers & discoverers, 486
World factbk 1991-92, 105
World fishes important to N Americans, 1559
World gd to abbrevs of orgs, 9th ed, 2
World hist for children & young adults, 561
World in turmoil, 550
World list of social sci pers 1991, 101
World lit criticism 1500 to the present, 1118
World of W. E. B. Du Bois, 99
World of winners, 2d ed, 1314
World quality of life indicators, 2d ed, 95
World racism & related inhumanities, 618
World radio TV hndbk, 1992 ed, 1000
World resources 1992-93, 1776
World Resources Institute, 1776
World retail dir & sourcebk 1991, 262
World trade resources gd, 265
World trade system, 266
World War II: America at war 1941-45, 556
World wildlife habitats, 1535
World's greatest brands, 275
World's master paintings from the early Renaissance to the present day, 1045
World's news media, 953
Worldwide bibliog of art exhibition cats 1963-87, 1020
Worldwide govt dir 1992, 724
Woroby, Maria, 980
Woy, James, 206
Wright, Christopher, 1045
Wright, Elizabeth, 801
Wright, H. Stephen, 1271
Wright, Nicola, 476
Wright, Peter, 787
Write to the heart, 944
Writers after WW II, 1945-60, 1198
Writers dir 1992-94, 1119
Writers from the S Pacific, 1229

Writers of ...
   the Caribbean & Central America, 1226
   the middle ages & renaissance before 1660, 1199
   the restoration & 18th century, 1660-1789, 1200
   the romantic period, 1789-1832, 1201
Writing for the ethnic markets, 962
Wynar, Bohdan S., 8, 22

X-rated videotape gd 2, 1332

Yaakov, Juliette, 673
Yachmetz, Kathy A., 351
Yakima, Palouse, Cayuse, Umatilla, Walla Walla, & Wanapum Indians, 435
Yale Daily News, staff of, 372
Yamada, Nanako, 1043
Yamada, Osamu, 1206
Yang, Hiyol, 215
Yannone, Mark J. A., 586
Yarwood, Doreen, 1011
Year bk of labour stats 1991, 314
Yearbook of intl orgs 1991/92, 75
Yearbook of Soviet foreign relations, 1991 ed, 788
Yearbook on intl communist affairs 1991, 780
Yoell, John H., 1262
Yogacara school of Buddhism, 1414
Yolton, John W., 555
Young adult 1991 annual bklist, 1136
Young adult reader's adviser, 1137
Young, Cheryl G., 1521
Young, Copeland H., 102
Young, James A., 1521
Young, Michael L., 103
Young, Millie M., 1684
Young people's bks in series, 1133
Youngberg, Harold W., 1510
Yount, Lisa, 1443

Zalucky, Henry K., 1097
Zeleny, Robert O., 58, 64
Zeleznik, Karen, 1462
Zepper, John T., 383
Zera, Richard S., 219
Zezulin, Alexandra, 1079
Zhao, Yu-tang, 1507
Zikopoulos, Marianthi, 389, 390
Zimmerman, Dorothy Wynne, 1222
Zimmerman, Julie N., 846
Zimmerman, Marc, 1166
Ziring, Lawrence, 776
Zorc, R. David, 1099, 1103
Zubatsky, David S., 1233
Zurick, Tim, 717

Subject Index
Reference is to entry number.

ABBREVIATIONS
Acronyms, initialisms & abbrevs dict 1992, v.1, 1
Oxford dict of abbrevs, 3
Stedman's abbrev., 1623
World gd to abbrevs of orgs, 9th ed, 2

**ABBREVIATIONS, RUSSIAN—
DICTIONARIES—ENGLISH**
Compressed Russian, 1097

ABORTION
Abortion: a ref hndbk, 851
Abortion & family planning bibliog for 1989-90, 850

ABSTRACTING & INDEXING SERVICES
Guide to current indexing & abstracting servs in the Third World, 652

ABSTRACTS
Matter of fact: statements containing stats on current social, economic & pol issues, v.14-15, 910

ACACIA
Field gd to the acacias of Kenya, 1516

ACADIENSIS (FREDERICTON, N.B.)
Acadiensis index, 1971-91, 526

ACCIDENTS
Vocabulary of safety & security equipment, 1601

ACCOUNTING
European accountancy yrbk 1992/93, 271

ACHIEVEMENT TESTS
ETS test collection cat, v.6, 329

ACQUIRED IMMUNE DEFICIENCY SYNDROME. *See* **AIDS**

ACRONYMS. *See also* **ABBREVIATIONS**
Acronyms, initialisms & abbrevs dict 1992, v.1, 1
New intl dict of acronyms in lib & info sci, 2d ed, 621
Stedman's abbrev., 1623
World gd to abbrevs of orgs, 9th ed, 2

ACTIVITY PROGRAMS IN EDUCATION
Literature-based moral educ, 351
More creative uses of children's lit, v.1, 671

ACTORS. *See also* **MOTION PICTURE ACTORS & ACTRESSES**
Edwin Booth: a bio-bibliog, 1379
Jessica Tandy: a bio-bibliog, 1315
Joseph Chaikin: a bio-bibliog, 1376
Richard Burton: a bio-bibliog, 1322

ADA (COMPUTER PROGRAM LANGUAGE)
Ada lang vocabulary, 1677

ADMINISTRATIVE AGENCIES
Prune bk: the 60 toughest sci & tech jobs in Washington, 757

ADOPTION
Adoption lit for children & young adults, 868
Encyclopedia of adoption, 866

ADOPTION AGENCIES
Adoption choices, 869

ADULT EDUCATION
Guide to academic travel, 2d ed, 407

ADVENTURE STORIES. *See* **DETECTIVE & MYSTERY STORIES**

ADVERTISING
Shipping lit of the Great Lakes, 1778

AERONAUTICS, COMMERCIAL
Encyclopedia of American bus hist & biog: the airline industry, 248

AERONAUTICS, MILITARY
United States air force, 709

AFGHANISTAN
Afghanistan, 122
Historical dict of Afghanistan, 121

AFRICA
African music, 1241
Conservation atlas of tropical forests: Africa, 1484
Post-harvest & processing techs of African staple foods, 1478
Urban informal sector in Africa in retrospect & prospect, 277

AFRICA, NORTH
Biographical dict of the Middle East, 161
Peoples of the world: the Middle East & N Africa, 160

AFRICA, SUB-SAHARAN
Peoples of the world: Africans south of the Sahara, 117
Political leaders in Black Africa, 761
Who's who in Africa, 760

AFRICAN-AMERICANS. *See* **AFRO-AMERICANS**

AFRO-AMERICAN ARTISTS
Black artist in America, 1033
Black authors & illustrators of children's bks, 2d ed, 1139

AFRO-AMERICAN AUTHORS
Black authors & illustrators of children's bks, 2d ed, 1139

AFRO-AMERICAN COMPOSERS
String music of black composers, 1260

AFRO-AMERICAN LIBRARIANS
Directory of ethnic professionals in LIS (lib & info sci), 625

AFRO-AMERICAN SCIENTISTS
Black scientists, 1443

AFRO-AMERICAN WOMEN
Notable black American women, 52

AFRO-AMERICAN WOMEN ATHLETES
Black American women in Olympic track & field, 843

AFRO-AMERICAN WOMEN COMPOSERS
Piano music by black women, 1264

AFRO-AMERICANS
African American biogs, 423
Black bk publishers in the US, 679
Black resource gd, 10th ed, 422
Encyclopedia of African-American civil rights, 616
Hippocrene USA gd to black America, 424
Kaiser index to black resources, 1948-86, 425
World of W. E. B. Du Bois, 99

AFRO-AMERICANS IN LITERATURE
Masterpieces of African-American lit, 1164
Out of the woodpile, 1151

AGED
Bibliography of seniors & the family research 1980-91, 852
Creativity in the later yrs, 856
Encyclopedia of aging & the elderly, 858
Families & aging, 854
Late achievers, 43
Palliative care of the elderly, 857
Pastoral responses to older adults & their families, 859
Second 50 yrs: a ref manual for sr citizens, 853
Senior movement, 861
U.S. aging policy interest groups, 860

AGING
Encyclopedia of aging & the elderly, 858
Women & aging, 928

AGRICULTURAL PRODUCTIVITY
Commodity review & outlook 1990-91, 1466

AGRICULTURE
Agriculture dict, 1468
Biological & agricultural index, 1458
French-English agricultural dict, 1465
Who's who in sci in Europe, 7th ed, 1442

AIDS (DISEASE)
AIDS: abstracts of the psychological and behavioral lit 1983-91, 3d ed, 1650
AIDS funding, 1653
Directory of current HIV/AIDS research in Canada 1988-91, 1651
How to find info about AIDS, 1652

AIKIDO
Aiki News ency of aikido, 838

AIR POWER
Jane's all the world's aircraft 1992-93, 1780

AIR TRANSPORT. *See* **AERONAUTICS, COMMERCIAL**

AIRCRAFT INDUSTRY
Encyclopedia of American bus hist & biog: the airline industry, 248

AIRLINES
Encyclopedia of American bus hist & biog: the airline industry, 248

AIRPLANES
Guide to 475 aircraft museums, 224 city-displayed aircraft, 37 restaurants with aircraft, 6 WWI landmarks, 10th ed, 1779

ALASKA
Checklist of beetles of Canada & Alaska, 1560
Nature of SE Alaska, 1528

ALBERTA
Alberta bibliog, 135
From the past to the future, 527
Place names of Alta., v.2, 492

ALDISS, BRIAN W.
Work of Brian W. Aldiss, 1154

ALIENS
Hein's cum index to interim precedent decisions of the Board of Immigration Appeals, 599

ALMANACS
Texas almanac & state industrial gd, 1992-93, 111
Webster's 2 New Riverside desk ref, home & office ed, 5
Whitaker's almanac 1992, 6

ALPINE FAUNA
Illustrated gd to the mountain stream insects of Colo., 1568

ALTERNATIVE MEDICINE
Complete hndbk of natural healing, 1648

AMERICA—DISCOVERY & EXPLORATION
Columbus' dict, 517
Shedding the veil: mapping the European discovery of America & the world, 470

AMERICAN DRAMA
American drama criticism, suppl.3 to the 2d ed, 1168
American drama 1918-60, 1380

American women playwrights, 1900-30, 1167
Drama by women to 1990, 1146
Political left in the American theatre of the 30's, 1375

AMERICAN FICTION
Genreflecting, 3d ed, 1147
Protestant sensibility in the American novel, 1170
War & peace through women's eyes, 1169

AMERICAN ISRAELITE
Index to Fla. Jewish hist in the American Israelite 1854-1900, 446

AMERICAN LITERATURE. See also names of individual authors
American literary mags, 1163
Bibliography of American lit, v.9, 1162
Humor in American lit, 1189
Literature of the Great Lakes region, 1165
Masterpieces of African-American lit, 1164
Recent studies in myths & lit, 1970-90, 1301

AMERICAN LITERATURE – MEXICAN AMERICAN AUTHORS
U.S. Latino lit, 1166

AMERICAN PERIODICALS
American literary mags, 1163

AMERICAN POETRY
Concordance to the minor poetry of Edward Taylor (1642?-1729), 1181
Critical survey of poetry: English lang series, rev ed, 1236
Index of American per verse: 1990, 1187

AMERICAN PROSE LITERATURE
Sourcebook of American literary journalism, 976

AMERICAN PSYCHOLOGICAL ASSOCIATION
APA membership register, 1991, 802

AMERICAN WIT & HUMOR
American pol prints 1766-1876, 735
Humor in American lit, 1189

AMERICANISMS
Dictionary of American regional English, v.2, 1062

AMPHIBIANS
Amphibians & reptiles of the W Indies, 1579
Peterson 1st gd to reptiles & amphibians, 1577
Reptiles & amphibians of Austr., 5th ed, 1575

ANARCHISM
Anarchist thinkers & thought, 778

ANARCHISTS
Anarchist thinkers & thought, 778

ANGLO-AMERICAN CATALOGING
AACR2 decisions & rule interpretations, 5th ed, 639

ANGLO-INDIAN DIALECT See **HOBSON-JOBSON**

ANGOLA
Historical dict of Angola, 2d ed, 112

ANIMALS
Animals around the world, 1530
Macmillan animal ency for children, 1532
Natural hist from A to Z, 1523
Visual dict of animals, 1534
Wild animals of W Canada, 1533

ANIMALS, FOSSIL. See **PALEONTOLOGY**

ANIMALS, TREATMENT OF
National gd to funding for the environment & animal welfare, 881

ANIMATED FILMS
Encyclopedia of animated cartoons, 1347

ANTHROPO-GEOGRAPHY
Cultural atlas of France, 143
World Bk ency of people & places, 490

ANTHROPOLOGY
Anthropology in use, 417

APOCRYPHAL BOOKS
Catalogue of English Bible translations, 1427

AQUACULTURE
Elsevier's dict of aquaculture, 1467

AQUARIUM FISHES
Dr. Axelrod's atlas of freshwater aquarium fishes, 6th ed, 1553
Dr. Burgess's mini-atlas of marine aquarium fishes, 1554

AQUATIC INSECTS. See **INSECTS, AQUATIC**

ARAB COUNTRIES
Education in the Arab Gulf states & the Arab world, 384

ARCHAEOLOGY
Archaeology hndbk, 507

ARCHITECTS
Illustrated ency of architects & architecture, 1040

ARCHITECTURE
Art & architecture thesaurus, suppl.1, 635
Directory of intl pers & newsletters on the built environment, 2d ed, 1036
Home building & woodworking in colonial America, 1612
Illustrated ency of architects & architecture, 1040
Penguin dict of architecture, 4th ed, 1038
RAIC dir of scholarships & awards for architecture, 1039

ARCHIVES
Sources in European pol hist, v.3, 766

ARCTIC REGIONS
Directory of arctic sci & tech research in Canada, 118
Passages: a treasure trove of N American exploration, 485

ARGENTINA
Argentina, 152

ARIZONA
Arizona legal research gd, 596

ARMENIAN MASSACRES, 1915-1923
Armenian genocide, 530

ARMENIAN QUESTION
Armenian genocide, 530

ART
Art & architecture thesaurus, suppl.1, 635
Art index, 1030
Art on screen, 1016
Bulfinch pocket dict of art terms, 3d ed, 1023
Contemporary masterworks, 1028
Fine art index, 1992 N American ed, 1031
Fine arts pers, 1034
HarperCollins dict of art terms & techniques, 2d ed, 1025
Worldwide bibliog of art exhibition cats 1963-87, 1020

ART, CLASSICAL
Guide to research in classical art & mythology, 1029

ART CRITICISM
Bibliography of salon criticism in Paris from the ancien regime to the Restoration, 1699-1827, 1018
Bibliography of salon criticism in Paris from the July Monarchy to the Second Republic, 1831-51, 1019

ART, MODERN
Annual bibliog of modern art, 1990, 1015

ARTHURIAN ROMANCES
Encyclopaedia of Arthurian legends, 1190

ARTIFICIAL INTELLIGENCE
Dictionary of artificial intelligence & neuronal networks, 1671

ARTIFICIAL SATELLITES
International satellite dir, 1992, 1696

ARTISTS
Encyclopedia of living artists in America, 6th ed, 1024

ARTISTS' MATERIALS
American artists' materials, v.2, 1027

ARTS, BLACK
Black arts annual 1989/90, 1026

ASIA. *See also names of countries*
Who's who in Asian & Australasian pols, 762

ASIAN-AMERICAN LIBRARIANS
Directory of ethnic professionals in LIS (lib & info sci), 625

ASIAN-AMERICANS
Asian Americans info dir, 421

ASSOCIATIONS, INSTITUTIONS, ETC. *See also* TRADE & PROFESSIONAL ASSOCIATIONS
Associations Canada 1992, 65
Encyclopedia of medical orgs & agencies 1992-93, 1632
IMF glossary, 254

ASTRONOMY
Astronomer's sourcebk, 1701
Astronomy & astrophysics ency, 1704
Children's space atlas, 1703
HarperCollins dict of astronomy & space sci, 1702
Space atlas, 1700
Space words, 1706

ASTROPHYSICS
Astronomy & astrophysics ency, 1704

ATHLETES
Biographical dict of American sports, 1989-92 suppl, 817
Great athletes, 816
Neal-Schuman index to sports figures in collective biogs, 824

ATLANTIC COAST (CANADA)
Guide to the marine sport fishes of Atlantic Canada & New England, 1555

ATLANTIC PROVINCES
Acadiensis index, 1971-91, 526

ATLASES
Hammond gold medallion world atlas, 474
Macmillan 1st atlas, 476
New cosmopolitan world atlas, census/environmental ed, 477
New state of the world atlas, 4th ed, 475
Rand McNally world atlas, 478
Random House compact world atlas, rev ed, 479
Reader's Digest children's world atlas, 480
Today's world: a new world atlas, 481
Troll student atlas, 482
World Bk atlas, 483

ATLASES, CANADIAN
Macmillan school atlas, 3d ed, 471

ATOMIC ENERGY. *See* NUCLEAR ENERGY

AUDIOCASSETTES
Words on cassette 1992, 984

AUDIO-VISUAL AIDS. *See* AUDIO-VISUAL MATERIALS

AUDIO-VISUAL LIBRARY SERVICE
School lib media annual, v.10, 672

AUDIO-VISUAL MATERIALS
AV market place 1992, 991
Educators gd to free guidance materials, 30th ed, 400
Elementary school lib collection, 18th ed, 667

AUGUSTINE, SAINT, BISHOP OF HIPPO
Augustine's De Civitate Dei: an annot bibliog of modern criticism, 1960-90, 1416

AUSTRALASIA
Major cos of the Far East & Australasia 1991/92, 8th ed, v.1, 281
Who's who in Asian & Australasian pols, 762

AUSTRALIA
Australian pers in print 1991, 81
Australian ref dict, 131
Reptiles & amphibians of Austr., 5th ed, 1575

AUSTRIA
Where once we walked: a gd to the Jewish communities destroyed in the Holocaust, 494

AUSTRIAN LITERATURE
Companion to 20th-century German lit, 1223

AUTHORITY FILES (CATALOGING)
ERIC identifier authority list (IAL) 1992, 636

AUTHORS. *See also* CHILDREN'S LITERATURE; *names of individual authors*
Author profile collection, 1138
Biographical index to children's & young adult authors & illustrators, 1144
Bookpeople: a multicultural album, 1142
Contemporary authors, v.133, 1108
Contemporary authors, v.134, 1109
Who's who in writers, eds & poets, 1992-93, 974
Writers dir 1992-94, 1119

AUTHORS, AFRICAN
Twentieth-century Caribbean & black African writers, 1st series, 1110

AUTHORS, AMERICAN. *See also names of individual authors*
Grants & awards available to American writers, 17th ed, 960
Hemingway: an annot chronology, 1174

AUTHORS, BLACK
Black authors & illustrators of children's bks, 2d ed, 1139
Black lit criticism, 1115

AUTHORS, BRITISH
Children's fiction sourcebk, 1125

AUTHORS, CANADIAN
Who's who in Canadian lit 1992-93, 1220

AUTHORS, CARIBBEAN
Twentieth-century Caribbean & black African writers, 1st series, 1110

AUTHORS, DUTCH
Dutch Filipiniana, 169

AUTHORS, ENGLISH
British writers, suppl.2, 1191
Writers of the middle ages & renaissance before 1660, 1199

AUTHORS, ENGLISH – 18TH CENTURY
British Romantic novelists, 1789-1832, 1196

AUTHORS, ENGLISH – 19TH CENTURY
Late Victorian & Edwardian writers, 1890-1914, 1194

AUTHORS, ENGLISH – 20TH CENTURY
Contemporary writers, 1960 to the present, 1192
Modern writers, 1914-45, 1195

AUTHORSHIP. *See also* PUBLISHERS & PUBLISHING
Children's writer's & illustrator's market, 1992, 957
Fiction writers gdlines, 2d ed, 963
Handbook for scholars, rev ed, 973
High-technology editorial gd & stylebk, PC ed, 969
Novel & short story writer's market, 1992, 966
Writing for the ethnic markets, 962

AUTOMOBILES
Lemon-aid new car gd 1992, 1781
New car buying gd, 1992-93 ed, 1784
Visual dict of cars, 1787

AVIATION INDUSTRY. *See* AIRLINES

BACALL, LAUREN
Lauren Bacall: a bio-bibliog, 1321

BALI ISLAND (INDONESIA)
Bibliography of Bali, 123

BAND MUSIC
American Wind Symphony commissioning project, 1284
Heritage ency of band music, 1283

BANGLADESH
South Asian hndbk, 1992, 502

BANKS & BANKING
American Banker's banking factbk 1991, 236
Corporate finance sourcebk 1991, 238

BANKS & BANKING, INTERNATIONAL
International business dict & ref, 255

BARBADOS
Supplement to a gd to source materials for the study of Barbados hist, 1627-1834, 541

BASEBALL
Baseball file, 825

BASEBALL FILMS
Baseball in the movies, 1351

BASEBALL PLAYERS
Baseball nicknames, 826

BASKETBALL
NCAA basketball's finest, 827

BAXTER, ANNE
Anne Baxter: a bio-bibliog, 1318

BEAUVOIR, SIMONE DE
Simone de Beauvoir: a bibliog, 930

BEETLES
Checklist of beetles of Canada & Alaska, 1560

BHUTAN
South Asian hndbk, 1992, 502

BIBLE
Almanac of the Bible, 1435
Bible & modern literary criticism, 1432
Literary-critical approaches to the Bible, 1430
New treasury of Scripture knowledge, 1434
Revell concise Bible dict, 1433

BIBLE AS LITERATURE
Bible & modern literary criticism, 1432

BIBLE—CONCORDANCES, ENGLISH
Nelson's concordance of Bible phrases, 1431

BIBLE. N.T.
Exegetical dict of the N.T., v.2, 1426

BIBLE. N.T. GOSPELS
Dictionary of Jesus & the Gospels, 1428

BIBLE. O.T.
Citations & allusions to Jewish scripture in early Christian & Jewish writings through 180 CE, 1429

BIBLE—VERSIONS
Catalogue of English Bible translations, 1427

BIBLIOGRAPHY
B&T link module 2, world ed, 27
Books in print 1991-92, 29
Books in print plus with bk reviews plus, 28
Checklist of American imprints for 1842, 32
Cumulative bk index [CD-ROM], 25
Cumulative bk index 1991, 23
Cumulative bk index, v.95, no.2, 24
Design of bibliogs, 690
Guide to ref materials for Canadian libs, 8th ed, 16
Index to reviews of bibliographical pubs, v.10, 949
International legal bibliogs, 567
Paperbound bks in print, spring 1992, 31

BIBLIOGRAPHY—BEST BOOKS
Best in children's bks, 1134
Best ref bks 1986-90, 8
Distinguished classics of ref publishing, 18
Guide to ref bks for school media centers, 4th ed, 670
Kister's best dicts for adults & young people, 1048
New, completely rev, greatly expanded, Madam Audrey's mostly cheap, all good, useful list of bks for speedy ref, 5th ed, 13
Newbery & Caldecott awards, 1992 ed, 1128
Recommended ref bks in paperback, 2d ed, 15
Supernatural fiction for teens, 2d ed, 1156
Walford's gd to ref material, 5th ed, v.3: generalia, 21
Young adult reader's adviser, 1137

BIBLIOGRAPHY, NATIONAL
American bk publishing record cum 1991, 26

BIOGRAPHY
American literary biographers, 2d series, 50
American originals, 54
Biography index [CD-ROM], 34
Biography index: Sept 1990-Aug 1991, 33
Biography today, v.1, issue 1, 35
Contemporary heroes & heroines, bk 2, 45
Current biog yrbk 1991, 37
Dictionary of 20th century world biog, 38
Distinguished shades, 49
Encyclopedia of world biog, 20th century suppl, v.17, 39
Faces in the news, 40
Icons, 42
Nobel prize winners: suppl 1987-91, 41
Prospect researcher's gd to biographical research collections, 675
Supplement to Who's Who in America 1991-92, 53
Who was who: a cum index 1897-1990, 47
Who was who 1981-90, 46
Who's who in America: jr & sr high school version, v.5-v.8, 55
Who's who of American women 1991-92, 56

BIOLOGY
Biological & agricultural index, 1458

BIOMEDICAL MATERIALS
Szycher's dict of biomaterials & medical devices, 1639

BIOTECHNOLOGY
Vocabulary of cell engineering, v.1, 1600

BIRDS
Birds alternative names, 1544
Birds in jeopardy, 1541
Cambridge ency of ornithology, 1540

BIRDS—BLUE RIDGE MOUNTAIN REGION
Birds of the Blue Ridge Mountains, 1545

BIRDS, EXTINCT
Birds in jeopardy, 1541

BIRDS—JAPAN
Birds of Japan, 1538

BIRDS—KANSAS
Birds in Kans., v.2, 1546

BIRDS—MICHIGAN
Atlas of breeding birds of Mich., 1539

BIRDS—NEPAL
Guide to the birds of Nepal, 1543

BIRDS—NORTH AMERICA
Audubon Society ency of N American birds, 1537

BIRDS—ROCKY MOUNTAINS
Watchable birds of the Rocky Mountains, 1542

BIRTH CONTROL
Abortion & family planning bibliog for 1989-90, 850

BLACK AMERICANS. *See* **AFRO-AMERICANS**

BLACK ART. *See* **ARTS, BLACK**

BLACKS
Contemporary black biog, v.1, 426
Kaiser index to black resources, 1948-86, 425

BOARD OF GOVERNORS OF THE FEDERAL RESERVE SYSTEM (U.S.)
Biographical dict of the board of governors of the Fed Reserve, 240

BOATS & BOATING
Marine atlas of the Hawaiian Islands, 466

BOCCACCIO, GIOVANNI
Giovanni Boccaccio: an annot bibliog, 1224

BODY, HUMAN
Visual dict of the human body, 1492

BONES
Dictionary of evolutionary fish osteology, 1558

BOOK DESIGN
Design of bibliogs, 690

BOOK INDUSTRIES & TRADE
Books & mags: a gd to publishing & bkselling courses in the US, 681
Fanfare for words: bkfairs & bk festivals in N America, 682

BOOKS—CONSERVATION & RESTORATION
Library, media, & archival preservation glossary, 663

BOOKS—REVIEWS
B&T link module 2, world ed, 27
Book review digest, 76
Booklist's gd to the yr's best bks, 1992 ed, 9
Books in print plus with bk reviews plus, 28
Canadian bk review annual 1990, 10
Children's bk review index, v.16, 1145
New, completely rev, greatly expanded, Madam Audrey's mostly cheap, all good, useful list of bks for speedy ref, 5th ed, 13

BOOKS & READING
Reader's quotation bk, 403

BOOKSELLERS & BOOKSELLING
Books & mags: a gd to publishing & bkselling courses in the US, 681
Bowker annual lib & bk trade almanac, 37th ed, 629
Colorado bk gd, 683
Multilingual dict of publishing, printing & bkselling, 680

BOOTH, EDWIN
Edwin Booth: a bio-bibliog, 1379

BORDEN, LIZZIE
Borden murders, 605

BOSWELL, JAMES
Boswellian studies, 3d ed, 1231
Boswell's literary art, 1232

BOTANY
Cleveland herbal, botanical, & horticultural collections, 1493
Green plants, 1498
Vascular plants of Ky., 1494

BOTANY—CANADA, EASTERN
Manual of vascular plants of NE US and adjacent Canada, 2d ed, 1500

BOTANY—ECOLOGY
Elsevier's dict of terrestrial plant ecology, 1497

BOTANY—NORTHEASTERN STATES
Manual of vascular plants of NE US and adjacent Canada, 2d ed, 1500

BOTANY—PRE-LINNEAN WORKS
Cleveland herbal, botanical, & horticultural collections, 1493

BOYS IN LITERATURE
English schoolboy stories, 1135

BRANDS (COMMERCE). *See* **BUSINESS NAMES**

BRAZIL
Brazil in ref bks, 1965-89, 153

BREWERS
North American brewers resource dir 1992-93, 1477

BRIDGES, ROBERT SEYMOUR
Robert Bridges: an annot bibliog, 1873-1988, 1205

BRITISH COLUMBIA
Adventuring in B.C., 503

BROADCASTING
Broadcasting & cable market place 1992, 992

BROWN, GEORGE MACKAY
Contribution to lit of Orcadian writer George Mackay Brown, 1206

BUDDHISM
Dictionary of Buddhist terms & terminologies, 1413
Yogacara school of Buddhism, 1414

BUILDING
Construction tech info sources, 1586
Directory of building & equipment grants, 2d ed, 1035
Directory of intl pers & newsletters on the built environment, 2d ed, 1036
Means illus construction dict, new ed, 1037

BURMA
Burma, 124

BURTON, RICHARD
Richard Burton: a bio-bibliog, 1322

BUSINESS. *See also* **CORPORATIONS**
Business info sourcebk, 200
Business pers index, 216
Business rankings annual, 1992, 202
China business dir 1992, 278
Directory of business info resources, 1992, 192
Encyclopedia of bus info sources, 9th ed, 206
Little black bk of business words, 186
McGraw-Hill dict of bus acronyms, initials, & abbrevs, 170
NTC's French & English bus dict, 182
Quotable business, 218
Who's who in bus & industry in the UK 1991, 298
Wilson bus abstracts, 176

BUSINESS COMMUNICATION
1001 quips & quotes for bus speeches, 219

BUSINESS CONSULTANTS
European consultants dir, 287

BUSINESS CYCLES
Handbook of economic cycles, 201

BUSINESS—DATA BASES
Books & pers online, 1992 ed, 187
Online manual, 203

BUSINESS—DIRECTORIES
Directory of business to business cats, 1991, 194

BUSINESS EDUCATION
Directory to intl bus educ in Canada, 230

BUSINESS ENTERPRISES
Business connexions 1992, 228
Contemporary entrepreneurs, 178
Directory, 1991-92: Japanese-affiliated cos in USA & Canada, 279
Eastern European business dir, 284
Hoover's hndbk of American bus 1992, 208
McGraw-Hill pocket gd to bus finance, 241
National bk of lists 1992, 211
Ward's bus dir of US private & public cos 1992, 198
Western European economic orgs, 290
Work-at-home sourcebk, 4th ed, 308

BUSINESS FORECASTING
Book of European forecasts, 282

BUSINESS NAMES
Brands & their cos 1992, 188
Companies & their brands 1992, 189
Corporate eponymy, 184
World's greatest brands, 275

BUSINESS—PERIODICALS
Books & pers online, 1992 ed, 187
Business pers index: Aug 1990-July 1991, 215

BUSINESS RELOCATION
Craighead's intl bus, travel, & relocation gd to 71 countries 1992-93, 264

BUSINESS—RESEARCH
Business info: how to find it, how to use it, 2d ed, 209

BUSINESSMEN
Contemporary entrepreneurs, 178
Corporate eponymy, 184

BUTTERFLIES
Butterflies & moths, 1547
Butterfly bk, 1551
Common names of N American butterflies, 1548
Field gd to E butterflies, 1549

BUYERS' GUIDES. *See* **CONSUMER EDUCATION**

BYELORUSSIAN LANGUAGE—DICTIONARIES—ENGLISH
Byelorussian-English, English-Byelorussian dict with complete phonetics, 1079

CABLE TELEVISION
Broadcasting & cable market place 1992, 992

CAD/CAM SYSTEMS
CAD/CAM abstracts annual 1991, 1690

CALDECOTT MEDAL BOOKS
Newbery & Caldecott awards, 1992 ed, 1128
Newbery & Caldecott medal & honor bks in other media, 1121
Newbery & Caldecott medalists & honor bk winners, 2d ed, 1120

CALIFORNIA
California initiatives & referendums 1912-90, 793
Legal asst's notebk, 595
Prime sources of Calif. & Nev. local hist, 511
Trade & professional assns in Calif., 5th ed, 67

CAMPAIGN FUNDS
Handbook of campaign spending, 749
Open secrets, 2d ed, 752

CAMP-MEETINGS
Holy ground: a study of the American camp meeting, 1398

CANADA
Acadiensis index, 1971-91, 526
ACCC dir of Canadian colleges & insts, 362
Almanac of Canadian pols, 764
Annotated list of Ont. lepidoptera, 1550
Associations Canada 1992, 65
Best doctors in America 1992-93, 1644
Birds in jeopardy, 1541
Business connexions 1992, 228
Canada: a reader's gd, 19
Canada legal dir 1992, 583
Canadian bk review annual 1990, 10
Canadian law symposia index, 598
Canadian lit index: cum index to 1986 pubs, 1218
Canadian master tax gd, 1992, 229
Canadian media list 1992/93, 952
Canadian medical device dir, 1642
Canadian studies: foreign pubs & theses, 4th ed, 134
Checklist of beetles of Canada & Alaska, 1560
Common & botanical names of weeds in Canada, 1992 ed, 1511
Common names of N American butterflies, 1548

Construction tech info sources, 1586
Descriptive cat of the Glenn Gould papers, 1255
Dictionary of Canadian quotations, 90
Directory, 1991-92: Japanese-affiliated cos in USA & Canada, 279
Directory of special collections of research value in Canadian libs, 646
Directory to intl bus educ in Canada, 230
Drug file, 1667
Ethnic cookbks & food marketplace, 3d ed, 1472
From the past to the future, 527
Glenn Gould cat, 1253
Guide to docs relating to French & British N America in the archives of the sacred congregation "de Propaganda Fide," 1424
Guide to MBA programs in Canada, 376
Guide to ref materials for Canadian libs, 8th ed, 16
Guide to the Canadian financial servs industry 1991, 232
Guide to the marine sport fishes of Atlantic Canada & New England, 1555
In search of your roots: a gd for Canadians, rev ed, 456
International dir of Canadian studies, 132
Jewish museums of N America, 444
Legal desk bk 1992, 597
Lemon-aid new car gd 1992, 1781
Lemon-aid used car gd 1992, 1782
Lieutenant-governors of the NW territories & Alta. 1876-1991, 765
Maritime provinces atlas, new ed, 472
Money for performing artists, 1326
NFB film gd, 1342
North American horticulture, 2d ed, 1487
RAIC dir of scholarships & awards for architecture, 1039
Reruns on file, 994
Sears list of subject headings: Canadian companion, 4th ed, 643
Statistics & surveys vocabulary, 905
Unemployment insurance glossary, 252
Vocabulary of cell engineering, v.1, 1600
Vocabulary of free trade, 233
Vocabulary of safety & security equipment, 1601
Weeds of the woods, 1515
Who's who in Canadian film & TV 1991-92, 1341
Wild animals of W Canada, 1533

CANADA—ARMED FORCES
Courage in the air, 697

CANADA—BIOGRAPHY
1000 brave Canadians, 36

CANADA—HISTORY, MILITARY
Courage in the air, 697

CANADA—NATIVE RACES
Annotated bibliog of aboriginal-controlled justice programs in Canada, 569
Breaking down the walls, 568

CANADA. PARLIAMENT
Almanac of Canadian pols, 764
Canadian parliamentary hndbk, 763

CANADIAN LITERATURE
Canadian lit index: cum index to 1986 pubs, 1218
Canadian lit index: cum index to 1987 pubs, 1219
Who's who in Canadian lit 1992-93, 1220

CANCER
Everyone's gd to cancer therapy, 1655

CARDIOVASCULAR AGENTS
Handbook of heart drugs, 1657

CAREER CHANGES
Encyclopedia of career change & work issues, 409

CAREER DEVELOPMENT
Focus on careers, 408
Professional careers sourcebk, 2d ed, 411

CAREER EDUCATION
Chronicle career index, 405

CARIBBEAN AREA
Latin America & the Caribbean: a critical gd to research sources, 148
Political & economic ency of S America & the Caribbean, 774
Statistical yrbk for Latin America & the Caribbean, 1991 ed, 151

CARIBBEAN AREA—LIBRARY RESOURCES
Scholars' gd to Washington, DC for Latin American & Caribbean studies, 2d ed, 149

CARIBBEAN LITERATURE
Writers of the Caribbean & Central America, 1226

CARING
Prosocial dvlpmt in children, 894

CAROLINIAN LANGUAGE—DICTIONARIES—ENGLISH
Carolinian-English dict, 1080

CARS (AUTOMOBILES). See **AUTOMOBILES**

CARTOGRAPHY
Shedding the veil: mapping the European discovery of America & the world, 470

CARTOONS, ANIMATED. See **ANIMATED FILMS**

CATALAN LITERATURE
Spanish, Catalan, & Galician literary authors of the 20th century, 1233

CATALOGING OF MOTION PICTURES
Subject access to films & videos, 640

CATALOGING OF VIDEO RECORDINGS
Subject access to films & videos, 640

CATALOGS, COMMERCIAL
Catalogue of Canadian catalogues, 3d ed, 227

CATALOGS, ON-LINE
Dial in 1992, 662
Search sheets for OPACs on the Internet, 661

CATALOGS, UNION
Shipping lit of the Great Lakes, 1778

CATHOLIC CHURCH
Guide to docs relating to French & British N America in the archives of the sacred congregation "de Propaganda Fide," 1424

CATHOLIC SCHOOLS
Catholic school educ in the US, 348

CATTLE BREEDS
Cattle: a hndbk to the breeds of the world, 1491

CD-ROM
Books & pers online, 1992 ed, 187
CD-ROM dir 1992, 1691
CD-ROMS in print, 1692

CD-ROM INDUSTRY
CD-ROM per index, 82

CD-ROM PROFESSIONAL
Cumulative index to ONLINE, DATABASE & CD-ROM Professional 1986-91, 1669

CELEBRITIES
American originals, 54
Icons, 42
Late achievers, 43

CELLS
Vocabulary of cell engineering, v.1, 1600

CEMETERIES
American military cemeteries, 706

CENSUS
1920 fed population census: cat of microfilm available, 901
State census records, 899

CENTRAL AFRICAN REPUBLIC
Historical dict of the Central African Republic, 2d ed, 113

CENTRAL AMERICA
Pines of Mexico & Central America, 1519

CENTRAL AMERICAN LITERATURE
Writers of the Caribbean & Central America, 1226

CENTRAL MEXICO
Latin American serial pubs available by exchange, 633

CHAIKIN, JOSEPH
Joseph Chaikin: a bio-bibliog, 1376

CHAMBER MUSIC
Piano music by black women, 1264

CHANNELING (SPIRITUALISM)
Channeling: a bibliographic exploration, 806

CHARACTERS & CHARACTERISTICS IN LITERATURE
Characters from young adult lit, 1143
Dictionary of fictional characters, rev ed, 1148

CHARITABLE USES, TRUSTS, & FOUNDATIONS
AIDS funding, 1653

CHARITIES
Charitable orgs of the US 1992-92, 878

CHARTS, DIAGRAMS, ETC.
Charts, graphics & stats index 1988-91, 916

CHEMICAL ELEMENTS
Elements, 2d ed, 1712

CHEMICAL ENGINEERING
Handbook of molecular sieves, 1584

CHEMICAL ENGINEERS
Directory of chemical engineering consultants, 9th ed, 1583

CHEMICAL LABORATORIES
Illustrated chemistry lab terminology, 1708

CHEMICALS—ADDITIVES
Handbook of industrial chemical additives, 1709

CHEMISTRY
Current chemical reactions (CCR), v.14, no.2, 1718
Index chemicus, v.125, no.1, 1719
Lange's hndbk of chemistry, 14th ed, 1716

CHEMOTHERAPY
AARP Pharmacy Serv prescription drug hndbk, 2d ed, 1660

CHILD CARE
Guide to fed funding for child care & early childhood dvlpmt, 893

CHILD DEVELOPMENT
Best of Bkfinder, 1123
Guide to fed funding for child care & early childhood dvlpmt, 893
Help for children from infancy to adulthood, 5th ed, 896
Prosocial dvlpmt in children, 894

CHILD HEALTH SERVICES
Maternal & child health legislation: 1991, 594

CHILDHOOD. *See* **CHILDREN**

CHILDREN
Literature-based moral educ, 351
Reflections on childhood, 895

CHILDREN—BOOKS & READING
Information bks for children, 7
Library serv to children, 665
More exciting, funny, scary, short, different, & sad bks kids like, 1122

Sensitive issues: an annot gd to children's lit K-6, 1130
Using children's bks in reading/lang arts programs, 402

CHILDREN—CARE. *See* **CHILD CARE**

CHILDREN—MEDICAL CARE. *See* **CHILD HEALTH SERVICES**

CHILDREN—PSYCHIC ABILITY
Parapsychological research with children, 808

CHILDREN'S ENCYCLOPEDIAS & DICTIONARIES
Childcraft: the how & why lib, 58
New Grolier student ency, 61
New bk of knowledge, 60

CHILDREN'S LIBRARIES. *See* **LIBRARIES, CHILDREN'S**

CHILDREN'S LITERATURE. *See also* **CHILDREN'S STORIES**
Adoption lit for children & young adults, 868
Author profile collection, 1138
Best in children's bks, 1134
Best of Bkfinder, 1123
Biographical index to children's & young adult authors & illustrators, 1144
Black authors & illustrators of children's bks, 2d ed, 1139
Bookpeople: a multicultural album, 1142
Children's bk review index, v.16, 1145
Children's fiction sourcebk, 1125
Children's lit review, v.25, 1141
Children's ref plus, 11
Children's writer's & illustrator's market, 1992, 957
E for environment, 1752
Elementary school lib collection, 18th ed, 667
From page to screen, 1359
Hispanic heritage, series 4, 150
Indian subcontinent in lit for children & young adults, 1126
More creative uses of children's lit, v.1, 671
More exciting, funny, scary, short, different, & sad bks kids like, 1122
Newbery & Caldecott awards, 1992 ed, 1128
Newbery & Caldecott medal & honor bks in other media, 1121
Newbery & Caldecott medalists & honor bk winners, 2d ed, 1120
Our family, our friends, our world, 1127
Sensitive issues: an annot gd to children's lit K-6, 1130
Through Indian eyes, 433
University pr bks for public & secondary school libs 1991, 664
Using children's bks in reading/lang arts programs, 402
Wordless/almost wordless picture bks, 1131

CHILDREN'S LITERATURE IN SERIES
Young people's bks in series, 1133

CHILDREN'S MUSEUMS
Doing children's museums, 78

CHILDREN'S PERIODICALS
Magazines for young people, 2d ed, 84

CHILDREN'S PERIODICALS, AMERICAN
Magazines for children, 2d ed, 87

CHILDREN'S REFERENCE BOOKS
Children's ref plus, 11
Guide to ref bks for school media centers, 4th ed, 670
Reference bks for children, 4th ed, 1129

CHILDREN'S STORIES
English schoolboy stories, 1135
Portraying persons with disabilities: an annot bibliog of fiction, 3d ed, 1132
Portraying persons with disabilities: an annot bibliog of nonfiction, 2d ed, 1124

CHINA
Bibliography of Sun Yat-sen in China's Republican Revolution, 1885-1925, 521
Cambridge ency of China, 2d ed, 125
China business dir 1992, 278
Forage resources of China, 1510
Historical dict of revolutionary China, 1839-1976, 523
Iris of China, 1507

CHINESE LANGUAGE—DICTIONARIES—ENGLISH
Chinese-English dict of the Wu dialect, 1081

CHIROPRACTIC
National dir of chiropractic, 3d ed, 1645

CHORAL MUSIC
Choral music of Latin America, 1267

CHRISTIAN ETHICS
Encyclopedia of biblical & Christian ethics, rev ed, 1419

CHRISTIAN FICTION
Protestant sensibility in the American novel, 1170

CHRISTIAN LITERATURE
Encyclopedia of the early church, 1406

CHRISTIAN SECTS
Encyclopedia of religions in the US, 1407

CHRISTIANITY
Almanac of the Christian world, 1415
Dictionary of Judaism & Christianity, 1405
Resources in ancient philosophy, 1393

CHRONOLOGY, HISTORICAL
Asimov's chronology of the world, 549
People's chronology, rev ed, 554

CHURCH HISTORY
Encyclopedia of the early church, 1406

CHURCH MUSIC
Dictionary of W church music, 1269

CHURCH OF JESUS CHRIST OF LATTER-DAY SAINTS
Encyclopedia of Mormonism, 1420
Encyclopedia of Mormonism [CD-ROM], 1421

CHURCH SCHOOLS
NCEA/Ganley's Catholic schools in America 1992, 353

CINEMATOGRAPHERS
Cinematographers, production designers, costume designers & film eds gd, 3d ed, 1371
Masters of lens & light, 1343

CINEMATOGRAPHY
Film-video terms & concepts, 1345

CITATION OF LEGAL AUTHORITIES
User's gd to the Bluebk, 590

CITIES & TOWNS
Facts about the cities, 918
Instant natl locator gd, 955

CIVIL AVIATION. *See* **AERONAUTICS, COMMERCIAL**

CIVIL ENGINEERING
Elsevier's dict of civil engineering, 1585

CIVIL RIGHTS MOVEMENT
Encyclopedia of African-American civil rights, 616

CLASSICAL LITERATURE
Recent studies in myths & lit, 1970-90, 1301

CLASSIFICATION – ARCHIVES
FIAF cataloguing rules for film archives, 638

CLERKS OF COURT
BNA's dir of state & fed courts, judges, & clerks, 4th ed, 582

COCAINE HABIT
Treatment of cocaine abuse, 889

COGNITIVE PSYCHOLOGY
Blackwell dict of cognitive psychology, 798

COINS
Commemorative coins of the US, 1002
Comprehensive US silver dollar ency, 1003

COLLECTION AGENCIES
Collection agency dir, 2d ed, 237

COLLECTION DEVELOPMENT (LIBRARIES)
Collection evaluation in academic libs, 677

COLLEGE, CHOICE OF
Barron's top 50, 366

COLOR PRINTS
Guide to modern Japanese woodblock prints, 1900-75, 1043

COLORADO
Illustrated gd to the mountain stream insects of Colo., 1568

COLUMBIA PICTURES TELEVISION
Screen gems: a hist of Columbia Pictures TV from Cohn to coke, 1948-83, 996

COLUMBUS, CHRISTOPHER
Columbus' dict, 517

COMEDIANS
Quinlan's illus dir of film comedy actors, 1338
Who's who in comedy, 1325

COMMERCIAL POLICY
National trade policies, 320

COMMERCIAL PRODUCTS
Eastern European business dir, 284

COMMERCIAL STATISTICS
Business rankings annual, 1992, 202

COMMODITY EXCHANGES
Handbook of world stock & commodity exchanges, 1992, 222

COMMODITY FUTURES
Commodity review & outlook 1990-91, 1466

COMMONWEALTH OF INDEPENDENT STATES
Eastern Europe & the Commonwealth of Independent States 1992, 141

COMMONWEALTH OF NATIONS – PERIODICALS
Index to Commonwealth little mags 1987-89, 83

COMMUNICATION
Communication serials, 1992/1993 ed, 982
Human communication behavior & info processing, 956
Index to jls in communication studies through 1990, 954
World's news media, 953

COMMUNICATION IN LIBRARY ADMINISTRATION
Directory of computer conferencing in libs, 656

COMMUNICATION IN LIBRARY SCIENCE
Directory of computer conferencing in libs, 656

COMMUNICATION POLICY
Control of the media in the US, 951

COMMUNISM
International Trotskyism 1929-85, 777
Revolutionary orgs & revolutionaries in interbellum Poland, 779
Yearbook on intl communist affairs 1991, 780

COMMUNIST PARTIES
Revolutionary orgs & revolutionaries in interbellum Poland, 779

COMMUNITY COLLEGES
AACJC membership dir 1992, 359

COMPACT DISC READ-ONLY MEMORY. *See* **CD-ROM**

COMPARATIVE LAW
Dictionary of intl & comparative law, 577

COMPOSERS
Contemporary composers, 1254
Listener's musical companion, new ed, 1251

COMPOSERS, AFRO-AMERICAN. *See* **AFRO-AMERICAN COMPOSERS**

COMPOSERS – AUSTRIA
Hans Rosbaud: a bio-bibliog, 1257

COMPOSERS – CANADA
Descriptive cat of the Glenn Gould papers, 1255
Glenn Gould cat, 1253

COMPOSERS – CZECHOSLOVAKIA
Antonin Dvorak on records, 1262

COMPOSERS – SPAIN
Enrique Granados: a bio-bibliog, 1259

COMPOSERS – UNITED STATES
George Rochberg: a bio-bibliographic gd to his life & works, 1256

COMPOSITE MATERIALS
Composite materials hndbk, 2d ed, 1606

COMPUTER CONFERENCING
Computer mediated communication, 345
Directory of computer conferencing in libs, 656

COMPUTER GRAPHICS
Dictionary of computer graphics tech & applications, 1688
Graphics file formats, 1687

COMPUTER INTERFACES
Computer professional's quick ref, 1685
Virtual reality: a selected bibliog, 1672

COMPUTER MUSIC
Dictionary of electronic & computer music terminology, 1247
Dictionary of musical tech, 1246

COMPUTER NETWORKS
Computer professional's quick ref, 1685

COMPUTER SCIENCE
Magill's survey of sci: physical sci series, 1699

COMPUTER SIMULATION
Concise ency of modelling & simulation, 1674

COMPUTER SOFTWARE
Computer catalogs, 1673
Electric utility industry sftwr dir, 1992, 1590

COMPUTER-ASSISTED INSTRUCTION
Computer mediated communication, 345

COMPUTERS. *See also* **INFORMATION STORAGE & RETRIEVAL SYSTEMS; MICROCOMPUTERS**
Computer catalogs, 1673
Computer dict, 3d ed, 1681
Computer glossary, 5th ed, 1676
Computer publishers & pubs, 1992-93 ed, 684
Dictionary of computer terms, 3d ed, 1675
Guide to free computer materials, 10th ed, 401
Macmillan ency of computers, 1678
McGraw-Hill dict of info tech & computer acronyms, initials, & abbrevs, 1679
New hacker's dict, 1680

CONCERTS
Music lover's gd to Europe, 1250

CONFEDERATE STATES OF AMERICA. ARMY
Compendium of the Confederate armies: Ala., 711
Compendium of the Confederate armies: Fla. & Ark., 712
Compendium of the Confederate armies: N.C., 713
Compendium of the Confederate armies: Tenn., 714
Compendium of the Confederate armies: Va., 715

CONFERENCE FACILITIES. *See* **CONVENTION FACILITIES**

CONFLICT MANAGEMENT
Conflict & culture, rev ed, 419

CONRAD, JOSEPH
Annotated critical bibliog of Joseph Conrad, 1207

CONSERVATION OF NATURAL RESOURCES
Conservation atlas of tropical forests: Africa, 1484
North American horticulture, 2d ed, 1487

CONSOLIDATION & MERGER OF CORPORATIONS
Directory of merger & acquisition firms & professionals 1992, 193

CONSTRUCTION INDUSTRY
Construction tech info sources, 1586

CONSUMER EDUCATION
Consumer Reports 1992 buying gd issue, 234
Consumer sourcebk 1992-93, 235
Lemon-aid new car gd 1992, 1781
Lemon-aid used car gd 1992, 1782
New car buying gd, 1992-93 ed, 1784
Toxics A to Z, 1769

CONTEMPORARY CHRISTIAN MUSIC
Paul Baker's topical index of contemporary Christian music, 1268

CONTINUING EDUCATION
Guide to academic travel, 2d ed, 407

CONVENTION FACILITIES
Guide to campus & non-profit meeting facilities 93, 207

CONVERTS
Conversion experience in America, 1418

COOKERY
Health-related cookbks, 1471
Specialty cookbks, v.1, 1470

COOKERY, MIDDLE EASTERN
Ethnic cookbks & food marketplace, 3d ed, 1472

COOKING. *See* **COOKERY**

COOPER, JAMES FENIMORE
James Fenimore Cooper: an annot bibliog of criticism, 1171

COOPERATION
Prosocial dvlpmt in children, 894

COPYRIGHT – DEPOSITORY COPIES. *See* **LEGAL DEPOSIT (OF BOOKS, ETC.)**

CORAL SEA, BATTLES OF THE, 1942
Battles of Coral Sea & Midway, 1942, 695

CORPORATE SPONSORSHIP
IEG dir of sponsorship mktg, 1991, 258

CORPORATIONS
Brands & their cos 1992, 188
Companies & their brands 1992, 189
Corporate tech dir 1992, 246
Corporate yellow bk, v.8, no.3, 191
Hoover's hndbk of American bus 1992, 208
International dir of co hists, v.4, 260
Major cos of the Far East & Australasia 1991/92, 8th ed, v.1, 281
United States corporation hists, 2d ed, 174
Walker's manual of W corps 1992, 214

CORPORATIONS – FINANCE
McGraw-Hill pocket gd to bus finance, 241

CORPORATIONS, NONPROFIT
National dir of nonprofit orgs 1992, v.1, 195

COSMETICS
Formulary of cosmetic preparations, v.1, 1715

COSTA RICA
Costa Rica, 154

COSTUME
Chronicle of W fashion, 1010

COSTUME DESIGNERS
Cinematographers, production designers, costume designers & film eds gd, 3d ed, 1371

COUNTY GOVERNMENT
Municipal yellow bk, v.2, no.1, 741

COURTS
BNA's dir of state & fed courts, judges, & clerks, 4th ed, 582
National dir of courts of law 1991, 586

CRAFTS (HANDICRAFTS). *See* **HANDICRAFT**

CRANE, STEPHEN
Stephen Crane: an annot bibliog of secondary scholarship, 1172

CREATION
Rediscovery of creation, 1417

CREATIVE ABILITY
Creativity in the later yrs, 856

CRICKET
Padwick's bibliog of cricket, v.2, 828

CRIME & CRIMINALS
Comparative criminology, 602
Crimes & criminals, 614
Criminology: a reader's gd, 606
World ency of organized crime, 610

CRIMINAL JUSTICE, ADMINISTRATION OF
Annotated bibliog of aboriginal-controlled justice programs in Canada, 569
Breaking down the walls, 568
Dictionary of crime, 608

CRIMINAL LAW
Dictionary of crime, 608

CRIMINAL STATISTICS
USSR crime stats & summaries, 613

CRIMINOLOGY. *See* **CRIME & CRIMINALS**

CRITICISM
Concise glossary of contemporary literary theory, 1112
Dictionary of concepts in literary criticism & theory, 1111
Encyclopedia of lit & criticism, 1116
Glossary of contemporary literary theory, 1113
World lit criticism 1500 to the present, 1118

CROQUET
Croquet: an annot bibliog from the Rendell Rhoades croquet collection, 829

CRUELTY TO ANIMALS. *See* **ANIMALS, TREATMENT OF**

CUBAN LITERATURE
U.S. Latino lit, 1166

CULTS
Encyclopedic hndbk of cults in America, rev ed, 1410

CULTURAL GEOGRAPHY. *See* **ANTHROPO-GEOGRAPHY**

DANCING
Dance film & video gd, 1328
Music & dance in Puerto Rico from the age of Columbus to modern times, 1243

DATA BASES
CD-ROM per index, 82
CD-ROM research collections, 660
Directory of online databases, v.13, no.2, 1682
Directory of portable databases, v.3, no.2, 1670
Directory to fulltext online resources 1992, 626

DATA LIBRARIES
CD-ROM research collections, 660

DATABASE
Cumulative index to ONLINE, DATABASE & CD-ROM Professional 1986-91, 1669

DE CIVITATE DEI
Augustine's De Civitate Dei: an annot bibliog of modern criticism, 1960-90, 1416

DEAFNESS
Encyclopedia of deafness & hearing disorders, 1656

DEGREES, ACADEMIC
Campus-free college degrees, 5th ed, 378

DEMOGRAPHY
Demographic stats 1991, 897

DENOMINATIONS, CHRISTIAN. See **CHRISTIAN SECTS**

DEPOSITORY LIBRARIES. See **LIBRARIES, DEPOSITORY**

DESCRIPTION (RHETORIC)
Descriptionary, 1072

DESKTOP PUBLISHING
Design of bibliogs, 690

DETECTIVE & MYSTERY FILMS
Screen sleuths, 1350

DETECTIVE & MYSTERY STORIES
Locked room murders & other impossible crimes, 1150
Murder ... by category, 1152
Out of the woodpile, 1151
Twentieth-century crime & mystery writers, 3d ed, 1153

DEVELOPING COUNTRIES
Dictionary of Third World terms, 136
Encyclopedia of the Third World, 4th ed, 137
Guide to current indexing & abstracting servs in the Third World, 652
Guide to the info activities of European dvlpmt networks, 630
Third World tourism research 1950-84, 504
Urban informal sector in Africa in retrospect & prospect, 277
World debt tables 1991-92, 244

DEWEY, JOHN
John Dewey: the collected works, 1882-1953: index, 342

DIAGNOSIS
Concise ency of biological & biomedical measurement systems, 1635

DICTIONARIES. See **ENCYCLOPEDIAS & DICTIONARIES**

DICTIONARIES, POLYGLOT
Dictionary of evolutionary fish osteology, 1558
Elsevier's dict of aquaculture, 1467
Elsevier's dict of civil engineering, 1585
Elsevier's dict of hydrology & water quality mgmt, 1724
Elsevier's dict of office automation, 323
IMF glossary, 254

DIET THERAPY
Health-related cookbks, 1471

DIGITAL ELECTRONICS
Digital systems ref bk, 1596

DINOSAURS
Dinosaurs: a gd to research, 1731
Macmillan children's gd to dinosaurs & other prehistoric animals, 1732

DIPLOMATS
World dir of diplomatic representation, 723

DIPTERA
Catalogue of palaearctic diptera, v.7, 1567
Flower flies of the subfamily syrphinae of Canada, Alaska, and Greenland, 1564

DISABLED. See **HANDICAPPED**

DISASTER FILMS
Nuclear movies, 1349

DISCRIMINATION
Discrimination & prejudice, 845
World racism & related inhumanities, 618

DISSENTERS
Revolutionary & dissident movements, 3d ed, 728

DISSERTATIONS, ACADEMIC
Canadian studies: foreign pubs & theses, 4th ed, 134

DIVIDENDS
Moody's hndbk of dividend achievers 1992, 224

DOCUMENTARY FILMS
NFB film gd, 1342

DOCUMENTS LIBRARIANS
Directory of govt doc collections & librarians, 6th ed, 676

DOGS
Complete dog bk, 18th ed, 1552

DOPING IN SPORTS
Drug file, 1667

DRAMA
Back Stage theater gd, 1389
Dramatic re-visions, 1333
International dict of theatre, v.1, 1391

DRAMATIC CRITICISM
American drama criticism, suppl.3 to the 2d ed, 1168

DRUG ABUSE. *See* **SUBSTANCE ABUSE**

DRUG THERAPY. *See* **CHEMOTHERAPY**

DRUG TRAFFIC
Handbook of research on the illicit drug trade, 892

DRUGS
AARP Pharmacy Serv prescription drug hndbk, 2d ed, 1660
Canadian Medical Assn gd to prescription & over-the-counter drugs, 1661
Complete drug ref, 1992 ed, 1662
Drug info for the health care professional 1992, 1663
Drug interactions gd bk, 1664
Encyclopedia of drug abuse, 2d ed, 890
Quick look drug bk with indications index, 1665

DRUGS IN SPORTS. *See* **DOPING IN SPORTS**

DU BOIS, W. E. B. (WILLIAM EDWARD BURGHARDT)
World of W. E. B. Du Bois, 99

DVORAK, ANTONIN
Antonin Dvorak on records, 1262

EAR
Encyclopedia of deafness & hearing disorders, 1656

EARLY CHILDHOOD EDUCATION
Encyclopedia of early childhood educ, 332

EARTH SATELLITES. *See* **ARTIFICIAL SATELLITES**

EARTH SCIENCES. *See also* **GEOGRAPHY; GEOLOGY**
Chambers earth scis dict, 1720
Encyclopedia of earth system sci, 1721
Nature in America, 1526

EAST (U.S.)
Population hist of E US cities & towns, 1790-1870, 900

EAST ASIA
Major cos of the Far East & Australasia 1991/92, 8th ed, v.1, 281

EAST ASIA—LIBRARY RESOURCES
Guide to E Asian collections in N America, 120

ECOLOGY
Dictionary of environmental quotations, 1777

ECOLOGY IN LITERATURE
E for environment, 1752

ECONOMIC ASSISTANCE, DOMESTIC
Assistance & benefits info dir, 887
Federal domestic outlays 1983-90, 745
Government assistance almanac 1992-93, 874

ECONOMIC ASSISTANCE, JAPANESE
Inside Japanese support 1992, 280

ECONOMIC FORECASTING
Handbook of economic cycles, 201

ECONOMIC GEOGRAPHY. *See* **GEOGRAPHY, ECONOMIC**

ECONOMIC INDICATORS
Economic indicators hndbk, 204
Measuring global values, 729

ECONOMIC POLICY
Economist atlas, 172
Short-term economic stats: Central & E Europe, 292

ECONOMICS. *See also* **BUSINESS; STATISTICS; TAXATION**
Bibliography of law & economics, 564
Dictionary of economics, 185
Encyclopedic dict of economics, 4th ed, 180
Lexicon of economics, 181
Macrothesaurus for info processing in the field of economic & social dvlpmt, 641
MIT dict of modern economics, 4th ed, 183

ECONOMISTS
Biographical dict of dissenting economists, 177

EDDY, NELSON
Nelson Eddy: a bio-discography, 1277

EDITORS
Who's who in writers, eds & poets, 1992-93, 974

EDUCATION
American educators' ency, 330
Education in the Arab Gulf states & the Arab world, 384
Education index, 341
Encyclopedia of educl research, 6th ed, 331
European educ thesaurus, 1991 ed, 385
Higher educ in India, 391
Higher educ in the UK 1992-93, 386
Public schooling in America, 354
Publication sources in educl leadership, 343
Russian & Soviet educ 1731-1989, 383

EDUCATION—CURRICULA
Handbook of research on curriculum, 334

EDUCATION, HIGHER
Almanac of higher educ 1992, 355
Encyclopedia of higher educ, 358

EDUCATION OF ADULTS. *See* **ADULT EDUCATION**

EDUCATIONAL LITERATURE
Educators gd to free videotapes, 39th ed, 396
Educators index of free materials, 101st ed, 328

EDUCATIONAL MEDIA CENTERS. *See* **INSTRUCTIONAL MATERIALS CENTERS**

EDUCATIONAL TECHNOLOGY
Educational media & tech yrbk, v.18, 398
Emerging techs & instruction, 344

EDUCATIONAL TESTING SERVICE
ETS test collection cat, v.6, 329

EDUCATIONAL TESTS & MEASUREMENTS
ETS test collection cat, v.6, 329
Test critiques, v.9, 337
Tests: a comprehensive ref for assessments in psychology, educ, & bus, 3d ed, 338

EGYPT
Gamal Abdel Nasser: a bibliog, 543
Nile notes of a howadji, 163

ELASTOMERS
Handbook of plastics, elastomers, & composites, 2d ed, 1714

ELECTION DISTRICTS
Almanac of Canadian pols, 764

ELECTIONEERING
World almanac of presidential campaigns, 732

ELECTIONS
British electorate, 1963-87, 772
Historic docs on presidential elections 1787-1988, 753

ELECTRIC APPARATUS & APPLIANCES
Pocket gd to electrical equipment & instrumentation, 2d ed, 1599

ELECTRIC CABLES
Lineman's & cableman's hndbk, 8th ed, 1598

ELECTRIC ENGINEERING
American electricians' hndbk, 12th ed, 1587
Dictionary of measurement engineering & units, 1597
History of electrical tech, 1593
Pocket gd to electrical equipment & instrumentation, 2d ed, 1599

ELECTRIC INDUSTRIES
Electric utility industry sftwr dir, 1992, 1590

ELECTRIC LINES
Lineman's & cableman's hndbk, 8th ed, 1598

ELECTRIC UTILITIES
EL&P US electric utility industry dir, 1992, 1589

ELECTRONIC DATA PROCESSING
Computer dict, 3d ed, 1681
High-technology editorial gd & stylebk, PC ed, 969
New hacker's dict, 1680

ELECTRONIC MUSIC
Dictionary of musical tech, 1246

ELECTRONIC PUBLISHING
Directory of electronic jls, newsletters & academic discussion lists, 2d ed, 72

ELECTRONIC SYSTEMS
International defense electronic systems hndbk, 718

ELECTRONICS
HarperCollins dict of electronics, 1595

ELEMENTARY SCHOOL LIBRARIES – BOOK LISTS
Elementary school lib collection, 18th ed, 667

EMBLEMS
Reverse symbolism dict, 1311

EMBLEMS, NATIONAL
Our natl symbols, 1309

EMERGENCIES. *See* **ACCIDENTS**

EMERGING NATIONS. *See* **DEVELOPING COUNTRIES**

EMIGRATION & IMMIGRATION
Passenger & immigration lists index, 1992 suppl., 460

EMIGRATION & IMMIGRATION LAW
Hein's cum index to interim precedent decisions of the Board of Immigration Appeals, 599
Insider's gd to successful US immigration, 589

EMPLOYEE FRINGE BENEFITS
Companies that care, 312

EMPLOYEES' MAGAZINES, HANDBOOKS, ETC.
Corporate mags of the US, 217

EMPLOYEES, TRAINING OF
Training & dvlpmt orgs dir, 5th ed, 307

EMPLOYER-SUPPORTED DAY CARE
Companies that care, 312

EMPLOYMENT (ECONOMIC THEORY)
European employment & industrial relations glossary: Spain, 295
European employment & industrial relations glossary: UK, 297
Urban informal sector in Africa in retrospect & prospect, 277

ENCYCLOPEDIAS & DICTIONARIES. *See also* **CHILDREN'S ENCYCLOPEDIAS & DICTIONARIES**
Academic American ency, 57
Australian ref dict, 131
Encyclopedia Americana, intl ed, 59
From archetype to zeitgeist, 1060
New bk of knowledge, 60
New standard ency, 62
Webster's new world ency, 63
Webster's 2 New Riverside desk ref, home & office ed, 5
World Bk ency, 64

END OF THE WORLD
Millennialism: an intl bibliog, 1399

ENDOWMENTS
America's new fndns 1992, 870
EHR dir of awards: fiscal yr 1990, 875
Guide to funding for intl & foreign programs, 880
Inside Japanese support 1992, 280
National data bk of fndns, 16th ed, 879
National gd to funding for the environment & animal welfare, 881
National gd to funding in religion, 1411

ENERGY POLICY
Energy balances of OECD countries 1980-89, 1746
Energy stats of OECD countries 1980-89, 1747

ENGINEERING
Comprehensive dict of measurement & control, 2d ed, 1607
Encyclopedia of applied physics, v.2, 1733
Encyclopedia of applied physics, v.3, 1734
Scientific & technical pers of the 17th & 18th centuries, 1463

ENGINEERS
Biographies of scientists for sci-tech libs, 1440

ENGLAND
Dictionary of English place names, 493
Dictionary of English law, 575
Historical dict of Tudor England, 1485-1603, 532
London stage 1940-49, 1386

ENGLISH DRAMA
Caroline drama, 2d ed, 1202
Drama by women to 1990, 1146
Scott dramatized, 1210

ENGLISH FICTION
English Renaissance prose fiction, 1500-1660, 1203
Genreflecting, 3d ed, 1147

ENGLISH LANGUAGE
Merriam-Webster concise hndbk for writers, 964
Oxford companion to the English lang, 1054
Penguin dict for writers & eds, 968
Scientific English, 958

ENGLISH LANGUAGE – DIALECTS
Dictionary of American regional English, v.2, 1062
Index to dialect maps of Great Britain, 1067

ENGLISH LANGUAGE – DICTIONARIES
American Heritage dict, 2d college ed, 1055
American Heritage dict of the English lang, 3d ed, 1056
British English for American readers, 1068
Chambers concise dict, 1057
Kister's best dicts for adults & young people, 1048
Merriam-Webster concise school & office dict, 1058
Random House Webster's college dict, 1059
Vocabulary of free trade, 233

ENGLISH LANGUAGE – DICTIONARIES – BYELORUSSIAN
Byelorussian-English, English-Byelorussian dict with complete phonetics, 1079

ENGLISH LANGUAGE – DICTIONARIES – DUTCH
International illus vocabulary of English-French fingerprint terminology..., 607

ENGLISH LANGUAGE – DICTIONARIES – ESTONIAN
Estonian-English, English-Estonian dict, 1082

ENGLISH LANGUAGE – DICTIONARIES – FRENCH
Ada lang vocabulary, 1677
French-English agricultural dict, 1465
Glossary geotextiles, 1609
International illus vocabulary of English-French fingerprint terminology..., 607
NTC's French & English bus dict, 182
Space station glossary, 1581
Statistics & surveys vocabulary, 905
Unemployment insurance glossary, 252
Vocabulary of cell engineering, v.1, 1600
Vocabulary of safety & security equipment, 1601

ENGLISH LANGUAGE – DICTIONARIES – GEORGIAN
Georgian-English, English-Georgian dict, 1084

ENGLISH LANGUAGE – DICTIONARIES – GERMAN
Dictionary of terms in music, 4th ed, 1248
International illus vocabulary of English-French fingerprint terminology..., 607

ENGLISH LANGUAGE – DICTIONARIES – HAWAIIAN
New pocket Hawaiian dict, 1086

ENGLISH LANGUAGE – DICTIONARIES – HEBREW
Webster's new world Hebrew dict, 1087

ENGLISH LANGUAGE – DICTIONARIES – IRISH
Irish/English, English/Irish dict & phrasebk, 1088

ENGLISH LANGUAGE – DICTIONARIES – ITALIAN
International illus vocabulary of English-French fingerprint terminology..., 607

ENGLISH LANGUAGE – DICTIONARIES – JAPANESE
International illus vocabulary of English-French fingerprint terminology..., 607

ENGLISH LANGUAGE – DICTIONARIES – PORTUGUESE
Random House Portuguese dict, 1091

ENGLISH LANGUAGE – DICTIONARIES – RUSSIAN
English-Russian dict with phonetics, 1094
Lexical semantics, 1092

ENGLISH LANGUAGE – DICTIONARIES – SERBIAN
International illus vocabulary of English-French fingerprint terminology..., 607

ENGLISH LANGUAGE – DICTIONARIES – SPANISH
Collins Spanish-English/English-Spanish dict, 3d ed, 1100
Elsevier's dict of terrestrial plant ecology, 1497
International illus vocabulary of English-French fingerprint terminology..., 607

ENGLISH LANGUAGE – DICTIONARIES – YIDDISH
English-Yiddish, Yiddish-English dict, 1105
Transliterated English-Yiddish, Yiddish-English dict, 1106

ENGLISH LANGUAGE – DICTIONARIES, JUVENILE
Troll young people's dict, 1063

ENGLISH LANGUAGE – GLOSSARIES, VOCABULARIES, ETC.
Dickson's word treasury, 1073

ENGLISH LANGUAGE – GRAMMAR
Handbook of good English, rev ed, 1061

ENGLISH LANGUAGE – GREAT BRITAIN – DICTIONARIES
British/American lang dict, 1069
British English for American readers, 1068

ENGLISH LANGUAGE – NEW WORDS
Fifty Yrs "Among the New Words," 1064
Oxford dict of new words, 1065

ENGLISH LANGUAGE – PUNCTUATION
Lauther's complete punctuation thesaurus of the English lang, 1051

ENGLISH LANGUAGE – RHETORIC
Handlist of rhetorical terms, 2d ed, 1071

ENGLISH LANGUAGE – STUDY & TEACHING – FOREIGN SPEAKERS
English lang & orientation programs in the US, 10th ed, 1053

ENGLISH LANGUAGE – SYNONYMS & ANTONYMS
Descriptionary, 1072
Merriam-Webster concise school & office thesaurus, 1074
Roget's 21st century thesaurus, 1076
Roget's intl thesaurus, 5th ed, 1075

ENGLISH LANGUAGE – TERMS & PHRASES
Concise glossary of contemporary literary theory, 1112
Dictionary of concepts in literary criticism & theory, 1111
Glossary of contemporary literary theory, 1113

ENGLISH LITERATURE
Recent studies in myths & lit, 1970-90, 1301

ENGLISH LITERATURE – MIDDLE ENGLISH, 1100-1500
Writers of the middle ages & renaissance before 1660, 1199

ENGLISH LITERATURE – EARLY MODERN, 1500-1700
Writers of the restoration & 18th century, 1660-1789, 1200

ENGLISH LITERATURE – 18TH CENTURY
Writers of the restoration & 18th century, 1660-1789, 1200

ENGLISH LITERATURE – 19TH CENTURY
Victorian writers, 1832-1890, 1197
Writers of the romantic period, 1789-1832, 1201

ENGLISH LITERATURE – 20TH CENTURY
British writers, suppl.2, 1191
Contemporary writers, 1960 to the present, 1192
Writers after WW II, 1945-60, 1198

ENGLISH POETRY. *See also names of individual poets*
Critical survey of poetry: English lang series, rev ed, 1236

ENGLISH PROSE LITERATURE
British Romantic prose writers, 1789-1832, 2d series, 1193

ENLIGHTENMENT
Blackwell companion to the enlightenment, 555

ENTREPRENEURSHIP
Government giveaways for entrepreneurs, 3d ed, 210
Pratt's gd to venture capital sources, 1992 ed, 197

ENVIRONMENTAL EDUCATION
Business & the environment, 249
Wilderness U: opportunities for outdoor educ in the US & abroad, 335

ENVIRONMENTAL HEALTH
Livable cities almanac, 920
Toxics A to Z, 1769

ENVIRONMENTAL LAW
Environmental hazards: toxic waste & hazardous material, 1770

ENVIRONMENTAL LITERATURE
E for environment, 1752

ENVIRONMENTAL MONITORING
Environment on File, 1767

ENVIRONMENTAL POLICY
Earth jl, 1992, 1765
Environment abstracts annual 1991, 1766
Environment on File, 1767
Environmental telephone dir 1992-93, 1756
Gale environmental sourcebk, 1768
Green almanac, 1751
Green co resource gd, 1774
HarperCollins dict of environmental sci, 1753
National gd to funding for the environment & animal welfare, 881
Statistical record of the environment, 1764
U.S.A. oil industry's environmental dir, 1993, 1762
Who is who at the Earth Summit, Rio de Janeiro, 1992, 1763
Who is who in serv to the earth, 1775
World dir of environmental orgs, 4th ed, 1773

ENVIRONMENTAL PROTECTION
E for environment, 1752
Environmental address bk, 1760
Environmental industries marketplace, 1755
Nature dir, 1759
Nature projects on file, 1527
World resources 1992-93, 1776

ENVIRONMENTAL PROTECTION AGENCY
EPA headquarters telephone dir, 1991 ed, 1757

ENVIRONMENTALISTS
Environmental address bk, 1760

EPONYMS
Corporate eponymy, 184

EQUATORIAL GUINEA
Equatorial Guinea, 114

EROTIC FILMS
X-rated videotape gd 2, 1332

ESPIONAGE
Spycatcher's ency of espionage, 787

ESSAYS
Essay & general lit index, rev ed, 77

ESTONIAN LANGUAGE—DICTIONARIES—ENGLISH
Estonian-English, English-Estonian dict, 1082

ETHICS
Encyclopedia of ethics, 1395

ETHICS IN THE BIBLE
Encyclopedia of biblical & Christian ethics, rev ed, 1419

ETHNIC GROUPS. *See also* **MINORITIES**
Directory of ethnic professionals in LIS (lib & info sci), 625
Peoples of the world: Africans south of the Sahara, 117
Writing for the ethnic markets, 962

ETHNIC GROUPS IN LITERATURE
Our family, our friends, our world, 1127

ETHNIC RELATIONS
Conflict & culture, rev ed, 419

ETHNIC STUDIES
Peoples of the world: the Middle East & N Africa, 160

ETHNOBOTANY
Medicinal wild plants of the prairie, 1514

ETHNOLOGY
Cultural anthropology of the Middle East, v.1, 416
Dictionary of concepts in cultural anthropology, 418
Encyclopedia of world cultures, 413
Multicultural aspects of lib media programs, 669
People atlas, 414

ETHNOMUSICOLOGY
Ethnomusicology research, 1242

ETIQUETTE
Emily Post's etiquette, 15th ed, 1307

EUROPE
Annotated index of medieval women, 933
Bibliography of law & economics, 564
Book of European forecasts, 282
Directory of European sports orgs, 821
European accountancy yrbk 1992/93, 271
European advertising mktg & media data 1992, 285
European compendium of mktg info, 286
European dir of consumer brands & their owners 1992, 288
European wholesalers & distrs dir, 257
International histl stats: Europe 1750-1988, 3d ed, 911
Music lover's gd to Europe, 1250
Scientific traveler, 1456
Spaghetti westerns, 1367

EUROPE—CENSUS
Handbook of natl population censuses: Europe, 898

EUROPE, EASTERN
Comecon data 1990, 907
Consumer E Europe 1992, 283
Directory of E European film-makers & films 1945-91, 1348
Eastern Europe: a dir & sourcebk 1992, 140
Eastern Europe & the Commonwealth of Independent States 1992, 141
Eastern European business dir, 284
Handbook of reconstruction in E Europe & the Soviet Union, 536
Handbook of Soviet & E European films & film-makers, 1340
New pol parties of E Europe & the Soviet Union, 770
Short-term economic stats: Central & E Europe, 292
Where once we walked: a gd to the Jewish communities destroyed in the Holocaust, 494

EUROPE—HISTORY—20TH CENTURY
Columbia dict of European pol hist since 1914, 529

EUROPE—POLITICS & GOVERNMENT
Sources in European pol hist, v.3, 766

EUROPEAN COMMUNITIES
Modern companion to the European Community, 767

EUROPEAN FEDERATION
Directory of pan-European orgs 1992, 138

EVALUATIONS
Evaluation thesaurus, 4th ed, 642

EXCAVATIONS (ARCHAEOLOGY)
Spain: 1001 sights, 506

EXECUTIVE DEPARTMENTS. *See* **ADMINISTRATIVE AGENCIES**

EXHIBITIONS
Books of the fairs, 1306
Tradeshow week data bk, 1992, 322

EXPLORERS
Who was who in world exploration, 488
Who's who in Pacific navigation, 487
World explorers & discoverers, 486

EXPORT MARKETING
Global Tex.: intl trade info sourcebk, 267
Global trade white pages 1992, 268
International business dict & ref, 255
World trade resources gd, 265

EXPORTS
American export register 1992, 318
Ukraine top 100 exporters, 294

EXTINCT BIRDS. *See* **BIRDS, EXTINCT**

EXTRATERRESTRIAL LIFE. *See* **LIFE ON OTHER PLANETS**

FABLES
Brewer's dict of 20th-century phrase & fable, 1294

FACTS, MISCELLANEOUS. *See* **ALMANACS**

FALKLAND ISLANDS WAR, 1982
Falklands/Malvinas campaign, 694

FAMILY
Families & aging, 854
Statistical hndbk on the American family, 867

FAMILY RECREATION
National parks, 498

FANTASTIC FICTION
British sci fiction, 1204
Reference gd to sci fiction, fantasy, & horror, 1155
Supernatural fiction for teens, 2d ed, 1156

FANTASTIC LITERATURE
Reginald's sci fiction & fantasy awards, 2d ed, 1157

FARMING. *See* **AGRICULTURE**

FASHION
Chronicle of W fashion, 1010
Fashion in the W world 1500-1990, 1011

FAULKNER, WILLIAM
Faulkner in the 80s, 1173

FAUNA. *See* **ANIMALS**

FEDERAL AID. *See* **ECONOMIC ASSISTANCE, DOMESTIC**

FEDERAL GOVERNMENT
Government dir of addresses & telephone nos, 740

FEDERAL GRANTS. *See* **GRANTS-IN-AID**

FEMINISM
Feminist movement: a bibliog, 929
Goddesses & wise women, 923
Simone de Beauvoir: a bibliog, 930
Women's studies ency, v.3, 939

FEMINISM & LITERATURE
Shakespeare & feminist criticism, 1212

FEMINISM & THEATER
Dramatic re-visions, 1333

FEMINIST CRITICISM
Dramatic re-visions, 1333

FERMENTED MILK
Encyclopedia of fermented fresh milk products, 1475

FESTIVALS
Fanfare for words: bkfairs & bk festivals in N America, 682
Folklore of American holidays, 2d ed, 1297
Folklore of world holidays, 1298
Multicultural projects index, 1312

FETUS
Catalog of prenatally diagnosed conditions, 2d ed, 1654

FICTION. *See also* **DETECTIVE & MYSTERY STORIES; SCIENCE FICTION**
Classic cult fiction, 1149
Fiction writers gdlines, 2d ed, 963
Genreflecting, 3d ed, 1147
Unreal! Hennepin County lib subject headings for fictional characters & places, 2d ed, 644

FIGURES OF SPEECH
Descriptionary, 1072
Handlist of rhetorical terms, 2d ed, 1071

FILIPINOS
Ang mahalaga sa buhay, 1102

FILM ADAPTATIONS
Books & plays in films 1896-1915, 1344
From page to screen, 1359

FINANCE. *See also* **INVESTMENTS**
Corporate finance sourcebk 1991, 238
Financial yellow bk, v.5, no.2, 239
Glossary of finance & debt, 231
Guide to the Canadian financial servs industry 1991, 232
New Palgrave dict of money & finance, 242
Who's who in finance & industry 1992-93, 179
World debt tables 1991-92, 244

FINANCE, PERSONAL
Dictionary of personal finance, 243

FINANCIAL AID
Scholarships, fellowships & loans 1992-93, 377

FINE ARTS. *See* **ART**

FINGER PLAY
Creative fingerplays & action rhymes, 340

FIREARMS
Standard cat of firearms, 2d ed, 1004

FISHES
Dictionary of evolutionary fish osteology, 1558
Field gd to the freshwater fishes of Tanzania, 1556
Guide to the marine sport fishes of Atlantic Canada & New England, 1555
World fishes important to N Americans, 1559

FLIES. *See* **DIPTERA**

FLORA. *See* **BOTANY**

FLORIDA
Florida almanac 1992-93, 106
Florida statistical abstract 1991, 107
Index to Fla. Jewish hist in the American Israelite 1854-1900, 446
Parasites & diseases of wild mammals in Fla., 1569

FLOWERS. *See* **WILD FLOWERS**

FLY FISHING
Fly patterns, 2d ed, 837

FOLKLORE
Folklore & folklife, 1300
Folklore of American holidays, 2d ed, 1297
Folklore of world holidays, 1298

FONDA, HENRY
Henry Fonda: a bio-bibliog, 1323

FOOD. *See also* **NUTRITION**
Codex alimentarius, v.1, 1479
Corinne T. Netzer ency of food values, 1476
How many calories? how much fat?, 1481
Post-harvest & processing techs of African staple foods, 1478

FOOD INDUSTRY & TRADE
Encyclopedia of food sci & tech, 1473

FOOD RELIEF
Food aid in figures, v.8/2, 1480

FOOTBALL
Football coach quotes, 830
NCAA football's finest, 831

FORAGE PLANTS
Forage resources of China, 1510

FOREIGN AGENTS
Washington representatives 1992, 744

FOREIGN STUDY
Academic yr abroad, 392
Vacation study abroad, 42d ed, 393

FOREIGN TRADE. *See* **INTERNATIONAL TRADE**

FOREIGNERS. *See* **ALIENS**

FOREST ECOLOGY
Book of forest & thicket, 1518

FOREST FLORA
Book of forest & thicket, 1518

FOREST PRODUCTS
FAO yrbk: forest products 1979-90, 1483

FORESTRY
Bibliography, 1988-90, 1482

FORESTS & FORESTRY
Parks dir of the US, 500

FORTIFICATION
Military fortifications, 692

FOSSILS. *See* **PALEONTOLOGY**

FOUNDATION FOR PUBLIC AFFAIRS (WASHINGTON, D.C.)
Public interest profiles 1992-93, 795

FOUNDATIONS (ENDOWMENTS). *See* **ENDOWMENTS**

FOUNDATIONS (PHILANTHROPY). *See* **ENDOWMENTS**

FOWLES, JOHN
John Fowles: a ref companion, 1208

FOX, CHARLES JAMES
Charles James Fox 1749-1806: a bibliog, 773

FRANCE
Cultural atlas of France, 143
French women writers, 1222
Historical dict of the French 4th & 5th Republics, 1946-91, 537

FREE MATERIAL
Educators gd to free videotapes, 39th ed, 396
Educators index of free materials, 101st ed, 328
Free resource builder for librarians & teachers, 2d ed, 70

FREE TRADE & PROTECTION
Vocabulary of free trade, 233

FRENCH LANGUAGE – DICTIONARIES
Vocabulary of free trade, 233

FRENCH LANGUAGE – DICTIONARIES – ENGLISH
Ada lang vocabulary, 1677

French-English agricultural dict, 1465
Glossary geotextiles, 1609
International illus vocabulary of English-French fingerprint terminology..., 607
NTC's French & English bus dict, 182
Oxford gd to the French lang, 1083
Space station glossary, 1581
Statistics & surveys vocabulary, 905
Unemployment insurance glossary, 252
Vocabulary of cell engineering, v.1, 1600
Vocabulary of safety & security equipment, 1601

FRENCH LANGUAGE—GRAMMAR
Oxford gd to the French lang, 1083

FRENCH LITERATURE
French women writers, 1222
Guide to French lit: 1789 to the present, 1221

FUNCTION TESTS (MEDICINE)
Concise ency of biological & biomedical measurement systems, 1635

FUND RAISING
Fund raiser's gd to religious philanthropy, 5th ed, 1425

GALLEGAN LITERATURE
Spanish, Catalan, & Galician literary authors of the 20th century, 1233

GAMES
Multicultural projects index, 1312

GARDENING
Garden lit, v.1, no.2, 1485
New gardener's hndbk & dict, 1486
North American horticulture, 2d ed, 1487

GAS INDUSTRY
Financial Times oil & gas intl yr bk 1993, 1748

GAWAIN (LEGENDARY CHARACTER)
Sir Gawain & the Green Knight: an annot bibliog, 1978-89, 1217

GAY MEN
Big gay bk, 886

GAYNOR, JANET
Janet Gaynor: a bio-bibliog, 1316

GAZETTEERS
Omni gazetteer of the USA [CD-ROM], 495

GENEALOGY
A-Z gd to tracing ancestors in Britain, 4th ed, 461
Address bk for Germanic genealogy, 4th ed, 454
Ancestry's red bk, rev ed, 455
First American Jewish families, 3d ed, 458
German-English genealogical dict, 453
In search of your roots: a gd for Canadians, rev ed, 456
State census records, 899

GENERALS
Concise dict of military biog, 699

GENOCIDE
First-person accounts of genocidal acts in the 20th century, 548

GEOGRAPHICAL NAMES. *See* **NAMES, GEOGRAPHICAL**

GEOGRAPHY. *See also Maps under names of places*
Concise Oxford dict of geography, 489

GEOGRAPHY—ATLASES. *See* **ATLASES**

GEOGRAPHY—COMPUTER PROGRAMS
International GIS sourcebk, 1993, 491

GEOGRAPHY, ECONOMIC
New state of the world atlas, 4th ed, 475
World economic data, 3d ed, 273

GEOGRAPHY—15TH-16TH CENTURIES
Shedding the veil: mapping the European discovery of America & the world, 470

GEOGRAPHY, HISTORICAL
Atlas of world affairs, 9th ed, 720

GEOLOGY
Elsevier's dict of geoscis, 1723

GEOGRAPHY, HISTORICAL
Rand McNally atlas of world hist, 1992 ed, 545

GEORGIAN LANGUAGE—DICTIONARIES—ENGLISH
Georgian-English, English-Georgian dict, 1084

GEOTEXTILES
Glossary geotextiles, 1609

GERMAN LANGUAGE—DICTIONARIES—ENGLISH
Dictionary of terms in music, 4th ed, 1248
NTC's dict of German false cognates, 1085

GERMAN LITERATURE
Companion to 20th-century German lit, 1223

GERMAN REUNIFICATION QUESTION (1949-1990)
Big Powers & the German question, 1941-90, 538

GERMANY
Nazi-retro film, 1362
Where once we walked: a gd to the Jewish communities destroyed in the Holocaust, 494

GERMANY—GENEALOGY
Address bk for Germanic genealogy, 4th ed, 454

GERMPLASM RESOURCES, PLANT
Elsevier's dict of plant genetic resources, 1496

GERONTOLOGY
Encyclopedia of aging & the elderly, 858

GETTYSBURG (PA.), BATTLE OF, 1863
Gettysburg: a battlefield atlas, 691

GHOSTS
Encyclopedia of ghosts & spirits, 810

GIFTED CHILDREN
Gifted & talented info resources, 339

GILA MONSTER
Venomous reptiles of N America, 1576

GILBERT, W. S. (WILLIAM SCHWENCK)
How quaint the ways of paradox!, 1274

GODDESSES
Guide to the gods, 1305

GODS
Guide to the gods, 1305

GOLD COINS
Gold bk: a gd to commonly traded gold bullion coins & bars, 226

GOLF
Encyclopedia of golf, 832
Golfers almanac, 833
Guide to golf schools & camps, 834

GOULD, GLENN
Descriptive cat of the Glenn Gould papers, 1255
Glenn Gould cat, 1253

GOVERNMENT AGENCIES. *See* **ADMINISTRATIVE AGENCIES**

GOVERNMENT EXECUTIVES
Prune bk: the 60 toughest sci & tech jobs in Washington, 757

GOVERNMENT PUBLICATIONS. *See also under names of countries*
Introduction to US govt info sources, 4th ed, 73
Using govt docs, 668

GOVERNMENT PURCHASING
Government contracts ref bk, 580

GRAINGER, PERCY
Source gd to the music of Percy Grainger, 1261

GRAMMAR, COMPARATIVE & GENERAL
Theoretical syntax 1980-90, 1049

GRANADOS, ENRIQUE
Enrique Granados: a bio-bibliog, 1259

GRANTS-IN-AID
America's new fndns 1992, 870
Awards almanac 1992, 871
Directory of building & equipment grants, 2d ed, 1035
Directory of corporate & fndn givers 1992, 872
Directory of grants in the humanities 1992/93, 946
Directory of research grants 1992, 873
Federal domestic outlays 1983-90, 745
Government giveaways for entrepreneurs, 3d ed, 210
Grants & awards available to American writers, 17th ed, 960

GRAPHIC ARTS
Graphic arts ency, 1042

GREAT BRITAIN
A-Z gd to tracing ancestors in Britain, 4th ed, 461
Biographical dict of life peers, 462
British electorate, 1963-87, 772
British English for American readers, 1068
British literary publishing houses, 1881-1965, 689
Contemporary Britain: an annual review 1992, 144
Encyclopedia of romanticism, 531
Famous trials, 604
Index to dialect maps of Great Britain, 1067
Music in British libs, 650
Reruns on file, 994
Richard Burton: a bio-bibliog, 1322
Sport in Britain, 814
Trade union hndbk, 5th ed, 305
Victorian studies, 533

GREAT BRITAIN—HISTORY—TUDORS, 1485-1603
Historical dict of Tudor England, 1485-1603, 532

GREAT BRITAIN—POLITICS & GOVERNMENT
Charles James Fox 1749-1806: a bibliog, 773
William Wilberforce 1759-1833: a bibliog, 771

GREAT LAKES
Literature of the Great Lakes region, 1165
Shipping lit of the Great Lakes, 1778

GREEK LANGUAGE, BIBLICAL
Exegetical dict of the N.T., v.2, 1426

GREELEY, HORACE
Horace Greeley: a bio-bibliog, 979

GREENHOUSE PLANTS
Ball field gd to diseases of greenhouse ornamentals, 1499

GREENLAND
Greenland, 119

GROCERY TRADE
Ethnic cookbks & food marketplace, 3d ed, 1472

GUMS & RESINS
Water-soluble resins, 2d ed, 1713

HABITAT (ECOLOGY)
World wildlife habitats, 1535

HALLS OF FAME
Sports halls of fame, 820

HAMLET
Hamlet in the 1960s, 1211

HAND WEAVING
Weaver's bk of 8-shaft patterns, 1009

HANDBOOKS, VADE-MECUMS, ETC.
Guinness bk of answers, 8th ed, 4
Macmillan visual dict, 1077

Matter of fact: statements containing stats on current social, economic & pol issues, v.14-15, 910
Pocket ref, 1454

HANDICAPPED. *See also* **PHYSICALLY HANDICAPPED**
Complete dir for people with disabilities, 1992, 862
Disability, sexuality & abuse, 865
Portraying persons with disabilities: an annot bibliog of fiction, 3d ed, 1132
Portraying persons with disabilities: an annot bibliog of nonfiction, 2d ed, 1124

HANDICAPPED CHILDREN
Individuals with disabilities educ act 1980-91, 394

HANDICRAFT
Crafts index for young people, 1005
Fun for kids 2, 1006
Multicultural projects index, 1312

HARDING, WARREN G.
Warren G. Harding: a bibliog, 509

HARDWARE
Illustrated hrdwr bk, 1611

HAWAII
Hawaiian insects & their kin, 1565
Insects of Hawaii, v.15, 1561
Marine atlas of the Hawaiian Islands, 466

HAWAIIAN LANGUAGE – DICTIONARIES – ENGLISH
New pocket Hawaiian dict, 1086

HAZARDOUS WASTES
Environmental hazards: toxic waste & hazardous material, 1770

HEALTH
Marshall Cavendish ency of family health, 1617

HEALTH CARE. *See* **MEDICAL CARE**

HEAVY MINERALS
Heavy minerals in colour, 1726

HEBREW LANGUAGE – DICTIONARIES – ENGLISH
Webster's new world Hebrew dict, 1087

HELPING BEHAVIOR IN CHILDREN
Prosocial dvlpmt in children, 894

HEMINGWAY, ERNEST
Hemingway: an annot chronology, 1174

HERBALS
Cleveland herbal, botanical, & horticultural collections, 1493

HEROES
Contemporary heroes & heroines, bk 2, 45
Courage in the air, 697

HEROINES
Contemporary heroes & heroines, bk 2, 45

HIGH TECHNOLOGY INDUSTRIES
Hidden job market, 303

HIGHER EDUCATION. *See* **EDUCATION, HIGHER**

HIKING
Essential gd to hiking in the US, 835

HISPANIC-AMERICAN LIBRARIANS
Directory of ethnic professionals in LIS (lib & info sci), 625

HISPANIC-AMERICANS
Extraordinary Hispanic Americans, 51
Hispanic Americans info dir 1992-93, 428
Hispanic heritage, series 4, 150
Hispanic presence in N America from 1492 to today, 427
Hispanic resource dir 1992-94, 429

HISPANIC-AMERICANS IN MOTION PICTURES
Hispanic image on the silver screen, 1363

HISTORIC SHIPS
Great American ships, 1788

HISTORIC SITES
Hippocrene USA gd to black America, 424
Parks dir of the US, 500

HISTORICAL GEOGRAPHY. *See* **GEOGRAPHY, HISTORICAL**

HISTORIOGRAPHY
Selected bibliog of modern historiography, 546

HISTORY. *See also History under names of countries, states, etc.*
First-person accounts of genocidal acts in the 20th century, 548
Longman hndbk of world hist since 1914, 559
Timetables of hist, 3d ed, 560
Walford's gd to ref material, 5th ed, v.2: social & histl scis, 98

HOBSON-JOBSON
Sahibs, nabobs & boxwallahs, 1070

HOLIDAYS
Folklore of American holidays, 2d ed, 1297
Folklore of world holidays, 1298
Holidays & special days project index for young people, 1308
Our natl holidays, 1313

HOLOCAUST, JEWISH (1939-1945)
Catalogue of audio & video collections of Holocaust testimony, 2d ed, 528
World in turmoil, 550

HOLOGRAPHY
Holography market place, 3d ed, 1012

HOME CARE SERVICES
Home health care, 1620

HOME CONSTRUCTION. *See* **HOUSE CONSTRUCTION**

HOME-BASED BUSINESSES
Work-at-home sourcebk, 4th ed, 308

HONDURAS
Honduras, 155

HORROR FILMS
Critical gd to horror film series, 1354
Television horror movie hosts, 985

HORROR TELEVISION PROGRAMS
Television horror movie hosts, 985

HORTICULTURE
North American horticulture, 2d ed, 1487

HOSPICE (TERMINAL CARE)
Palliative care of the elderly, 857

HOUSE CONSTRUCTION
Home building & woodworking in colonial America, 1612

HOUSE ORGANS
Corporate mags of the US, 217

HOUSEHOLD SUPPLIES
Consumer's dict of household, yard & office chemicals, 1754

HOUSING & HEALTH
Consumer's dict of household, yard & office chemicals, 1754
Tackling toxics in everyday products, 1761

HUMAN CHROMOSOMES
Mendelian inheritance in man, 10th ed, 1624

HUMAN ECOLOGY
Rediscovery of creation, 1417

HUMAN GEOGRAPHY. *See* **ANTHROPO-GEOGRAPHY**

HUMAN REPRODUCTION
Language of sex, 883
Reproduction: a gd to materials in the Women's Educl Resource Centre, 885

HUMAN RIGHTS
Great events from hist 2: human rights series, 617
Human rights: 60 major global instruments, 615
World dir of human rights research & training insts, 2d ed, 619
World dir of peace research & training insts, 7th ed, 792
World racism & related inhumanities, 618

HUMAN-COMPUTER INTERACTION
Virtual reality: a selected bibliog, 1672

HUMANITIES
American humanities index for 1991, v.27, 945
Directory of grants in the humanities 1992/93, 946
Humanities index, 948
Persian & English glossary for humanities & social scis, 1090

HUNGARY
Hippocrene insider's gd to Hungary, 505

HUNTING
Hunting quotations, 836

HYDROLOGY
Elsevier's dict of hydrology & water quality mgmt, 1724

HYGIENE, SEXUAL
A-to-Z of women's sexuality, rev ed, 884
Language of sex, 883

HYPERMEDIA SYSTEMS
Emerging techs & instruction, 344

HYPERTEXT SYSTEMS
Emerging techs & instruction, 344

ILLUSTRATED BOOKS
Photography & lit, 1013

ILLUSTRATED BOOKS, CHILDREN'S
Artists of the page, 1022
Newbery & Caldecott awards, 1992 ed, 1128
Newbery & Caldecott medal & honor bks in other media, 1121
Newbery & Caldecott medalists & honor bk winners, 2d ed, 1120

ILLUSTRATORS
Artists of the page, 1022
Author profile collection, 1138
Biographical index to children's & young adult authors & illustrators, 1144
Talking with artists, 1021

IMAGE TRANSMISSION
AIIM speakers dir 1992-93, 1668

IMAGING SYSTEMS
International imaging source bk 1992, 1693

IMMIGRANTS
Complete bk of emigrants 1700-50, 452
Immigrant experience, 420

IMPORTS
Bergano's register of intl importers 1992/93, 256
Global Tex.: intl trade info sourcebk, 267
Global trade white pages 1992, 268
World trade resources gd, 265

INCOME TAX
Guide to income tax preparation, 326

INDEPENDENT SCHOOLS. *See* **PRIVATE SCHOOLS**

INDEXING
Indexing from A to Z, 653

INDIA
Handbook of libs, archives & info centres in India, v.9, 647
Handbook of libs, archives & info centres in India, v.11, pt.1, 648
Higher educ in India, 391
Indian music lit, 1239
Limca bk of records 1991, 1310
South Asian hndbk, 1992, 502

INDIANA
Indiana factbk 1992, 108

INDIANS
Biographical dict of Indians of the Americas, 430

INDIANS OF NORTH AMERICA
Discover Indian reservations USA, 434
Encyclopedia of Native American religions, 432
Field gd to rock art symbols of the greater southwest, 508
Fighting men of the Indian wars, 515
Indians along the Oregon Trail, expanded ed, 436
Medicinal wild plants of the prairie, 1514
Native America, 431
Through Indian eyes, 433
Yakima, Palouse, Cayuse, Umatilla, Walla Walla, & Wanapum Indians, 435

INDOCHINA
America & the Indochina wars, 1945-90, 733

INDOCHINA—RELATIONS—UNITED STATES
America & the Indochina wars, 1945-90, 733

INDOOR AIR POLLUTION
Indoor air quality dir 1992-93, 1758
Tackling toxics in everyday products, 1761

INDUSTRIAL ENGINEERING
Industrial engineering terminology, rev ed, 1602
Maynard's industrial engineering hndbk, 4th ed, 1603

INDUSTRIAL MANAGEMENT
Business & the environment, 249

INDUSTRIAL MOBILIZATION
International defense electronic systems hndbk, 718

INDUSTRIAL PROMOTION
Directory of incentives for bus investment & dvlpmt in the US, 3d ed, 221

INDUSTRIALISTS
Corporate eponymy, 184

INDUSTRY
Industrial research in the UK, 14th ed, 296
Manufacturing USA, 2d ed, 247
Service industries USA, 250
Who knows about industries & markets, 13th ed, 251
Who's who in bus & industry in the UK 1991, 298
Who's who in finance & industry 1992-93, 179

INFORMAL SECTOR (ECONOMICS)
Informal economy, 173

INFORMATION NETWORKS
Guide to the info activities of European dvlpmt networks, 630

INFORMATION RESOURCES MANAGEMENT
AIIM speakers dir 1992-93, 1668
Burwell dir of info brokers 1992, 654

INFORMATION SCIENCE
Annotated bibliog of faculty status in lib & info sci, 634
Annual review of info sci & tech, v.26, 628
Dictionary of info sci & tech, 622
Librarianship & info work worldwide 1991, 631
Library lit, 632
New intl dict of acronyms in lib & info sci, 2d ed, 621

INFORMATION SERVICES
Directory of Japanese technical resources in the US 1992, 655
Directory to fulltext online resources 1992, 626
Information marketplace dir, 1993, 685

INFORMATION STORAGE & RETRIEVAL SYSTEMS
Encyclopedia of bus info sources, 9th ed, 206
Handbook of libs, archives & info centres in India, v.9, 647
Macrothesaurus for info processing in the field of economic & social dvlpmt, 641
Online manual, 203

INFORMATION TECHNOLOGY
Dictionary of info sci & tech, 622
Handbook of libs, archives & info centres in India, v.11, pt.1, 648
McGraw-Hill dict of info tech & computer acronyms, initials, & abbrevs, 1679

INJURIES. See ACCIDENTS

INSECTS
Catalogue of palaearctic diptera, v.7, 1567
Hawaiian insects & their kin, 1565
Insects of Hawaii, v.15, 1561

INSECTS, AQUATIC
Illustrated gd to the mountain stream insects of Colo., 1568

IN-SERVICE TRAINING. See EMPLOYEES, TRAINING OF

INSTITUTIONS, ASSOCIATIONS, ETC.. See ASSOCIATIONS, INSTITUTIONS, ETC.

INSTRUCTIONAL MATERIALS CENTERS
Educational media & tech yrbk, v.18, 398
School lib media annual, v.10, 672

INSURANCE
Who's who in world insurance, 253

INSURANCE, UNEMPLOYMENT
Unemployment insurance glossary, 252

INTEGRATED CIRCUITS
International ency of integrated circuits, 2d ed, 1594

INTELLIGENCE OFFICERS
Soviet security & intelligence orgs 1917-90, 769

INTELLIGENCE SERVICE
American intelligence, 1775-1990, 785
Soviet security & intelligence orgs 1917-90, 769

INTERCULTURAL EDUCATION
Multicultural projects index, 1312

INTER-LIBRARY LOANS
Interlibrary loan policies dir, 4th ed, 657
WLN interlib loan policies dir, 658

INTERNAL SECURITY
Information security hndbk, 315
Soviet security & intelligence orgs 1917-90, 769

INTERNATIONAL AGENCIES
International orgs & world order dict, 781
Who's who in intl orgs, 784
Who's who in the UN & related agencies, 2d ed, 782
Yearbook of intl orgs 1991/92, 75

INTERNATIONAL BUSINESS ENTERPRISES
CIFAR's global co hndbk, 1992 ed, 263
European advertising mktg & media data 1992, 285
European business rankings, 291
European consultants dir, 287
European dir of consumer brands & their owners 1992, 288
European markets: a gd to co & industry info sources, 4th ed, 289
International corporate yellow bk, v.5, no.1, 259
Major cos of the Far East & Australasia 1991/92, 8th ed, v.1, 281
SIBD 92-93, 293
Transnational corps in S Africa, 276
World business dir, 261
World class business, 272

INTERNATIONAL COOPERATION
Guide to funding for intl & foreign programs, 880

INTERNATIONAL ECONOMIC RELATIONS
International business dict & ref, 255

INTERNATIONAL EDUCATION
Access to UK higher educ, 380
International exchange locator, 387
International higher educ, 381
Open doors 1990/91, 389
Profiles 1989-90, 390
Where walls once stood, 388

INTERNATIONAL FINANCE
IMF glossary, 254
International business dict & ref, 255

INTERNATIONAL LAW
Dictionary of intl & comparative law, 577
International business dict & ref, 255

INTERNATIONAL MONETARY FUND
IMF glossary, 254

INTERNATIONAL NUCLEAR INFORMATION SYSTEM
INIS: thesaurus, 1735

INTERNATIONAL ORGANIZATIONS. *See* **INTERNATIONAL AGENCIES**

INTERNATIONAL RELATIONS
International business dict & ref, 255
International orgs & world order dict, 781

INTERNATIONAL TRADE
Directory to intl bus educ in Canada, 230
Henry Holt intl desk ref, 269
International trade, 270
Who knows about foreign industries & markets, 13th ed, 274

INTERSTELLAR COMMUNICATION
Extraterrestrial ency, rev ed, 805

INVENTIONS
Great inventions through hist, 1447
Great modern inventions, 1448
Nineteenth-century inventors, 1439
Oxford illus ency of invention & tech, 1451

INVENTORS
Nineteenth-century inventors, 1439
Radio & TV pioneers: a patent bibliog, 983

INVESTMENTS
Business One Irwin bus & investment almanac, 1992, 220
Corporate finance sourcebk 1991, 238
Guide to the Canadian financial servs industry 1991, 232
McGraw-Hill dict of Wall St acronyms, initials, & abbrevs, 171
NASDAQ yellow bk, v.4, no.1, 225

INVISIBLE WORLD. *See* **SPIRITS**

IRAN
Persian & English glossary for humanities & social scis, 1090

IRAQ
BBC World Service Gulf Crisis chronology, 542

IRELAND
Companion to Irish hist 1603-1921, 539

IRIS (PLANT)
Iris of China, 1507

IRISH LANGUAGE – DICTIONARIES – ENGLISH
Irish/English, English/Irish dict & phrasebk, 1088

IRISH-AMERICANS
Irish in America, 437

ISRAEL
Glossary of Jewish life, 449

ITALIAN-AMERICANS
Italian American material culture, 438

ITALIAN-CANADIANS
Italian American material culture, 438

JAPAN
Birds of Japan, 1538
Directory, 1991-92: Japanese-affiliated cos in USA & Canada, 279
Directory of Japanese technical resources in the US 1992, 655
Guide to modern Japanese woodblock prints, 1900-75, 1043
Japanese studies from pre-hist to 1990, 126
Who's who in Japan 1991-92, 48
Women in Japanese society, 925

JAPAN—ARMED FORCES
Handbook on Japanese military forces, 705

JAZZ MUSIC
Best rated CDs 1992: jazz, popular, etc., 1275
Fire music, 1286
Jazz discography, v.1, 1287
Jazz discography, v.2, 1288
Jazz discography, v.3, 1289
Sarah Vaughan: a discography, 1285

JEFFERSON, THOMAS
Thomas Jefferson, 1981-90: an annot bibliog, 512

JERUSALEM
Jerusalem, the holy city, v.2, 544

JEWISH ART & SYMBOLISM
Encyclopedia of Jewish symbols, 443

JEWISH MUSEUMS
Jewish museums of N America, 444

JEWISH TRAVELERS
Traveling Jewish in America, 3d ed, 441

JEWS
American Jewish yr bk 1992, 439
Encyclopedia of Jewish symbols, 443
First American Jewish families, 3d ed, 458
Glossary of Jewish life, 449
Index to Fla. Jewish hist in the American Israelite 1854-1900, 446
Jewish museums of N America, 444
Jewish profiles, 450
Jewish wisdom, 445
Jewish-American hist & culture, 442
New standard Jewish ency, 7th ed, 448
Soviet Jewish hist, 1917-91, 447
Traveling Jewish in America, 3d ed, 441
Where once we walked: a gd to the Jewish communities destroyed in the Holocaust, 494

JEWS—GERMANY
World in turmoil, 550

JEWS—HISTORY—70-1789—MAPS
Atlas of medieval Jewish hist, 440

JEWS IN MOTION PICTURES
Jewish film dir, 1357

JOB HUNTING
Hidden job market, 303
Job hunter's gd to 100 great American cities, 304
Job seeker's gd to private & public cos, 310
100 best job$ for the 1990s & beyond, 311

JOB TRAINING. *See* **OCCUPATIONAL TRAINING**

JOHN D. CRUMMEY PEACE COLLECTION (HOOVER INSTITUTION ON WAR, REVOLUTION, & PEACE)
Guide to the John D. Crummey peace collection in the Hoover Inst, 790

JORDAN
Historical dict of the Hashemite kingdom of Jordan, 164

JOURNALISM
Sourcebook of American literary journalism, 976

JOURNALISTS
Horace Greeley: a bio-bibliog, 979

JUDAISM
Dictionary of Judaism & Christianity, 1405
Encyclopedia of Jewish symbols, 443
Glossary of Jewish life, 449
Jewish profiles, 450
Jewish wisdom, 445

JUDGES
BNA's dir of state & fed courts, judges, & clerks, 4th ed, 582

JUNG, C. G. (CARL GUSTAV)
Cross-currents of Jungian thought, 796

JUNIOR COLLEGES
AACJC membership dir 1992, 359
Chronicle 2-yr college databk for 1991-92 school yr, 369

JUTLAND, BATTLE OF, 1916
Battle of Jutland, 693

KANSAS
Kansas hist, 513

KENTUCKY
Kentucky ency, 109
Vascular plants of Ky., 1494

KENYA
Field gd to the acacias of Kenya, 1516

KOSINSKI, JERZY
Jerzy Kosinski: an annot bibliog, 1175

KURDS
Kurds: a concise hndbk, 165

KUWAIT
BBC World Service Gulf Crisis chronology, 542

LABOR & LABORING CLASSES
Encyclopedia of career change & work issues, 409
Year bk of labour stats 1991, 314

LABOR MARKET
100 best job$ for the 1990s & beyond, 311

LABOR POLICY
Labour & population programme, 299

LABRADOR (NFLD.)
Atlas of Nfld. & Lab., 473
Encyclopedia of Nfld. & Lab., v.3, 133

L'AMOUR, LOUIS
Work of Louis L'Amour, 1176

LANDSCAPE GARDENING
Shade & color with water-conserving plants, 1520

LANGUAGE ARTS
Using children's bks in reading/lang arts programs, 402

LAOS
Historical dict of Laos, 128
Laos, 127

LARGE TYPE BOOKS
Complete dir of large print bks & serials 1992, 30

LASERS
Laser video disc companion, updated ed, 997

LASERS IN MEDICINE
Understanding lasers, 1646

LATIN AMERICA
Choral music of Latin America, 1267
Hispanic heritage, series 4, 150
Latin America & the Caribbean: a critical gd to research sources, 148
Statistical yrbk for Latin America & the Caribbean, 1991 ed, 151

LATIN AMERICA – LIBRARY RESOURCES
Scholars' gd to Washington, DC for Latin American & Caribbean studies, 2d ed, 149

LATIN AMERICA – RELATIONS – UNITED STATES
United States in Latin America, 786

LAW
Bibliography of law & economics, 564
Bowker's law bks & serials in print 1991, 565
Canadian law symposia index, 598
Dictionary of English law, 575
Historic US court cases 1690-1990, 578
Index to legal pers [CD-ROM], 601
Index to legal pers: Sept 1990-Aug 1991, 600
International legal bibliogs, 567
Law bks in print 1990, 570
Law lib ref shelf, 2d ed, 572
Legal asst's notebk, 595
Legal desk bk 1992, 597
Legal thesaurus, 2d ed, 574
Mellinkoff's dict of American legal usages, 579
Mexican legal system, 563
Recommended pubs for legal research 1990, 573
West's tax law dict, 1992 ed, 581
World dict of legal abbrevs, 562

LAW ENFORCEMENT
Dictionary of crime, 608

LAW FIRMS
Law firms yellow bk, v.2, no.1, 584

LAWYERS
Canada legal dir 1992, 583
Tennessee attorneys dir, 1992, 585

LEADERSHIP
Thoughts on leadership, 316

LEBANON
Lebanon, rev ed, 166

LEGAL DEPOSIT (OF BOOKS, ETC.)
International gd to legal deposit, 651

LEGAL ETHICS
Resources for research in legal ethics, 592

LEGAL RESEARCH
Arizona legal research gd, 596
Legal researcher's desk ref 1992, 591
Mexican legal system, 563

LEGISLATIVE BODIES
Directory of legislative leaders 1991-92, 739

LEPIDOPTERA
Annotated list of Ont. lepidoptera, 1550

LIBRARIES. *See also specific types, e.g.,* **PUBLIC LIBRARIES**
American lib dir 1992-93, 623
Interlibrary loan policies dir, 4th ed, 657
Library lit, 632
WLN interlib loan policies dir, 658

LIBRARIES – PERIODICALS
Magazines for libs, 7th ed, 85

LIBRARIES – SPECIAL COLLECTIONS
CD-ROM research collections, 660
Directory of special collections of research value in Canadian libs, 646
Free resource builder for librarians & teachers, 2d ed, 70

LIBRARIES, CHILDREN'S
Library serv to children, 665
Using children's bks in reading/lang arts programs, 402

LIBRARIES, CHILDREN'S—BOOK LISTS
Reference bks for children, 4th ed, 1129

LIBRARIES, DEPOSITORY
International gd to legal deposit, 651

LIBRARIES, SPECIAL
Tools of the profession, 2d ed, 674

LIBRARIES, UNIVERSITY & COLLEGE
Collection evaluation in academic libs, 677
Search sheets for OPACs on the Internet, 661

LIBRARY ASSOCIATION INDUSTRIAL GROUP
Industrial group index, 649

LIBRARY CATALOGS & READERS
Search sheets for OPACs on the Internet, 661

LIBRARY COOPERATION
Latin American serial pubs available by exchange, 633

LIBRARY INFORMATION NETWORKS
Directory of computer conferencing in libs, 656

LIBRARY RESOURCES
Directory of special collections of research value in Canadian libs, 646
Scholars' gd to Washington, DC for Latin American & Caribbean studies, 2d ed, 149

LIBRARY RESOURCES ON GOVERNMENT PUBLICATIONS
Directory of govt doc collections & librarians, 6th ed, 676

LIBRARY SCIENCE
Advances in librarianship, v.15, 627
Annotated bibliog of faculty status in lib & info sci, 634
Bowker annual lib & bk trade almanac, 37th ed, 629
Dictionary of info sci & tech, 622
FID dir 1991-92, 624
Librarianship & info work worldwide 1991, 631
Library lit, 632
Library serv to children, 665
New intl dict of acronyms in lib & info sci, 2d ed, 621

LIBYA
Historical dict of Libya, 2d ed, 115

LIEUTENANT-GOVERNORS
Lieutenant-governors of the NW territories & Alta. 1876-1991, 765

LIFE CARE COMMUNITIES
99 best residential & recreational communities in America for vacation, retirement & investment planning, 919

LIFE ON OTHER PLANETS
Extraterrestrial ency, rev ed, 805

LINGUISTICS
International ency of linguistics, 1050
Linguistics ency, 1052

LITERACY
International hndbk of reading educ, 404

LITERARY AGENTS
Guide to literary agents & art/photo reps, 1992, 961

LITERARY CHARACTERS. *See* **CHARACTERS & CHARACTERISTICS IN LITERATURE**

LITERATURE
Black lit criticism, 1115
Concise glossary of contemporary literary theory, 1112
Dictionary of concepts in literary criticism & theory, 1111
Encyclopedia of lit & criticism, 1116
Essay & general lit index, rev ed, 77
Glossary of contemporary literary theory, 1113
MLA intl bibliog, 1107
Photography & lit, 1013
Writers dir 1992-94, 1119

LITERATURE PUBLISHING
British literary publishing houses, 1881-1965, 689

LIVERWORTS
Guide to the liverworts of N.C., 1512

LIZARDS
Giant lizards, 1580

LOBBYISTS
Directory of pressure groups in the European Community, 768
Washington representatives 1992, 744

LOBSTERS
FAO species cat, v.13: marine lobsters of the world, 1557

LOCAL GOVERNMENT
Government dir of addresses & telephone nos, 740

LOCUSTS
Locust neurobiology, 1566

LONDON (ENGLAND)
Times London hist atlas, 534

LOUISIANA
Louisiana almanac 1992-93, 110

MAGIC
Magic, witchcraft, & paganism in America, 2d ed, 811

MAGNETIC MATERIALS
Concise ency of magnetic & superconducting materials, 1591

MAHICAN LANGUAGE
Schmick's Mahican dict, 1089

MAIL-ORDER BUSINESS
Catalogue of Canadian catalogues, 3d ed, 227

MALDIVES
South Asian hndbk, 1992, 502

MAMMALS. *See also* **MARINE MAMMALS**
Mammals of the neotropics: the S cone, v.2, 1570
Parasites & diseases of wild mammals in Fla., 1569
Walker's mammals of the world, 5th ed, 1572

MAN—INFLUENCE ON NATURE
Conservation atlas of tropical forests: Africa, 1484
Random House atlas of the oceans, 1730

MANAGEMENT
Concise dict of mgmt, 317
Quotable business, 218

MANNERS & CUSTOMS
People atlas, 414

MANPOWER POLICY
Plant closings, 300

MANUFACTURES
Brands & their cos 1992, 188
Companies & their brands 1992, 189
Manufacturing USA, 2d ed, 247
Official museum products & servs dir 1992, 80

MANUSCRIPTS, AMERICAN
Union cat of letters to Clemens, 1183

MANUSCRIPTS, CANADIAN
From the past to the future, 527

MAO, TSE-TUNG
Mao Zedong: a bibliog, 522

MARINE ALGAE
Seaweeds of the SE US, 1513

MARINE BIOLOGY
Random House atlas of the oceans, 1730

MARINE FISHES
Guide to the marine sport fishes of Atlantic Canada & New England, 1555

MARINE MAMMALS
Sierra Club hndbk of seals & sirenians, 1571

MARINE RESOURCES CONSERVATION
Random House atlas of the oceans, 1730

MARITIME PROVINCES
Maritime provinces atlas, new ed, 472

MARKETING
Book of European forecasts, 282
Consumer E Europe 1992, 283
European advertising mktg & media data 1992, 285
European compendium of mktg info, 286
European dir of consumer brands & their owners 1992, 288
European wholesalers & distrs dir, 257
IEG dir of sponsorship mktg, 1991, 258
$upertrader's almanac, 2d ed, 321
Tradeshow week data bk, 1992, 322
World retail dir & sourcebk 1991, 262
World trade system, 266

MARTIAL ARTS
Aiki News ency of aikido, 838
Dictionary of the martial arts, 839

MASS COMMUNICATION. *See* **COMMUNICATION**

MASS MEDIA
Control of the media in the US, 951
Facts on File dict of film & broadcast terms, 987
Reruns on file, 994

MASS SPECTRONOMETRY
Important peak index of the registry of mass spectral data, 1717

MASTER OF BUSINESS ADMINISTRATION DEGREE
Guide to MBA programs in Canada, 376

MATHEMATICAL MODELS
Concise ency of modelling & simulation, 1674

MATHEMATICS
Biographical dict of mathematicians, 1736
Combined membership list 1992-93, 1737
HarperCollins dict of mathematics, 1739
Mathematical bk review index 1800-1940, 1738
Mathematical jls, 1741
Numbers you need, 1740

MAURITIUS
Historical dict of Mauritius, 2d ed, 147
Mauritius, 146

MCCARTHY, MARY
Mary McCarthy: an annot bibliog, 1177

MEASURING INSTRUMENTS
Economist desk companion, 205

MEDIA PROGRAMS (EDUCATION)
Brown's dir of instructional programs, 1992: K-8, 346
Brown's dir of instructional programs, 1992: 7-12, 347
Guide to ref bks for school media centers, 4th ed, 670
School lib media annual, v.10, 672

MEDICAL CARE
Consumer health & nutrition index, v.8, no.1, 1614
Glossary of health care terms, 2d ed, 1615
Glossary of health servs, 1616
Health care terms, 2d ed, 1621
Medical & health care bks & serials in print 1992, 1625
Minority health resources dir, 1618

MEDICAL GENETICS
Mendelian inheritance in man, 10th ed, 1624

MEDICAL INSTRUMENTS & APPARATUS
Canadian medical device dir, 1642
Szycher's dict of biomaterials & medical devices, 1639

MEDICAL LITERATURE
Information sources in the medical scis, 4th ed, 1626

MEDICINAL PLANTS
Cleveland herbal, botanical, & horticultural collections, 1493

MEDICINE
Black's medical dict, 37th ed, 1629
Charles Press hndbk of current medical abbreviations, 3d ed, 1622
Consumer's gd to medical lingo, 1633
Davies' medical terminology, 5th ed, 1630
Encyclopedia of medical orgs & agencies 1992-93, 1632
Information sources in the medical scis, 4th ed, 1626
Medical & health care bks & serials in print 1992, 1625
Medical word bk A-Z, 1631
Morton's medical bibliog, 5th ed, 1627
Stedman's abbrev., 1623
Stedman's medical speller, 1637
Stedman's pathology lab medicine words, 1638
Who's who in sci in Europe, 7th ed, 1442

MEDICINE, POPULAR
Home ency of symptoms, ailments & their natural remedies, 1640

MELANESIA
Indigenous navigation & voyaging in the Pacific, 1789

MELVILLE, HERMAN
Checklist of Melville reviews, 1178

MENTAL DISORDERS. *See* **MENTAL ILLNESS**

MENTAL ILLNESS
Female psychology, 797

MENTAL TESTS. *See* **EDUCATIONAL TESTS & MEASUREMENTS**

MERMAN, ETHEL
Ethel Merman: a bio-bibliog, 1317

MERRICK, DAVID
David Merrick: a bio-bibliog, 1377

METALS
ASM hndbk, v.18, 1604

METAL-WORK
Complete metalsmith, rev ed, 1008

METROPOLITAN AREAS
Livable cities almanac, 920
Moving & relocation sourcebk, 917

MEXICAN LITERATURE
Mexican lit, 2d ed, 1227

MEXICO
Latin American serial pubs available by exchange, 633
Mexican legal system, 563
Mexican pol biogs, 1884-1935, 775
Pines of Mexico & Central America, 1519

MICHIGAN
Atlas of breeding birds of Mich., 1539

MICROCOMPUTERS
High-technology editorial gd & stylebk, PC ed, 969
Microcomputer index, v.12, 1686
Pocket PCref, 1684

MICROFORMS
Guide to microforms in print 1991: author-title, 1694
Guide to microforms in print 1991: subject, 1695

MICRONESIA
Indigenous navigation & voyaging in the Pacific, 1789

MIDDLE AGE
Late achievers, 43

MIDDLE EAST
Bibliographic gd to Middle Eastern studies 1990, 159
Bibliography on temples of the ancient Near East & Mediterranean world, 1402
Biographical dict of the Middle East, 161
Cultural anthropology of the Middle East, v.1, 416
Kurds: a concise hndbk, 165
Middle East: a pol dict, 776
Middle East bibliog, 162
Peoples of the world: the Middle East & N Africa, 160

MIDWAY, BATTLE OF, 1942
Battles of Coral Sea & Midway, 1942, 695

MILITARY ART & SCIENCE
Army dict & desk ref, 717
International military ency, v.1, 702

MILITARY AVIATION. *See* **AERONAUTICS, MILITARY**

MILITARY BIOGRAPHY
Concise dict of military biog, 699
Harper ency of military biog, 698

MILITARY UNIFORMS. *See* **UNIFORMS, MILITARY**

MILK
Encyclopedia of fermented fresh milk products, 1475

MILLENNIALISM
Millennialism: an intl bibliog, 1399

MILLER, WALTER M.
Walter M. Miller, Jr.: a bio-bibliog, 1179

MINERALOGY
Heavy minerals in colour, 1726
Minerals of the world, 1729
Rocks & minerals, 1728

MINERALS IN HUMAN NUTRITION
Essential gd to vitamins & minerals, 1647

MINORITIES
Immigrant experience, 420
Substance abuse among ethnic minorities in America, 891

MINORITIES IN LIBRARY SCIENCE
Directory of ethnic professionals in LIS (lib & info sci), 625

MINORITIES IN LITERATURE
Our family, our friends, our world, 1127

MINORITY STUDENTS
Multicultural aspects of lib media programs, 669

MINORITY WOMEN
Women, race, & ethnicity, 931

MODEMS
Modem USA, 1683

MOLECULAR SIEVES
Handbook of molecular sieves, 1584

MONEY
New Palgrave dict of money & finance, 242

MONEY RAISING. See **FUND RAISING**

MONTSERRAT
Montserrat, 156

MOON
Moons of the solar system, 1707

MORAL EDUCATION
Literature-based moral educ, 351

MORMON CHURCH
Encyclopedia of Mormonism, 1420
Encyclopedia of Mormonism [CD-ROM], 1421

MOTHS
Butterflies & moths, 1547

MOTION PICTURE ACTORS & ACTRESSES
Anne Baxter: a bio-bibliog, 1318
Cult movie stars, 1337
Henry Fonda: a bio-bibliog, 1323
International dict of films & filmmakers, v.3, 2d ed, 1335
John Wayne: a bio-bibliog, 1320
Lauren Bacall: a bio-bibliog, 1321
Resources for writers, 971
Sweethearts of the sage, 1361
Who's who in Hollywood, 1339

MOTION PICTURE AUTHORSHIP
Film writers gd, 3d ed, 1368

MOTION PICTURE EDITORS
Cinematographers, production designers, costume designers & film eds gd, 3d ed, 1371

MOTION PICTURE MUSIC
Cinema sheet music, 1272
Film & TV composers, 1258
Keeping score: film & TV music, 1980-88, 1271

MOTION PICTURE PRODUCERS & DIRECTORS
Directory of E European film-makers & films 1945-91, 1348
Handbook of Soviet & E European films & film-makers, 1340
Michael Singer's film directors, 9th ed, 1372
Who's who in Canadian film & TV 1991-92, 1341

MOTION PICTURE REMAKES
Haven't I seen you somewhere before?, 1358

MOTION PICTURE SEQUELS
Haven't I seen you somewhere before?, 1358

MOTION PICTURE SERIALS
Motion picture serial, 1364

MOTION PICTURES
Chambers concise ency of film & TV, 1346
Chambers film quotes, 1374
Contemporary theatre, film, & TV, v.9, 1324
Directory of E European film-makers & films 1945-91, 1348
Family video gd, 1329
FIAF cataloguing rules for film archives, 638
Film & video finder, 3d ed, 1330
Film annual 1992, 1369
Great Spanish films: 1950-90, 1365
Guinness bk of movie facts & feats, 1370
Handbook of Soviet & E European films & film-makers, 1340
Hispanic image on the silver screen, 1363
International film index 1895-1990, 1373
Laser video disc companion, updated ed, 997
Masters of lens & light, 1343
Movie classics, 1356
Nazi-retro film, 1362
NFB film gd, 1342
Picture this! a gd to over 300 environmentally, socially, & politically relevant films & videos, 1355
Sound films, 1927-39, 1352
Viewers' choice gd to movies on video, 1334

MOTION PICTURES & CHILDREN
Family video gd, 1329

MOTION PICTURES IN EDUCATION
AFVA evaluations 1991, 395
Educators gd to free films, 52d ed, 397
Films for learning, thinking, & doing, 399

MOVING, HOUSEHOLD
Moving & relocation sourcebk, 917

MOZAMBIQUE
Historical dict of Mozambique, 116

MULTICULTURALISM. See **PLURALISM (SOCIAL SCIENCES)**

MUNICIPAL GOVERNMENT
Municipal yellow bk, v.2, no.1, 741

MURDER
Borden murders, 605
World ency of 20th century murder, 611

MUSEUMS
Guide to 475 aircraft museums, 224 city-displayed aircraft, 37 restaurants with aircraft, 6 WWI landmarks, 10th ed, 1779
Official museum dir 1992, 79
Official museum products & servs dir 1992, 80

MUSEUMS FOR CHILDREN. See **CHILDREN'S MUSEUMS**

MUSHROOMS
Texas mushrooms, 1509

MUSIC
African music, 1241
American Wind Symphony commissioning project, 1284
Baker's biographical dict of musicians, 8th ed, 1244
Dictionary of terms in music, 4th ed, 1248
Handbook of research on music teaching & learning, 1252
Historical research in music educ, 2d ed, 1240
Indian music lit, 1239
Music & dance in Puerto Rico from the age of Columbus to modern times, 1243
Music for oboe, 1650-1800, 2d ed, 1263
New American dict of music, 1249
Opera performances in video format, 1273

MUSIC APPRECIATION
Listener's musical companion, new ed, 1251

MUSIC FESTIVALS
Music lover's gd to Europe, 1250

MUSIC, HINDUSTANI
Indian music lit, 1239

MUSIC, INDIC
Indian music lit, 1239

MUSIC LIBRARIES
Music in British libs, 650

MUSICAL FILMS
Great Hollywood musical pictures, 1360

MUSICAL INSTRUMENTS
Indian music lit, 1239

MUSICAL LANDMARKS
Music lover's gd to Europe, 1250

MUSICAL REVUE, COMEDY, ETC.
American musical theatre: a chronicle, 2d ed, 1385

MUSICIANS
Baker's biographical dict of musicians, 8th ed, 1244
Contemporary musicians, v.6, 1245

MYTHOLOGY
Mythology, 1302

MYTHOLOGY, CELTIC
Dictionary of Celtic mythology, 1304

MYTHOLOGY, CLASSICAL, IN ART
Guide to research in classical art & mythology, 1029

MYTHOLOGY, EGYPTIAN
Concise dict of Greek, Roman, Norse, & Egyptian mythology, 1303

MYTHOLOGY, GREEK
Concise dict of Greek, Roman, Norse, & Egyptian mythology, 1303

MYTHOLOGY IN LITERATURE
Recent studies in myths & lit, 1970-90, 1301

MYTHOLOGY, NORSE
Concise dict of Greek, Roman, Norse, & Egyptian mythology, 1303

MYTHOLOGY, ROMAN
Concise dict of Greek, Roman, Norse, & Egyptian mythology, 1303

NAMES, ENGLISH
Penguin dict of proper names, 464

NAMES, GEOGRAPHICAL
Dictionary of English place names, 493
Omni gazetteer of the USA, 495

NAMES, PERSONAL
Dictionary of Russian personal names, 463
Tuttle dict of 1st names, 465

NARCOTICS, CONTROL OF
Handbook of research on the illicit drug trade, 892

NASSER, GAMAL ABDEL
Gamal Abdel Nasser: a bibliog, 543

NATIONAL CEMETERIES
American military cemeteries, 706

NATIONAL LIBRARY OF CANADA
Passages: a treasure trove of N American exploration, 485

NATIONAL PARKS & RESERVES
Easy access to natl parks, 499
National park gd 1992, 496
National parks, 498
U.S. outdoor atlas & recreation gd, 497

NATIONAL SCIENCE FOUNDATION
EHR dir of awards: fiscal yr 1990, 875

NATIONAL SOCIALISM IN MOTION PICTURES
Nazi-retro film, 1362

NATIVE PLANTS. See **BOTANY**

NATURAL HISTORY
Birds of the Blue Ridge Mountains, 1545
Nature in America, 1526
Nature of SE Alaska, 1528
Nature projects on file, 1527

NATURAL HISTORY ILLUSTRATION
Index to illus of animals & plants, 1525

NATURAL HISTORY MUSEUMS
Natural hist museums, v.1, 1524

NATURE
Dictionary of environmental quotations, 1777
Rediscovery of creation, 1417

NATURE CONSERVATION
Nature dir, 1759

NATURE IN LITERATURE
E for environment, 1752

NATURE STUDY
Wilderness U: opportunities for outdoor educ in the US & abroad, 335

NATUROPATHY
Encyclopedia of natural medicine, 1634

NAUTICAL CHARTS
Marine atlas of the Hawaiian Islands, 466

NAVAL MUSEUMS
Great maritime museums of the world, 1791

NAVIGATION
Maritime affairs: a world hndbk, 2d ed, 1790

NAVIGATION, PRIMITIVE
Indigenous navigation & voyaging in the Pacific, 1789

NEBULAE
Messier's nebulae & star clusters, 2d ed, 1705

NEPAL
Guide to the birds of Nepal, 1543
Hippocrene insiders' gd to Nepal, 9th ed, 501
South Asian hndbk, 1992, 502

NEVADA
Nevada printing hist, 678
Prime sources of Calif. & Nev. local hist, 511

NEW ENGLAND
Guide to the marine sport fishes of Atlantic Canada & New England, 1555

NEWBERY MEDAL BOOKS
Handbook for the Newbery medal & honor bks, 1980-89, 1140
Newbery & Caldecott awards, 1992 ed, 1128
Newbery & Caldecott medal & honor bks in other media, 1121
Newbery & Caldecott medalists & honor bk winners, 2d ed, 1120

NEWFOUNDLAND
Atlas of Nfld. & Lab., 473
Encyclopedia of Nfld. & Lab., v.3, 133

NEWSLETTERS
Newsletters in print 1993-94, 978

NEWSPAPER SYNDICATES. *See* **SYNDICATES (JOURNALISM)**

NEWSPAPERS
Horace Greeley: a bio-bibliog, 979
Newspapers online, 975
1992-1993 gd to newspaper syndication, 977

NOBEL PRIZES
Nobel prize winners: suppl 1987-91, 41

NOBILITY
Biographical dict of life peers, 462

NONFERROUS METALS
Non-ferrous metal data 1990, 1727

NON-FORMAL EDUCATION
Campus-free college degrees, 5th ed, 378

NORM-REFERENCED TESTS
Consumer's gd to tests in print, 2d ed, 333

NORRIS, FRANK
Frank Norris: a descriptive bibliog, 1180

NORTH AMERICA – DISCOVERY & EXPLORATION
Passages: a treasure trove of N American exploration, 485

NORTH CAROLINA
Guide to the liverworts of N.C., 1512

NORTHERN IRELAND
Northern Ireland, 145

NORWEGIAN-AMERICANS
Guide to collections relating to S.D. Norwegian-Americans, 451

NOVELISTS, ENGLISH
British Romantic novelists, 1789-1832, 1196
John Fowles: a ref companion, 1208

NUCLEAR ENERGY
Chambers nuclear energy & radiation dict, 1742

NUCLEAR REACTORS
Nuclear power reactors in the world, 1991 ed, 1749

NUCLEAR WARFARE IN MOTION PICTURES
Nuclear movies, 1349

NUDIBRANCHIATA
Pacific coast nudibranchs, 1573

NURSES
American nursing, v.2, 1659

NUTRITION
Consumer health & nutrition index, v.8, no.1, 1614

OBOE MUSIC
Music for oboe, 1650-1800, 2d ed, 1263

OCCUPATION APTITUDE TESTS
ETS test collection cat, v.6, 329
Tests: a comprehensive ref for assessments in psychology, educ, & bus, 3d ed, 338

OCCUPATIONAL TRAINING
Chronicle vocational school manual for 1991-92 school yr, 406

OCCUPATIONS
Dictionary of occupational titles, 4th ed, 301
Vocational careers sourcebk, 412

OCEAN
Random House atlas of the oceans, 1730

OCEANIAN LITERATURE
Writers from the S Pacific, 1229

OFFICE PRACTICE
Elsevier's dict of office automation, 323
Professional Secretaries Intl complete office hndbk, 324

OIL & GAS JOURNAL
Oil & Gas Jl exploration index, 1750

OILS & FATS
Minor oil crops, 1464

OLYMPICS
Black American women in Olympic track & field, 843
Complete bk of the Olympics, 1992 ed, 841
Olympics factbk, 840

ONLINE
Cumulative index to ONLINE, DATABASE & CD-ROM Professional 1986-91, 1669

ON-LINE BIBLIOGRAPHIC SEARCHING
Newspapers online, 975
Search sheets for OPACs on the Internet, 661

ON-LINE DATA PROCESSING
Directory of online databases, v.13, no.2, 1682
Modem USA, 1683

OPENING SENTENCES. *See* **OPENINGS (RHETORIC)**

OPENINGS (RHETORIC)
In the beginning: great 1st lines from your favorite bks, 1117

OPERAS
Music lover's gd to Europe, 1250
Opera performances in video format, 1273

OPERATING SYSTEMS (COMPUTERS)
Computer professional's quick ref, 1685

OPTICAL DISKS – LIBRARY APPLICATIONS
CD-ROM reviews 1987-90, 659

OPTICAL STORAGE DEVICES – LIBRARY APPLICATIONS
CD-ROM reviews 1987-90, 659

ORAL HISTORY
Catalogue of audio & video collections of Holocaust testimony, 2d ed, 528

ORDER STATISTICS
Chronological annot bibliog of order stats, v.4, 902

OREGON TRAIL
Indians along the Oregon Trail, expanded ed, 436

ORGANIC GARDENING
Prentice-Hall pocket ency [of] organic gardening, 1488
Rodale's all-new ency of organic gardening, 1489

ORGANIZATIONAL EFFECTIVENESS
Organization charts, 212

ORGANIZATIONS. *See* **ASSOCIATIONS, INSTITUTIONS, ETC.**

ORKNEY IN LITERATURE
Contribution to lit of Orcadian writer George Mackay Brown, 1206

ORNITHOLOGY. *See* **BIRDS**

OUTDOOR EDUCATION
Wilderness U: opportunities for outdoor educ in the US & abroad, 335

OUTDOOR RECREATION
Adventuring in B.C., 503

OUTER SPACE
Children's space atlas, 1703
Space atlas, 1700
Space words, 1706

OUTLAWS
Encyclopedia of W lawmen & outlaws, 609

PACIFIC AREA
Who's who in Pacific navigation, 487
Who's who of the Asian Pacific Rim, 1992 ed, 168

PACIFIC COAST (NORTH AMERICA)
Pacific coast nudibranchs, 1573

PACS. *See* **POLITICAL ACTION COMMITTEES**

PAGANISM
Magic, witchcraft, & paganism in America, 2d ed, 811

PAINTING
World's master paintings from the early Renaissance to the present day, 1045

PAINTING, BRITISH
Handbook of modern British painting 1900-80, 1044

PAKISTAN
South Asian hndbk, 1992, 502

PALEONTOLOGY
Macmillan children's gd to dinosaurs & other prehistoric animals, 1732

PALMISTRY
Palmist's companion, 809

PANAMA
Latin American serial pubs available by exchange, 633
Mammals of the neotropics: the S cone, v.2, 1570

PAPERBACKS
Recommended ref bks in paperback, 2d ed, 15
Supernatural fiction for teens, 2d ed, 1156

PAPP, JOSEPH
Joseph Papp: a bio-bibliog, 1378

PARAPSYCHOLOGY. See PSYCHICAL RESEARCH

PARKS
Easy access to natl parks, 499
Parks dir of the US, 500

PARSIFAL
Parsifal on record, 1270

PATENTS
Information sources in patents, 587
Radio & TV pioneers: a patent bibliog, 983

PATHOLOGY
Directory of pathology training programs in the US & Canada 1993-94, 1643

PEACE
American peace movement, 791
Guide to the John D. Crummey peace collection in the Hoover Inst, 790
Peace: abstracts of the psychological & behavioral lit 1967-90, 789
World dir of peace research & training insts, 7th ed, 792

PEACE IN LITERATURE
War & peace through women's eyes, 1169

PEACE OFFICERS
Encyclopedia of W lawmen & outlaws, 609

PEARL HARBOR (HAWAII), ATTACK ON, 1941
Pearl Harbor, 1941, 696

PENSIONS
Index to US invalid pension records 1801-15, 459

PENSIONS, MILITARY
Pension lists of 1792-95, 457
Veterans benefits manual, 708

PERENNIALS
Encyclopedia of perennials, 1508

PERFORMING ARTS
Communication serials, 1992/1993 ed, 982
Money for performing artists, 1326
Popular entertainment research, 1327

PERIODICALS
Australian pers in print 1991, 81
Canadian media list 1992/93, 952
CD-ROM per index, 82
Directory of electronic jls, newsletters & academic discussion lists, 2d ed, 72
Directory of humor mags & humor orgs in America (& Canada), 3d ed, 1188
Index of American per verse: 1990, 1187
Index to Commonwealth little mags 1987-89, 83
Index to legal pers: Sept 1990-Aug 1991, 600
Journal of Women's Hist gd to per lit, 943
Magazines for libs, 7th ed, 85
Mathematical jls, 1741
New per title abbrevs, 86
Ulrich's intl pers dir 1992-93, 88
World list of social sci pers 1991, 101

PERSIAN GULF WAR, 1991
BBC World Service Gulf Crisis chronology, 542

PERSIAN LANGUAGE
Persian & English glossary for humanities & social scis, 1090

PERSONAL COMPUTERS. See MICROCOMPUTERS

PERSONAL NAMES. See NAMES, PERSONAL

PERSONNEL MANAGEMENT
Human resources glossary, 302

PETAWAWA NATIONAL FORESTRY INSTITUTE
Bibliography, 1988-90, 1482

PETROLEUM
Dictionary for the petroleum industry, 1743

PETROLEUM INDUSTRY & TRADE
International petroleum ency, 1744
Oil & Gas Jl exploration index, 1750
U.S.A. Gulf Coast oil & gas industry dir, 1992, 1745
U.S.A. oil industry's environmental dir, 1993, 1762

PHILANTHROPY. See CHARITIES; ENDOWMENTS

PHILIPPINE LITERATURE
Dutch Filipiniana, 169

PHILIPPINES
Dutch Filipiniana, 169

PHILOSOPHERS
Simone de Beauvoir: a bibliog, 930
Spinoza in English, 1394

PHILOSOPHY
Great thinkers of the W world, 950

Leo Spitzer on lang & lit, 1046
Philosopher's index thesaurus, 1397
Walford's gd to ref material, 5th ed, v.2: social & histl scis, 98
Women philosophers, 1392

PHILOSOPHY, ANCIENT
Resources in ancient philosophy, 1393

PHOTOGRAPHERS
Guide to literary agents & art/photo reps, 1992, 961
Photographers: a sourcebk for histl research, 1014

PHOTOGRAPHY
Photography & lit, 1013

PHYSICAL ANTHROPOLOGY
Dictionary of concepts in physical anthropology, 415

PHYSICALLY HANDICAPPED
Illustrated dir of handicapped products 1991-92, 863

PHYSICIANS
Best doctors in America 1992-93, 1644

PHYSICS
Encyclopedia of applied physics, v.2, 1733
Encyclopedia of applied physics, v.3, 1734

PHYSICS, ASTRONOMICAL. See ASTROPHYSICS

PIANISTS
Glenn Gould cat, 1253

PIANO MUSIC
Descriptive cat of the Glenn Gould papers, 1255
Piano music by black women, 1264
Source gd to the music of Percy Grainger, 1261

PICTURE DICTIONARIES
Macmillan visual dict, 1077
Visual dict of animals, 1534
Visual dict of cars, 1787
Visual dict of everyday things, 1078
Visual dict of military uniforms, 703
Visual dict of plants, 1502
Visual dict of ships & sailing, 1792
Visual dict of the human body, 1492

PICTURE DICTIONARIES, SPANISH
Facts on File English/Spanish visual dict, 1101

PICTURE TRANSMISSION. See IMAGE TRANSMISSION

PICTURE-BOOKS FOR CHILDREN
Wordless/almost wordless picture bks, 1131

PICTURE-WRITING
Dictionary of symbols, 1041

PINES
Pines of Mexico & Central America, 1519

PLANNED COMMUNITIES
99 best residential & recreational communities in America for vacation, retirement & investment planning, 919

PLANT DISEASES
Ball field gd to diseases of greenhouse ornamentals, 1499

PLANT ENGINEERING
Plant engineer's ref bk, 1608

PLANT SHUTDOWNS
Plant closings, 300

PLANT VIRUSES
Dictionary of plant virology, 1495

PLANTS. See also WILD FLOWERS
Cultivated plants of the tropics & subtropics, 1469
Green plants, 1498
Handbook of Rocky Mountain plants, 1501
Manual of vascular plants of NE US and adjacent Canada, 2d ed, 1500
Visual dict of plants, 1502

PLANTS, ORNAMENTAL
Ball field gd to diseases of greenhouse ornamentals, 1499
New gardener's hndbk & dict, 1486

PLASTICS
Handbook of plastic compounds, elastomers, & resins, 1710
Handbook of plastics, elastomers, & composites, 2d ed, 1714
Plastics additives & modifiers hndbk, 1711

PLURALISM (SOCIAL SCIENCES)
Bookpeople: a multicultural album, 1142

POETRY
Masterplots 2: poetry series, 1237
Poetry index annual 1990, 1238

POETS
Who's who in writers, eds & poets, 1992-93, 974

POETS, AMERICAN
American poets since WW II, 3d series, 1186
Critical survey of poetry: English lang series, rev ed, 1236

POETS, ENGLISH
Critical survey of poetry: English lang series, rev ed, 1236

POISONOUS SNAKES
Poisonous snakes of the world, 1578
Venomous reptiles of N America, 1576

POLAND
Polish biographical dict, 44
Revolutionary orgs & revolutionaries in interbellum Poland, 779

POLITICAL ACTION COMMITTEES
Open secrets, 2d ed, 752

POLITICAL PARTIES
Minor presidential candidates & parties of 1992, 748
New pol parties of E Europe & the Soviet Union, 770

POLITICAL PLANNING
Washington almanac, 731

POLITICAL PLAYS, AMERICAN
Political left in the American theatre of the 30's, 1375

POLITICAL SCIENCE
Chambers dict of pol biog, 721
Dictionary of pols, 7th ed, 722

POLITICAL STATISTICS
Political data hndbk: OECD countries, 727

POLITICIANS
Horace Greeley: a bio-bibliog, 979
Political leaders in Black Africa, 761
Who's who in Asian & Australasian pols, 762

POLITICS & LITERATURE
Political left in the American theatre of the 30's, 1375

POLLUTION
Environmental hazards: toxic waste & hazardous material, 1770
Statistical record of the environment, 1764

POLLUTION CONTROL INDUSTRY
Statistical record of the environment, 1764

POLYMERS & POLYMERIZATION
Concise ency of polymer processing & applications, 1582

POLYNESIA
Indigenous navigation & voyaging in the Pacific, 1789

POPULAR CULTURE
Communication serials, 1992/1993 ed, 982

POPULAR LITERATURE
Classic cult fiction, 1149

POPULAR MUSIC
Best rated CDs 1992: jazz, popular, etc., 1275
Billboard top 1000 singles 1955-90, 1282
Billboard's hottest hot 100 hits, 1276
Popular music, v.15, 1279
Trouser Press record gd, 4th ed, 1281
World beat: a listener's gd to contemporary world music on CD, 1280

POPULATION
Labour & population programme, 299

PORTUGUESE LANGUAGE
Random House Portuguese dict, 1091

POSTAL ADDRESSES. *See* **STREET ADDRESSES**

PRECIOUS STONES
Larousse ency of precious gems, 1725

PREHISTORIC ANIMALS. *See* **PALEONTOLOGY**

PREJUDICES
Discrimination & prejudice, 845

PRENATAL CARE
Catalog of prenatally diagnosed conditions, 2d ed, 1654

PRESBYTERIAN CHURCH
Encyclopedia of the reformed faith, 1422

PRESIDENTIAL CANDIDATES
Minor presidential candidates & parties of 1992, 748

PRESIDENTS
Almanac of American presidents from 1789 to the present, 519
Complete bk of US presidents, 3d ed, 514
Warren G. Harding: a bibliog, 509
World almanac of presidential campaigns, 732

PRESSURE GROUPS
Public interest profiles 1992-93, 795
U.S. aging policy interest groups, 860

PRINCETON UNIVERSITY—ALUMNI
Princetonians 1784-90, 356
Princetonians 1791-94, 357

PRINTING
Graphic arts ency, 1042
Multilingual dict of publishing, printing & bkselling, 680
Nevada printing hist, 678

PRINTS
Print price index '93, 1032

PRISONS
Prison slang, 603

PRIVATE COMPANIES
Owners & officers of private cos, 1992, 196

PRIVATE SCHOOLS
Catholic school educ in the US, 348
Handbook of private schools, 73d ed, 349
NCEA/Ganley's Catholic schools in America 1992, 353

PROCESS CONTROL
Comprehensive dict of measurement & control, 2d ed, 1607

PROSTITUTION
Prostitution: a gd to sources, 1960-90, 882

PROTESTANTISM & LITERATURE
Protestant sensibility in the American novel, 1170

PROVERBS
Cassell bk of proverbs, 1295

Concise Oxford dict of proverbs, 2d ed, 1296
Dictionary of American proverbs, 1299
Jewish wisdom, 445

PSYCHIATRY
Comprehensive glossary of psychiatry & psychology, 1649

PSYCHICAL RESEARCH
Encyclopedia of ghosts & spirits, 810
Parapsychological research with children, 808

PSYCHOANALYSIS
Cross-currents of Jungian thought, 796
Feminism & psychoanalysis, 801

PSYCHOANALYTIC INTERPRETATION
Female psychology, 797

PSYCHOLOGICAL LITERATURE
Library use, 2d ed, 804

PSYCHOLOGICAL TESTS
Tests: a comprehensive ref for assessments in psychology, educ, & bus, 3d ed, 338

PSYCHOLOGY
Comprehensive glossary of psychiatry & psychology, 1649
Encyclopedic dict of psychology, 4th ed, 800
Thesaurus of psychological index terms, 6th ed, 645

PSYCHOLOGY—LIBRARY RESOURCES
Library use, 2d ed, 804

PSYCHOMETRICS
Eleventh mental measurements yrbk, 803

PUBLIC ADMINISTRATION
Public admin research gd, 794

PUBLIC CONTRACTS
Government contracts ref bk, 580

PUBLIC HEALTH
Health care terms, 2d ed, 1621

PUBLIC HEALTH ADMINISTRATION
National health dir, 1992, 1619

PUBLIC INTEREST LAW
Public interest law, 566

PUBLIC LIBRARIES
University pr bks for public & secondary school libs 1991, 664

PUBLIC OPINION POLLS
Dictionary of polling, 103

PUBLIC SCHOOLS
Public schooling in America, 354
Public schools USA, 2d ed, 350

PUBLIC SPEAKING
1001 quips & quotes for bus speeches, 219

PUBLIC WORSHIP
ABCs of worship, 1423

PUBLICATION LISTS. *See* BIBLIOGRAPHY

PUBLISHERS & PUBLISHING
Black bk publishers in the US, 679
Books & mags: a gd to publishing & bkselling courses in the US, 681
British literary publishing houses, 1881-1965, 689
Colorado bk gd, 683
Computer publishers & pubs, 1992-93 ed, 684
Information marketplace dir, 1993, 685
Multilingual dict of publishing, printing & bkselling, 680
Publishers dir, 1992, 687

PUERTO RICAN LITERATURE
U.S. Latino lit, 1166

PUERTO RICO
Birds in jeopardy, 1541
Music & dance in Puerto Rico from the age of Columbus to modern times, 1243

PUNJAB
Settlement lit of the Greater Punjab, 524

PYM, BARBARA
Barbara Pym: a ref gd, 1209

QUAILS
Atlas of quails, 1536

QUALITY OF LIFE
Livable cities almanac, 920
World quality of life indicators, 2d ed, 95

QUESTIONS & ANSWERS
Guinness bk of answers, 8th ed, 4

QUOTATIONS
Columbia Granger's dict of poetry quotations, 1235
Dictionary of Canadian quotations, 90
Dictionary of environmental quotations, 1777
Dictionary of quotations from Shakespeare, 1213
Familiar quotations, 16th ed, 89
Jewish wisdom, 445
Merriam-Webster dict of quotations, 91
Oxford dict of quotations, 4th ed, 92
Power quotes, 730
Reader's quotation bk, 403
Reflections on childhood, 895
Thoughts on leadership, 316
Treasury of religious quotations, 1412
Tuttle dict of quotations for speeches, 93
Webster's 2 New Riverside desk quotations, 94
World of W. E. B. Du Bois, 99

RACISM
World racism & related inhumanities, 618

RADIO
Broadcasting & cable market place 1992, 992
Canadian media list 1992/93, 952
Radio & TV pioneers: a patent bibliog, 983
World radio TV hndbk, 1992 ed, 1000

RADIO STATIONS
Traveler's gd to world radio, 1992 ed, 999

RAIN FORESTS
Conservation atlas of tropical forests: Africa, 1484

RAPE
Rape: a bibliog 1976-88, 620

RARE BIRDS
Birds in jeopardy, 1541

RATIONAL EXPECTATIONS (ECONOMIC THEORY)
Reader's gd to rational expectations, 175

READING
International hndbk of reading educ, 404

REAL ESTATE. *See* **REAL PROPERTY**

REAL ESTATE BUSINESS
Handbook of real estate terms, rev ed, 325

REAL PROPERTY
Handbook of real estate terms, rev ed, 325

RECLAMATION OF WATER. *See* **WATER REUSE**

RECREATION AREAS
Parks dir of the US, 500
U.S. outdoor atlas & recreation gd, 497

REFERENCE BOOKS
Best ref bks 1986-90, 8
Business info: how to find it, how to use it, 2d ed, 209
Canada: a reader's gd, 19
Distinguished classics of ref publishing, 18
Government ref bks 90/91, 74
Guide to ref bks, suppl to the 10th ed, 12
Guide to ref materials for Canadian libs, 8th ed, 16
New, completely rev, greatly expanded, Madam Audrey's mostly cheap, all good, useful list of bks for speedy ref, 5th ed, 13
Recommended ref bks 1992, 22
Reference sources for small & medium-sized libs, 5th ed, 17

REFERENCE BOOKS FOR CHILDREN. *See* **CHILDREN'S REFERENCE BOOKS**

REFERENCE SERVICES (LIBRARIES)
Recommended ref bks 1992, 22

REFERENDUM
California initiatives & referendums 1912-90, 793

REFORMED CHURCH
Encyclopedia of the reformed faith, 1422

REGULATORY AGENCIES. *See* **ADMINISTRATIVE AGENCIES**

RELIGION
Fund raiser's gd to religious philanthropy, 5th ed, 1425
National gd to funding in religion, 1411
Reference works for theological research, 3d ed, 1400
Religious bodies in the US, 1408
Religious info sources, 1401
Religious leaders, 1403
Treasury of religious quotations, 1412
Walford's gd to ref material, 5th ed, v.2: social & histl scis, 98

RELIGION, PRIMITIVE
Encyclopedia of Native American religions, 432

RELIGIONS
Eliade gd to world religions, 1409

RELIGIOUS BIOGRAPHY
Who's who of world religions, 1404

REPORT WRITING
College style sheet, 3d ed, 959

REPTILES
Amphibians & reptiles of the W Indies, 1579
Peterson 1st gd to reptiles & amphibians, 1577
Reptiles & amphibians of Austr., 5th ed, 1575

RESEARCH
International research centers dir 1992-93, 68
Prospect researcher's gd to biographical research collections, 675
Scientific traveler, 1456

RESEARCH GRANTS
GRANTS subject authority gd, 637
Peterson's grants for grad study, 3d ed, 374
Peterson's grants for postdoctoral study, 375
Scholarships, fellowships & loans 1992-93, 377

RESEARCH LIBRARIES
CD-ROM research collections, 660

RESINS. *See* **GUMS & RESINS**

RESORTS
99 best residential & recreational communities in America for vacation, retirement & investment planning, 919

RETIREMENT
Henry Holt retirement sourcebk, 855

RETIREMENT COMMUNITIES
50 fabulous places to retire in America, 921
99 best residential & recreational communities in America for vacation, retirement & investment planning, 919

REVOLUTIONS
Historical dict of revolutionary China, 1839-1976, 523
Revolutionary orgs & revolutionaries in interbellum Poland, 779

REWARDS (PRIZES, ETC.)
Awards, honors, & prizes, 9th ed, 66
World of winners, 2d ed, 1314

RHODODENDRON
Rhododendron portraits, 1506
Rhododendron species, v.3, 1504

RHYMING GAMES
Creative fingerplays & action rhymes, 340

RIGHT & LEFT (POLITICAL SCIENCE)
Political left in the American theatre of the 30's, 1375

ROAD MAPS
Gousha new deluxe rd atlas, 467
Rand McNally road atlas, 67th ed, 468

ROCHBERG, GEORGE
George Rochberg: a bio-bibliographic gd to his life & works, 1256

ROCK MUSIC
Doo-wop: the forgotten 3d of rock 'n roll, 1290
50 yrs of rock music, 1291
Off the record, v.1, 1292

ROCK PAINTINGS
Field gd to rock art symbols of the greater southwest, 508

ROCKS
Rocks & minerals, 1728

ROCKY MOUNTAINS
Handbook of Rocky Mountain plants, 1501
Meet the natives: the amateur's field gd to Rocky Mountain wildflowers, trees & shrubs, 9th ed, 1505

ROMANTICISM
Classic cult fiction, 1149
Encyclopedia of romanticism, 531

ROME – HISTORY – EMPIRE, 284-476
Rome in the 4th century AD, 547

ROOSEVELT, ELEANOR
Roosevelt research, 516

ROOSEVELT FAMILY
Roosevelt research, 516

ROOSEVELT, FRANKLIN D. (FRANKLIN DELANO)
Roosevelt research, 516

ROOSEVELT, THEODORE
Roosevelt research, 516

ROSBAUD, HANS
Hans Rosbaud: a bio-bibliog, 1257

ROUSSEAU, JEAN-JACQUES
Rousseau dict, 1396

RURAL DEVELOPMENT
Rural dvlpmt, 922

RUSSIAN LANGUAGE
Dictionary of Russian personal names, 463
Elsevier's dict of geoscis, 1723

RUSSIAN LANGUAGE – ACRONYMS
Compressed Russian, 1097

RUSSIAN LANGUAGE – DICTIONARIES – ENGLISH
Compressed Russian, 1097
Lexical semantics, 1092
Supplementary Russian-English dict, 1096
Vocabulary of Soviet society & culture, 1095

RUSSIAN LANGUAGE – SOCIAL ASPECTS
Vocabulary of Soviet society & culture, 1095

RUSSIAN LITERATURE
Women & writing in Russian & the USSR, 1230

SAFETY APPLIANCES
Vocabulary of safety & security equipment, 1601

SAILING
A-Z of sailing terms, 842
Visual dict of ships & sailing, 1792

SALES MANAGEMENT
Ward's sales prospector, 199

SALON (EXHIBITION: PARIS, FRANCE)
Bibliography of salon criticism in Paris from the ancien regime to the Restoration, 1699-1827, 1018
Bibliography of salon criticism in Paris from the July Monarchy to the Second Republic, 1831-51, 1019

SANITATION
Statistical record of the environment, 1764

SATELLITES
Moons of the solar system, 1707

SAUDI ARABIA
Western lang lit on pre-Islamic central Arabia, 167

SCHIZOPHRENIA
Encyclopedia of schizophrenia & the psychotic disorders, 799

SCHOLARSHIPS
America's new fndns 1992, 870
Awards almanac 1992, 871
Directory of grants in the humanities 1992/93, 946
Directory of research grants 1992, 873
EHR dir of awards: fiscal yr 1990, 875
Inside Japanese support 1992, 280
Money for performing artists, 1326
Peterson's grants for grad study, 3d ed, 374
Peterson's grants for postdoctoral study, 375
RAIC dir of scholarships & awards for architecture, 1039
Scholarships, fellowships & loans 1992-93, 377

SCHOOL CHILDREN IN LITERATURE
English schoolboy stories, 1135

SCHOOL DISTRICTS
Public schools USA, 2d ed, 350

SCHOOL EXCURSIONS
Encyclopedia of field trips & educl destinations, 352

SCHOOL LIBRARIES
Book Report & Library Talk dir of sources, 666
Multicultural aspects of lib media programs, 669
School lib media annual, v.10, 672
University pr bks for public & secondary school libs 1991, 664
Using children's bks in reading/lang arts programs, 402
Using govt docs, 668

SCHOOL LIBRARIES—ACTIVITY PROGRAMS
More creative uses of children's lit, v.1, 671

SCHOOL LIBRARIES—BOOK LISTS
Guide to ref bks for school media centers, 4th ed, 670
Reference bks for children, 4th ed, 1129
Senior high school lib cat, 14th ed, 673

SCHOOL MEDIA CENTERS. *See* **INSTRUCTIONAL MATERIALS CENTERS**

SCHWEITZER, ALBERT
Guide to Albert Schweitzer collections, 2d ed, 947

SCIENCE
Academic Press dict of sci & tech, 1444
American men & women of sci 1992-93, 1438
Applied sci & tech index, 1457
Black scientists, 1443
Dictionary of scientific literacy, 1445
Encyclopedia of physical sci & tech 1991 yrbk, 1453
General sci index, v.14, no.7, 1459
General sci index [CD-ROM], 1460
Great scientific discoveries, 1449
Great thinkers of the W world, 950
Henry Holt hndbk of current sci & tech, 1455
History of sci, 1437
McGraw-Hill ency of sci & tech, 7th ed, 1446
New bk of popular sci, 1450
Science fair project index 1985-89, 1462
Science sources 1991, 1452
Scientific & technical pers of the 17th & 18th centuries, 1463
Scientific traveler, 1456
Who's who in sci in Europe, 7th ed, 1442
Women scientists, 1441

SCIENCE & STATE
Prune bk: the 60 toughest sci & tech jobs in Washington, 757

SCIENCE—EXPERIMENTS
Science experiments index for young people update 91, 1461

SCIENCE FICTION
British sci fiction, 1204
Reference gd to sci fiction, fantasy, & horror, 1155
Reginald's sci fiction & fantasy awards, 2d ed, 1157
Science fiction & fantasy bk review annual 1990, 1158
Walter M. Miller, Jr.: a bio-bibliog, 1179
Work of Brian W. Aldiss, 1154

SCIENCE FICTION—BIOGRAPHY
Twentieth-century sci-fiction writers, 3d ed, 1159

SCIENCE PROJECTS
Nature projects on file, 1527
Science fair project index 1985-89, 1462

SCIENCES
Magill's survey of sci: physical sci series, 1699

SCIENTISTS
Biographies of scientists for sci-tech libs, 1440

SCOTLAND
Contribution to lit of Orcadian writer George Mackay Brown, 1206

SCOTT, SIR WALTER
Scott dramatized, 1210

SCOTTISH LITERATURE
Boswellian studies, 3d ed, 1231

SEA LIFE. *See* **MARINE BIOLOGY**

SEALS (ANIMALS)
Sierra Club hndbk of seals & sirenians, 1571

SEAMANSHIP
A-Z of sailing terms, 842

SEASHORE BIOLOGY
Peterson 1st gd to seashores, 1574

SEASHORE FLORA
Peterson 1st gd to seashores, 1574

SEAWEED. *See* **MARINE ALGAE**

SECOND CAREERS. *See* **CAREER CHANGES**

SECRET SERVICE
Soviet security & intelligence orgs 1917-90, 769

SECRETARIAL PRACTICE. *See* **OFFICE PRACTICE**

SECTS
Encyclopedic hndbk of cults in America, rev ed, 1410

SECURITIES
McGraw-Hill dict of Wall St acronyms, initials, & abbrevs, 171

SELF-CARE, HEALTH
Complete hndbk of natural healing, 1648

SELF-HELP DEVICES FOR THE DISABLED
Resource dir for the disabled, 864

SEMANTICS
Semantics: a bibliog, 1986-91, 1047

SEMICONDUCTORS
Concise ency of semiconducting materials & related techs, 1592

SENIOR CITIZENS. *See* **AGED**

SENIOR POWER
Senior movement, 861

SERIAL MURDERS
Women serial & mass murderers, 612

SERIAL PUBLICATIONS
Communication serials, 1992/1993 ed, 982
Directory of electronic jls, newsletters & academic discussion lists, 2d ed, 72
Latin American serial pubs available by exchange, 633
Ulrich's intl pers dir 1992-93, 88

SERIES (PUBLICATIONS)
Young people's bks in series, 1133

SET DESIGNERS
Scenic design on Broadway, 1384
Theatrical designers, 1382

SEX
A-to-Z of women's sexuality, rev ed, 884
Language of sex, 883

SEX BIAS. *See* **SEXISM**

SEX CRIMES
Disability, sexuality & abuse, 865

SEX ROLE
Womanwords, 938

SEX ROLE IN LITERATURE
Shakespeare & feminist criticism, 1212

SEXISM
She said, he said, 914

SEXISM IN LANGUAGE
Womanwords, 938

SHADE TREES
Shade & color with water-conserving plants, 1520

SHAKESPEARE, WILLIAM
Dictionary of quotations from Shakespeare, 1213
Hamlet in the 1960s, 1211
Shakespeare: an annot bibliog, 1214
Shakespeare & feminist criticism, 1212
Shakespeare index, 1215

SHAREWARE (COMPUTER SOFTWARE)
PC-SIG ency of shareware, 4th ed, 1689

SHAW, BERNARD
Bernard Shaw: a gd to research, 1216

SHELLS
Field gd to shells of the Tex. coast, 1522

SHIPPING
Shipping lit of the Great Lakes, 1778

SHIPS
Visual dict of ships & sailing, 1792

SHIPS—PASSENGER LISTS
Passenger & immigration lists index, 1992 suppl., 460

SHORT STORIES
Latin American short story, 1225
Short story writers & their work, 2d ed, 1160

SHORT STORY
Twentieth-century short story explication: an index, 1161

SHRUBS
Meet the natives: the amateur's field gd to Rocky Mountain wildflowers, trees & shrubs, 9th ed, 1505
Weeds of the woods, 1515

SEA COWS. *See* **SIRENIA**

SIBERIA (R.S.F.S.R.)
Siberia & the Soviet Far East, 139

SIGN LANGUAGE
Perigee visual dict of signing, rev ed, 1098

SIGNS & SYMBOLS
Dictionary of symbols, 1041

SIKHS
Sikhs in N America, 1436

SIKHS—CANADA
Sikhs in N America, 1436

SILENT FILMS
Resources for writers, 971

SINATRA, FRANK
Frank Sinatra: a complete recording hist, 1265

SINGAPORE
Historical dict of Singapore, 129

SIR GAWAIN & THE GREEN KNIGHT
Sir Gawain & the Green Knight: an annot bibliog, 1978-89, 1217

SIRENIA
Sierra Club hndbk of seals & sirenians, 1571

SLANG
Brewer's dict of 20th-century phrase & fable, 1294

SLOGANS
Brewer's dict of 20th-century phrase & fable, 1294

SMALL BUSINESS
Pratt's gd to venture capital sources, 1992 ed, 197
Small business sourcebk, 5th ed, 213

SMALL LIBRARIES—BOOK LISTS
Reference sources for small & medium-sized libs, 5th ed, 17

SMITHSONIAN INSTITUTION. LIBRARIES
Books of the fairs, 1306

SOCIAL HISTORY
Macrothesaurus for info processing in the field of economic & social dvlpmt, 641

SOCIAL INDICATORS
Livable cities almanac, 920
Measuring global values, 729

SOCIAL INTERACTION IN CHILDREN
Prosocial dvlpmt in children, 894

SOCIAL PROBLEMS
New state of the world atlas, 4th ed, 475

SOCIAL PROBLEMS IN LITERATURE
Sensitive issues: an annot gd to children's lit K-6, 1130

SOCIAL PROBLEMS IN MOTION PICTURES
Picture this! a gd to over 300 environmentally, socially, & politically relevant films & videos, 1355

SOCIAL SCIENCES
Handbook of research on social studies teaching & learning, 336
Inventory of longitudinal studies in the social scis, 102
Persian & English glossary for humanities & social scis, 1090
Social scis index: April 1990-March 1991, 96
Social scis index [CD-ROM], 97
Walford's gd to ref material, 5th ed, v.2: social & histl scis, 98
World list of social sci pers 1991, 101

SOCIAL SCIENCES—PERIODICALS
Social scis: an intl bibliog of serial lit, 1830-1985, 100

SOCIOLOGY
Encyclopedia of sociology, 847
Encyclopedic dict of sociology, 4th ed, 849
HarperCollins dict of sociology, 848
Sociology in govt, 846

SOLAR SYSTEM
Children's space atlas, 1703
Space atlas, 1700

SOLDIERS
Fighting men of the Indian wars, 515

SOMALI LANGUAGE—DICTIONARIES—ENGLISH
Somali-English dict, 2d ed, 1099

SONGWRITERS. *See* **COMPOSERS**

SOUL MUSIC
Soul music A-Z, 1293

SOUND MOTION PICTURES
Sound films, 1927-39, 1352

SOUND RECORDINGS
Dictionary of musical tech, 1246
Trouser Press record gd, 4th ed, 1281

SOUTH AFRICA
Transnational corps in S Africa, 276

SOUTH AMERICA
Atlas of S America, 484
Political & economic ency of S America & the Caribbean, 774

SOUTH ASIA IN LITERATURE
Indian subcontinent in lit for children & young adults, 1126

SOUTH CAROLINA
Books & articles on S.C. hist, 2d ed, 510

SOUTH DAKOTA
Guide to collections relating to S.D. Norwegian-Americans, 451

SOUTHWEST, NEW
Shade & color with water-conserving plants, 1520

SOVIET UNION
Rise & fall of the Soviet Union, 535
Russian & Soviet educ 1731-1989, 383
SIBD 92-93, 293
Soviet Jewish hist, 1917-91, 447
Soviet security & intelligence orgs 1917-90, 769
Soviet stats since 1950, 142
USSR crime stats & summaries, 613
Women & writing in Russian & the USSR, 1230

SOVIET UNION—FOREIGN RELATIONS
Yearbook of Soviet foreign relations, 1991 ed, 788

SPACE SCIENCES
HarperCollins dict of astronomy & space sci, 1702

SPACE STATIONS
Space station glossary, 1581

SPAIN
European employment & industrial relations glossary: Spain, 295
Great Spanish films: 1950-90, 1365
Hispanic heritage, series 4, 150
Historical dict of the Spanish empire, 1402-1975, 540
Spain: 1001 sights, 506

SPANISH AMERICAN POETRY
Contemporary Spanish American poets, 1228

SPANISH LANGUAGE
Facts on File English/Spanish visual dict, 1101

SPANISH LANGUAGE—DICTIONARIES—ENGLISH
Collins Spanish-English/English-Spanish dict, 3d ed, 1100
Elsevier's dict of terrestrial plant ecology, 1497

SPANISH LITERATURE
Spanish, Catalan, & Galician literary authors of the 20th century, 1233

SPECIAL LIBRARIES. *See* **LIBRARIES, SPECIAL**

SPIDERS
Ground Spiders of Canada and Alaska, 1564

SPINOZA, BENEDICTUS DE,
Spinoza in English, 1394

SPIRITS
Encyclopedia of ghosts & spirits, 810

SPITZER, LEO
Leo Spitzer on lang & lit, 1046

SPORTING NEWS
Index to the Sporting News, 823

SPORTS
College admissions index of majors & sports 1992-93, 379
Directory of European sports orgs, 821
Drug file, 1667
Encyclopedia of N American sports hist, 819
Norm Hitzges histl sports almanac, 812
Sport in Britain, 814
Sports fan's connection, 822
Sports Illustrated 1992 sports almanac, 813

SPORTS FOR WOMEN
Outstanding women athletes, 818

SPORTS MUSEUMS
Sports halls of fame, 820

SPORTS STORIES
Index to the Sporting News, 823

SRI LANKA
South Asian hndbk, 1992, 502

STAGE LIGHTING
Lighting design on Broadway, 1383

STAR TREK (TELEVISION PROGRAM)
Star Trek: an annot gd to resources, 1331

STAR TREK FILMS
Star Trek: an annot gd to resources, 1331

STARS
Messier's nebulae & star clusters, 2d ed, 1705

STATE GOVERNMENTS
Directory of legislative leaders 1991-92, 739
Government dir of addresses & telephone nos, 740
Inside the legislative process, 1991 ed, 751
State issues 1992, 755
State legislative sourcebk 1992, 750
State legislative staff dir 1991, 738
State ref pubns 1991-92, 734

STATESMEN
Mexican pol biogs, 1884-1935, 775
Who's who in Africa, 760

STATISTICS
Almanac of the 50 states, 1992 ed, 909
Charts, graphics & stats index 1988-91, 916
County & city extra, 1992, 908
Demographic stats 1991, 897
Dictionary of US govt statl terms, 903
HarperCollins dict of stats, 904
Index to intl stats 1990, 915
International histl stats: Europe 1750-1988, 3d ed, 911
Official gd to the American marketplace, 906
Political data hndbk: OECD countries, 727
She said, he said, 914
Short-term economic stats: Central & E Europe, 292
Statistics & surveys vocabulary, 905
Statistics sources 1993, 913

STEROIDS
Anabolic steroids & sports, 1666

STEWART, JAMES
James Stewart: a bio-bibliog, 1319

STOCK-EXCHANGE
Handbook of world stock & commodity exchanges, 1992, 222
McGraw-Hill dict of Wall St acronyms, initials, & abbrevs, 171

STOCKS. *See also* **INVESTMENTS**
Moody's hndbk of common stocks, spring 1992, 223

STREET ADDRESSES
National dir of addresses & telephone nos, 69

STUDENT AID
Chronicle financial aid gd for 1991-92 school yr, 367
Complete college financing gd, 2d ed, 371
Fund your way through college, 373

STUDENT LOAN FUNDS
Complete college financing gd, 2d ed, 371

STUDENTS, FOREIGN
Open doors 1990/91, 389
Profiles 1989-90, 390

STUDENTS' SONGS
School songs of America's colleges & univs, 1278

SUBJECT HEADINGS
Art & architecture thesaurus, suppl.1, 635
GRANTS subject authority gd, 637
Sears list of subject headings: Canadian companion, 4th ed, 643
Subject access to films & videos, 640
Thesaurus of psychological index terms, 6th ed, 645
Unreal! Hennepin County lib subject headings for fictional characters & places, 2d ed, 644

SUBSTANCE ABUSE
Drug abuse bibliog for 1988, 888

Encyclopedia of drug abuse, 2d ed, 890
Substance abuse among ethnic minorities in America, 891

SULLIVAN, ARTHUR, SIR
How quaint the ways of paradox!, 1274

SUMMER THEATER
Summer theatre dir 1992, 1387

SUN, YAT-SEN
Bibliography of Sun Yat-sen in China's Republican Revolution, 1885-1925, 521

SUPERCONDUCTORS
Concise ency of magnetic & superconducting materials, 1591

SUPERNATURAL IN LITERATURE
Supernatural fiction for teens, 2d ed, 1156

SURFACES (TECHNOLOGY)
Encyclopedia of materials characterization, 1605

SVOBODA
Select index to Svoboda, v.1, 980
Select index to Svoboda, v.2, 981

SWISS LITERATURE (GERMAN)
Companion to 20th-century German lit, 1223

SYMBOLISM
Reverse symbolism dict, 1311

SYNDICATES (JOURNALISM)
1992-1993 gd to newspaper syndication, 977

SYNDROMES
Dictionary of medical & surgical syndromes, 1658

TAGALOG LANGUAGE
Ang mahalaga sa buhay, 1102
Tagalog slang dict, 1103

TALK SHOWS
Talk shows & hosts on radio, 990

TANDY, JESSICA
Jessica Tandy: a bio-bibliog, 1315

TANZANIA
Field gd to the freshwater fishes of Tanzania, 1556

TAX INCENTIVES
Directory of incentives for bus investment & dvlpmt in the US, 3d ed, 221

TAX RETURNS
Canadian master tax gd, 1992, 229
Guide to income tax preparation, 326
J. K. Lasser's your income tax 1993, 327

TAXATION
West's tax law dict, 1992 ed, 581

TAYLOR, EDWARD
Concordance to the minor poetry of Edward Taylor (1642?-1729), 1181

TEACHERS' UNIONS
Directory of faculty contracts & bargaining agents in institutions of higher educ, v.18, 360

TEACHING—AIDS & DEVICES
Brown's dir of instructional programs, 1992: K-8, 346
Brown's dir of instructional programs, 1992: 7-12, 347

TECHNICAL EDITING
Oxford dict for scientific writers & eds, 967
Technical editing, 972

TECHNICAL WRITING
Oxford dict for scientific writers & eds, 967
Science & technical writing: a manual of style, 970
Technical editing, 972

TECHNOLOGY
Academic Press dict of sci & tech, 1444
Applied sci & tech index, 1457
Corporate tech dir 1992, 246
Encyclopedia of physical sci & tech 1991 yrbk, 1453
General sci index, v.14, no.7, 1459
Henry Holt hndbk of current sci & tech, 1455
McGraw-Hill ency of sci & tech, 7th ed, 1446
New bk of popular sci, 1450
Oxford illus ency of invention & tech, 1451
Who's who in sci in Europe, 7th ed, 1442

TECHNOLOGY & STATE
Prune bk: the 60 toughest sci & tech jobs in Washington, 757

TELECOMMUNICATION
Telecommunications fact bk & illus dict, 1697
Telecommunications dir, 5th ed, 1698

TELECOMMUNICATION IN LIBRARIES
Directory of computer conferencing in libs, 656

TELEPHONE—AREA CODES
Instant natl locator gd, 955

TELEPHONE—DIRECTORIES
Business connexions 1992, 228
National dir of addresses & telephone nos, 69

TELEVISION
Canadian media list 1992/93, 952
Chambers concise ency of film & TV, 1346
Contemporary theatre, film, & TV, v.9, 1324
FIAF cataloguing rules for film archives, 638
Radio & TV pioneers: a patent bibliog, 983
Television engineering hndbk, rev ed, 1588
World radio TV hndbk, 1992 ed, 1000

TELEVISION AUTHORSHIP
Television writers gd, 2d ed, 965

TELEVISION BROADCASTING
Les Brown's ency of TV, 3d ed, 986
TV ency, 988

TELEVISION MUSIC
Film & TV composers, 1258

TELEVISION PERSONALITIES
Television horror movie hosts, 985

TELEVISION PLAYS, AMERICAN
Television drama series programming, 993

TELEVISION PRODUCERS & DIRECTORS
Who's who in Canadian film & TV 1991-92, 1341

TELEVISION PROGRAMS
Fifty yrs of TV, 998
Television drama series programming, 993
Television yrbk, 995

TELEVISION PROGRAMS. PUBLIC SERVICE
Transcript/video index, 1991, 1001

TELEVISION SCRIPTS
Transcript/video index, 1991, 1001

TEMPLES
Bibliography on temples of the ancient Near East & Mediterranean world, 1402

TENNESSEE
Tennessee attorneys dir, 1992, 585
Tennessee govt officials dir, 1991, 742

TERATOGENIC AGENTS
Catalog of teratogenic agents, 7th ed, 1628

TEXAS
Field gd to shells of the Tex. coast, 1522
Texas almanac & state industrial gd, 1992-93, 111
Texas mushrooms, 1509

TEXTILE FABRICS
Encyclopedia of textiles, 1007

THEATER. *See also* **DRAMA**
American drama criticism, suppl.3 to the 2d ed, 1168
American drama 1918-60, 1380
American theatre hist, 1381
Back Stage theater gd, 1389
Contemporary theatre, film, & TV, v.9, 1324
International dict of theatre, v.1, 1391
Joseph Papp: a bio-bibliog, 1378
London stage 1940-49, 1386
Regional theatre dir 1992-93, 1388

THEATER CRITICISM. *See* **DRAMATIC CRITICISM**

THEATER—STUDY & TEACHING
Directory of theatre training programs, 3d ed, 1390

THEATRICAL PRODUCERS & DIRECTORS
David Merrick: a bio-bibliog, 1377
Joseph Chaikin: a bio-bibliog, 1376

THEOLOGY
Dictionary of Judaism & Christianity, 1405
Great thinkers of the W world, 950
Reference works for theological research, 3d ed, 1400

THERAPEUTICS
Prevention how-to dict of healing remedies & techniques, 1636

THIRD WORLD. *See* **DEVELOPING COUNTRIES**

THOREAU, HENRY DAVID
Henry David Thoreau: an annot bibliog of comment & criticism before 1900, 1182

TIBET
Tibet, 130

TIME
Time: a bibliographic gd, 14

TOURISM. *See* **TOURIST TRADE**

TOURIST TRADE
Third World tourism research 1950-84, 504

TOXICOLOGY
Toxics A to Z, 1769

TRADE & PROFESSIONAL ASSOCIATIONS
Associations yellow bk, v.2, no.1, 319
Business orgs, agencies, & pubs dir, 6th ed, 190
State & regional assns of the US, 1992 ed, 71
Trade & professional assns in Calif., 5th ed, 67

TRADE CATALOGS. *See* **CATALOGS, COMMERCIAL**

TRADE NAMES. *See* **BUSINESS NAMES**

TRADE-UNIONS
American dir of organized labor, 306
Trade union hndbk, 5th ed, 305
Trade unions of the world 1992-93, 313

TRAFFIC ACCIDENTS
Statistics of road traffic accidents in Europe 1991, 1785

TRAFFIC ENGINEERING
Concise ency of traffic & transportation systems, 1613

TRANSPORTATION
Concise ency of traffic & transportation systems, 1613

TRANSPORTATION ENGINEERING
Concise ency of traffic & transportation systems, 1613

TREATIES
United States treaty index: 1776-1990 consolidation, 759

TREE CROPS
Seeds of woody plants in N America, rev ed, 1521

TREES
Meet the natives: the amateur's field gd to Rocky Mountain wildflowers, trees & shrubs, 9th ed, 1505
Trees of the west, 1517

TRIALS
Famous trials, 604

TROPICAL PLANTS
Cultivated plants of the tropics & subtropics, 1469

TROPICS
Cultivated plants of the tropics & subtropics, 1469

TROTSKY, LEON
International Trotskyism 1929-85, 777

TRUCKING
Trucksource 1992, 1783

TUDOR, HOUSE OF
Historical dict of Tudor England, 1485-1603, 532

TURKS & CAICOS ISLANDS
Turks & Caicos Islands, 157

TWAIN, MARK
Union cat of letters to Clemens, 1183

TWENTIETH CENTURY
Chronicle of the 1st World War, v.2, 551
Dictionary of 20th century hist 1914-90, 557

UFO'S. *See* **UNIDENTIFIED FLYING OBJECTS**

UKRAINE
Ukraine top 100 exporters, 294

UKRAINIAN NEWSPAPERS
Select index to Svoboda, v.1, 980
Select index to Svoboda, v.2, 981

UNDERDEVELOPED AREAS. *See* **DEVELOPING COUNTRIES**

UNEMPLOYMENT BENEFITS. *See* **INSURANCE, UNEMPLOYMENT**

UNIDENTIFIED FLYING OBJECTS
UFO ency, v.2, 807

UNIFORM SYSTEM OF CITATION
User's gd to the Bluebk, 590

UNIFORMS, MILITARY
Visual dict of military uniforms, 703

UNITED KINGDOM
Access to UK higher educ, 380
European employment & industrial relations glossary: UK, 297
Higher educ in the UK 1992-93, 386
Who's who in bus & industry in the UK 1991, 298

UNITED NATIONS
Who's who in the UN & related agencies, 2d ed, 782

UNITED NATIONS – ARCHIVAL RESOURCES
Directory of UN documentary & archival sources, 783

UNITED STATES
United States, 520

UNITED STATES. AIR FORCE
United States air force, 709

UNITED STATES – ANTIQUITIES
Archaeology hndbk, 507

UNITED STATES – ARMED FORCES
Guide to military installations, 3d ed, 704

UNITED STATES – ARMED FORCES – WOMEN
American women & the US armed forces, 707

UNITED STATES. ARMY
Army dict & desk ref, 717
U.S. military logistics, 1607-1991, 710
Vietnam battle chronology, 716

UNITED STATES – CIVILIZATION
Gay 90s in America, 518
Jewish-American hist & culture, 442

UNITED STATES – CIVILIZATION – SPANISH INFLUENCES
Extraordinary Hispanic Americans, 51

UNITED STATES. CONGRESS
CIS 4-yr cum index, 1987-90, 758
Congressional Quarterly's gd to Congress, 4th ed, 747
Congressional voting gd: a 10 yr compilation, 4th ed, 746
Handbook of campaign spending, 749
Vital stats on congress, 1991-92, 754

UNITED STATES – CONSTITUTIONAL LAW
Encyclopedia of the American Constitution, suppl.1, 576
Language of the Constitution, 593

UNITED STATES – ECONOMIC POLICY
Washington almanac, 731

UNITED STATES – EMIGRATION & IMMIGRATION
Immigrant experience, 420

UNITED STATES – EXECUTIVE DEPARTMENTS
Washington info dir 1992-93, 743

UNITED STATES – FOREIGN RELATIONS – TREATIES
Consolidated treaties & intl agreements, 756
United States treaty index: 1776-1990 consolidation, 759

UNITED STATES – GOVERNMENT PUBLICATIONS
Government ref bks 90/91, 74

UNITED STATES – HISTORY – CIVIL WAR, 1861-1865
Compendium of the Confederate armies: Ala., 711
Compendium of the Confederate armies: Fla. & Ark., 712
Compendium of the Confederate armies: N.C., 713
Compendium of the Confederate armies: Tenn., 714
Compendium of the Confederate armies: Va., 715

UNITED STATES—HISTORY, MILITARY
Military hist of the US, 700

UNITED STATES—IMPRINTS
American bk publishing record cum 1991, 26
Checklist of American imprints for 1842, 32

UNITED STATES—MAPS
United States atlas for young people, 469

UNITED STATES. MARINE CORPS
Vietnam battle chronology, 716

UNITED STATES—OCCUPATIONS
Career connection, rev ed, 410

UNITED STATES—POLITICS & GOVERNMENT
Almanac of American presidents from 1789 to the present, 519
American pol prints 1766-1876, 735
Congressional voting gd: a 10 yr compilation, 4th ed, 746
Encyclopedic dict of American govt, 4th ed, 737
HarperCollins dict of American govt & pols, 736
Minor presidential candidates & parties of 1992, 748
Washington almanac, 731
Washington representatives 1992, 744

UNITED STATES—RELATIONS—INDOCHINA
America & the Indochina wars, 1945-90, 733

UNITED STATES—RELATIONS—LATIN AMERICA
United States in Latin America, 786

UNITED STATES—RELIGION
Encyclopedia of religions in the US, 1407
Religious bodies in the US, 1408

UNITED STATES—RURAL CONDITIONS
Sociology in govt, 846

UNITED STATES—STATISTICS
Almanac of the 50 states, 1992 ed, 909
State rankings, 1991, 912

UNITED STATES. SUPREME COURT
How to research the Supreme Court, 571
Supreme Court yrbk 1990-91, 588

UNIVERSITIES & COLLEGES
ACCC dir of Canadian colleges & insts, 362
American univs & colleges, 14th ed, 363
Barron's best buys in college educ, 2d ed, 364
Barron's profiles of American colleges, 19th ed, 365
Barron's top 50, 366
Chronicle financial aid gd for 1991-92 school yr, 367
Chronicle 4-yr college databk for 1991-92 school yr, 368
College admissions data hndbk 1992-93, 370
Guide to the univs of Europe, 382
Insider's gd to the colleges 1993, 372
School songs of America's colleges & univs, 1278

UNIVERSITIES & COLLEGES—CURRICULA
College admissions index of majors & sports 1992-93, 379

UNIVERSITIES & COLLEGES—FACULTY
Directory of faculty contracts & bargaining agents in institutions of higher educ, v.18, 360
Faculty white pages 1991, 361

UNIVERSITY EXTENSION
Campus-free college degrees, 5th ed, 378

UNIVERSITY OF ALBERTA
From the past to the future, 527

UNIVERSITY PRESSES
MLA dir of scholarly presses in lang & lit, 686

URBAN HEALTH
Livable cities almanac, 920

USED CARS
Lemon-aid used car gd 1992, 1782
Used car buying gd, 1992-93 ed, 1786

VAMPIRE FILMS
Cinematic vampires, 1353

VAUGHAN, SARAH
Sarah Vaughan: a discography, 1285

VENTURE CAPITAL
Pratt's gd to venture capital sources, 1992 ed, 197

VETERANS IN MOTION PICTURES
Vietnam vet films, 1366

VETERINARY MEDICINE
Black's vet dict, 17th ed, 1490

VIDEO DISCS
Bowker's complete video dir 1992, 989
Laser video disc companion, updated ed, 997

VIDEO RECORDINGS
Family video gd, 1329
Viewers' choice gd to movies on video, 1334
X-rated videotape gd 2, 1332

VIDEO TAPE RECORDERS & RECORDING
Bowker's complete video dir 1992, 989
Film-video terms & concepts, 1345

VIDEO TAPES
Bowker's complete video dir 1992, 989
Educators gd to free videotapes, 39th ed, 396
Film & video finder, 3d ed, 1330

VIDEO TAPES IN EDUCATION
AFVA evaluations 1991, 395
Films for learning, thinking, & doing, 399

VIDEOCASSETTES
Transcript/video index, 1991, 1001

VIETNAMESE CONFLICT, 1961-1975
America & the Indochina wars, 1945-90, 733
Vietnam battle chronology, 716
Vietnam bk list, 525
Vietnam vet films, 1366

VIETNAMESE LANGUAGE—DICTIONARIES—ENGLISH
Vietnamese-English dict, 1104

VIRGIN ISLANDS
Virgin Islands, 158

VIRTUAL REALITY
Virtual reality: a selected bibliog, 1672

VISUAL ARTS. See **ART**

VITAL STATISTICS
Indiana factbk 1992, 108

VITAMINS IN HUMAN NUTRITION
Essential gd to vitamins & minerals, 1647

VOCABULARY
Dickson's word treasury, 1073

VOCATIONAL EDUCATION
Chronicle vocational school manual for 1991-92 school yr, 406

VOCATIONAL GUIDANCE
Educators gd to free guidance materials, 30th ed, 400
Encyclopedia of career change & work issues, 409
Encyclopedia of career choices for the 1990s, 309
Focus on careers, 408
Professional careers sourcebk, 2d ed, 411
Vocational careers sourcebk, 412

VOCATIONAL QUALIFICATIONS
Career connection, rev ed, 410
Encyclopedia of career choices for the 1990s, 309

VOCATIONAL TRAINING. See **OCCUPATIONAL TRAINING**

VOLUNTARISM
Guide to fed funding for volunteer programs, 876
Nonprofit almanac 1992-93, 877

VOLUNTARY ORGANIZATIONS. See **ASSOCIATIONS, INSTITUTIONS, ETC.**

VOTING
British electorate, 1963-87, 772

WAGNER, RICHARD
Parsifal on record, 1270

WAR IN LITERATURE
Vietnam bk list, 525

WAR STORIES, AMERICAN
War & peace through women's eyes, 1169

WARFARE, CONVENTIONAL
Penguin ency of modern warfare, 701

WASHINGTON (D.C.)
Washington info dir 1992-93, 743

WASTE WATER RECLAMATION. See **WATER REUSE**

WATER
Dictionary of water & wastewater treatment trademarks & brand names, 1772

WATER CHEMISTRY
Groundwater chemicals field gd, 1771

WATER QUALITY MANAGEMENT
Elsevier's dict of hydrology & water quality mgmt, 1724

WATER REUSE
Dictionary of water & wastewater treatment trademarks & brand names, 1772

WATER SOLUBLE POLYMERS
Water-soluble resins, 2d ed, 1713

WATER, UNDERGROUND
Groundwater chemicals field gd, 1771

WAYNE, JOHN
John Wayne: a bio-bibliog, 1320

WEATHER
Weather almanac, 6th ed, 1722

WEDDING MUSIC
Wedding music, 1266

WEEDS
Common & botanical names of weeds in Canada, 1992 ed, 1511

WEST (U.S.)
Encyclopedia of W lawmen & outlaws, 609
Fighting men of the Indian wars, 515
Trees of the west, 1517
Wildflowers of the west, 1503
Women in the west, 941

WEST INDIES
Amphibians & reptiles of the W Indies, 1579

WESTERN FILMS
Spaghetti westerns, 1367
Sweethearts of the sage, 1361

WESTERN STORIES
Work of Louis L'Amour, 1176

WHOLESALE TRADE
American wholesalers & distrs dir, 245

WILBERFORCE, WILLIAM
William Wilberforce 1759-1833: a bibliog, 771

WILBUR, RICHARD
Richard Wilbur: a ref gd, 1184

WILD FLOWERS
Meet the natives: the amateur's field gd to Rocky Mountain wildflowers, trees & shrubs, 9th ed, 1505
Wildflowers of the west, 1503

WILDERNESS AREAS
U.S. outdoor atlas & recreation gd, 497

WILDERNESS SURVIVAL
Wilderness U: opportunities for outdoor educ in the US & abroad, 335

WILDLIFE. *See* **ANIMALS**

WILDLIFE DISEASES
Parasites & diseases of wild mammals in Fla., 1569

WILLIAMS, TENNESSEE
Tennessee Williams: a bibliog, 2d ed, 1185

WIND ENSEMBLES
American Wind Symphony commissioning project, 1284

WINE & WINE MAKING
Hugh Johnson's pocket ency of wine 1992, 1474

WIT & HUMOR
Directory of humor mags & humor orgs in America (& Canada), 3d ed, 1188
1001 quips & quotes for bus speeches, 219

WITCHCRAFT
Magic, witchcraft, & paganism in America, 2d ed, 811

WOMEN
A-to-Z of women's sexuality, rev ed, 884
Book of women, 935
Female psychology, 797
Journal of Women's Hist gd to per lit, 943
Lesser-known women, 934
Portraits of American women, 932
Victorian American women 1840-80, 927
Who's who of American women 1991-92, 56
Womanwords, 938
Women & aging, 928
Women in the west, 941
Women's studies ency, v.3, 939

WOMEN & LITERATURE
American women playwrights, 1900-30, 1167
Shakespeare & feminist criticism, 1212
War & peace through women's eyes, 1169

WOMEN & RELIGION
Goddesses & wise women, 923

WOMEN & THE MILITARY
American women & the US armed forces, 707

WOMEN ATHLETES
Great women athletes of the 20th century, 815
Outstanding women athletes, 818

WOMEN AUTHORS
Bloomsbury gd to women's lit, 942
Confidence woman, 936
Drama by women to 1990, 1146

WOMEN AUTHORS, FRENCH
French women writers, 1222
Simone de Beauvoir: a bibliog, 930

WOMEN AUTHORS, JAPANESE
Women in Japanese society, 925

WOMEN COMPOSERS, AFRO-AMERICAN. *See* **AFRO-AMERICAN WOMEN COMPOSERS**

WOMEN DRAMATISTS
American women playwrights, 1900-30, 1167

WOMEN – EDUCATION
Education of women in the US, 926

WOMEN – EUROPE
Annotated index of medieval women, 933

WOMEN – HISTORY – MIDDLE AGES, 500-1500
Annotated index of medieval women, 933

WOMEN IN LITERATURE
Bloomsbury gd to women's lit, 942

WOMEN IN POLITICS
Who's who of women in world pols, 937

WOMEN IN SCIENCE
Women scientists, 1441

WOMEN IN THE THEATER
Dramatic re-visions, 1333

WOMEN – JAPAN
Women in Japanese society, 925

WOMEN MURDERERS
Women serial & mass murderers, 612

WOMEN PHILOSOPHERS
Women philosophers, 1392

WOMEN – QUOTATIONS
Write to the heart, 944

WOMEN SCIENTISTS
Women scientists, 1441

WOMEN – SOCIETIES & CLUBS
NWO: a dir of natl women's orgs, 940

WOMEN SOCIOLOGISTS
Women in sociology, 844

WOMEN – SOVIET UNION
Women & writing in Russian & the USSR, 1230

WOMEN TRACK & FIELD ATHLETES
Black American women in Olympic track & field, 843

WOMEN'S HEALTH SERVICES
Maternal & child health legislation: 1991, 594

WOMEN'S STUDIES
WIP: a dir of work-in-progress & recent pubs, 924
Women, race, & ethnicity, 931

WOODWORK
Home building & woodworking in colonial America, 1612

WOODWORKING TOOLS
Illustrated ency of woodworking handtools instruments & devices, rev ed, 1610

WOODY PLANTS
Seeds of woody plants in N America, rev ed, 1521
Weeds of the woods, 1515

WORLD HISTORY. *See also* **GEOGRAPHY**
Guinness bk of records 1492, 558
Illustrated almanac of histl facts, 553
World factbk 1991-92, 105
World hist for children & young adults, 561

WORLD LITERATURE. *See* **LITERATURE**

WORLD POLITICS
Annual register 1991, 725
Big Powers & the German question, 1941-90, 538
Facts on File world pol almanac, 2d ed, 719
Federal systems of the world, 726
Names of countries & their capital cities, 104
New state of the world atlas, 4th ed, 475
Revolutionary & dissident movements, 3d ed, 728
World factbk 1991-92, 105
Worldwide govt dir 1992, 724

WORLD POLITICS—1945
Atlas of world affairs, 9th ed, 720

WORLD RECORDS
Guinness bk of records 1492, 558
Limca bk of records 1991, 1310

WORLD WAR, 1914-1918
Chronicle of the 1st World War, v.2, 551
Pivotal conflict: a comprehensive chronology of the 1st world war, 1914-19, 552

WORLD WAR, 1939-1945
Battles of Coral Sea & Midway, 1942, 695
Nazi-retro film, 1362
Pearl Harbor, 1941, 696
World in turmoil, 550
World War II: America at war 1941-45, 556

XERISCAPING
Shade & color with water-conserving plants, 1520

YIDDISH LANGUAGE—DICTIONARIES—ENGLISH
English-Yiddish, Yiddish-English dict, 1105
Transliterated English-Yiddish, Yiddish-English dict, 1106

YOUNG ADULT FICTION
Portraying persons with disabilities: an annot bibliog of fiction, 3d ed, 1132
Supernatural fiction for teens, 2d ed, 1156

YOUNG ADULT LITERATURE. *See also* **CHILDREN'S LITERATURE**
Adoption lit for children & young adults, 868
Author profile collection, 1138
Biographical index to children's & young adult authors & illustrators, 1144
Characters from young adult lit, 1143
From page to screen, 1359
Indian subcontinent in lit for children & young adults, 1126
Our family, our friends, our world, 1127
Portraying persons with disabilities: an annot bibliog of nonfiction, 2d ed, 1124
University pr bks for public & secondary school libs 1991, 664
Young adult 1991 annual bklist, 1136
Young adult reader's adviser, 1137
Young people's bks in series, 1133

YOUTH PERIODICALS
Magazines for young people, 2d ed, 84

YUGOSLAV LITERATURE
Second suppl to a comp bibliog of Yugoslav lit in English 1986-90, 1234

ZIP CODE
Instant natl locator gd, 955

ZOOGEOGRAPHY
Children's animal atlas, 1531

ZOOLOGY
Concise Oxford dict of zoology, 1529
Wild animals of W Canada, 1533

Contributors' Index

Reference is to entry number.

Aby, Stephen H., 347, 399, 851, 853, 889, 892
Adamshick, Robert D., 174, 190, 192, 194, 228
Allen, Walter C., 1783
Aman, Mary Jo, 332, 340
Anderson, Byron P., 23, 24, 91, 100, 101, 103, 632, 1454
Anderson, Frank J., 510, 681, 1041, 1791
Anderson, James D., 626, 636, 641, 652, 886
Anderson, Robert T., 1303, 1406, 1427, 1431, 1432, 1435
Andrews, Charles R., 89, 718
Andrews, Theodora, 1655
Ardis, Susan B., 265, 587, 1585, 1600, 1605
Attinson, Roslyn, 234, 268, 360, 921
Auld, Lawrence W. S., 655

Bailey, Bill, 45, 146, 608, 609, 610, 611, 612, 613, 1025, 1033, 1071, 1077, 1111, 1119, 1149, 1188
Baird-Joshi, Susan D., 257, 287
Bales, Jack, 17, 1162, 1164
Ballard, Robert M., 5, 725
Barber, Gary D., 132, 588, 757, 793, 1155
Barber, Helen M., 1500, 1524
Barchers, Suzanne I., 330, 331, 339, 352, 402, 1120, 1121, 1145
Barclay, Donald A., 682
Bardack, David, 1720
Baxter, Pam M., 807, 808, 1098, 1649
Beard, Craig W., 448, 1405, 1409, 1410, 1419, 1428, 1429
Beck, Maureen A., 71, 196, 326, 1008, 1171
Belanger, Sandra E., 188, 189, 260, 308, 311, 564, 579, 897, 984
Bell, Carol Willsey, 437, 452, 456, 460, 901
Bell, George H., 1525, 1526, 1533, 1536, 1537, 1538, 1539, 1540, 1541, 1542, 1543, 1545, 1546, 1555, 1556, 1558, 1559, 1575, 1576, 1577, 1579, 1580, 1662, 1663
Bergup, Bernice, 529, 1067, 1072, 1118, 1168, 1202, 1392
Beston, John B., 914, 1094, 1167, 1198, 1262
Biley, Kerranne G., 54, 198, 215, 269, 297, 303, 304
Bilhartz, Terry D., 370, 908, 931, 934, 1416, 1418
Blazek, Ron, 106, 107, 223
Blewett, Daniel K., 105, 488, 619, 727, 728, 792
Bloss, Marjorie E., 621, 622, 627, 1024
Bobinski, George S., 779
Bordelon, Bobray, 195, 206, 207, 211, 218, 219, 239, 243, 254, 312
Bowie, Melvin M., 52, 426, 760, 1312
Bracken, James K., 982, 1181, 1211, 1697
Bright, William, 1047, 1089
Broadus, Robert N., 1150, 1213

Bronner, Simon J., 418, 424, 439, 440, 444, 445, 450, 528, 1005, 1105, 1106, 1294, 1297, 1300
Brown, Barbara E., 231, 232, 275, 276
Brugger, Judith M., 121, 124, 438, 589, 637
Buchan, Ronald L., 679, 1012, 1609, 1696
Buckingham, Betty Jo, 346, 348, 350, 1063
Burkhardt, Joanna M., 415
Buttlar, Lois J., 343, 351, 419, 625, 669
Bynagle, Hans E., 1395, 1396, 1422

Calabrese, Diane M., 846, 881, 939, 1442, 1462, 1467, 1485, 1548, 1551
Campbell, John Lewis, 179, 225, 240, 244, 1670
Campbell, Robert A., 902, 904, 912
Carrier, Esther Jane, 658
Casada, James A., 138, 147, 814, 821, 836, 837, 839, 1004, 1761
Cevasco, G. A., 9, 39, 1184, 1206, 1424
Chapman, Bert, 383, 516, 576, 717, 737, 748, 753, 759, 769, 771, 787
Cheung, John Y., 1587, 1590, 1593, 1597, 1686, 1694, 1695
Childress, Boyd, 176, 216, 813, 819, 820, 824, 831
Christianson, Eric H., 1349, 1749
Clark, Paul F., 247, 306, 313, 314
Cluxton, Harriette M., 850, 1616, 1617, 1618, 1622, 1626, 1629, 1630, 1631, 1641, 1654, 1659
Cocozzoli, Gary R., 235, 988, 1367, 1591, 1592, 1594, 1596, 1598, 1601
Collins, Donald E., 3, 455, 514, 520, 899
Conroy, Barbara, 309, 405, 406, 409, 410, 412, 857, 861
Cornelius, Kay O., 711, 712, 713, 714, 715, 1055, 1062, 1187, 1298, 1308
Cors, Paul B., 1224, 1269, 1751, 1754
Coutts, Brian E., 110, 155
Cox, Richard J., 2
Craver, Kathleen W., 84, 345, 629, 668, 670, 1144, 1147
Crouch, Milton H., 974, 1279, 1569
Curtis, Gregory, 497, 1013, 1014, 1022, 1043, 1785, 1790

Darrell, C. B. (Bob), 374, 375, 1203, 1214, 1301
Dauben, Joseph W., 521, 522, 1044, 1417, 1738
Davis, Elisabeth B., 1496, 1513
Davis, Estelle A., 1715
Davis, Jr., Donald G., 1415

de Lerma, Dominique-Rene, 1026, 1241, 1293, 1317, 1360
Dede, Bonnie A., 639
DeMiller, Anna L., 847
Dick, Elie M., 166, 199, 220, 258, 322
Dickinson, Donald C., 38, 92, 675, 1073, 1107
Dillon, John B., 1223
Doll, Carol A., 433, 666, 672, 1138
Dominy, Margaret F., 1003, 1702, 1706, 1735, 1736
Dorenfeld, Edith M., 1656
Dority, G. Kim, 13, 85, 180, 200, 209, 210, 992, 1078, 1492, 1534, 1792
Drabenstott, Karen Markey, 644, 654, 661
Dunn, Joe P., 22, 109, 416, 525, 692, 698, 700, 701, 716, 1366

Ebershoff-Coles, Susan, 830, 1552, 1667, 1732
Eggenberger, David, 542, 691, 693, 706
Ellis, Marie, 954, 976, 1146, 1344, 1389
England, Claire, 1135
Erlen, Jonathon, 856, 887, 947, 1625, 1627, 1632, 1635, 1639, 1664
Evans, G. Edward, 413, 430, 431, 432, 434, 435, 436, 451
Ezergailis, Andrew, 139, 293, 554

Fairclough, Ian, 66, 68, 650, 828, 1248, 1252, 1271, 1283, 1284
Falk, Joyce Duncan, 143, 548
Farago, Kathleen, 43, 53, 508
Farber, Evan Ira, 15, 33, 355, 358, 977
Farrell, Megan S., 1030
Fasick, Adele M., 665, 1049, 1142
Fast, Robin Riley, 936, 1238
Ferrall, Eleanor, 871, 872, 875, 879, 917
Fiscella, Joan B., 251, 256
Fischer, Virginia S., 471, 472, 473, 485, 526, 763, 764, 765, 1218, 1219
Flack, Jerry D., 41, 55, 1006
Fleming, Patricia, 10, 19
Foley, Michael A., 567, 591, 598, 602, 616, 618, 930
Forshey, Harold O., 544, 1434
Franklin, A. David, 1275, 1285, 1286, 1287, 1288, 1289
Frasier, David K., 993, 1001, 1329, 1341, 1342, 1356, 1361, 1365, 1369, 1373
Frayser, Suzanne G., 797, 801, 865, 882, 883, 884
Freegard, Sarah A., 1461
Freiband, Susan J., 429, 446, 447, 940, 1243
Friedrichs, David O., 604, 606, 607, 614
Friedrichs, Jeanne, 30, 394
Fritze, Ronald H., 486, 531, 533, 558, 560, 772, 773, 1352

Gamaluddin, Ahmad, 159, 160, 163, 164, 384, 776, 880, 1472
Garner, Joan, 1042, 1335
Geary, Gregg S., 1267, 1278
Gleaves, Edwin S., 154, 484, 633, 1174
Gokhale, Maya B., 1677
Goldberg, Lisha E., 441, 1331
Goldwhite, Harold, 1709, 1713, 1716, 1766
Gothberg, Helen M., 953, 985, 994

Goudy, Allie Wise, 1239
Graham, M. Patrick, 443, 1394, 1399, 1408, 1426
Green, Marilynn, 885, 1465, 1615
Greenspoon, Leonard J., 167, 442, 449, 494, 1433
Grefrath, Richard W., 1290, 1292
Gribben, Arthur, 1302, 1304
Grift, Margaret A., 65, 90, 134, 1244, 1268, 1280
Griggs, Janice M., 37, 46, 47, 205, 1447, 1448, 1451
Grossman, Jacqueline L., 590, 595
Grotzinger, Laurel, 1699

Haenel, Stephen, 684, 969, 1010, 1676, 1679, 1682, 1692
Hall, Blaine H., 82, 1074
Hammer, Deborah, 469, 496, 1179
Hannibal, Joseph, 1452, 1522, 1731
Haro, Roberto P., 156, 379, 511, 774
Harris, Chauncy D., 474, 491
Harris, Marvin K., 1466, 1468, 1527
Harrison, S. L., 735, 755, 978
Hartness, Ann, 152, 1091
Hastings, Joy, 1153, 1481, 1490
Havlik, Robert J., 635, 967, 972, 1035, 1037, 1038, 1039, 1040, 1455, 1779
Hay, Fred J., 99, 102, 151, 417, 422, 423, 425, 1110, 1115
Heller, James S., 571, 580, 586
Henige, David, 112, 113, 114, 115, 116, 277, 761
Herold, Jean, 267, 299, 300, 301, 327
Herring, Mark Y., 559, 561, 585, 592, 617, 719, 742, 998, 1060, 1183, 1186, 1393, 1401
Herring, Susan Davis, 927, 938, 942, 944, 1438, 1441
Hill, Janet Swan, 638
Hodges, Robert Clyde, 726, 754
Holl, Richard E., 556, 747, 756
Hollis, Deborah D., 1157
Hollis, Susan Tower, 923, 1029, 1402
Hopkinson, Shirley L., 104, 120, 168, 380, 391, 392, 393, 487
Horowitz, Renee B., 259, 288, 291, 295, 970
Hotchkiss, Valerie R., 50, 1057, 1085, 1199, 1305
Howard, Helen, 302, 316
Huestis, Carmel A., 407
Hug, William E., 328, 344, 956
Hunter, John H., 14, 1633, 1637, 1638, 1658, 1727, 1746, 1747, 1752, 1762
Hurt, C. D., 1236, 1237, 1599, 1606, 1608

Ilyina, Ludmila N., 1528, 1756, 1764, 1768
Isaacson, David, 1048, 1114, 1163, 1177, 1192, 1208
Ittner, Barbara, 64

Jackman, John A., 1499, 1561, 1566, 1674
Jackson, Eugene B., 649, 685, 1588, 1595, 1613, 1710
Johnson, D. Barton, 463, 1092, 1093, 1095, 1096, 1230
Johnson, Jennie S., 498, 935, 1470
Johnson, Richard D., 72, 628, 674, 1668
Jones, Dorothy E., 1411
Jones, Raymond E., 7, 671, 1122, 1125, 1133, 1134

Jones, Robert L., 1636
Jordan, Rebecca, 335, 373, 1193, 1320, 1333, 1336, 1379
Jurgens, J. C., 130, 458, 501, 502, 707, 1207

Karel, Thomas A., 142, 283, 535, 723, 724, 740, 788, 789, 790, 791, 1191, 1195
Keiser, Jr., Edmund D., 1523, 1578
Kelland, John Laurence, 1483, 1486, 1510, 1517, 1518, 1573
Keller, Dean H., 8, 32, 680
Kemp, Barbara E., 1221, 1222, 1318, 1350
Kern-Simirenko, Cheryl, 141, 536
Kesler, Jackson, 1381, 1382, 1383, 1384
Killion, Vicki J., 1493, 1514
Kincaide, Norman L., 703
King, Christine E., 6, 83, 144, 371, 386, 532, 534, 1377
Kollar, Mary Ellen, 170
Koltay, Zsuzsa, 18, 505, 1052
Koren, Johan, 97, 382, 385, 387, 388, 634, 948, 1249, 1404
Kraus, Betsy J., 1665
Krikos, Linda A., 924, 929, 932
Kullman, Colby H., 699, 1173, 1175, 1185
Kutner, Peter B., 479, 481, 741

Lam, R. Errol, 421, 965
Langworthy, Sharon, 42, 739, 968
LaPerriere, Renee J., 1242
Larsgaard, Mary, 466, 470, 476, 478, 482, 1282
Lawrence, John R. M., 523, 540, 545, 547, 705, 1046, 1503
Le, Binh P., 75, 127, 128, 720, 1104
Leck, Charles, 1531, 1574
LeCompte, Mary Lou, 812, 818, 840, 841, 843
Lee, Hwa-Wei, 125, 278, 315, 1081
Lee, Joann H., 31, 1128, 1136
Lehmann, R. S., 825, 826, 1351
Leiter, Richard A., 512, 562, 574, 596
Lewis, Bart, 1166
Li, Tze-chung, 95, 577
Lindgren, Charlotte, 1170, 1178, 1180, 1182, 1194, 1196, 1205, 1209, 1232
Lockhart, Koraljka, 1017, 1234, 1250, 1251, 1256, 1270, 1340
Loertscher, David V., 11, 27, 28, 336, 403, 467, 468, 642, 659, 660, 667, 1129, 1137, 1330, 1420, 1421
Logan, Elisabeth, 173, 185, 213, 662
Lonergan, David, 35
Luttrell, Jeffrey R., 949, 1116, 1161, 1204, 1210

MacArthur, Marit S., 249, 310, 573, 582, 584, 600, 601, 975
Mack, Sara R., 67, 86, 664
Maggio, Theresa, 1643, 1647
Main, Linda, 506, 539, 656, 1669
Malone, Cheryl Knott, 552, 744, 870, 876, 877, 878
Matthews, Judy Gay, 507, 690, 1031, 1553, 1554
Mattil, J. Francis, 362
Mayer, George Louis, 1260, 1263, 1375, 1385
McDonald, James R., 480, 483, 500, 537, 1742, 1759
McKee, Robert B., 1602, 1604, 1780

McKimm, Susan V., 182, 203, 204, 237, 253, 255, 296, 325
McKimmie, T., 817, 1443, 1444, 1469, 1497, 1582, 1583, 1712, 1755, 1758, 1771, 1772, 1776
McKinley, Margaret, 645, 678, 905, 915, 979
McLeod, Marian B., 158, 541
Mead, Margo B., 34, 499, 863
Mesner, Lillian R., 1456, 1471, 1473, 1476, 1482, 1494, 1614
Messina, Michael G., 1484, 1773
Metzger, Philip A., 686, 689, 957
Mieczkowski, Bogdan, 48, 140, 208, 248, 270, 272, 274, 279, 284, 285, 289, 1778
Mieczkowski, Seiko, 126, 280, 925
Mieczkowski, Zbigniew, 292, 504
Miller, Edward P., 70, 794, 860, 1412, 1581, 1607, 1775
Miller, Jerome K., 651
Miller, Richard A., 178, 183, 186, 193, 202, 212, 214, 217, 241, 250
Mongan, Janet, 926, 943, 1723, 1739, 1740, 1741
Mood, Terry Ann, 76, 77, 145, 493, 1117, 1148, 1160
Moran, Gerald D., 1398, 1589
Morein, P. Grady, 238
Mulliner, K., 123, 1229, 1675
Murray, James M., 172, 273, 946, 1623

Naru, Linda A., 509, 657, 920, 922, 1165, 1172, 1343, 1345, 1357, 1364
Neuringer, Charles, 338, 802, 1325, 1327, 1378, 1380, 1390
Nitecki, Danuta A., 951
Nitecki, Joseph Z., 44
Nitschke, Eric R., 695, 696, 702, 704, 708, 709, 710
Nolan, Christopher W., 377, 1439, 1440, 1446
Noll, Carol L., 58, 1501, 1502, 1509, 1642, 1644, 1666
Norman, O. Gene, 245, 262, 318, 319, 1058
Noronha, Marilyn Strong, 367, 806, 809, 810, 866, 1245, 1272, 1634, 1640, 1648
Nunn, Marshall E., 169, 359, 372, 1102, 1103

Ockerman, Herbert W., 263, 290, 298, 1475, 1478, 1479, 1480
Olinger, Heidi Ann, 1051, 1059
Owen, Berniece M., 565, 566, 570, 572, 605, 1315, 1316, 1326, 1353, 1358
Oxley, John Howard, 694, 697, 1672, 1781, 1782, 1784

Padnos, Mark, 453, 454, 550
Palmer, Joseph W., 396, 397, 640, 663, 989, 1319, 1323, 1332, 1354, 1371
Palmieri, Robert, 1253, 1255, 1259, 1261
Patterson, Anna Grace, 1, 20, 26, 29, 57, 623, 673, 687, 1108, 1109
Patterson, Elizabeth, 796, 804, 1314
Patzwald, Gari-Anne, 135, 492, 527, 594, 603, 620, 928, 1645
Pence, Harry E., 1708, 1711, 1717, 1763, 1767, 1769, 1770, 1774
Pendle, Karin, 1264, 1273
Posey, Edwin D., 958
Potter, Daphne Fallieros, 1291

Powell, Phillip P., 56, 364, 489
Prentice, Ann E., 1007, 1671, 1698, 1725, 1726, 1728, 1729
Proudfoot, William S., 184
Pukkila, Marilyn R., 1126, 1143

Rafferty, Randall, 1786, 1787
Ramsdell, Kristin, 941, 1141, 1156, 1266
Rasmussen, Lise, 1152
Ray, Jack, 578, 593, 599
Reinharz, Shulamit, 854, 858, 937
Rettig, James, 960, 1197
Rhodes, Diane B., 1529, 1535, 1544, 1547, 1549, 1550, 1557, 1560, 1562, 1563, 1564, 1565, 1568, 1570, 1571, 1572
Ricardo, Henry J., 464, 1056, 1064, 1065, 1066, 1075, 1076, 1299, 1678, 1680, 1681, 1737
Ricca, Jo Anne H., 88, 324, 955
Roberts, Anne F., 408, 1127, 1188
Robison, William B., 555
Rockman, Ilene F., 78, 389, 390, 400, 404, 873, 893, 896, 1124, 1132
Roess, Anne C., 1449, 1453, 1721, 1743, 1744, 1745, 1748, 1750
Rogers, JoAnn V., 171, 221
Rollins, Deborah V., 69, 329, 333, 368, 369, 1322, 1370
Rothschild, Bertram H., 337, 798, 799, 800, 803
Rothschild, D. A., 51, 61, 62, 361, 557, 683, 688, 805, 961, 963, 966, 1016, 1061, 1068, 1069, 1347, 1450, 1519, 1646
Rothschild, Marilyn, 894
Rothstein, Samuel, 36, 503, 833
Rudolph, Emanuel D., 118, 119
Ruybal, Louis R., 653, 964, 973

Sabadell, Gabriel P., 1584, 1724
SantaVicca, Edmund F., 4, 79, 80, 363, 945, 1020, 1231, 1311, 1376, 1388, 1391, 1650, 1651, 1652, 1653
Schafer, Jay, 1610
Schmidt, Diane, 1458, 1460, 1511, 1515
Schmidt, Steven J., 108, 1009
Schmidt, Willa, 420, 538, 551, 1112, 1113, 1235
Schmitt, John P., 1176, 1216, 1338, 1368, 1372
Schon, Isabel, 1101
Scott, Ralph Lee, 842, 983, 999, 1000, 1457, 1505, 1521, 1673, 1683, 1700, 1730, 1788, 1789
Scott, Richard A., 334
Seal, Robert A., 1703, 1704, 1705, 1707
Seashore, Margretta Reed, 1624, 1628
Seavey, Charlie, 1107
Sharma, Ravindra Nath, 624, 647, 648, 1070
Sharp, Patricia Tipton, 87
Shuman, Bruce A., 1054, 1083, 1158, 1337, 1346, 1348, 1355, 1359, 1362, 1374
Sigala, Stephanie C., 1018, 1019, 1023, 1034, 1045
Skinner, Robert, 25, 495, 1246, 1247, 1258, 1687, 1688, 1691, 1693
Smith, Jeanette C., 74, 903
Smith, Linda Sue, 1489
Smith, Nathan M., 906, 909, 913, 916, 1488
Sonevytsky, Natalia, 1328
Soudek, Lev I., 1053

Stabler, Karen Y., 320, 563, 775, 888, 890, 891, 910
Stanley, Mary J., 852, 862, 869, 874
Staver, Allen E., 1722
Stephenson, James Edgar, 1386
Stevens, Norman D., 131, 226, 816, 822, 827, 829, 832, 1002, 1295, 1296, 1611, 1612
Stierman, John P., 518, 950
Storey, John W., 1403, 1407, 1425, 1430
Struning, William C., 136, 222, 236, 246, 266, 281, 286, 323, 630
Stuart, Bruce, 1657, 1660, 1661
Sullivan, Timothy E., 175, 181, 187, 201, 907
Swain, Richard H., 129, 133, 191, 224, 282, 1306, 1397, 1413, 1414
Sweetland, James H., 519, 677, 848

Tappin, Nigel, 197, 229, 233, 252, 305, 568, 569, 575, 581, 583, 597, 762, 770
Taylor, Deborah A., 49, 60
Taylor, Lori Elaine, 987
Thomas, Glynys R., 986, 990, 995, 1321, 1387
Thompson, Christine E., 738, 749, 752, 785, 811, 1151
Thompson, Mary Ann, 855, 1619, 1620, 1621
Thor, Angela Marie, 1487, 1530, 1532, 1753, 1760, 1765
Tiffney, Bruce H., 1495, 1504, 1506, 1507, 1508, 1512, 1516
Torok, Andrew G., 838, 1459, 1714
Trefny, John U., 1437, 1463, 1733, 1734
Trotter, Ben B., 271
Truett, Carol, 395, 398, 401, 1131, 1139
Tucker, John Mark, 381
Tudor, Dean, 227, 230, 646, 952, 959, 991, 996, 997, 1220, 1281, 1474, 1477
Turner, Diane J., 96, 341, 1036, 1445, 1586, 1603, 1757, 1777
Turner, Jr., Robert L., 461, 845, 867, 868

Upgren, Arthur R., 898, 900, 911, 918, 919, 1254, 1257, 1701

Van Orden, Phyllis J., 1123, 1130, 1140, 1307
VanMeter, Vandelia L., 517, 549, 553, 557, 1309, 1313
Veitch, Carol J., 729, 844, 859
Villa, Dario J., 51, 137, 148, 149, 150, 153, 157, 427, 428, 1363
Voigt, Kathleen J., 1011, 1015, 1021, 1027, 1028, 1032

Wahid, Abu N. M., 321
Walker, Mary Jo, 63, 93, 342, 365, 1189
Wasylenko, Lydia W., 317
Weihs, Jean, 643
Weinberg, Bella Hass, 1087
Weingand, Darlene E., 971
Whalen, Lucille, 615
Wharton, Robert A., 1567
Wheeler, Carol, 73, 676, 731, 758, 782, 783, 795
Whitaker, Cathy Seitz, 117, 750, 786, 1169
White, David L., 122, 161, 162, 165, 524, 543, 1310, 1436
White, George M., 1684, 1685

Wiese, William H., 513, 1464, 1498, 1520
Williams, Dorothy M., 81
Williams, Lynn F., 933, 1154, 1159, 1190, 1200, 1201, 1212, 1215, 1217
Williams, Robert V., 631
Williams, Wiley J., 307, 730, 745
Willis, Liz, 411
Wilson, Frank L., 721, 722, 736, 766, 767, 768, 777, 778
Wilson, Patricia S., 1491, 1718, 1719
Wilson, Wayne, 815, 823, 834
Wintz, Celia J., 895
Wittig, Glenn R., 1400, 1423
Wood, Randy M., 111, 349, 353, 378
Wood, Raymund F., 40, 457, 459, 462, 465, 515, 835
Woodbridge, Hensley C., 1225, 1226, 1227, 1228, 1233
Woodson, Dorothy C., 477

Wright, Kieth C., 864
Wynar, Bohdan S., 12, 21, 59, 98, 294, 414, 490, 980, 981
Wynar, Lubomyr R., 546, 962

Yazhari, Martha Miller, 1090, 1240
Yerkey, A. Neil, 1689, 1690
York, Henry E., 732, 733, 734, 743, 746, 751, 781, 784
Young, Arthur P., 16, 94, 354, 356, 357, 366, 376

Zelenka, Louis G., 1265, 1274, 1276, 1277
Zgusta, L., 1050, 1079, 1080, 1082, 1084, 1086, 1088, 1099
Zinam, Oleg, 177, 242, 261, 264, 475, 530, 780, 849, 1097, 1100
Zutis, Anita, 1324, 1334, 1339